SECOND EDITION
Sexuality Now

EMBRACING DIVERSITY

JANELL L. CARROLL
University of Hartford

THOMSON

WADSWORTH

Australia • Brazil • Canada • Mexico • Singapore • Spain
United Kingdom • United States

Sexuality Now: Embracing Diversity, Second Edition
Janell L. Carroll

PUBLISHER	Vicki Knight	TEXT DESIGNER	Diane Beasley
SENIOR ACQUISITIONS EDITOR, PSYCHOLOGY	Marianne Taflinger	PHOTO RESEARCHER	Roman A. Barnes
DEVELOPMENT EDITOR	Kristin Makarewycz	COPY EDITOR	Mary Anne Shahidi
ASSISTANT EDITOR	Jennifer Alexander	ILLUSTRATORS	Rolin Graphics and Adam Miller
EDITORIAL ASSISTANT	Lucy Faridany	COVER DESIGNER	Denise Davidson
TECHNOLOGY PROJECT MANAGER	Darin Derstine	COVER IMAGES (clockwise, left to right)	Dex/Getty Images, Cheryl Maeder/ Getty Images, Friends/Digital Vision/Getty Images, Jim Arbogast/ Getty Images, Thinkstock/Getty Images, Friends/Digital Vision/ Getty Images
MARKETING MANAGER	Dory Schaeffer		
MARKETING COMMUNICATIONS MANAGER	Kelley McAllister		
PROJECT MANAGER, EDITORIAL PRODUCTION	Lori Johnson		
CREATIVE DIRECTOR	Rob Hugel		
ART DIRECTOR	Vernon Boes	COVER PRINTER	Phoenix Color Corp
PRINT BUYER	Barbara Britton	COMPOSITOR	Graphic World
PERMISSIONS EDITOR	Sarah Harkrader	PRINTER	Courier Corporation/Kendallville
PRODUCTION SERVICE	Ellen Brownstein, Chapter Two		

Printed in the United States of America
3 4 5 6 7 10 09 08 07

Library of Congress Control Number: 2005933545
ISBN 978-0-495-09108-0
ISBN 0-495-09108-1

THOMSON HIGHER LEARNING
10 Davis Drive
Belmont, CA 94002-3098
USA

For more information about our products, contact us at:
Thomson Learning Academic Resource Center
1-800-423-0563
For permission to use material from this text or product,
submit a request online at
http://www.thomsonrights.com.
Any additional questions about permissions
can be submitted by email to
thomsonrights@thomson.com.

This book is dedicated to
my very supportive husband,
Gregory Paul,
and our three wonderfully bright,
loving, and curious children,
Reagan, MacKenzie,
and Sammy.

About the Author

An AASECT-certified sexuality educator, Dr. Janell L. Carroll received her Ph.D. in Human Sexuality Education in 1989 from the University of Pennsylvania. A dynamic educator, speaker, and author, she has published many articles, authored a syndicated sexuality column, and written two college-level textbooks on human sexuality. She has lectured extensively, hosted two of her own radio talk shows, appeared as an expert on numerous television talk shows and networks, and has been mentioned in several national publications, Internet news media outlets, and cyber-press articles.

On a personal level, Dr. Carroll feels it's her mission to educate students and the public at-large about their sexuality—to help people think *and* feel through the issues for themselves. Dr. Carroll's success as a teacher comes from the fact that she loves her students as much as she loves what she teaches. She sees students' questions about sex as the foundation for her course, and has brought that attitude—along with her enthusiasm for helping them find answers—to this text.

Dr. Carroll has won several teaching awards, including the Gordon Clark Ramsey Award for Creative Excellence, given to professors at the University of Hartford who demonstrate sustained excellence and creativity in the classroom. She also has been recognized by Planned Parenthood as a Sexuality Educator of the Year. Prior to teaching at University of Hartford, Dr. Carroll was a tenured psychology professor at Baker University, where she was honored with awards for Professor of the Year and Most Outstanding Person on Campus. Dr. Carroll maintains her own sexuality website (http://www.drjanellcarroll.com) where people can learn about sexuality and ask questions.

Brief Contents

Contents

1

Exploring Human Sexuality: Past and Present   1

2

Understanding Human Sexuality: Theory and Research 29

3

Gender Development, Gender Roles, and Gender Identity 64

4

Female Sexual Anatomy and Physiology 101

5

Male Sexual Anatomy and Physiology 135

Communication: Enriching Your Sexuality   157

7

Love and Intimacy 180

8

Childhood and Adolescent Sexuality 210

9

Adult Sexual Relationships 253

10

Sexual Expression: Arousal and Response   290

11

Sexual Orientation 327

12

Pregnancy and Birth 366

13

Contraception and Abortion 406

14

Challenges to Sexual Functioning 458

15

Sexually Transmitted Infections and HIV/AIDS   493

16

Varieties of Sexual Expression   534

17

Power and Sexual Coercion 567

18

Sexual Images and Selling Sex 603

Preface

The human sexuality course is one of my favorite courses to teach, and I look forward to it each semester. I believe that students and teachers have a unique relationship, learning and teaching as a team. My approach to teaching is similar to a line in a Phil Collins song that says *"in learning you will teach, and in teaching you will learn."* While it's true that students have so much to learn about sexuality, they also are wonderful teachers. I learn a lot in class just by listening to my students open up and share their own attitudes and thoughts about issues related to sexuality. It is through these conversations with students that I learn what students really want to know about sexuality and what things cause problems in their relationships. All that I have learned throughout my many years of teaching I bring to you in the Second Edition of *Sexuality Now: Embracing Diversity.*

For me, the decision to write this book was an easy one. After teaching this course for more than 16 years, I was aware that a student-centered approach and students' voices were missing from the majority of sexuality textbooks on the market. Don't get me wrong, there are a lot of good books out there, but I think some authors wrote what they thought the students needed to know, without asking the students what gaps they felt needed to be filled. Of course, I too have many ideas about what I think students should know, but I also spend a great deal of my time listening and talking to students about sexuality issues. Students are really the foundation of *Sexuality Now*, and I keep this student-centered approach throughout the text.

The Second Edition of this book builds upon the successes of the First Edition and maintains many of the original features. Large-scale changes include a new art and photo program, an increased multi-cultural focus, and completely updated research with hundreds of new research citations. You will find updated material on issues such as same-sex marriages, contraception, sexually transmitted infections, pornography, love, pheromones, and brain chemistry. The field of sexuality has been changing rapidly during the last decade, and I have worked hard in this revision to keep up with these many changes.

NEW TO THIS EDITION

There are many new changes to the Second Edition. We have totally reworked the majority of figures—including all new sex position art in Chapter 10—and added many new photos throughout the textbook. This gives the Second Edition a wonderfully fresh and contemporary feel.

We have added a new feature entitled Sex in Real Life to this edition. This feature highlights changing practices and cutting-edge research, and some are drawn from material that appeared in the What Do Women Think? What Do Men Think? and Sex Facts & Fantasies features from the First Edition. Students and professors alike both thought these features didn't work as well as I had hoped and, in reworking them, I realized one feature that concentrated on important current issues was critical and a wonderful addition to the Second Edition.

Other new additions include historical timelines, pronunciation guides, active summaries, links to videos by chapter, and movie recommendations. Three new **historical timelines**—on the history of sexuality and television (Chapter 1), key developments in sex research (Chapter 2), and assisted reproduction (Chapter 12)—help facilitate student learning and provide visual material to maintain student interest (see Chapter 1, page 6; Chapter 2, page 40; and Chapter 12, page 376). A new **pronunciation guide** helps students understand how to pronounce difficult words—helping to improve student communication about sexuality. **Active Summaries** now appear at the end of each chapter, so that students can easily study and review material contained in each chapter. A variety of **video links**—including video panel discussions on GLB and transgendered/transsexual individuals—also appear throughout the text, highlighting video segments by chapter geared to stimulate classroom discussion. Finally, we've also added a current or classic **movie recommendation** to the end of each chapter, which helps tie the material to popular culture for students. Clips of these movies may also be shown in class to facilitate class discussion.

As I look over the many changes made to the Second Edition, I think that one of the most important changes is the focus on multicultural diversity both within and outside the United States. You will find many new references to the importance of culture and ethnicity/race. This is an important addition and critical in the teaching of this material, especially given the rapidly changing ethnicity of Americans today (for examples, see Chapter 8, page 292; Chapter 9, pages 257, 258, 264, 270; and Chapter 10, page 292). Research on cross-cultural sexuality from Francoeur & Noonan's (2004), *The Continuum Complete International Encyclopedia of Sexuality* is extensively reviewed and discussed throughout the text. Also see pages xxxviii–xxxix for indexes of cultural and gender coverage throughout the book.

IMPORTANT FEATURES

sexbyte

This feature is consistently rated by students as a favorite. It developed out of my experiences in the classroom. I noticed that students loved to learn "fun facts" about sexuality and they would talk to their friends after class about them. I loved this! My students had become teachers and were taking the facts they had learned outside the classroom. Many long discussions were born out of these fun facts. The majority of SexBytes in the Second Edition have been updated with new and cutting-edge research. They are placed where appropriate throughout the book and contain information from both current and classic research studies.

For example, Chapter 3 contains SexBytes about Turner's syndrome and age of diagnosis (see page 73); transsexual athletes and professional sports (see page 88); and parenting and gender (see page 95). Chapter 6 contains SexBytes about the menstrual cycle and nonverbal communication (see page 166); gender and Internet usage (see page 168); and teenagers and tanning bed usage (see page 175). Chapter 10 contains SexBytes about the psychosocial aspects of orgasmic pleasure (see page 295); gender differences in sexual behaviors (see page 303); and masturbation and sperm concentration (see page 313). Chapter 11 contains SexBytes about civil unions and stress (see page 329); children and same-sex couple households (see page 332); and male homosexuality and family size (see page 334).

SEX Talk Questions

Throughout my many years of teaching this course, I have collected thousands of questions about sexuality from students. I have visited colleges and universities all over the world to better understand the questions that college students have today and how these questions might vary in the United States and farther afield. My search for these student questions has taken me as far away as New Zealand, Australia, Egypt, and Europe. I also receive questions about sexuality on my website—http://www.drjanellcarroll.com. Student questions are helpful in understanding what information students need. Examples include, *"Can you breastfeed if your nipples are pierced?"* and *"Do any animal species exhibit homosexual behaviors?"* These types of questions are the backbone of *Sexuality Now*.

In addition, the online student study tool *SexualityNow*™ (go to www.thomsonedu.com) includes an audio version of one Sex Talk question per chapter. These audio versions have a "student" audio response to a question, and then each individual student user has the ability to submit his or her own response.

Personal Voices

First-person accounts from both students and published sources appear in the Personal Voices feature. Personal Voices are included in most chapters to give students access to personal experiences of a variety of sexuality issues and their effects on people's lives—learning about sex, first intercourse, coming out, abortion, rape, sexual variations, and sex after a heart attack.

Human Sexuality in a Diverse World

One way students can challenge their assumptions about sexuality is by understanding how attitudes and practices vary across and among cultures. In addition to cross-cultural and multicultural information integrated into chapter material, Human Sexuality in a Diverse World features present accounts, some lighthearted and some serious, of topics such as Internet-based sex research, how we talk about love, sex education in Brazil and Europe, and reasons for divorce in several cultures.

Book Companion Website

On the book companion website for *Sexuality Now* you'll find a variety of polls and quizzes that students can take to evaluate their knowledge about topics such as nonverbal communication, homosexuality, and marriage. There are also inventories to measure attitudes and values about a variety of sexual issues, including abortion, communication patterns between partners, birth control, and rape.

Also on the website are interactive practice tests for each chapter to allow students to check their knowledge level after completing each chapter. The website also includes flashcards, an InfoTrac Reader, Web links, and Active Summary activities. Go to www.thomsonedu.com/carroll.

DISTINCTIVE CONTENT AND CHANGES BY CHAPTER

Chapter 1: Exploring Human Sexuality: Past and Present This chapter presents an in-depth look at the early evolution of human sexuality, including how sexuality was viewed by ancient Hebrews, Greeks, Romans, and throughout ancient Asian cultures. It also traces sexuality throughout history and examines how Christianity, the Middle Ages, Islam, the Renaissance, the Reformation, and the Victorian Era all have affected our views of sexuality. Chapter 1 also explores the impact of slavery, the free love movement, the social hygiene movement, feminism, and queer theory. It also:

- Introduces U.S. and global cultural diversity issues, including Gail Wyatt's groundbreaking work on African-American female sexuality and features cross-cultural research on Asian sexuality.
- Features a newly revised visual timeline that reviews the history of sexuality and television to provide students an overview of major television changes.

Chapter 2: Understanding Human Sexuality: Theory and Research This chapter contains comprehensive coverage of theories, research methods and issues, and landmark sexuality studies, which gives students the necessary background for understanding the theoretical basis of sexuality research, for evaluating that research, and for sorting out the "pop psychology" so prevalent in our society. It contains discussions of changing societal attitudes and how these attitudes have affected sexuality research; classic early researchers and theorists as well as less widely-known contributors—particularly female researchers; and modern trends, including Internet-based sexuality research. Chapter 2:

- Reviews major studies, both in the U.S. and worldwide, from age-specific studies such as the National Survey of Adolescent Males (NSAM) and more recent, broader studies, particularly the Pfizer Global Study of Sexual Attitudes and Behavior, the most comprehensive global study of sexuality ever done with responses from men and women in 28 countries (see page 55).
- Includes a newly revised visual timeline that reviews important developments in the history of sex research to provide students an overview of major developments, and a summary table of the major theories and a list of questions that each theorist would ask to help students conceptualize theoretical differences (see page 40).
- Contains a comprehensive exploration of the future of sexuality research, including current setbacks by governmental and religious institutions.

Chapter 3: Gender Development, Gender Roles, and Gender Identity
This chapter begins with prenatal sexual development and theories of gender development, which provides a springboard for the nature–nurture debate, including discussion of intersexuality. In addition, this chapter offers a comprehensive look at gender development, gender roles, and gender identity and contains a full review of important psychological theories and a newly designed summary table of the major theories. In this chapter you will find:

- Newly designed figures to help students understand complicated material.
- A complete review of congenital adrenal hyperplasia, including updated research and information.
- Inclusion of current large-scale studies, including the Land et al. study on gender and well-being, which reviewed data from various large and ongoing studies, federal surveys, and census and crime statistics from 1985–2001.
- Reviews of current, groundbreaking work on transgenderism and transexualism and the success of sex reassignment surgery, with cross-cultural information on sex reassignment surgery.

Chapter 4: Female Sexual Anatomy and Physiology
This chapter contains comprehensive coverage of the female sexual and reproductive system and includes information on diseases and conditions that affect the female reproductive organs—endometriosis, toxic shock syndrome, urinary tract infections, uterine fibroids, vulvodynia, vaginal infection, and the various cancers that affect the female reproductive organs.

- In response to reviewer and professor recommendations, female sexual anatomy and physiology is now presented before the male material.
- A review of polycystic ovarian syndrome is presented, including a Personal Voices feature from a student who was recently diagnosed (see page 125).
- Newly designed art presents clearer figures on the ovarian and menstrual cycle (page 116).
- Updated information is included on a variety of other current issues related to female sexual and reproductive health, including menstrual manipulation and suppression, vulvodynia, pubic hair removal, tattooing, female genital mutilation, and hormone replacement therapy.

Chapter 5: Male Sexual Anatomy and Physiology
This chapter contains comprehensive coverage of the male sexual and reproductive system and includes information on diseases and conditions that affect the male reproductive organs—testicular

torsion, cryptorchidism, priapism, Peyronie's disease, and the various cancers that affect the male reproductive organs. Other key changes include:

- Newly designed art and figures present clearer figures on the cycle of male hormones (page 143) and cryptorchidism (page 48).
- Exploration of the circumcision debate and cross-cultural and multicultural information on the impact of ethnicity and religion on circumcision.
- Updated information on body image problems in men, testicular cancer, and long- and short-term effects of anabolic–androgenic steroid use.

Chapter 6: Communication: Enriching Your Sexuality

Sexuality Now devotes an entire chapter to communication. In this chapter, you will find full coverage of learning to communicate, theories of communication, gender differences in communication, and nonverbal and computer-mediated communication. In addition, at the request of students, we have also included an in-depth section on enriching personal sexuality. *Sexuality Now* doesn't shy away from exploring intimate questions about personal sexuality. This chapter's coverage includes:

- A newly designed feature exploring gender and communication patterns (page 162).
- A new section exploring computer-mediated communication. It explores the use of the Internet, e-mails, chat rooms, and instant messaging and the impact of this technology on communication patterns (see page 166).
- New information on the influence of the menstrual cycle on a woman's ability to interpret nonverbal communication (page 166).

Chapter 7: Love and Intimacy

This chapter contains a review of theories of attraction and love, including life-span coverage and cross-cultural ideas of love and attraction. The chapter also addresses the relationship between love and sex, as well as trust, intimacy, respect, jealousy, compulsiveness, and possessiveness. Other new topics in this chapter include:

- New research on the major histocompatibility complex, pheromones, and brain imaging and their roles in the development of love (see pages 191 and 194).
- New research on neuroscience and a review of research on love and brain physiology and neurotransmitters (see page 198).
- New research on love and technology, exploring how the Internet, chat rooms, and instant messaging have changed love relationships on college campuses today (see page 201).

Chapter 8: Childhood and Adolescent Sexuality

This chapter explores physical and psychosexual development and sexual behavior from birth through early and middle childhood, preteen, and adolescent years. The discussion of adolescence also addresses the influence of family, peers, and religion. The last part of the chapter is devoted to sexuality education in the United States and elsewhere, describing various approaches and reviewing social and political influences, heterosexual bias, government mandates, and research measuring the effectiveness of sexuality education programs. This chapter also includes:

- Current ongoing governmental research into childhood sexuality, including the National Survey of Family Growth, National Longitudinal Study of Adolescent Males, National Longitudinal Study of Adolescent Health, and the Youth Risk Behavior Surveillance System, with a summary table that shows students the target populations and data methods these four studies used.
- Updated coverage of gay and lesbian teens, the coming-out process, and other experiences (see page 228).
- Research by the *National Campaign to Prevent Teenage Pregnancy* on the increasing popularity of oral sex in teenage populations and the risks of these behaviors (see page 233).

- Increased coverage of sexuality education, including abstinence-only education, and a review of sexuality education programs outside the United States (see page 247).

Chapter 9: Adult Sexual Relationships

This chapter explores dating, cohabitation, marriage, domestic partnerships, same-sex marriage, and divorce, as well as adult sexual relationships such as arranged marriages. It contains up-to-date material on same-sex marriage, including information on recent laws and changes in domestic partnerships and civil unions across the United States, as well as same-sex marriage policies in other countries and recent changes in the legalization of same-sex marriage. Other changes include:

- Updated information on marriage rates and ethnicity/race (see page 264), marital status by age (see page 269), and living arrangements by age and ethnicity/race (see page 270).
- Highlights of new changes in dating practices on college campuses, including hooking up, buddy sex, and casual dating (see page 256).
- Research on polyamory and a review of various types of polyamory (see page 272).

Chapter 10: Sexual Expression: Arousal and Response

Beginning with an in-depth look at the importance of hormones in sexual arousal and response, this chapter explores the factors that have been found to affect sexual expression and challenges assumptions about sexual behavior and attitudes. This chapter contains information on the sexual response cycle and research by Masters and Johnson, Helen Singer Kaplan, David Reed, and Leonore Tiefer. A variety of sexual behaviors are reviewed, including foreplay, manual sex, oral sex, masturbation, sexual intercourse, anal sex, and sexual fantasy. Information on physiological changes that occur with age and how these changes affect the sexual response cycle, and thus sexual functioning, is also presented. This chapter contains:

- Newly designed position art that gives this chapter a contemporary feel and generates more student interest.
- An exploration of hormones, ethnicity, religion, culture, and other factors that influence our sexuality and sexual behavior (see page 292).
- A review of contemporary criticisms of Masters & Johnson's sexual response cycle, including work by noted sex therapist, Leonore Tiefer (see page 300).
- Cross-cultural and multicultural coverage including information about Asian-American sexuality and how ethnicity affects the practice and frequency of sexual behaviors, sexual attitudes, and the ability to communicate about sex.

Chapter 11: Sexual Orientation

This chapter includes discussions of same-sex parents, transgenderism, and related issues, including our society's tendency toward heterocentrism. This chapter evaluates the biological research (genetics, hormones, birth order, and physiology), developmental theories (Freud, gender-role nonconformity, peer group interaction, and behaviorist theories), sociological, and interactional theories. Taking an essentialist and constructivist approach, the chapter provides a comprehensive review and comparison of theories. Also included are:

- Updated statistics on GLB behaviors, including updated information about heterosexism, homophobia, hate crimes, the coming-out process, and the coming out of Sheryl Swoopes (see page 357).
- An updated section exploring homosexuality and bisexuality in other cultures, and the important lessons that can be learned from these cultures. This includes a complete section on minority homosexuals, including Asian Americans and African Americans (see page 341).

Chapter 12: Pregnancy and Birth

This chapter reviews conception, sex selection, pregnancy signs, pregnancy testing, problems during pregnancy, and fetal development throughout the trimesters, with information on delivery and problems during the birth process. This chapter includes:

- A new visual timeline that summarizes the history of assisted reproduction (see page 376).
- New art throughout the chapter, helping students comprehend complicated materials. It also includes updated statistics on ethnicity/race with new figures on ethnicity/ race and birth (see page 368) and postpartum depression (see page 400).
- An updated Personal Voices feature from a single woman who underwent assisted reproduction and successfully gave birth (see page 380).

Chapter 13: Contraception and Abortion

Contraception and abortion are covered after pregnancy and birth so students have a clear understanding of hormonal and developmental physiological processes. Information on historical development in contraceptive research and a review of barrier, hormonal, chemical, natural, permanent, emergency, and ineffective methods is included. A review of the abortion debate and surgical and medical procedures is also included. Chapter 13 includes:

- Comprehensive coverage of contraceptive methods with updated statistics and information from the 18th Edition of *Contraceptive Technology*. An extensive section covers emergency contraception and methods being developed for men, along with updated information on the use of nonoxynol-9.
- A new table illustrating important events in the history of contraceptive development (see page 409) and a reworked figure providing at-a-glance statistics on contraceptive effectiveness, helping students understand effectiveness rates of various methods (see page 408). New figures illustrate U.S. and global contraceptive method choices (see page 414) and ethnicity/race and contraceptive choices (see page 411).
- Updated research on medical abortion, including research on the use of Mifepristone and Methotrexate (see page 447).

Chapter 14: Challenges to Sexual Functioning

Chapter 14 includes a thorough review of sexual dysfunction including DSM-IV-TR information with details on symptoms, causes, and treatment options, and updated information on pharmaceutical treatments for erectile functioning, including the newest Viagra competitors. It also includes a full review of illness, disability, and sexual functioning. In Chapter 14 you will find:

- A newly designed table summarizing the various sexual dysfunctions (see page 463).
- Groundbreaking new research into female sexual dysfunction with an exploration of the pros and cons of pharmaceutical treatment of female dysfunctions.
- Updated research and information about women and sexual dysfunction, including Leonore Tiefer's *New View of Female Sexuality* (see page 462).
- Updated material on the treatment of sexual dysfunction outside the United States (see page 465).

Chapter 15: Sexually Transmitted Infections and HIV/AIDS

This chapter contains information on attitudes about sexually transmitted infections and reviews the various infections. A complete review of HIV and AIDS is also included, and a section on the global aspects of AIDS looks at worldwide issues. This chapter:

- Presents current information on sexually transmitted infections and HIV, including the September 2005 *Centers for Disease Control Surveillance Report* on sexually transmitted infections and the November 2005 *UNAIDS Global Survey*. A review of STI vaccine development is also included.
- Reviews current research into microbicides and the importance of these products in reducing sexually transmitted infections and includes the 2005 *Centers for Disease Control Fact Sheets and Treatment Guidelines for STDs*.
- Updates the impact of ethnicity/race and sexually transmitted infections (see pages 497, 502, 503, 506, and 520).

- Updates global coverage of the AIDS epidemic, including current information on infections in women and children (see page 525).

Chapter 16: Varieties of Sexual Expression

Chapter 16: Varieties of Sexual Expression This chapter explores how sexual behaviors are classified, beginning with a review of typical and atypical sexual behaviors that includes an extensive theoretical explanation of paraphilias, including biological, psychoanalytic, developmental, behavioral, and sociological theories. Chapter 16:

- Updates all the DSM-IV-TR diagnoses for paraphilias and sexual addiction.
- Contains updated coverage of sexual offender registries, pedophilia, and Megan's Law.
- Helps students relate to the chapter material with Personal Voices of college students who discuss variations in sexual behavior and one student's masochism. Personal Voices are also included from a cross-dresser, a victim of an obscene phone caller, a pedophile, and a rubber fetishist.

Chapter 17: Power and Sexual Coercion

Chapter 17: Power and Sexual Coercion Beginning with definitions and an overview of rape and sexual assault, this chapter reviews theories of rape. It also examines gender differences in attitudes about rape, rape on campus, date-rape drugs, and the rape of men; offers guidance on reporting and avoiding rape; explores partner reaction to rape; and describes rapist treatment. This chapter also has:

- A comprehensive discussion of rape on college campuses, using data from the 2005 *U.S. Criminal Victimization Statistical Tables*, published by the U.S. Bureau of Justice Statistics. It reviews the incidence of rape, how rape occurs on campus, and the relationship between alcohol use and rape. It also discusses fraternities and athletics and how these variables are related to rape on college campuses.
- Material on the evolutionary theory of the practice of rape and a review of research from Randy Thornhill and Craig Palmer, authors of *Natural History of Rape: Biological Bases of Sexual Coercion*.
- A new table on ages of consent both within and outside the United States. It also contains updated information and review of date-rape drugs, the incidence and effects of rape and sexual abuse, and post-traumatic stress disorder.
- An exploration of issues of intimate partner violence in both heterosexual and same-sex relationships, stalking, sexual harassment, and cyber-harassment on college campuses.

Chapter 18: Sexual Images and Selling Sex

Chapter 18: Sexual Images and Selling Sex Chapter 18 presents full historical coverage of erotic representations and the invention of pornography, erotic literature, television and films, advertising, and the sex industry. This chapter reviews the portrayal of minority and GLBTQ, sexuality in the media and contains full coverage of prostitution, including definitions, types of prostitution, predisposing factors, and prostitution and the law. Cross-cultural and global coverage reviews prostitution both inside and outside the United States. Chapter 18 includes:

- Material from the 2005 Henry J. Kaiser Family Foundation study *Sex on TV4*, which identifies and analyzes the messages about sex and sexual behavior that are presented on television today (see pages 607–608).
- Updated information on online pornography and pornography on portable devices including cell phones, iPods, and other devices (see pages 614 and 622).
- The Henry J. Kaiser Family Foundation 2005 report entitled *Generation M: Media in the Lives of 8–18-Year-Olds*, which detailed the use of various media in 2,000 8 to 18-year-olds (see page 610).
- Research from Pamela Paul's 2005 *Pornified: How Pornography Is Transforming Our Lives, Our Relationships, and Our Families* (see pages 621, 623, and 642).
- Increased coverage of global prostitution including a feature exploring sexual trafficking (see page 636).

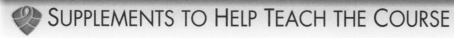

SUPPLEMENTS TO HELP TEACH THE COURSE

SexualityNow™

0-495-17089-5

Empower your students with the first assessment-centered student tutorial system for Human Sexuality. Seamlessly tied to the new edition of this text, this powerful and interactive Web-based learning tool helps students gauge their unique study needs, then gives them a Personalized Learning Plan that focuses their study time on the concepts they most need to master. Within the learning modules are animations, video panels for review, and Sex Talk Questions with audio responses from students. *SexualityNow* quizzes were written by Margit Berman, University of Minnesota. Visit www.thomsonedu.com.

WebTutor™ Advantage

WebTutor Advantage on WebCT: 0-495-17087-9
WebTutor Advantage on Blackboard: 0-495-17088-7

Creating an engaging e-learning environment is easier than ever with *WebTutor Advantage*. Save time building or Web-enhancing your course, posting course materials, incorporating multimedia, tracking progress, and more with this customizable, engaging course management tool. *WebTutor Advantage* saves you time and enhances your students' learning—pairing advanced course management capabilities with text-specific learning tools. View a demo at http://webtutor.thomsonlearning.com.

JoinIn™ on TurningPoint®

0-495-17097-6

Turn your lecture into an interactive experience for your students, using "clickers." Thomson Wadsworth is pleased to offer you book-specific *JoinIn*™ content from *Sexuality Now: Embracing Diversity, Second Edition* for classroom response systems, allowing you to transform your classroom and assess your students' progress with instant in-class quizzes and polls. Our exclusive agreement to offer *TurningPoint®* software lets you pose book-specific questions and display students' answers seamlessly within the Microsoft® PowerPoint® slides of your own lecture, in conjunction with the "clicker" hardware of your choice. Enhance your students' interactions with you, your lecture, and each other. It includes questions specifically written on the Virtual Safer-Sex kit and Centers for Disease Control and Prevention STD Clinical Slides. Students can also "participate" in polls and surveys from the text. *For college and university adopters only. Contact your local Thomson representative to learn more.*

Study Guide written by Shirley Ogletree, University of Texas, San Marcos
0-495-17086-0

For each chapter of Janell Carroll's text, the *Study Guide* contains a chapter summary, a list of learning objectives, a detailed chapter outline, personal assessments and activities, a paper assignment, 15 fill-in-the-blank and 5 short-answer questions per main subhead, labeling of anatomic art in appropriate chapters, and a post-test consisting of 10 true/false, 30 multiple-choice, and 10 matching quiz questions covering the entire chapter. The answers, rejoinders, and main text page references for all quiz items will be included at the end of each chapter.

InfoTrac® College Edition

Free with this text! InfoTrac College Edition is an ideal way to give your students access to scholarly, peer-reviewed, advertising-free research sources. This extensive resource includes some of the most highly respected journals in human sexuality, such as *Archives of Sexual Behavior, Journal of Sex Research, Sex Roles, Canadian Journal of Human Sexuality,* and a number of AIDS-specific and other health journals (such as *AIDS Weekly*).

Book Companion Website

www.thomsonedu.com/carroll

There is a substantial collection of online resources, featuring:

- "Where Do I Stand?" polls for each chapter. These attitude polls are scored and compared against national averages.
- Other polls including "What Would You Do?," "Personal Sexual Expression," and "Variations in Sexual Behaviors."
- A Practice Quiz with online scoring for each chapter, including multiple-choice, true-false, and short essay questions, as well as a final exam. Engaging critical thinking questions are also included.
- Active Summary activities using the active summaries from the book.
- Chapter outlines and objectives.
- An online Pronunciation Glossary of all margin terms from the main text.
- Web links, flashcards, and InfoTrac® College Edition activities.
- PowerPoint® Lecture Slides—a sample of what's available on the Multimedia Manager Instructor's Resource CD.

Instructor's Manual with Test Bank

0-495-17091-7

This comprehensive, easy-to-customize three-ring binder gives you all the support you need to run an effective course, including:

Instructor's Manual written by Teri Tomatich, Kennesaw State University.

- A comprehensive film and video guide that provides extensive listings of what Wadsworth provides as well as descriptions of suggested videos with their running times and suppliers.
- A resource integration guide that shows, at a glance, how all of this text's supplements can be used with each chapter of the text.
- A detailed outline and learning objectives for each chapter of the text.
- Two to four classroom activities or demonstrations per text chapter, some of which use websites and other resources.
- Two questions designed for online discussions and two to five additional annotated Web links per text chapter.
- Opposing Viewpoints Resource Center activities and writing assignments.
- InfoTrac Virtual Reader exercises.
- Lecture and discussion tie-ins for the text's SexBytes and Sex Talk questions that get students to think critically about sexuality.

Test Bank written by Debra Hull, Wheeling Jesuit University and John H. Hull, Bethany College. The *Test Bank* features 50 multiple-choice questions, 15 true/false items, and 8–15 short-answer/essay questions for every chapter of the text. Answers, with text page references, are provided for all items.

Examview®

0-495-17092-5

Quickly create customized tests that can be delivered in print or online. *Examview's* simple "what you see is what you get" interface allows you to generate tests of up to 250 items easily. All *Test Bank* questions are electronically pre-loaded.

Multimedia Manager Instructor's Resource CD-ROM written by Alishia Huntoon, Oregon Institute of Technology.

This CD-ROM contains customizable Microsoft PowerPoint® presentations that include detailed lecture outlines, artwork from the text, Centers for Disease Control and Prevention STD Clinical Slides, video clips and animations, as well as a Virtual Safer-Sex Kit that lets you easily show contraceptive devices in class. To make course preparation even easier, the CD-ROM contains simple instructions on how to embed the animations and videos into your PowerPoint Slides. It also contains the entire contents of the *Instructor's Manual with Test Bank* binder in an electronic format!

New to this edition of the Multimedia Manager:

- Images of various types of sex toys.
- Animations and panel-discussion videos.
- Centers for Disease Control and Prevention STD Clinical Slides to supplement your STI lectures.
- Animations of the sexual response cycle for lectures of biological processes.

 ## NOTE TO THE STUDENT

Campus life is different today than it was when I was in college. I graduated from college in 1982 and, although that really wasn't all that long ago (I realize that many of you reading this weren't even born yet, but it honestly doesn't feel as though it was that long ago), my experience in college was probably very different from yours. For one thing, you have the Internet. While we had computers (although no one owned his or her own), we didn't have access to all the information that you have on the Web. The Internet has forever changed how we view sexuality. Instant messaging, chat rooms, and cyber-relationships weren't around in the early '80s. I overhear my students deciphering and explaining their IMs from various friends and lovers. My friends and I didn't have VCRs, DVDs, or iPods so, unlike the majority of students today who tell me they've seen at least one pornographic tape, we never watched any in college. Times were different—we didn't pierce our navels, use tanning beds, talk on cell phones, use emergency contraception, watch reality television, or know what a Brazilian wax was!

College *is* different today and college textbooks also need to reflect these changes. The book you are holding in your hands is contemporary and fun. I think you'll find it easy to keep up with the reading in this class because I've really worked hard to keep the material fresh and thought-provoking. I've included lots of personal stories from students just like you to help in your exploration and understanding of human sexuality. The result is a book that talks to students like yourself, answering questions *you* have about sexuality.

As you read through the book, if you have any questions, thoughts, or opinions you'd like to share with me, I'd love to hear from you. Many students email me and suggest additions, changes, or just share their thoughts about this book. You can email me at jcarroll@hartford.edu, or contact me through my website, http://www.drjanellcarroll.com. You can also send snail mail to Dr. Janell L. Carroll, University of Hartford, Department of Psychology, 200 Bloomfield Avenue, West Hartford, CT 06117.

 ## ACKNOWLEDGMENTS

Undertaking a book such as this is a huge task and one that I could never have done without the help of many smart, creative, and fun people. Recognition should first go to all my students who, over the years, have opened themselves up to me and felt comfortable enough to share intimate, and sometimes painful, details of their lives. I know that their voices throughout this book will help students truly understand the complexity of human sexuality.

Second, and of equal importance, a big thank you goes to my family, who helped me pull off the Second Edition. I couldn't have done it without their support and encouragement. They understood my crazy schedule and worked hard to help make life manageable in our household. My husband was an endless support in a million ways and allowed me to constantly interrupt him for statistical and mathematical clarifications. My children also helped me pull this together and through the process have continued to learn—I am certain they will all grow up with a true understanding of the importance of sexuality in their lives. In addition, my extended family deserves a great deal of thanks, including Susanne, Bob and Janice, Rheta and Gordon, and other family members and relatives who provided a wealth of long-distance support throughout the entire project. As in all projects of such magnitude, there are hundreds of others who supported me with friendship, advice, information, laughter, and a focus on the "big picture."

The Second Edition of *Sexuality Now* is truly the result of a team effort—and the team was fantastic. My Senior Editor, Marianne Taflinger, deserves more thanks than I can ever give her. Her vision of *Sexuality Now* helped give it new life. Marianne has been a constant source of support and encouragement throughout both editions of this book. She also helped assemble one of the best Second Edition teams ever put together. A big thank you goes to Kristin Makarewycz, Developmental Editor, who has been terrific— her tireless efforts, insights, and suggestions helped make *Sexuality Now* all it could be. Lori Johnson, Editorial Production Project Manager, was at the helm, calmly and gracefully keeping everything and everyone on track. Mary Anne Shahidi was by far the best copyeditor I have ever worked with. Ellen Brownstein, Chapter Two Editoral Production Services, was the cherry on the top of the sundae. She also helped manage the details, gently keeping us all on track under tremendous time pressures. There are numerous others whose help was invaluable, including Chris Caldeira, Dory Schaeffer, Vernon Boes, Darin Derstine, Jennifer Alexander, Lucy Faridany, Roman Barnes, Sarah Harkrader, Gary Clark of Graphic World, and Diane Beasley of Diane Beasley Design. You guys are the best. I will look forward to a long and productive relationship with everyone at Wadsworth/Thomson Learning.

And thank you to the many others who so willingly gave their time and/or support, especially students, Kareem Allwood, Caitlin Bailey, Kevin Ball, Lisa Belval, Becky Czlapinski, Rachel Gearhart, Jillian Goldberg, Jamie Graves, Cherry Hodges, Alan Kelley, Joanna Melon, Steve Michaud, Elizabeth Murphy, Robert Oswald, Todd Rice, Kris Rochette, Ashley Seiffert, Kara and Krista Tesoriero, Pricilla Thorn, Christianne Wolfson, Ebony Wright, and Christine Zuendt. A big thanks goes to Lisa Belval and Kris Rochette for their special contributions to this Second Edition. Also thank you to my colleagues and friends, without whom this would not have been possible, including Kim Acquaviva, Genevieve Ankeny, Demetrius Bagley, Caryn Christensen, Maxine Chuck, Bob Conover, Barb Curry, Keith D'Angelo, Ken Decker, Karen Hicks, David Holmes, Peg Horne, Will Hosler, Petra Lambert, Lisa Lepito, Carole Mackenzie, Megan Mahoney, Konnie McCaffree, Mike Morrow, Kirsten Neptun, Leslie Obrizzo, Robyn Oches, Monica Rodriguez, Debbie Schiltz, Maryann Schuppe, Diana Shanley, Bill Stayton, Toby, Peterson Toscano, the Tsacoyeanes family, Meghan Waskowitz, Laurie Watters, Gracemarie Welter, John and Nina Whitnah, and Rand Ziegler.

I also want to thank Maxine Effensen Chuck and Paul Root Wolpe whose original hard work helped lay some of the groundwork for this textbook. Maxine has been an endless support system throughout all of our years of friendship and it would have been hard to have done this Second Edition without her. I also am grateful to Paul for his support and understanding in this ongoing endeavor.

I would also like to thank all the authors of our Second Edition supplements: Shirley Ogletree, Teri Tomatich, Debra Hull, John H. Hull, Margit Berman, and Alishia Huntoon. As good as a textbook can be, it is only one piece of the teaching puzzle.

Finally, it is important to acknowledge the contributions of the reviewers who have carefully read my manuscript and offered many helpful suggestions. I would like to thank them all for their time and dedication to this project.

Second Edition Reviewers

Katherine Allen, Virginia Polytechnic Institute and State University; Glenn Carter, Austin Peay State University; Cindi Ceglian, South Dakota State; Nancy Daley, University of Texas; Joe Fanelli, Syracuse University; Jorge Figueroa, University of North Carolina, Wilmington; Anne Fisher, New College of Florida; Lois Goldblatt, Arizona State University; Helen Hoch, New Jersey City University; Susan Horton, Mesa Community College; Alicia Huntoon, Washington State University; Bobby Hutchison, Modesto Junior College; Ingrid Johnston-Robledo, SUNY at Fredonia; Jody

Martin de Camilo, St. Louis Community College, Meramec; Laura Miller, Edinboro University; Jennifer Musick, Long Beach City College; Robin Musselman, Lehigh Carbon Community College; Shirley Ogletree, Texas State University, San Marcos; Lisabeth Searing, University of Illinois, Urbana-Champaign; Kandy Stahl, Stephen F. Austin State University; Dana Stone, Virginia Polytechnic Institute and State University; Karen Vail-Smith, East Carolina University; Mary Ann Watson, Metropolitan State College of Denver; Tanya Whipple Missouri State University; Susan Wycoff, California State University, Sacramento.

Second Edition Specialist Reviewers

Talia Ben-Zeev, Ph.D., University of California, San Francisco; Leah Millheiser Ettinger, M.D., Stanford University; Cheryl Walker, M.D., University of California, Davis; Vicki Mays, Ph.D., University of California, Los Angeles.

First Edition Reviewers

Michael Agopian, Los Angeles Harbor College; Veanne Anderson, Indiana State University; Amy Baldwin, Los Angeles City College; Sharon Ballard, East Carolina University; Jim Backlund, Kirtland Community College; Sally Conklin, Northern Illinois University; David Corbin, University of Nebraska, Omaha; Michael Devoley, Northern Arizona University; Jim Elias, California State University, Northridge; Sussie Eshun, East Stroudsburg University; Linda Evinger, University of Southern Indiana; Randy Fisher, University of Central Florida; Sue Frantz, Highline Community College; David Gershaw, Arizona Western College; Lois Goldblatt, Arizona State University; Anne Goshen, California Polytechnic State University, San Luis Obispo; Kevin Gross, East Carolina University; Gary Gute, University of Northern Iowa; Shelley Hamill, Winthrop University; Robert Hensley, Iowa State University; Roger Herring, University of Arkansas, Little Rock; Karen Hicks, CAPE; Karen Howard, Endicott College; Lisa Hoffman-Konn, The University of Arizona; Kathleen Hunter, SUNY College at Brockport; Shelli Kane, Nassau Community College; Joanne Karpinen, Hope College; Chrystyna Kosarchyn, Longwood College; Holly Lewis, University of Houston–Downtown; Kenneth Locke, University of Idaho; Betsy Lucal, Indiana University, South Bend; Laura Madson, New Mexico State University; Sue McKenzie, Dawson College; Mikki Meadows, Eastern Illinois University; Corey Miller, Wright State University; Carol Mukhopadhyay, San Jose State University; Jennifer Musick, Long Beach Community College; Missi Patterson, Austin Community College; Julie Penley, El Paso Community College; Robert Pettit, Manchester College; Judy Reitan, University of California, Davis; William Robinson, Purdue University Calumet; Jeff Wachsmuth, Napa Valley College; Mary Ann Watson, Metropolitan State College of Denver; Kelly Wilson, Texas A & M University; and Midge Wilson, DePaul University.

First Edition Specialist Reviewers

In-depth reviewers of Chapter 15, Sexually Transmitted Infections and HIV/AIDS: Thomas Coates, University of California San Francisco AIDS Research Institute; and Linda Koenig, Centers for Disease Control and Prevention.

In-depth reviewer of Chapter 12, Pregnancy and Birth, and Chapter 13, Contraception and Abortion: Valerie Wiseman, University of Connecticut Medical Center, Department of Obstetrics and Gynecology.

First Edition Focus Group Participants

Also thanks to all the Focus Group participants, including: Jennifer Musick, Long Beach City College; Jonathan Karpf, San Jose State University; Kathie Zaretsky, San Jose State University; Beverly Whipple, Rutgers University; and Lisa Schwartz, St. Joseph's College.

Culture Index

Gender Index

1

Exploring Human Sexuality: Past and Present

Sexuality Now Go to www.thomsonedu.com to link to
SexualityNow, your online study tool.

*S*exuality is mysterious and exciting. How come as you read this page you feel more excitement about this course than any other course you have this semester? Everyone likes to learn about sex, especially when you consider that we live in a sex-saturated society that uses sexuality to sell everything from cologne to automobiles. But we also live in a time when there is a taboo against good, honest information about human sexuality. Some people believe that providing sexuality information can cause problems—including increased teenage sexual activity and adolescent pregnancy rates. Others believe that learning about sexuality can empower students to make healthy decisions both today and in the future. Although human sexuality courses were rare on college campuses even 20 years ago, today they are not only common but popular as well.

Many recent events have profoundly affected the way we view sexuality. From the overwhelming popularity of Viagra™, to the horror and shock of the terrorist attacks and natural disasters, our newspapers have been full of stories relating to our sexuality and relationships with others. The pain and sadness of 9/11 and the devastating South Asia tsunami of 2004 taught us much about survival, relationships, intimacy, love, and grief. The continuing controversy over same-sex marriage and child pornography along with ever increasing HIV/AIDS rates also help to shape our sexuality. In addition, we live in a society full of sexual images and events. All of these factors influence our sexuality.

In this opening chapter, we begin by exploring human sexuality, both present and past. First we will define sexuality and look at the goals both you and your professor have for this course. Then we will examine sexual images in our culture and the effect of the media's preoccupation with sex. A historical exploration of sexuality will follow, in which we will explore the early evolution of human sexuality from walking erect to ancient civilizations. Following that, we will look at religion's role in sexuality and examine some of the early sexual reform movements.

HUMAN SEXUALITY IN A DIVERSE WORLD

Human sexuality is grounded in biological functioning, emerges in each of us as we develop, and is expressed by cultures through rules about sexual contact, attitudes about moral and immoral sexuality, habits of sexual behavior, patterns of relations between the sexes, and so on.

Only Human: What Is Sexuality?

The sexual nature of human beings is unique in the animal kingdom. Although many of our fellow creatures also display complex sexual behaviors, only human beings have gone beyond instinctual mating rituals to create ideas, laws, customs, fantasies, and art around the sexual act. In other words, although sexual intercourse is common in the animal kingdom, **sexuality** is a uniquely human trait.

Sexuality is studied by "sexologists," who specialize in understanding our sexuality, but also by biologists, psychologists, physicians, anthropologists, historians, sociologists, political scientists, those concerned with public health, and many other people in scholarly disciplines. For example, political scientists may study how sexuality reflects social power; powerful groups may have more access to sexual partners or use their legislative power to restrict the sexual behaviors of less powerful groups.

There are few areas of human life that seem as contradictory and confusing as sexuality. We come from a society that is often called sexually "repressed," yet images of sex-

sexbyte

When praying mantises mate, the male jumps on the back of the female. The female will often turn around and eat the head of the male during copulation. The male's body will complete copulation, after which the female will eat the remainder of the male (Watkins & Bessin, 2005).

sexuality
A general term for the feelings and behaviors of human beings concerning sex.

uality are all around us. We tend to think that everyone else is "doing it"; still, we are often uncomfortable talking about sex. Some feel that we should all be free to explore our sexuality; others believe that there should be strong moral restrictions around sexual behavior. To some, only sex between a man and a woman is natural and acceptable; others believe that all kinds of sexual expression are equally "natural" and valid. Many people find it puzzling that others find sexual excitement by wearing rubber, exposing themselves in public, or by being humiliated or spanked. Although parents teach their children about safe driving, fire safety, and safety around strangers, many are profoundly uncomfortable instructing their children on safe sexual practices.

Review Question

Explain how sexuality can be both contradictory and confusing, and provide one example of how this might be so.

Why Are We Here? Goals for the Human Sexuality Course

Think for a moment about your goals for taking this course. Are you here because you want to learn more about sex? Could it be that you've had a less-than-ideal sex life so far and you want to improve it? Is it because you want to learn to be a good lover? Students come to sexuality courses for a variety of different reasons. What are your reasons? Like you, instructors have goals for this course. They want you to:

- develop a broad and accurate knowledge base about sexuality
- be willing to examine your own beliefs, assumptions, and opinions, and compare and contrast them to relevant facts using a critical thinking paradigm
- understand the various influences on the development of your sexual knowledge, attitudes, relationships, and behaviors
- have a clear understanding of society's attempts to regulate your sexuality
- identify trends and changes that have influenced your sexual attitudes and values
- understand the biological basis and the complex political, media-related, and ethical issues of sexuality
- become more comfortable talking about sex

As you go through this semester, keep these goals in mind to help you understand the rationale for some of the activities, lectures, guest speakers, and videos you'll see.

Sneak Peek

"Before you draw conclusions about Republicans and Democrats, keep in mind that this survey could be more about gender than about political party."—*Politics, Religion, and Sexual Expression*

Sexuality Now

Sex Sells: The Impact of the Media

Modern life is full of visual media. Magazines, newspapers, book covers, CD and DVD packaging, cereal boxes, and food products—even medicines are adorned with pictures of people, scenes, or products. Advertisements peer at us from billboards, buses, matchbook covers, and anywhere else that advertisers can buy space. Television, movies, computers, and other moving visual images surround us almost everywhere we go, and we will only depend upon them more as information technology continues to develop. We live in a visual culture whose images we simply cannot escape.

Many of these images are subtly or explicitly sexual. Barely clothed females and shirtless, athletic males are so common in ads that we scarcely notice them anymore. The majority of movies today, even some of those directed at children, have sexual scenes that would not even have been permitted in movie theaters 50 years ago. The humor in television situation comedies has become more and more sexual, and nudity has begun to appear on prime-time network television shows. American media are the most sexually suggestive in the Western hemisphere (Kunkel et al., 2005).

Sex is all over television today—from *The O.C.* to *The Real World*. Shows use sex to lure viewers in. The basis of "dating" reality shows, such as *The Bachelor* and *The Bachelorette*, is sex. Talk show hosts such as Jerry Springer and Maury Povich seek out unconventional guests, many of whom have sexual issues (common show themes include topics such as *Don't Deny It, You're Sleeping Around* or *I Had Sex with Two Sisters, Am I Their Babies' Daddy?*). Other shows, like *Real Sex, Taxicab Confessions*, and even *Sex in the City* reruns, don't beat around the bush—they talk about graphic sexual issues. A newer genre of reality shows such as *The Swan, Extreme Makeover*, or *Dr. 90210* show us that we can achieve physical perfection through plastic surgery. What messages do these types of shows send? What do they teach us about sexuality?

sex byte

Significant gender differences have been found in teenage magazine content. The majority of magazines for teen girls are about beauty, cosmetics, people, and relationships, whereas magazines for teen boys focus on video games, sports, cars, music, and other hobbies (Kaiser Family Foundation, 2004).

How Do You Decide What Sex You'll Engage In?

All sexually active human beings make decisions about when, where, and with whom they will engage in sexual activity. For most people, at least part of that decision is based on their views of what behaviors are morally acceptable, which may be derived from their religious beliefs, their upbringing, or personal decisions about the kind of person they want to be. For example, some people would not have sex with a partner they did not love, perhaps because they feel it is meaningless, immoral, or against God's wishes; others find it acceptable if both partners are willing and go into the encounter openly and freely. There are few areas of life in which moral principles are so clearly and commonly debated. Why is it that sexuality evokes so strong a moral response in us?

The sexual behavior of human beings differs from all other animals in part because of our moral, religious, legal, and interpersonal values. How simple it seems for animals, who mate without caring about marriage, pregnancy, or hurting their partner's feelings! Human beings are not (typically) so casual about mating; every culture has developed elaborate rituals, rules, laws, and moral principles that structure sexual relations. The very earliest legal and moral codes archaeologists have uncovered discuss sexual behavior at great length, and rules about sexual behavior make up a great part of the legal and ethical codes of the world's great civilizations and religions.

Sexuality is a basic drive, and it is one of the few that involves intimate, one-on-one interaction with another person's basic needs. We may eat next to each other, but we each feed only ourselves. Conflicts may arise when our own needs, feelings, fears, and concerns are not the same as our partner's. People can be hurt, used, and taken advantage of sexually, or be the victim of honest miscommunication, especially because sex is so difficult for many people to discuss.

Sexuality is also closely related to the formation of love bonds and to procreation. Every society has a stake in procreation, for without adequate numbers of people a society can languish, and with too many people a society can be overwhelmed. Most societies create rules to prevent accidental births and births that do not fit conventional family structures (such as "illegitimate" births). Societies also formulate sexual rules to control the size of their population (such as the outlawing of contraception or abortion in cultures that want to encourage childbirth, or distributing free contraception and free abortions, as they do in modern China, when the population gets too high).

Another reason sexuality and ethics are so closely linked is because the sexual drive emerges relatively late in life. Think about it—you've been eating, sleeping, loving, communicating, and otherwise exercising most of your basic drives since you were an infant. However, genital-based sexuality did not emerge in its present form until somewhere around puberty. You had to learn to cope with these new feelings at the very time that you were learning to cope with being an adult, establishing independence from parents, and forming your own identity.

There are certainly other possible explanations for the moral and ethical standards that have developed around sexual behavior. Why do you think morality and sexuality are so closely bound?

Reality makeover shows, such as Dr. 90210, The Swan, *and* Extreme Makeover *play upon our physical insecurities. Television, movies, and advertising often brainwash us into believing that we can achieve the perfect body and look with a little help from a plastic surgeon. How far would you go to look like this woman?*

We know what makes you feel good.

What message do you get from this advertisement? Can you tell what product they are trying to sell? Do you think sex helps sell this product?

Sexuality is an important component of each of us, but it is also one of the most difficult aspects for us to express and explore (McKenna, Green, & Smith, 2001). Social norms, embarrassment, and fear hold us back from expressing many of our sexual needs and desires. However, the Internet is changing patterns of social communication and relationships (Griffiths, 2001). People now have access to sexual information and are able to express various aspects of their sexuality online without the fear of negative responses. The popularity of the Internet for gathering sex information continues to grow.

Countless websites offer information, provide advice, and answer questions on sexuality today. Sexual paraphernalia (such as vibrators or sex toys), pornographic picture libraries, videos and video clips, and access to a variety of personal webcam sites can be purchased online (Griffiths, 2000), and a variety of chat rooms cater to just about any conceivable fantasy. More than 8,000 chat rooms devoted to sex can be found at any given time of day or night (McKenna et al., 2001). The Internet allows for anonymity and provides the freedom to ask questions, seek answers, and talk to others about sexual issues.

Teenagers rate the media as one of their leading sources of sex information (behind school sex education programs; Kunkel et al., 2005), yet much of this information is not very educational. Each year the average American adolescent is exposed to nearly 14,000 sexual references in the media, but very few of these references have anything to do with contraception, **sexually transmitted infections (STIs),** or pregnancy risk. Even though sexual information in the media is often inaccurate, unrealistic, and misleading, many young people accept it as fact.

What is the effect of living in a society that is so saturated with sexual references and images? How do these messages subtly affect the way we think about our own sexuality? The sexuality of others? As you read about various aspects of sexuality covered in this text, keep this media saturation in mind.

sexually transmitted infection (STI)
Infection that is transmitted from one person to another through sexual contact. This used to be called sexually transmitted disease (STD) or venereal disease (VD).

Review Question

Identify some of the ways we learn about sexuality, and give two reasons for questioning the accuracy of these sources.

SEX Talk

Question: *The other day as I was reading a* Details *magazine, I was amazed at how sexual the advertising was. Sometimes when I look at ads like these, all I see is half-naked women straddling some guys. Don't get me wrong, I don't mind looking at that kind of stuff, but many times I can't even tell what the ad is for. Sometimes the ad is for jeans but no one in the picture has jeans on! Just how does an ad like this sell jeans?*

Ahhh, you ask a very important question. Advertisers know that consumers are emotional beings. When half-naked men or women in ads wear a pair of jeans, it arouses us and helps us to associate the jeans with passion. Suddenly we need the jeans because we want to be sexy too, just like the model in the ad. So, even when the advertised item isn't in the ad, we associate the feeling the ad generates with a particular item or brand name.

We will now turn our attention to the history of human sexuality, from prehistoric times to the present. Of course, in the space of one chapter, we cannot begin to cover the variety and richness of human sexual experience. Hopefully this overview will give you an idea of how varied human cultures are, while also showing that human beings throughout history have had to grapple with the same sexual issues that confront us in American society today.

◈ THE EARLY EVOLUTION OF HUMAN SEXUALITY

Our ape ancestors began walking upright over 3 million years ago, according to recent fossil records. Before that, our ancestors were mostly **quadrupeds** (KWA-drew-peds) who stood only for brief moments—as baboons do now—to survey the terrain. The

quadruped
Any animal that walks on four legs.

evolution of an upright posture changed forever the way the human species engaged in sexual intercourse.

Stand Up and Look Around: Walking Erect

In an upright animal, eyesight becomes more important than the sense of smell. When the male genitals and female breasts became more visible, sexual attraction began shifting from the sense of smell to visual stimuli. In an upright posture, the male genitals are rotated to the front of the body, so merely approaching someone involves displaying the genitals. The human male has the largest penis of all primates—the chimpanzee penis averages about three inches, and the gorilla's half that (Margulis & Sagan, 1991). Because male confrontation often involved acts of aggression, the **phallus**—the male symbol of sex and potency—became associated with displays of aggression. In other words, upright posture may have also contributed to a new tie between sexuality and aggression (Rancour-Laferriere, 1985).

The upright posture of the female also emphasized her breasts and hips, and the rotation of the female pelvis forward (the vagina faces the rear in most quadrupeds) also resulted in the possibility of face-to-face intercourse. Because more body area is in contact in face-to-face intercourse than in rear entry, the entire sensual aspect of intercourse was enhanced, manipulation of the breasts became possible (the breasts are sexual organs only in humans), and the female clitoris was much more easily stimulated. Only in human females does orgasm seem to be a common part of sexual contact.

phallus
Term used to refer to the penis as a symbol of power and aggression.

SEXTalk

Question: *Do female primates experience orgasm?*

Yes, some do, though it is relatively rare compared to human females. Female primates rarely masturbate, though occasionally they stimulate themselves manually during intercourse. Bonobos (pygmy chimpanzees) do have face-to-face intercourse on occasion and may reach orgasm. However, most chimpanzees engage in rear-entry intercourse, a position that does not favor female orgasm (Margulis & Sagan, 1991).

homo sapiens
The technical name for the species that all human beings belong to.

About 200,000 years ago, **Homo sapiens** appeared on the scene. We do not know much about how these early ancestors behaved or what they believed. However, anthropological evidence suggests that they developed monogamous relations and lived in fairly stable sexual pairings (Margulis & Sagan, 1991).

Timeline: Television

1927	1930	1939	1946	1947	1950
Philo T. Fransworth develops the first black-and-white television set.	*The Association of Motion Pictures* devises a rating code to govern events portrayed in motion pictures.	Television makes its debut when the Radio Corporation of America (RCA) brings it to the World's Fair in New York City. Here the first televised presidential debate with Franklin D. Roosevelt is shown.	First color television set is presented to the Federal Communications Commissions (FCC).	Sitcom *Mary Kay and Johnny* shows first married couple in bed together.	Sitcom *I Love Lucy* shows married couples in separate beds.

© Bettmann/Corbis

© Bettmann/Corbis

Life among early humans tended to be exceedingly difficult, with high infant mortality, disease, malnutrition, and a harsh environment. Living conditions began to improve about 11,000 years ago, when human beings discovered agriculture and began to settle down into permanent communities. Because women typically did the gathering, they understood plant life better than men. Women therefore probably first discovered how to cultivate plants, generally considered one of the two greatest discoveries—with harnessing fire—in the history of humankind.

Sexuality in the Ancient Mediterranean

Laws give us a glimpse into the world of sexuality in early cultures. As the first Western civilizations were established, cities began to grow and people began living together in larger and larger groups. Cities require a more formal way of structuring social life, and so the first codes of law began to develop. Codes of law and other legal sources, however, tend to tell us only about what was forbidden.

From writings and art we know a bit about ancient accounts of sexually transmitted infections (some ancient medical texts discuss cures), menstruation (there were a variety of laws surrounding menstruation), circumcision (which was first performed in Egypt and possibly other parts of Africa), and contraception (Egyptian women inserted sponges or other objects in the vagina). Because a great value was put on having as many children as possible—especially sons, for inheritance—abortion was usually forbidden. Prostitution was common, and **temple prostitutes** often greeted worshippers. Egypt was the first civilization to eliminate sexual intercourse and prostitution as part of temple worship, though prostitution was not uncommon in the cities and towns.

It is important to remember that throughout history men dominated public life and women's voices were effectively silenced; we know far more about what men thought, how men lived, and even how men loved than we do about the lives and thoughts of women. In fact, it was only relatively recently in human history that women's voices have begun to be heard on a par with men's in literature, politics, art, and other parts of public life.

It may seem that ancient civilizations were very different from ours, yet some societies had surprisingly modern attitudes about sex. Though the Egyptians condemned adultery, especially among women, there is evidence that it was still fairly common. A woman in Egypt had the right to divorce her husband, a privilege, as we will see, that was not allowed to Hebrew women. Egyptians seem to have invented male circumcision, and Egyptian workers left behind thousands of pictures, carvings, and even cartoons of erotic scenes. All told, ancient Egyptians had sexual lives that do not seem all that different from the way humans engage in sex throughout the world today.

Of all the ancient civilizations, modern Western society owes the most to the interaction of three ancient cultures: Hebraic, Hellenistic (Greek), and Roman. Each made a contribution to our views of sexuality, so it is worthwhile to examine each culture briefly.

Review Question

How have prehistoric changes in our posture influenced human sexuality?

temple prostitutes
Women in ancient cultures who would have sex with worshippers at pagan temples to provide money for the temple or as a form of worshipping the gods.

1953	1953	1956	1957	1961	1962
First network children's show, *Captain Kangaroo*, debuts.	Color broadcasting on television begins after FCC approves modified version of RCA system.	Elvis Presley appears on the *Ed Sullivan Show* and is broadcast from the waist up because his dance moves are thought to be too suggestive.	First remote control for television is introduced.	*Dick Van Dyke Show* begins and airs until 1966. The show is a hit, and unlike most '60s sitcoms, viewers see a father both in the home and at work.	First satellite transmission of a televised program. Eliminates delays in programming and allows for instant reporting of events around the world.

© John Springer Collection/Corbis

© Bettmann/Corbis

© Bettmann/Corbis

The Hebrews

The Hebrews rejected the common religious thinking of their day, which included idol worship and local gods that ruled only over a particular group of people. The Hebrews believed a single deity had a supreme place in the universe and ruled over all tribes and peoples. With a single, universal God came the idea of an absolute set of truths, given by God, that instructed people how to live.

The Hebrew Bible, which was put into written form some time between 800 and 200 B.C., contains very explicit rules about sexual behavior, such as forbidding adultery, male homosexual intercourse, and sex with various family members and their spouses. The Bible includes tales of sexual misconduct—ranging from incest, to sexual betrayal, to sex outside of marriage, to sexual jealousy—even by its most admired figures. Yet, the Bible also contains tales of marital love and acknowledges the importance of sexuality in marital relations.

The legacy of the Hebrew attitude toward sexuality has been profound. The focus on marital sexuality and procreation and the prohibition against such things as homosexuality were adopted by Christianity and formed the basis of sexual attitudes in the West for centuries thereafter. On the other hand, as opposed to the Greeks, the Hebrew Bible sees the marital union and its sexual nature as an expression of love and affection, as a man and woman "become one flesh."

The Greeks (1000–200 B.C.)

The Greeks were more sexually permissive than the Hebrews. Their stories and myths were full of sexual exploits, incest, rape, and even **bestiality** (beest-ee-AL-i-tee; as when Zeus, the chief god, takes the form of a swan to rape Leda). The Greeks clearly distinguished between love and sex in their tales, even giving each a separate god: Aphrodite was the goddess of sexual intercourse; Eros (her son) was the god of love.

Greece was one of the few major civilizations in Western history to institutionalize homosexuality successfully, though the practice was widespread only among the upper class. In Greek **pederasty** (ped-er-AST-ee), an older man would befriend a postpubescent boy who had finished his orthodox education and aid in the boy's continuing intellectual, physical, and sexual development. In return, the boy would have sex with his mentor. The mentor was always the active partner, the penetrator; the student was the passive partner. Socrates, for example, was supposed to have enjoyed the sexual attentions of his (all male) students, and his students expressed jealousy when he paid too much physical attention to one or another. Many Greek leaders had young boys as lovers, and, in fact, more than a few were assassinated by boys they had seduced.

In Greece, men and the male form were idealized. When the ancient Greek philosophers spoke of love, they did so almost exclusively in **homoerotic** terms. Man's nonsex-

Review Question

What sources provide information on sexuality in early cultures?

bestiality
The act of having intercourse with an animal.

pederasty
Sexual contact between adult men and (usually) postpubescent boys.

homoerotic
Artistic or literary works that focus on the sexual or love relations between members of the same sex.

Scala/Art Resource, NY

Greek cups, plates, and other pottery often depicted erotic scenes, such as this scene from the 5th century B.C.

Timeline: Television

1965	1969	1975	1983	1987	1987
I Dream of Jeannie airs from 1965 to 1970. Jeannie's harem costume is controversial for exposing too much flesh. Bellybutton is filled in with flesh-colored putty plug.	*The Brady Bunch* airs, inspired by the growing statistics of blended families with children from previous marriages.	*The Jeffersons* is the first show to include an interracial couple.	*Bay City Blues* is the first television series to show bare buttocks in locker room scene.	Playtex shows first television commercials with live models wearing bras and underwear.	*StarTrek* introduces alien race named "Ferengi" who require females to be naked and subservient to males.

Hulton Archive/Getty Images   CBS-TV/The Kobal Collection

ual love for another man was seen as the ideal love, superior to the sexual love of women. Plato discussed such an ideal love, and so we have come to call friendships without a sexual element **platonic.**

platonic
Named after Plato's description, a deep, loving friendship that is devoid of sexual contact or desire.

SEX Talk

Question: *I've heard that the Greeks believed that sex between men and boys was a "natural" form of human sexuality. Couldn't they see that it was perverted?*

One society's perversion is another society's normal sexual practice. Every culture sees its own forms of sexuality as natural and obvious—including ours. Not too long ago in our own society, it seemed "obvious" to most people that things like oral sex and anal sex were perversions (they are still technically illegal in many states) and that masturbation was a serious disease that could lead to mental illness. Now most people see these acts as part of healthy sexual life. Sexual beliefs and practices change over time and are different in various cultures.

Pederasty was only a small part of Greek sexual life. In the great stories of Homer, such as the *Iliad* and the *Odyssey,* we find descriptions of deep heterosexual love, of caring marriages, of tenderness for children, and of conjugal and maternal affections (Flacelière, 1962). Coupled with the obvious admiration Greeks had of the feminine form—such as the Venus de Milo—it is a mistake to see Greek pederasty as the basic form of Greek sexuality.

Contemporary historians of sexuality, following the work of philosopher Michel Foucault (1978, 1987, 1988), have been writing about sexuality in society as a reflection of social power. In the ancient Greek city of Athens, for example, only a small group of men were considered "citizens," and they held all the political and social power. Sex became a symbol of that power, and it was therefore acceptable for citizens to have sex with any of the other, less powerful groups in society—women, slaves, foreigners, or children. In other words, a powerful male, wielding the symbol of masculine power (the penis), could penetrate any one of his social inferiors, thus reinforcing his place in the social order.

The Romans (5th Century B.C.–7th Century A.D.)

In Rome, marriage and sexual relations were viewed as a means to improve one's economic and social standing; passionate love almost never appears in the written accounts handed down to us. Bride and groom need not love each other, for that kind of rela-

1991	1992	1993	1994	1995	1996	1997
LA Law shows lesbian kiss by characters C.J. Lamb and Abby Perkins.	Mariel Hemingway bares her breasts in an episode of *Civil Wars* on ABC.	David Caruso and Sherry Stringfield are shown nude while making love in a scene from *NYPD Blue.*	Rosanne Barr and Mariel Hemingway kiss on *Roseanne.*	Drew Barrymore bares her breasts on David Letterman.	*Friends* airs episode of lesbian wedding, even though vows are not sealed with a kiss.	Ellen DeGeneres comes out on the air, making *Ellen* the first openly gay sitcom. Several advertisers withdraw all commercials from this episode.

20th Century Fox Television/Courtesy of Getty Images

© Reuters/Corbis

tionship would grow over the life of the marriage; more important was fair treatment, respect, and mutual consideration. Wives even encouraged their husbands to have slaves (of either gender) for the purposes of sexual release. Rome had few restrictions about sexuality until late in the history of the empire, so early Romans had very permissive attitudes toward homosexual and bisexual behaviors, which were entirely legal until the 6th century A.D. (Boswell, 1980).

In Rome, as in Greece, adult males who took the passive sexual position in homosexual encounters were viewed with scorn, whereas the same behavior by youth, foreigners, slaves, or women was seen as an acceptable means to try to please a person who could improve one's place in society. Still, long-term homosexual unions did exist.

Sexuality in Ancient Asia

Chinese and Indian civilizations also had unique views of sexuality. In Chinese culture, people work to live in harmony with the Tao, which is made up of **yin** and **yang.** In Indian culture, Hinduism and rebirth give life direction.

China

Chinese civilization never developed a Western-style concept of God, a conscious being who determines correct behavior. Instead, Chinese philosophy emphasizes the interdependence of all things, unified in the Tao, which represents the basic unity of the universe. The Tao is usually translated as "The Way" or "The Path" but is itself unknowable (much like the Western view that God is unknowable). The Tao itself is made up of two principles, yin and yang, which represent the opposites of the world: yin is feminine, passive, and receptive; yang is masculine, active, and assertive. Sexuality in Chinese thought is not a matter of moral or allowable behavior but, rather, is a natural procreative process, a joining of the yin and yang, the masculine and feminine principles. The goal of Taoist life is harmony, the effortless, natural blending of yin and yang.

Because sex itself was part of the basic process of following the Tao, sexual instruction and sex manuals were common and openly available in early Chinese society. These texts were very explicit, with pictures of sexual positions and instructions on how to stimulate partners, and were often given to brides before their weddings.

Because women's essence, yin, is inexhaustible, whereas man's essence, yang (embodied in semen), is limited, man should feed his yang through prolonged contact with yin. In other words, intercourse should be prolonged as long as possible, without the man ejaculating, to release all the woman's accumulated yin energy. (The man may experience orgasm without ejaculation, however, and techniques were developed to teach men how to do so). Men should try to have sex with many different women to prevent the yin energy of any single woman from getting depleted. It was also important for the man to experience the woman's orgasm, when yin is at its peak, in order to maximize his contact with yin energy. The Chinese were unique in stressing the importance of female orgasm.

yin and yang
According to a Chinese belief, the universe is run by the interaction of two fundamental principles: yin, which is negative, passive, weak, yielding, and female; and yang, which is positive, assertive, active, strong, and male.

Timeline: Television

1998	1998	1999	1999	1999	2000
Network and broadcast executives design a rating system to help parents monitor what their children watch on television.	First episode of NBC hit show *Will & Grace*, wherein a gay male lives with his female friend.	*Naked News*, a Toronto-based Internet show, features anchors who strip completely while reporting the news. Billed as the program with "nothing to hide."	FCC passes law that all television sets 13 inches or larger must have a V-chip installed.	Debut of *Queer as Folk*, which follows the lives of five gay men and two lesbians.	Popular teen drama *Dawson's Creek* discusses gay character coming out of the closet.

Jim Watson/AFP/Getty Images

Showtime/The Kobal Collection/Mark Seliger

Same-sex relations were not discouraged, but because semen was seen as precious and primarily for impregnation (we will discuss Chinese views of homosexuality more in Chapter 9), male homosexuality was viewed as a wasteful use of sperm. Aphrodisiacs were developed, as were drugs for all kinds of sexual problems. Also common were sexual devices to increase pleasure, such as penis rings to maintain erection, balls and bells that were grafted under the skin of the head of the penis to increase its size, and "ben-wa" balls (usually two or three) containing mercury and other substances that were inserted in the vagina and bounced against each other to bring sexual pleasure.

Taoists believed that yin and yang were equally necessary complements of all existence, so one might guess that men and women were treated more equally in China than in the West. Yet because yin is the passive, inferior principle, women were seen as subservient to men throughout their lives: first to their fathers, then to their husbands, and finally to their sons when their husbands died. **Polygamy** (pah-LIG-ah-mee) was practiced until very late in Chinese history, and the average middle-class male had between three and a dozen wives and concubines, with those in nobility having thirty or more. A husband's adultery was tolerated, and only men could initiate divorce.

India

Hinduism, the religion of India for most of its history, concentrates on an individual's cycle of birth and rebirth, or **karma.** *Karma* involves a belief that a person's unjust deeds in this life are punished by suffering in a future life, and suffering in this life is undoubtedly punishment for wrongs committed in previous incarnations. The goal, then, is to live a just life now to avoid suffering in the future. One of the responsibilities in this life is to marry and procreate, and because sex is an important part of those responsibilities, it was generally viewed as a positive pursuit, and even a source of power and magic.

There are legends about great women rulers early in India's history, and women had important roles in ceremonies and sacrifices. Still, India's social system, like others we have mentioned, was basically **patriarchal** (pay-TREE-arc-al), and Indian writers (again, mostly male) shared many of the negative views of women that were characteristic of other civilizations. Being born a woman was seen as a punishment for sins committed in previous lives. In fact, murdering a woman was not seen as a particularly serious crime, and **female infanticide** (in-FAN-tis-side) was not uncommon (V. L. Bullough, 1973).

By about the 3rd or 4th century B.C., the first and most famous of India's sex manuals, the *Kamasutra* (CAH-mah-SUH-trah), appeared. India is justifiably famous for this amazing book. The *Kamasutra* discusses not just sex but also the nature of love, how to make a good home and family, and moral guidance in sex and love. The *Kamasutra*

polygamy
The practice of men or women marrying more than one partner.

karma
The idea that there is a cycle of birth, death, and rebirth and that deeds in one's life affect one's status in a future life.

patriarchal
A society ruled by the male as the figure of authority, symbolized by the father's absolute authority in the home.

female infanticide
The killing of female infants; practiced in some countries that value males more than females.

© Archivo Iconografico, S.A./Corbis

Indian sculptors followed the tradition of tantric art, which is famous for its depictions of eroticism. Of the 85 temples originally built, 22 still stand today.

2000	2001	2003	2004	2004	2004
All My Children features character coming out of the closet, the first major homosexual role in a soap opera.	*Naked News* begins airing on television. An all-nude cast of females delivers both the serious and lighter side of the news on cable.	Bravo network begins airing the popular show *Queer Eye for the Straight Guy*.	Reality shows such as *The Bachelor, Survivor, Blind Date,* and *Extreme Makeover* flood the market.	Janet Jackson exposes her breast during halftime Super Bowl show. The federal communications commission fines CBS over $500,000.	During ABC's *Monday Night Football*, Nicollette Sheridan *(Desperate Housewives)* attempts to lure Philadelphia Eagles Terrell Owens into sex by dropping her towel and appearing nude in the locker room.

Peter Kramer/Getty Images

© Steve Azzara/Corbis

Giulio Marcocchi/Getty Images

© Pierre Ducharme/Reuters/Corbis

is obsessive about naming and classifying things. In fact, the *Kamasutra* categorizes men by the size of their penis (hare, bull, or horse man) and women by the size of their vagina (deer, mare, or cow-elephant woman). A good match in genital size was preferred, but barring that, a tight fit was better than a loose one (Tannahill, 1980). The *Kamasutra* recommends that women learn how to please their husbands, and it provides instructions on sexual techniques and illustrations of many sexual positions, some of which are virtually impossible for anyone who cannot twist his or her body like a pretzel. The *Kamasutra* proposes that intercourse should be a passionate activity that includes scratching, biting, and blows to the back, accompanied by a variety of animal noises (the book details eight kinds of nail marks and eight different animal sounds).

Question: *Wasn't the original* Kamasutra *pretty sexist? I don't understand how it could still be popular today when we work so hard for equality.*

Although the original *Kamasutra* has been criticized for its heterosexist and oppositional male and female power imbalances, there have been several translations over time. Today we understand that the *Kamasutra* may have a more balanced power structure than originally thought and also provides women more power to say no (Kong, 2004). Perhaps these new understandings account for the *Kamasutra's* continued popularity today.

Review Question

Explain how the moral standards of past civilizations influence our own judgments about modern events today.

In India, marriage was an economic and religious obligation; families tried to arrange good marriages by betrothing their children at younger and younger ages, though they did not live with or have sex with their future spouses until after puberty. Because childbearing began so young, Indian women were still in the prime of their lives when their children were grown, and they were often able to assert themselves in the household over elderly husbands. However, when a husband died, his wife was forbidden to remarry, and she had to live simply, wear plain clothes, and sleep on the ground. She was to devote her days to prayer and rituals that ensured her remarriage to the same husband in a future life. Many women chose (or were forced to) end their lives as widows by the ritual act of *sati*, which consisted of a woman throwing herself on her husband's burning funeral pyre to die.

SEXUALITY FROM ST. PAUL TO QUEEN VICTORIA

Throughout history, religion has influenced many of our views about sexuality. Perhaps no single system of thought had as much impact on the Western world as Christianity, and nowhere more so than in its views on sexuality. We will explore early Christianity and the Middle Ages, and also look at the influence of Islam and Islamic law and the views of sexuality that developed during the Renaissance.

Early Christianity: Chastity Becomes a Virtue

Christianity began as a small sect following the teachings of Jesus. It was formalized into a religious philosophy by Paul and by other early leaders who were influenced by the Roman legal structure. Within a few hundred years, this little sect would become the predominant religion of the Western world and would influence the attitudes of people toward sexuality until the present day.

Jesus himself was mostly silent on sexual issues such as homosexuality or premarital sex. Jesus was born a Jew and was knowledgeable in Jewish tradition, and many of his attitudes were compatible with mainstream Jewish thought of the time. However, he was liberal in his thinking about sexuality, preaching, for example, that men should be held to the same standards as women on issues of adultery, divorce, and remarriage (V. L. Bullough, 1973). The Gospels also show that Jesus was liberal in his recommendations for punishing sexual misadventurers. When confronted with a woman who had committed adultery, a sin for which the Hebrew Bible had mandated stoning, Jesus replied with one of his more famous comments, "Let he who is without sin cast the first stone."

But it was Paul and later followers, such as St. Jerome and St. Augustine, who established the Christian view of sexuality that was to dominate Western thought for the next 2,000 years. St. Paul condemned sexuality in a way found neither in Hebrew nor Greek thought—nor anywhere in the teachings of Jesus. Paul suggested that the highest love was love of God and that the ideal was not to allow sexual or human love to compete with love for God. Therefore, though sexuality itself was not sinful when performed as part of the marital union, the ideal situation was **celibacy** (SEH-luh-buh-see). **Chastity,** for the first time in history, became a virtue; abstaining from sexual intercourse became a sign of holiness (Bergmann, 1987). Paul suggested that those unable to make a commitment to chastity could engage in marital sex, occasionally abstaining for periods of prayer and devotion.

As Christianity developed, Greek, Roman, and other philosophies influenced the Church's developing views on sexuality. St. Jerome (347–420 A.D.) and St. Augustine (died 604 A.D.) were both powerful influences on the early church's views of sexuality. Both had been sexually active before converting to a life of chastity, and both felt ongoing sexual temptation; perhaps that is why they were so strong in condemning sexual activity, as they themselves were struggling with their erotic feelings. St. Augustine prayed to God: "Give me chastity—but not yet!" St. Jerome declared sexuality itself unclean and even taught that one who feels ardent (erotic) love for his own wife is committing adultery (Bergmann, 1987). Throughout early Christianity there were sects (such as a group known as the Gnostics) and individual theologians and clerics who denounced sexuality and even renounced marriage as an institution in order to try and form a purer relationship to God, unsullied by sexual thoughts or behaviors (V. Bullough, 1977).

The legacy of early Christianity was a general association of sexuality with sin. All nonprocreative sex was strictly forbidden, as were contraception, masturbation, and sex for pleasure's sake. The result was that the average Christian associated the pleasure of sexuality with guilt. Christianity's view of sex has been one of the harshest of any major religious or cultural tradition.

The Middle Ages: Eve the Temptress, Mary the Virgin

In the early Middle Ages, the church's influence slowly began to increase. Christianity had become the state religion of Rome, and though the church did not have much formal power, its teachings had an influence on law. For example, homosexual relations (even homosexual marriage) had been legal for the first 200 years that Christianity was the state religion of Rome, and the church was very tolerant of homosexuality. Eventually, however, church teachings changed and became much stricter.

Between about 1050 and 1150 (the High Middle Ages) sexuality once again became liberalized. For example, a gay subculture was established in Europe that produced a body of gay literature that had not been seen since the Roman Empire and would not emerge again until the 19th century (Boswell, 1980).

However, the homosexual subculture disappeared in the 13th century when the church cracked down on a variety of groups—including Jews, Muslims, and homosexuals (Boswell, 1980). In the year 1215, the Church instituted **confession,** and soon guides appeared to teach priests about the various sins **penitents** (PENN-it-tunce) might have committed. The guides seem preoccupied with sexual transgressions and used sexual sins more than any other kind to illustrate their points (Payer, 1991). All sex outside of marriage was considered sinful, and even certain marital acts were forbidden. But penance also had to be done for such things as nocturnal emissions and violations of modesty (looks, desires, touches, kisses).

celibacy
The state of remaining unmarried; often used today to refer to abstaining from sex.

chastity
The quality of being sexually pure, either through abstaining from intercourse or by adhering to strict rules of sexuality.

confession
A Catholic practice of revealing one's sins to a priest.

penitents
Those who come to confess sins (from the word penance, meaning "to repent").

European women in the early Middle Ages were only slightly better off than they had been under the ancient Greeks or Romans. By the late Middle Ages, however, new ideas about women were brought back by the Crusaders from Islamic lands (see the section on Islam that follows). Women were elevated to a place of purity and were considered almost perfect. Eve, who caused Adam's downfall, was replaced as the symbol of ideal womanhood by Mary, the mother of God (Tannahill, 1980). Woman was no longer a temptress but a model of virtue. The idea of romantic love was first created at this time, and it spread through popular culture as balladeers and troubadours traveled from place to place, singing songs of pure, spiritual love, untroubled by sex.

At the same time that women were seen to be virtuous, however, they were also said to be the holder of the secrets of sexuality (Thomasset, 1992). Before marriage, men would employ the services of an **entremetteuse** (on-TRAY-meh-toose) to teach them the ways of love. These old women procured young women (prostitutes) for the men and were said to know the secrets of restoring potency, restoring virginity, and concocting potions. It was a small step from the scary accounts of these old women's powers to the belief in witches. By the late 15th century, the church began a campaign against witchcraft, which they said was inspired by women's insatiable "carnal lust" (Covey, 1989).

Perhaps no person from the Middle Ages had a stronger impact on subsequent attitudes toward sexuality than the theologian (and later saint) Thomas Aquinas (1225–1274). Aquinas established the views of morality and correct sexual behavior that form the basis of the Catholic Church's attitudes toward sexuality, even today. Aquinas drew from the idea of "natural law" to suggest that there were "natural" and "unnatural" sex acts. Aquinas argued that the sex organs were "naturally" intended for procreation, and other use of them was unnatural and immoral; in fact, he argued that semen and ejaculation were intended only to impregnate, and any other use of them was immoral. But Aquinas recognized a problem: if the reason that, for example, homosexual intercourse was wrong was because it was an unnatural use of the sex organs, then was it not wrong to use other parts of the body for other uses? Is it immoral, for example, to walk on one's hands, which were not naturally designed for that (Boswell, 1980)? Aquinas solved that problem by arguing that the sin was that misuse of sexuality got in the way of procreation. But he himself had argued that individuals are not obligated to reproduce, for the Christian church thought celibacy and voluntary virginity were the highest virtue. Aquinas's own logic led him to admit that certain sex acts are immoral simply because of popular sentiment. Yet Aquinas's strong condemnation of sexuality—and especially homosexuality, which he called the worst of all sexual sins—set the tone for Christian attitudes toward sexuality for many centuries.

Islam: A New Religion

In the 6th century, a man named Muhammad began to preach a religion that drew from Jewish and Christian roots and added Arab tribal beliefs. Islam became a powerful force that conquered the entire Middle East and Persian lands; swept across Asia, and so touched China in the East; spread through Northern Africa and, from there, north into Christian Europe, particularly Spain. Between about the 8th and 12th centuries, Islamic society was the most advanced in the world, with a newly developed system of mathematics (Arabic numbers) to replace the clumsy Roman system and having the world's most sophisticated techniques of medicine, warfare, and science.

Many Muslim societies have strong rules of *satr al-'awra*, or modesty, that involve covering the private parts of the body (which for women means almost the entire body). Muhammad had tried to preserve the rights of women. There are examples in the **Koran** (koe-RAN), the Muslim Bible, of female saints and intellectuals, and powerful women often hold strong informal powers over their husbands and male children. Still, women in many Islamic lands are subjugated to men, are segregated and not permitted to venture out of their homes, and are forbidden to interact with men who are not family members.

In Islamic law, as in Christian law, sexuality between a man and a woman is legal only when the couple is married or when the woman is a concubine (Coulson, 1979).

entremetteuse
Historically, a woman who procures sexual partners for men or one who taught men about lovemaking.

Koran
The holy book of Islam. Also spelled Quran or Qur'an.

Human Sexuality in a Diverse World

What's It Like to Be a Woman in China?

It is often difficult to imagine how sexuality and gender are viewed outside the United States. We become accustomed to norms, practices, and behaviors where we live and may not understand how other cultures may view the same practices differently. For example, sexuality and gender in China are very different from in the United States.

Taking a historical look at China, we find that in its earliest history, China was a matriarchal society. Women ruled the majority of families and were highly respected. During Confucius's reign, however, things changed. Women were seen as inferior to men. They were taught to be respectful and obedient to their fathers and older brothers when they were young, to their husbands when they were married, and to their sons when their husbands died. Women's importance during this time was in their reproductive role—and in their role to reproduce male descendents. A woman's position within her family was "temporary and of

© Alison Wright/Corbis

no great importance" (Ruan & Lau, 2004, p. 184). Because of this, a woman's education and skills training was not encouraged. Her responsibilities centered on childcare, cooking, cleaning, and other household tasks.

In 1950 the People's Republic of China passed a marriage law that contained a statement on the equality of men and women. This law enabled women to obtain work and education so that by 1988, women accounted for 37% of the workforce, up from 7.5% in 1949.

Even with these changes, however, many would say that men and women are far from equal in China. Some employers refuse to hire women, and various graduate schools reject female students. Today, 70% of China's illiterate population is female.

SOURCE: Much of this information was adapted from Ruan, F., & Lau, M. P. (2004). China: Demographics and a brief historical perspective. In R. T. Francoeur & R. J. Noonan (Eds.), *International encyclopedia of sexuality.* New York: Continuum International.

Sexual intercourse in marriage is a good religious deed for the Muslim male, and the Koran likens wives to fields that men should cultivate as frequently as they want. All forms of sexuality, including anal and oral sex, are permissible. A man with a strong sex drive is advised to marry many wives, even more than the normal limit of four (Bürgel, 1979). Islam restricts sex to the marital union exclusively, and when this is not adhered to, extreme measures are taken.

In traditional Islamic communities, women who were married to wealthy men usually lived in secluded areas in their husbands' homes, called **harems.** Harems were not the dens of sex and sensuality that are sometimes portrayed but, rather, were self-contained communities where women learned to become self-sufficient in the absence of men. Among the middle and lower classes, men had less wealth to offer potential wives, which gave women more power.

Islamic society has had a much freer, more open attitude to sexuality than Christian society. Erotic and love writings from medieval Islam are very common, and some of the books are quite explicit. There are many Arab love poems that are clearly sexually charged poems about the love of boys (Roth, 1991), for, like Greeks, Arabs celebrated young boys as the epitome of beauty and allowed sexual contact between men and boys.

The Sultans of the Ottoman Empire, which ruled most of the Islamic world from the 15th to the 20th century, had between 300 and 1,200 concubines, mostly captured or bought slaves. The Sultan's mother ruled the harem and even sometimes ruled the empire itself if she was strong and her son was weak-willed (Tannahill, 1980). Because each woman might sleep with the Sultan once or twice a year at most, **eunuchs** (YOU-niks) were employed to guard against the women finding sexual satisfaction elsewhere. Some eunuchs had their testicles removed, some their penises, and some both; young eunuchs might have their testicles crushed. Many died under the surgeon's knife.

harem
Abbreviation of the Turkish word harêmlik (harâm in Arabic), meaning "women's quarters" or "sanctuary."

eunuch
Castrated male (or less often, man with his penis removed) who guarded a harem. At times, children were also made eunuchs in childhood in order to sing soprano in church choirs.

asceticism
The practice of a lifestyle that rejects sensual pleasures such as drinking alcohol, eating rich food, or engaging in sex.

The Renaissance: The Pursuit of Knowledge

The Renaissance, which began in Italy in the late 1300s, may be summed up as a time when intellectual and artistic thought turned from a focus on God to a focus on human beings and their place in the world; from the sober and serious theology of the Middle Ages to a renewed sense of joy in life; from **asceticism** (ah-SET-ah-siz-um) to sensuality; from religious symbolism to a focus on naturalness; and from a belief in tradition to experimentation in the pursuit of knowledge (New, 1969). Part of the cultural shift of the Renaissance was new views of sexuality and, to some degree, the roles of women in society.

During the Renaissance, women made great strides in education and began to become more prominent in political affairs (Bornstein, 1979). Antifemale tracts still had wide circulation, but they gave rise to profemale tracts, and a lively debate arose on the worth and value of women. Henricus Cornelius Agrippa published a tract in 1532 arguing that each of God's creations in Genesis is superior to the one before, and because the human female is the last thing God created, she must be his most perfect creation. In the Bible, Agrippa continues, a male is the first sinner; men introduce polygamy, drunkenness, and murder into the world; and men are aggressive and tyrannical. Women, on the other hand, are more peaceful, chaste, refined, and faithful. Agrippa concludes that what holds women back is the tyranny of men and that women should be liberated and educated (Bornstein, 1979).

Human Sexuality in a Diverse World

The Fear of Female Sexuality

Many images of women have been created by men throughout history, some of which have expressed male fears of female sexuality and helped to keep women subjugated. The woman as whore, temptress, shrew, simple-minded, virtuous, and image of perfection—all have prevented men from seeing women as simply the other half of the human species. But perhaps none has been so dangerous to women's lives as the image of the witch.

Though the idea of witchcraft has been around at least since the Bible (which mandates killing witches), the Catholic Church did not take witches seriously until the 13th century, when Aquinas suggested they still existed. Witch hunting became an obsession in Europe when Pope Innocent VIII decreed in 1486 that witches should be wiped out. A pamphlet released in that year (which went through 13 editions) claimed witches were more likely to be female because women were the source of all evil, had defective intelligence, tried to dominate men, and "[knew] no moderation whether in goodness or vice" (V. L. Bullough, 1973).

From the 1500s through the 1700s in Germany over 100,000 people (mostly women) were executed for witchcraft (Roach, 2004). One visitor wrote of his trip to Cologne: "A horrible spectacle met our eyes. Outside of the walls of many towns and villages, we saw numerous stakes to which poor, wretched women were bound and burned as witches"

(quoted in V. L. Bullough, 1973, p. 224). In England, where most of the women accused were married, executions for witchcraft continued until 1712.

Witchcraft trials seemed to happen at times of social disruption, religious change, or economic troubles. At such times, it is easier to blame evil forces, and women, than to look to causes in the greater society. Such was the case in Salem, Massachusetts, in 1692, where three young girls began acting strangely, running around, falling to the ground in convulsions, and barking like dogs. Soon the other girls of Salem began to follow suit, and the doctors decided that the girls had been bewitched. Forced to identify the witches that had put spells on them, the girls began to name the adults they did not particularly like and went on to name names from every corner of the village. Not one suspect dragged before the courts was acquitted, and 22 women were executed or died in prison. When the tide finally turned, 150 people were in prison awaiting trial, and another 200 stood accused. All were finally released (K. Erikson, 1986).

Accusations of witchcraft were often used as a way to punish women who did not conform to the social expectation of appropriate female behavior. It was also a means to reaffirm men's dominance over women. Even in many contemporary tribal cultures in which witchcraft is very much a part of the cultural beliefs, women are seen as potentially more malevolent and evil creatures than men (Janeway, 1971).

But, as seems to happen so often in history when women make modest gains, there was a backlash. By the 17th century, witchcraft trials appeared once again in Europe and in the New World, symbols of the fears that men still held of women's sexuality. Thousands of women were killed, and the image of the evil witch became the symbol of man's fear of women for centuries to come (see the accompanying Human Sexuality in a Diverse World: The Fear of Female Sexuality for more information about witch hunts).

The Reformation: The Protestant Marital Partnership

In the early 16th century, Martin Luther challenged papal power and founded a movement known as Protestantism. Instead of valuing celibacy, Luther saw in the Bible the obligation to reproduce, saw marital love as blessed, and considered sexuality a natural function. John Calvin, the other great Protestant reformer, suggested that women were not just reproductive vessels but men's partners in all things.

To Luther, marriage was a state blessed by God, and sexual contact was sinful primarily when it was done out of wedlock, just as any indulgence was sinful. Marriage was inherent in human nature, had been instituted in paradise, and was confirmed in the fifth commandment and safeguarded by the seventh (V. L. Bullough, 1973). Because marriage was so important, a bad marriage should not continue, and so Luther broke away from the belief of the Catholic Church and allowed divorce.

Sexuality was permissible only in the marital union, but it had other justifications besides reproduction, such as to reduce stress, avoid cheating, and increase intimacy—a very different perspective on sex than was preached by the Catholic Church. Calvin, in fact, saw the marital union as primarily a social and sexual relationship. Though procreation was important, companionship was the main goal of marriage.

Luther did accept the general subjugation of women to men in household affairs and felt that women were weaker than men and should humble themselves before their fathers and husbands. He excluded women from the clergy because of standards of "decency" and because of women's inferior aptitudes for ministry. Though Calvin and Luther tried to remove from Protestantism the overt disdain of women they found in some older Christian theologians, they did not firmly establish women's equal place with men.

Review Question

Explain how views of sexuality changed from the Reformation through the Renaissance.

THE ENLIGHTENMENT AND THE VICTORIAN ERA

The Enlightenment, an intellectual movement of the 18th century, prized rational thought over traditional authority and suggested that human nature was to be understood through a study of human psychology. Enlightenment writers argued that human drives and instincts are part of nature's design, so one must realize the basic wisdom of human urges and not fight them (Porter, 1982). Sexual pleasure was therefore considered natural and desirable. In fact, of all the earthly pleasures, enlightenment thinkers praised sexuality as supreme. Sexuality had become so free that there was an unprecedented rise in premarital pregnancy and illegitimate births; up to one-fifth of all brides in the late 17th century were pregnant when they got married (Trumbach, 1990).

The Enlightenment

As liberal as the Enlightenment was, many sexual activities, such as homosexuality, were condemned and persecuted. For example, starting in 1730, there was a 2-year "sodomite panic" in the Netherlands, and hundreds of men accused of homosexual acts were executed while hundreds more fled the country. France burned homosexuals long after it stopped burning witches. Yet there were also times of relative tolerance. Napoleon so eased laws against homosexuality that by 1860 homosexuality was tolerated, and male prostitutes were very common in France (Tannahill, 1980).

In the late 19th and early 20th centuries, many doctors taught that masturbation was harmful, and so devices, such as the two barbed rings and the shock box shown here, were created to keep children—especially boys—from achieving unwanted erections.

The Wellcome Trust, London

Review Question

How did the Enlightenment and the Victorian era influence the modern development of ideas of sexuality?

sex byte

In the 1800s, Sylvester Graham (a Presbyterian minister and vegetarian) recommended that in order to be healthy a person needed loose clothing, vigorous exercise, a hard mattress, cold night air, chastity, and cold showers. In 1829 he invented the graham cracker, which he believed could reduce sexual desire and increase physical health.

Puritan
Refers to a 16th- and 17th-century Protestant group from England that wanted to purge the church of elaborate ceremonies and simplify worship; has come to mean any person or group that is excessively strict in regard to sexual matters.

The Victorian Era

The Victorian era, which lasted into the 20th century, was a time of great prosperity in England. Propriety and public behavior became more important, especially to the upper class, and sexual attitudes became more conservative. Sex was not to be spoken of in polite company and was to be restricted to the marital bed, in the belief that preoccupation with sex interfered with higher achievements. Privately, Victorian England was not as conservative as it has been portrayed, and pornography, extramarital affairs, and prostitution were common. Still, the most important aspect of Victorian society was public propriety, and conservative values were often preached, though not always practiced.

During this period, the idea of male chivalry returned, and women were considered to be virtuous, refined, delicate, fragile, vulnerable, and remote; certainly, no respectable Victorian woman would ever admit to a sexual urge. The prudery of the Victorian era sometimes went to extremes. Victorian women were too embarrassed to talk to a doctor about their "female problems" and so would point out areas of discomfort on dolls. Women were supposed to be interested in music but were not supposed to play the flute because pursing the lips was unladylike; the cello was unacceptable because it had to be held between the legs; the brass instruments were too difficult for the delicate wind of the female; the violin forced the woman's neck into an uncomfortable position. Therefore, only keyboard instruments were considered "ladylike" (V. L. Bullough, 1973; see the accompanying Personal Voices: Instruction and Advice for the Young Bride for more information about "ladylike" behavior).

Sexuality was repressed in many ways. Physicians and writers of the time often argued that semen was precious and should be conserved; Sylvester Graham (see accompanying Sexbyte) recommended sex only 12 times a year. He argued that sexual indulgence led to all sorts of ailments and infirmities, such as depression, faintness, headaches, blindness—the list is almost endless.

The Victorian era had great influence on sexuality in England and the United States. Many of the conservative attitudes that people of Western countries have held until the modern day are holdovers from Victorian standards.

SEX IN AMERICAN HISTORY

American society has been influenced most strongly by Europe, particularly England. Yet it also developed its own unique mix of ideas and attitudes, tempered by the contributions of the many cultures that immigrants brought with them. Let us look at some of these influences.

The Colonies: The Puritan Ethic

The **Puritans** were a religious group that fled England and tried to set up a biblically based society in the New World. They had severe sanctions for sexual transgressions: in New England, for example, the death penalty was applied for sodomy, bestiality, adultery, and rape. In Puritan ideology, the entire community was responsible for upholding morality (D'Emilio & Freedman, 1988). However, the Puritans were not as close-minded about sex as their reputation suggests, and they believed that sexuality was good and proper within marriage. In fact, men were obligated to have intercourse with their wives. The Puritans also tolerated most mild sexual transgressions as long as people accepted their punishments and repented.

As the New World began to grow, it suffered from a lack of women, and the speculation in Europe was that any woman seeking a man should come to America, which offered women greater independence than Europe. On the island of Nantucket, for exam-

ple, whaling kept the men at sea for months. The women took over the island's businesses, and prestige was granted to those who managed to make the money grow while their husbands were away (V. L. Bullough, 1973). Still, women were generally expected to tend to their domain of the home and children.

Sexuality was also a bit freer, and courting youth would wander into barns or look for high crops in the field to obscure their necking and groping. There was also a custom called **bundling,** in which young couples were allowed to share a bed as long as they were clothed, wrapped in sheets or bags, or had a wooden "bundling board" between them. The large number of premarital pregnancies suggests that couples found ways to get around their bundling impediments, but in most such cases, the couple would quickly marry (D'Emilio & Freedman, 1988).

bundling
An American practice of placing a wooden board or hanging sheets in the middle of the bed, or wrapping the body in tight clothes, in order to allow an unmarried couple to spend the night together without having sex.

The United States: Freedom—and Slavery—in the New World

After the Revolutionary War, the church's power began to diminish in the United States, and this led to more liberal sexual conduct. This liberalization, along with the continuing slave influx from Africa, had powerful effects on our culture's developing sexuality.

The Liberalization of Sex

The church's power began to wane in the late 1700s, and communities began abolishing church courts, which had previously heard cases of divorce and sexual crimes. The United States entered a period of practical, utilitarian philosophy (as exemplified in Benjamin Franklin's maxims, such as "Early to bed and early to rise . . ."), which stressed the individual's right to pursue personal happiness. People began to speak more openly about sexuality and romantic love, and women began to pay more attention to appearance and sexual appeal. Children stopped consulting parents about marriage, and some young women simply became pregnant when they wanted to marry. By the late 18th century, as many as one-third of all brides in some parts of New England were pregnant (D'Emilio & Freedman, 1988).

This newfound sexual freedom had many results. In 1720, prostitution was relatively rare, but by the late 18th century, angry mobs were attacking brothels in cities all over the eastern seaboard (D'Emilio & Freedman, 1988). Contraception, such as early condoms, was now readily available (Gamson, 1990), and newspapers and almanacs often advertised contraceptive devices and concoctions to induce abortion. The birth rate dropped, and abortion rates rose through the use of patent medicines, folk remedies, self-induced abortion by inserting objects into the uterus, and medical abortions. Within marriage, sexuality was much celebrated, and in many surviving diaries and letters from that era, couples speak of passion and longing for each other. Extramarital affairs were not uncommon, and some of the diaries quite explicitly record extramarital sexual passion.

Slavery

Before the influx of slaves from Africa, the southern colonies had made use of **indentured servants.** Sexual contact with and even rape of female indentured servants was fairly common. Interracial sex was legal, and southern white men often took black slaves as wives. After 1670, African slaves became common in the South, and many states passed **antimiscegenation** (an-TEE-miss-seg-jen-nay-shun) **laws.** At first the laws were largely ignored. Sexual relations between whites and blacks continued, ranging from brutal rape to genuinely affectionate, long-term relationships. By the end of the 18th century, mixed-race children accounted for one-fifth of the children born out of wedlock in Virginia (D'Emilio & Freedman, 1988).

The sex lives of slaves were different from those of colonists due to the relative lack of female slaves, the restrictions put on contact with members of the other sex, and the different cultural traditions of Africa. African slaves were accused by whites of having loose morals because women tended to have children by different fathers and children slept in the same rooms as their copulating parents. These sexual habits of slaves were used as an excuse to rape them, break up their families, and even, at times, kill them. Of course, slave owners did not consider that they were responsible for forcing slaves to live that way. The fear that freed black men would rape white women (or accusations that they had) was often used as justification to keep blacks segregated or to lynch them, even though it was far more common for white men to rape black slaves and servants. White women, on the other hand, had their movements and freedoms restricted for fear that they would "lose their virtue" to black males. The paradox was that the sexual availability of female black slaves severely damaged the sexual relations between white men and women.

The slaves themselves developed a social system to protect their few freedoms. Adults formed and tried to maintain stable unions when possible, although marriage was officially illegal between slaves. Despite harsh conditions, there was a strong sense of morality within the slave community, and slaves tried to regulate sexual behavior as much as possible, forcing men to take care of the women they impregnated and sanctioning girls who were too promiscuous. The myth of slave sexual looseness is disproved by the lack of prostitution and very low venereal disease (STI) rates among slaves (D'Emilio & Freedman, 1988). It is difficult, however, to maintain sexual unions when the woman's body is legally owned by the white master or when sexual favors might free one from harsh labor in the cotton fields. Despite the fact that plantation owners often condemned the promiscuity of the blacks (and therefore excused their own sexual exploitation of them), slaves' premarital sexual activity was probably not much different from that of poor whites.

Settlers throughout early American history used the sexuality of minorities as an excuse to disdain or oppress them. Native Americans had their own cultural system of sexual morality; nonetheless, they were branded as savages for their acceptance of premarital sex and their practice of polygamy, which existed primarily because of the large

Human Sexuality in a Diverse World

Sex in Black America

Although there has been significant growth in the scientific study of sexuality within the last 20 years, many specific populations, such as African American men and women, have not been equally studied (Lewis & Kertzner, 2003). Because of this, there have been many myths about the sexuality of African American men and women. Black women have typically been portrayed as overly sexed women with uncontrollable lust. Black men and women are often viewed as "super sexperts" because they are supposed to know a lot about sexuality and engage in a lot of sex (Wyatt, 1999). They have been portrayed as sexually promiscuous, unable to control their sex drives or satisfy their sexual urges, and as "baby makers" (Grimes, 1999). Many of these myths surfaced during slavery out of the desire to scare white women away from black men, while allowing white men to sexually exploit black women (Leavy, 1993).

© Rob Levine/Corbis

One of the most prominent early sexuality researchers, Alfred Kinsey, did include African Americans in his study, but his sample size was small and select (Kinsey, Pomeroy, Martin, & Gebhard, 1953; we will discuss more of Kinsey's work in Chapter 2). Studies that followed Kinsey focused on the differences between black and white sexuality and ignored the diversity and richness of black sexuality. Many of these studies supported the myths about black sexuality.

Studies on African American sexuality have found that black men and women are very conservative in their sexual behavior (Bowser, 2001; Leavy, 1993; Lewis & Kertzner, 2003). Gail Wyatt, a sex therapist, researcher, and professor of psychiatry at UCLA, has been researching black sexuality for over 15 years. In 1998, she published *Stolen Women: Reclaiming Our Sexuality, Taking Back Our Lives.* Although we will discuss her book more throughout this textbook, here let me cite some of her interesting findings:

- 83% of black women did not masturbate during childhood.
- 74% of white women and 26% of black women (between the ages of 18 and 36) had 13 or more sexual partners.
- 56% of black women had only one sexual partner from the time they initiated sexual intercourse until age 17, whereas only 36% of white women reported a long-term relationship during adolescence.
- Black men (72%) are more likely to use condoms for birth control and STI protection than white men (37%).
- 93% of white women and 55% of black women have had oral sex performed on them, whereas 93% of white women and 65% of black women have performed oral sex on a man.

Other studies have found that African American gay and bisexual men who have integrated their identification as both African American and gay have higher levels of self-esteem, greater levels of life satisfaction, and lower levels of male gender-role distress than those who have not integrated these identities (Crawford, Allison, Zamboni, & Sotot, 2002).

number of males killed in war. White men freely raped female Native Americans, for whites could not be convicted of rape, or any crime, solely on the testimony of a "savage Indian." Similarly, Americans used sexual imagery to criticize the Mexicans they encountered in the West and Southwest; one writer claimed that all "darker colored" races were "inferior and syphilitic" (D'Emilio & Freedman, 1988). Mexicans, who were religious Catholics with strict sexual rules, were considered promiscuous by the Protestants because they did not consider it wrong to dance or show affection in public. The settlers often criticized others for sexual behaviors, such as homosexuality and premarital sex, that were not uncommon in their own communities.

The 19th Century: Polygamy, Celibacy, and the Comstock Laws

The 19th century saw the rise of a number of controversial social movements focusing on sexuality. The **free love movement,** which began in the 1820s, preached that love, not marriage, should be the prerequisite to sexual relations. Free love advocates criti-

free love movement
A movement of the early 19th century that preached that love should be the factor that determines whether one should have sex (not to be confused with the free love movement of the 1960s).

cized the sexual "slavery" of women in marriage, often condemned the sexual exploitation of slaves, and condemned uncontrolled sexuality unconnected to love (though their critics often claimed that they preached promiscuity).

Another controversial group, the Church of Jesus Christ of Latter Day Saints, or Mormons, announced in 1852 that many of its members practiced polygamy, which almost cost Utah its statehood. As with the free love movement, Americans accused the Mormons of loose morals even though, despite their acceptance of polygamy, they were very sexually conservative (Iverson, 1991). A number of small communities that practiced alternative forms of sexual relations also began during this time. The Oneida community preached group marriage, whereas the Shakers, frustrated with all the arguments over sexuality, practiced strict celibacy.

By the close of the 19th century, the medical model of sexuality began to emerge. Americans became obsessed with sexual health, and physicians and reformers began to advocate self-restraint, abstention from masturbation, and eating "nonstimulating" foods. Doctors also argued that women were ruled by their wombs, and many had their ovaries surgically removed to "correct" masturbation or sexual passion. An influential group of physicians even argued that women were biologically designed for procreation and destined only for marriage, for they were too delicate to work or undergo the rigors of higher education. These theories completely ignored the fact that lower-class women often worked difficult labor 12 and 15 hours a day. Male sexuality, however, was viewed as normative.

In the 19th century, homosexuality was underground, though there were some open same-sex relationships that may or may not have been sexual. For example, there are a number of recorded cases in which women dressed and passed as men and even "married" other women (we will discuss this more in Chapter 3). There were also men who wrote of intimate and loving relationships with other men, without an explicit admission of sexual contact. The great poet Walt Whitman, now recognized as a homosexual, at times confirmed his erotic attraction to men, while at other times he denied it. In accordance with the developing medical model of sexuality, physicians began to argue that homosexuality was an illness rather than a sin, a view that lasted until the 1970s (Hansen, 1989; see Chapter 11).

The movements for more open sexual relationships were countered by strong voices arguing for a return to a more religious and chaste morality, an argument that continues more than a century later. In the 1870s, Anthony Comstock, a dry-goods salesman, single-handedly lobbied the legislature to outlaw obscenity. The resulting Comstock Act of 1873 prohibited the mailing of obscene, lewd, lascivious, and indecent writing or advertisements, including articles about contraception or abortion. Comstock himself was the act's most vigorous enforcer, and he reported hundreds of people to the authorities, even for such things as selling reprints of famous artwork containing nudity or famous books that mentioned prostitution. Literally thousands of books, sexual objects, and contraceptive devices were destroyed, denying many people sophisticated contraceptive devices or information for almost 60 years (D'Emilio & Freedman, 1988).

The 20th Century: Sexual Crusaders and Sexologists

In a study of 1,000 women born shortly before the turn of the 20th century, 74% used some form of contraception (despite Comstock), most made love at least once a week, and 40% acknowledged masturbating during childhood or adolescence (although others began after marriage; D'Emilio & Freedman, 1988). These statistics reflect the freedom women found as they moved to the cities, lived on their own, and began working more outside the home (Irvine, 1990). Yet fewer than half the women polled considered sex crucial to their mental or physical health, and an overwhelming majority still considered reproduction the primary goal of sex. In part, this may be because information about sex was generally unavailable; there was a high correlation between lack of sexual instruction, distaste for sex, and unhappiness in marriage.

By the turn of the 20th century, moral crusaders trying to curb newfound sexual freedoms and those trying to further liberalize sexuality were in a serious struggle, trying to guide the rapid changes taking place in American sexual behaviors. Moral crusaders

Review Question

Identify five influences on the developing views of sexuality in early American society.

pointed to the spread of prostitution, high rates of sexually transmitted infections (STIs), and youth who rejected traditional morality for nightclubs, dances, and long-delayed marriages. Liberalizers argued that modern industrial society could not sustain the coercive sexual standards of past centuries. In one guise or another, these battles are still being fought today, more than 100 years later.

The Social Hygiene Movement

In response to high STI rates, a New York physician, Prince Morrow, started a movement in 1905 that was a curious mixture of both liberal and traditional attitudes. The social hygiene movement convinced legislators that scores of "virtuous" women were catching STIs from husbands who frequented prostitutes, and so laws were passed mandating blood tests before marriage, and a number of highly publicized police actions were brought against prostitutes. On the other hand, although the movement accepted that sex in marriage was for pleasure, not just reproduction, followers were against premarital sex and warned that masturbation harmed one's future sex life. Most importantly, they were early (if unsuccessful) advocates for sex education in the schools for all students, male and female (D'Emilio & Freedman, 1988).

Sexology

Beginning in the early part of the century and increasingly by midcentury, the pioneers of sexual research were beginning to make scientific advances into the understanding of sexuality. Rejecting the religious and moral teachings about how people "should" behave, researchers brought sex out into the open as a subject worthy of medical, scientific, and philosophical debate. We discuss these researchers at length in the following chapter, but here we should note that they had a profound impact on the way people began to talk and think about sexuality.

For example, by midcentury Kinsey's large-scale surveys of American sexual behavior were promising to settle some of the debates and confusion about sexuality by providing scientific solutions to questions about how people behaved. Masters and Johnson were trying to do the same for the physiology of the sexual response. The work of these sexologists helped to demystify sex and to make it more respectable to publicly discuss the sexual behaviors and problems of real people. Much of this work was condemned by moral crusaders, who criticized its lack of connection to traditional standards of morality (Irvine, 1990).

Feminism

There have always been women who protested against the patriarchy of their day, argued that women were as capable as men in the realms of work and politics, and defied their culture's stereotypes about women. Yet the 20th century saw the most successful feminist movement in history. The **women's suffrage** movement of the early 20th century first put women's agendas on the national scene, but it was Margaret Sanger who most profoundly influenced women's sexuality in the first half of the 20th century.

women's suffrage
The movement to get women the right to vote.

Sanger, a 30-year-old homemaker, attended a lecture on socialism that transformed her into an advocate for the rights of workers and their children. Sanger defied the Comstock laws by arguing that poor workers, who were having child after child, needed birth control. Her statement "It is none of society's business what a woman shall do with her body" has remained the centerpiece of feminist views on the relation between the state and sexuality ever since. Because she published information about birth control, Sanger was forced to flee to England to avoid arrest for violating the Comstock laws. She finally returned when a groundswell of support in the United States convinced her to come back and face trial. Intellectuals from across Europe wrote to President Woodrow Wilson on her behalf, and the public was so outraged by her arrest that the prosecutors dropped the case. She then opened a birth control clinic in Brooklyn (which eventually evolved into the Planned Parenthood organization) and was repeatedly arrested, evoking much protest from her supporters.

After Sanger, organized feminism entered a quiet phase, not reemerging until the 1960s. In the middle of the 20th century, women increasingly entered institutions of higher education and entered the labor force in great numbers while men were off fighting World War II. At the same time, divorce rates were rising, many women widowed by war were raising children as single parents, and the postwar baby boom relegated middle class women to their suburban homes. Social conditions had given women more power just as their roles were being restricted again to wife and mother. A backlash was soon to come.

The modern feminist movement can best be summarized by the work of three women authors (Ferree & Hess, 1985). In her 1949 book, *The Second Sex*, Simone de Beauvoir showed that women were not granted an identity of their own but were considered the objects of men's wishes and anxieties. Betty Friedan followed in 1963 with *The Feminine Mystique*, a 10-year follow-up of the lives of her graduating class from Smith College, in which she found that these educated, bright women felt trapped in the role of housewife and wanted careers in order to have happier, more fulfilled lives. Finally, at the height of the Vietnam War, Kate Millet's (1969) *Sexual Politics* argued that patriarchy breeds violence and forces men to renounce all that is feminine in them. According to Millet, rape is an act of aggression aimed at keeping women docile and controlling them, and men see homosexuality as a "failure" of patriarchy, so it is violently repressed.

Feminists of the 1960s argued that they were entitled to sexual satisfaction, that the existing relations of the sexes were exploitative, and that women had a right to control their lives and their bodies. Some of the more radical feminists advocated lesbianism as the only relationship not based on male power, but most feminists fought for a transformation of the interpersonal relationship of men and women and of the male-dominated political structure. Part of the freedom women needed was the freedom to choose when to be mothers, and the right to choose abortion became a firm part of the feminist platform.

Feminism has made great cultural and political strides and has changed the nature of American society and sexual behavior. The pursuit of sexual pleasure is now seen as a woman's legitimate right, and men are no longer expected to be the sexual experts relied upon by docile, virginal mates. Feminists were at the forefront of the abortion debate and hailed the legalization of abortion as a great step in achieving women's rights over their own bodies. More recently, women have begun entering politics in record numbers, and the Senate, Congress, and governorships are increasingly counting women among their members. Even so, women still have many struggles. Men are paid more than women for the same work, poverty is increasingly a problem of single mothers, and rape and spousal abuse are still major social problems in the United States. Still, feminism as a movement has had a major impact on the way America views sexuality.

Gay Liberation

Following World War II was a period of challenge to homosexuals. Senator Joseph McCarthy, who became famous for trying to purge America of communists, also relentlessly hunted homosexuals. Homosexuals were portrayed as perverts, lurking in schools and on street corners ready to pounce on unsuspecting youth, and many were thrown out of work or imprisoned in jails and mental hospitals. The news media participated in this view, as in a 1949 *Newsweek* article that identified all homosexuals as "sex murderers." Doctors tinkered with a variety of "cures," including lobotomies and castration. Churches were either silent or encouraged the witch hunts, and Hollywood purged itself of positive references to homosexuality. Many laws initiated during this period, such as immigration restrictions for homosexuals and policies banning gays from the military, have lasted in some form until today (Adam, 1987).

In 1951, an organization for homosexual rights, the Mattachine Society, was founded in the United States by Henry Hay. The Daughters of Bilitis, the first postwar lesbian organization, was founded by four lesbian couples in San

The gay liberation movement has argued that all sexual minorities have a right to sexual happiness.

© Don Mason/Corbis

Francisco in 1955. Though these groups began with radical intentions, the vehement antihomosexuality of American authorities forced the groups to lay low throughout the late 1950s.

Though gay activism had been increasing in America with protests and sit-ins throughout the 1960s, modern gay liberation is usually traced to the night in 1969 when New York police raided a Greenwich Village gay bar called Stonewall. For the first time, the gay community erupted in active resistance, and the police were greeted by a hail of debris thrown by the gay patrons of the bar. Though there had been previous acts of resistance, the Stonewall riot became a symbol to the gay community and put the police on notice that homosexuals would no longer passively accept arrest and police brutality.

Following Stonewall, gay activism began a strong campaign against prejudice and discrimination all over the country. Groups and businesses hostile to gays were picketed, legislators were lobbied, committees and self-help groups were founded, legal agencies were formed, and educational groups tried to change the image of homosexuality in America. For example, in 1973 strong gay lobbying caused the American Psychiatric Association to remove homosexuality from the *Diagnostic and Statistical Manual* (DSM), the official reference of psychiatric disorders. Almost overnight, people who had been considered "sick" were suddenly "normal." The DSM change removed the last scientific justification for treating homosexuals any differently than other citizens and demonstrated the new national power of the movement for homosexual rights. Soon the gay movement was a powerful presence in the United States, Canada, Australia, and Western Europe (Adam, 1987).

The 1970s were, in many ways, the golden age of gay life in America. In cities like San Francisco and New York, gay bathhouses and bars became open centers of gay social life, and gay theater groups, newspapers, and magazines sprang up. In 1979, the National March on Washington for Lesbian and Gay Rights was a symbolic step forward for the gay movement (Ghaziani, 2005). Other marches would follow in 1987, 1993, and 2000. The gradual discovery of the AIDS epidemic in the United States and Europe in the beginning of the 1980s ended the excitement of the 1970s, as thousands of gay men began to die from the disease (see Chapter 15). Historically, when such fearsome epidemics arise, people have been quick to find a minority group to blame for the disease, and homosexuals were quickly blamed by a large segment of the public (Perrow & Guillén, 1990; Shilts, 2000).

In 1990, queer theory developed and grew out of lesbian and gay studies. We will discuss queer theory more in Chapter 2. In summary, the gay rights movement has been at the forefront of trying to change sexual attitudes in the country, not only by pressing for recognition of homosexuality as a legitimate sexual choice, but also by arguing that all sexual minorities have a right to sexual happiness. Although a handful of states allow gay couples to register as "domestic partners" and allow them certain health and death benefits that married couples have, the issue of gay marriage is still controversial in American society. In 2004 Massachusetts became the first U.S. state to grant marriage licenses to same-sex couples. Still, gays and lesbians are subject to prejudices in America, and some states are passing laws making it illegal for homosexuals to be considered a minority group worthy of special protections.

We are the sum total of our history. Our attitudes and beliefs reflect all of our historical influences, from the ancient Hebrews and Greeks to the Christianity of the Middle Ages to the modern feminist and gay liberation movements. The great difficulty most of us have is in recognizing that our own constellation of beliefs, feelings, and moral positions about sex are a product of our particular time and place, and are in a constant state of evolution. It is important to keep this in mind as we explore the sexual behaviors of other people and other cultures throughout this book.

In 2004 Massachusetts became the first state in the United States to grant marriage licenses to same-sex couples.

Review Question

What are the two most important movements to change sexuality in the latter part of the 20th century? What did each contribute?

ACTIVE SUMMARY

1. Intercourse in the animal kingdom is common and necessary for species survival, whereas sexuality is a uniquely **(a)** _____ _____. This is because only human beings have developed ideas, **(b)** _____, and **(c)** _____ around the sexual act. Human sexuality is grounded in **(d)** _____ _____. Few areas of life are as **(e)** _____ and **(f)** _____ as sexuality.

2. American media are the most **(a)** _____ _____ in the Western Hemisphere. Many shows popular with college students today use sex to **(b)** _____ _____. Makeover reality shows play on our **(c)** _____ _____ and decrease our feelings of **(d)** _____.

3. Social norms, **(a)** _____, and **(b)** _____ hold us back from expressing many of our sexual needs and desires. Teenagers today rate the **(c)** _____ as one of their leading sources of sex information. Sex sells in advertising because we **(d)** _____ the feelings generated in a sexual advertisement with a particular product.

4. The evolution from quadrupeds to an upright posture forever changed the way humans engaged in **(a)** _____ _____. This is because **(b)** _____ became more important than the sense of smell. It also increased the possibility of **(c)** _____ _____. This, in turn, increased the **(d)** _____ _____ of intercourse.

5. Men dominated **(a)** _____ _____ in early history and we know far more about men's **(b)** _____ than women's. The **(c)** _____ _____ contained very explicit rules about sexual behavior. The focus on marital sexuality and **(d)** _____ formed the basis of sexual attitudes in the West for centuries.

6. The Greeks were **(a)** _____ sexually permissive than the Hebrews. In Greek culture, **(b)** _____ was considered a natural form of sexuality. Rome had **(c)** _____ restrictions about sexuality until late in the history of the empire. Chinese civilization's belief in **(d)** _____ taught people how to maximize their sexuality.

7. A woman's essence, or yin, was viewed as **(a)** _____, whereas a man's essence, yang, embodied in semen, was **(b)** _____. Hinduism concentrates on an individual's cycle of birth and rebirth, also known as **(c)** _____. India's most famous sex manual, the **(d)** _____, appeared sometime during the 3rd or 4th century.

8. Perhaps no single system of thought had as much impact on the Western world as **(a)** _____. According to this belief, sexuality itself was not sinful when performed as part of the **(b)** _____ _____, but the ideal situation was **(c)** _____. In fact, for the first time in history, **(d)** _____ became a virtue.

9. In the early Middle Ages, the influence of the **(a)** _____ began to increase. Its teachings began to influence **(b)** _____, which became much **(c)** _____. Perhaps no person from the Middle Ages had a stronger impact on attitudes toward sexuality than the theologian **(d)** _____ _____.

10. Muhammad began to preach a religion in the 6th century called **(a)** _____. Many Muslim societies have strong rules of **(b)** _____ for women that involve covering private parts of a woman's body. According to the Muslim bible, the **(c)** _____, marital sexual intercourse was a good **(d)** _____ _____ , and men were encouraged to frequently engage in such behavior. All forms of sexuality were permissible.

11. The Renaissance witnessed a new **(a)** _____ of sexuality and of the roles of women in society. Women made great strides in **(b)** _____ and became more prominent in political affairs. Profemale tracts began to circulate, and lively debates about the **(c)** _____ of women ensued. However, by the 17th century, **(d)** _____ trials appeared, symbolizing the fear that men held of women's sexuality.

12. In the early 16th century, Martin Luther started Protestantism, and Luther saw in the Bible the obligation to **(a)** _____, saw marital love as **(b)** _____, and considered sexuality a(n) **(c)** _____ _____. Sexuality was permissible only in the **(d)** _____ _____, although it had other justifications besides reproduction.

13. Three great movements that influenced modern sexuality were the **(a)** _____, the **(b)** _____, and the **(c)** _____.

14. After the Revolutionary War the **(a)** _____'s power began to diminish in the United States. People began to **(b)** _____ more openly about sexuality, and the **(c)** _____ of sexual conduct had many results. Prostitution flourished, and contraception became more **(d)** _____ _____.

15. Slavery had a(n) **(a)** _____ effect on post–Revolutionary America. Many slaves developed a social system and formed stable unions, although **(b)** _____ was officially illegal between slaves. There was a strong sense of **(c)** _____ within the slave community, and **(d)** _____ _____ was regulated as much as possible.

16. The 19th century saw the rise of a number of controversial social movements focusing on human sexuality, including the **(a)** _____ _____ movement. Strong voices argued against this movement and proposed a more **(b)** _____ morality. The **(c)** _____ _____ movement followed in response to increasing rates of STIs.

17. In the 20th century, three major trends profoundly influenced sexuality: **(a)** _____, **(b)** _____, and the **(c)** _____ _____ _____. Today we know that we are the sum total of our **(d)** _____.

Critical Thinking Questions

1. Explain your goals for this class and how you developed each of these goals. Do you think this class will help you in the future? If so, in what ways?

2. Why do you think "sex sells" when our culture traditionally has had a problem openly talking about sexuality?

3. The Bible has had a profound impact on our attitudes toward sexuality. Do you think that it is still influential? In what ways?

4. Is it acceptable to judge the morality of a civilization's sexuality by modern standards? Was ancient Greece's pederasty "immoral"?

5. How different do China's and India's sexual histories seem to you today? Are they different from our Western views of sexuality?

6. Compare and contrast both the role of women and the views of sexuality in modern society and Islam.

CHAPTER RESOURCES

Check It Out

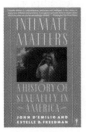

D'Emilio, J., & Freedman, E. B. (1988). **Intimate matters: A history of sexuality in America.** New York: HarperCollins.

This book reveals how we have moved from sexual repression to sexual freedom. In each era sexuality has been reshaped due to factors such as the economy, family structure, and politics. The media and Internet also exert influences and shape sexuality. The authors explore topics such as racial sex-stereotyping, Chinese slave rings, abortion, same-sex relationships, women's rights, and AIDS-engendered conservatism.

The Virgin Diaries (2002; 57 minutes; NR). Available from First Run/Icarus Films, 32 Court St., 21st Floor, Brooklyn, New York 11201 (718) 488-8900.

An important movie for understanding contemporary Islam and traditional Middle Eastern cultures, *The Virgin Diaries* is the story of an Islamic woman on the verge of marrying the man her grandfather has chosen for her. She embarks on a journey for answers about virginity, sex, and Islam. This quest takes her to ancient Islamic schools, camel markets, city doctors' offices (the most common minor surgery in Morocco is the repair of the hymen), and beachside resorts.

InfoTrac® College Edition

If your instructor ordered InfoTrac with this book, explore InfoTrac College Edition, your online library, for additional readings and review. Go to: **www.thomsonedu.com,** and enter these search terms:

Victorian era   Comstock   history of sex

Web Resources

SexualityNow Companion Website
Go to **http://thomsonedu.com/carroll** for practice quiz questions, interactive activities, Internet links, critical thinking exercises, discussion forums, and more. You can also access sites from the Wadsworth Psychology Study Center **(http://psychology.wadsworth.com)** or you can connect directly to the following sites:

The Kinsey Institute
This is the official website for the Kinsey Institute, founded by Dr. Alfred Kinsey (1894–1956) in 1947. The Institute is one of only a handful of centers in the world that conducts interdisciplinary research exclusively on sex. The Institute is housed within Indiana University in Bloomington, Indiana, and has a large library that includes books, films, video, fine art, artifacts, photography, archives, and more.

The Journal of the History of Sexuality
The *Journal of the History of Sexuality* illuminates the history of sexuality in all its expressions, recognizing various differences of class, culture, gender, race, and sexual orientation. The journal provides a forum for historical, critical, and theoretical research in this field. Its cross-cultural and cross-disciplinary character brings together original articles and critical reviews from historians, social scientists, and humanities scholars worldwide. The website offers a look at recently published articles in the journal.

Salem Witch Trials Documentary Archive
This website offers information on the Salem witch trials, including transcripts of court records and maps. Also included are links to Salem witchcraft papers from a variety of sources.

Sexuality Information and Education Council of the United States
The Sexuality Information and Education Council of the U.S. (SIECUS) is a national, nonprofit organization that affirms that sexuality is a natural and healthy part of living. SIECUS develops, collects, and disseminates information; promotes comprehensive education about sexuality; and advocates the right of individuals to make responsible sexual choices. This link to SIECUS offers information specifically on religion, including topics such as morality, spirituality, and sexuality, and sexuality education in faith communities, as well as links to a variety of organizations with projects in religion and sexuality.

Go to **www.thomsonedu.com** to link to **SexualityNow,** your online study tool. First take the **Pre-Test** for this chapter to get your **Personalized Study Plan,** which will identify topics you need to review and direct you to online resources. Then take the **Post-Test** to determine what concepts you have mastered and what you still need work on.

Videos in SexualityNow
For additional information on topics discussed in this chapter, check out the videos in **SexualityNow** on the following topics:

• **Politics, Religion, and Sexual Expression**—Answers questions about the frequency and nature of sexual practices among churchgoers, nonchurchgoers, Republicans, and Democrats in the United States.

2 Understanding Human Sexuality: Theory and Research

Sexuality ⬤ **Now** Go to www.thomsonedu.com to link to **SexualityNow,** your online study tool.

*Y*ou might wonder why reviewing theory and research in a sexuality textbook is important. Because theories guide our understanding of sexuality, and research helps answer our many questions, learning how theories are formulated and research is pursued will give you insight into the information that is provided in the chapters to come. Recently I asked my students to imagine that they were sexuality researchers who were designing a new study. What topic would they be interested in studying? Students have a wide range of interests: some wanted to examine gender differences; others were interested in specific aspects of sexual behavior. If you were to do a study in some area of sexuality, what would you be most interested in?

How should you frame your questions? Do you need to understand theory to decide what you are interested in? Once you have decided your area of interest, what comes next? How is a research study done? What are some of the obstacles to doing sexuality research, and how can these difficulties be avoided?

The results of sexuality studies seem to appear everywhere today—in magazines, newspapers, and on television. But how do you know whether the research is reliable, that it has been carried out properly? In this chapter, we will explore both the major theories and the research methods that underlie the study of sexuality. We will also examine information on some of the most influential sexuality studies that have been done. Theoretical development and ongoing research combine to provide a foundation on which to build further understanding of sexuality.

THEORIES ABOUT SEXUALITY

The study of sexuality is multidisciplinary. Psychologists, sexologists, biologists, theologians, physicians, sociologists, anthropologists, and philosophers all perform sexuality research. The questions each discipline asks and how its practitioners transform those questions into research projects can differ greatly. However, the insights of these disciplines complement each other, and no single approach to the study of sexuality is better than another.

A **theory** is a set of assumptions, principles, or methods that help a researcher understand the nature of the phenomenon being studied. A theory provides an intellectual structure to help conceptualize, implement, and interpret a topic, such as human sexuality. The majority of researchers begin with theories about human behavior that guide the kind of questions they ask about sexuality. For example, suppose a researcher sub-

theory
A set of assumptions, principles, or methods that helps a researcher understand the nature of the phenomenon being studied.

SEXTalk

Question: When scientists come up with new theories, how do they know they are true?

They don't. Theories begin as ideas to explain observed phenomena, but must undergo testing and evaluation. Many early theories of sexuality were developed out of work with patients, such as Sigmund Freud's work, whereas others base their theories on behaviors they observe or the results of experiments they conduct. However, researchers never really know whether their theories are true or not. Some scientists become so biased by their own theories that they have trouble seeing explanations other than their own for certain behaviors. That is why scientific findings or ideas should always be tested and confirmed by other scientists.

scribes to the theory that sexuality is innate and biologically determined; he or she would probably design studies to examine such things as how the hypothalamus in the brain influences our sexual behavior, or the monthly cycle of hormones. It is unlikely he or she would be interested in studying how society influences sexuality. A person who believes sexuality is determined by environmental influences, on the other hand, would be more likely to study how the media influences sexuality rather than genetic patterns of sexual behavior.

There are several theories—often clashing—that guide much of our thinking about sexuality. These include psychological, biological, sociological, and evolutionary theoretical views of human sexuality. In addition, over the last few years, feminist and queer theories have also become important models for exploring and explaining sexual behavior. We will first explore each of these and look at how they influence sexuality research. While we do, however, it is important to remember that many theorists borrow from multiple theoretical perspectives, and that these categories often overlap and learn from each other.

Psychological Theories

Of the psychological theories of sexuality, the most influential has been Sigmund Freud's psychoanalytic theory. Freud felt that the sex drive was one of the most important forces in life, and he spent a considerable amount of time studying sexuality.

Psychoanalytic Theory

Sigmund Freud (1856–1939) spent most of his life in Vienna, Austria. In the early 1900s, Sigmund Freud gathered a group of psychologists together to further his ideas, and he became the founder of the psychoanalytic school. He is also indirectly responsible for many concepts that form the foundation of other theories that followed psychoanalytic theory. Some of these theories will be presented in the following sections. For now, we explore two of Freud's most controversial concepts—personality formation and psychosexual development.

Personality Formation According to Freud, human behavior is motivated by instincts and drives. The two most powerful drives are **libido** (la-BEED-oh), which is the sexual motivation, and **thanatos** (THAN-uh-toes), which is the aggressiveness motivation. Of these two, the libido is the more powerful.

Freud believed that there were two divisions to the personality. In the first division, he identified three levels in which the personality operates. These included the conscious, preconscious, and unconscious. The **conscious** level contains information that we are aware of—for instance, right now as you are reading this page you are aware of the fact that you are doing so, and you might also be aware of other things going on around you. You are *consciously* aware of all of this information. However, there are some things that you might not be aware of, but you could recall them if you wanted to or someone asked you to. For instance, what did you have for dinner two nights ago? This information is stored in your **preconscious** level. The third level of the personality, the **unconscious**, Freud believed, was the most important part. The unconscious level contains information that we have no conscious access to, such as conflicts or anxiety-producing memories. However, even though we have no access to the unconscious, it is responsible for much of our behavior. For example, perhaps there are unconscious reasons why we choose the partners we do.

The second division of the personality contains the id, ego, and superego. At birth, a child has only the **id** portion of the personality, which functions as the pleasure center. A child is interested only in things that bring immediate satisfaction; for example, when a child is hungry, he or she cries. The id operates totally within the unconscious part of the mind. If the id were the only part of the personality that developed, we would always be seeking pleasure and fulfillment with little concern for others; in other words, the way most animals operate. As humans get older, however, the id balances its desires with other parts of the personality.

Review Question

What is a theory? How does a theory help guide research?

sex byte

Throughout most of history, religion provided the standards for appropriate sexual and social behaviors. However, from the 20th century on, social scientists (relying on their own beliefs, expectations, personal experiences, and social circumstances) have become the experts (Ericksen, 1999).

libido
According to Freud, the energy generated by the sexual instinct.

thanatos
According to Freud, the self-destructive instinct, often turned outward in the form of aggression.

conscious
The part of the personality that contains information of which we are currently aware.

preconscious
The part of the personality that contains thoughts that can be brought into awareness with little difficulty.

unconscious
All the ideas, thoughts, and feelings to which we have no conscious access.

id
The collection of unconscious urges and desires that continually seek expression.

Sigmund Freud (1856–1939), the father of psychoanalysis, set the stage for all other psychological theories.

ego
The part of the personality that mediates between environmental demands (reality), conscience (superego), and instinctual needs (id).

superego
The social and parental standards an individual has internalized; the conscience.

psychoanalysis
System of psychotherapy developed by Freud that focuses on uncovering the unconscious material responsible for a patient's disorder.

psychosexual development
The childhood stages of development during which the id's pleasure-seeking energies focus on distinct erogenous zones.

erogenous zones
Areas that are particularly sensitive to touch and are associated with sexual pleasure.

fixation
The tying up of psychic energy at a particular psychosexual stage, resulting in adult behaviors characteristic of the stage.

oral stage
A psychosexual stage in which the mouth, lips, and tongue are the primary erogenous zone.

anal fixation
The result of unresolved conflict in the anal stage, characterized by anal character traits, such as excessive stubbornness, orderliness, or cleanliness.

phallic stage
A psychosexual stage in which the genital region is the primary erogenous zone and in which the Oedipus or Electra complex develops.

Oedipus complex
A male child's sexual attraction for his mother and the consequent conflicts.

By the 2nd year of life, the **ego** develops as the child begins to interact with his or her environment. The ego constitutes the reality part of the personality, and it keeps the id in check by being realistic about what the child can and cannot have. Because the majority of the id's desires may be socially unacceptable, the ego works to restrain it. The ego can move among the conscious, preconscious, and unconscious.

By 5 years of age, the last portion of the personality, the **superego,** develops. It contains both societal and parental values and puts more restrictions on what we can and cannot do. It acts as our conscience, and its most effective weapon is guilt. For example, let's say that a woman was raised in a very religious family and learned that premarital sexual activity was wrong. One night she becomes passionate with her long-term boyfriend (an id action). This activity feels pleasurable, and the id is being fulfilled. Suddenly, reality kicks in (the ego), and she realizes that she is engaging in sexual activity with her boyfriend in the back seat of a car, which is parked at a busy convenience store—she could be discovered at any moment! This causes her to evaluate the situation, because she has been taught that premarital sexual activity is wrong. As a result, she begins to feel guilty (a superego action). Throughout our lives, the id, ego, and superego are in a constant struggle with each other, but it is the ego, or the realistic portion of our personality, that keeps the other two parts balanced.

Two things can occur if the ego does not keep things in balance. First, if the superego takes over, the person might be paralyzed by guilt. If, on the other hand, the id takes over, the person might constantly search for pleasure with little concern for others. Freud believed that the only way to bring these conditions into balance was for the person to undergo **psychoanalysis,** which allows the individual to bring unconscious thoughts into consciousness.

Psychosexual Development   One of Freud's most controversial ideas was his theory of **psychosexual development.** He believed that one's basic personality was formed by events that happened in the first 6 years of life. During each stage of development, Freud identified a different **erogenous (uh-RAJ-uh-nus) zone** where libidinal energy was directed. If the stage was not successfully completed, the libidinal energy was tied up in that zone, and the child could experience a **fixation.** We will discuss this more in a moment.

The first stage of psychosexual development, known as the **oral stage,** lasts through the first 18 months of life. The erogenous zone is the mouth, and most babies in this age range put everything in their mouths. Enjoyment comes from eating, sucking, and biting. However, if a traumatic event happens during this time (for instance, if a child is not allowed to eat when he or she is hungry), the child may develop an oral fixation later in life. According to Freud's theory, this would lead the individual to desire oral satisfaction, such as cigarette smoking, overeating, fingernail chewing, or alcohol abuse. Freud believed that people with these problems had oral personalities and exhibited this through personality traits such as dependency or aggression.

After 18 months, children enter into the second stage, the **anal stage.** During this stage most children are being toilet trained, and the erogenous zone is the anus. Children realize that parents are pleased when the children learn to use the toilet. Many parents will cheer and clap when their child has his or her first bowel movement in the toilet. Usually, the parents' glee is due to the fact that they won't have to deal with diapers anymore, but the child believes that the feces must be valuable. For what other reason would his or her parents become so excited? If there are any traumatic experiences with toilet training (such as taking an excessive period of time to learn), the child could develop an **anal fixation.** Traits of an anal personality include stubbornness, orderliness, or cleanliness.

According to Freud, the most important stage is the next one, the **phallic stage,** which occurs between the ages of 3 and 6. During this stage, the genitals (the penis in boys and the clitoris in girls) become the erogenous zone, and masturbation begins or increases. Freud believed that during the phallic stage, boys go through the **Oedipus (ED-uh-puss) complex** (which derives its name from the Greek story of Oedipus, who unknowingly killed his father and married his mother), which causes them to fall in love with their mother. Although they want her all to themselves, to do so would mean having to kill their father, which causes castration anxiety, a fear that the father might retaliate by cutting off their penis, and they may lose it (as girls "obviously" did). The Oedipus complex is resolved when the child realizes he cannot have his mother, and he renounces his desire for her.

Freud was less clear about what happened to girls. He believed that girls go through an **Electra complex,** in which they love their father and want to be impregnated by him. However, they realize they cannot have this, and eventually come to identify with the mother. During this time, Freud believed that women develop penis envy. When a girl sees a boy's penis, she realizes that she is lacking one and feels inferior. Freud believed that the Electra stage for girls is never fully resolved and that women are less psychologically mature than men.

Electra complex
The incestuous desire of a daughter for her father.

SEXTalk

Question: Why did Freud call it "penis envy" when guys are always trying to hook up? Shouldn't we call it "vagina envy"?

Karen Horney, a follower of Freud, believed that it could be argued that men have "womb envy" rather than women having "penis envy." Many modern feminists—some who are psychoanalysts—have reframed psychoanalytic theory to be less biased against women and women's experiences. Freud chose the penis because it fit with his theory—and perhaps because he had one.

The resolution of the phallic stage is important for both boys and girls because by identifying with the same-sex parent, they learn to adopt masculine or feminine characteristics. The superego begins to develop during this time as well, and most children adopt their parents' values. Keep in mind, however, that the conflicts associated with the Oedipus and Electra complexes are **repressed,** and how they are resolved affects future behavior.

Prior to puberty, the child passes through the **latency stage,** in which all libido and sexual interest go underground. The fear and strength of the previous stage makes all sexual urges and interests disappear. In fact, during this stage, little boys often think little girls have "cooties" (and vice versa), and childhood play primarily exists in same-sex groups. Puberty marks the **genital stage,** which is the final stage of psychosexual development. The erogenous zone once again becomes the genitals. During this stage, sexuality becomes less internally directed and more directed at others as erotic objects.

Freud believed that if there were no trauma or fixation in any of the above-mentioned stages, a child would be heterosexual. To Freud, homosexuality and bisexuality were the result of atypical psychosexual development (we'll discuss this more in Chapter 11).

Freud's ideas were controversial in the Victorian time period in which he lived. His claims that children were sexual from birth and that children lusted for the other-sex parent caused tremendous shock in the conservative community of Vienna. Among modern psychologists, Freud and the psychoanalytic theory have received a considerable amount of criticism. The predominant criticism is that his theory is unscientific and does not lend itself to testing. How could a researcher study the existence of the phallic stage? If it is indeed unconscious, then it would be impossible to hand out surveys to see when a child was in each stage. Because Freud based his theories on his patients, he has been accused of creating his theories around people who were sick; consequently, they may not apply to healthy people (we will discuss this more in the section on research methodology). Finally, Freud has also been heavily criticized because of his unflattering psychological portrait of women.

repression
A coping strategy by which unwanted thoughts or prohibited desires are forced out of consciousness and into the unconscious mind.

latency stage
A psychosexual stage in which libido and sexual interest are repressed.

genital stage
Final psychosexual stage in which a person develops the ability to engage in adult sexual behavior.

Review Question

Describe the influence of Freud's theories on sexuality.

Behavioral Theory

Behaviorists believe that it is necessary to observe and measure behavior in order to understand it. Psychological states, emotions, the unconscious, and feelings are not measurable and therefore are not valid for study. Only overt behavior can be measured,

behaviorists
Theorists who believe that behavior is learned and can be altered.

operant conditioning
Learning resulting from the reinforcing response a person receives following a certain behavior.

behavior modification
Therapy based on operant conditioning and classical conditioning principles, used to change behaviors.

aversion therapy
A technique that reduces the frequency of maladaptive behavior by associating it with aversive stimuli.

sexbyte

Gender differences have been found to cause more substantial variations in sexual attitudes and behaviors than either racial or ethnic differences (Laumann & Michaels, 2001).

cognitive theory
A theory that proposes that our thoughts are responsible for our behaviors.

observed, and controlled by scientists. Radical behaviorists (those who believe that we do not actually choose how we behave), such as B. F. Skinner (1953), claim that environmental rewards and punishments determine the types of behaviors in which we engage. This is referred to as **operant conditioning.**

We learn certain behaviors, including most sexual behaviors, through reinforcement and punishment. Reinforcements encourage a person to engage in a behavior by associating it with pleasurable stimuli, whereas punishments make it less likely that a behavior will be repeated, by associating it with unpleasant stimuli. For instance, if a man decided to engage in extramarital sex with a colleague at work, it may be because of the positive reinforcements he receives, such as the excitement of going to work. If, on the other hand, a man experiences an erection problem the first time he has sexual intercourse outside of his marriage, it may make it less likely he will try the behavior anytime soon. The negative experience reduces the likelihood that he will engage in the behavior again.

To help change unwanted behavior, behaviorists use **behavior modification.** For example, if a man engages in sex only with adolescent boys, a behavioral therapist might use **aversion therapy.** To do so, the therapist might show the man slides of young boys; when he responds with an erection, an electrical shock is administered to his penis. If this is repeated several times, behaviorists believe the man will no longer respond with an erection. The punishment will have changed the behavior. Contrast this form of therapy to that of a psychoanalytic therapist, who would probably want to study what happened to this man in the first 6 years of his life. A behavior therapist would primarily be concerned with changing the behavior and less concerned with its origins. Much of modern sex therapy uses the techniques developed by behaviorists.

Social Learning Theory

Social learning theory actually grew out of behaviorism. Scientists began to question whether or not behaviorism was too limited in its explanation of human behavior. Many believed that thoughts and feelings had more influence on behaviors than the behaviorists claimed. A noted social learning theorist, Albert Bandura (1969), argued that both internal and external events influence our behavior. By this, he meant that external events, such as rewards and punishments, influence behavior, but so do internal events, such as feelings, thoughts, and beliefs. Bandura began to bridge the gap between behaviorism and cognitive theory, which we will discuss next.

Social learning theorists believe that imitation and identification are also important in the development of sexuality. For example, we identify with our same-sex parent and begin to imitate him or her, which helps us develop our own gender identity. In turn, we are praised and reinforced for these behaviors. Think for a moment about a young boy who identifies with his mother and begins to dress and act like her. He will probably be ridiculed or even punished, which may lead him to turn his attention to a socially acceptable figure, most likely his father. Peer pressure also influences our sexuality. We want to be liked, and therefore we may engage in certain behaviors because our peers encourage it. We also learn what is expected of us from television, our families, even from music.

Cognitive Theory

So far, the theories we have looked at emphasize that either internal conflicts or external events control the development of personality. Unlike these, **cognitive theory** holds that people differ in how they process information, and this creates personality differences. We feel what we think we feel, and our thoughts also affect our behavior. Our behavior does not come from early experiences in childhood or from rewards or punishments; rather, it is a result of how we perceive and conceptualize what is happening around us.

As far as sexuality is concerned, cognitive theorists believe that the biggest sexual organ is between the ears (Walen & Roth, 1987). What sexually arouses us is what we *think* sexually arouses us. We pay attention to our physical sensations and label these reactions. For example, if a woman does not have an orgasm during intercourse, she could perceive this in one of two ways. She might think that having an orgasm during sexual intercourse is not really all that important and maybe next time she will have one; or she could think that she is a failure because she did not have an orgasm during sexual intercourse and feel depressed as a result. What has caused the depression, however, is not the lack of an orgasm but her perception of it.

Humanistic Theory

Humanistic (or person-centered) psychologists believe that we all strive to develop ourselves to the best of our abilities and to achieve **self-actualization** (Raskin & Rogers, 1989). This is easier to do if we are raised with **unconditional positive regard,** which involves accepting and caring about another person without any stipulations or conditions. In other words, there are no rules a person must follow in order to be loved. An example of unconditional positive regard would be a child being caught playing sexual games with her friends and her parents explaining that they loved her but disapproved of her behavior.

If, on the other hand, the parents responded by yelling at the child and sending her to her room, she learns that when she does something wrong, her parents will withdraw their love. This is referred to as **conditional love.** The parents make it clear that they will love their child only when she acts properly.

Children who grow up with unconditional positive regard learn to accept their faults and weaknesses, whereas children who have experienced conditional love may try to ignore those traits because they know others would not approve. Accepting our faults and weaknesses leads us toward self-actualization.

Self-actualization occurs as we learn our own potential in life. We want to do things that make us feel good about ourselves. For the majority of us, casual sex with someone we don't know would not make us feel good; therefore, it does not contribute to our own growth. Sexual intimacy in a loving and committed relationship does feel good and helps contribute to our own self-actualization.

self-actualization
Fulfillment of an individual's potentialities, including aptitudes, talents, and the like.

unconditional positive regard
Acceptance of another without restrictions on their behaviors or thoughts.

conditional love
Conditional acceptance of another, with restrictions on their behaviors or thoughts.

Biological Theory

The biological theory of human sexuality emphasizes that sexual behavior is primarily a biological process. The acts of sexual intercourse, hormonal release, ovulation, ejaculation, conception, pregnancy, and birth are controlled physiologically. Sexual function evolved over thousands of years and is deeply embedded in our physiology. Those who advocate this theory also point out that human sexual behavior, including gender roles and sexual orientation, are primarily due to inborn, genetic patterns and are not functions of social or psychological forces. Sexual problems are believed to be due to physiological causes, and intervention often includes medications or surgery.

SEX Talk

Question: How can the biological theory explain sexual behavior?

A person who adopts a biological theory of sexuality would explain differences in sexuality as a result of brain anatomy, hormones, neurochemicals, or other physical explanations. For example, if a male college student had a problem with premature ejaculation, the biological theorist would look to physical reasons for the problem, such as hormonal or neurological causes. If, on the other hand, a biological theorist were trying to explain sexual orientation, he or she might look at hormones, genetics, or brain anatomy for an explanation.

Evolutionary Theory

Evolutionary theory incorporates both evolution and sociology to understand sexual behavior. In order to understand sexual behavior in humans, evolutionary theorists study animal sexual patterns and look for evolutionary trends. They believe that sexuality ex-

evolutionary theory
A theory that incorporates both evolution and sociology and looks for trends in behaviors.

ists for the purpose of reproducing the species, and individual sexuality is designed to maximize the chances of passing on one's genes. According to evolutionary theorists, the winners in the game of life are those who are most successful at transmitting their genes to the next generation.

Think about the qualities you look for in a partner. Students often tell me that they are looking for someone who is physically attractive, monogamous, has a sense of humor, and is intelligent, honest, extroverted, fun, and sensitive. An evolutionary theorist would argue that these qualities have evolved to ensure that a person would be able to provide healthy offspring and care for them well. A physically attractive person is more likely to be physically fit and healthy. Could this be important to us because of their reproductive capabilities? Evolutionary theorists would say so. They would also argue that qualities such as monogamy, honesty, and sensitivity would help ensure that a partner will be reliable and help raise the offspring.

Some sexual activities have evolved to ensure the survival of the species. Evolutionary theorists believe that premarital sex is resisted because pregnancy in a single woman would be much less desirable for the species (because there would be only one parent for the offspring). They also believe that orgasms have evolved to make sexual intercourse pleasurable; this, in turn, increases the frequency that people engage in it and therefore the possibility of reproduction is increased. In Chapter 1 we discussed how the evolution of an upright posture changed the way the human species engaged in sexual intercourse.

Differences between the sexes in sexual desire and behavior are also thought to have evolved. The double standard, which states that men are free to have casual sex whereas women are not, exists because men produce millions of sperm per day and women produce only one viable ovum per month. Males try to "spread their seed" in order to ensure the reproduction of their family line, whereas females need to protect the one ovum they produce each month. When women become pregnant, they have a 9-month biological commitment ahead of them (and some would argue a lifelong commitment as well).

Evolutionary theory has received a considerable amount of criticism, however, particularly because evolutionary theorists tend to ignore the influence of both prior learning and societal influences on sexuality.

Sociological Theories

Sociologists are interested in how the society in which we live influences sexual behavior. Even though the basic capacity to be sexual might be biologically programmed, *how* it is expressed varies greatly across societies, as we saw in the last chapter. For instance, there are differences in what societies tolerate, men's and women's roles, and how sexuality is viewed. A behavior that may be seen as normal in one society may be considered abnormal in another. For instance, on the island of Mangaia in the South Pacific, women are very sexually assertive and often initiate sexual activity (D. S. Marshall, 1971). From an early age, they are taught by elders how to have multiple orgasms. However, in Inis Beag in Ireland, sexuality is repressed and is considered appropriate only for procreation (Messenger, 1993). Couples engage in sexual intercourse fully clothed, with only the genitals exposed. Each society has regulated its sexual behaviors.

Sociologists believe that many institutions influence a society's rules about sexual expression (DeLamater, 1987). These institutions include the family, religion, economy, medicine, law, and the media. Each of these dictates certain beliefs about the place of sexuality in one's life, and these beliefs can determine what is seen as normal within the society.

The family is the first institution that influences our values about what is sexually right and wrong. Our parents and family provide strong messages about what is acceptable and unacceptable. Religion also influences how a society views sexuality. As we discussed in Chapter 1, Christian doctrine stated that sex before marriage was wrong because sex was primarily for procreation. Some religions provide strong opinions on issues such as premarital and extramarital sex, homosexuality, sexual variations, abortion, masturbation, contraception, and sex education. Many people within society look to religious institutions and leaders for answers to their questions about sexuality.

The economy is another institution that affects the societal view of sexuality. The U.S. economy is based on capitalism, which involves an exchange of services for money. This influences the availability of sex-related services such as prostitution, pornography, and sex shops. They exist because they generate money. If people did not purchase these services, they probably would not exist in our society.

The medical community also affects the societal views of sexuality. For example, many years ago physicians taught that masturbation was a disease that could lead to permanent mental illness. This attitude influenced societal opinions of masturbation. Other behaviors that physicians urged people not to engage in included anal intercourse, extramarital sex, homosexuality, and bisexuality. In turn, society's values about these behaviors were guided by the medical community's attitudes and beliefs.

A fifth institution that regulates sexual behavior in the United States is the law. The law establishes what sexual behaviors are "officially" right and wrong. For instance, laws regulate things like the practice of sodomy (or anal intercourse), the availability of certain contraceptive methods, and abortion. In turn, this affects how society feels about these practices. Laws help establish societal norms.

As we discussed in Chapter 1, the media constitute another institution that influences societal attitudes about sexuality. Television, magazines, and popular music portray who are desirable sexual partners and what is acceptable sexual behavior. Even though the media have been more inclusive over the last few years, a heterosexual bias still exists (the media tell us that heterosexuality is the most acceptable form of sexual behavior). To be homosexual or even **abstinent** (AB-stin-nent) is less acceptable. All of these influence the social views of sexuality and what practices we believe are right and wrong.

Feminist Theory

Many feminist researchers believe that **sexology** in the United States is still dominated by white, middle-class, heterosexist attitudes, which permeate sexuality research (Ericksen, 1999; Irvine, 1990). Others add that sexuality research has been based on a model of male sexuality, which also promotes heterosexuality as the norm (M. Jackson, 1984). Feminist researchers often claim that they have a different view of sexuality that enables them to see things not seen by men (Ericksen, 1999). Many feminist researchers have been leaders in the effort to redefine sexual functioning and remove the medical and biological aspects that permeate sexuality today. Leonore Tiefer, a feminist researcher, has written extensively about the overmedicalization of sexuality. Tiefer argues that there may not be any biological sex drive at all—it may be that our culture is what influences our sexual desire the most (Kaschak & Tiefer, 2001; Tiefer, 2001). We will talk more about Tiefer's work in Chapter 14.

Typically there are a number of different variations of feminism with some more liberal or radical than others. Overall, however, feminist scholars believe that the social construction of sexuality is based on power, which has been primarily in the hands of men for centuries (Collins, 1998; Schwartz, 2000). They believe there is sexual gender inequality that, for the most part, sees women as submissive and subordinate (Collins, 2000). This power over women is maintained through acts of sexual aggression such as rape, sexual abuse, sexual harassment, pornography, and prostitution (M. Jackson, 1984; MacKinnon, 1986). In addition, feminists argue that male sexuality consistently views sex as an act that involves only a penis in a vagina. For "sex" to occur, the erect penis must penetrate the vagina and thrust until the male ejaculates. Catharine MacKinnon (1987, p. 75) suggests that male-dominated views of sexuality have resulted in a society that believes that "what is sexual gives a man an erection." Andrea Dworkin (1987), one of the more radical feminists, took this one step further; she believed that sexual intercourse itself was a women's punishment by men. Thrusting during sexual intercourse was meant to be painful for women, Dworkin claimed, and this pain was to prove to the woman that the man was in charge and possessed the power. All of this led to the repression of female sexuality and, as a result, the lack of attention to the female orgasm.

abstinent
The state of not engaging in sexual activity.

Review Question

Differentiate between behavioral, social learning, cognitive, humanistic, biological, evolutionary, and sociological theories.

sexology
The scientific study of sexuality.

Feminist researchers also believe that there is much to be gained from collaborative or group research, which uses interviews to gain information, because they can provide rich, qualitative data. Controlled laboratory experiments, which have been viewed as more "masculine" in structure (due to the rigid nature of experiments), remove the study from the social context, which affects the outcome of the study (Peplau & Conrad, 1989). We will discuss this more later in the chapter.

Queer Theory

The feminist and queer theories share a common political interest—a concern for women's and gay, lesbian, bisexual, and transsexual rights. Queer theory was developed in the 1990s; it grew out of lesbian and gay studies. Its premise is the belief that domination and its related characteristics, such as heterosexism and homophobia, should be resisted. Resisting the model of sexuality that claims heterosexuality as its origin, queer theory focuses on mismatches between sex, gender, and desire (Schlichter, 2004). Queer theorists believe that studies need to examine how a variety of sexualities are constructed and to abandon the category of "homosexual" (Rudy, 2000). Categories are cultural constructions that limit and restrain. Overall, queer theorists and some feminists believe that meaningful societal change can come about only through radical change and cannot be introduced into a society in a piecemeal way (Turner, 2000). (The accompanying Sex in Real Life presents examples of studies that researchers with different theoretical backgrounds might be interested in doing.) Now let's turn our attention to some of the important sexuality studies that have been done.

Review Question

Explain how feminist and queer theories have asked a different set of questions about sexuality.

sex byte

In 1907, a Berlin dermatologist named Iwan Bloch was the first to coin the new term for sexology, *Sexualwissenschaft.*

SEX in Real Life

What Questions Would They Ask?

Because theorists from different perspectives are interested in different types of studies, they ask different types of questions. Following are a few questions that theorists from different schools of thought might ask.

Psychoanalytic: How are sexual problems later in life related to early childhood experiences? How do children resolve the Oedipal and Electra complexes? Does an overactive superego cause college students to feel guilt about sexual behavior?

Behavioral: What reinforces a person's attraction to partners of the same sex? What reinforces a college student to use contraception? What are the attractions and hesitancies around the decision to lose one's virginity?

Social Learning: How does peer group pressure influence our sexuality? What effects do the media have on our sexuality? Are children influenced by sexual messages on television?

Cognitive: What is the decision-making process related to contraceptive choice? Do children cognitively understand sexuality? How do men view erectile dysfunction?

Humanist: How do negative parental reactions to first sexual experience affect teenagers? How does self-actualization affect sexuality?

Biological: How does genetics influence sexuality? What are the effects of hormone levels on sexual desire? Does menstruation affect sexual desire in women?

Evolutionary: Why are women the ones who usually control the level of sexual activity? How has monogamy developed?

Sociological: How does religion influence sexuality? How does the threat of HIV/AIDS affect society? Do laws affect sexual behavior?

Feminist: What is the role of rape in repressing female sexuality? How do the media reinforce a male view of sexuality?

Queer: How do homosexual individuals move from a state of identity confusion about their homoerotic feelings to a point at which they accept their lesbian or gay identity? How are same-sex and heterosexual desires interrelated?

As you read through these various questions, which seem of most interest to you? Perhaps these questions can give you insight into which theory makes the most sense to you. Do you lean toward a biological explanation for why people do what they do, or does another theory make more sense to you?

SEXUALITY RESEARCH: PHILOSOPHERS, PHYSICIANS, AND SEXOLOGISTS

The ancient Greeks, through physicians like Hippocrates and philosophers such as Aristotle and Plato, may actually be the legitimate forefathers of sex research, because they were the first to elaborate theories regarding sexual responses and dysfunctions, sex legislation, reproduction and contraception, and sexual ethics. But it wasn't until the 18th century that there was increased discussion of sexual ethics and that the first programs of public and private sex education and classifications of sexual behavior were established.

Early Sex Research

In the 19th century researchers from a variety of disciplines (such as Darwin, Kaan, Charcot, and others) laid the foundations of sex research in the modern sense. It was during this time that the study of sex began to concentrate more on the bizarre, dangerous, and unhealthy aspects of sex. In 1843, Heinrich Kaan, a Russian physician, wrote *Psychopathia Sexualis*, which presented a classification of sexual mental diseases. This system was greatly expanded and refined over 40 years later by Richard von Krafft-Ebing in another book with the same title. Sex research during this time almost exclusively focused on people believed to be sick (see timeline).

During the Victorian period in the 19th century, the majority of sex research was thwarted. Some researchers found that they suddenly lost their professional status, were accused of having the very sexual disorders they studied, or were viewed as motivated solely by lust, greed, or fame. However, as interest in medicine in general grew, researchers began to explore how to improve health and peoples' lives, which included researching various aspects of sexuality.

Physicians were the primary sexuality researchers in the late 19th century (keep in mind that nearly all physicians were men at that time). Because physicians were experts in biology and the body, they were also viewed as the experts of sexuality (V. Bullough, 1994). Interestingly, although the majority of physicians had little or no specialized knowledge of sexual topics, most spoke with authority about human sexuality anyway.

The majority of the early sexuality studies were done in Europe, primarily in Germany (V. Bullough, 1994). At the time, sex research was protected because it was considered part of medical research, even though holding a medical degree did not always offer complete protection. Some researchers used pseudonyms to publish their work, some were verbally attacked, and others had their data destroyed.

At the turn of the 20th century it was the pioneering work of Sigmund Freud, Havelock Ellis, and Iwan Bloch that established the study of sexual problems as a legitimate endeavor in its own right. It is interesting to note that many of the early researchers of sexology were of Jewish background. The Nazis persecuted many German-Jewish physicians who specialized in sexuality, calling them "decadent." The Jewish roots of much of modern sexology have certainly added to its controversial nature in certain countries. As a result of all the negative reactions and problems with sexuality research in Europe, it gradually moved from Germany to the United States, which has led the way in sexuality research ever since.

In 1921, several prominent European doctors attempted to set up an organization called the Committee for Research in Problems of Sex. After much hard work, the organization established itself but experienced problems in low membership rates and a lack of research and publishing support. However, because of strong beliefs and persistence by the founders, the group continued.

Systematic research into sexuality in the United States began in the early 1920s, motivated by pressures from the social hygiene movement, which was concerned about sexually transmitted infections and their impact on marriage and children. American society was generally conservative and viewed the "sex impulse" as a potential threat to societal stability, and research into sexuality was viewed as one way to help "cure" these threats. Funding for sexuality research was minimal. It wasn't until the beginnings of philanthropy from the fortunes of men such as John D. Rockefeller and Andrew Carnegie that researchers were able to afford to implement large-scale, interdisciplinary projects.

Recent Studies on Sexuality

In the late 1980s and early 1990s there was an unprecedented surge in sexuality research, predominantly driven by concerns over human immunodeficiency virus (HIV) and acquired immune deficiency syndrome (AIDS). Researchers were anxious to understand more about specific sexual behaviors that might contribute to the spread of these diseases. In fact, since this time, the majority of research into human sexuality has been "problem-driven," meaning that most of the research that has been done has focused on a specific problem. The research areas of priority include HIV and AIDS, adolescent sexuality, gender, sexual orientation, and sexual coercion (Bancroft, 1996). A review of ongoing research projects at the National Institutes of Health in 2002 revealed several "problem-driven" types of studies ("Sex and Unintended Pregnancy Among Low-Income Adolescents," "Initiation of Sexual Behavior in Early Adolescence in African American Mothers"; National Institutes of Health, 2002). However, a focus on problems doesn't allow researchers to obtain funds to research topics on healthy sexuality and answer questions such as "How does normal child sexual development progress?" or "How is sexuality expressed in loving long-term relationships?"

There are many people who are opposed to sexuality research today, and some believe that the mystery surrounding sexuality will be taken away by increasing scientific knowledge. Conservative groups believe that research done on topics such as adolescent sexuality would encourage young people to have more sex. Sex researchers are used to pressure from conservative groups that oppose their work. In fact, after Alfred Kinsey published his two famous studies about male and female sexuality (which were funded by the Rockefeller Foundation), Congress pushed the Foundation to withdraw its financial support from Indiana University, which it did (J. H. Jones, 1997).

Sexuality research in the United States has also become very fragmented, with researchers coming from several different disciplines, such as psychology, sociology, medicine, social work, and public health, to name a few. Researchers tend to be unaware of research being published in other disciplines. Journal articles are often inaccessible to a general audience or to researchers outside the discipline from which the research originated (diMauro, 1995). What tends to happen, therefore, is that the popular media become responsible for disseminating information about sexuality, which is often distorted and/or sensationalistic.

Sexologists—researchers, educators, and clinicians who specialize in sexuality—are usually PhD-level scientists who engage in sophisticated research projects and pub-

sexologist
A professional who studies sexuality.

Timeline: Important Developments in the History of Sex Research

1843	1886	1892	1896	1897
Russian physician Heinrich Kaan publishes *Psychopathia Sexualis*, a classification system of sexual diseases.	Richard von Krafft-Ebing, a German psychiatrist, expands and refines Kaan's earlier work in *Psychopathia Sexualis*.	American physician Clelia Mosher begins a survey among educated middle-class women concerning sexual attitudes and experiences.	English private scholar Havelock Ellis begins *Studies in the Psychology of Sex*. Because they cannot be published in England, they appear in the United States and in Germany.	Berlin physician Magnus Hirschfeld founds the Scientific Humanitarian Committee, the world's first "gay rights" organization. 

Courtesy of Erwin J. Haeberle, Magnus Hirschfeld Archive for Sexology, Humboldt Universitat du Berlin

© Hulton-Deutsch Collection/Corbis

Courtesy of Erwin J. Haeberle, Magnus Hirschfeld Archive for Sexology, Humboldt Universitat du Berlin

lish their work in scientific journals. Unfortunately, they are sometimes ridiculed, not viewed as "real" scientists, and accused of studying sexuality because of their own sexual hang-ups or because they are voyeurs. Geer and O'Donohue (1987) claim that, unlike other areas of science, sex research is often evaluated as either moral or immoral. Some groups believe that marital sex for procreation is the only acceptable sexual behavior and that many sexual practices (such as masturbation, homosexuality, and premarital and extramarital sex) are immoral. Researchers are often encouraged not to invade the privacy of intimate relationships or to study the sexuality of certain age groups (either young or old). People often resist participating in sexuality research because of their own moral or psychological attitudes toward sex. Methodological problems also have made it difficult for the field of sexuality research. We will discuss these issues more later in this chapter.

Academic programs that specialize in human sexuality appeared in the 1970s, and many still flourish today. There are many programs offering advanced degrees in sexology across the United States (for more information about these programs, see our website listing at the end of this chapter). In addition, several groups exist today to promote sexuality research and education, including: the Kinsey Institute for Research in Sex, Gender, and Reproduction; the Society for the Scientific Study of Sexuality (SSSS); American Association for Sexuality Educators, Counselors and Therapists (AASECT); Society for Sex Therapy and Research (SSTAR); and the Sexuality Information and Education Council of the United States (SIECUS). Many medical schools and universities now teach sexuality courses as a part of the curriculum.

Because the study of sexuality has become so fragmented among disciplines, it is possible that universities will eventually form a separate discipline of "sexual science." Departments of Sexual Science would include specialists from different disciplines providing students with a comprehensive, multidisciplinary grounding in human sexuality. In addition, they would enable the field to acquire appropriate dedicated research funds (because funding sources are usually unaware of whom and where the researchers of sexuality are). Steady funding for sexuality research is needed to attract new students to the field of sexuality, to continue the work of senior researchers, and to expand research agendas (diMauro, 1995). Some researchers have gone so far as to claim that because the field of sexuality has many excellent gay, lesbian, and feminist scholars, we now need find a way to attract bright, straight, young academics to enter the field, especially men (Bancroft, 1999).

Although sexuality research is still in its early stages, it has begun to help remove the stigma and ignorance associated with discussing human sexual behavior. Ignorance and fear can contribute to irresponsible behavior. Sexuality research has helped sex become a topic of discussion rather than a taboo subject. Today, understanding sexuality has become increasingly important to the work of psychologists, physicians, educators, theologians, and scientists.

Review Question

Describe the early beginnings of sexuality research, and trace how sex research progressed.

sex byte

In 2002, the University of Wisconsin was denied a request for government funding to establish a doctoral program in human sexuality research because there was no focus on abstinence. Some lawmakers suggested that even at the doctorate level, educational courses on sexuality must include a focus on abstinence as a way to prevent STIs and HIV.

1897	1899	1903–04	1905	1907	1908
Berlin physician Albert Moll publishes *Investigations Into Sexuality*.	Magnus Hirschfeld begins editing the *Yearbook for Sexual Intermediate Stages* for the Scientific Humanitarian Committee.	Magnus Hirschfeld begins his statistical surveys on homosexuality. They are quickly terminated by legal action.	Sigmund Freud publishes *Three Essays on the Theory of Sex*, based on his theory of psychoanalysis.	Berlin dermatologist Iwan Bloch coins the term Sexualwissenschaft (sexology) and publishes *The Sexual Life of Our Time*.	Magnus Hirschfeld publishes the first issue of *The Journal for Sexology*.

© Hulton-Deutsch Collection/Corbis

Courtesy of Erwin J. Haeberle, Magnus Hirschfeld Archive for Sexology, Humboldt Universitat du Berlin

Of all these researchers, the most influential early promoters of sexology were Iwan Bloch, Albert Moll, Magnus Hirschfeld, and Richard von Krafft-Ebing. All four were German and were working around the turn of the 20th century. Another researcher, Havelock Ellis, was working in London to establish the field of sexology.

Early Promoters of Sexology

Several people were responsible for the early promotion of sexology, including Iwan Bloch, Albert Moll, Magnus Hirschfeld, Richard von Krafft-Ebing, Havelock Ellis, Katharine Bement Davis, Clelia Mosher, Alfred Kinsey, Morton Hunt, William Masters, and Virginia Johnson. All of these researchers made a tremendous contribution to the study of sexology.

Iwan Bloch: The Journal of Sexology

Iwan Bloch (1872–1922), a Berlin dermatologist, believed that the medical view of sexual behavior was shortsighted and that both historical and anthropological research could help broaden it. He hoped that sexual science would one day have the same structure and objectivity as other sciences. Along with Magnus Hirschfeld, Bloch and several other physicians formed a medical society for sexology research in Berlin. It was the first sexological society, and it exercised considerable influence (we will talk more about this society below). Starting in 1914, Bloch published the *Journal of Sexology*, a scientific journal about sexology. For almost 2 decades this journal collected and published many important sexological studies. Bloch planned to write a series of sexological studies, but due to World War I and his untimely death at the age of 50, he never did.

Albert Moll: Investigations Concerning the Libido Sexualis

Albert Moll (1862–1939), a Berlin physician, was another big promoter of sexology. He was a very conservative man who disliked both Freud and Hirschfeld and tried to counter their research at every opportunity. Moll formed the International Society for Sex Research in 1913 to counter Hirschfeld's Medical Society of Sexology. He also organized an International Congress of Sex Research in Berlin in 1926.

Moll wrote several books on sexology, including *Investigations Concerning the Libido Sexualis* in 1897. Unfortunately, it was probably Moll's disagreements with Freud that caused him to be ignored by the majority of English-speaking sexuality researchers, because Freud's ideas were so dominant during the first half of the 20th century (V. Bullough, 1994). Moll stayed in Germany and eventually had his memoirs published. He

Timeline: Important Developments in the History of Sex Research

1909	1911	1912	1913	1914	1919	1933
Albert Moll publishes *The Sexual Life of the Child*, which challenges Freud's psychoanalytic theory.	Albert Moll publishes the *Handbook of Sexual Sciences*.	Iwan Bloch begins publication of the *Handbook of Sexology*.	Magnus Hirschfeld, Iwan Bloch, and others found the Society of Sexology in Berlin. Albert Moll founds the International Society of Sex Research in Berlin.	Magnus Hirschfeld publishes *Homosexuality in Men and Women*.	Magnus Hirschfeld opens the first Institute for Sexology in Berlin.	Nazis close the Institute for Sexology.

avoided being sent to a concentration camp only by dying of natural causes in September of 1939 (ironically, on the same day Sigmund Freud died).

Magnus Hirschfeld: The Institute for Sexology

Magnus Hirschfeld (1868–1935) was born in Kolberg, Germany. His work with patients inspired him and convinced him that negative attitudes toward homosexuals were inhumane and unfounded. Because Hirschfeld was independently wealthy, all of his work was supported by his own funds (V. Bullough, 1994).

Using a pseudonym, Hirschfeld wrote his first paper on sexology in 1896. In this paper, he argued that sexuality was the result of certain genetic patterns that could result in a person being homosexual, bisexual, or heterosexual. He fought for a repeal of the laws that made homosexuality and bisexuality punishable by prison terms and heavy fines. In 1899, he began the *Yearbook for Sexual Intermediate Stages*, which was published for the purpose of educating the public about homosexuality and other sexual "deviations."

Thousands of people came to him for his help and advice about sexual problems; and, in 1900, Hirschfeld began distributing questionnaires on sexuality. By this time, he had also become an expert in the field of homosexuality and sexual variations and testified as an expert witness in court cases of sexual offenders. Hirschfeld used only a small amount of his data in the books he published because he hoped to write a comprehensive study of sexuality at a later date. Unfortunately, his data were destroyed by the Nazis before they could be published.

Even though many books had been published by Krafft-Ebing, Havelock Ellis, and others, Hirschfeld was the first to develop an Institute for Sexology, which contained his libraries, laboratory, and lecture halls. Over the next few years the Institute continued to grow in size and influence. In 1933, as the political climate heated up, Hirschfeld left Germany and soon learned that his Foundation in Berlin had been destroyed by the Nazi government, its contents publicly burned, and those who were working there sent to concentration camps. Hirschfeld stayed in France, continuing his work until his death in 1935. In 1994, after the reunification of Berlin, the Robert Koch Institute opened a sexological information and resource center in Berlin, with the goal of protecting sexual health by providing education.

Richard von Krafft-Ebing: Psychopathia Sexualis

Richard von Krafft–Ebing (1840–1902) was one of the most significant medical writers on sexology in the late 19th century (V. Bullough, 1994). His primary interest was what he considered "deviant" sexual behavior. Krafft-Ebing believed that deviant sexual behavior was the result of engaging in nonreproductive sexual practices, including masturbation. In 1886, he published an update of a book entitled *Psychopathia Sexualis*, which explored approximately 200 case histories of individuals who had experienced

Magnus Hirschfeld (1868–1935) worked hard to establish sexuality as a legitimate field of study.

Courtesy of Erwin J. Haeberle, Magnus Hirschfeld Archive for Sexology, Humboldt Universtat de Berlin

1938	1947	1948	1949	1951	1953	1957	1964
Alfred Kinsey begins his studies of human sexual behavior.	Alfred Kinsey founds the Institute for Sex Research at Indiana University.	Alfred Kinsey and colleagues publish *Sexual Behavior in the Human Male*.	Simone de Beauvoir publishes *The Second Sex*, which helps awaken the feminist movement.	Clellan S. Ford and Frank A. Beach publish *Patterns of Sexual Behavior*, in which they compare sexual behavior in 200 human societies.	Alfred Kinsey and colleagues publish *Sexual Behavior in the Human Female*.	American gynecologist Hans Lehfeldt founds the Society for the Scientific Study of Sexuality (SSSS).	American MD Mary Calderone founds the Sexuality Information and Education Council of the United States (SIECUS).

© Bettmann/Corbis

© Michel Philipott/Sygma/Corbis

AP/World Wide Photos

sexual pathology, including people who had had sex with children (pedophiles) and homosexuals.

Although Krafft-Ebing supported sympathetic concern for those who expressed "deviations" and worked to help change existing laws that discriminated against them, he also increased suspicion about differences in sexuality by lumping all forms of sexual variations together as deviant.

Havelock Ellis: Studies in the Psychology of Sex

Havelock Ellis (1859–1939), another important sex researcher, was an English citizen who grew up in Victorian society but began to rebel against the secrecy surrounding sexuality. In 1875, when he was 16 years old, he decided to make sexuality his life's work. In fact, it is reported that Ellis sought a medical degree primarily so he could legitimately and safely study sexuality (V. Bullough, 1994). Upon publication of his famous six-volume *Studies in the Psychology of Sex* (1897–1910; Ellis, 1910), Ellis established himself as an objective and nonjudgmental researcher. In his collection of case histories from volunteers, he reported that homosexuality and masturbation were not abnormal and should not be labeled as such (Reiss, 1982). In 1901, *The Lancet*, a prestigious English medical journal, reviewed his early volumes and wrote:

> [*Studies in the Psychology of Sex*] must not be sold to the public, for the reading and discussion of such topics are dangerous. The young and the weak would not be fortified in their purity by the knowledge that they would gain from these studies, while they certainly might be more open to temptation after the perusal of more than one of the chapters. (Grosskurth, 1980, p. 222)

Unfortunately, Ellis's book was also fairly dry and boring, and as a result, and much to his dismay, Ellis never found the fame and fortune that Freud did.

All of the aforementioned researchers and their publications helped give credibility to the area of sexual research. Some of the researchers adopted Freud's psychoanalytic theory, whereas others developed their research without adopting specific theories of sexuality. Though they had introduced scientific principles into the study of sexual behavior, their influence was mostly limited to the field of medicine.

The rise of behaviorism in the 1920s added a new dimension to the research. The idea of studying specific sexual behaviors became more acceptable. The formulation of more sophisticated scientific research techniques provided researchers with more precise methods for sexual research. Many researchers attempted to compile data on sexual behavior, but the results were inconsistent, and the data were poorly organized. This led Alfred Kinsey, an American researcher, to undertake a large-scale study of human sexuality.

Havelock Ellis (1859–1939) was a key figure in the early study of sexuality.

© Hulton-Deutsch Collection/Corbis

Timeline: Important Developments in the History of Sex Research

1965	1967	1970	1971	1974	1974	1976
SSSS publishes the first issue of the *Journal of Sex Research*.	The American Association of Sex Educators, Counselors and Therapists (AASECT) is founded.	William Masters and Virginia Johnson publish *Human Sexual Inadequacy*.	American psychiatrist Richard Green founds The International Academy of Sex Research. This organization publishes the journal *Archives of Sexual Behavior*.	The first World Health Organization convenes in Geneva. Participants include sexologists and public health experts. The following year it publishes *Education and Treatment in Human Sexuality: The Training of Health Professionals*.	Hans Lehfeldt organizes the first World Congress of Sexology. *Journal of Homosexuality* is published.	The Institute for Advanced Study of Sexuality is founded in San Francisco.

Courtesy of The Society for the Scientific Study of Sexuality   © Bettmann/Corbis

Although Alfred Kinsey was mainly responsible for moving large-scale sexuality research to the United States, we also have to give credit to two hard-working female researchers, Clelia Mosher and Katharine Bement Davis, both of whom were working in the United States. Much of their work remained unpublished, although they are also responsible for paving the way for later researchers.

Clelia Mosher: Important Female Questions

By now you have probably realized that men were doing much of the early research into human sexuality. Male sexuality was viewed as normative, and therefore female sexuality was approached through the lens of male sexuality. Clelia Mosher (1863–1940) was ahead of her time, asking questions about sexuality that were quite different from those of her male predecessors. She was actually the first researcher to ask Americans about their sexual behavior (Ericksen, 1999).

In 1892, while Mosher was a student at the University of Wisconsin, she began a research project that lasted 28 years. Her main motivation was to help married women have more satisfying sex lives. She asked upper-middle-class women whether they enjoyed sexual intercourse, how often they engaged in it, and how often they wanted to engage in it (MaHood & Wenburg, 1980). One of the questions that Mosher asked the women in her study was, "What do you believe to be the true purpose of intercourse?" (Ericksen, 1999). Although a few women claimed that sexual intercourse was only for procreation, the majority of women said that intercourse was for both sexual pleasure and procreation. However, many of these women felt guilty for wanting or needing sexual pleasure. Ericksen (1999) suggests that this guilt reflected the transition from the repressive Victorian era to the more progressive 20th century view of sex as an important component of marriage. Much of Mosher's work was never published and never became part of the sex knowledge that circulated during her time.

Katharine Bement Davis: Defending Homosexuality

Another female researcher, Katharine Davis (1861–1935), began her sexuality research along a slightly different path. In 1920, Davis was appointed superintendent of a prison, and she became interested in prostitution and sexually transmitted infections. Her survey and analysis were the largest and most comprehensive to date (Ericksen, 1999).

Davis believed that lesbianism was not pathological, and she defended homosexuality as no different from heterosexuality. This idea was considered a threat in the early 1900s because it could mean that women did not need men (Faderman, 1981). Her ideas about lesbianism were largely ignored, but the idea that women might have sexual appetites

Special Collections/Vassar College Libraries

Katharine Bement Davis (1861–1935) conducted some of the largest and most comprehensive sexuality studies to date.

1978	1986	1988–1989	1990	1993	1994	1994	2002
The World Association for Sexology is founded in Rome.	The American Board of Sexology organizes in Washington, D.C.	German *Journal of Sex Research* is published. The European Federation of Sexology is founded in Geneva.	The Asian Federation for Sexology is founded in Hong Kong.	*Janus Report on Sexual Behavior* is published.	Robert Koch Institute opens Archive for Sexology in Berlin.	*The National Health and Social Life Study* is published.	Pfizer Pharmaceuticals publishes the *Pfizer Global Study of Sexual Attitudes and Behaviors.*

Hulton Archive/Getty Images

equal to men's worried many male researchers. Soon the researchers of the day began to turn their attention toward strengthening the family unit. Researchers began to include married couples and turn away from studying single men and women (Ericksen, 1999).

Alfred Kinsey: Large-Scale Sexuality Research Begins in the United States

Alfred Kinsey (1894–1956) was probably the most influential sex researcher of the 20th century. His work was a decisive factor in changing many of the existing attitudes about sexuality. By training, Kinsey was a biologist with a PhD from Harvard who was an internationally known expert on gall wasps. In 1938, when Kinsey was a professor of zoology at Indiana University, he was asked to coordinate a new course on marriage and the family. Before courses like this appeared on college campuses, human sexuality had been discussed only in hygiene courses, in which the focus was primarily on the dangers of STIs and masturbation (V. L. Bullough, 1998).

Soon after the course began, students came to Kinsey with sexuality questions that he could not answer, and the existing literature was little help. This encouraged him to begin collecting data on his students' sex lives. His study grew and before long included students who were not in his classes, faculty members, friends, and nonfaculty employees. Soon he was able to obtain grant money that enabled him to hire research assistants. By this time, Kinsey's research had become well established in the scientific community. Kinsey had received a grant in 1941 from the Committee for Research in the Problems in Sex (CRPS), which was so impressed by his work that it awarded Kinsey half of its total research budget in the 1946–1947 academic year (V. L. Bullough, 1998).

In his early work, Kinsey claimed to be **atheoretical.** He felt that because sexuality research was so new, it was impossible to construct theories and hypotheses without first having a large body of information to base them on.

Kinsey's procedure involved collecting information on each participant's sexual life history, with an emphasis on specific sexual behaviors. Kinsey chose to interview participants, rather than have them fill out questionnaires, because he believed that questionnaires would not provide accurate responses. He was also unsure about whether participants would lie during an interview and because of this he built into the interview many checks to detect false information. Data collected from husbands and wives were compared for consistency, and the interview was done again 2 and 4 years later to see whether the basic answers remained the same.

Kinsey was also very worried about **interviewer bias** (which we will discuss later in this chapter). To counter interview bias, only Kinsey and three colleagues conducted the interviews. Of the total 18,000 interviews, Kinsey himself conducted 8,000 (Pomeroy, 1972). Participants were asked a minimum of 350 questions, and each interviewer memorized each question so he or she could more easily build rapport with each participant and wouldn't have to continually consult a paper questionnaire. Interviewers used appropriate terminology that participants would understand during the interview. Interviews lasted several hours, and participants were assured that the information they provided would remain confidential. A total of 13 areas were covered in the interview, including demographics, physical data, early sexual knowledge, adolescent sexual behaviors, masturbation, orgasms in sleep, heterosexual petting, sexual intercourse, reproductive information, homosexual activity, sexual contact with animals, and sexual responsiveness. See Table 2.1 for information on some of Kinsey's early findings.

The sampling procedures Kinsey used were also strengths of his research. He believed that he would have a high refusal rate if he used **probability sampling.** Because of this, he used what he called "quota sampling accompanied by opportunistic collection" (Gebhard & Johnson, 1979, p. 26). In other words, if he saw that a particular group—such as young married women—was not well represented in his sample, he would find organizations with a high percentage of these participants and add them.

Overall, he got participants from colleges and universities; hospitals; prisons; mental hospitals; institutions for young delinquents; churches and synagogues; groups of people with sexual problems; settlement houses; homosexual groups in Chicago, Los Angeles, New York, Philadelphia, and San Francisco; and members of various groups including the YMCA and the YWCA. Within these groups, every member was strongly

atheoretical
Research that is not influenced by a particular theory.

interviewer bias
The bias of a researcher caused by his or her own ideas about the research.

probability sampling
A research strategy that involves acquiring a random sample for inclusion in a study.

TABLE 2.1   What Did Kinsey Find in His Early Research?

Kinsey's groundbreaking research and the publication of his 1948 and 1953 books revealed many new findings about sexuality. Following are a few of these statistics. Keep in mind that these statistics are based on people's lives in the middle of the 20th century. For more information, visit the Kinsey Institute online at http:www.indiana.edu/~kinsey/.

- Nearly 46% of the males have engaged in both heterosexual and homosexual activities or have "reacted to" persons of both sexes in the course of their adult life.
- 21% of males had lost their virginity by the age of 16, whereas only 6% of females had.
- Married couples reported engaging in sexual intercourse 2.8 times per week in their late teens and only once per week by the age of 50.
- As much as 70% of the adult population used only the male-above position during sexual intercourse.
- 40% of males and 19% of females preferred to have the lights on during sexual activities.
- 50% of married males had engaged in sexual activity outside of their marriage, whereas 26% of women had.
- 37% of males and 13% of females reported engaging in same-sex behavior to orgasm.
- 92% of males and 62% of females reported having engaged in masturbation.
- 69% of white males reported at least one sexual experience with a prostitute.
- 68% of males and 40% of females reached their first orgasm during masturbation.

SOURCE: Kinsey, Pomeroy, & Martin, 1948; Kinsey, Pomeroy, Martin, & Gebhard, 1953.

---

encouraged to participate in the project to minimize volunteer bias. Kinsey referred to this procedure as **100% sampling.**

Institute for Sex Research   In 1947, Kinsey and his associates established the Institute for Sex Research primarily to maintain the confidential data that had been collected and also to claim royalties from any published work (Gebhard & Johnson, 1979). Not coincidentally, two of Kinsey's most popular and lucrative works were published soon afterward—in 1948, *Sexual Behavior in the Human Male* appeared, and in 1953, *Sexual Behavior in the Human Female*. These books were overnight best-sellers and provided the Institute with the financial ability to continue its work. Both books helped to break down the myths and confusion surrounding sexuality, while providing scientifically derived information about the sexual lives of men and women.

Many practices that had previously been seen as perverse or unacceptable in society (such as homosexuality, masturbation, and oral sex) were found to be widely practiced; as you might guess, such findings were very controversial and created strong reactions from conservative groups and religious organizations. Eventually, continued controversy about Kinsey's work resulted in the termination of several research grants. The lack of funds was very frustrating for Kinsey, who did not like to ask people for money because he felt that to do so would be self-serving (Pomeroy, 1982).

Kinsey's research challenged many of the assumptions about sexuality in the United States, and he stirred up antagonisms; in this sense, Kinsey was truly a pioneer in the field of sexuality research (V. L. Bullough, 1998). Just prior to his death in 1956, Kinsey feared his life's work on sexuality had been a failure. The accompanying Personal Voices feature presents some comments made in his obituary from the *New York Times*.

Morton Hunt: Playboy *Updates Dr. Kinsey*

In the early 1970s, the Playboy Foundation commissioned a study to update Kinsey's earlier work on sexual behavior. Morton Hunt eventually published these findings in his book *Sexual Behavior in the 1970s* (Hunt, 1974). In addition, he reviewed his findings in a series of articles in *Playboy* magazine.

Hunt gathered his sample through random selection from telephone books in 24 U.S. cities. Although Hunt's sampling technique was thought to be an improvement over Kinsey's techniques, there were also drawbacks. People without listed phone numbers, such as college students or institutionalized persons, were left out of the study. Each person in Hunt's sample was called and asked to participate in a group discussion about sexuality. Approximately 20% agreed to participate.

People participated in small group discussions about sexuality in America and, after doing so, were asked to complete questionnaires about their own sexual behavior and at-

100% sampling
A research strategy in which all members of a particular group are included in the sample.

Review Question
Explain the work done by early promoters of sexology.

Alfred Kinsey (1894–1956) implemented the first large-scale survey of adult sexual behavior in the United States.

Personal Voices

The Death of Alfred Kinsey

*M*any people believe that Kinsey's early death at the age of 62 was caused by the stress of the constant criticism and struggle he lived under as he tried to legitimize the field of sexuality research. In fact, Kinsey's colleagues believed he literally worked himself to death trying to do all he could with his limited money and time (Pomeroy, 1982). Kinsey was also frustrated by the lack of respect many had for his controversial findings in sexuality research, which was then still considered taboo. After Kinsey's death in 1956, the *New York Times* wrote:

The untimely death of Dr. Alfred C. Kinsey takes from the American scene an important and valuable, as well as controversial, figure. Whatever may have been the reaction to his findings—and to the unscrupulous use of some of them—the fact remains that he was first, last, and always a scientist. In the long run it is *probable that the values of his contribution to contemporary thought will lie much less in what he found out than in the method he used and his way of applying it. Any sort of scientific approach to the problems of sex is difficult because the field is so deeply overlaid with such things as moral precept, taboo, individual and group training, and long established behavior patterns. Some of these may be good in themselves, but they are no help to the scientific and empirical method of getting at the truth. Dr. Kinsey cut through this overlay with detachment and precision. His work was conscientious and comprehensive. Naturally it will receive a serious setback with his death. Let us earnestly hope that the scientific spirit that inspired it will not be similarly impaired.*

SOURCE: Pomeroy (1982, p. 441).

---

volunteer bias
A slanting of research data caused by the characteristics of participants who volunteer to participate.

generalizable
Findings that can be taken from a particular sample and applied to the general population.

gender bias
The bias of a researcher caused by his or her gender.

titudes. A total of 982 males and 1,044 females participated in his study. However, because his sample was such a small percentage of those he contacted, **volunteer bias** (which we'll discuss in more detail later in this chapter) prevents his results from being **generalizable** to the population as a whole.

William Masters and Virginia Johnson: Measuring Sex in the Laboratory

Although Alfred Kinsey first envisioned doing physiological studies on sexual arousal and orgasm (and had actually requested funds for a physiologist and a neurologist prior to his death), it was Masters and Johnson who were actually the first modern scientists to observe and measure the act of sexual intercourse in the laboratory. William Masters, a gynecologist, and Virginia Johnson, a psychology researcher, began their sex research in 1954. They were primarily interested in the anatomy and physiology of the sexual response and later also explored sexual dysfunction. Masters and Johnson were a dual sex-therapy team, representing both male and female opinions, which reduced the chance for **gender bias.** Much of the work done by Masters and Johnson was supported by grants, the income from their books, and individual/couple therapy.

Virginia Johnson and William Masters were the first to bring sexuality into the laboratory.

Masters and Johnson's first study, published in 1966, was entitled *Human Sexual Response*. In an attempt to understand the physiological process that occurs during sexual activity, the researchers actually brought 700 people into the laboratory to have their physiological reactions studied during sexual intercourse. The volunteers participated for financial reasons (participants were paid for participation), personal reasons, and even for the release of sexual tension (Masters and Johnson both stated that they felt some volunteers were looking for legitimate and safe sexual outlets). Because Masters and Johnson were studying behaviors they felt were normative (i.e., they happened to most people) they did not feel they needed to recruit a **random sample.**

When a volunteer was accepted as a participant in the study, he or she was first encouraged to engage in sexual activity in the lab without the investigators present. It was hoped that this would make him or her feel more comfortable with the new surroundings. My students often ask me how sex could be "natural" in the sterile conditions of such a lab. Many of the volunteers reported that after a while they did not notice that they were being monitored. During the study they were monitored for physiological changes with an electrocardiograph to measure changes in the heart and an electromyograph to measure muscular changes. Measurements were taken of penile erection and vaginal lubrication with **penile strain gauges** and **photoplethysmographs** (FOH-toh-pleth-iss-mo-grafs).

Through their research, Masters and Johnson discovered several interesting aspects of sexual response, including women's potential for multiple orgasms and the fact that sexuality does not disappear in old age. They also proposed a four-stage model for sexual response, which we will discuss in more detail in Chapter 10.

In 1970, Masters and Johnson published another important book, entitled *Human Sexual Inadequacy,* which explored sexual dysfunction. Again they brought couples into the laboratory, but this time only those who were experiencing sexual problems. They evaluated the couples physiologically and psychologically and taught them exercises to improve their sexual functioning. Frequent follow-ups were done to measure the therapeutic results—some participants were even contacted 5 years after the study was completed.

Masters and Johnson found that there is often dual sexual dysfunction in couples (i.e., males who are experiencing erectile problems often have partners who are also experiencing sexual problems). Their studies also refuted Freud's theory that women are capable of both vaginal and clitoral orgasms and that only vaginal orgasms result from intercourse. According to Masters and Johnson, all female orgasms result from direct or indirect clitoral stimulation.

It's important to point out that Masters and Johnson's books were written from a medical, not a psychological, perspective. They also used clinical language and many professionals speculate this was a tactic to avoid censorship of the books. But even with this scientific and medical base, their work was not without controversy. Many people viewed Masters and Johnson's work as both unethical and immoral.

Research Studies on Homosexuality

Although many studies have been done on homosexuality, as you will see in Chapter 11, there have been very few actual, wide-scale studies. As we stated earlier in this chapter, Katharine Bement Davis researched lesbianism, but her results were largely ignored because they posed a threat to male researchers. Let's now review two classic studies on gay and lesbian sexual behavior.

Evelyn Hooker: Comparing Gay and Straight Men

In the early 1950s, a researcher named Evelyn Hooker (1907–1996) undertook a study on male homosexuality. Hooker compared two groups of men, one gay and the other straight, who were matched for age, education, and IQ levels. She collected information about their life histories, personality profiles, and psychological evaluations and asked professionals to try to distinguish between the two groups on the basis of their profiles and evaluations. They could not, demonstrating that there was little fundamental psychological difference between gay and straight men. Hooker's research helped challenge the widely held view that homosexuality was a mental illness. Today, many studies have shown that there is no psychological difference between heterosexual and homosexual men and women.

Courtesy Farrall Instruments, Inc.

Changes in penile erection and vaginal lubrication were measured with penile strain gauges and photoplethysmographs.

random sample
A number of people taken from the entire population in such a way as to ensure that any one person has as much chance of being selected as any other.

sexbyte

In the beginning of their research, Masters and Johnson had difficulty recruiting volunteers. They hired prostitutes but soon realized that because many prostitutes do not orgasm regularly during their work, they experienced a condition known as **chronic pelvic congestion.** This congestion interfered with normal physiological functioning and convinced the researchers to include several middle-class volunteers in the study.

chronic pelvic congestion
A vasocongestive buildup in the uterus that occurs when arousal does not lead to orgasm.

penile strain gauge
A device used to measure penile engorgement.

photoplethysmograph
A device used to measure vaginal lubrication.

Review Question

Differentiate between Alfred Kinsey's work and Masters and Johnson's. What did these researchers contribute to our understanding of human sexuality?

Dr. Evelyn Hooker published the first empirical study to challenge the psychiatric view that homosexuality was a mental illness. Her work ultimately led to the removal of homosexuality from the Diagnostic and Statistical Manual of Mental Disorders (DSM).

sex byte

The *National Health and Social Life Survey* found that 93% of those who were married in the last 10 years chose marriage partners of the same race or ethnicity (Mahay et al., 2001).

Review Question

Discuss the wide-scale research studies that have been done on homosexuality.

sex byte

The *Janus Report* found that 22% of men and 17% of women reported having had experienced at least one same-sex encounter in their lives. Of those responding, 9 percent of males and 5 percent of females identified themselves as homosexual or bisexual (Janus & Janus, 1993).

Alan Bell and Martin Weinberg: Homosexualities

Alfred Kinsey's death prevented him from publishing a book on homosexuality as he had hoped. He had collected a large number of case histories from homosexuals and had learned that a large number of people had participated in homosexual behavior in childhood and adulthood. Homosexuality, to Kinsey, was not as "abnormal" as society had thought.

In 1967, a task force was established within the National Institute of Mental Health to examine homosexuality. A total of 5,000 homosexual men and women were interviewed, and 5,000 heterosexual men and women were used for comparison. The interviews contained 528 questions and took 2 to 5 hours to complete. In 1978, Alan Bell and Martin Weinberg published *Homosexualities*, which explored the results of this study.

Prior to this research, many people believed that homosexuals were sexually irresponsible and had psychological problems that needed to be cured (Bell & Weinberg, 1978). However, Bell and Weinberg revealed that the majority of homosexuals do not conform to stereotypes. They do not generally push unwanted sexual advances onto people, nor do they seduce children. In fact, heterosexual men were found to be more likely to sexually abuse children than were homosexual men. The homosexual community was also found to be similar to the heterosexual community in its types of intimate relationships.

Other Sexuality Studies

A number of other studies have had an impact on how we think about sexuality today. The *Janus Report* and the *National Health and Social Life Survey* each tried to update Kinsey's large-scale survey of sexual behavior. Let's look at each in turn.

The Janus Report

In 1993 Drs. Samuel and Cynthia Janus published *The Janus Report on Sexual Behavior* (Janus & Janus, 1993). It was touted as the most comprehensive study of sex in America since Kinsey's work in the 1950s. *The Janus Report* was based on data obtained from nearly 3,000 questionnaires. Overall, the authors claimed that since Kinsey, there had been redistribution of sexual values in American society. They found that people were more willing to engage in a variety of sexual behaviors and that there had been an increase in sexual interest and behavior in elderly Americans. In addition, the report examined the sexual behavior of people according to where they lived—the South, Northeast, West, and the Midwest.

Although one study cannot fill in all the gaps in knowledge about sexual attitudes and behaviors in the United States, this study did yield valuable information on sexuality, such as:

- Americans in their 60s and 70s reported experiencing greatly heightened levels of sexual activity.
- Married couples reported the highest level of sexual activity and satisfaction.
- Three out of five married people said their sex lives improved after marriage.
- Areas in which people live influenced overall sexual attitudes and behaviors. Midwesterners were found to have the least sexual activity, whereas those in the South reported the earliest ages of sexual initiation and the highest rates of premarital sex.
- People who are ultraconservative were more likely to be involved in frequent or ongoing extramarital affairs than are those who are ultraliberal.
- Men and women were both initiating sexual activity.

The Janus Report was widely criticized for many reasons. The biggest problems were that the sample was not randomly selected from the general population and also that many sexual behaviors were overestimated (Greely, 1994).

SEX RESEARCH METHODS AND CONSIDERATIONS

Now that we have explored some of the findings of studies in sexuality, let us look at the specifics of how these studies are conducted. Each study that we have discussed in this chapter was scientific, yet researchers used different experimental methods depending on the kind of information they were trying to gather. For example, Freud relied on a case study methodology, whereas Kinsey used questionnaires to gather data. There are other ways that researchers collect information, such as interviews, laboratory experiments, direct observation, participant observation, and **correlations.**

Whatever techniques they use, researchers must be certain that their experiment passes standards of validity, reliability, and generalizability. Tests of **validity** determine whether or not a question or other method actually measures what it is designed to measure. For example, the people who read the question need to interpret it the same way as the researcher who wrote it. **Reliability** refers to the consistency of the measure. If we ask a question today, we would hope to get a similar answer if we ask it again in two months. Finally, **generalizability** refers to the ability of samples in a study to have wide applicability to the general population. A study can be generalized only if a random sample is used. All of the methods we review below must fit these three criteria.

Case Studies

When a researcher describes a **case study,** he or she attempts to explore individual cases to formulate general hypotheses. Freud was famous for his use of this methodology. He would study hysteria in only one patient, because he didn't have several patients with similar complaints. Using this method, however, does not allow researchers to generalize to the general public because the sample is small. Even so, the case study method may generate hypotheses that can lead to larger, generalizable studies.

Questionnaire Versus Interview

Questionnaire or survey research is generally used to identify the attitudes, knowledge, or behavior of large samples. For instance, Kinsey used this method to obtain information about his many participants, though questions have since been raised about Kinsey's validity and reliability. Kinsey recognized these problems and tried to increase the validity by using interviews to supplement the questionnaires.

Some researchers prefer to use interviews instead of questionnaires; there are advantages and disadvantages to each method. An interview allows the researcher to establish a rapport with each participant and emphasize the importance of honesty in the study. In addition, the researcher can vary the order of questions and skip questions that are irrelevant. However, there are some limitations to interviews. First, they are more time consuming and expensive than questionnaires. Also, it has been argued that questionnaires provide more honesty because the participant may be embarrassed to admit things to another person that he or she would be more likely to share with the anonymity of a questionnaire. Research has revealed that when people answer sexuality questionnaires, they are likely to leave out the questions that cause the most anxiety, especially questions about masturbation (Catania et al., 1986).

Direct Observation

Masters and Johnson used direct observation for their research on sexual response and physiology. This method is the least frequently used because it is difficult to find participants who are willing to come into the laboratory to have sex while researchers monitor their bodily functions. However, if direct observation can be done, it does provide information that cannot be obtained elsewhere. Researchers can actually monitor behavior as it happens, which gives the results more credibility. A man may exaggerate

correlation
A statistical measure of the relationship between two variables.

validity
The property of a measuring device measuring what it is intended to measure.

reliability
The dependability of a test as reflected in the consistency of its scores on repeated measurements of the same group.

generalizability
The ability of samples in research studies to have wide applicability to the outside population.

case study
A research methodology that involves an in-depth examination of one participant or a small number of participants.

the number of erections per sexual episode in a self-report, but he cannot exaggerate in a laboratory.

Direct observation is much more expensive than any of the other methods and may not be as generalizable, because it would be impossible to gather a random sample. In addition, direct observation focuses on behaviors and, as a result, ignores feelings, attitudes, or personal history.

Participant Observation

Participant observation research involves researchers going into an environment and monitoring what is happening naturally. For instance, a researcher who wants to explore male and female flirting patterns and alcohol might watch interactions between men and women in bars. This would entail several visits and specific note taking on all that occurs. However, it is difficult to generalize from this type of research because the researcher could subtly, or not so subtly, influence the research findings. Also, much of sexual behavior occurs in private, where researchers have no access.

Experimental Methods

Experiments are the only research method that allows us to isolate cause and effect. This is because in an experiment, strict control is maintained over all variables so that one variable can be isolated and examined.

For example, let's say you want to teach high school students about AIDS, but you don't know which teaching methodology would be most beneficial. You could design an experiment to examine this more closely. First, you choose a high school and **randomly assign** all the students to one of three groups. You might start by giving them a questionnaire about AIDS to establish baseline data about what they know or believe. Group 1 then listens to a lecture about AIDS, group 2 is shown a video, and group 3 listens to a person with AIDS talk about his or her experience. Strict care is taken to make sure that all of the information that is presented in these classes is identical. The only thing that differs is the teaching method. In scientific terms, the type of teaching method is the **independent variable,** which is manipulated by the researcher. After each class, the students are given a test to determine what knowledge they have gained about AIDS. This measurement is to determine the effect of the independent variable on the **dependent variable,** which in this case is knowledge about AIDS. If one group shows more learning after one particular method was used, we might be able to attribute the learning to the type of methodology that was used.

Experiments can be more costly than any of the other methods discussed, both in terms of finances and time commitment. It is also possible that in an attempt to control the experiments, a researcher may cause the study to become too sterile or artificial (nothing like it would be outside of the laboratory), and the results may be faulty or inapplicable to the real world. Finally, experiments are not always possible in certain areas of research, especially in the field of sexuality. For instance, what if we wanted to examine whether or not early sexual abuse contributed to adult difficulties with intimate relationships? It would be entirely unethical to abuse children sexually in order to examine whether or not they develop these problems later in life.

Correlations

Correlations are often used when it is not possible to do an experiment. For example, because it is unethical to do a controlled experiment in a sexual abuse study, we would study a given population to see whether there is any correlation between past sexual abuse and later difficulties with intimate relationships. The limitation of a **correlational study** is that it doesn't provide any information about cause. We would not learn whether past sexual abuse causes intimacy difficulties, even though we may learn that these factors are related. The intimacy difficulties could occur for several other reasons, including factors such as low self-esteem or a personality disorder.

SEX in Real Life

Kiss and Tell

Could it be that the questions researchers ask about sexuality are more important than the answers? Some researchers believe so, and research indicates that our questions about sexuality may indeed shape our thoughts (Ericksen, 1999). The following is an excerpt from Julia Ericksen's *Kiss and Tell,* a book that explores human sexuality research.

> *Sexual behavior is a volatile and sensitive topic, and surveys designed to reveal it have both great power and great limits. By revealing the private behavior of others, they provide a way for people to evaluate their own behavior and even the meaning of information the surveys produce. And they provide experts with information they urgently seek to understand society and develop social policy. Social scientists often view surveys as providing hard facts about be-*

> *havior, yet results are limited by researchers' often unrecognized preconceptions about what the important questions are and also by respondents' ability and willingness to reveal what they have done. (p. 2)*

We learned in Chapter 1 that for most of Western history, our religion determined the appropriate standards for sexual behavior. However, sexuality researchers became the experts in the 20th century as they helped define what was considered "normal." Sexuality researchers have great power over the research they are involved in. Do you think that sexuality researchers approach their studies with ideas of what they will find? Where do these ideas come from? Could these ideas bias their research? Are researchers shaped by past research?

SOURCE: Ericksen (1999).

PROBLEMS AND ISSUES IN SEX RESEARCH

Many problems in sexuality research are more difficult to contend with than in other types of research. These include ethical issues, volunteer bias, sampling problems, and reliability.

Ethical Issues

Ethical issues affect all social science—and sexuality research in particular. Prior to a person's participation in a study of sexuality, researchers must obtain the participant's **informed consent.** This is especially important in an area such as sexuality because it is such a personal subject. Informed consent means that the person knows what to expect from the questions and procedures, how the information will be used, that his or her **confidentiality** will be assured, and to whom he or she can address questions. Some things that people reveal in a study, such as their acknowledgment of an affair or a sexual dysfunction, can cause harm or embarrassment if researchers are careless enough to let others find out. Another ethical question that has generated controversy is whether or not children should be asked questions about sexuality. Overall it is standard procedure in sexuality research to maintain confidentiality and obtain informed consent from all participants, regardless of age.

informed consent
Informing participants about what will be expected of them before they agree to participate in a research study.

confidentiality
Keeping all materials collected in a research study private and confidential.

Volunteer Bias

Earlier in this chapter we touched on the topic of volunteer bias in our discussion of Morton Hunt's *Sexual Behavior in the 1970s.* Because Hunt's sample was such a small percentage of those he contacted, volunteer bias prevents his results from being generalizable to the population as a whole.

Imagine that we wanted to administer a questionnaire about college students' attitudes toward sexuality, and we recruited volunteers from your biology class. Do you think those who volunteer would be different from those who do not? Research indicates that they may indeed differ.

As early as 1969, Rosenthal & Rosnow (1975) claimed that those who volunteer for psychological studies often have a special interest in the studies in which they participate. Studies that have examined volunteer bias in sexuality research conducted with college students generally support the finding that volunteers differ from nonvolunteers (Catania et al., 1995; Gaither et al., 2003). Volunteers have been found to be more sexually liberal, more sexually experienced, more interested in sexual variety, and more likely to have had sexual intercourse and to have performed oral sex; and they report less traditional sexual attitudes than nonvolunteers (Bogaert, 1996; Gaither, 2000; Plaud et al., 1999; Wiederman, 1999). Research has also found that overall, men are more likely than women to volunteer for sexuality studies (Gaither et al., 2003).

You might be wondering how a researcher would know whether his or her volunteer sample is different from the nonvolunteer sample. After all, how can the researcher know anything about the nonvolunteers who are not in the study? Researchers have designed ways of overcoming this problem. Prior to asking for volunteers to take part in a sexuality study, researchers ask all participants to fill out a questionnaire that contains personality measures and sexuality questions. Participants are then asked whether or not they would volunteer for a sexuality study. Because the researchers already have information from both volunteers and nonvolunteers, they simply compare these data.

Because volunteers appear to differ from nonvolunteers, it is impossible to generalize the findings of a study that used a volunteer sample. The Kinsey studies attempted to decrease volunteer bias by obtaining full participation from each member of the groups they studied.

Sampling Problems

Sexuality studies routinely involve the use of college-age populations. Brecher and Brecher (1986) refer to these populations as **samples of convenience,** because the participants used are convenient for researchers who tend to work at universities. Kinsey used such samples in his initial research at Indiana University. The question is, can these studies be generalized to the rest of the population? Are college students similar to noncollege students of the same age, or people who are older or younger? Probably not. These samples also miss certain groups, such as those who do not go to college, and may also underrepresent minorities and the disabled.

samples of convenience
A research methodology that involves using samples that are easy to collect and acquire.

Reliability

How reliable is sex research? Some studies have found that couples who are sexually satisfied tend to overestimate their frequency of sexual behavior, whereas those who are unsatisfied underreport it (James, 1971). In 1967, a study was done to evaluate the reliability of the reporting of sexual activity. Men were required to keep daily logs of when they engaged in sexual activity and also to provide daily urine samples. These samples were microscopically evaluated for semen to substantiate their logs of sexual activity. Reports were found to be consistent with their written logs.

Some critics claim that changes in frequency of sexual behavior over time may be due more to changes in the *reporting* of behavior than to actual changes in frequency (Kaats & Davis, 1971). For instance, if we had done a study in 1995 about the number of college students that engaged in premarital sex and compared this to data collected in 1963, we would undoubtedly find more people reporting having had premarital sex in 1995. However, it could be that these higher numbers are due in part to the fact that more people felt comfortable talking about premarital sex in 1995 than they did in 1963. To ensure that we know the increase in numbers is actually due to an increase in behavior, it is necessary to take into account the time period of the study when evaluating the results.

Another problem affecting reliability involves the participant's memory. Because many sexuality researchers ask questions about behaviors that might have happened in one's adolescence, people may not always have the capacity to accurately remember information. For instance, if we were to ask a 52-year-old man the age at which he first masturbated, chances are good that he would not remember exactly how old he was. He would probably *estimate* the age at which he first masturbated. Estimates are not adequate for scientific study.

Review Question

Identify the problems and issues that affect sex research. What can be done to avoid these problems?

SEX Talk

Question: *How do you know that what people tell you is true?*

The fact is that we just don't know, and we hope that people are being honest. Sometimes researchers build into studies little tricks that can catch someone who is lying, such as asking the same questions in different wording again later in a survey. Researchers also anticipate that participants will understand the questions asked and be able to provide the answers. In actuality, researchers may take many things for granted.

SEXUALITY RESEARCH ACROSS CULTURES

Many studies examine sexuality in cultures outside the United States. Some have been general studies that examine knowledge levels and attitudes in different populations; others have evaluated specific areas such as pregnancy, rape, homosexuality, or sex education. Many times these studies are done by researchers in other countries, but some have also been done by American researchers.

Of all the topics that have been studied cross-culturally, we have probably learned the most about how societies' values and culture influence sexuality. Every culture develops its own rules about which sexual behaviors are encouraged and which will not be tolerated. In 1971, Donald Marshall and Robert Suggs published a classic anthropological study, entitled *Human Sexual Behavior*, which examined how sexuality was expressed in several different cultures. This study remains one of the largest cultural studies ever done on sexuality. Following are some of its interesting findings:

- Masturbation is rare in preliterate cultures (those without a written language).
- In the majority of societies, foreplay is engaged in prior to sexual intercourse.
- Foreplay is usually initiated by males.
- Sexual intercourse is most commonly engaged in at night prior to falling asleep.
- Female orgasmic ability varies greatly from culture to culture.

More recent studies on cross-cultural sexuality have yielded other interesting results. A comprehensive study of sexual behavior entitled the *Analyse des Comportements Sexuels en France* (ACSF) was done in 1992. Funded by a $2.5 million grant from France's Health Ministry and the National AIDS Research Agency, it examined the sexual practices of over 20,000 people between the ages of 18 and 69. Interviews were done primarily by telephone, and the majority of those people contacted agreed to participate (an impressive response rate of 76.5% was obtained). Findings revealed that many teenagers do not use condoms during sexual intercourse because they are too expensive; that rates of extramarital sexual behavior are decreasing; and that the average French heterosexual engages in sex approximately two times per week. This was the largest study done in France in over 20 years.

In 2001, results gathered from the ACSF were compared to the *National Health and Social Life Study* (NHSLS) done in the United States. Overall, patterns of sexual conduct were similar (Gagnon, 2001). However, there were some areas of difference. The French were found to form monogamous sexual partnerships earlier and to remain in these partnerships for a longer time period than the Americans. The French also had fewer sexual partners over their lifetime and higher frequencies of sexual behavior.

Human Sexuality in a Diverse World

The Pfizer Global Study of Sexual Attitudes and Behaviors

*T*he Pfizer Global Study of Sexual Attitudes and Behaviors (Pfizer, 2002) was the first global survey to study sexual behavior, attitudes, beliefs, and relationship satisfaction among more than 26,000 men and women age 40 to 80. Interviews and surveys were conducted in 29 countries representing all world regions.

This study found that more than 80% of men and 60% of women claimed sex was an important part of their overall lives. The highest ratings for the importance of sex came from Korea, whereas the lowest ratings came from Hong Kong. The survey also found that physical and emotional satisfaction in a relationship was higher among those who reported better health. This supported Pfizer's conclusions that sexual health and satisfaction have an impact on men's and women's emotional and physical health (see Figures 2.1 and 2.2). Note that 37% of respondents from Hong Kong and 87% of respondents from Korea rated sex "very," "extremely," or "moderately important." Why might these differences exist?

SOURCE: Pfizer, *The Pfizer Global Study of Sexual Attitudes and Behavior,* 2002. Used by permission.

Percent responding "very," "extremely," or "moderately important"

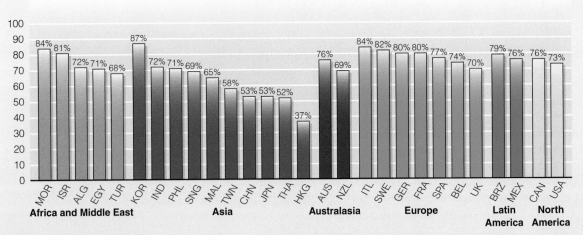

Figure 2.1
How important is sex in your overall life?

Percent responding "yes"

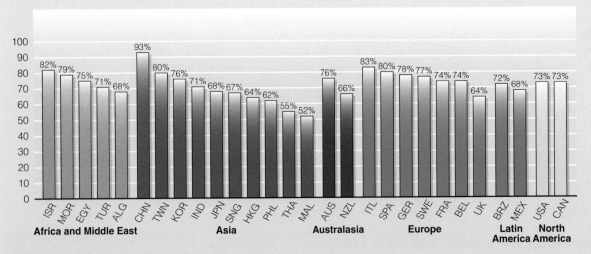

Figure 2.2
Have you had sexual intercourse in the last 12 months?

In 2002, Pfizer Pharmaceuticals did the most comprehensive global study of sexuality to date (see the accompanying Human Sexuality in a Diverse World). The *Pfizer Global Study of Sexual Attitudes and Behaviors* surveyed over 26,000 men and women in 28 countries. This study was the first global survey to assess behaviors, attitudes, beliefs, and sexual satisfaction. Surveys assessed the importance of sex and intimacy in relationships, attitudes and beliefs about sexual health, and treatment-seeking behaviors for sexual dysfunctions, and provided an international baseline regarding sexual attitudes to compare various countries and also monitor cultural changes over time.

SEX Talk

Question: *How could an entire culture's attitudes about sex differ from those of another culture? I can understand how there might be individual variations, but could there really be significant cultural differences?*

Yes, there could. It makes more sense when you think about two very different types of cultures (Triandis et al., 1990). A collectivist culture (e.g., India, Pakistan, Thailand, or the Philippines) emphasizes the culture as a whole and thinks less about the individuals within that society. In contrast, an individualistic culture (e.g., United States, Australia, or England) stresses the goals of individuals over the culture as a whole. This cultural difference can affect the way that sexuality is viewed. For example, a culture such as India may value marriage because it is good for the social standing of members of the society, whereas a marriage in the United States is valued because the two people love each other and want to spend their lives together.

Human Sexuality in a Diverse World

Internet-Based Sexuality Research

In 2000 it was estimated that two-thirds of Americans used the Internet, and this number continues to grow today (A. C. Nielsen, 2000). It is estimated that the average Internet user in the United States spends 3 hours per day online (Markoff, 2004). The popularity of the Internet has led to an increase in Internet-based social science research (Baron & Siepmann, 2000), and sexuality researchers have been relying on the Internet for data collection in many of their studies (Mustanski, 2001). The accessibility and sense of anonymity of the web have given sexuality researchers access to a wider group of diverse participants.

However, there are disadvantages and risks to Internet-based sexuality research. As in other research methods, participants can lie and sabotage research. Because surveys are anonymous, participants could submit multiple responses. To lessen the possibility of this happening, researchers could collect e-mail addresses to check for multiple submissions, but this would negate participants' anonymity. One study that checked for multiple submissions found that participants rarely submitted more than one response (Reips, 2000).

Although as much as 75% of Americans have access to the Internet (Markoff, 2004), some caution that Internet users are not representative of all Americans—a variety of minorities are not well represented, nor are those with low socioeconomic status or education (NTIA & USDC, 1999). Wealthier, Caucasian, and better-educated individuals are well represented on the Internet, and this can bias research results. However, some researchers claim that even though these differences exist, the participants pool available online may be more representative of the general population than a group of typical college students (who are the most common research participants; Mustanski, 2001; Reips & Bachtiger, 2000).

Finally, one more concern is that minors may access Internet-based sexuality research studies. However, researchers must ask for informed consent, and participants must agree that they are over the age of 18 before participating.

Even with these cautions, however, Internet-based sexuality research is a dynamic and exciting new frontier for sexuality researchers. It is anticipated that more studies will be done using web-based research methodology in the future.

SOURCE: Mustanski (2001).

Review **Question**

Discuss the sexuality research that has been done outside the United States.

sex byte

Sex surveys in magazines, such as *Cosmopolitan,* create new dangers for sex researchers in that they tell readers things that they want to hear. Selected voices that are used in these "analyses" promote sexual joy and passion above all else (Ericksen, 1999).

Societal influences affect all aspects of sexuality. Throughout this book we will explore more details from cross-cultural studies on sexuality and examine how cultures vary from each other.

SEX RESEARCH IN THE FUTURE: BEYOND PROBLEM-DRIVEN RESEARCH

Many view America as a country "obsessed with sex." As we discussed in Chapter 1, sex is used to sell everything from blue jeans to cologne and is oozing from television sitcoms, advertising, music videos, and pop lyrics. However, even with this openness and sex all around us, there is a painful lack of solid sexuality research. Our "problem-driven" approach to sex research has limited what we really know about relationships, love, and human development. Often funding for sexuality research comes from private foundations or governmental agencies. Over the past few years, however, there has been a lack of adequate funding.

Overall, it is a trying time for sexuality researchers. Congressional attacks on sexuality research continue, and in 2003 an amendment was proposed that would have cut funding for many grants given to study sexual behaviors. In response, the Coalition to Protect Research (CPR) was organized to support federal investments in biomedical and behavioral research into human sexual development, sexual health, and sexually transmitted infections (Studwell, 2004).

Religious institutions may also work to impede sexuality research. In fact, in 2003, the Traditional Values Coalition (consisting of over 43,000 churches) publicly objected to $100 million of government-backed research, much of it focusing on sexual behavior (Carey, 2004). Conservative groups pressure federal agencies to cut funding for sexuality studies, which forces many researchers to turn to pharmaceutical companies for financial support (Clark, 2005). Some researchers claim that a reliance on drug company money will reduce sexual functioning to purely physical functions and the important questions about the psychological and emotional aspects of sexuality will be ignored.

The opinion of many conservatives is that the key to sexual health lies in a lifelong monogamous relationship and because of this, no research is needed on any sexual behaviors (Carey, 2004). In fact, according to such beliefs, if researchers *do* study behaviors outside of this formula, the research will "normalize" deviant behaviors. All of these pressures affect sexuality researchers' ability to do their work. In fact, it has been said that because of these pressures, many sex researchers today operate in a type of "scientific underground," fearing suppression and censure (Carey, 2004).

Our "problem-driven" approach has resulted in a lack of information in several key areas in human sexuality. We know very little about sexual desire and arousal and what makes couples happy long term, or about childhood and adolescent sexuality, which has long been a taboo area of research. We also know little about the development of sexual identity, sexual risk-taking, and how the increase in sexual material on the Internet affects people's sexual behaviors (Carey, 2004). Infidelity, sexual trauma, and various sexual variations, including sexual predators and people who engage in sex with children, also have been poorly researched.

Funding for sexuality education has also been controversial. In fact, to get federal funds for sexuality education, a program must discuss abstinence and is often barred from discussing condoms or other contraceptive methods (Kristof, 2005). Today we know that these abstinence-only sex education programs are not successful (we'll discuss this more in Chapter 8).

The goal of sex research in the future will be to understand the emotional and relational aspects of human sexuality. Instead of overly focusing on what doesn't work in sexual relationships, such as problems with erections or orgasms, it will help us understand what does work and what keeps couples happy and satisfied. In the future, an increased willingness on the part of the federal government to consider sexuality-related research will help improve our knowledge about sexuality and will aid in bringing sexuality researchers together. An improved collaboration between researchers of various disciplines would help us more fully understand the influences that affect our sexuality and, in turn, would help build the field of sexual science research strives to answer.

In the following chapters of this book, keep in mind the importance of theory and how it guides the questions we have about sexuality. The scientific method helps sexologists find answers to the varied questions we have about human sexual behavior. We will be discussing the results of many more of these scientific studies.

Review Question

Describe what the future might hold for sexuality research.

Chapter Review

ACTIVE SUMMARY

1. A(n) **(a)** _____ is a set of assumptions, principles, or methods that help a researcher understand the nature of the phenomenon being studied. The most influential psychological theory has been the **(b)** _____ theory, developed by Sigmund Freud. He discussed **(c)** _____ formation (the development of the id, ego, and superego) and also **(d)** _____ development (oral, anal, phallic, latency, and genital stages).

2. **(a)** _____ theory believes that only overt behavior can be measured, observed, and controlled by scientists. **(b)** _____ uses rewards and punishments to control behavior. A treatment method called **(c)** _____ is used to help change unwanted behaviors.

3. Social learning theory looks at reward and punishment in controlling behavior but also believes that **(a)** _____ events, such as feelings, thoughts, and beliefs, can also influence behavior. Another theory, **(b)** _____ theory, holds that people differ in how they process information, and this creates **(c)** _____. Our behavior is a result of how we **(d)** _____ and conceptualize what is happening around us.

4. Humanistic theory purports that we all strive to develop ourselves to the best of our abilities and to become **(a)** _____. Biological theory claims that sexual behavior is primarily a(n) **(b)** _____ _____, whereas **(c)** _____ theories are interested in how the society in which we live influences sexual behavior. Evolutionary theory incorporates both **(d)** _____ and sociology to understand sexual behavior.

5. Feminist theory looks at how the social construction of **(a)** _____ is based on power and the view that women are submissive and **(b)** _____ to men. **(c)** _____ theory, another politically charged theory, asserts that domination, such as **(d)** _____ and homophobia, should be resisted.

6. The legitimate forefathers of sexuality research may be **(a)** _____ and **(b)** _____, because they were the first to elaborate theories regarding sexual responses and dysfunctions, sex legislation, reproduction, contraception, and sexual ethics. The majority of the early sex research was done in Europe, primarily in **(c)** _____. It wasn't until the 1900s that sexual-

ity research moved from Germany to the United States, which has **(d)** _____ sexuality research ever since.

7. The majority of sexuality research has been **(a)** _____ _____, and because of this, we know very little about what constitutes **(b)** _____ sexuality. The research has also become **(c)** _____, with researchers coming from several disciplines, many unaware of the work being done by others.

8. The most influential early promoters of **(a)** _____ were Iwan Bloch, Albert Moll, Magnus **(b)** _____, and Richard von Krafft-Ebing. Clelia Mosher did a great deal of sexuality research in the 1800s, but most of her work was **(c)** _____. Katherine Bement Davis found that homosexuals were no different from heterosexuals, but her work was **(d)** _____ because it caused fear among male researchers. The focus of sexuality research began to change after her research.

9. **(a)** _____ _____ was probably the most influential sex researcher of the 20th century. He was the first to take the study of sexuality away from the **(b)** _____ model and move it toward other **(c)** _____ disciplines. Kinsey established the Institute for **(d)** _____ _____ at Indiana University. Morton **(e)** _____ updated Kinsey's earlier work on human sexuality.

10. **(a)** _____ and **(b)** _____ were the first scientists to observe and measure the act of **(c)** _____ _____ in the laboratory. They discovered several interesting aspects of sexuality, including a model called the **(d)** _____ _____ _____.

11. Adolescent health and risk behaviors were the focus of a study by **(a)** _____. The **(b)** _____ studied adolescent males, collecting data between 1988 and 1995. Because seniors were underrepresented in Kinsey's studies, **(c)** _____ and **(d)** _____ studied sexuality in 60- to 91-year-olds. Edward Brecher et al.'s (1984) study confirmed earlier findings that older adults are indeed **(e)** _____.

12. The **(a)** _____ *Report* was published in 1993, based on data obtained from nearly from 3,000 **(b)** _____. The *National Health and Social Life Survey* (NHSLS), published in

(c) _____, was the most (d) _____ study of sexual attitudes and behaviors since Kinsey.

13. (a) _____ can use several methods to study sexuality, including case study, questionnaire, (b) _____, (c) _____ _____, (d) _____ observation, experimental methods, and correlations.

14. Researchers must be certain that their experiment passes standards of (a) _____, (b) _____, and (c) _____.

15. Several problems can affect sexuality research, such as (a) _____ issues, (b) _____ bias, and (c) _____ and reliability problems. Of all the topics that have been studied cross-culturally, we have learned the most about how societies' values and (d) _____ influence sexuality.

16. Sexuality researchers should maintain (a) _____ and acquire informed (b) _____ from all participants. Volunteers have been found to differ from (c) _____ in sexuality studies and many studies use college students, which may (d) _____ the results.

17. The most comprehensive global study of sexuality was funded by (a) _____ _____ in 2002. This study (b) _____ over 26,000 men and women from over 28 coun-

tries and provided a baseline of sexual (c) _____ in a variety of different countries.

18. Pressure from (a) _____ groups has resulted in less (b) _____ and acceptance of sexuality research. Our (c) _____ _____ approach to sexuality research has interfered with what we really know and understand about relationships, love, and human development.

Critical Thinking Questions

1. Is sexuality research as valid and reliable as other areas of research? Explain.

2. Do you think that people would be more honest about their sex lives if they were filling out an anonymous questionnaire or if they were being interviewed by a researcher? Which method of research do you think yields the highest degree of honesty? With which method would you feel most comfortable?

3. Why do you think couples might have volunteered to be in Masters and Johnson's study? Would you have volunteered for this study? Why, or why not?

4. If you could do a study on sexuality, what area would you choose? What methods of data collection would you use? Why? How would you avoid the problems that many sex researchers face?

CHAPTER RESOURCES

Check It Out

Laumann, E. O., and Michael, R. T. (Eds.). (2001). **Sex, love, and health in America.** Chicago: University of Chicago Press.

Based on data collected from the *National Health and Social Life Survey* (1994), this book delves deeper into the original findings. Sixteen researchers explore controversial topics, including teenage sexuality and pregnancy; sexual contact between children and adults; race, ethnicity, and sexuality; abortion; circumcision; sexual dysfunction; the role of cohabitation in the sexual satisfaction of couples; and how sexual behavior has changed in response to AIDS. In addition, there is a lengthy section on private sex and public policy.

Kinsey (2004; 1 hour, 58 minutes; Rated R)

Based on the life of Alfred Kinsey (played by Liam Neeson), one of the most influential sex researchers of the 20th century, this movie discusses the issues and controversies that arose throughout Kinsey's time. It allows the viewer to take a deeper look at his life and career and the criticism both received. Because of Kinsey's publications, he received great scrutiny from his colleagues, who often referred to his works as the "atom bomb." The movie exposes the censorship of and controversy surrounding sex research that to some extent still exists today.

InfoTrac® College Edition

If your instructor ordered InfoTrac with this book, explore InfoTrac College Edition, your online library, for additional readings and review. Go to: **www.thomsonedu.com,** and enter these search terms:

sexuality research	sampling	theories
sex research methods	sexology	

Web Resources

SexualityNow Companion Website
Go to **http://thomsonedu.com/carroll** for practice quiz questions, interactive activities, Internet links, critical thinking exercises, discussion forums, and more. You can also access sites from the Wadsworth Psychology Study Center (**http://psychology.wadsworth.com**) or you can connect directly to the following sites:

American Association of Sexuality Educators, Counselors, and Therapists (AASECT)
AASECT is devoted to the promotion of sexual health through the development and advancement of the fields of sex therapy, counseling, and education. AASECT also encourages research related to sex education, counseling, and therapy, and supports the publication and dissemination of professional materials related to these fields.

Electronic Journal of Human Sexuality
This website is intended to disseminate knowledge to the international community about all aspects of human sexuality. There are peer-reviewed research articles, dissertations, and theses on sexuality, and general-interest articles by qualified authors.

Sexuality Information and Education Council of the United States (SIECUS)
SIECUS is a national, private, nonprofit advocacy organization that promotes comprehensive sexuality education and HIV/AIDS prevention education in the schools and advocates for sexual and reproductive rights.

Society for the Scientific Study of Sexuality (SSSS)
SSSS is an interdisciplinary, international organization for sexuality researchers, clinicians, educators, and other professionals in related fields.

Go to **www.thomsonedu.com** to link to **SexualityNow,** your online study tool. First take the **Pre-Test** for this chapter to get your **Personalized Study Plan,** which will identify topics you need to review and direct you to online resources. Then take the **Post-Test** to determine what concepts you have mastered and what you still need work on.

Videos in SexualityNow
For additional information on topics discussed in this chapter, check out the videos in **SexualityNow** on the following topics:

- **American Sex Lives: 2004 Survey**—Listen to how this poll of 1,500 Americans about their sex lives was conducted.
- **Studying Sexual Response**—Dr. David Barlow and staff psychologists explain how research on sexual dysfunctions is conducted.

3

Gender Development, Gender Roles, and Gender Identity

Sexuality■Now Go to www.thomsonedu.com to link to
SexualityNow, your online study tool.

I magine that right now, as you are reading this page, an alien walks into the room. The alien tells you that "zee" (not he or she) is only on Earth for a short time and would like to learn as much as possible about life here during this visit. One of the things "zee" would like to learn about is **gender,** specifically, "What are a man and woman?" How would you answer such a question? You might try to explain how a man and woman look, act, think, or feel. But what is a man, and what is a woman?

When a baby is born, new parents are eager to hear whether "It's a Girl" or "It's a Boy," but what if it were neither? What if a newborn child had ambiguous genitalia and it was impossible to tell whether it was a boy or a girl? A child with the **gonads** (testes or ovaries) of one gender but with ambiguous external genitalia is often referred to as **intersexed.** Intersexed girls and boys are often reared as members of their chromosomal sex. Throughout history most parents have opted for immediate surgery to quickly assign the child's gender to either male or female (Neergaard, 2005). But isn't gender more than anatomy or hormones? What is gender?

Gender raises many issues. For example, does your university allow you to have a roommate who is the other gender? Over the last couple of years, many universities across the country have established "gender neutral" housing (Marklein, 2004), which means it doesn't matter what gender you are when it comes to living quarters on campus. These efforts are part of a national movement aimed at helping students who may feel confused or who have questions about their gender.

Before we go any further, let's talk about how people tend to use the words **sex** and gender synonymously, even though they have different meanings. When you fill out a questionnaire that asks you "What is your sex?" how do you answer? When you apply for a driver's license and they ask, "What gender are you?" how do you respond? Although your answers here might be the same, researchers usually use the word *sex* to refer to the biological aspects of being male or female and *gender* to refer to the behavioral, psychological, and social characteristics of men and women (Pryzgoda & Chrisler, 2000).

You might wonder why exploring gender is important to our understanding of sexuality. How does gender affect sexuality? Gender stereotypes shape our opinions about how men and women act sexually. For example, if we believe that men are more aggressive than women, we might believe that these gender stereotypes carry over in the bedroom as well. Traditionally, men are viewed as the initiators in sexual activity, and they are the ones who are supposed to make all the "moves." Stereotypes about women, on the other hand, hold that women are more emotional and connected when it comes to sex—more into "making love" than "having sex." Do gender stereotypes really affect how we act and interact sexually? We will explore the relationship between gender and sexuality later in this chapter.

So, let's ask again, what is a man? A woman? Are we really made of sugar and spice or snails and puppy dog tails? For many years scientists have debated whether gender is more genetics and biology ("nature") or social environment and upbringing ("nurture"), or is it a combination of the two? A real-life story[1] from 1965 can help us understand more about the nature versus nurture debate. A young Canadian couple brought their two identical twin boys (Bruce and Brian) to the hospital for routine circumcisions when the boys were 8 months old. A surgical mistake was made during Bruce's circumcision, and his penis was destroyed. At the time, a well-known sexologist from Johns Hopkins University, Dr. John Money, was promoting his ideas about gender identity. Money believed that gender could be changed through child rearing and was not contingent upon **chromosomes,** genitals, or even sex hormones (Money, 1975).

---

[1]In 2001, John Colapinto wrote the details of this real-life story in a book called *As Nature Made Him: The Boy Who Was Raised as a Girl* (New York: Harper Perennial).

gender
The behavioral, psychological, and social characteristics of men and women.

gonads
The male and female sex glands—ovaries and testes.

intersexed
A person who has the gonads (testes or ovaries) of one gender but ambiguous external genitalia; also referred to as a pseudohermaphrodite.

sex
The biological aspects of being male or female.

chromosome
A threadlike structure in the nucleus of a cell that carries the genetic information.

After meeting with Dr. Money and discussing their options, the Canadian couple decided to have their son, Bruce, undergo castration (removal of the testicles) and have surgery to transform his genitals into those of an anatomically correct female. Bruce became Brenda and was put on hormone treatment beginning in adolescence to maintain his feminine appearance. For many years, this Brenda/Bruce case stood as "proof" that children were psychosexually "neutral" at birth and that gender could be assigned, no matter what the genetics or biology indicated. As a result, many children who were born with ambiguous genitals or who had experienced genital trauma were advised to undergo gender reassignment. It is estimated that one in 2,000 births involves a baby with ambiguous genitals or reproductive structures that are both male and female in physiology (D. A. Lewis, 2000).[2]

However, even though Money paraded the Brenda/Bruce story as a success, and around the globe intersexed children began reassignments, no one paid much attention to the fact that Brenda was struggling with her gender identity. Once she reached puberty, despite her hormone treatments, her misery increased and Brenda became depressed and suicidal. She never felt that she was a girl, and she was relentlessly teased by peers. At 15 years old she stopped hormonal treatments and changed her name to David. Although David eventually married and adopted children, his struggles continued. He battled depression his entire life and felt "brainwashed" by physicians (Burkeman & Younge, 2005). In 2004, he took his own life.

This case illustrates the fact both nature *and* nurture are important in the development of gender. **Evolutionary theory** argues that there are many behaviors in men and women that have evolved in the survival of the species and that gender differences between men and women may be at least partially a result of heredity.

In this chapter we will explore the nature versus nurture debate as it relates to gender in hopes of finding answers to the questions "What is a man?" and "What is a woman?" We'll start by reviewing prenatal development and sexual differentiation. We will also look at atypical sexual differentiation and chromosomal/hormonal disorders. Although these disorders are not exceedingly common, their existence and how scientists have dealt with them help us learn more about gender. Our biological exploration of gender will help set the foundation on which we can understand how complex gender really is. We will also explore gender roles, theories about gender, and socialization throughout the life cycle.

PRENATAL DEVELOPMENT: X AND Y MAKE THE DIFFERENCE

Human beings have a biological urge to reproduce and so are in some sense "designed" to be sexual beings; any species that does not have good reproductive equipment and a strong desire to use it will not last very long. Simpler organisms, such as amoebas, simply split in two, creating a pair genetically identical to the parent amoeba. More complex organisms, however, reproduce through **sexual reproduction,** in which two parents each donate a **gamete** (GAM-meet), or **germ cell,** which combine to create a new organism.

The tiny germ cells from the male (sperm) and the much larger but also microscopic cell from the female (egg, or ovum) each contain half of the new person's genes and determine his or her sex, hair and eye color, general body shape, the likely age at which he or she will reach puberty, and literally millions of other aspects of the new person's physiology, development, and emotional nature. The genes direct the development of the genitals and the reproductive organs and set the biological clock running to trigger puberty and female **menopause** or male **andropause.** We will discuss both of these in the next two chapters.

---

[2]Today, the Intersex Society of North America (ISNA) is working to end the shame, secrecy, and unwanted genital surgery for people who experience such a trauma or who are born with ambiguous genitalia (http://www.isna.org).

evolutionary theory
Theory that emphasizes the gradual process of development of species through biological adaptation.

sexual reproduction
The production of offspring from the union of two different parents.

gamete
A male or female reproductive cell; the spermatozoon or ovum; also referred to as a germ cell.

germ cell
A male or female reproductive cell; the spermatozoon or ovum; also referred to as a gamete.

Review Question

Differentiate between *sex* and *gender,* and explain how the Bruce/Brenda case shed light on the nature versus nurture debate.

menopause
The cessation of menstruation in life.

andropause
A period of time in a man's life, usually during his 70s or 80s, when testosterone decreases, causing a decrease in spermatogenesis, a thinner ejaculate, a decrease in ejaculatory pressure, decreased muscle strength, increased fatigue, and mood disturbances.

Most cells in the human body contain 46 chromosomes: 23 inherited from the mother and 23 from the father, arranged in 23 pairs. Twenty-two of the pairs look almost identical and are referred to as **autosomes;** the exception is the 23rd pair, the sex chromosomes. The two **sex chromosomes,** which determine whether a person is male or female, are made up of an X chromosome donated by the mother through the ovum and either an X or a Y chromosome donated by the father's sperm. In normal development, if the male contributes an X chromosome, the child will be female (XX); if he contributes a Y, the child will be male (XY).

All the cells of the body (somatic cells), except gametes, contain all 23 pairs of chromosomes (46 total) and are called diploid (meaning *double*). But if a merging sperm and egg also had 23 pairs each, they would create a child with 46 pairs, which is too many (remember that most cells contain only 23 pairs of chromosomes). So gametes are haploid, meaning they contain half the number of chromosomes (23) of a somatic cell (46). During **fertilization,** a haploid sperm and a haploid egg join to produce a diploid **zygote** (ZIE-goat) containing 46 chromosomes, half from each parent. The zygote can now undergo **mitosis,** reproducing its 46 chromosomes as it grows.

The 46 chromosomes are threadlike bodies made up of somewhere between 20,000 to 25,000 genes, each of which contains **deoxyribonucleic (dee-OCK-see-rye-bow-new-KLEE-ik) acid (DNA;** Human Genome Project, 2003). DNA acts as a blueprint for how every cell in the organism will develop. At first, the zygote reproduces exact copies of itself. Soon, however, the cells begin a process of differentiation. Differentiation is one of the great mysteries of human biology—suddenly, identical cells begin splitting into liver cells, brain cells, skin cells, and all the thousands of different kinds of cells in the body. The DNA determines the order in which cells differentiate, and a cell's position may de-

autosome
Any chromosome that is not a sex chromosome.

sex chromosomes
Rod-shaped bodies in the nucleus of a cell at the time of cell division that contain information about whether the fetus will become male or female.

fertilization
Occurs when a haploid sperm and a haploid egg join to produce a diploid zygote, containing 46 chromosomes.

zygote
The single cell resulting from the union of sperm and egg cells.

mitosis
The division of the nucleus of a cell into two new cells such that each new daughter cell has the same number and kind of chromosomes as the original parent.

deoxyribonucleic acid (DNA)
A nucleic acid in the shape of a double helix, in which all genetic information in the organism is encoded.

SEX Talk

Question: *Does the father's sperm really determine the sex of the child?*

Yes, it is the sperm that determines the sex of the child, but the woman's body does have a role to play; there are differences between X and Y sperm (X's are heavier and slower but live longer; Y's are faster but die more quickly), and a woman's vaginal environment or ovulation cycle may favor one or the other. But the sex of the child does depend on whether an X chromosome sperm or a Y chromosome sperm, donated by the father, joins with the ovum (which is always an X). The irony is that for many years, in many cultures, men routinely blamed and even divorced women who did not produce a child of a certain sex (usually a boy), when in fact the man's sperm had much more to do with it.

Sneak Peek

"Scientists stained the sperm and marked them through a laser, so the X chromosomes may be separated from the Y chromosomes."—*Choosing Your Child's Gender*

Sexuality ◗ Now

It is hard to tell infant boys and girls apart, which is why so many parents dress them in pink or blue.

VLC/Getty Images

gestation
The period of intrauterine fetal development.

testes
Male gonads inside the scrotum that produce testosterone.

ovaries
Female gonads that produce ova and sex hormones.

testosterone
A male sex hormone that is secreted by the Leydig cells of mature testes and produces secondary sex characteristics in men.

Müllerian duct
One of a pair of tubes in the embryo that will develop, in female embryos, into the Fallopian tubes, uterus, and part of the vagina.

Wolffian duct
One of a pair of structures in the embryo that, when exposed to testosterone, will develop into the male reproductive system.

Müllerian inhibiting factor (MIF)
A hormone secreted in male embryos that prevents the Müllerian duct from developing into female reproductive organs.

androgen
A hormone that promotes the development of male genitals and secondary sex characteristics. It is produced by the testes in men and by the adrenal glands in both men and women.

homologous
Corresponding in structure, position, or origin but not necessarily in function.

termine to some degree what type of cell it will become. Researchers in evolutionary developmental biology explore how and when cells differentiate.

Whether the zygote will develop into a male or female is determined at the moment of conception, and part of the process of differentiation includes the development of our sexual characteristics. If sexual differentiation proceeds without a problem, the zygote will develop into a fetus with typically male or typically female sexual characteristics. However, a variety of things can happen during development that can later influence the person's own sense of being either male or female.

Sexual Differentiation in the Womb

A human embryo normally undergoes about 9 months of **gestation.** At about 4 to 6 weeks, the first tissues that will become the embryo's gonads develop. Sexual differentiation begins a week or two later and is initiated by the sex chromosomes, which control at least four important aspects of sexual development: (1) the internal sexual organs (for example, whether the fetus develops ovaries or testicles); (2) the external sex organs (such as the penis or clitoris); (3) the hormonal environment of the embryo; and (4) the sexual differentiation of the brain (Money & Norman, 1987).

Internal Sex Organs

In the first few weeks of development, XX (female) and XY (male) embryos are identical. Around the 5th to 6th week, the primitive gonads form, and at this point they can potentially develop into either **testes** or **ovaries.** Traditional developmental models claim that the "default" development is female; without the specific masculinizing signals sent by the Y chromosome and the SRY gene, the gonads will develop as female. The SRY is a Y chromosome-specific gene that plays a central role in sexual differentiation and development in males (Knower et al., 2003). However, it may not be only **testosterone** or the SRY gene that differentiates males from females—it may also be the presence of ovarian hormones (Fitch & Bimonte, 2002).

In most males, the testes begin to differentiate from the primitive gonad by the 7th to 8th week following conception. In most females, the development of the primitive gonad begins to differentiate into ovaries by the 10th or 11th week. The primitive duct system, the **Müllerian** (myul-EAR-ee-an) **duct** (female) or the **Wolffian** (WOOL-fee-an) **duct** (male), also appear at this time (Warne & Kanumakala, 2002). Once the gonads have developed, they then hormonally control the development of the ducts into either the female or male reproductive system.

In female embryos, the lack of male hormones results in the regression and disappearance of the Wolffian ducts, and the Müllerian duct fuses to form the uterus and inner third of the vagina. The unfused portion of the duct remains and develops into the two oviducts or Fallopian tubes (see Figure 3.1).

In the presence of a Y chromosome, the gonads develop into testes, which soon begin producing Müllerian inhibiting factor (MIF) and **testosterone.** MIF causes the Müllerian ducts to disappear during the 3rd month, and testosterone stimulates the Wolffian duct to develop into the structures surrounding the testicles. The body converts some testosterone into another **androgen,** called dihydrotestosterone (DHT), to stimulate the development of the male external sex organs.

External Sex Organs

External genitals follow a pattern similar to internal organs, except that male and female genitalia all develop from the same tissue. Male and female organs that began from the same prenatal tissue are called **homologous** (HOE-mol-lig-gus). Until the 8th week, the undifferentiated tissue from which the genitalia will develop exists as a mound of skin, or tubercle, beneath the umbilical cord. In females, the external genitalia develop under the influence of female hormones produced by the placenta and by the mother and also the lack of influence from the Y chromosome. The genital tu-

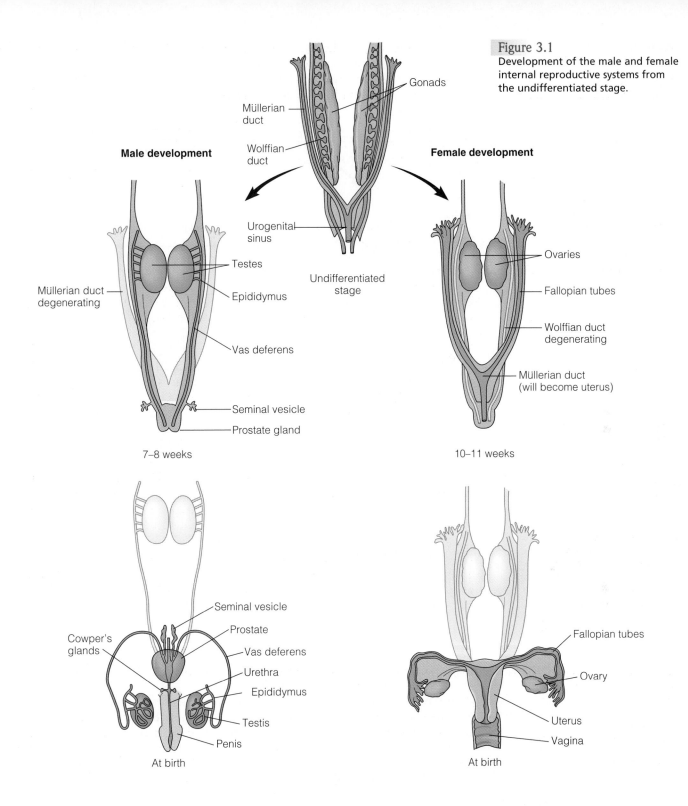

Figure 3.1
Development of the male and female internal reproductive systems from the undifferentiated stage.

bercle develops into the clitoris, the labia minora, the vestibule, and the labia majora (see Figure 3.2).

In males, by the 8th or 9th week the testes begin androgen secretion, which begins to stimulate the development of male genitalia. The genital tubercle elongates to form the penis, in which lies the urethra, culminating in an external opening called the urethral meatus. Part of the tubercle also fuses together to form the scrotum, where the testicles will ultimately rest when they descend.

Review Question

Describe sexual differentiation in a developing fetus.

Figure 3.2
Development of the male and female external genitalia from the undifferentiated genital tubercle.

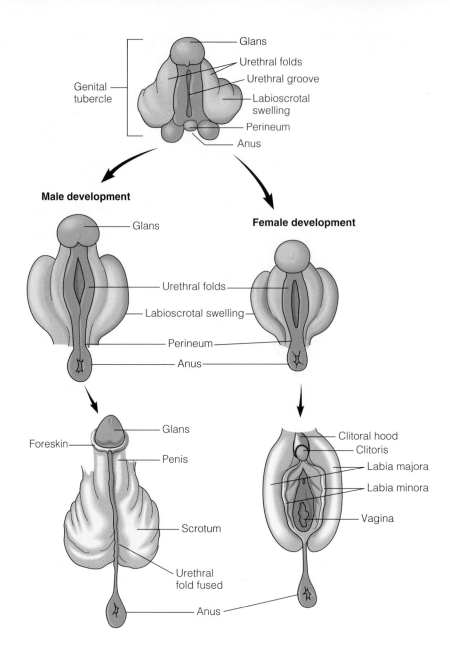

endocrine gland
Gland that secretes hormones into the blood.

estrogen
A hormone that produces female secondary sex characteristics and affects the menstrual cycle.

progesterone
A hormone that is produced by the ovaries and helps to regulate the menstrual cycle.

TABLE 3.1	Homologous Tissue

Male and female organs that began from the same prenatal tissue are called homologous. Below are some of the homologous tissues.

Female	Male
clitoris	head of the penis (glans)
clitoral hood	foreskin
labia minora	penis
labia majora	scrotum
ovaries	testes

Hormonal Development and Influences

Hormones play an important role in human development. Table 3.2 lists the various sex hormones and the roles they play. **Endocrine glands,** such as the gonads, secrete hormones directly into the bloodstream to be carried to the target organs. The ovaries, for example, produce the two major female hormones, **estrogen** and **progesterone.** Estrogen is an important influence in the development of female sexual characteristics throughout fetal development and later life, while progesterone regulates the menstrual cycle and prepares the uterus for pregnancy. The testicles produce androgens, which are quite important to the male, because even a genetically male embryo will develop female characteristics if androgens are not secreted at the right time or if the fetus is insensitive to androgens (see the following section, Atypical Sexual Differentiation).

Brain Differentiation

Most hormonal secretions are regulated by the brain, in particular by the hypothalamus, which is the body's single most important control center. Yet hormones also affect the development of the brain itself, both in the uterus and

TABLE 3.2   The Sex Hormones

HORMONE	PURPOSES
Androgens	A group of hormones that control male sexual development and include testosterone and androsterone. Androgens stimulate the development of male sex organs and secondary sex characteristics such as beard growth and a deepening voice. Testosterone also plays an important part (in both sexes) in stimulating sexual desire. The testes produce androgens in men (stimulated by luteinizing hormone), though a little is also produced by the adrenal glands. Women's ovaries also produce a small amount of androgens, which helps stimulate sexual desire; too much production by the ovaries causes masculinization in women.
Estrogens	A group of hormones that control female sexual development and include estriol, estrone, and estradiol. Estrogen controls development of the female sex organs, the menstrual cycle, parts of pregnancy, and secondary sex characteristics such as breast development. The ovaries produce most of the estrogen in women, although the adrenal glands and the placenta also produce small amounts. Testes also produce a small amount of estrogen in men; if they produce too much, feminization may occur.
Progesterone	A female hormone secreted by the ovaries. Progesterone helps to prepare the lining of the uterus for the implantation of the fertilized ovum, to stimulate milk production in the breasts, and to maintain the placenta. Progesterone works in conjunction with estrogen to prepare the female reproductive system for pregnancy.
Gonadotropin-releasing hormone (GnRH)	A hormone that affects the nervous system. It is produced in the hypothalamus of the brain and transported through the bloodstream to the pituitary gland. Gonadotropin means "gonad stimulating," and GnRH stimulates the pituitary to release hormones, such as follicle-stimulating hormone (FSH) and luteinizing hormone (LH), which themselves induce the ovaries and testes (as well as other glands) to secrete their hormones.
Follicle-stimulating hormone (FSH)	A hormone released by the pituitary gland when stimulated by GnRH, which stimulates the follicular development in females and the formation of sperm in the male.
Luteinizing hormone (LH)	A hormone released by the pituitary gland when stimulated by GnRH that stimulates ovulation and the release of other hormones, notably progesterone in the female and testosterone in the male. It also stimulates the cells in the testes to produce testosterone.
Prolactin	A pituitary hormone that stimulates milk production after childbirth and also production of progesterone.
Oxytocin	A pituitary hormone that stimulates the ejection of milk from the breasts and causes increased contractions of the uterus during labor.
Inhibin	A hormone produced by the cells of the testes that signal the anterior pituitary to decrease FSH production if the sperm count gets too high.

after birth. Male and female brains have different tasks and so undergo different development. For example, female brains control menstruation and therefore must signal the release of hormones in a monthly cycle, whereas male brains signal release continuously. With the brain, as with sexual organs, the presence of androgens during the appropriate critical stage of development may be the factor that programs the central nervous system to develop male sexual behaviors.

Review Question

Explain the role that hormones and brain differentiation play in human development.

Atypical Sexual Differentiation: Not Always Just X and Y

Prenatal development depends on carefully orchestrated developmental stages. At any stage, sex hormone irregularities, genetic abnormalities, or exposure of the fetus to inappropriate maternal hormones can result in atypical sexual differentiation. The result can be a child born with ambiguous genitals or with the external genitals of one sex and the genetic makeup of the other sex.

Sex Chromosome Disorders

Sometimes a person's sex chromosomes will include an extra X or Y chromosome or will be missing one. Though medical researchers have identified over 70 such abnormalities of the sex chromosomes, we will discuss the three most common.

Klinefelter's syndrome, which occurs in about 1 in 700 live male births, occurs when an ovum containing an extra X chromosome is fertilized by a Y sperm (designated XXY), giving a child 47 chromosomes altogether. The Y chromosome triggers the development of male genitalia, but the extra X prevents them from developing fully. Men with Klinefelter's syndrome are tall, with feminized body contours, small testicles, low levels of testosterone, **gynecomastia,** and are infertile. In fact, Klinefelter's syndrome is

Klinefelter's syndrome
A genetic disorder in men in which there are three sex chromosomes, XXY, instead of two; characterized by small testes, low sperm production, breast enlargement, and absence of facial and body hair.

gynecomastia
Abnormal breast development in the male.

the most common genetic cause of male infertility (Lanfranco et al., 2004). These men often show low levels of sexual desire, probably due to the lack of testosterone. **Testosterone therapy,** especially if it is begun during adolescence, can enhance the development of **secondary sexual characteristics.**

Turner's syndrome is another chromosomal disorder. It is among the most common of the chromosomal disorders, occurring in 1 of every 2,500 live female births. Turner's syndrome results from an ovum without any sex chromosome being fertilized by an X sperm (designated XO), which gives the child only 45 chromosomes altogether (if an ovum without a chromosome is fertilized by a Y sperm and so contains no X sex chromosome, it will not survive). Though the external genitalia develop to look like a normal female's, the woman's ovaries do not develop fully, causing **amenorrhea** (aye-men-uh-REE-uh) and infertility. In addition, Turner's syndrome is characterized by short stature, immature breast development, and abnormalities of certain internal organs (Moreno-Garcia et al., 2005). Therapeutic administration of estrogen and progesterone, especially during puberty, can help enhance some sexual characteristics and slightly increase height (Turner's Syndrome Society, 2002).

TABLE 3.3	Some Prenatal Sex Differentiation Syndromes				
SYNDROME	CHROMOSOMAL PATTERN	EXTERNAL GENITALS	INTERNAL STRUCTURES	DESCRIPTION	TREATMENT
CHROMOSOMAL					
Klinefelter's syndrome	47, XXY	Male	Male	Testes are small; breasts may develop; low testosterone levels, erectile dysfunction, and mental retardation are common; these people have unusual body proportions and are usually infertile.	Testosterone during adolescence may help with body shape and sex drive.
Turner's syndrome	45, XO	Female	Uterus and oviducts	There is no menstruation or breast development; a broad chest with widely spaced nipples, loose skin around the neck, nonfunctioning ovaries, and infertility.	Androgens during puberty can help increase height, and estrogen and progesterone can help breast development and menstruation.
XYY syndrome	47, XYY	Male	Male	There is likelihood of slight mental retardation, some genital irregularities, and decreased fertility or infertility.	None
Triple X syndrome	47, XXX	Female	Female	There is likelihood of slight mental retardation and decreased fertility or infertility.	None
HORMONAL					
Congenital adrenal hyperplasia (CAH)	46, XX, XY	Some male and some female traits	Internal organs are normal; external organs may be fused together. Fertility is unaffected.	Surgery can correct external genitals.	
Androgen-insensitivity syndrome (AIS)	46, XY	Female	Male gonads in the abdomen	Usually AIS children are raised female. Breasts develop at puberty, but menstruation does not begin. Such a person has a shortened vagina, no internal sexual organs, and is sterile.	Surgery can lengthen vagina to accommodate a penis for intercourse if necessary.

XYY syndrome and **triple X syndrome** are very rare disorders. As the names imply, these syndromes occur when a normal ovum is fertilized by a sperm that has two Y chromosomes or two X chromosomes or when an ovum with two X chromosomes is fertilized by a normal X sperm. The XYY individual may grow up as a normal male and the XXX as a normal female, and so often their unusual genetic status is not detected. However, many do suffer from some genital abnormalities, fertility problems, and possible learning difficulties later in life. There is no effective treatment for XYY or XXX syndrome.

Hormonal Irregularities

A **hermaphrodite** (her-MAFF-fro-dite) is born with fully formed ovaries and fully formed testes, which is very, very rare. In fact, true hermaphroditism is the rarest form of intersex variations (Krstic et al., 2000). Most people who are called hermaphrodites are actually **pseudohermaphrodite**s, those whose external genitals resemble to some degree the genitals of both sexes.

Congenital adrenal hyperplasia (CAH) is a hormonal irregularity that occurs when a genetically normal female (XX) is exposed to large amounts of androgens during crucial stages of prenatal development. It is estimated that 1 in 10,000 to 18,000 children are born with CAH (MedlinePlus, 2004b). All women produce some androgens in their adrenal glands, and if the adrenal glands produce too much, CAH may develop. A similar syndrome can also develop if the mother takes male hormones or drugs whose effects mimic male hormones (a number of pregnant women were prescribed such drugs in the 1950s, resulting in a group of CAH babies born during that time).

Depending on the amount of male hormones or drugs, different degrees of masculinization can occur. Though the internal organs remain female and are not affected, the clitoris enlarges, even sometimes developing into a true penis containing a urethra. Underneath the penis, the two labia may fuse to resemble a scrotum, but it contains no testicles.

If the adrenal glands continue to produce excessive androgens, masculinization can continue throughout the CAH female's development. When a child is born with the genital traits of CAH today, a chromosomal analysis is usually performed, so CAH females are typically diagnosed at birth. Corrective surgery can be done to

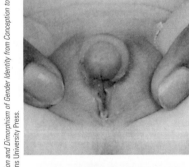

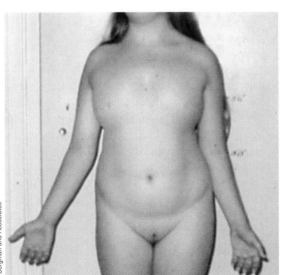

Female with Turner's syndrome.

Money, John and Anke A. Ehrhardt. Man and Woman, Boy and Girl: Differentiation and Dimorphism of Gender Identity from Conception to Maturity. p. 115 (fig 6.2). © 1975. Reprinted with permission of The Johns Hopkins University Press.

Genitalia of fetally androgenized female and androgen-insensitive male with feminized genitals.

© Bergman and Associates

form female genitalia, and drugs can be prescribed to control adrenal output (Warne et al., 2005). Because the internal organs are unaffected, even pregnancy is possible in many CAH females. Overall, research has shown that CAH females have good long-term psychological health and social functioning (Morgan et al., 2005). Interestingly, some research has found that CAH girls choose more male-typical toys than girls without CAH (Pasterski et al., 2005).

CAH may also appear in newborn boys, although it is less common. No obvious abnormalitis are often present, but 2 to 3 years prior to the onset of typical puberty, a CAH boy often experiences increased muscular strength, penile growth, an increase in pubic hair, and a deepening in the voice. The testicles, however, remain small.

Androgen-insensitivity syndrome (AIS) is, in some ways, the opposite of CAH. It is often first detected when a seemingly normal teenage girl fails to menstruate and chromosomal analysis discovers that she is XY, a genetic male. It is estimated that 1 in 20,000 boys are born each year with AIS (Medline Plus, 2004a). In this syndrome, although the gonads develop into testes and produce testosterone normally, for some reason the AIS individual's cells cannot absorb it; in other words, the testosterone is there but has no effect on the body. Because the Wolffian ducts did not respond to testosterone during the sexual differentiation phase, no male genitalia developed; but because the gonads, which are male, did produce Müllerian inhibiting factor, the Müllerian ducts did not develop into normal female internal organs either. The AIS individual ends up with no internal reproductive organs except two testes, which remain in the abdomen producing testosterone that the body cannot use.

The AIS infant has the "default" female genitals, but because the Müllerian ducts also form the last third of the vagina, the infant has only a very shallow vagina. Usually the syndrome is undetected at birth, and the baby is brought up female. Because males do produce a small amount of estrogen, the breasts do develop, so it is only when the teen fails to menstruate that AIS is usually diagnosed. Surgery can then be initiated to lengthen the vagina to accommodate a penis for intercourse, though without any female internal organs, the individual remains infertile. Even though they are genetically male, most AIS individuals seem fully feminized and live as females.

Now that we have discussed the various chromosomal and hormonal conditions that may affect gender, the important question becomes, what can a parent do after a child is born with ambiguous genitals or the genitals of one sex and the genetic makeup of the other? Today's experts recommend that no surgery be performed until the child can consent to it (Neergaard, 2005) because there is too much uncertainty in infancy about intersex conditions (Lorio, 2004; Thyen et al., 2005). This would mean waiting until a child is perhaps 3–5 years old or even older to determine whether to proceed with gender reassignment.

GENDER ROLES AND GENDER TRAITS

Let's go back, for a moment, to that alien you met earlier in the chapter. When you describe what is male and female for the alien, chances are you will talk about stereotyped behavior. You might say, "Men are strong, independent, and assertive, and often have a hard time showing emotion," or "Women are sensitive, nurturing, emotional, and soft." Descriptions like these are based on gender stereotypes. Gender stereotypes are fundamental to our ways of thinking, which makes it difficult to realize how thoroughly our conceptions of the world are shaped by gender issues. For example, when a baby is born, the very first question we ask is, "Is it a boy or a girl?" The parents proudly display a sign in their yard or send a card to friends, proclaiming "It's a girl!" or "It's a boy!" as the sole identifying trait of the child. The card does not state "It's a redhead!" From the moment of birth onward, the child is thought of first as male or female, and all other characteristics—whether the child is tall, bright, an artist, Irish, disabled, gay—are seen in light of the person's gender.

Overall, we expect men to act like men and women to act like women, and we become confused and uncomfortable when we are denied knowledge of a person's gender.

It is very difficult to know how to interact with someone whose gender we do not know because we are so programmed to react to people first according to their gender. If you walked into a party tonight and found yourself face-to-face with someone whom you couldn't tell was male or female, how would you feel? Most likely you'd be confused and search for gender clues. Often our need to categorize people by gender is taken for granted. But why is it so important?

Even our language is constructed around gender. English has no neutral pronoun (neither do many other languages, including French, Spanish, German, and Italian), meaning that every time you refer to a person, you must write either "he" or "she." Therefore, every sentence you write about a person reveals his or her gender, even if it reveals nothing else about that person. Gender-specific pronouns, in turn, can affect recall of material. For example, girls have higher recall when stories contain the pronoun "she" instead of "he" (Conkright et al., 2000). This is noteworthy given the fact that the pronoun "he" has historically often been used generically.

In the gender variant community, a new language for gender-neutral pronouns has emerged. "Sie" or "ce" (pronounced "see") is proposed for she/he and "hir" (pronounced "here") for hers/his (Feinberg, 1999). So "he is wearing a blue hat" would become "ce is wearing a blue hat," whereas "her book is over there" would become "hir book is over there."

Many of our basic assumptions about gender are open to dispute. Gender research has been growing explosively over the past 30 years, and many of the results challenge long-held beliefs about gender differences. Still, research into gender runs into some serious problems. For example, even gender researchers are socialized into accepted **gender roles** from birth, which may make it very difficult for them to avoid projecting their own gender biases onto the research (K. Hamberg, 2000). Despite these problems, the data do seem to report certain findings consistently.

Gender roles are culturally defined behaviors that are seen as appropriate for males and females, including the attitudes, personality traits, emotions, and even postures and body language that are considered fundamental to being male or female in a culture. Gender roles also extend into social behaviors, such as the occupations we choose, how we dress and wear our hair, how we talk (see Chapter 6 for a description of gender differences in communication), and the ways in which we interact with others.

Note that by saying that gender roles are *culturally* defined, we are suggesting that such differences are not primarily due to biological, physiological, or even psychological differences between men and women but, rather, are due to the ways in which we are taught to behave. Yet many people believe that many gender differences in behavior are biologically programmed. Who is correct?

Another way to ask the question is: Which of our gender-specific behaviors are gender roles (that is, culturally determined), and which are **gender traits** (innate or biologically determined)? If gender-specific behaviors are biologically determined, then they should remain constant in different societies; if they are social, then we should see very different gender roles in different societies. In fact, there are some gender-specific behaviors that seem to be universal and therefore are probably gender traits related to differences in biology; still others may have biological bases. The majority of gender-specific behaviors, however, differ widely throughout the world and are determined primarily by culture.

It is common today for parents to announce the gender of their newborn child. What if instead of gender, the sign announced, "It's a 10-Pound Baby!" or "It's a Redhead!"?

gender roles
Culturally defined behaviors seen as appropriate for males and females.

gender traits
Innate or biologically determined gender-specific behaviors.

Review Question

Differentiate between gender roles and gender traits, and explain how cross-cultural research helps us identify each.

Girls Act Like Girls, Boys Act Like Boys

Typically, we expect that boys and girls will follow stereotypic gender roles and traits. However, the models of femininity and masculinity are quickly changing in our society. Let's now explore our cultural expectations.

Masculinity and Femininity

What is masculine? What is feminine? Not too long ago, the answers would have seemed quite obvious: men naturally have masculine traits, meaning they are strong, stable, aggressive, competitive, self-reliant, and emotionally undemonstrative; women are naturally feminine, meaning they are intuitive, loving, nurturing, emotionally expressive, and gentle. Even today, many would agree that such traits describe the differences between the sexes. These gender stereotypes, however, are becoming less acceptable as our culture changes.

Masculinity and **femininity** refer to the ideal cluster of traits that society attributes to each gender. Most societies have cultural heroes and heroines who are supposed to embody the traits of masculinity and femininity and serve as models for socializing youths into their gender roles. In some societies, these models are provided by gods and goddesses, religious leaders, warriors, or mythical figures. In modern American society, entertainers and sports figures serve the purpose of providing gender models of behavior. For example, Halle Berry and Brad Pitt both embody many of the stereotypic feminine and masculine traits we hold today.

Some studies have documented less gender role stereotyping in African American than Caucasian populations. This is probably due to the fact that African Americans are less sex-role restricted than Euro-American groups and believe that they possess both masculine and feminine traits (Dade & Sloan, 2000). In fact, African Americans often view others through a lens of age and competency *before* gender. There are also some geographic differences in sex-role expectations. In the United States, the South has more traditional sex-role expectations than the North does (Suitor & Carter, 1999).

Even so, models of masculinity and femininity are changing rapidly in modern American society. It's not uncommon today to see women police officers directing traffic or women CEOs in the boardroom, nor is it uncommon to find stay-at-home dads at the park with kids or men librarians at the public library shelving books. Avril Lavigne wears combat boots and neckties, and many men today wear two earrings and keep their hair long.

But gender role change can also result in confusion, fear, and even hostility in society. Gender roles exist, in part, because they allow comfortable interaction between the sexes. If you know exactly how you are supposed to behave and what personality traits you are supposed to assume in relation to the other sex, interactions between the sexes go more smoothly. When things change, determining correct behaviors becomes more difficult.

---

masculinity
The ideal cluster of traits that society attributes to males.

femininity
The ideal cluster of traits that society attributes to females.

SEX Talk

Question: *I've always wondered why so many men are into acting tough. It seems that the majority of women want a guy who is tough and they don't give the nice guys a chance. Guys on the other hand, tend to look for hot girls instead of thinking about how nice or intelligent the girls are. Why is this?*

Men and women always seem to wonder why people of the other sex behave the way they do. Yet society itself supports those kinds of behaviors. Is it really any surprise that men often seem to pursue appearance over substance in women when advertising, television, and women's and men's magazines all emphasize women's appearance? Is it surprising conversely, that some women pursue the "tough guys" when society teaches them to admire male power?

Women have been found to value many qualities in their partners, and sometimes it depends on the relationship. For example, women are more likely to rate "niceness" as an important quality for guys with whom they are considering having long-term relationships (Urbaniak & Kilmann, 2003). In the end, it is society that determines the way we view gender relationships, and each of us is responsible to some degree for continuing those attitudes.

For example, when construction sites were the exclusive domains of men, a very male-oriented culture arose that included sexual joking, whistling at passing women, and the like. Now that women have become part of the construction team, men complain that they do not know how to behave anymore: Are sexual jokes and profanity still okay, or are they considered sexual harassment? Some people yearn for the old days when male and female behaviors were clearly defined, and they advocate a return to traditional gender roles. Other people still see inequality in American society and argue that women need to have more freedom and equality.

Review Question

Explain the three ways that the terms *masculinity* and *femininity* are used in society.

Are Gender Roles Innate?

As gender stereotypes evolve, a trait may no longer be seen as the exclusive domain of a single gender. For example, many people have been trying to change our current stereotypes of men as "unemotional" and women as "emotional." The constellation of traits that has been traditionally seen as masculine and feminine may be becoming less rigid. For many centuries, these types of gender traits were seen as innate, immutable, part of the biological makeup of the sexes. Few scientists suggested that the differences between men and women were primarily social; most believed that women and men were fundamentally different.

Not only did they believe that the differences in the sexes were innate, but they also believed that men were superior—having developed past the "emotional" nature of women (Gould, 1981). Unfortunately, these attitudes still exist, both subtly in cultures like our own and overtly in cultures where women are allowed few of the rights granted to men.

How many of our gender behaviors are biological, and how many are socially transmitted? The truth is that the world may not split that cleanly into biological versus social causes of behavior. Behaviors are complex and are almost always interactions between one's innate biological capacities and the environment in which one lives and acts. Behaviors that are considered innately "male" in one culture may be assumed to be innately "female" in another. Even when modern science suggests certain gender traits that seem to be based on innate differences between the sexes, culture can contradict that trait or even deny it.

For example, most researchers accept the principle that males display more aggression than females; adult males certainly demonstrate this tendency, which is probably the result, in part, of higher levels of testosterone. When female bodybuilders, for example, take steroids, they often find themselves acquiring male traits, including losing breast tissue, growing more body hair—and becoming more aggressive. However, the difference is also demonstrated in early childhood, when boys are more aggressive in play whereas girls tend to be more compliant and docile.

Yet Margaret Mead's (1935) famous discussion of the Tchambuli tribe of New Guinea shows that such traits need not determine gender roles. Among the Tchambulis, the women performed the "aggressive" occupations such as fishing, commerce, and politics, whereas the men were more sedentary and artistic and took more care of domestic life. The women assumed the dress appropriate for their activities—plain clothes and short hair—whereas the men dressed in bright colors. So even if we accept biological gender differences, societies like the Tchambuli show that human culture can transcend biology.

There are some gender differences that are considered purely biological. Physically, males tend to be larger and stronger, with more of their body weight in muscles and less in body fat than females (Angier, 1999). Females, however, are born more neurologically advanced than males, and they mature faster. Females are also biologically heartier than males; more male fetuses miscarry, more males are stillborn, the male infant mortality rate is higher, males acquire more hereditary diseases and remain more susceptible to disease throughout life, and men die at younger ages than women. Males are also more likely to have developmental problems such as learning disabilities. It has long been believed that males are better at mathematics and spatial problems, whereas females are better at verbal tasks; for example, female children learn language skills earlier than males. Yet many of these differences may be the result of socialization rather than biology.

Another aspect of gender that is said to be in some sense innate in females is "mothering" or the "maternal instinct." Do women really have a maternal instinct that men lack? For example, is there a psychological or physical bonding mechanism that happens to women who carry babies in their wombs, one that fathers are unable to experience? Historians have pointed out examples (such as France and England in the 17th and 18th centuries) in which maternal feelings seemed almost nonexistent; children were considered a nuisance, and breast-feeding was seen as a waste of time. Poor children were often abandoned, and the children of the wealthy were sent to the countryside for care by a **wet nurse.**

Studies on surrogate mothering have challenged the notion of a maternal instinct, because surrogate mothers relinquish a baby for payment (Baslington, 2002). In animal species, lionesses are known for abandoning and even eating their first litter, and female bears that have lost one cub in a litter often leave the second to starve (Allport, 1997). So the question of an innate female desire for childrearing is far from settled.

Boys and girls do show some behavioral differences that appear to be universal. For example, in a study of six different cultures, Whiting and her colleagues (Whiting & Edwards, 1988; Whiting & Whiting, 1975) discovered that certain traits seemed to characterize masculine and feminine behavior in 3- to 6-year-olds. In almost all countries, boys engaged in more insulting behavior and rough-and-tumble play, and boys "dominated egoistically" (tried to control the situation through commands), whereas girls more often sought or offered physical contact, sought help, and "suggested responsibly" (dominated socially by invoking rules or appealing to greater good).

Interestingly, though their strategies were different, both boys and girls often pursued the same ends; for example, rough-and-tumble play among boys and initiation of physical contact among girls are both strategies for touching and being touched. However, Whiting suggests that even these behaviors might be the result of different kinds of pressures put on boys and girls; for example, in their sample, older girls were expected to take care of young children more often than boys, and younger girls were given more responsibility than younger boys. These different expectations from each gender may explain later differences in their behaviors. So even gender behaviors that are spread across cultures may not prove to be innate differences.

There has always been evidence that men's and women's brains were different; autopsies showed that men's brains were more asymmetrical than women's, and women seemed to recover better from damage to the left hemisphere of the brain (as in strokes), where language is situated. Yet it has always been unclear what facts such as these mean. Recently, newer techniques in brain imaging have provided evidence that women's and men's brains not only differ in size, but that women and men use their brains differently during certain activities (DeBellis et al., 2001; K. Hamberg, 2000; Schneider et al., 2000). Although it is too early to know what these differences mean, future studies may be able to provide clearer pictures of the different ways men and women think and shed some light on the biological and social influences of these differences.

Aside from the above behaviors and physical attributes, almost no differences between the sexes are universally accepted by researchers. This does not mean that there are not other biological gender differences; we simply do not know for sure. We must be careful not to move too far in the other direction and suggest that there are no innate differences between the sexes. Many of these differences remain controversial, such as relative levels of activity and curiosity and facial recognition skills. But these are relatively minor differences. Even if it turns out, for example, that female infants recognize faces earlier than males, as has been postulated, or that male children are more active than females, would that really account for the enormous gender role differences that have developed over time? Though biologists and other researchers still study innate differences between the sexes, today more attention is being paid to gender similarities.

This brings up another important concept to keep in mind. Articles on differences between the sexes tend to be easier to publish. For example, which article do you think most people would find more exciting: "Large Differences Found in Men's and Women's Math Skills" or "Insignificant Gender Differences Found in Math Skills"? Therefore, it may just be that the articles on male/female differences are more likely to be published than those that find no differences.

wet nurse
A woman who is able to breast-feed children other than her own.

Review Question

Which gender behaviors/traits are considered to be biologically based? Are any gender differences universal?

Studying Gender

During much of the 1970s and 1980s the focus of gender research was on girls (Warrington & Younger, 2000). Researchers looked at girls' career expectations, how educational curricula reinforced male areas of interest and the effects on girls, and how educators responded less frequently to girls in the classroom. Even in the 1990s this research continued by examining how adolescent girls were losing their sense of self (Pipher, 1994) and how girls have trouble finding peace with their bodies (Brumberg, 1997). Over the past few years, research has expanded to focus on both boys and girls and has examined areas such as alcohol use (Green, 2004), body image (Phares et al., 2004; K. A. Phillips & Castle, 2002), eating disorders (Wiseman, 2004), mathematics (Mendick, 2005; J. S. Hyde & Kling, 2001), attitudes toward work (Tinklin et al., 2005), and athletics (Hammermeister & Burton, 2004).

sex byte

Men who report more gender role flexibility and liberal social attitudes are more likely to choose women-dominated occupations, such as nursing or teaching (Lease, 2003).

Review Question

What is the focus of recent research on gender?

GENDER ROLE THEORY

In Chapter 2 we reviewed general theories of sexuality, and the debates there centered on how much of human sexuality is programmed through our genes and physiology, and how much is influenced by culture and environment. Gender role theory struggles with the same issues, and different theorists take different positions. Social learning theorists believe that we learn gender roles almost entirely from our environment, whereas cognitive development theorists believe that children go through a set series of stages that correspond to certain beliefs and attitudes about gender. Earlier in this chapter we discussed biological gender differences. Here we will talk about evolutionary, social learning, cognitive development, gender schema, and gender hierarchy theories.

When a baby is born, he or she possesses no knowledge and few instinctual behaviors. But by the time the child is about 3 or 4, he or she can usually talk, feed him- or herself, interact with adults, describe objects, and use correct facial expressions and body language. The child also typically exhibits a wide range of behaviors that are appropriate to his or her gender. The process whereby this infant who knows nothing becomes a toddler who has the basic skills for functioning in society is called **socialization.**

As we saw in the last chapter, different types of sexual socialization occur at different ages and levels of development. The same is true of gender role socialization, which is closely related to sexual socialization. Many boys dress and act like other boys and play with traditionally male toys (guns, trucks); whereas many girls insist on wearing dresses and express a desire to do traditionally "female" things, such as playing with dolls and cooking toys. Is this behavior innate, or are gender stereotypes still getting through to these children through television and in playing with their peers? The answer depends on which theory of gender role development you accept.

socialization
The process in which an infant is taught the basic skills for functioning in society.

Evolutionary Theory: Adapting to Our Environment

Recently we have begun to understand more about the biological differences between men and women through the field of evolutionary theory. Evolutionary theory takes into account evolution and our physical nature. Gender differences are seen as ways in which we have developed in our adaptation to our environment.

For example, later in this book we will explore how the double standard in sexual behavior developed, in which a man with several partners was viewed as a "player," whereas a woman with several partners was viewed as a "slut." An evolutionary theorist would explain this gender difference in terms of the biological differences between men and women. A man can impregnate several women at any given time, but a woman, once pregnant, cannot become pregnant again until she gives birth. The time investment of these activities varies tremendously. If evolutionary success is determined by how many offspring we have, the men win hands down.

Social Learning Theory: Learning From Our Environment

Social learning theory suggests that we learn gender roles from our environment, from the same system of rewards and punishments that we learn our other social roles. For example, research shows that many parents commonly reward gender-appropriate behavior and disapprove of (or even punish) gender-inappropriate behavior. Telling a boy sternly not to cry "like a girl," approving a girl's use of makeup, taking a Barbie away from a boy and handing him Spider-Man, making girls help with cooking and cleaning and boys take out the trash—these little, everyday actions build into powerful messages about gender.

Children learn to model their behavior after the same-gender parent to win parental approval. They may learn about gender-appropriate behavior from parents even if they are too young to perform the actions themselves; for example, they see that Mommy does the sewing, whereas Daddy fixes the car. Children also see models of the "appropriate" ways for their genders to behave in their books, on television, and when interacting with others. Even the structure of our language conveys gender attitudes about things, such as the dominant position of the male; for example, the use of male words to include men and women (using "chairman" or "mankind" to refer to both men and women) or the differentiation between Miss and Mrs. to indicate whether or not a woman is married. However, people are trying to amend these inequalities today, as evidenced by the growing acceptance of words like "chairperson" and "humankind," and the title "Ms."

Cognitive Development Theory: Age-State Learning

Cognitive development theory assumes that all children go through a universal pattern of development, and there really is not much parents can do to alter it. As the child's brain matures and grows, the child develops new abilities and new concerns; and, at each stage, his or her understanding of gender changes in predictable ways. This theory follows the ideas of Piaget (1951), the child development theorist who suggested that social attitudes in children are mediated through their processes of cognitive development. In other words, children can process only a certain kind and amount of information at each developmental stage.

As children begin to be able to recognize the physical differences between girls and boys and then to categorize themselves as one or the other, they look for information about their genders. Around the ages of 2 to 5, they form strict stereotypes of gender based on their observed differences—men are bigger and stronger and are seen in aggressive roles like policeman and superhero; women tend to be associated with motherhood through their physicality (e.g., the child asks what the mother's breasts are and is told they are used to feed children) and through women's social roles of nurturing and emotional expressiveness. These "physicalistic" thought patterns are universal in young children and are organized around ideas of gender.

As the child matures, he or she becomes more aware that gender roles are, to some degree, social and arbitrary, and cognitive development theory predicts therefore that rigid gender role behavior should decrease after about the age of 7 or 8. So cognitive development theory predicts what set of gender attitudes should appear at different ages; however, the research is still contradictory on whether its predictions are correct (see Albert & Porter, 1988).

Newer theories of gender role development try to combine social learning theory and cognitive development theory, seeing weaknesses in both. Cognitive development theory neglects social factors and differences in the ways different groups raise children. On the other hand, social learning theory neglects a child's age-related ability to understand and assimilate gender models, and portrays the child as too passive; in social learning theory, the child seems to accept whatever models of behavior are offered without passing them through his or her own thought processes.

Gender Schema Theory: Our Cultural Maps

Sandra Bem's (1974, 1977, 1981) theory is a good example of a theory that tries to overcome the difficulties posed by the other theories. According to Bem, children (and, for that matter, all of us) think according to **schemas** (SKI-muz), which are cognitive mech-

Review Question

Describe the differences between the evolutionary, social learning, and cognitive development theories.

schema
Cognitive mechanism that helps to organize our world.

anisms that organize our world. These schemas develop over time and are universal, like the stages in cognitive development theory; the difference lies in Bem's assertion that the contents of schemas are determined by the culture. Schemas are like maps in our heads that direct our thought processes.

Bem suggests that one schema we all have is a **gender schema,** which organizes our thinking about gender. From the moment we are born, information about gender is continuously presented to us by our parents, relatives, teachers, peers, television, movies, advertising, and the like. We absorb the more obvious information about sexual anatomy, "male" and "female" types of work and activities, and gender-linked personality traits. But society also attributes gender to things as abstract as shapes (rounded, soft shapes are often described as "feminine," and sharp, angular shapes as "masculine") and even our drinks (champagne is seen as more feminine, whereas beer is seen as more masculine; Crawford et al., 2004).

Gender schemas are very powerful in our culture. When we first meet a man, we immediately use our masculine gender schema and begin our relationship with an already-established series of beliefs about him. For example, we may believe that men are funny or assertive. Our gender schema is more powerful than other schemas and is used more often, Bem argues, because our *culture* puts so much emphasis on gender and gender differences. This is where she parts company with cognitive development theorists, who argue that gender is important to children because of their naturally physicalistic ways of thinking.

The gender schema becomes so ingrained that we do not even realize its power. For example, some people so stereotype gender concepts that it would never occur to them to say, "My, how strong you are becoming!" to a little girl, whereas they say it easily to a little boy. We do not see girls on one end and boys on the other of a weak-to-strong continuum; rather, Bem argues, "strong" as a feminine trait does not exist in the female schema for many people, so they rarely invoke the term "strong" to refer to women.

Gender Hierarchy Theories: Power and Subordination

Men tend to be more frequently assigned to formal positions of power and authority in society, creating what we might call a **gender hierarchy.** Though women have held formal positions of power across cultures and tend to wield power in more subtle ways than men, it is still indisputable that, viewed as a whole, women have been restricted from roles of formal power in most societies.

Why are women's roles considered subordinate to, and often inferior to, those of men in many societies? For example, have you noticed that when a girl is told she plays "like a boy" it's an empowering compliment, but when a boy is told he "plays like a girl," it's a put-down? In those societies, men seem to be the standard against which women are judged. In other words, masculinity is held up as the basic model from which femininity is a deviation.

Why is this so? Why are masculine traits in our society more valued than feminine traits? Why is being a female "tomboy" considered admirable, whereas a male "sissy" is subject to taunting and cruelty? Of course, finding a satisfactory answer to such a complex question, one that will explain every society throughout all of history, is unlikely. Nevertheless, let us briefly examine a few of the many theories that try to get at the basic reasons societies might value traits they see as male over traits they see as female.

Chodorow's Developmental Theory

One example of a psychological theory of gender hierarchy is found in the work of Nancy Chodorow (1978). Chodorow draws from psychoanalytic theory to argue that girls and boys undergo fundamentally different psychological developmental processes. Because females have always been the primary child rearers, Chodorow suggests, we must explore what it means to boys and girls to be brought up by women. Both boys and girls create a powerful bond with their mothers; the mother becomes the source of personal identification for both. But, argues Chodorow, boys have a dilemma: they must separate themselves from their mothers and reidentify themselves as males. This is a very difficult

gender schema
Cognitive mechanism that helps us to understand gender.

gender hierarchy
Differences in how the men and women are treated based solely on gender.

TABLE 3.4	Summary of Major Theories
Theory	**Key Characteristics**
Biological	Gender differences between men and women are caused by biological factors such as hormones, chromosomes, or brain differences.
Evolutionary	Gender differences between men and women may be at least partially a result of heredity, and these differences have evolved in the survival of the species.
Social Learning	Gender differences between men and women come from a complex system of rewards and punishments in our interactions with parents, friends, television shows, magazines, books, and even through our language.
Cognitive Development	Gender differences come from our categorization of ourselves as male or female and our search for more information about our gender. Our thought patterns about gender organize our ideas about what is male and what is female.
Gender Schema	In this combination of social learning and cognitive development theories, we use cognitive gender schemas to help to organize our world and that these schemas are developed by our culture.
Gender Hierarchy	Gender differences are the result of the power differentials in society between men and women. As a whole, women have restricted roles of formal power, which helps create these power differentials.
Chodorow's Developmental	In this gender hierarchy theory, boys and girls undergo a different process of personal identity, in which boys must learn to separate themselves from their mothers and re-identify themselves as men. In doing so, they learn to devalue the female role.
Ortner's Culture/Nature	In this gender hierarchy theory, society is seen as a whole and things are divided into male and female. Male things such as going out with the tribe or making war are seen as having to do with "culture," whereas things like childbirth and breast-feeding are seen as female and more associated with "nature."
MacKinnon's Dominance	In this gender hierarchy theory, gender differences are the result of men's attempt to dominate social life. It is this system of dominance, rather than any biological or social differences, that causes gender differences.

process, and boys do it by devaluing the female role. Because their attachment to the mother is so profound, the only way they can overcome it and adopt a male role is to decide that being female is inferior to being male.

On the other hand, girls have a different problem: they can continue to identify with their mothers, but they cannot continue to love their mothers as they mature into heterosexual adults. Boys can carry over their original love for their mothers into adulthood, but heterosexuality in adult girls to some extent involves the loss of the mother. Girls cope with that separation by idealizing the qualities of the father (and therefore all men).

This brief description of Chodorow's rich and complex theory shows how the psychological needs of boys and girls both result in a devaluation of the female and an overvaluation of the male. Perhaps, Chodorow suggests, the overall social gender hierarchy can be traced back to these important psychological processes.

Ortner's Culture/Nature Theory

Whereas Chodorow draws from the experiences of individuals, Sherry Ortner's (1974) theory looks at society as a whole. Ortner argues that a universal tendency in cultural thought is to align things male and masculine with "culture" and things female and feminine as closer to "nature." Men are outwardly oriented, going out from the tribe or group to hunt, make war and the like, whereas women's concerns with childbirth, breast-feeding, and the like are more biological and inward. Because culture, in the broad sense, sets human beings apart from animals, whereas childbirth and child rearing are traits of all animals, men's cultural roles are valued over women's more biological roles.

Other theorists have taken that idea and developed it (Ortner & Whitehead, 1981). For example, both Strathern (1981), who studied the Mt. Hegeners of New Guinea, and Llewelyn-Davies (1981), who studied the Massai in Africa, differentiate between women's involvement in "self-interest" and men's in the "public good." Women are seen in these two cultures as more involved with local, parochial, and private concerns of the family and children, whereas men are more concerned with the welfare of society as a whole. Another way to put it is that women are concerned with the "domestic domain" and men with the "public domain." The public domain includes the domestic domain, which means that women's sphere of influence—the family—is subordinate to men's. Ortner and Whitehead conclude their discussion of these kinds of oppositions with:

> It seems clear to us that all of the suggested oppositions—nature/culture, domestic/ public, self-interest/social good—are derived from the same central sociological insight: that the sphere of social activity predominantly associated with males encompasses the sphere predominantly associated with females and is, for that reason, culturally accorded higher value. (1981, pp. 7–8)

MacKinnon's Dominance Theory

Catharine MacKinnon (1987), a feminist scholar, believes that the gender hierarchy is the result of men's attempt to dominate social life. MacKinnon dismisses biological arguments about gender and argues that gender itself is fundamentally a system of dominance rather than a system of biological or social differences. She suggests that back in ancient times men assumed the power to define "difference" in society and especially the "difference gender makes."

MacKinnon believes that men define what is male, what is female, and what difference that makes, but try to present these ideas as though they were scientifically or objectively true rather than a result of male dominance. "Male" and "female" are therefore not biological categories, MacKinnon suggests, but social and political categories, "a status socially conferred upon a person because of a condition of birth." MacKinnon can see no end to this fundamental inequality except through wholesale social change.

Review Question

Which of the gender role theories do you feel makes the most sense, and why?

sex byte

Playing with "masculine," rather than "feminine," toys and games has been found to be related to a woman's future participation in college athletics (Giuliano et al., 2000).

VARIETIES OF GENDER

Culture and social structure interact to create **sex typing,** a way of thinking that splits the world into two basic categories—male and female—and suggests that most behaviors, thoughts, actions, professions, emotions, and so on fit one gender more than the other (Liben & Bigler, 2002; Maccoby, 2002). Today we are finding that although there are fewer sex-typed assignments and attitudes than there were years ago, sex typing still exists (Lueptow et al., 2001).

These stereotypes become so basic to our way of thinking that we do not even realize the powerful hold they have over our conceptions of the world. Many cultures build their entire world views around masculinity and femininity. Some cultures have taken these ideas and created models of the universe based on masculine and feminine traits.

The Chinese concept of yin and yang, which we discussed in Chapter 1, is a good example of this type of world view. The male/female dimension of yin and yang are represented by a series of traits that are considered associated with each. Yang represents the masculine, firm, strong side of life, and yin represents the feminine, weak, yielding side. There are thousands of other yin/yang polarities, and the goal of Chinese life is to keep these forces in balance.

Gender is socially constructed; that is, societies decide how gender will be defined and what it will mean. Williams & Best (1994) collected data about masculinity and femininity in 30 different countries and found that throughout the world, people largely agree on gender role stereotypes. In a study of 37 countries, Buss (1994) found that women and men value different qualities in each other. Women place a higher value on the qualities of being "good financial prospects" and "ambitious and industrious" for their mates. This finding was true in all 37 countries, showing that throughout the world masculinity is judged, at least in part, in terms of a man's ability to succeed as a provider and as an aggressive worker.

sex typing
Cognitive thinking patterns that divide the world into male and female categories and suggest the appropriate behaviors, thoughts, actions, professions, and emotions for each.

Sneak Peek

"Inside, I just knew I was a boy."— *Female-to-Male Transsexual: Teo*

Sexuality Now

In American society, conceptions of "masculinity" and "femininity" have been seen as mutually exclusive; that is, a person who is feminine cannot also be masculine and vice versa (Spence, 1984). But research has shown that masculinity and femininity are independent traits that can exist in people separately (Bem, 1977; Spence, 1984). Bem (1978) suggests that this can lead to four types of personalities: those high in masculinity and low in femininity; those high in femininity and low in masculinity; those low in both ("undifferentiated"); and those high in both ("androgynous"). Such categories may challenge traditional thinking about gender. So may examples of ambiguous gender categories, such as transsexualism or asexuality, which we'll discuss later in this chapter. In fact, the more one examines the categories of gender that really exist in the social world, the clearer it becomes that gender is more complicated than just splitting the world into male and female.

Masculinity: The Hunter

From the moment of a baby's birth, almost every society has different expectations of its males and females. In many societies, men must go through trials or rights of passage in which they earn their right to be men; few societies have such trials for women.

For example, the !Kung bushmen have a "rite of the first kill" that is performed twice for each boy—once after he kills his first large male animal and once after he kills his first large female animal (Collier & Rosaldo, 1981). During the ceremony, a gash is cut in the boy's chest and filled with a magical substance that is supposed to keep the boy from being lazy. Hunting prowess is ritually connected with marriage, and men acquire wives by demonstrating their ability at the hunt (Lewin, 1988). For example, a boy may not marry until he goes through the rite of first kill, and, at the wedding, he must present a large animal he has killed to his bride's parents. Even the language of killing and marrying is linked; !Kung myths and games equate marriage with hunting and talk of men "chasing," "killing," and "eating" women just as they do animals.

In American society, men are often judged by their "prowess" in business, with successful men receiving society's admiration. Although in many societies men tend to have privileges that women do not, and despite the fact that male traits in many societies are valued more than female traits (which we discuss in further detail soon), it is not easy for men to live up to the strong social demands of being male in a changing society.

Great contradictions are inherent in the contemporary masculine role: the man is supposed to be the provider and yet is not supposed to live entirely for his work; he is often judged by his sexual successes and yet is not supposed to see women as sexual objects to be conquered; he is supposed to be a strong, stable force yet must no longer cut his emotions off from his loved ones; and he is never supposed to be scared, inadequate, sexually inexperienced, or financially dependent on a woman.

Men in all societies live with these types of gender role contradictions. In some cases, men simplify their lives by exaggerating the "macho" side of society's expectations and becoming hypermasculine males (Farr et al., 2004). To these macho men, violence is manly, danger is exciting, and sexuality must be pursued callously.

Another side of the masculine way of being must also be addressed, however. David Gilmore (1990) notes that men often must go through trials to prove their masculinity, except in those few societies in which people are totally free of predators and enemies and food is plentiful. In those societies, there is no stress on proving "manhood" and little pressure to emphasize differences between men and women. Gilmore concludes that in most societies masculine socialization prepares men to adopt the role of safeguarding the group's survival, to be willing to give their own lives in the hunt or in war to assure the group's future by protecting the women's ability to reproduce. Gilmore's point is that men are not concerned with being macho as an end in itself but are concerned with the ultimate welfare of society. In fact, Gilmore argues, men are as much nurturers as women, concerned with society's weaker and more helpless members, willing to give their energy and even their lives for the greater social good.

Though masculinity has its privileges, it has its downside too. Men do not live as long as women, in part because of the demands of the male role. For example, men are more likely to die of stress-related illnesses, including lung cancer (men smoke more than women), motor vehicle accidents (men drive more than women, often because of work), suicide (women attempt suicide more often, but men are more successful at actually killing themselves), other accidents (men do more dangerous work than women), and cirrhosis of the liver (there are more male alcoholics and drug addicts; Courtenay, 2000; Nicholas, 2000). Men also die more often in wars. School-aged boys are twice as likely as girls to be labeled as "learning disabled" and constitute up to 67% of "special education" classes (Pollack, 1998).

In fact, with all the attention on how gender stereotypes harm women, men are equally the victims of society's expectations. Male stereotypes tend to be narrower than female stereotypes, and men who want to conform to society's ideas of gender have less flexibility in their behavior than women.

For example, it is still unacceptable for men to cry in public except in the most extreme circumstances. Crying is the body's natural response to being upset. Boys are taught not to cry, but that is difficult when they are emotionally moved; so they stop allowing themselves to be moved emotionally—and then are criticized for shutting themselves off (S. K. Resnick, 1992). Interestingly, when men *do* cry, their emotions are often seen as more genuine than a woman's (Kallen, 1998). This is probably because a behavior that is inconsistent with a gender stereotype is often seen as more legitimate and "real."

Femininity: The Nurturer

When someone says, "She is a very feminine woman," what image comes to mind? The president of a corporation? A woman in a frilly pink dress? A soldier carrying her gear? In American culture, we associate femininity with qualities such as beauty, softness, empathy, concern, and modesty. In fact, in almost every culture, femininity is defined by being the opposite of masculinity.

On the other hand, ideas of femininity are not static. Sheila Rothman (1978) has argued that modern American society has gone through a number of basic conceptions of what "womanhood" (and, by extension, femininity) should be. For example, the 19th century emphasized the value of "virtuous womanhood," whereby women instilled "morality" in society by starting women's clubs that brought women together and eventually led to the battling of perceived social ills. The Women's Christian Temperance Union, for example, started a movement to ban alcohol that eventually succeeded.

By the early part of the 20th century, the concept of the ideal woman shifted to what Rothman calls "educated motherhood," whereby the woman was supposed to learn all the new, sophisticated theories of child rearing and was to shift her attention to the needs of children and family. Over the next few decades, the woman's role was redefined as a "wife-companion," and she was supposed to redirect her energy away from her children and toward being a sexual companion for her husband. Finally, Rothman argues, the 1960s began the era of "woman as person," in which a woman began to be seen as autonomous and competent and able to decide the nature of her own role in life independent of gender expectations.

Among feminist scholars, ideological battles rage about the meaning of being a woman in today's society. For example, many have faulted feminism for its attitude, at least until recently, that women who choose to stay in the home and raise children are not fulfilling their potential. Yet women with young children who do work often report feelings of guilt about not being with their children (Crittenden, 2001; Lerner, 1998). Many argue that the idea of femininity

Review Question

Describe the stereotypic views of masculinity, and identify the risks associated with these stereotypes.

sex byte

One study found that only 1 in 3 women who accepts a tenure-track university job before having a baby will ever become a mother (Mason & Goulden, 2004).

Today, men are often judged by how well they do at work, whereas women are often judged by how pretty and thin they are.

itself is an attempt to mold women in ways determined by men. In fact, such feminist theorists as Catherine MacKinnon (1987) argue that men have always set the definitions of what gender, sexual difference, and masculinity and femininity are, and so gender itself is really a system of dominance rather than a social or biological fact.

For example, the pressure on women to stay thin, to try to appear younger than they are, and to try to appear as beautiful as possible can be seen as reflections of male power (Wolf, 1991). Sexually, as well, women are supposed to conform to feminine stereotypes and be passive, naïve, and inexperienced. The media reinforce the ideals of feminine beauty, and the pressures on women to conform to these ideals lead to eating disorders and the surge in cosmetic surgery (Wolf, 1991). We will talk more about the powerful influences of the media in Chapter 18.

The messages a woman receives from modern North American culture are contradictory; she needs a job for fulfillment, but should be home with her children; she is more than her looks, but she had better wear makeup and stay thin; she has every opportunity men have, but only on men's terms. Though femininity has moved away from classic portrayals of women as docile and subservient to men, the pressures are still strong to appeal to those outdated stereotypes.

Androgyny: Feminine and Masculine

Up until the 1970s, masculinity and femininity were thought to be on the same continuum. The more masculine you were, the less feminine you were, and vice versa. However, in the 1970s, researchers challenged this notion by suggesting that masculinity and femininity were two separate dimensions and a person could be high or low on both dimensions.

The breakdown of traditional stereotypes about gender has refocused attention on the idea of **androgyny.** Bem (1977), as we mentioned earlier, suggested that people have different combinations of masculine and feminine traits. She considers those who have a high score on both masculinity and femininity to be androgynous. Androgyny, according to Bem, allows greater flexibility in behavior because people have a greater repertoire of possible reactions to a situation. Bem (1974, 1977, 1981) has tried to show that androgynous individuals can display "masculine" traits (such as independence) and "feminine" traits (such as playfulness with a kitten) when situations call for them.

Due to Bem's early research on masculinity, femininity, and androgyny, some suggested that androgyny was a desirable state and androgynous attitudes were a solution to the tension between the sexes. There has been more research on gender roles and androgyny since, and androgyny may not be the answer to the world's gender problems. Suggesting that people should combine aspects of masculinity and femininity may simply reinforce and retain outdated ideas of gender.

Newer research has questioned whether the masculine and feminine traits that Bem used are still valid nearly 30 years later. One study found that although 18 of 20 feminine traits still qualified as feminine, only 8 of 20 masculine traits qualified as masculine (Auster & Ohm, 2000). Traits originally associated with masculinity, such as *analytical, individualistic, competitive, self-sufficient, risk-taking,* and *defends own beliefs,* were no longer viewed as strictly masculine traits. These findings reflect recent societal changes that render some masculine traits desirable for both men and women.

Transgenderism: Living as the Other Sex

In the last few years there has been an active increase in attention paid to **transgenderism.** The transgendered community includes those who live full or part time in the other gender's role, **transsexuals,** and **transvestites** (we will talk more about transvestites in Chapter 16. See Table 16.2 for more information about transgendered groups). Some professional actors, such as **drag queens** or **female impersonators,** may or may not be transgendered.

A transgendered person is often happy as the biological sex in which he or she was born, yet enjoys dressing up and acting like the other sex (e.g., a man who works during

Review Question

Describe the stereotypic views of femininity, and identify the risks associated with these stereotypes.

androgyny
Having high levels of both masculine and feminine characteristics.

Review Question

Define androgyny, and give one example of androgynous behavior.

transgenderism
Living full or part time in the other gender's role and derive psychosocial comfort in doing so.

transsexual
A person who feels he or she is trapped in the body of the wrong gender.

transvestite
A person who dresses in the clothing of the other gender and derives sexual pleasure from doing so.

drag queen
Professional actor, typically a gay man, who, for a variety of reasons, performs in flamboyant women's clothing.

female impersonator
Professional male actor who dresses in women's clothing for a variety of reasons.

the day as a man and dresses and acts like a man, but who goes home and puts on women's clothing and acts like a woman at night). Although a transvestite often derives sexual pleasure from dressing as a member of the other sex, the majority of transgendered men and women do so for psychosocial pleasure rather than sexual pleasure. Many transgendered people report that they feel more "relaxed" and "at peace" while cross-dressed (Author's files).

Some of the earliest work on transgenderism was done by Magnus Hirschfeld (see Chapter 2). Hirschfeld wrote a book in 1910 called *The Transvestites: An Investigation of the Erotic Desire to Cross Dress*. In this book Hirschfeld explained that there were men and women who thought, felt, or acted like the other sex. John Money, whom we discussed earlier in this chapter, suggested that the majority of people are "gender congruent," which means that their biologic sex, gender identity, and gender behaviors are all in sync and there is no transgender behavior (Money, 1955). However, it is estimated that 10 to 15% of the population fails to conform to prescribed gender roles (V. L. Bullough, 2001). One 45-year-old transgendered male said:

Billy Tipton was a well-known jazz musician who was discovered to be a female when he died in 1989.

> Being transgendered has given me the chance to see life from both sides, male and female. It is not something I chose. I feel like I was drawn to it much like a moth to a flame. I started dressing at age 5, and by the time I reached puberty, it became an active part of my life because it made me feel better about myself. Interestingly, each little dose of euphoria was quickly sublimated by hours, days, and weeks of guilt. No one could exert greater guilt on me than myself. The personal disgrace I felt was at times paralyzing. In my adult life, cross-dressing is much more than just part of my sexuality, it is part of the way I define myself. I have overcome most of the shame and guilt I grew up with, and I have learned to accept myself no matter who I see looking back at me in the mirror. (Author's files)

At some points in history, transgendered behavior was chosen out of necessity. Billy Tipton (1914–1989), a well-known jazz musician, was discovered to be a female when he died in 1989 (Middlebrook, 1999). He was married to a woman and was the father of three adopted boys who did not learn of his biological gender until after his death. It is believed that Dorothy Tipton changed herself into Billy Tipton sometime around 1934 for professional reasons. Dorothy had been having trouble being taken seriously as a musician and felt that if she were a man, she would have more opportunities to prove herself. Although many people believed that Tipton pretended to be a man out of necessity, some believe that she really had a desire to become a man and was unhappy being a woman.

Transsexualism: When Gender and Biology Don't Agree

Transsexualism has profound implications for our conceptions of gender categories. In the Western world, we tend to think of gender in terms of biology; if you have XX chromosomes and female genitalia, you are female, and if you have XY chromosomes and male genitalia, you are male. This is not universally true, however. A male transsexual is convinced that he is really a female "trapped" in a man's body. Another way to put it is that a transsexual's gender identity is inconsistent with his or her biological sex. This is called **gender dysphoria** (dis-FOR-ee-uh). Overall, more males than females experience gender dysphoria, though the exact degree of difference in men and women is in dispute (H. Bower, 2001).

Some cases of transsexualism have received great publicity. In 1952, George Jorgenson, an ex-Marine, went to Denmark to have his genitals surgically altered to resemble those of a female. George changed his name to Christine, went public, and became the first highly publicized case of a transsexual who underwent **sex reassignment surgery (SRS).** Jorgenson desired to be a girl from an early age, avoided rough sports, and was a small, frail child with underdeveloped male genitals (Jorgenson, 1967). Jorgenson's story is typical of other transsexuals, who knew from an early age that they were somehow different.

Another famous case was that of Richard Raskind, an eye doctor and tennis player, who had sex reassignment surgery and then tried to play in a professional women's ten-

transsexualism
The condition of feeling trapped in the body of the wrong gender.

gender dysphoria
A condition in which one's gender identity is inconsistent with one's biological sex.

sex reassignment surgery (SRS)
Anatomical surgery to change genitalia on a transsexual; also referred to as gender reassignment.

nis tournament as Renee Richards. When it was discovered that she was a genetic male, Richards was barred from playing on the women's tennis tour.

More recently, in the early 1990s, the case of Barry Cossey received much publicity. Cossey, who was passing as a female showgirl by the age of 17, eventually underwent sex reassignment surgery, and became known as "Tula."[3] For a long time, Cossey kept her sex change a secret and went on to become a well-known model, even appearing in bathing suit and brassiere advertisements. After she received a role in the James Bond spy thriller *For Your Eyes Only* (in which she appeared primarily in a skimpy bathing suit), a British tabloid uncovered her past and announced: "James Bond Girl Was a Boy!" Cossey then wrote an autobiography and began appearing on the talk-show circuit as a crusader for the rights of transsexuals. She even appeared fully nude in *Playboy* in 1991.

Today in the United States, transsexualism is viewed as an identifiable and incapacitating disease, which in selected patients can be successfully treated through reassignment surgery (Harish & Sharma, 2003). However, outside the United States, transsexualism is not as socially acceptable. For example, Japan approved sex reassignment surgery in 1996, and by 2001 a total of seven patients had undergone SRS in Japan (Ako et al., 2001; Matsubara, 2001). Even though Japan has always been considered a leader in many areas (such as technology and education), the country has been very reluctant to deal with issues of gender dysphoria.

Most transsexuals report a lifelong desire to be a member of the other sex. The desire is often temporarily satisfied by cross-dressing, but, unlike transgenderists, transsexuals do not find cross-dressing satisfying in itself. The personal accounts of transsexuals are usually tales of suffering and confusion over who they are and what gender they belong to, and therapy is useful only in establishing for them that they do, in fact, deeply believe themselves to be emotionally and psychologically of the other sex. Gender reassignment surgery was developed to help bring transsexuals' biology into line with their inner lives.

The process of seeking gender reassignment is long and complicated. The first step is psychological counseling to confirm that the individual is truly gender dysphoric; one cannot just see a doctor and ask for a sex change. The next step is to live as a member of the other sex, and if a person does so successfully for a designated period, hormones are then administered to masculinize or feminize his or her appearance. Finally, sex reassignment surgery (SRS) is performed. It may take two or more surgeries to complete the transition.

For male-to-female (MtoF or M2F) transsexuals, the scrotum and testicles are removed. The penis is removed, but the penile skin, with all its sexually sensitive nerve endings, remains attached. This skin is then used to form the inside of the vagina, which is constructed along with a set of labial lips to simulate female genitalia as closely as possible. Finally, silicone implants create breasts. MtoF transsexuals can engage in sexual intercourse as females and achieve orgasm. Many also report that their male lovers cannot tell they have had SRS.

Female-to-male (FtoM or F2M) transsexuals have a number of choices to make. First, the female internal sex organs are usually removed. Because the testosterone they take enlarges their clitoris, many do not have artificial penises constructed but make do with an enlarged clitoris (which can be anywhere from one to three inches long). Others have an artificial penis constructed from their abdominal skin, and a scrotum is made from the labia, into which are placed prosthetic testicles. The surgical building of a penis (also known as phalloplasty) is still a difficult procedure and, as of 2003, no ideal technique had been developed (Harish & Sharma, 2003). Although the penises may look fairly real, they cannot achieve a natural erection, so penile implants of some kind are usually used (we will discuss these implants more in Chapter 14). The results of female-to-male SRS are rarely as good as that of male-to-female.

In fact, SRS in general is controversial, with some studies showing healthy postoperative functioning (Y. L. S. Smith et al., 2001), and others showing no alleviation of the psychological suffering that many male and female transsexuals feel (Cohen-Ketteris

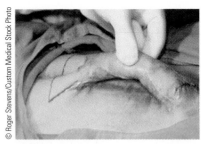

Doctors shape a penis from abdominal skin.

A completed female-to-male transsexual.

---

[3]It should be noted that Cossey was born with a chromosomal abnormality, XXXY chromosomes, compared to XX for a normal female and XY for a normal male. In most cases of transsexualism, however, no abnormal chromosomes are found.

& Gooren, 1999). Some clinics have stopped performing transsexual surgery altogether. But some people seeking gender reassignment have longed for years to bring their bodies into line with their sense of gender identity, and SRS is their ultimate goal. As surgical techniques improve, some SRS problems may be resolved.

SEXTalk

Question: *It seems like there has been very little written over the years about the transgendered experience. Is it true that transgendered men and women were too afraid to write articles or research studies?*

Historically, the transgendered community has been relatively quiet in terms of actively publishing research. Prior to 1990, transgendered men and women made very few research contributions to the professional literature (with the exceptions of Magnus Hirschfeld, whom we discussed in Chapter 2). Transsexuals were even quieter—in fact, not one transsexual authored a research study or textbook prior to 1990 (Denny & Wiederman, 2004). Even so, we have learned much about the transgendered experience through various autobiographies. It is estimated that over 100 such autobiographies were published from 1952 to 2000 (Denny & Wiederman, 2004). Today the transgendered community is actively engaged in research and continues to contribute rich autobiographies that help us more fully understand the transgendered experience.

Third Genders: Other Cultures, Other Options

Transsexuals stretch our usual concepts of gender by suggesting that there can be a fundamental and irreconcilable break between our psychological and biological genders. However, some cultures challenge our notions and even have a gender category that is neither male nor female—a third gender.

Many traditional Native American societies had a category of not-men/not-women, known as berdaches. The **berdache** (or "two-spirit") was usually (but not always) a biological male who was effeminate or androgynous in behavior and who took on the social role of female (Blackwood, 1984; W. L. Williams, 1986). The berdache often married a male Native American (and adopted children), though not all married or engaged in sexual behavior with males. Berdachism was considered a vocation, like being a hunter or warrior, which was communicated to certain boys in their first adult vision. In all social functions, the berdache was treated as a female. The berdache held a respected, sacred position in society and was believed to have special powers.

berdache
A type of Native American third gender who takes on the social role of the other gender; also referred to as a "two-spirit."

Biologically female berdaches also lived in Native American tribes. Female berdaches began showing interest in boys' activities and games during childhood (Blackwood, 1984). Adults, recognizing this desire, would teach the girls the same skills the boys were learning. (In one tribe, a family with all girl children might select one daughter to be their "son," tying dried bear ovaries to her belt to prevent conception!)

These females were initiated into puberty as men, and thereafter they were essentially considered men. They hunted and trapped, fought in battle, and performed male ceremonial tasks. Among the Alaskan Ingalik, for example, these biological women would even participate in nude, men-only sweat baths, and the men would ignore the female genitalia and treat the berdache as a man. The female berdache could marry a woman, though the unions remained childless, and the berdache would perform the appropriate rituals when her partner menstruated but would ignore her own menses. Female berdaches became prominent members of some Native American societies, and, in at least one case, a female berdache became chief of the tribe (Whitehead, 1981).

Other cultures have similar roles. The Persian Gulf country of Oman has a class of biological males called the *xaníth* (Wikan, 1977). The *xaníth* are exempt from the strict Islamic rules that restrict men's interaction with women, because they are not considered men. They sit with females at weddings and may see the bride's face; they may not sit with men in public nor do tasks reserved for men. Yet the *xaníth* are not considered females either; for example, they retain men's names.

Another important example are the *hijra* of India. The *hijra* are men who undergo ritual castration in which all or part of their genitals are removed, and they are believed to have special powers to curse or bless male children. *Hijra* dress as women, though they do not really try to "pass" as women; their mannerisms are exaggerated, and some even sport facial hair. In India, the *hijra* are considered neither men nor women but inhabit a unique third social gender (Nanda, 2001).

In Thailand, there is a group of people called the *kathoey*, who are very similar to Oman's *xaníth*. Two other examples are the *aikane* of native Hawaii, who were attached to the court of the chiefs and served sexual, social, and political functions (Morris, 1990), and the *mahu* of Tahiti (Herdt, 1990). The belief in these societies that it is neither obvious nor natural that there are only two genders should make us carefully reconsider our own assumptions about gender.

Asexualism: The Genetics but Not the Sex

asexuality
Often refers to the lack of sexual desire, but can also refer to a lack of maleness or femaleness.

A final type of gender category is **asexuality.** On occasion, usually due to a mother's hormone use during pregnancy, a child is born without sexual organs of any kind. This means that the child has no ovaries, uterus, or vagina; has no penis or testicles; and usually has only a bladder and a urethra ending in an aperture for the elimination of urine.

Personal Voices

Toby: An Asexual Person

Toby was born without any internal or external reproductive organs: Toby has no penis, scrotum, or testicles, and Toby has no vagina, ovaries, or uterus. Therefore, Toby also has no male or female sex hormones, except the small amount secreted by the adrenal glands on the kidneys. Though at a chromosomal level Toby is either XX or XY, it has no impact on Toby's life; therefore, Toby has no real gender and has adopted the term "neuter" rather than male or female. Because Toby has no gender, terms like "he" or "she" are also inappropriate. Toby therefore uses the word "xe," instead, to signify those who have neither a male nor female gender.

Toby was assigned a female gender at birth because the doctor saw no penis. Toby was raised as a girl until the age of about 12, when Toby began refusing female hormones because xe did not "feel" like the girl everyone thought xe was. Of course, without hormones, Toby could not begin puberty at all. During Toby's early teens, xe also spent some time taking male hormones. But that did not feel right either. Between the ages of 13 and 18, the doctors began to experiment with Toby's gender. Finally, at 18, when Toby was no longer a minor, xe refused to take any more hormones and has been living as a neuter ever since.

When official or school forms ask for the person's sex, Toby writes in "neuter"; Toby has the first driver's license in the state of Kansas with the designation "O" under sex. Toby uses whichever restroom is less crowded, dresses in jeans and other unisex, casual clothes, and has close friends of both sexes. Toby also taught Sunday school, where, after a period of intense interest, the children decided that the fact that their teacher was neither a male nor a female was no big deal. Toby talks about what it means to be a neuter and to be asexual:

I conclude that I'm neuter because I don't see anything in being male or being female that I can relate to. It's partly a matter of anatomy; the basic medical definitions of maleness and femaleness involve the presence of body parts which I don't have. Most people who don't have those body parts still somehow relate to the idea that there are these things called maleness and femaleness, and everybody has to be one or the other, and therefore I must be one or the other because everyone is. Therefore there has to be something wrong with me that has to be "fixed." I have to be "repaired"— I have to have hormones, I have to have surgery, I have to pretend, or acquire somehow these characteristics that I didn't start out with. I didn't do that. I started out saying, "I don't know what being male or female means; I read the definitions, I looked at myself, they didn't match, and my conclusion was, therefore: I must not be either male or female, therefore it must not be true that everyone has to be one or the other." And that is what I mean when I say that I am neuter. (Author's files)

Though such a child has a genetic gender (that is, has XX or XY chromosomes), the child has no *biological* gender. Most are assigned a gender in childhood, are given hormones, and live as male or female. The Personal Voices on page 90 tells the story of an asexual named Toby, who chose to live without any social gender at all.

Review Question

Differentiate between transgenderism, transsexualism, gender dysphoria, third genders, and asexuality.

GENDER ROLE SOCIALIZATION FROM INFANCY THROUGH OLD AGE

Socialization into gender roles begins at birth and, nowadays, may begin even before! Parents can now know months before birth whether the fetus is a boy or a girl and can begin to prepare accordingly. Parents even speak to the unborn child—a mother simply by talking and the father by putting his mouth close to the mother's belly—and communicate ideas about their "little boy" or "little girl." In a real sense, then, these parents may begin trying to communicate gender-specific messages before the child is even born (whether the child actually is influenced by these sounds diffusing into the womb is, of course, another question). Parents awaiting the birth of a child are filled with gender expectations, stereotypes, and desires.

SEXTalk

Question: I don't think there anything wrong with letting boys and girls act like boys and girls! Why try to discourage boys from playing with guns and girls with dolls? Everyone I know grew up that way, and they are okay.

The same people who believe that they "grew up okay" are often the first to complain about the nature of gender relations in the United States. Perhaps we should not forbid boys from ever playing with toy guns (anyway, they would probably just make other toys into guns) or forbid girls to play with dolls, but trying to encourage children to appreciate the activities of the other sex can only help matters. Research has found that parents allow their girls more flexibility in toy choices, whereas they limit the toys that boys play with to mainly masculine toys (Wood, 2002).

Childhood: Learning by Playing

From the moment parents find out the sex of their baby a child's life is largely defined by his or her gender. From the baby's name, to how he or she is dressed, to how his or her room is decorated, gender suffuses the newborn's life. Not only do parents construct different environments for boys and girls from birth, they tend to treat them differently as well.

As early as age 2, **modeling behavior** begins to emerge, and children begin to realize that objects and activities are appropriate to specific genders. The rules that a child develops at this point are not flexible but universal; to the child, only women can wear skirts, and only men can use electric razors. In fact, cross-gender humor is very funny to young children; a television program that shows a man dressed up in a woman's clothes or a woman who appears on TV sporting a mustache will elicit bursts of laughter.

As the child begins to show more complex behaviors, he or she is usually rewarded for displaying gender-stereotyped behavior and discouraged or punished for nonstereotyped behaviors. A boy picks up a bat and hits a ball and hears his parents call "Good boy!" whereas no such encouragement is forthcoming when he mimics his mother sewing. A daughter watches her father fix the car and although her father might not take

modeling behavior
Gender-appropriate behavior that usually emerges in childhood from watching others.

Children learn much of their gender-role behavior from modeling.

© Tony Freeman/PhotoEdit

gender-identity disorder
A disorder in which a child has a strong and persistent identification with the other sex or the gender role of the other sex and is uncomfortable with his or her own biological sex or gender role.

homosocial play
Gender-segregated play.

the time to teach her the specific car parts, he would teach his son. Similarly, when a daughter wanders into the kitchen, the mother who is cooking may begin instructing her on how to mix ingredients, while a son gets no such guidance.

Overall, boys are treated more harshly than girls when they adopt cross-gender characteristics (Sandnabba & Ahlberg, 1999). Children who have a strong and persistent identification with the other sex or the gender role of the other sex and are uncomfortable with their own biological sex or gender role may be diagnosed with a **gender-identity disorder.** Overall, the prevalence of gender-identity disorder ranges from .003 to 3% in boys and .001 to 1.5% in girls (Bartlett et al., 2000).

Early in childhood, gender segregation in play, also known as **homosocial play,** begins. Children tend to gravitate to same-sex friends, and as early as $2\frac{1}{2}$ to 3 years old, children play more actively and more interactively with same-sex playmates (Maccoby, 1987). This tendency is universal. Researchers have tried rewarding children for playing with the other sex, but as soon as the reward is discontinued, play reverts back to same-gender groupings. This gender segregation may be due to the different playing styles of boys and girls, the attraction of children to others like themselves, or to learned social roles; most probably, it involves a combination of all these factors.

During the school years, gender roles become the measure by which children are judged by their peers. Children who violate sex-typed play are usually rejected (and not kindly) by their peers (Blakemore, 2003). This is especially true of boys, who experience more rejection from their peers when they violate gender stereotypes than girls do.

The classroom itself can also strongly reinforce gender stereotypes. Even though teachers believe they show equal attention to boys and girls, research shows that teachers spend more time with boys, give them more attention, both praise and criticize boys more, use more follow-up questions to boys, and tolerate more bad behavior among boys than girls (Duffy et al., 2001). Girls are also steered away from math and science courses and use biased textbooks that reinforce gender stereotypes (Keller, 2002). Boys who question the teacher are considered curious, whereas girls who question are considered aggressive. Also, teachers stereotype the tasks they ask boys and girls to do; boys may be asked to help move desks, whereas girls are asked to erase the blackboard.

One of the most comprehensive studies on the well-being of male and female children found that both genders enjoy a higher quality of life than they did in 1985 and that boys and girls are fairly equally well (Meadows et al., 2005). This study reviewed

Play Like a Boy! Play Like a Girl!

For a child, playing is not a game, it is serious business. Play is what teaches the child physical coordination, eye–hand coordination, the rules of gravity and cause and effect, and other physical and motor skills. As a child matures, playing with peers also teaches a child lessons of social interaction, sharing, letting go of things he or she wants, winning and losing, and compromise. Strong gender messages are also typically communicated to children during play, even in infancy.

Boys and girls are provided different toys and different play environments from birth. One study, comparing the physical environment of 120 infant girls and boys, found that boys were provided with more sports equipment, tools, and large and small vehicles, whereas girls had more dolls, fictional characters, and children's furniture (Pomerleau et al., 1990). Parents send a powerful message by the way they decorate nurseries and stock them with playthings, and the message is, "There are boy toys and girl toys. You will play with the appropriate toys."

In a study of the toys children request for Christmas, Etaugh and Liss (1992) found that children requested, wanted, received, and best liked sex-appropriate toys. When a child did request a gender-inappropriate toy, the parent was likely to give him or her something else. So even when a child wants to escape from toy stereotypes, parents generally do not cooperate. This is applicable more for boys than girls. Parents have been found to spend more time using masculine toys when playing with boys but have much more flexibility in toys when playing with girls (Wood et al., 2002).

Walk through a toy store one day. Even though the aisles may not be marked "for boys" and "for girls," it is very clear for which gender an aisle is intended. Boys' toys are often geared toward aggression and destruction, whereas girls' toys are geared toward domestic life and appearance. Toys have been found to be gender stereotyped for all ages, with the exception of infant and toddler toys (Campenni, 1999).

The same patterns tend to hold true in other countries too. In a study of play differences between Canada and Poland, Stephen Richer (1990) found that boys tended to draw pictures of competitive activities and situations, whereas girls did not; even when shown the same picture, such as children shooting basketballs, boys would set up a competitive situation (such as someone trying to block the shot), whereas girls would describe more noncompetitive situations.

Almost every culture has its own gender-appropriate toys. In Russia, the dolls available to the average child are bulky and have simple, bland clothes. But they also have pink or blue hair to indicate whether they are girl or boy dolls. In fact, when Barbie came to Russia, complete with sequined outfits and blond hair and toy Ferrari cars, the Russians would often spend over a month's salary for the doll. When some mothers who were staring longingly at the Barbie in the store window were asked by a reporter whether Barbie might not teach their daughters bad lessons, such as the idea that blond hair and Ferraris bring happiness, they looked confused. It seems that Americans are not the only ones who overlook the gender messages of their toys.

data from various large and ongoing studies, including federal surveys, the census, crime statistics, and other research projects. Between 1985 and 2001 girls and boys were evaluated from childhood through their early 20s. This research comes after several studies that claim that each gender is being shortchanged in society for a variety of different reasons. Gender researchers often disagree about whether there are advantages or disadvantages to being one gender or the other and although the findings of this study were widely criticized from both sides of the argument, it is encouraging to see that the quality of life for girls and boys is improving in U.S. society.

Adolescence: Practice Being Female or Male

By adolescence, gender roles are firmly established, and they guide adolescents through their exploration of peer relationships and different "love styles" with potential partners. Part of the task of adolescence is to figure out what it means to be a "man" or a "woman" and to try to adopt that role. Boys quickly learn that to be popular they should be interested in and good at sports, should express interest in sex and in women, should not be overly emotional, and should not display interests that are seen as feminine or girlish. Girls, on the other hand, seem to have more latitude in their behavior but are supposed

Review Question

How are children socialized about gender roles throughout childhood?

to express interest in boys and men, show concern with their appearance, and exercise a certain amount of sexual restraint. When boys deviate from gender role behavior, the consequences are more severe than when girls deviate. However, girls have traditionally been sanctioned more than boys when they violate gender stereotypes of sexuality (such as being promiscuous). We will discuss some reasons that masculine roles are narrower than feminine roles in a later section.

Adolescence can be a particularly difficult time for those who are transgendered, homosexual, or bisexual. There tends to be little tolerance for these behaviors in adolescence because they are viewed as the opposite of what the teenagers are "supposed" to do. Teenage males are supposed to be striving for genuine "masculinity." Though female homosexuality is also seen as deviant and lesbians can be the subject of taunts, females tend to discover their sexual orientation later than males, so fewer "come out" in adolescence.

The life of an emerging gay, lesbian, or bisexual adolescent may be fraught with tension and gender role confusion, which contributes to the high suicide rate among these adolescents. Many gay, bisexual, and transgendered youth survive the adolescent years by concealing their sexual orientation or gender identity (Human Rights Watch, 2001). Many learn that if they don't, they may be subjected to violence and/or verbal harassment. We will discuss the physical and emotional harassment of gay, lesbian, and bisexual students more in Chapter 11.

Teenage gender roles have been changing over the last few years. For example, girls today are much more willing to assert themselves and call boys on the phone or ask them out than they were 25 years ago, when they would have been considered either "desperate" or "sluts."

Yet such changing roles are also confusing; adolescent girls and boys still receive contradictory messages. Traditional male attitudes value sexual achievement, control of the sexual relationship, and suppression of emotions. However, today, as teenaged boys are being approached by girls, they are not necessarily more sexually experienced than the girls they date, and they are expected to be sensitive to issues of female equality. Teenage girls, on the other hand, have often been taught to be dependent on males but now are expected to assert their independence. In addition, opportunities for achievement have opened up to the point that many girls who express a wish to become mothers and stay at home may be denigrated for lacking ambition. So, even with all the changes that have leveled the playing field between the sexes, it is still not easy for adolescents to negotiate their way into sexual adulthood.

Review Question

How are teenagers socialized about gender roles throughout adolescence?

Adulthood: Careers and Families

As men and women grow into adulthood, they tend to derive their gender identity primarily in two realms—their careers and their family lives. Although many believe that ideas about gender are firmly established by the time we reach adulthood, recent social changes in sex roles show that adults do have the capacity to revise their thoughts about gender roles.

One area of research that has been tracking gender differences is in television commercials (Bartsch et al., 2000). These studies have found that women are overrepresented in commercials of domestic products and are underrepresented in commercials of all other product types. Characters in television commercials are portrayed as having more authority if they are white or male. In fact, there are well-established stereotypes in today's commercials—white men have been viewed as powerful; white women as sex objects; African American men as aggressive; and African American women as inconsequential (Coltrane & Messineo, 2000). Interestingly, women and men with traditional gender roles (who score higher on measures of masculinity and femininity) have been found to respond more favorably to gender-stereotyped advertising (Morrison & Shaffer, 2003).

For many years in Western society, men were encouraged to develop careers, whereas women (insofar as they have been encouraged to work at all) were taught to get a job that would occupy their time until marriage and children remove them from the workforce. The tendency still exists, especially in traditional women who are more feminine, to choose low-prestige occupations and/or subordinate their careers to their husbands'. One study found that a woman's career intentions have been found to be influenced by her gender role attitudes and her perceptions of both her parents' and her boyfriend's career preferences for her (Vincent et al., 1998).

Men are also socialized into career choices. Society teaches men that career achievement is, in large part, the measure of their worth. Being the breadwinner is a crucial part of male identity, and a man's success is often measured in dollars earned. This is also changing, however, although not as quickly as women's roles in the workplace are changing. In the past few years, men have been entering more female-dominated fields, such as physical therapy and library science, and have also been taking on more child-care responsibilities (U.S. Bureau of the Census, 1999).

Although women comprise close to 50% of the workforce and 30% of management in large American corporations, less than 5% of senior managers are women (Powell, 1999). Women's roles in the workplace have slowly been changing and more women are pursuing careers and are holding positions of responsibility and leadership. For example, although the percentage of working mothers was about 40% in 1970, it rose to over 70% by the late 1990s (U.S. Bureau of the Census, 1999). Women have also been moving into more traditionally male-dominated fields, such as law, engineering, and architecture.

More and more women are pursuing professions and looking toward careers for at least part of their personal fulfillment. Although women received 5% of law degrees in 1970, they were awarded over 40% of law degrees by the mid-1990s (U.S. Bureau of the Census, 1999). Yet powerful pressures still exist for women to retain primary responsibility for home life, which means that women in high-pressure jobs may have more responsibility than men in similar jobs. One study found that although there are more women who are commercial air pilots today, many report experiencing discrimination and sexism on the job (Davey & Davidson, 2000).

Women and Family Life

Throughout most of history, women worked outside the home; and even today, in most countries, women (especially the poor) are a major part of the workforce. Yet most women in the United States and elsewhere are still taught that their primary sense of satisfaction and identity should be derived from their roles as wives and mothers.

Women receive two conflicting messages from American society: the first is the conservative message that a woman must be married and have children to be fulfilled; the second, a feminist message, is that to be fulfilled, women must have a career outside the home. Women who try to do both find themselves with two full-time jobs. Researchers of domestic life point out that "housework" involves far more than its stereotype of dusting and ironing and includes creating an atmosphere of good family relations, planning the budget, and educating oneself in consumer skills, evaluating educational options, being the liaison between the family and outside services (such as appliance repair) and so on (Epstein, 1988). Single working women with children must assume both roles; but even when a working woman has a working (male) partner, research shows that the woman tends to do a significantly larger percentage of household tasks (Bianchi et al., 2000).

Many women therefore live with a double sense of guilt. If they work, they feel they are not spending the time they should with their children and are leaving the important task of child rearing to a nanny, day care center, or other relatives. If they decide to stay at home and raise their children, they may feel guilty for not being productive members of the workforce. Many women do not even have that choice because economic circumstances require that they work, and most would not be able to stay at home full-time without public assistance.

This dispute has been called the "mommy wars," as working mothers and stay-at-home mothers each try to defend their decisions. Nearly half the stay-at-home mothers in one survey said employed mothers did not spend enough time with their children; whereas half of employed mothers said they would keep their jobs even if they got the same salary without working. The debates over working mothers will not end soon, for

Review Question

How are adults socialized about gender roles throughout adulthood, and how does this socialization affect career choice?

Review Question

Describe the conflicting messages that women receive about career and family life.

sex byte

Even with the increase of women in the workforce, research has found that American women spend more time participating in parenting and housework activities, whereas American men spend more time participating in career and leisure activities (Perrone et al., 2005).

Today, more men are choosing to stay at home with the children while their partners go to work.

Review Question

How has the role of the husband/father in the family changed over the last few years?

As men and women age, gender roles become less restrictive.

Review Question

Explain how gender roles change as people enter later life.

women are continuing to enter the workforce in great numbers. As long as society portrays a woman's "real" job as that of mother, women will feel guilty when they choose to be productive outside the family (Warner, 2005).

Men and Family Life

Because of the traditional view that women's primary domain is the family and men's primary domain is the workplace, we have relatively few studies of men's roles in the home. For example, enormous amounts of literature have been dedicated to discussing the "unmarried mother," but it is only relatively recently that research has begun to look at the fathers of children born outside of marriage. A growing field of men's studies looks at the role of being a "man" in modern society, including the changing domestic demands on men as more women enter the workforce.

Studies do show that men with working wives have begun to share more responsibility for home life. When men become fathers, they begin to carry out many tasks that are stereotypically female, such as feeding and dressing the baby. Even so, fathers have been found to spend less time in direct interaction with infants than do mothers (Laflamme et al., 2003). Women still tend to retain primary responsibility for organizing the daily household and for physical chores like preparing meals and doing laundry. Men tend to take on other types of chores, such as heavy-lifting chores and specific projects in the home. Although working women spend more hours on household chores than men do, this too has been slowly changing. Today, research suggests that many men are taking more responsibility for childcare and are assuming more domestic chores (Auster & Ohm, 2000).

Because of the changing workforce, the numbers of unemployed men whose wives are the primary wage earners are increasing (Fitch, 2003). These stay-at-home dads assume domestic chores and become the primary caretakers for the children. It is interesting, however, that we consider men who choose to keep house "unemployed," whereas women who do the same tasks are usually considered outside the wage-earning workforce. There is still an assumption that a man "should" be working, whereas women have the choice to stay home.

The Senior Years

In families with children, the parents can experience either a great sense of loneliness or a newfound freedom as their children grow and leave the home. A few women, especially those with traditional roles as wife and mother, become depressed about losing their primary roles as caretakers and mothers. The phrase "empty nest syndrome" identifies the feelings of sadness and loss that many women experience when their children leave home or no longer need day-to-day care (Raup & Myers, 1989). Men and women both may have trouble adjusting to retirement if they derived a large sense of their identity from their work. In other words, whether a career or family life is the source of a person's gender identity, significant changes are common in the senior years that may involve difficult adjustments.

As people age, gender roles relax and become less restrictive. For example, older men tend to do more housework than younger men. Many are retired and spend more time at home, and some find that their wives are less able to handle the household by themselves. Similarly, women who are widowed or whose husbands become disabled must learn to care for their finances or learn other skills that their husbands may have previously handled.

DIFFERENT, BUT NOT LESS THAN: TOWARD GENDER EQUALITY

Can we create a society that avoids gender stereotypes, a society of total gender equality? Would you want to live in such a society? Does a gender-equal society mean that we must have unisex bathrooms, or is it something subtler, referring to a sense of equal opportunity and respect? Epstein (1986, 1988) believes that gender distinctions begin with basic, human, dichotomous thinking—the splitting of the world into opposites like good–bad, dark–light, soft–hard, and male–female. This very basic human process tends to exaggerate differences between things, including the sexes, and society invests a lot of energy in maintaining those distinctions.

Many religious and cultural systems clearly define gender roles. Advocates of such systems deny that differentiating gender roles means that one gender is subordinate to the other. For example, Susan Rogers (1978) has argued that we cannot apply Western notions of gender equality to countries with fundamentally different systems. She argues that inequality can exist in society only when women and men are seen in that society as fundamentally similar.

In Oman, for example, women are subject to strict social rules that we in the West would clearly see as subordination. Yet Rogers argues that women in Oman see themselves as quite different from men and are uninterested in the male role and male definitions of power. Is it appropriate for us to impose our categories on their society and suggest that women in Oman are exploited and subordinate even though they themselves do not think so? Such questions go to the heart of the discussion of power in society.

The goal for many is not a society without gender distinctions; a world without differences is boring. Yet a world that restricts people's ability to express difference because of the color of their skin, their religious beliefs, or the type of genitalia they happen to have (or not have!) is unjust. It is the content of gender roles, not their existence, that societies can alter to provide each person an opportunity to live without being judged by stereotypes of gender.

Review Question

Do you think there could ever be a society without gender distinctions? Why, or why not?

Chapter Review

ACTIVE SUMMARY

1. Human beings use (a) _____ reproduction to combine 23 chromosomes in the mother's gamete with the 23 in the father's. The (b) _____ then begins to undergo cell differentiation. If the 23rd chromosome pair is (c) _____, the fetus will develop typically female sexual characteristics.

2. Female genitalia develop from the (a) _____ duct. Both male and female external genitalia develop from the same (b) _____ so that many male and female genital structures are (c) _____.

3. A number of prenatal problems can develop, usually due to the fetus's inability to (a) _____ or (b) _____ to hormones or due to the mother ingesting (c) _____.

4. Atypical sexual differentiation can be caused by (a) _____ or (b) _____ disorders. Klinefelter's, Turner's syndrome, XYY, and triple X are examples of (c) _____ disorders, whereas congenital adrenal hyperplasia and androgen-insensitivity syndrome are (d) _____ disorders.

5. (a) _____ roles are the culturally determined pattern of behaviors that societies prescribe to the sexes. Gender traits are the (b) _____ determined characteristics of gender.

Little agreement exists on which gender (c) _____ are innate and which are (d) _____.

6. (a) "_____" and "femininity" are used in three ways in society: first, a masculine or feminine person is said to (b) _____ characteristics that differentiate the sexes; second, the terms refer to the extent to which adults adhere to (c) _____ prescribed gender roles; and third, masculinity and femininity refer to (d) _____ characteristics.

7. Most people agree that males are larger, stronger, and more (a) _____, whereas females are neurologically more advanced than males, (b) _____ faster, and are biologically (c) _____. Some also cite evidence that males have better (d) _____ abilities, whereas females have better verbal abilities.

8. Three types of theories about gender role (a) _____ have been offered: (b) _____ _____ theories, which postulate that almost all gender knowledge is dependent on what children are taught; (c) _____ _____ theories, which suggest that children go through a universal set of stages during which they can learn only certain types of information about gender; and newer theories, such as Bem's gender

(d) _____ theory, which suggests that children do go through developmental stages and that the kinds of things they learn at each stage are largely culturally determined.

9. Gender **(a)** _____ theories try to explain why masculine traits tend to be valued in society over feminine traits. Nancy Chodorow's developmental theory suggests that boys must switch from **(b)** _____ with their mothers to identifying with their fathers, which is a very difficult process, and they must **(c)** _____ feminine traits in order to reject them. Ortner suggests that women's domain is nature because women perform the biological functions of **(d)** _____, whereas men's domain is "culture." MacKinnon argues that men get to define what is fundamentally "male" and "female" in society and what the implications of those differences are; therefore, men **(e)** _____ gender definitions in society.

10. **(a)** _____ is socially constructed, and societies decide how it will be defined and what it will mean. In American society, masculinity and femininity are seen as **(b)** _____ exclusive. Masculine **(c)** _____ include being a good provider, strong, stable, unemotional, fearless, sexually experienced, and financially independent.

11. Men have been found to have several **(a)** _____-_____ illnesses related to the narrow focus of their gender role. Feminine traits include being beautiful, soft, empathetic, modest, and **(b)** _____. Many traits of femininity are considered to be the **(c)** _____ of masculinity.

12. **(a)** _____ is high levels of masculine and feminine characteristics, and some advocate it as a way to transcend gender **(b)** _____. Transsexuals believe their biological and psychological **(c)** _____ are incompatible, showing us that gender is more complex than simply determining biological gender. Some societies assign gender **(d)** _____ that are neither male or female.

13. The **(a)** _____ community includes three groupings; those who live full time or part time in the other gender's **(b)** _____; transsexuals; and **(c)** _____.

14. Infants are socialized into gender roles early through the way they are **(a)** _____ and treated, and through the **(b)** _____ in which they are brought up. They are reinforced for **(c)** _____ gender activity through ridiculing children who violate gender boundaries. Adolescents "try on" adult **(d)** _____ _____ and attitudes.

15. In adulthood, **(a)** _____ have been seen as the domain of men, and women have gravitated to **(b)** _____-paying jobs and to subordinate their careers to their husbands. Family life has traditionally been the domain of women, but as women enter the workforce in greater numbers, more men are assuming a larger portion of the **(c)** _____ and household duties.

16. As people age, gender roles become more **(a)** _____, and the elderly may have to make **(b)** _____ to their stereotypes once they retire or their children leave the home. Gender **(c)** _____ are not necessarily bad. In fact, the goal for many societies is not being **(d)** _____ by gender stereotypes.

Critical Thinking Questions

1. What questions does the case study example on Brenda/Bruce raise about the nature of gender? Do you feel that gender is innate, socially learned, or a combination of both?

2. How are definitions of masculinity and femininity changing in society? Are many of the old stereotypes still powerful?

3. Why do you think a woman considers the phrase "She's one of the guys" to be a compliment, whereas a man considers the phrase "He's one of the girls" to be a put-down?

4. Which theory of gender development do you favor? Can you relate this theory to your own gender development? What are the theory's strengths and weaknesses?

5. If you met someone at a party tonight who was transgendered, what kind of emotions or thoughts do you think you would have? Would you be interested in pursuing a relationship with him or her? Why, or why not?

Check It Out

Nanda, S. (2001). **Gender diversity: Crosscultural variations.** Prospect Heights, IL: Waveland Press.

In this exploration of sex, gender, and sexuality, Nanda looks at the relationships between culture and gender diversity and how sex/gender diversity are experienced in several different cultures. Her arguments help us to evaluate our own definitions of what we consider natural, normal, and morally right. Nanda explores gender diversity, sexual orientation, transgenderism, sex/gender identity, and the concept of multiple genders.

What Women Want (2000; 1 hour, 7 minutes; PG-13)

In this humorous exploration of gender roles and how men and women think, Mel Gibson plays a hypermasculine "man's man" who is clueless about what women want. His female friends, colleagues, ex-wife, and daughter all dislike him. A fateful accident involving a blow-dryer and a bathtub turn him into a man who can hear what women think. This ability ultimately teaches him to treat people with kindness and respect.

InfoTrac® College Edition

If your instructor ordered InfoTrac with this book, explore InfoTrac College Edition, your online library, for additional readings and review. Go to: **www.thomsonedu.com,** and enter these search terms:

masculinity   femininity   gender
sexual orientation   stereotypes

Web Resources

SexualityNow Companion Website
Go to **http://thomsonedu.com/carroll** for practice quiz questions, interactive activities, Internet links, critical thinking exercises, discussion forums, and more. You can also access sites from the Wadsworth Psychology Study Center **(http://psychology.wadsworth.com)** or you can connect directly to the following sites:

FTM International
FTM International is an Internet contact point for the largest, longest-running educational organization serving F2M transgendered people and transsexual men. Information on history, law, transitioning, helplines, and a variety of links about transgenderism are available.

International Foundation for Gender Education
The International Foundation for Gender Education (IFGE), founded in 1987, is an advocacy and educational organization for promoting the self-definition and free expression of individual gender identity. IFGE maintains the most complete bookstore on transgenderism. It also publishes the leading magazine, providing discussion of issues of gender expression and identity, including information on issues such as cross-dressing, transsexualism, F2M and M2F issues spanning health, family, medical, legal, and workplace issues.

Intersex Society of North America
The Intersex Society of North America (ISNA) is devoted to ending the shame, secrecy, and unwanted genital surgeries for people born with nonstandard sexual anatomy. This organization offers information and support for both intersexed people and their friends and family members. A variety of links to related materials are available.

National Transgender Advocacy Coalition (NTAC)
The National Transgender Advocacy Coalition (NTAC) is a political advocacy coalition working to establish and maintain the right of all transgendered, intersexed, and gender-variant people to live and work without fear of violence or discrimination. The site contains information on gender studies, gender rights, and a variety of links to related materials.

SexualityNow   **Sexuality ⚙ Now**

Go to **www.thomsonedu.com** to link to **SexualityNow,** your online study tool. First take the **Pre-Test** for this chapter to get your **Personalized Study Plan,** which will identify topics you need to review and direct you to online resources. Then take the **Post-Test** to determine what concepts you have mastered and what you still need work on.

Videos in SexualityNow

For additional information on topics discussed in this chapter, check out the videos in **SexualityNow** on the following topics:

- **Female-to-Male Transsexual: Teo**—An interview with a female-to-male transsexual about his experiences.
- **Transgendered: Liz**—A transgendered woman discusses her experiences and challenges.
- **Male-to-Female Transsexual: Rachel**—An interview with a male-to-female transsexual about her experiences.
- **Choosing Your Child's Gender**—Although it's possible to stain sperm and to separate X and Y chromosomes with 90% accuracy, hear the arguments for and against doing so.

- **Which Is the Real Me? One Woman With Many Hats**—Listen to how one woman has many aspects and roles in her identity.
- **Perceiving Gender Roles: Ages 0–2**—Although research shows that there are early sex differences in behavior, see how these differences are small but accentuated by environmental influences.
- **Perceiving Gender Roles: Ages 2–5**—Hear how children in the preschool years have acquired many gender stereotypes and have different gender role expectations.
- **Perceiving Gender Roles: Ages 5–11**—Learn how children have a strong sense of gender identity and gender role expectations by middle childhood.
- **Gender Identity Disorder: Jessica**—Hear how Jessica describes her life both before and after her sex reassignment surgery.
- **As Nature Made Him**—Meet David Reimer, the real John/Joan who's described in this book, as he and his biographer discuss his botched sexual reassignment.

4

Female Sexual Anatomy and Physiology

Sexuality Now Go to www.thomsonedu.com to link to SexualityNow, your online study tool.

*F*or many years, only physicians were thought to be privileged enough to know about the human body. Today we realize how important it is for all of us to understand how our bodies function. Considering the number of sex manuals and guides that line the shelves of American bookstores, it may seem surprising that the majority of questions that students ask about human sexuality are fundamental, biological questions.[1] Yet it becomes less surprising when we realize that many parents are still uncomfortable about discussing sexual biology with their children, and younger people often do not know whom to approach or are embarrassed about the questions they have (we will talk more about this in Chapter 8). But questions about sexual biology are natural, for the reproductive system is complex, and there are probably more myths and misinformation about sexual biology than any other single part of human functioning.

Children are naturally curious about their genitals and spend a good deal of time touching and exploring them. However, they are often taught that this exploration is something to be ashamed of. Because girls' genitals are more hidden and recessed, and girls are often discouraged from making a thorough self-examination, they tend to be less familiar with their genitals than boys. This may be reinforced as females mature and are taught that menstruation is "dirty." These attitudes are reflected in ads for "feminine hygiene" products, which suggest that the vagina is unsanitary and has an unpleasant smell.

In this chapter we will explore female anatomy and physiology. Although there are many similarities to male anatomy and physiology, as you will soon learn, female anatomy and physiology are a bit more complicated. Unlike males, females have fluctuating hormone levels, monthly menstruation cycles, and menopause. In Chapter 5 we will explore male sexual anatomy and physiology.

THE FEMALE SEXUAL AND REPRODUCTIVE SYSTEM

It is important for women (and men) to understand the structure of the female reproductive system, which is really a marvel of biological engineering. Women who have not done a thorough genital self-examination should do so, not only because it is an important part of the body to learn to appreciate but also because any changes in genital appearance should be brought to the attention of a **gynecologist** or other health care provider. See the accompanying Sex in Real Life for instructions on performing a genital self-exam.

External Sex Organs

Though many people refer to the female's external sex organs collectively as the "vagina," this is technically incorrect; the more accurate term for the whole region is **vulva,** or **pudendum** (pue-DEN-dum). The vulva, as we will see, is made up of the mons veneris, the labia majora and labia minora, the vestibule, the perineum, and the clitoris (see Figure 4.1). Though the vagina does open into the vulva, it is mainly an internal sex organ and will be discussed in the next section.

gynecologist
A physician who specializes in the study and treatment of disorders of the female reproductive system.

vulva
The collective designation for the external genitalia of the female, also referred to as the pudendum.

pudendum
The collective designation for the external female genitalia, also called the vulva.

---

[1]Consider the questions two students asked during a lecture on human sexual biology: Can a woman pee with a tampon in? (yes) Can a man pee with an erection? (not that well) If you didn't know the answers to these questions, this chapter and the next can help!

SEX in Real Life

Female Genital Self-Examination

genital self-examination can teach a woman about her body and make her more comfortable with her genitals. Many female health problems can be identified when changes are detected in the internal or external sexual organs; therefore, self-examination has an important health function as well.

Begin by examining the outside of your genitals; using a hand mirror can help. Using your fingers to spread open the labia majora, try to identify the other external structures—the labia minora, the prepuce, the introitus (opening) of the vagina, and the urethral opening. Look at the way your genitals look while sitting, lying down, standing up, squatting. Feel the different textures of each part of the vagina, and look carefully at the coloration and size of the tissues you can see. Both coloration and size can change with sexual arousal, but such changes are temporary, and the genitals should return to normal within a couple of hours after sexual activity. Any changes over time in color, firmness, or shape of the genitals should be brought to the attention of a health professional.

If it is not uncomfortable, you may want to move back the prepuce, or hood, over the clitoris and try to see the cli-

© Thomas Michael Corcoran/PhotoEdit

Genital self-examination can help a woman become more comfortable with her own body.

toral glans. Though the clitoris is easier to see when erect, note how it fits beneath the prepuce. Note also if there is any whitish material beneath the prepuce; fluids can accumulate and solidify there, and so you should gently clean beneath the prepuce regularly.

If you place a finger inside your vagina, you should be able to feel the pubic bone in the front inside part of your vagina. It is slightly behind the pubic bone that the G-spot is supposed to be, but it is hard for most women to stimulate the G-spot with their own fingers. Squat and press down with your stomach muscles as you push your fingers deeply in the vagina, and at the top of the vagina you may be able to feel your cervix, which feels a little like the tip of your nose. Note how it feels to touch the cervix (some women have a slightly uncomfortable feeling when their cervix is touched). Feeling comfortable inserting your fingers into your vagina will also help you if you choose a barrier method of birth control, such as the contraceptive sponge or cervical cap, all of which must be inserted deep within the vagina at the cervix (see Chapter 13).

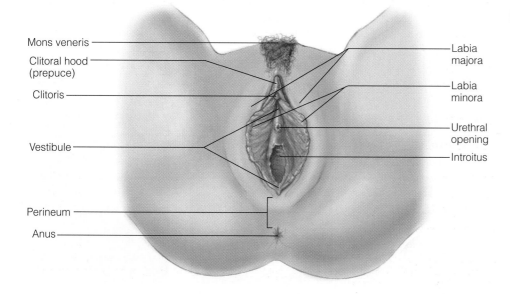

Mons veneris

Clitoral hood (prepuce)

Clitoris

Vestibule

Perineum

Anus

Labia majora

Labia minora

Urethral opening

Introitus

Figure 4.1
The external genital structures of the mature female.

Mons Veneris

mons veneris or mons pubis
The mound of fatty tissue over the female pubic bone, also referred to as mons pubis, meaning "pubic mound."

The fatty cushion resting over the front surface of the pubic bone is called the **mons veneris** or **mons pubis.** The mons veneris becomes covered with pubic hair after puberty, and though it is considered a stimulating place to caress during lovemaking, it serves largely as a protective cushion for the genitals, especially during sexual intercourse. (See Personal Voices, "Pubic Hair: Shaving, Waxing, and Zapping.")

Labia Majora

labia majora
Two longitudinal folds of skin extending downward and backward from the mons pubis of the female.

The **labia majora** (outer lips) (LAY-bee-uh muh-JOR-uh) are two longitudinal folds of fatty tissue that extend from the mons, frame the rest of the female genitalia, and meet at the perineum. The skin of the outer labia majora is pigmented and covered with hair, whereas the inner surface is hairless and contains sebaceous (oil) glands. During sexual excitement, the labia majora fill with blood and engorge, which makes the entire pubic region seem to swell. Because the labia majora are homologous to the male scrotum, the sensation of caressing this area may be similar to that of caressing the scrotum for a male.

Labia Minora

labia minora
Two small folds of mucous membrane lying within the labia majora of the female.

The **labia minora** (inner lips) (LAY-bee-uh muh-NOR-uh) are two smaller pink skin folds situated between the labia majora and the vestibule. They are generally more delicate, shorter, and thinner than the labia majora and join at the clitoris to form the prepuce, the "hood" over the clitoris. The labia minora contain no hair follicles, although they are rich in sebaceous glands. They also contain some erectile tissue and serve to protect the vagina and urethra. During sexual arousal the labia minora will darken although the appearance can differ considerably in different women.

sexbyte

Exposure to the pheromones of male perspiration has been found to improve a woman's mood, reduce tension, increase relaxation, and affect luteinizing hormone (LH) levels (Preti et al., 2003). Changes in LH levels can, in turn, affect the length and timing of menstruation.

The Clitoris

clitoris
An erectile organ of the female located under the prepuce; an organ of sexual pleasure.

prepuce
A loose fold of skin that covers the clitoris.

The **clitoris** (KLIT-uh-rus) is a small cylindrical erectile tissue located under the **prepuce** (PREE-peus). Homologous to the penis, the clitoris is richly supplied with blood vessels as well as nerve endings, and the glans is a particularly sensitive receptor and transmitter of sexual stimuli. In fact, the clitoris, though much smaller, has twice the number of nerve endings as the penis and has a higher concentration of nerve fibers than anywhere else on the body, including the tongue or fingertips (Angier, 1999). In addition, the clitoris is the only human organ whose sole function is to bring sexual pleasure.

The clitoris is difficult to see in many women unless the prepuce is pulled back, though in some women the clitoris may swell enough during sexual excitement to emerge from under the prepuce (see Sex in Real Life, "Female Genital Self-Examination"). It is easy to feel the clitoris, however, by gently grasping the prepuce and rolling it between

The female vulva comes in various sizes and shapes, and the color and quantity of pubic hair differ as well.

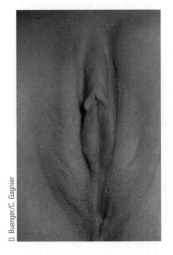

D. Buenger/C. Gagnier

© Susan Lerner/Joel Gordon Photography

Personal Voices

Pubic Hair: Shaving, Waxing, and Zapping

A relatively new development in the sexuality of female college students is pubic hair removal. Products that promote shaving, such as creams, powders, or waxing products, play into the fear that pubic hair is "dirty" or "smelly" and needs to be removed. Changing fashions, such as thong underwear and microscopic bathing suit bottoms, have also contributed to this practice. Outside the United States, perceptions of pubic hair often differ. In fact, women often undergo pubic hair transplants in Korea because pubic hair is seen as a sign of fertility ("Pubic Hair Transplants," 2005).

However, today many students tell me that they have either removed their pubic hair at some point or have decided to remove it forever. Some who have tried it say they like it, but others claim it's uncomfortable because of the new hair growth. There are many ways in which to remove pubic hair. Some women shave, others wax or undergo electrolysis (using electricity to permanently destroy the hair follicle). A "Brazilian" wax removes all of a woman's pubic hair, whereas a traditional "bikini" wax removes hair that grows outside the bikini line. Many of these procedures are painful, but the level of discomfort depends on a woman's skin sensitivity. Some gynecological healthcare providers have noted an increase in pubic hair trimming or removal in their offices (Ursus, 2004).

Following are some opinions on the subject of shaving pubic hair:

"I always thought that pubic hair was like the hair on your head, it grows there, so it was meant to be there. The first time I did it, I thought I looked like a 10-year-old little girl, but I thought it looked cool! Now I always shave and think it's a lot "neater" and looks pretty! I have become very good at designing my pubic hair. I can make hearts, and a "J" for my first name. If I'm not seeing anyone, you can bet that it hasn't seen the Bic in a while! Sometimes I do that on purpose, because I know that if I'm not trimmed up all nice then there is no way that I will let anyone go near there!"—*20-year-old female*

"I have never shaved my pubic hair, nor will I ever. I think it would be too strange and would feel gross. My partners have never complained."—*21-year-old female*

"My girlfriend always shaves her pubic hair, and I love it. I can't imagine her being hairy down there, it would be gross. We've experimented with me shaving, but it's really not the same. I think sex feels better for her with no hair to get in the way."—*20-year-old male*

"I have a Brazilian wax once every couple months and I love it. It feels so clean and I think it lets my partner know I care about good hygiene."—*21-year-old female*

"I have no desire to shave my pubic hair. I think my husband would probably like it, but that's too bad, because it's my body and I don't have the energy to maintain a shaved pussy."—*38-year-old female*

---

the fingers. In fact, most women do not enjoy direct stimulation of the clitoris and prefer stimulation through the prepuce. It is important to clean under the prepuce, for secretions can accumulate underneath as a material known as smegma. As in men, smegma can harden and cause pain and, if left uncleaned, can produce an unpleasant odor.

In some cultures, the clitoris is removed surgically in a ritual **circumcision,** often referred to as a **clitorectomy.** Other parts of the vulva can also be removed in a procedure known as **infibulation** (in-fib-you-LAY-shun). We will discuss the controversy over this practice later in this chapter.

The Vestibule

The **vestibule** is the name for the entire region between the labia minora and can be clearly seen when the labia are held apart. The vestibule contains the opening of the urethra and the vagina and the ducts of Bartholin's glands.

The Urethral Meatus The opening, or meatus (mee-AYE-tuss), to the urethra (yoo-REE-thruh) lies between the vagina and the clitoris. The urethra, which brings urine from the bladder to be excreted, is much shorter in women than in men, where it

circumcision
Surgical removal of the clitoris in women; also referred to as clitorectomy.

clitorectomy
Surgical removal of the clitoris; also referred to as circumcision.

infibulation
The ritual removal of the clitoris, prepuce, and labia and the sewing together of the vestibule. Although this is practiced in many African societies, today many are working to eliminate the practice.

vestibule
The entire region between the labia minora, including the urethra and introitus.

Urinary Tract Infections

Sexually active young women are one of the most at-risk populations for the development of urinary tract infections (UTIs; Orenstein & Wong, 1999), and many women experience one or more UTIs while in college (Ellen-Rinsza & Kirk, 2005). It is estimated that 1 in 5 women will develop a UTI in her lifetime (Hooton, 2003) and that 20% of these women will experience a recurrence of the UTI after treatment.

There are several physiological and behavioral reasons this is so. Physiologically, women have shorter urethras than men, which allows bacteria to enter into the bladder (Azam, 2000; Kunin, 1997). Bacteria can be present in the rectum or around the vaginal tissues and during sexual intercourse, this bacteria is often forced up into the urethra. College-aged women may also have several sexual partners, which also increases the risk of developing a UTI (Sobel, 1997). Other factors that have been found to be related to the development of UTIs includes retaining urine for an extended time period (i.e., not going to use the bathroom when a woman first feels the need to urinate), wearing thong underwear, frequent bubble baths, and the use of scented feminine hygiene products.

Normal urine is free from bacteria and viruses. When bacteria do get into the urethra they can quickly multiply and cause an infection. The majority of UTIs are caused by *Escherichia coli* (E. coli; Walsh et al., 1997). Common symptoms include an increased urge to urinate and pain and/or burning in the urethra or bladder. Most of the time there is also pain during urination and, even though frequency of urinating increases, the volume of urine decreases significantly. The urine may look cloudy and, in severe cases, may even have blood in it.

Any woman who experiences any of these symptoms of UTI should immediately seek medical care. If the pain is severe and a healthcare provider is unavailable, an over-the-counter medication called Uristat® can help lessen the painful symptoms associated with the infection. However, Uristat will not cure a UTI. It is imperative that women who suspect a UTI undergo urine testing for bacteria. If bacteria are present, UTIs are most often treated with antibacterial drugs (such as Bactrim™, Amoxil™, or Cipro™). Additional medications may be prescribed to treat the pain during urination; but, if caught early, most UTIs can be cured within a few days. Women who have had three UTIs are likely to continue experiencing them. If you do have frequent UTIs, you should talk to your healthcare provider about options. Scientists are currently working on a vaccine to prevent UTIs (Schmidhammer et al., 2002).

To help decrease the likelihood that you or someone you know acquires a UTI, it is important to:
1. Drink plenty of water
2. Urinate before and after sexual intercourse
3. Urinate as soon as you have the urge to go
4. Wipe the vulva from front to back to avoid bringing bacteria from the anus
5. Avoid feminine hygiene sprays, douches, and frequent bubble baths
6. Avoid thong and noncotton underwear
7. Change damp clothing immediately after exercise
8. Increase intake of unsweetened cranberry juice and/or vitamin C. Both of these can increase the acidity of urine and interfere with the ability of the bacteria to adhere to bladder tissue ("Cranberry and urinary tract infection," 2005).

---

urinary tract infection
Infection of the urinary tract, often resulting in a frequent urge to urinate, painful burning in the bladder or urethra during urination, and fatigue.

introitus
Entrance to the vagina.

hymen
A thin fold of vascularized mucous membrane at the vaginal opening.

imperforate hymen
An abnormally closed hymen that usually does not allow the exit of menstrual fluid.

goes through the penis. This is the reason that women are much more susceptible to **urinary tract infections** (see Sex in Real Life, "Urinary Tract Infections").

The Introitus and the Hymen   The entrance, or **introitus** (in-TROID-us), of the vagina also lies in the vestibule. The introitus is usually covered at birth by a fold of tissue known as the **hymen** (HIGH-men). The hymen varies in thickness and extent and is sometimes absent. The center of the hymen is usually perforated, and it is through this perforation that the menstrual flow leaves the vagina and that a tampon is inserted. If the hymen is intact, it will usually rupture easily and tear at several points during the first intercourse, often accompanied by a small amount of blood. If the woman is sexually excited and well lubricated, the rupture of the hymen usually does not cause more than a brief moment's discomfort. In rare cases a woman has an **imperforate hymen,** which is usually detected because her menstrual flow is blocked. A simple surgical procedure can open the imperforate hymen.

An intact hymen has been a symbol of "purity" throughout history, a sign that a woman has not had sexual intercourse. Lady Diana Spencer was required to undergo a physical examination to certify that her hymen was intact before her engagement to

Female Genital Mutilation

Female genital mutilation, also known as female circumcision or infibulation, is practiced in many parts of Africa and in a few other countries around the world. This operation has been performed throughout history to distinguish "respectable" women from prostitutes or slaves. Controlling "excessive" female sexual desire is one of the major reasons cited (Ugboma et al., 2004). Many cultures believe that unless the source of female pleasure is removed, women will become promiscuous or cheat on their husbands. As of 2004, it was estimated that 132 million women worldwide had undergone female genital mutilation (Daley, 2004). The procedure is usually done between the ages of 4 and 8, though in some cultures it is performed later (Dare et al., 2004).

Female genital mutilation is often done without anesthesia or antiseptic. In female circumcision the clitoris is removed, whereas infibulation involves the removal of the clitoris and the sewing of the labia tissues. The least severe form of circumcision involves lightly cutting the clitoris in order to cause bleeding but not excessive damage (Magoha & Magoha, 2000). The tip of the clitoris may also be removed, but the body of the clitoris is left intact.

The most severe type of circumcision involves the complete removal of the clitoris and labia minora and also the scraping of the labia majora with knives, broken bottles, or razor blades (Carcopino et al., 2004). The remaining tissue is sewn together, leaving a matchstick-sized hole to allow for the passing of urine and menstrual blood. The young girl's legs are then bound together with rope, and she is immobilized for anywhere from 14 to 40 days for the circumcision to heal. The tighter the girl's infibulation, the higher the bride price will be for her. The majority of these procedures are performed by medically untrained personnel (Dare et al., 2004).

Female genital mutilation can cause pain, urinary complications and/or dysfunction, shock, hemorrhage, infection, scarring, recurrent urinary infections, retention of menses at menarche, vulval cysts, and pelvic inflammatory disease (Nour, 2004). Of these symptoms, severe pain and bleeding are most common (Dare et al., 2004). A woman who has been infibulated will require surgery during childbirth delivery (Carcopino et al., 2004).

The day that a woman is circumcised is thought to be the most important day in her life, and it is accompanied in most cultures by rituals. Because menstruation is often very difficult through the pinhole opening, marriage usually takes place soon after menstruation begins. Marital penetration of the infibulation can take anywhere from 3 to 4 days to several months, and, in 15% of cases, men are unable to penetrate their wives at all. Often penetration results in severe pain, hemorrhaging, or infection, which may lead to death (Morrone et al., 2002). Anal intercourse is common in some of these cultures, because the vagina may not be penetrable. Approximately one-fifth of all women who undergo genital mutilation report wanting their daughters to also undergo the surgery (Dare et al., 2004).

Recently, there has been controversy over what Americans and others should do to try to discourage this practice. The United States has been strongly opposed to the practice of female genital mutilation and has worked hard to help reduce the practice. However, the rate at which women continue to undergo the procedure has not declined as rapidly as experts had hoped (Adams, 2004). Female circumcision is actually illegal in many of the countries where it is practiced, but it is hard to end a deeply ingrained social practice, especially among the rural and tribal peoples who have been performing the ritual for many centuries. The most common reason given for undergoing such procedures is culture and tradition (Carcopino et al., 2004; Dare et al., 2004). Some argue that those outside of Africa have no right to comment on a religious ritual, just as Africans have no right to oppose the circumcision of American males. However, African governments and other groups are beginning to make some headway in decreasing the prevalence of this practice.

Prince Charles was made public. In reality, many activities can shred the hymen, including vigorous exercise, horseback or bike riding, masturbation, or the insertion of tampons or other objects into the vagina. Still, in many cultures during many historical eras, the absence of bloodstained sheets on the wedding night was enough to condemn a woman as "wanton" (promiscuous), and some knowing mothers encouraged their newlywed daughters to have a little vial of blood from a chicken or other animal to pour on the sheet of their bridal bed, just in case. Although virginity "testing" (to check for an intact hymen) has been against the law in some countries, illegal virginity tests are routinely performed (Pelin, 1999). Reconstructive surgery to repair a ruptured hymen is practiced in some countries (such as Turkey), but because of fear of repercussions, many physicians are afraid to perform these surgeries (Cindoglu, 1997).

There has been enough demand from women who desire "hymen-plasty" that today a handful of physicians offer the procedure. Hymen reconstruction is a procedure in which the mucous membranes in the vagina are sewn together to make a woman appear to be a virgin (Azam, 2000). Women from Middle Eastern cultures and many American and Canadian women have undergone such procedures.

Bartholin's Glands   The "greater vestibular glands," or **Bartholin's** (BAR-tha-lenz) **glands,** are bean-shaped glands whose ducts empty into the vestibule in the middle of the labia minora. Historically, Bartholin's glands have been presumed to provide lubrication for penile penetration of the vagina; however, they do not actually secrete enough lubrication for intercourse (Blumstein, 2001). It is also thought that they might be responsible for creating a genital scent. The Bartholin's glands can become infected and form a cyst or abscess. When this happens, a woman experiences pain and swelling in the labial and vaginal areas. This is most common in women between the ages of 20 and 29 years old (Aghajanian et al., 1994).

The Perineum   The **perineum** (pear-uh-NEE-um) is the tissue between the vagina and the anus. During childbirth, the baby can stretch the perineum, and in some women, it may tear or a doctor may do an **episiotomy** to allow more room for the baby's head to emerge (we will discuss this more in Chapter 12).

Bartholin's glands

A pair of glands on either side of the vaginal opening that open by a duct into the space between the hymen and the labia minora; also referred to as the greater vestibular glands.

perineum

Area between the vagina and the anus.

episiotomy

A surgical incision made in the perineum toward the end of labor to allow the baby to pass through.

Review Question

Identify and discuss the functions of the external female sexual organs.

sex byte

Approximately 1 baby girl in 4,000 is born without a vagina (Hamilton, 2002).

SEX Talk

Question: *I've always been worried about the size and shape of my vaginal lips. They just seem too big and floppy. At this point, I'm so embarrassed about them that I can't imagine ever being comfortable showing them to anyone. Is there anything I can do to fix them?*

It's important to remember that vulvas come in a variety of different shapes and sizes. Some women have long labial lips, whereas others have shorter ones. With the introduction of smaller swimsuits, bikini waxes, and exposure to various pornographic images, many women today are feeling increased pressure to have the "perfect vulva." Concerns like yours are common and it's important to know that what you describe is perfectly normal.

However, there are some women that are so concerned about their vulva that they opt for vaginal plastic surgery. Vaginoplasty (tightening of the vaginal muscles) and labiaplasty (reduction of the labia minora) are two of the most popular vaginal procedures, even though they can cost up to $8,000. Research indicates these procedures are not without risk—reduced sensation and/or impaired sexual functioning are common side effects (Navarro, 2004). My advice would be to make peace with your vulva and don't be brainwashed into believing there is a perfect vulva!

Internal Sex Organs

Now that we've covered the female's external sex organs, let's move inside and explore the internal sex organs. The internal female sex organs include the vagina, uterus, Fallopian tubes, and the ovaries (see Figures 4.2 and 4.3).

The Vagina

vagina

A thin-walled muscular tube that leads from the uterus to the vestibule and is used for sexual intercourse, a passageway for menstrual fluid, sperm, and a newborn baby.

The **vagina** is a thin-walled tube extending from the cervix of the uterus to the external genitalia and serves as the female organ of intercourse, a passageway for the arriving sperm, and a canal through which menstrual fluid and babies can pass from the uterus. It is tilted toward the back in most women and so forms a 90-degree angle with the uterus, which is commonly tilted forward (see Figure 4.2). The vagina is approximately 4 inches in length when relaxed but contains numerous folds that help it expand some-

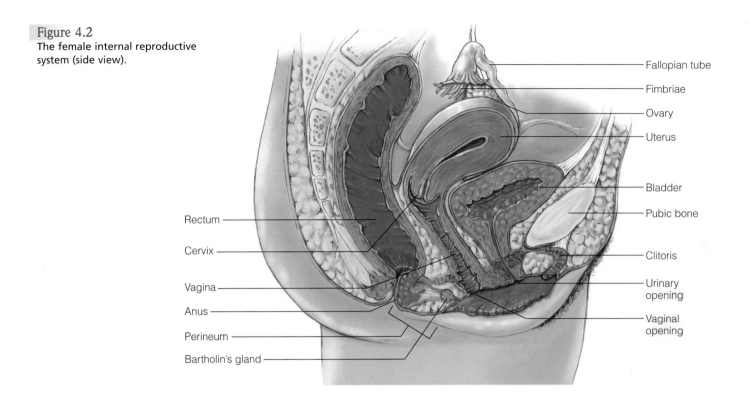

Figure 4.2
The female internal reproductive system (side view).

Fallopian tube

Fimbriae

Ovary

Uterus

Bladder

Pubic bone

Clitoris

Urinary opening

Vaginal opening

Rectum

Cervix

Vagina

Anus

Perineum

Bartholin's gland

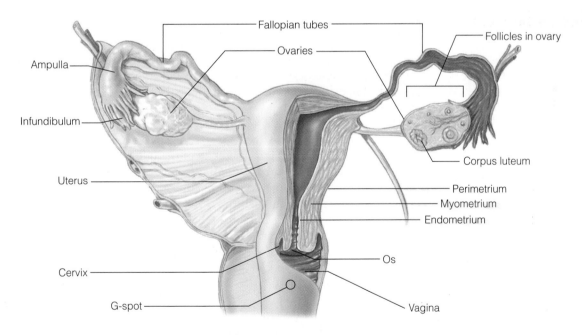

Figure 4.3
The female internal reproductive system (front view).

Fallopian tubes

Ovaries

Follicles in ovary

Ampulla

Infundibulum

Uterus

Cervix

G-spot

Corpus luteum

Perimetrium

Myometrium

Endometrium

Os

Vagina

what like an accordion. The vagina can expand to accommodate a penis during intercourse and can stretch four to five times its normal size during childbirth.

The vagina does not itself contain glands but lubricates through small openings on the vaginal walls during engorgement, almost as if the vagina is sweating, and by mucus produced from glands on the cervix. Although the first third of the vaginal tube is well endowed with nerve endings, the inner two-thirds are practically without tactile sensation; in fact, minor surgery can be done on the inner part of the vagina without anesthesia.

The Grafenberg Spot and Female Ejaculation

The **Grafenberg spot (G-spot)** and female ejaculation are two controversial issues in the field of human sexuality. The G-spot, first described by Ernest Grafenberg in 1950, is a spot about the size of a dime or quarter in the lower third of the front part of the vagina and is particularly sensitive to stimulation (Whipple, 2000). The G-spot is found about 2 or 3 inches up the anterior (front or stomach) side of the vagina, just past the pubic bone (see Figure 4.3). There is some controversy over whether this spot is a separate physiological entity, with some arguing that the entire anterior wall (and even parts of the posterior wall) of the vagina is generally sensitive (Alzate & Hoch, 1986). Others argue that the G-spot is homologous to the male prostate.

Stimulating the G-spot causes pleasant vaginal sensation in some women and can result in powerful orgasms accompanied by the forceful expulsion of fluid (female ejaculation). Women may ejaculate up to 4 ounces of fluid, which may come from the Skenes glands on either side of the urethra (Heath, 1984); however, some researchers argue that female ejaculate is chemically indistinguishable from urine (Alzate, 1985).

The Uterus

The **uterus** is a thick-walled, hollow, muscular organ in the pelvis sandwiched between the bladder in front and the rectum behind. It is approximately the shape of an inverted pear, with a dome-shaped top (fundus), a hollow body, and the doughnut-shaped cervix at the bottom. The uterus provides a path for sperm to reach the **ovum,** undergoes a cycle of change every month that leads to menstruation, nourishes and protects the fetus during gestation, and provides the contractions for expulsion of the mature fetus during labor. The uterus is about 3 inches long and flares to about 2 inches wide, but it increases greatly in size and weight during and after a pregnancy and atrophies after menopause.

The uterine wall is about 1 inch thick and is made up of three layers (see Figure 4.3). The outer layer, or **perimetrium,** is part of the tissue that covers most abdominal organs. The muscular layer of the uterus, the **myometrium,** contracts to expel menstrual fluid and to push the fetus out of the womb during delivery. The inner layer of the uterus, the **endometrium,** responds to fluctuating hormonal levels, and its outer portion is shed with each menstrual cycle.

The Cervix. The **cervix** (SERV-ix) is the lower portion of the uterus that contains the opening, or **os,** leading into the body of the uterus. It is through the os that menstrual fluid flows out of the uterus and that sperm gain entrance. Glands of the cervix secrete mucus with varying properties during the monthly cycle; during **ovulation,** the mucus helps sperm transport through the os, and during infertile periods, it can block the sperm from entering. During childbirth, the cervix softens and the os dilates to allow the baby to pass through. The cervix can be seen with a mirror during a pelvic exam, and women should not hesitate to ask their gynecologist or other medical professional to show it to them. The cervix can also be felt at the top end of the vagina.

The Fallopian Tubes

Fallopian (fuh-LOH-pee-un) **tubes,** also called **oviducts,** are 4-inch-long trumpet-shaped tubes that extend laterally from the sides of the uterus. From the side of the uterus, the tube expands into an ampulla, or widening, which curves around to a trumpet-shaped end, the **infundibulum** (in-fun-DIB-bue-lum). At the end of the infundibulum there are fingerlike projections that curl around the ovary, poised to accept ova when they are released (see Figure 4.3).

Once a month an ovary releases an ovum that is swept into the Fallopian tube by the waving action of the **fimbriae** (FIM-bree-ee). The fimbriae sense the chemical messages released from the ovary that signal the release of the ovum and begin a series of

Grafenberg spot (G-spot)
A structure that is said to lie on the anterior (front) wall of the vagina and is reputed to be a seat of sexual pleasure when stimulated.

uterus
The hollow muscular organ in females that is the site of menstruation, implantation of the fertilized ovum, and labor; also referred to as the womb.

ovum
The female reproductive cell or gamete; plural is ova.

perimetrium
The outer wall of the uterus.

myometrium
The smooth muscle layer of the uterus.

endometrium
The mucous membrane lining the uterus.

cervix
The doughnut-shaped bottom part of the uterus that protrudes into the top of the vagina.

os
The opening of the cervix that allows passage between the vagina and the uterus.

ovulation
The phase of the menstrual cycle in which an ovum is released.

Fallopian tubes
Two ducts that transport ova from the ovary to the uterus; also referred to as oviducts.

oviducts
Another name for the Fallopian tubes.

infundibulum
The funnel- or trumpet-shaped open end of the Fallopian tubes.

fimbriae
The branched, fingerlike border at the end of each Fallopian tube.

muscular contractions to help move the ovum down the tube. If the Fallopian tube is long and flexible, it may even be able to catch the released ovum from the opposite ovary; some women with a single active ovary on one side and a single functioning Fallopian tube on the other have been known to get pregnant (Nilsson, 1990).

The inner surface of the Fallopian tubes are covered by cilia (hairlike projections) whose constant beating action creates a current along which the ovum is conducted toward the uterus. The entire transit time from ovulation until arrival inside the uterus is normally about 3 days. Fertilization of the ovum usually takes place in the ampulla because, after the first 12 to 24 hours, postovulation fertilization is no longer possible. Occasionally, the fertilized ovum implants in the Fallopian tube instead of the uterus, causing a potentially dangerous ectopic pregnancy (see Chapter 12).

The Ovaries

The mature ovary is a light-gray structure most commonly described as the size and shape of a large almond shell. With age, the ovaries become smaller and firmer, and after menopause they become difficult for gynecologists to feel. The ovaries have a dual responsibility—to produce ova and to secrete hormones.

The ovary is the repository of oocytes, also known as ova, or eggs, in the female. A women is born with approximately 250,000 ova in each ovary, each sitting in its own primary follicle (Rome, 1998). Approximately 300 to 500 of these will develop into mature eggs during a woman's reproductive years (Macklon & Fauser, 2000). The primary follicle contains an immature ovum surrounded by a thin layer of follicular cells. Follicle stimulating hormone (FSH) and luteinizing hormone (LH) are released in sequence by the pituitary gland during each menstrual cycle, causing about 20 primary follicles at a time to begin maturing. Usually only one follicle finishes maturing each month, which is then termed a secondary follicle, containing a secondary oocyte. At ovulation, the secondary follicle bursts, and the ovum begins its journey down the Fallopian tube. The surface of a mature ovary is thus usually pitted and dimpled at sites of previous ovulations.

Ovulation can occur each month from either the right or left ovary. No one knows why one or the other ovary releases an ovum any given month; sometimes they take turns, and sometimes they do not. It seems to be mostly a matter of chance. If one ovary is removed, however, the other ovary will often ovulate every month (Nilsson, 1990). The ovaries are also the female's most important producer of female sex hormones, such as estrogen, which we will discuss later in this chapter.

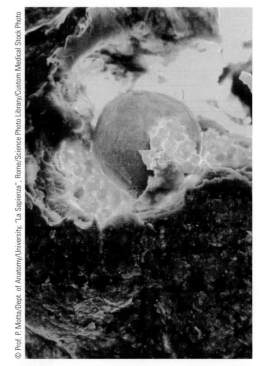

© Prof. P. Motta/Dept. of Anatomy/University, "La Sapienza," Rome/Science Photo Library/Custom Medical Stock Photo

This photo shows the release of a mature ovum at ovulation. The ovum (red) is surrounded by remnants of cells and liquid from the ruptured ovarian follicle. Mature ova develop in the ovaries from follicles that remained dormant until sexual maturity.

Review Question

Identify and discuss the functions of the internal female sexual organs.

SEX Talk

Question: *My girlfriend told me that my penis is too large for her vagina and that it causes her pain during intercourse. How far can the vagina expand?*

Although it is true that the vagina expands and lengthens during sexual arousal, not every vagina expands to the same degree. If a man's penis is very large, it can bump against the woman's cervix during thrusting, which can cause discomfort. In such cases it is particularly important to make sure the woman is fully aroused before attempting penetration and to try a variety of positions to find which is most comfortable for her. The female superior position or the rear entry positions (see Chapter 10) may help her control the depth of penetration. Either partner's hand around the base of the penis (depending on the position) may also prevent full penetration, as will some devices such as "cock rings," which are sold through adult catalogues or in adult stores. If the woman's pain continues, she should consult with her gynecologist to rule out a physiological problem and to get more advice and information.

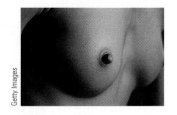
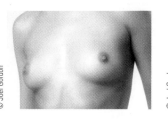

The female breast is mostly fatty tissue and can take various shapes and sizes.

Getty Images

© Joel Gordon

© Joel Gordon

Other Sex Organs

Reproductive organs are not the only organs involved in a woman's sex life. The secondary sex characteristics of a woman also contribute to sexual pleasure. Although most people consider the breast a sexual part of the body, other erogenous zones may not be as obvious.

SEX Talk

Question: *I recently had both my nipples pierced and I'm wondering how this might affect my ability to breast-feed in the future. Is there any research on nipple piercing and breast-feeding?*

Body piercing has experienced a resurgence over the last few years (Armstrong et al., 2004; Caliendo et al., 2005). Men and women today pierce their navels, eyebrows, noses, lips, tongues, nipples, and even genitals! Although the research is sparse, it appears that there are no long-term breast-feeding issues in women with pierced nipples. Each nipple has several milk ducts, so even if there were scarring in one area, other areas could potentially make up for it. In addition, the majority of nipple piercings are done horizontally, which is better for future breast-feeding (Martin, 1999). Many piercers recommend not piercing within 1 year of giving birth because piercings need time to heal. Generally this can take anywhere from 3 to 6 months. Jewelry should be removed prior to breast-feeding, although some women choose to breast-feed with jewelry intact. Doing so, however, increases the risk of injury to the child.

nipple
A pigmented, wrinkled protuberance on the surface of the breast that contains ducts for the release of milk.

areola
The pigmented ring around the nipple of the breast.

lactation
The collective name for milk creation, secretion, and ejection from the nipple.

prolactin
A hormone secreted by the pituitary gland that initiates and maintains milk secretion.

oxytocin
A hormone secreted by the hypothalamus that stimulates contraction of both the uterus for delivery of the newborn and the mammary gland ducts for lactation.

The Breasts

Breasts, or mammary glands, are modified sweat glands that produce milk to nourish a newborn child. The breasts contain fatty tissue and milk-producing glands and are capped by a **nipple** surrounded by a round, pigmented area called the **areola** (ah-REE-oh-luh). Each breast contains between 15 and 20 lobes, made up of a number of compartments that contain alveoli, the milk-secreting glands. Alveoli empty into secondary tubules, which in turn pass the milk into the mammary ducts and then into the lactiferous sinuses, where the milk is stored until the lactiferous ducts release it from the nipple (Figure 4.4). When **lactation** begins, infant suckling stimulates the posterior pituitary gland to release **prolactin,** which signals milk synthesis, and **oxytocin,** which allows the milk to be ejected.

Most people see the breasts as an erogenous zone and include stimulation of the breasts in sexual arousal and masturbation. Some women can even experience orgasm from breast and nipple stimulation alone. But many women in American society are uncomfortable about the size and shape of their breasts. Because breasts are a constant source of attention in our society and are considered an important part of a woman's attractiveness, women may worry that their breasts are unattractive, too small, or too large. Yet the ideal breast differs in other cultures. For example, large breasts are valued in the United States, and so over 80% of breast surgeries are performed to increase the size of the bust. In France, however, the majority of surgical alterations of the breasts are to decrease their size! Although there has been a cultural emphasis on larger breasts in

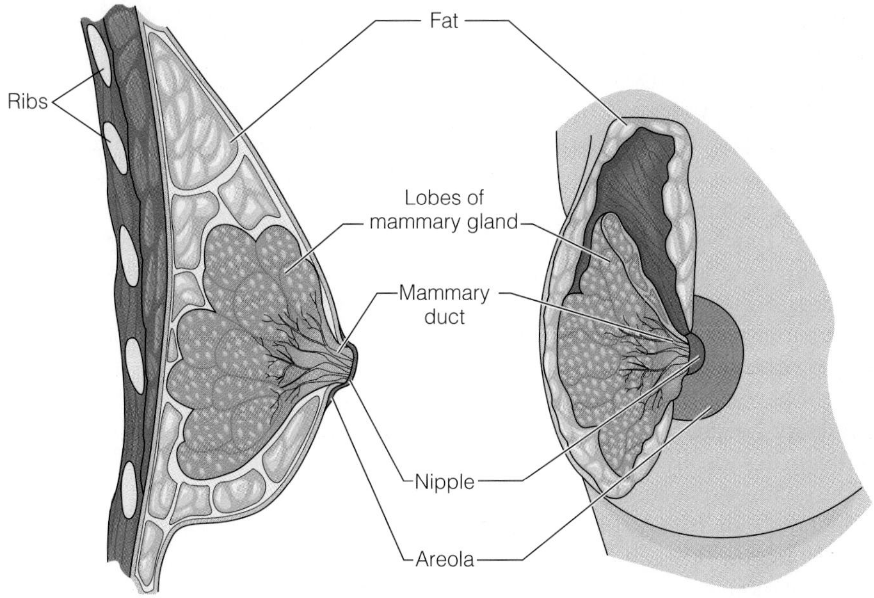

Figure 4.4
The female breast.

the United States, there has been a significant decrease in the chest size preferred by women overall (Tantleff-Dunn, 2001).

Other Erogenous Zones

There are many other erogenous zones on the body that can be considered part of a woman's sexual organ system. In fact, the largest sexual organ of all is the skin, and there is no part of it that cannot be aroused if caressed in the right way at the right time during lovemaking. Some of the more common erogenous areas include the lips or the ears, but others, such as the back of the knee, the armpit, or the base of the neck, for example, may be stimulating to certain people. Some people find stimulation of the anus, or anal intercourse, extremely erotic, whereas others do not. Of course, the most important sexual organ is one that you can stimulate only indirectly—the brain.

🌀 THE FEMALE MATURATION CYCLE

Now that we've discussed the female sexual and reproductive system, let's explore female maturation. The female reproductive system undergoes cyclic hormonal events that lead to pubertal changes, menstruation, and eventually, menopause.

Female Puberty

After birth, the female's sexual development progresses slowly until puberty. The first stirrings of puberty, usually begin at about age 8, but can begin as late as 14 or 15. Puberty lasts from 3 to 5 years on average.

No one really knows how the body knows its own age or that it is time for puberty to begin. Newer research suggests that the onset of puberty may be related to weight—girls who are overweight begin menstruating earlier than those who are average or underweight (Biro et al., 2003). The onset of puberty can also vary with race. For example, African American girls reach puberty earlier than Caucasian girls (Kaplowitz et al., 2001). African American girls begin puberty between 8 and 9 years of age, a good 1 to 1-$\frac{1}{2}$ years earlier than Caucasian girls (Herman-Giddens & Slora, 1997). No one really understands why this is, although some researchers believe it could be due to weight differences (Adair & Gordon-Larsen, 2001).

sex byte

The Brava™ Breast Enhancement system, a battery-operated microprocessor connected to domes that a woman wears under her bra, creates a suction that stretches the breast cells and encourages them to grow (C. J. Smith et al., 2002). This expensive device (around $1,000) must be worn for at least 10 hours per day for 10 to 16 weeks to result in an average one-cup gain in size. Some women use the device to improve symmetry in asymmetrical breasts.

Review **Question**

Discuss female erogenous zones.

When puberty begins, a girl's internal clock signals the pituitary gland to begin secreting the hormones FSH and LH, which stimulate the ovaries to produce estrogen while the girl sleeps. Between the ages of 11 and 14, FSH and LH levels begin to increase during the day as well.

As puberty continues, the ovaries, in response to stimulation by the pituitary gland, begin to release more and more estrogen into the circulatory system. Estrogen is responsible for the development and maturation of female primary and secondary sexual characteristics. Under its influence, the Fallopian tubes, the uterus, and the vagina all mature and increase in size. The breasts also begin to develop as fat deposits increase and the elaborate duct system develops. The pelvis broadens and changes from a narrow funnel-like outlet to a broad oval outlet, flaring the hips. The skin remains soft and smooth under estrogen's influence, fat cells increase in number in the buttocks and thighs, and pubic hair develops. The growing end of certain longer bones in the body, which are responsible for height, fuses with the bone shaft, and growth stops. (In the absence of estrogen, females usually grow several inches taller than average.)

The changes that accompany puberty prepare the woman for mature sexuality, pregnancy, and childbirth. At some point during puberty, usually at about the age of 11 or 12, the woman will begin to ovulate. Most women are unable to feel any internal signs during ovulation. In a few women, however, a slight pain or sensation accompanies ovulation, referred to as **mittelschmerz.** The pain may result from a transitory irritation caused by the small amount of blood and fluid released at the site of the ruptured follicle. An increase in female sexual interest around this time may be triggered by a rise in various hormones, most notably testosterone (Halpern et al., 1997).

The beginning of ovulation often closely corresponds to **menarche** (MEN-are-kee) in most girls, though some may begin menstruating a few months before their first ovulation, whereas others may ovulate a few times before their first full menstrual cycle. In the first year after menarche, 80% of menstrual cycles are anovulatory (do not involve ovulation; Oriel & Schrager, 1999).

In some cultures in the past, as soon as a girl reached menarche, she was considered ready to marry and begin bearing children. In our culture, the age of menarche has been steadily falling, and most people believe that there is a difference between being physiologically capable of bearing children and being psychologically ready for sexual intercourse and childbearing. In Chapter 8, we will discuss the psychological and emotional changes of female puberty.

Menstruation

Menstruation (also referred to as a "period") is the name for the monthly bleeding that the majority of healthy women of reproductive age experience. The menstrual cycle lasts from 24 to 35 days, but the average is 28 (meaning there are 28 days from the first day of bleeding to the next first day of bleeding). During the cycle, the lining of the uterus builds up and prepares for a pregnancy. When there is no pregnancy, menstruation occurs, and the lining of the uterus is released in the form of blood and tissue. A cycle of hormones controls the buildup of the uterine lining and the release of fluid. The main reason for a menstrual cycle is to enable a woman to become pregnant.

Earlier we discussed how African American girls often enter puberty earlier than Caucasian girls, so it should come as no surprise that African American girls begin menstruating earlier than Caucasian girls (Herman-Giddens & Slora, 1997). The Add Health data, which we discussed in Chapter 2, enabled researchers to compare racial and ethnic differences in menarche onset. African American and Hispanic girls experienced menarche before the age of 11, whereas Asian girls reached menarche at 14 or later (Adair & Gordon-Larsen, 2001). Girls who have earlier menarche have been found to be shorter and heavier than those who have later menarche, presumably due to the fact that heavier girls have higher estrogen levels (see Sex in Real Life, "Age of Menarche").

The menstrual cycle can be divided into four general phases: the follicular phase, ovulation, the luteal phase, and the menstrual phase (see Figure 4.5). The **follicular phase** begins after the last menstruation has been completed and lasts anywhere from 6 to 13 days. Only a thin layer of endometrial cells remains from the last menstruation. As

---

mittelschmerz
German for "middle pain." A pain in the abdomen or pelvis that some women feel at ovulation.

menarche
The start of menstrual cycling, usually during early puberty.

Review Question

Identify and explain the physiological changes that signal the onset of puberty.

sex byte

The menstrual cycle has been found to affect women's mate preferences (Clark, 2005). During ovulation (high fertility), research has found that women prefer a handsome and/or creative partner, whereas during low fertility points in the menstrual cycle, she is more likely to prefer earning power over looks and creativity.

follicular phase
First phase of the menstrual cycle that begins after the last menstruation has been completed.

Age of Menarche

Menarche is the "hallmark maturation event" in young girls (Towne et al., 2005). In the United States, the average age of first menarche is 12.7 years, but the age has been steadily decreasing each decade (Remsberg et al., 2005). One hundred years ago, the average age of first menstruation was about 16 years old. Over the last 20 to 30 years, however, decreases in age of first menarche have been small (Whincup et al., 2001). In other, less-developed countries, the age of menarche is later. For example, in rural Chile, the average age of first menarche is close to 14 years old (Dittmar, 2000). Environmental factors, such as high altitudes and poor nutrition, can delay the age at which a girl begins menstruating. In fact, girls with poor nutrition and with substandard living conditions begin menstruating later than girls with either adequate nutrition or adequate living standards (Dittmar, 2000). It is hard to say exactly why this is. There is also a heritability component to the age at which a woman menstruates—many girls reach menarche and menopause at approximately the same age as their biological mothers (Towne et al., 2005).

Severe exercise regimens, such as long distance running or intense ballet dancing, may delay puberty in young girls. The onset of puberty is triggered by the acquisition of a certain body weight and appropriate fat-to-muscle ratio (Warren et al., 2002). Research has also found that family stress may be associated with an earlier entrance into puberty for girls (K. Kim & Smith, 1999; Ravert & Martin, 1997). Moderate to high levels of stress tend to stimulate early maturation in girls.

There is some evidence to suggest that girls who reach menarche earlier may be at risk for developing physical problems, including high blood pressure and/or glucose intolerance (Remsberg et al., 2005). In addition, those girls who reached menarche before the age of 11 have been found to be more "norm breaking," having earlier sexual experiences, less academic education in adulthood, and less body satisfaction (Johansson & Ritzen, 2005).

---

the follicles in the ovaries begin to ripen with the next cycle's ova, estrogen released by the ovaries stimulates regrowth of the endometrium's outer layer, to about 2 to 5 millimeters thick.

During the **ovulation phase,** an ovum is released, usually about the 14th day of the cycle. The particulars of ovulation were described in the preceding section on the ovaries and Fallopian tubes. The third phase is the **luteal phase.** Immediately following ovulation, a small, pouchlike gland, the **corpus luteum,** forms on the ovary. The corpus luteum secretes additional progesterone and estrogen for 10 to 12 days, which causes further growth of the cells in the endometrium and increases the blood supply to the lining of the uterus. The endometrium reaches a thickness of 4 to 6 millimeters during this stage (about a quarter of an inch) in preparation to receive and nourish a fertilized egg.

ovulation phase
The second stage of the general menstrual cycle, when the ovum is released.

luteal phase
Third phase of the menstrual cycle, following ovulation, when the corpus luteum forms.

corpus luteum
A yellowish endocrine gland in the ovary formed when a follicle has discharged its secondary oocyte.

SEX Talk

Question: When I started college, I began having very severe menstrual cramps—often to the point of nausea, fatigue, and backache. What causes bad cramps, and how can I reduce them?

Menstrual cramps are usually caused by prostaglandins, which stimulate the uterus to contract and expel the endometrial lining during menstruation. The uterine muscles are powerful (remember that the muscles help push an infant out at birth), and the menstrual contractions can be strong and are sometimes quite painful. However, there are many things that can make the cramps worse. Poor eating habits, an increase in stress, alcohol use, insufficient sleep, and a lack of exercise can aggravate the problem. Reducing salt, sugar, and caffeine intake; moderate exercise; warm baths; and gentle massage of the lower back sometimes help, as do antiprostaglandin pain relievers, such as ibuprofen. Orgasm, either through masturbation or with a partner, also helps many women relieve menstrual cramps.

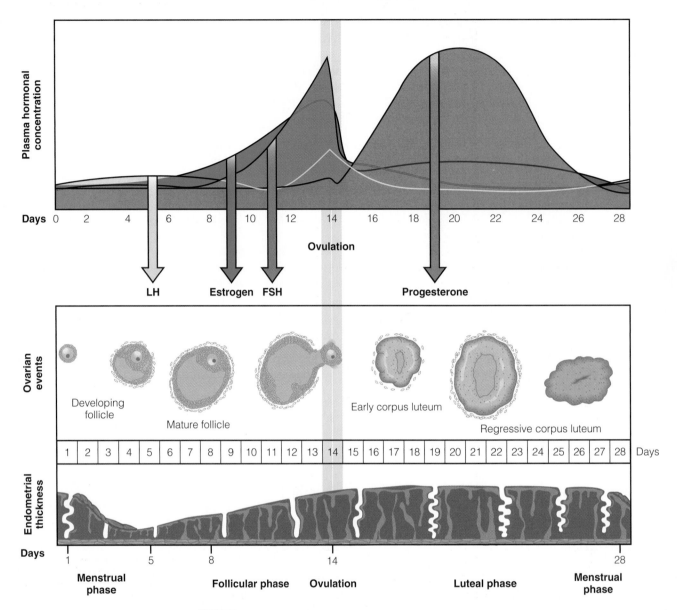

Figure 4.5
The ovarian and menstrual cycles.

If fertilization does not occur, however, the high levels of progesterone and estrogen signal the hypothalamus to decrease LH and other hormone production. The corpus luteum begins to degenerate as LH levels decline. Approximately 2 days before the end of the normal cycle, the secretion of estrogen and progesterone decreases sharply as the corpus luteum becomes inactive, and the menstrual stage begins.

In the **menstrual phase,** the endometrial cells shrink and slough off (this flow is referred to as **menses** (MEN-seez). The uterus begins to contract in an effort to expel the dead tissue along with a small quantity of blood (it is these contractions that cause menstrual cramps, which can be painful in some women). During menstruation, approximately 35 milliliters of blood, 35 milliliters of fluid, some mucus, and the lining of the uterus (about 2 to 4 tablespoons of fluid in all) are expelled from the uterine cavity through the cervical os and ultimately the vagina. (If a woman is using oral contraceptives, the amount may be significantly smaller; see Chapter 13.) Some women lose too

menstrual phase
Final stage of the general menstrual cycle, when the endometrial cells shrink and slough off.

menses
The blood and tissue discharged from the uterus during menstruation.

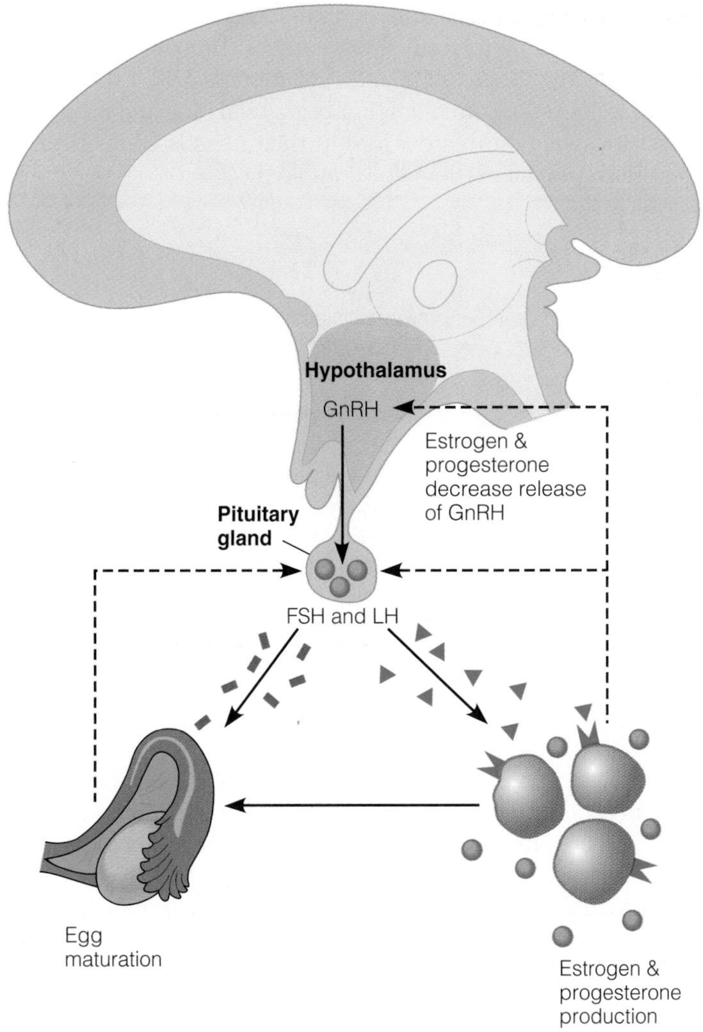

Figure 4.6
The cycle of female hormones.

Hypothalamus

GnRH

Estrogen & progesterone decrease release of GnRH

Pituitary gland

FSH and LH

Egg maturation

Estrogen & progesterone production

much blood during their menstruation and may develop **anemia.** Menses usually stops about 3 to 7 days after the onset of menstruation.

This monthly cyclical process involves a **negative feedback loop,** in which one set of hormones controls the production of another set, which in turn controls the first (see Figure 4.6). In women, the negative feedback loop works like this: Estrogen and progesterone are produced by the ovaries at different levels during different parts of the menstrual cycle. As these levels increase, the hypothalamus is stimulated to decrease its production of GnRH, which sends a message to the pituitary to decrease levels of FSH and LH. The decrease in FSH and LH signals the ovaries to decrease their production of estrogen and progesterone, so the hypothalamus increases its level of GnRH, and it all begins again. This process is similar to a thermostat; when temperatures go down, the thermostat kicks on and raises the temperature, until the rising heat turns off the thermostat and the heat begins slowly to fall.

Variations in Menstruation

Amenorrhea, the absence of menstruation, can take two forms. In **primary amenorrhea** a woman never even begins menstruation, whereas in **secondary amenorrhea,** previously normal menses stop before the woman has gone through menopause. Primary amenorrhea may result from malformed or underdeveloped female reproductive organs, glandular disorders, general poor health, emotional factors, or excessive exercise. The most common cause of secondary amenorrhea is pregnancy, although it can also occur with excessive ex-

anemia
A deficiency in the oxygen-carrying material of the blood, often causing symptoms of fatigue, irritability, dizziness, memory problems, shortness of breath, and headaches.

negative feedback loop
When one set of hormones controls the production of another set, which in turn controls the first, thus regulating the monthly cycle of hormones.

amenorrhea
The absence of menstruation.

primary amenorrhea
The lifelong absence of menstruation.

secondary amenorrhea
The absence of menstruation after a period of normal menses.

ercise, eating disorders, emotional factors, certain diseases, surgical removal of the ovaries or uterus, or hormonal imbalance caused naturally or through the ingestion of steroids. For example, almost all women with anorexia nervosa will experience amenorrhea. When they regain weight, they often will not begin ovulating and menstruating and may need drugs to induce ovulation in order to start their periods again (Biro et al., 2003). If amenorrhea persists, a physician should be consulted.

SEX Talk

Question: Someone once told me that women who live together often experience menstruation at the same time. Why does this happen?

Menstrual synchronicity, as this phenomenon is called, is common, and women who live in the same apartment or house often notice that they begin to cycle together (however, this will only happen if the women are not using hormonal forms of birth control). Menstrual synchronicity occurs because of pheromones, chemicals that are produced by females (more powerfully in animals) during their fertile periods that signal their reproductive readiness. Women who live together detect each other's pheromones (unconsciously), and slowly their fertile periods begin to converge.

menorrhagia
Excessive menstrual flow.

Some women suffer from **menorrhagia** (men-or-RAY-gee-uh), or excessive menstrual flow. Often oral contraceptives are prescribed to make menses lighter and more regular. Later in this chapter we will discuss some newer options that women have to avoid menstruation altogether.

dysfunctional uterine bleeding (DUB)
Menstrual bleeding for long periods of time or intermittent bleeding throughout a cycle.

Dysfunctional uterine bleeding (DUB), when a woman bleeds for long periods of time or intermittently bleeds throughout her cycle, is another common disorder. DUB is usually caused by conditions such as hormonal imbalance, significant weight loss, eating disorders, stress, chronic illness, and excessive exercise (Oriel & Schrager, 1999). A woman who bleeds throughout her menstrual cycle should see her healthcare provider. Untreated DUB can lead to medical problems, such as anemia, and can also cause social embarrassment, because some women need to change their sanitary pads and tampons as often as once an hour.

dysmenorrhea
Painful menstruation.

Dysmenorrhea (dis-men-uh-REE-uh), or painful menstruation, may be caused by a variety of inflammations, by constipation, or by psychological stress. In the past there was a tendency to believe that cramps were always the result of an organic problem, and some women even had operations in an attempt to stop the pain, but such strategies usually failed. Today, doctors recommend medication, relaxation, stress relief, yoga, and massage, all of which can bring some relief from dysmenorrhea.

Premenstrual Syndrome

The term **premenstrual syndrome (PMS)** refers to physical or emotional symptoms that appear in some women during the latter half of the menstrual cycle that can affect their relationships and/or ability to function. Estimates of PMS vary widely depending on how it is defined, but only a small number of women find it debilitating. In fact, although close to 75% of reproductive-aged women report premenstrual symptoms, less than 10% have symptoms that would necessitate a diagnosis of PMS (Born & Steiner, 2001; Elliott, 2002; Stanford, 2002).

Women who experience PMS often report feeling "out of control," "sad," and "cranky." Their partners often do not understand how to handle their PMS, and many report not knowing what to say. Overall a woman who suffers from this syndrome needs a partner to take her symptoms seriously and be loving and supportive. Women who experience PMS may also experience depression, insomnia, excessive sleepiness, restlessness, and feelings of hopelessness (Strine et al., 2005).

The existence of PMS has been controversial. The term became well known in the early 1980s when two separate British courts reduced the sentences of women who had killed their husbands on the grounds that severe PMS reduced their capacity to control their behavior (Rittenhouse, 1991). Though this defense never succeeded in a U.S. trial, publicity over the British trials led to much discussion about PMS. Some women objected to the idea of PMS, suggesting that it would reinforce the idea that women were "out of control" once a month and were slaves to their biology, whereas others supported it as an important biological justification of the symptoms they were experiencing each month. The extreme views of PMS have calmed down somewhat, and women who suffer from it can now find sympathetic physicians and a number of suggestions for coping strategies.

In 1994 the American Psychiatric Association introduced the diagnosis of **premenstrual dysphoric disorder (PMDD),** the most debilitating cases of PMS (Limosin & Ades, 2001). PMDD is now listed in the DSM-IV-TR (American Psychiatric Association, 2000), the latest guide to the accepted disorders of the American Psychiatric Association. In order to accurately diagnose PMDD, a woman needs to chart her symptoms for at least two menstrual cycles to establish a typical pattern of symptoms (Born & Steiner, 2001; Elliott, 2002).

There are four main areas of PMDD symptoms—mood, behavioral, somatic, and cognitive. Mood symptoms include depression, irritability, mood swings, sadness, and/or hostility. Behavioral symptoms include becoming argumentative, increased eating, and a decreased interest in activities. Somatic symptoms include abdominal bloating, fatigue, headaches, hot flashes, insomnia, backache, constipation, breast tenderness, and a craving for carbohydrates. Cognitive symptoms include confusion and poor concentration. PMDD symptoms seem to have both biological and lifestyle components, and so both medication and lifestyle changes can help.

PMDD is often blamed on serotonin dysregulation (Limosin & Ades, 2001). Serotonin is a neurotransmitter in the brain that is involved in the expression of irritability, anger, depression, and specific food cravings. There is also some evidence that PMDD may have a genetic component—that is, it may run in families (Treloar et al., 2002).

Once documented, the first treatment for PMS or PMDD usually involves lifestyle changes. Dietary and vitamin/nutritional changes such as decreasing caffeine, salt, and alcohol intake; maintaining a low-fat diet; increasing calcium, magnesium, and vitamin E (to decrease negative mood and fluid retention); and taking primrose oil have been found to be helpful. Stress management, increased regular exercise, improved coping strategies, and drug therapy can also help (Stearns, 2001; Yonkers, 1999). It's important to point out that these lifestyle changes would make the majority of us happier, regardless of PMS!

One of the most promising pharmacological treatments has been the selective serotonin reuptake inhibitors (SSRIs), such as fluoxetine (Prozac; Pearlstein & Yonkers, 2002). Fluoxetine has yielded some promising results in the treatment of PMDD, al-

premenstrual dysphoric disorder (PMDD)
The most debilitating and severe cases of PMS.

SEX Talk

Question: My roommate has been on a strict diet (she might be anorexic), and recently she stopped having her periods. Could this be due to her eating disorder?

Absolutely. Once a woman drops below a certain percentage of body fat, she will cease to menstruate. This is common in women with eating disorders or those who are malnourished because of starvation or disease. It also occurs in female athletes who train so hard that they reduce their body fat to a point below the critical level for menstruation. It is probably an evolutionary mechanism that prevents women from getting pregnant when there is too little food available to support the pregnancy. Over long periods of time, this loss of menstruation and ovulation can lead to infertility.

though it can cause side effects, such as headaches and sexual dysfunction (Carr & Ensom, 2002). Overall, the majority of women who suffer from PMS and PMDD do respond well to treatment (Stanford, 2002).

Women who have a history of major depression, **posttraumatic stress disorder,** sexual abuse, or those who smoke cigarettes tend to be more at risk for developing PMS or PMDD (Koci, 2004; Cohen et al., 2002; Wittchen et al., 2002). In addition, ethnic variations have also been found. For example, compared to Caucasian women, Hispanic women have been found to have more severe symptoms, whereas Asian women have less (Sternfeld et al., 2002).

Menstrual Manipulation and Suppression

Many years ago, women had fewer periods than they do today. Because of poorer health and nutrition, shorter life spans, more pregnancies, and longer periods spent breast-feeding, women had 50 to 150 periods during their lifetime (Ginty, 2005; Thomas & Ellertson, 2000), whereas today, they have up to 450. Many women today wish they could schedule their periods around certain events in their lives (e.g., beach weekends, dates, or even weddings and honeymoons).

Over the last few years, **menstrual manipulation** has become more popular, and in the future it is likely that periods may become optional (**menstrual suppression;** Ginty, 2005). Although we'll discuss birth control pills in more detail in Chapter 13, it's important to understand that birth control pills have been used to reduce menstrual bleeding and to delay the onset of menstruation. Some physicians prescribe continuous birth control pills (in which a woman takes birth control pills with no break), progesterone **intrauterine devices,** and injections to suppress menstrual periods.

In 2003 Barr Laboratories unveiled a new oral contraceptive, called Seasonale™, which is used for 84 consecutive days instead of the usual 21-day birth control regimen. Users of Seasonale experience only 4 periods a year, compared to the usual 13. Many women are excited about the option of reducing the number of menstrual periods; one study found that given a choice of having a period or not, 90% of women would choose not to have periods (Sulak et al., 2002). Continuous-use birth control pills are also on the horizon. Wyeth pharmaceuticals applied for FDA approval for its first continuous-use oral contraceptive, called Librel (Lambert, 2005), which is designed to let women stop menstruating altogether.

These methods suppress the growth of the uterine lining, leaving little or nothing to be expelled during menstruation (Druff, 2000). Actually this treatment has been used for years to treat a menstrual condition known as **endometriosis** (en-doe-mee-tree-OH-sus), which can cause severe menstrual cramping and irregular periods.

Women with painful periods, intense cramps, heavy menses, migraines, PMS, epilepsy, asthma, rheumatoid arthritis, irritable bowel syndrome, and diabetes all can benefit from menstrual suppression (Chollar, 2000). In addition, menstrual disorders are the number one cause of gynecological disease and affect nearly 2.5 million American women yearly (Kjerulff et al., 1996). Some experts suggest that amenorrhea may be healthier than monthly periods because menstrual suppression also avoids the sharp hormonal changes that occur throughout the menstrual cycle.

Originally, birth control pills were designed to mimic the normal menstrual cycle, which is why the cycle includes a period of time for a woman to bleed. This bleeding, called "withdrawal bleeding," is a result of stopping birth control pills for 1 week or taking placebo pills (Willis, 2001). The bleeding itself bears little biological resemblance to a menstrual period; this is because there is very little built-up endometrium to be shed (Thomas & Ellertson, 2000). Even so, most women link having their period with health and fertility. Bleeding has "psychological importance" to many women; it lets a woman know that everything is fine and working the way it should. In fact, abnormal bleeding (spotting or clotting) or an absence of bleeding are important to report to a healthcare provider promptly.

posttraumatic stress disorder
A stress disorder that follows a traumatic event, causing flashbacks, heightened anxiety, and sleeplessness.

ReviewQuestion

Explain what is known about the existence of PMS/PMDD. What treatments are available?

menstrual manipulation
The ability to plan and schedule the arrival of menstruation.

menstrual suppression
The elimination of menstrual periods.

intrauterine devices
Devices that are inserted into the uterus for contraception. Progesterone IUDs often inhibit menstruation.

endometriosis
The growth of endometrial tissue outside the uterus.

ReviewQuestion

Differentiate between menstrual manipulation and menstrual suppression.

© Corbis

Female athletes who significantly reduce their body fat will often stop menstruating.

Sexual Behavior and Menstruation

Many cultures have taboos about engaging in sexual intercourse, or any sexual behaviors, during menstruation. Orthodox Jewish women are required to abstain from sexual intercourse for 1 week after their menstrual period. After this time they engage in a mikvah bath, following which sexual activity can be resumed.

Although many sexually active couples report avoiding sexual intercourse during menstruation (Hensel et al., 2004), research has found that this might have to do with personal comfort. Couples who feel more comfortable with their sexuality report higher levels of sexual intercourse during menstruation (Rempel & Baumgartner, 2003). From a medical standpoint, there is no reason to avoid sexual intimacy during a woman's period. Of course, menstruation can make things a little messy, so a little preplanning is often needed. Some women use diaphragms or other specially designed products, such as the Instead Softcup™, to contain menstrual fluid. Others insert a tampon just prior to sexual activity and then engage in oral or manual sex.

How do you feel about sex during menstruation? It's important to talk to your partner about this issue and decide what works best for you as a couple. As we've mentioned earlier, however, menstrual suppression might make this question obsolete.

Photo courtesy of Instead, Inc.

The Instead Softcup can be used during a woman's period to make sexual activity less messy.

Review Question

What are some of the reasons that couples might avoid sexual intimacy during menstruation?

Menopause

The term **menopause** refers to a woman's final menstrual period but is often (incorrectly) used as a synonym for the **climacteric.** These terms refer to the period in which the woman's estrogen production begins to wane, culminating in the cessation of menstruation, usually between the ages of 40 and 58, with the average age at about 51 (North American Menopause Society, 2003). Smoking, being separated/widowed/divorced, nonemployment, lower educational attainment, and a history of heart disease have all been found to be related to an earlier onset of menopause (Brett & Cooper, 2003; Whiteman et al., 2003).

As women age, their ovaries become less responsive to hormonal stimulation from the anterior pituitary, resulting in decreased hormone production. The first sign of the climacteric is often a menstrual cycle that does not include ovulation, followed by irregular cycles. Amenorrhea may occur for 2 or 3 months, followed by a menstrual flow. In most cases, menstruation does not stop suddenly.

Diminishing estrogen production also results in atrophy of the primary sexual glands. The clitoris and labia become smaller, and degenerative changes occur in the vaginal wall. At the same time, the ovaries and uterus also begin to shrink. Estrogen reduction can also cause changes in the secondary sex characteristics, including pubic hair loss, thinning of head hair, growth of hair on the upper lip and chin, drooping of the breasts and wrinkling of skin due to loss of elasticity, and **osteoporosis** (ah-stee-oh-po-ROW-sus), resulting in brittle bones.

Decreasing levels of estrogen accelerate bone loss during menopause. It is estimated that 70% of women over the age of 80 will have osteoporosis (Stanford, 2002). Incidentally, "osteopenia" (a thinning of the bones) also can occur in younger women and is a precursor to osteoporosis. If you smoke, use Depo Provera, have an eating disorder or a family history of osteoporosis, you might ask your doctor for a bone-density test. Today, women in their 20s and 30s are advised to get at least 1,000 milligrams of calcium each day and to engage in frequent exercise to maintain bone strength (Lloyd et al., 2004; Manson, 2004).

Many women go through menopause with few problems and find menopause to be a liberating time, signaling the end of their childbearing years and a newfound freedom from contraception. In some women, however, the hormonal fluctuations can cause **hot flashes,** headaches, and insomnia. Sexual complaints include a change in levels of sexual desire, decreased frequency of sexual activity, painful intercourse, and diminished sexual responsiveness; sometimes this is associated with dysfunction in the male partner as well (Sarrel, 1990). The most prevalent psychosexual problems of older women are not these classic complaints but rather the lack of tenderness and sexual contact with a partner (von Sydow, 2000). In fact, for many menopausal women, life satisfaction is

menopause
The cessation of menstrual cycling.

climacteric
The combination of physiological and psychological changes that develop at the end of a woman's reproductive life; usually includes menopause.

osteoporosis
An age-related disorder characterized by decreased bone mass and increased susceptibility to fractures as a result of decreased levels of estrogens.

hot flashes
A symptom of menopause in which a woman feels sudden heat, often accompanied by a flush.

Review Question

Explain what causes the physical and emotional changes of menopause.

hormone replacement therapy (HRT)
Medication containing one or more female hormones, often used to treat symptoms of menopause.

Review Question

Explain the benefits and risks of hormone replacement therapy.

speculum
An instrument for dilating the vagina to examine the cervix and other internal structures.

Papanicolaou (Pap) smear
A microscopic examination of cells scraped from the cervix. Named for its inventor.

more closely related to relationship with a partner, stress, and lifestyle than menopause status, hormone levels, or hormone replacement therapy (Dennerstein et al., 2000).

Certain surgeries, such as removal of the ovaries, can result in a surgically induced menopause because of estrogen deprivation. For this reason, surgeons try to leave at least one ovary in premenopausal women to allow these women to enter menopause naturally.

Hormone Replacement Therapy

Overall, **hormone replacement therapy (HRT)** has been found to help maintain vaginal elasticity and lubrication, reduce hot flashes, reduce depression, and restore regular sleep patterns (North American Menopause Society, 2003). It has also been found to decrease the risk of developing colorectal cancer and osteoporosis (Brinton & Schairer, 1997). However, it has also been found to increase the risks of heart attacks, strokes, blood clots, and breast cancer.

It was this increased risk of breast cancer that caused researchers to finally halt a study in 2002 that compared two groups of menopausal women—one taking HRT and the other taking placebos (Rubin, 2002). The study involved more than 16,000 postmenopausal women and hoped to shed light on the ability of hormone therapy to reduce osteoporosis and heart disease. Researchers concluded that the long-term risks of taking hormones may outweigh the benefits for certain women. Some women who choose HRT eventually discontinue the treatment for a variety of reasons, including fear of breast cancer, bloating, and/or breakthrough bleeding (Lie, 2000).

Many healthcare providers stopped prescribing hormones to their menopausal patients; others began prescribing hormone replacement only for those women with severe menopausal symptoms. Menopausal women need to weigh the risks and benefits of HRT. It is important to discuss these issues with a trusted healthcare provider. There is no single treatment option that is best for all women.

Today, some women continue to choose to use hormone replacement therapy. Others use nutritional and/or vitamin therapy or use herbal remedies containing natural estrogens, such as black cohosh, ginseng, or soy products, to help lessen symptoms (although the use of these products is controversial and may lead to a variety of side effects). HRT has been approved for symptom relief and osteoporosis prevention. In addition, HRT has been found to lessen the symptoms associated with menopause and also to decrease the risk of colorectal cancer.

FEMALE REPRODUCTIVE AND SEXUAL HEALTH

It is a good idea for every woman to examine and explore her own sexual anatomy. A genital self-exam (see Sex in Real Life, "Female Genital Self-Examination") can help increase a woman's comfort with her genitals. In addition, to maintain reproductive health, all women should undergo routine gynecological examinations once they begin menstruating and certainly before they begin having sexual intercourse. Routine gynecological exams include a general medical history and a general checkup, a pelvic examination, and a breast examination. During the pelvic examination, the healthcare provider inspects the genitals, both internally and externally, and manually examines the internal organs.

In a pelvic exam, the health professional will often use a **speculum** to hold open the vagina to examine the cervix (though there is a sense of stretching, this is not generally painful). Many women report discomfort with speculums, and research is currently being done to find alternatives that would allow healthcare providers access to the cervix. One such product, the FemSpec™, is an inflatable device that comes in three sizes (small, medium, and large). A **Papanicolaou (Pap) smear** will be taken from the cervix (see the discussion on cervical cancer, following). The practitioner will then insert two fingers in the vagina and press down on the lower abdomen to feel the ovaries and uterus for abnormal lumps or pain. A recto-vaginal exam may also be performed, in which the practitioner inserts one finger into the rectum and one into the vagina to feel the membranes in between.

It is important to choose a gynecologist or nurse practitioner with care, for they should be a resource for sexual and birth control information as well. Referrals from friends or family members, college health services, women's health centers, and Planned Parenthood Centers can direct you to competent professionals. Do not be afraid to change practitioners if you are not completely comfortable.

Gynecological Health Concerns

There are several conditions that can interfere with gynecological health. We will discuss some of the most prevalent, including endometriosis, toxic shock syndrome, uterine fibroids, vulvodynia, polycystic ovarian syndrome, and vaginal infections.

Endometriosis

Endometriosis occurs when endometrial cells begin to migrate to places other than the uterus. They may implant on any of the reproductive organs or other abdominal organs and then engorge and atrophy every month with the menstrual cycle, just like the endometrium does in the uterus. The disease ranges from mild to severe, and women may experience a range of symptoms or none at all.

Endometriosis is most common in women between 25 and 40 years of age who have never had children; it has been called the "career woman's disease" because it is more common in professional women (Simsir et al., 2001). Women who have not had children and those who experience short and heavy menstrual cycles have also been found to be more at risk for endometriosis (Vigano et al., 2004). Among women of childbearing age, the estimated prevalence of endometriosis is as high as 10%; and among infertile women, between 20 and 40% (Vigano et al., 2004; Frackiewicz, 2000). If you or someone you know has had symptoms of endometriosis, it is important that complaints are taken seriously.

The cause of endometriosis is still unknown, though some have suggested that it is due to retrograde menstrual flow (a process in which parts of the uterine lining are carried backward during the menstrual period into the Fallopian tubes and abdomen; Frackiewicz, 2000; Leyendecker et al., 2004). The symptoms of endometriosis depend on where the endometrial tissue has invaded but commonly include painful menstrual periods, pelvic or lower back pain, and pain during intercourse; some women also experience pain on defecation (Prentice, 2001). Symptoms often wax and wane with the menstrual cycle, starting a day or two before menstruation, becoming worse during the period, and gradually decreasing for a day or two afterward. The pain is often sharp and can be mistaken for menstrual cramping. Many women discover their endometriosis when they have trouble becoming pregnant. The endometrial cells can affect fertility by infiltrating the ovaries or Fallopian tubes and interfering with ovulation or ovum transport through the Fallopian tube.

Endometriosis is diagnosed through biopsy or the use of a **laparoscope.** Treatment consists of hormone therapy, surgery, or laser therapy to try to remove endometrial patches from the organs. Endometriosis declines during pregnancy and disappears after menopause.

© Joel Gordon

During a pelvic examination, a device such as a speculum is used to view the cervix.

Review Question

Explain what is done in a yearly pelvic exam, and why.

sex byte

A woman who is scheduled for a yearly pelvic examination with Pap testing should abstain from sexual intercourse, douching, and yeast infection medication for at least 2 days prior to her pelvic exam. These can all interfere with the reading of a Pap test and make the results difficult to interpret (Globerman, 2005; Obrizzo, 2005).

© Coris

Although tattoos are popular among college students today, there are no safety regulations in the United States for the inks that are used (Marris, 2005). Some of the inks have been found to have high levels of lead, lithium, and copper, which may lead to health problems.

laparoscope
A small instrument through which structures within the abdomen and pelvis can be viewed.

Toxic Shock Syndrome

Toxic shock syndrome (TSS) first hit the news in the early 1980s, when a number of women died or lost limbs to the disease. Many of the infected women used a brand of tampons called Rely™, which was designed to be kept in the vagina over long periods of time. Using a single tampon for a long period of time allows bacteria to build up and can result in infection, and the TSS cases of the 1980s were believed to be due to a buildup of toxins produced by an infection of vaginal *Staphylococcus aureus* bacteria (Reingold, 1991).

TSS is an acute, fast-developing disease that can cause multiple organ failure. Symptoms of TSS usually include fever, sore throat, diarrhea, vomiting, muscle ache, and a scarlet-colored rash. It may progress rapidly from dizziness or fainting to respiratory distress, kidney failure, shock, and heart failure and can be fatal if medical attention is not received immediately.

TSS can occur in persons of any age, sex, or race, but most reported cases have occurred in younger menstruating women using tampons. There has been a substantial reduction in the incidence of TSS in the last 10 years, which is primarily attributed to the changes in absorbency and composition of tampons available to the consumer (Meadows, 2000). Today, TSS is most common in women who forget to remove a tampon, which becomes a breeding ground for bacteria over a few days. TSS can be avoided by using less absorbent tampons, changing tampons regularly, or using sanitary pads instead of tampons.

Polycystic Ovarian Syndrome

Polycystic ovarian syndrome (PCOS) is an endocrine disorder that affects 5 to 10% of premenopausal women (Polson et al., 1988). PCOS causes cyst formation on the ovaries during puberty, which causes estrogen levels to decrease and androgen levels (including testosterone) to increase. A girl with PCOS typically experiences irregular or absent menstruation; a lack of ovulation; excessive body/facial hair or hair loss; obesity; acne, oily skin, or dandruff; and/or infertility. Many women with PCOS experience fertility issues, and research is ongoing to find ways to help these women achieve successful pregnancies (Stadtmauer & Oehninger, 2005).

There are many possible long-term health concerns associated with PCOS, such as an increased risk of diabetes, high blood pressure, and increased cholesterol levels. A variety of treatment options are available, including oral contraception to regulate the period and inhibit testosterone production. Many women find that some of the symptoms associated with PCOS decrease with weight loss (Clark et al., 1995).

Because many of the symptoms, including increased body/facial hair, acne, and weight gain, affect a woman's sense of self, many women with PCOS experience emotional side effects, including mild depression and/or self-esteem issues. In the accompanying Personal Voices, "Living With Polycystic Ovarian Syndrome," one woman talks about her struggle with PCOS.

Uterine Fibroids

Uterine fibroids, or hard tissue masses in the uterus, affect from 20 to 40% of women 35 and older, and as many as 50% of African American women (Laval, 2002). Newer imaging techniques suggest that the prevalence of uterine fibroids may be as high as 77% (Stewart, 2001). Symptoms include pelvic pain and pressure, heavy cramping, prolonged or heavy bleeding, constipation, abdominal tenderness or bloating, infertility, recurrent pregnancy loss, frequent urination, and painful sexual intercourse.

Of all of these symptoms, excessive menstrual bleeding is the most common complaint. Some fibroids can become very large (up to the size of a basketball) and can make a woman look as though she is in her sixth month of pregnancy. Treatment for uterine fibroids is hormone or drug therapy, laser therapy, surgery, or **cryotherapy** (Stewart, 2001). It is important to point out that the majority of uterine fibroids are not cancerous and do not cause any problems.

Personal Voices

Living With Polycystic Ovarian Syndrome

Following is an excerpt from a 23-year-old woman who was diagnosed with polycystic ovarian syndrome when she was 22.

From the time I started puberty I knew something wasn't right. I could have counted on my fingers and toes the number of times I'd had a period between the first one and the age of 22. I honestly had no problem with not having periods—it didn't make me feel like "less of a woman." I figured it couldn't be anything too serious, and the fear of finding out what was really wrong would probably mean more than I was willing to know. I knew that I should get it checked out, but because I wasn't sexually active I didn't get my first Pap smear until I was 19. It wasn't until I was 22 that I went to find out what was going on with my periods. I finally went to the university health clinic the first year of graduate school. It had been 3 years since my last Pap and I told myself I needed to know what was going on with my body. I needed answers and I was finally willing to accept them. I was diagnosed with polycystic ovarian syndrome (PCOS) and although I'd never heard of it, I found out it was common in women.

I'm glad I didn't wait any longer. With my diagnosis, things made more sense. I'd always been overweight and it was mostly in my middle. No one had ever said anything, but I always felt I had more facial hair than a girl "should." I had even questioned having more testosterone than most women because I have very well-developed calf muscles that look more like a man's. After some accompanying blood work I found out I was also nearly diabetic. I had NEVER thought that not having periods would be related to developing diabetes or high blood pressure. Research is finding that insulin is connected to PCOS, which explains why many women will become diabetic who have the condition. With that tends to come the obesity. PCOS, if not managed, can also lead to hypertension and endometrial cancer. Also because of the insulin and other hormones, it's often hard for women with PCOS to lose weight. I feel betrayed by my body; like it is working against me.

In a society where body image is everything, I grew up being overweight. Now I have more of an explanation of why, but people don't know that when they see me. Despite how attractive I feel on the outside, I've

also felt unattractive on the inside because my "girl parts" just don't work right. When I didn't know what was wrong with me, I assumed I was a rare case, no one would really understand what was going on with me, or if they found out, it'd be a quick fix that I could ignore for the rest of my life. Yet, PCOS isn't curable. It can be managed, and managed well enough that symptoms virtually disappear, but there is and was no magic quick fix I had hoped for.

Hearing a diagnosis can be comforting in a "they know what's wrong" sort of way. Yet, if you've never heard of the syndrome you're being diagnosed with, because it's only recently gaining much attention, it can be an isolating and scary experience. I'm finding there are a lot of women with PCOS and they've formed communities and groups to talk about how to advocate for themselves and their medical care.

Because my body doesn't work quite right and because it leaves me with some side effects I'm less than thrilled about (with the potential for more as I age!), I'm self-conscious about my body and consequently self-conscious about sex. I'm afraid it'll be hard to find someone willing to learn about how PCOS makes my life different and somewhat challenging. I'm afraid that I won't be able to find someone who is attracted to me that I am equally attracted to who because of how I look because of my syndrome. I'm afraid I won't be able to find someone who is all of these things and is OK with not having children or having to work for them [using fertility specialists].

Honestly, even though I'm quite hopeful about my prognosis, I can't help but think that PCOS has robbed me of some of my self-esteem. I basically have to take some sort of medication to make my body create a period for the rest of my fertile days, though it doesn't necessarily mean I'm ovulating. I can't just quit taking birth control and get pregnant whenever I want (if that's even what I wanted). I can't just exercise enough in a few weeks to slim down enough to look good in a bikini. I can't guarantee that I won't become very obese and get high blood pressure down the line; not because I'm lazy, but because of my ovaries. I can't always choose what PCOS does to my body, but I can choose to take comfort in the fact that I'm not alone.

Source: Author's files.

Vulvodynia

At the beginning of the 21st century, many physicians were unaware that a condition known as **vulvodynia** (vull-voe-DIN-nia) even existed. Vulvodynia refers to chronic vulval pain and soreness. Although a burning sensation in the vagina is the most common symptom, women also report itching, burning, rawness, stinging, or stabbing vaginal/vulval pain (Innamaa & Nunns, 2005; Lotery et al., 2004). Vulvodynia pain is either intermittent or constant and can range from mildly disturbing to completely disabling. Women who suffer from vulvodynia experience higher levels of psychological distress and depression than those who do not (Wylie et al., 2004).

No one really knows what causes vulvodynia, but there have been several speculations, including injury or irritation of the vulval nerves, hypersensitivity to vaginal yeast, allergic reaction to environmental irritants, or pelvic floor muscle spasms (R. K. Jones et al., 2002). Treatment options include biofeedback, diet modification, drug therapy, oral and topical medications, nerve blocks, vulvar injections, surgery, and/or pelvic floor muscle strengthening (Glazer et al., 1998). Newer research indicates that using birth control pills for more than 2 years may increase the risk for vulvar pain during intercourse (Berglund et al., 2002; Bouchard et al., 2002).

Infections

A number of different kinds of infections can afflict the female genital system, and those that are sexually transmitted are discussed in Chapter 15. However, some infections of the female reproductive tract are not necessarily sexually transmitted. For example, as we discussed earlier in this chapter, the Bartholin's glands and the urinary tract can become infected, just as any area of the body can become infected when bacteria get inside and multiply. These infections may happen because of poor hygiene practices and are more frequent in those who engage in frequent sexual intercourse. When infected, the glands can swell and cause pressure and discomfort and can interfere with walking, sitting, or sexual intercourse. Usually a physician will need to drain the infected glands with a catheter and will prescribe a course of antibiotics (Blumstein, 2001).

Douching may put a woman at risk for vaginal infections because it changes the vagina's pH levels and can destroy healthy bacteria necessary to maintain proper balance. Those who reported using douches said they were concerned about vaginal odor and cleanliness. This is typically what drives women to use a variety of feminine hygiene products (see Sex in Real Life, "Feminine Hygiene," on page 127).

sex byte

Women should change out of their workout clothes—including their underwear—within an hour of exercise (Nardone, 2004). Sweat glands from the bikini area can lead to dampness, which increases the risk of itching and yeast or bacterial infections. In addition, thong underwear should never be worn during a workout because it can help spread bacteria from the rectum to the vagina.

Cancer of the Female Reproductive Organs

Cancer is a disease in which certain cells in the body don't function properly—they divide too fast and/or produce excessive tissue that forms a tumor. There are a number of different cancers that can affect the female reproductive organs. In this section, we will look at breast, uterine, cervical, endometrial, and ovarian cancers. We will also review preventive measures for detecting or avoiding common female health problems. In Chapter 14, we will discuss how these illnesses affect women's lives and sexuality.

Breast Cancer

Breast cancer is the most prevalent cancer in the world (Parkin et al., 2005). One in seven American women will develop breast cancer in her lifetime (American Cancer Society, 2005a). In the United States, an estimated 211,240 new cases of invasive breast cancer were expected to occur in 2005, and approximately 40,410 women were expected to die (American Cancer Society, 2005b).

White women are more likely to develop breast cancer than African American women; however, white women are less likely to die from it. African American women have a 20% higher death rate from all cancers (Chlebowski et al., 2005; Jemal et al., 2005). Deaths from breast cancer have significantly decreased since the 1990s, probably due to earlier detection and improved treatment procedures.

Feminine Hygiene

*W*omen have been brainwashed into thinking that somehow their vaginas and vulvas are bad, dirty, or ugly. One trip down the feminine hygiene aisle will convince you. How do feminine hygiene products affect young women today? What is the impact on us as we age and develop into sexual beings? Do our negative feelings about our bodies affect our sexuality? You bet.

The following statements are from actual products that line drugstore shelves. As you read the statements, pay attention to your thoughts.

Feminine Cleansing Cloths

"Lets you feel feminine fresh. Anytime, Anywhere . . ."

"Perfect for whenever you need to feel confident or refreshed . . ."

"Neutralizes odors, not just covers them up."

"Comes in Shower Fresh, White Blossoms, and Baby Powder scents."

Cleansing Foam

"Fresh, clean scent!"

"Slim design fits in your purse or gym bag . . . so you can feel confidently clean and fresh wherever you go."

Floral Fresh Feminine Wash

"A woman's special cleansing needs call for . . ."

"Washes away odor to leave you feeling fresh, clean and confident."

"You may want to use it all over!"

"Comes in Country Flowers, Fresh Mountain Breeze, Spring Rain Freshness, and Fresh Baby Powder."

Feminine Deodorant Spray

"Spray it directly on yourself."

"Spray it on your underwear."

"Spray it on your pantyliners."

"Spray it on your pantyhose."

Worldwide, breast cancer rates have been found to correlate with variations in diet, especially fat intake. Even with these variations, however, the specific dietary factors that affect breast cancer have not been established. Breast-feeding, on the other hand, has been found to reduce a woman's lifetime risk of developing breast cancer (Eisinger & Burke, 2002). A woman's chance of acquiring breast cancer significantly increases as she ages. In fact, 77% of breast cancers appear in women who are 50 years old or older, whereas less than 5% appear in women under the age of 40 (Jemal et al., 2005).

Unfortunately, there is no known method of preventing breast cancer, so it is extremely important to detect it as early as possible. Every woman should regularly perform breast self-examinations (see the accompanying Sex in Real Life, "Breast Self-Examination"), especially after the age of 35. Women should also have their breasts examined during routine gynecological checkups, which is a good time to ask for instruction on self-examination if you have any questions about the technique.

Another important preventive measure is **mammography,** which can detect tumors too small to be felt during self-examination. There is some controversy about when a woman should begin going for regular mammography examinations, with some claiming that the research shows no significant benefit in women under 50; others suggesting mammograms every 2 years from age 40; still others recommending regular mammograms for women of all ages. The American Cancer Society recommends that a woman begin yearly mammograms every year after the age of 40. However, you should discuss with your healthcare provider whether mammography is appropriate for you, and if so, how often.

All women are at risk for breast cancer, even if they have no family history of the disease. Most commonly, breast cancer is discovered by a postmenopausal woman who discovers a breast lump with no other symptoms. However, breast cancer can also cause breast pain, nipple discharge, changes in nipple shape, and skin dimpling. It should be noted here that the discovery of a lump or mass in your breast does not mean you have cancer; most masses are **benign,** and many do not even need treatment. If it is **malignant**

mammography
A procedure for internal imaging of the breasts to evaluate breast disease or screen for breast cancer.

benign
A nonmalignant, mild case of a disease that is favorable for recovery.

malignant
A cancerous growth that tends to spread into nearby normal tissue and travel to other parts of the body.

Breast Self-Examination

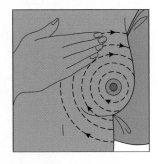

A breast self-examination (BSE), along with mammography and a clinical breast exam from a healthcare provider, can help reduce breast cancer in women. Before the age of 40 years old, BSE is most helpful to help a woman become familiar enough with her breasts so that any irregularity will be easily detectable. If a woman does detect a thickening or a lump, however, she should not panic; 80 to 90% of all lumps are noncancerous and can be easily treated. After the age of 40, mammography and clinical breast exams become more useful, although a monthly BSE is still recommended.

Because the shape and feel of the breasts change during ovulation and menstruation, it is best to perform a BSE about 1 week after menstruation. BSE should be done at the same time during each cycle.

In the Mirror

The first step of a BSE is inspection. Look at your breasts in a mirror to learn their natural contours. With arms relaxed, note any elevation of the level of the nipple, dimpling, bulging, or *peau d'orange* ("orange peel skin," which results from edema, or swelling). Compare the size and shape of the breasts, remembering that one (usually the left) is normally slightly larger. Next, press the hands down firmly on the hips to tense the pectoral muscles, and then raise the arms over the head looking for a shift in relative position of the two nipples. These maneuvers also bring out any dimpling, bulging, or peau d'orange. After doing BSEs over time, any changes will become obvious, which is why it is best to begin BSEs early rather than later in life.

Thinkstock/Getty Images

In the Shower

The shower is a good place to do a breast palpation (pressing)—fingers glide well over wet or soapy skin. Press the breast against the chest wall with the flat of the hand, testing the surface for warmth, and moving the hand to test mobility. Pay close attention to increased heat or redness of the overlying skin, tenderness, dilated superficial veins, peau d'orange, and retraction (dimpling, asymmetry, decreased mobility). Feel the tissue carefully in all four quadrants of the breast, being sure to include the tissue that extends up toward the armpit, and examine the armpit itself for any lymph node enlargement (see photo). Finally, gently squeeze the nipple inward and upward to see if there is any discharge.

Lying Down

Finally, lie down and put a folded towel or a pillow under your left shoulder. Placing your left hand behind your head, use your right hand to press firmly in small, circular motions all around the left breast, much as you did in the shower. Imagine a clock: Start at the top of the breast, 12 o'clock; move to 1 o'clock, 2 o'clock, and so on, on the outside rim of the breast; and then move in 1 inch toward the nipple and repeat (see the figure). Make at least three circles, and end on the nipple itself. You will feel the normal structures of the breast beneath your fingers, but look for a distinct lump or hardness. Repeat the entire procedure for your other breast.

Finally, squeeze each nipple again gently, looking for any discharge, whether clear or bloody. Any discharge or any other irregularities or lumps should be reported to your healthcare provider without delay.

Source: The American Cancer Society, 2003.

and left untreated, however, breast cancer usually spreads throughout the body, which is why it is very important that any lump be immediately brought to the attention of your physician or other medical practitioner.

radical mastectomy
A surgical procedure that involves removal of the breast, its surrounding tissue, the muscles supporting the breast, and underarm lymph nodes.

Treatment   In the past, women with breast cancer usually had a **radical mastectomy.** Today, few women need such drastic surgery. More often, a partial or modified mastectomy is performed, which leaves many of the underlying muscles and lymph nodes in place (see photo). This procedure, combined with radiation therapy, has similar long-term survival rates as mastectomy (American Cancer Society, 2003). If the breast must be removed, many women choose to undergo breast reconstruction, in which a new breast is formed from existing skin and fat (see Chapter 14).

If the tumor is contained to its site and has not spread, a **lumpectomy** may be considered. A lumpectomy involves the removal of the tumor, along with some surrounding tissue, but the breast is left intact. Radiation therapy and/or chemotherapy are often used in conjunction with a lumpectomy.

Risk Factors   A number of risk factors have been identified for breast cancer. An early onset of puberty and menarche may increase the chances of developing breast cancer, probably due to prolonged estrogen exposure (Breast Cancer Coalition, 2002). However, newer research claims that obesity, low levels of physical activity, and alcohol consumption may have more to do with the development of breast cancer than do early onsets of puberty or menarche (Verkasalo et al., 2001).

Family history also may be a risk factor in breast cancer; however, about 90% of women who develop breast cancer do not have any family history of the disease (Breast Cancer Coalition, 2002). No study has been large enough to reliably show how the risk of breast cancer is influenced by familial patterns of breast cancer. Although women who have a first-degree relative with breast cancer may have an increased risk of the disease, most of these women will never develop breast cancer (Collaborative Group on Hormonal Factors in Breast Cancer, 2001).

Medical researchers are working on targeting abnormal breast tissues that could potentially develop into breast cancer. It is possible that in the future doctors will be able to determine a woman's breast cancer risk from a simple blood test, which in turn will help determine treatment and options prior to any breast cancer formation (American Cancer Society, 2001). Some women who have been found to have a high risk of developing breast cancer choose to undergo prophylactic (preventive) mastectomies before breast cancer can develop (Sakorafas, 2005; D. A. Levine & Gemignani, 2003).

Early pregnancy (having a first child before the age of 30) seems to have a protective effect against getting breast cancer, though no one understands exactly why. There has also been some controversy over the effect of oral contraceptives on breast cancer rates, with many contradictory studies, some finding an increased risk (Cabaret et al., 2003; Narod et al., 2002), and others finding no increased risk. Although there have been slightly more breast cancers found in women who use oral contraceptives, these cancers have been less advanced and less aggressive (Fraser, 2000). A comprehensive study conducted by the FDA concluded that there is no concrete evidence that the pill causes or influences the development of breast cancer; however, the long-term effects of using oral contraception are not yet certain, and those with a family history of breast cancer might want to use other forms of contraception.

Uterine Cancer

There are different types of cancer that can affect the uterus. The most common forms are cervical and endometrial cancer.

Cervical Cancer

It is estimated that 1 in 130 American women will develop cervical cancer (American Cancer Society, 2005b). In 2005, approximately 10,370 new cases of cervical cancer were expected in the United States. A Pap smear, taken during routine pelvic exams, can detect early changes in the cervical cells. A few cells are painlessly scraped from the cervix and are examined under a microscope for abnormalities.

Cervical cancer has high cure rates because it starts as an easily identifiable lesion, called a **cervical intraepithelial neoplasia (CIN),** which usually progresses slowly into cervical cancer. Better early detection of cervical cancer has led to a sharp decrease in the numbers of serious cervical cancer cases. Screening for cervical cancer should begin

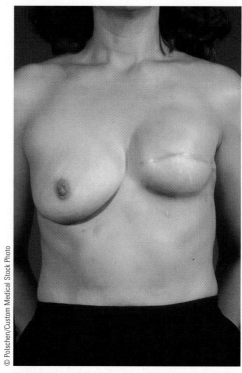

© Polscher/Custom Medical Stock Photo

Partial or modified mastectomies are more common today than radical mastectomies.

lumpectomy
A modern surgical procedure for breast cancer in which only the tumorous lump and a small amount of surrounding tissue are removed.

Review Question

Identify and explain the risk factors that have been identified for breast cancer.

sex byte

Many women today take herbal supplements, which are unregulated by the FDA. Many of these supplements can interfere with menstrual cycles and the effectiveness of birth control pills (Roan, 2004). For example, St. John's Wort can decrease the pill's effectiveness, and black cohosh has been found to interfere with estrogen levels. It's best to check with your healthcare provider before taking any herbal supplements.

cervical intraepithelial neoplasia (CIN)
A change in the cells on the surface of the cervix that may signal early beginnings of cervical cancer; sometimes referred to as cervical dysplasia.

no later than age 21 and should be done every year. But for some women in poor countries, routine pelvic examinations and Pap smears are not available. It is for this reason that approximately 80% of the 500,000 new cases of cervical cancer are diagnosed every year in poor countries such as sub-Saharan Africa and Latin America (Nebehay, 2004). In Chapter 15 we will discuss vaccine development for sexually transmitted infections that have been found to contribute to cervical cancer.

Cervical intraepithelial neoplasia (CIN) occurs more frequently in women who have had sexual intercourse early in their lives as well as women with multiple sexual partners (American Cancer Society, 2003). Women who begin to have children at an early age, such as teenage mothers, are also at increased risk. Chronic inflammation of the cervix (cervicitis) has also been found to be frequently associated with cervical cancer (American Cancer Society, 2003). Because a number of viral infections of the genitals can lead to low-grade cervicitis, it is particularly important for those with a diagnosis of genital warts or herpes to have annual Pap smears. Oral contraceptive users have two to four times the risk for developing cervical cancer, particularly if they have used oral contraceptives for more than 5 to 10 years; and so there, too, annual Pap smears are important. Of course, good gynecological health care requires that all women have annual Pap smears.

There are simple and effective treatments for CIN, such as surgery, radiation, or both, which have resulted in cure rates up to 90% in early-stage disease and a dramatic decline in mortality rate for cervical cancer. If the disease has progressed, treatment commonly includes a **hysterectomy** followed by radiation and chemotherapy.

Endometrial Cancer

Cancer of the lining of the uterus is the most frequent gynecological cancer. It is estimated there would be 40,880 new cases of endometrial cancer in the United States in 2005 (American Cancer Society, 2005b). Symptoms include abnormal uterine bleeding and/or spotting. Because a Pap smear is rarely effective in detecting early endometrial cancer, a **D&C (dilation and curettage)** is more reliable. Treatment options for endometrial cancer include surgery, radiation, hormones, and/or chemotherapy.

Endometrial cancer generally affects women over 50 and is a major reason for hysterectomies in that age group. If detected at an early stage, over 90% will survive at least 5 years. Use of birth control pills has been found to decrease the incidence of endometrial cancer.

hysterectomy
The surgical removal of the uterus.

dilation and curettage (D&C)
The surgical scraping of the uterine wall with a spoon-shaped instrument.

Review Question

Identify and describe the two most common forms of uterine cancer.

SEX Talk

Question: Is it true that the United States has a really high rate for hysterectomy? Are some being done unnecessarily?

The United States has one of the highest rates of hysterectomy in the world (Bren, 2001). In fact, today hysterectomy is the most common major gynecologic operation in the United States (Thakar et al., 2002). It is estimated that every 10 minutes, 12 hysterectomies are performed in the United States alone. A hysterectomy may be performed for a variety of medical problems, including uterine fibroids, endometriosis, cancer, chronic pelvic pain, abnormal uterine bleeding, and pelvic infection, or if there is abnormal bleeding after a delivery of a baby. Today there are several new options—medications and various procedures—to treat uterine conditions, which has decreased the overall hysterectomy rate. Rates have also been falling because of increased patient involvement (A. Kennedy et al., 2002).

Ovarian Cancer

It is estimated there would be 22,220 new cases of ovarian cancer in the United States in 2005 (American Cancer Society, 2005b). Though not as common as uterine or breast cancer, it is the most deadly of all gynecologic cancers; 61% of women die within 5 years of developing it. Ovarian cancer is more common in Northern European and North American countries than in Asia or developing countries.

Ovarian cancer invades the body silently, with few warning signs or symptoms until it reaches an advanced stage. A woman in whom an ovarian lump is detected need not panic, however, for most lumps turn out to be relatively harmless **ovarian cysts;** about 70% of all ovarian tumors are benign.

The cause of ovarian cancer is unknown. An increased incidence is found in women who are childless, undergo early menopause, eat a high-fat diet, or who are from a higher socioeconomic status. Women who are lactose-intolerant or who use talc powder (especially on the vulva) have also been found to have higher rates of ovarian cancer. A decreased incidence is associated with having children, using oral contraceptives, or undergoing late menopause (American Cancer Society, 2003). Women who take birth control pills, who were pregnant at an early age, or who had several pregnancies, have particularly low rates of ovarian cancer (Modan et al., 2001). One study demonstrated that women who undergo tubal ligation (have their tubes tied to prevent pregnancy) also reduce the risk of ovarian cancer (Narod et al., 2001).

The most important factor in the survival rate from ovarian cancer is early detection and diagnosis. It is estimated that two-thirds of cases of ovarian cancer are diagnosed late (Mantica, 2005). Because the ovary floats freely in the pelvic cavity, a tumor can grow undetected without producing many noticeable symptoms (i.e., there is little pressure on other organs; see Figure 4.2).

There are several screening techniques for detecting ovarian cancer. These include blood tests, pelvic examinations, and ultrasound. Unfortunately, pelvic examinations are not effective in the early diagnosis of ovarian cancer, and both blood tests and ultrasound have fairly high **false negatives.** This is why many women with ovarian cancer are diagnosed after the cancer has spread beyond the ovary. Although there are a variety of screening tests available for ovarian cancer, including CA-125 and YKL-40, the United States Preventive Services Task Force recommends against routine screening for ovarian cancer, because the potential benefits of these tests remains low (Mantica, 2005; U.S. Preventive Services Task Force, 2005).

Early symptoms of ovarian cancer, if there are any, include vague abdominal discomfort, loss of appetite, indigestion, and anorexic symptoms, and later a patient may become aware of an abdominal mass or diffuse abdominal swelling. At this stage, nausea and vomiting may also occur due to intestinal obstruction. The only treatment is removal of the ovaries (with or without accompanying hysterectomy) and radiation and chemotherapy. As we stated earlier, early detection is crucial to maximizing the chance of a cure. Preventive surgery to remove the ovaries in women with a genetic risk has been found to decrease the risk of ovarian and other gynecologic cancers (American Cancer Society, 2003).

As you have learned throughout this chapter, understanding anatomy and physiology is an important piece in learning about human sexual behavior. It is important to understand all of the physiological and hormonal influences and how they affect the female body before we can move on to the emotional and psychological issues involved in human sexuality. Anatomy and physiology, therefore, are really the foundations of any human sexuality class. We will continue laying this foundation in the following chapter when we move on to "Male Sexual Anatomy and Physiology."

ovarian cysts
Small, fluid-filled sacs, which can form on the ovary, that do not pose a health threat under most conditions.

false negatives
Incorrect result of a medical test that wrongly shows the lack of a finding, condition, or disease.

Review Question

Explain why ovarian cancer is the most deadly gynecologic cancer.

Chapter Review

ACTIVE SUMMARY

1. Endocrine glands produce **(a)** _____. Female reproductive hormones include **(b)** _____ and **(c)** _____, whereas the primary male reproductive hormone is **(d)** _____.

2. The women's external sex organs, collectively called the **(a)** _____, include a number of separate structures, including the mons veneris, labia **(b)** _____, and labia **(c)** _____. The **(d)** _____ is cylindrical erectile tissue, located under the prepuce, that becomes erect during sexual excitement and is the seat of female sexual arousal. The space between the labia minora is referred to as the **(e)** _____. The opening of the vagina is also referred to as the **(f)** _____.

3. The female's internal sexual organs include the **(a)** _____, the **(b)** _____, the Fallopian tubes, and the **(c)** _____. The **(d)** _____ serves as the female organ of intercourse and the passageway to and from the uterus.

4. The **(a)** _____ is a thick-walled, hollow, muscular organ that provides a path for sperm to reach the ovum and provides a home for the developing fetus. On the sides of the uterus lie two **(b)** _____ _____, and their job is to bring the **(c)** _____ from the ovary into the uterus. The mature ovary contains a woman's **(d)** _____ and are the major producers of female **(e)** _____ hormones.

5. The **(a)** _____ are modified sweat glands that contain fatty tissue and produce **(b)** _____ to nourish a newborn. Milk creation, secretion, and ejection from the nipple is referred to as breast-feeding, or **(c)** _____.

6. Female puberty occurs when the ovaries begin to release **(b)** _____, which stimulates growth of the woman's sexual organs and menstruation. Menstruation can be divided into four general phases: the **(b)** _____ phase, **(c)** _____, the **(d)** _____, and the **(e)** _____ phase.

7. A number of menstrual problems are possible, including **(a)** _____, which involves a lack of menstruation, **(b)** _____, which involves excessive menstrual flow, and **(c)** _____, which is painful menstruation. The physical and emotional symptoms that may occur late in the menstrual cycle are called **(d)** _____ _____. The most debilitating and severe cases of PMS are referred to as **(e)** _____ _____ _____.

8. Menstrual **(a)** _____, the ability to schedule menstrual periods, and menstrual **(b)** _____, the ability to completely eliminate menses, are becoming more popular. There

are cultural **(c)** _____ against sexual intercourse during menstruation. However, engaging in sexual intercourse during menstruation is a personal decision; and although there is no **(d)** _____ reason to avoid intimacy during this time, couples need to talk about what they are comfortable with.

9. As women age, **(a)** _____ or **(b)** _____ production wanes, leading to **(c)** _____, or the cessation of menstruation. Some women use **(d)** _____ therapy to help lessen menopausal symptoms, whereas others use **(e)** _____ _____ _____, which has its advantages and disadvantages.

10. Regular **(a)** _____ examination is recommended for all women to help detect uterine, ovarian, and cervical **(b)** _____. Genital **(c)** _____-_____ is also an important part of women's health behavior.

11. There are several gynecological health concerns. Endometriosis is a condition in which the **(a)** _____ cells begin to migrate to places other than the **(b)** _____. Toxic shock syndrome is a(n) **(c)** _____, usually caused by the use of **(d)** _____. Symptoms of TSS include high fever, vomiting, diarrhea, and sore throat. If left untreated it can result in **(e)** _____.

12. Uterine fibroids are hard tissue **(a)** _____ in the uterus, and symptoms include pelvic **(b)** _____, heavy **(c)** _____, and prolonged **(d)** _____.

13. The most prevalent cancer in the world is **(a)** _____ cancer. Breast self-examination can help **(b)** _____ breast cancer early. The most common forms of uterine cancer are **(c)** _____ and **(d)** _____. The most deadly of all gynecologic cancers is **(e)** _____.

ANSWERS

1. (a) hormones; **(b)** estrogen; **(c)** progesterone; **(d)** testosterone. **2. (a)** vulva; **(b)** majora; **(c)** minora; **(d)** clitoris; **(e)** vestibule; **(f)** introitus. **3. (a)** vagina; **(b)** uterus; **(c)** ovaries; **(d)** vagina. **4. (a)** uterus; **(b)** Fallopian tubes; **(c)** ovum; **(d)** oocytes; **(e)** reproductive. **5. (a)** breasts; **(b)** milk; **(c)** lactation. **6. (a)** estrogen; **(b)** follicular; **(c)** ovulation; **(d)** luteal; **(e)** menstrual. **7. (a)** amenorrhea; **(b)** menorrhagia; **(c)** dysmenorrheal; **(d)** premenstrual syndrome; **(e)** premenstrual dysphoric disorder. **8. (a)** manipulation; **(b)** suppression; **(c)** taboos; **(d)** medical. **9. (a)** hormone; **(b)** estrogen; **(c)** menopause; **(d)** nutritional; **(e)** hormone replacement therapy. **10. (a)** gynecological; **(b)** cancers; **(c)** self-examination. **11. (a)** uterine; **(b)** uterus; **(c)** infection; **(d)** tampons; **(e)** death. **12. (a)** masses; **(b)** pain; **(c)** cramping; **(d)** bleeding. **13. (a)** breast; **(b)** detect; **(c)** cervical; **(d)** endometrial; **(e)** ovarian.

Critical Thinking Questions

1. What were the early messages that you received (as a man or a woman) about menstruation? Did you receive any information about it when you were growing up? What do you wish would have been done differently?

2. Do you think that PMS really exists? Provide a rationale for your answer.

3. How would you feel about engaging in sexual intercourse during menstruation? Why do you think you feel this way? Trace how these feelings may have developed.

4. If you are a woman, have you ever practiced a breast self-exam? If so, what made you decide to perform one? If you have never performed one, why not? If you are a man, do you encourage the women in your life to perform breast self-exams? Why, or why not?

CHAPTER RESOURCES

Check It Out

Stewart, E. G., and Spencer, P. (2002). **The V book: A doctor's guide to complete vulvovaginal health.** New York: Bantam Doubleday Dell Publishers.

This is an excellent, must-read book for women of all ages and their partners. Using user-friendly language, the authors discuss vulvovaginal anatomy and functions, changes through the life cycle, routine self-care, sexual issues affecting the vulvovaginal area, pelvic exams, bothersome symptoms, and 13 chapters for specific vulvovaginal problems. The authors believe that "your private parts shouldn't be private to you."

The Vagina Monologues (2002; 1 hour, 16 minutes)

The Vagina Monologues, created and performed by Eve Ensler, debuted off-Broadway in 1996. This controversial work soon received national acclaim and continues to be performed around the world. It has been translated into 14 different languages and has been performed in over 30 different countries.

InfoTrac® College Edition

If your instructor ordered InfoTrac with this book, explore InfoTrac College Edition, your online library, for additional readings and review. Go to: **www.thomsonedu.com,** and enter these search terms:

PMDD	clitoris	G-spot
vagina	female ejaculation	female genitalia
hormone replacement therapy	menopause	vaginitis
hysterectomy	female genital mutilation	menstruation
Pap smear	breast cancer	gynecologist

Web Resources

SexualityNow Companion Website
Go to **http://thomsonedu.com/carroll** for practice quiz questions, interactive activities, Internet links, critical thinking exercises, discussion forums, and more. You can also access sites from the Wadsworth Psychology Study Center **(http://psychology.wadsworth.com)** or you can connect directly to the following sites:

Museum of Menstruation & Women's Health (MUM)
An online museum that illustrates the rich history of menstruation and women's health. Contains information on menstruation's history and various aspects of menstruation, including products, exhibits, patents, religion, menstrual products, shame, synchrony, tampons, and much more. Links to a variety of sources are included.

The American College of Obstetricians and Gynecologists (ACOG)
ACOG was founded in 1951 and is the nation's leading group of professionals providing health care for women. Based in Washington, D.C., ACOG is a private, voluntary, nonprofit membership organization. This site contains information on recent news releases relevant to women's health, educational materials, and links to various other health-related websites.

National Women's Health Information Center (NWHIC)
This website, operated by the Department of Health and Human Services, provides a gateway to women's health information services. Information is available on pregnancy, cancer in women, eating disorders, nutrition, exercise and diet, menopause and hormone replacement therapy, and many other health-related areas.

The National Vulvodynia Association (NVA)
The National Vulvodynia Association (NVA) is a nonprofit organization created in 1994 to improve the lives of women who experience vulvodynia. The NVA educates women, provides support, works with other health organizations to educate the public about vulvodynia, coordinates a central source of information, and encourages further research

Cancernet
This site contains material for health professionals, including cancer treatments, prevention, and CANCERLIT, a bibliographic database.

Forward USA
Forward USA is a nonprofit organization that works to eliminate female genital mutilation (FGM) and provide support services for those young girls and women who are victims of FGM. Founded in 1996, Forward USA provides education and supports legislation aimed at preventing FGM.

Go to **www.thomsonedu.com** to link to **SexualityNow,** your online study tool. First take the **Pre-Test** for this chapter to get your **Personalized Study Plan,** which will identify topics you need to review and direct you to online resources. Then take the **Post-Test** to determine what concepts you have mastered and what you still need work on.

Videos in SexualityNow
For additional information on topics discussed in this chapter, check out the videos in **SexualityNow** on the following topics:
- **Breast Cancer: Education and Support Groups**—Is providing group support or group education more effective in prolonging the lives of women with breast cancer?

5 Male Sexual Anatomy and Physiology

The Male Sexual and Reproductive System
External Sex Organs
- SEX IN REAL LIFE Penis Size and Male Anxiety
- HUMAN SEXUALITY IN A DIVERSE WORLD Ethnicity, Religion, and Circumcision
Internal Sex Organs
Other Sex Organs

The Male Maturation Cycle
Male Puberty
Andropause

Male Reproductive and Sexual Health
Diseases of the Male Reproductive Organs

- SEX IN REAL LIFE Testicular Self-Examination
Other Conditions That Affect the Male Reproductive Organs
Cancer of the Male Reproductive Organs
- SEX IN REAL LIFE Testicular Cancer

Chapter Review

Chapter Resources

Sexuality Now Go to www.thomsonedu.com to link to
SexualityNow, your online study tool.

*I*n the last chapter we discussed female anatomy and physiology, and here we begin our discussion of male sexual anatomy and physiology. Although there are many similarities between the two, there are also many important differences. One obvious difference is the fact that the male gonads (the testes) lie outside of the body, whereas the female gonads (ovaries) are located deep within the abdomen. Because of the location of the male genitalia, boys are often more comfortable than girls with their genitalia. In addition to this, boys usually hold the penis during urination, which further increases comfort levels. In this chapter we will explore the male reproductive system, maturation, and sexual health issues.

THE MALE SEXUAL AND REPRODUCTIVE SYSTEM

Most men are fairly familiar with their penis and scrotum. Boys learn to hold their penises while urinating, certainly notice them when they become erect, and generally talk more freely about their genitals among themselves than girls do. Yet the male reproductive system is a complex series of glands and ducts, and few men have a full understanding of how the system operates physiologically.

External Sex Organs

The external sex organs of the male include the penis (which consists of the glans and root) and the scrotum. Here we will discuss these organs and the process of penile erection.

The Penis

The **penis** is the male sexual organ. It contains the urethra, which carries urine and semen to the outside of the body. The penis has the ability to engorge with blood and stiffen, which evolutionary theorists would tell us allows for easier penetration of the vagina in order to deposit sperm near the cervical os for its journey toward the ovum. Though there is no bone and little muscle in the human penis, the root of the penis is attached to a number of muscles that help eject **semen** and that allow men to move the penis slightly when erect. Throughout history men have experienced anxiety about penis size. In the accompanying Sex in Real Life, "Penis Size and Male Anxiety," we'll discuss this anxiety.

penis
The male copulatory and urinary organ, used both to urinate and move spermatozoa out of the urethra through ejaculation; it is the major organ of male sexual pleasure and is homologous to the female clitoris.

semen
A thick, whitish secretion of the male reproductive organs, containing spermatozoa and secretions from the seminal vesicles, prostate, and bulbourethral glands.

The human penis can be various sizes and shapes and may be circumcised or uncircumcised.

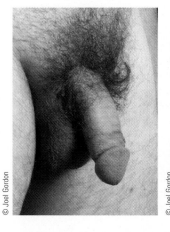

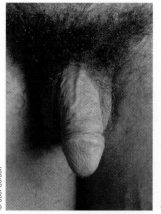

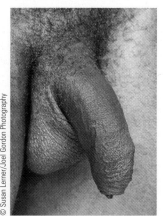

(flah-GEL-lum), which propels the mature spermatozoon. Human sperm formation requires approximately 72 days, yet because sperm is in constant production, the human male produces about 300 million sperm per day.

Testosterone Production   Testosterone is produced in the testicles in **interstitial** (in-ter-STIH-shul) or **Leydig cells** and is synthesized from cholesterol. Testosterone is the most important male hormone; we will discuss its role when we examine male puberty, later in this chapter.

The Epididymis   Once formed, immature sperm enter the seminiferous tubule and migrate to the **epididymis** (ep-uh-DID-uh-mus; see Figure 5.5), where they mature for about 10 to 14 days and where some faulty or old sperm are reabsorbed. The epididymis is a comma-shaped organ that sits atop the testicle and can be easily felt if the testicle is gently rolled between the fingers. If uncoiled, the epididymis would be about 20 feet in length. After sperm have matured, the epididymis pushes them into the vas deferens, where they can be stored for several months.

The Ejaculatory Pathway

The **vas deferens** (vass DEH-fuh-renz), or ductus deferens, is an 18-inch tube that carries the sperm from the testicles, mixes it with fluids from other glands, and propels the sperm toward the urethra during ejaculation (see Figure 5.6). **Ejaculation** is the physiological process whereby the seminal fluid is forcefully ejected from the penis. During

interstitial cells
Cells responsible for the production of testosterone; also referred to as Leydig cells.

Leydig cells
The cells in the testes that produce testosterone; also referred to as interstitial cells.

epididymis
A comma-shaped organ that sits atop the testicle and holds sperm during maturation.

vas deferens
One of two long tubes that convey the sperm from the testes and in which other fluids are mixed to create semen.

ejaculation
The reflex ejection or expulsion of semen from the penis.

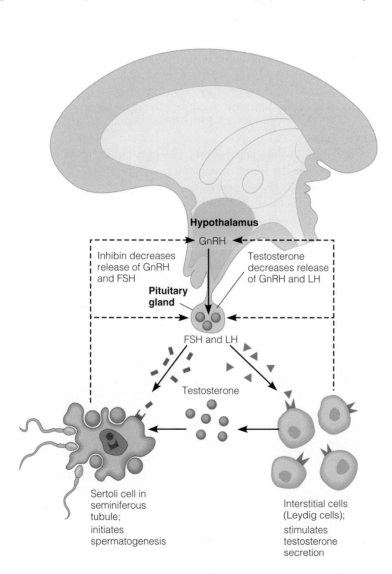

Figure 5.6
The cycle of male hormones.

ejaculation, sperm pass successively through the epididymis, the vas deferens, the ejaculatory duct, and the urethra, picking up fluid along the way from three glands—the seminal vesicles, the prostate gland, and the bulbourethral gland.

The Seminal Vesicles   The vas deferens hooks up over the ureter of the bladder and ends in an **ampulla.** Adjacent to the ampulla are the **seminal vesicles.** The seminal vesicles contribute rich secretions, which provide nutrition for the traveling sperm and make up about 60 to 70% of the volume of the ejaculate. The vas deferens and the duct from the seminal vesicles merge into a common **ejaculatory duct,** a short straight tube that passes into the prostate gland and opens into the urethra.

The Prostate Gland   The **prostate** (PROSS-tayt) **gland,** a walnut-sized gland at the base of the bladder, produces several substances that are thought to aid sperm in their attempt to fertilize an ovum. The vagina maintains an acidic pH to protect against bacteria, yet an acidic environment slows down and eventually kills sperm. Prostatic secretions, which comprise about 25 to 30% of the ejaculate, effectively neutralize vaginal acidity almost immediately following ejaculation.

The prostate is close to the rectum, so a doctor can feel the prostate during a rectal examination. The prostate gland can cause a number of physical problems in men, especially older men, including prostate enlargement and the development of prostate cancer (see the section later in this chapter on "Male Reproductive and Sexual Health"). Annual prostate exams are recommended for men over 35 years of age.

Cowper's Glands   The **bulbourethral** or **Cowper's glands** are two pea-sized glands that flank the urethra just beneath the prostate gland. The glands have ducts that open right into the urethra and produce a fluid that cleans and lubricates the urethra for the passage of sperm, neutralizing any acidic urine that may remain in the urethra. The drop or more of pre-ejaculatory fluid that many men experience during arousal is the fluid from the Cowper's glands. Be aware, however, that the fluid may contain some live sperm, especially in a second act of intercourse if the male has not urinated in between.

Ejaculation   Earlier in this chapter, we discussed erection as a spinal reflex. Ejaculation, like erection, also begins in the spinal column; however, unlike erection, there is seldom a "partial" ejaculation. Once the stimulation builds to the threshold, ejaculation usually continues until its conclusion.

When the threshold is reached, the first stage of ejaculation begins: the epididymis, seminal vesicles, and prostate all empty their contents into the urethral bulb, which swells up to accommodate the semen. The bladder is closed off by an internal sphincter so that no urine is expelled with the semen. Once these stages begin, some men report feeling that ejaculation is imminent, that they are going to ejaculate and nothing can stop it; however, others report that this feeling of inevitability can be stopped by immediately ceasing all sensation.

If stimulation continues, strong, rhythmic contractions of the muscles at the base of the penis squeeze the urethral bulb, and the ejaculate is propelled from the body, usually accompanied by the pleasurable sensation of orgasm. Most men have between 5 and 15 contractions during orgasm, and many report enjoying strong pressure at the base of the penis during orgasm. This may be an evolutionary way of encouraging deep thrusting at the moment of ejaculation to deposit semen as deeply as possible within the woman's vagina.

Once orgasm subsides, the arteries supplying the blood to the penis narrow, the veins taking the blood out enlarge, and the penis usually becomes limp. Depending on the level of excitement, the person's age, the length of time since the previous ejaculation, and his individual physiology, a new erection can be achieved anywhere from immediately to an hour or so later.

Ejaculate   The male ejaculate, or semen, averages about 2 to 5 milliliters—about 1 or 2 teaspoons. Semen normally contains secretions from the seminal vesicles and the prostate gland and about 50 to 150 million sperm per milliliter. If there are fewer than

---

ampulla
Base of the vas deferens, where the vas hooks up over the ureter of the bladder.

seminal vesicles
The pair of pouchlike structures lying next to the urinary bladder that secrete a component of semen into the ejaculatory ducts.

ejaculatory duct
A tube that transports spermatozoa from the vas deferens to the urethra.

prostate gland
A doughnut-shaped gland that wraps around the urethra as it comes out of the bladder, contributing fluid to the semen.

bulbourethral gland
One of a pair of glands located under the prostate gland on either side of the urethra that secretes a fluid into the urethra; also called a Cowper's gland.

Cowper's gland
One of a pair of glands located under the prostate gland on either side of the urethra that secretes a fluid into the urethra; also called a bulbourethral gland.

sex byte

In his lifetime, a man will ejaculate approximately 18 quarts of semen, containing approximately 500 billion sperm (Welch, 1992).

Review Question

Identify and discuss the functions of the internal male sexual organs.

sex byte

Each ejaculation contains between 300 to 500 million sperm, and it is estimated that 10 to 20 ejaculations contain enough sperm to populate the earth (T. Hamilton, 2002).

Question: *Can a male have an orgasm without an ejaculation?*

Yes. Before puberty, boys are capable of orgasm without ejaculation. In adulthood, some men report feeling several small orgasms before a larger one that includes ejaculation, whereas other men report that if they have sex a second or third time, there is orgasm without ejaculatory fluid. There are also some Eastern sexual disciplines, like Tantra, that try to teach men to achieve orgasm without ejaculation because they believe that retaining semen is important for men.

20 million sperm per milliliter, the male is likely to be infertile—even though the ejaculate can have almost 100 million sperm altogether! Sperm is required in such large numbers because only a small fraction ever reach the ovum. Also, the sperm work together to achieve fertilization; for example, many die to plug up the os of the cervix for the other sperm, and the combined enzyme production of all sperm are necessary for a single spermatozoon to fertilize the ovum.

During vaginal intercourse, after ejaculation the semen initially coagulates into a thick mucuslike liquid, probably to keep it from leaking back out of the vagina. After 5 to 20 minutes, the prostatic enzymes contained in the semen cause it to thin out and liquefy. If it does not liquefy normally, coagulated semen may be unable to complete its movement through the cervix and into the uterus.

Other Sex Organs

Like women, men have other **erogenous zones,** or areas of the body that may be responsive to sexual touch. This is often an individual preference, but it can include the breasts and other erogenous zones, including the scrotum, testicles, and anus.

The Breasts

Men's breasts are mostly muscle, and though they do have nipples and areolae, they seem to serve no functional purpose. Transsexual males, who want to change their sex (see Chapter 3), can enlarge their breasts to mimic the female breast by taking estrogen. Some men experience sexual pleasure from having their nipples stimulated, especially during periods of high excitement, whereas others do not.

There are some breast disorders that occur in men, including gynecomastia (guy-neck-oh-MAST-ee-uh), or breast enlargement. Gynecomastia is common both in puberty and old age and usually lasts anywhere from a few months to a few years. It is caused by drug therapy, excessive marijuana use, hormonal imbalance, and certain diseases. Generally gynecomastia disappears in time, and surgical removal is not necessary. However, some men choose to undergo a new surgical technique that removes the excessive tissue through suction, which is usually followed by cosmetic surgery.

Breast cancer does affect men, although it is rare and accounts for less than 1% of all cases (Kahla et al., 2005). Because it is uncommon, it often progresses to an advanced stage prior to diagnosis (Frangou et al., 2005). Treatment for breast cancer involves radiation or chemotherapy, and, if the cancer has spread to other parts of the body, surgical removal of the testes may be necessary to eliminate the hormones that may support the growth of the cancer (we will talk about this more later in this chapter).

Other Erogenous Zones

Besides the penis, many men experience pleasure from stimulation of the scrotum, testicles (usually through gentle squeezing), and anus. As with women's erogenous zones, there is no part of the male body that is not erogenous if

Review Question

Describe the path taken by a sperm from the moment it is a spermatogonium until it is ejaculated. What other internal male organs donate fluids to the semen along the way?

erogenous zone
Any part of the body which, when stimulated, induces a sense of sexual excitement or desire.

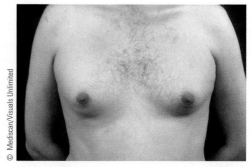

© Mediscan/Visuals Unlimited

Gynecomastia is common in puberty and old age and can be caused by a variety of factors.

caressed in the right way and at the right time during lovemaking. When the body is sexually stimulated, almost all moderate sensation can enhance excitement—which is why gentle pinching, scratching, and slapping can be exciting for some lovers.

THE MALE MATURATION CYCLE

Now that we've discussed the male sexual and reproductive system, let's explore male maturation. In the following section we will discuss the physical changes that accompany male puberty. Many of these changes are controlled by hormonal changes that occur and contribute to physical changes in a young boy's body. In Chapter 8 we will discuss the psychosexual changes of male puberty.

Male Puberty

During a boy's early life, the two major functions of the testes—to produce male sex hormones and to produce sperm—remain dormant. No one knows exactly what triggers the onset of puberty or how a boy's internal clock knows that he is reaching the age in which these functions of the testes will be needed. Still, at an average of 10 years of age, the hypothalamus begins releasing gonadotropin releasing hormone (GnRH), which stimulates the anterior pituitary gland to send out follicle-stimulating hormone (FSH) and luteinizing hormone (LH; see Table 3.2 in Chapter 3).

These flow through the circulatory system to the testes, where LH stimulates the production of the male sex hormone, testosterone, which, together with LH, stimulates sperm production. A negative feedback system regulates hormone production; when the concentration of testosterone in the blood increases to a certain level, GnRH release from the hypothalamus is inhibited, causing inhibition of LH production and resulting in decreased testosterone production. Alternately, when testosterone levels decrease below a certain level, this stimulates GnRH production by the hypothalamus, which increases the pituitary's LH production and testosterone production goes up.

As puberty progresses, the testicles grow, and the penis begins to grow about a year later. The epididymis, prostate, seminal vesicles, and bulbourethral glands also grow over the next several years. Increased testosterone stimulates an overall growth spurt in puberty, as bones and muscles rapidly develop. This spurt can be dramatic; teenage boys can grow 3 or 4 inches within a few months. The elevation of testosterone and DHT affects a number of male traits: the boy develops longer and heavier bones, larger muscles, thicker and tougher skin, a deepening voice due to growth of the voice box, pubic hair, facial and chest hair, increased sex drive, and increased metabolism.

Spermatogenesis begins at about 12 years of age, but ejaculation of mature sperm usually does not occur for about another 1 to 1-½ years. At puberty, the hormone FSH begins to stimulate sperm production in the seminiferous tubules, and the increased testosterone induces the testes to fully mature. The development of spermatogenesis and the sexual fluid glands allows the boy to begin to experience his first wet orgasms, though, at the beginning, they tend to contain a very low live sperm count.

Andropause

As men age, their blood testosterone concentrations decrease. Hormone levels in men have been found to decrease by about 1% each year after the age of 40 (Daw, 2002). Men do not go through an obvious set of stages, as menopausal women do, but experience a less well-defined set of symptoms in their 70s or 80s called **andropause.** Though men's ability to ejaculate viable sperm is often retained past the age of 80 or 90, spermatogenesis does decrease, the ejaculate becomes thinner, and ejaculatory pressure decreases. The reduction in testosterone production results in decreased muscle strength, decreased libido, easy fatigue, and mood disturbances. Men can also experience **osteoporosis** and **anemia** from the decreasing hormone levels (Bain, 2001). Although some men are prescribed testosterone therapy (Morales, 2004), hormonal treatment for men is still controversial today.

Review Question

Describe the two major functions of the testes, and explain the negative feedback loop in males.

andropause
The hormonal changes accompanying old age in men that correspond to menopause in women.

osteoporosis
A disease in which bones become fragile and more likely to break.

anemia
A condition in which there is a deficiency in the oxygen-carrying material of the blood.

Review Question

What effect do the decreasing levels of testosterone have on men?

It is a good idea for every man to examine and explore his own sexual anatomy. A genital self-exam can help increase a man's comfort with his genitals (see Sex in Real Life, "Testicular Self-Examination"). It can also help a man know what his testicles feel like just in case something were to change. We will now discuss diseases and other conditions that may affect the male reproductive organs, in addition to cancer of the male reproductive organs.

Diseases of the Male Reproductive Organs

There are several conditions that can affect the male reproductive organs, including cryptorchidism, testicular torsion, priapism, and Peyronie's disease. It's important for both men and women to have a good understanding of what these conditions are and what symptoms they might cause.

Cryptorchidism

The testicles of a male fetus begin high in the abdomen near the kidneys, and, during fetal development, descend into the scrotum through the **inguinal canal** (Hutson et al., 1994). In approximately 3 to 5% of full-term male infants, the testes fail to descend into the scrotum, a condition called **cryptorchidism** (krip-TOR-kuh-diz-um; Docimo et al., 2000). (A similar condition can occur in males with an inguinal hernia, in which the intestine enters the scrotum through the inguinal canal and may fill it completely, leaving no room for the testicles.) The temperature of the abdomen is too high to support sperm production, so if the testes remain in the abdomen much past the age of 5, the male is likely to be infertile. Cryptorchid testes also carry a 30 to 50 times increased risk of testicular cancer. In most infants, cryptorchidism can be identified and corrected

inguinal canal
Canal through which the testes descend into the scrotum.

cryptorchidism
A condition in which the testes fail to descend into the scrotum.

SEX in Real Life

Testicular Self-Examination

© Joel Gordon

Although there are no obvious symptoms of testicular cancer, when detected early, it is treatable. The only early detection system for testicular cancer is testicular self-examination (TSE). Yet most men do not do regular TSEs. Just like breast self-examinations in women, men should examine their testicles at least monthly. This will enable them to have an understanding of what things feel like under normal conditions, which will help them to find any lumps or abnormal growths, should they appear.

Let's talk about how to do a testicular exam. First, compare both testicles simultaneously by grasping one with each hand, using thumb and forefinger. This may be best done while taking a warm shower, which causes the scrotum to relax and the testicles to hang lower. Determine their size, shape, and sensitivity to pressure.

As you get to know the exact shape and feel of the testicles, you will be able to notice any swelling, lumps, or unusual pain. Report any such occurrence to your physician without delay, but do not panic; most lumps are benign and nothing to worry about.

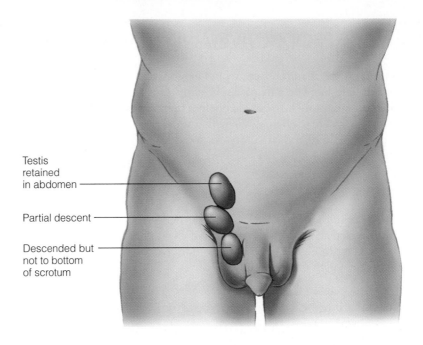

Figure 5.7
Although the testicles of a fetus begin high in the abdomen, they must descend into the scrotum during fetal development. If they do not, the male may become infertile.

Testis retained in abdomen

Partial descent

Descended but not to bottom of scrotum

through laparoscopy to find the undescended testis and then surgery to relocate the testis in the scrotum (Hack et al., 2003). It is recommended that this surgery be done by 6 months of age (Hutson & Hasthorpe, 2005).

Testicular Torsion

testicular torsion
The twisting of a testis on its spermatic cord, which can cause severe pain and swelling.

Testicular torsion refers to a twisting of a testis on its spermatic cord (see Figure 5.8). Usually it occurs when there is abnormal development of the spermatic cord or the membrane that covers the testicle. It is most common in men from puberty to the age of 25, although it can happen at any age. Testicular torsion can occur after exercise, sexual intercourse, or even while sleeping.

Severe pain and swelling are two of the most common symptoms of testicular torsion, although there can also be abdominal pain, tenderness, and aching. A physician must diagnose this condition quickly because the twisted cord can cut off the blood supply to the testicle, and surgery to untwist the cord must be done within 24 hours or else the testicle may be lost.

Figure 5.8
Testicular torsion can occur after exercise, sexual intercourse, or even while sleeping.

Normal anatomy

Testicular torsion

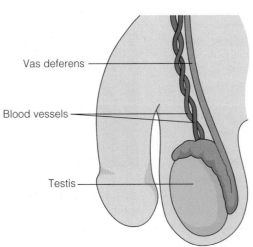
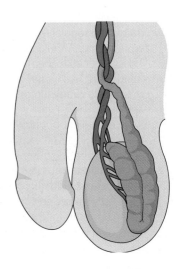

Vas deferens

Blood vessels

Testis

Question: If a right-handed man's penis curves to the right when he gets an erection, does this mean he masturbated too much as a child?

No, although many men worry about this during their adolescent years. The fact is that erect penises are rarely straight or smooth—some curve left or right, and some go up or down upon erection. All of these variations are normal. A man may be able to influence the angle of his erect penis by the way he places his penis in his underwear. Pointing the flaccid penis up, down, or sideways in one's underwear can affect the penis's tendency to point in a certain direction when erect (T. Hamilton, 2002).

Priapism

Priapism (pry-AE-pizm) is a painful and persistent erection that is not associated with sexual desire or excitement (Van der Horst et al., 2003). Blood becomes trapped in the erectile tissue of the penis and is unable to get out. The most common cause of priapism is drug use (erection drugs, cocaine, marijuana, or anticoagulants), but in many causes the cause is unknown.

Treatment for priapism depends on the cause. Draining the blood from the penis is possible with the use of a needle and syringe. If it is related to drug use, the drugs need to be discontinued immediately. If there is a neurologic or other physiological cause for the priapism, anesthesia or surgery may be necessary. Future sexual functioning may suffer if this condition is not treated effectively.

priapism
A condition in which erections are long-lasting and often painful.

Peyronie's Disease

Every male has individual curves to his penis when it becomes erect. These curves and angles are quite normal. However, in approximately 1% of men, painful curvature makes penetration impossible, leading to a diagnosis of a condition known as **Peyronie's** (pay-ra-NEEZ) **disease** (C. J. Smith et al., 2005). Typically this happens between the ages of 45 and 60, although a younger or older man could also experience Peyronie's.

Peyronie's disease occurs in the connective tissue of the penis, and although some cases are asymptomatic, others develop penile nodules, which can cause severe erectile pain (Gelbard, 1988). No one knows what causes Peyronie's disease. It is possible that crystal deposits in the connective tissue, trauma, excessive calcium levels, or calcification may contribute to this disorder (Gelbard, 1988). Usually this disease lasts approximately 2 years and may go away just as suddenly as it appears. It is often treated with medication or surgery (Austoni et al., 2005).

Peyronie's disease
Abnormal calcifications in the penis, which may cause painful curvature, often making sexual intercourse impossible.

sex byte

Laptop computers may pose a long-term threat to the fertility of young men. Research has found that keeping a laptop on a man's lap for 1 hour can raise the scrotal temperature enough to negatively impact male fertility (Sheynkin et al., 2005).

Other Conditions That Affect the Male Reproductive Organs

Other conditions may also affect the male reproductive organs, including steroid use, hernias, and hydoceles. Over the last few years, steroids have become a controversial topic as more and more male athletes disclose past steroid use. In 2005, congressional hearings began to evaluate steroid use in major league baseball. We will discuss this more in the following section.

Anabolic-Androgenic Steroid Use

Before we discuss diseases and cancer of the male reproductive organs, let's talk about the use of steroids (which occur naturally in the body and are known as **androgens**). During puberty in males, the release of androgens increases weight and muscle size, and can also increase endurance and aggressiveness. Some athletes, believing that additional androgens would further increase weight and muscle size and therefore enhance athletic performance, decided to use synthetic steroids.

androgen
The general name for male hormones such as testosterone and androsterone.

Accusations of steroid use in major league baseball circulated in 2005. Photos of before and after supported these claims. Here is Barry Bonds in 1989 (left) and in 2003 (right).

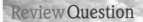

Review Question

Explain the side effects of anabolic-androgenic steroid use.

inguinal hernia
A condition in which the intestines bulge through a hole in the abdominal muscles of the groin.

hydrocele
A condition in which there is an excessive accumulation of fluid within the tissue surrounding the testicle, which causes a scrotal mass.

In the past 3 decades, the use of anabolic-androgenic steroid (AAS), also known as synthetic testosterone, in sport and exercise has increased notably, and it is no longer restricted to elite athletes or adult males. Estimates based on data from the National Household Survey on Drug Abuse indicated that there were more than 1 million current or former anabolic-androgenic steroid users in the United States, with more than half of the lifetime user population 26 years old or older. Approximately 12% of adolescent males admit to using AAS at some point in their lifetime, whereas 1 to 2% of adolescent females admit to using them (Yesalis & Bahrke, 2000). Another study found a significant number of female athletes who were using AAS (Gruber & Pope, 2000).

However, AAS use comes at a high price. It has been associated with many damaging changes in the physiologic characteristics of organs and body systems. The best documented effects are to the liver, serum lipids, and the reproductive system, including shrinkage of the testicles (Yesalis & Bahrke, 2000). Other areas of concern include cerebrovascular accidents (stroke), prostate gland changes, and impaired immune function (Friedl, 1993). In younger athletes, steroids can cause early fusion of the bone-growth plates, resulting in permanently shortened stature. Use of AAS has also been associated with changes in mood and behavior. Schizophrenia, increases in irritability, hostility, anger, aggression, depression, hypomania, psychotic episodes, and guilt have all been reported among AAS users (Millman & Ross, 2003).

The bottom line is this: steroids can cause erectile problems, overly aggressive behavior, mental problems, increased chances of various diseases, shrinkage of the testicles, and even masculinization in women. It is simply not worth the risk.

Inguinal Hernia

An **inguinal hernia** (ING-gwuh-nul HER-nee-uh) is caused when the intestine pushes through the opening in the abdominal wall into the inguinal canal (the inguinal canal was originally used by the testes when they descended into the scrotum shortly before birth). This can happen during heavy lifting or straining. When it does, the intestine pushes down onto the testicles and causes a bulge or lump in the scrotum. The bulge may change shape and size depending on what the man is doing, because it can slide back and forth within the testicle. Other symptoms include pain and possible blockage of the intestine. Depending on the size and the pain associated with the bulge, surgery may be necessary to remove the intestines and restore blood supply to the intestines.

Hydrocele

A **hydrocele** (HI-dra-seal) is a condition in which there is an excessive accumulation of fluid within the tissue surrounding the testicle, which causes a scrotal mass. This accumulation could be due to an overproduction of fluid or poor reabsorption of the fluid. Some men experience pain and swelling within the testicle. Treatment involves removing the built-up fluid.

Cancer of the Male Reproductive Organs

Cancer is a disease in which certain cells in the body don't function properly—they divide too fast and/or produce excessive tissue that forms a tumor. There are a number of different cancers that can affect the male reproductive organs. Let's now look at testicular, penile, and prostatic cancers. In this section we will also review preventive measures for detecting or avoiding common male health problems. In Chapter 14 we will discuss how these illnesses affect men's lives and sexuality.

Testicular Cancer

Testicular cancer is the most common malignancy in men aged 15 to 44 (Garner et al., 2005; McCullagh & Lewis, 2005). It was estimated that there would be 8,010 new cases of testicular cancer diagnosed in the United States in 2005 (American Cancer Society, 2005c). There are few symptoms until the cancer is advanced, which is why early detection is so important. Most men first develop testicular cancer as a painless testicular mass or a harder consistency of the testes. If there is pain or a sudden increase in testicular size, it is usually due to bleeding into the tumor. Sometimes lower back pain, gynecomastia, shortness of breath, or urethral obstruction may also be found.

Though the incidence of testicular cancer has continuously increased during the last few decades, cure rates have significantly improved (Kormann, 2001). In fact, testicular cancer is one of the most curable forms of the disease (American Cancer Society, 2005d). Treatment may involve radiation, chemotherapy, or the removal of the testicle (although radiation and chemotherapy can affect future fertility, the removal of a testicle does not). If removal of the testicle is necessary, many men opt to get a prosthetic testicle implanted, which gives the appearance of having two normal testicles. Early diagnosis is very important, as the treatment is less severe early on, and one's chance of being cured is greater (review Sex in Real Life, "Testicular Self-Examination").

 SEX in Real Life

Testicular Cancer

When Lance Armstrong was diagnosed with testicular cancer, his physicians advised sperm banking prior to treatment. He was able to father three children through assisted reproduction techniques.

We have already discussed the importance of testicular self-examination in the early detection of testicular cancer. Testicular cancer is the most common type of cancer found in young men between the ages of 15 and 34. Following are the stories of two men, both of whom were diagnosed with and treated for testicular cancer.

Lance Armstrong, who has won the Tour de France a record number of times, was diagnosed with testicular cancer when he was 25. A scan revealed that the cancer had spread from his testicle to his lungs and brain. Armstrong underwent aggressive surgery, first to remove the malignant testicle and later to remove the cancer that had spread throughout the rest of his body. He was also treated with an aggressive form of chemotherapy. At the time, his doctors gave him a 50/50 chance of survival. One year after his cancer ordeal, he began racing again. Even though Lance had to have a testicle removed and undergo chemotherapy, he was still able to have three children through in-vitro fertilization (see Chapter 12).

Armstrong is committed to his role as a spokesperson for testicular cancer. Had he known about the importance of early detection, he would have never ignored the swelling and pain in his testicle. Testicular cancer caught early has a 98% success rate. But many men ignore such pain, thinking that it will go away on its own.

Tom Green, a comedian and actor who was once married to Drew Barrymore, is another avid spokesperson on testicular cancer. Green was diagnosed with testicular cancer at the age of 28. Like Armstrong, Green ignored the testicular pain and swelling, convincing himself that he had somehow injured his testicle. Green's strange sense of humor pulled him through as he joked and laughed about his cancer. He started a fund to raise money for testicular cancer, calling it the *Nuts Cancer Fund.* He also went public with a show called *The Tom Green Cancer Special,* which included taped footage of his hospital stay and the surgery to remove his testicle.

Both Armstrong and Green urge all men to regularly check their testicles for swelling, pain, and any changes in structure or size. Remember, early detection is key!

Question: *Can a man who has been treated for testicular cancer still have children?*

Many men with testicular cancer also have fertility problems. Cancer treatments can cause scarring or ejaculation problems that will interfere with later fertility. During radiation or chemotherapy, sperm production does drop off significantly, and some men have no sperm in their semen. However, for the majority of men, sperm production generally returns to normal within 2 to 3 years. Because many men with testicular cancer are in their reproductive prime, waiting 2 or more years might not be an option. For this reason, many healthcare providers recommend sperm banking before cancer treatment. Many men who have been treated for testicular cancer do have children after their cancer treatment, as you'll see in Sex in Real Life, "Testicular Cancer."

benign prostatic hypertrophy
The common enlargement of the prostate that occurs in most men after about age 50.

prostate-specific antigen (PSA)
Blood test that measures levels of molecules that are overproduced by prostate cancer cells, enabling physicians to identify prostate cancer early.

Penile Cancer

A wide variety of cancers involving the skin and soft tissues of the penis can occur, though cancer of the penis is not common (Mosconi et al., 2005). Any lesion on the penis must be examined by a physician, for benign and malignant conditions can be very similar in appearance, and STIs can appear as lesions. Even though most men handle and observe their penis daily, there is often significant delay between a person's recognition of a lesion and seeking medical attention. Fear and embarrassment may contribute most to this problem, yet almost all of these lesions are treatable if caught early.

Prostate Cancer

As men age, their prostate glands enlarge. In most cases, this natural occurrence, **benign prostatic hypertrophy (BPH),** causes few problems. Because of its anatomical position surrounding the urethra, BPH may block urination, and surgeons may need to remove the prostate if the condition becomes bad enough. Of far more concern than BPH is prostate cancer, which is one of the most common types of cancer found in American men (Postma & Schroder, 2005). It was estimated that there would be approximately 232,090 new cases of prostate cancer in 2005, and that 30,350 men would die of this disease (American Cancer Society, 2005e).

Although men of all ages can get prostate cancer, it is found most often in men over the age of 50. In fact, more than 80% of the men with prostate cancer are 65 or older (American Cancer Society, 2005e). For reasons not clearly understood, cancer is about twice as common among African American men as it is among Caucasian Americans (Shaver & Brown, 2002). In fact, African American men have the highest prostate cancer rates in the world. Interestingly, prostate cancer is relatively rare in Asia, Africa, and South America (Brawer, 1999).

Even so, it's important to also realize that there are researchers who believe that prostate cancer is not as common as some suggest. For example, one study found that 29 to 44% of men diagnosed with prostate cancer were actually "overdiagnosed" (Etzioni et al., 2002). This is primarily because current testing methods (see below) have been yielding high false positive results.

Although we don't know exactly what causes prostate cancer, we do know that there are several risk factors that have been linked to prostate cancer. These include aging, race, a diet high in fat, and a genetic risk. Signs of possible prostate cancer (or BPH) include lower back, pelvic, or upper thigh pain; inability to urinate; loss of force in the urinary stream; urinary dribbling; pain or burning during urination; and frequent urination, especially at night. Many deaths from prostate cancer are preventable, because a simple 5- or 10-second rectal examination by a physician, to examine for hard lumps on the prostate, detects over 50% of cases at a curable stage.

In 1986 the U.S. Food and Drug Administration approved the **prostate-specific antigen (PSA)** blood test that measures levels of molecules that are overproduced by prostate cancer cells. This enables physicians to identify prostate cancer and is recommended yearly for men over the age of 50. The PSA test has been one of the most important advances in the area of prostate cancer (Brawer, 1999). Though not all tumors will show up on a PSA test, a high reading does indicate that something (such as a tumor) is releasing prostatic material into the blood, and a biopsy or further examination is warranted.

There are many treatments for prostate cancer, and almost all are controversial. Some argue that, in older men especially, the best thing is "watchful waiting" in which the cancer is simply left alone, because most men will die of other causes before the prostate cancer spreads. Men who are unmarried, have a history of poor health, or are living in a geographically undesirable location for medical treatment often opt for these more conservative treatments (Harlan et al., 2001).

Others choose **radical prostatectomy** or **radiation** treatment, each of which can contribute to erectile disorder or incontinence (Potosky et al., 2000). **Cryosurgery** uses a probe to freeze parts of the prostate and has had good success in reducing the occurrence of postsurgical erectile disorder and incontinence (Onik et al., 2002). Newer treatments include drugs that attack only cells with cancer, unlike radiation and chemotherapy, which both kill healthy cells in addition to those cells with cancer. Research has found that these drugs hold much promise in the treatment of prostate cancer (Bonaccorsi et al., 2004; Ryan & Small, 2005).

Two of the most common surgical side effects of prostate cancer treatment include erectile dysfunction and the inability to hold one's urine. However, the likelihood of these problems depends on several things, including the extent and severity of the cancer and a man's age at the time of surgery (Stewart et al., 2005). Although younger men who experienced satisfactory erections prior to any prostate cancer treatments have fewer erectile problems after surgery, for most men erections will improve over time. Difficulty holding urine or urinary leakage may also occur; however, there are treatments available to lessen these symptoms.

As you have learned throughout this chapter and the last, understanding anatomy and physiology is an important part of learning about human sexual behavior. We must understand all of the physiological and hormonal influences and how they affect both the female and male body before we can move on to the emotional and psychological issues involved in human sexuality. Anatomy and physiology, therefore, are really the foundations of any human sexuality class. With that in mind, in Chapter 6, we discuss "Communication: Enriching Your Sexuality."

radical prostatectomy
The surgical removal of the prostate.

radiation
The use of radioactivity in the treatment of cancer.

cryosurgery
Surgery that uses freezing techniques to destroy part of an organ.

Review Question

Describe the cancers that can affect the male reproductive organs.

Chapter Review

ACTIVE SUMMARY

1. The **(a)** _____ has the ability to fill with blood during sexual arousal. It contains the **(b)** _____ and three cylinders—two corpora cavernosa and one corpus spongiosum. These cylinders are bound together with **(c)** _____ tissue.

2. In many cultures, the **(a)** _____ of the penis is removed during circumcision. Although it is the single most **(b)** _____ surgical procedure performed on male patients in the United States, medical professionals have questioned the health value of **(c)** _____.

3. A/An **(a)** _____ is a spinal reflex, and many types of sexual stimulation can lead to this response. When stimulation stops, the penis returns to its **(b)** _____ state. Most men have regular erections during their sleeping cycle and often **(c)** _____ _____ with an erection.

4. The **(a)** _____ sits outside the man's body and contains the testicles. **(b)** _____ survival requires a temperature that is a few degrees lower than the body's temperature. The **(c)** _____ muscle is responsible for the scrotum's positioning. When it's too hot, the muscle allows the scrotum to hang farther **(d)** _____ from the body. When it is too cold, the muscle elevates the scrotum so that it is **(e)** _____ to the body.

5. The **(a)** _____ have two main functions: spermatogenesis and **(b)** _____ production. One testicle usually hangs **(c)** _____ than the other so that they do not hit each other when compressed. Testosterone is produced in the **(d)** _____ cells.

6. **(a)** _____ is the physiological process whereby the seminal fluid is ejected from the penis. The **(b)** _____ _____, seminal vesicles, prostate, and Cowper's glands all work together during ejaculation. Most men experience between 5 and 15 **(c)** _____ during orgasm. After orgasm, the **(d)** _____ that has been trapped in the penis is released, and the penis becomes **(e)** _____.

7. **(a)** _____, or abnormal breast development, is common during male **(b)** _____ and again in older age. It can be caused by drug therapy, drug abuse, hormonal imbalance, and certain diseases. It will often disappear on its own without surgical intervention. Some men do get **(c)** _____ cancer and, because it is rare, men who are diagnosed are often in **(d)** _____ stages prior to their diagnoses.

8. At about the age of **(a)** _____, a boy enters the first stages of puberty. A/An **(b)** _____ feedback system regulates **(c)** _____ production. As puberty progresses, the testicles increase in size, and the penis begins to grow. Increased **(d)** _____ stimulates an overall growth spurt in puberty, and the bones and muscles grow rapidly. **(e)** _____ usually begins about the age of 12, but it takes another year or so for an ejaculation to contain mature sperm.

9. Blood testosterone levels **(a)** _____ as a man ages; and, although it is not as defined as menopause, men experience a condition known as **(b)** _____. During this time, **(c)** _____ production slows down, the ejaculate becomes **(d)** _____, and ejaculatory pressure decreases.

10. There are several diseases of the male **(a)** _____ organs, including **(b)** _____, testicular torsion, **(c)** _____, Peyronie's disease, inguinal hernia, and hydrocele. Fortunately, all of these are **(d)** _____ conditions.

11. Athletes' use of **(a)** _____ has increased notably over the past 3 decades, even though it had been associated with several damaging changes in the body. This can cause **(b)** _____ and **(c)** _____ gland changes, **(d)** _____ shrinkage, and impaired immune function. Research has also found an increased risk of **(e)** _____ accidents and for young people, early fusion of bone growth plates.

12. Testicular cancer is difficult to catch early because there are few **(a)** _____. It is one of the most **(b)** _____ forms of the disease. Penile cancer is relatively uncommon, but it usually appears as a lesion on the penis. **(c)** _____ cancer is more common in men over age 50 and is the most common cause of cancer deaths among men over age 60. For unknown reasons, this type of cancer is twice as common in **(d)** _____ _____ men as it is among Caucasians.

Critical Thinking Questions

1. We don't seem to need to know how the digestive system works to eat. Why is detailed knowledge of the sexual functioning of men important in human sexuality?

2. If you have a baby boy in the future, would you have him circumcised? Why, or why not?

3. Why do you think some men use the "blue balls" excuse to encourage their partners to have sex? What is the physiological basis for this?

4. Why do you think men are uncomfortable talking about their own body image issues? Why aren't men encouraged to explore these issues?

Check It Out

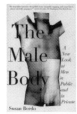

Bordo, S. (2000). **The male body: A new look at men in public and private.** New York: Farrar, Strauss & Giroux.

Susan Bordo takes a close look at men's bodies and changing cultural perceptions over time. One section of the book is devoted to men's genitals in various contexts, including penis size and penile enlargements. Chapters include information on gay men, masculinity, and sexual harassment.

The Last Samurai (2003; 2 hours, 34 minutes; Rated R)

In this 2003 movie, Captain Nathan Algren (Tom Cruise) is a man adrift. The battles he once fought now seem distant and futile. He had risked his life for honor and country, but, in the years since the Civil War, the world has changed. Another soldier, Katsumoto (Ken Watanabe), sees his way of life and war about to disintegrate. He is the last leader of an ancient line of warriors, the venerated Samurai, who dedicated their lives to serving emperor and country. The paths of these two warriors converge when the two must face off to determine the ways of war. Along the way, Algren discovers the man he is. Wonderful exploration of friendship, war, and masculinity.

InfoTrac® College Edition

If your instructor ordered InfoTrac with this book, explore InfoTrac College Edition, your online library, for additional readings and review. Go to: **www.thomsonedu.com,** and enter these search terms:

penis	urethra	spongy body
cavernous bodies	glans	male genitals
penile cancer	testicular cancer	prostate cancer

Web Resources

SexualityNow Companion Website
Go to **http://thomsonedu.com/carroll** for practice quiz questions, interactive activities, Internet links, critical thinking exercises, discussion forums, and more. You can also access sites from the Wadsworth Psychology Study Center **(http://psychology.wadsworth.com)** or you can connect directly to the following sites:

Testicular Cancer Resource Center
The Testicular Cancer Resource Center is a charitable organization devoted to helping people understand testicular cancer. This website provides accurate information about testicular self-exam, the diagnosis and treatment of testicular cancer, male anatomy and physiology, and biological functioning. Links are also provided for other cancers and additional websites.

Medical Education Information Center (MEdIC™)
The University of Texas–Houston Department of Pathology and Laboratory Medicine's worldwide medical education information center contains information about health and has a special link to men's health issues. The site has information on cancer screening, PSA testing, prostate concerns, and other health issues.

MedlinePlus Health Information: Men's Health Topics
This is an excellent site for researching men's health, containing information on STIs, prostate cancer, circumcision, reproductive health concerns, gay and bisexual health, Klinefelter's syndrome, and male genital disorders.

Lance Armstrong Foundation
The Lance Armstrong Foundation (LAF) was founded in 1997 by cancer survivor and champion cyclist Lance Armstrong. The Foundation focuses its activities in the following areas: survivorship education and resources, community programs, national advocacy initiatives, and scientific and clinical research grants. LAF provides information, services, and support, and strives to help all cancer patients through the challenging phases of diagnosis and treatment, encouraging each to adopt the same positive attitude that Lance Armstrong adopted in his own battle with cancer.

National Organization of Circumcision Information Resource Centers (NOCIRC)
NOCIRC is a nonprofit educational organization founded in 1986. It is the first national clearinghouse in the United States for information about circumcision and claims that it owns one of the largest collections of information about circumcision in the world. Today NOCIRC is an international network and has more than 110 centers worldwide.

SexualityNow

Go to **www.thomsonedu.com** to link to **SexualityNow,** your online study tool. First take the **Pre-Test** for this chapter to get your **Personalized Study Plan,** which will identify topics you need to review and direct you to online resources. Then take the **Post-Test** to determine what concepts you have mastered and what you still need work on.

6 Communication: Enriching Your Sexuality

*D*id you ever notice that there are certain rules to communicating with others? Let's say you meet someone new tonight. Your eyes find each other across the room and slowly you make your way over to talk to each other. What would you say? What wouldn't you say? How do you decide? Most likely you make a comment like, "Pretty loud in here, huh?" or "I can't believe how crowded it is!" The first unwritten rule about communication early in a relationship is that you talk about something relevant but impersonal. You wouldn't walk up to someone you don't know and say, "Do you get along with your parents?" or "Do you ever get acne?" No, these questions are too personal to discuss with a stranger.

When do you start to talk about personal things in relationships? Social psychologists talk about the "onion" theory of communication. We all are onions with many, many layers, and when we first meet someone we are careful about what we say—our onion layers stay in place. However, as more and more time goes by (and the amount of time differs from person to person), we begin to take off our layers. We take turns sharing personal information.

At first we might talk about the weather ("I can't believe it's still so hot in October") and then progress to certain classes or professors ("I really enjoyed my psychology teacher last semester"). These comments are low risk and really don't involve sharing too much personal information. However, the next layer may include information about politics or family relationships, and the information gets more personal. The key to the onion theory is that as you begin to peel off your layers, so too does your partner. If you share something personal about yourself, your partner will probably do the same. If your partner tells you something about a bad experience he or she had, you share a negative experience you've been through.

Have you ever met someone who shared really personal information early, maybe within the first few days of meeting you? Some people are notorious for peeling off their layers prematurely. They talk about personal issues very early in the relationship, which often makes their partner feel uncomfortable. There are exceptions to this—for example, have you ever sat next to a stranger on an airplane and shared information that you later realized you've never shared with people you know well? This happens all the time. On an airplane you might be a little nervous, and talking might help lessen your anxiety. But more importantly, you assume you'll never see this person again, so talk is cheap. There are relatively few risks to sharing so much so soon. When you arrive at your destination, you both go off in different directions and probably won't ever see each other again.

Whether you are involved in an intimate relationship now or plan to be at some point in the future, communication is one of the most important elements in a healthy, satisfying relationship. In this chapter we will talk about the importance of communication and improving interpersonal communication, including the ability to communicate about sexual issues. Improving communication has been found to enrich personal sexuality. We will discuss other ways to enrich your personal sexuality by learning to feel good about yourself, your skills as a lover, and improving your relationships with others. No one is born a good lover; it takes learning and patience. The information in this chapter may be valuable to you throughout your life, as your relationships change and mature.

Overall, the research has shown that couples who know how to communicate with each other are happier, more satisfied, and

Partners who know how to communicate with each other have a better chance of their relationship working out.

have a greater likelihood of making their relationship last (Hahlweg et al., 2000). However, learning to really communicate with your partner isn't easy. In fact, students often tell me that it's easier to just "do it" than talk about "doing it." Why is it so hard to talk to your partner? How can you share yourself physically with someone but feel unable to talk about things that are important to you? Why is it difficult to listen to someone when they want to talk about something you don't want to hear about?

THE IMPORTANCE OF COMMUNICATION

Good communication is the hallmark of a healthy, developing relationship. These skills can be applied to all aspects of life, such as improving family relationships, being more effective in relationships at school or work, developing a love relationship, or discussing relationship issues and sexuality with a partner. Communication fosters mutual understanding, increases emotional intimacy, and helps deepen feelings of love and intimacy. For love and intimacy to grow, each partner must know how the other feels. In fact, good communication is one of the most important factors in a satisfying relationship (Fowers, 1998). Note that having good communication skills and using them are two different things. Partners who have no trouble talking about their feelings in general, for example, may still have trouble telling each other how they want to change certain things in their relationship.

Many relationship problems stem from misunderstandings and poor communication, which lead to anger and frustration. In fact, communication problems are a major source of trouble in relationships. Communication experts have also found that a lack of communication skills contributes to many serious marital problems, including violence and abuse (Burleson & Denton, 1997). Misunderstandings, anger, and frustration can all lead to a downward spiral in which communication becomes less and less effective.

Relationships between two people inevitably run into difficulties. It's nearly impossible not to experience difficulties when you are sharing your space with another person. This is precisely why many forms of therapy emphasize learning communication skills and why communication self-help books overflow from bookstore shelves. Communication problems usually occur when partners have poor communication skills, feel unable to self-disclose, and/or have trouble listening. It is also important to point out, however, that not all relationship problems are caused by a lack of communication or poor communication. Sometimes the problems come from an unwillingness to acknowledge a problem or issue that needs to be worked out. In other cases, issues such as poor health or economic stresses can create problems that hinder communication and intimacy.

It Takes Some Learning to Communicate

Students often tell me they wish they could improve their communication skills. Before we talk about how to do this, let's discuss how we learn to communicate with others. Are we born with the ability to communicate with others, or do we learn it as we grow? If you've ever been around babies, you know that even though they don't have the ability to speak, they know how to communicate with their caregivers. When they are hungry, tired, or just want to be held, they cry. Crying communicates to their caregiver that they need something. As children acquire language, they learn more effective ways of communicating. Yet as we learn to communicate, a whole host of issues surface and interfere with our ability to talk to others. We worry about what others might think, we feel selfish for asking for things we want and need, and we don't know how to talk about ourselves and our needs.

When we communicate with other people, we have three competing goals (Vanfossen, 1996). The first is to "get the job done"—we have a message for someone, and we want to communicate that message. Second, we also have a "relational goal"—we want to maintain the relationship and not hurt or offend someone with our message. Finally, we have an "identity management goal"—that is, we want our communication

Human Sexuality in a Diverse World

I Love Peanut Butter!

I was born in Regensburg, Germany, and I have lived there all of my life up until now. For the past year I have been living in the United States, and during this time, I have learned a lot about cross-cultural differences in communication. When I first came to the States I was so surprised that foreigners would greet me on the street and ask me, "How are you doing?"—I was not used to people I didn't know asking me how I was feeling! Americans have a very emotional way of using language. They "love" strawberries—what does this mean? When someone says "I love you," does this mean that a person loves you as much as the strawberries? Or is it a different kind of love? This was really confusing for me.

When I went back to Germany for a visit I said, "I love peanut butter" in German, and all the people looked at me strangely. They would say, "I like peanut butter." Saying "I love" is too exaggerated. Can you really "love" strawberries or peanut butter?

I love the enthusiasm that Americans use when talking to each other. It makes their language so lively. However, I think that special expressions or words lose their real meanings when you use them all the time. This is especially true when it comes to relationships. Americans say "I love you," but I'm not sure what that really means. A little boy tells his mother he loves her, good friends say it, you hear it being said in advertisements, and everyone loves everyone! But how can you express real deep feelings if you are using the phrase "I love you" all the time? Does it still mean the same thing? How do you know if Americans really love you, if they also love their peanut butter? What does "I love you" really mean?

In Germany, we say something that is between "I love you" and "I like you," maybe it means more, "You are in my heart." You would use the phrase *Ich hab' dich lieb* to tell your mother and father, your friends, or your new boyfriend how you feel about them. But when someone says *Ich liebe Dich,* the German "I love you," then your relationship is really serious. This phrase is reserved only for relationships in which you know your partner really well. Saying *Ich liebe Dich* is very hard for some people, because it can make you more vulnerable. When a man would say *Ich liebe Dich* after three months of dating, it would make me wonder whether he could be taken seriously. Germans only use these words when they really mean it, and this gives the phrase much more respect.

I like how Americans are so open about letting someone know that they care about them. The first time an American told me they loved me I was touched. It felt great to have someone feel that strongly about me. But I knew that the way the phrase was used was very different than in Germany. It's hard to tell when it's really serious. I wish that the English language had an expression for real emotions between two people who are really in love with each other. Why is there no phrase in the English language that means something between liking and loving someone? Every culture and every country has its own ways of communicating and expressing ideas. What is most important is learning how to accept and learn from the differences.

Source: Author's files.

Review Question

Identify and describe the three competing goals for good communication.

to project a certain image of ourselves. All of these goals compete with one another, making the job of communicating our thoughts, needs, or desires even that much tougher. We'll discuss these goals in more detail later in this chapter, but for now, let's explore the nature of communication between the sexes and perhaps we can uncover guidelines to good communication.

How Women and Men Communicate

Conversations between women and men are often more difficult than conversations that occur in same-sex groups (Athenstaedt et al., 2004; Edwards & Hamilton, 2004). Why is this? Do men and women communicate differently? Is part of the communication problem incompatibility between how men and women communicate, so that the content of the communication gets lost in the form it takes?

Deborah Tannen (1990) has done a great deal of research in the area of communication and gender differences. She has termed the fundamental differences between the way men and women communicate as **genderlects** (JEN-der-lecks; which derives from the word "dialect" and not "derelict"!). Men tend to see the world as a place of hierarchical order in which they must struggle to maintain their position. Therefore, they interpret comments more often as challenges to their position and attempt to defend their

genderlect
Coined by Deborah Tannen, this term refers to the fundamental differences between the way men and women communicate.

independence. Women, on the other hand, see the world more as a network of interactions, and their goal is to form connections and avoid isolation. Women have been found to use more *rapport-talk*, which establishes relationships and connections, whereas men use more *report-talk*, which imparts knowledge (Eckstein & Goldman, 2001). Tannen (1990) asserts that women use conversations to establish and maintain intimacy, whereas men use conversations to establish status. She believes that there are a "male" and a "female" mode of communication.

A male mode of communication uses more report-talk, which imparts knowledge and helps to establish status.

Before we go into more detail about other gender differences in communication, it's important to note that often when a gender difference is revealed, it's common to view the male way as normative and the female way as deviating from the norm. When we say "different," it means that there are gender differences in ways of speaking that need to be understood. If they are not, the contrasting conversational styles can lead to frustration, disappointment, and misunderstandings. This is not to imply that one way is better than another—they are simply "different."

Language flow is different for men and women. Men believe that women constantly interrupt them, but women claim that men interrupt them more than other women do. The research shows that men are more likely than women to interrupt when others are speaking (Athenstaedt et al., 2004). Tannen responds that, in keeping with a report-talk style, men tend to speak one at a time, and so another comment is seen as an interruption. Women use more overlapping talk, in which it is all right for a second person to speak over the first, as long as that second person does not change the subject to try to take over as the primary speaker. When men interrupt women, they expect to become the primary speaker; when women interrupt, they overlap without expecting that the conversation will turn to them. Men are also more likely to answer questions that are not specifically addressed to them.

Question: I am really confused about my relationship with my girlfriend. I thought we communicate really well, but now I don't know what to think. She told me about a problem she is having with another friend. I listened for hours and tried to offer some solutions to help her improve the situation. To my surprise, she became angry with me! What's going on?

Men and women also differ in how they respond to problems. Men tend to view conversations as ways to exchange information or fix problems (Gard, 2000). Women tend to try to confirm the other person's feelings and empathize. In your case, you listened to your girlfriend and moved on to trying to fix the problem. Perhaps she was looking for your emotional support and some TLC, instead of concrete answers to her dilemma. This is a common problem that couples make in conversation. Women resent men's tendencies to try to fix their emotional problems, and men complain that women refuse to take action to solve their problems.

Men use more nonstandard forms of speech (slang); talk more about money and business; refer more to time, space, quantity, destructive actions, physical movements, and objects; and use more hostile verbs than women. Women are more supportive in speech, are more polite and expressive, talk more about home and family, and use more words implying feelings, evaluations, interpretations, and psychological states (Tannen, 1990). When stating an opinion, women often end their statement with **tag questions** (e.g., "It's really cold in here, isn't it?" or "That's an interesting idea, isn't it?") in order to invite discussion and minimize disagreements. They also use **disclaimers** (e.g., "I may be wrong, but . . ."), **question statements** ("Am I off base here?"; Vanfossen, 1996), and **hedge words** such as "sort of," "kind of," "aren't you," or "would you mind?" All of these

tag question
A way of speaking in which the speaker renounces or denies the validity of what he or she is saying by adding a questioning statement at the end of his or her statement.

disclaimer
A way of speaking in which the speaker renounces or denies the validity of what he or she is saying by including a negative statement.

question statement
A way of speaking in which the speaker renounces or denies the validity of what he or she is saying by adding a question at the end of his or her statements.

hedge word
A way of speaking in which the speaker renounces or denies the validity of what he or she is saying by using certain words to decrease his or her perceived assertiveness.

TABLE 6.1 Gender and Communication

Although communication styles can vary widely within each gender, there are some general similarities. Following are some findings on typical gender differences in both verbal and nonverbal communication. The question is, do these potential differences mean anything? Researchers suggest that the differences may contribute to a perception that men are more self-confident and authoritative.

Women	Men
Use language to increase intimacy	Use language for information
Engage in "rapport" talk	Engage in "report" talk
Use tag questions, disclaimers, and question statements	Use few tag questions, disclaimers, and question statements
Use hedge words	Use few hedge words
Use verbal strategies to build group morale (framing questions such as "Should we . . .?" or "Can we . . .?")	Use verbal strategies to dictate what should and can be done ("We should . . ." or "We can . . .")
Interpret men's verbal strategies as bossy and impolite	Interpret women's verbal strategies as "wishy-washy" and based on an inability to be decisive
Use compliments	Use playful insults and teasing
Listen to gain better understanding of speaker's experience	Listen to solve problems
Relate similar experiences to match speakers' troubles	Do not engage in trouble-matching
Seek agreement and an avoidance of disagreement	Enjoy disagreement and argument
Are more likely to interrupt other women if interrupting at all	Are more likely to interrupt
Are more likely to allow an interruption to be successful	Are less likely to allow an interruption to be successful
In formal group settings, talk less often and for shorter time periods	In formal group settings, talk more often and talk for longer time periods
Spend less time talking in mixed-gender groups	Spend more time talking in mixed-gender groups
Head-nod and smile when listening	Furrow brow and/or squint when listening
Display facial expressions and emotional reactions	Display few facial expressions in listening feedback
Pay more attention to nonverbal communication cues	Are less sensitive to communication cues
Assume more forward positions when sitting; lean forward when listening	Assume more reclined positions when sitting; lean backward when listening
Gesture toward the body	Gesture away from the body
Take up less physical space, sitting with arms and legs toward their body	Take up more physical space when sitting or standing, with arms and legs stretched out away from their body
Maintain direct eye contact during conversation	Tend to avoid direct eye contact during conversation
Misinterpret men's lack of eye contact as disinterest	Misinterpret women's direct eye contact as flirtatious or sexual
Talk more about how they feel and more about relationships with others	Talk more about what they did, where they went, and less about relationships with others
Tend to take verbal rejection more personally	Tend to take verbal rejection less personally

Source: Adapted from Coates, 1986; Glass, 1992; Lawhorn, 2005; Tannen, 1990; Uman, 2004; Vanfossen, 1996.

A female mode of communication uses more rapport-talk, which establishes relationships and maintains intimacy.

tend to decrease the speaker's perceived assertiveness of speech. Although tag questions are used frequently in English, they are not used as much in other languages. In fact, the French and Swedish languages lack an equivalent feature (Cheng & Warren, 2001).

There have been criticisms of Tannen's genderlect theory. One of the biggest criticisms has been in her unidimensional approach of studying gender differences in communication. To Tannen, gender is based on *biological* sex. Therefore, all women communicate one way and all men another way. Another model agrees there are gender differences, but these differences are based on one's *gender role* instead of biological sex (Edwards & Hamilton, 2004). So, not all men use dominance in their speech and not all women use cooperative speech. Men who are higher in nurturance engage in more cooperative speech, whereas women who are lower in nurturance engage in less (Edwards & Hamilton, 2004).

With all of these differences, men and women are not necessarily destined to try to communicate over a giant chasm of misunderstanding. First of all, these ways of communicating are only tendencies, and plenty of men and women are good at different techniques of communication. Second, understanding and patience play a key role. Those willing to work at improving their communication skills can significantly enhance their intimate relationships both with members of their own and the other gender.

Theories in Gender Differences

In the preceding section we discussed gender differences in communication, but why do these differences exist? Is it biology? Society? We discussed earlier that researchers often disagree about whether there are gender differences, but it's also true that researchers who agree that there are differences disagree on the reasons for these differences. There may be a biological basis—physically innate differences between men and women that cause gender differences in communication. There may be psychological reasons—men and women have experienced different reinforcements for communicating, and these have shaped their patterns of communication. There may also be societal reasons for the differences. Social role theory explains the differences in terms of role expectations about masculinity and femininity in society, whereas societal development theories focus on male dominance in society and its effects on communication patterns.

Although it's true that all of these theories can explain some of the gender differences in communication, gender communication can often be best understood as a form of cross-cultural communication (A. M. Johnson, 2001; Mulvaney, 1994). If you were suddenly in a conversation with a person from another country who had no experience with your culture, you might find this conversation difficult. You wouldn't know the subtleties of that person's communication style, and he or she wouldn't know yours. It's hypothesized that even though men and women grow up in similar environments, they learn different ways of communicating, which resembles a form of cross-cultural communication.

Maltz & Borker (1982) believe that American men and women come from different "sociolinguistic subcultures" and learn different communication rules. They interpret conversations and use language differently. This all begins as children in same-sex play groups, which are often organized very differently. The majority of young girls play in small groups and have "best friends." They negotiate friendships and pay attention to subtle cues of "who likes who." Reaching higher levels of intimacy is the goal, and their games, such as playing house, less often have winners and losers. Boys, on the other hand, learn to use speech for the expression of dominance and play in hierarchically organized groups that focus on directing and winning (Maltz & Borker, 1982). Boys often jockey for status by telling jokes, showing off, or claiming they are the best at things. In their conversations, a "leader" tends to emerge. Girls tend to focus more on negotiation.

According to Maltz & Borker (1982), during same-sex conversations, girls and boys learn the rules and assumptions about communication, and these rules follow them through life. As adolescents, they begin to communicate in mixed-sex groups with the rules they learned from same-sex communication, which can cause problems. For example, girls learn to nod their head during conversations with other girls. This lets the talker know that she is being listened to. When a woman nods her head during a conversation with a man, he thinks she agrees with him (when she might not agree or disagree—her head nod may simply be showing him that she is listening). When a man doesn't nod his head when a woman is talking to him, she may think he isn't listening to her. All of this can lead to feeling misunderstood and poor communication. Understanding the differences in communication styles won't automatically prevent disagreements, but it will help keep the disagreements manageable. We will talk more about nonverbal communication techniques in a moment.

One more point deserves mention before leaving our discussion of gender and communication. Many of the studies on gender differences in communication have studied only young, well-educated, middle-class Americans (Mortenson, 2002). Because of this, we do not know whether these findings are generalizable to different groups inside the United States or in different countries. Cultures differ in many ways, but one important dimension that has been extensively studied is the degree to which a culture encourages individual needs in relation to group needs. *Individualistic cultures* encourage their members to have individual goals and values and an independent sense of self

Review Question

What is a "genderlect"? Describe the research on gender and communication styles.

sex byte

Although same-sex conversations are often easier, women report more difficulties in same-sex conversations than men. Researchers suggest that this is due to the fact that conversations between women tend to be complex and multilayered, requiring more effort and listening (Edwards & Hamilton, 2004).

Gossiping and Complaining

Recently I asked a group of students what it would be like to spend 24 hours with their partner but be able to use only nonverbal communication. Students thought about it, and many didn't know what to make of the question. Would it really be possible for them to be alone with their partner but not (verbally) speak to each other for 24 hours?

Several of the women who were asked this question said that, although they'd be willing to try, they didn't think it would work out well. They weren't sure they could be with their partner without verbal communication. The men, on the other hand, enthusiastically responded to my question. "Sure!" many of them said. When pressed for their reasoning, several of the men said, "I wouldn't have to hear her complaining!" This made me think—what exactly is "complaining," and do women do this more than men? The answer depends on your definition. Many women say that it's not really "complaining," but rather "discussing" important issues.

Women do more complaining than men and are more likely to commiserate with each other about their complaints (Boxer, 1996). Women report they enjoy engaging in this type of communication with other women. In fact, these types of communication have been found to be an important bonding tool in women's friendships (Sotirin, 2000). Many times women complain to each other in an ef-

fort to cope with their disappointments, whereas men address troubles by responding with solutions instead of talking at length about the injustice of it all.

Verbal communication is very important in women's lives. Some women like to gossip, talk about daily events, rehash scenarios and issues. Researchers have found that women's informal talk includes gossip, complaining, "troubles talk," and "bitching" (Sotirin, 2000). Although at first glance these types of talk might seem similar, each appears to have its own structure and function. The focus of gossip is on an absent target and includes contributions from several participants. Gossiping may also have an aggressive component to it, wherein the gossip is meant to hurt or harm a particular relationship (Conway, 2005; Ferguson, 2004). Complaining is usually brief and to the point. "Bitching," in contrast, relates an in-depth account of events, usually about an injustice or something negative that has happened to the speaker, allowing her to express her dissatisfaction (Sotirin, 2000). In "troubles talk," there is one "troubles teller" and the focus of the conversation stays on the teller the entire length of the conversation.

Next time you stroll through the mall or even your student union, take a look around you. What kinds of communication are the women around you engaging in? What do you think the purpose of the communication is?

Communication patterns begin when children play in same-sex groups.

(Matsumoto, 1996), whereas *collectivist cultures* emphasize the needs of their members over individual needs.

Communication patterns have been found to vary depending on cultural orientation (Cai et al., 2000). Men and women raised in collectivist cultures have a greater concern for the feelings of those around them, whereas those raised in individualist cultures are less concerned with emotions and feelings in communication. For example, none of the gender differences in communication we discussed above were found among Chinese men and women (a collectivist culture; Mortenson, 2002). For this reason, it is important to realize that cultural orientations, gender, and communication styles are all interconnected, and it may be impossible to look at gender without also looking at cultural influences.

Types of Communication: More Than Words

It's important to realize that there is much more to communication than words alone. We use nonverbal communication to get our message across, and many of us communicate with others online. Both of these methods of communication raise other important issues.

Nonverbal Communication

The other day a floral delivery truck passed me on the highway, and the sign on its side said, "Increase your vocabulary: Say it with flowers." What does this mean? What does it mean when you send flowers? What does it mean to receive them? Truth is, it can mean several things: "I love you," "I'm sorry," "I'll never do it again," "I'm a jerk," "You're a jerk," "Sorry I made such a mess." There are many different meanings, but what's important to realize is that sending flowers is a **nonverbal communication** technique. In fact, the majority of our communication with others is nonverbal (Guffey, 1999). This is because, even when we say nothing, we are communicating. We communicate through flowers, with periods of silence, and also by the way we move our body. We may change our facial expression, tilt our head, or move closer or further away from a person. All of these nonverbal communication techniques tell our partner something.

Nonverbal communication behavior differs widely from culture to culture. For example, in Arab cultures, it's common for people to stand very close to one another when conversing, regardless of their gender (Mulvaney, 1994). Although smiling is often a sign of happiness in the United States and many other countries, in many Asian countries smiling is a way to cover up emotional pain (Gunawan, 2001). Another common, nonverbal form of communication in the United States is to gesture with a palm up to call another person to come join the group. However, in Korea, the Philippines, and in certain parts of Latin America, this nonverbal behavior is viewed as rude and objectionable (Gunawan, 2001).

Nonverbal communication varies within the United States as well. When a friend tells you, "You're the best" with a smile on her face and a relaxed body posture, you'll probably believe her. But the same statement coming from a person who has arms crossed, teeth clenched, and eyebrows furrowed has a completely different message. Most likely, in this second situation, you'll think that your friend is angry and being sarcastic. Body language helps fill in the gaps in verbal communication. When a man is uncomfortable, he may have a hard time maintaining eye contact, be unable to sit still, pick his fingernails, or play with his hair (Perry, 2000). When a woman feels positively about you she will maintain eye contact, smile, or touch you during the conversation. As humans, we are uniquely designed to read these nonverbal cues and respond accordingly.

How well can you read the nonverbal cues people around you share? Are you better at reading your partner's nonverbals than those of, say, a friend? Can you ever know exactly what another person is saying nonverbally? The ability to do so is an important ingredient in successful interpersonal relationships. You might be better at reading your best friend's nonverbal behavior than someone you have known only a short time. Overall, women are better at decoding and translating nonverbal communication (DeLange, 1995). Women's nonverbal communication techniques include more eye contact and head nods, whereas men have fewer head nods, less eye contact, and minimal "encouragers" (nonverbal cues to let their partner know they are listening; Pearson et al., 1991). Women have also been found to smile, gaze, lean forward, and touch more often than men in conversation (Wood, 1999).

Review Question

Describe the theories that have been proposed to explain gender differences in communication styles.

nonverbal communication
Communication without words (includes eye contact, head nodding, touching, and the like).

What do the nonverbal cues in this photo tell you?

---

sex byte

Research has found that the menstrual cycle may influence women's ability to pick up on certain nonverbal cues (Pearson & Lewis, 2005). The accuracy to recognize certain emotions was highest just before ovulation, which may be due to an increase in estrogen.

Review Question

What is nonverbal communication? What can you learn from your partner's nonverbal behavior? Provide one example.

---

sex byte

Researchers have found several gender differences in instant messaging. Women take longer turns, have longer overall conversations, and take longer to say goodbye than men (Baron, 2004).

---

computer-mediated conversation
Communication produced when people interact with one another by transmitting messages via networked computers.

---

emoticons
Facial symbols used when sending text messages online; an example would be :-) .

In one study that looked at first meetings between men and women, women were found to "flirt" using nonverbal cues (such as hair-flipping and head-nodding) in order to encourage men to reveal more about themselves, which would in turn allow the women to formulate an impression of the men (W. E. Martin, 2001). Men, on the other hand, view flirting as a way to show interest in a potential relationship (Henningsen, 2004).

When it comes to sex, verbal communication about your likes and needs is far better than nonverbal. Yet nonverbal communication can express your sexual desires, and it can be much less threatening than verbal communication. For example, if you would like your partner to touch your breasts more during foreplay, show this by moving your body more when he or she is doing what you like, or moving his or her hands to your breasts. You can moan, or even move more, to communicate your pleasure to your partner. You might also try performing the behavior on your partner that you wish she or he would do to you. However, there are problems with some types of nonverbal communication. As this couple demonstrates, it can often be misunderstood:

> One woman attempted to communicate her preference for being kissed on the ears by kissing her partner's ears. However, [she] found that the more she kissed her partner's ears, the less he seemed to kiss hers. Over a period of time her kissing of his ears continued to increase, while his kissing of her ears stopped altogether. Finally she asked him why he never kissed her ears anymore, only to discover that he hated having his ears kissed and was trying to communicate this by not kissing hers. After their discussion, he began to kiss her ears, she stopped kissing his, and both were happier for the exchange. (Barbach, 1982, p. 105)

Computer-Mediated Communication

Computer-mediated communication (CMC) includes communication tools for conveying written text via the Internet. This would include instant messaging, chat rooms, e-mailing, and other forms of online communication. How does online communication compare to face-to-face communication? Are gender differences readily apparent in online conversation? Does online communication foster emotionally disconnected or superficial relationships? There is research that indicates that there are indeed gender differences in communication styles on the Internet (Baron, 2004; Sussman & Tyson, 2000).

Women have been found to have an easier time making their voices heard online than in a face-to-face conversation, and use more "smileys" and other **emoticons** (e-MOTE-ick-cons) online than men (Baron, 2004; B. P. Bailey et al., 2003). These often serve to express emotion but may deflect from the seriousness of the women's statements. Emoticons can be compared to tag questions during face-to-face conversations. It's also important to point out that researchers who study online communication have no sure way of knowing the gender of the people online. In fact, it has been suggested that people create "virtual identities" online (McAdams, 1996). A man can claim to be a woman or a child could claim to be an adult. Our "virtual identities" are temporary but they affect our online personae.

Online communication can help establish intimate relationships. It can reduce the role that physical characteristics play in the development of attraction and enhance rapport and self-disclosure. These conditions promote erotic connections that develop out of emotional intimacy rather than physical attraction. Online communication may also reduce the overly constraining gender roles that are automatically in place in face-to-face conversation.

What about meeting Mr. or Ms. Right online? Some students who like to use chat rooms have told me that they find it easier to meet people online than in a bar or at a party. It almost seems hard to believe that it would be possible to meet a partner online, given the fact that conversation is reduced to a monitor and a keyboard, yet computer-

Personal Voices

Internet Romance

Vicki and Russ met online through instant messaging [IMs]. Both believed that the self-disclosure they made earlier promoted connections out of emotional intimacy rather than physical attraction. Vicki and Russ talk about how they met and share their first IMs:

Russ: *I found that it was easier to interact with women by computer, since my work took up a good deal of my time. Besides, it was a lot less expensive than going to a bar every night.*

Vicki: *I ignored Russ's early IMs because I don't accept IMs from unfamiliar people. However, one day he had some comment that was pretty witty and entertaining so I actually replied.*

Russ: *Our senses of humor were very similar. I quickly realized that Vicki was a very nice person, and I was very interested in following this through.*

Vicki: *Conversations with Russ were very relaxed, and he always made me laugh. Since he always found me whenever I logged on, we'd chat, and I got to know a lot about him without sharing much about me (I kept thinking "what if he is one of those Internet psychos?"). Soon he offered his phone number. He warned me that he had caller ID, which meant he would get my phone number automatically, if I called him from home. I thought this was very honest of him to tell me that. I was convinced he was a nice guy.*

Russ: *While I did want to, I never pressed Vicki to meet or even to speak on the phone, because I was enjoying the repartee that was happening. I know that this could be deceiving, as you can type anything, but from the beginning I recognized the honesty in what she was saying.*

Vicki: *Our first telephone conversation lasted about 3 hours. We talked on the phone about a week, and then I e-mailed him accepting his dinner offer.*

Russ: *I felt that Vicki was someone worth waiting for. After finally meeting, we did not encounter a lot of the normal dating problems, like learning about each other's likes and dislikes, since we had discussed these at length long before meeting. Dating Vicki was like dating a long-time friend, since we knew so much about each other. Our relationship progressed at that point in what would be considered a more "mainstream" fashion. Two years later I asked Vicki to marry me, and we were wed the following year.*

Here is a copy of Vicki and Russ's first instant message:

V: *What do you look like?*

R: *6'0", 175 pounds, red hair, somewhat athletic build, clean shaven.*

V: *red huh? Watch out for the sun!*

R: *Yeah, I know ... gotta be careful.*

R: *My turn, what do you look like? or should I just ask if you have a picture?*

V: *ummm . . . don't have a pix-so, let's see . . . I'm 5'7", light brown hair, kinda unruly curly hair, blue eyes, freckles*

R: *I have blue eyes too*

V: *I used to have red hair as a kid. how cool is that?*

V: *no chance I'm giving you my weight. Let's just say, not as athletic as I should have been over the last year. But heading in the right direction again.*

R: *I'm a gentleman. No chance I will be asking for it.*

V: *I wear glasses*

R: *Me too!! Then I don't have to play like I don't need them and walk into walls!*

V: *you remind me of my friend's husband, Mark*

R: *nope, just checked my license and it says Russell*

V: *good because if you were Mark, I would have to call the marriage police*

R: *At the risk of seeming eager, may I offer you my phone number?*

V: *at the risk of making you think I am not sincere . . . can I say, not yet?*

R: *Honesty is one of the most important things in the world to me Vic. I appreciate your response and respect it.*

V: *I gotta get some sleep*

R: *I have really enjoyed this meeting Vic*

V: *nice meeting up with you too*

V: *sweet dreams*

R: *Thank you! I'll look for you again.*

V: *cya soon*

Source: Author's files.

mediated conversation can be very intimate, and couples can potentially become acquainted faster online than in face-to-face contact. One woman said:

> I found that our relationship progressed very quickly. We became intimate very early on and told each other things about ourselves that "bonded" us. It seemed that there was less risk, since we weren't face-to-face and didn't have to worry about what each other would think. We could also talk all the time—it wasn't unusual for us to find each other online in the wee hours of the morning. (Author's files)

However, it's also important to point out that there also is a risk of "eroticized pseudointimacy" online (Cooper & Sportolari, 1997). When couples overindulge and are compulsive on the Internet, the results can be destructive (i.e., a person may become obsessed with the Internet and unable to stop the behavior).

The key to online relationships is to take it slow and, because you are not meeting the person face-to-face, really get to know your partner as much as you can. Communicate the things that are important to you, and "listen" as your partner talks. Be realistic about the chances the relationship will work out.

Review Question

How can the Internet reduce some of the common communication problems that couples experience in face-to-face conversations?

SEX Talk

Question: My partner spends a lot of time on the Internet. The other night I discovered that he was in a chat room having a very "intimate" conversation with another man. I was heartbroken. Do you think an online relationship constitutes cheating? It sure feels that way to me.

This is an interesting question. Many people believe that if their partner is having an intimate relationship with someone on the Internet, this is indeed cheating. But this really depends on how you define "intimate." Many online relationships involve sharing personal information about yourself and learning personal information about the person you are chatting with. One study that was done on "online infidelity" found that usually people who engage in these behaviors are not unhappy with their present relationships (Aviram, 2005). Typically, it has more to do with personality variables, such as a high degree of narcissism. Communication is key here—see if he can help you understand why he was drawn to engaging in such conversation on the Internet and with the other person. Remember, though, that unless he is proven guilty, he didn't do anything wrong.

Communicating More Effectively

Earlier in this chapter we discussed the three competing goals of communication. Do you remember what they were? When we communicate with another person we have a task, a relational, and an identity management goal. How can we be successful in reaching these various goals?

The first goal is to get the job done. Often men and women are too afraid to share their thoughts with their partner. They do have a message that they would like to share with their partner, but something holds them back. Remember how good communication can make a relationship even better? It is important to put aside your vulnerability and fears and learn to communicate your thoughts to your partner. Get the job done!

The second goal isn't always easy either. How can we maintain our relationship and not upset the applecart by communicating our thoughts and desires? Think through what you want to say, and realize the impact your message will have on your partner. How would you feel if your partner shared a similar thought? What might make it easier for you or your partner? Often timing is everything. Make sure that you have the time

Being a More-Effective Communicator

A number of techniques can help us to communicate more effectively. Following we highlight some of the most important ways to become a more effective communicator.

1. **Talk about good communication.** When you need a good icebreaker to move into a conversation that will allow you to talk about intimate issues, a safe place to start is to talk about talking. This will let each of you discuss how it is sometimes difficult to talk about things. From there you can move into more personal and sexual areas.

2. **Learn to accommodate the style of the other sex.** Tannen (1990) notes that when groups of men meet or when groups of men and women are together, the conversation tends to adopt men's conversational and body-language styles. Only when women are alone do they feel able to relax their posture and assume their natural style. Understanding the style of the other sex and accepting it (that is, not seeing it as selfish, stupid, or a threat) will go a long way to improving communication.

3. **Give helpful, supportive feedback.** A good listener tries to understand what the speaker is really trying to say and what he or she really wants in return. Knowing your partner means knowing when your partner wants advice and when he or she just wants a sympathetic ear.

4. **Do not wait until you're angry.** According to an ancient Chinese book of wisdom, the truly wise person handles things when they are small, before they grow too big. Let this guide you in your relationships. Discuss problems when you first realize them, while they are still small, and avoid the big, blowout fights.

5. **Let go of the need to be right.** In relationships, establishing who is "right" and "wrong" is never fruitful. What is fruitful is establishing how to improve communication and how to increase intimacy.

6. **Ask questions.** Remember to ask questions so that you can really understand your partners' needs, desires, and thoughts.

7. **Be responsible.** Most people cannot read their partner's mind. What is obvious to you may not be obvious to your partner. If you want something, ask for it, and be direct. For example, suppose you want your partner to be more romantic. "You never do anything romantic" is a challenge, whereas "let's plan a romantic evening together" is a more direct and less threatening way to request the same thing.

8. **Be supportive.** Mix praise with your criticism; say things in positive rather than negative ways. In the previous example, an even better way to put it would be, "I love being alone with you, together, just talking. Let's go out for a candlelight dinner tonight, just the two of us."

9. **Learn to say no, gently.** People sometimes get into relationship trouble because they do not know how to say "no" to their partners and end up resenting that they are doing things they do not want to do. Every person has a right to say no; in fact, it is a sign of trust and respect for your partner to believe that you can say no and still retain his or her love and affection. But saying no to a request is different from rejecting the person making it. "No" must be said in a way that reassures the partner that it is only the requested action you are refusing.

10. **Be forgiving.** In love relationships, we all make mistakes. We hurt our partners, we do something thoughtless, and we do a thousand little things we wish we could change. We are all human. Bringing up slights from the past is never helpful. When communication is done in a spirit of unconditional positive regard (which, we realize, is a very difficult state to achieve), all the other qualities of good communication will fall into place.

and energy to talk to your partner before you start. Five minutes before class is probably not the best time to start a conversation.

The identity management goal involves projecting a certain image of ourselves. We might want to tell our partner that we need more space or more time alone, but we don't want to hurt his or her feelings. We certainly don't want him or her to think we're a "weirdo" for needing some alone time! How can we best share this message with our partner?

Finally, we must also consider the importance of other communication tools. The use of tag questions, which indicate uncertainty in conversation, should be limited (Vanfossen, 1996). Using tag questions can make a partner form an opinion about a person that might not be correct. Nonverbal language is also important. Pay attention to the nonverbal cues that you notice in other people as well as the nonverbal cues that you are sending. What messages are you receiving/sending? Is the other person paying attention? How can you tell? Let's talk about the importance of self-disclosure and asking for what you need.

Self-Disclosure

Self-disclosure is critical in maintaining healthy and satisfying relationships. Talking with your partner and sharing feelings helps deepen intimacy. feelings of love, and even sexual satisfaction (Macneil, 2004). In addition, opening up and sharing your thoughts and feelings with your partner helps you to grow together as a couple. Self-disclosure lets your partner know what is wrong and how you feel about it, and enables you to ask for specific change (Fowers, 1998). To make it a bit easier, communication experts recommend editing during self-disclosure. Editing means that you decide which comments are the most courteous, polite, and sincere before disclosing. Overall, women have been found to engage in more self-disclosure than men (Dindia, 2000).

Keeping silent about your true feelings and thoughts or criticizing your partner instead of talking is much easier and puts you in a much less vulnerable position. Opening up and talking about yourself makes you vulnerable. Ideally, an intimate partner is one who can hear what you are all about and still love you.

One final note about self-disclosure: it is risky to disclose too much before the relationship is stable and communication skills are in place. This can cause the relationship to deteriorate. This is what we discussed in the onion theory earlier in this chapter. Problems and issues that are brought up before a couple knows how to communicate and discuss them may only get worse (Butler & Wampler, 1999).

Asking for What You Need

Even though communication is important, it is not always easy. Telling your partner what you really want and need during sexual activity can be very difficult. This is because sexuality is an area in which many people feel insecure. People may wonder if they are good lovers and worry that their partners do not think they are. At the same time, however, they may be hesitant to make suggestions to improve their partner's techniques because they worry that their partner will become insulted and think that their lovemaking is being criticized. Anxieties like these do not foster a sense of open and mutual communication. Ultimately, not being open about your likes or dislikes is self-defeating because you may end up feeling resentful of your partner or unhappy in your relationship.

SEX Talk

Question: I have been in a relationship with my boyfriend for almost 1 year. We love each other very much, but most of the time I feel that we don't communicate well with each other, mainly because I'm just too afraid to talk about things. I love him very much and want our relationship to last. How can we learn to communicate better?

Communicating our thoughts, needs, hopes, dreams, and desires isn't always easy. Usually intimate or personal information is difficult to share. It's natural to worry about what your boyfriend might think or say. It's best to start slowly. Don't try to tell him everything at one time. You might try sharing a few small details about what you're thinking and feeling. Remember that asking for what you need involves self-disclosure. If you can open up and share your thoughts and listen to what your boyfriend is saying, this can help you grow together as a couple.

CRITICISM: CAN YOU TAKE IT? (AND ALSO DISH IT OUT?)

The majority of couples spend too much time criticizing each other and not enough time really listening and making affectionate comments (P. Coleman, 2002). One partner often becomes defensive and angry when the other says something he or she doesn't want to hear. For example, if your partner told you that he felt you weren't giving enough to your relationship, you could hear this message with an open mind, or you could get angry and think, "What do you know about my time?" Let's now talk about the importance of listening, constructive and nonconstructive communication, and verbal disagreements.

The Fine Art of Listening

One of the most important communication skills is **nondefensive listening,** which involves focusing your attention on what your partner is saying without being defensive (Gottman, 1994). Nondefensive listening relies on self-restraint, which is often absent in distressed couples, who have a difficult time hearing and listening to each other. It can be very difficult to listen fully, but this skill reduces your inclination to interrupt or to defend yourself. **Active listening** involves using nonverbal communication to let your partner know that you are attentive and present in the conversation. For example, as your partner talks, you can maintain eye contact to let him or her know you are actively listening.

Poor listeners often think that they understand what their partner is trying to say, but they rarely understand. Instead they try to find a way to circumvent the discussion and talk about something else. It's very difficult to really listen to someone when you are angry or defensive. However, by really listening to your partner, you can learn to make the relationship stronger. Sometimes good listening skills can reduce the desire to change each other (M. P. Nichols, 1995)!

Being a More Effective Listener

It's tough to be a good listener these days. We all have so many things going on at one time that it makes it difficult to really focus on what our partner is saying. Because we all have "buttons" that our partners can push, it's important to know what these buttons are. For instance, two students of mine, Linda and Steve, told me that when they get into a disagreement, Steve often brings up the fact that Linda acts "just like her mother." This infuriates Linda because she has unresolved feelings about her relationship with her mother. Instead of listening to what Steve has to say, she gets defensive and angry because he compared her to her mother. Knowing in advance what these "buttons" are in your own relationship can help reduce conflict and misunderstandings.

Listening and really paying attention can also help you learn important things about your partner. John Gottman, a relationship expert, gives couples a relationship quiz to see if they have been paying attention to each other's likes and dislikes (Gottman, 1999). His questions include the following:

- What is the name of your partner's best friend?
- Who has been irritating your partner lately?
- What are some of your partner's life dreams?
- What are three of your partner's favorite movies?
- What are your partner's major current worries?
- What would your partner want to do if he or she suddenly won the lottery?

We don't ever realize how important it is to have others listen to us until someone we really care about doesn't listen to us (Coleman, 2002). When others really listen, we are often able to see more clearly what it is that upsets us. Being listened to can make us feel worthy, protected, and cared about. As we mentioned earlier, encouraging your partner through active listening, such as eye contact, nodding, and/or saying "um hum"

nondefensive listening
Listening strategy in which the listener focuses attention on what his or her partner is saying without being defensive.

active listening
Communication/listening technique wherein the listener uses nonverbal communication, such as nodding or eye contact, to let the partner know that the listener is attentive.

When our partner listens to us, we feel worthy and cared about, which, in turn, strengthens our relationship.

(Fowers, 1998), shows your partner that you are "tuned in." It also shows that you believe he or she has something worthwhile to say and it encourages him or her to continue talking.

When your partner is finished talking, it is important to summarize what your partner has told you as accurately as possible. This lets your partner know that you heard what he or she was saying and also enables your partner to correct any misunderstandings. Finally, it is also very important when listening to validate your partner's statement. Saying "I can understand why you might feel that way" or "I know what you mean" can help you show your partner that you think what he or she is saying is valid. This doesn't necessarily mean that you agree, but that you can accept your partner's point of view.

Message Interpretation

When walking across campus one day, you trip and fall down. Your partner sees you and says, "Please be careful!" How do you interpret that? Does it mean that you're moving too fast? You need to slow down? Does it mean that your partner is genuinely worried you might hurt yourself? In all conversations, the recipient of the message must interpret the intended meaning of the message (P. Edwards, 1998), which is dependent on several factors, such as the nature of the relationship with the person and your mood at the time.

If you are angry or upset, you may perceive more hostility in ambiguous or benign comments than someone who is not angry or upset (Epps & Kendall, 1995). If you are worried about something or preoccupied with an issue, this can also bias how you interpret a message. In one study, women who were preoccupied with their weight were more likely to interpret ambiguous sentences with negative or "fat" meanings, whereas women who were not preoccupied with their weight did not (Jackman et al., 1995). For example, if a woman who was preoccupied with her weight heard someone say, "You look much better today!" she would probably interpret this to mean that she looked fat yesterday. However, couldn't she also interpret the message in other ways? Perhaps she looked tired yesterday or even stressed out.

Gender Differences in Listening

Men and women have been found to listen for different things when they engage in conversation (DeLange, 1995). As we mentioned earlier, men typically listen for the bottom line or to find out what action needs to be taken to improve the situation, whereas women listen for details. This helps explain why men and women might respond differently in conversation. Men may listen for ways to "fix" the problem, whereas women are listening to listen. It's important to keep this in mind when you are communicating with your partner.

Negative Feelings and Criticism

We all get angry sometimes, and we know that not all conversations have happy, peaceful endings. However, the key is in managing the tension. When we disagree with our partner, the opening minutes of a disagreement can indicate whether or not the conversation will turn angry or simply be a quiet discussion (P. Coleman, 2002). If harsh words are used, chances are the disagreement will build and the tension will escalate. However, if softer words are used, there is a better chance the disagreement can be resolved.

Negative feelings may also involve sharing or accepting criticism. Accepting criticism isn't an easy thing to do—we are all defensive at times. Although it would be impossible to eliminate all defensiveness, it's important to reduce defensiveness in order to resolve disagreements. If you are defensive while listening to your partner's criticism, chances are good that you will not be able to hear his or her message. Common defensive techniques are to deny the criticism (e.g., "That is just NOT TRUE!"), make excuses without taking any responsibility (e.g., "I was just exhausted!"), deflecting respon-

Review Question

Why is listening one of the most important communication skills? What is nondefensive listening?

Review Question

Describe one gender difference in listening behavior.

sibility (e.g., "Me? What about your behavior?"), and righteous indignation (e.g., "How could you possibly say such a hurtful thing?"; P. Coleman, 2002). All of these techniques interfere with our ability to really understand what our partner is trying to tell us. Keeping our defensiveness in check is another important aspect of good communication.

John Gottman, whom we mentioned earlier, found that happy couples experienced 20 positive interactions for every negative one (Nelson, 2005). Couples who were in conflict experienced only 5 positive interactions for every negative one, and those couples soon to be divorced experienced only 0.8 negative interactions for every negative one. This research suggests that positive and negative interactions can shine light on a couple's relationship happiness.

Nonconstructive Communication: Don't Yell at Me!

Couples often make many mistakes in their communication patterns that can lead to arguments, misunderstandings, and conflicts. **Overgeneralizations,** or making statements such as "Why do you always ...?" or "You never ...," generally exaggerate an issue. Telling your partner that they "always" (or "never") do something can cause defensiveness and will often lead to complete communication shutdown. Try to be specific about your complaints and help your partner to see what it is that is frustrating you.

Try to stay away from **name-calling** or stereotyping words, such as calling your partner a "selfish bastard" or a "nag." These derogatory terms will only help escalate anger and frustration and will not lead to healthy communication. Digging up the past is another nonconstructive communication pattern wherein one partner continually brings up events about the other partner's past. It's also important to stay away from old arguments and accusations. The past is just that—the past. So try to leave it there and move forward. Dwelling on past events won't help to resolve them.

Another common mistake that couples make in conversations is to use **overkill.** When you are frustrated with your partner and threaten the worst (e.g., "If you don't do that, I will leave you"), even when you know it is not true, you reduce all communication. Don't make threats that you can't follow through with. In the same vein, it's important to focus on your frustration in conversation.

Try not to get overwhelmed and throw too many issues in the conversation at once (e.g., the fact that your partner didn't take the trash out last night, forgot to kiss you goodbye, and ignored you when he or she was with friends). This approach makes it really difficult to focus on resolving any one issue because there is just too much happening. Also, avoid yelling or screaming, which can cause your partner to be defensive and angry, and less likely to be rational and understand what you are saying. Even though it's not easy, it's important to stay calm during conversation.

Clinging to any of these communication patterns can interfere with the resolution of problems and concerns. If you recognize any of these patterns in your own relationship, try talking to your partner about it and try to catch yourself before you engage in them.

Fighting

Overall, verbal disagreements aren't a bad thing in relationships. In fact, couples who disagree are usually happier than those who say "We never, ever fight!" Disagreements are a common part of relationships. (It's important to point out, however, that verbal disagreements are different from physical disagreements. We will discuss domestic violence in Chapter 17.) As we discussed earlier in this chapter, it is nearly impossible not to experience difficulties when you are sharing your space with another person. How you handle such disagreements is what is important. Research has shown that happier couples think more positive thoughts about each other during their disagreements, whereas unhappy couples think negatively about each other (P. Coleman, 2002). Even though a happy couple is disagreeing about an issue, they still feel positively about each other.

What happens after an argument? Generally, women are more likely to demand a reestablishment of closeness, whereas men are more likely to withdraw (Noller, 1993). Some couples have developed unique ways to end arguments. One couple told me that

overgeneralization
Making statements that tend to exaggerate a particular issue.

name-calling
Using negative or stereotyping words when in disagreement.

overkill
A common mistake that couples make during arguments, in which one person threatens the worst but doesn't mean what he or she says.

when they want to stop arguing, they have agreed that whoever is ready first holds up a pinky finger. This signals to the other that they are ready to end the fight. The other partner must touch his or her pinky to the partner's pinky to acknowledge that the fight is over. This isn't always easy, but it has helped this couple to end arguments amicably.

Other suggestions include taking a time out and coming back to finish a discussion later, learning to compromise, or validating each others' differences in opinions. Also remember that in every relationship, there are some issues that may simply be unresolvable. It's important to know which issues can be worked out and which cannot. The question is: can you live with the irresolvable issues? How can you work on improving these issues?

Let's continue to look at how improved communication can enrich personal sexuality and examine the importance of self-esteem and the qualities we look for in our partners.

Review Question

Describe two nonconstructive communication strategies, and explain why they could lead to a communication shutdown.

ENRICHING YOUR SEXUALITY

So far we've been talking about how difficult it can be to communicate with the people in our lives. What about talking to our intimate partner about sex? Sex can be one of the hardest topics to discuss. Let's talk about why this might be so.

Talking With Your Partner About Sex

How do you let your partner know that you are interested in having sex? The majority of couples show their consent to engage in sexual intercourse by saying nothing at all (Hickman & Muehlenhard, 1999). Let's face it: it *is* hard to talk about sex. This is probably because sexuality seems to magnify all the communication problems that exist in any close relationship. We grow up in a society instilled with a sense of shame about our sexuality and are taught at an early age that talking about sex is "dirty." Approaching the subject of sex for the first time in a relationship implies moving on to a new level of intimacy, which can be scary. It also opens the way for rejection, which can be painful.

Too often, we assume that being a good lover also means being a mind reader. Somehow, our partner should just know what arouses us. In reality, nothing could be further from the truth. Good lovers are not mind readers—they are able and willing to listen and communicate with their partners.

I Like You, and I Like Myself

Healthy sexuality depends on feeling good about yourself. If you have a poor self-image or do not like certain aspects of your body or personality, how can you demonstrate to a lover why you are attractive? Imagine a man or woman who is overly concerned about his or her body while in bed with a partner. Maybe a woman is worried that her partner will not be attracted to the size or shape of chest, thighs, stomach, or her inverted nipples. Perhaps a man is consumed with anxiety over the size of his penis, worrying that his partner won't find it appealing. All of these fears interfere with our ability to let go, relax, and enjoy the sexual experience. Before anyone else can accept us, we need to accept ourselves.

In American society, learning to like our bodies is often difficult. Magazines, television, and advertisers all play into our insecurities with their portrayals of the ideal body. The beauty images that the media present to us are often impossible to live up to, and leave many of us feeling unattractive by comparison. We are encouraged to buy products that will make us look more attractive or sexy. To sell products, advertisers must first convince us that we are not okay the way we are, that we need to change our looks, our smells, or our habits. The endless diet products currently on the market also help to increase our dissatisfaction with our bodies. In turn this has led to a preoccupation with weight and the development of eating disorders such as anorexia and bulimia. Many young women who are convinced that they are overweight consciously starve themselves (sometimes to death) in an attempt to be thin.

In the United States in particular, we put a high value on physical attractiveness throughout the life cycle, and our body image greatly affects how attractive we feel. The media are primarily responsible for shaping our ideas of the "ideal body." Today, the desired body is young, slim, tanned, and pimple-free (Barker & Barker, 2002). Because of this, many American women go on diet after diet, have breast augmentation (or, less often, reduction surgery), or endure liposuction or other types of cosmetic surgery to correct what they see as "flaws" (thighs, eyelids, chests, necks, cheekbones). Men and women use makeup, lie in tanning beds, acquire tattoos and piercings, and undergo surgical procedures to feel more comfortable with their bodies. Many Americans spend hours in gyms lifting weights—some boosting the effects with steroids—to achieve the "perfect" body.

Evan Agostini/Getty Images

Many women and men agree that Johnny Depp is a sexy and attractive man.

Jo Hale/Getty Images

Many men and women agree that Jennifer Lopez is a sexy and beautiful woman.

We all have parts of our bodies we wish we could change. In fact, most of us are much more critical of our bodies than our partners would ever be. Not all of us are blessed with the good looks of Jennifer Lopez or Johnny Depp!

Self-esteem is related to our emotional and mental health. Therapists agree that improving mental health includes improving one's self-acceptance, autonomy, and self-efficacy (being able to function in the world), resilience (not to get overburdened by anger, depression, or guilt), interest in one's own career and life, and close relationships with others. All of these are important in establishing not only good mental health, but good sexual relationships as well.

What Makes a Good Lover?

It would be impossible to list all the qualities that make people good lovers. People look for many different things in a partner, and what makes someone a good lover to you might not make that person a good lover to someone else. Overall, good lovers are sensitive to their partner's needs and desires, can communicate their own desires, and are patient, caring, and confident. Being nervous or feeling silly can interfere with lovemaking abilities. It is hard to concentrate when you are worried about performing.

Men and women sometimes have different views of the same sexual behaviors. In the classic movie *Annie Hall*, the lead characters, Annie and Albey, each go to see their respective therapists, and are each asked how often they have sex. Annie replies, "Oh, all the time, at least three times a week," whereas Albey says, "Hardly ever, maybe three times a week." Do you think this reflects a gender difference?

Even sexual techniques can be viewed differently. One man recounts an early sexual experience:

> I'll never forget the first time. She was lying on her parent's bed with the lamplight shining on her, naked and suntanned all over. . . . I climbed on that bed and I lifted her up onto my thighs—she was so light I could always pick her right up—and I opened up her [vagina] with one hand and I rammed my [penis] up there like it was a Polaris missile. Do you know, she screamed out loud, and she dug her nails in my back, and without being too crude about it I [screwed] her until she didn't know what the hell was happening. . . . She loved it. She screamed out loud every single time. I mean I was an active, aggressive lover. (Masterton, 1987, p. 70)

Yet his partner viewed the sexual activity very differently:

What did I think about it? . . . I don't know. I think the only word you could use would be "flabbergasted." He threw me on the bed as if he were Tarzan, and tugged off all of my clothes, and then he took off his own clothes so fast it was almost like he was trying to beat the world record. . . . He took hold of me and virtually lifted me right up in the air as if I were a child, and then he pushed himself right up me, with hardly any foreplay or any preliminaries or anything. (Masterton, 1987, p. 73)

This is another reason that communication is so important. Here is a man thinking he is doing exactly what a woman wants and a woman wondering why he's doing it. Eventually, this couple's relationship ended, mainly due to a lack of communication, which left both feeling confused and frustrated. As we discussed earlier, communication is one of the most important aspects of a healthy and satisfying relationship.

Review Question

Identify the ways that good communication can improve your sex life.

sex byte

Both men and women misjudge which body shape the other sex would rate as most attractive. Women guess that men prefer thinner shapes, whereas men guess that women prefer bulkier shapes. Overall, African American women have the most accurate perception of what men find attractive, whereas Caucasian women have the most distorted view (Demarest & Allen, 2000).

SEX Talk

Question: Are looks more important to men or women?

Men often report that when looking for a partner, physical attractiveness is important. Women are less likely to identify looks as one of the most important characteristics. However, women are more likely than men to report that a person's career is very important. In essence, it seems that men value looks more, whereas women place more value on success.

We must keep in mind, however, that these differences may be due to the fact that men and women feel more comfortable saying that these characteristics are important. In the past, women have not been socialized to value attractiveness in men, whereas men have not been socialized to value success in women (see Chapter 3).

As for body type, lesbian and bisexual women have been found to prefer a heavier figure than heterosexual men, perhaps because they are more comfortable with heavier figures and are unwilling to accept the media's fixation on thinness in women (Cohen & Tannenbaum, 2001).

Good lovers are sensitive to their partner's needs and desires, and can communicate their own desires.

Enriching Your Sexuality: It's Not Mind Reading

Throughout this chapter we have discussed the importance of communication and its role in the development of healthy, satisfying relationships. Good communication skills are an integral part of all healthy relationships, and couples who know how to communicate with each other are happier, more satisfied, and have a better chance of making their relationship last. Many relationship problems stem from poor communication. When it comes to sexual relationships, good communication skills are vital. By talking to your partner, you can share your sexual needs and desires and learn what your partner's sexual needs are. In turn, this can strengthen your overall relationship. It's important to be honest and open and ask for what you need.

Understanding gender differences in communication can help you minimize disagreements and misunderstandings. It's also important to pay attention to nonverbal cues because we know that much of our communication is interpreted through our nonverbal behavior. Talking about sex isn't easy. We live in a society that believes sex talk is dirty or bad, but talking about sex is one of the best ways to move a relationship to a new level of intimacy and connection.

Chapter Review

ACTIVE SUMMARY

1. Good communication skills are an integral part of all **(a)** _____ _____, and couples who know how to communicate with each other are **(b)** _____, more satisfied, and have a better chance of making their relationship **(c)** _____. Many relationship problems stem from **(d)** _____ _____.

2. Communication fosters mutual understanding, increases **(a)** _____ _____, and helps deepen feelings of love and **(b)** _____. However, a lack of communication skills is a major source of **(c)** _____ in relationships. Having poor communication skills, an inability to self-disclose, and/or trouble **(d)** _____ can all lead to communication problems.

3. The three goals of communication include: getting the **(a)** _____ _____, maintaining the **(b)** _____, and managing our **(c)** _____. All of these three goals **(d)** _____ with each other, making communication difficult.

4. Deborah Tannen proposed that there are fundamental differences between the way men and women communicate, and she called these differences **(a)** _____. Men see the world as a place of **(b)** _____ order, whereas women see the world more as a network of **(c)** _____. Men attempt to defend their **(d)** _____, whereas women work to establish **(e)** _____ and avoid isolation.

5. Women engage in more **(a)** _____-talk, whereas men engage in more **(b)** _____-talk. Men also tend to use more **(c)** _____ in their communication, whereas women are more **(d)** _____ and use more words implying **(e)** _____.

6. Many theories have been proposed to explain gender differences in communication. However, gender communication is often best understood as a form of **(a)** _____-_____ communication. Research suggests that men and women may come from different **(b)** _____ _____ and learn different communication rules. Young girls play in small groups and have **(c)** _____ _____, whereas boys play in hierarchically organized groups that focus on **(d)** _____ and/or **(e)** _____.

7. Individualistic cultures encourage their members to have **(a)** _____ goals and values and a(n) **(b)** _____ sense

of self. Collectivist cultures emphasize the needs of their **(c)** _____ over **(d)** _____ needs. Communication patterns have been found to vary depending on **(e)** _____ orientation.

8. The majority of our communication with others is **(a)** _____. This form of communication is often done through **(b)** _____ _____, **(c)** _____, or **(d)** _____. Research has found that **(e)** _____ are better at decoding and translating nonverbal communication.

9. During computer-mediated conversation, **(a)** _____ have an easier time making their voices heard than in face-to-face communication. They have also been found to use more **(b)** _____ online. One of the risks of online communication is **(c)** _____ _____, but if things progress **(d)** _____, there is a better chance of a relationship working out.

10. There are several ways to communicate more effectively. One of these involves increasing **(a)** _____-_____. However, it's important not to disclose too much before the relationship is stable and communication skills are in place. It's also important to **(b)** _____ _____ _____ _____ _____, which can be very difficult. Partners often worry about hurting feelings or worry that their partner will feel differently about them.

11. The majority of couples spend too much time **(a)** _____ each other and not enough time really **(b)** _____ and making affectionate comments. One of the most important communication skills involves **(c)** _____ _____, which involves focusing your attention on what your partner is saying without being defensive. Active listening involves using **(d)** _____ communication to let your partner know that you are attentive and present in the conversation.

12. Researchers have found some gender differences in listening. Men tend to listen for the **(a)** _____ _____, to find out what **(b)** _____ needs to be taken. Women tend to listen for **(c)** _____. This results in men typically listening to **(d)** _____ the problem, and women listening to **(e)** _____.

13. When we express negative feelings, it's important not to use **(a)** _____ _____ because tension will escalate. It's also important to learn how to accept **(b)** _____ without becoming defensive. Mistakes in communication patterns that can get couples into trouble include **(c)** _____, name-calling, and **(d)** _____. Overall, verbal disagreements aren't a(n) **(e)** _____ thing in a relationship.

14. One of the hardest topics to discuss in an intimate relationship is **(a)** _____. The majority of couples show their consent to engage in sexual intercourse by saying **(b)** _____. Most of us grow up learning that talking about sex is **(c)** _____. Too often we assume that being a good lover means being a(n) **(d)** _____ _____.

15. Healthy sexuality depends on feeling good about **(a)** _____. The fact is, before anyone can accept us, we need to accept **(b)** _____; however, one thing that makes this difficult is the **(c)** _____'s portrayal of the perfect body.

16. Good lovers are **(a)** _____ to their partners' needs and desires, and can **(b)** _____ their own desires. They are also **(c)** _____, caring, and confident. Overall, we know that communication is one of the most **(d)** _____ aspects of a healthy and satisfying relationship.

ANSWERS

1. (a) healthy relationships; (b) happier; (c) last; (d) poor communication. 2. (a) emotional intimacy; (b) intimacy; (c) trouble; (d) listening. 3. (a) hierarchical; (c) interactions; (d) independence; (e) connections. 5. (a) rapport; (b) report; (c) slang; (d) supportive; (e) feelings. 6. (a) cross-cultural; (b) sociolinguistic subcultures; (c) best friends; (d) directing; (e) winning. 7. (a) individual; (b) independent; (c) members; (d) individual; (e) cultural. 8. (a) nonverbally; (b) eye contact; (c) smiling; (d) touching; (e) women. 9. (a) women; (b) emoticons; (c) eroticized pseudointimacy; (d) slowly. 10. (a) Self-disclosure; (b) ask for what you need. 11. (a) Criticizing; (b) listening; (c) non-defensive listening; (d) nonverbal. 12. (a) bottom line; (b) action; (c) details; (d) fix; (e) listen. 13. (a) harsh words; (b) criticism; (c) overgeneralizations; (d) overkill; (e) bad. 14. (a) sex; (b) nothing; (c) dirty; (d) mind reader. 15. (a) yourself; (b) ourselves; (c) media. 16. (a) sensitive; (b) communicate; (c) patient; (d) important.

Critical Thinking Questions

1. Have you ever met someone on an airplane and talked about issues that you had never discussed with a friend? How did you feel about this? Why do you think it's easy for strangers to communicate on an airplane?

2. The research shows that couples who know how to communicate have a greater likelihood of making their relationship last. Apply this to a relationship that didn't work out for you, and explain how poor or absent communication may have affected your relationship.

3. Do you think that men and women have different communication styles and may, in fact, have cross-cultural styles of communication? Explain why or why not, and give examples.

4. Do you agree with the findings that claim that women gossip, complain, and bitch more than men? Why, or why not? Give one example.

5. Have you ever communicated with someone online and then met later face-to-face? If so, how did your online communication affect your face-to-face communication? What was your online impression of him or her before you met in person?

6. Can you think of any incidence in which a lack of self-esteem on your part negatively affected a relationship? Explain.

CHAPTER RESOURCES

Check It Out

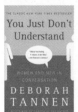

Tannen, Deborah (2001). **You just don't understand: Women and men in conversation.** New York: Quill.

In this book, Tannen argues that women tend to be more relational, whereas men are more likely to interpret the same messages according to the perceived use of power in the message. Although her argument is largely supported by anecdotal evidence, she presents additional work to support her conclusions about gender differences.

The Upside of Anger (2005; 118 minutes; Rated R)

The Upside of Anger tells the story of a woman and her four daughters coping with the loss of a husband and father. Terry Wolfmeyer's (Joan Allen) husband runs away with his secretary, leaving Terry angry and bitter. She uses alcohol to help reduce the pain of his loss and befriends Denny Davies (Kevin Costner). Wolfmeyer's daughters (Erika Christensen, Alicia Witt, Keri Russell, and Evan Rachel Wood) try to help take care of their mother, and at the same time try to understand the breakup of their family. Although Wolfmeyer, her children, and Davies try to communicate with each other as best they can, there are several fumbled attempts at connecting. An interesting ending helps explore the importance of communication and human relationships and the destructive nature of anger.

InfoTrac® College Edition

If your instructor ordered InfoTrac with this book, explore InfoTrac College Edition, your online library, for additional readings and review. Go to: **www.thomsonedu.com,** and enter these search terms:

unconditional positive regard   paraphrasing   validating

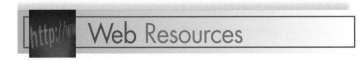

Web Resources

SexualityNow Companion Website
Go to **http://thomsonedu.com/carroll** for practice quiz questions, interactive activities, Internet links, critical thinking exercises, discussion forums, and more. You can also access sites from the Wadsworth Psychology Study Center **(http://psychology.wadsworth.com)** or you can connect directly to the following sites:

The American Communication Association
The American Communication Association (ACA) was created to promote academic and professional research, criticism, teaching, and exchange principles and theories of human communication. This website has links to the *American Communication Journal* and the Communication Studies Center, which contains a collection of online resources.

The Positive Way
Founded by relationship experts, The Positive Way is a resource for helping enhance relationships through communication. Information is available for single people who are looking for a relationship and also for people who would like to improve relationships with a spouse, family members, friends, or coworkers. This website contains questionnaires and information about communication.

The Journal of Communication
The Journal of Communication is an interdisciplinary journal in the field of communication studies. Focusing on communication research, practice, policy, and theory, it includes the most up-to-date and important findings in the communication field. It contains research, book reviews, and a search engine for communication-based studies.

More Self-Esteem
This website contains information on how to subscribe to monthly self-esteem newsletters, tips on how to build self-esteem, inspirational words/quotes, information about attitudes and moods and how to cope with them, help with depression, self-confidence tips, articles, and free resources on self-esteem.

Go to **www.thomsonedu.com** to link to **SexualityNow,** your online study tool. First take the **Pre-Test** for this chapter to get your **Personalized Study Plan,** which will identify topics you need to review and direct you to online resources. Then take the **Post-Test** to determine what concepts you have mastered and what you still need work on.

Videos in SexualityNow
For additional information on topics discussed in this chapter, check out the videos in **SexualityNow** on the following topics:
• **Marriage: "Me" Versus "We"**—Listen to one couple argue about relocating for the husband's job.
• **Communication and Compromise: Planning a Wedding**—See how one couple's understanding of each other's point of view helps them compromise on their wedding plans.

7 Love and Intimacy

Sexuality ⬤ Now Go to www.thomsonedu.com to link to SexualityNow, your online study tool.

*M*any years ago in a small Pennsylvania town named Roseto, medical professionals discovered that the townspeople had significantly lower rates of heart attacks than the people of any of the neighboring towns (Egolf et al., 1992). The people in the town were of similar age as people living in nearby towns. They smoked cigarettes, ate similar foods, and saw the same healthcare professionals. People wondered what was happening. It turns out the town of Roseto was founded in 1882 by Italian immigrants and had many three-generation families. As such, the town had a strong sense of community, love, loyalty, and ties to one another. These connections were found to reduce stress and improve the health and well-being of all of Roseto's townspeople. The "Roseto Effect," as it was known, continued until the 1960s, when early family tradition began to diminish and the rates of heart disease began to increase.

This study illustrates the power of intimacy and love and the impact these have on our health (Ornish, 1999). When people love each other, talk to each other, and share their inner selves, their immune systems may actually become stronger than people who isolate themselves or are emotionally withdrawn (see the accompanying Sex in Real Life, "What Does Love Have to Do With It?" for more information). This works in reverse as well. In the last chapter we talked about communication problems and negativity in intimate relationships. Arguments between intimate partners have been found to weaken the immune system and render the couple more at risk for illness (Caldwell, 2003).

You might be wondering why we begin the chapter with such a story. Love and the ability to form loving, caring, and intimate relationships with others are important for our emotional health but also for our physical health. In this chapter, we will talk about the forms and measures of love, where love comes from, love throughout the life cycle, and building intimate relationships. Before we do, try answering this question: What exactly is *love*?

SEX in Real Life

What Does Love Have to Do With It?

*I*n his 1999 best-selling book, *Love and Survival: Scientific Basis for the Healing Power of Intimacy,* Dean Ornish discusses the importance of love and intimacy. He points to a variety of research studies that claim that when people open up to each other, talk to each other, and love each other, they become physically healthier. Following are just a few of these findings from longitudinal research:

- College students who had distant and nonemotional relationships with their parents had significantly higher rates of high blood pressure and heart disease years later than did students who reported close and emotionally connected relationships.
- Heart patients who felt "loved" had 50% less arterial damage than those who said they did not feel "loved."

- Men and women who reported the least social contact died at the rate of three times those who reported the most social contact.
- Women who said they felt "lonely and isolated" were three-and-a-half times more likely to die of breast, ovarian, or uterine cancer.
- Men who said their wives did not show them "love" suffered 50% more chest pain.
- People with heart disease who have a dog have been found to have four times fewer sudden cardiac deaths than those without dogs.

SOURCE: Ornish (1999).

romantic love
Idealized love, based on romance and perfection.

unrequited love
Loving another when the love will never be returned.

WHAT IS LOVE?

Love. One of the great mysteries of humankind is the capacity to love, to make attachments with others that involve deep feeling, selflessness, and commitment. Throughout history, literature and art have portrayed the saving powers of love. How many songs have been written about its passion, and how many films have depicted its power to change people's lives? Yet, after centuries of writers discussing love, philosophers musing over its hold on men and women, and religious leaders teaching of the necessity to love one another, how much do we really know about love? Are there different, separate kinds of love—friendship, passion, love of parents—or are they all simply variations on one fundamental emotion? Does love really "grow"? Is love different at 15 than at 50? What is the relationship between love and sexuality?

We go through life trying to come to terms with loving, trying to figure out why we are attracted to certain types or why we fall in love with all the wrong people. The mystery of love is part of its attraction. We are surrounded with images of love in the media and are taught from the time we first listen to fairy tales that love is the answer to most of life's problems. Why should we not try to understand what love is?

Love in Other Times and Places

The desire for love is as old as humanity. Each new generation somehow imagines that it was the first, the inventor of "true love"; but look at this poem from the Late Egyptian empire, over 3,000 years ago:

> I found my lover on his bed, and my heart was sweet to excess.
> I shall never be far away (from) you while my hand is in your hand,
> and I shall stroll with you in every favorite place.
> How pleasant is this hour, may it extend for me to eternity;
> since I have lain with you, you have lifted high my heart.
> In mourning or in rejoicing be not far from me.
> (Quoted in Bergmann, 1987, p. 5)

The Hebrew Bible speaks of God's love of Israel, and the metaphorical imagery in the Song of Solomon, usually interpreted as depicting God and Israel as lovers, is highly erotic and sexual. Jacob had to work for 7 years to win Rachel's hand, but these 7 years "seemed to him to be but a few days, for the love he had for her" (Genesis 29:20). The Middle Ages glorified the modern idea of **romantic love,** including loving from afar, or loving those one could not have (**unrequited** (un-ree-KWI-ted) **love**).

Not until the 19th century did people begin to believe that romantic love was the most desirable form of loving relations. Through most of Western history, marriage was an economic union, arranged by the parents. Once wed, husbands and wives were encouraged to learn love for one another, to develop love. How different that is from the modern romantic ideal of love preceding marriage.

THE FORMS AND MEASURE OF LOVE

We must admire those researchers who are willing to tackle a difficult subject such as the origins of love or the different forms of love. We all love, and one of the characteristics of love is that we often believe that the intensity of the emotion is unique to us, that no one else has ever loved as we have loved. We also feel many different kinds of love, such as love of a friend, love of a parent, love of a celebrity, or love of a pet. Philosophers, historians, social scientists, and other scholars have made attempts to untangle these types of love.

Romantic Versus Companionate Love

Romantic love is the all-encompassing, passionate love of romantic songs and poetry, of tearjerker movies and romance novels, and has become the prevailing model of sexual relationships and marriage in the Western world. Romantic love is also sometimes called passionate love, infatuation, obsessive love, and even lovesickness, and with it comes a sense of ecstasy and anxiety, physical attraction, and sexual desire. We tend to idealize the partner, ignoring faults in the newfound joy of the attachment. Passionate love blooms in the initial euphoria of a new attachment to a sexual partner, and it often seems as if we're swept away by it; that is why we say we "fall" in love, or even fall "head over heels" in love.

Companionate love involves deep affection, trust, loyalty, attachment, and intimacy; and, although passion is often present, companionate love lacks the high and low swings of romantic love.

There are few feelings as joyous or exciting as romantic love. The explosion of emotion is often so intense that people talk about being unable to contain it; it feels as if it spills out of us onto everything we see, making the flowers a bit more beautiful and birds' songs a little sweeter. Some people joke that there is nothing quite as intolerable as those in love; they are just so annoyingly happy all the time! It is not surprising that such a powerful emotion is celebrated in poetry, story, and song. It is also not surprising that such a powerful emotion seems as though it will last forever. After all, isn't that what we learn when the couples in fairy tales "live happily ever after," and when the couples in movies ride off into the sunset?

Unfortunately, perhaps, passion of that intensity fades after a time. If the relationship is to continue, romantic love usually develops into **companionate love,** or **conjugal** (CONN-jew-gull) **love.** Companionate love involves feelings of deep affection, attachment, intimacy, and ease with the partner as well as the development of trust, loyalty, a lack of criticality, and a willingness to sacrifice for the partner (Critelli et al., 1986; Shaver & Hazan, 1987). Though companionate love does not have the passionate high and low swings of romantic love, passion is certainly present for many companionate lovers. Companionate love may even be a deeper, more intimate love than romantic love.

It can be difficult for couples to switch from passionate love to the deeper, more mature companionate love (Peck, 1978). Because the model of love we see on television and in movies is the highly sexual, swept-off-your-feet passion of romantic love, some may see the mellowing of that passion as a loss of love rather than a development of a different kind of love. Yet the mutual commitment to develop a new, more mature kind of love is, in fact, what we should mean by "true love."

companionate love
An intimate form of love that involves friendly affection and deep attachment based on a familiarity with the loved one. (Also referred to as conjugal love.)

conjugal love
An intimate form of love that involves friendly affection and deep attachment based on familiarity with the loved one. (Also referred to as companionate love.)

Review Question

What is the difference between romantic and companionate, or conjugal, love? What kind of love relationship do you hope to have with your mate?

SEX Talk

Question: *Why is love so confusing?*

Love is confusing because it often evokes a host of other emotions and personal issues, such as self-worth and self-esteem, fears of rejection, passion and sexuality, jealousy and possessiveness, great joy and great sadness. Dealing with those emotions is confusing enough; but in love, we try to communicate and share intimacies with another person who is going through the same kinds of confused feelings that we are. When so many emotions are fighting for attention, it comes as no surprise that the mind doesn't seem to work that well!

The Colors of Love: John Alan Lee

"How do I love thee? Let me count the ways . . ." wrote Elizabeth Barrett Browning, who seemed to agree that there is more than one way to love, that even within one person love can take many forms. Psychologist John Alan Lee (1974, 1988, 1998)

TABLE 7.1	Lee's Colors of Love
1. Eros: The Romantic Lover	Eros is like romantic love. Erotic lovers speak of their immediate attraction to their lover, to his or her eyes, skin, fragrance, or body. Most have the picture of an ideal partner in their mind, which a real partner cannot fulfill; that is why purely erotic love does not last. In childhood, erotic lovers often had a secure attachment style with their caregivers.
2. Ludus (LOO-diss): The Game-Playing Lover	Ludic lovers play the "game" of love, enjoying the act of seduction. Commitment, dependency, and intimacy are not valued, and ludic lovers will often juggle several relationships at the same time. In childhood, ludic lovers often had an avoidant attachment style with their caregivers.
3. Storge (STOR-gay): The Quiet, Calm Lover	Storgic love is a quiet, calm love that builds over time, similar to companionate love. Storgic lovers don't suddenly "fall in love," and do not dream of some idealized, romantic lover; marriage, stability, and comfort within love are the goal. Should the relationship break up, the storgic partners would probably remain friends, a status unthinkable to erotic lovers who have split.
4. Mania: The Crazy Lover	Manic lovers are possessive and dependent, consumed by thoughts of the beloved and are often on a roller coaster of highs and lows. Each encouraging sign from the lover brings joy; each little slight brings heartache, which makes their lives dramatic and painful. Manic lovers fear separation; they may sit by the phone waiting for the beloved to call, or they may call their beloved incessantly. They tend to wonder why all their relationships ultimately fail. In childhood, manic lovers often had an anxious/ambivalent attachment style with their caregivers.
5. Pragma: The Practical Lover	Pragmatic lovers have a "shopping list" of qualities they are looking for in a relationship. They are very practical about their relationship and lovers. Pragmatic lovers want a deep, lasting love but believe the best way to get it is to assess their own qualities and make the best "deal" in the romantic marketplace. They tend to be planners—planning the best time to get married, have children, and even when to divorce ("Well, in two years the house will be paid for and Billy will be in high school, so that would be a good time to get divorced …").
6. Agape (AH-ga-pay): The Selfless Lover	Altruistic, selfless, never demanding, patient, and true is agapic love. Never jealous, not needing reciprocity, agapic love tends to happen in brief episodes. Lee found very few long-term agapic lovers. Lee gives the example of a man whose lover was faced with a distressing choice between him and another man, and so he gracefully bowed out.

As you read through these descriptions, where do you think your love style fits in? Are you a pragmatic lover, planning all the details of your love affair? Do you feel stir-crazy in a relationship and end up juggling lovers and playing games? Or do you have a romantic and sensitive love style? It is possible that more than one style will fit you, and also that your love style may change throughout your lifetime. What influences in your life do you think contributed to your love style today?
Source: John Alan Lee, "The Styles of Loving," *Psychology Today*, 8(5), 43–51. Reprinted with permission from *Psychology Today*. Copyright © 1974 by Sussex Publishers, Inc.

Review Question

Identify and describe John Alan Lee's six colors of love.

suggests that in romantic relationships, there are more forms of love than just romantic and companionate love. Lee collected statements about love from hundreds of works of fiction and nonfiction, starting with the Bible and including both ancient and modern authors. He gathered a panel of professionals in literature, philosophy, and the social sciences, and had them sort into categories the thousands of statements he found. Lee's research identified six basic ways to love, which he calls "colors" of love, to which he gave Greek and Latin names. Lee's categories are described in Table 7.1.

Lee's colors of love have generated a substantial body of research, much of which shows that his love styles are independent from one another and that each can be measured to some degree (Hendrick & Hendrick, 1989). Lee points out that two lovers with compatible styles are probably going to be happier and more content with each other than two with incompatible styles. Couples who approach loving differently often cannot understand why their partners react the way they do or how they can hurt their partners unintentionally. Imagine how bored an erotic lover would be with a pragmatic lover, or how much a ludic lover would hurt a manic lover. Each would consider the other callous or even cruel, suggests Lee, when people simply tend to love differently. Higher levels of manic and ludic love styles are associated with poorer psychological health, whereas higher levels of storge and eros love styles are associated with higher levels of psychological health (Blair, 2000).

Incidentally, certain types of love styles are more socially desirable for men or women (Davies, 2001). It's more socially desirable for men to have eros (passionate love) or ludus (game-playing love) and women to have agape (selfless love); and less socially desirable for men to have agape and women to have ludus.

Personal Voices

Love in Song

J ust by turning on the radio you can learn popular views on love and romance. Read through the following lyrics. What do the words make you think about romance? How do you think popular music helps shape our views of love?

"Fallin'"

I keep on fallin' in and out of love with you

sometimes I love you, sometimes you make me blue

sometimes I feel good, at times I feel used

Loving you darlin' makes me so confused

I never loved someone the way that I'm loving you

oh, oh, I never felt this way,

how do you give me so much pleasure and cause me so much pain

just when I think I've taken more than would a fool

I start fallin' back in love with you.

SOURCE: Words and music by Alicia Keys. © 2001 EMI APRIL MUSIC INC. and LELLOW PRODUCTIONS. All rights controlled and administered by

SEX Talk

Question: How do I know the difference between love and infatuation? How do I know if it's real love or just sexual attraction?

Each individual must struggle with these questions as he or she matures, particularly in the teenage and early adulthood years, before gaining much experience with romantic love. There is no easy answer, but there are some indications that a relationship may be infatuation rather than love when it involves a compulsion (rather than a desire) to be with the person, a feeling of lack of trust (such as a need to check up on the partner), extremes of emotions (ecstatic highs followed by depressing lows), and a willingness to take abuse or behave in destructive ways that one would not have before the relationship. Some questions to ask yourself about your love relationship are: Would I want this person as a friend if he or she were not my partner? Do my friends and family dislike this person or think he or she is not right for me? (Friends and family are often more level-headed judges of character than the infatuated individual.) Do I really know this person, or am I fantasizing about how he or she is with little confirmation by his or her actual behavior? It's not always easy to tell the difference between infatuation and love—many couples have a hard time differentiating between the two (Aloni & Bernieri, 2004)!

Love Triangles: Robert Sternberg

Robert Sternberg (1998, 1999) suggests that different strategies of loving are really different ways of combining the basic building blocks of love. He has proposed that love is made up of three elements—passion, intimacy, and commitment—that can be combined in different ways. Sternberg refers to a total absence of all three components as nonlove.

Passion is sparked by physical attraction and sexual desire and drives a person to pursue a romantic relationship. Passion instills a deep desire for union, and, though it is often expressed sexually, self-esteem, nurturing, domination, submission, and self-actualization may also contribute to the experience. Passion is the element that identities romantic forms of love; it is absent in the love of a parent for a child. Passion fires up quickly in a romantic relationship but is also the first to fade.

TABLE 7.2   Sternberg's Triangular Theory of Love

Robert Sternberg, a professor of psychology at Yale University, believes that love is made up of three elements: passion, intimacy, and commitment, each of which may be present or absent in a relationship. The presence or absence of these components produces eight triangles (seven of these involve at least one component; the eighth represents the absence of any components, referred to as nonlove). Problems can occur in a relationship if one person's triangle significantly differs from the other's. This can happen when one person has more or less of one of the three elements of love. Following are the various types of love proposed by Sternberg.

	Type	Description
	Nonlove	In most of our casual daily relationships, there is no sense of intimacy, passion, or commitment.
	Liking	When there is intimacy without (sexual) passion and without strong personal commitment, we are friends. Friends can separate for long periods of time and resume the relationship as if it had never ended.
	Infatuation	Passion alone leads to infatuation. Infatuation refers to physiological arousal and a sexual desire for another person. Casual hookups and one-night stands would fall into this category. Typically, infatuation quickly fades, often to be replaced with infatuation for someone else!
	Empty love	Empty love involves only commitment, as in a couple who stays together even though their relationship long ago lost its passion and intimacy. However, relationships can begin with commitment alone and develop intimacy and passion.
	Romantic love	Passion and intimacy lead to romantic love, which is often the first phase of a relationship. Romantic love is often an intense, joyful experience.
	Companionate love	Companionate love ranges from long-term, deeply committed friendships to married or long-term couples who have experienced a decrease in the passionate aspect of their love.
	Fatuous (FAT-you-us) love	Love is fatuous (which means silly or foolish) when one does not really know the person to whom one is making a commitment. Hollywood often portrays two people who meet, become infatuated, and make a commitment by the end of the movie. However, a committed relationship continues even after passion fades, so it makes sense to know one's partner before making a commitment.
	Consummate love	Consummate, or complete, love has all three elements in balance. Even after achieving consummate love, we can lose it: passion can fade, intimacy can stagnate, and commitment can be undermined by attraction to another. But it is consummate love we all strive for.

Source: Robert J. Sternberg, "A Triangle Theory of Love," *Psychological Review, 93*(2): 119–135. Reprinted by permission of the author.

Intimacy involves feelings of closeness, connectedness, and bondedness in a loving relationship. It is the emotional investment one has in the relationship and includes such things as the desire to support and help the other, happiness, mutual understanding, emotional support, and communication. The intimacy component of love is experienced in many loving relationships, such as parent–child, sibling, friendship, and the like.

Commitment, in the short term, is the decision to love someone; in the long term, it is the determination to maintain that love. This element can sustain a relationship that is temporarily (or even permanently) going through a period without passion or intimacy. The marriage ceremony, for example, is a public display of a couple's commitment to each other.

Sternberg combines these elements into seven forms of love, which are described in Table 7.2. A person may experience different forms of love at different times; romantic love may give way to companionate love, or the infatuated lover may find a person to whom he or she is willing to commit and settle down. In the emotionally healthy person, as we shall see, love evolves and changes as we mature (Sternberg, 1998).

Can We Measure Love?

Based on these types of theories, theorists have tried to come up with scales that measure love. However, you can't just ask people, "How deeply do you love [your partner]?" Each participant will interpret love in his or her own way. One strategy is to create a scale that measures love by measuring something strongly associated with love. Zick Rubin (1970, 1973) was one of the first to try to scientifically measure love. Rubin thought of love as a form of attachment to another person, and created a "love scale" that measured what he believed to be the three components of attachment: degrees of needing ("If I could never be with _____, I would feel miserable"); caring ("I would do almost anything for _____"); and trusting ("I feel very possessive about _____"). Rubin's scale proved to be an extraordinarily powerful tool to measure love. For example, how a couple scores on the "love scale" is correlated not only with their rating of the probability that they will get married, but their score even predicts how often they will gaze at each other!

Others have since tried to create their own scales. Keith Davis and his colleagues (Davis & Latty-Mann, 1987; Davis & Todd, 1982) created the Relationship Rating Scale (RRS), which measures various aspects of relationships, such as intimacy, passion, and conflict. Hatfield and Sprecher (1986) created the Passionate Love Scale (PLS), which tries to measure the degree of intense passion or "longing for union."

Will measures of love eventually tell us what love is made of? Well, as you can imagine, many problems are inherent in trying to measure love. Most love scales really focus on romantic love and are not as good at trying to measure the degree of companionate love (Sternberg, 1987). Also, measuring degrees of love, or types of love, is different from saying what love actually is. Finally, when you ask people questions about love, they can answer only with their conscious attitudes toward love. Many theorists suggest that we don't consciously know why we love, how we love, or even how much we love. Other theorists argue that people do not realize to what degree love is physiological (see the section on physiological arousal theories later in this chapter). So we may be measuring only how people think they love.

Review Question

Identify and describe the three elements of love, according to Robert Sternberg. Explain how these elements combine to make seven different forms of love.

Review Question

Is it possible to measure love? What problems have researchers run into when attempting to do so?

THEORIES: WHERE DOES LOVE COME FROM?

Why do we love in the first place? What purpose does love serve? After all, most animals mate successfully without experiencing "love." Researchers' theories on why we form emotional bonds in the first place can be grouped into four general categories: behavioral reinforcement, cognitive, physiological arousal, and evolutionary.

Behavioral Reinforcement Theories

One group of theories suggests that we love because another person reinforces positive feelings in ourselves. Lott & Lott (1961) suggested that a rewarding or positive feeling in the presence of another person makes us like them, even when the reward has nothing to do with the other person. For example, they found that children who were rewarded continually by their teachers came to like their classmates more than children who were not equally rewarded. The opposite is also true. Griffitt & Veitch (1971) found that people tend to dislike people they meet in a hot, crowded room, no matter what those people's personalities are like. Behavioral reinforcement theory suggests that we like people we associate with

The behavioral reinforcement theory suggests that we love people we associate with feeling good. Our love for them grows out of doing things together that are mutually reinforcing.

feeling good and love people if the association is very good. Love develops through a series of mutually reinforcing activities.

Cognitive Theories

Cognitive theories of liking and loving are based on an interesting paradox: the less people are paid for a task, the more they tend to like it. In other words, a person tends to think, "Here I am painting this fence, and I'm not even getting paid for it. Why am I doing this? I must like to paint!" The same goes for relationships. If we are with a person often and find ourselves doing things for them, we ask, "Why am I with her so often? Why am I doing her laundry? I must like her—I must even love her!" This theory suggests the action comes first, and the interpretation comes later (Tzeng, 1992). Studies have also found that when we think someone likes us, we're more likely to be attracted to them (Ridge & Reber, 2002).

Physiological Arousal Theories

How does love feel? Most people describe physiological sensations: "I felt so excited I couldn't breathe"; "My throat choked up"; "I felt tingling all over." If you look at those descriptions, couldn't they also be descriptions of fear, anger, or excitement? Is there a difference between being in love and being on a roller coaster?

Perhaps not. In a famous experiment, Schachter & Singer (1962) gave students a shot of epinephrine (adrenaline) that causes general arousal, including sweaty palms, increased heart rate, increased breathing, and so on. They split the students into four groups: one was told exactly what was happening and what to expect, another was told the wrong set of symptoms to expect (itching, numbness, a slight headache), a third group was told nothing, and a fourth group got an injection of saline solution (saltwater) rather than epinephrine.

Each group was put into a waiting room with a student who was actually part of the study. In half the cases, the confederate acted happy, and in half, angry. The interesting result was that the students in the informed group, when they felt aroused, assumed they were feeling the effects of the epinephrine. However, the uninformed groups tended to believe they were experiencing the same emotion as the other person in the room. They thought they were happy, or they thought they were angry. Schachter & Singer concluded that an emotion happens when there is general physiological arousal for whatever reason and a label is attached to it—and that label might be any emotion. In other words, people should be vulnerable to experiencing love (or another emotion) when they are physiologically aroused for whatever reason (Schachter & Singer, 2001).

Another experiment by Dutton & Aron (1974) found similar results. Male participants were asked to walk across one of two bridges. The first was a very high bridge that hung over a gorge, had low handrails, and swayed in the wind. The second bridge was close to the ground and didn't sway. As the men crossed the bridge, they were met by an attractive male or female research assistant who asked them to answer a few questions and tell a story based on a picture. The assistant also mentioned that the men could call him or her at home for more information. The result was that those men who met the female on the high bridge, where they were more physiologically aroused by the sense of danger, told stories with more erotic content and were most likely to call the female assistant at home. The men had a physiological response to the danger and interpreted this response as arousal to the attractive research assistant. (Male participants in this study were assumed to be heterosexual. How do you think this assumption could affect the results of the study?)

So, is love just a label we give to sweaty palms? The idea may explain why we tend to associate love and sex so closely; sexual excitement is a state of intense physiological arousal. Certainly arousal of some sort is a necessary component of love. Would you want to be in love with someone who wasn't the least bit excited when you entered the room? Love, however, is almost certainly more than arousal alone. Perhaps arousal has a stronger connection to initial attraction than to love. Maybe that is why lust is so often confused with love.

However, this being said, it's also important to point out that the original Schachter & Singer (1962) study has often been challenged and is difficult to replicate. There is very little support for the claim that arousal is a necessary condition for an emotional state, and the role of arousal has been overstated (Reisenzein, 1994).

Evolutionary Theories

Evolutionary theorists try to understand the evolutionary advantages of human behaviors. Love, they believe, developed as the human form of three basic instincts: the need to be protected from outside threats, the instinct of the parent to protect the child, and the sexual drive. Love is an evolutionary strategy that helps us form the bonds we need to reproduce and pass our genes on to the next generation. We love in order to propagate the species.

To evolutionary theorists, that would explain why we tend to fall in love with people whom we think have positive traits; we want to pass those traits along to our children. In fact, evolutionary theorists argue that their perspective can explain why heterosexual men look for attractive women, and heterosexual women look for successful men, the world over (see the section on cultural influences on attraction on page 194). Heterosexual men want a fit, healthy woman to carry their offspring, and heterosexual women want a man with the resources to protect them and help care for the infant in the long period they devote to reproduction. For most of history, that included 9 months of pregnancy and over a year of breast-feeding. Love creates the union that maximizes each partner's chance of passing on their genes to the next generation.

Review Question

Compare and contrast the four theories about where love comes from.

LOVE FROM CHILDHOOD TO MATURITY

Throughout our lives, we love others. First we love our parents or caretakers and then siblings, friends, and lovers. At each stage of life we learn lessons about love that help us mature into the next stage. Love gets more complex as we get older. Let us walk through the different stages of individual development and look at the different ways love manifests itself as we grow.

Childhood

In infancy, the nature and quality of the bond with the caregiver can have profound effects on the ability of the person to form attachments throughout life (we will discuss this more in the next chapter, "Childhood and Adolescent Sexuality"). Loving, attentive caregivers tend to produce secure, happy children. Our parents, or the adults who raised us, are the very first teachers of love and intimacy. In fact, we tend to relate to others in our love relationships much as we did when we were young. If you grew up in a family in which your parents were unemotional and distant, you learn that love is dangerous. Researchers used to believe that mother love was more important than father love, but today we know that both are equally important to the development of healthy, intimate relationships (Rohner & Veneziano, 2001).

Those who do not experience intimacy growing up may have a harder time establishing intimate relationships as adults (Perry, 1998). Of course, it is also true that many people who had difficult upbringings are successful at developing deep and intimate relationships.

The type of intimate relationships you form as an adult may be due primarily to the type of attachment you formed as a child (Burton, 2005; Mikulincer & Shaver, 2005). Hazan & Shaver (1987) and Shaver and colleagues (1988), building on the work of Ainsworth and her colleagues (Ainsworth et al., 1978), suggest that infants form one of three types of attachment behaviors that follow them throughout life. *Secure* infants tolerate caregivers being out of their sight because they believe the caregiver will respond if they cry out or need care. Similarly, the secure adult easily gets close to others and is not threatened when a lover goes away. *Anxious/ambivalent* babies cry more than secure

Review Question

Identify the various attachment styles. Which of these styles is most like yours?

sex byte

Men and women who use online dating services may find that they prematurely establish intense relationships, based on the anticipation of finding a "soul mate" online (Houran & Lange, 2004).

babies and panic when the caregiver leaves them. Anxious/ambivalent lovers worry that their partner doesn't really love them or will leave them, and that their need for others will scare people away. They tend to desire more closeness than their partners are willing to allow. *Avoidant* babies often have caregivers who are uncomfortable with hugging and holding them and tend to force separation on the child at an early age. In the adult, the avoidant lover is uncomfortable with intimacy and finds trusting others difficult.

Hazan & Shafer (1987) found that adults report the same types of behavior as Ainsworth found in infants. People with secure attachment styles also reported more positive childhood experiences and had higher self-esteem than others (Feeney & Noller, 1990). We may develop an attachment style as a child that reemerges as we begin to form romantic attachments in adolescence. College students who are securely attached to their parents have an easier time establishing intimate relationships (Neal & Frick-Horbury, 2001).

SEX Talk

Question: I have always had a tough time trusting in relationships. Could this have anything to do with the fact that my parents divorced when I was quite young?

It is possible that the divorce of your parents has made it difficult for you to trust your intimate partners. Research has found that divorce affects a young adult's level of trust in intimate relationships (Ensign et al., 1998). Women whose parents have divorced (compared to women whose parents maintained stable marriages) typically report less trust and satisfaction in intimate relationships (Jacquet & Surra, 2001). Men whose parents have divorced are less likely to experience problems in their intimate relationships unless their female romantic partner is also from a divorced family (because women with divorced parents tend to have less trust). Overall, parental divorce may affect trust and intimacy in a close relationship, but it does not put children at an overall disadvantage in the development of love relationships (Sprecher et al., 1998). It may not be the divorce itself that interferes with people's ability to form intimate relationships, but rather the quality of the relationships they have with their mother and father. If they have a good relationship with at least one of their parents, the negative effects in intimate relationships may be reduced (Ensign et al., 1998).

Adolescence

There is something attractive about young love, which is why it is celebrated so prominently in novels and movies. The love relationship seems so important, so earnest, and so passionate at the time, and yet so innocent and bittersweet in retrospect. Why are the dips and rises of our loves so important to us in adolescence? Adolescent love is to adult love what a child's play is to adult work: it teaches us how to react to love, to manage our emotions, and to handle the pain of love. It also lays the groundwork for adult intimacy. Adolescents must learn to establish a strong personal identity separate from their family. Experimentation with different approaches to others is very natural; and, during adolescence, we develop the **role repertoire** that follows us into adulthood. Similarly, we experiment with different intimacy styles (J. Johnson & Alford, 1987) and develop an **intimacy repertoire,** a set of behaviors that we use to forge close relationships throughout our lives.

The process of establishing our repertoires can be a difficult task. This helps explain why adolescent relationships can be so intense and fraught with jealousy and why adolescents often are unable to see beyond the relationship (J. Johnson & Alford, 1987). Our first relationships often take the form of a "crush" or infatuation and are often directed toward unattainable partners such as teachers or movie stars. Male movie stars provide adolescent girls with a safe outlet for developing romantic love before dating and sexual activity begin (Karniol, 2001).

role repertoire
A set of behaviors that we use in our interactions with others. Once we find what works, we develop patterns of interacting with others.

intimacy repertoire
A set of behaviors that we use to forge intimate relationships throughout our lives.

Sometimes the first lessons of love are painful, as we learn that love may not be returned, that feelings of passion fade, that love itself does not preclude conflict. Yet managing such feelings helps us develop a mature love style. Many factors have been found to be associated with the ability to find romantic love in adolescence, such as marital status of the parents, the quality of the parental relationship, and comfort with one's body (Seiffge-Krenke et al., 2001). In fact, as we discussed earlier, difficulties with attachments in college students' intimate relationships are often caused by poor attachments to one's parents (see the Sex Talk question on page 190).

The emotions of adolescent love are so powerful that adolescents may think that they are the only ones to have gone through such joy, pain, and confusion. They may gain some comfort in knowing that almost everyone goes through the same process to some degree. Confusion about love certainly does not end with adolescence.

Young love lays the groundwork for adult intimacy.

SEX Talk

Question: Someone told me I'm attracted to my boyfriend because of how he smells. That sounds completely crazy. Is there any truth to this idea?

Although controversial, there may be some truth to it (Baum, 2004). We register the "smells" of people through their pheromones (FAIR-oh-moans)—odorless chemicals secreted by both humans and animals (Rodriguez, 2004; Thorne & Amrein, 2003). Pheromones have been found to influence attraction, mating, and bonding (Wright, 1994), and have also been found to promote the bond between a mother and her infant (Kohl & Francoeur, 2002). You might remember that we talked about the influence of pheromones in Chapter 4 when we discussed menstrual synchronicity (Hays, 2003; see page 118).

As for how pheromones influence our mate choice, it may be that our odor preferences are influenced by our major histocompatibility complex (MHC; Santos et al., 2005). The MHC is a group of genes that helps the body recognize invaders such as bacteria and viruses. Because humans are protected by the broadest array of disease resistance, we may be programmed to mate with a partner whose MHC differs from our own (Milinski & Wedekind, 2001). This way, any offspring have a more complete MHC. In one study, women were given several soiled T-shirts from a variety of men and asked which scents they preferred. The women preferred the T-shirts with odors from men who had different MHC systems (Milinski & Wedekind, 2001). This doesn't mean that we can't bond and mate with someone whose smell we dislike. Over time, we adjust to these smells and can learn to love them.

Review Question

What makes love relationships so difficult and unstable for many adolescents? Why do you think those highs and lows even out as we get older?

💠 ADULT LOVE AND INTIMACY

Love relationships can last many years. As time goes by, relationships grow and change, and love grows and changes. Trying to maintain a sense of stability and continuity while still allowing for change and growth is probably the single greatest challenge of long-term love relationships.

Attaining intimacy is different from loving. We can love from afar, and we can love anonymously; we can love our cat, our favorite musician, or a great leader. Intimacy requires reciprocity: it takes two. Intimacy is a dance of two souls, each of whom must reveal a little, risk a little, and try a lot. In some ways, therefore, true intimacy is more difficult to achieve than true love because the emotion of love may be effortless, whereas the establishment of intimacy always requires effort.

Does fate determine whom you will fall in love with, or are there other factors at work? We will now talk about physical attraction, proximity, common interests, and other factors that contribute to adult love and intimacy.

Attraction

Imagine that you are in a public place, such as a bar, a museum, or a sports event. Suddenly you see someone and feel an immediate attraction. As you approach him or her with your favorite opening line, you muse to yourself, "I wonder why I am so attracted to this person and not to someone else?" What might be going on?

"Haven't I Seen You Here Before?"

One of the most reliable predictors of whom a person will date is proximity: people are most likely to find lovers among the people they know or see around them. The vast majority of people have sex with, love, and marry people who are very much like them in ethnic, racial, and religious background (Michael et al., 1994). This is, in part, because we tend to meet many more such people as we go through our normal lives. We have a cultural myth about seeing a stranger across a crowded room, falling in love, and finding out that the stranger is from an exotic place and has lived a much different life. In fact, such a scenario is rare. We are much more likely to meet our mates at a party, religious institution, or friend's house, where the other guests are likely to come from backgrounds very similar to our own.

"You Know, We Really Have a Lot in Common"

Folklore tells us both that "birds of a feather flock together" and that "opposites attract." Yet only the first saying is supported by the evidence; people tend to be attracted to those who think like they do (Byrne & Murnen, 1988). The majority of people who fall in love share similar educational levels, social class, religion and degree of religiousness, desired family size, attitudes toward gender roles, physique and physical attractiveness, family histories, and political opinions (Rubin, 1973).

"You Have Such Beautiful Eyes"

Physical attractiveness has been found to be one of the most importance influences in forming love relationships for both gay and straight men and women (Sangrador & Yela, 2000). Physically attractive people are assumed by others to have more socially desirable personalities and to be happier and more successful (Zebrowitz et al., 1998). As we talked about in Chapter 6, men have traditionally rated physical attraction as the single most important feature in potential mates (Buss, 1989b). However, over the last few years, both men and women have increased the importance they attach to physical attractiveness in an intimate partner (Lacey et al., 2004; Buss et al., 2001). The "matching hypothesis" claims that people are drawn to others with similar traits and attractiveness to themselves. However, it may be that both men and women would really prefer highly attractive partners, but they go through a mental probability calculation (i.e., thinking that they don't have a chance with the most attractive partner so they choose the next attractive partner and so on; Takeuchi, 2000).

Physical appearance is usually the first thing we perceive about a potential lover, though it tends to fade in importance over the life of the relationship. When considering a romantic partner, both men and women may be willing to compromise on some qualities they are looking for in a partner, but not on physical attractiveness (Sprecher & Regan, 2002). As we discussed in Chapter 6, the media have put such a premium on physical appearance that the majority of people in the United States report they are unhappy with their appearance and would change it if they could.

Personal Voices

If You Love Something, Set It Free

Following is a personal account of a love relationship between two college students. Meghan and Sebastian decided to take a break from each other to see whether their relationship was really working. Do you think most students would be willing to take a break and put their relationship on hold, or are Meghan and Sebastian unique? Do you think many college students today fear being alone? Why, or why not?

Meghan: Sebastian and I had our first class together my sophomore year, and there was definitely chemistry between us. I thought he was gorgeous. We caught each other's eyes on a few occasions during class, each time maintaining eye contact. I knew that the butterflies in my stomach had to be telling me something. Our romance grew into an incredible relationship. Not only were we in love with each other, but we were also best friends. As time passed, I saw my future with Sebastian more and more. I knew he felt the same way, although we rarely talked about it. We felt that to talk about future plans would be putting too much pressure on the relationship. It was clear though, through moments of vulnerability, that we both wanted to be with the other for the rest of our lives. It was perfect, a little too perfect.

However, I soon began to question our relationship. Here I was, at 20 years old, with the man I wanted to marry (who was 24). I realized that, since my first boyfriend at age 14, I had never been single for more than two weeks at a time. I always knew I was "the relationship type" but never thought about the consequences of never having been on my own. Was I the type of person to get lonely? How would I cope without affection and intimacy? Love? These are things that I never had the opportunity to learn about myself.

I believe that we all need a period to be by ourselves, and I had never had that. Whether I wanted it or not, I felt that it was necessary. Breaking the news to Sebastian was one of the hardest things I have ever done. I began by telling him how much I loved him and wanted to spend my life with him. A thrilled reaction turned sour when the next sentence out of my mouth was, "I can't be with the man I am going to marry at 20 years old." Needless to say, he was shocked.

I explained that I did not want it to be a permanent end. It was simply a break; a time for me to get to know myself. Since it is something that inevitably needed to happen, I would have rather done it one year into the relationship than down the line, when I had a ring on my finger or a child on the way.

I was aware of the monumental risk I took. But overriding all doubt is a certainty that I cannot explain. We spoke many times after that night, and even saw each other once. Not only did we not become emotionally distant from one another, but our feelings grew even stronger. Never again will we take each other, or our relationship, for granted. I sincerely believe that this made us stronger.

It's so ironic, because the same thing that made me sad, missing him and wanting to be with him, is what brought me comfort. I believed that things would work out for us. If I had any doubt I don't think I would have been able to do what I did.

Sebastian: I remember when Meghan walked into class the first day. We never spoke, and I never really thought much about her being interested in me.

One night, we met up at a party on campus and went back to her room. We talked for hours. I left that morning with not even so much as a kiss—I wasn't going to ruin the moment. I ended up calling her, and we started the whole dating ritual. I was a little hesitant at first because I had just had a miserable streak of relationships. However, with Meghan I learned to share myself fully and be honest and carefree. I had never in my life trusted another person with my deepest emotions, secrets, fears, and anxieties.

One day something changed. So I confronted her and was floored when she told that she needed to figure things out. Unlike my past relationships, though, I wasn't angry: I was confused, hurt, and disappointed. I could never be angry with her. In fact, I respected the fact that she had the ability to tell me. She was honest!!!

The funny thing is that people get mad when they break up to cover up the rest of their emotions, but we faced them, and we dealt with them. That in itself is fascinating for people our age. Actually I thought that we were too young to have a love so deep. We hit a level that even adults who have been married for years haven't achieved. I can't really explain it, because I don't have the vocabulary to do so.

We were two people who were very much in love with each other. We firmly believed we would be together again. I supported her decision and respected her wishes as she did with me. We were honest with each and would never put pressure on one another.

Update: After 7-½ months of separation, Meghan knew that she was ready to go back and be with Sebastian. Though the separation was difficult, she believed that it was for the best. They both grew closer through the separation than they ever were before. Meghan said, "The result of this very hard decision and process is a certainty and relief that I cannot explain. Now all he needs to do is propose!"

SOURCE: Author's files.

"You Seem So Warm and Understanding"

On the other hand, it should be some relief to those of us not blessed with cover-model looks that a large percentage of people cite personality as the most important factor in choosing their partners. Though people tend to be attracted to others with personalities like theirs, the general traits cited as most important are openness, sociability, emotional stability, a sense of humor, and receptivity (willing to favorably accept behaviors and/or emotions).

"By the Way, Have I Shown You My Porsche?"

For many years, women were found to rate men's economic resources as one of the most important requirements in a partner (Buss, 1989b). This was consistent across cultures. However, newer research has shown that men want their female partners to have financial resources as well (Buss et al., 2001). Perhaps this has changed as women have gained greater access to increasing their own financial resources.

"So, Can I See You Again?"

What is it, finally, that we really look for in a mate? Men and women report that at the top of their list is mutual attraction and love (Buss et al., 2001). In addition to this, people are in surprising agreement on what other factors they want in an ideal partner. A study of homosexual, heterosexual, and bisexual men and women showed that, no matter what their sexual orientation, gender, or cultural background, all really wanted the same thing. They wanted partners who had similar interests, values, and religious beliefs, who were honest, trustworthy, intelligent, affectionate, warm, kind, funny, financially independent, dependable, and physically attractive (Amador et al., 2005; Toro-Morn & Sprecher, 2003). Now that doesn't seem too much to ask, does it?

Review Question

What do we know about why we are attracted to certain people? Explain what factors might be involved.

sex byte

Research on brain imaging has found that the emotional experience of grief following a relationship breakup is physiologically different from the emotional experience of either sadness or depression, both in intensity and quality of emotional experience (Najib et al., 2004).

Attraction in Different Cultures

Do men and women in every culture look for the same traits? For example, are more males than females looking for physically attractive mates in Nigeria? Is earning potential more important in males than females in China? David Buss (1989b) did an ambitious study comparing the importance of, among other things, physical attractiveness, earning potential, and age difference to men and women in 37 different cultures. His results confirmed what we have been claiming about the nature of mate attraction (although Buss assumed all his respondents were heterosexual and therefore assumed they were all talking about the other sex). He found that across all 37 cultures, men valued "good looks" in a partner more than women did, and in all 37 cultures, women valued "good financial prospect" in a partner more than men did. Also interesting is that in all 37 cultures, men preferred mates who were younger than they were, whereas women preferred mates who were older. Selected results of Buss's study appear in Human Sexuality in a Diverse World, "Good Looks or Prospects? What Do You Want in a Partner?"

This young girl is from a Longneck tribe in Mae Hong Son, Thailand. In this culture, an elongated neck is viewed as physically attractive.

© Corbis

Intimate Relationships

What exactly is intimacy? Think about the word; what does it imply to you? The word intimacy is derived from the Latin word *intimus*, meaning "inner" or "innermost" (Hatfield, 1988). Keeping our

Human Sexuality in a Diverse World

Good Looks or a Good Prospect?
What Do You Want in a Partner?

*I*n a classic study on cultural differences in what men and women look for in a mate, David Buss (1989) found that, almost universally, men value good looks more in a mate, and women value good financial prospects. More recent research has found that in the United States, good looks and financial stability are important partner qualities for both men and women (Amador et al., 2005; Lacey et al., 2004). As for age, almost universally, men want their mates to be a few years younger than they are, and women want their mates to be a few years older. After taking a look at these graphs, if you were a young, poor, handsome male, what country would you want to live in?

SOURCE: Adapted from David Buss, "Sex Differences in Human Mate Preferences: Evolutionary Hypotheses Tested in 37 Cultures." *Behavioral and Brain Sciences, 12,* 149, 1989. Reprinted with permission from Cambridge University Press.

In the accompanying graphs, males and females from different countries rate the importance of a mate's looks, financial prospects, and their ideal age difference. In the "Good Looks" and "Good Financial Prospects" graphs, participants rated importance from 0 (unimportant) to 3 (very important). In the "Age Difference" graph, participants rated the importance of age difference in potential mates. A negative number refers to a desire for a mate who is younger by a certain number of years, whereas a higher number refers to a desire for a mate who is older by a certain number of years.

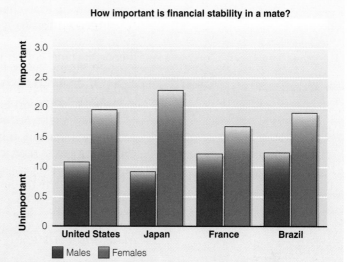

How important is financial stability in a mate?

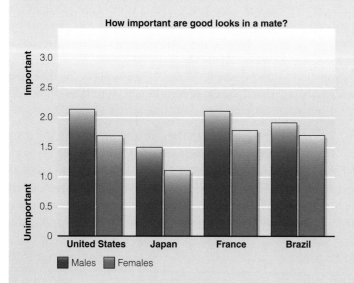

How important are good looks in a mate?

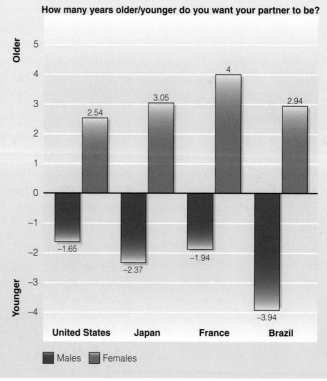

How many years older/younger do you want your partner to be?

innermost selves hidden is easy; revealing our deepest desires, our longings and insecurities can be scary. As we discussed in Chapter 6, intimate partners reveal beliefs and ideas to each other, disclose personal facts, share opinions, admit to their fears and hopes. In fact, self-disclosure is so important to intimacy that early researchers thought that willingness to self-disclose was itself the definition of intimacy (Clark & Reis, 1988). True self-disclosure, however, involves sharing feelings, fears, and dreams, not just facts and opinions. Individuals who can self-disclose have been found to have higher levels of self-esteem and confidence in their relationship and rate their relationships as more satisfying (Sprecher & Hendrick, 2004).

Intimacy involves a sense of closeness, bondedness, and connectedness (Popovic, 2005; Sternberg, 1987). People who value intimacy tend to express greater trust in their friends, are more concerned for them, tend to disclose more emotional, personal, and relational content, and have more positive thoughts about others. They also tend to be seen as more likable and noncompetitive by peers, smile, laugh, and make eye contact more often, and report better marital enjoyment (Clark & Reis, 1988).

However, all types of disclosures are risky; the other person may not understand or accept the information offered or may not reciprocate (Beach & Tesser, 1988). Thus, risk-taking and trust are crucial to the development of intimacy. Because intimacy makes us vulnerable, and because we invest so much in the other person, intimacy can also lead to betrayal and disappointment, anger, and jealousy. We will explore the dark side of intimacy later in this chapter.

Male and Female Styles of Intimacy

If any area of research in love and intimacy has yielded conflicting findings, it is the question of gender differences. Research has found that women tend to give more importance to the future of intimate relationships than men do (Oner, 2001). Women think more about whether a romantic relationship will develop into a long-term committed relationship. However, Clark & Reis (1988) suggest that the subject remains murky because many other variables are at work.

Perhaps the most important factor is culturally transmitted gender roles. Men and women report equally desiring and valuing intimacy, some suggest, but men grow up with behavioral inhibitions to expressing intimacy. We are taught how to be male and female in society, and, from a very young age, boys are discouraged from displaying vulnerability or doubt about intimacy. As one man's experience reveals in the accompanying Personal Voices, "In the Men's Locker Room," it is acceptable for men to talk about sex, but talk of intimacy is taboo. Although the author's experience may have been extreme, exaggerated by the all-male atmosphere of the athletic team, such attitudes are communicated in subtle ways to most men. Therefore, men may remain unexpressive about intimacy, however strongly they may desire it. However, it could also be that men simply express intimacy differently; either they express intimacy more through action than words (Gilmore, 1990) or they use a language of intimacy that women do not always recognize (Tannen, 1990).

One study compared men and women who scored high on a scale of masculinity or femininity to those who scored high on both (androgyny; Coleman & Ganong, 1985). In Chapter 3 we discussed androgyny. Androgynous people have been found to be more aware of their love feelings, more expressive, and more tolerant of their partner's faults than those who scored high only on the masculinity scale; they were also more cognitively aware, willing to express faults, and tolerant than those who scored high only on the femininity scale.

The importance of accepting traditional gender roles is also reflected in comparisons of homosexual and heterosexual men. Though homosexual and heterosexual men agree on the ideal characteristics of love partners and express the same amounts and kinds of love, gay men are more likely to believe that "you should share your most intimate thoughts and feelings with the person you love" (Engel & Saracino, 1986, p. 242). This may be because gay men tend to adopt fewer stereotyped beliefs about gender roles than heterosexual men.

Personal Voices

In the Men's Locker Room

I played organized sports for 15 years, and they were as much a part of my growing up as Cheerios, television, and homework. My sexuality unfolded within this all-male social world of sport, where sex was always a major focus. I remember, for example, when we as prepubertal boys used the old "buying baseball cards" routine as a cover to sneak peeks at Playboy and Swank magazines at the newsstand. We would talk endlessly after practices about "boobs" and what it must feel like to kiss and neck. Later, in junior high, we teased one another in the locker room about "jerking off" or being virgins, and there were endless interrogations about "how far" everybody was getting with their girlfriends.

Eventually, boyish anticipation spilled into real sexual relationships with girls, which, to my delight and confusion, turned out to be a lot more complex than I ever imagined. While sex (kissing, necking, and petting) got more exciting, it also got more difficult to figure out and talk about. Inside, most of the boys, like myself, needed to love and be loved. We were awkwardly reaching out for intimacy. Yet publicly, the message that got imparted was to "catch feels," be cool, and connect with girls but don't allow yourself to depend on them. Once when I was a high school junior, the gang in the weight room accused me of being wrapped around my girlfriend's finger. Nothing could be further from the truth, I assured them; and, in order to prove it, I broke up with her. I felt miserable about this at the time, and I still feel bad about it.

Within the college jock subculture, men's public protests against intimacy sometimes became exaggerated and ugly. I remember two teammates, drunk and rowdy, ripping girls' blouses off at a mixer and crawling on their bellies across the dance floor to look up skirts. Then there were the Sunday morning late breakfasts in the dorm. We jocks would usually all sit at one table and be forced to listen to one braggart or another describe his sexual exploits of the night before. Though a lot of us were turned off by such kiss-and-tell, ego-boosting tactics, we never openly criticized them. Real or fabricated, displays of raunchy sex were also assumed to "win points." A junior fullback claimed to have defecated on a girl's chest after she passed out during intercourse. There were also some laughing reports of "gang-bangs."

When sexual relationships were "serious," that is, tempered by love and commitment, the unspoken rule was silence. It was rare when we young men shared our feelings about women, misgivings about sexual performance, or disdain for the crudeness and insensitivity of some of our teammates. I now see the tragic irony in this: we could talk about superficial sex and anything that used, trivialized or debased women, but frank discussions about sexuality that unfolded within a loving relationship were taboo. Within the locker room subculture, sex and love were seldom allowed to mix. There was a terrible split between inner needs and outer appearances, between our desire for the love of women and our feigned indifference toward them.

SOURCE: Adapted from Sabo & Runfola, 1980.

However, some evidence indicates that the differences in attitudes between the genders may be changing. The women's movement and, more recently, the men's movement have tried to challenge old stereotypes of gender and intimacy. Although in the past women were more comfortable with intimate encounters and men were more comfortable taking independent action, now a new, more androgynous breed of men and women may be emerging who are more comfortable in both roles (Choi, 2004). If so, maybe we can expect greater ease in intimacy between and among the genders in the upcoming generations of men and women.

Review Question

Explain what the research has found with respect to gender differences in intimacy styles.

Intimacy in Different Cultures

Love seems to be a basic human emotion. Aren't "basic human emotions" the same everywhere? Isn't anger the same in Chicago and Timbuktu, and sadness the same in Paris and Bombay? Although there is evidence that the majority of worldwide cultures experience romantic love (see Sex in Real Life below), we do know that one's culture has been found to have a more powerful impact on love beliefs than one's gender (Sprecher & Toro-Morn, 2002). For example, passionate love as we conceive of it is unknown in Tahiti (Peele, 1988). Although we in the United States consider dependency to be a sign of a problem in a relationship, in Japan dependency on another is seen as a key aspect of love, a positive trait that should be nurtured.

In China, people's sense of self is entirely translated through their relationships with others. "A male Chinese would consider himself a son, a brother, a husband, a father, but hardly himself. It seems as if . . . there was very little independent self left for the Chinese" (Chu, 1985, quoted in Dion & Dion, 1988, p. 276). In China, love is thought of in terms of how a mate would be received by family and community, not in terms of one's own sense of romance. Because of this, the Chinese have a more practical approach to love than do Americans (Sprecher & Toro-Morn, 2002).

Culture has a large part in determining how we view love. In a study of France, Japan, and the United States, intimacy style was directly related to whether the culture was individualistic (United States), collectivistic (Japan), or mixed (France) and also to how much the culture had adopted stereotypical views of gender roles (how much it tended to see men as assertive and women as nurturing; Ting-Toomey, 1991). The Japanese, with a collectivistic culture and highly stereotypical gender roles, had lower scores in measures of attachment and commitment and were less likely to value self-

SEX in Real Life

Love—It's All in Your Head

What does our brain have to do with our feelings of love and romance? New research into brain physiology has found that our brain is more involved than you might think. Magnetic resonance imaging (MRI) of brain functioning revealed that certain areas of the brain experience increases in blood flow when a newly in love man or woman looks at a photograph of his or her romantic partner (Aron et al., 2005). Over 2,500 brain images from 17 men and women who rated themselves as "intensely in love" were analyzed using MRI technology (which monitors increases in blood flow indicating neural activity). Strong activity was noted in the motivation areas of the brain, where an overabundance of cells produce or receive the neurotransmitter dopamine (Aron et al., 2005).

Dopamine has been found to be critical for motivation. In fact, neuroscientists have found that men and women who gamble have increased dopamine when they are winning (Carey, 2005). The researchers concluded that romantic love serves as a motivation for a man or woman to reach a goal. In this case, the goal is to spend time with the love interest.

The area of our brain responsible for sexual arousal was also found to be stimulated in these newly in love participants, but it was the motivation area that received the most stimulation. There is a biological urge that comes from sexual arousal, but also from new love (Carey, 2005). The researchers hypothesized that when the motivation area is stimulated, a person is motivated to get rewards with his or her love interest above all else. Think about it for a minute.

When we are hungry, thirsty, or tired, the motivation area of our brain is stimulated, motivating us to find food, water, or a place to sleep. When we are romantically in love, this same area motivates us to make the connection and seek out the person we wish to be with.

This may also explain why new love often feels so crazy. Feelings of euphoria, sleeplessness, a preoccupation of thoughts of the partner, and an inability to concentrate are all common when a person is newly in love. Some college students describe new love as a "drug," one that often leads them to do things they wouldn't normally do. Perhaps it is a result of the increased blood flow to our motivation center—and the increases in dopamine—that motivate us to get more of what we desire.

Although more research is needed on neuroscience, brain activity, and emotions, it has been suggested that this research might help us understand why people with autism often are indifferent to romantic relationships (Carey, 2005). It could be due to the atypical brain development in the motivation areas of brain, which is typical in those with autism. In addition, this research may also help us understand why love changes as the years go by. The strength of activity in the motivation section of the brain has been found to weaken as the length of the relationship increases (Carey, 2005). In the future, research into brain physiology will continue to teach us more about the physiology of romantic love.

SOURCE: Aron et al., 2005.

disclosure than the French or Americans. Americans also have stereotypical gender roles; but, because of the highly individualistic culture in the United States, Americans tend to have high levels of confusion and ambivalence about relationships. Interestingly, the French, who have a culture with high individual motivation yet with a strong group orientation, and who also have a more balanced view of masculine and feminine gender roles, had the lowest degree of conflict in intimate relationships. Thus, culture plays a role in how we experience and express both love and intimacy.

A cross-cultural study of college students from Brazil, India, Philippines, Japan, Mexico, Australia, the United States, England, Hong Kong, Thailand, and Pakistan studied the perceived significance of love for the building of a marriage. Researchers found that love is given highest importance in Westernized nations and the lowest importance in the less developed Asian nations (Levine et al., 1995). We will talk more about marriage in Chapter 9.

Long-Term Love and Commitment

The ability to maintain love over time is the hallmark of maturity. Many people regard love as something that happens to them, almost like catching the flu. This attitude hides an important truth about love: it takes effort and commitment to maintain love—not only commitment to the other person but commitment to continually build on and improve the quality of the relationship. Most long-term relationships that end do so not because the couple "fell out of love," but because, somewhere down the line, they stopped working together on their relationship. In this sense, the old saying is true: the opposite of love is not hate, but indifference.

Couples going through hard times, as Christopher Reeve and his wife Dana did, can build even stronger relationships in the face of adversity.

Sternberg (1985), you may recall, claimed that passion, intimacy, and commitment are the three elements of love; in consummate love, he says, all three are present. Yet one tends to hear very little talk of commitment in our culture, with its great emphasis on passionate love. In the account of the man and woman in Personal Voices, "Murray and Frances," it is this sense of commitment that is the test of love. Couples going through hard times can persevere and build even stronger and more intimate relationships when their commitment reflects such a deep sense of trust.

If you observe an older couple who have been together for many years, you may have a strong sense of their ease with each other. Couples who continue to communicate with each other, remain committed to each other and the relationship, and remain interested in and intimate with each other build a lasting bond of trust. Those who don't may feel

SEX Talk

Question: How can you stay with only one person your whole life and not get bored?

Love grows and changes when two people commit themselves to work on a relationship. Are you the person you were 10 years ago? What makes you think you'll be the same 10 years from now? When two people allow each other to grow and develop, they find new experiences and new forms of love all the time. People get bored primarily when they lose interest, not because the other person has no mysteries left.

Personal Voices

Murray and Frances: A Tale of Committed Love

At the time of the publication of the photo and following text, Frances had multiple sclerosis and was living at a home for severely physically disabled persons called Inglis House. Her husband, Murray, was working full time.

Frances: *I know there are a lot of things to be thankful for . . . but after all there are women here whose husbands just put them in here and forgot about them. And I think that's sad. In fact, when I told my husband how worried I was about him once when he wasn't feeling well, he said: "Don't worry"—not to "worry about me"—and all that business—and I said to him: "Don't you dare deprive me of that! That's one of my privileges." The people for whom I feel sorry are the people that have nobody to worry about. . . . It's a reciprocal thing.*

Murray: *When I married Frances, I swore that I would stay with her till death do us part, see, and I'm keeping my word—that's all. This is what I wanted; now, I wouldn't want any other woman. Even if she'd give me a divorce today, I wouldn't want any other woman. I've had a marvelous—a beautiful—life with her, even with*

© Bernard F. Stehle

her handicaps. She's humorous, she's smart—and we talk the same language: we don't even have to come out with the exact words. I can say one word, and she knows what I'm thinking about . . . because [of] living with me that length of time [50 years of marriage, the last 35 with multiple sclerosis, the last 15 of these at Inglis House]. I come here four or five times a week. Her love draws me out here. When I come here I feel good; I look for the moment when I have to get in the car to come out here.

So it must be in me to want to do that. And we can have an argument, we can have a difference of opinion. And I can leave her in a huff here, but the next time I come—it's just like nothing happened. And I daren't walk in that room without kissing her! . . . So, we're still on our honeymoon, even though she's incapacitated to the point where she's not really a wife to me. But as far as a companion? She's all I want.

SOURCE: Text and photo from "Murray and Frances," in *Incurably Romantic* (Temple University Press), by Bernard F. Stehle. Copyright © 1985 by Bernard F. Stehle. Reprinted by permission.

Review Question

Explain how the ability to maintain love over time is the hallmark of maturity.

isolated and lonely in marriages that nevertheless endure for many years. Men report feeling lonelier in marriages in which there is less intimacy, less liking, and less communication, whereas women report more loneliness in marriages in which there is less liking, less marital satisfaction, less self-disclosure, and less love (Sadava & Matejcic, 1987). Although passionate love may fade over time, love itself does not necessarily diminish. The decline of passion can allow the other components of love to flourish in the relationship.

Loss of Love

Popular songs are often about the loss of love; "the blues" is a whole genre of music built on the experience of losing love, and country-western music is well known for its songs of lost love. People experience loss of love in many ways. The couple may realize that their relationship was based on passion and cannot develop into long-term love. One partner may decide, for his or her own reasons, to end a relationship that is still valued by the other partner. Also, a partner may be lost to disease or may die.

The loss of love is a time of mourning, and going through a period of sadness and depression, as well as anger at the partner, is natural. Most people are also very vulnerable after the loss of a love relationship—vulnerable to rushing into another relationship

Love in Times of E-mail, Chat Rooms, and Instant Messaging

Technology has changed the mating habits and strategies of establishing love relationships. Years ago, someone who wanted to ask for a date agonized over when and how to phone, what to say, and how to say it. Today, that person can send an e-mail quickly and without fear of stumbling over his or her words or worrying about reading the body language of rejection. The person can meet people, set up dates or "hookups," and even break up online today. In addition, a number of new websites let college students connect to each other through their computers.

Students all over the country are gaining access to online college dating services (Han, 2004). Today students can check to see whether the cute guy/girl sitting next to them in class is single, straight, or gay. *The FaceBook* is one of these services. Available only to students with valid university e-mail addresses, students can post photos, relationship status, phone numbers, and instant messenger screen names. As of 2004, there were over 1 million members from over 293 schools (Weiss, 2004). But how do these technological changes affect our view of love and relationships?

In many ways, this changing technology has made dating and finding love relationships easier. Men and women who are uncomfortable about meeting people, or who are new to a school or area, often find online dating beneficial. Online dating services can also be beneficial for people who work unusual hours or those who have children or handi-

caps that might interfere with their ability to meet people. Emotional and intellectual connections are made prior to any physical interactions. Men and women can get to know specifics about a person, such as hobbies and interests, and before they decide whether they want to meet in person.

There are also risks, however. People can present themselves differently online, and what you read may not be what you'll actually get! In Chapter 6, we discussed eroticized pseudointimacy and the risks of moving too quickly online (see page 168). Following is a list of suggestions for dating online:

1. **Guard your anonymity.** Don't give any personal information that would allow someone to find you until you're ready to give this information out.
2. **Watch for red flags.** Pay attention to inconsistencies and stories that just sound too good to be true. If the story sounds too good to be true, it probably is.
3. **Take your time.** There is no reason to rush into anything. The longer you communicate online, the better your opportunity to really get to know each other.
4. **Meet in a public place.** If you do decide to meet, make sure you meet in a public place and tell a friend or relative where you're going and whom you'll be with.
5. **Realize that it's easy to be seduced.** The informality of e-mail, instant messaging, and chat rooms can lead to things becoming too serious too fast.

---

to replace the lost partner and vulnerable to self-blame, loss of self-esteem, and distrust of others (Timmreck, 1990).

No easy solutions exist to decreasing the pain of a breakup. Often being good to yourself can help, taking some time to do the things that make you happy. Readjusting your schedule can be difficult, especially if your day revolved around the other person. You may feel the greatest sense of loss at just those times that you used to be together (dinnertime, bedtime). Try to find new activities and new patterns in your day. Call on your family and friends for support. As you go through the grieving process, remember: almost everyone has experienced what you are feeling at one time or another, and you will pull through.

sexbyte

After a breakup, feelings of sadness, anger, and relief are the most common emotional reactions, and contact with former partners often slows the feelings of sadness (Sbarra & Emery, 2005).

LOVE, SEX, AND HOW WE BUILD INTIMATE RELATIONSHIPS

One way to express deep love and intimacy is through sexual behavior, but sexual behavior itself is not necessarily an expression of love or intimacy. How do we make the decision to have sex? There are many levels of relationships that can lead to sex. Casual sex and "hooking up" can happen between people who barely know each other, generated by excitement, novelty, and pure physical pleasure.

Love and Sex

Sex can be an expression of affection and intimacy without considering it an expression of passionate love; sex can also be engaged in purely for procreation; or sex can be an extension of a loving relationship, an expression of love. Problems can develop when one partner has one view of the developing sexual relationship, and the other partner takes a different perspective.

Because the decision to engage in sexual contact involves the feelings and desires of two people, examining your own motivations as well as your partner's is important. When making the decision to initiate a sexual relationship with another person, consider the following:

1. Clarify your values. At some point, each of us needs to make value decisions regarding intimacy, sex, and love. How do you feel about casual sexual contact? What role does love play in your sexual decisions? How will you reconcile these values with those you have learned from your family, friends, and religion?

2. Be honest with yourself—which is often more difficult than being honest with others. Entering a relationship with another person takes close self-examination. What do you really want out of this encounter? Out of this person? Are you hoping the sexual contact will lead to something deeper, or are you in it simply for the sex? What will you do if you (or your partner) gets pregnant? If you find that you (or your partner) have a sexually transmitted infection? Will you feel better or worse about yourself tomorrow? Are you in this because you want to be, or because you feel some kind of pressure to be sexual—from yourself or from your partner? Could you say "no" comfortably? Are you ready for a sexual relationship with this person?

3. Be honest with your partner. Another person's feelings and needs are always at issue in any relationship, and part of our responsibility as caring human beings is not to hurt or exploit others. Why is your partner interested in sex with you? Do his or her expectations differ from yours? Will she or he be hurt if your relationship does not develop further? Have you discussed your feelings? Does your partner really want to do this, or is she or he afraid of losing your love or friendship?

The decision to engage in a sexual relationship may or may not be related to feelings of love. Casual sex has become much more common and accepted than it was 35 or 40 years ago, when young people (especially women) were strongly advised to save their "greatest asset," their virginity, for marriage. One can enter a sexual relationship too casually, without a close examination of how both partners will feel afterward. Sex can be used as a substitute for intimacy or love. Overall the importance of love as an essential condition for sexual relations has diminished. Yet casual sex has become more physically risky with the spread of sexually transmitted infections (we will discuss this more in Chapter 15).

When we begin to feel attracted to someone, we begin to act intimate; we gaze longer at each other, lean on each other, and touch more (Hatfield, 1988). People meeting each other for the first time tend to reveal their levels of attraction by their body language. Perper (1985) observed strangers approaching each other in bars. The first stage he called the initial contact and conversation (which, by the way, Perper found to be commonly initiated by the female). If the couple is mutually attracted, they will begin to turn their bodies more and more toward each other, until they are facing one another. The first tentative touches begin, a hand briefly on a hand or a forearm, for example, and increase in duration and intimacy as the evening progresses (again, also often initiated by the female). Finally, the couple shows "full body synchronization"; their facial expressions, posture, and even breathing begin to mirror their partner's. As we discussed in Chapter 6, women smile, gaze, lean forward, and touch more often than men in conversation. Women also "flirt" with their nonverbal cues (such as hair-flipping and head-nodding) in order to encourage men to reveal more about themselves, which would in turn allow the women to formulate an impression of the men (W. E. Martin, 2001).

Sexual desire has been found to be related to "relational maintenance"; that is, the higher the sexual desire for the partner, the less likely the couple has thoughts about ending the relationship or being unfaithful (Regan et al., 2000). There are some gender differences in attitudes toward sexual intimacy in heterosexual relationships. In one study, men said they would have intercourse with someone they had known for only 3 hours, with two different people within a 6-hour period, and with someone they didn't love or have a good relationship with (Knox et al., 2001). Women, on the other hand, considered a number of variables before making the decision to have sex with a partner. They thought about whether their partner might love them and how interested he seemed in continuing the relationship (Knox et al., 2001). We have to keep in mind that these responses are more socially acceptable for each gender to report, so we don't actually know what their behavior in a given situation might be.

Review Question

What factors might a couple consider when making the decision to initiate a sexual relationship?

SEX Talk

Question: *How can I tell the difference between being in love and just deeply liking someone?*

Unfortunately, no one has come up with a foolproof way of making that distinction. Being "in love" can feel a lot like being "in deep like." One would hope we deeply like those whom we love; and, in fact, we probably love those we deeply like. The element that may be missing from those we deeply like is sexual passion; but sometimes we don't realize that we are not in love with them until after we develop a sexual relationship. The discovery can be painful to both parties, which is why it is advisable to be very careful before initiating a sexual relationship with a friend.

Developing Intimacy Skills

There are many ways to improve our intimacy skills. As we discussed in Chapter 6, developing intimacy often begins with understanding and liking ourselves—self-love. Other important skills we can develop to enhance our ability to form relationships include receptivity, listening, showing affection, trust, and respect.

Self-Love

Self-love is different from conceit or **narcissism;** it is not a process of promoting ourselves but of being at ease with our positive qualities and forgiving ourselves for our faults. If you are not willing to get to know yourself and to accept your own faults, why would others think you are any more interested in them or that you would judge them any less harshly? Many people look to others for indications of their own self-worth. Making others the guardians of our self-worth is not fair to them. We must first take responsibility to know ourselves (self-intimacy) and then to accept ourselves as we are. Once we like ourselves, we can reach out to others.

self-love
Love for one's self; the instinct or desire to promote one's own well-being.

narcissism
Excessive admiration of oneself.

Receptivity

Many of us think we are receptive to others when actually we are sending subtle signals that we do not want to be bothered. Receptivity can be communicated through smiling, eye contact, and a warm, relaxed posture. This allows the other person to feel comfortable and makes us approachable. Taking 5 minutes a day to sit and reconnect with your partner may improve your relationship and help preserve intimacy and passion.

Listening

We discussed in Chapter 6 how true communication begins with listening. Nothing shows you care about another person quite as much as your full attention. Who is more of a bore than a person who talks only of him- or herself, who sees any comment made by another person primarily in terms of how it relates to him or her? Learning to truly listen enhances intimacy.

Affection

Do you want to learn to display affection? Watch a loving parent with his or her child. Parents attend to their children, smile at them, touch them in affectionate ways, look in their eyes, and hug and kiss them. Most people want the same things from their intimate friends and lovers. Affection shows that you feel a sense of warmth and security with your partner.

Trust

To trust another is an act of courage because it grants that person the power to hurt or disappoint you. However, intimacy requires trust. Usually trust develops slowly. You trust your partner a little bit at the beginning of your relationship and begin to trust him or her more and more as he or she proves to be dependable and predictable. Trusting behaviors lead to greater trust in the relationship and more confidence that the relationship will last. When a couple trusts each other, each expects the partner to care and respond to his or her needs, now and in the future (Zak et al., 1998).

Remember earlier we talked about women from divorced families being less able to trust in intimate relationships? Perhaps it is because these women have seen firsthand what happens in unsuccessful marriages, and they fear intimate relationships just don't work. Men, too, may feel less able to trust when their partner is ambivalent or cautious about trust. The important thing to remember is that a close relationship has a "curative" function—the longer it exists, the more trust can build (Jacquet & Surra, 2001).

Respect

We enter into relationships with our own needs and desires, which sometimes cloud the fact that the other person is different from us and has his or her own special needs. Respect is the process of acknowledging and understanding that person's needs, even if you don't share them.

The Dark Side of Love

Love evokes powerful emotions; this is both its strength and its weakness. Many of the emotions that can come from strong feelings about another person can also be destructive to a relationship and may require great maturity or a strong act of will to overcome. Let's now examine three of the dark sides of love: jealousy, compulsiveness, and possessiveness.

Jealousy: The Green-Eyed Monster

Jealousy is a common experience in intimate relationships. Imagine you are at a party with a person with whom you are in an exclusive, sexual relationship. You notice that person standing close to someone else, talking and laughing, and occasionally putting his or her hand on the other person's arm. At one point, you notice your partner whispering in the other person's ear, and they both laugh. They walk out to the dance floor, where they dance together, still talking and laughing.

How does that make you feel? Are you jealous? But wait, I forgot to tell you: The person your partner was talking to and dancing with was of the same sex as your partner (if you are heterosexual) or the opposite sex (if you are homosexual). Are you still jealous? Oh yes, one more thing. The other person was your partner's younger sibling. Now are you jealous?

Jealousy is an emotional reaction to a relationship that is being threatened (Knox et al., 1999; Sharpsteen & Kirkpatrick, 1997). A threat is a matter of interpretation; people who deeply trust their partners may not be able to imagine a situation in which the relationship is really threatened. We are most jealous in the situation just described, when the person flirting with our partner has traits we ourselves want (or we fantasize that they do). Maybe we imagine our partner will find the other person more desirable than us, sexier or funnier. A correlation has been found between self-esteem and jealousy; the lower the self-esteem, the more jealous a person feels and in turn the higher his or her insecurity (Knox et al., 1999). We imagine that the partner sees in the other person all those traits we believe that we lack.

We are often jealous when we think, fantasize, or imagine that another person has traits we ourselves want.

Men and women experience similar levels of jealousy in intimate relationships, yet there is controversy over what triggers jealousy (Fleischmann et al., 2005). Some research supports the fact that men are more jealous when they believe that their female partner has had a sexual encounter with another man, whereas women are often more focused on the emotional or relationship aspects of infidelity (Buss, 2003). However, according to research that has attempted to replicate these findings, it may have to do with whether the relationship is short or long term. In short-term relationships, both men and women are more threatened by sexual infidelity, whereas emotional infidelity is often more threatening in a long-term relationship (Mathes, 2005). Other studies have found physiological responses (e.g., increased high blood pressure) in both men and women when they imagined scenarios of their partner committing either emotional or sexual infidelity (DeSteno et al., 2002; Harris, 2003; Turner, 2000). Cheating, either emotional or sexual, can lead to jealousy in both men and women.

Research on heterosexual couples has found that men report male–female sexual infidelity would make them most jealous, whereas women report that male–male sexual infidelity would make them most jealous (Wiederman & LaMar, 1998). Female–female sexual infidelity was rated the least jealousy-producing—some theorists claim this may be due to the fact that there is no risk of conception (Sagarin et al., 2003). Unfortunately we know very little about infidelity in same-sex relationships and marriages because the majority of the research has been done on heterosexual relationships (Blow & Hartnett, 2005). People who do not experience jealousy have been found to be more secure, and this security in intimate relationships tends to increase as the couple's relationship grows (Knox et al., 1999). That is, the longer we are in a relationship with someone, the more our vulnerability to jealousy decreases.

Jealousy exists in all cultures, but what evokes jealousy may be very different. In Yugoslavia, for example, having your partner flirt with another evokes a strong jealousy response, whereas having your partner kiss another, or hearing your partner's sexual fantasies about another person had the lowest jealousy response of all nations studied. The Dutch, on the other hand, seem to have a hard time with sexual fantasies about other people (Buunk et al., 1996).

Though many people think that jealousy shows that they really care for a person, in fact it shows a lack of trust in the partner. Jealousy is not a compliment, but a demonstration of lack of trust and low self-esteem (Puente & Cohen, 2003). Jealousy is also a self-fulfilling prophecy; jealous individuals can drive their mates away, even into the arms of another lover, which convinces them that they were right to be jealous in the first place. Jealousy can be contained by trying to improve one's own self-image; by turning it around into a compliment (not "she's flirting with other men" but "look at how lucky I am—other men also find her attractive"); and by trust of one's partner. Communicating with your partner about your jealous feelings can often help to maintain your relationship (Guerrero & Aff, 1999). Opening up and talking about your uncertainty about the relationship or reassessing the relationship can help restore and strengthen the relationship.

Compulsiveness: Addicted to Love

Being in love can produce a sense of ecstasy, euphoria, and a feeling of well-being, much like a powerful drug. In fact, when a person is in love, his or her body releases the drug phenylethylamine, which produces these feelings (Sabelli et al., 1996). (Phenylethylamine

Review Question

What can we learn from the fact that although sexual jealousy is found in almost all cultures, the things that make people jealous can be completely different in different societies? Explain where jealousy may come from.

is also present in chocolate, which may be why we love it so much, especially during a breakup!) Some people do move from relationship to relationship as if they were love-addicted, trying to continually recreate that feeling, or else they obsessively hang on to a love partner long after his or her interest has waned. (See Lee's description of mania in the Colors of Love, page 183.)

Love addiction is reinforced by the popular media's portrayals (even as far back as Shakespeare's Romeo and Juliet) of passionate love as all-consuming. It fosters the belief that only one person is fated to be your "true love," that love is always mutual, and that you'll live "happily ever after." Some people feel the need to be in love because society teaches that only then are they really whole, happy, and fulfilled in their role as a woman or a man. Yet love based solely on need can never be truly fulfilling. In Peele & Brodsky's (1991) book *Love and Addiction*, they argue that love addiction is more common than most believe, and that it is based on a continuation of an adolescent view of love that is never replaced as the person matures. Counseling or psychotherapy may help the person come to terms with his or her need to constantly be in love relationships.

Possessiveness: Every Move You Make, I'll Be Watching You

Because love also entails risk, dependency to some degree, and a strong connection between people, there is always the danger that the strength of the bond can be used by one partner to manipulate the other. Abusive love relationships exist when one partner tries to increase his or her own sense of self-worth or to control the other's behavior through withdrawing or manipulating love.

For intimacy to grow, partners must nurture each other. Controlling behavior may have short-term benefits (you might get the person to do what you want for a while); but, long-term, it smothers the relationship. No one likes the feeling of being manipulated, whether it is subtle, through the use of guilt, or overt, through physical force. Part of love is the joy of seeing the partner free to pursue his or her desires and appreciating the differences between partners. Though every relationship has its boundaries, freedom within those agreed-upon constraints is what encourages the growth and maturation of both partners.

Possessiveness indicates a problem of self-esteem and personal boundaries and can eventually lead to **stalking.** Most states have passed stalking laws, which enable the police to arrest a person who constantly shadows someone (usually, but not always, a woman) or makes threatening gestures or claims (we will discuss this more in Chapter 17). Thinking about another person with that level of obsession is a sign of a serious psychological problem, one that should be brought to the attention of a mental health professional.

We started this chapter talking about the importance of love in our lives. The ability to form loving, caring, and intimate relationships with others is important for our emotional health and also our physical health. Love and intimacy are two of the most powerful factors in well-being. Love might not always be easy to understand, but it is a powerful force in our lives, and intimacy is an important component of mature love in our culture.

stalking
Relentlessly pursuing someone, shadowing him or her, or making threatening gestures or claims toward the person when the relationship is unwanted.

Review Question

Compare and contrast compulsiveness and possessiveness.

Chapter Review

ACTIVE SUMMARY

1. We go through life trying to come to terms with **(a)** _____, trying to figure out why we are **(b)** _____ to certain types, or why we fall in love with all the wrong people. The **(c)** _____ of love is part of its attraction.

2. Not until the **(a)** _____ century did people begin to believe that romantic love was the most desirable form of loving relations. Through most of **(b)** _____ history, marriage was a(n) **(c)** _____ union arranged by the parents. Once wed, husbands and wives were encouraged to **(d)** _____ love for one another, to *develop* love.

3. **(a)** _____ love comes with a sense of ecstasy and anxiety, physical attraction, and **(b)** _____ desire. We tend to idealize the partner, ignoring faults in the newfound joy of the attachment. **(c)** _____ love blooms in the initial euphoria of a new attachment to a sexual partner. If a(n) **(d)** _____ is to continue, romantic love must develop into companionate love.

4. Romantic love is the passionate, highly **(a)** _____ part of loving. **(b)** _____ love involves feelings of affection, **(c)** _____, and attachment to another person. In many cultures, marriages are based on companionate love, assuming that **(d)** _____ will grow as the couple does.

5. John Alan Lee suggests there are **(a)** _____ basic types of love, and Robert Sternberg suggests that love is made up of **(b)** _____ elements: passion, **(c)** _____, and decision/commitment, which can combine in different ways in relationships, creating seven basic ways to love and an eighth state, called **(d)** _____, which is an absence of all three elements.

6. Where does love come from? Behavioral reinforcement theorists argue that we love those who make us feel good, who reinforce positive **(a)** _____ in ourselves. **(b)** _____ theorists suggest love is our interpretation of being with someone a lot or thinking about them a lot; the action comes first, the interpretation later. **(c)** _____ arousal theorists argue that love happens when we enter a general state of arousal in the presence of a potential love object. **(d)** _____ theorists suggest that love is a combination of our sexual drive and our instincts to protect and to procreate.

7. The behavioral reinforcement theories suggest that we love because another person **(a)** _____ positive feelings in ourselves. Positive **(b)** _____ in the presence of another person make us like him or her, even when the **(c)** _____ has nothing to do with the other person.

8. The cognitive theories propose that we love because we **(a)** _____ we love. This theory suggests that the **(b)** _____ comes first and the **(c)** _____ comes later.

9. In the physiological arousal theory, people are **(a)** _____ to experiencing love (or another emotion) when they are **(b)** _____ aroused for whatever reason. A(n) **(c)** _____ happens when there is general physiological arousal for whatever reason and a label is attached to it—and that label might be **(d)** _____ emotion.

10. Evolutionary perspectives of love believe that love developed out of our need to be protected from outside **(a)** _____, to protect children, and from our sexual drive. **(b)** _____ is an evolutionary strategy that helps us form the bonds we need to **(c)** _____ and pass our genes on to the next generation.

11. Love develops over the life cycle. In **(a)** _____, we develop attachments to our caregivers; receiving love in return has an influence on our capacity to love later in life. In adolescence, we deal with issues of **(b)** _____ from our parents, and begin to explore adult ways of loving. Adolescents tend to experience romantic love. **(c)** _____ styles we learn in infancy, such as secure, avoidant, and ambivalent styles, may last through life and **(d)** _____ how we begin to form adult attachment in adolescence.

12. As we mature and enter adulthood, forming **(a)** _____ relations becomes important. Developing intimacy is risky, and men and women have different styles of intimacy, but intimacy is seen as an important component of **(b)** _____ love in our culture. As we grow older, **(c)** _____ in love becomes more important, and passion may decrease in importance.

13. **(a)** _____ take effort, and when a couple stop working on the relationship, they can become very lonely, love can fade, and intimacy can evaporate. When **(b)** _____ is lost, for whatever reason, it is a time of pain and mourning. The support of family and friends can help us let go of the lost love and try to form new **(c)** _____.

14. Men and women may have **(a)** _____ intimacy styles. For example, men may learn to suppress **(b)** _____ about intimacy as they **(c)** _____, or they may learn to express it in different ways.

15. The decision to be **(a)** _____ is often confused with the decision to **(b)** _____. **(c)** _____ need to be clarified before a(n) **(d)** _____ relationship is begun.

16. Developing intimacy begins with understanding ourselves and **(a)** _____ ourselves. Receptivity, listening, showing affection, trusting in your **(b)** _____, and respecting him or her are **(c)** _____ in the development of **(d)** _____.

17. Love also has its **(a)** _____ side. **(b)** _____ plagues many people in their love relationships, whereas others seem **(c)** _____ to love, going in and out of love relationships. Some people also use love as a means to **(d)** _____ and control others.

18. **(a)** _____ indicates a problem of self-esteem and personal boundaries and can eventually lead to **(b)** _____. Most states have passed stalking laws, which enable the police to **(c)** _____ a person who constantly shadows someone or makes threatening gestures or claims.

Critical Thinking Questions

1. Using John Alan Lee's colors of love, examine a relationship that you are in (or were in), and analyze the styles of love that you and your partner use(d). Which love style do you think would be hardest for you to deal with in a partner, and why?

2. Think of a love relationship that you have been in. Describe how each of the theories proposed in this chapter would explain why you loved your partner. Which theory do you think does the best job, and why?

3. Explain what gender differences have been found in love, and tie this research to an example from one of your past relationships.

4. How long do you think is appropriate to wait in a relationship before engaging in sexual activity? Why?

5. Have you ever been involved with a partner who was jealous? What was the hardest part of this relationship? How did you handle the jealousy?

CHAPTER RESOURCES

Check It Out

Brown, N. M., & Amatea, E. S. (2000). **Love and intimate relationships: Journeys of the heart.** Philadelphia: Brunner/Mazel.

This book provides a synthesis of theories and data that attempts to explain the mysteries of love, intimacy, and relationships. It includes investigations of the life cycle of relationships, influences that affect them, and ways to improve them. Stories from students about relationships are interspersed throughout the book, and there is also information on children of divorce, same-sex relationships, and the importance of understanding gender socialization.

The Notebook (2004; 2 hours, 4 minutes; Rated PG-13)

Based on a Nicholas Sparks novel, this drama chronicles an enduring love that withstands both war and disease. It begins in a nursing home, where a man (James Garner) arrives every day armed with a notebook from which he reads stories about a couple, Noah and Allie (played by Ryan Gosling and Rachel McAdams), to an unresponsive woman (Gena Rowlands). Explores the nature of love and importance of relationships.

InfoTrac® College Edition

If your instructor ordered InfoTrac with this book, explore InfoTrac College Edition, your online library, for additional readings and review. Go to: **www.thomsonedu.com,** and enter these search terms:

passionate love   companionate love   jealousy

Web Resources

SexualityNow Companion Website
Go to **http://thomsonedu.com/carroll** for practice quiz questions, interactive activities, Internet links, critical thinking exercises, discussion forums, and more. You can also access sites from the Wadsworth Psychology Study Center **(http://psychology.wadsworth.com)** or you can connect directly to the following sites:

Love Is Great
This website is all about love, dating, romance, and relationships. The website contains information about how to find and express love. There are also links to single/dating websites and a question-and-answer feature about love.

Loving You
This website is devoted to love, life, and romance. The site contains advice, love poems, and free romantic love notes and quotes. There are also links to dating services, love libraries, and gift shops.

Love Test
A nonscientific but fun website that offers a multitude of different "love" tests. Compatibility analysis, astrology reports, fortune tellers, and relationship rating tests are available.

Queendom
This site offers the largest online battery of professionally developed and validated psychological assessments. This website is a fun place to find a variety of different quizzes on topics such as jealousy, relationships, commitment readiness, romantic personality, honesty, and the ability to self-disclose. There are links to many more tests on topics such as forgiveness, fatal attraction, first dates, breakups, and love. Although none of these tests are scientifically based, they are fun to explore and may even help inspire some conversations with your friends and lovers.

SexualityNow

Go to **www.thomsonedu.com** to link to **SexualityNow,** your online study tool. First take the **Pre-Test** for this chapter to get your **Personalized Study Plan,** which will identify topics you need to review and direct you to online resources. Then take the **Post-Test** to determine what concepts you have mastered and what you still need work on.

Videos in SexualityNow
For additional information on topics discussed in this chapter, check out the videos in **SexualityNow** on the following topics:
- **Emotions, Stress, and the Immune System**—Learn how social relationships can literally keep you safe from physical ailments.
- **How Do I Love Thee? Expressions of Love Styles**—Listen to these personal videos and use Lee's love styles to match potential mates.

8 Childhood and Adolescent Sexuality

Sexuality ⬤ Now Go to www.thomsonedu.com to link to
SexualityNow, your online study tool.

I *magine yourself as a little kid again. Can you remember the first thing you ever thought about being a boy or a girl? About sex? When did you learn that little boys and girls had different parts? Where did you think babies came from?*

I often ask my students to try to remember the funniest thing they ever thought about sexuality. Their answers never fail to make me smile. One student told me that he really thought girls had cooties and was sure he'd never, ever want to kiss one, whereas another said that she really believed people died after they had sex. Another student told me he believed all girls got their periods at the same time each month.

A friend of mine, the mother of two young girls, told me that when one daughter was 3 years old, she asked my friend about a little boy's body. "Why does Brian have a finger sticking out of his bottom?" she asked. Trying her best to keep a straight face and answer the question with as much dignity and respect as she could muster, my friend sat her daughter down and explained that it was a penis, not a finger. She then went on to explain the physiological differences in male and female genitalia.

It's interesting to think about these early questions we all have about sexuality and how we find answers to all of our questions. In this chapter, we will look at childhood sexuality from infancy through adolescence. We will examine how sexuality develops throughout childhood and the various influences on adolescent sexuality today. We will look at adolescent sexual behavior, contraceptive use, and pregnancy. Finally, we will discuss the importance of sexuality education and the controversies surrounding it.

It is important to first realize that the idea of "childhood" is a recent invention. Throughout most of history, children were treated simply as miniature adults, and concepts such as "childhood"—and certainly "adolescence"—did not exist (Aries, 1962). Most children worked, dressed, and were expected to behave (as much as they were capable) like adults. The one area in which children were considered clearly different from adults was their sexuality. Children were considered presexual and referred to as "innocents," meaning that they had no knowledge of, nor desire for, sexual contact. Some people still view children as sexual innocents who can be "corrupted" if exposed to sexual information or images.

Today, we think of children as undergoing their own, exclusive stage of development. Children are not just "little adults," and though they can be sexual, children's sexuality is not adult sexuality (Gordon & Schroeder, 1995). Children want love, appreciate sensuality, and engage in behaviors that set the stage for the adult sexuality to come. But we must be careful not to attribute adult motives to childhood behaviors. When a 5-year-old boy and a 5-year-old girl sharing a bath reach out to touch each others' genitals, the meaning that they ascribe to that action cannot be considered "sexual" as adults use the term. As Plummer (1991) notes, a child having an erection shows simply that his physiology functions normally; seeing the erection as "sexual" is to overlay an adult social meaning onto the physiology. The child is probably not even aware of the "sexual" nature of his erection and, indeed, may not even be aware that his penis is erect.

Every society distinguishes between young and old; every society also creates rules around the sexuality of the young. Sexual growth involves a host of factors—physical maturation of the sexual organs, psychological dynamics, familial relations, and peer relations, all within the social and cultural beliefs about gender roles and sexuality.

Historically, children were considered sexually innocent and pure.

As we discussed in Chapter 2, it is very difficult to carry out research on children's sexuality in American society. Many people oppose questioning children about sexuality, often believing that research on child sexuality will somehow encourage promiscuity. Others seem to believe that if we do not talk about children's sexuality, it will just go away. The truth about American society, however, is that teenagers and even preteens today are often sexually active, with high pregnancy, birth, and abortion rates.

Some researchers have been forging ahead in their study of children's sexual behavior, despite the opposition. The U.S. government has sponsored four large-scale studies to examine adolescent behaviors. These studies include the National Survey of Family Growth (1973–2001), the National Longitudinal Study of Adolescent Males (1988, 1990–1991, 1995), the National Longitudinal Study of Adolescent Health (1994–1995, 1996, 2000), and the Youth Risk Behavior Surveillance System (YRBS, which collects new data every 2 years; see Table 8.1).

The National Survey of Family Growth (NSFG) is the only one of these studies not limited to teenagers. It provides information on first intercourse, birth control, childbearing, cohabitation, and divorce, among other things, and has examined the behaviors of over 45,000 females between the ages of 14 and 44 (males were included in their analysis beginning in 2001). The NSFG is a household-based survey and uses personal in-home and phone interviews to access information. The National Longitudinal Study of Adolescent Males (NSAM), which was originally designed to correlate with the NSFG study, was the first nationally representative survey of the sexual and risk-related behavior of young, never-married men in the United States. Over 6,600 males between the ages of 15 and 27 were surveyed through face-to-face interviews in conjunction with questionnaires. In 1995, the NSAM included urine testing for those over 18 years old to test for chlamydia and gonorrhea to collect information about the prevalence of these two STIs.

The National Longitudinal Study of Adolescent Health (Add Health) is a nationally representative sample of over 126,000 adolescents in grades 7 through 12 and has included over 18,000 parent and school administrators. Interviews and questionnaires are used to gather information. This study provides a comprehensive view of the health behaviors of adolescents (parents and school administrators are included to collect information on various adolescent influences). The Add Health study was designed to explore the causes of these behaviors, with an emphasis on the influence of social context. Families, friends, schools, and communities play roles in the lives of adolescents that may encourage healthy choices or may lead to unhealthy, self-destructive behavior, and this study explores these influences.

The Youth Risk Behavior Surveillance System (YRBS) is another ongoing, longitudinal study that explores the prevalence of certain behaviors that put young people at

TABLE 8.1	Studies of Childhood Sexuality		
Study Name	Years	Participants	Method
National Survey of Family Growth (NSFG)	1973–2001	Not limited to teens; females only for 1973–2000; began including males in 2001; 45,000 females, 14–44 years old	Household-based, in-home interviews and phone interviews
National Longitudinal Study of Adolescent Males (NSAM)	1988; 1990–1991; 1995	Young, never-married males; 6,600 males, 15–27 years old	In-person interviews and questionnaires; originally designed to correlate with NSFG study
National Longitudinal Study of Adolescent Health (Add Health)	1994–1995; 1996; 2000	School-based sample; 126,000 students in grades 7–12; 18,000 parents and school administrators	Interviews and questionnaires
Youth Risk Behavior Surveillance System (YRBS)	Conducted every 2 years	Students in grades 9–12; 15,000 respondents in 1999 survey	Questionnaires

risk, including sexual behaviors that may result in STIs and unintended pregnancies. This national study is conducted every 2 years and includes students in grades 9 through 12. The 1999 survey included more than 15,000 respondents.

In 2002, the Alan Guttmacher Institute released a report from a multiyear study, conducted with researchers from Canada, Great Britain, France, and Sweden. This study explored teenage pregnancy and birth rates both in the United States and in comparable developed countries. We will discuss findings from this study throughout this chapter. Finally, the National Health and Social Life Survey also provided some information on childhood sexuality (see Chapter 2 for more information on the National Health and Social Life Survey).

Together, these studies have helped to shed some light on trends in adolescent sexual behavior. As we discussed in Chapter 2, sexuality research has always been problem driven (i.e., many studies are aimed at decreasing rates of STI or teenage pregnancy), and nowhere is this more apparent than the research on adolescent sexuality, yet the research has also helped us to understand adolescent sexuality. Although methodologies and populations varied for each of the aforementioned studies, adolescents between the ages of 15 and 17 were a common subpopulation. Overall, the data have revealed comparable trends in many adolescent sexual behaviors (Santelli et al., 2000). We will discuss many of these findings later in this chapter and in upcoming chapters.

In the future, more research is needed on frequency of sexual behaviors other than intercourse; differences in gender, ethnicity, race, religion, and social class; same-sex preferences and behavior; cross-cultural research; and the meaning of eroticism and sexuality in young people's lives. The data that do exist show some things about childhood sexuality that you might find surprising.

Review Question

Explain why there has been opposition to childhood sexuality research.

BEGINNINGS: BIRTH TO AGE 2

Let's first take a look at physical and psychosexual changes from birth to age 2. We would not label behavior as "sexual" during this time; however, there are many behaviors that arise out of curiosity.

Physical Development: Fully Equipped at Birth

Our sexual anatomy becomes functional even before we are born; ultrasound has shown male fetuses with erections in the uterus, and some babies develop erections shortly after birth—even before the umbilical cord is cut (Masters et al., 1982). Female babies are capable of vaginal lubrication from birth (Martinson, 1981). Infant girls produce some estrogen from the adrenal glands before puberty, whereas infant boys have small testes that produce very small amounts of testosterone. Young children are even capable of orgasm!

Kinsey and his colleagues (1948, 1953) established that one-half of boys between the ages of 3 and 4 could achieve the urogenital muscle spasms of orgasm (though no fluid is ejaculated), and almost all boys could do it 3 to 5 years before puberty. Kinsey did not collect systematic data on the abilities of young girls to reach orgasm, though he did include some anecdotal stories on the subject. Still, there is no reason to think that girls should be any less able than boys to orgasm.

Psychosexual Development: Bonding and Gender Identification

The single most important aspect of infant development is the child's relationship to his or her parents or caregivers. The infant is a helpless creature, incapable of obtaining nourishment or warmth or relieving pain or distress. The bond between the mother and child is more than psychological; a baby's crying actually helps stimulate the secretion of the hormone **oxytocin** in the mother, which releases her milk for breast-feeding (Rossi, 1978; we'll discuss this more in Chapter 12).

Pheromones are also important. Remember that in Chapter 7, we discussed how pheromones promote the bond between a mother and her infant (Kohl & Francoeur,

oxytocin
A hormone secreted by the hypothalamus that may contribute to the physical bond between a mother and her infant (we'll discuss this more in Chapter 12).

2002). Equally as important as the infant's need for nourishment is the need for holding, cuddling, and close contact with caregivers. An infant's need for warmth and contact was demonstrated in Harlow's (1959) famous experiment, in which rhesus monkeys were separated at birth from their mothers. When offered two surrogate mothers, one a wire figure of a monkey equipped with milk bottles and one a terrycloth-covered figure, the monkeys clung to the terrycloth figure for warmth and security and ventured over to the wire figure only when desperate for nourishment. The need for a sense of warmth and security in infancy overwhelms even the desire to eat.

As we discussed in Chapter 3, infants between 1 and 2 years of age begin to develop their gender identity (Lewis, 1987). After about the age of 2, it becomes increasingly difficult to change the child's gender identity (which is occasionally done when, for example, a female with an enlarged clitoris is mistakenly identified at birth as a boy). It takes a little longer to achieve **gender constancy,** whereby young children come to understand that they will not become a member of the other sex sometime in the future. By this age there is usually strong identification with one gender, which becomes a fundamental part of a child's self-concept. Along with this identification begins knowledge of gender role behavior, the behaviors that society teaches are appropriate for a person of that gender. Though gender role behavior undoubtedly has some biological component, it is primarily a product of modeling and direct teaching by the parents and other caretakers (Finan, 1997).

gender constancy
The realization in the young child that one's gender does not normally change over the life span.

Young girls and boys are curious about their bodies and bodily functions.

Sexual Behavior: Curiosity

In infancy, the child's body is busy making sure all of his or her organs work and learning to control them. The sexual system is no exception. Male babies sometimes have erections during breast-feeding (which can be very disconcerting to the mother), whereas girls have clitoral erections and lubrication (though that is less likely to be noticed). The baby's body (and mind) has not yet differentiated sexual functions from other functions, and the pleasure of breast-feeding, as well as the stimulation from the lips, mouth, and tongue, create a generalized neurological response that stimulates the genital response.

Self-stimulation is common in infancy, as many infants touch their genitals as soon as their hands are coordinated enough to do so, after about 3 or 4 months (Casteels et al., 2004). Some babies only occasionally or rarely touch themselves, whereas others masturbate frequently. Infants and babies do not masturbate to achieve orgasm, though they clearly derive pleasure from the activity; it is soothing to the baby and may serve as a means of tension reduction and distraction. In fact, in some cultures, it is a common practice for mothers to calm a baby down by stroking the baby's genitals. Self-stimulation is normal and common at this age, and parents should be more concerned if babies show absolutely no curiosity about exploring their world and their bodies than if they touch themselves.

Review Question

Explain physical and psychosexual development in infancy. What sexual behaviors are common in infancy?

EARLY CHILDHOOD: AGES 2 TO 5

Children continue to develop physically, and in early childhood they begin to understand what it means to be a boy or girl. Curiosity still is the basis for their sexuality during this time. Children also learn that their genitals are private during these years, and they often begin to associate sexuality with secrecy.

Physical Development: Mastering Coordination

Early childhood is a crucial period for physical development. Children of this age must learn to master the basic physical actions, such as eye-hand coordination, walking, talking, and generally learning to control their bodies. Think of all the new things a child must learn: all the rules of speaking and communicating; extremely complex physical skills such as self-feeding, walking, and running; how to interact with other children and adults; control of bodily wastes through toilet training; and handling all the frustrations of not being able to do most of the things they want to do when they want to do them. Though this period of childhood is not a particularly active one in terms of physical sexual development, children may learn more in the first few years of childhood about the nature of their bodies than they learn in the entire remainder of their lives. It is truly a time of profound change and growth.

Psychosexual Development: What It Means to Be a Girl or Boy

Young boys develop strong relationships with same-sex and other-sex friends and relatives, and these relationships set the stage for adult intimate relationships.

In early childhood, children begin serious exploration of their bodies. It is during this period that children are usually toilet trained, and they go through a period of intense interest in their genitals and bodily wastes. They begin to ask the first, basic questions about sex, usually about why boys and girls have different genitals and what they are for. They begin to explore what it means to be "boys" or "girls" and turn to their parents, siblings, or television for models of gender behavior. Sometimes children at this age will appear flirtatious or engage in sexual behaviors such as kissing in an attempt to understand gender roles. However, it is almost certainly wrong to suggest that these behaviors are motivated by sexual desire at this young age.

Sexual Behavior: Curiosity and Responsibility

Toddlers are not yet aware of the idea of sexuality or genital sexual relations. Like infants, toddlers and young children engage in many behaviors that involve exploring their bodies and doing things that feel good. Both girls and boys engage in self-stimulation. Over 70% of mothers in one study reported that their children under age 6 self-stimulated (Okami et al., 1997). Almost all research reports that boys do so more than girls, though girls may self-stimulate more than is reported, because they can often do it more subtly (e.g., by rubbing their legs together). One mother commented about her 5-year-old daughter:

> Jessica would masturbate every night just before she fell asleep. She would lie on her stomach with her hands between her legs and rock back and forth. She didn't seem embarrassed or uptight about me walking in and finding her. She'd just smile and tell me that it felt really good. (Author's files)

Self-stimulation is actually more common in early childhood than later childhood, though it picks up again after puberty (Friedrich et al., 1991). The act may be deliberate and obvious and may even become a preoccupation; some children insist on keeping their pants and underwear off to have easy access to their genitals. Boys at this age are capable of erection, and some proudly show it off to visitors. Parental reaction at this stage is very important; strong disapproval may teach their children to hide the behavior and to be secretive and even ashamed of their bodies, whereas parents who are tolerant of their children's emerging sexuality can teach them to respect and take pride in their bodies. It is perfectly appropriate to make rules about the times and places that such behavior is acceptable, just as one makes rules about other childhood actions, such as the correct time and place to eat or to urinate.

Child sex play often begins with games exposing the genitals ("I'll show you mine if you show me yours . . .") and, by the age of 4, may move on to undressing and touching, followed by asking questions about sex around the age of 5. Sometimes young children will rub their bodies against each other, often with members of the same sex, which seems to provide general tactile pleasure. In one study, 48% of parents reported that their children under 6 years old had engaged in sex play with another child (Okami et al., 1997).

Question: Is it damaging to a child to see his or her parents naked? What about accidentally seeing them making love?

For many years in Western society, it has been thought that children would be somehow traumatized by seeing their parents naked. In fact, nudity is natural and common in many cultures, such as Scandinavian countries, which have a reputation for physical health and beauty. Parents' casual nudity, openness to sexual questions, and willingness to let their children sleep at times in their beds has been found to be correlated with generally positive overall effects on the well-being of children (Lewis & Janda, 1988; Okami et al., 1998). If parents are caught making love, their best tactic is not to be upset but to tell the child calmly that the parents are showing each other how much they love each other and would prefer to do it in private. Then they should teach the child to knock on their bedroom door in the future. More trauma can come from the parents' overreaction than from the sight of lovemaking.

Sexual Knowledge and Attitudes: Sex Is Different

During this period of early childhood, children learn that the genitals are different from the rest of the body. They remain covered up, at least in public, and touching or playing with them is either discouraged or to be done only in private. This is the beginning of the sense of secrecy surrounding sexuality. Children are usually taught about their genitals in order to teach them about elimination, not sexuality, and young children often confuse eliminative and sexual functions (Chilman, 1983).

As we discussed in Chapters 4 and 5, children this age rarely learn the anatomically correct names for their genitals. In one study, young children knew the correct anatomical terms for body parts like eyes, arms, and legs, but only 6.3% knew the term "penis" and only 3% "vagina" (Wurtele et al., 1992). Children are easily capable of learning the correct terminology when taught at home by their parents. Why is it that we teach our children the correct names for all the body parts except their genitalia? What message do you think it might send children when we use cute play words like "dinkle" or "piddlewiddle" for their genital organs?

In our culture, boys are taught very early a name for their focus of sexual pleasure, the penis, but girls rarely are taught about the focus of their sexual pleasure, the clitoris. Typically, girls are often taught incorrect terminology for their genitals, which in turn discourages them from learning more about their sexuality (Ogletree & Ginsburg, 2000). Boys often know more sexual words than girls, even though girls, in general, have larger vocabularies than boys (Bem, 1989). In addition, the appearance of the penis seems to fascinate both girls and boys, and although boys tend to be relatively uninterested in girls' genitals, girls are quite interested in boys' penises (Gundersen et al., 1981). Parents must make an extra effort to introduce girls to their genital anatomy. One mother was dismayed when her 6-year-old daughter commented about her 2-year-old brother and asked, "Why does he have such a nice big thing there and I have a boring nothing?" (Author's files).

ReviewQuestion

Explain physical and psychosexual development in early childhood. How is sexual behavior different in early childhood than in infancy?

MIDDLE CHILDHOOD TO PRETEEN: AGES 6 TO 12

Between the ages of 6 and 12, the first outward signs of puberty often occur, and both boys and girls become more private about their bodies. Children begin building a larger knowledge base about sexual information—and acquire information from many sources, including their parents/caregivers, peers, and siblings. During the middle childhood to preteen years, children often play in same-sex groups and may begin masturbating, engaging in sexual fantasy, and/or sexual contact.

Physical Development: Puberty

Until a child's body starts the enormous changes involved in puberty, the sexual organs grow in size only to keep up with general body growth and change very little in their physiological activity. Though the body begins internal changes to prepare for puberty as early as age 6 or 7, the first outward signs of puberty begin at 9 or 10. In girls, **breast buds** appear, and pubic hair growth may begin. In boys, pubic hair growth generally starts a couple of years later than in girls, and, on average, girls experience menarche (which we discussed in Chapter 4) before boys experience their first ejaculation (often referred to as **semenarche**; SEM-min-ark). Preadolescent boys experience frequent erections, even to nonerotic stimuli. Common reactions to semenarche include surprise, curiosity, confusion, and pleasure—and typically most boys don't tell anyone about this event (Frankel, 2002; Stein & Reiser, 1994). Pubertal changes can be frightening for both boys and girls if they are not prepared for them, and, even if prepared, the onset of puberty can be emotionally, psychologically, and physically difficult for many children.

Psychosexual Development: Becoming More Private

Freud believed that children enter a sexual "latency" period after about age 6, when sexual issues remain fairly unimportant; they reemerge with the coming of puberty (see Chapter 2). The latency thesis may have been formulated because as the child matures, overt sexual behavior lessens. However, such behavior may lessen because it becomes less tolerated by parents and adults as the child grows older. For example, it is common to see a 3-year-old happily holding or stroking her genitals in public; such behavior would be shocking in a 9-year-old. Children are quickly socialized into correct sexual behaviors and learn to restrict them to moments of privacy (Friedrich et al., 1991).

Most researchers disagree with Freud today; in fact, research seems to show that sexual interest and activity in societies across the world steadily increases during childhood. However, it appears that children engage in more "sexual" types of behaviors up until the age of 5 and then this behavior decreases. One study found that 2-year-old children of both sexes were more overtly sexual than were children in the 10- to 12-year-old range (Friedrich, 1998). Presumably this is due to the fact that children get better at hiding their sexual behaviors.

Sexual Behavior: Learning About the Birds and Bees

Children through the middle and late childhood years continue to masturbate, engage in heterosexual and homosexual contact, enjoy displaying their genitals and seeing those of other children, and sometimes even attempt intercourse. Prepubescence is the age of sexual discovery; most children learn about adult sexual behaviors such as intercourse at this age and assimilate cultural taboos and prejudices concerning unconventional sexual behavior. For example, it is at this age that children (especially boys) first begin to use sexual insults with each other, questioning their friends' desirability and/or sexual orientation. Both boys and girls at this age tend to play in same-sex groups and learn about sexuality in their discussions with each other (Lorber, 1994). As children enter the later years of preadolescence, frequency and sophistication of sexual activity often increases.

Sexual Fantasies

Children as young as 4 or 5 have fantasies with erotic content, and children between the ages of 6 and 10 can become physically aroused by thinking about these fantasies (Langfeldt, 1981a). Children are sometimes fearful of their fantasies, worrying that thinking about certain acts would lead them to actually perform them (Langfeldt, 1981b). As children grow older, their fantasies have more and more erotic content and are more often used during masturbation.

breast buds
The first swelling of the area around the nipple that indicates the beginning of breast development.

semenarche
The experience of first ejaculation.

Review Question

Explain physical and psychosexual development in middle childhood through the preteen years.

sex byte

When 4- to 6-year-old children from China, Germany, and the United States were asked to select their favorite movie videos, boys showed a strong preference for videos with aggressive themes, whereas girls preferred peaceful and/or nurturing videos (Knobloch et al., 2005).

Childhood Sexuality Among the Muria

The Muria, a non–Hindu tribal people, live in the state of Basar in the central hill country of India. Their view of childhood sexuality differs from ours in the West.

Beautiful Jalaro, twelve years old, slips out of her parents' thatched-roof hut, heading for the ghotul compound at the edge of the village. . . . Tonight Jalaro hopes to sleep with Lakmu, her favorite of all the ghotul boys. Only last week, she had her first menstrual period, and now all the village boys are eager to sleep with her. She has made love to many of them during her years in the ghotul, but now beautiful Jalaro is a real woman at last. . . .

With a rush of noise and laughter, the girls swarm through the gate, assembling first in front of their own fire and then dispersing to mingle with the boys. One group of boys and girls pairs off and begins singing sexual, taunting songs. Another group settles down by the fire, talking and joking. From a third group, in a different part of the compound, there is the sudden beat of a drum, and halfnaked bodies begin to bob and weave in the darkness.

Later on, when the singing and dancing have died down and the smaller children have begun to fall asleep, the Belosa (the girls' headmistress) tells each one whom she will massage and with whom she will sleep. These assignments are made arbitrarily by the headmistress, but Jalaro smiles and lowers her eyes when the Belosa, wise and fair for her seventeen years, orders her to massage Lakmu and then share his sleeping mat.

Before long, Jalaro is kneeling on the ground a short distance from the fire; Lakmu sits on the ground between her thighs. She takes one of the beautiful hand-carved combs from her head and begins to comb out his long, black tangles, talking softly as she works.

When this is done, she massages his back, chest, arms, and legs—slowly at first, but building up to a violent intensity. Then she runs the teeth of her comb all over his body to stimulate his skin. Finally, she finishes by taking each of his arms in turn and cracking every joint from shoulder to fingertip.

This same scene is repeated in a great many other places throughout the compound. Soon the sleeping mats will be unrolled, and the unmarried young of the Muria will be well engrossed in the lovemaking and sexual play. The adults like this arrangement because it gives them privacy in their small, crowded huts at night. And to the [adult] Muria, the enjoyment of sex—in private and without interference from children—is one of the supreme pleasures of married life.

In this technologically simple society, where privacy is all but impossible to find and where sex—like work, play, food, and sleep—is openly accepted as a normal and natural part of life, children of three or four are already familiar with the basic facts of sexual behavior. And by the time a Muria child is twice that age, sexual innocence is a thing of the past. The traditional cultures of the West generally take the attitude that children are not naturally sexual creatures, should not be sexual creatures, and should at all costs be kept away from sexual knowledge and ideas lest they somehow become sexual creatures before their appointed hour arrives. Yet the members of relatively few cultures studied by anthropologists would have anything but derision for such notions. Indeed, the overwhelming majority of preindustrial cultures consider sex to be an inevitable and harmless aspect of childhood.

Source: Richard Currier, "Juvenile Sexuality in Global Perspective," in L. L. Constantine and F. M. Martin (Eds.), *Children and Sex: New Findings, New Perspectives,* 1981, pp. 9–19. Used by permission of Little, Brown and Co.

Masturbation

Generally, by the end of this time period, most children have the ability to stimulate themselves to orgasm. A consistent finding about childhood and adolescent masturbation is that boys masturbate more than girls (boys about twice a week, girls about once a month) and that boys reach orgasm more frequently (I. M. Schwartz, 1999; Sorenson, 1973). Boys often learn masturbation from each other and sometimes masturbate in groups, whereas girls often discover masturbation by accident.

Boys and girls masturbate a variety of different ways. Boys masturbate manually or by rubbing their penis against soft objects like their bedsheets or stuffed animals. Girls also masturbate manually by pelvic rubbing and thrusting; they may also put objects such as pillows between their legs. Many girls experience pleasure and even orgasm by rhythmically rubbing their legs together. Some children find creative ways to masturbate:

> I used to love to take "rides" on the washing machine during the wash and rinse cycles, when the whole machine was whirring. I don't know if my parents ever realized it—I'm sure they thought I was pretending to ride a horsey—but the vibrations of the machine were some of my earliest sexual feelings. (Author's files)

In their relationships with each other, boys and girls in middle childhood often imitate adults.

Sexual Contact

Children from the age of 6 to puberty engage in a variety of heterosexual and homosexual play. It is common during this period to engage in sex games, such as "spin the bottle" (spinning a bottle in a circle while asking a question such as, "Who is going to kiss Lisa?"; then the person whom the bottle points to must perform the task), allowing children to make sexual contact under the guise of a game. Play, in a sense, is the "work" of childhood, teaching interpersonal and physical skills that will be developed as we mature. Sex play helps the child discover the differences and similarities between the sexes and is tolerated to a greater or lesser degree in different cultures. Children at this age have some knowledge about sex and are curious about it, but they often have incomplete or erroneous ideas, as expressed by the 12-year-old in the accompanying Personal Voices, "My Sex Life, Chapter One."

Rates of sexual contact among school-age children are difficult to come by, and most experts still cite Kinsey's data of 1948 and 1953. Kinsey found that 57% of men and 46% of women remembered engaging in some kind of sex play in the preadolescent years. By the age of 12, about 1 boy in 4 reported having at least attempted heterosexual intercourse, and about 10% had their first ejaculation in sex play with a girl. Girls' activity tended to taper off as they approached preadolescence, and they reported the majority of their experiences before the age of 8. Greenwald & Leitenberg (1989) found that, of 526 undergraduates questioned about sexual activity prior to age 13, about 5% reported having had a sibling sexual encounter; 12% reported having had both a sibling and a nonsibling childhood sexual experience; and 45% reported having had only a nonsibling sexual experience. Thirty-nine percent reported no sexual experience with another child prior to age 13. Both the Kinsey and the Greenwald & Leitenberg studies suffer from being retrospective (i.e., they asked older adults to remember what they did when they were young), and there are many reasons to think people's recollections of childhood sexuality may not be entirely accurate.

Both boys and girls exhibit a range of same-sex sexual behaviors as they move through childhood, from casual rubbing and contact during horseplay to more focused attention on the genitals. The figures for prepubescent contact are difficult to obtain, both because it is difficult at this age to define homosexual behavior and because there is sensitivity among parents in asking children about it. Although girls' heterosexual activity declines as they reach puberty, they report a steadily increasing rate of same-sex activity as they approach adolescence.

Review Question

Identify and discuss the types of sexual behaviors that are common in middle childhood through the preteen years.

Sexual Knowledge and Attitudes: Our Sexual Scripts

Children get information from many different sources, much of it contradictory. They use this information to construct a **sexual script** (Plummer, 1991). The sexual script can have different themes, depending on the sexual ideas and values communicated to the child by the culture and his or her specific environment.

Sexual scripts refer to explicit things we communicate to children, such as "Sex is dirty" or "Save it for someone you love," or they can be subtle, such as what Plummer (1991) calls the scripting of "absence." Because of the reluctance parents have about talking frankly about sex, children may have gaps of knowledge and of vocabulary and may have to create these words or ideas for themselves. Another example is the "script of utility," or ways in which sexuality can be used in a social context. For example, chil-

sexual script
The sum total of a person's internalized knowledge about sexuality.

My Sex Life, Chapter One

The writings of a 12-year-old boy, published in Harper's Magazine, show the struggles of trying to understand sexuality as he emerges from preadolescence.

At school I've had some formal sex ed. In health class, at the beginning of the year, we had a discussion about it, and we watch movies—The Miracle of Life and The Miracle of Birth. People make lots of jokes about those movies because they show a man and a woman having sex and they have a close-up of the in-and-out. But you don't learn much about the details of sex in school. It's what most of the boys talk about, telling each other how they do it and who they do it with. What I've found is most girls have experienced this stuff before most boys have. There are only a few boys in my school who I've heard talking about kissing someone with the tongue and I've actually believed them. Some of the boys talk about feeling certain parts of the girlfriends' bodies, but I don't believe most of it.

I'm not sure why, but in conversations I've had with my parents they've made requests like "not until you're sixteen." I think it might become a possibility for me at the age of fourteen. I don't think I'll be having sex regularly until I'm fifteen or sixteen. It's not something I'm dying to do, because I question what you're supposed to do. I've seen it on the video, the in-and-outing, but how does that start? I'd say that's the main thing that makes most people my age not quite ready

to have sex. Trying to figure out or make up how it works or could work. First there's the question of how girls have sex with you, and then there's the question of how to get girls to have sex with you. The first one is one of the most important things I think about now, how it happens. I've seen enough and heard enough to understand how kissing works, but I don't know how to get from that to having sex. I suppose that's the next bridge to cross, how to turn kissing into sexual intercourse. At school it's perfectly all right to talk about it happening, but there's no way of coming out and asking your friends how it happens. It's one of those things that everyone thinks about, but no one's able to admit it. You think, maybe everyone else understands this, maybe they're going to think less of me.

On some of the late-night TV shows, I've seen people making out on the couch, and then it cuts off right where the guy unbuttons the girl's top button, and it begins again in the morning, where they're lying in bed. There's no way to figure out how it starts. I don't think girls know either, but I have the feeling that it doesn't matter what the girl does, it's all because of the boy. I can see on TV that the girl doesn't start unbuttoning the boy's shirt, it's always the boy unbuttoning the girl's shirt. They always go home to the boy's apartment. That just gives me the idea the boy is the person who starts it.

SOURCE: Maurer, 1994, p. 34.

dren learn that sexuality can be used to intimidate other children, to defy authority with adults, as a form of play, or, in the cases of abuse, as a means to gain love. See the accompanying Sex in Real Life, "What Do Children Want to Know, and What Are They Ready For?" for the kinds of questions that children have at different stages in their development.

Sexuality and Relationships: What We Learn

All of our intimate relationships influence our sexuality in one way or another. We learn different aspects of sexuality from these varied influences; for example, we may learn taboos from our parents, information from our siblings, or techniques from our peers.

Relationships With Parents and Caretakers

Parents and children often have very different views about how open the parents are to discussions of sexuality and how often the topic is discussed (Jaccard et al., 1998; King & Lorusso, 1997). Parents also have conflicting ideas about sexuality in their children. In a study of parental attitudes toward masturbation, for example, Gagnon (1985) found about 60% of parents accepted the fact that their children masturbated and said that it

What Do Children Want to Know, and What Are They Ready For?

Because developmental differences influence children's ability to comprehend sexuality education, educators often evaluate what types of questions students ask in order to develop programs that can meet the needs of different age levels (we will discuss sex education at greater length later in this chapter). Many proponents of sexuality education programs believe that these programs should be sequential (i.e., there should be a logical order in the curriculum) and comprehensive (i.e.,

they should include information on biological, psychological, social, and spiritual components). Following are some typical questions students ask at various ages and suggestions for what to include in sexuality education programs at these levels. Although we've presented these general guidelines for sexuality education programs, it is important to keep in mind that any particular program must be designed according to the needs of the specific group to which it will be presented.

Age Range	Developmental Issues	Questions Children Might Ask	Suggestions for Sexuality Educators
3 to 5 years	Shorter attention spans.	What is that? (referring to specific body parts) What do mommies do? What do daddies do? Where do babies come from?	At this level, sexuality education can focus on the roles of family members, the development of a positive self-image, and an understanding that living things grow, reproduce, and die.
5 to 8 years	Very curious about how the body works.	Where was I before I was born? How does my mommy get a baby? Did I come from an egg?	Sexuality education can include information on plant and animal reproduction, gender similarities and differences, growth and development, and self-esteem.
9 to 12 years	Curiosity about their bodies continues, and children are often interested in the other sex and reproduction.	How does the reproductive system work? Why do some girls have larger breasts than others? Do boys menstruate? Why don't some women have babies?	Sexuality education can include focus on biological topics such as the endocrine system, menstruation, masturbation and wet dreams, sexual intercourse, birth control, abortion, self-esteem, and interpersonal relationships.
12 to 14 years	Pre-teens may be concerned and/or confused about the physical changes of puberty, including changes in body shape, body control, reproductive ability, menstruation, breast and penis development, and voice changes.	How can you keep yourself looking attractive? Should your parents know if you're going steady? Why are some people homosexual? Does a girl ever have a wet dream? Does sexual intercourse hurt? Why do people get married?	Sexuality education can focus on increasing knowledge of contraception, intimate sexual behavior (why people do what they do), dating, and variations in sexual behaviors (homosexuality, transvestism, transsexualism).
15 to 17 years	Increased interest in sexual topics and curiosity about relationships with others, families, reproduction, and various sexual activity patterns. Many teenagers begin dating at this time.	What is prostitution? What do girls really want in a good date? How far should you go on a date? Is it good to have sexual intercourse before marriage? Why is *sex* considered a dirty word?	Sexuality education can include more information on birth control, abortion, dating, premarital sexual behavior, communication, marriage patterns, sexual myths, moral decisions, parenthood, sexuality research, sexual dysfunction, and the history of sexuality.

SOURCE: Based on Breuss & Greenberg, 1981, pp. 223–231.

was all right. Ironically, fewer than half wanted their children to have a positive attitude toward masturbation, and that attitude was transmitted to their children.

Parents can be extremely upset and confused when they discover that their children are engaged in sexual play. As one parent said, "I don't mind if he walks around with his hands in his pants, but when he starts touching other kids' penises, then I have to step in" (Author's files). Even parents who want their children to grow up with a healthy view of sexuality often are not sure of the best way to respond to children's sex play. Sex play in children is perfectly normal, and parents should probably be more concerned if their children show no interest in their own or other children's bodies than if they want to find out what other children have "down there."

Relationships With Peers

As children age and try to determine how they will fare in the world outside the family, their peer groups increase in importance. Learning acceptable peer-group sexual standards (acceptable attitudes and moral values) is as important as learning all the other attitudes and behaviors. Children learn acceptable attitudes and behaviors for common games, sports, and even the latest media trends. Friends are very important to adolescents.

Same-Sex Peers   During middle childhood, adolescents overwhelmingly prefer same-sex to other-sex friends (Hendrick & Hendrick, 2000). Although other-sex friendships do develop, the majority of early play is done in same-sex groupings (Fabes et al., 2003). Early on these friendships tend to be activity based (friends are made due to shared interests or proximity); but, by early adolescence, affective qualities (such as trust, loyalty, honesty) replace the activity-based interests (Bigelow, 1977). With these qualities in place, friendships can tolerate differences in interests or activities and reasonable distance separations (such as not being in the same classroom). As a result, friendships in adolescence become more stable, supportive, and intimate than they were prior to this time (B. B. Brown et al., 1997).

Peers are a major catalyst in the decision to partake in voluntary sexual experimentation with others. Sexual communication and contact are carefully negotiated, as both participants are usually a little frightened and nervous about the initiation of sexuality. Often initial sexual experimentation takes place among preadolescents of the same sex. Same-sex experimentation is quite common in childhood, even among people who grow up to be predominantly heterosexual. As one boy relates:

> I was at summer camp, about 11 or 12 years old, and I went for a walk with a friend. We were in the woods, and we began to dare each other to do things. My friend was always considered a bit effeminate, and I dared him to take off his clothes, which he did. I ended up daring him to put my penis in his mouth, which he resisted initially but finally did for a few seconds. We then got dressed and left and remained friends and never spoke of that experience again. (Author's files)

Other-Sex Peers   For most American children, preadolescence is when they begin to recognize their sexual nature and to see peers as potential boyfriends and girlfriends. Although this doesn't happen until the very end of this time period, children as early as 11 begin to develop interest in the other gender and may begin pairing off within larger groups of friends, or at parties. Preadolescence has traditionally been a time of early sexual contact, such as kissing and petting, but for many this doesn't occur until later.

Sibling Sex   Another fairly common childhood experience is sexual contact (fondling or engaging in sex games) with siblings or close relatives, such as cousins. Sometimes this occurs as abuse, with an older relative coercing a younger one into unwanted sexual activity. However, more often it involves mutual sexual curiosity. Greenwald and Leitenberg (1989) found that among a sample of college students, 17% reported having sibling sexual contact before age 13. Only a small percentage involved force or threat, and intercourse was rare.

Sibling sex is common among diverse family types, involving children of all ages, from age 3 through adolescence. Research on sibling sex suggests that it can be harmful when there is a large difference between the ages of siblings or when coercive force is used (Finkelhor, 1980; Rudd & Herzberger, 1999). It is probably not a good idea, therefore, to encourage boys going through puberty to bathe with their younger sisters or to share a bedroom with a brother 4 or 5 years younger. Yet normal sexual experiences, such as minor touching and looking at siblings of approximately the same age, are usually innocent and harmless.

Review Question

Discuss the importance of relationships with parents, peers, and siblings in childhood through preadolescence.

ADOLESCENCE: AGES 12 TO 18

Adolescence begins after the onset of puberty and is, in part, our emotional and cognitive reactions to puberty. Adolescence ends when the person achieves "adulthood," signified by a sense of individual identity and an ability to cope independently with internal and external problems (Lovejoy & Estridge, 1987). People reach adulthood at different times; adolescence can end at around the age of 17 or 18, or it can drag out into a person's 20s. It is recognized the world over as a time of transition, as the entrance into the responsibilities and privileges of adulthood. Most societies throughout history have developed rites of passage around puberty; the Jewish Bar or Bat Mitzvah, Christian confirmation, and the Hispanic Quinceanera come to mind—and other cultures have other rites. The Quinceanera—a 15th birthday celebration for Latina girls—has traditionally been used as an opportunity to discuss female adolescent developmental tasks and challenges, including teenage pregnancy and sexuality (Stewart, 2005).

We know the most about this developmental period because, as we discussed earlier in this chapter, we do have ongoing research studies on adolescent sexual behavior. Overall, we know that adolescence is a time of physical, emotional, and cognitive change. There is no other time in the life cycle that so many things happen at once: the body undergoes rapid change; the individual begins a psychological separation from the parents; peer relationships, dating, and sexuality increase in importance; and attention turns to job, career, or college choices. The relationships an adolescent has with his or her mother and father are important during this time (Nickerson & Nagle, 2005). Typically, adolescents report being closer to their mothers than their fathers during adolescence (Williams & Kelly, 2005).

Many young people have their first experience with heterosexual intercourse during this time, and some others confirm or discover same-sex attractions. It is no wonder that many adults look back on their adolescence as both a time of confusion and difficulty and a time of fond memories. However, though some researchers portray adolescence as a time of great stress, others argue that really only a small proportion of adolescents find it to be a particularly difficult period (Chilman, 1983).

© Bill Aron/PhotoEdit

Many cultures have rituals of passage that signify the entry of the child into adulthood. Here a young Jewish boy reads from the Torah at his Bar Mitzvah.

SEX Talk

Question: I keep reading about how terrible people's adolescence was, and mine was fine—I mean I had the normal problems, but it was no big deal. Am I weird?

Adolescence is a time of great change and development, and how people handle it depends on a host of factors, including their biology (such as fluctuating hormone levels), their family, their personality, and their social relationships. Adolescence, in general, may not be as upsetting or disturbing to most people as theorists tend to portray it (Brooks-Gunn & Furstenburg, 1990). If you had (or are having) a wonderful adolescence, that makes you fortunate, not "weird." Be sympathetic to others who may not have had your resources—whether biological, psychological, or social—as they went through adolescence.

Physical Development: Big Changes

Puberty is one of the three major stages of physiological sexual development, along with prenatal sexual differentiation and menopause. Puberty marks the transition from sexual immaturity to maturity and the start of reproductive ability. In Chapters 4 and 5, we discussed the physiological and hormonal changes that accompany puberty, so here we will review only those physical changes that have an effect on the nature of adolescent sexuality.

Puberty begins anywhere between the ages of 8 and 13 in most girls and 9 and 14 in most boys. In fact, the age of puberty has been steadily declining, especially among girls, probably due to better nutrition during childhood. American girls reach menarche at the mean age of 12 (Steiner et al., 2003), and boys experience first semenarche at about the age of 13 (Stein & Reiser, 1994). In other countries, the age at which children reach puberty may differ. A study in Israel, for example, found the age of semenarche of about 14 (Reiter, 1986). Girls' maturation is, in general, about $1\frac{1}{2}$ to 2 years ahead of boys (Gemelli, 1996).

Parents are often shocked at the extreme changes that puberty can bring; a boy can grow up to 5 or 6 inches in less than a year and develop pubic hair, a lower voice, and a more decidedly adult physique. Girls begin to develop breasts, pubic hair, and an enlargement of the genitals. Though we tend to concentrate on the development of the sexual organs, biological changes take place in virtually every system of the body and include changes in cardiovascular status, energy levels, sexual desire, mood, and personality characteristics (Hamburg, 1986). If those changes are difficult for a parent to cope with, imagine how much more difficult it is for the person going through it!

The physiological changes of puberty almost seem cruel. At the time when attractiveness to potential sexual partners begins to become important, the body starts growing in disproportionate ways; fat can accumulate before muscles mature, feet can grow before the legs catch up, the nose may be the first part of the face to begin its growth spurt, and one side of the body may grow faster than the other (Diamond & Diamond, 1986). Add acne, a voice that squeaks at unexpected moments, and unfamiliarity with limbs that have suddenly grown much longer than one is accustomed to, and it is no wonder that adolescence is often a time of awkwardness and discomfort. Fortunately, the rest of the body soon catches up, so the awkward phase does not last too long.

Maturing early or late can also be awkward for boys or girls. Because girls' growth spurts happen earlier than boys', there is a period when girls will be at least equal in height and often taller than boys; this reversal of the cultural expectation of male height often causes both sexes to be embarrassed at dances. Being the last boy (or the first) in the locker room to develop pubic hair and have the penis develop can be a humiliating experience that many remember well into adulthood. Similarly, girls who are the first or last to develop breasts often suffer the cruel taunts of classmates, though the messages can be mixed. It may be this combination of beginning of sexual exploration, changing bodies, and peer pressure that results in the average adolescent having a negative **body image** (Brumberg, 1997).

sexbyte

The age at which a girl experiences menarche has been found to be highly correlated with the age at which her biological mother began menstruating (Ersoy et al., 2005).

body image
A person's feelings and mental picture of his or her own body's beauty.

Females

As we discussed earlier, for most girls, the first signs of puberty are the beginnings of breast buds, the appearance of pubic hair, the widening of the hips, and the general rounding of the physique. Increased estrogen levels stimulate the growth of the breasts, labia, and clitoris; the enlargement of the uterus; widening of the vaginal canal; an increase in body fat and in the activities of the sweat glands. In other words, the adolescent's body is adding oily skin, fat, sweat, and odor—is it any wonder that girls become self-conscious during this period, when the entire advertising industry advises us that these are the most undesirable traits of the human body?

Menarche is the hallmark of female puberty and is often viewed as one of the most important events in a woman's life (Ersoy et al., 2005). It usually begins fairly late in the sequence of changes after the peak of the growth spurt and generally (but not always) before regular ovulation. However, ovulation does sometimes occur early in puberty, so unprotected intercourse before menarche can result in pregnancy. Menarche can be a scary time for a girl who is uninformed about what to expect and an embarrassing time if she is not taught how to correctly use tampons or pads.

Menarche can mean different things to an adolescent girl depending on how her family or her culture explains it to her. It can signify the exciting beginning of adulthood, sexuality, and the ability to have babies—but with all the potential problems that brings as well. Girls who are prepared for menstruation and who are recognized for their intellectual or creative capabilities are more likely to describe pleasurable reactions to the onset of menstruation, whereas girls who are not recognized for other abilities often experience more fear and shame associated with first menstruation (Teitelman, 2004).

Girls often worry that their maturation is too fast or too slow. Common fears include the fear that their breasts will not grow or will be extremely large, that one breast will be much different than the other, or that their first menstrual period occurs too soon or too late. Girls who consider themselves to be "on time" feel more attractive and positive about their bodies than those who consider themselves "early" or "late" (Hamburg, 1986). Although boys' first sign of sexual maturity—ejaculation—is generally a pleasurable experience that is overtly associated with sexuality, girls' sign of maturity is not associated with sexual pleasure and may be accompanied by cramps and discomfort, as well as embarrassment if the onset is at an inopportune time (such as in the middle of gym class). As one girl commented:

> I started my period in April of my 8th grade year. All my friends had already started, and my Mom had talked to me about it, so I wasn't really scared. I thought it was really gross and painful because of the cramps. I was scared to use a tampon because I thought it would hurt. I wore a pad for my first period, and I was really embarrassed because I had to go church and I thought people could see my pad. (Author's files)

Unfortunately, some girls begin menstruation with little idea of what is happening or with myths about it being bad to bathe, swim, exercise, or engage in sexual activities. Many are unfamiliar with their genital anatomy, making tasks such as inserting tampons difficult and frustrating (Diamond & Diamond, 1986).

Males

Male puberty is different from female puberty in many ways. Unlike ovulation, which occurs late in female puberty, spermatogenesis and ejaculation occur early in male puberty; ejaculation may even precede secondary sexual characteristics such as body hair and voice changes. Some boys become capable of impregnating a female even while appearing sexually immature (Lancaster, 1986). Boys' voices change more drastically than girls', and their growth spurts tend to be more extreme and dramatic, usually accompanied by an increase in appetite. Because boys' pubertal growth tends to be more uneven and sporadic than girls', the adolescent boy will often appear gangly or awkward. As a boy's testicles begin to increase their production of testosterone, his scrotum darkens and the testes and penis enlarge. As puberty progresses, pubic hair appears, the larynx enlarges, bones grow, and the frame takes on a more adult appearance.

For the most part, early development in boys is usually not as embarrassing as it is in girls; a larger penis may be a symbol of status, and beginning to shave may be seen as a sign of maturity and adulthood. However, adolescent boys do experience frequent spontaneous erections, which may have no association with sexuality but are nonetheless quite embarrassing. Their increased sexual desire is released through **nocturnal emissions** and increased masturbation.

nocturnal emission
Involuntary ejaculation during sleep, also referred to as a "wet dream."

Psychosexual Development: Emotional Self-Awareness

Puberty is, by far, the most psychologically and socially difficult of the life cycle changes. There are a number of tasks that adolescents struggle with: achieving comfort with their bodies, developing an identity separate from their parents', trying to prove their capacity to establish meaningful intimate and sexual relationships, beginning to think abstractly and futuristically, and establishing emotional self-awareness (Gemelli, 1996).

Figure 8.1

This graph illustrates the average ages when boys and girls go through the major bodily changes of puberty.

Source: From *School Age Pregnancy and Parenthood* by Jane Lancaster, p. 20, Aldine de Gruyter, 1986. Reprinted by permission.

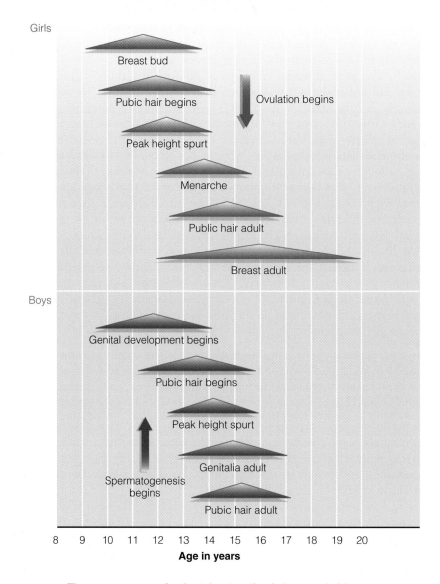

The age sequence of pubertal maturation in boys and girls

We will examine these stages by splitting adolescence into three general stages: early adolescence, middle adolescence (or "adolescence proper"), and late adolescence (Lawlis & Lewis, 1987).

Early Adolescence (Ages 12 to 13)

In early adolescence, preteens begin to shift their role from child to adolescent, trying to forge an identity separate from their family by establishing stronger relationships with peers. Perhaps you remember developing a close friendship at this age—another adolescent with whom you became extremely close (and from whom you may have moved apart later on). Such same-sex friendships are common by the eighth grade, and may develop into first same-sex sexual contacts as well (Diamond, 2000; Lawlis & Lewis, 1987). Supportive friendships during this time are crucial to the adolescent's emotional well-being (B. B. Brown et al., 1997). The importance of a best friend grows as an adolescent matures. In fact, by the end of high school, both girls and boys rated their relationship with their best friend as their most important relationship (B. B. Brown et al., 1997; see Figure 8.2).

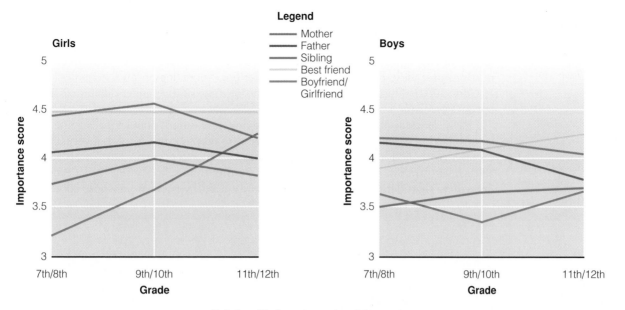

Legend
— Mother
— Father
— Sibling
— Best friend
— Boyfriend/ Girlfriend

Girls

Boys

Importance score (y-axis, both graphs): 3, 3.5, 4, 4.5, 5

Grade (x-axis, both graphs): 7th/8th, 9th/10th, 11th/12th

Relationship importance in adolescence

Figure 8.2
This graph shows the age differences in mean ratings of the importance of each type of relationship to one's life during adolescence (1 = not at all important; 5 = extremely important).
Source: Brown, Dolcini, & Leventhal, "Transformations in peer relationships at adolescence," p. 169, in Schulenberg et al. (Eds.), *Health Risks and Developmental Transitions During Adolescence*, 1997. Reprinted by permission of Cambridge University Press.

Early adolescence, as most of us remember, is filled with "cliques," as people look to peers for validation and standards of behavior. Dating also often begins at this age, which drives many adolescents to become preoccupied with their bodily appearance and to experiment with different "looks." Perhaps surprisingly, girls' body images tend to improve as they progress through adolescence, whereas boys' tend to worsen (Petrie, 2001; Whitsel-Anderson, 2002); this may be attributed to the positive image of the youthful female in our culture. On the other hand, girls' general self-images tend to worsen as they grow older, whereas boys' improve.

Young adolescents are often very concerned with body image at this time. Many young girls, in an attempt to achieve the perfect "model" figure, will endlessly diet, sometimes to the point of serious eating disorders. As we discussed in Chapter 5, today many young boys are also developing eating disorders and may turn to steroids in an attempt to achieve the athletic image so popular for boys at this age (B. B. Brown et al., 1997).

In early and middle adolescence, teens try on different looks, from trendy to rebellious, as they develop an identity separate from their families.

Middle Adolescence (Ages 14 to 16)

For heterosexual youths, the onset of puberty sparks an increasing interest in relationships with the other gender. The social environment also helps build this interest through school-sponsored dances and private, mixed-sex parties (B. B. Brown et al., 1997). Even the media sell images of teenagers in love. These messages are so powerful that even those adolescents who have not yet reached puberty or those who feel they might be gay or lesbian feel intense pressure to express interest in other-sex relationships (K. M. Cohen & Savin-Williams, 1996). Many adolescents increase the frequency of dating as they try to integrate sexuality into their growing capacity for adult-to-adult intimacy. This does not mean they will achieve the goal; rather, in various ways, they will "try on" different roles and different ways of being intimate with others (J. Johnson & Alford, 1987).

For the average middle adolescent, dating consists of going to movies, eating lunch together at the school cafeteria, or spending time together after school or on weekends.

During this period, couples develop longer-term and more exclusive relationships, and early sexual experimentation (deep kissing, fondling) may also begin. Many couples exchange rings, bracelets, necklaces, or some other token to signify exclusivity. These relationships are typically short lived. As a consequence of their involvement in romantic relationships, adolescent females tend to experience more depression than males (Joyner & Udry, 2000). This depression may account for some of the gender differences in adolescent depression levels.

Early dating is often quite informal, and double-dating is popular, as is going out in groups. Dating among the very poor, or those who drop out of school, is a very different experience than it is among the middle class. Adolescents who have been sexually abused, who are runaways, or who go to work rather than school often have needs more immediate than dating. They may not be surrounded by peers as are those adolescents

Personal Voices

Don't Forget to Breathe

*T*he following is a personal account from Jackson, a college student who struggled with sexual orientation issues as a child and adolescent. His inability to open up and share his feelings led to a traumatic rape.

I grew up in a very strict Catholic household—we attended church every Sunday and my parents had many expectations of me. One expectation was that I was supposed to like girls. Since I was the only boy, my parents they pounded the idea into me that I was responsible for passing on the family name. I was to get married and have children one day.

In 7th grade someone in my gym class thought I was gay. He began making fun of me and calling me "gay." Then he slammed my head into my locker and shut the locker door on my head. I didn't know what I did to upset him—I wasn't even looking at him or anything. This was when I realized something was up. I straightened up and decided it was time for a girlfriend.

I had my first girlfriend in 8th grade. At that time I identified myself as a bisexual because I still was attracted to guys. But I was just too afraid to express my true feelings. My girlfriend and I never did anything sexually. She was my FIRST kiss though, and although I didn't see fireworks, it wasn't bad.

Now, here was the changing point in my life. I was still alone, and unable to talk to anyone about my feelings about being gay, especially my parents. All of the feelings I had were kept deep inside. I thought I did a pretty good job at suppressing them; however, things change, and so did I.

When I was 16 years old, I decided to go into a gay chat room just to see what it was like. I used it as an op-portunity to start to "act" on my gay feelings and test the waters. Well, at first I thought the chat rooms were awesome. . . . it was a great way to experiment without anyone knowing. Was I wrong. It seemed like everyone was just looking for a hookup. I felt confused, because I expected it to be somewhere that I could meet people like myself—new and ready to explore a whole new life. I was 16 at the time, and it clearly stated that in my profile that anyone could view. I left the chat room. But it was too late. . . . I had been snatched.

All of a sudden I had received an instant message saying "Jackson?? I know you!" My heart sank! The fact that someone knew who I was scared the crap out of me. But he did know me. A month earlier I had won a contest at a local club and I had to give my name and address to claim my prize. Turns out this was the guy I had given my information to. Now he knew my phone number and where I lived.

He threatened to tell my parents I was gay. Since I had never been able to talk to them, I was terrified. He said, "How would mommy and daddy like finding out that their son is a little homo, hanging out in a gay chat room?!" My heart was pounding, and he continued. "I know where you live, and I can 'out' you to your parents in a heartbeat." I believed him. I said, "I don't want you to out me to my parents. They would kill me. I will meet you only for dinner so that we can talk things out but I will not hook up with you." I explained that I had never been with a guy before. He agreed to meet me at the movies the next night.

My father dropped me off the next evening. I was terrified, but didn't even dream of talking to my dad about it, I knew that if either of my parents found out my life would be over. The thought never even crossed my mind

who are in school together, or they may be preoccupied with concerns related to survival, something from which most adolescents are shielded.

The pattern for young adolescents who have identified their homosexual feelings may be quite different from that of their heterosexual counterparts. Often, gay and lesbian adolescents feel that they don't really fit into the dating scene and may try to hide their disinterest in the discussions of the other sex that so fascinate their friends (Faulkner & Cranston, 1998). Rates of depression, loneliness, drug and alcohol abuse, and suicide are significantly higher for gay, lesbian, and bisexual youths (Westefeld et al., 2001). The suicide attempt rate among these youths is much higher than for adolescents in general (B. K. Jackson, 2000; McDaniel et al., 2001). Though life can still be difficult for the homosexual adolescents today, there is evidence that young people are becoming more accepting of their gay, lesbian, and bisexual peers. Typically, gay and lesbian youths who feel

that if something were to happen to me no one would ever know. I was hoping that this guy would accept the fact that I wouldn't hook up with him and would leave me alone. Soon my cell phone rang and he said he was looking for me. My legs were shaking as I got in his car.

Turns out, he drove me to a hotel and he told me he wanted a hookup and was going to get one. He forced me to perform oral sex on him, and later he had anal sex with me. It was a scary experience for me, and I felt dirty and used. After that night I promised myself I would never go online again. I felt that it was my own fault, and that I should have done something to change what could have happened that night. I started to doubt my sexuality, and went back to playing it "straight." But that didn't last long, because I was drawn back to men. As much as I didn't want to like men, and as bad as my first experience was, there was something deep down inside that made me attracted to men. I didn't know any other way to find others who were going through a similar experience. I was very much in the closet and needed someone that could relate to what I was going through. I always considered talking to close friends and family about my sexuality, but felt like I would be rejected. Still feeling completely alone, I felt my only resort was the online chat room, hoping that just maybe my "knight in shining armor" would arrive.

Things didn't get any better for me. When I was a freshman in college I thought it would be great to be on my own and to maybe experience coming out of the closet. But don't think that happened smoothly. I didn't even have a chance to tell my parents that I was bi/gay. During the fall of my freshman year, my parents were cleaning my room and found a note written by my first boyfriend. My mother and father were so upset with me and I felt like a failure to the family. When I got home my parents had left a paper on HIV/AIDS on my bed. I guess

it was a scare tactic to remind me of the risks of being gay. So, as hard as it was for me, I went back in the closet.

My mom said that it was just a phase. But I knew it was more than that, but I went along with what she said. She actually started to treat me more like her SON and not some alien. Since then (3 years later) I have remained in the closet with them. I have talked about it once or twice with them, because my parents often ask me if I am "happy." My response to that is NO because of who I really am. So I'm still in the closet with my family. It is something that I have to do, and I accept it. I plan on coming out completely to my family after I move out and begin a life of my own. So until then, I have no problem remaining in the closet.

At school I'm out to some of my friends. It has taken a lot of getting used to because I remembered how I felt when that guy in middle school thought I was gay. When I used to go to parties on campus up at school, I was always worried that people thought I was gay. For the most part I have ALWAYS put on a "straight face." It seems pretty difficult, but it's not.

If people could learn anything from reading this, it's this: you only live life once. If you are struggling with your sexuality, don't be afraid to actually talk to a friend or close relative about it because it is not fun to go through it alone. Whatever you do, don't visit chat rooms. If you're not ready to act on certain feelings, then don't! You'd rather be safe then sorry, and in the long run the most important thing is that you are HAPPY! I am able to live by my own words because I realized what is important to me—my happiness, health, and above all, family. There is one saying that I put in my back pocket every day I step foot out into the real world, and that is . . . "Just Breathe. . . ."

SOURCE: Author's files.

Figure 8.3

Men and women experience important sexual and reproductive events at similar ages.
Source: Alan Guttmacher Institute, *In Their Own Right: Addressing the Sexual and Reproductive Health Needs of Men,* 2002, page 8.

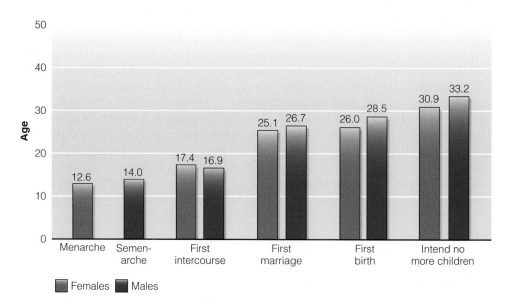

Sexual and reproductive timeline

they can talk to their parents about their sexual orientation have a much easier time accepting themselves (D'Augelli et al., 2005). We will discuss this more in Chapter 11.

Because developing the adolescent sense of self is a delicate process, adolescents may be very sensitive to perceived slights and threats to their emerging ideas of "manhood" or "womanhood." There is an unfortunate tendency among adolescents to portray certain partners as "desirable" (football captain, cheerleader) and others as undesirable or outcast, which as you can imagine (or remember) can be extremely painful if you are on the wrong side of that judgment. Also, for gay, lesbian, and bisexual youths, family reactions or self-expectations may result in depression or confusion. The development of a gay identity may challenge long-held or socially taught images of the acceptable way to be a man or a woman.

Late Adolescence (Ages 17 to Adulthood)

There is no clear line between adolescence and adulthood. Almost all cultures allow marriage and other adult privileges in late adolescence, though there still may be certain restrictions (such as needing parental permission to marry). Late adolescence was, until recently, the stage during which people in Western cultures were expected to begin their search for marital partners through serious dating. With the increased sexual freedoms of the last 30 years, however, young adults have been pushing marriage further back and spending more time in temporary sexual relationships.

Sexual Behavior: Experimentation and Abstinence

Almost every survey shows that U.S. sexual activity has increased overall among teens over the past 50 years, although it may be slowing down somewhat today. Teenagers have become more independent and autonomous than in past generations. Whereas in the past colleges and universities would set curfews and rules for students regarding the other sex, today there are college dorms where males and females are allowed to room together. Additionally, as we discussed in Chapter 1, society itself has become eroticized, with sexual images commonly used in advertising, movies, music, and other media—much of it directed at teens.

Teens engage in sex for many reasons, but studies show that teens link love and sex more than teens did 20 years ago and tend to be more committed to sexually exclusive relationships (McCabe & Cummins, 1998).

Review Question

Explain physical and psychosexual development in adolescence.

sex byte

Even though intimacy in male friendships increases during adolescence, adolescent females spend more time with friends and report more closeness in these relationships than males (Johnson, 2004).

Sexual Fantasies

Sexual fantasies are often used as a means to test sexual situations for their potential erotic content and to help determine emotional reactions to sexual situations. Most research shows that boys use more visual imagery in their sexual fantasies, and that their fantasies include explicit sexual behavior and interchangeable partners. Girls' fantasies focus more on emotional involvement, romance, committed partners, and physical touch, and they also tend to be more complex and vivid (Chick & Gold, 1987–88; Ellis & Symons, 1990). Both men and women tend to fantasize about adults they know, such as teachers, and famous people, such as celebrities. However, 84% of university students in one study also reported at least occasional fantasies that were obtrusive and unwanted (Renaud & Byers, 1999). We will explore more about college students and sexual fantasy in Chapter 10.

SEX Talk

Question: I am 19 years old, and I masturbate at least twice a week, but not as much if I am having good sex with my girlfriend. But she tells me that she never masturbates as much as I do. Why do teenage men masturbate so much more than teenage women?

There are interesting differences in masturbation patterns between the sexes. Though women masturbate more now than they did in years past, girls are less likely than boys to report enjoying masturbation. Also, boys tend to reinforce the social acceptability of masturbation by talking about it more freely among themselves and even engaging occasionally in group masturbation. This is important because both girls and boys report feeling guilty about their masturbatory activities. Girls are socialized not to pay attention to their sexual feelings, and this may also affect masturbation rates. Finally, there may also be biophysical reasons for more frequent male masturbation, such as the obvious nature of the male erection and levels of testosterone.

Masturbation

Masturbation is one of the most underreported sexual behaviors in adolescence. This is mainly because adolescent masturbation is a sensitive topic, and adolescents are often somewhat reluctant to admit to doing it (C. J. Halpern et al., 2000a). Masturbation during adolescence is more likely to be reported during adulthood than during adolescence itself.

As boys and girls enter adolescence, masturbation sharply increases, and the activity is more directed toward achieving orgasm than simply producing pleasurable sensations. Kinsey and his colleagues (1953) found a sharp increase between the ages of 13 and 15 in boys, with 82% of boys having masturbated by age 15. The girls' pattern was more gradual, with 20% having masturbated by age 15 and no sharp increase at any point. A study by Leitenberg and colleagues (1993) found that twice as many college-age males as females had ever masturbated, and men who masturbated during adolescence did so three times more frequently than women who masturbated. The authors also note that no relationship was found between the frequency of masturbation as an adolescent and later experience with sexual intercourse, sexual satisfaction, sexual arousal, or sexual difficulties in relationships.

Masturbation is a very common sexual behavior for adolescent males (Laumann et al., 1994). In fact, almost all studies find that at every age from adolescence into adulthood, more males masturbate and masturbate more frequently than females. Many boys worry that they masturbate more than other boys, but studies of male adolescents show that the average male teen masturbates between three and five times a week (Lopresto et al., 1985; Schwartz, 1999). Boys' masturbatory activities decrease when they are having regular sexual intercourse, whereas girls' increase; this may be because boys mastur-

sex byte

Gay and lesbian adults tend to label a greater number of sexual behaviors as "sex" than do a comparable sample of heterosexuals (Mustanski, 2000).

bate significantly more than girls in general or because girls are less likely to reach orgasm during intercourse than boys and supplement it with masturbation.

Abstinence

What does **abstinence** really mean? This is a question many researchers have tried to answer. Some would argue that to be abstinent means to abstain from sex. Does this mean that a person who is abstinent doesn't engage in any type of sex? Or does this mean he or she refrains from penile-vaginal intercourse but can engage in all other types of sexual behavior? The answer depends on the person. Some people who decide to become abstinent choose to refrain from all sexual behaviors, whereas others may engage in a variety of sexual behaviors but choose not to engage in penile-vaginal intercourse.

The majority of people believe that to be abstinent means to maintain virginity. The Sexuality Information and Education Council of the United States (SIECUS) encourages adolescents to delay sexual intercourse until they are physically, cognitively, and emotionally ready for mature sexual relationships and their consequences. Today, groups advocating abstaining from sex until marriage are cropping up across the country, with mottos like "Save Sex, Not Safe Sex" and "Trust Me, I'm a Virgin." In Chapter 9, we will take a look at athletes, like A. C. Green, who support abstinence before marriage. Later in this chapter we will review sexuality education and abstinence-based programs.

Some heterosexual teens do, in fact, decide to delay sexual activity, or at least intercourse, until marriage. About 20% of people never have sex while in their teens (Darroch & Singh, 1999). Even those who have had intercourse may have long periods during which they don't engage in sexual intercourse. When asked why they thought they should delay intercourse, teens cited the dangers of disease and of pregnancy most often, followed by what their parents would do and what their peers would think (Blinn-Pike, 1999). One study found that nearly half of nonvirgin students wished they had waited longer to initiate intercourse (deGaston et al., 1995). Adolescents with positive self-images are more likely to delay sexual experience than those with poor self-images (Carvajal et al., 1999).

Adolescents often think about many factors when making this important decision. Some decide they are not ready because they haven't met the "right" person, while others delay intercourse because of fears of STIs or pregnancy. There are a few factors that have been found to be related to waiting to have sexual intercourse. Those who tend to wait live with both biological parents (Upchurch et al., 2001), feel a personal connection to their family (Meschke et al., 2000; Resnick et al., 1997), have discussed sex and abstinence with their parents (Sprecher & Regan, 1996), believe that their mother disapproves of premarital sex and have higher intelligence levels (C. J. Halpern et al., 2000a). Those who tend to engage in early sexual intercourse have sexually active friends and siblings, have no religious affiliation (Meschke et al., 2000; Davis & Lay-Yee, 1999), grow up in economically disadvantaged neighborhoods (Baumer & South, 2001), live with only one parent (Meschke et al., 2000), have overcontrolling parents (Upchurch et al., 1999), and have experienced depression (Whitbeck et al., 1999). All of these factors were also identified as important in the National Longitudinal Study of Adolescent Health (Dailard, 2001a).

Girls who decide to remain virgins often feel more positive about this decision than do boys who make the same decision (Sprecher & Regan, 1996). Overall, boys feel more embarrassment and guilt about their virginity than do girls. This may be due to societal standards that support the idea that sex is an important part of masculinity. Differences in levels of adolescent sexual activity across developed countries are quite small.

Sexual Contact

Adolescents may engage in a variety of sexual behaviors, including kissing, oral sex, sexual intercourse, anal intercourse, and homosexual sexual behaviors.

Kissing and Petting   Kissing and touching are the first sexual contact that most people have with potential sexual partners. Coles and Stokes (1985) reported that 73%

of 13-year-old girls and 60% of 13-year-old boys had kissed at least once. Because younger girls tend to date older boys, they have higher rates of these kinds of activities at earlier ages than boys do, but the differences diminish over time. For example, 20% of 13-year-old boys reported touching a girl's breast, whereas 35% of 13-year-old girls reported having their breasts touched, a difference that disappears within a year or two. By age 18, about 60% of boys and girls report vaginal touching, and about 77% of boys and girls report penile touching (Coles & Stokes, 1985).

Oral Sex   Today's teens report engaging in oral sex more than sexual intercourse. It is estimated that 1 in 4 virgin teens (those who had never engaged in intercourse) between the ages of 15 to 19 report having engaged in oral sex (Flanigan et al., 2005). More adolescents have had and intend on having oral sex with a partner than vaginal sex (Halpern-Felsher et al., 2005). In fact, over 50% of teens view oral sex as less risky than vaginal sex and less of a threat to their values and morals (Halpern-Felsher et al., 2005). They believe that if they limit their sexual behavior to oral sex, they are less likely to get a bad reputation or feel bad or guilty about their behavior (Halpern-Felsher et al., 2005). Female teens have argued that oral sex is something a girl can do to a boy (unlike intercourse that is described as something a boy does to a girl; Remez, 2000).

In any event, how much oral sex are adolescents having? The truth is that oral sex has increased in acceptance among young people. Kinsey and his colleagues (1948, 1953) reported that 17% of adolescents reported engaging in **fellatio** (fil-LAY-she-oh) and 11% in **cunnilingus** (kun-nah-LING-gus). More current research from the National Survey of Family Growth (see Chapter 2) found that among teenagers between the ages of 15 and 19, 54% of girls and 55% of boys reported having engaged in oral sex (Flanigan et al., 2005). See the accompanying Sex in Real Life, "Teenagers and Oral Sex," for more information about these findings.

Why has the incidence of oral sex been increasing among adolescents? There are several possible reasons. First, oral sex is more prevalent and acceptable today—there is more exposure to it on television and in the media. Teenagers have also been warned

fellatio
The act of sexually stimulating the male genitals with the mouth.

cunnilingus
The act of sexually stimulating the female genitals with the mouth.

SEX in Real Life

Teenagers and Oral Sex

Over the years there has been speculation about the increasing incidence of oral sex in the U.S. teenage population, but there have been no scientific studies to rely on for valid information. We know that Kinsey and his colleagues (1948, 1953) found that 17% of adolescents reported engaging in fellatio, and 11% reported engaging in cunnilingus. The *National Campaign to Prevent Teen Pregnancy* analyzed the 2002 data from the *National Survey of Family Growth* (NSFG) to get more information on teenage sexual behavior. As you might remember from Chapter 2, the NSFG included data from people aged 15 to 44 years old, so researchers at the *National Campaign* included only the data from the 10,000 adolescents between the ages of 15 and 19 years old.

This analysis revealed that 54% of girls and 55% of boys reported engaging in oral sex and that teenagers' experience with oral sex increased as teens got older (Flanigan et al., 2005). Teenagers who had already engaged in sexual intercourse also reported engaging in oral sex—88% of boys and 83% of girls who had experienced sexual intercourse had also engaged in oral sex (Flanigan et al., 2005). Oral sex was more common than sexual intercourse for teens—at least one-quarter of teenagers who had never engaged in sexual intercourse had engaged in oral sex.

Although some researchers were skeptical about these proposed increases in oral sex activity and believed that they represented an increased comfort level in talking about these issues and not actual increases in activity, others believed these statistics represented real changes in teenage sexual activity. What we do know is that educators and parents of teenagers can use this information to help teach teenagers about sexuality and the risks involved with specific sexual behaviors. Because many teens view oral sex as less risky than vaginal sex (Halpern-Felsher et al., 2005) they still need to be aware of the risks involved. Only 9% of teenagers who reported engaging in oral sex said they used barrier protection, such as condoms and dental dams (we'll discuss these in Chapter 15), during oral sex (Maugh, 2005).

sex byte

The Boy Scout movement originally started as an to attempt to control sexuality and decrease "self-abuse" or masturbation (Pryke, 2005).

about the dangers of heterosexual intercourse (pregnancy and sexually transmitted infections), and many believe that oral sex is a safe alternative (Halpern-Felsher et al., 2005). It may also have to do with the increase in virginity pledgers (adolescents who pledge to remain virgins until marriage), many of whom may view oral sex as an acceptable behavior because it maintains virginity status (Brückner & Bearman, 2005).

SEX Talk

Question: Sometimes I feel I should have intercourse just to get it over with—being a virgin is embarrassing! It's pretty hard to resist when everybody else seems to be doing it.

It used to be that it was shameful (especially for women) to admit to having had sexual intercourse; now it often seems equally shameful to admit to being a virgin. The decision to have sex is a serious one. Too often this step is taken without consideration of its consequences—for example, whether we feel psychologically or emotionally ready and whether our partner does. Sex should never be the result of pressure (by our partner, our friends, or ourselves). There may be many reasons that we want to delay sexual experimentation—including moral or religious reasons. Also, teens usually overestimate the numbers of their friends who are engaging in intercourse.

Sexual Intercourse   The decision to have intercourse for the first time is difficult for many teens. Those who think carefully about their decision may worry about pregnancy, about whether it will change their relationship with their partner, about their skills and techniques, or about moral and ethical questions of sexuality. (The accompanying Personal Voices, "First Sexual Experiences," takes a look at some people's recollections of first intercourse.)

Boys and girls tend to react differently to their first intercourse. The National Health and Social Life Survey found that more than 90% of men said they wanted to have intercourse the first time they did it; more than half were motivated by curiosity, whereas only a quarter said they had intercourse out of affection for their partner (see Chapter 2 for more information on the National Health and Social Life Survey). About 70% of women, too, reported wanting to have intercourse. Nearly half of women said they had sex the first time out of affection for their partner, whereas a quarter cited curiosity as their primary motivation. Twenty-four percent said they just went along with it (fewer than 8% of men said that); 4% reported being forced to have sex the first time, whereas only about 3 men in 1,000 (0.3%) reported being forced.

Teenagers report that their first intercourse is usually unplanned, although the decision to engage in sexual intercourse is rarely spontaneous (DeLamater, 1989). In one survey of adolescents, almost two-thirds of girls said that their first intercourse "just happened," one-fifth said that sex was "unplanned but not entirely unexpected," and only 15% said that they had planned to have intercourse (Brooks-Gunn & Furstenberg, 1990). For many, the first sexual intercourse is a monumental occasion. This experience contributes to the redefining of self and the reconfiguration of relationships with friends, family members, and sexual partners (Upchurch et al., 1998).

The number of teenagers who have engaged in sexual intercourse has fluctuated since 1965. In the late 1990s, rates decreased for the first time since the early 1970s (Althaus, 2001). In contrast, in the 40 years between 1925 and 1965, rates of intercourse changed very little, remaining at about 10% for high school females and 25% for high school males (Chilman, 1986). In the United States, the majority of adolescents become sexually active during their teenage years—63% of teens have had sexual intercourse by their 18th birthday (Boonstra, 2002b).

Other studies have found that the average age at which teenagers engage in sexual intercourse is 16.9 years old, with African American males often being younger (15 years old) and Asian American males older (18 years old; Upchurch et al., 1998). Approximately 12%

Personal Voices

First Sexual Experiences

Following, college students recall their first sexual experience. Note how varied the memories are; to some it was scary, to others wonderful, to others no big deal.

Female: *I was 21 years old when I lost my virginity. It turned out to be an OK situation, but was mainly something I set out to do. I was sick of hearing about it and wanted to do it. It was positive in that I wanted to do it, but wasn't really special in any way. Now when my boyfriend and I look back, he always says he wished he had made it more special for me. We ended up falling in love and have been together for almost 2 years.*

Male: *I was 15 when I lost my virginity. It was in my bedroom with my girlfriend who was 14. I had a permanent smile on my face for about 2 weeks. It was very positive.*

Female: *My first sex was when I was 14 years old. It was a negative experience because I was not sure why I was doing it or what I was doing. I was overtaken by the moment and thought that it was just supposed to happen.*

Male: *I was 13 years old when I lost my virginity to a 36-year-old woman. It was an awkward experience, since I knew nothing and she took control of everything. But I'm happy it happened!*

Female: *I lost my virginity at 18, and I felt as if I were an entirely different person. I often hear horror stories that people were drunk or regret who they had sex with for the first time. I am glad to say I didn't then and don't regret who I was with. I had this plastered grin on my face for at least two days straight. I wasn't so sure I did the right thing but the good feelings I had seemed to overwhelm the wondering.*

Female: *I had sex the first time when I was 16. I hated it. It was painful and certainly not enjoyable. I felt ashamed and regretted the entire experience. Now that I think back to that time, I recall that I really didn't know any facts or biological information concerning sex. I think that was a bigger mistake than having sex itself.*

SOURCE: Author's files.

of males and 3% of females report that they engaged in sexual intercourse by the age of 12 (Meschke et al., 2000). Compare these ages to Japan, where the majority of men and women wait until they are at least 20 years old to begin having sex and use contraception when they do (Althaus, 1997). In most of the developed world, the majority of men and women engage in sexual intercourse during their teen years (Alan Guttmacher Institute, 2002b; see Figure 8.4). In fact, the age at which teenagers become sexually active is similar across comparable developed countries, such as Canada, France, Sweden, and the United States (see Figure 8.5).

The first partner a female adolescent engages in sexual intercourse with is usually slightly older (1 to 3 years older, 61%) or much older (at least 4 years older, 20%); 15% of partners are the same age (Althaus, 2001). Adolescent males, on the other hand, are likely to have sexual intercourse the first time with a partner who is slightly older (1 to 3 years older, 36%) or the same age (33%); 24% of partners are 1 to 3 years younger, and 2% of partners are at least 4 years older. Overall, when first intercourse does occur, boys are generally more satisfied and have a more positive reaction than do girls, presumably because they are able to reach orgasm during the experience, whereas girls often do not (Sprecher et al., 1995). In fact, for some girls, first intercourse is painful:

I lost my virginity when I was 16 years old. I had been intimate with other guys but never had intercourse. I hadn't expected it at all. My boyfriend was 21, and I thought he was my first love. The experience was both positive and negative. I thought I was ready but the pain was SO unbearable. (Author's files)

Figure 8.4

Percentage of American teenagers who have sexual intercourse at different ages.

Source: Facts in Brief: Teen Sex and Pregnancy (Alan Guttmacher Institute, 1999).

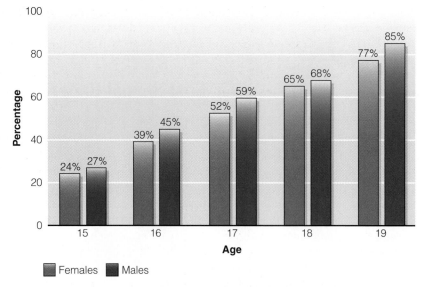

Percentage of teenagers who have had sexual intercourse

Figure 8.5

Half of young women in Canada, France, Great Britain, Sweden, and the United States begin sexual intercourse between the ages of 17 and 18.

Source: Reproduced with the permission of The Alan Guttmacher Institute from *Teenage Sexual and Reproductive Behavior in Developed Countries: Can More Progress Be Made?* New York: AGI, 2001, Microsoft® PowerPoint® presentation.

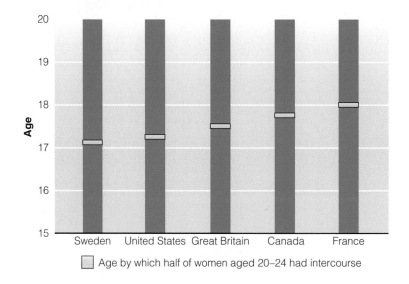

Age by which half of women aged 20–24 had intercourse

Cross-cultural age of first intercourse

There are also some adolescents who engage in anal sexual intercourse. Although studies of the rates of anal intercourse among youths are rare, one study of 350 heterosexual African American youths between the ages of 9 and 15 found that about one-third were sexually active; and, of those, about one-third had engaged in anal intercourse at least once (Stanton et al., 1994). Newer research indicates that the rates of anal intercourse may be increasing in adolescents who make virginity pledges (Brückner & Bearman, 2005). This may be because they believe that engaging in anal intercourse would maintain their virginity status (we will discuss virginity pledges in greater detail later in this chapter).

Homosexual Sexuality Same-sex contact is common in adolescence, both for those who will go on to have predominantly heterosexual relationships and those who will have predominantly homosexual relationships. In fact, some adolescents change their self-identification as heterosexual, lesbian, gay, or bisexual a number of times during adolescence (L. M. Diamond, 2000; Rosario et al., 1996). Until recently, adolescent homosexuality was not treated seriously and was considered simply a "phase"; it was not until 1983 that the American Academy of Pediatrics formally acknowledged the existence of adolescent homosexuality and called on pediatricians to recognize and to address the needs of homosexual youths (Bidwell & Deisher, 1991). Many gay and lesbian adolescents experience heterosexual relationships and heterosexual intercourse during their teenage years, before they identify themselves as lesbian, gay, or bisexual (Saewyc et al., 1998).

It is difficult to determine actual figures for adolescent same-sex contact. Studies of high-school students find that about 10 to 13% report being "unsure" about their sexual orientation, whereas 1 to 6% consider themselves homosexual or bisexual; still, anywhere from 8 to 12% report sexual contact with same-sex partners (Faulkner & Cranston, 1998). Such research, however, relies on self-reports; people may define homosexual differently, deny experiences, or lie due to the stigma on homosexuality that continues to prevail in our society. Many people also do not consider same-sex contact—even repeated contact—indications of homosexuality; they see it as a "passing phase," and thus they do not report it (Bolton & MacEachron, 1988).

Although many homosexual adolescents, especially today, establish healthy and accepting gay identities, discovering one's homosexuality during adolescence can be a painful and difficult process. Even those who report having felt "different" from their peers from as early as 4 or 5 years old may not label that difference as homosexual attraction until adolescence (H. P. Martin, 1991). Many hide their orientation due to fears of being taunted by classmates or rejected by family members; gay adolescents are at higher risk for suicide, substance abuse, and being victimized (S. T. Russell & Joyner, 2001). However, gay students today are also taking more pride in their identity, starting support groups, and suing their schools when the schools fail to protect them from anti-gay harassment. In Chapter 11 we will explore specialized schools for gay, lesbian, bisexual, and transgendered youths.

Other Sexual Situations There are many other types of sexual situations that adolescents can experience. Some teenagers, especially runaways—both male and female—engage in prostitution. Others make money by becoming involved in child pornography, posing nude for pictures, or performing sexual acts. Although there are few comprehensive studies of the results of engaging in prostitution or pornography as an adolescent (or younger), there is every clinical indication that it results in many sexual and psychological difficulties later on (we will discuss coercive sexuality in Chapter 17).

Many of the sexual variations seen in adults, such as transvestism, exhibitionism, and voyeurism, may begin in adolescence, though it is more common for these desires to be expressed in early adulthood. We discuss these sexual variations in depth in Chapter 16.

Ethnic and Racial Differences in Sexual Activity

Several racial and ethnic differences have been found in the age of first sexual intercourse (Blum et al., 2000). African American males were more likely to have lost their virginity and to have had more lifetime partners than were non-African American males (Ku et al., 1998). In fact, in one study the median age (or middle of the range of ages) for African American males to engage in sexual intercourse was 11 years old (Stanton et al., 1994), but other studies have found different results. Other ethnic differences include findings that Native American adolescents show more same-sex behavior than whites (Saewyc et al., 1998), whereas African American adolescents engage in more sexual behavior than Asian adolescents (Upchurch et al., 1998).

The Youth Risk Behavior Surveillance (YRBS), which we discussed earlier in this chapter, found that among 9th- through 12th-grade boys, 72.7% of black students, 52.2% of Latino students, and 43.6% of white students reported having had sexual intercourse (Brener et al., 2002). Among 9th- through 12th-grade girls, the numbers were 65.6% for black students, 45.7% for Latinos, and 44% for whites.

Another study on rates of sexual intercourse found that 30% of over 1,300 Philadelphia 6th graders, averaging under 12 years old, reported having already initiated

Adolescents who have a secure sense of themselves in their ethnic group have been found to have higher self-esteem and better mental health overall (Greig, 2003).

sex byte

Researchers have found a connection between childhood tomboy behavior and later lesbianism (Safir et al., 2003).

Review Question

Explain what we know about the specific sexual behaviors that often occur during adolescence.

sexual intercourse (Grunbaum et al., 2002). Most studies find that females have sex later than males throughout the teen years in all racial groups (O'Connor, 1999). It is important to realize that all such studies rely on self-report and are made more difficult because definitions of sexuality (even intercourse!) differ among young people (Sanders & Reinisch, 1999).

Influences: Peers, Family, and Religion

The decision to engage in sexual contact with another person is a personal one, yet it is influenced by many social factors, including peers, family, and religion. There are a number of other social factors that influence sexual behavior as well, and we will discuss a few of the more important ones.

Peer Influences

Peer pressure is often cited as the most important influence on teen sexual behavior, and adolescence is certainly a time when the influence of one's friends and peers is at a peak. Many adolescents base their own self-worth on peer approval (Rudolph et al., 2005). Even among preadolescents, peer influences are strong; among sixth graders who have had intercourse, students were more likely to initiate intercourse if they thought that peers were having sex and that it would bring them some kind of social gain—that peers would like them more, for example. Those who did not initiate sex were more likely to believe that their behavior would be stigmatized or disapproved of by their peers (Grunbaum et al., 2002).

However, there are two sides to the peer-influence story. On the one hand, there is evidence that a person's perceptions of what his or her peers are doing have a greater influence over sexual behavior than peers' actual behavior, but there is also evidence that has found that adolescents with strong family relationships tend to be less influenced by peers (Kotchick et al., 1999). Among those subject to and applying peer pressure, adolescent males feel the need to "prove" their masculinity, leading to early sexual activity. However, many adolescents cite peer pressure as the number one reason they do not wait to engage in intercourse. The relationship between peer influences and sexual activity in teens is complex.

Relationship With Parents

In general, good parental communication, an atmosphere of honesty and openness in the home, a two-parent home, and reasonable rules about sexuality are among the most important factors associated with adolescents delaying their first intercourse. This may be attributed to the fact that close families are more likely to transmit their sexual values and integrate their children into their religious and moral views. Researchers have also found a correlation between adolescents from close families and the likelihood that they will use contraception when they do have intercourse (Halpern-Felsher et al., 2004). In fact, this is the case among almost all races and ethnic groups (Baumeister et al., 1995; Brooks-Gunn & Furstenberg, 1989; Kotchick et al., 1999).

Overall, it is mothers who tend to be the primary communicators about sexuality to children of both sexes; in one study of Latino youths, mothers did 92% of all communication about sexuality to their teenagers (L. M. Baumeister et al., 1995). The National Longitudinal Study of Adolescent Health (Add Health, 2002) has also found that there is a maternal influence on the timing of first sexual intercourse for adolescents, especially for females. A mother's satisfaction with her relationship with her daughter, disapproval of her daughter having sex, and frequent communication about sex was found to be related to a delay of first sexual intercourse (McNeely et al., 2002).

Research has found that children of both overly strict and overly permissive parents engage in sexual intercourse earlier and more frequently than parents who are moderately strict. Family influences do not stop with parents, however; younger children with sexually active older siblings are also more likely to become sexually active themselves (Werner-Wilson, 1998).

Religion

The National Longitudinal Study of Adolescent Health has found that although the relationship between religiosity and sexual activity is complex, in general, more religious youths tend to delay first sexual intercourse (Hardy & Raffaelli, 2003) and have fewer incidents of premarital sexual activity and fewer sexual partners (Nonnemaker et al., 2003). This correlation may be due to the fact that young people who attend church frequently and who value religion in their lives have less permissive attitudes and are less sexually experienced (White & DeBlassie, 1992). Not only do major Western religions and many other world religions discourage premarital sex, but religious adolescents also tend to develop friendships and relationships within their religious institutions and thus have strong ties to people who are more likely to disapprove of early sexual activity. However, newer research indicates that once sexual intercourse occurs, religious affiliation and frequency of religious attendance has little impact on sexual behaviors (R. Jones et al., 2005).

Review Question

Identify and explain the influences on adolescent sexuality.

Contraception and Pregnancy: Complex Issues

Sexually active American adolescents tend to be erratic users of contraception, as are their likely role models, American adults (see Chapter 13). This may be, in part, because Americans are exposed to mixed messages about contraceptive use. Until recently, words like "condom" have been taboo on television, and contraception is not generally advertised in magazines or other media. Access to contraceptive devices (except condoms) is difficult for teens, and many forms of birth control are expensive. Most other industrialized countries provide free or low-cost birth control to adolescents. Providing free condoms in America has been a very controversial issue. As a result of this erratic use of contraception and the mixed messages, teen pregnancy continues to be a problem in this country.

Contraceptive Use

Teenagers in the United States have the highest rates of pregnancy, childbearing, and abortion among developed countries, and this is primarily because they do not use contraception as reliably (Alan Guttmacher Institute, 2001a). However, data from the National Survey of Family Growth found that contraceptive use among teenagers increased from 1995 to 2002 (Centers for Disease Control and Prevention, 2002b). Over the last decade, condom use among teenagers has increased, whereas use of the birth control pill has decreased (Alan Guttmacher Institute, 1999a). Other data from the National Survey of Family Growth found that 13% of teenagers used long-acting hormonal contraceptive methods, such as implants and injectables (we will discuss these methods more in Chapter 13).

Several factors have been found to be related to contraceptive use in adolescence. An adolescent who is able to talk to his or her mother about sexuality is more likely to use contraception than an adolescent who cannot (Meschke et al., 2000). High satisfaction between adolescents and their mothers has been found to be associated with a lower probability of sexual intercourse and a higher usage of contraception when sexual intercourse does take place (Jaccard & Dittus, 2000). Those who do not use contraception are more likely to be engaging in early sexual intercourse (U.S. Department of Health and Human Services, 1995), be younger than 17, be in an unstable relationship, or engage in infrequent intercourse. Many teens also do not have adequate information about STI risks. However, there have been studies that have found that a substantial majority of teenagers use contraception without interruption for extended periods (Glei, 1999).

Although gay, lesbian, and bisexual youths may not need contraception for birth control purposes, they do need it for STI protection. Research has found that gays and lesbians are less likely to use condoms than straight youths or those who are unsure about their sexual orientation (Saewyc et al., 1998). Birth control responsibilities among teens, as among adults, often fall on the females. The prevailing attitude seems to be that females become pregnant; therefore, females must either carry the baby for 9 months or undergo abortion.

It is often difficult to impress on teenage boys the need for shared contraceptive responsibility. Misinformation about contraception is widespread among teens, and parents seem to be doing little to correct it. Most studies find relatively low rates of parental communication about sex in general and contraception in particular, with children reporting far fewer and less involved discussions about it than their parents report (Jaccard et al., 1998; King & Lorusso, 1997). Baker and colleagues (1988) found that parents who communicated to their children about sex did have significant influence on whether or not adolescents used contraception when they had sex. We will discuss contraceptive use in more detail in Chapter 13.

Teenage Pregnancy

Teen pregnancy is probably the most studied aspect of adolescent sexual behavior because of its many impacts on the life of the teenager, the teenager's family, and society as a whole. Although the number of sexually active adolescents is increasing, teenage pregnancy rates have declined over the last few years. The primary reason for this has been an increase in contraceptive use (Alan Guttmacher Institute, 2001b; J. G. Kahn et al., 1999).

However, as we pointed out earlier, the United States still has the highest rates of teenage pregnancy, abortion, and childbirth of any Western country. Studies have found that the likelihood of a child of 14 or younger becoming pregnant in the United States is 7 times higher than in the Netherlands, 9 times higher than in Europe as a whole, and 17 times higher than in Japan (Meschke et al., 2000; Society for Adolescent Medicine, 1991; see Figure 8.6).

Teen pregnancies do not preclude teen mothers from living healthy, fulfilling lives. In fact, there are many examples of teenagers who become pregnant and raise healthy babies while pursuing their own interests. However, the problems a teenage mother faces are many, especially if there is no partner participating in the child's care. Babies born to teens tend to have lower birth weight, and the mothers have more difficult labors and are more likely to die in childbirth.

Teen mothers are more likely to drop out of school, have poorer physical and mental health, and be on welfare than their nonchildbearing peers, and their children tend have poorer health and cognitive abilities, more behavioral problems, and fewer educational opportunities (Meschke et al., 2000). Teen parenting also has an impact on others, such as the parents of the teens (who may end up having to take care of their children's children), and on society in general, because these parents are more likely to need government assistance. Finally, children raised by a teenage mother are more likely to engage in earlier sexual intercourse and to face pregnancy than do children raised by older mothers (O'Connor et al., 1999; Woodward et al., 2001).

Pregnancy Rates Although there have been dramatic decreases in teenage pregnancy rates in the United States in the last decade, the United States still has higher levels of adolescent pregnancy than other Western industrialized countries (Bennett & Assefi, 2005). More than three-quarters of pregnancies to teens each year are unintended. Nationwide, the 1996 pregnancy rate was 97 pregnancies per 1,000 women aged 15 to 19, down from 107 per 1,000 in 1986 and a drop of 17% from its peak of 117 per 1,000 teens in 1990 (Alan Guttmacher Institute, 2001b). Among teenagers 14 and younger, the rate in 1996 was 13 pregnancies per 1,000 females, down from about 17 per 1,000 from the mid-1980s until 1993. U.S. teenagers are more likely than teenagers in other developed countries to become pregnant unintentionally (Alan Guttmacher Institute, 2001a).

Birth Rates Birth rates in the United States have been declining since about 1957, even as pregnancy rates have risen, because a high per-

Figure 8.6

Birth and abortion rates per 1,000 women aged 15–19.

Source: Reproduced with the permission of The Alan Guttmacher Institute from *Teenage Sexual and Reproductive Behavior in Developed Countries: Can More Progress Be Made?* New York: AGI, 2001, Microsoft® PowerPoint® presentation.

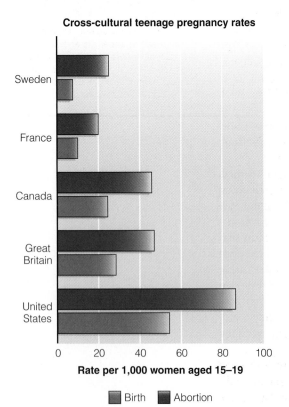

Cross-cultural teenage pregnancy rates

Rate per 1,000 women aged 15–19

■ Birth ■ Abortion

Note: Data are for mid-1990s.

centage of teen pregnancies end in abortion. Teen birth rates actually reached close to an all-time low in 1978! Then why all the concern over teen pregnancy? The problem is that, due to the post–World War II baby boom, there are many more teenagers. In 1970, there were 43% more teenagers in the United States than in the previous decade, so even though rates fell, the numbers of babies born to teenagers rose (C. W. Williams, 1991). Recently, however, the numbers of births to teenagers have been declining. In 1986, there were 50 births per 1,000 women aged 15 to 19. The rate rose rapidly to 62 per 1,000 in 1991, an increase of 24%, before declining over the next 5 years until, in 1996, 54 births occurred per 1,000 teenage women (still a higher rate than that in 1986; Alan Guttmacher Institute, 2001a).

In studies of teen pregnancy, most of the focus has been on the mothers, who often bear the brunt of the emotional, personal, and financial costs of childbearing. Adolescent fathers are more difficult to study. Teenage fathers may run as soon as they learn of their mate's pregnancy or become uninvolved soon after, and thus the problem of single mothers raising children can be traced in part to the lack of responsibility of teen fathers. Society asks little of the teenage male, and there are few social pressures on him to take responsibility for his offspring.

Yet many of these fathers also feel isolated or rejected or are treated punitively (Bolton & MacEachron, 1988). Today many adolescent fathers do accept their role in both pregnancy and parenthood and realistically assess their responsibilities toward the mother and child. Many feel both stress over the birth and guilt. Ideally, fathers should be reintegrated into the lives of their children and should be expected to take equal responsibility for the results of their sexual activities. However, if teen fathers neglect their partners and children, it is at least in part due to the fact that society does not demand or even encourage that they do otherwise.

Abortion   The legalization of abortion in America in 1973 had the greatest impact on the ratio of teen pregnancies to births. Teenagers accounted for more than a quarter of all abortions in the United States in 1985 (Hudson, 1991). Yet although teenage abortion rates varied little during the 1980s, they began a steady decline in the 1990s. By 1996, the rate was 31% lower than the teenage abortion rate a decade earlier (Alan Guttmacher Institute, 1999a). In 2000, one-third of pregnancies among 15- to 18-year-olds was terminated through abortion (Alan Guttmacher Institute, 2004). However, there are state-by-state variations in these numbers. For example, 50–60% of teenage pregnancies in New Jersey, New York, Massachusetts, and the District of Columbia ended in abortion, whereas only 13% in Kentucky and Utah ended in abortion (Alan Guttmacher Institute, 2004). We will discuss the emotional and personal aspects of the abortion decision in Chapter 13.

The Effects of Race and Poverty   Adolescent parenthood affects every race, every income group, and every part of American society; it is not just a problem of the inner-city poor. Historically, white teenagers have had lower birthrates than African American adolescents or Latino adolescents, a trend that continued in the 1990s. Though through much of the 1990s, African American teenagers had the highest rates of pregnancy, birth, and abortion, all three rates dropped by about 20% between 1990 and 1996. Because the birthrate declined more steeply among African American than among white teenagers, the gap between these two groups narrowed. By contrast, birthrates among Latino teenagers increased through the early 1990s, only taking a small dip after 1994, even though pregnancy and abortion rates declined slightly. As a result, Latino teenagers now have the highest birthrates of the three groups (Alan Guttmacher Institute, 1999a).

Unmarried mothers and their children of all races are more likely to live in poverty than any other segment of the population. Even though only about one-third of teen pregnancies happen to people officially listed as "poor," many others are to people just above the official poverty line. For these mothers, pregnancy may carry with it the end of her educational history and decreased job opportunities. Society has become less willing to grant benefits to teenage and single mothers, believing (despite most data to the contrary) that such aid simply perpetuates dependency on welfare and leads to the children of teenage mothers becoming teenage mothers themselves.

What Should Be Done About Teen Pregnancy? What is it about American society that seems to foster such high rates of teenage pregnancy? A complex series of factors is at work. American society is extremely conflicted about the issue of sexuality in general. Our teens are exposed to sexual scenes in movies and television, yet we hesitate to discuss sex frankly with them. We allow advertising to use blatantly sexual messages and half-dressed models, yet we will not permit advertising for birth control; and there is significant resistance to sex education in the schools.

Today, when teenagers do become pregnant, opportunities may be limited; it is difficult to have a baby and attend high school all day or work at a job. The United States is far behind most other Western countries in providing day care services that would help single or young parents care for their children. Better counseling, birth control, day care services, and hope for the future can help assure that the teenagers who are at risk for unwanted pregnancies and the children of those unwanted pregnancies are cared for by our society.

Sexually Transmitted Infections: Education and Prevention

Although we will discuss sexually transmitted infections in great detail in Chapter 15, here we will briefly talk about adolescent rates of STIs. In the United States, approximately 4 million teenagers are infected with an STI every year (Boonstra, 2002b). Adolescents between 15 and 19 years old account for one-third of all gonorrhea and chlamydia cases in the United States. It is estimated that in the United States, two teenagers are infected with an STI every hour of every day (Boonstra, 2002b). Preventing STIs and teenage pregnancy are both important goals of sex education programs. In the following section we will discuss the importance of sexuality education and what is being taught in schools today.

Review Question

Identify and discuss the reasons that adolescents are erratic users of contraception.

WHAT CHILDREN NEED TO KNOW: SEXUALITY EDUCATION

Sexuality education inspires powerful emotions and a considerable amount of controversy. In fact, it may be one of the most heated topics in the field of sexuality, as different sides debate whether and how sexuality education programs should be implemented in the schools.

Hygiene and Sexuality Education: Then and Now

People have always been curious about sex. However, it was only in the 20th century that the movement to develop formal and effective sexuality education programs began. Public discussion of sexuality was due, in part, to the moral purity movement of the late 19th century and the medicalization of the sex movement in the early 20th century.

Several developments in the United States set the stage for sexuality education. Concern over skyrocketing rates of venereal diseases (what we now refer to as sexually transmitted infections) in the early 1900s resulted in the formation of two groups, the American Society of Sanitary and Moral Prophylaxis and the American Federation for Sex Hygiene. Although these groups helped to further the cause of sexuality education, they concentrated their attention on STIs. Their approach was to use sexuality education to explain biology and anatomy and to address adolescents' natural sexual curiosity. School sexuality education was very scientific and avoided all discussions of interpersonal sexuality.

Starting in the early 1900s, sexuality education was implemented by various national youth groups, including the YMCA, YWCA, Girl Scouts, Boy Scouts, and 4-H Clubs (see the SexByte about the Boy Scouts on page 234). These programs were developed mainly to demonstrate to young people the responsibilities required in parenting and to discourage early childbearing. More controversial, however, has been whether to include sexuality education as part of the public school curriculum.

In the United States, for example, the opposition to sexuality education has often been due to two complementary attitudes: first, that sexuality is private, should be discouraged in children, and is best discussed in the context of a person's moral and religious beliefs; and second, that public schools are by their nature public, cannot discuss sex without giving children implicit permission to be sexual, and should not promote the moral or religious beliefs of any particular group. The result of these conflicting attitudes was the belief that sexuality education was best performed by parents in the home. However, today we know that the majority of families do not know how to teach adequate sex education to their children (Kakavoulis, 2001).

Attitudes toward sexuality, however, began to change, and people began having sex earlier and more frequently. Sexuality education was seen as more important, due not only to the high teenage pregnancy rate (which shatters the illusion that kids are not actually having sex) but also due to AIDS. Television and other media contributed by being so sex saturated that sexuality was no longer a private topic. Yet, even with all these changes, many still believe that public educational institutions will present a view of sexuality that they object to, and so they still oppose sexuality education in the United States.

Today, the majority of states either recommend or require sexuality education in public schools. However, the content that each state allows often varies. For example, there is little guidance for teachers in North Dakota, yet in South Carolina there are severe restrictions. Contraception cannot be mentioned outside of marriage and homosexuality cannot be taught unless the teaching is about sexually transmitted infections (Sexuality Information and Education Council of the United States, 2004b).

In the 1950s, sexuality education courses began appearing in colleges and universities in the United States. One of the first sexuality education and counseling programs in the United States was initiated at Yale University. It was very popular, and, as a result, similar programs were implemented at other institutions. Do you know how long the sexuality course you are taking has been taught at your institution? It might be interesting to find out the background and history of the course.

Evolving Goals of Sexuality Education

Sexuality education can have different goals. Knowledge acquisition, improving personal psychological adjustment, and improving relationships between partners are popular goals. Early sexuality education programs focused primarily on increasing knowledge levels and educating students about the risks of pregnancy (Kirby, 1992), believing that if knowledge levels were increased, then students would understand why it was important for them to avoid unprotected sexual intercourse. Soon sexuality education programs added values clarification and skills, including communication and decision-making skills. These second-generation sexuality education programs were based on the idea that if knowledge levels were increased and if students became more aware of their own values and had better decision-making skills, they would have an easier time talking to their partners and evaluating their own behavior.

Today, **comprehensive sexuality education** tries to help students develop a positive view of sexuality. The Guidelines for Comprehensive Sexuality Education (Sexuality Information and Education Council of the United States, 2004a) are a framework designed to help promote the development of comprehensive sexuality education programs nationwide. Originally developed in 1990, the guidelines were revised again in 2004 and include four main goals for sexuality education:

1. To provide accurate information about human sexuality.
2. To provide an opportunity for young people to question, explore, and assess their sexual attitudes.
3. To help young people develop interpersonal skills, including communication, decision making, peer refusal, and assertiveness skills that will allow them to create satisfying relationships.
4. To help young people develop the ability to exercise responsibility regarding sexual relationships.

comprehensive sexuality education programs
Programs that often begin in kindergarten and continue through 12th grade, presenting a wide variety of topics to help students develop their own skills while learning factual information.

The guidelines have also been adapted for use outside the United States and are being used in both Cairo and Beijing to help design and implement a variety of sexuality education programs.

Why Sexuality Education Is Important

Although many people claim that knowledge about sexuality may be harmful, studies have found that it is the lack of sexuality education, ignorance about sexual issues, or unresolved curiosity that is harmful (S. Gordon, 1986). Students who participate in comprehensive sexuality education programs are less permissive about premarital sex than students who do not take these courses. Accurate knowledge about sex may also lead to a more positive self-image and self-acceptance. Sexuality affects almost all aspects of human behavior and relationships with other persons. Therefore, if we understand and accept our own sexuality and the sexuality of others, we will have more satisfying relationships. Some experts believe that not talking to children about sex prior to adolescence is a primary cause of sexual problems later in life (Calderone, 1983).

Another reason to support sexuality education is that children receive a lot of information about sex through the media, and much of it is not based on fact. The media and peers are often primary sources of information about sexuality. Sex is present in the songs children listen to, the magazines they read, the shows they watch on television, and on the Internet. Although it is true that there are a growing number of educational sites on the Internet dedicated to sexuality education (Goldman & Bradley, 2001), there are also many poor sources of information on the web.

Proponents of sexuality education believe that sexual learning occurs even when there are no formalized sexuality education programs. When teachers or parents avoid children's questions or appear embarrassed or evasive, they reinforce children's ideas that sex is secret, mysterious, and bad (Milton et al., 2001). Sexuality education does not push teenagers to engage in sexual behavior earlier, nor does it increase the frequency of sexual behavior or number of sexual partners (Sexuality Information and Education Council of the United States, 2001).

As adolescents approach puberty, they may feel anxious about their bodily changes or their relationships with other people. Many teenagers feel uncomfortable asking ques-

SEX in Real Life

Parents and Anxiety: Where Does It Come From?

When parents discuss the concept of sexuality education for their children, many report feeling very anxious and insecure about their own abilities. Pamela Wilson suggests that anxiety comes from many places, including:

- *Fear:* Many parents worry that something bad will happen to their children if they start talking to them about sex. They might be impregnated or impregnate their partner; be raped or rape someone; or even become infected with an STI such as AIDS. Parents also worry that they will wait too long, start too early, say the wrong thing, or give misinformation. The biggest fear is that providing sexuality education will take away a child's innocence.
- *Lack of comfort:* Because most parents did not talk to their parents about sex, many feel uncomfortable in pre-

senting it themselves. Those who did talk about it usually talked with their mothers. This causes many fathers to feel especially uncomfortable facing the prospect of educating their sons and daughters.
- *Lack of skills:* Parents often do not know how to say what they want to say. Some resort to a lecture about the "birds and bees," whereas others simply ask their children, "Do you have any questions?"
- *Misinformation:* Many parents do not have the necessary facts about sexuality education. Having received little sexuality education themselves, many believe in the myths about sexuality.

SOURCE: Adapted from Wilson (1994, pp. 1–2).

tions and may be pressured by their peers to engage in sexual activity when they do not feel ready. Giving teenagers information about sex can help them to deal with these changes. The majority of parents, teachers, and students want sexuality education to be taught in secondary schools and high schools (Sexuality Information and Education Council of the United States, 2005a). Many students, however, believe that school-based sex education programs are usually "too late" for them because they have already learned information from other sources or have become sexually active by the time the programs start (Buston & Wight, 2002).

Sexuality Education Programs

In the United States, each state is responsible for developing its own sexuality educational programs. Therefore, the programs vary greatly. There are four main types of sexuality programs: comprehensive; abstinence-based HIV-prevention; abstinence-only; and abstinence-only-until-marriage. Comprehensive sexuality programs, which we've already been discussing, are those that begin in kindergarten and continue through 12th grade—they include a wide variety of topics and help students to develop their own skills and learn factual information. There are also a variety of different abstinence-based programs. **Abstinence-based HIV-prevention programs** emphasize the importance of abstinence but also include information about sexual behavior, contraception, and disease prevention. **Abstinence-only programs** emphasize abstinence from all sexual behaviors and do not provide information about contraception or disease prevention. Finally, **abstinence-only-until-marriage programs** are similar to abstinence-only programs but present marriage as the only morally acceptable context for all sexual activity.

Abstinence-only programs began in the early 1990s when there was a proliferation of sexuality education programs that used fear to discourage students from engaging in sexual behavior. These programs include mottos such as "Control your urgin'—be a virgin," "Don't be a louse—wait for your spouse," "Do the right thing—wait for the ring," or "Pet your dog—not your date." Critical information about topics such as anatomy or STIs is omitted from these programs, and there is an overreliance on religion, the need to avoid sexual behavior, and the negative consequences of sexual behavior. These negative consequences are often exaggerated, and sexual behavior is portrayed as dangerous and harmful. It is estimated that fewer than half of all U.S. public schools offer information on contraception, and the majority of public schools today teach abstinence-only education (Starkman & Rajani, 2002).

Federal funding for abstinence-based sexuality education has grown significantly since 1996. Federal funds can only be used for sexuality education if they teach abstinence only until marriage, which often excludes information about contraception and sexually transmitted diseases. In fiscal year 2005, the federal government proposed spending approximately $170 million on abstinence-only sexuality education programs, which was more than twice the amount that was spent in fiscal year 2001 (Waxman, 2004a). Since 1996, the U.S. government has spent over 1 billion dollars on abstinence-only educational programs (Boonstra, 2004), but as of 2005 there was no federal funding for comprehensive sexuality education (Sexuality Information and Education Council of the United States, 2005a). In 1996, the federal government also passed a law outlining the federal definition of abstinence education. These programs teach:

- abstinence from sexual activity outside marriage as the expected standard for all school-age children
- that sexual activity outside of the context of marriage is likely to have harmful psychological and physical effects
- that bearing children out of wedlock is likely to have harmful consequences for the child, the child's parents, and society

The majority of Americans believe that sexuality education should emphasize abstinence but also include contraception and STI information (Dailard, 2001b). Some of

abstinence-based HIV-prevention sexuality education programs
Sexuality education programs that emphasize abstinence but also include information about sexual behavior, contraception, and disease prevention.

abstinence-only programs
Sexuality education programs that emphasize abstinence from all sexual behaviors; no contraceptive or disease prevention is provided.

abstinence-only-until-marriage programs
Sexuality education programs that emphasize abstinence but present marriage as the only morally acceptable context for sexual activity.

the abstinence-only programs use scare tactics to encourage abstinence, such as Teen-Aid, which claims the consequences of premarital sexual behavior to be:

> [L]oss of reputation; limitations in dating/marriage choices; negative effects on sexual adjustment; negative effects on happiness (premarital sex, especially with more than one person, has been linked to the development of emotional illness [and the] loss of self-esteem); family conflict and possible premature separation from the family; confusion regarding personal value (e.g., "Am I loved because I am me, because of my personality and looks, or because I am a sex object?"); and loss of goals. (Kantor, 1992, p. 4)

A happy and healthy future is also promoted as a reason for not engaging in sexual behavior. Facing Reality, a program for senior high school students, claims that there are rewards for those who avoid premarital sexual behavior. These include:

> continuing education, being able to serve others, mastering emotions and impulses, sharing family values for a lifetime, making more friends, becoming a leader, concentrating on important tasks, remaining physically healthy, raising a healthy family, making a clearheaded marriage choice, pursuing spiritual goals, making permanent commitments, excelling in athletics, giving example to others, creating positive peer pressure, enjoying a beautiful time of life, taking on greater responsibilities, [and] having piece of mind. (Kantor, 1992, p. 4)

Do abstinence-only programs work? This is the important question, and the responses will differ depending on whom you ask. Supporters of abstinence-only programs often have very strong feelings about comprehensive sexuality education programs and claim that talking only about abstinence lets children and young adults know that this is the only choice. Those who believe in these programs would say that they are effective.

On the other hand, your author, along with many sexuality education experts, believes that strictly abstinence-only programs may do more harm than good. They often fail to provide necessary factual information, and they support many myths and stereotypes about various topics in human sexuality (such as sexual assault, gender differences, sexual orientation, pregnancy options, and STIs). Over 80% of abstinence-only educational programs contain "false, misleading, or distorted" information about reproductive health (including false information about contraceptive effectiveness, misrepresented abortion risks, and a high degree of scientific error; Waxman, 2004b). Overall, abstinence-only programs have not been found to significantly change adolescents' values and attitudes about, or their intentions to engage in, premarital sexual activity (Sather, 2002; Starkman & Rajani, 2002). In fact, the research has also shown that when students who have had abstinence-based sexuality programs do become sexually active, they often fail to use condoms or any type of contraception (Brückner & Bearman, 2005; Walters, 2005).

Before we move on to heterosexism in sexuality education, one more comment deserves your attention. Sexuality educators routinely discuss the importance of communication in their sexuality courses; however, isn't it interesting that many educators are not permitted to discuss many aspects of human sexuality in high schools today (Fields, 2001b)? For example, in Utah (which has the strictest state policies on sexuality education), a teacher is not allowed to answer a student's questions about contraception (Alan Guttmacher Institute, 2001c). What message does this send about the importance of communication?

A Heterosexual Bias in Sexuality Education

A recent criticism of sexuality education programs is that there is an underlying assumption that human sexuality is "heterosexual" sexuality (Petrovic, 2002). If same-sex behavior is left out of the sexuality education curriculum, in essence this is saying that gays, lesbians, and bisexuals are "not fully sexual human beings" (M. Ellis, 1984). A discussion of same-sex issues is often left out in elementary, junior high, and high school sex education, and in college-level sexuality

Review Question

Identify and discuss the various types of sexuality education programs.

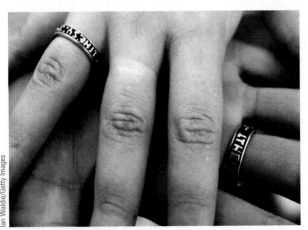

Celibacy rings are often worn by those who pledge not to engage in sexual intercourse until marriage.

Human Sexuality in a Diverse World

Sexuality Education in Other Cultures

In a study done by the Alan Guttmacher Institute, the United States led nearly all developed countries in the world in the rates of teenage pregnancy, abortion, and teenage childbearing (see Figures 8.3 through 8.6). Overall, countries that have liberal attitudes toward sexuality, easily accessible birth control services for teenagers, and formal and informal sexuality education programs have the lowest rates of teenage pregnancy, abortion, and childbearing. Following, we review sexuality education in a variety of places.

The Netherlands

The Netherlands has the world's lowest rates of teenage pregnancy, abortion, and childbearing. This may be due to the liberal attitudes toward sexuality education, high quality of information in sexuality classes, and widely available and confidential contraceptive services. It is estimated that 80% of Dutch secondary schools offer at least 4 to 5 hours of AIDS education (Drenth & Slob, 2004). The Dutch government also supports a variety of sexuality organizations and finances mass-media campaigns aimed at educating the public about sexuality. A Dutch broadcasting company runs a weekly sexuality talk radio show, and it is estimated that there are over 250,000 listeners (Drenth & Slob, 2004).

Sweden

Over the years, Sweden has become known as the world leader in sexuality education. In 1897, the first sex education courses were organized by a female physician (Trost, 2004), and in 1956 sex education became mandatory in all schools. There are national requirements for all sexuality education courses, a national curriculum, and a national handbook to guide teachers' training for these courses. Starting at age 7, students learn about menstruation, intercourse, masturbation, contraception, pregnancy, and childbirth. From ages 10 to 13 they are taught about puberty, sexually transmitted infections, homosexuality, and pedophilia. At the next level of learning, students are taught about sex roles, premarital sex, abortion, pornography, HIV/AIDS, and prostitution. Finally, at the college level, students are taught about sexual desire, sexual orientation, and sexual dysfunction. Sweden also has approximately 150 youth clinics, offering information, education, and contraceptive services (Trost, 2004). These clinics began forming in an attempt to reduce the teenage abortions rates (a law passed in 1975 allows for free abortions).

England

Sex education in England is a compulsory part of the National Curriculum—Science, and throughout England students participate in a comprehensive sex education program (Hilton, 2003). Studies have found that the programs have effectively prepared students and increased their skills (Douglas et al., 2001).

Brazil

Brazil's annual Carnival is a time of liberation from the sexually repressive ways of Brazilian society. During Carnival, television stations become much less conservative and air naked men and women, many engaging in public sexual activities. Yet, even with the open attitudes about sexuality during Carnival, it has been difficult to establish sexuality education in Brazilian schools. The culture is highly patriarchal and has rigid gender roles. There are few sexuality education programs in public schools today, but they first appeared in some of the private schools in the late 1980s (Freitas, 2004).

Japan

In 1974, the Japanese Association for Sexuality Education (JASE) was founded to help establish comprehensive sexuality education in the schools, although abstinence education was very popular in Japan. As in the United States, popular sources of sex information in Japan include friends and older same-sex peers, magazines, and television.

In 1986, a new sexuality education curriculum was distributed to all middle and high schools in Japan (Kitazawa, 1994). In 1992, the Japanese Ministry of Education revised the sexuality curriculum and approved the discussion of secondary sex characteristics in coeducational fifth-grade classes. In fact, 1992 was called the "First Year of Sexuality Education," and sexuality education was required in schools. Prior to this time, there was no discussion of sexuality in elementary schools at all (Hatano & Shimazaki, 2004).

Many teachers in the elementary schools felt very uncomfortable with these changes. Talking about sexuality is very anxiety producing, both for teachers and many Japanese citizens. In addition, there is no formal sexuality training for these teachers.

Today, however, the number of educators interested in teaching sexuality education is increasing. Teacher workshops and educational programs add to the increasing comfort levels with sexuality. Overall, however, these open attitudes toward sexuality education have not been met without opposition. In fact, sexuality education has been blamed for the changing norms in sexuality that resulted in an increase in divorce and a destruction of the family.

Russia

Although the majority of Russian teenagers and their parents and teachers favor sex education in the schools, Russia has no formal sexuality education program (Kon, 2004). Conservative forces, along with various churches, are adamantly opposed to sex education and have instituted an aggressive campaign against the implementation of sex education programs in the schools. A national opinion poll in 1990 found that only 13% of parents in Russia have ever talked to their children about sexuality (Kon, 2004).

education courses same-sex behavior is often discussed during only one or two class periods. The rest of the semester is spent exploring various aspects of heterosexuality (such as premarital, marital, and extramarital sex, contraception, and abortion). Textbooks on human sexuality typically offer one chapter on sexual orientation, discussing primarily what causes it. Conversely, very little, if any, attention is paid to what causes heterosexuality. Heterosexism is a problem in almost all topics in academia today, but it creates particular problems in the field of sexuality education.

Studying Effects and Results

The main way that researchers determine whether or not a sexuality program is successful is by measuring behavioral changes after a program has been presented. Currently, the standard behavioral measures include vaginal intercourse, pregnancy, and contraceptive use (Remez, 2000). If the rates of vaginal intercourse increase after sexuality education, a program is judged to be ineffective. If, on the other hand, rates of intercourse and pregnancy decrease, a program is successful. So, what are the effects of sex education programs? Do sexuality education courses change people's actual sexual behavior? It is difficult to measure and evaluate these behavioral changes after a sexuality education program, but it appears that there are some limited changes.

Comprehensive sexuality programs have been found to be the most successful at helping adolescents delay their involvement in sexual intercourse (Kirby, 2001) and help protect adolescents from STIs and unintended pregnancies (Starkman & Rajani, 2002; UNAIDS, 1997). In addition, sexuality education programs that teach contraception and communication skills have been found to delay the onset of sexual intercourse or reduce the frequency of sexual intercourse, reduce the number of sexual partners, and increase the use of contraception (Sexuality Information and Education Council of the United States, 2001). Abstinence-only programs, on the other hand, have not yielded successful results in delaying the onset of intercourse (Sexuality Information and Education Council of the United States, 2001). Overall, there have been no published reports of abstinence-based programs providing significant effects on delaying sexual intercourse (Kirby, 2001). Although many who teach abstinence-only classes claim that these programs are successful, outside experts have found the programs to be ineffective and methodologically unsound (B. Wilcox et al., 1996).

Over the last few years, "virginity pledges," whereby teens sign pledge cards and promise to remain a virgin until marriage, have become popular. The Add Health Study, which we discussed earlier in this chapter, found that teenagers who took a virginity pledge were less likely to become sexually active in the months that follow the pledge than students who didn't take a pledge (Dailard, 2001). However, these types of programs have also been found to put teenagers at higher risk of pregnancy and sexually transmitted infections (Brückner & Bearman, 2005).

Why do you think this might be? Researchers believe that it is because signing the pledge may make a teenager unable to accept the responsibilities of using contraception when he or she decides to engage in sexual intercourse. One study found that 88% of students who pledged virginity engaged in premarital sex, and when they did they were less likely to use contraception (Brückner & Bearman, 2005; Planned Parenthood Federation of America, 2005).

Some other questions deserve our attention before we end our discussion about sexuality education. Do you think that sex education should be concerned with the attitudes and values of the students who take these courses? Of course. But measuring attitudes or changes in attitudes and values is difficult at best. Behavioral changes are easier to measure, and this is why they are often the only measures used. Also, it's important to realize that researchers need to measure long-term behavioral and attitude changes, not simply the short-term changes (Kirby, 1999). Do the students maintain the behavioral changes a month after a program? What about a year later? Two years? We need to track students in order to evaluate the behavioral changes. All of these are important questions that sexuality researchers need to address.

Overall, we do know that students of comprehensive sex education programs can increase knowledge levels, affect the attitudes, and/or change their behaviors (Dailard,

2001). The most successful programs were those in which schools and parents worked together in developing the program. However, many effects of sexuality education programs may not be quantifiable. Programs may help students to feel more confident, be more responsible, improve their mental health, and increase their communication skills. We rarely measure for these changes.

It will be interesting to monitor the changes in sexuality education over the next few years. In 2001, Surgeon General David Satcher issued his Call to Action to Promote Sexual Health (U.S. Surgeon General, 2001). This report stressed the importance of finding "common ground" to promote sexual health and responsible sexual behavior. Since this report, many organizations have joined forces to support the Family Life Education Act, which is a new comprehensive sexuality education policy. This act would help ensure that sexuality education provides information not only about abstinence, but also about contraception and STIs. Abstinence is a key component of sexuality education, and supporters of this act believe that we need to help adolescents understand the consequences of sexual behavior. Your author is hopeful that in the future all sexuality education will be comprehensive and will help adolescents to understand themselves and their choices more fully.

In summary, childhood sexuality is an evolving phenomenon. Sexual knowledge and sexual behavior are common among children in today's society, in which sexuality is so much a part of our culture. But knowledge does not necessarily mean that children must act on it; there are still very good reasons to encourage children and teenagers to think carefully about sexuality and to advise them to refrain from expressing their sexual feelings physically until the time is right for them.

What we do know is that a close and open parent–adolescent relationship that allows for open communication about sexuality has been found to decrease adolescent sexual behaviors and reduce the influence of peers with regard to sexual issues (Meschke et al., 2000). This is an important finding and is partially responsible for the later ages of first intercourse, fewer teenage pregnancies, and fewer numbers of sexual partners. Open communication about sexuality, along with a good, solid sexuality education, encourages this kind of responsible sexual behavior.

Review Question

Discuss research findings on the effects of sexuality education.

Chapter Review

ACTIVE SUMMARY

1. Throughout most of history, children were treated as miniature adults and concepts such as (a) _____ did not exist. Children were considered (b) _____. Four large-scale (c) _____ studies have been done on adolescent sexuality. These include the National Survey of Family Growth, the National Longitudinal Study of (d) _____ _____, the National Longitudinal Study of (e) _____ Health, and the Youth Risk Behavior Surveillance System.

2. Sexual anatomy is (a) _____ even before we are born. Male babies are capable of (b) _____, whereas female babies are capable of (c) _____ _____. The single most important aspect of infant development is the child's (d) _____ with his or her caretakers. Gender identity develops between the ages of (e) _____ and (f) _____. It takes a little longer to develop (g) _____ _____, which is the realization that gender will not change during their lifetime. Self-stimulation is (h) _____ at this age.

3. In early childhood, physical development continues. In fact, children may learn more in the first few years of childhood about the nature of their bodies than they learn in the (a) _____ of their lives. Child sex play is common at this age and many parents or caregivers need to teach that this behavior is (b) _____. Children learn that their genitals are private and must be (c) _____ _____ in public. Boys are often taught about the (d) _____, yet it is rare for girls to be taught about the (e) _____.

4. Sometime between the ages of 6 and 12, a child experiences the first outward signs of (a) _____. In girls the first sign of puberty is the appearance of (b) _____ _____, and soon they will experience (c) _____. Preadolescent boys experience frequent erections, and soon they will experience (d) _____. Typically boys don't (e) _____ anyone about this event. Prepubescence is the age of (f) _____ _____.

5. During preadolescence, it is common to participate in (a) _____, sexual fantasies, and sex (b) _____. A sexual script is the sum total of a person's (c) _____ knowledge about sexuality and it can have different themes. All of our intimate relationships influence our sexuality. We learn from our parents and our (d) _____. Sexual contact with siblings is (e) _____ at this age and has been found to be harmful only when there is (f) _____ _____ used or a large age difference between siblings.

6. Puberty prepares the body for adult sexuality and reproduction. Adolescence often includes our (a) _____ and (b) _____ reactions to puberty. There are many (c) _____, emotional, and cognitive changes during this time. The three major stages of physiological sexual development include (d) _____ _____ _____, puberty, and (e) _____. Some of the first signs of female puberty include the development of breast buds, the appearance of (f) _____ _____, a widening of the hips, a rounding of the physique, and the onset of (g) _____.

7. Unlike ovulation, which occurs (a) _____ in female puberty, spermatogenesis and ejaculation occur (b) _____ in male puberty. Some of the first signs of male puberty include body changes, increased (c) _____ _____, a growth spurt, and (d) _____ deepening. For the most part, early development in boys is usually not as (e) _____ as it is in girls.

8. Adolescents tend to fantasize about sex, and (a) _____ sharply increases, especially for boys. Mature sexual experimentation begins, often with (b) _____. Girls' body image tends to (c) _____ as they progress through adolescence, whereas boys' tends to (d) _____. However, girls' general self-image tends to (e) _____ as they grow older, whereas boys' tends to (f) _____.

9. First intercourse is usually (a) _____ but rarely spontaneous. Adolescents are (b) _____ users of contraception, which, coupled with increasing sexual activity, results in high (c) _____ rates. The United States has the highest rates of pregnancy, (d) _____, and (e) _____ of any Western country.

10. Opposition to sexuality education has often been due to two attitudes: one says that sexuality is (a) _____ and two that public schools cannot discuss sex without giving children implicit permission to be (b) _____ and should not promote certain (c) _____. Individual states can (d) _____ that schools provide sexuality education.

11. The most common goals for sexuality education include increasing (a) _____, understanding one's own (b) _____ and (c) _____, reducing unhealthy (d) _____ behavior, and respecting the (e) _____ and values of others.

12. Sexuality education programs are often either (a) _____ or (b) _____-based. Although many Americans believe that (c) _____ should be included in sexuality education, they also believe that information on (d) _____ and (e) _____ should be included.

13. Sexuality education often has a strong (a) _____ bias, and educators must be knowledgeable about this bias. Overall, sexuality programs can increase (b) _____ levels, affect (c) _____, and/or change the (d) _____ of the students who take them.

Critical Thinking Questions

1. Should masturbation in young children be encouraged, ignored, or discouraged? What message do you think it sends to a child when parents encourage their child to discover and play with toes, ears, and fingers, but pull the child's hands away when he or she discovers his or her genitals?

2. Young children often play sex games, like "doctor," with each other. What age differences do you think pose the biggest problems? Are sex games acceptable? Why or why not? How should a parent respond?

3. Where should children get their sexual knowledge? Should children learn everything from their parents, school, or the church? Are some things actually better coming from a particular place? Explain.

4. Why do you think adolescence is a difficult time for many people? What can be done to make the transition through adolescence easier?

5. People today are having sex relatively early in life, often in their middle or early teens. Do you think this is a good time to experiment with intercourse, or do you think it is too early? What do you think is the "ideal" age to lose your virginity, and why?

Check It Out

Levine, Judith. (2002). **Harmful to minors: The perils of protecting children from sex.** Minneapolis: University of Minnesota Press.

In this book Levine argues that society needs to accept the fact that children and teenagers can have sexual pleasure and be safe. She also discusses campaigns against "sex-positive thinking" that interfere with our ability to protect children from sex. Our efforts to protect children from sex may do more harm than good, and Levine suggests that parents need to accept and recognize their children as sexual beings. Talking to teenagers about sexual pleasure scares most people. Why is this? Can we teach teenagers about the pleasurable aspects of sexuality? In the past few years, Levine believes that sexuality education has been transformed into "no-sex" education. Desire in this education is a "hidden discourse." Levine argues that if we could find a way to talk about pleasure and sexuality, we might find that fewer women experience sexual problems and dysfunctions later on in life.

The Holy Girl (2004; 1 hour, 46 minutes; Rated R)

This subtitled movie (*La Niña Santa*) explores the developing adolescent sexuality and religious fervor of two teenage girls: Amelia and her best friend, Josefina. Amelia is 16 and lives with her mother in a hotel. After choir rehearsals at church, she and the other girls get together in the church to discuss faith and vocation, and secretly discuss kissing and sex. When a visiting doctor presses himself up against Amelia, she find herself secretly drawn to him. Caught between her religious education and her developing sexuality, Amelia attempts to save the doctor from sin. Understanding the temptation of good, and the potential evils it causes, *The Holy Girl* explores sin, frustration, sexuality, and desire.

InfoTrac® College Edition

If your instructor ordered InfoTrac with this book, explore InfoTrac College Edition, your online library, for additional readings and review. Go to: **www.thomsonedu.com,** and enter these search terms:

puberty	puberty rites	precocious puberty	
sex education	sexual intercourse	teenaged sexual behavior	teenage pregnancy

Web Resources

SexualityNow Companion Website
Go to **http://thomsonedu.com/carroll** for practice quiz questions, interactive activities, Internet links, critical thinking exercises, discussion forums, and more. You can also access sites from the Wadsworth Psychology Study Center (**http://psychology.wadsworth.com**) or you can connect directly to the following sites:

The Sexuality Information and Education Council of the United States (SIECUS)
SIECUS is a national, nonprofit organization that develops, collects, and disseminates information; promotes comprehensive education about sexuality; and advocates the right of individuals to make responsible sexual choices.

Alan Guttmacher Institute (AGI)
The mission of the Alan Guttmacher Institute is to provide information and services about issues of sexuality. The Institute does important research on adolescent and child sexual issues.

All About Sex Discussions
This website provides information for preteens, teens, and parents and gives good information on how to talk about and explain such topics as sex, masturbation, sexual orientation, gender, and virginity.

Society for Research on Adolescence
The Society for Research on Adolescence was formed in 1984 as an international, multidisciplinary, nonprofit professional association whose goal is to promote the understanding of adolescence through research and dissemination. Members conduct theoretical studies, basic and applied research, and policy analyses to understand and enhance adolescent development. Links to research and publications on adolescence are provided.

The National Longitudinal Study of Adolescent Health
This is the official website for the Add Health study on adolescent sexuality. Information is available on the research design of the study, the research team, publications, data sets, statistics, and research details.

SexualityNow

Go to **www.thomsonedu.com** to link to **SexualityNow,** your online study tool. First take the **Pre-Test** for this chapter to get your **Personalized Study Plan,** which will identify topics you need to review and direct you to online resources. Then take the **Post-Test** to determine what concepts you have mastered and what you still need work on.

Videos in SexualityNow

For additional information on topics discussed in this chapter, check out the videos in **SexualityNow** on the following topics:

- **Adolescence: Sexual Risk Taking**—Listen to teens talk about the reasons adolescents have unprotected sex.
- **Teen Slang for Having Sex**—Hear the slang terms that teenagers use to describe sexual activity.
- **Adolescence: Body Image**—Hear interviews with teens about body image, dieting, and eating disorders.

9 Adult Sexual Relationships

Sexuality ❂ Now Go to www.thomsonedu.com to link to
SexualityNow, your online study tool.

*L*et's imagine that you meet someone at a campus party tonight. The two of you joke, laugh, and talk the night away. Although you've just met this person, it feels like you've known him/her forever. You wish the night would never end, but eventually it does. What will your next move be? Will you call him/her? Email? Instant message? Hope to run into each other again? The relationship rules have been changing on campuses across the country. Today couples "hook up" and "hang out," and dating relationships often aren't as clear as they once were.

We know that every society has rules to control the ways that people develop sexual bonds with other people. Until recently, in many parts of the world, parents or other family members arranged for their children to meet members of the other sex, marry them, and begin their sexual lives together. The expectation was that couples would remain sexually faithful and that marital unions would end only in death. In such societies, adult sexual relationships were clearly defined, and deviating from the norm was frowned upon.

In our society today, people openly engage in a variety of adult sexual relationships, including premarital, marital, extramarital, gay, lesbian, bisexual, and transgendered relationships. (Note that a term like "premarital sex" assumes eventual marriage; for people who never marry, their entire lives' sexualities are considered "premarital"!) These relationships can change and evolve over the course of a lifetime, and at different times a person might live alone and date, cohabit with a partner or partners, marry, divorce, or remarry. In this chapter, we will look at adults' sexual relationships with others.

sex byte

"Hooking up," engaging in sex with no promise of future commitment, is popular on college campuses today, and men report more comfort engaging in hooking up behavior than women (Lambert et al., 2003).

patriarchy
A social system in which the father is the head of the family and men have authority over women and children.

DATING: FUN OR SERIOUS BUSINESS?

We can understand a lot about a society just by examining the customs and rules it sets up for choosing a partner. For example, just from looking at dating patterns, we can learn about: the level of **patriarchy** (PAY-tree-ark-kee) in a society; its ideals about masculinity and femininity; the roles of women and men; the value placed on conformity; the importance of childbearing; the authority of the family; attitudes toward childhood, pleasure, responsibility; and a host of other traits.

The process of dating—meeting people socially for possible partner selection—may seem like a casual and fun process, but it is, in fact, serious business. Sociologists view dating as a "marriage market," or a way for prospective mates to compare the assets and liabilities of eligible partners to choose the best available mates (Benokraitis, 1993). Dating serves an important recreational function in that many teens spend a good deal of their free time having fun on dates. For most people, however, this leads to progressively more serious dating and eventually to final partner selection.

Today, it is not uncommon for men and women to date many people prior to settling down into their first serious relationship. This is not to say that a relationship cannot work if the partners have not dated others, but dating helps clarify what we look for in a partner. In fact, many people feel uncomfortable making a lifetime commitment to one person without having spent some time dating others first. If a couple meets each other, and 2 weeks later they decide to get married, do you feel they have dated long enough? Today, probably not. But consider that not too long ago, parents arranged marriages between people who had known each other for only a few hours, days, or weeks.

In Chapter 7, we discussed the physical benefits of love and intimacy. Dating has been found to provide similar benefits. Steady dating in adolescence has also been found to be associated with higher self-esteem and sex-role identity (Samet & Kelly, 1987). Relationships provide companionship, emotional support, and even, at times, economic support. Of course, the key may be the kind of dating relationships people have. Both the pressure to have sex and engaging in sex before the person is ready may turn a healthy dating experience into a detrimental one.

Young gay and lesbian people have a much harder time finding dates and developing sexually than their heterosexual counterparts because of the stigma of homosexuality and the difficulty in determining who are potential sexual partners. Some communities are tolerant of gay and lesbian teen dating, whereas others still severely stigmatize gay youth and make it difficult for them to admit their sexual orientation. As we discussed in Chapter 8, many gay, lesbian, and bisexual youths feel drawn to the Internet in search of available partners.

Overall, the research has found that commitment in relationships, whether the relationships are between college students in dating relationships or cohabiting or married gay and straight adults, is dependent on how much individual satisfaction there is in the relationship and the cost-benefit ratio of the relationship (Impett et al., 2001). If the benefits of the relationship outweigh the costs, the couple is generally more satisfied.

Review Question

What differences have been found between those who date and those who do not?

SEX Talk

Question: Is an email or an instant message (IM) an acceptable way to ask someone out?

Today email and instant messaging are common forms of communication, and research supports that they can help promote intimacy (Hu et al., 2004). As long as you understand the risks (we talked about some of these in Chapter 7, page 201), Internet communication can provide a good way to contact someone. It would probably be a good idea, however, to follow up with a phone call just to be sure your message was received.

Types of Dating

The problem with discussing dating behavior is that there are no agreed-on words for different levels of commitment. "Dating," "going out," "hanging out," "seeing each other"—these terms mean different things to different couples. Even a term such as "engaged" can mean different things—to some it means the wedding date is set; to others it simply means that they have decided that someday they will marry each other, although they are in no rush to say when.

On college campuses today there have been many changes in dating practices. Some researchers argue that college "dating" doesn't exist (see the accompanying Sex in Real Life, "Is Dating Dead on Campus?"). Overall, we know that the dating years in American society begin in earnest in high school, and how they develop depends on whether the person goes to college or directly to work. People with more free time tend to date more, and so college students pursue dating behaviors longer than those who begin working. (Of course, now that people are delaying marriage later and later, they can continue to date for many more years—even into their 30s and 40s—and dating may even begin again after a divorce.) But the late teens and early 20s are a special time for dating, for then dating patterns become more firmly established and sexual maturity is reached.

In traditional dating, which occurred before the 1970s, the boy would pick up the girl at her house, the father and mother would meet with or chat with the boy, and then the boy and girl would go to a well-defined event (a "mixer"—a chaperoned, school-sponsored dance—or a movie), and she would be brought home by the curfew her parents imposed (Benokraitis, 1993). Today, however, formal dating has given way to more casual dating, in part because of teenagers'

The dating years usually begin in high school in the United States.

Is Dating Dead on College Campuses?

Do students are your university go on "dates"? One study found that only half of female seniors reported being asked out by a man on six or more dates while at college; and one-third of respondents said they had been on only two or fewer dates (Glenn & Marquardt, 2001). Today, it is much more common for men and women to "hang out" rather than go out on a date. Typically, men and women go out with friends and plan on meeting up at a party on campus and going home together, rather than prearranging a date.

Why might there be less "dating" today and more "hooking up," or casual affairs? Researchers suggest that there are several possible reasons (Glenn & Marquardt, 2001). The sexual revolution has changed society's attitudes about sexuality, making hooking up, casual sex, one-night stands, and "friends with benefits" more acceptable. In addition, college dormitories today are often coed, meaning that men and women are living in close proximity to each other, which promotes intimacy. Students today are also busy and stressed, and perhaps they are too busy for romance, settling instead for casual, quick affairs. We also can't deny the influence of alcohol, which is commonly used on college campuses today and may serve to legitimize casual sex.

In a preliminary study I did on college hookups, I found that over 88% of students reported engaging in a hookup. Ninety-percent said that they had had a "really good" hookup. They rated it good for many reasons, including good sex, no interruptions, or a resulting relationship. However, 78% reported they had also had a "bad" hookup because of bad sex, interruptions, or a partner wanting more out of the hookup than they did. Following are some of their best and worst hookups.

What Made the Hookup Good?

We will probably get married. (female)

We were both really drunk, and it was really fun. (female)

The sex was good, and the girl didn't bug out and get psycho on my ass. (male)

Two words: simultaneous orgasm. (male)

She was from another school, and I didn't have to worry about being awkward and seeing her again. (male)

What Made the Hookup Bad?

He took advantage of me when I was drunk. (female)

I took one for the team, since my friend wanted his friend. (female)

She wasn't shaved. (male)

The guy didn't want a relationship, and I thought he cared. (female)

We were both drunk and didn't stop making out even after he vomited. (female)

Our sex was videotaped and shown all over campus. (male)

SOURCE: Author's files.

almost universal access to cars and parents' more permissive attitudes toward the early mixing of the sexes. Teenagers still go to movies and dances, but just as often they will get together at someone's house or go for a drive. In casual dating, there are more opportunities for couples to find time alone away from parents or chaperones, which is one reason that the age of first intercourse has steadily decreased over the last 30 years.

The most difficult part of dating is the initial invitation; it is difficult to ask someone out and risk rejection. Whether a person is straight, or gay, or lesbian, asking someone out can be risky. The ego can be bruised if the desired person is not interested. The problems of dating change as one gets older, as there are fewer organized ways to meet other single people. Socializing and going out to bars and clubs may work for some, but others are uncomfortable with this approach. Perhaps the best way to meet others as one gets older is to get involved in community, religious, and singles groups and to find community events and programs where other single people go. Evening classes at local universities are also a good way to meet people. As we discussed in Chapter 7, the Internet has provided a new way to meet people, through websites, chat rooms, and dating services.

Review Question

Differentiate between traditional dating and current dating patterns.

Interracial Dating

We live in a multicultural world. As a result, dating someone of a different race, religion, or culture is more common today. This is especially true on college campuses, where close to 25% of students said they were currently in an interracial relationship, and 50% said they'd be open to dating someone of a different race (Knox et al., 2000). However, interracial relationships weren't always acceptable. In fact, it wasn't until 1967 that the Supreme Court struck down state antimiscegenation laws, which outlawed interracial relationships (we discussed these laws in Chapter 1).

Despite these trends, there are still very strong social forces that keep the races separate and make it difficult for people of different races to meet or maintain relationships. Overall, African Americans are twice as likely as Caucasians to report being open to the possibility of an interracial relationship (Knox et al., 2000; Rosenblatt et al., 1995), possibly due to the fact that there are more whites to choose from and a greater exposure of blacks to white culture. For African-American women who want to date within their race, this may lead to less dating and fewer marriages (Crowder & Tolnay, 2000). In the accompanying Sex in Real Life feature, "Marriage and African-American Women," we discuss African-American women and marriage.

In our multicultural world, race is not the only criterion on which a couple's suitability is judged: there are also issues of different religions, ages, social classes, and disabilities. Couples with these issues may also face some of the same challenges that interracial couples do.

Although the attitudes of college students toward interracial dating are more open, overall there are strong social forces that make it harder for people of different races and cultures to meet.

Review Question

Explain how the increased frequency of interracial relationships between African-American men and Caucasian women has affected African-American women.

SEX Talk

Question: Why is it that people stare at interracial couples? I just don't understand what the big deal is if they really love each other.

Americans have a history of disapproving of relationships that take place between people of different races. In many other countries, interracial couples are not unusual. Latino-white relationships, as well as Asian-white, Native American-white, Latino-black, and other combinations—although still often looked upon negatively—are more acceptable in the United States than black-white. Unfortunately, these negative feelings can lead to discrimination against such couples and their children.

Dating After Divorce or Widowhood

After a divorce or the death of a spouse, it can be very difficult to get back into the dating scene. Many of these people have been involved in committed relationships for many years; consequently, they find that the dating environment has changed drastically since they were younger. For example, consider a 54-year-old man and woman who have been married since 1975. In 2006 they decide to divorce. Dating in 2006 is very different from dating in 1975. The relationship between the sexes has changed, casual dating is more common, women initiate dates and sexual activity, sexual activity may be more frequent, and one has to be more worried about sexually transmitted infections. It is not uncommon for newly divorced people to feel frustrated or confused about this unfamiliar environment.

In fact, men and women who have been divorced or widowed often have a difficult time dating again. Research has found that widowhood is a major barrier to repartnering (Wu & Schimmele, 2005). One widowed 49-year-old man explains:

It was very hard for me to get into the dating scene again. I had married very young. Honestly, there is no one to match my late wife. I don't know if I am still responding

SEX in Real Life

Marriage and African-American Women

Although marriage rates have been dropping for several years now, there has been a significant decline in marriage among African-American women (Tucker & Mitchell-Kernan, 1995). From 1970 to 1990, the percentage of African-American women over age 18 who were married went from 62% to 43% (Crowder & Tolnay, 2000). In 1990, only 35% of African-American women under the age of 35 were married. This change has been accompanied by a substantial increase in interracial marriage, especially between African-American men and non-African-American women. Are these events related?

Perhaps so. As more and more African-American men marry non-African-American women, this reduces the pool of available African-American partners for the African-American women. This is even more true for highly educated African-American women whose marriage prospects are most likely to choose interracial marriage. However,

when African-American women are asked which ethnicity they prefer their partner to be, the majority would prefer an African American (Wyatt, 1998).

African-American women, in general, often experience a shortage of marriageable men because African-American men have higher mortality and incarceration rates (Bennett et al., 1992). African-American men have also been found to have higher rates of unemployment, lower earnings, and lower levels of education than Caucasian men, which further reduces the numbers of appropriate African-American men for African-American women to marry (Tucker & Mitchell-Kernan, 1995).

Some researchers have proposed that rates have dropped because African-American women are reluctant to marry. However, the evidence doesn't support this theory. African-American men, rather than African-American women, have been found to have the strongest reservations about marriage (South, 1993).

to the wonderful life I had in my marriage or have just lost all interest in romance. I meet quite a few young women and can see that they are attractive, and to someone else may be desirable, but I hardly give it a blink. (Janus & Janus, 1993, p. 8)

But people in this situation need not be discouraged. Today, more and more groups and organizations are being created to help divorced and widowed people ease back into the dating scene.

As couples age, one partner eventually dies, and the other may find him- or herself single again for the first time in many years. Even though many of these people are not interested in marrying again, they may still be interested in dating (Bulcroft & Bulcroft, 1991). Some older couples decide to live with their partner instead of marrying. It is estimated that 4% of older couples live together (Chevan, 1996). This same study found that the likelihood that an older man will choose to date is predicted by his age and social involvement, whereas older women are influenced more by their health and mobility. Some older men decide to marry younger spouses (e.g., Paul McCartney and Heather Mills or Pierce Brosnan and Keely Shaye Smith). Later in this chapter we will discuss dating after the death of a spouse among the elderly in more detail (see the section "Marriages in Later Life").

Sexuality in Dating Relationships

Sexual practices have been changing on college campuses today. "Hooking up" or having a "friend with benefits" or a "sex buddy" have become more common. Although both men and women report these behaviors are often engaged in purely for the physical pleasures they provide, the research isn't so clear cut (Lambert et al., 2003).

I once had two students in my class who I thought didn't know each other because they never talked or sat next to each other. However, in reading papers they had handed in, I learned they had been "hooking up" almost every weekend for over 8 months. What was interesting to me, however, was how they each described their relationship. Blye wrote that she was sure Laizon was looking for a commitment because he had sex with her every weekend, whereas Laizon wrote that he was relieved that Blye understood their relationship was only sexual because he never talked to her during the week. Both Blye

sex byte

Although years ago, many women were looking for financial security that led them toward older, more established partners, today one-third of women between the ages of 40 and 69 are involved with men who are 10 or more years younger (high-profile examples include Demi Moore and Ashton Kutcher or Susan Sarandon and Tim Robbins; Lawrence, 2003).

Review Question

Identify some of the issues that make dating difficult after a divorce or death of a spouse.

Personal Voices

Sports and Virginity

A. C. Green, a former professional basketball player for teams including the Los Angeles Lakers and the Phoenix Suns, has dedicated his life to teaching youths about abstinence. In 2002 the deeply religious Green married Veronique Green, fulfilling a lifelong vow of celibacy until marriage. Green's promotion of abstinence and his belief in celibacy until marriage are at the core of the A. C. Green Youth Foundation. About his marriage to Veronique, Green said, "My beautiful wife has been well worth the wait." His new wife replied, "A. C. is the man I have waited for my whole life. To know he has also been faithful in waiting for me is the best wedding present I could ever imagine." Prior to his marriage, A. C. Green spoke openly about his desire to remain a virgin until marriage.

As a professional athlete, I have to deal with groupies in many cities. It seems as though my teammates and I are often confronted by young women wanting to meet us from the time we arrive to the time we depart. They hang out everywhere—airports, hotel lobbies, restaurants and sports arenas—always trying to catch our eyes.

Not many resist their advances. I don't know how many virgins there are in the NBA, but you can probably count them on one hand. Pro basketball players have this larger-than-life image, and it doesn't help when a former player such as Wilt Chamberlain boasts about bedding 20,000 women in his lifetime.

While I've remained sexually pure, I still hear the locker-room talk about the latest sexual conquests. But I don't let that weaken my resolve because I have cho-

sen to follow God's standard. I've communicated my stand to my teammates. Some—in a humorous vein—have threatened to set me up with women who would make themselves available to me; "Let's see how strong you really are," they joke.

Don't get me wrong. Sex itself isn't bad. It's just a matter of when to experience it. I want young people to hear this message: It is possible to wait. Not everybody is doing it. I started the A. C. Green Youth Foundation in Los Angeles. We put together basketball camps, help kids find summer jobs, and try to give inner-city youth some direction. As part of that outreach, last summer several pro athletes—including Daryl Green and David Robinson—along with a Christian rap group called Idol King joined me to make a video called "It Ain't Worth It." It's a rap song dealing with teenage love, broken hearts, the dilemma of abortion, and the fallacy of the "safe sex" message.

Of course, some young kids listening to me have been sexually active for years. That's when I tell them about the concept of secondary virginity. "You may have had sex in the past and think you don't have a reason to wait now," I say. "But there's a better way, and that's following God's way. Perhaps you feel guilty or not worthy, but the Lord can forgive you. After that, you can commit yourselves to remaining pure until your wedding day."

SOURCE: From *Focus on the Family* magazine (June 1993, pp. 2–3).

and Laizon were evaluating the same behavior differently. It might be easy to assume that it's always the female who is looking for more commitment in these "hookups," but that wouldn't be entirely true. There are many men who hope for more out of a "hookup" but settle for what they can get (see the Sex Talk Question on page 260).

There are some couples who decide to abstain from sex. These couples tend to hold more conservative attitudes about sex and have less prior sexual experience. Today more and more adults are standing up for their virginity instead of being embarrassed by it. Even some famous athletes have spoken out about their virginity in their youth (see the accompanying Personal Voices, "Sports and Virginity"). When both partners have been sexually active in the past, they are very likely to continue to be sexually active in their present relationship (Peplau et al., 1977).

For couples in which one partner has been sexually active in the past and the other is a virgin, the woman's past experience is a stronger predictor of the sexual behavior of the couple. Virginal men often do not resist the opportunity to have sexual intercourse with an experienced woman. Peplau and colleagues (1977) found in a study of college students that every male virgin who dated a sexually experienced female engaged in sexual intercourse. However, when a virginal female dated a sexually experienced man, only one-third of couples had sexual intercourse.

Review Question

Explain how sexuality has changed on college campuses today. What factors influence whether an intimate relationship will become sexual?

SEX Talk

Question: *I have a "sex buddy" that I hook up with at least once a week, sometimes more. We don't ever talk about us or what is going on, but the sex is great. I'd like to take this to the next level and become a "couple," but I just don't know how. I guess we've become very accustomed to the way things are. I'm scared to death that maybe she doesn't want anything more than we already have. I'd be devastated.*

Moving from a hookup into a more serious dating situation can be difficult primarily because there is often a significant lack of communication between the partners. Although it is possible for a serious relationship to develop out of a hookup, many do not make it past the hookup stage. Your best bet would be to find a time when the two of you can talk about your feelings and hope for a more committed relationship. Students have different motivations for hooking up and engaging in casual sex, and you won't know your partner's motivations unless you ask.

Sexuality in Elderly Relationships

When we picture people making love, we rarely think of two people over the age of 60. In fact, when I show a film on elderly sexuality, many of my students cover their eyes and feel repulsed. Why is this? Why are we so averse to the idea that older people have healthy and satisfying sex lives? It is probably because we live in a society that equates sexuality with youth. Even so, the majority of elderly persons maintain an interest in sex and sexual activity, and many engage in sexual activity, including those who live in nursing homes (B. W. Walker & Ephross, 1999). In fact, half of all Americans who are 60 years old or older report their sex is as good as, or better than, when they were younger (N. K. Edwards, 2000).

A study by the American Association of Retired Persons (AARP) and *Modern Maturity* magazine found that even though the frequency of sexual intercourse drops with age, 67% of men and 61% of women rated their physical relationship with their partner as "extremely" or "very" satisfying (*Modern Maturity,* 1999). In another study, nearly half of the respondents age 60 and older were found to engage in sexual behavior at least once a month, and 40% wanted sex more often (National Council on Aging, 1998). In addition, 43% reported that sex is physically and emotionally "just as good or better" than in their youth. The most common sexual behaviors for men and women over the age of 80 are touching and caressing, masturbation, or sexual intercourse (Bretschneider & McCoy, 1988). There are many similarities in aging among gay, lesbian, and heterosexual populations. In fact, the physical changes of aging affect all men and women, regardless of sexual orientation (Woolf, 2002).

Older Americans may find that their preferences for certain types of sexual behaviors change as they age—they may engage in sexual intercourse less and oral sex more, for example. These changes happen because many women do not discover their own sexual desires or try new sexual behaviors until later in life. Whether or not a man or woman remains sexually interested and active has to do with a variety of factors, including his or her age, physical health, medications, level of satisfaction with life, and the availability of a partner (Metz & Miner, 1998). One's attitude about all these changes also makes a big difference (Woolf, 2002).

Throughout time, many researchers believed that medical and health issues were two of the biggest issues affecting female sexuality later in life. Although these factors are important, the most prevalent sexual problems in older women are not medical complaints (e.g., insufficient lubrication or painful intercourse), but rather a lack of tenderness and sexual contact (vonSydow, 2000). Hormonal changes associated with menopause are less influential than the effects of societal, psychological, and partner-related issues.

One of the most important factors dictating whether or not a woman continues sexual activity is whether she has an available and interested partner. When sexual intercourse stops in a marital relationship, it is usually because of the male's refusal or inability to continue, rather than the wife's disinterest. This is often due to the existence of an erectile problem, which may be caused by physiological aging, illness, medication, or psychological issues (we will discuss this more extensively in Chapter 14).

Many older couples who experience problems in sexual functioning may not understand that they may have some options. In fact, some may give up on sex at the first signs of any sexual difficulties, believing that "sex is over." After raising a family, one or both of the partners may also feel that recreational sex is inappropriate; as a result, they may stop having sex. For these reasons, it is important to educate aging populations about sex to help them understand the implications of any physiological changes they may be experiencing.

Many people, young and old, are not aware of the physical changes that can affect sexual functioning. One 79-year-old man understands the limitations but has come to accept them: "These days, my erections tend to come and go a bit unpredictably, but it doesn't particularly matter. It usually comes back again pretty soon if stimulation is continued. And in any case, it only affects vaginal intercourse, and sex can be very good by other techniques" (Hite, 1981, pp. 883–884).

We've been talking about various types of dating, the importance of dating, and sexuality. Before we leave this discussion, there is one more important point to make. Many men and women who date each other for a significant time period have ideas about where they would like the relationship to go. Although they might not openly talk about these ideas, they think about it often. Because of this, couples enter into what is known as "silent agreements" wherein they believe they know what the other wants because they base it on what they themselves want (A. M. Johnson, 2001).

For example, two students of mine, Jason and Charene, have been dating for a year now. Charene has made it clear to Jason that she would like to get married and have a family one day. Jason, on the other hand, has made it clear to Charene that he doesn't want marriage or kids. Yet they continue to see each other and avoid any discussions about this. The more they see each other, the more Charene believes that he'll change his mind and come around. Jason, however, is thinking Charene must have let go of her fantasies of marriage because she's still with him. Can you see how this silent agreement can lead to trouble? It's important to talk about issues like these in relationships and consider moving on when your needs are not being met.

Review Question

Describe how sexuality and relationships may change as people age.

SEX Talk

Question: Do most people tell their partners about all of their past lovers?

Knowing whether your partners have been exposed to sexually transmitted infections and whether you are at risk is important. However, knowing the specifics of their past love lives is really a personal matter. Some couples insist on knowing everything, whereas others believe the past should stay in the past. The biggest risk of sharing information about past lovers is jealousy. Many men and women who think they want to know everything about their partner's past are consumed with jealousy or negative feelings after hearing the facts.

One study found that 25% of women who find out their partner had more sexual partners than they would have liked are significantly bothered by this, whereas 52% are bothered somewhat (Milhausen & Herold, 1999). My advice? Because it really depends on the couple, think it through before you and your partner share past history. Although many couples find that this kind of sharing brings them closer, others are driven apart.

Cohabitation: Instead of, or on the Way to, Marriage?

Like dating, the terminology of cohabiting is also interesting. Is it "living together," "shacking up," "living in sin," "a test drive," or "a trial run"? In recent years **cohabitation** has increased dramatically (Bumpass & Lu, 2000). Today, cohabitation has become so

cohabitation
Living together in a sexual relationship when not legally married.

common that many sociologists regard it as a stage of courtship (Seltzer, 2000). More than half of first marriages in the early 1990s began with cohabitation (Bumpass & Lu, 2000).

Forty percent of U.S. couples live together without being married (Allen, 2005), and typically the pattern is for young couples to live together as a prelude to marriage, and not *instead* of marriage (King & Scott, 2005; Cummins, 2002). But the United States still does not compare with Sweden, where 90% of married couples lived together before marriage, or Denmark, where 80% cohabit. In 2000, more than 5.2 million U.S. couples were cohabiting (U.S. Bureau of the Census, 2000). Compare this to the 430,000 couples living together in 1960 and the 2.8 million living together in 1990 (Benokraitis, 1993). Of these 5.2 million couples, 87% were male/female couples, 6% were male/male couples, and 6% were female/female couples (U.S. Bureau of the Census, 2000).

Cohabiting couples tend to differ from married couples in several ways. For example, 21% of females who live with their partner are 2 or more years older than their partner, but only 12% of wives are 2 or more years older than their husband (Fields & Casper, 2001). Most of the married couples are the same race, but cohabiting partners were twice as likely to be a different race than married couples.

There are advantages and disadvantages to cohabitation. Cohabitation allows couples to learn more about each other and not be legally or economically bound. It allows a couple who love one another to become more mature and more financially stable if they do eventually marry. It can be more realistic than dating because it gives couples the opportunity to learn of their partners' bad habits and idiosyncrasies.

Yet there are also problems. Parents and relatives may not support the union, and society as a whole tends not to recognize people who live together for purposes of health care, taxes, and the like. Also, partners may want different things out of living together, such as when one partner sees it taking the relationship to another level, whereas the other sees it as a way to have a more accessible sexual partner. People who live together may feel cut off from their friends and the couple can become too enmeshed in each other (Benokraitis, 1993).

Some people believe that when couples live together, they can smooth out the rough spots in their relationships and see whether they would be able to be happily married. Research indicates, however, that the reverse may be true. Half of all couples that live together break up within a year or less (Bumpass & Lu, 2000). Those who marry are at increased risk of divorce, and longer cohabitation has been found to be associated with higher likelihood of divorce (Cohan & Kleinbaum, 2002; Seltzer, 2000). The research has found that these problems are more common among non-Hispanic white women but not among non-Hispanic Mexican American or African American women (Phillips & Sweeney, 2005). Even in Sweden, couples who cohabited before marriage had almost an 80% higher rate of marital dissolution than those who did not (Benokraitis, 1993).

Why might couples who live together be less successful as marriage partners? Perhaps these couples develop as separate individuals during that time (because they are not married, they maintain their own "life" outside of the relationship), and this may lead to a higher risk for divorce (Seltzer, 2000). Without the legal commitment of marriage, couples may just be "playing house," unprepared for the real problems of married couples. Also, most cohabiting couples do not get joint checkbooks, have expensive mortgages, and so on, and may not be prepared for the financial pressures of marriage (money fights are a major reason for divorce).

However, there are several possible shortcomings of the foregoing findings. It may not be that living together itself increases the chance of divorce, but that the type of people who are willing to live together are also the type who are more likely to divorce when marriage gets difficult. Couples who live together may feel that they would not be happy in a marriage; they may be more accepting of divorce; they may be less religious and less traditional in the first place; or they may be less committed in the beginning of the relationship. Because we do not know about the samples in the studies on cohabiting couples, it is difficult to generalize their findings. Some studies have found no correlation between living together and future marital disruption (Teachman, 2003).

A couple's reasons for living together may indicate whether their marriage will be successful. The reasons a couple decides to live together may have a lot to do with whether or not the relationship survives marriage. If a couple lives together for economic reasons or because of timing (say they are planning to marry in the near future), this will generally result in a healthy marital relationship. However, complications arise when couples live together because they are nervous about committing to marriage or they want to "test" their relationship. Obviously, if they need to test a relationship to see whether it will work, they are not ready for marriage.

As of 2005, 13 states recognize **common-law marriage,** which means that if a couple lives together for a certain number of years, they are considered married. Typically a couple must present themselves as a married couple (refer to each other as husband and wife and/or file a joint tax return). There are also cases of individuals who have successfully sued partners they lived with for **alimony** or shared property (called **palimony**), claiming that their partner promised them marriage or lived together with them as though married. If the couple has a baby, of course, both partners are responsible for his or her upbringing, even if they separate afterward. So living together may entangle a couple in legal issues they did not anticipate.

Cohabitation in Other Cultures

Cohabitation is rarer in more traditional societies where, even if a couple has sex before or instead of marriage, social customs would never tolerate an unmarried heterosexual couple living together openly. Asian societies still frown on it, although it is sometimes allowed, and it is severely discouraged in Islamic societies. Living together has become more common today in China, although it is difficult to determine exactly how many couples live together because there is no formal definition of cohabitation (Ruan & Lau, 2004).

Most Western countries have substantial numbers of couples who live together. In France, for example, the number of cohabitating couples rose from 67,000 in 1968 to 589,000 in 1985, and by 1990, 1 out of 5 couples was living together outside of marriage (Forsé et al., 1993). In Sweden, the majority of couples live together before marriage (Trost, 2004). In fact, half of all Swedish children are born to couples who are living together.

In some countries, cohabitation is often a step toward marriage or is seen as a "lower form" of marriage. As one female student in the former Yugoslavia put it: "I have nothing against living together out of wedlock, but marriage is something more elevated" (Blagojevic, 1989, p. 226).

Although having more than one wife is illegal in the United States, it is still practiced in some conservative Mormon communities.

common-law marriage
A marriage existing by mutual agreement between a man and a woman, or by the fact of their cohabitation, without a civil or religious ceremony.

alimony
An allowance for support made under court order to a divorced person by the former spouse, usually the chief provider during the marriage.

palimony
An allowance for support made under court order and given usually by one person to his or her former lover or live-in companion after they have separated.

Review Question

Identify the differences between cohabiting and married couples, and explain why couples who live together and then marry have higher rates of divorce compared to those of couples who didn't live together prior to marrying.

Review Question

Explain what we know about cohabitation outside the United States.

sex byte

Approximately 50% of straight couples who live together will marry within 5 years, 40% will break up, and 10% will continue to live together (Cummins, 2002).

MARRIAGE: HAPPY EVER AFTER?

Throughout history, people have had a long-standing love–hate relationship with the institution of marriage. Writers have often cursed it and praised it, but no matter what their attitude toward it, almost all have done it. Even today, the majority of young people say they are planning and expecting to marry at some point in their lives (Thornton & Young-DeMarco, 2001). In fact, compared to the 1970s, young men and women in the United States were more committed to a good marriage in the 1990s, and men reported an increased desire for marriage. Moreover, 93% of Americans say that a happy marriage is one of their most important life goals (M. Gallagher & Waite, 2000). A survey in 2000 found that marriages in the United States are as happy today as they were 20 years ago (Amato et al., 2003).

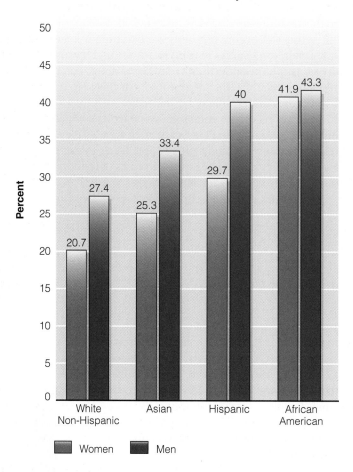

Never married rates by race

White Non-Hispanic — Women 20.7, Men 27.4
Asian — Women 25.3, Men 33.4
Hispanic — Women 29.7, Men 40
African American — Women 41.9, Men 43.3

Women ◻ Men ◼

Over time, many married couples experience changes in their sex lives, even though sexuality remains an essential part of the majority of marriages.

In almost all societies on Earth, women are more likely to marry partners older than themselves, whereas men are more likely to marry younger women (Mackay, 2000). In adolescence, these age preferences are less strong, but they increase as one ages. Evolutionary explanations suggest that men want to ensure conception and pregnancy (more likely with a younger, healthy wife), whereas women want to be sure they will be taken care of (more likely with an older, more established husband). Sociological models say instead that social gender roles value wealth and power in men (more likely in older men) and physical beauty in women (more likely in younger women).

Over the last 30 years, the age at first marriage has been increasing, though this number leveled off in the 1990s (Fields & Casper, 2001; see Figure 9.1). In 1970, the median age for first marriage for men and women was 23 and 21, respectively. In 2002 the age at first marriage went to 27 and 25 for men and women, respectively.

What do married couples think is important for a good marriage? Marital satisfaction for men has been found to be related to the frequency of pleasurable activities (doing fun things together) in the relationship, whereas for women it was related to the frequency of pleasurable activities that focus on emotional closeness. Other important variables, including being able to talk to each other and self-disclose, physical and emotional intimacy, and personality similarities, are all instrumental in achieving greater relationship quality.

John Gottman, whom we discussed in Chapter 7, found that the quality of the friendship with one's spouse is the most important factor in marital satisfaction for both men and women (Gottman & Silver, 2000). High rewards, such as emotional support and a satisfying sex life, and low costs (such as arguing, conflicts, and financial burdens) are also important in marital satisfaction (Impett et al., 2001). If a marriage has high costs but low rewards, a person might end the relationship or look outside the marriage for alternative rewards. We will discuss Gottman's research more in Chapter 10.

Question: What is a "prenuptial" agreement?

If a couple divorces, their marriage contract is governed by state law, which determines how assets are divided. However, some couples decide to implement nuptial agreements, or financial plans that couples agree on in marriage, that supersede state laws (Philadelphia, 2000).

These agreements can be either prenuptial (drawn up before a marriage) or postnuptial (drawn up after a couple has wed). It is estimated that 20% of couples who plan to marry pursue a prenuptial agreement (A. Dickinson, 2001). These agreements are more common in second marriages (Freedman, 2001). A postnuptial agreement is usually drawn up when there is a major change in finances, such as an inheritance.

Some couples feel prenuptials are unromantic and don't want to implement one before they are married, but decide to wait until after the wedding to implement a postnuptial agreement. Prenuptial agreements also have a predetermined expiration date, and couples will update their original plans with a postnuptial agreement. All of these nuptial agreements should be revised if a couple moves to a new state.

Proponents of prenuptial agreements believe that because many couples have a hard time talking about financial issues, a prenuptial agreement can help them to sort through these important issues before marriage (Daragahi & Dubin, 2001). However, these types of agreements can also cause problems because they are often initiated by the financially stronger partner and may involve issues of power (Margulies, 2003).

Marital quality tends to peak in the first few years of a marriage and then declines until midlife, when it rises again (Weigel & Ballard-Reisch, 1999). This often leads to a decline in marital satisfaction in the early years of marriage, which is primarily due to the fact that couples tend to work harder early in the marriage to maintain a high level of satisfaction (Kurdek, 1999).

Over time these maintenance behaviors decrease. Ragsdale (1996) found that couples married more than 25 years were less likely to be open and use positive affirmations than couples who had been married only a few years. Long-time married couples also spend less time and energy on communication strategies with their partners because they have developed unique "relational codes" to help them communicate nonverbally (Sillars & Wilmot, 1989). One woman who has been married 10 years comments:

> I know when he's not in a good mood because I can see it in his eyes. He looks at me a little differently and his look tells me to "stay away." When this happens I just wait for him to come around. It took me a few years of marriage to really realize this, but now it's not a big deal at all. (Author's files)

The majority of married couples report that their marriages are happy and satisfying. In fact, in one study more than 60% of couples reported that their marriages were happy (Greeley, 1991). This study also found that slightly more women than men report being happy in their marriages, although the difference has been declining since the early 1970s.

Why do some marriages last, whereas others end in divorce? Lauer et al. (1990) asked 351 married couples why their marriages have lasted. They found that marriages seem to last most when both partners have a positive attitude toward the marriage, view their partner as a best friend, and like their partner as a person. Another important aspect of marriage is the belief that marriage is a long-term commitment. To make it work, couples need to be willing to work through the difficulties that are part of any relationship. Relationships are a challenge and take work to succeed. Disagreements and misunderstandings are a part of all relationships.

As we discussed in Chapter 7, researchers have found that marriage is good for a person's health. People who are married tend to be happier and healthier and have longer lives than either widowed or divorced persons of the same age (Zheng & Hart, 2002). Marriage has also been found to reduce the impact of several potentially traumatic events, including job loss, retirement, and illness. In single men, suicide rates are twice

Sexual activity and relationship satisfaction have been found to be positively correlated.

as high as those of married men, and single men have been found to experience more psychological problems, such as depression and nightmares (Faludi, 1991).

Overall, marriage provides more health benefits to men than women. For instance, although married men have better physical and mental health and more self-reported happiness and experience fewer psychological problems than either divorced, single, or widowed men (Joung et al., 1995), married women tend to be less healthy than married men (Benokraitis, 1993). This may be because women have multiple role responsibilities; for example, working women still tend to do the bulk of the housework and disproportionately take care of the children. Men's improved health in marriage may also have to do with the fact that married women are more likely to monitor their husbands' health behaviors than vice versa (Depner & Ingersoll-Dayton, 1985). One final note deserves mention here: Over the last few years there has been a trend in the mental health benefits of marriage applying equally to men and women (R. W. Simon, 2002). This is probably a result of an increased equality in marriages today.

Having Children or Remaining Childless

Children can be born at any period before or during a marriage or outside of marriage, and the timing of having children has effects on the relationship quality. Some people get married in order to have children, others get married because the woman is pregnant, others decide to get married even though neither partner wants children, and some couples remain single and have children. In any case, the decision to have or raise children is one that most people face at one time or another.

Data from the Commonwealth Survey of Parents with Young Children, which looked at over 2,000 parents with children younger than 3 years old, reported that many parents with young children find themselves with little time to work on their relationship (Halfon et al., 2002). In fact, married couples with children report lower marital satisfaction than those without children (Twenge et al., 2003). Satisfaction levels fall lower as the number of children increases. Typically, relationship happiness is higher before the children come, declines steadily until it hits a low when the children are in their teens, and then begins to increase once the children leave the house (P. H. Collins, 1988). Why is this? Many couples may not have agreed on roles after childbearing, and the female may find, for example, that her partner assumes that she will take primary care of the children (Benokraitis, 1993).

Review Question

How do married couples stay happily together over many years?

sex byte

Although engagement rings for men are becoming more popular in the United States, they have been standard in other countries, such as Sweden (which is more socially liberal) and Syria (where it is considered shameful for an engaged man not to wear a ring for fear he might cheat on his beloved; O. Barker, 2002).

SEX in Real Life

Eye-Rolling, Marriage, and Divorce

John Gottman, a renowned marriage and family therapist, claims that he can predict whether a couple's marriage will succeed or fail from watching and listening to them for just 5 minutes (Gottman, 1999). And 91% of the time, he's right.

Gottman and his colleagues believe that in order for marriages to succeed, they need to be "emotionally intelligent." They find ways for couples to keep the negative thoughts about each other from overtaking their positive ones. Strong marriages have a 5:1 ratio of positive to negative interactions; and, when this ratio starts to drop, a cou-

ple is headed for divorce. Gottman has also found that certain facial expressions during communication are also important. For example, eye-rolling after a spouse's comments can be a strong predictor for divorce (Parker-Pope, 2002b).

Gottman holds workshops all over the United States for couples who want to improve their relationships. He has recently started offering workshops for gay and lesbian couples as well. He has found that same-sex couples tend to manage relationship conflict in more positive than negative ways. However, not all gay and lesbian couples can maintain these strengths.

The introduction of children can affect relationship quality.

Marital Sex Changes Over Time

Sexuality is an essential part of most marriages. Many young people see marriage as an unproblematic feast of sexual pleasure; after all, you have your partner there all the time, and you just make love anytime you want to. (Figure 9.2 illustrates frequency of sex in marriage as compared to other types of relationships.) But others wonder whether sex with the same person might not become boring after a while. The number of books promising to teach couples how to put zing back into the marital bedroom indicates that marriage is not always an unending string of sexual encounters.

Although many marriages start out high on passion, these feelings slowly dissipate over time (Starling, 1999). Laumann and colleagues (1994) found that 40% of married people have sexual intercourse two or more times a week, whereas 50% engage in it a few times each month. No matter how often couples had sex, most reported a decline over time—only 6% reported an increase in sexual frequency over time. More than a third reported that they made love less than 60% as often as they did in the first year of marriage.

When one partner is unhappy with the amount of sex in a relationship there can be trouble (Deveny, 2003). The reason it decreases in long-term relationships has less to do with getting bored with one's partner than it has to do with the pressures of children, jobs, commuting, housework, and finances. However, even with these life changes, after

Review Question

Explain how children may affect relationship quality.

sex byte

The number of sons a white couple has heightens the probability of divorce, whereas the number of daughters has been found to have no affect on the marital union (Christie-Mizell, 2003). Interestingly, offspring gender has not been found to be related to divorce in African-American families.

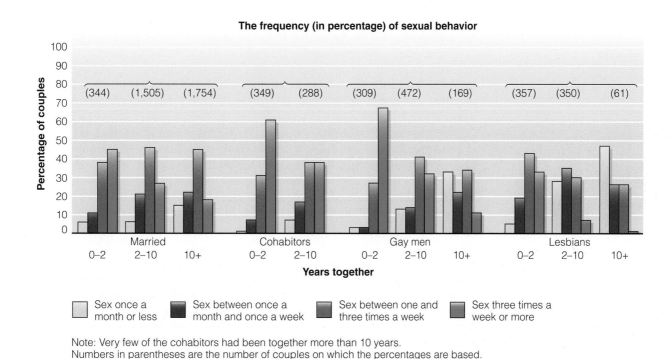

The frequency (in percentage) of sexual behavior

Note: Very few of the cohabitors had been together more than 10 years.
Numbers in parentheses are the number of couples on which the percentages are based.

Figure 9.2 Frequency of sexual behavior in various types of relationships by years. The numbers above each category represent the total number of respondents.
Source: From Philip Blumstein and Pepper Schwartz, "Sexual Imitation, p. 196, in *American Couples.* Copyright © 1983 by Philip B. Blumstein and Pepper S. Schwartz. Reprinted by permission of HarperCollins Publishers, Inc.

10 years or more of marriage only 15% of married couples have sex less than once a month, and 63% report having sex once a week or more (Heiman & LoPiccolo, 1992). Another study found that 40% of married women have sex once every few weeks; 22% have it once a week or so; and 34% have it two to three times a week (J. Carroll, 2002).

The frequency of sexual activity and satisfaction with a couple's sex life have been found to be positively correlated (Blumstein & Schwartz, 1983); that is, the more frequent the sexual behavior, the greater the sexual satisfaction. However, it is not known whether increased sexual frequency causes more satisfaction, or whether increased marital satisfaction causes increased sexual behavior. Some couples feel that decreasing frequency of sexual behavior is a positive change:

> Maybe it's not a necessity anymore. We have other ways of expressing our feelings, and intercourse is one of the ways. When we first got married we thought it was the only way, and now we realize it is not. And the quality of our sex life has improved. Now it gives us so much satisfaction, it's not really necessary that we have it every single night. (Greenblat, 1989, p. 187)

Ellen Frank and Carol Anderson (1989) studied 100 couples and found that sexuality changes as one moves through different stages of marriage. During the early years, about the first 5 years, sex is more frequent and generally satisfying, with both partners feeling that they can satisfy the other. During the next 15 or so years, the middle stage, other aspects of life take precedence over sex, and the couple may experience difficulty in maintaining sexual interest in each other. In this stage, the couple begins to report more sexual dissatisfaction, with husbands troubled by an increasing interest in other women and wives troubled by a decreasing interest in sex itself. In the later years, 20 or more, sex gets more difficult as frequency and potency decline; still, men report being generally satisfied with their sex lives. Women, on the other hand, report being much less satisfied, saying they feel a sense of resignation that their sex lives are not exciting to them anymore.

Frequency and type of marital sex have been found to differ by social class (R. Collins, 1988). The upper classes tend to have marital sex more frequently, use more sexual positions, and practice more oral sex and other varieties of sexual contact. This may be because of more leisure time, because of more space and privacy, or perhaps because lower classes tend to have more traditional gender roles. Still, class differences in marital sexuality have been decreasing in recent years.

asexual relationship
A type of intimate relationship in which the partners do not engage in sexual intercourse.

Some marriages are **asexual relationships,** which means the partners do not engage in sexual behavior (we discussed a slightly different definition of asexuality in Chapter 3, which dealt with the concept of having no assigned gender). This is usually a mutual decision, and it may be because the partners do not have sexual desire for each other anymore.

Finally, masturbation is often taboo in marital relationships. The myth is that if a married man masturbates, his wife cannot be satisfying him sexually. However, this is not true. Forty-four percent of American husbands masturbate weekly or more often, whereas only 16% of wives do (Janus & Janus, 1993). Michael and colleagues (1994, p. 165) found that masturbation is often stimulated by other sexual behavior—"[T]he more sex you have of any kind, the more you may think about sex and the more you may masturbate." (We will discuss masturbation more in Chapter 10.)

Marriages in Later Life

In 2003, older men were more likely than older women to be married. This is because women live longer than men and widowhood is more common among older women. Three-quarters of men between the ages of 65 to 74 were married in 2003, whereas only one-half of women in the same age group were married (Federal Interagency Forum on Aging-Related Statistics, 2004). However, although 59% of men over the age of 85 were still married, only 14% of women were (see Figure 9.3 for more information).

For those who are still married, most report that their marriages improved over time and that the later years are some of the happiest. Elderly men often report more satisfaction with marriage than do women, who complain of increased responsibilities in car-

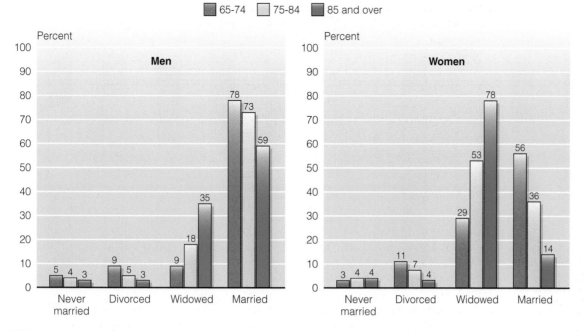

Marital status of the population age 65 and over

■ 65-74　□ 75-84　■ 85 and over

Men

Percent

	Never married	Divorced	Widowed	Married
65-74	5	9	9	78
75-84	4	5	18	73
85 and over	3	3	35	59

Women

Percent

	Never married	Divorced	Widowed	Married
65-74	3	11	29	56
75-84	4	7	53	36
85 and over	4	4	78	14

Figure 9.3 Marital status of the population age 65 and over, by age group and sex, 2003.
Source: Federal Interagency Forum on Aging-Related Statistics, 2004.

ing for a sick husband or planning activities if he is retired. This is further complicated by the fact that older persons usually have very few places to turn to for emotional assistance. They have fewer relatives and friends and no coworkers, and they often feel uncomfortable sharing problems with their children. In addition, counseling services are limited.

Many older people who experience the death of a spouse will remarry. Older men are twice as likely to remarry, however, because women outnumber men in older age and also because older men often marry younger women (M. Coleman et al., 2000). White males remarry more often than other groups; the remarriage rates for African Americans are lower, and they have longer intervals between marriages (South, 1991). Marriages that follow the death of a spouse tend to be more successful if the couple knew each other for a period of time prior to the marriage, if their children and peers approve of the marriage, and if they are in good health, financially stable, and have adequate living conditions. Remarriages for couples older than 40 tend to be more stable than first marriages (Wu & Penning, 1997). One 73-year-old man describes his experience:

> I can't begin to tell you how happy I am. I am married to a wonderful woman who loves me as much as I love her. My children gave me a hard time of it at first, especially because she is a bit younger than me, but they finally accepted the relationship and came to our wedding. In fact, they gave me away at the ceremony. That's a switch, isn't it? I put some humor into this situation when my oldest son, who is in the business with me, objected. He was telling me that marrying again and trying to have a lot of sex—imagine that, saying to me trying to have sex—could be dangerous to the marriage. So, I said to him with a straight face, "Do you think she'll survive it?" He was so shocked, he laughed. (Janus & Janus, 1993, p. 8)

Although an estimated 500,000 people over the age of 65 remarry in the United States every year (M. Coleman et al., 2000), as we discussed earlier in this chapter, a small percentage of older couples live together in place of marriage (Chevan, 1996). See Figure 9.4 for more information on living arrangements in men and women aged 65 and over.

Older couples may experience increased happiness and intimacy when children grow up and leave home.

Review Question

Explain what we know about marital satisfaction in older couples.

Adult Sexual Relationships **269**

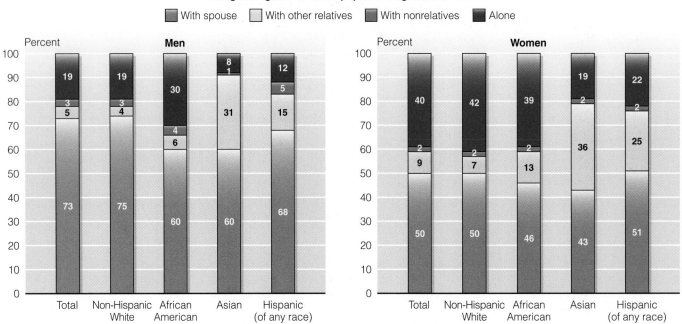

Living arrangements of the population age 65 and over

■ With spouse   □ With other relatives   ■ With nonrelatives   ■ Alone

Men

Total: With spouse 73, 5, 3, Alone 19
Non-Hispanic White: 75, 4, 3, 19
African American: 60, 6, 4, 30
Asian: 60, 31, 1, 8
Hispanic (of any race): 68, 15, 5, 12

Women

Total: With spouse 50, 9, 2, Alone 40
Non-Hispanic White: 50, 7, 2, 42
African American: 46, 13, 2, 39
Asian: 43, 36, 2, 19
Hispanic (of any race): 51, 25, 2, 22

Figure 9.4 Living arrangements of the population age 65 and over, by sex and race and Hispanic origin, 2003.
Source: Federal Interagency Forum on Aging-Related Statistics, 2004.

Extramarital Affairs: "It Just Happened"

All societies regulate sexual behavior and use marriage as a means to control the behavior of their members to some degree. Our society is one of the few that have traditionally forbidden sexual contact outside of marriage; research estimates that less than 5% of all societies are as strict about forbidding extramarital intercourse as ours has been (Leslie & Korman, 1989). Our opposition to sex outside of marriage stems from our Judeo-Christian background, and although today it is not as shocking as it used to be, there is still a strong feeling among Americans that extramarital sex is wrong.

Almost all couples, whether dating, living together, or married, expect sexual exclusivity from each other. Although extramarital sex refers to sex outside of marriage, we are also referring here to extra-relationship sex, or dating couples who have sex with someone other than their partner. Not surprisingly, adults in the United States are more likely to cheat while living together than while married (Treas & Giesen, 2000). Those who cheat in intimate relationships have been found to have stronger sexual interests, more permissive sexual values, less satisfaction in their intimate relationship, and more opportunities for sex outside the relationship (Treas & Giesen, 2000).

Half the states in the United States have laws against sex outside of marriage, although these laws are rarely enforced. If they were enforced, a cheating spouse would be unable to vote, practice law, adopt children, or even raise his or her own children. Even though many of these laws aren't enforced, attitudes about extramarital sex in the United States remain fairly negative. Over the last few years, attitudes about extramarital sex have become even more negative (Thornton & Young-DeMarco, 2001).

Laumann and colleagues (1994) found that 20% of women and 15% to 35% of men of all ages reported that they had engaged in extramarital sex while they were married. Even for those couples who never consider sex outside of marriage, the possibility looms, and people wonder about it—what it would be like, or if their partners are indulging in it.

How does an extramarital affair begin? In the first stage, a person might become emotionally close to someone at school, work, a party, or even on the Internet. As they get to know each other, there is chemistry and a powerful attraction. This moves into the second stage, in which the couple decides to keep the relationship secret. They don't tell their closest friends about their attraction. This secret, in turn, adds fuel to the passion. In the third stage, the couple starts doing things together, even though they would not refer to it as "dating." Each still believes that the relationship is all about friendship. Finally, in the fourth stage, the relationship becomes sexual, leading to an intense emotional and sexual affair (Layton-Tholl, 1998).

Extra-relationship affairs can have a similar effect on a dating relationship. Overall, married couples are the most deceptive about sexual affairs outside of their relationship. Both nonmarried heterosexual couples and lesbians who live together have been found to be less deceptive and secretive than married couples.

There appear to be some gender and racial differences in acceptance of extramarital affairs. Males tend to be more accepting of extramarital sex than females (Wilson & Medora, 1990). Overall, women have been found to experience more emotional distress about infidelity than men do, although a woman is more likely to be upset about emotional infidelity, whereas a man is more likely to be upset about his partner's sexual infidelity (see Chapter 7 for more information about gender differences in jealousy; Nannini & Meyers, 2000). Interestingly, men and women often accept more responsibility for their partner's infidelity when it was emotional in nature. Perhaps this is because they feel their own emotional unavailability led their partner to seek emotional comfort somewhere else (Nannini & Meyers, 2000). Overall, women have been found to have more emotional, rather than physical, affairs.

Although many people think that sexual desire drives an extramarital affair, research has found that over 90% of extramarital affairs occur because of unmet emotional needs within the marital relationship (Layton-Tholl, 1998). Those who cheat may be looking for the original spark and passion from earlier in their marriage. In fact, when asked, the majority of people claim that marital dissatisfaction is a justifiable reason for engaging in an extramarital affair (Taylor, 1986). Laumann and colleagues (1994) found that, overall, couples are faithful to each other as long as the marriage is intact and satisfying.

Most people who engage in extramarital affairs feel intense guilt about their behavior. Some do go on to marry their new partner, but these relationships are often fraught with turmoil because the relationship was based on a lie from the beginning. A. P. Thompson (1984) claims that there are three types of extramarital affairs: sexual but not emotional; sexual and emotional; and emotional but not sexual. Twenty-one percent of respondents having extramarital sex were involved in predominantly sexual affairs; 19% in both sexual and emotional affairs; and 18% in affairs that were emotional but not sexual (the remaining affairs did not fit clearly into any of these categories). Affairs that are both emotional and sexual appear to affect the marital relationship the most, whereas affairs that are primarily sexual affect it the least.

Gender differences play a role in the type of extramarital sexual relationships that occur. Women are more likely than men to have emotional but not sexual affairs, and twice as many men have sexual affairs. Research has also found that the more positive a woman's attitude is toward sexuality, the longer she will stay in a primarily sexual extramarital affair. However, attitudes about sex are often unrelated to the length of the emotional type of extramarital affair. Age differences have also been found—men are more likely to have extramarital affairs when they are younger, whereas women are more likely to do so when they are older. In addition, women who have extramarital affairs are less sex typed and are more independent and assertive than women who do not (Hurlbert, 1992).

Can a marital relationship continue after an extramarital affair? Yes, but it can be difficult. Often the male partner who has an extramarital affair adds further distress to his wife by mislabeling her reactions and emotions (Gass & Nichols, 1988). For example, he may try to distort reality so that his wife thinks she is imagining things. All in all, regaining trust and reestablishing a relationship will often take time after an affair.

Open Marriages: Sexual Adventuring

Some married couples open up their relationships and encourage their partners to have extramarital affairs or to bring other partners into their marital beds, believing that sexual variety and experience enhance their own sexual life. This has been referred to as

Review Question

Explain the gender differences that have been found in reactions to infidelity.

sex byte

Couples in long-term relationships are far less likely to have heart attacks while having sex than those having affairs or one-night stands (G. Jackson, 2002).

SEX in Real Life

What Is Polyamory?

If you're in a relationship, do you expect monogamy from your partner? Most of us would answer this question with a resounding "YES"! We live in a society that expects monogamy from our sexual partners. Serial monogamy, a form of monogamy in which partners have only one sexual partner at any one time, is common on college campuses today. The majority of men and women have more than one sexual partner in their lifetime, but they are monogamous while in these relationships.

A "polyamorous" man or woman has intimate, loving relationships with more than one person at a time, but he or she also has a consensual and agreed-on context to these affairs (Weitzman, 1999). Polyamorous couples are gay and straight, and they are honest with each other about their relationships. These types of relationships are very different from a monogamous couple that cheats while claiming to maintain his or her faithfulness.

Polyamorous individuals are not swingers because the emphasis is on a relationship rather than on recreational sex. Polyamorous relationship could take many forms, including:

1. *Primary-Plus:* One couple in a primary relationship agrees to pursue outside relationships. New lovers are "secondary lovers," and the primary relationship remains the most important relationship.
2. *Triad:* Three people involved in a committed intimate relationship. All three relationships are equal and there is no primary relationship.
3. *Individual with Multiple Primaries:* This relationship resembles a "V," with one partner at the pivot point with two additional partners who may not relate to each other.

SOURCE: Davidson, 2002.

---

comarital sex
The consenting of married couples to sexually exchange partners.

swinger
A man, woman, or couple who openly exchanges sexual partners (also called a polyamorist).

polyamorist
A man, woman, or couple who openly exchanges sexual partners (also called a swinger).

Review Question

Explain the concept and rules of open marriage.

open marriage, in which couples engage in **comarital sex** (the consenting of married couples to sexually exchange partners), and the partners are often referred to as **swingers** or **polyamorists** (pah-lee-AM-more-rists). It is estimated that there are about 3 million married, middle-aged swingers in the United States today. Years ago, these swingers found each other in swingers' magazines, but today many support groups exist, and the Internet is the main source of contact (Rubin, 2001). Overall, the majority of swingers are white, middle class, middle aged, and church going (Bergstrand & Williams, 2000).

In 1972, George & Nena O'Neill published a book entitled *Open Marriage* (O'Neill & O'Neill, 1972). In this book, they explained that "sexual adventuring" was fine, as long as both spouses knew about it. In open marriages, each partner is free to seek out sexual partners outside of the marriage. Many swingers engage in "safe-sex circles" in which they have sex only with people who have tested negative for STIs.

Most couples who allow this, however, have strict rules meant to protect the marriage; sex in those cases is seen as separate from the loving relations of marriage. The marriage is always viewed as the primary relationship, and sex outside this relationship is thought only to strengthen the marriage (Rubin, 2001). In fact, swingers have been found to report happier marriages and a higher life satisfaction than nonswingers (Bergstrand & Williams, 2000). However, many couples also find that maintaining that kind of openness is more difficult than they anticipated.

Marriages in Other Cultures

Dating, cohabitation, and marriage are often viewed differently outside the United States. Let's now take a look at courtship, arranged marriages, extramarital sex, and various customs and practices common outside the United States.

Courtship and Arranged Marriages

In most industrialized countries, partner selection through dating is the norm. However, in some countries there are no dating systems. For example, in Sweden, there is no Swedish term for what Americans call "dating"—couples meet at dance clubs, bars, schools, or through friends (Trost, 2004).

Human Sexuality in a Diverse World

Arranged Marriage

How would you feel about your mother or father choosing a partner for you to marry? Don't they know you better than anyone else? Although arranged marriages aren't common in the United States today, a significant proportion of all marriages are arranged in large parts of Africa, Asia, and the Middle East (M. Moore, 1994). Marriage partners are chosen by parents, relatives, friends, and matchmakers based on the prospective partner's finances, family values, status, and perceived compatibility (Batabyal, 2001).

Some of the women who are offered as brides come with a dowry (cash or gifts for the groom's family). Although giving and accepting a dowry is illegal in many countries, it is still widely practiced. Some families are willing to pay up to $500,000 cash to find a husband for an Indian daughter (Easley, 2003).

The Manhattan-based *India Abroad Weekly*, which can be accessed online, runs about 125 classified ads every week for families or others searching for Indian brides and grooms (Easley, 2003). The ads are very specific about what qualities the potential bride or groom has to offer. For example, a recent search yielded the following results:

[bride] PARENTS seek professional/Doctor match below 27, minimum 5'4''; for USMD fellow son, 27/6'.

BRIDE needed for well-settled Punjabi boy in US, 42/5'11'' Ph.D. Healthcare, teetotaler, issueless divorcee; from family-oriented girls.

[groom] AFFLUENT, Hindu Punjabi parents seek v. tall, v. good-looking, US raised, v. well educated & settled professionals/businessmen match; for v. beautiful, slim, v. fair 29yrs/5'8'', Dentist daughter.

[groom] UNMARRIED established young Californians who would like to get married to an established educated Hindu Bengali girl 27/ 5'4'', US citizen. Please respond with your accomplishments, family background & photograph.

SOURCE: Retrieved October 21, 2005, from http://www.indiaabroad.com/CLASSIFIED/current-listing/2910.shtml.

There are still a few industrialized cultures in which **arranged marriages** take place. In Iran all marriages are arranged, even those that are based on love (Drew, 2004). A young man will visit the home of the woman he wishes to marry accompanied by three members of his family. The woman is not allowed to speak unless directly questioned. A contract is signed and although the couple is not formally married, this contract is legally binding. A formal marriage ceremony usually takes place a year later. (For more information about arranged marriage, see the accompanying Human Sexuality in a Diverse World, "Arranged Marriage.")

In some cultures, courtship is a highly ritualized process in which every step is defined by one's kin group or tribe (Hutter, 1981). For example, the marriages of the Yaruros of Venezuela are arranged and highly specified; a man must marry his "cross-cousin"—that is, the daughter of either his father's sister or his mother's brother. The marriages are arranged by the shaman or religious leader in consultation with one of the boy's uncles.

The Hottentots of South Africa also marry their cross-cousins, but here the boy can choose which cousin he wants to marry; once he does, he informs his parents, who send someone to seek permission from the girl's parents. Tradition dictates that they must refuse. The youth then approaches the girl, going to her house late at night once everyone is asleep and lying down next to her. She then gets up and moves to the other side of the house. The next night he returns, and if he finds her back on the side where he first lay next to her, he lies down again with her, and the marriage is consummated (Hutter, 1981).

For 2,000 years, marriages in China were arranged by parents and elders, and emotional involvement between prospective marriage partners was frowned upon; if a couple appeared to like having their marriage arranged, the marriage was called off! In China, the primary responsibility of each person was supposed to be to his or her extended family. If there was a marriage bond that was very strong outside of that extended family, it could jeopardize the cohesiveness of the group.

arranged marriage
Marriage that is arranged by parents or relatives and is often not based on love.

This all began to change with the communist revolution of 1949. Through contact with the West, these customs began to erode. Only 8 months after coming to power, the communist leaders established the Marriage Law of the People's Republic of China, in which, among other things, they tried to end arranged marriages and establish people's right to choose their spouse freely. Today in China, although arranged marriages still take place in the rural areas, people date and meet each other in public places—a condition that was virtually unknown a few generations before.

In many parts of Africa, too, parents used to be involved in mate selection (Kayongo-Male & Onyango, 1984). Marriages were arranged between families, not really individuals, and each family had a set of expectations about the other's role. Courtship was highly ritualized, with the groom's family paying a "bride wealth" to the bride's family. The rituals that preceded marriage were intended to teach the couple what their particular tribe or culture believed married couples needed to know in order to keep their marriage successful. However, young people did have some say in who they were to marry; in many cases, young people would reject their parents' choices or meet someone they liked and ask their parents to arrange a marriage. One Egyptian boy commented:

> We all know the girls of our village. After all, we played together as kids, and we see them going back and forth on errands as they get older. One favorite place for us to get a glimpse of girls is at the village water source. The girls know that and like to linger there. If we see one we like and think she might be suitable, we ask our parents to try to arrange a marriage, but usually not before we have some sign from the girl that she might be interested. (Rugh, 1984, p. 137)

Today, however, mate selection in most places is a much more individual affair. However much we in the West believe in the right of individuals to choose their own mates, there were some advantages to parental participation in mate selection, and the transition to individual mate selection in traditional societies is often difficult.

An alarming practice has been on the rise, especially in places such as Afghanistan, Africa, and Bangladesh. Many poor families have been selling their young daughters for a "bride price" (Hinshelwood, 2002). Usually the girls are sold between the ages of 8 and 12 years old, for anywhere from $300 to $800. These young girls can stay with their families until their future husband comes to claim them, usually around their first menstrual period. Although this practice is against the law, poverty has contributed to its increased popularity. Today many women's groups in the West have become very concerned about the sale of these girls and are working to stop this practice.

Extramarital Sex

Extramarital sex is forbidden in many cultures but often tolerated—even in cultures in which it is technically not allowed. For example, infidelity is considered a grave transgression in Islam and is punishable, according to the Koran, by 100 lashes for both partners (Farah, 1984). However, there are a number of Muslim societies, such as many in Africa (Kayongo-Male & Onyango, 1984) and Pakistan (Donnan, 1988) in which adultery is tacitly accepted as a fact of life.

Those countries that tolerate extramarital sex often find it more acceptable for men than for women. In Zimbabwe, for example, women were asked what they would do if they found out their partners were engaging in extramarital sex: 80% reported they would confront their partners, 15% said they would caution their husbands, and 5% were indifferent. But when men were asked the same question, 60% replied they would divorce their wives, 20% would severely beat their wives, 18% would severely caution her, and 2% would express disappointment and ask their partner to change (Mhloyi, 1990). In China, elderly neighborhood women keep watch in "neighborhood committees" and report suspicious extramarital activities (Ruan & Lau, 2004).

In some cultures, extramarital relations are replacing polygamy. In some African societies in which having multiple wives is becoming less accepted, men may set up a secret second household in which a woman is kept as his wife without a ceremony—and without any of the legal rights that accrue to a wife (Kayongo-Male & Onyango, 1984).

Customs and Practices

Marriage ceremonies take place in every society on Earth, but marriage customs vary widely from culture to culture. In some cultures, girls can be married as young as 9 years old (although they do not have sex with their husbands until puberty). Other cultures mandate marriages between certain relatives, and still other cultures allow multiple spouses.

Most cultures celebrate marriage as a time of rejoicing and have rituals or ceremonies that accompany the wedding process. Among different Berber tribes in Morocco, for example, wedding rituals can include performing a sacrifice, painting the heels of the couple's feet with goat's blood, having a feast, having fish cast at the feet of the bride, or feeding bread to the family dog (Westermarck, 1972). In Iranian culture a "temporary marriage" allows a Muslim man an opportunity for female companionship outside of legal marriage when he travels or is employed by the military (Drew, 2004). Temporary marriages were formally approved by the Iranian government in 1990.

In many preliterate cultures (and in some literate ones, too) there is a tendency to believe that the main purpose of being female is to get married and have babies. Among the Tiwi, a group of Australian aborigines, this was taken to its logical conclusion; a woman was to get married, and there was no word in their language for a single woman, for there was, in fact, no female—of any age—without at least a nominal husband. The Tiwi believed that pregnancy happens because a spirit entered the body of a female, but one could never be sure exactly when that happened; so the best thing to do was to make sure that the woman was married at all times. Therefore, all Tiwi babies were betrothed before or as soon as they were born, and widows were required to remarry at the gravesides of their husbands, no matter how old they were (Hart & Pilling, 1960).

As we discussed earlier in this chapter, 60% of marriages worldwide are arranged (Mackay, 2000), so for many the concept of "loving" one's partner may be irrelevant. In Japan, for example, "love" marriages are often frowned upon because a couple can fall out of love and split up (Kristof, 1996). Some would argue that Japanese men and women actually love each other less than American couples do. Yet the secret to a strong family, claim the Japanese, is not in love but rather low expectations, patience, and shame (Kristof, 1996). These factors lead to couples staying together through thick or thin, rather than splitting up when the going gets rough. When one Japanese man, married for 33 years, was asked whether he loved his wife, he replied, "Yeah, so-so, I guess. She's like air or water. You couldn't live without it, but most of the time, you're not conscious of its existence" (Kristof, 1996). This is probably why Japanese couples scored the lowest on what they have in common with each other, compared to couples in 37 other countries (see Figure 9.5).

Some countries allow the practice of **polygamy** (pah-LIGG-uh-mee). Usually, this takes the form of **polygyny** (pah-LIDGE-uh-nee), or having more than one wife, which is a common practice in many areas of Africa and the Middle East, among other places. Although it is rarely practiced in the United States, there are some small Mormon fundamentalist groups that do practice polygyny. Most commonly, a polygynous marriage involves two or three wives, though in Islam a man is allowed up to four.

Some have suggested that polygyny began as a strategy to increase fertility, but the suggestion is controversial. In fact, a number of stud-

polygamy
The condition or practice of having more than one spouse at one time.

polygyny
The condition or practice of having more than one wife at one time.

Figure 9.5 In a survey by the Dentsu Research Institutes and Leisure Development Center in Japan, spouses answered questions about politics, sex, social issues, religion, and ethics. A score of 500 would indicate perfect compatibility.
Source: "Who Needs Love! In Japan, Many Couples Don't," *New York Times,* February 11, 1996, p. A1. Copyright © 1996 by New York Times Co. Reprinted by permission.

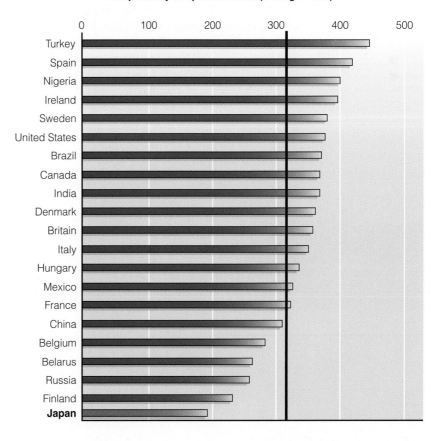

Compatibility of spouses index (average = 316)

ies have found that polygyny is associated with lower fertility among wives (Anderton & Emigh, 1989), although other studies have found no differences and a few have even found higher rates of fertility (Ahmed, 1986). However, the majority of the research supports the conclusion that wives in polygynous marriages have lower fertility rates. This is because husbands in polygynous marriages must divide their time between each of their wives, which decreases the chance of impregnation for each individual wife. Therefore, it may be more likely that polygyny developed as a strategy for men to gain prestige and power by having many wives, whereas women could gain the protection of a wealthy man.

In Islam, a woman may have sex with only one man, but a man may marry up to four wives. Al-Ghazali, the great Islamic thinker and writer of the 11th century, believed that polygyny was permitted due to the desires of men. What determines whether a Muslim man has multiple wives in most Islamic countries today is his wealth more than anything else, for he usually sets up a different household for each wife. Another reason for polygyny in many Muslim countries is the desire for a male child; if one wife does not deliver a male heir, the man may choose a second and third wife to try for a boy (Donnan, 1988).

Polygamy also occurs in France, where primarily African couples have practiced it for many years (M. Simons, 1996). As of 1996, it was estimated that there were 200,000 people living in polygamous families in France. But the practice has met with much resistance. In 1996, the French government ruled that France will recognize only one-spouse marriages, and all other types of marriage will be annulled.

One woman commented on the negative aspects of polygamy: "You hear everything, your husband and the other wives. You hear how he behaves with his favorite, usually the new one. The women end up hating the man. Everyone feels bad inside" (M. Simons, 1996, p. A1). However, polygamous husbands have a different view. One polygamous husband says:

> My father did it, my grandfather did, so why shouldn't I? When my wife is sick and I don't have another, who will care for me? Besides, one wife on her own is trouble. When there are several, they are forced to be polite and well behaved. If they misbehave, you threaten that you'll take another wife. (M. Simons, 1996, p. A1)

Polyandry (PAH-lee-ann-dree), in which a woman has more than one husband, is much less common than polygyny, and it is usually used to keep together inheritance. For example, in Tibet, a woman may marry several brothers in order to avoid cutting up the inherited property. The same rationale is used in many **consanguineous** (con-san-GWIN-ee-us) **marriages,** in which a woman marries her own relative to maintain the integrity of family property.

In the majority of U.S. states, consanguineous marriage is illegal and has been since the late 19th century. However, in many Muslim countries in northern Africa; western and southern Asia; north, east, and central India; and the middle Asian republics of the former Soviet Union, marriages take place between relatives between 20% and 55% of the time (Bittles et al., 1991). In Islamic societies marriages between first cousins are most common, whereas in Hindu states of south India uncle–niece and first-cousin marriages are equally common. Incidentally, marriages between certain cousins are legal in many U.S. states.

Finally, there are also some interesting postmarriage practices that take place outside the United States. For example, in Iran the bride's mother and mother-in-law will sleep close to the marriage bed on the wedding night and both will inspect a special handkerchief that provides evidence of virginity (Drew, 2004). Family members often travel together with the couple on the honeymoon, and the groom's mother remains with the newlywed couple for the first few weeks of marriage. It is her job to set the household guidelines and rules.

polyandry
The condition or practice of having more than one husband at one time.

consanguineous marriage
A type of marriage between blood relatives, usually to maintain the integrity of family property.

Review **Question**

Explain what is known about courtship, arranged marriages, extramarital sex, and other customs and practices outside the United States.

SAME-SEX RELATIONSHIPS

Although we have been discussing both gay and straight relationships throughout this chapter, in many ways, gay and lesbian relationships have changed more than heterosexual relationships over the last few decades. First, these relationships came out of the closet in the 1960s and 1970s, when there was a blossoming of a gay subculture. Then, the advent of AIDS resulted in fewer sexual partners and more long-term, monogamous relationships, especially in the gay community. Although we will discuss many aspects of same-sex relationships in Chapter 11, here we will explore sexuality in these relationships and the advent of same-sex marriages.

Sexuality in Same-Sex Relationships

Earlier in this chapter, we discussed gender differences in initiating sexual activity in heterosexual relationships: men often do more of the initiating. Does this mean that lesbians may be uncomfortable initiating sex or that gay men never have problems doing so? According to a classic study done by Blumstein & Schwartz (1983), this may be the case. They found that some lesbians do have difficulty initiating or balancing sex in their relationships. As with heterosexual relationships, often one partner initiates more than the other. One woman explains:

> The problem is that I want more than she does. And she feels guilty about wanting less. Recently, we've been to a counselor to talk about it. I think we've come to a point of deciding that we probably are not going to be able to solve it . . . that we've gone around in circles long enough. (Blumstein & Schwartz, 1983, p. 214)

Problems with initiating sex in lesbian relationships may be due to the social pressures women have while growing up. According to one 33-year-old woman:

> Women have a hesitancy to initiate. My forthrightness makes sex happen. [Lesbians] don't ask; they wait. All that "boy asking them to dance" stuff. It's not alright for women to ask for things for themselves. . . . Sometimes I have gotten these messages from my partner. It's very subtle. Subtly to imply I am too intense. If you're the only person asking, you get to feel pretty weird. I ask, "What do you want?" and they say, "Whatever you want." So I start to pull back on asking for what I want. (Blumstein & Schwartz, 1983, p. 215)

In lesbian couples, it is often the more emotionally expressive partner who is responsible for maintaining the couple's sex life.

Similarly, in relationships between gay men the more emotionally expressive partner is usually the one who initiates sexual activity. However, gay men are much less bothered by their role of initiator. Again, this may lead to other problems, with one partner feeling he is always the initiator. One gay man explains:

> I don't want sex enough, according to him. He would like me to be more aggressive. But sometimes I'm just beat and I don't feel like having sex. . . . I used to be more dominant, but he would turn me off because he felt so uncomfortable about [receiving anal intercourse], and although we never articulated it, it embedded itself as a memory that he felt he wouldn't be able to satisfy me, so we'd better not start. I have to remind him occasionally that I've gotten used to his not wanting it and now I don't want it so much. (Blumstein & Schwartz, 1983, p. 216)

Gay men engage in sexual behavior more often than lesbian women do. Lower rates of sexual behavior in lesbian couples have been explained in many ways. It could be that the biological nature of the sex drive is lower in women, that females typically do not initiate sexual activity and may not be comfortable doing so, or that women are less likely than men to express their feelings through sex. Finally, it also must be pointed out that perhaps lesbian lovemaking lasts longer than heterosexual lovemaking (focusing more on foreplay), and a longer duration of lovemaking could lead to a decrease in the actual number of occurrences.

Same-Sex Marriage

In 1996, the U.S. Congress enacted the Defense of Marriage Act, which allows each state to recognize or deny any marriage relationship between same-sex couples, recognizes marriage as a "legal union of one man and one woman as husband and wife," refers

The families of same-sex couples often include children and grandchildren.

to a "spouse" only as a person of the other sex. In 2000, Vermont passed a civil union statute that grants same-sex couples the same benefits and responsibilities given to heterosexual couples (allows couples to share employee benefits, including health insurance, family and medical leave, bereavement leave, and other family workplace benefits that help employees handle job and family responsibilities; Mason et al., 2001). However, civil unions performed in Vermont have no legal weight once the couple leaves Vermont.

In 2004 Massachusetts became the first state in the nation to give full marriage rights to lesbian and gay couples. As of 2005, Massachusetts is the only state in which same-sex marriage is recognized. Seven states, including California, Connecticut, the District of Columbia, Hawaii, Maine, New Jersey, and Vermont, grant legal status to same-sex couples through civil unions or domestic partnerships. All other states have constitutional amendments or legal statutes that define marriage as only between a man and a woman. As of late 2005, same-sex marriage was legal only in the Netherlands, Belgium, Canada, Spain, and South Africa (we will discuss this more later in this chapter).

Why should marriage be allowed only for heterosexual couples and not for gay and lesbian couples? Shouldn't same-sex marriages be legalized (or an equivalent marriage-like status)? The answers to these questions go back many years. Aristotle discussed the importance of legislators to establish rules regulating marriage (Dixit & Pindyck, 1994).

Societies have always given preference to heterosexual couples, presumably because of the benefits that heterosexual marriages provide to society (benefits to the couples but also to their offspring). Wardle (2001) discusses eight social interests for marriage, including

1. Safe sexual relations
2. Responsible procreation
3. Optimal child rearing
4. Healthy human development
5. Protecting those who undertake the most vulnerable parenting roles (i.e., mothers/wives)
6. Securing the stability and integrity of the basic unit of society
7. Fostering civic virtue and social order
8. Facilitating interjurisdictional compatibility

As you can see, heterosexual marriage is strongly linked to procreation, childbirth, and child rearing (Wardle, 2001). The United States has long regulated marriage in an attempt to protect procreative health. This is precisely why marriages between relatives are illegal (birth defects are more prevalent in couples who are related), and marriages between "unfit" or mentally challenged partners are regulated.

Even with all this controversy, many gay and lesbian couples "marry" their partners in ceremonies that are not recognized by the states in which they live. Gay marriages, whether legally recognized or not, often suffer from the same jealousies, power struggles, and "divorces" as heterosexual marriages; they may even be more unstable because of the added pressures of social disapproval (P. H. Collins, 1988). Gay and lesbian couples interviewed by Blumstein & Schwartz (1983) complained about their partners' lack of attention, sexual incompatibility, and the same mundane, day-to-day struggles that straight couples deal with. In addition, these couples often have to cope with the disapproval of their families and, sometimes, the stress of hiding their relationship. See the accompanying Personal Voices, "Same-Sex Marriage," for a moving personal story about the legality of same-sex marriage.

As we just discussed, many groups have been working to get states to set up **domestic partner** acts, whereby same-sex couples who live together in committed relationships can have some of the benefits granted to married couples. Many same-sex couples across the United States are challenging existing laws that regulate issues such as same-sex marriage, separation, child custody, and gay adoption. These court cases will continue, some say, until same-sex couples are given the same marital rights as their heterosexual counterparts. We will discuss these issues more in Chapter 11.

domestic partner

A person other than a spouse with whom one cohabits. Domestic partners can be either same or other sex.

Review Question

Explain what we know about same-sex relationships and same-sex marriage.

Personal Voices

Same-Sex Marriage

I am a 39-year-old gay man. Robert, my childhood sweetheart, and I came out as gay at the age of 13. The purity of that relationship, juxtaposed with the trauma of his death, far too young (the result of what today would be called a gay bashing), have doubtless shaped who I am today.

I define my marital status as widowed, principally as the result of the death of my lover, Ken, in 1994; his death brought to a close a relationship which had spanned close to seven years. The cause of death was heart failure, the result of a congenital lung condition. Soon after we started dating, he told me of his health condition and of its eventually fatal consequences. He did so not to scare me away, but to prepare me for what lay ahead.

One of my greatest regrets was my inability to place my lover on my health care plan. He was self-employed and found premiums prohibitively expensive. When his health declined to the point that he required around-the-clock care, I lost my job. My employer informed me that a leave of absence would not be

granted as care for a dying lover failed to meet guidelines for such consideration. Survival necessitated liquidating, one after another, all of my assets. Upon his death, the estate being insolvent, household items were sold to cover just debts. For those who've experienced the death of a legally defined spouse, if you feel that my relationship with my lover does not equate to the loss that you've sustained, let me tell you this. I remember every restless night, waking up screaming, trembling, and crying; I've lived with the overwhelming loneliness associated with birthdays, anniversaries, and the countless private rituals now remembered only by one; and I can state, unequivocally, that the worst part of widowhood is sleeping alone again—and it has nothing to do with sex—it is literally just sleeping alone again.

The one thing that no one can take away are the last words that Ken spoke, some 20 minutes before he breathed his last, addressed to me, "My beautiful boy, I love you very much."

SOURCE: Author's files.

Same-Sex Relationships in Other Cultures

Rob Melnychuk/Getty Images

Many gay and lesbian couples in the United States would like to wed someday. As of 2005, only Massachusetts allows gay and lesbian couples to legally wed.

Same-sex relationships outside the United States are supported in some countries and ignored in others. For example, in Australia, equal rights legislation gives gay and lesbian couples equal rights as heterosexual couples (Coates, 2004). Larger cities, such as Sydney, contain the largest population of gay couples. Gay and lesbian relationships are acceptable in France, where a law in 1985 made it illegal to discriminate against gays and lesbians (Meignant, 2004). Other countries, such as Ireland, are not as supportive of same-sex relationships.

Same-sex marriage and the adoption of children by same-sex couples were both legalized in the Netherlands in 2001. At least one partner must have Dutch nationality or live in the Netherlands in order to marry. As of September of 2005, there had been 2,100 men and 1,700 women married in same-sex ceremonies in the Netherlands. In Belgium, same-sex marriage was legalized in 2003, although adoption by same-sex couples is not allowed. Originally Belgium allowed foreign same-sex couples to marry only if their country of origin allowed same-sex marriage. However, in 2004 new rulings allowed any couple to marry if one of the partners had lived in Belgium for at least 3 months. As of 2005, a total of 2,442 same-sex couples mar-

Review Question

Explain what we know about same-sex relationships in other cultures.

ried there. Canada legalized same-sex marriage countrywide in 2005. Prior to that, it had been legalized only in certain provinces and territories. Spain also legalized same-sex marriage in 2005 and allowed for same-sex couples to adopt. Finally South Africa became the fifth country to legalize same-sex marriage in late 2005.

DIVORCE: WHOSE FAULT OR NO-FAULT?

There have been substantial changes in the institution of marriage over the last 30 years. During most of U.S. history, a married couple was viewed as a single, legal entity (M. A. Mason et al., 2001). However, over the last 3 decades there has been a shift in how marriage is viewed. Today, marriage is seen more as a partnership between a man and a woman. This shift in perception of marriage also brought with it a shift in how marriage was dissolved. The liberalization of divorce laws made it easier to obtain a divorce and made it a less expensive process.

By 1985, all states offered couples some type of **no-fault divorce** (Krause, 1986). In an attempt to reduce the skyrocketing divorce rates, some states have instituted **covenant marriages,** which revolve around restrictive agreed-on rules and regulations for ending a marriage and also involve premarital counseling and an agreement to pursue additional counseling if marital problems develop. In addition, the wait time for a divorce is extended, in some cases to 2 years or more, unless there is domestic violence involved. We will talk more about covenant marriages later in this chapter.

What causes a couple to end their marriage? The question is complicated because not all unstable or unhappy marriages end in divorce. Couples stay together for many reasons—for the children, because of lack of initiative, because of religious prohibitions against divorce—even though they have severe problems in their marriages. Similarly, couples with seemingly happy marriages separate and divorce, sometimes to the surprise of one of the partners who did not even know the marriage was in trouble.

The current divorce rate in the United States remains high compared to earlier times in the century and other countries (Goldstein, 1999; South et al., 2001). If current levels persist, half of the current marriages in the United States will end in divorce. In 1970 there were 4.3 million divorced Americans, but this number jumped to 20 million by 2000 (Fields & Casper, 2001).

Divorce rates vary among age groups. They are at their highest in women in their teens and decline with increasing age. Perhaps the most consistent finding about divorce is that those who marry early are more likely to divorce eventually. Generally, divorce occurs early in the marriage; the median duration of marriage at divorce in 1988 was 7.1 years. First marriages have been found to last approximately 2 years longer before divorce than second marriages, which last 2 years longer than third or subsequent marriages (Centers for Disease Control, 1991).

African Americans, Native Americans, and Puerto Ricans show the highest separation and divorce rates in the United States; Korean, Asian Indian, and Chinese Americans have the lowest rates; and Mexican Americans, Cubans, and whites lie somewhere in between (Skolnick, 1992). Interracial marriages also have higher divorce rates than marriages within racial groups (Zinn & Eitzen, 1993).

The marital instability of African Americans has received considerable attention, in part because it has increased dramatically over the last 30 years. In 1960, 65% of African American women aged 30 to 34 were in intact marriages, whereas by 1990, the percentage dropped to 39% (Zinn & Eitzen, 1993). Although many cultural factors contribute to the high rates of divorce, such as the unwillingness of black women to put up with male-dominated marriages, the main reasons for the increased divorce rates are probably the unemployment, economic dislocation, and increasing poverty within the African American community.

A mutually shared decision to divorce is actually uncommon. Usually, one partner wants to terminate a relationship more than the other partner, who is still strongly attached to the marriage and who is more distraught at its termination. In fact, the declaration that a partner wants a divorce often comes as a shock to his or her spouse. When

no-fault divorce
A divorce law that allows for the dissolution of a marriage without placing blame on either of the partners.

covenant marriage
A marriage that is preceded by premarital counseling and has strict rules about divorce.

Human Sexuality in a Diverse World

Reasons for Divorce in Four Cultures

Following are the reasons given for divorce in four cultures: among the men of the Muria, a tribal group in India; among couples in the African country of Cameroon; among Chinese couples registering for divorce in Shanghai, China; and among couples in the United States.

Rank of Reasons for Divorce Among Men of the Muria Tribe

1. She ran away.
2. I could not satisfy her (sexually).
3. My older wife could not stand it when I married a second wife.
4. My elder wife drove out the second.
5. We quarreled over work.
6. She was a bitch.
7. We did not like each other.
8. Impotence.
9. She did not like me.
10. I was ill and she didn't like to stay with me. (Stephens, 1963)

Reasons for Divorce in Cameroon, Africa

1. Ill treatment of wife by husband.
2. Marriage forced by parents against daughter's wishes.
3. Extensive neglect of wife by husband.
4. Marriage of husband to a second wife.
5. The husband was a Muslim, and the parents did not like him.

6. The wife delivered the child in a hospital and had it baptized.
7. The wife's parents hated the husband.
8. The mother-in-law quarreled with the wife a lot.
9. The husband wanted sexual relations with his wife when the baby was only three months old.
10. One of the children died suddenly, and people blamed the wife. (Kayongo-Male & Onyango, 1984)

Rank of Reasons Given in Shanghai, China, for Divorce

1. Insufficient premarital foundation.
2. Don't get along in style, personality, or moral values.
3. Inadequate or no sex life.
4. Economic problems.
5. Other. (Class of 1978, 1983–84)

The Top Ten Reasons Behind Divorces in America

1. Communication problems.
2. Spouse's infidelity.
3. Constant fighting.
4. Emotional abuse.
5. Falling out of love.
6. Unsatisfactory sex.
7. Spouse didn't make enough money.
8. Physical abuse.
9. Falling in love with somebody else.
10. Boredom. (Patterson & Kim, 1991)

---

one partner is the initiator, it is usually the female. One study found that women initiated 75% of divorces (J. B. Kelly, 1989). The individual who wants his or her marriage to end is likely to view the marriage totally differently from the individual who wants the marriage to continue (Wang & Amato, 2000). In addition, the partner who initiated the divorce has often completed the mourning of the relationship by the time the divorce is complete, unlike the partner whose mourning begins once the divorce is finalized.

Why Do People Get Divorced?

It is very difficult to determine why some marriages fail; every couple has its own story. Sometimes the spouses themselves are at a loss to understand why their marriage failed. We will now explore some of the social, predisposing, and relationship factors that may contribute to divorce.

Social Factors Affecting Divorce

Divorce rates in the United States are influenced by changes in legal, political, religious, and familial patterns. For example, states have all instituted some type of no-fault divorce, whereby neither partner needs to be found guilty of a transgression (such as hav-

Review Question

Describe the differences between traditional and covenant marriages.

sex byte

Men have been found to mourn divorce differently from women (Baum, 2003). They tend to mourn the loss of their home and children more than the loss of their wife, and men's pain over divorce is expressed more through action, rather than words or emotions.

SEX in Real Life

Point-and-Click Divorce

It is estimated that half of all marriages that take place today will end in divorce. Because of this, many entrepreneurial types have found ways to cash in. One of the newest methods to enter this market is the "point-and-click" divorce found on the Internet. At many of these sites, men and women can find divorce forms and state-by-state divorce information. For $250 or so, couples can begin the divorce process online in the privacy of their own homes! Completed divorce forms are simply faxed to the state court.

States have various rules about divorce proceedings. Some states have a 90-day waiting period before a divorce to be granted (such as Connecticut); some require spouses to have lived in the state for at least 3 months (Utah and Minnesota), 6 months (Mississippi), or 1 year (Nebraska and

New Jersey). States also vary with respect to what constitutes "fault" in a divorce. Factors that might be included are adultery, conviction of a felony, erectile dysfunction, willful desertion, drunkenness, or drug use.

Such websites guide couples through the tedious process of "who gets what" in the divorce. Forms are also available to help sort through issues of child custody, financial support, and visitations. Founders of such divorce websites argue that they save couples money by not requiring each partner to hire a lawyer to guide him or her through the divorce process. However, lawyers counter that divorces are not as easy as this and that couples need to protect themselves and their interests when they are divorcing.

Do you think it should be possible to obtain a divorce through the Internet? Why, or why not?

ing sex outside marriage) in order to dissolve the marriage. The growth of low-cost legal clinics and the overabundance of lawyers have made divorce cheaper and thus more accessible (see the accompanying Sex in Real Life, "Point-and-Click Divorce"). Additionally, the more equitable distribution of marital assets has made some people less apprehensive about losing everything to their spouses.

As we discussed earlier in this chapter, a few states have recently passed laws allowing people to choose a new type of marriage—a covenant marriage. Because a covenant marriage involves premarital counseling and makes divorce more difficult even if the couple decides later they want one (Wardle, 1999), couples who choose them tend to be more conservative, religious, and have stronger gender-role ideologies than those who choose a traditional marriage (A. J. Hawkins et al., 2002). When people were asked whether they would consider a covenant marriage for themselves, over two-fifths of people said they would (Henry J. Kaiser Family Foundation, 2000a).

In recent years, divorce has become generally more acceptable in American society. Although 30 or 40 years ago it was very difficult for a divorced person to attain high political office, Ronald Reagan's divorce was not even an issue in his presidential campaign. Also, many religious groups are less opposed to divorce than they used to be; many Catholic parishes, for example, no longer ostracize parishioners who divorce (Benokraitis, 1993).

Predisposing Factors for Divorce

Certain situations may predispose a couple to more marital problems. Couples who marry at a young age often suffer more marital disruption than older couples (S. P. Morgan & Rindfuss, 1985), due in part to emotional immaturity. Also, couples who marry because of an unplanned pregnancy are more likely to divorce (G. Becker et al., 1977). Marital stability increases as couples have children but then decreases if the couple has more than five (Zinn & Eitzen, 1993). The interval between marriage and the arrival of children is also an important factor; waiting

Supershoot Images/Getty Images

Communication avoidance may be one of the first signs that a marriage is in trouble.

longer promotes marital stability by giving couples time to get to know each other prior to the arrival of children and may also allow them to become more financially secure (S. P. Morgan & Rindfuss, 1985). Catholics and Jews are less likely to divorce than Protestants, and divorce rates tend to be high for marriages of mixed religions. Marriages between people having no religious affiliation at all have particularly high divorce rates (Skolnick, 1992).

People who have been divorced before or whose parents have divorced have more accepting attitudes toward divorce than those who grew up in happy, intact families (Amato, 1996). In addition, people who have divorced parents are significantly more likely to report marital problems in their own relationships than people from intact families, and they also tend to be more skeptical about marriage, feeling insecure about the permanence of these relationships (Jacquet & Surra, 2001).

Relationship Factors in Divorce

In general, couples who divorce have known for a long time that there were difficulties in their marriage, although they may not have contemplated divorce. These problems are made worse, in most cases, by communication problems. Some warning signs are communication avoidance (not talking about problems in the relationship); demand and withdrawal patterns of communication, whereby one partner demands that they address the problem and the other partner pulls away; and little mutually constructive communication (Christensen & Shenk, 1991).

A California divorce study demonstrated that women and men tend to complain about different things about their mates (J. B. Kelly, 1989). Women's most frequent complaint was that they were feeling unloved by their partners. That was followed by a feeling that their competence and intelligence were belittled by their husbands and that their husbands were hypercritical of them. Men, on the other hand, complained most that their wives were inattentive or neglectful of their needs and that they and their wives had incompatible interests, value, or goals. Both sexes mentioned sexual incompatibility or loss of sexual interest as a problem.

Many problems in people's marriages are there before they decide to get married. As one woman put it:

> I had a queasy feeling before the marriage. There were signs. When we were studying for the Bar [both are lawyers], he became critical of me in ways he hadn't been before. "Whoa! Where did this come from? I don't need this!" We had discussions about it before the marriage. He'd say, "That's the way I am." It didn't get settled. (Blumstein & Schwartz, 1983, p. 357)

Many couples make poor assessments of their partner, or believe that the little annoyances or character traits that they dislike in their potential spouses will disappear or change after marriage (Neff & Karney, 2005). Marrying a person with the intention to change his or her personality or bad habits is a recipe for disaster.

Adjusting to Divorce

One year after a divorce, 50% of men and 60% of women reported being happier than they were during the marriage (Faludi, 1991). Even 10 years later, 80% of the women and 50% of the men said that their divorce was the right decision. However, for some, divorce can be very painful, both emotionally and physically. Depression is common in those who believe that marriage is permanent (R. W. Simon & Marcussen, 1999). One recently divorced 27-year-old man explains:

> My mind is unclear, my body aches, my dreams run rampant, and I feel a loss like I've never felt before. Maybe I'm old-fashioned, but I have always dreamed of a wife, a home, and a decent job. I spent time with her, I sent her flowers for no reason, a movie, dinner, and our sex life was very satisfying on both accounts. I can honestly say that I would rather she had died in an accident than to be facing and feeling this type of hurt for the rest of my life. (Author's files)

sex byte

Adult children of divorce are more likely to divorce than are adult children from intact families. (Jacquet & Surra, 2001)

Review Question

Identify some of the factors that research has found might predispose a couple to divorce.

Women often have an increase in depression after a divorce, whereas men experience poorer physical and mental health (Zheng & Hart, 2002). Illness in men is often attributed to the fact that wives often watch out for their husband's physical health. Depression and sadness also surface when divorced men and women find that they have less in common with married friends as many friends separate into "hers" and "his." Older individuals experience more psychological problems because divorce is less common in older populations and because there are fewer options for forming new relationships in older age (Wang & Amato, 2000). Divorced older women are more likely to feel anger and loneliness than are younger divorced women. Finally, some racial differences have also been found. Divorced black men and women adjust more easily and experience less negativity from peers than do whites (Kitson, 1992).

Another area that is impacted after divorce is economics. Financial adjustment is often harder for women because after a divorce a woman's standard of living declines more than a man's (Wang & Amato, 2000). Many women who previously lived in a middle-class family find themselves slipping below the poverty line after divorce. The situation is made worse when the ex-husband refuses to pay his alimony or child support; about 20% of divorced fathers never provide any form of assistance for their children (Benokraitis, 1993). Many states are trying to find ways to deal with "deadbeat dads," fathers who do not pay child support. For example, in Iowa the names of delinquent fathers are published in a statewide paper, and the public is asked to help locate them.

On the other hand, some women's careers improve after a divorce, even more than men's do. Some women who divorce find they have improved performance evaluations and feel more motivated and satisfied with their jobs because they put the time and energy they had invested in their relationship into their work instead. Men tend to be more work focused, and so divorce may not give them as much free time—instead, some men may have to learn how to cook, clean, do their own laundry, and so on. Women may also get more emotional support from their friends and coworkers than men do. Over time, the majority of people seem to adjust to divorce. Often, social support from friends and family can be very helpful.

Approximately 75% of divorced people remarry (Furstenberg & Cherlin, 1991) and some remarry, divorce, and remarry again (often referred to as **serial divorce**). Typically the length of time between divorce and remarriage is less than 4 years (B. Wilson & Clark, 1992). Men remarry at higher rates than women, and Hispanics and African Americans remarry at lower rates than whites (M. Coleman et al., 2000). Today, increasing numbers of couples are cohabiting as an alternative to remarriage.

Divorce and Sex

Few studies have focused on sexual behavior among people who are divorced. Common sense tells us that a person who is depressed or angry about a divorce may have a decrease in both levels of sexual activity and sexual satisfaction. Steven Stack and Jim Gundlach (1992) found that age was inversely related to sex among the divorced: the older a person was at divorce, the less sexual activity occurred afterwards. Another relationship was found between religiosity and sex: the more religious a divorced person was, the less likely he or she was to have another sex partner.

Whether or not a person has sexual partners after a divorce also depends on whether his or her attitudes are liberal toward sex and the presence or absence of children. Divorced persons without children are more likely to have sexual partners than those with children. After a divorce, men are more likely to have one or more partners, whereas women are less likely to find new partners, especially if they are middle-aged or older (Laumann et al., 1994).

Divorce in Other Cultures

Divorce is common in almost all societies, but cultural views about it are changing as societies develop. In societies such as the United States, Sweden, Russia, and most European countries, divorce is relatively simple and has little stigma. The exceptions are countries that are largely Roman Catholic; because Catholicism does not allow divorce,

serial divorce
The practice of divorce and remarriage, followed by divorce and remarriage.

Review Question

Explain how men and women adjust to divorce.

it can be difficult to obtain in Catholic countries. Ireland legalized divorce in 1995; prior to this time, Ireland was the only country in the Western world to constitutionally ban divorce (Pogatchnik, 1995). The last country in South America to legalize divorce was Chile, where legalization took place in late 2004.

To assure that divorce did not disrupt the community, many traditional societies, including some in Africa, performed rituals for peacefully dissolving marriages. But today divorces can be disruptive and messy as couples fight in court over marital assets and custody (Kayongo-Male & Onyango, 1984).

Traditional laws about divorce can still be enforced, especially in more patriarchal cultures. Islamic law, like traditional Jewish law, allows a man to divorce his wife simply by repudiating her publicly three times. A wife, on the other hand, must go to court to dissolve a marriage (Rugh, 1984). In Egypt, it is far easier for men to divorce than for women, and because of this only about 33% of divorces in Egypt are initiated by females. In Israel, women need their husband's permission for a divorce, and councils have been set up to try to convince men to let their wives have a divorce.

In 2001, China's government revised its 20-year-old marriage law and included the concept of fault in marriage (Dorgan, 2001; Ruan & Lau, 2004). Before this law was implemented, Chinese couples had an equal division of family property regardless of the reasons for the divorce. Under this new law, however, if a partner is caught engaging in extramarital sex, he can lose everything (research has found that it is mostly men who cheat in China). To catch the cheating spouses, many entrepreneurial types have started detective firms where women pay them to catch their cheating spouses.

The reasons that people get divorced are numerous, although different patterns emerge in different societies. In Egypt, the most common reason given for divorce is infidelity by the husband, whereas among the Hindus of India, the most common reason is cruelty (either physical or mental) from their partner (Pothen, 1989). Arab women's main reasons for divorce include the husband's physical, sexual, or verbal abuse; alcoholism; mental illness; and in-law interference (Savaya & Cohen, 2003). In China, more than 70% of divorces are initiated by women and the main reason given is an extramarital affair of the husband (Ruan & Lau, 2004). This is also the main reason for divorce in Brazil and many other countries (de Freitas, 2004). See Human Sexuality in a Diverse World, "Reasons for Divorce in Four Cultures," on page 281 for more information about cross-cultural reasons for divorce.

Overall, divorce rates seem to be increasing worldwide as countries modernize and as traditional forms of control over the family lose their power. Only time will tell, however, whether a backlash will stabilize marriage rates, as they seem to be doing in the United States.

Review Question

Identify how dating, cohabitation, marriage, extramarital sex, and divorce are viewed outside the United States.

Chapter Review

ACTIVE SUMMARY

1. Sociologists describe dating as a **(a)** "_____ _____," in which prospective spouses compare the **(b)** _____ and liabilities of eligible partners to choose the best available mates. By examining the **(c)** _____ and rules a culture sets up for choosing a mate, we can learn about the level of **(d)** _____ in that particular society, ideals about masculinity and femininity, roles of women and men, the value placed on conformity, the importance of **(e)** _____, the authority of the family, and attitudes toward childhood, pleasure, and responsibility.

2. On college campuses today there have been many changes in **(a)** _____ practices. Some researchers argue that college dating doesn't exist. Overall, we know that dating begins in

earnest in **(b)** _____ _____. In traditional dating, the boy would pick up the girl at her **(c)** _____, giving her father and mother time to meet with the boy, and then they would go to a **(d)** _____-_____ event. The most difficult part of dating is the initial **(e)** _____.

3. We are living in a **(a)** _____ world. As a result, it is not uncommon to date someone of a different race, religion, or culture. There are still strong social forces that keep the races **(b)** _____ and make it difficult for people to meet. It can be difficult to begin dating again after the end of a marriage or the **(c)** _____ of a spouse. Oftentimes this has to do with the fact that the dating environment has **(d)** _____. Widowhood is a major barrier to **(e)** _____.

4. Sexual **(a)** _____ have changed on college campuses today. **(b)** _____ _____, or having a friend with benefits, has become more common. Some couples decide to abstain from sex; these students have been found to have more conservative **(c)** _____ about sex and less prior sexual experience. As people age their sexual **(d)** _____ changes and this can affect their relationships. Sexual **(e)** _____ has been found to be a major cause of decreases in sexual functioning.

5. In recent years **(a)** _____, or living together outside of marriage, has increased dramatically. In the United States, the typical pattern is to live together before marriage and not in **(b)** _____ of marriage. Advantages of cohabitation are that it allows couples to move into marriage more **(c)** _____, learn more about each other, and not be legally or **(d)** _____ tied together. Couples are often older, more mature, and more financially stable when they finally marry. It also allows couples to learn of their partners' bad habits and idiosyncrasies before marriage. Cohabitating couples tend to either marry or separate after just a few years. **(e)** _____ of all couples who live together break up within a year or less, and those who marry are at increased risk of divorce. Longer cohabitation has been found to be associated with higher likelihood of divorce.

6. The majority of young people say they are planning and **(a)** _____ to marry at some point in their lives. The median age for first marriage has been increasing, and in 2000 the age at first marriage went to 27 and 25 for men and women respectively. Marital **(b)** _____ has been found to be related to the quality of the **(c)** _____, frequency of pleasurable activities, being able to talk to each other and **(d)** _____-_____, physical and emotional intimacy, and personality similarities. High rewards/low costs are also important.

7. Marital quality tends to **(a)** _____ in the first few years of a marriage and then declines until **(b)** _____, when it rises again. However, the majority of married couples report that their marriages are happy and satisfying. People who are married tend to be happier, **(c)** _____, and have longer lives than either widowed or divorced persons of the same age. Marriage has also been found to **(d)** _____ the impact of several potentially traumatic events including job loss, retirement, and illness. Overall, marriage provides more health **(e)** _____ to men than women.

8. Marital happiness is higher **(a)** _____ having children, declines steadily until it hits a low when the children are in their **(b)** _____, and then begins to increase once the children leave the house. Many couples do not realize how time consuming children are, and they find themselves with **(c)** _____ time to work on their marriage.

9. The **(a)** _____ the frequency of sexual behavior in marriage, the **(b)** _____ the sexual satisfaction. During the early years, sex is more **(c)** _____ and generally satisfying. During the next 15 or so years, other aspects of life take precedence over sex, and the couple may experience difficulty in maintaining sexual **(d)** _____ in each other. In the later years, sex gets more difficult as frequency and potency decline; still, men report being generally **(e)** _____ with their sex lives.

10. Almost all couples, whether dating, living together, or married, expect sexual **(a)** _____ from each other. Those who cheat have stronger sexual **(b)** _____, more **(c)** _____ sexual values, less **(d)** _____ in their intimate relationship, and more **(e)** _____ for sex outside the relationship.

11. Women experience more **(a)** _____ distress about infidelity than men do. A woman is also more likely to be upset about **(b)** _____ infidelity, whereas a man is more likely to be upset about his partner's **(c)** _____ infidelity. Some couples engage in **(d)** _____ sex, but the sex is viewed as separate from the marriage.

12. In many ways, same-sex relationships have changed more than **(a)** _____ relationships over the last few decades. Overall, research has found that gay men engage in sexual behavior more often than **(b)** _____ women do. Societies have always given preference to heterosexual couples, presumably because of the **(c)** _____ that heterosexual marriages provides. The United States has long regulated marriage in an attempt to protect **(d)** _____ health. Even with all this controversy, many same-sex couples "marry" their partners in ceremonies that are not **(e)** _____ by the states in which they live.

13. Today, marriage is seen as a **(a)** _____ between a man and a woman. This shift in perception of marriage has brought with it a shift in divorce. The **(b)** _____ of divorce laws has made it easier to **(c)** _____ a divorce and made it an easier and less expensive process. The current **(d)** _____ rate remains high compared to earlier times in the century and to other countries. African Americans, Native Americans, and Puerto Ricans show the highest separation and divorce rates in the United States; Korean, Asian Indian, and Chinese Americans have the lowest rates.

14. Certain factors increase the **(a)** _____ of divorce. These include marrying at a young **(b)** _____, marrying because of a(n) **(c)** _____ pregnancy, having no religious affiliation, being Protestant or a mixed-religion couple, having many communication problems, having divorced before, or having parents who have **(d)** _____. Women often have an increase in depression after a divorce, whereas men experience poorer physical and mental health. Men **(e)** _____ at

higher rates than women, and Hispanics and African Americans remarry at lower rates than whites. Today, increasing numbers of couples are cohabiting as an alternative to remarriage.

15. In most industrialized countries, **(a)** _____ is the norm. There are still a few industrialized cultures in which **(b)** _____ marriages take place, although those are often in the upper classes. Mate selection in most places is a much more individual affair. However as much we in the West believe in the right of **(c)** _____ to choose their own mates, there were some advantages to parental **(d)** _____ in mate selection, and the transition to individual mate selection in traditional societies is often difficult.

16. Cohabitation is **(a)** _____ in more traditional societies where, even if a couple has sex before or **(b)** _____ of marriage, social customs would never tolerate an unmarried heterosexual couple living together openly. In some countries, cohabitation is often a step toward marriage or is seen as a "lower form" of **(c)** _____.

17. Marriage **(a)** _____ take place in every society on Earth, but marriage customs vary widely from culture to culture. Some cultures mandate marriages between certain relatives, whereas other cultures allow **(b)** _____ spouses. Usually, this takes the form of **(c)** _____, or having more than one wife, which is a common practice in many areas of Africa and the Middle East. Attitudes toward marriage vary in different cultures in different times. Same-sex marriages are **(d)** _____ in some countries outside of the United States. **(e)** The

_____ was the first country to allow same-sex marriages. **(f)** _____ sex is forbidden in many cultures, but it is often tolerated even in cultures in which it is technically not allowed.

18. **(a)** _____ is common in almost all societies, but cultural views about it are changing as societies **(b)** _____. In societies such as the United States, Japan, Sweden, Russia, and most European countries, divorce is relatively **(c)** _____ and has little stigma. The exceptions are countries that are largely Roman Catholic, because Catholicism does not allow **(d)** _____.

Critical Thinking Questions

1. What are the qualities that you look for in a partner? Why do you think these qualities are important to you? Which could you live without? Which are nonnegotiable?

2. How long do you think you would want to date someone before settling down for life? Do you think you would be ready to make a lifelong commitment after a few days? Weeks? Months? Years? How will you know?

3. How would you feel if your partner cheated on you and engaged in sex outside of your relationship? What would you say to him or her? Have you ever had a conversation about monogamy?

4. Suppose this morning when you woke up, you realized your roommate had another "hookup" last night. How do you feel about his or her frequent hooking up activity? What do you think encourages or discourages hookups on your campus?

5. Pretend you live in a country that practices arranged marriage, and write an informational paragraph about yourself to give to a matchmaker. What would you want the matchmaker to look for in your marriage partner?

6. Jeff and Steve have been dating for 3 years and are ready to commit to each other for life. Do you think their "marriage" should be formally recognized by the law? Why, or why not?

7. There have been many changes in the institution of marriage and the liberalization of divorce laws. Do you think that divorce has become too easy today? Do couples give up on their marriages too soon because of this?

Check It Out

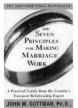

Gottman, John. (1999). **The seven principles for making marriage work.** New York: Three Rivers Press.

John Gottman, the director of the Gottman Institute, discusses the concept of emotionally intelligent marriages and what makes marital relationships work. This book includes chapters on the truth about happy marriages, how Gottman predicts divorce, nurturing relationships, marital conflict, solving problems, overcoming gridlock, and improving relationships. Quizzes, checklists, and exercises, similar to those Gottman uses in workshops across the country, are included.

Closer (2004; 1 hour, 44 minutes; Rated R)

In this movie, Dan (played by Jude Law), an aspiring writer, meets Alice (Natalie Portman), who becomes his girlfriend. Through her, he becomes confident enough to approach the woman he believes he's in love with, Anna (Julia Roberts), a successful photographer and recent divorcée. After meeting and flirting with Dan, Anna marries Larry (Clive Owen), a handsome, self-assured dermatologist, while carrying on a secret affair with Dan. This movie explores love, relationships, divorce, extramarital sexuality, and deception.

 InfoTrac® College Edition

If your instructor ordered InfoTrac with this book, explore InfoTrac College Edition, your online library, for additional readings and review. Go to: **www.thomsonedu.com,** and enter these search terms:

alimony	arranged marriage	unmarried couples
common law marriage	domestic partnerships	no-fault divorce
palimony	polygamy	

 Web Resources

SexualityNow Companion Website
Go to **http://thomsonedu.com/carroll** for practice quiz questions, interactive activities, Internet links, critical thinking exercises, discussion forums, and more. You can also access sites from the Wadsworth Psychology Study Center (**http://psychology.wadsworth.com**) or you can connect directly to the following sites:

The Gottman Institute
This website provides information on the work of John Gottman and his wife, Julie Schwartz Gottman, who have revolutionized the study of marriage. For 3 decades, they have conducted research on all facets of married life, including parenting issues. The Gottmans have developed an approach that strengthens happy marriages and committed relationships, and supports and repairs troubled ones. The Gottman Institute provides information and training workshops for both gay and straight couples.

Divorce Service Center
CompleteCase.com is an online uncontested divorce service center. This site offers assistance with divorce documents without the expenses of a personal lawyer. For $250 a couple can file divorce documents. This is an interesting website that illustrates the changing attitudes about divorce today.

Queendom Tests
This Internet magazine, started in 1996, includes interactive tests to explore personality, relationships, intelligence, and health. Jealousy, honesty, and various relationship tests appear in four formats—for lesbians, gay men, heterosexual women, and heterosexual men. Although these tests allow you to explore important issues related to relationships, they are not scholarly or scientific.

Romance 101
Hosted by womensforum.com, this website contains humorous information about relationships, including information about men and women's views on dating, romance, and the "dating bill of rights." This is a fun place to visit for a lighthearted look at romance.

Go to **www.thomsonedu.com** to link to **SexualityNow,** your online study tool. First take the **Pre-Test** for this chapter to get your **Personalized Study Plan,** which will identify topics you need to review and direct you to online resources. Then take the **Post-Test** to determine what concepts you have mastered and what you still need work on.

Videos in SexualityNow

For additional information on topics discussed in this chapter, check out the videos in **SexualityNow** on the following topics:

- **Same-Sex Marriage**—Hear a lesbian talk about her "civil union" with her partner and how it is perceived by others.
- **Sex After 45**—Do people become more or less attracted to their partners as they age?
- **American Sex Lives: 2004 Poll**—Learn the truth about your sex life and everyone else's sex life in this summary of a poll.
- **How Frequently Do People Have Sex?**—Compare how much sex Americans are having depending on their age, marital status, and whether they have children.
- **Who's Cheating?**—Hear how differently men and women perceive what cheating is, and how people pursue cheating.
- **Initiating Sex**—Check your intuitions about how and when people initiate sex against the survey data.
- **Orgasm: For Real or Not?**—Dr. Jennifer Berman and people on the street discuss the whys and hows of orgasms—fake and real.
- **Discussing Marriage While Dating**—Listen to a young couple discuss whether they are ready for marriage.
- **Meeting a Partner's Family**—Hear a young man describe his anxiety about meeting his girlfriend's family for the first time.

10 Sexual Expression: Arousal and Response

*H*uman sexuality is a complex part of life, with cultural, psychological, and biological influences shaping how people choose to express their sexuality. Because of the varied influences, it is important to view sexual behaviors in an open, nonjudgmental fashion. In this chapter, we will discuss adult sexual behaviors from early adulthood through the senior years. After a brief discussion of the role of hormones, ethnicity, and religion, we will explore the human sexual response cycle and various ways that adults express their sexuality.

INFLUENCES ON SEXUALITY

There are many powerful influences on our sexuality. Here we discuss three of the biggest influences: hormones, ethnicity, and religion.

Hormones

As we discussed in Chapters 4 and 5, hormones have a powerful effect on our bodies. The various endocrine glands secrete hormones into the bloodstream, which carries them throughout the body. The most influential hormones in sexual behavior are estrogen and testosterone. Both men and women produce these hormones, though in different quantities. For example, in men testosterone is produced in the testes and adrenal glands, and in women testosterone is produced in the adrenal glands and ovaries. Even so, men produce much more testosterone than women: men produce 260 to 1,000 nanograms per deciliter of blood plasma (a nanogram is one-billionth of a gram), whereas women produce around 15 to 70. The amount also varies and decreases with age.

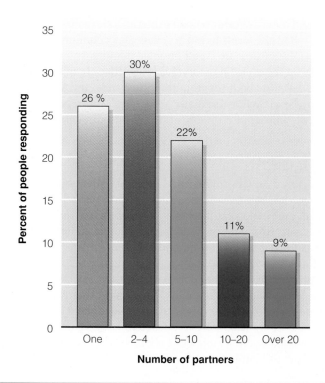

"How many sexual partners have you had?" (18–59 years old)

Figure 10.1

Number of sexual partners reported by females and males, 18–59 years old.
Source: National Health and Social Life Survey, as reported in Laumann et al., 1994.

sexbyte

In general, whites have been found to be more sexually permissive than African Americans or Hispanics—white men and women are more accepting of premarital and oral sex and less likely to cite religion as a factor in shaping one's sexual behavior (Mahay et al., 2001).

Review Question

Identify the most influential hormones in sexual behavior, and explain their roles in sexual behavior.

During menopause, women's estrogen levels fall, which can lead to slower growth in the vaginal cells, resulting in thinner vaginal walls, vaginal dryness, and decreased vaginal sensitivity. Despite this decrease in estrogen, testosterone levels often remain constant, which may result in an increase in sexual desire even though the above physical changes can negatively affect sexual functioning.

Although controversial, hormone replacement therapy (estrogen or a combination of estrogen and progesterone) can help alleviate some of these physical changes and increase sexual desire (see Chapter 4 for more information about hormone replacement therapy). In men, decreases in testosterone can lead to lessening sexual desire and decreases in the quality and quantity of erections. We will discuss aging and sexuality more later in this chapter.

In most animals, the brain controls and regulates sexual behavior chiefly through hormones. In humans, hormones have an enormous effect on sexual behavior as well, but people are also very strongly influenced by learned experiences and their social, cultural, and ethnic environment.

Ethnicity

How does our ethnic group and our race affect our sexuality? First, ethnicity and sexuality join together to form a barrier, a "sexualized perimeter," which helps us decide who we let in and who we keep out (Nagel, 2003). Ethnicity can also affect which sexual behaviors we engage in, the frequency of these behaviors, our sexual attitudes, and our ability to communicate about sex (Quadagno et al., 1998).

For example, white and Hispanic women are more likely than African-American women to engage in sexual acts besides sexual intercourse, and white women are more likely to give or receive oral sex than are African-American or Hispanic women (Laumann et al., 1994). Heterosexual Hispanic women are more likely to engage in anal sex than are white or African-American women (Van Oss Marin & Gomez, 1994). When it comes to numbers of partners, African-American men and women have the most (Eisenberg, 2001), whereas Hispanic women have been found to have the least (Dolcini et al., 1993).

Ethnicity also affects our sexual attitudes. For example, the sexual attitudes of Mexican-American men and women and African-American women are more traditional, whereas the attitudes of whites are less traditional, and those of African-American men are the least traditional of all (Mahay et al., 2001). In addition, Asian students have been found to be significantly more conservative than non–Asian students in their sexual behavior (Okazaki, 2002). We discuss Asian-American sexual behavior more in Human Sexuality in a Diverse World, "Asian-American Sexuality," on page 306.

Finally, ethnicity has also been found to affect our communication patterns about sex. For example, in cultures that are based on male dominance in relationships, women are less likely to bring up the topic of sex or have knowledge about sexual topics. Hispanic women are expected to learn about sex from their husbands, and a Hispanic woman who knows about sex may be viewed as "sexually permissive" (Forrest et al., 1993). We will continue to explore the impact of ethnicity and sexuality throughout this chapter.

Review Question

Explain how ethnicity can affect sexual behavior.

Religion

We have already discussed how hormones and ethnicity affect our sexual behavior, but there are many other variables to consider. Our culture, our religion, and social, economic, psychological, and biological factors all contribute to the way we behave sexually. As we grow, we learn strong messages about acceptable and unacceptable behaviors from the culture at large, our social classes, and even our language.

Religiosity and strength of religious beliefs also influence sexual behavior. Generally, the more religious people are, the more conservative their sexual behavior tends to be. For example, studies on religion and sexuality have found that people with high levels of religiosity are more likely to hold conservative attitudes about sex, engage in less premarital sexual intercourse, are less likely to engage in risky sexual behavior, are less approving of oral sex, and experience more guilt about sexual behavior (Bridges & Moore, 2002; Davidson et al., 2004; Janus & Janus, 1993).

Review Question

Explain how religion may influence sexual behavior.

STUDYING SEXUAL RESPONSE

There is a series of physiological and psychological changes that occur in the body during sexual behavior; this is referred to as our **sexual response.** Over the years, several models of this behavior have been proposed to explain the exact progression and nature of the human sexual response. These models are beneficial in helping physicians and therapists identify how dysfunction, disease, illness, and disability affect sexual functioning. The most well-known model has been Masters and Johnson's sexual response cycle. We will review some critiques of this model, most notably, the "new view" of female sexuality proposed by Leonore Tiefer and colleagues.

Masters and Johnson's Four-Phase Sexual Response Cycle

Based on their laboratory work (see Chapter 2), William Masters and Virginia Johnson proposed a four-phase model of physiological arousal known as the **sexual response cycle** (see Figure 10.2). This cycle occurs during all sexual behaviors in which a person progresses from excitement to orgasm, whether it is through oral or anal sex, masturbation, or vaginal intercourse. These physiological processes are similar for all sexual relationships, whether they are between heterosexual or homosexual partners.

The four phases of the sexual response cycle are **excitement, plateau, orgasm,** and **resolution.** The two primary physical changes that occur during the sexual response cycle are **vasocongestion** (VAZ-oh-conn-jest-shun) and **myotonia** (my-uh-TONE-ee-uh), which we will discuss in greater detail shortly.

The Sexual Response Cycle in Women

Sexual response patterns vary among women (and in the same woman depending on her menstrual cycle). These variations can be attributed to the amount of time spent in each phase. For example, more time spent during arousal in foreplay may result in a greater orgasmic response. The intensity of the response may also be affected by factors such as menstrual cycle and previous childbearing. However, even with these differences, the basic physical response is always the same.

Excitement Phase   The first phase, excitement, begins with vasocongestion, an increase in the blood concentrated in the genitals and/or breasts. Vasocongestion is the principle component of sexual arousal (Frohlich & Meston, 2000). Many different circumstances can induce excitement, including hearing your partner's voice, seeing an erotic picture, having a fantasy, or being touched a certain way. Within 30 seconds, vasocongestion causes the vaginal walls to begin lubricating, a process called **transudation** (trans-SUE-day-shun). If a woman is lying down (which is common during foreplay), the process of lubricating the vaginal walls may take a little longer than if she is standing up. This may help explain why it takes most women longer than men to get ready to have sexual intercourse. During the excitement phase, the walls of the vagina, which usually lie flat together, expand. This has also been called the **tenting effect** (see Figure 10.3).

The breasts also experience changes during this phase. Nipple erections may occur in one or both breasts, and the areolas enlarge (see Figure 10.4). The breasts enlarge, which may cause an increased definition of the veins in the breasts, especially if a woman has large breasts and is fair skinned.

During sexual arousal in women who have not had children, the labia majora (see Chapter 4, p. 104) thin out and become flattened, and may pull slightly away from the **introitus.** The labia minora often turn bright pink and begin to increase in size. The increase in size of the vaginal lips adds an average of ½ to 1 inch of length to the vaginal canal.

Because of increased blood flow to the genitals, women who have had children have a more rapid increase in vasocongestion and enlargement of both the labia majora and minora, which may become two to three times larger by the end of the excitement

---

sexual response
Series of physiological and psychological changes that occur in the body during sexual behavior.

sexual response cycle
Four-stage model of sexual arousal proposed by Masters and Johnson.

excitement
The first stage of the sexual response cycle, in which an erection occurs in males and vaginal lubrication occurs in females.

plateau
The second stage of the sexual response cycle, occurring prior to orgasm, in which vasocongestion builds up.

orgasm
The third stage of the sexual response cycle, which involves an intense sensation during the peak of sexual arousal and results in a release of sexual tension.

resolution
The fourth stage of the sexual response cycle, in which the body returns to the prearoused state.

vasocongestion
An increase in the blood concentrated in the male and female genitals, as well as in the female breasts, during sexual activity.

myotonia
Involuntary contractions of the muscles.

transudation
The lubrication of the vagina during sexual arousal.

tenting effect
During sexual arousal in females, the cervix and uterus pull up, and the upper third of the vagina balloons open, making a larger opening in the cervix.

introitus
Entrance to the vagina.

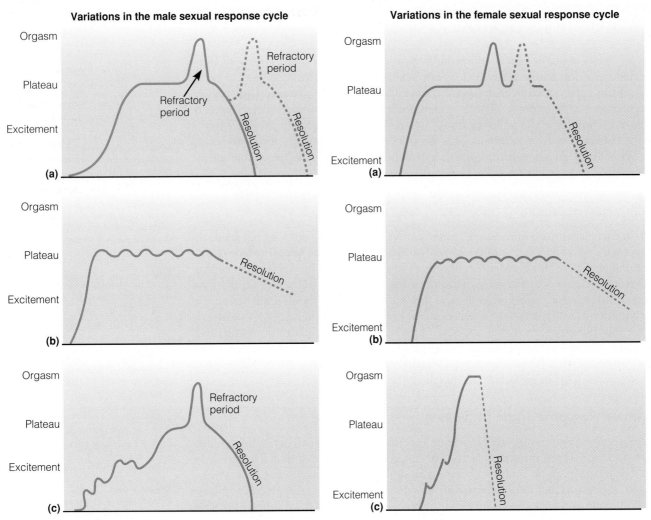

Variations in the male sexual response cycle

Variations in the female sexual response cycle

(a) Refractory period / Refractory period / Resolution / Resolution

(b) Resolution

(c) Refractory period / Resolution

(a) Resolution

(b) Resolution

(c) Resolution

Figure 10.2
Variations within male and female sexual response cycles.

Source: From W. Masters, V. Johnson, and R. Kolodny, *Heterosexuality,* pp. 51–52. Copyright © 1994 by William H. Masters, Virginia E. Johnson, and Robert C. Kolodny. Reprinted by permission of HarperCollins Publishers, Inc.

sex flush

A temporary reddish color change that sometimes develops during sexual excitement.

phase. Vasocongestion may also cause the clitoris to become erect, depending upon the type and intensity of stimulation. Generally, the more direct the stimulation, the more erect the clitoris will become. It is possible that serotonin, a neurotransmitter, participates in producing sexual arousal as well (Frohlich & Meston, 2000). (We discussed serotonin in Chapter 4.)

The excitement phase can last anywhere from a few minutes to hours. Toward the end of the excitement phase, a woman may experience a **sex flush,** which resembles a rash. This usually begins on the chest and, during the plateau stage, spreads from the breasts to the neck and face, shoulders, arms, abdomen, thighs, buttocks, and back. Women report varied sensations during the excitement phase, which are often felt all over the body, rather than being concentrated in one area.

Plateau Phase   Breast size continues to increase during the plateau phase, and the nipples may remain erect. The clitoris retracts behind the clitoral hood anywhere from 1 to 3 minutes before orgasm, and, just prior to orgasm, the clitoris may not be visible at all. Masters and Johnson claim that it is the clitoral hood rubbing and pulling over the clitoris that is responsible for the orgasm during sexual intercourse.

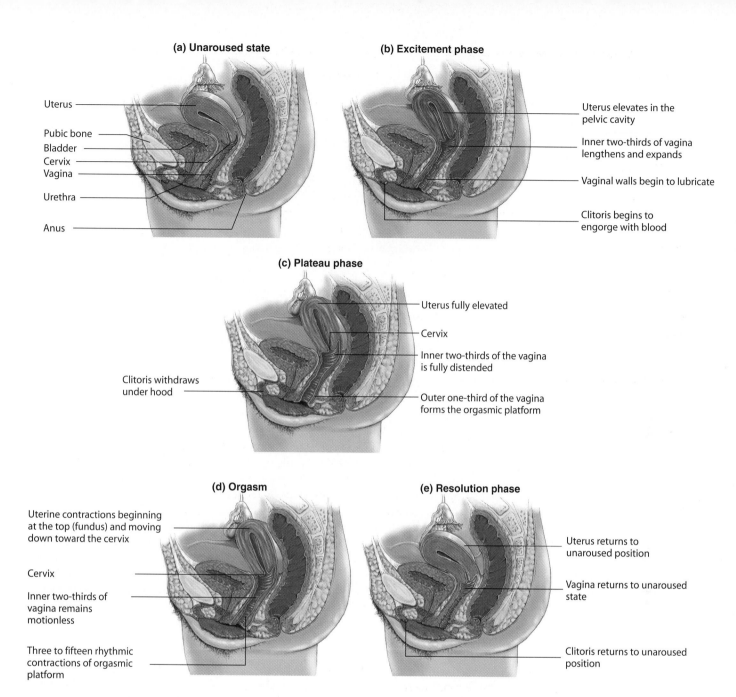

Figure 10.3
Internal changes in the female sexual response cycle.

Source: From W. Masters, V. Johnson, and R. Kolodny, *Heterosexuality,* p. 58. Copyright © 1994 by William H. Masters, Virginia E. Johnson, and Robert C. Kolodny. Reprinted by permission of HarperCollins Publishers, Inc.

During sexual arousal in women who have not had children, the labia majora are difficult to detect, due to the flattened-out appearance. The labia minora, on the other hand, often turn a brilliant red. In women who have had children, the labia majora become very engorged with blood and turn a darker red, almost burgundy. At this point, if sexual stimulation were to stop, the swelling of the clitoris and labia, which can continue for anywhere from a few minutes to hours, can be very uncomfortable. Orgasm helps to relieve this pressure, whether through masturbation or sexual activity with another person. Overall, the plateau stage may last anywhere from 30 seconds to 3 minutes.

Figure 10.4
Breast changes in the female sexual response cycle.

Source: From W. Masters, V. Johnson, and R. Kolodny, *Heterosexuality,* p. 59. Copyright © 1994 by William H. Masters, Virginia E. Johnson, and Robert C. Kolodny. Reprinted by permission of HarperCollins Publishers, Inc.

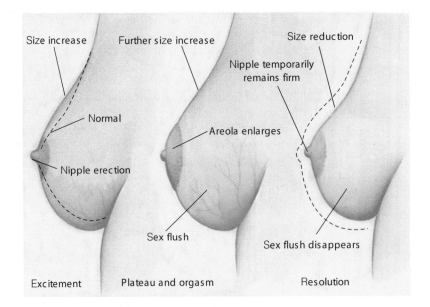

orgasmic platform
The thickening of the walls of the outer third of the vagina.

Orgasm Phase At the end of the plateau phase, vasocongestion in the pelvis creates an **orgasmic platform** in the lower third of the vagina, labia minora (and labia majora in women who have had children), and the uterus (see Figure 10.3). When this pressure reaches a certain point, a reflex in the surrounding muscles is set off, causing vigorous contractions. These contractions expel the blood that was trapped in the surrounding tissues and, in doing so, cause pleasurable orgasmic sensations. Myotonia of the uterine muscles is primarily responsible for these contractions; without these muscles, the orgasmic response would be significantly reduced.

Muscular contractions occur about every 0.8 seconds during orgasm. In total, there are about 8 to 15 contractions, and the first 5 or 6 are felt most strongly. In women, contractions last longer than in men, possibly because vasocongestion occurs in the entire pelvic region in women and is very localized in men (mainly in the penis and testicles). Because of this, women need more muscle contractions to remove the built-up blood supply. In Chapter 2, we discussed Freud's two types of orgasms, the clitoral and the vaginal. Today we know that all orgasms in women are thought to be the result of direct or indirect clitoral stimulation, even though orgasms might feel different at different times.

During orgasm, there is a release of vasocongestion and muscle tension. The body may shudder, jerk uncontrollably, or spasm. In addition, orgasms may involve facial grimacing, groans, spasms in the hands and feet, contractions of the gluteal and abdominal muscles, and contractions of the orgasmic platform. Peaks in blood pressure and respiration patterns have been found during both male and female orgasms.

Question: Why would a person fake orgasm?

Many women have faked orgasms at some point in their lives. Some women who never have orgasms rely on faking them. It could be that either the woman or her partner is unaware of what would help her to reach orgasm, and so faking becomes habitual. Other women claim that they fake orgasm in order to end a sexual encounter or to make their partners feel good. Men are also able to fake orgasm—if a man is losing his erection during sexual intercourse, he may fake orgasm in order to avoid a confrontation with his partner. In all of these instances a man or woman is giving false information to his or her partner; and, even though they are probably doing it under the guise of good intentions, open, honest communication about sexual needs and feelings is a far better strategy.

Resolution Phase   During the last phase of the sexual response cycle, resolution, the body returns to preexcitement conditions. The extra blood leaves the genitals, erections disappear, muscles relax, and heart and breathing rates return to normal.

During resolution, women are able to be restimulated to orgasm (and some women can experience **multiple orgasms**). Kinsey reported that 14% of women regularly experienced multiple orgasms, and although Masters and Johnson believed all women were capable of such orgasms, the majority of women they studied did not experience them. If they did, multiple orgasms were more likely to occur from manual stimulation of the clitoris, rather than from penile thrusting during sexual intercourse. There has also been some research into the female **G-spot** that indicates that some women may have an area inside the vagina that, when stimulated, causes intense orgasms and possibly female ejaculation of fluid (see Chapter 4).

After orgasm, the skin is often sweaty, and the sex flush slowly disappears. The breasts begin to decrease in size, usually within 5 to 10 minutes. Many women appear to have nipple erections after an orgasm because the breast as a whole quickly decreases in size while the areola are still engorged. The clitoris returns to its original size but remains extremely sensitive for several minutes. Many women do not like the clitoris to be touched during this time due to the increased sensitivity.

Earlier we mentioned that a woman's menstrual cycle may influence her sexual responsiveness. Research has found that sexual excitement occurs more frequently during the last 14 days of a woman's menstrual cycle (Sherfey, 1972). During this time, more lubrication is produced during the excitement phase, which may be due to the increased vasocongestion. As we discussed in Chapter 4, orgasms can be very helpful in reducing cramps during menstruation, presumably because they help to relieve **pelvic congestion** and vasocongestion.

The Sexual Response Cycle in Men

The sexual response cycle in males is similar to that of females, with vasocongestion and myotonia leading to physiological changes in the body (see Figure 10.5). However, in men the four phases are less well defined. During the excitement phase, the penis, like the clitoris in women, begins to fill with blood and become erect. Erection begins very quickly during excitement, generally within 3 to 5 seconds (although the speed of this response lengthens with age).

Excitement Phase   The excitement phase of the sexual response cycle in men is often very short, unless a man uses deliberate attempts to lengthen it. Often this causes a gradual loss of **tumescence** (too-MESS-cents; the swelling of the penis due to vasocongestion), which is referred to as **detumescence** (dee-too-MESS-cents). Distractions during the excitement phase (such as a roommate walking into the room) may also cause detumescence. However, once the plateau stage is reached, an erection is often more stable and less sensitive to outside influences. It takes men less time to reach the plateau phase than women because women have more intense pelvic congestion.

During the excitement phase, the testicles also increase in size, becoming up to 50% larger. This is both a vasocongestive and myotonic response. The dartos and cremastic muscles pull the testicles closer to the body to avoid injury during thrusting (see Chapter 5 for more information about these muscles). If sexual stimulation were to stop at this point, the swelling in the testicles could be uncomfortable.

Plateau Phase   All of these physical changes continue during the plateau phase. Some men may experience a sex flush, which is identical to the sex flush women experience. In addition, it is not uncommon for men to have nipple erections. Just prior to orgasm, the glans penis becomes engorged (this is comparable to the engorgement of the clitoris in women). At this point, a few drops of preejaculatory fluid may appear on the head of the penis.

Orgasm Phase   Orgasm and ejaculation do not always occur together (see Figure 10.5). In fact, there are men who are able to have orgasms without ejaculating and can

multiple orgasms
More than one orgasm experienced within a short period of time.

G-spot
Grafenberg spot. A controversial structure that is said to lie on the anterior (front) wall of the vagina and is reputed to be a seat of sexual pleasure when stimulated.

pelvic congestion
Pelvic congestion occurs when blood pools in the veins in the uterus, ovaries, and vulva, causing cramping and general discomfort. Typically this pain is lessened after orgasmic release.

Review Question

Identify and describe the four stages of Masters and Johnson's female sexual response cycle.

tumescence
The swelling of the penis due to vasocongestion, causing an erection.

detumescence
The return of an erect penis to the flaccid state.

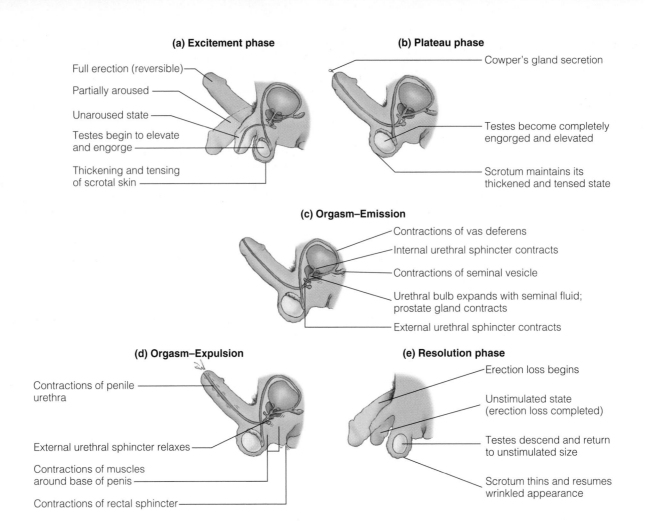

(a) Excitement phase

- Full erection (reversible)
- Partially aroused
- Unaroused state
- Testes begin to elevate and engorge
- Thickening and tensing of scrotal skin

(b) Plateau phase

- Cowper's gland secretion
- Testes become completely engorged and elevated
- Scrotum maintains its thickened and tensed state

(c) Orgasm–Emission

- Contractions of vas deferens
- Internal urethral sphincter contracts
- Contractions of seminal vesicle
- Urethral bulb expands with seminal fluid; prostate gland contracts
- External urethral sphincter contracts

(d) Orgasm–Expulsion

- Contractions of penile urethra
- External urethral sphincter relaxes
- Contractions of muscles around base of penis
- Contractions of rectal sphincter

(e) Resolution phase

- Erection loss begins
- Unstimulated state (erection loss completed)
- Testes descend and return to unstimulated size
- Scrotum thins and resumes wrinkled appearance

Figure 10.5

External and internal changes in the male sexual response cycle.

Source: From W. Masters, V. Johnson, and R. Kolodny, *Heterosexuality,* p. 60. Copyright © 1994 by William H. Masters, Virginia E. Johnson, and Robert C. Kolodny. Reprinted by permission of HarperCollins Publishers, Inc.

SEX Talk

Question: *Does the condition "blue balls" really exist?*

The concept of blue balls refers to a pain in the testicles that is experienced by men if sexual arousal is maintained for a significant period but is not followed by an orgasm. It is true that the pressure felt in the genitals, which is caused by vasocongestion, can be uncomfortable at times. However, this discomfort can easily be relieved through masturbation. Women also experience a similar condition if they are sexually aroused and do not reach orgasm. There can be pressure, pain, or a bloating feeling in the pelvic region, which can also be relieved through masturbation.

have several orgasms prior to ejaculating. Although it is rare, some men are capable of anywhere from 2 to 16 orgasms prior to ejaculation, though the ability to have them decreases with age (Chia & Abrams, 1997; J. Johnson, 2001).

If orgasm and ejaculation occur at the same time, ejaculation can occur in two stages. During the first stage, which lasts only a few seconds, there are contractions in

the vas deferens, seminal vesicles, and prostate gland. These contractions lead to **ejaculatory inevitability,** whereby just prior to orgasm there is a feeling that ejaculation can no longer be controlled. Next, the semen is forced out of the urethra by muscle contractions (the same set of muscles that contract in female orgasm).

The first three or four contractions are the most pleasurable and tend to be the most forceful (various herbal and drug products have recently appeared on the market claiming to increase male orgasmic contractions; see Sex in Real Life, "Sexual Performance Scams"). The force of the ejaculation can propel semen up to 24 inches; this distance is generally longer in younger men (Welch, 1992). After these major contractions, minor ones usually follow, even if stimulation stops. As with women, the muscular contractions during orgasm occur about every 0.8 seconds.

Some men are able to experience multiple orgasms, whereby the orgasm phase leads directly into another orgasm without a refractory period. Research has found that some men are able to teach themselves how to have multiple orgasms (Chia & Abrams, 1997; J. Johnson, 2001). The Chinese were the first to learn how to achieve multiple orgasm by delaying and withholding ejaculation. Some men learn to separate orgasm and ejaculation, thereby allowing themselves to learn to become multiorgasmic. The average number of orgasms a multiorgasmic man can have varies between two and nine orgasms per sexual interaction (Chia & Abrams, 1997; Dunn & Trost, 1989).

Resolution Phase   Directly following ejaculation, the glans of the penis decreases in size, even before general penile detumescence. During the resolution phase of sexual response, when the body is returning to its prearousal state, men go into a **refractory stage,** during which they cannot be restimulated to orgasm for a certain time period. The refractory period gets longer as men get older (we discuss this more later in this chapter). Younger men, on the other hand, may experience another erection soon after an ejaculation.

Masters and Johnson's model of sexual response is the most comprehensive model sexologists use. It has not been without controversy, however. Many feminist therapists believe that Masters and Johnson's sexual response cycle should not be used universally for classification and diagnosis of sexual dysfunctions (we will discuss this more in a moment). What has happened is that the definition of healthy sexuality has been focused on orgasm and has given less importance to emotions and relationships (Tiefer, 2001). Other researchers would say that the model of sexuality that values performance, pene-

ejaculatory inevitability
A feeling that ejaculation can no longer be controlled.

refractory stage
The period of time after an ejaculation in which men cannot be stimulated to further orgasm.

Review Question

Identify and describe the four stages of Masters and Johnson's male sexual response cycle, noting any differences between the male and female cycles.

triphasic model
A model of sexual response proposed by Helen Singer Kaplan, in which there are three phases.

tration, and orgasm is a male model of sexuality (Burch, 1998). Often this belief leads to a view of female sexuality that is passive and even nonexistent.

Other Models of Sexual Response

There have been several other, less comprehensive, models proposed, such as noted sexologist Helen Singer Kaplan's **triphasic model** (Kaplan, 1979), David Reed's Erotic Stimulus Pathway (ESP), and Tiefer's New View model. Kaplan's triphasic model has only three stages, whereas Reed's ESP has four.

Kaplan believed sexual response included sexual desire, excitement, and orgasm (see Figure 10.6). Sexual desire is a psychological phase, whereas excitement and orgasm involve physiological processes, including genital vasocongestion and muscular contractions during orgasm. Originally Kaplan's model included only excitement and orgasm, but she added the desire phase in response to the numbers of people who came to therapy with sexual desire problems. Sexual desire was of paramount importance to Kaplan because, without sexual desire, the other two physiological functions would not occur.

Many factors can block sexual desire, such as depression, pain, fear, medications, or past sexual abuse. We discuss the importance of the desire phase and disorders associated with it in Chapter 14. An advantage to Kaplan's model is that the triphasic model is easier to conceptualize than Masters & Johnson's model. For example, most of us can recognize and differentiate desire, excitement, and orgasm but may have a difficult time recognizing when we are in Masters & Johnson's plateau phase.

David Reed's (1998) ESP model blends features of Masters and Johnson's and Kaplan's models and uses four phases, including seduction, sensation, surrender, and reflection (see Figure 10.7). Seduction includes all those things that we might do to entice someone to have sex with us—what we wear, perfume or cologne, flowers, and so on. In the next stage of sensation, our senses take over. What we hear, smell, taste, touch, and fantasize about all have the potential to turn us on and enhance our excitement. This, in turn, moves us into the plateau phase. Both the seduction and sensation phase are psychosocial, and they contribute to our physiological response.

In the third phase, surrender, orgasm occurs. Reed believes that we need to be able to let go and let ourselves reach orgasm. Too much control or not enough may interfere with this response. The final phase of Reed's model is the reflection phase, in which we reflect on the sexual experience. Whether or not the experience was positive or negative will affect future sexual functioning.

Another model has been proposed by noted sex therapist Leonore Tiefer. Tiefer originated the "New View" of women's sexual problems, and although we will discuss

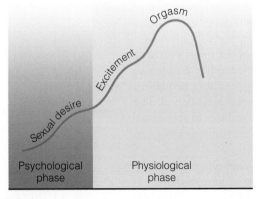

Figure 10.6
Helen Singer Kaplan's three-stage model of sexual response includes the psychological phase of sexual desire and two physiological stages of excitement and orgasm.

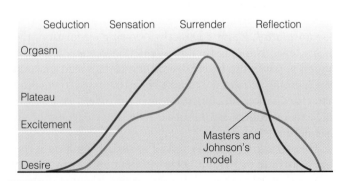

Figure 10.7
David Reed's Erotic Stimulus Pathway (ESP) model blends features of Masters and Johnson's and Kaplan's models using four phases: seduction, sensation, surrender, and reflection.

this model more in Chapter 14, we will introduce it here. Tiefer suggests that because both Masters and Johnson's and Kaplan's models are based on the medical model, they leave out important aspects of sexual functioning (Tiefer, 2001). The medical model of sexual functioning focuses solely on adequate genital functioning—vasocongestion, myotonia, physical excitement, and orgasm. As Tiefer characterizes the perspective of the medical model, "if it's wet and hard and works, it's normal; if it's not, it's not" (Tiefer, 2001).

Tiefer believes that there are many important aspects of sexual functioning that are left out of these models, including pleasure, emotionality, sensuality, cultural differences, power issues, and communication. Women's sexual experiences do not fit neatly into Masters and Johnson's four stages, according to Tiefer, and as a result women complain of desire and arousal issues and other difficulties in emotionality, sensitivity, or connectedness (Tiefer, 2001). Although there has been some controversy over Tiefer's model, for the most part her views have been widely praised. Her work has begun a much-needed dialogue about the importance of gender and sexual functioning.

Review Question
Compare and contrast the various models of sexual response that have been proposed.

 ## SOLITARY SEXUAL BEHAVIOR

Adult sexual behavior includes a range of different sexual activities. There are some adults who choose not to engage in sexual behavior, whereas others may choose to experiment with sexual partners and behaviors. **Celibacy,** or **abstinence,** occurs when a person chooses not to engage in sexual intercourse. One 18-year-old man said:

> I just don't take my virginity lightly. I want to be sure that the time is right and my partner is right before I decide to have sex. I want to feel completely comfortable and in love with someone before sex enters into the picture. It's that important to me. (Author's files)

In Chapter 9 we discussed abstinence and A. C. Green's Youth Foundation. People may choose abstinence for many reasons (e.g., to wait for marriage or the right partner, because of a fear of sexually transmitted infections, or for religious convictions). In the past decade, abstinence has become more popular in the United States. Some college students who have become frustrated with past sexual relationships have decided to become abstinent and spend time working on healthy relationships without sex (Elliot & Brantley, 1997). Some people remain abstinent their whole lives and have no sexual partners, whereas others may go through life with just one partner, and still others have multiple partners.

celibacy
The state of remaining unmarried; often used today to refer to abstaining from sex.

abstinence
The refraining from intercourse and often other forms of sexual contact.

Sexual Fantasy: Enhancement or Unfaithfulness?

Over the last few decades, views about sexual fantasy have been changing. Sigmund Freud believed that only sexually unsatisfied people fantasized about sex. Today, many researchers believe that not only are sexual fantasies normal and healthy, but they may be a driving force behind human sexuality. Liberal attitudes and more sexual experience have been found to be associated with longer and more explicit sexual fantasies (Gold & Chick, 1988; Person et al., 1992). Conversely, those who do not have sexual fantasies have been found to experience a greater likelihood of sexual dissatisfaction and sexual dysfunction (Cado & Leitenberg, 1990).

Both men and women may use sexual fantasies both during sexual intercourse and outside of sexual activity, although men tend to have these fantasies more often (Leitenberg & Henning, 1995). Men have also been found to have more **sexual cognitions,** or thoughts about sex, than women (Renaud & Byers, 1999). The sexual fantasies of homosexuals and heterosexuals have also been found to be more similar than different, except for the sex of the fantasized partner (Leitenberg & Henning, 1995).

Overall, research on men's and women's sexual fantasies has shown the fantasies are becoming more similar (Block, 1999). In fact, women have been reporting more graphic

sexual cognition
Thoughts about sex.

and sexually aggressive fantasies than they have had in the past. Overall, however, most men and women have a select few fantasies that are their favorites. These fantasies can arouse them over and over again, and sexual fantasies are used for a variety of different reasons. They can help enhance masturbation, increase sexual arousal, help a person reach orgasm, and allow a person to explore various sexual activities that he or she might find taboo or too threatening to engage in.

College Students and Sexual Fantasy

The majority of college students use sexual fantasy (Strassberg & Lockerd, 1998). Many feel little guilt about it and believe it is normal, moral, common, socially acceptable, and more beneficial than harmful. Others, however, feel a considerable amount of guilt about using sexual fantasies. This guilt can cause a person to be less likely to engage in more intimate types of sexual behavior. In one study, college students felt a considerable amount of jealousy about their partner's sexual fantasies and believed that engaging in sexual fantasy was equivalent to unfaithfulness in the relationship (Yarab & Allgeier, 1998). Let's now explore both women's and men's sexual fantasies.

Women's Sexual Fantasies

Many women report that they use sexual fantasy to increase their arousal, self-esteem, and sexual interest, or to relieve stress and cope with past hurts (Maltz & Boss, 2001). Overall, women's sexual fantasies tend to be more passive and submissive than men's and include more touching, feeling, partner response, and ambiance than men's (Zurbriggen & Yost, 2004). The five most common sexual fantasies for women include sex with current partner, reliving a past sexual experience, engaging in different sexual positions, having sex in rooms other than the bedroom, and sex on a carpeted floor (Maltz & Boss, 2001).

Female sexual fantasies tend to be more romantic than male fantasies, as illustrated by this 21-year-old woman's fantasy:

> My ultimate fantasy would be with a tall, strong man. We would spend a whole day together—going to a beach on a motorcycle, riding horses in the sand, and making love on the beach. Then we'd ride the motorcycle back to town, get dressed up and go out to dinner. After dinner we'd come home and make love by the fire. Or we could make love in a big field of tall grass while it is raining softly. (Author's files)

Lesbian and bisexual women also use sexual fantasy. Research has found that relationship quality affects the content of sexual fantasy (J. D. Robinson & Parks, 2003). One 20-year-old lesbian shares her favorite sexual fantasy:

> She has black hair and I stop the car and motion her to get in. She walks quickly, with a slight attitude. She gets in with silence—her hands and eyes speak for her. I take her home, and she pulls me in. I undress her, and she is ready for me. Down on the bed she goes, and down on her I go. With legs spread, her clitoris is swollen and erect, hungry for my touch. I give her what she wants. She moans as orgasm courses through her body. (Author's files)

Sexual fantasies are commonly used by women over the age of 50. In fact, using fantasies may help women experience arousal and orgasm (Maltz & Boss, 2001). Studies have shown that age is unrelated to what types of sexual fantasies a person has (Block, 1999). One 50-year-old woman reveals her fantasies at this point in her life:

> One big change in my imaginary sex life since I was a young woman: I no longer have those fluffy romantic fantasies where most of the story is about pursuit and the sex at the end is NG, no genitals, in view. Now I picture the genitals, mine and his, and I watch them connect in full juicy color. I see a big penis, always a big penis, and every detail, including the little drops of pre-ejaculate like dew on the head. (Block, 1999, p. 100).

Over the years, there has been some exploration of women's sexual fantasies in which force is used. In one study, more than 50% of the respondents reported using sexual force fantasies (Strassberg & Lockerd, 1998), and these force fantasies are also found in lesbian couples (J. D. Robinson, 2001). Why would a woman incorporate force into her sexual fantasies? Researchers claim it is a way to reduce the guilt women feel for having sexual desires; a way for women to show their "openness" to a variety of sexual experiences; or a result of past sexual abuse (Barner, 2003; Strassberg & Lockerd, 1998).

Women who incorporate force in their sexual fantasies have been found to be less sexually guilty and open to more variety of sexual experiences than those who do not. However, it is important to keep in mind that even though a woman fantasizes about being forced to engage in certain sexual behaviors, being forced in real life is a very different thing. In a fantasy, the woman is in control. In her fantasy she is able to transform something fearful into something pleasurable (Maltz & Boss, 2001).

Men's Sexual Fantasies

Men's sexual fantasies tend to be more active and aggressive than women's (Zurbriggen & Yost, 2004). They are often more frequent and impersonal, dominated by visual images. These fantasies move quickly to explicit sexual acts and often focus on the imagined partner as a sex object. They generally include visualizing more body parts, specific sexual acts, group sex, a great deal of partner variety, and less romance.

Men use more sexual fantasies that involve someone other than their current partner than women do (Hicks & Leitenberg, 2001). Unlike female fantasies, male sexual fantasies often involve doing something to someone else. The five most common sexual fantasies for men include engaging in different sexual positions; having an aggressive partner; getting oral sex; having sex with a new partner; and having sex on the beach (Maltz & Boss, 2001). Here is a sexual fantasy from a 20-year-old male:

> My sexual fantasy is to be stranded on an island with beautiful women from different countries (all of them horny, of course). I'm the only male. I would make all of them have multiple orgasms, and I would like to have an everlasting erection so I could please them all nonstop. (Author's files)

Sexual fantasy is used by heterosexual, homosexual, and bisexual men. For gay and bisexual men, the most common sexual fantasies were receiving oral sex from another man, being manually stimulated by another man, engaging in anal intercourse, and kissing another man's lips. When asked about his favorite sexual fantasy, one 21-year-old gay man reports:

> My favorite sexual fantasy consists of a purely coincidental meeting between myself and an old friend from high school, Jason. We would eventually end up at my house and talk for hours about what each of us had been up to for the last few years. Eventually, the conversation would become one of his talking about trouble with a girlfriend or something of that nature. Jason tells me that he was always aware that I was gay and that he had been thinking about that a lot lately. He tells me that he has always wondered what it would be like to have sex with another man. I offer to have sex with him. He agrees and we engage in passionate, loving sex. (Author's files)

Like older women, older men also use sexual fantasy. For some older men, fantasy is necessary to reach orgasm. One 60-year-old man says he fantasizes about

> . . . the person I met at a party, the hitchhiker picked up on a long trip, the teenager wanting an adult to take her to an R-rated movie. . . . Such things don't happen to me except in fantasies. . . . Yet the excitement about it all has enough power to suggest yes, I'd like to try it—and know I never will! (Brecher et al., 1984, p. 387)

© Corbis

Sexual fantasies play a role in many people's lives, and may or may not be shared with a partner.

Personal Voices

The Best and the Worst of Times

I asked some of my students to identify both positive and negative sexual experiences they have had. Following are some of their responses to the question, "What, in your opinion, constitutes your best and worst sexual experience?" Students decided for themselves how to define "sexual experience." For some it meant first sexual intercourse, and for others it did not.

The Best Sexual Experience

Female: *When my boyfriend and I spent the whole night together in a hotel room. We exchanged presents, ate food, and, of course, had sex. It didn't matter how long it was for or what we did because since we were alone we didn't have to worry about parents walking in the room. After we had sex we took a bath together and then fell asleep together.*

Male: *The Monday Night Maddog Special!! We would have dinner when Monday Night Football started, give each other a massage with hot oil and then have sex every quarter of the game!*

Female: *The first time my boyfriend gave me oral sex. We had both just learned about the clitoris. He made the alphabet on my clitoris with his tongue, starting with the letter A and ending with Z. Then he started all over again.*

Male: *When I realized there was a difference between "making love" and "having sex." I've never been the same since.*

Female: *A guy I was getting to like called me one night and told me how much he wanted me and how gorgeous I was. When he finished telling me all these great things he told me to touch myself, and I did. That was the first time I ever had an orgasm with my own hands.*

Male: *When I gave my boyfriend oral sex, because it was the first time he had received pleasure like that from a guy.*

Male: *When I lost my virginity. We had such an open and easy relationship that when we had sex again it was totally fine. We tried a variety of positions to learn what was best for both of us.*

Male: *A threesome with two girls on New Year's Eve.*

The Worst Sexual Experience

Female: *When my boyfriend and I had sex in the car. We were so excited that he forgot to turn the car off. Somehow we pushed the car down and it started rolling down the hill. We didn't know until we hit a tree and crashed up my Dad's car.*

Female: *When I had a one-night stand that I didn't want to have happen. He kept trying, and I finally gave in. It sucked, and he sucked.*

Female: *I had sex with one guy that everyone wanted in high school. He was the most gorgeous guy in our school. I found out he was also the worst kisser ever. He slobbered all over me and then he couldn't get it up.*

Male: *Having sex with a girl I really had no interest in. I just felt dirty and wrong for having sex just for the sake of having sex.*

Male: *Having sex with someone much older who later confessed that she lied about her age and was really 20 years older than me.*

Male: *When I called my girlfriend the wrong name during sex. This resulted in a huge fight and it was a mess.*

SOURCE: Author's files.

Are there gender differences in sexual fantasy? On the surface, it appears so. But we have to be careful in interpreting these findings. It could be that men have an easier time discussing their sexual fantasies than women. In one study, almost every woman reported using sexual fantasy on a regular basis (Strassberg & Lockerd, 1998).

Try thinking for a moment about your own sexual fantasies. Where do they take place? With whom? What activities do you engage in? (Remember that having a fantasy does not necessarily mean you want to engage in that particular activity or be with that particular person.) If you feel comfortable, you might try sharing your fantasies with your partner.

SEX Talk

Question: *I've always had a fantasy about having sex in a very public place, with lots of people watching. I don't really want to try this, but the thought turns me on. Am I weird?*

Fantasies are private mental experiences that involve sexually arousing thoughts or images. They are used for many different reasons, but primarily to heighten sexual arousal. Having sexual fantasies does not mean you want certain events to happen. It can be a turn-on to think about having sex with a lot of people watching, even though you would never do it in real life. Researchers today have found that sexual fantasies are a concern only if they interfere with healthy sexual expression or the development of partner intimacy (Block, 1999).

Review Question

Describe the research on sexual fantasy, noting any gender differences.

sex byte

A Swedish online questionnaire found that one-third of men and women reported engaging in cybersex (sexual behaviors while online; Ross et al., 2005).

Masturbation: A Very Individual Choice

For a period in the 19th and early 20th centuries in the United States and Europe, there was a fear that masturbation caused terrible things to happen. Myth had it that masturbation resulted in insanity, death, or even sterility. Parents would go to extremes to protect their children from the sins of masturbation. In fact, aluminum gloves were sold to parents for the purpose of covering children's hands at bedtime so that children wouldn't be able to masturbate.

Many of these beliefs have persisted, even to the present day. However, today masturbation is beginning to be viewed as one way to promote sexual health and well-being (Coleman, 2002; Wood, 2005). In fact, men who ejaculated more than five times per week during their 20s, 30s, and 40s are less likely to develop prostate cancer later in life (Giles et al., 2003). Researchers suggest that this is because frequent ejaculation prevented build-up of semen in the ducts, where it may be carcinogenic (of course these ejaculations could be a result of frequent sexual activity or masturbation or both).

Masturbation fulfills a variety of different needs for people at different ages, and it can decrease sexual tension and anxiety and provide an outlet for sexual fantasy. It allows people the opportunity to experiment with their bodies to see what feels good and where they like to be touched. It can provide information on what kind of pressure and manipulation give a person the greatest pleasure and orgasmic response. In addition, masturbation can be exciting for couples to use during sexual activity. They may masturbate themselves or each other, either simultaneously or one at a time. **Mutual masturbation** can be very pleasurable, although it may make reaching orgasm difficult because it can be challenging to concentrate both on feeling aroused and pleasuring your partner.

mutual masturbation
Simultaneous masturbation of sexual partners by each other.

For the majority of American boys, their first ejaculation results from masturbation, and it is often the main sexual outlet during adolescence (see Chapter 8). Janus & Janus (1993) found that 48% of single men masturbate weekly or more, whereas 28% of women do so. Choosing to masturbate is an entirely personal decision. You do not need to masturbate to be a good lover; in fact, some people who never masturbate are terrific lovers. For some people, masturbation may be unacceptable for personal or religious reasons.

College students are among the populations who have been found to masturbate, and research indicates that the largest gender difference in sexual behavior is in the incidence of masturbation—college men masturbate more than women (Hyde & Oliver, 2000; I. M. Schwartz, 1999). Men who masturbate do so three times more frequently than women do during the same periods. Interestingly, the National Health and Social Life Survey found that people who are having regular sex with a partner masturbate more than people who are not having regular sex (Laumann et al., 1994).

Many men and women feel guilty and inadequate about masturbating because of the lasting cultural taboos against this behavior. In relationships, masturbation is the most commonly kept sexual secret between the partners (M. Klein, 1988). Outside of the United States, however, attitudes toward masturbation differ. In some cultures, masturbation is acceptable and may be practiced openly and casually in public (as in certain ar-

Human Sexuality in a Diverse World

Asian-American Sexuality

In most Asian cultures, sexuality is linked to procreation. However, throughout the years erotic sexuality has been portrayed in Asian paintings, sculptures, and books (e.g., the *Kama Sutra*). There is even Japanese and Chinese erotica that dates back to ancient times. What is noticeably absent is open discussion about sexuality. Sex education in the schools is minimal, and many Asian parents are unwilling to talk to their children about sex, believing that to do so would encourage premarital sexual activity (Kulig, 1994).

It is estimated that 4% of the U.S. population is Asian American (Okazaki, 2002). But because this group includes people from many different countries, it is difficult to characterize the group as a whole. In 1990, the largest proportions of Asian Americans were (in descending order): Chinese, Filipino, Japanese, Korean, Asian Indian, and Vietnamese (Reeves & Bennett, 2003). Generally speaking, compared to other U.S. ethnic groups, Asian Americans have been found to:

- Be more sexually conservative.
- Initiate sexual intercourse later.
- Believe the family is of utmost importance.
- Believe that sexuality is most appropriate within the context of marriage.
- Link sexuality with procreation.
- Be more reluctant to obtain sexual and reproductive care.

But beliefs and behaviors are changing. As Asian Americans become more acculturated to the mainstream American culture, their sexual attitudes and behaviors become more consistent with the Caucasian American norms (Okazaki, 2002).

eas of Melanesia), whereas in others, it is prohibited. Prohibition often simply relegates masturbation to private locations. In China, Taoist manuals describe masturbation as an essential way to circulate sexual energy in the body (Chia & Abrams, 1997).

In some religious traditions, masturbation is discouraged or forbidden. These cultural views toward masturbation have much to do with whether masturbation is perceived to be "normal" in a particular culture. For example, Asian American women have been found to masturbate significantly less than non–Asian women (Meston et al., 1996). Although masturbation is becoming more acceptable in African American women, research has found that the majority of black women feel uncomfortable with self-pleasuring (Wyatt, 1998).

Female Masturbation

The average woman is able to reach orgasm in 95% or more of her masturbatory attempts (Kinsey et al., 1953), and female masturbation has been found to produce the most intense orgasms in women (Masters & Johnson, 1970). Even so, women report masturbating much less than men (Cornog, 2003; Larsson & Svedin, 2002). This may not be entirely true, however, because many women are embarrassed to admit they masturbate. There is a strong masturbation taboo that makes women feel it is not acceptable to admit they masturbate or can reach orgasm alone. This goes back to the double standard and the stereotype that women are not supposed to enjoy and take pleasure in sexual activities. This is also the reason that women are more likely to report guilt about their masturbatory activity than men (Davidson & Darling, 1986).

This guilt may interfere with physiological and psychological sexual satisfaction in general (Davidson & Darling, 1993). Although women often feel more guilt than men about masturbation, white women overall have less guilt and feel less conflicted about their masturbation than African American women (Wyatt, 1998). In Chapter 14 we'll discuss how masturbation is being used in therapy for women who are unable to have orgasms.

Although some women feel comfortable with masturbating, there are others who still feel guilt and discomfort. Two women discuss their feelings about masturbation:

I felt so scared when I masturbated the first time. But it felt so great and soon, I couldn't stop. Now I masturbate a couple of times a week. I love it.

I feel a little uncomfortable when I masturbate. It feels like I should be with a partner or else I'm a total loser. I try to relax and enjoy it, but sometimes it's hard to do so. (Author's files)

Many women (and some men) use vibrators or dildos during masturbation. A vibrator uses batteries and can vibrate at different speeds. Some women like to use a vibrator directly on their clitoris, whereas other women move the vibrator around the entire vulva, or insert it into their vagina or anus. A dildo, which is a flexible plastic penis-shaped object that comes in a variety of shapes and sizes, can also be inserted into the vagina or anus but does not use batteries. Vibrators and dildos can also be used during partner sex. In Chapter 14, we will discuss how vibrators are being used in sex therapy today by women who have difficulty reaching orgasm.

Male Masturbation

Like women, some men feel very comfortable with masturbating, whereas others do not. Here are some comments from men:

I used to never masturbate because she always did such a good job on me. Also, I guess all the things drilled in your head before you can think made me think that it was degrading, selfish, a waste of time, and why do it yourself when a woman is much better. (Hite, 1981, pp. 488, 491)

I know other guys do it, but it doesn't feel right for me. I just think I should be with a partner when I have an orgasm! (Author's files)

One final word about masturbation: Some may choose not to do it for personal or religious reasons. Others may enjoy the release of sexual tension. This is an individual choice that each person needs to make for himself or herself.

Figure 10.8
Female masturbation.

Review Question

Explain the differences in frequency of male versus female masturbation.

Figure 10.9
Male masturbation.

SEX in Real Life

Sexual Expression on Spring Break

Over the years there has been a great deal of research on the sexual behavior of college students. As we discussed in Chapter 2, many of the published studies use college students as participants in their research. What we don't know much about, however, is college students' sexual behaviors in specific contexts, such as spring break. Colleges and universities provide students with a 1-week spring break vacation, usually sometime in March. It is estimated that 1 million U.S. students participate in some form of spring break vacation (Maticka-Tyndale et al., 1998).

Today the most popular spring break locations are Florida, South Padre Island, Texas, Cancun, Costa Rica, Jamaica, and cruises. These vacations often consist of several friends traveling together and sharing rooms, with unlimited partying, high alcohol consumption, and many sexually oriented contests (such as wet T-shirt contests). Overall, vacations have been found to be times that people

AP/World Wide Photos

break from typical routines—they might try new things and adopt a more laissez-faire attitude (Eiser & Ford, 1995).

Research has shown that students on spring break have more permissive attitudes about casual sex than they do when they are in school (Maticka-Tyndale et al., 1998). In addition, students who drink alcohol are seven times more likely to have sexual intercourse than those who don't drink (Center on Addiction and Substance Abuse, 2002), and more likely to engage in risky sexual behaviors (O'Hare, 2005).

Although more men say that they *intend* to engage in casual sex while on spring break than do women, the number of students that actually do are pretty similar for both sexes. Approximately 15% of men and 13% of women say that they engage in casual sex during spring break (Maticka-Tyndale et al., 1998). Why do you think college students might have more permissive attitudes about casual sex on spring break than the rest of the year?

SEXUAL BEHAVIOR WITH OTHERS

We have already discussed the influence of hormones, ethnicity, and religion on sexual behavior. It is also important to understand that cultural factors, such as sex-role stereotypes, may influence sexual behavior. Our culture helps us define what is considered acceptable and unacceptable sexual behavior. Some people experiment with different techniques, whereas others accept a smaller set of sexual behaviors. Overall, research has shown that not only is sexual satisfaction an important component to a happy marriage (Henderson-King & Veroff, 1994), but it is also linked to satisfaction, love, and commitment in sexually active dating couples as well (Sprecher, 2002).

Foreplay: The Prelude?

It is interesting to consider how people define "foreplay." Is foreplay all of the sexual behaviors that take place before sexual intercourse? What if sexual intercourse doesn't occur? For the majority of heterosexuals, foreplay is often defined as everything that happens before vaginal penetration (touching, kissing, massage, oral sex, etc.). It has been viewed as something a man has to do to get a woman ready for sexual intercourse. Interestingly, many lesbians do not even use the term foreplay because all sexual behavior is simply "sex."

Caressing, fondling, and snuggling are all important parts of good sex. Hugging is also an important aspect in caring relationships but also one that is often neglected. In fact, research has shown that married couples have deeper, more relaxed hugs with their young children than they do with each other (Schnarch, 1997).

Question: I'm happily involved in a very serious relationship with a wonderful woman. We have both had other partners, but I have found that over the last few months my girlfriend is reluctant to talk to me about the things she has done with other men. Are women ashamed to talk, or is it just something they are afraid of? What can I do to get her to talk more? I would be a very good listener.

Your girlfriend's reluctance to share her past sexual history with you probably has very little to do with the fact that she fears you wouldn't be a good listener. Chances are, it has more to do with the fact that she worries about your reactions to her past behaviors. It can be very difficult for some men and women to talk about their past, and this is complicated by the fact that hearing about your lover's past can often stir up jealousy and strong emotions. Talk to your girlfriend about your thoughts and ask her what holds her back. Do remember, though, that sometimes the past is best left in the past.

Manual Sex: A Safer-Sex Behavior

Manual sex (also referred to as a "hand job") refers to the physical caressing of the genitals during solo or partner masturbation. Generally, people think of manual sex as something that happens before sexual intercourse, but it has become more popular over the years as a form of safer sex. This is because during manual sex, there is no exchange of body fluids (we will discuss safer sex later in this chapter). In order for partners to learn how best to stimulate each other manually, it may help to watch each other masturbate. After all, most people know best how to stimulate their own bodies. This can be very anxiety-producing for some couples and in situations in which one partner is hesitant, the other partner can go first or they can try it again another time.

manual sex
The physical caressing of the genitals during solo or partner masturbation.

Manual Sex on Women

Many men (and women too) do not know exactly what to do with the female genitals. What feels good? Rubbing? Can rubbing hurt? Can anything break? When does a woman like to have her clitoris touched? Where do women like to be touched? Men and women who worry about these questions may become overly cautious or eager in touching a woman's clitoris and vulva.

Because each woman differs in how she likes her clitoris stroked or rubbed, it is important that partners talk openly. The majority of women enjoy a light caressing of the shaft of the clitoris, along with an occasional circling of the clitoris, and maybe digital (finger) penetration of the vagina. Other women dislike direct stimulation and prefer to have the clitoris rolled between the lips of the labia. Women report that clitoral stimulation feels best when the fingers are well lubricated. K-Y Jelly or a woman's own lubrication can be used. Some women like to have the entire area of the vulva caressed, whereas others like the caressing to be focused on the clitoris.

Some women like it when their partners begin by lightly caressing their thighs, stomach, and entire mons area. Other women like to have their partners gently part the labia and softly explore the inner vulva. As a woman gets more excited she may breathe more deeply and/or moan, and her muscles may become tense. Stopping stimulation when a partner is close to orgasm can be very frustrating for her. It is best for partners to communicate openly about what is most enjoyable.

Manual Sex on Men

Many women (and men too) do not know exactly what to do with the penis. Does rubbing feel good? How do men like to have their penis stroked? Will it hurt? Can something break? When do men like to have their penis touched? Because of these concerns, many partners become overly cautious in touching the penis. To reach orgasm, however, many men like to have the penis stimulated with strong and consistent strokes.

Review Question

Explain why manual sex can be a form of safer sex.

cunnilingus
The act of sexually stimulating the female genitals with the mouth.

fellatio
The act of sexually stimulating the penis with the mouth.

sixty-nine
Oral sex that is performed simultaneously between two partners.

anilingus
Oral stimulation of the anus.

At the beginning of sexual stimulation, most men like soft, light stroking of the penis and testicles. The testicles can be very responsive to sexual touch, although out of fear of hurting them oftentimes partners avoid touching them at all. It is true that the testicles can be badly hurt by rough handling, but a light stroking can be pleasurable. A good rule to follow is that most men do not like to have their testicles squeezed any harder than a woman would like to have her breasts squeezed. Remember, also, that the friction of a dry hand can cause irritation, so hand lotion, baby oil, or K-Y Jelly can be used while manually stimulating the penis. However, if manual stimulation leads to vaginal or anal intercourse, any lotion or oil should be washed off, because these products can be difficult for the body to expel and can weaken the strength of latex condoms or diaphragms.

Switching positions, pressures, and techniques often can be very frustrating for a man who feels almost at the brink of an orgasm. Another common mistake is to grasp the penis far down near its base. Although this can feel pleasurable, there are fewer nerve endings in the base of the penis than there are in the tip. The most sensitive parts of the male penis are the glans and tip, which are very responsive to touch. In fact, some men can masturbate by rubbing only the glans of the penis. For others, stimulation at the base may help bring on orgasm because it mimics deep thrusting.

All men have their own individual techniques for masturbating. However, the most common techniques involve a quick up-and-down motion that is applied without a great deal of pressure. To emulate this motion, partners should try varying the pressure every once in awhile (harder and then softer). Prior to orgasm, a stronger and deeper stroke that focuses on the glans of the penis should be used. At the point of orgasm, it is important to continue firm stroking on the top and sides of the penis but not on the underside. Firm pressure on the underside (the underside is the part of the penis that is "under" when the penis is not erect) of the penis during orgasm can restrict the urethra, which can be very uncomfortable during ejaculation.

Oral Sex: Not So Taboo

Oral sex, also called **cunnilingus** (oral sex on a woman) and **fellatio** (oral sex on a man), has been practiced throughout history. Ancient Greek vases, 10th-century temples in India, and even 19th-century playing cards, all portrayed couples engaging in different types of oral sex. Over the years, however, there have been many taboos associated with oral sex. For some people, oral sex is not an option. It may be against their religion or beliefs or they may simply find it disgusting or sickening. However, for many people, oral sex is an important part of sexual behavior.

The majority of Americans report that they engage in oral sex at least occasionally. Many men and women begin engaging in oral sex prior to their first experience with sexual intercourse (and many teenagers experiment with oral sex, as we discussed in Chapter 8). In one study, 70% of males reported performing cunnilingus prior to their first sexual intercourse, whereas 57% of females reported performing fellatio prior to their first coitus (I. M. Schwartz, 1999). Research into racial differences has found that African-American women engage in less fellatio and/or cunnilingus than white women (Wyatt, 1998). African-American women who did engage in these behaviors were more likely to be married, whereas white women were more likely to be single if they engage in fellatio. Differences have also been found in educational levels. As educational levels increase, so does experience with oral sex (Laumann et al., 1994).

Those who enjoy oral sex usually do so as a form of foreplay. Others like to have oral sex instead of other sexual behaviors, and some may engage in **sixty-nine** (see Figure 10.10). This position, however, can be very challenging for some couples and may not provide the best stimulation for either of them. **Anilingus** (ain-uh-LING-gus; or "rimming"), another form of oral sex, involves oral stimulation of the anus. However, it's essential to keep in mind that hygiene is important to avoid the spread of intestinal infections, hepatitis, and various sexually transmitted infections by an infected partner.

One note of caution here: a partner should never force another partner to engage in oral sex. This can be very detrimental to a relationship. As one man recalls:

I really want my girlfriend to go down on me. I keep trying to put myself in a position in bed where my cock is close to her lips, but she doesn't seem to take the hint. Once I actually took hold of her hair and tried to push her down there, but she got upset and after that I didn't know what else to do. (Masterton, 1987, p. 9)

Some people feel that engaging in oral sex is less intimate than sexual intercourse and may not like it for this reason. Because there is little face-to-face contact during cunnilingus or fellatio, it may make partners feel emotionally distant. Other people report that engaging in oral sex is one of the most intimate behaviors that a couple can engage in because it requires total trust and vulnerability. Not surprisingly, the majority of men and women are more interested in receiving oral sex rather than giving it (Laumann et al., 1994). When there is a conflict in a relationship concerning oral sex, partners should talk about it and try to compromise. However, if an agreement cannot be reached, couples should try to find a mutually satisfying alternative.

One more thing deserves mention before we discuss the types of oral sex. If the person giving oral sex has a cold sore in his or her mouth or lips, it is possible to transmit this virus to the person on whom they are performing oral sex. In Chapter 15 we will discuss how sexually transmitted infections are spread.

Figure 10.10
The sixty-nine position.

Question: Do women like their partners to kiss them right after they have performed cunnilingus on them?

Some women do; some do not. For some women, sharing a kiss after cunnilingus can be very erotic and sensual. However, other women feel uncomfortable with the taste of their own genitals. It would be best to ask your partner to see what her individual pleasure is.

Cunnilingus

In the United States, women have historically been inundated with negative messages about their vaginas—though never more so than today. Many makers of feminine powders, douches, creams, jellies, and other scented items try to persuade women that their products will make the vagina smell "better" (see Sex in Real Life, "Feminine Hygiene," in Chapter 4). For this reason, many women express concern about the cleanliness of their vaginas during cunnilingus. When their partners try to have oral sex with them, fears and anxieties often prevent women from enjoying the sexual experience. This, coupled with many women's lack of familiarity with their own genitals, contributes to many women's strong discomfort with oral sex.

Many men find cunnilingus to be erotic. They report that the taste of the vaginal secretions is arousing to them, and they find the female vulva beautiful and sexy, including its smell and taste. Generally, when we are highly aroused, we are less alert to sensory impressions than when we are not stimulated. This means that when we are aroused, the flavor of the vagina or of semen may be more appealing than it would be if we were not aroused. However, for those who do not find the odor and taste of the vagina arousing, taking a bath or shower together before engaging in oral sex is recommended.

Women report that they like oral sex to begin in a slow and gradual way. They dislike an immediate concentration on the clitoris. Usually the best approach is to begin kissing a woman's lips and mouth and then slowly move down her body to her neck and shoulders, to her breasts, stomach, and finally, her vulva. Kiss the outer lips and caress the mons. A persistent rhythmic caressing of the tongue on the clitoris will cause many women to reach orgasm. During cunnilingus, some women enjoy a finger being inserted into their vagina or anus for extra stimulation. In performing cunnilingus with a pregnant woman, never blow air into her vagina. This can force air into her uterine veins, which can cause a fatal condition known as an air embolism, in which an air bubble travels through the bloodstream and can obstruct the vessel.

Cunnilingus is the most popular sexual behavior for lesbian and bisexual women. In fact, the more oral sex a woman-to-woman couple has, the happier the relationship and the less they fight (Blumstein & Schwartz, 1983). Although women in heterosexual relationships often worry that their partners may find the vagina unappealing, this is not so in women-to-women relationships. Perhaps this is due to the fact that each is more accepting of the other's genitals because they are both women. As one woman said: "Gay women are very much into each other's genitals. . . . Not only accepting, but truly appreciative of women's genitals and bodies. . . . Lesbians are really into women's bodies, all parts" (Blumstein & Schwartz, 1983, p. 238).

Fellatio

The majority of men enjoy having their genitals orally stimulated, and many are displeased if their partners do not like to perform fellatio (Blumstein & Schwartz, 1983). In gay couples, the more oral sex occurs, the more sexually satisfied the couple is (Blumstein & Schwartz, 1983). Fellatio is the most popular sexual behavior for gay men. However, some men do not even desire such stimulation. These two men have very different views:

> This is by far my favorite sexual activity. I always orgasm and it is more intense for me than an intercourse orgasm.

> I have never had fellatio. I have no desire to have it done, it is repulsive to me. (Hite, 1981, p. 532)

Prior to fellatio, many men enjoy having their partners stroke and kiss various parts of their bodies, gradually getting closer to their penis and testicles. Some men like to have their partner take one testicle gently into the mouth and slowly circle it with the tongue. They may also like to have the head of the penis gently sucked while their partner's hand is slowly moving up and down the shaft. When performing fellatio, partners must be sure to keep their teeth covered with their lips, as exposed teeth can cause pain. Some men like the sensation of being gently scratched with teeth during oral sex, but this must be done very carefully.

Pornographic movies tend to show a sex partner who takes the entire penis into his or her mouth, but this is not necessary. In fact, it may be uncomfortable due to the gagging response. Some men make the mistake, during fellatio, of holding their partners' heads during orgasm. This makes it impossible for the partner to remove the penis and to control the ejaculate. In fact, a bad experience in which a man forces his partner to swallow can negatively affect the partner for a long time.

SEX Talk

Question: Do men want their partners to swallow the ejaculate after their orgasms?

Some men do; some don't care. Again, there is more than one way to perform fellatio. Swallowing the ejaculate can be a very intimate experience for both partners. Unless a man has a STI, there is nothing in the ejaculate that could harm a person. However, some people find it uncomfortable to swallow and prefer to either remove the penis prior to ejaculation or spit the ejaculate out.

To avoid a gagging response, it is often very helpful to place a hand around the base of the penis while performing fellatio. By placing a hand there, the penis will be kept from entering the back of the mouth, thus reducing the urge to gag. In addition, the hand can be used to provide more stimulation to the penis.

Some partners are concerned about having their partners' ejaculate in their mouths after fellatio. If your partner is HIV negative and free from all sexually transmitted infections, swallowing the ejaculate is fine. Some enjoy the taste, feel, and idea of tasting and swallowing ejaculate, whereas others do not. If swallowing is unacceptable, another option may be to spit the ejaculate out after orgasm.

How much semen a man ejaculates during fellatio often depends on how long it has been since his last ejaculation. If a long period of time has gone by, generally the ejaculate will be larger. An average ejaculation is approximately 1 to 2 teaspoons, consists mainly of fructose, enzymes, and different vitamins, and contains approximately 5 calories. The taste of the ejaculate can vary, depending on a man's use of drugs and/or alcohol, stress level, and diet. Coffee and alcohol can cause the semen to have a bitter taste, whereas fruits (pineapple in particular) can result in sweet-tasting semen. Men who eat lots of red meat often have very acid-tasting semen. The taste of semen also varies from day to day.

Some men and women dislike performing fellatio. There have been some ethnic differences found as well. For example, in Gail Wyatt's study of African American female sexuality, over half of the hundreds of women in her sample had never engaged in fellatio and had no desire to do so (Wyatt, 1998). If you dislike performing fellatio on your partner, try talking about it. Find out if there are things that you can do differently (using your hands more) or that your partner can vary (ejaculating outside of your mouth).

Review Question

Describe the differences that have been found in how men and women view oral sex.

sex byte

The more turned on a man is during masturbation, the higher the concentration of sperm in his ejaculate (Pound et al., 2002).

SEX Talk

Question: I have heard that you can get genital herpes if your partner performs oral sex on you and has a cold sore on his or her lip. Is this true?

Although we will discuss herpes in more depth in Chapter 15, it appears that even though oral herpes (a cold sore) is caused by a different strain of the virus, this virus can be passed on during oral sex and lead to genital herpes. Therefore, it is best to avoid performing oral sex when you have a cold sore.

Heterosexual Sexual Intercourse

People have always wondered how much sex everyone else is having. Overall, Americans fall into three groups: those who have sexual intercourse at least twice a week (one-third); those who engage in sexual intercourse a few times a month (one-third); and those who engage in sexual intercourse a few times a year or have no sexual partners (one-third; Laumann et al., 1994). Newer research has found that the national average for frequency of sexual activity is about once a week (Robinson & Godbey, 1998).

Most heterosexual couples engage in sexual intercourse almost every time they have sex, and when most of us think about "sex," we think of vaginal intercourse (Sanders & Reinisch, 1999). Sexual intercourse involves inserting the penis into the vagina. However, there are a variety of ways in which couples perform this action. We will discuss the various positions for sexual intercourse shortly.

It is important for couples to delay vaginal penetration until after lubrication has begun. We discussed the sexual response cycle earlier in this chapter, and how, during arousal, the vagina becomes lubricated, making penetration easier and providing more pleasure for both partners. Penetrating a dry vagina, forcefully or not, can be very uncomfortable for both partners. If the woman is aroused but more lubrication is needed, a water-based lubricant (such as K-Y Jelly) should be used.

sex byte

Physically attractive men have been found to have more short-term sexual partners, whereas physically attractive women have been found to have more long-term sexual partners (Rhodes et al., 2005).

Many men believe that women want hard and fast thrusting during sexual intercourse. One man explains:

> I believe women want huge, hard ramming. Part of me thinks that if I do it real slow, she'll be totally mine. But when I'm having sex, I listen to my primal self, and my primal self says I must do it hard, and not just at the climax either—because there's some guy out there who can do it even harder, all night long. I never fantasize that I can do it more "feathery" than the next guy. (Jake, 1993)

Pornography helps reinforce the idea that women like thrusting to be fast and rough during sexual intercourse. Video after video shows men engaged in hard and fast thrusting—and women asking for more. In reality, many women like a slower pace for intercourse. It can be very intimate and erotic to make love very slowly, circling the hips, varying pressure and sensations, while maintaining eye contact. Men, too, enjoy a woman who can move her hips, squeeze the penis with her vaginal muscles, and vary the pace and strength of intercourse.

Some women do not find thrusting during sexual intercourse comfortable; in this case, the partners might try to slow each other down. When one partner works up to a quicker pace, he can be stopped by holding his or her hips or buttocks. This nonverbal communication can be very helpful, although verbal communication is also needed to ensure that both partners are happy with the pace of intercourse.

Although many men try to delay ejaculation until their partners are satisfied with the length of thrusting, it's important to point out that longer thrusting does not always mean that a woman will be close to orgasm. If intercourse lasts for too long, the vagina may become dry, and this can be very uncomfortable. Couples should communicate what is best for them.

Each time a couple engages in sexual intercourse, there are a variety of needs, feelings, and desires the partners bring together. They may want to stretch out the time and make it last longer, or they may desire a "quickie." Various ointments have long been sold to men to allow them to lengthen their thrusting time. However, these are often counterproductive in that they tend to psychologically separate the man and his penis and may desensitize the woman's genitals as well. In Chapter 14 we will discuss erectile dysfunction.

The majority of couples do not have eye contact during sexual intercourse, regardless of their positions (Schnarch, 1997). Schnarch proposed that eye contact during sexual intercourse intensifies intimacy, and this is difficult for most couples. In addition, over time, we have learned to close our eyes during intimate interactions (such as kissing, making love, or oral sex). To increase the intensity of sexual behavior, try keeping your eyes open (it's not as easy as you might think).

Review Question

Identify any gender differences that have been found in the experience of sexual intercourse.

Leslie Sponseller/Getty Images

There are many ways that couples engage in sexual intercourse.

Positions for Sexual Intercourse

According to the *Complete Manual of Sexual Positions* (Stewart, 1990), there are 116 vaginal entry positions, and, in *The New Joy of Sex* (Comfort & Rubenstein, 1992), 112 positions are illustrated. Of course, we don't have enough room to describe all of these positions, so we will limit this discussion to the four main positions for sexual intercourse: male-on-top, female-on-top, rear entry, and side-by-side. There are advantages and disadvantages to each of these positions, and each couple must choose the sexual positions that are best for them.

Male-on-Top   The male-on-top (also called the "missionary" or "male superior") position is one of the most common positions for sexual intercourse. In this position, the woman lies on her back and spreads her legs, often bending her knees to make penetration easier. The man positions himself on top of the woman, between her legs (see Figure 10.11). Because his full weight is usually uncomfortable and perhaps even

Figure 10.11
The male-on-top position for sexual intercourse.

painful for the woman, he should support himself on his arms or elbows and knees. Either partner may guide the penis into the vagina, although in this position the male controls thrusting.

The male-on-top position allows deep penetration during intercourse and enables the partners to look at each other, kiss, and hug during sexual intercourse. The woman can move her legs up around her partner or even put them on his shoulders. She can also use a pillow under her hips to increase clitoral stimulation. For some couples, this posi-

Human Sexuality in a Diverse World

Sex Is Against the Law

Swaziland, a small African nation, has the world's highest HIV infection rate. Over one-third of the total population is infected with HIV (Cullinan, 2003). Today, the life expectancy in Swaziland is 38 years. There are many factors contributing to the high HIV rate, including a high rate of sexually transmitted infections and the practice of having multiple wives (polygamy). The king of Swaziland, a 35-year-old man, currently has nine wives and two fiancées (it is estimated that his father had at least 120 wives; (GenderAIDS, 2003). The king believes that the practice of polygamy and having multiple sex partners is unrelated to the skyrocketing AIDS rate, even though HIV testing is not routine.

In an attempt to fight HIV infection, in 2002 the king resurrected an ancient chastity custom that prohibits single Swazi women from engaging in sexual intercourse or marrying for 5 years (Haworth, 2002). All single women in Swaziland are required to wear tasseled headdresses to signify their compliance with this ban. Virgins under the age of 19 must wear blue and yellow tassels, and women over 19, regardless of sexual status, must wear red and black tassels. These headdresses are meant to warn men to stay away.

If this law is not followed, the women face penalties ranging from surrendering one cow to a cash fine of up to $150. Violators must also live with the shame of being labeled a "lawbreaker." So far, many women have taken this new law very seriously. One woman said, "I don't think abstaining from sex is a sacrifice if it saves your life."

SOURCE: Adapted from Haworth, 2002.

tion is the most comfortable because the male is more active than the female. This position may also be the most effective for procreation. In the male-on-top position, the penis can be thrust deep into the vagina, which allows the semen to be deposited as deeply as possible; and, because the woman is lying on her back, the semen does not leak out as easily.

However, there are also some disadvantages to the male-on-top position. If either partner is obese, or if the female is in the advanced stages of pregnancy, this position can be very uncomfortable. Also, the deep penetration that is possible in this position may be uncomfortable for the woman, especially if her partner has a large penis, which can bump the cervix. This position also makes it difficult to provide clitoral stimulation for the female and may prevent the woman from moving her hips or controlling the strength and/or frequency of thrusting. Finally, in the male-on-top position, it may be difficult for the man to support his weight (and his arms and knees may get tired), and he may experience difficulties controlling his erection and ejaculation. For these reasons, sex therapists often advise couples with erectile difficulties to use different positions.

Female-on-Top   The female-on-top position (also called "female superior") has become more popular in the last decade. In this position, the man lies on his back while his partner positions herself above him (see Figure 10.12). She can either put her knees on either side of him or lie between his legs. By leaning forward, she has greater control over the angle and degree of thrusting and can get more clitoral stimulation. Other variations of this position include the woman sitting astride the man facing his feet or the woman sitting on top of her partner while he sits in a chair. Because **intromission** (the insertion of a penis) can be difficult in this position, many couples prefer to begin in the male-on-top position and roll over.

In the female-on-top position, the female can control clitoral stimulation either by manual stimulation or through friction on her partner's body. She can also control the depth and rhythm of thrusting. Her partner's hands are also free so that he can caress her body during sexual intercourse. Because this position is face-to-face, the partners are able to see each other, kiss, and have eye contact.

intromission
Insertion of the penis into the vagina or anus.

Figure 10.12
The female-on-top position for sexual intercourse.

Sex therapists often recommend this position for couples who are experiencing difficulties with premature ejaculation or a lack of orgasms, because the female-on-top position can extend the length of erection for men and facilitates female orgasm. It also doesn't require a man to support his weight. For women who are in the advanced stages of pregnancy, the female-on-top position may be a very good position.

There are, however, some drawbacks to the female-on-top position. Some women may feel shy or uncomfortable about taking an active role in sexual intercourse, and this position puts the primary responsibility on the female. Some men may feel uncomfortable letting their partners be on top and may not receive enough penile stimulation in this position to maintain an erection.

Figure 10.13
The side-by-side position for sexual intercourse.

Side-by-Side   The side-by-side position takes the primary responsibility off both partners and allows them to relax during sexual intercourse. In this position, the partners lie on their sides, and the woman lifts one leg to facilitate penile penetration (see Figure 10.13). This is a good position for playful couples who want to take it slow and extend sexual intercourse. Both partners have their hands free and can caress each other's bodies. In addition, they can see each other, kiss, and talk during sexual intercourse.

Disadvantages include the fact that sometimes couples in this position have difficulties with penetration. It can also be difficult to get a momentum going, and even more difficult to achieve deep penetration. Women may also have a difficult time maintaining contact with the male's pubic bone during sexual intercourse, which often increases the chances of orgasm.

Rear-Entry   There are many variations to the rear-entry position of sexual intercourse. Intercourse can be fast or slow depending on the variation chosen. One variation involves a woman on her hands and knees (often referred to as "doggie style"), while her partner is on his knees behind her. The female can also be lying on her stomach with a pillow under her hips while the male enters her from behind. Another variation is to use the side-by-side position, in which the male lies behind his partner and introduces his penis from behind (see Figure 10.14).

The rear-entry positions provide the best opportunity for direct clitoral stimulation, either by the male or the female. It may also provide direct stimulation of the G-spot. The rear-entry position also can be good for women who are in the later stages of pregnancy or who are overweight.

Review Question

Identify various positions for sexual intercourse. Name some advantages and disadvantages of each.

Figure 10.14
The side-by-side (rear entry) position for sexual intercourse.

Anal Intercourse   During anal intercourse, the man's penis enters his partner's anus. Although many people think of anal sex as a gay male activity (with the anus being used as a substitute for the vagina), anal stimulation is very pleasurable for many people and so is practiced by heterosexual, gay, lesbian, and bisexual men and women. There are many nerve endings in the anus, and it is frequently involved in sexual response, even if it is not directly stimulated. Some men and women experience orgasm during anal intercourse, especially with simultaneous penile or clitoral stimulation.

Studies generally show that approximately 25% of adults have engaged in anal sex at least once (Seidman & Rieder, 1994), despite the fact that in the United States, 69% of men and 74% of women believe that anal sex is unusual or kinky (Janus & Janus, 1993).

Because the anus is not capable of producing lubrication and the tissue is so fragile, it is important that additional water-soluble lubrication (such as K-Y Jelly) be used. Oil-based lubricant (such as Vaseline) may cause problems later because the body cannot easily get rid of it, and it can damage latex condoms. Without lubrication, there may be pain, discomfort, and possibly tearing of the tissue in the anus.

During anal intercourse, the **anal sphincter** muscle must be relaxed, which can be facilitated by gentle stroking and digital penetration of the anus. If it is not, intercourse can be very painful. If a couple decides to engage in anal sex, it is important to take it very slowly. A condom is a must (unless partners are absolutely sure that both are free from STIs and are HIV-negative). Anal intercourse is one of the riskiest of all sexual behaviors and has been implicated in the transmission of HIV. Research has shown that the risk of contracting HIV through unprotected anal intercourse is greater than the risk of contracting HIV through unprotected vaginal intercourse (Silverman & Gross, 1997; we will discuss this more in Chapter 15).

In addition, any couple who decides to engage in anal sex should never transfer the penis from the anus to the vagina without changing the condom or washing the penis (sex toys should also be washed with antibacterial soap). The bacteria in the anus can cause vaginal infections in women.

Before engaging in anal sex, couples should make sure that they have discussed and agreed upon it. Forcing anal sex can be very painful and even dangerous. The anal sphincter is delicate tissue that can tear if not treated gently. One man recalls:

> One night I got kind of carried away and tried to penetrate my girlfriend up the backside. That was virtually the end of our relationship. I hurt her quite badly and she said I was brutal and clumsy and an animal. It's not only broken up our relationship, it's also destroyed my confidence in myself as a lover. (Masterton, 1987, p. 9)

anal sphincter
A ringlike muscle that surrounds the anus; it usually relaxes during normal physiological functioning.

Review Question

Identify the risks of engaging in anal sex.

Same-Sex Sexual Techniques

Though the similarities between heterosexual and same-sex sexual behavior are many, there are some differences. The differences have to do with frequency and types of sexual behaviors in which couples engage.

Gay Men

Gay men use a variety of sexual techniques, which refutes the stereotype that most gay men assume only one role (either passive or active) in their relationships. The most frequent techniques used by gay males are fellatio, followed by mutual masturbation, anal intercourse, and body rubbing. Overall, gay and bisexual men engage in oral sex more often than heterosexual or lesbian couples.

Although many gay men practice anal sex, not all gay men do. Findings indicate that approximately 30% rarely engage in it; 27% regularly engage in it, reciprocally; and another 43% regularly engage in it, with one partner as the dominant one (Blumstein & Schwartz, 1983). However, it is important to note that this study was done prior to the AIDS crisis. Today, oral sex is more common than anal sex among gay males.

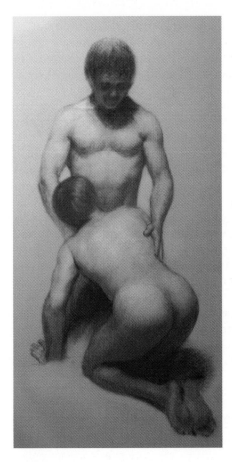

Figure 10.15
Gay men use a variety of sexual techniques in their lovemaking.

Another sexual technique gay men use is **fisting** (also called "hand-balling"), which involves the insertion of the fist and even part of the forearm into the anus. Fisting is still practiced today, although it is common to use gloves during fisting activity (Richters et al., 2003). Gay men also enjoy hugging, kissing, and body caressing; **interfemoral** (in-ter-fem-OR-ull) **intercourse** (thrusting the penis between the thighs of a partner); and **buttockry** (BUT-ock-ree; rubbing of the penis in the cleft of the buttocks).

Gay male sexual behavior changed significantly after AIDS arrived. Undoubtedly due to the massive education efforts initiated in the gay community, in the early 1990s safe sex practices had increased (at least in the major cities) among male homosexuals (Catania et al., 1989). However, today, researchers believe that STI increases among sexually active gay men are due to a decreased fear of acquiring HIV, an increase in high-risk sexual behaviors (including, for example, oral sex), a lack of knowledge about diseases, and increased Internet access to sexual partners (Ciesielski, 2003). We will discuss this more in Chapter 15.

fisting
Sexual technique that involves inserting the fist and even part of the forearm into the anus.

interfemoral intercourse
Thrusting the penis between the thighs of a partner.

buttockry
Rubbing of the penis in the cleft of the buttocks.

Lesbians

I think about sex during the day, staring at my computer screen, while I'm supposed to be writing. Sometimes I call Dana up at work, she picks up the phone, I say, "I'll meet you at home in fifteen minutes, and I'm going to rip off your clothes and throw you down on the couch, and I'm going to eat your pussy. That's what I'm having for lunch." (S. E. Johnson, 1996, p. i)

Lesbians tend to enjoy body contact, kissing, and caressing before beginning stimulation of the breasts or genitals. Manual stimulation of the genitals is the most common sexual practice among lesbians, though lesbians tend to use a variety of techniques in their lovemaking. Two-woman couples kiss more than man–woman couples, and two-man couples kiss least of all. After manual stimulation, the next most common practice is cunnilingus, which most lesbians report is their favorite sexual activity. Another common practice is **tribadism,** (TRY-bad-iz-um) also called the genital apposition technique, in which the women rub their genitals together. As we noted earlier, some lesbians engage in fisting and also may use dildos or vibrators, often accompanied by manual or oral stimulation.

A nonscientific survey was done of over 100 members of a lesbian social organization in Colorado

tribadism
Rubbing genitals together with another person for sexual pleasure.

Figure 10.16
Lesbians have been found to be more sexually responsive and more satisfied with their sexual relationships than heterosexual women.

(Munson, 1987). When asked what sexual techniques they had used in their last 10 lovemaking sessions, 100% reported kissing, sucking on breasts, and manual stimulation of the clitoris; over 90% reported French kissing, oral sex, and fingers inserted into the vagina; and 80% reported tribadism. Lesbians in their 30s were twice as likely as other age groups to engage in anal stimulation (with a finger or dildo). About one-third of women used vibrators, and there were a small number who reported using a variety of other sex toys, such as dildo harnesses, leather restraints, and handcuffs. Sexual play and orgasm are important aspects of lesbian sexuality (Bolso, 2005).

There has been some preliminary research done on the existence of **lesbian erotic role identification** [or the roles of "butch" (masculine) and "femme"(feminine) in lesbian relationships]. Some scholars believe that such roles are simply social contracts, whereas others believe they are natural expressions of lesbian sexuality. One study examined physiological and behavioral differences of women in these self-identified roles. Butch lesbians were found to have higher saliva testosterone levels, higher waist-to-hip ratios, and recalled more childhood behavior atypical for their gender (Singh et al., 1999). What's important to remember here is that there is no "typical" lesbian couple. Some lesbian couples may engage in role identification, but many others do not.

Overall, lesbians have been found to be more sexually responsive and more satisfied with their sexual relationships and to have lower rates of sexual problems than heterosexual women. On the other hand, research also suggests that the frequency of sexual contact among lesbians declines dramatically in their long-term, committed relationships (Nichols, 1990).

lesbian erotic role identification
The roles of "butch" and "femme" in lesbian relationships.

Review Question

Compare and contrast gay and lesbian sexual behavior.

SEXUAL BEHAVIOR LATER IN LIFE

As men and women age, a variety of physical changes affect sexual functioning and behavior. We will now discuss these physical changes and their affect on sexual behavior. (We will discuss more of the challenges of aging and health concerns in Chapter 14.)

Physical Changes

As people age, they inevitably experience changes in their physical health, some of which can affect normal sexual functioning (see Table 10.1). Many of these decreases in sexual functioning are exacerbated by sexual inactivity. In fact, the research clearly reveals that elderly men and women who have remained sexually active throughout their aging years have a greater potential for a more satisfying sex life later in life (Weeks & Hof, 1987). Better knowledge of these changes would help the elderly anticipate changes in their lovemaking.

TABLE 10.1	Physical Changes in Older Men and Women

In Men	In Women
1. Delayed and less firm erection.	1. Reduced or increased sexual interest.
2. More direct stimulation needed for erection.	2. Possible painful intercourse due to menopausal changes.
3. Extended refractory period (12 to 24 hours before rearousal can occur).	3. Decreased volume of vaginal lubrication.
4. Reduced elevation of the testicles.	4. Decreased expansive ability of the vagina.
5. Reduced vasocongestive response to the testicles and scrotum.	5. Possible pain during orgasm due to less flexibility.
6. Fewer expulsive contractions during orgasm.	6. Thinning of the vaginal walls.
7. Less forceful expulsion of seminal fluid and a reduced volume of ejaculate.	7. Shortening of vaginal width and length.
8. Rapid loss of erection after ejaculation.	8. Decreased sex flush, reduced increase in breast volume, and longer postorgasmic nipple erection.
9. Ability to maintain an erection for a longer period.	
10. Less ejaculatory urgency.	
11. Decrease in size and firmness of the testes, changes in testicle elevation, less sex flush, and decreased swelling and erection of the nipples.	

One 50-year-old woman explains how her sex life has improved with age:

When I was in my twenties and early thirties I almost never had an orgasm during intercourse, but I still enjoyed it because of the feeling of the closeness you can't get from anything else. Now, at fifty, I am often orgasmic during intercourse, partly because I have orgasms easier, but mostly because I am more comfortable with stroking my clitoris. (Block, 1999, p. 65)

Changes in Sexual Behavior

Two of the most frequent complaints among elderly men are decreases in sexual desire and also in the ability to perform. Because of these changes, masturbation increases, and rates of sexual intercourse decrease (C. B. White, 1982). Research on older homosexual men has found that they continue to be sexually active; however, they tend to engage in less anal sex than younger homosexual men (Van de Ven et al., 1997).

Masturbation may continue among the elderly so that they can reassure themselves that they are not the asexual persons that society labels them (Catania & White, 1982). Also, when an older adult finds that his or her partner is no longer interested in sexual activity, masturbation often becomes an important outlet. This can also be an important activity for elderly people who have lost their sexual partners because it offers a sexual release that may help decrease depression, hostility, or frustration. Other physical prob-

Personal Voices

The Best Sex I Ever Had

The following excerpt is from an article that appeared in the September–October 1999 issue of Modern Maturity *magazine.*

Recently I was talking to my girlfriend, who is a sextuple heart-bypass veteran, about my husband. She had been calling me to help support me during my husband's hospitalization with chest pain. He was scheduled for an angiogram and possible angioplasty.

"You know, Carolyn, you will have sex again." I was shocked. She said it so quietly that it just slipped into the conversation. At that point I hadn't even thought about sex. I just wanted to know how to keep him alive. I figured my best contribution would be in the kitchen. Once I started preparing healthier foods for him, clogged arteries would be a thing of the past.

"All Mike has to do," said Millie, "is walk up two flights of stairs without getting winded. As soon as he can do that, it's all right." "No treadmill test to pass first?" I asked. "Two flights of stairs, and he can have sex."

I saw him that afternoon, and he was still miffed at his bad luck. He was 52 and the cause of his trouble had been stress and genes. I relayed Millie's news to him. Despite being drugged and sporting tubes connected to an IV and assorted monitors, he nevertheless gave me a smile.

A week later, after undergoing an angioplasty to open an artery that had been 95 percent blocked, Mike was discharged. The only directions he had been given,

other than which medications to take, was that he could not drive for two days. He refused to take it easy and grew antsy whenever I drove him anywhere. Precisely 48 hours after being released, he got into his Jeep and drove around until dinnertime.

On day four, Mike said, "I want to show you something," and led me to the stairwell. He jogged down the stairs, then back up. I started to ask what he was doing, but he held up his finger. Then he went back down and jogged up again. He was breathing easily. That's when it dawned on me. At the top of the stairs, he took my hand and led me to the bedroom.

"No!" I cried. "This is way too soon." He looked me in the eyes. "I've gotta know."

There are a lot of things that crowd into a woman's mind at a time like this. "Forget it. Call 911 if anything happens." Fear gripped me. Then I said something that contravened my 25 years of feminist thinking: "Don't try to please me, okay? Just get it over with as fast as you can."

My memory of the occasion is clouded by the chant that washed through my mind: Call 911 . . . call 911 . . . call 911. It seemed like an eternity. All I wanted was for it to be over safely. I got my wish. Just at the right moment, he whispered in my ear, "I'm still alive!"

Looking back, I'd say that was probably the worst sex we've ever had. Yet, in my heart, it was also the best.

SOURCE: From Dobel, 1999.

lems, such as arthritis, diabetes, and osteoporosis can also interfere with sexual functioning. We will discuss many other physical problems, such as illness, surgery, and injuries that can affect sexual functioning in Chapter 14.

The stereotype that sex worsens with age is not inevitably true. A key to sexual enjoyment later in life is for partners to learn more about each other and to be patient and understanding with each other. Physical fitness, good nutrition, adequate rest and sleep, a reduction in alcohol intake, and positive self-esteem can all enhance sexuality throughout the life span. As one man notes:

> The age of one's mind and spirit is the determiner that affects all relationships and sex at any age. Age is irrelevant, our culture has made too much of this. We must ignore the public relations commercials in regard to age and sex (always young male and female couples) and begin to see each other as loving persons who need, desire, and can give love—whatever our ages. (Hite, 1981, p. 900)

Review Question

Identify and explain some of the physiological changes that occur with aging. How might these affect the sexual response cycle?

safe sex
Sexual behaviors that do not pose a risk for the transmission of sexually transmitted infections.

safer sex
Sexual behaviors that reduce the risk of sexually transmitted infections.

SAFER-SEX BEHAVIORS

What exactly is **safe sex**? Does it mean wearing a condom? Limiting sex partners? Not engaging in oral, anal, vaginal, or casual sex? Although safe sex does include condom use, it also refers to specific sexual behaviors that are "safe" to engage in because they protect against the risk of acquiring sexually transmitted infections. However, there are no sexual behaviors that protect a person 100% of the time (with the exception of abstinence, solo masturbation, and sexual fantasy). Therefore, maybe the real question is, "Is there really any such thing as safe sex?" In response to that question, it may be more appropriate to refer to **safer-sex** behaviors, because we do know there are some sexual behaviors that are safer than others (see Sex in Real Life, "Safer-Sex Behavior Guidelines"). In Chapter 15 we will discuss high-risk sexual behaviors.

All sexually active people should be aware of the risks associated with various sexual behaviors. Not only should people decrease the number of sexual partners, they must learn more about the backgrounds of their partners, avoid unprotected vaginal and anal intercourse and other risky activities, and use barrier contraception. In Chapter 13 we will discuss what types of lubricants to use with condoms.

Research has shown that college students are aware of their partner's prior sexual history, past condom use, and HIV status only about half the time (Buysse, 1998). In one study, male college students were more likely to ignore past sexual history with partners who were physically attractive (Agocha & Cooper, 1999).

Even though most people feel anxious about the possibility of acquiring an STI, casual sexual activity has increased in the past several years, and there have been very few increases in heterosexual safer-sex behaviors (Moore, 1999). Although there has been a gradual increase in condom use, there have been very few changes in the heterosexual behavior of male and female college students; in fact, no significant changes in sexual behavior have been noted. Overall, effective safer-sex negotiation is more an exception than the rule in dating couples (Buysse & Ickes, 1999).

One item worth mentioning in the promotion of safer sex is the dental dam, which is a square piece of thin latex, similar to the latex used in condoms, that can be used to prevent the transmission of sexually transmitted infections. It is stretched across the vulva or anus to prevent the exchange of bodily fluids. It is available without a prescription in many drugstores across the United States and now comes in a variety of flavors and colors.

One behavior that has been clearly linked to unsafe sexual behaviors is drinking alcohol. As pointed out earlier in this chapter, drinking alcohol can cause impaired judgment. In one study, 75% of college students had made decisions while under the influence of alcohol that they later regretted (Poulson et al., 1998). In fact, alcohol use is one of the most important factors that is repeatedly linked to unsafe sexual behavior (Wechsler & Issac, 1992). Young men and women who drink alcohol are seven times

SEX in Real Life

Safer-Sex Behavior Guidelines

Following are some sexual activities that are rated for safety. Remember that engaging in hookups (casual sex) and alcohol use are two activities that can increase your risk of acquiring a sexually transmitted infection. Typically, unsafe behaviors involve contact with semen, blood, or other body fluids. Those behaviors that are considered safe include activities that involve no exchange of bodily fluids. Contact your local health clinic or AIDS organization for more information.

Safe
massage
hugging
dry kissing
body rubbing, dry humping
sexual fantasy
masturbation (self only)
watching erotica
phone/computer sex
sex toys (provided condoms are used if toys are shared)
taking a bath together

Possibly Safe
French kissing
anal intercourse with condom

vaginal intercourse with condom
fisting with glove
cunnilingus with dental dam
fellatio with condom
anal rimming or analingus with dental dam
vaginal or anal stimulation with fingers using latex glove

Possibly Unsafe
cunnilingus without a dental dam
vaginal or anal stimulation with fingers without latex glove
fellatio without a condom
sharing sex toys without cleaning or changing condoms in between uses
fisting without a glove
anal rimming or analingus without a dental dam

Unsafe
anal intercourse without condom
vaginal intercourse without condom
blood contact
cunnilingus without a dental dam during menstruation

SOURCE: Adapted from "Safer Sex Basics," 2005.

more likely to engage in sexual intercourse (and have more sexual partners) than those who do not drink (Center on Addiction and Substance Abuse, 2002).

In Chapter 6, we talked about the importance of communication. Communication is key to safer sex relationships. When there is talk about safe sex, women are more likely than men to bring up the topic (M. Allen et al., 2002). But it's important for all couples to talk about each other's past sexual relationships prior to engaging in sexual intercourse or sexual activity. Not only will such openness result in safer sex, it will also result in a healthier relationship.

Throughout this chapter you have learned that human sexuality is shaped by cultural, ethnic, religious, psychological, and biological influences. All of these factors help us to determine what sexual behaviors we will engage in and which are unacceptable for us. These influences also shape our sexual attitudes and our ability to talk about sexuality.

Review Question

Define "safe sex" and give some guidelines for safe sex behaviors.

Chapter Review

ACTIVE SUMMARY

1. Our hormones have a powerful effect on our bodies. The **(a)** _____ glands secrete hormones into the bloodstream. The most influential hormones in sexual behavior are **(b)** _____ and **(c)** _____. In most animals, the **(d)** _____ controls and regulates sexual behavior chiefly through hormones, although in humans, learned experiences and social, cultural, and ethnic influences are also important. Hormone levels **(e)** _____ as we age, and this can cause a variety of different problems, such as vaginal dryness and decreased vaginal sensitivity in women and slower and less frequent **(f)** _____ in men.

2. Our ethnic group affects the types of sexual behaviors we engage in, our sexual **(a)** _____, and our ability to **(b)** _____ about sexuality. Differences have been found between African Americans, Hispanics, Caucasians, and Asian Americans. Religiosity also influences sexual behavior. The more religious people are, the more **(c)** _____ their sexual behavior tends to be.

3. There are a series physiological and psychological changes that occur during sexual behavior. Masters and Johnson's sexual response cycle involves four **(a)** _____ phases, including excitement, plateau, orgasm, and resolution. During these phases, there are changes in both **(b)** _____ and **(c)** _____. In men, there is a(an) **(d)** _____ period during resolution, and generally the stages are less well-defined. In women, the menstrual cycle may affect the sexual response cycle.

4. Kaplan's model of sexual response has three stages—**(a)** _____, excitement, and orgasm. It is easier to **(b)** _____ when a person is going through Kaplan's stages. Reed's ESP model encompasses features of both Kaplan's and Masters and Johnson's models. Phases include seduction, sensation, surrender, and reflection. Tiefer argues that these models are all based on the **(c)** _____ model and because of this, they leave out important aspects of sexual **(d)** _____.

5. The majority of heterosexuals define **(a)** _____ as "anything that happens before penetration" or something a man does to get a woman in the mood. Many people use **(b)** _____ to help increase their sexual excitement, and people use them both during periods of sexual activity and **(c)** _____. Female sexual fantasies often reflect **(d)** _____ sexual experiences, whereas male fantasies are more dependent on erotica and images.

6. Adult sexual behavior includes a range of different sexual activities. Some adults choose to be **(a)** _____, or abstinent. Over the last decade, men's and women's sexual **(b)** _____ have become more similar. Men **(c)** _____ more than women, and women feel more **(d)** _____ about their masturbatory activity than do men. Masturbation fulfills a variety of different needs for different people at different ages. In manual sex no exchange of bodily **(e)** _____ occurs. Men and women both have concerns about how best to manually stimulate their partners. Fellatio and **(f)** _____ are becoming more popular as forms of sexual behavior. Both heterosexual and homosexual couples engage in oral sex.

7. Most heterosexual couples engage in sexual **(a)** _____ almost every time they have sex, and when most people think of **(b)** _____, they think of sexual intercourse. It is important to delay intercourse until after **(c)** _____ has begun. If a woman needs more lubrication, a(an) **(d)** _____ lubricant can be used. There are a variety of **(e)** _____ for sexual intercourse.

8. Same-sex couples engage in many of the same sexual **(a)** _____ as heterosexual couples do. Lesbians tend to be more sexually **(b)** _____ than heterosexual women and have lower rates of sexual **(c)** _____. There are more similarities than **(d)** _____ in the sexual behavior of homosexuals and heterosexuals. Both heterosexual and homosexual couples engage in anal sex, and some experience orgasm from this technique. After anal intercourse, the penis should never be transferred from the anus to the vagina because of the risk of **(e)** _____.

9. The majority of elderly persons maintain a(an) **(a)** _____ in sex and sexual activity, even though society often views them as **(b)** _____. A lack of **(c)** _____ about the physiological effects of aging on sexual functioning may cause an elderly person to think his or her sex life is **(d)** _____ when a sexual dysfunction is experienced.

10. There may be no such thing as **(a)** _____ sex; instead, we refer to "safer" sex. Other than abstinence, solo masturbation,

and sexual **(b)** _____, there are no 100% safe sexual behaviors. Very few changes in the heterosexual behavior of male and female college students have occurred as a result of the AIDS crisis. Men and women should learn the sexual histories of all their sexual partners and consistently use **(c)** _____ and **(d)** _____ _____.

Critical Thinking Questions

1. Why do you think so many people are hesitant to talk about sexual pleasure? There is no doubt that you talk about sex with friends, but why has it become so taboo and so difficult to talk about what brings you sexual pleasure?

2. Do you think your ethnicity affects your sexuality? In what ways? Why do you think this is?

3. Suppose that your sexual partner shares with you that he or she has been engaging in sexual fantasies during sexual activity with you. How would this make you feel? Would you want to talk to your partner about these fantasies? Why, or why not?

4. Susan has been masturbating regularly since the age of 15, although she feels very guilty about it. She realizes that she is un-

able to reach orgasm with her partner. After reading this chapter, explain to Susan what you've learned about masturbation, and offer her some advice.

5. Flash forward 30 years and imagine what your life will be like in a committed, long-term relationship. How do you hope your sex life will be? What factors might contribute to any problems you might experience?

6. Suppose you are in a new relationship and have just begun engaging in sexual activity. How can you communicate your desires to keep the sex safe? What problems might come up in this discussion?

CHAPTER RESOURCES

Check It Out

Emmers-Sommer, T. M., & Allen, M. (2005). **Safer sex in personal relationships: The role of sexual scripts in HIV infection and prevention.** Mahwah, NJ: Erlbaum.

In this book, the authors discuss sexual attitudes and practices related to sex both within and outside of intimate relationships. They address safe sex issues and explore how to practice safe sex within intimate relationships, including information on negotiating condom use, communicating about sexual disease and sexual history issues, and extrarelationship sexuality.

The Mother (2003; 1 hour, 52 minutes; Rated R)

At the beginning of the film, the mother (May) and father prepare for a trip to London to visit their grown children. The father is ill but wants to make the trip. When he dies suddenly, the wife's world spins out of control. Saddened by the loss of her husband, May decides to stay at her daughter's home to watch her grandson. She soon begins having a sexual affair with her daughter's lover. Her passion is reignited, and she transforms herself. Suddenly she is an attractive, sexual woman, instead of the aging woman she was before the loss of her husband. The film explores aging and sexuality, relationships, deception, and sexual well-being.

InfoTrac® College Edition

If your instructor ordered InfoTrac with this book, explore InfoTrac College Edition, your online library, for additional readings and review. Go to: **www.thomsonedu.com,** and enter these search terms:

aphrodisiac	male orgasm	female orgasm
multiple orgasms	sexual abstinence	celibacy
sexual excitement	oral sex	G-spot
safe sex	safer sex	sexual intercourse
hormones, sex	homosexual sex	sexual fantasies

Web Resources

SexualityNow **Companion Website**
Go to **http://thomsonedu.com/carroll** for practice quiz questions, interactive activities, Internet links, critical thinking exercises, discussion forums, and more. You can also access sites from the Wadsworth Psychology Study Center **(http://psychology.wadsworth.com)** or you can connect directly to the following sites:

Electronic Journal of Human Sexuality
This online publication of the Institute for Advanced Study of Human Sexuality in San Francisco disseminates information about all aspects of human sexuality. The site offers a database of research articles, dissertations, and theses on human sexuality, book reviews, and posters from faculty and student conference presentations.

San Francisco Sex Information Organization
San Francisco Sex Information (SFSI) is a free information and referral switchboard providing anonymous, accurate, nonjudgmental information about sex. If you have a question about sex, they will answer it or refer you to someone who can. They also offer training in sex education.

Healthy Sex
HealthySex.com is an educational site, designed by Wendy Maltz, to promote healthy sexuality based on caring, respect, and safety. The site contains information on sexual health, intimacy, communication, sexual abuse and addiction, sexual fantasies, and midlife sex, and links to a variety of different sexuality sites.

Go Ask Alice!
Go Ask Alice! is a question-and-answer format website produced by Columbia University's Health Education Program. The mission of Go Ask Alice! is to increase access to, and use of, health information by providing factual, in-depth, straightforward, and nonjudgmental information to assist the people's decision making about many issues, including sexual health. You can visit recently asked questions or search the database for past questions. Links are also provided to several valuable websites. Although this site was originally designed only for Columbia University students, today it is available to everyone.

Go to **www.thomsonedu.com** to link to **SexualityNow,** your online study tool. First take the **Pre-Test** for this chapter to get your **Personalized Study Plan,** which will identify topics you need to review and direct you to online resources. Then take the **Post-Test** to determine what concepts you have mastered and what you still need work on.

Videos in SexualityNow
For additional information on topics discussed in this chapter, check out the videos in **SexualityNow** on the following topics:
- **Styles of Sexually Traditional and Adventurous People**—Explore the question of sex's importance within a relationship, and the styles of sexual expression.

11

Sexual Orientation

Sexuality ⊙ Now Go to www.thomsonedu.com to link to SexualityNow, your online study tool.

*S*exual orientation refers to the gender(s) that a person is attracted to emotion-ally, physically, sexually, and romantically. Heterosexuals are predominantly attracted to members of the other gender; homosexuals to members of the same gender; and bisexuals are attracted to all individuals (the word "gay" is often used to refer to a male homosexual, whereas "lesbian" is often used to refer to a female homosexual).

GLBTQ
Acronym for gay, lesbian, bisexual, transgen-dered, and questioning (or queer) adults or youths.

Although such distinctions may seem simple, as you will soon see, human sexual be-havior does not always fit easily into such neat boxes. Today many people use the acronym **GLBTQ** to refer to people whose identity is gay, lesbian, bisexual, transgen-dered, or questioning, and we will use this acronym throughout this chapter (we dis-cussed transgender issues in Chapter 3 and here we will focus only on gay, lesbian, and bisexual issues—often referred to as GLB. The "Q" in this acronym includes those who are either questioning their sexual orientation, or queer.)

Before the 1980s most of published research on homosexuality focused on the causes or on associated mental disorders (because homosexuality was classified as such until 1973—see Chapter 1), and in the 1990s HIV and AIDS dominated the research studies (Boehmer, 2002). Today we are learning more about the development of gay, lesbian, and bisexual identities; coming out issues; aging; and health care, to name a few areas. We will discuss this research throughout this chapter.

WHAT DETERMINES SEXUAL ORIENTATION?

sexual orientation
The gender(s) that a person is attracted to emo-tionally, physically, sexually, and romantically.

How should we categorize a person's **sexual orientation**? Take a moment to read Personal Voices, "Defining Sexual Orientation." Here you will see that the simplest way to categorize a person's sexual orientation seems to be through sexual behavior: with whom does he or she have sex? However, if that were our sole criterion, we would have to call Peter gay—after all, he has sex exclusively with other men. But because Peter fan-tasizes only of sex with women, can we really call him gay?

Maybe, then, the secret life of sexual fantasies determines sexual orientation. Bill, however, sometimes fantasizes about sex with men, even though he considers himself **straight** and has sex only with women. Allie is having sex only with men now but has slept with women in the past.

straight
Slang for heterosexual.

Perhaps we should consider romantic love instead of sex to determine a person's sexual orientation. Whom do you love, or whom could you love? Anthony loves his wife romantically and would never consider an emotional attachment to the men he picks up. Would you consider Anthony 100% **heterosexual** just because he loves only his wife? Maybe we should just let people decide for themselves; if they believe they are het-erosexual, they are, no matter how they behave. Yet when people's behavior and beliefs about themselves are in conflict (such as Anthony's), social scientists usually define them by their behavior.

heterosexual
Man or woman who is sexually attracted to members of the other sex.

The problem may be that we tend to think of sexual orientation in discrete cate-gories: you are either **homosexual** or heterosexual (or, occasionally, **bisexual**). The full variety and richness of human sexual experience, however, cannot be easily captured in such restrictive categories. People can show enormous variety in their sexual behavior, sexual fantasies, emotional attachments, and sexual self-concept, and each contributes to a person's sexual orientation.

homosexual
Man or woman who is sexually attracted to members of the same sex.

bisexual
Person who is erotically attracted to members of either sex.

In this chapter, we will explore the nature of sexual orientation and the ways re-searchers and scholars think about it. Heterosexuality is a sexual orientation, and the question "Why is he or she heterosexual?" is no less valid than "Why is he or she ho-

Personal Voices

Defining Sexual Orientation

*R*ead through the following descriptions of different sexual lifestyles. How would you categorize these people? Who is heterosexual? Who is homosexual? Who is bisexual?

Susan, 45 years old: *I have been in an exclusive, monogamous lesbian relationship with Michele for 21 years. After 8 years with Michele, I decided I wanted a child and had sex a few times with a friend of mine, Jonathan. I now have a 13-year-old son. Seeing how much I enjoyed having a child, my partner decided she wanted one, too, but because she had no desire to have intercourse with a man she had herself artificially inseminated.*

Allie, 25 years old: *I had my first sexual experience with a guy when I was 16 years old. I loved sex and enjoyed being with guys. However, I fell madly in love with a woman during my junior year of college. Our sex life was awesome. We drifted apart after college, and now I am sleeping only with men again.*

Bill, 21 years old: *When I was in my teens, a friend of mine and myself stroked each other to orgasm on three occasions. Although I now date only women, every so often while masturbating I fantasize about those experiences, which enhances my orgasm. I consider myself heterosexual and feel a bit uneasy about my fantasies.*

Anthony, 31 years old: *I have been married for 15 years, and I have two children. My wife and I have a healthy sexual life, and I love her very much. I have never had sex with another woman since my marriage. However, about once every 2 or 3 months, I drive to a town about 2 hours away from where I live and pick up a man for quick, anonymous sex. I find these encounters to be the most exciting part of my sex life.*

Peter, 26 years old: *I have been in prison for 5 years for dealing drugs. While in prison, I've engaged in anal and oral sex with other men, usually fantasizing that they were women. I long for my scheduled release a few months from now, when I plan to resume having sex exclusively with women, as I did before being sent to prison.*

Kiko, 45 years old: *My partner and I enjoy engaging in group sex with other couples. In these group sex sessions, sexual contact is very free, and often I will give a guy a blow job while my partner engages in sexual contact with women. We are both are very comfortable with such contact, feeling that sexual pleasure is sexual pleasure no matter who is administering it.*

Are any of these people difficult to categorize? What about Bill, who is now exclusively heterosexual in his behavior but has fantasies of past homosexual behavior? Anthony has occasional sex with other men, whereas Peter and Susan both have had sex outside their usual lifestyles for purely practical reasons—Peter because he is in prison and women are not available to him, and Susan because she wanted to get pregnant. Allie has had sexual relationships with both men and women, whereas Kiko has an open relationship in which he and his partner are not restricted to only one gender.

mosexual?" "Bisexual?" Here, however, we focus our attention primarily on the research and writing about homosexuality and bisexuality.

SEX Talk

Question: *If I played sex games with a friend of the same sex when I was 15, am I gay?*

Sexual experimentation and sexual orientation are two different things. It is very common, especially in the teenage years and before, to experiment with same-sex contact (and for people who are predominantly gay or lesbian to experiment with the other sex). Yet only a fairly small percentage of people who experiment will become gay, lesbian, or bisexual (Fay et al., 1989).

Review Question

Describe the difficulties involved in our attempts to categorize sexual behavior.

sex byte

A study exploring civil unions during Vermont's first year of legislation found that gay couples experienced similar issues. However, lesbian couples reported more stress related to family reactions, whereas gay couples reported more stress related to HIV/AIDS and violence/harassment issues (Todosijevic et al., 2005).

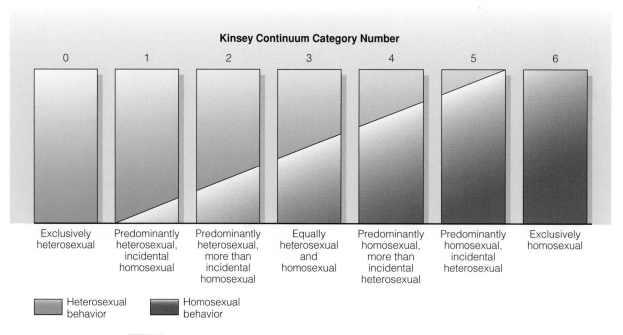

Kinsey Continuum Category Number

| 0 | 1 | 2 | 3 | 4 | 5 | 6 |

| Exclusively heterosexual | Predominantly heterosexual, incidental homosexual | Predominantly heterosexual, more than incidental homosexual | Equally heterosexual and homosexual | Predominantly homosexual, more than incidental heterosexual | Predominantly homosexual, incidental heterosexual | Exclusively homosexual |

Heterosexual behavior   Homosexual behavior

Figure 11.1

The Kinsey Continuum. The 7-point scale is based on behaviors ranging from exclusively heterosexual behavior to exclusively homosexual behavior.

From H. Kinsey, *Sexual Behavior in the Human Male*, 1948. Reprinted with permission of The Kinsey Institute for Research in Sex, Gender, and Reproduction, Inc.

© Arnold Gold/New Haven Register/The Image Works

Sexual orientation refers to the gender that a person is attracted to emotionally, physically, sexually, and romantically. Same-sex attraction has appeared in almost every society throughout history.

Models of Sexual Orientation: Who Is Homosexual?

Kinsey and his colleagues (1948) believed that relying on the categories "homosexual" and "heterosexual" to describe sexual orientation was inadequate. They also suggested that using a category such as "homosexual" was not as helpful as talking about homosexual behavior. Trying to decide who is a homosexual is difficult; trying to compare amounts or types of homosexual behavior (including fantasies and emotions) is easier.

So Kinsey introduced a 7-point scale (see Figure 11.1) ranging from exclusively heterosexual behavior (0) to exclusively homosexual behavior (6). The Kinsey continuum was the first scale to suggest that people engage in complex sexual behaviors that are not reducible simply to "homosexual" and "heterosexual." Many modern theorists agree that sexual orientation is a continuous variable rather than a categorical variable—that is, there are no natural cutoff points that would easily separate people into categories such as "heterosexual" or "homosexual" (Berkey et al., 1990; L. Ellis et al., 1987).

The Kinsey scale is not without its problems, however. First, Kinsey emphasized people's behavior (although he did consider other factors such as fantasies and emotions), but some researchers suggest that people's emotions and fantasies are the most important determinants of sexual orientation (Bell et al., 1981; Storms, 1980, 1981). Second, the scale is static in time; how recently must one have had homosexual contact to qualify for "incidents" of homosexual behavior? Or consider Anthony from Personal Voices, "Defining Sexual Orientation." If Anthony slept with 6 men over the last year and had sex with his wife once a week, is he in category 5 (because he had sex with 6 men and only 1 woman) or category 2 (because he had 52 experiences with a woman, but only 6 with men; F. Klein, 1990)?

Other models, such as the Klein sexual orientation grid (KSOG; see Figure 11.2), try to take the Kinsey continuum further by including 7 dimensions—attraction, behavior, fantasy, emotional preference, social preference, self-identification, and lifestyle (Horowitz et al., 2001). Each of these dimensions is measured for the past, the present, and the ideal. Take the KSOG to create a profile of your sexual orientation.

Review Question

Outline the Kinsey model of sexual orientation, and compare and contrast it with the KSOG.

The Klein Sexual Orientation Grid

	Past	Present	Ideal
A. Sexual attraction			
B. Sexual behavior			
C. Sexual fantasies			
D. Emotional preference			
E. Social preference			
F. Self-identification			
G. Heterosexual/homosexual lifestyle			

0 = other sex only
1 = mostly other sex, incidental same sex
2 = mostly other sex, more than incidental same sex
3 = both sexes equally
4 = mostly same sex, more than incidental other sex
5 = mostly same sex, incidental other sex
6 = same sex only

Figure 11.2

The Klein Sexual Orientation Grid was designed to examine seven dimensions of an individual's sexual orientation to determine whether these dimensions have changed over time and to look at a person's fantasy of his or her "ideal" sexual orientation. The KSOG gives a set of numbers that can be compared to determine rates of different sexual orientations. Use the Kinsey categories in this grid to rate yourself.

From Frtiz Klein, *Homosexuality/Heterosexuality*, p. 280. Reprinted with permission of The Kinsey Institute for Research in Sex, Gender, and Reproduction, Inc.

Measuring Sexual Orientation: How Many Are We?

How prevalent are homosexuality, heterosexuality, and bisexuality in society? Kinsey and his colleagues (1948) found that 37% of men and 13% of women reported that they had had at least one adult sexual experience with a member of the same sex that resulted in orgasm and that about 4% of men and 3% of women were lifelong homosexuals. He also reported that 10% of white men had been mostly homosexual for at least 3 years between the ages of 16 and 55, and this statistic became the one most people cited when estimating the prevalence of homosexuality in the United States. However, due to the problems with Kinsey's sampling (see Chapter 2), these figures may be unreliable.

There continues to be controversy about how many gays, lesbians, or bisexuals there are today. Estimates for homosexuality range from 2% to 4% to greater than 10% in males and 1% to 3% in females (Seidman & Rieder, 1994; Whitam et al., 1999), whereas estimates for bisexuality are approximately 3% (M. Diamond, 1993). Laumann and col-

SEX Talk

Question: Isn't it easy to tell a gay, lesbian, or bisexual from a heterosexual just by the way they talk and act?

No. Berger and colleagues (1987) showed videotapes of gay and straight men and women to participants (other gay and straight men and women) to see whether they could determine people's sexual orientation. No group did better than chance at determining who was gay, although the women (lesbian and straight) and gay men did a bit better than the straight men.

Although some gays enjoy dressing or acting like members of the other sex (as do many heterosexuals) and some adopt a style of speech or gait to identify themselves as gay, most are indistinguishable from heterosexuals. The idea that you can tell gays from straights was the premise for the Fox television show "Playing It Straight," in which a woman had to pick a straight man out of a group of gay and straight men. If a straight man was the last man standing, the couple split the money. However, if a gay man convinced the woman he was straight, he would win 1 million dollars.

sex byte

The 2000 U.S. Census found that at least a quarter of a million children live in same-sex couple households in the United States, and that San Francisco, Washington DC, and New York City have the highest concentration of gays and lesbians (Doyle, 2005).

Review Question

Describe the prevalence of gay, lesbian, and bisexual orientations. Explain why this research has been so controversial.

essentialist
Theorist who believes that homosexuals are innately different from heterosexuals, a result of either biological or developmental processes.

constructionist
Theorist who believes that homosexuality is a social role that has developed differently in different cultures and times.

leagues (1994) found that although 5.5% of women said they found the thought of having sex with another woman appealing, only about 4% said they had had sex with another woman after the age of 18, and fewer than 2% had had sex with another woman in the past year. Similarly, although 9% of men said they had had sex with another male since puberty, a little over 5% had had sex with a man since turning 18, and only 2% had had sex with a man in the past year. National studies in France, Britain, Norway, Denmark, and Canada all found same-sex behavior in 1% to 3% of men and a slightly lower percentage of women (Muir, 1993). Overall, when taken together, surveys indicate that the frequency of same-sex behavior in the United States has remained constant over the years in spite of the changes in the social status of homosexuality (Pillard & Bailey, 1998).

Although there are problems with each of the studies just cited—for example, they concentrate on homosexual sexual *behavior*, not fantasies or desires—scholars generally agree that between 3% and 4% of males are predominantly gay, 1.5% to 2% of women are predominantly lesbian, and about 2% to 5% are bisexual (Laumann et al., 1994; Mackay, 2000).

WHY ARE THERE DIFFERENT SEXUAL ORIENTATIONS?

In the 1930s and 1940s, a group of scientists tried to explain homosexuality by looking for "masculine" traits in lesbians and "feminine" traits in homosexual men. They claimed that gay men had broad shoulders and narrow hips (indicating "immature skeletal development") and lesbians had abnormal genitalia, including larger-than-average vulvas, longer labia minora, a larger glans on the clitoris, a smaller uterus, and higher eroticism, shown by their tendency to become sexually aroused when being examined (Terry, 1990)! Modern research has failed to find any significant nonneurological physical differences between homosexuals and heterosexuals, although some attempts to examine physical differences still exist.

Today's theories can be divided into two basic types: **essentialist** and **constructionist.** Essentialism suggests that homosexuals are innately different from heterosexuals, a result of either biological or developmental processes. Early essentialist theories implied that homosexuality was an abnormality in development, which contributed to the argument that homosexuality is a sickness. More recently, gay and lesbian scholars, in an attempt to prove that homosexuality is not a "lifestyle choice" as antihomosexual forces have argued, have themselves been arguing that homosexuality is a biologically based sexual variation. Constructionists, on the other hand, suggest that homosexuality is a social role that has developed differently in different cultures and times, and therefore nothing is innately different between homosexuals and heterosexuals. In Chapter 2 we discussed queer theory, which holds a constructionist view of homosexuality.

SEX Talk

Question: Why are men often turned on by watching two females having sex but turned off by watching two males?

Heterosexual men's magazines often feature two women together in sexual positions but almost never two men. In the United States, watching women interact sexually is much more socially acceptable. These pictorials always imply that the women are still attracted to men, waiting for them, just biding their time until a man arrives. An internalized fear of homosexuality in men also makes it difficult for many men to see two men being sexual with each other. It is much less threatening to watch two women. In Chapter 18 we'll discuss gender and the use of pornography.

Scholars in different fields tend to take different approaches to explain why some people are gay, lesbian, or bisexual. Note, however, that almost all the researchers we will discuss assume there are two, exclusive, nonoverlapping categories: homosexual and heterosexual. Most theories on sexual orientation ignore bisexuality or do not offer enough research to explain why bisexuality exists. We will discuss bisexuality throughout this chapter.

Biological Theories: Differences Are Innate

Biological theories are essentialist—that is, they claim that differing sexual orientations are due to differences in physiology. This difference can be due to genetics, hormones, birth order, or simple physical traits.

Genetics

In 1952, Franz Kallman tried to show that there was a genetic component to homosexuality. Kallman compared identical twins (who come from one zygote and have the same genes (see Chapter 3); with fraternal twins (who come from two zygotes and have about 50% of the same genes). Though Kallman found a strong genetic component to homosexuality, his study had a number of problems and is unreliable.

Bailey and his colleagues have done a number of studies of twins to determine the genetic basis of homosexuality. They report that in homosexual males, 52% of identical twins, 22% of fraternal twins, and 11% of adoptive brothers were also homosexuals, showing that the more closely genetically related two siblings were, the more likely they were to share a sexual orientation (J. M. Bailey & Pillard, 1993). Among females, 48% of identical twins, 16% of fraternal twins, and 6% of adoptive siblings of lesbians were also lesbians (J. M. Bailey et al., 1993). However, identical twins share much more than genetics. They also share many more experiences than do other kinds of siblings. So the studies cannot tell how much of the concordance is due to genetic factors and how much is due to the identical twins having grown up under similar environmental influences.

A more interesting finding is the one by Hamer and colleagues (1993) of the National Cancer Institute. Hamer found that homosexual males tended to have more homosexual relatives on their mother's side, and he traced that to the existence of a gene, passed through the mother, that he found in 33 of 40 gay brothers. Gay men have more gay brothers than lesbian sisters, whereas lesbians have more lesbian sisters than gay brothers (Pattatucci, 1998). This research has also found evidence of a "gay" gene on the X chromosome but not a "lesbian" gene. Newer genetic research has revealed that the frequency of homosexuality in twins may be much lower than previously reported (Kirk et al., 1999).

If homosexuality were solely a genetic trait, it should have disappeared long ago. Because homosexuals have been less likely than heterosexuals to have children, each successive generation of homosexuals should have become smaller, until genes for homosexuality disappeared from the gene pool. Yet rates of homosexuality have remained constant. Concordance rates for siblings, twins, and adoptees reveal that genes account for at least half of the variance in sexual orientation (Pillard & Bailey, 1998). Even so, Bailey and his colleagues agree that environmental factors are also very important.

Hormones

Hormonal theories can concentrate either on hormonal imbalances before birth or on hormone levels in adults. Here we look at both prenatal and adult hormonal levels.

Prenatal Factors   When certain hormones are injected into pregnant animals, such as rats or guinea pigs, at critical periods of fetal development, the offspring can be made to exhibit homosexual behavior (Dorner, 1976). Some researchers have found evidence that sexual orientation may be influenced by levels of prenatal hormones in human beings as well (Cohen-Bendahan et al., 2005; Rahman, 2005). (For more information about hormones, see Chapter 3.) In a retrospective study, L. Ellis and colleagues

sex byte

Homosexual and heterosexual men have been found to respond differently to two odors that may be involved in sexual arousal—gay men and heterosexual women respond to the odors in similar ways (Savic et al., 2005).

(1988) suggested that stress during pregnancy (which can influence hormonal levels) increased the chances of a homosexual offspring. Early hormone levels have also been found to influence both sexual orientation and related childhood sex-typed behaviors (Berenbaum & Snyder, 1995; Swaab, 2004).

However, other researchers have concluded that the evidence for the effect of prenatal hormones on both male and female homosexuality is weak (Whalen et al., 1990). A study of female rhesus monkeys who were given masculine hormones before birth revealed that their environment after birth was as important to their sexual behavior as the hormones (Money, 1987). In other words, even if prenatal hormones are a factor in sexual orientation, environmental factors may be equally important.

Adult Hormone Levels Many studies have compared blood androgen levels in adult male homosexuals with those in adult male heterosexuals, and most have found no significant differences (Green, 1988). Of five studies comparing hormone levels in lesbians and straight women, three found no differences between the two groups in either testosterone, estrogen, or other hormones, and the other two found higher levels of testosterone in lesbians (and one found lower levels of estrogen; Dancey, 1990). Thus, studies so far do not support the idea of adult hormone involvement.

Birth Order

Researchers have also examined effects of birth order. Many gay men have been found to be born later than their siblings and have older brothers, but not older sisters (Blanchard, 2004; Camperio-Ciani et al., 2004; Ridley, 2003). Overall it has been estimated that 1 in 7 gay men's sexual orientation was a result of fraternal birth order (the number of older brothers they have; Cantor et al., 2002).

Fraternal birth order could contribute to a homosexual orientation in two ways: first, the placenta cells of the uterine lining could influence later gestations; and children born later could develop an immune response. This immune response could influence the expression of key genes during brain development in a way that increases a boy's attraction to other boys (Ridley, 2003). This research is controversial, but nonetheless research in this direction continues to look for possible interactions. Interestingly, the relationship between sexual orientation and number of older brothers has been found to hold only for males (Blanchard, 2004).

Physiology

Two articles in the early 1990s reported differences between the brains of homosexual and heterosexual men (S. LeVay, 1991; Swaab & Hofman, 1990). Both studies found that certain areas of the hypothalamus, known to play a strong role in sexual urges, were either larger or smaller in homosexual men than in heterosexual men. Even though this research has been replicated (Kinnunen et al., 2004; Swaab, 2004), it has not yet been determined whether the differences were there from birth or developed later in life, and the research cannot prove that the differences were due primarily to the men's sexual orientation. Other studies that examined differences in ear structure and hearing in heterosexual, lesbian, and bisexual women found differences in these areas of the brain (Jensen, 1998).

Physiology studies have also looked at amount of facial hair, size of external genitalia, the ratio of shoulder width to hip width (Schuklenk et al., 1997), handedness (Lippa, 2003; Lalumiere & Blanchard, 2000), and finger length (Rahman, 2005; Bailey & Hurd, 2005). There has been limited scientific support for some of these physiological findings. For example, lesbian women have been found to have a male-type finger length pattern on the right hand (which is a shorter ring, than index, finger; Williams et al., 2000).

In summary, although there have been some biological differences found among homosexuals, heterosexuals, and bisexuals, findings are inconsistent, and in many cases the evidence is weak. Given the complexity of biological factors, it is impossible to make accurate individual predications because of the randomness of neural connections during development (Pillard, 1998). Because of this, it appears that sexual orientation is the result of a combination of genetic, biological, and social influences (Schuklenk et al., 1997). We will now examine some of the developmental and sociological theories about sexual orientation.

Review Question

Identify and describe the four physiological areas of research on the development of homosexuality.

Question: *Is homosexuality found only in humans, or do some animals also exhibit homosexual behavior?*

Same-sex activity has been found in 450 species of birds and mammals. In the summer months, killer whales spend one-tenth of their time engaging in homosexual activity (Mackay, 2000). Many mammal species, from rats to lions to cows to monkeys, exhibit same-sex mounting behavior. Males mount other males, and females mount other females (though they rarely do it when a male is present). Female rhesus monkeys probably mount each other to establish dominance hierarchies, and cows may mount to coordinate their reproductive cycles. Bonobo chimpanzees have been found to engage in all types of sexual behaviors, including same- and other-sex behaviors (Waal, 1995). Even so, no one has reliably reported on cases in which individual animals display exclusively homosexual behavior; that seems to be restricted to human beings. However, we should be very careful in extending animal analogies to humans.

Developmental Theories: Differences Are Learned

Developmental theories focus on a person's upbringing and personal history to find the origins of homosexuality. Developmental theories tend to be constructionist; that is, they see the development of homosexual behavior as a product of social forces rather than being innate in a particular individual. First we will discuss the most influential development theory, psychoanalytic theory, and then we will examine gender-role noncomformity, peer-interaction theories, and behavioristic theories of homosexuality.

Freud and the Psychoanalytic School

Sigmund Freud seemed to be of two minds about homosexuality (1953). On the one hand, he believed that the infant was "polymorphous perverse"—that is, the infant sees all kinds of things as potentially sexual. Because both males and females are potentially attractive to the infant, thought Freud, all of us are inherently bisexual. He therefore did not see homosexuals as being sick. In a famous letter to a concerned American mother, he wrote that homosexuality "is nothing to be ashamed of, no vice, no degradation, it cannot be classified as an illness" (1951, quoted in Friedman, 1986). He even found homosexuals to be "distinguished by specially high intellectual development and ethical culture" (1905, quoted in Friedman, 1986).

On the other hand, Freud saw male heterosexuality as the result of normal maturation and male homosexuality as the result of an unresolved Oedipal complex (see Chapter 2 for a more complete discussion). An intense attachment to the mother coupled with a distant father could lead the boy to fear revenge by the father through castration. Female genitalia, lacking a penis, could then represent this castration and evoke fear throughout his life. After puberty, the child shifts from desire for the mother to identification with her, and he begins to look for the love objects she would look for— men. Fixation on the penis allows the man to calm his castration fears, and by renouncing women he avoids rivalry with the father.

Like Freud's view of female sexuality in general, his theories on lesbianism were less coherent, but he basically argued that the young girl becomes angry when she discovers she lacks a penis and blames her mother (we discussed the Electra complex in Chapter 2). Unable to have her father, she defensively rejects him and all men and minimizes her anger at her mother by eliminating the competition between them for male affection.

Freud saw homosexuality as partly **autoerotic** and narcissistic; by making love to a body like one's own, one is really making love to a mirror of oneself. Freud's generally tolerant attitude toward homosexuality was repudiated by some later psychoanalysts, especially Sandor Rado (1949). Rado claimed that humans were not innately bisexual and that homosexuality was a psychopathological condition—a mental illness. This view (not Freud's) became standard for the psychiatric profession until at least the 1970s.

Another influential researcher who followed Rado's perspective was Irving Bieber. Bieber and colleagues (1962) studied 106 homosexual men and 100 heterosexual men who were in psychoanalysis. He claimed that all boys had a normal, erotic attraction to women. However, some had overly close and possessive mothers who were also overintimate and sexually seductive. Their fathers, on the other hand, were hostile or absent, and this **triangulation** (try-ang-gyuh-LAY-shun) drove the boy to the arms of his mother, who inhibited his normal masculine development. Bieber thus blamed homosexuality on a seductive mother who puts the fear of heterosexuality in her son. But Bieber's participants were all in psychoanalysis and thus may have been particularly troubled. Also, fewer than two-thirds of the homosexuals fit his model, and almost a third of heterosexuals came from the same type of family and yet did not engage in homosexual behavior.

The psychoanalytic views of homosexuality dominated for many years. Evelyn Hooker, a clinical psychologist, was a pioneer in gay studies who tried to combat the psychoanalytic view that homosexuality was an illness (see Chapter 2). Hooker (1957) used psychological tests, personal histories, and psychological evaluations to show that homosexuals were as well adjusted as heterosexuals and that no real evidence existed that homosexuality was psychopathological. Although it took many years for her ideas to take hold, many modern psychoanalysts have shifted away from the pathological view of homosexuality. Lewes (1988) demonstrated that psychoanalytic theory itself could easily portray homosexuality as a result of healthy development and that previous psychoanalytic interpretations of homosexuality were based more on prejudice than on science.

SEX Talk

Question: Is there any therapy that can change a person's sexual orientation?

Many Americans believe that sexual orientation is determined by social and environmental factors and that a homosexual can change his or her sexual orientation through therapy or religious faith (Newport, 1998). **Reparative** (rep-PEAR-at-tiv) **therapy,** or conversion therapy, has included techniques such as aversive conditioning, drug treatment, electroconvulsive shock, brain surgery, and hysterectomy (Haldeman, 1994). More recent forms of reparative therapy have led to the development of "ex-gay ministries," which use religion to change a gay or lesbian into a heterosexual (Christianson, 2005). Reparative therapy is based on the assumption that homosexuals must be cured or fixed.

Although the psychoanalyst Irving Bieber (Bieber et al., 1962) reported changing the sexual orientation of 27% of his sample of gay men, more recent psychoanalytic studies have had far less impressive success, and the duration of such "conversions" is questionable. Today reparative therapy is not supported by any reliable research (Bright, 2004), and the majority of professional organizations are opposed to the use of such therapies (Jenkins & Johnston, 2004).

Gender-Role Nonconformity

One group of studies that has begun to fuel debate about the role of early childhood in the development of homosexuality is **gender-role nonconformity** research. The studies are based on the observation that boys who exhibit cross-gender traits—that is, who be-

autoerotic
The arousal of sexual feeling without an external stimulus.

triangulation
The network of triangles that often occurs among three people (e.g., mother–father–child).

reparative therapy
Therapy to change sexual orientation; also called conversion therapy.

gender-role nonconformity
Theory that looks at the role of early childhood in the development of homosexuality and explores cross-gendered traits in childhood.

have in ways more characteristic of girls of that age—are more likely to grow up to be gay, whereas girls who behave in typically male ways are more likely to grow up to be lesbian. As children, gay men on average have been found to be more feminine than straight men, whereas lesbians have been found to be more masculine (J. M. Bailey et al., 1995; Pillard, 1991). Remember though that these findings are correlational, meaning that cross-gender traits and later homosexuality appear to be related, but do not have a cause-and-effect relationship.

Overall, cross-gender boys are viewed more negatively than cross-gender girls (Sandnabba & Ahlberg, 1999). In addition, cross-gender boys are more often thought to be gay than cross-gender girls are thought to be lesbian. One therapist who works with gay men reports that they saw themselves as

> . . . more sensitive than other boys; they cried more easily, had their feelings more readily hurt, had more aesthetic interests, enjoyed nature, art, and music, and were drawn to other "sensitive" boys, girls and adults. Most of these men also felt they were less aggressive as children than others of their age, and most did not enjoy participating in competitive activities. They report that they experienced themselves as being outsiders since these early childhood years. (Isay, 1989, p. 23)

Green (1987) did a prospective study by comparing 66 pervasively feminine boys with 56 conventionally masculine boys as they matured. Green calls the feminine boys "sissy-boys," an unfortunate term. However, he found that these boys cross-dressed, were interested in female fashions, played with dolls, avoided rough play, wished to be girls, and did not desire to be like their fathers from a young age. Three-fourths of them grew up to be homosexual or bisexual, whereas only one of the masculine boys became bisexual. The "sissy-boys," however, also tended to be harassed, rejected, and ignored more by their peers, were more sickly than other boys, and had more psychopathology (Zucker, 1990).

One cannot tell from these types of studies whether these boys are physiologically or developmentally different (an essentialist view of homosexuality) or whether society's reaction to their unconventional play encouraged them to develop a particular sexual orientation (a constructionist view of homosexuality). A constructionist might point out that girls are permitted to exhibit masculine play without being ridiculed, and gender nonconformity in girls—being a "tomboy"—does not correlate with later tendency to become a lesbian. Whether right or wrong, gender-role nonconformity theory cannot be the sole explanation of homosexuality, for many, if not most, gay men were not effeminate as children, and not all effeminate boys grow up to be gay.

Peer Group Interaction

Storms (1981) suggests a purely constructionist theory of development. Noting that a person's sex drive begins to develop in adolescence, Storms suggests that those who develop early begin to become sexually aroused before they have significant contact with the other sex. Because dating usually begins around the age of 15, boys who mature at the age of 12 still play and interact in predominantly same-sex groupings, and so their emerging erotic feelings are more likely to focus on boys.

Storms's theory is supported by the fact that homosexuals do tend to report earlier sexual contacts than heterosexuals. Also, men's sex drive may emerge at a younger age than women's, if such things as frequency of masturbation are any measure, which may explain why there are fewer lesbians than gay men.

Yet Storms's theory also has its problems. On page 345, we discuss the example of Sambian boys who live communally and have sex with other boys from an early age until they are ready to marry. If Storms is right and a male becomes homosexual because only males are available at the time of sexual awakening, then all male Sambians should be homosexuals. However, almost all go on to lead heterosexual lives.

Behaviorist Theories

Behavioral theories of homosexuality consider it a learned behavior, brought about by the rewarding or pleasant reinforcement of homosexual behaviors or the punishing or negative reinforcement of heterosexual behavior (Masters & Johnson, 1979). For example, a

sex byte

A study on genetically altered fruit flies found that changing one gene in the fruit fly could create a distinctive male or female pattern of sexual arousal and behavior (Demir & Dickson, 2005; Stockinger et al., 2005). Male fruit flies that were given the female version of the gene expressed sexual interest in other males, whereas female fruit flies given the male version expressed sexual interest in other females. Although this study gives support for a genetic component to sexual orientation, it is unclear whether the results could be applicable to humans.

person may have a same-sex encounter that is pleasurable, coupled with an encounter with the other sex that is frightening; in his or her fantasies, that person may focus on the same-sex encounter, reinforcing its pleasure with masturbation. Masters and Johnson (1979) believed that even in adulthood some men and women move toward same-sex behaviors if they have bad heterosexual encounters and pleasant homosexual ones.

It is interesting to point out, however, that in a society like ours that tends to view heterosexuality as the norm, it would seem that very few men and women would be societally reinforced for homosexual behavior, yet homosexuality exists even without this positive reinforcement from society.

Review Question

Identify and describe the four developmental theories of homosexuality development.

Sociological Theories: Social Forces at Work

Sociological theories are constructionist and try to explain how social forces produce homosexuality in a society. They suggest that concepts like homosexuality, bisexuality, and heterosexuality are products of our social imagination and are dependent on how we as a society decide to define things. In other words, we learn our culture's way of thinking about sexuality, and then we apply it to ourselves.

The idea of "homosexuality" is a product of a particular culture at a particular time; the idea did not even exist before the 19th century (though the behavior did). Some have argued that the use of the term "homosexuality" as a way to think about same-sex behavior arose only after the Industrial Revolution freed people economically from the family unit and urbanization allowed them to choose new lifestyles in the cities (Adam, 1987). Thus, the idea that people are either "heterosexual" or "homosexual" is not a biological fact but simply a way of thinking that evolves as social conditions change. In other countries, as we note later, these terms are not used, and a person's sexuality is not defined by who his or her partners are. Scientists often assume that homosexuality and heterosexuality are unproblematic categories, without considering whether they might be products of their particular culture.

Sociologists are interested in the models of sexuality that society offers its members and how individuals come to identify with one model or another. For example, maybe effeminate young boys begin to behave as homosexuals because they are labeled homosexual, are called "faggot" by their peers, are ridiculed by their siblings, and even witness the worry and fear on the faces of their parents. They begin to doubt themselves, search for homosexuality in their own behavior, and eventually find it. If American society did not split the sexual world into "homosexual" and "heterosexual," perhaps these boys would move fluidly through same-sex and other-sex contacts without having to choose between the "gay" and "straight" communities.

Interactional Theory: Biology and Sociology

Social psychologist Daryl Bem (1996) has proposed that biological variables, such as genetics, hormones, and brain neuroanatomy, do not cause certain sexual orientations, but rather they contribute to childhood temperaments that influence a child's preferences for sex-typical or sex-atypical activities and peers. Although this theory may seem a bit outdated to us today, his premise about sexual orientation is interesting to consider.

Bem believes that males who engage in "male typical activities," such as rough-and-tumble play or competitive team sports, prefer to be with other boys who also like these activities. Girls, on the other hand, who prefer "female typical activities," such as socializing quietly or playing jacks, prefer the company of other girls who like to do the same activities. Gender-conforming children (those who engage in activities typical for their gender) prefer the other gender for romantic interests, whereas nonconforming children prefer the same gender. Bem's "exotic-becomes-erotic" theory suggests that sexual feelings evolve from experiencing heightened arousal in situations in which one gender is viewed as more exotic, or different from oneself (Bem, 1996). Because this theory combines both biology and sociological issues, many refer to it as an interactional model.

Bem asserts that gay and lesbian children had playmates of the other sex while growing up, and this led them to see the same sex as more "exotic" and appealing. However, research has been contradictory and hasn't been supported by other research (Peplau et al., 1998). Many gay and lesbian children report playmates of both the same sex and the other sex while growing up.

Review Question

Identify and explain how the sociological and interactional theories explain the development of homosexuality.

HOMOSEXUALITY AND HETEROSEXUALITY IN OTHER TIMES AND PLACES

Homosexuality remains controversial in the United States. Some people see homosexuality as a mortal sin, others argue that homosexuals are a "bad influence" on society and children (and, for example, believe they should not be parents or teachers), and still others defend homosexual rights and attack America's whole view of sexuality.

Many other countries are much more tolerant of homosexuality than the United States, even other Western, predominantly Christian countries (such as Canada or parts of Europe). Western history has included many periods when homosexuality was generally accepted. In fact, Gilbert Herdt, a prominent scholar of homosexuality, states that the modern American attitude is much harsher toward homosexuality than most other countries throughout most of history (Herdt, 1988). The history of social attitudes toward homosexuality can teach us something about our own attitudes today.

Homosexuality in History

Homosexuality has been viewed differently throughout history. Although there have been times when homosexuality has been accepted, there have also been times it has been scorned. The influence of the church has greatly affected societal tolerance and acceptance of homosexuality.

The Ancient World

Before the 19th century, men who engaged in homosexual acts were accused of **sodomy** (SA-duh-mee), or **buggery,** which were simply seen as crimes and not considered part of a person's fundamental nature. Homosexual activity was common, homosexual prostitution was taxed by the state, and the writers of the time seemed to consider men loving men as natural as men loving women. Even after Rome became Christian, there was no anti-homosexual legislation for more than 200 years.

Lesbian love seems to have puzzled ancient writers (who were almost all men). The word *lesbian* itself comes from the island of Lesbos, in Greece, where the poet Sappho lived about 600 B.C. Lesbianism was rarely explicitly against the law in most ancient societies (in fact, two or more unmarried women living together has usually been seen as proper, whereas a woman living alone was viewed with suspicion; Bullough, 1979).

Contrary to popular belief, homosexuality was not treated with concern or much interest by either early Jews or early Christians. Neither ancient Greek nor Hebrew had a word for homosexual; in the entire Bible, same-gender sexual behavior is explicitly mentioned only in the prohibition in Leviticus (and here referring only to men); Saint Paul never explicitly condemned homosexuality, and Jesus made few pronouncements on proper or improper sexuality (except fidelity) and never mentioned homosexuality. Why, then, did Christianity become so antihomosexual?

The Middle Ages

By the 9th century, almost every part of Europe had some sort of local law code based on Church teachings, and although these codes included strong sanctions for sexual transgressions, including rape, adultery, incest, and fornication, homosexual relations were not forbidden in any of them (Boswell, 1980). Church indifference to homosexuality lasted well through

sodomy
Any of various forms of sexual intercourse held to be unnatural or abnormal, especially anal intercourse or bestiality (also called buggery).

buggery
Any of various forms of sexual intercourse held to be unnatural or abnormal, especially anal intercourse or bestiality (also called sodomy).

lesbian
Woman who is sexually attracted to women.

Ancient societies left evidence to show that same-sex behavior was not uncommon.

the 13th century; in other words, for the first 1,300 years of Christianity, the Church showed very little interest in homosexuality and did not generally condemn the behavior. Male brothels appeared, defenses of homosexual relations began to appear in print, and homosexuality became a fairly accepted part of the general culture until the late Middle Ages.

Homosexuality was completely legal in most countries in Europe in the year 1250. By 1300, however, there was a new intolerance of differences, and homosexuality was punishable by death almost everywhere. This view from the late Middle Ages has influenced the Western world's view of homosexuality for the last 700 years.

The Modern Era

From the 16th century on, homosexuals were subject to periods of tolerance and periods of severe repression. In the American colonies, for example, homosexuality was a serious offense. In 1656, the New Haven Colony prescribed death for both males and females who engaged in homosexual acts. The severe attitude toward homosexuality in America reflects its Puritan origins, and America remains, even today, more disapproving of homosexuality than Europe.

Even in times when homosexual acts were condemned, however, homoerotic poems, writings, and art were created. Openly homosexual communities appeared now and then. Other cultures also had periods of relative tolerance of homosexuality. In Japan, for example, the Edo period (1600–1868) saw a flourishing homosexual subculture, with openly gay clubs, geisha houses, and a substantial gay literature (Hirayama & Hirayama, 1986).

During the 19th and early 20th centuries in the United States, it was not uncommon for single, upper-middle-class women to live together in committed, lifelong relationships, although they may not all have engaged in genital sexuality (Nichols, 1990). At the same time, **passing women** disguised themselves as men, entered the workforce, and even married women—who sometimes never knew their husbands were female (remember the discussion of Billy Tipton, the famous jazz musician, from Chapter 3). In most cases, of course, the wife knew, and the couple probably lived as lesbians in a disguised heterosexual marriage. Some of these passing women held offices of great power, and their biological sex was not discovered until their death (Nichols, 1990).

passing woman
Woman who disguises herself as a man.

In the 19th and early 20th centuries, physicians and scientists began to suggest that homosexuality was not a sin but an illness, which, if left "untreated," would spread like a contagious disease (Hansen, 1989). The dangers of this perspective were realized in Nazi Germany, where homosexuals were imprisoned and murdered along with Jews, Gypsies, epileptics, and others as part of the program to purify the "Aryan race" (Adam, 1987). In America, psychiatry continued to view homosexuality as a mental disorder well into the 1970s—and some psychiatrists still do today.

Ironically, the medical model's view of homosexuality, which influenced modern ideas of sexual orientation, changed the politics of homosexuality. Because physicians saw homosexuality not as just a behavior but as a built-in trait, it became a primary part of the way people looked at each other (Risman & Schwartz, 1988). Homosexuals began to argue: "If homosexuality is something I am, not just something I do, then I should have a right to be 'who I am' just as blacks, women, and other groups have a right to be who they are." The new view of homosexuality encouraged homosexuals to band together and press for recognition of their civil rights as a minority group, which led to the modern gay and lesbian liberation movement we discussed in Chapter 1.

The history of homosexuality in the Western world has been strongly influenced both by the Judeo-Christian tradition of hostility to homosexuality and by the Western world's difficulty in incorporating minorities into its political structures. The study of history is instructive, for it shows that Western, predominantly Christian, societies have often existed without the hostility to homosexuality that characterizes modern America and that Christianity itself has had periods of tolerance. Equally important is that different attitudes toward homosexuality exist throughout the world today, and other cultural traditions do not view homosexuality with the suspicion and disapproval that characterize North America.

Review Question

Explain how our views on homosexuality have changed from ancient times through the Middle Ages to the modern era.

Homosexuality in Other Cultures

We all have a natural tendency to believe that others see the world the way we do. Yet what we call "homosexuality" is viewed so differently in other cultures that the word itself might not apply. In many societies, individuals have same-gender sexual relations as a normal part of their lives. This can be minor, as in Cairo, Egypt, where heterosexual men casually kiss and hold hands, or it can be fully sexual, as in the sequential homosexuality of Papua New Guinea, where young males have sexual contact exclusively with other males until getting married at the age of 18, after which they have sexual contact only with women (see page 345).

Applying American conceptions of "homosexuality" and "heterosexuality" to cultures for whom such ideas are meaningless can be extremely misleading. Theories of sexual orientation often neglect the experiences of other countries and just assume that there are "homosexuals" and "heterosexuals" everywhere.

Same-sex sexual behavior is found in every culture, and its prevalence remains about the same no matter how permissive or repressive that culture's attitude is toward it (Mihalik, 1988). Broude and Greene (1976) examined 42 societies for which there were good data on attitudes toward homosexuality. They found that a substantial number of

Human Sexuality in a Diverse World

Being Young and Gay, Lesbian, or Bisexual in Different Cultures

It's important to remember that although we have been exploring the gay, lesbian, and bisexual experiences in the United States, in different parts of the world GLB adolescents may have very different experiences. Here we take a look at adolescents in a variety of places around the globe.

English (male): *Between the ages of 13 and 15 I closed myself off from the outside world. I would rarely go out and would never dare to go places where other people of my own age would be. The only thing I knew was that homosexuality was bad. (Plummer, 1989, p. 204)*

East Indian (female): *My family holds Western culture somehow responsible for offbeat youth. They think my being a lesbian is my being young, and confused, and rebellious. They feel it has something to do with trying to fit into white culture. . . . They're waiting for me to stop rebelling and go heterosexual, go out on dates, and come home early. (Tremble et al., 1989, p. 260)*

Mexican (male): *I thought myself very bad, and many times I was at the point of suicide. I don't know if I really might have killed myself, but many times I thought about it and believed it was the only alternative. That caused me many problems with my friends. I felt they thought me to be different, homosexual, and really sick. It made me separate from them. I felt myself inferior and thought I was the only one these things happened to. (Carrier, 1989, p. 238)*

Chinese (male): *I am longing to love others and to be loved. I have met some other homosexuals, but I have doubt about this type of love. With all the pressure I was afraid to reveal myself and ruined everything. As a result, we departed without showing each other homosexual love. As I am growing older my homosexual desire increases. This is too troubling and depressing for anyone. I thought about death many times. When you are young you cannot fall in love and when you are old you will be alone. Thinking of this makes the future absolutely hopeless. (Ruan & Tsai, 1988, p. 194)*

Canadian (female): *I feel like I am the terrific person I am today because I'm a lesbian. I decided I was gay when I was very young. After making that decision, which was the hardest thing I could ever face, I feel like I can do anything. (Schneider, 1989, p. 123)*

Scottish (male): *I don't like being gay. I wouldn't choose to be gay, and I don't like the gay scene. It's too superficial. I've got high moral standards. Lust is a sin but love isn't. In the gay scene people use other people and throw them away again. (Burbidge & Walters, 1981, p. 41)*

Asian American (gender not identified): *I wish I could tell my parents—they are the only ones who do not know about my gay identity, but I am sure they would reject me. There is no frame of reference to understand homosexuality in Asian American culture. (Chan, 1989, p. 19)*

the cultures in the sample have an accepting or only mildly disapproving view of homosexual behavior, and less than half punished homosexuals for their sexual activities.

Remember too, that the relationship between sexual orientation and gender-related traits is moderated by culture. A culture that has more traditional gender roles tends to have larger homosexual–heterosexual differences in gender-related traits than cultures with less traditional gender roles (Lippa & Tan, 2001). With this in mind, research has found that, in the United States, Hispanic and Asian gays and lesbians show the largest homosexual–heterosexual differences and are more likely to cross gender boundaries (e.g., gay men tend to act more feminine, and lesbian women tend to act more masculine). Cultural factors play a very important role in moderating these gender-related differences. We will now explore a variety of cultures.

Latin American Countries

In many Central and South American countries, people do not tend to think in terms of homosexuality and heterosexuality, but rather in terms of masculinity and femininity. Male gender roles, for example, are defined by one's **machismo,** which, in terms of sexual behavior, is determined by being the active partner, or penetrator. Therefore, a man is not considered homosexual for taking the active, penetrating role in intercourse, even if he is penetrating other men. As long as he is penetrating, he is a man.

In Nicaragua, for example, penetrating another man does not make you homosexual; a man who is the active partner in same-sex anal intercourse is called *machista* or *hombre-hombre* ("manly man"), a term used for any masculine male (Murray & Dynes, 1999). In fact, penetrating other men is seen as a sign of manliness and prestige. In the Mexican state of Jalisco, where the *charro* (Mexican cowboy) originated and defending one's honor with a gun is common, being the active partner in anal sex with other men is seen as a sign of healthy sexuality (Carrier, 1989).

In other words, these Latin American countries look at sexuality in a fundamentally different way than we do; the basic categories of manhood are not homosexual or heterosexual but masculine and feminine. Masculine men sometimes penetrate other men and are admired, whereas feminine men allow themselves to be penetrated and are generally scorned.

Note that the implicit message of such cultures is that to mimic female behavior is disgraceful and shameful in a male. This attitude reflects the general nature of these societies, which tend to be patriarchal, with women lacking political and social power. Because women are, in general, considered inferior to men, men who mimic women are to be ridiculed.

In other Latin American countries, homosexuality may be viewed differently. For example, homophobia is widespread in Costa Rica, where prior to 1971 the punishment for engaging in sodomy was 1 to 3 years in prison (Arroba, 2004). In Brazil, homosexuality is acceptable only for those in the theater, movies, music, or television industry, and it is viewed negatively for those in all other professions (de Freitas, 2004).

Arabic Cultures

Although classic works of Arabic poetry use homoerotic imagery, and young boys were often used as the standard of beauty and sexuality in Arabic writing (Boswell, 1980), homosexuality in Arab countries, like sexuality in general, is usually not discussed. It is not uncommon to see men holding hands or walking down the street arm-in-arm on Arabic streets, but for the most part male homosexuality is taboo. Sexual relations in the Middle East are often about power and based on dominant and subordinate positions. Because of this, being the active partner with another man doesn't make a man gay (Sati, 1998).

Gay men in the Arabic world often limit their interactions with other men to sex, instead of emotionally based relationships. Although attitudes about homosexuality are slowly changing in Arabic cultures, many countries still view homosexuality as aberrant (Sherif, 2004). Overall, we know very little about lesbians in Arabic cultures mainly because Arabic and Jordanian women are very reserved and are uncomfortable talking about sex (Sherif, 2004).

machismo
Characterized or motivated by stereotypic masculine behavior or actions.

Ted Aijbe/AFP/Getty Images

The first-ever Hong Kong gay rights parade took place in 2005. Many participants wore a mask to symbolize the invisibility of gays and lesbians in Hong Kong.

Asian Countries

It wasn't until 2001 that the Chinese Psychiatric Association removed homosexuality from its list of mental disorders (Gallagher, 2001). This is a significant change for China, which as recently as 1994 openly opposed homosexuality. Homosexuality was seen as a result of Western influences, and it was considered a "Western social disease" (Ruan & Lau, 2004). In India, although homosexual sex is punishable by up to 10 years in jail, several homosexual couples have made headlines recently by publicly declaring themselves married in an attempt to overturn an existing law from 1861 (Predrag, 2005).

Other Asian societies have different views of homosexuality. Buddhism does not condemn homosexuality, and so Buddhist countries generally accept it. In Thailand, for example, there are no laws against homosexuality, and men may live sexually with boys over 13, who are considered old enough to make their own decisions (W. L. Williams, 1990). In fact, General Prem, Thailand's popular prime minister from 1980 to 1988, and Dr. Seri Wongmontha, one of the most famous and prominent people in the country, both live openly and freely as homosexuals (W. L. Williams, 1990). In Hong Kong the first-ever gay rights protest occurred in 2005 and drew over 350 men and women.

Sambia

A famous and much discussed example of a very different cultural form of sexual relations, called **sequential homosexuality,** is found in a number of cultures in the Pacific islands. The Sambia tribe of Papua New Guinea has been described in depth by Gilbert Herdt (Herdt, 1981; Stoller & Herdt, 1985). Life in Sambia is difficult because food is scarce and war is common; warriors, hunters, and many children are needed to survive. Sambians believe that mother's milk must be replaced by man's milk (semen) for a boy to reach puberty, and so, at the age of 7, all Sambian boys move to a central hut where they must fellate the postpubescent Sambian boys and drink their semen. After a boy reaches puberty, he no longer fellates others but is himself sucked by the prepubescent boys until he reaches the age of marriage at about 18. Despite his long period of same-sex activity, he will live as a heterosexual for the rest of his life.

sequential homosexuality
Situation in which heterosexual or bisexual men and women go through a period of homosexuality for a variety of reasons, including cultural and societal.

Review Question

Explain how homosexuality has been viewed in other cultures, citing as many examples as possible.

The Lesson of Cross-Cultural Studies of Homosexuality

With all these very different cultural forms of sexuality, trying to pigeonhole people or ways of life into our restrictive, Western "homosexuality–heterosexuality–bisexuality" model seems inadequate. This is a good time to think about your personal theory about homosexuality and to ask yourself: Can my theory account for the cross-cultural differences in sexual orientation that exist around the world today?

GAYS, LESBIANS, AND BISEXUALS THROUGHOUT THE LIFE CYCLE

Gays, lesbians, and bisexuals in America face particular problems that are not faced by most heterosexuals. Many struggle with discrimination, prejudice, laws that do not recognize same-sex unions, lack of spousal benefits for their partners, and families who may reject them. On the other hand, many gay and lesbian couples live together in stable, happy unions, leading lives not really that much different from the heterosexual couple next door. Gay and lesbian lifestyles are as varied and different as those of the rest of society; yet examining the special challenges and circumstances that gay and lesbian people face can be instructive.

Growing Up Gay, Lesbian, or Bisexual

Imagine what it must be like to be an adolescent and to either believe or know that you are gay, lesbian, or bisexual (a number of you reading this book do not have to imagine it). All your life, from the time you were a toddler, you were presented with a single model of sexual life: you were expected to be attracted to the other sex, to go on dates, and eventually to marry. No other scenario was seriously considered; if you are heterosexual, you probably have never even reflected on how powerfully this "presumption of heterosexuality" (Herdt, 1989) was transmitted by your parents, your friends, television and movies, newspapers and magazines, even the government. Advertisements on TV and in magazines always show heterosexual couples; your friends probably played house, doctor, or spin-the-bottle, assuming everyone was attracted to the other sex; your grade school, parties, and social activities were organized around this presumption of heterosexuality. There were open questions about many things in your life: what career you would pursue, where you might live, what college you would attend. But one thing was considered certain: you were going to marry (or at least date) someone of the other sex.

But imagine that while all your friends were talking about the other sex, dating, and sex, you were experiencing a completely different set of emotions. Why, you wondered, can't I join in on these conversations? Why can't I feel the attractions that all my friends feel? Then, at some point in your early teens, you began to realize why you felt differently from your friends. All of a sudden you understood that all the models you had taken for granted your whole life did not apply to you. You began to look for other models that described your life and your feelings—and they simply were not there. In fact, in hundreds of subtle and not-so-subtle ways, society taught you that you are different—and possibly perverted, sinful, illegal, and/or disgusting. Now what are you supposed to do? Whom do you turn to? How can you possibly tell anyone your deep, painful secret?

The experiences of many lesbians, gays, and bisexuals, at least until recently, followed this scenario, although the timing and intensity varied with individual cases. For example, many male homosexuals grew up with close male friends, enjoyed sports, and differed only in their secret attraction to other boys, whereas others remember feeling and acting differently from their friends as early as 4 or 5 years old (H. B. Martin, 1991). In those boys, atypical gender behavior often provoked anxiety from parents, teachers, and friends: "Why don't you act like other boys?"

This kind of pressure can lead to strong psychosocial problems (Plummer, 1989). Because group sports and heterosexual dating are focal to male adolescents forming peer group bonds, young gay or bisexual youths can feel unattached and alienated (Herdt,

1989). The same is true of young lesbians and female bisexuals, although the pressure and alienation may be slightly less early in life because same-sex affection and touching is more accepted for girls and because lesbians tend to determine their sexual orientation later than gay men. Overall, gay, lesbian, and bisexual youths have been found to experience higher levels of stigmatization and discrimination than heterosexual youths, which may be responsible for the higher levels of psychiatric disorders found in homosexual youths (Gilman et al., 2001).

SEX Talk

Question: Aren't gay men more creative than straight men and more likely to be in the arts? Aren't more female professional athletes lesbian?

If homosexuals are indeed overrepresented in certain professions, it may be because those professions were more accepting of gays and lesbians rather than because they have some "natural talents" in those areas. Jews entered the entertainment industry in the 20th century because the industry was accepting of them during a period when other professions were closed to them; the same may be true for homosexuals, although it has not yet been proven.

Coming Out to Self and Others

One of the most important tasks of adolescence is to develop and integrate a positive adult identity. This task is even a greater challenge for homosexual youths because they learn from a very young age the stigma of a homosexual or different identity (Ryan & Futterman, 2001). Special challenges confront the person who believes he or she is gay, lesbian, or bisexual, including the need to establish a personal self-identity and communicate it to others, known as **coming out** (see the accompanying Sex in Real Life, "Coming Out," and in Chapter 8, Personal Voices, "Don't Forget to Breathe," on page 228). A number of models have been offered to explain how this process proceeds.[*]

Coming out refers, first, to acknowledging one's sexual identity to oneself, and many homosexuals have their own negative feelings about homosexuality to overcome. The often difficult and anxiety-ridden process of disclosing the truth to family, friends, and eventually the public at large comes later. Although some researchers believe that the most stressful experience a gay, lesbian, or bisexual person faces is coming out to his or her parents (LaSala, 2000), others claim this process is not as traumatic as originally believed (Green, 2000). In any event, disclosure of identity plays an important role in identity development and psychological adjustment.

Gay men and lesbian women have been coming out at earlier ages in the past few years. Although first awareness of sexual orientation typically occurs between the ages of 8 and 9, gays and lesbians come out to others, on average, at around age 18 (Savin-Williams & Diamond, 2000). Some youths may come out early in their lives, whereas others remain closeted into late adolescence and adulthood (Taylor, 2000).

Coming out does not just happen overnight; being homosexual may mean for some a lifetime of disclosing different amounts of information to family, friends, and strangers in different contexts (Hofman, 2005). Deciding whether and how to tell friends and family are difficult decisions. Lesbian and gay adolescents usually come out to their friends before family members.

Discovering one's own homosexual identity can be painful and confusing. One woman explains:

> Here I was, with a good job, close friends who I knew would not abandon me when they learned I was gay. I had many gay friends, so I had a support network. My family is open, so I wasn't worried about them rejecting me. And still, I cried myself to sleep every night and woke up each morning feeling like I had been kicked in the solar plexus. (Author's files)

coming out
The process of establishing a personal self-identity and communicating it to others.

*See, for example, Cass, 1979, 1984; E. Coleman, 1982; H.P. Martin, 1991; M. Schneider, 1989; and Troiden, 1989.

A Model of Coming Out

A number of authors have created models of the process of coming out. For example, Vivienne Cass (1979, 1984) has proposed the following six-stage model of gay and lesbian identity formation. Not all gays and lesbians reach the sixth stage; it depends how comfortable one is at each stage with one's sexual orientation.

Stage 1: Identity confusion. The individual begins to believe that his or her behavior may be defined as gay or lesbian. There may be a need to redefine one's own concept of gay and lesbian behavior, with all the biases and misinformation that most people have. The person may accept that role and seek information, may repress it and inhibit all gay and lesbian behaviors (and even perhaps become an antihomosexual crusader), or may deny its relevance at all to his or her identity (like the man who has same-sex behavior in prison but doesn't believe he is "really" gay).

Stage 2: Identity comparison. The individual accepts potential gay and lesbian identity; he or she rejects the heterosexual model but has no substitute. The person may feel different and even lost. If willing to even consider a gay and lesbian self-definition, he or she may begin to look for appropriate models.

Stage 3: Identity tolerance. Here the person shifts to the belief that he or she is probably gay or lesbian and begins to seek out the homosexual community for social, sexual, and emotional needs. Confusion declines, but self-identity is still more tolerated than truly accepted. Usually, the person still does not reveal new identity to the heterosexual world but maintains a double lifestyle.

Stage 4: Identity acceptance. A positive view of self-identity is forged, and a network of gay and lesbian friends is developed. Selective disclosure to friends and family is made, and the person often immerses himself or herself in homosexual culture.

Stage 5: Identity pride. Homosexual pride is developed, and anger over treatment may lead to rejecting heterosexuality as bad. One feels validated in one's new lifestyle.

Stage 6: Identity synthesis. As the individual truly becomes comfortable with his or her lifestyle and as nonhomosexual contacts increase, the person realizes the inaccuracy of dividing the world into "good gays and lesbians" and "bad heterosexuals." No longer is sexual orientation seen as the sole identity by which an individual can be characterized. The person lives an open, gay lifestyle so that disclosure is no longer an issue and realizes that there are many sides and aspects to personality of which sexual orientation is only one. The process of identity formation is complete.

SOURCE: From Cass, 1979, 1984.

If a woman with all the support and advantages possible experienced such difficulties, imagine how much more difficult it is for youths who think their family and friends will reject them. Some gay, lesbian, and bisexual youths are rejected by friends and family and as a result are forced to run away or live on the streets. Approximately 26% of gay youths are forced to leave home because of their sexual orientation (A. T. Edwards, 1997), and more than 1 in 4 street youths are gay, lesbian, or bisexual (Kruks, 1991). One 16-year-old writes in her diary:

> Please help me. Oh shit, I have to talk to someone. Help me please. My feelings are turning into gnawing monsters trying to clamber out. Oh please, I want to just jump out that window and try to kill myself. Maybe I'll get some sympathy then. Maybe they'll try to understand. I have to tell someone, ask someone. Who?!! Dammit all, would someone please help me? Someone, anyone. Help me. I'm going to kill myself if they don't. (Heron, 1994, p. 10)

This young woman's threat to kill herself is not an idle one. The National Longitudinal Study of Adolescent Health found that homosexual and bisexual youths are more likely than heterosexual youths to think about and commit suicide (Russell & Joyner, 2001). Between 48% and 76% of homosexual and bisexual youths have thoughts of committing suicide, and 29% to 42% have attempted it (compared to estimated rates of 7% to 13% among high school students in general; Armesto, 2001; Cochran & Mays, 2000; S. L. Nichols, 1999; Russell & Joyner, 2001).

Other homosexual youths have more positive experiences. A 17-year-old male reports: "I like who I am. I have come to accept myself on psychological as well as physical terms. I not only like myself, I like everyone around me" (Heron, 1994, p. 15). Lesbian and gay youths who have a positive coming-out experience also have been found to have a higher self-concept, lower rates of depression, and better psychological adjustment than those who have a negative experience (Ryan & Futterman, 2001).

Parents of a homosexual child also often have a difficult time learning to accept their child's sexual orientation. Because we tend to think of homosexuality as something one "is," parents may suddenly feel they do not know the child, that he or she is a stranger, or worry that they did something wrong as a parent (Fields, 2001a; Strommen, 1989). Many parents of gay, lesbian, or bisexual youths tend to react with disappointment, shame, and shock when they learn about a son or daughter's sexual orientation (LaSala, 2000).

Parental rejection during the coming-out process is a major health risk for homosexual and bisexual youths (C. M. Mosher, 2001; Savin-Williams & Dube, 1998). Youths who are rejected by their parents have been found to have increased levels of isolation, loneliness, depression, suicide, homelessness, prostitution, and sexually transmitted infections (Armesto, 2001). The family must go through its own "coming out," as parents and siblings slowly try to accept the idea and then tell their own friends. The importance of positive resolution in the family has prompted the formation of a national organization, the Federation of Parents and Friends of Lesbians and Gays (PFLAG), which helps parents learn to accept their children's sexual orientation and gain support from other families experiencing similar events.

People may come out at different periods in their life, even after they are married. In 2004, New Jersey Governor James McGreevey announced his resignation after revealing that he was gay. McGreevy was married and the father of two children. He is not alone. It is estimated that between 14% and 25% of gay men and about a third of lesbians marry someone of the other sex at some point, either before they recognize that they are gay or lesbian or because they want to try to fit into heterosexual society. Many remain married, either with or without their spouses knowing that they are homosexual (Strommen, 1989).

Coming out to the family is very difficult on the spouse and the children of gay men and lesbians, and divorce is common. In some couples, though, the partners develop a platonic relationship and pursue sexual gratification outside the marriage (Hays & Samuels, 1989).

sex byte

A national survey of 1,139 self-identified lesbians found higher rates of alcohol use, alcohol intake, and self-reported alcoholism in lesbians than in women in general (Roberts et al., 2005). These findings are consistent with prior studies, and more research is needed to clarify the reasons for these differences.

Review Question

Identify the need for gay, lesbian, and bisexual youths to establish a personal self-identity, and describe the task of coming out.

SEX Talk

Question: Is homosexuality natural?

The question itself is biased: is heterosexuality "natural"? Also, the question seems to assume that if it is "natural," then it is okay; yet much that is natural, such as killing, is reprehensible. Some people suggest that a human behavior is "natural" if it is found in animals; other animals do display same-sex behavior, and so perhaps it is natural in that sense. Still, many human qualities—humor, language, religion—are not shared by animals and yet are considered "natural." Humans are so immersed in culture and so lacking in instincts that it is impossible to say what is natural. Perhaps the only measure we can use is to ask whether a behavior is found universally—that is, in all or almost all human cultures. By that measure, homosexuality is quite natural.

Life Issues: Partnering, Sexuality, Parenthood, and Aging

Although growing up and coming out can be difficult for many gay, lesbian, and bisexual youths, the next step is establishing intimate relationships. Let's now explore same-sex coupling, sexuality, parenting, and aging.

Looking for Partners

Meeting other gay, lesbian or bisexual partners in the heterosexual world can be difficult, so the gay community has developed its own social institutions to help people meet one another and socialize. As we discussed in Chapter 8, many homosexual youths have been turning to the Internet in search of partners. Today many schools and universities have clubs, support groups, and meeting areas for gay, lesbian, and bisexual students. Adults can meet others at **gay bars** or clubs that cater primarily to same-sex couples, gay support or discussion groups, and gay organizations, and also through the Internet. Some smaller towns that don't have gay bars offer gay night at certain bars once a week or so. Gay magazines like *The Advocate* carry personal ads and ads for dating services, travel clubs, resorts, bed and breakfasts, theaters, businesses, pay phone lines, sexual products, and other services to help gays and lesbians find partners. And of course, gay individuals are introduced through gay and straight friends.

Same-Sex Couples

Gay and lesbian couples often live together as happily as straight couples; their main challenge tends to be society's intolerance for their lifestyle. Contrary to the image of gay and lesbian couples having one dominant and one submissive partner, such relationships are actually characterized by greater role flexibility and partner equality (Risman & Schwartz, 1988) and lower levels of sexual jealousy (R. O. Hawkins, 1990) than are heterosexual relationships.

One interesting area of research has looked at differences between gay and lesbian couples. Because women are socialized to connect with others (Cross & Madson, 1997), female partners tend to have a better grasp of relationship problems (Gottman et al., 1998) and are often viewed as relationship "experts" (Kurdek, 2001). These relationship strengths benefit lesbian couples in that there is a double dose of relationship-enhancing influences in lesbian couples that may contribute to the higher levels of relationship satisfaction among lesbian couples (Kurdek, 2001).

On the other hand, because men have been socialized to be independent (Cross & Madson, 1997) and to withdraw from conflict (Heavey et al., 1995), they have been found to be more prone to distraction when relationship conflict exists (Buysse et al., 2000). These factors may put gay men at a disadvantage in relationships in that there is a double dose of relationship-destroying influences (Kurdek, 2001).

One more finding from this research deserves mention. Compared to heterosexual couples, gay and lesbian couples have a limited number of partners to choose from. Because of this, it's possible that they work harder on their relationships and make the best of them in times of crisis, unlike heterosexual couples who might think there is someone else out there (Kurdek, 2001). Research has also found that gay and lesbian couples reported higher levels of connection to ex-partners than heterosexuals after a breakup (Harkless & Fowers, 2005).

As we discussed in Chapter 9, although same-sex marriages are legal in the Netherlands, Belgium, Spain, South Africa, and parts of Canada, in the United States, only the state of Massachusetts gives full marriage rights to lesbian and gay couples. In some states same-sex couples can register as domestic partners or for civil unions, which may provide certain benefits.

In 2003, a United States Supreme Court decision, *Lawrence et al. v. Texas*, struck down the Texas "homosexual conduct" law that criminalized oral and anal sex by consenting gay couples. This decision has far-reaching consequences for same-sex couples and could help pave the way for the legalization of same-sex marriage or create a bigger storm of antigay protest throughout the nation. The majority of Americans support some relationship recognition for same-sex couples (Evans, 2004), and the American Psychiatric Association supports for legal recognition of same-sex marriage.

Gay and Lesbian Sexuality

Gays and lesbians, like heterosexuals, make love for a variety of reasons and use a variety of positions. Sexuality, for all people, heterosexual or homosexual, can be an expression of deep love, affection, or lust. Some gay and lesbian people have sexual experiences

sex**byte**

Proponents of same-sex marriage believe that same-sex couples should be given benefits similar to those of heterosexual married couples. It is estimated that there are 1,096 federal rights and benefits given to heterosexual married couples and an additional 300 rights provided by individual states (Johnson, 2005). These privileges include the right to sue for wrongful death or the right to family medical leave.

Sneak Peek

"All of a sudden I found myself completely smitten by this woman."— *Discovering Bisexuality*

Sexuality Now

with members of the other sex at some point in their lives and have considered themselves bisexual in the past (Rosario et al., 1996). Because most people identify the homosexual community primarily by its sexuality, sex is always close to the surface. However, gay men and lesbians view their community as broader, with sexuality as only one component.

As we discussed in Chapter 10, Masters and Johnson (1979) found that arousal and orgasm in homosexuals was physiologically no different than in heterosexuals. They also found, however, that homosexuals tend be slower, more relaxed, and less demanding with each other during sex. Male and female homosexual couples spend more time sexually "teasing" and caressing each other, bringing their partners to the brink of orgasm and then withdrawing, before beginning direct genital stimulation. Heterosexuals tend to be more goal oriented and spend less time at each phase of arousal than same-sex couples. Perhaps, Masters and Johnson suggest, this is because men and women know what pleases them, and so they have an immediate, intuitive understanding of what would please another member of their own sex.

Lesbian couples may find more sexual satisfaction over time than gay men or heterosexual couples.

Gay and Lesbian Parents

The 2000 U.S. Census Bureau revealed that there were 601,209 same-sex families, with approximately 301,000 gay male households and 293,000 lesbian households, in the United States (U.S. Bureau of the Census, 2001). However, it is estimated that actual numbers are significantly higher, because many gays and lesbians may be uncomfortable reporting their sexual orientation on the census forms.

Many gay and lesbian couples become parents, and they cite most of the same reasons for wanting to be parents that straight parents do (Bigner & Jacobsen, 1989). Fearing that same-sex parents might "make their children homosexual" or at least promote sex-role confusion, courts have often granted heterosexual parents more custody than same-sex parents. Research has found no significant differences between the offspring of lesbian and straight mothers, including their children's sexual orientation (Golombok & Tasker, 1996; Hicks, 2005). (See the accompanying Personal Voices, "Same-Sex Parents.") Yet some courts assume that lesbian mothers are emotionally unstable or unable to assume a maternal role. All of the scientific evidence suggests that children who grow up with one or two gay and/or lesbian parents do as well emotionally, cognitively, socially, and sexually as do children from heterosexual parents (Perrin, 2002).

Lesbian couples may become pregnant through intercourse or artificial insemination. It is not uncommon, in fact, for lesbians to ask gay friends to donate sperm for that purpose. However, gay male couples who want children do not have that option.

Some gay men and lesbian women have tried to adopt children, but many are refused adoption because of their homosexuality. Three states, Florida, Mississippi, and Utah, specifically bar homosexuals from adopting; several other states make it very difficult for same-sex couples to adopt (Price, 2001). Gay and lesbian adoptions are legal in California, Connecticut, District of Columbia, Illinois, Massachusetts, New Hampshire, New Jersey, New York, Ohio, Rhode Island, Vermont, and Washington. Some gay men have tried finding surrogate mothers to bear their children, whom they then adopt, but that can be very expensive, and surrogate mothers are difficult to find in general. Some organizations, such as PFLAG and LAMBDA (a national organization committed to the civil rights of gays, lesbians, and bisexuals), support gay and lesbian parents and are helping to make it easier for homosexuals to adopt.

Gay and lesbian couples encounter many problems that heterosexual parents do not face. Because same-sex marriages are not yet legally recognized nationally in the United States, gay couples may have trouble gaining joint custody of a child, and employers may not grant nonbiological parents parental leave or benefits for the child. A gay or lesbian couple may also experience discrimination and disapproval from family, friends, and the community. For the most part, our society assumes a heterosexist view of parenting. For example, most official forms ask about mothers and fathers (not mothers and mothers, or fathers and fathers). Yet gay and lesbian couples today are creating new kinds of families, and the social system is going to have to learn how to deal with them.

Personal Voices

Same-Sex Parents

Until recently, children raised by same-sex parents were almost always born during their parents' early heterosexual marriages. However, today there is a "Gayby Boom" underway, in which many same-sex couples are creating families through artificial insemination, surrogate mothers, or adoption. It is estimated that between 3 million and 6 million U.S. children have same-sex parents (Elias, 2001).

Do you think that gay or lesbian mothers or fathers parent differently from heterosexual mothers or fathers? Researchers who have examined this question have found that overall, there are no significant distinctions between children who are raised by same-sex parents and those raised in more traditional homes with a mother and a father. However, they have noted a few small differences.

Among these findings is the fact that sons of lesbian couples are more willing to discuss the range of sexual orientation and are more open in their definitions of masculine behavior (Drexler & Gross, 2005). In addition, daughters of lesbians have been found to have a stronger sense of their own identity. Children of same-sex parents have also been found to aspire to occupations less typical for their gender than do children of heterosexuals, and many children of same-sex parents have been raised with a less stereotypical view of how boys and girls should behave (Goode, 2001). Compared to straight fathers, gay fathers have stricter disciplinary guidelines and are more involved in their children's activities (Bigner & Jacobsen, 1992). In addition, same-sex couples have been found to share childcare and chores more evenly than do heterosexual couples.

But the news isn't all good. Many children of same-sex parents experience teasing and taunting during their school years, and some feel isolated because of this. Genevieve Ankeny, a 32-year-old woman, discusses her experiences of being raised by a lesbian mother:

It wasn't until recently that I realized the depth of my grief about the homophobia I endured in high school. Even today, after I've worked through so much of my many feelings about my Mom being lesbian—the old high school feelings still mow me down. I feel like I had been in the closet for my Mom for so, so long.

I never spoke to anyone whom I met in high school or outside of my old friends from the city, of my Mom being a lesbian—not until I was a junior in college. In my high school, I felt no room to be different. I cannot even imagine the isolation, loneliness, fear, and anger I might have felt as a GLB youth. Yet, my own feelings about being out of the norm with a gay parent stuck me hard. I felt displaced in a suburban high school, being from the city. I had always been so strong and assertive as a young person, but I could not stand up to this—to the undeniable, overt, and covert homophobia in my school.

Looking back, I would change a few things. I would ask my parents and all parents who are gay, lesbian, or bisexual to have consistent conversations with their children about sexuality and sexual orientation, and to acknowledge that the world where we live should all be okay with a family where there is love despite who loves whom. I would also encourage them to talk about homophobia and [the] complexity of being raised in a family that may be very out of the norm. I also would have accepted my mother unconditionally, without question.

SOURCE: Author's files.

Gay and Lesbian Seniors

It is estimated that there are anywhere from 1 to 3 million gay, lesbian, and bisexual seniors in the United States today, and this number will climb to over 4 million by the year 2030 (Cahill et al., 2000). Many studies have found that having "come out" prior to the senior years often helps a gay or lesbian senior to feel more comfortable with his or her life and sexuality (Quam & Whitford, 1992). Homosexual seniors who have not come out or come to terms with their sexual orientation may feel depressed or alone as they continue to age. In addition, they may experience depression and isolation from the years of internalized **homophobia** (Altman, 2000).

There are many issues that confront aging gay and lesbian seniors. In 2000 the National Gay and Lesbian Task Force released the first comprehensive report to address

homophobia
Irrational fear of homosexuals and homosexuality.

public policy facing these seniors (Cahill et al., 2000). Important issues include survivor benefits, health insurance, Social Security, and assisted living needs. Many older gay, lesbian, and bisexual seniors worry about where they will live once they require assisted living.

Studies have found that 52% of nursing home staff reported intolerant or condemning attitudes toward homosexual and bisexual residents (Cahill et al., 2000). Because of this, many groups are in the process of establishing retirement homes for aging gays, lesbians, bisexual, and transgendered individuals. The first GLBT retirement community, The Palms of Manasota, is located in Sarasota, Florida. In Boston, the Stonewall Community, a new retirement housing project for homosexual and bisexual seniors, is now open.

It is anticipated that GLBT retirement housing options will increase dramatically in coming years (Kirchofer, 1999). An advocacy organization called SAGE, or Services and Advocacy for Gay, Lesbian, Bisexual, and Transgendered Elders, has been helping aging gay, lesbian, bisexual, and transgendered individuals and couples (see the Web Resources at the end of this chapter for more information).

Specific Problems Facing Gays, Lesbians, and Bisexuals

We have already discussed the increased rates of depression and suicide in gay, lesbian, and bisexual populations. There are also higher rates of substance abuse and alcohol-related problems (Roberts et al., 2005), along with more widespread use of marijuana and cocaine than heterosexual youths and adults (Rosario et al., 2004; Ryan & Futterman, 2001); and higher rates of truancy, homelessness, and sexual abuse (H. E. Taylor, 2000).

For many years, psychiatrists and other therapists argued that this showed that homosexual and bisexual groups had greater psychopathology than heterosexuals. In fact, the problems of gay, lesbian, and bisexual life may not be due to psychopathology but to the enormous pressures of living in a society that discriminates against them (Lock & Steiner, 1999). Vulnerable and stigmatized groups in general have higher rates of these types of behaviors, and these problems often result from coping with stigma-related stress.

Homosexuals also face workplace discrimination. Gay men have been found to earn 11% to 27% less than heterosexual men with the same qualifications (Folbre, 1995), and lesbians tend to have even lower household incomes than gay men. (In this way, gender inequities among homosexuals mimic the inequities among heterosexuals.) In addition, homosexuals and bisexuals are particularly vulnerable to harassment and other forms of risk (S. E. James, 1998).

Gay, Lesbian, and Bisexual Organizations

Because many organizations misunderstand the needs of homosexuals and bisexuals, gay and lesbian social services, medical, political, entertainment, and even religious organizations have formed. For example, the National Gay and Lesbian Task Force (NGLTF) and its associated Policy Institute advocate for gay civil rights, lobbying Congress for such things as a Federal Gay and Lesbian Civil Rights Act, health care reform, AIDS policy reform, and hate-crime laws. In 1978 they successfully lobbied the Public Health Service to stop certifying all gay immigrants as "psychopathic personalities," and they helped establish the Hate Crimes Statistics Act in 1987, which identifies and records hate crimes. Also well known are the Lambda Legal Defense and Education Fund (for more information see the Web Resources at the end of this chapter) which pursues test-case litigation of concern to the gay and lesbian community, and the Human Rights Campaign Fund, which lobbies Capitol Hill on gay and lesbian rights, AIDS, and privacy issues.

Since the advent of the AIDS epidemic, many organizations have formed to help homosexuals and bisexuals obtain medical, social, and legal services. Local gay, lesbian, and bisexual organizations—including counseling centers, hotlines, legal aid, and AIDS information—have been established in almost every reasonably sized city in the United States.

sex byte

Many lesbian women engage in heterosexual relationships and intercourse during their early teenage years, before identifying themselves as lesbian or bisexual (Saewyc et al., 1999).

Review Question

Explain some of the tasks involved in living a gay, lesbian, or bisexual life, including looking for partners, sexuality, parenting, aging, and specific problems encountered by homosexual and bisexual individuals.

Gay and lesbian newspapers and magazines are published in almost all major U.S. cities.

Review Question

Explain why many gay, lesbian, and bisexual groups have set up their own organizations, and give one example of such an organization.

The Harvey Milk School in New York City is the first and largest accredited public school in the world devoted to the educational needs of lesbian, gay, bisexual, transgender, and questioning youths. The school was named after a gay San Francisco elected official who was murdered in 1978. Fourteen- to eighteen-year-old students from across the country come to the Harvey Milk School to study in an environment where their sexual orientation is accepted and where they will not be ridiculed, ostracized, or assaulted, as many were in the schools they came from. Universities and colleges have also begun to offer gay and lesbian students separate housing, and many high schools provide Gay–Straight Alliances (GSAs) that help encourage tolerance and provide a place for students to meet.

Gay and lesbian media, including countless magazines and newspapers across the country, have also developed over the last 30 years. The largest and best-known magazine, *The Advocate*, is a national publication that covers news of interest, entertainment reviews, commentaries, gay- and lesbian-oriented products and services, and hundreds of personal ads. Other publications include *Instinct* magazine for gay men, *QV* for gay Latino men, *BLK* for gay African American men, and *Noodle* for gay Asian and Pacific Islander men. *The Lesbian News* and *Off Our Backs* are two of the biggest lesbian newspapers; *BlackLace* is specifically for African American lesbians.

Many gay, lesbian, and bisexual magazines are also available online, and some, such as the *Triangle Journal News*, are published only on the web. Bisexual magazines, such as *Anything That Moves*, are also popular and help connect bisexuals with one another. Popular magazines for gay, lesbian, bisexual, and transgendered parents, *Gay Parent* and *Proud Parenting Magazine*, have both done well. Finally, travel magazines, such as *Out and About*, are also available for gay, lesbian, and bisexual persons.

Most major cities have their own gay newspaper, some of which get national exposure; some noteworthy examples are New York's *Next*, Philadelphia's *Gay News*, Chicago's *Free Press*, and the *Seattle Gay News*. These papers are often the best first sources for the young gay man or lesbian who is looking for the resources available in his or her community.

HOMOPHOBIA AND HETEROSEXISM

Gay, lesbian, and bisexual individuals have long been stigmatized. When homosexuality as an illness was removed from the *Diagnostic and Statistical Manual* in 1973 (see Chapter 1), negative attitudes toward homosexuality persisted. It was at this time that researchers began to study these negative attitudes and behaviors.

What Is Homophobia?

Many terms have been proposed to describe the negative, often violent, reactions of many people toward homosexuality—antihomosexualism, homoerotophobia, homosexism, homonegativism, and homophobia. The popularity of the term *homophobia* is unfortunate, for phobia is a medical term describing an extreme, anxiety-provoking, uncontrollable fear accompanied by obsessive avoidance. The word is also used to describe different negative views of homosexuality, including cultural, attitudinal, and personal biases (Fyfe, 1983). Still, the term is generally accepted, and so we will use it here to refer to strongly negative attitudes toward homosexuals and homosexuality.

Are people really homophobic? Some might accept homosexuality intellectually and yet still dislike being in the presence of homosexuals, whereas others might object to homosexuality as a practice and yet have acceptable personal relationships with individual homosexuals (Forstein, 1988). When compared with people who hold favorable views of gays, lesbians, and bisexuals, people with negative views are less likely to have had contact with homosexuals and bisexuals, and they are more likely to: be older and less well educated; be religious and to subscribe to a conservative religious ideology; have more traditional attitudes toward sex roles and less support for equality of the sexes; be less permissive sexually; and be authoritarian (Herek, 1984). Overall, heterosexual men have been found to be more negative toward gay men than heterosexual women (Davies, 2004), and African American college students have been found to be significantly more homophobic than Caucasian students (Waldner et al., 1999).

In 2001, Marshall Mathers (a.k.a. Eminem) released an album that contained many negative and hateful things about gay men (see the accompanying Sex in Real Life, "Gay Bashing and Hate Crimes"). Although some people believe that Eminem has the right to sing whatever he pleases, it is also important to note that much of his music encourages violence and hatred. It is interesting that Eminem's music is geared toward adolescent males—the very group that commits the most hate crimes (Gay and Lesbian Alliance Against Defamation, 2000). In addition, research has found that songs with violent lyrics increase aggression-related thoughts and emotions (C. A. Anderson et al., 2003).

It's important to point out that heterosexuals aren't the only people to experience homophobia. Homosexuals who harbor negative feelings about homosexuality experience internalized homophobia. Research has shown that homosexuals who have internalized homophobia also have decreased levels of self-esteem and increased levels of shame and psychological distress (Allen & Oleson, 1999; Szymanski et al., 2001).

An even bigger problem for most gay men and lesbians is **heterosexism** (he-tur-oh-SEK-si-zum). Heterosexism has a sociological rather than a medical implication: it describes the "presumption of heterosexuality" discussed earlier and the social power used

heterosexism
The "presumption of heterosexuality" that has sociological implications.

SEX in Real Life

Gay Bashing and Hate Crimes

In this chapter we are looking closely at sexual orientation and society's views of it, including homophobia, gay bashing, and hate crimes. Some musicians, such as Eminem, include antigay lyrics in their songs. Eminem's songs are filled with hate, violence, and negative comments about many groups, including gay, lesbian, and bisexual people. Here's a sample of his lyrics:

> You faggots keep egging me on 'til I have you at knifepoint, then you beg me to stop.
> My words are like a dagger with a jagged edge that'll stab you in the head whether you're a fag or les
> or the homosex, hermaph or trans-a-ves pants or dress.
> Hate fags? The answer's yes . . .
> Hey, it's me, Versace.
> Whoops, somebody shot me. And I was out checking the mail. Get it? Checking the male?
> (Eminem, 2000)

Many gay, lesbian, bisexual, and transgendered individuals have suffered from hate crimes and violence and, in some cases, been killed because of their assumed sexual orientation and gender identity. Here are a half-dozen examples of victims of various hate crimes:

Teena Brandon—Born female, Teena Brandon chose to live as a man without hormonal or surgical intervention (and changed his name to Brandon Teena). After discovering Brandon's physical sex, John Lotter and Marvin Thomas Nissen kidnapped, assaulted, raped repeatedly, and finally murdered Brandon on December 31, 1993. The movie *Boys Don't Cry* was based on Brandon Teena's life.

Matthew Shepard—This freshman at the University of Wyoming was beaten and left to die on October 12, 1998. Russell Henderson, 21, and Aaron McKinney, 22, beat Shepard and hung him spread-eagled on a fence. Shepard was later found by two bicyclists.

Billy Jack Gaither—This man was bludgeoned to death with an ax handle by Charles Monroe Butler, Jr., 21, and Steven Eric Mullins, 25, on February 19, 1999. They then threw the body of 39-year-old Gaither atop two burning tires.

Private First Class Barry Winchell—This soldier was beaten to death with a baseball bat, while sleeping, by a fellow soldier on July 4, 1999.

Arthur "J.R." Warren—This 26-year-old was murdered on July 4, 2000. Two teens, David Allen Parker and Jared Wilson, admitted that they physically assaulted Warren, including kicks to the head with steel-toed boots, and ran over Warren's body twice with a vehicle.

Danny Lee Overstreet—Overstreet was shot and killed at a bar on September 22, 2000, by 53-year-old Ronald Edward Gay, who eventually confessed to the murder.

to promote it (Neisen, 1990). Because only heterosexual relationships are seen as "normal," the heterosexist feels justified in suppressing or ignoring those who do not follow that model.

For example, even those with no ill feelings toward homosexuality are often unaware that businesses will not provide health care and other benefits to the partners of homosexuals. In other words, heterosexism can be passive rather than active, involving a lack of awareness rather than active discrimination:

> I remember there was a really cute guy in my psychology class. It took me all semester to walk up to him and talk. I was hoping to ask him out for coffee or something. As I walked up behind him to say hello I became aware of a button pinned to the back of his backpack. I was horrified when I read what it said, "How dare you assume I'm heterosexual!!" I nearly tripped and fell over backwards. (Author's files)

The gay rights movement has been successful at changing some of these assumptions, especially in larger cities, but today heterosexism still dictates a large part of the way the average American considers his or her world. Heterosexism can lead to a lack of awareness of issues that can harm gay, lesbian, and bisexual (GLB) individuals today. Let's now turn our attention to hate crimes against GLB people.

Hate Crimes Against Gay, Lesbian, and Bisexual People

Throughout history, persecution of minorities has been based on philosophies that portrayed those minorities as illegitimate, subhuman, or evil. Likewise, homophobia is not just a set of attitudes; it creates an atmosphere in which people feel they are permitted to harass, assault, and even kill homosexuals. **Hate crimes** are those motivated by hatred of someone's religion, sex, race, sexual orientation, disability, gender identity, or ethnic group. They are known as "message crimes" because they send a message to the victim's affiliated group (American Psychiatric Association, 1998).

The American Psychological Association reports that hate crimes against homosexuals are the most socially acceptable form of hate crimes. Homosexuals are victimized four times more often than the average American. It is estimated that 80% of gay, lesbian, and bisexual youths are verbally abused, and 17% are physically abused (Meyer, 1999). One woman in 8 and 1 man in 6 reports being assaulted, raped, robbed, or vandalized because of his or her sexual orientation (Brienza, 1998). When people are asked whether they have ever used threats or physical violence against a gay, lesbian, or bisexual person, 1 in 10 admit that they have, whereas another 24% acknowledge that they have used name-calling (Franklin, 2000). Many young adults believe that homosexual harassment is socially acceptable, mainly because of peer pressure.

After an assault, a homosexual may suffer from what is called "secondary victimization"—losing his or her job, being denied public services, or being harassed by the police in response to being the victim of an antigay attack (Berrill & Herek, 1990). For that reason, a large percentage of hate crimes against homosexuals go unreported (Herek et al., 2002). Whether or not they are reported, hate crimes have a more serious psychological impact on victims than other types of crime (Brienza, 1998).

hate crime
A criminal offense, usually involving violence, intimidation or vandalism, in which the victim is targeted because of his or her affiliation with a particular group.

SEX Talk

Question: Are people really homophobic because they fear that they themselves are homosexuals?

The question is difficult to answer, but many psychologists believe that fear of one's own sexual desires is a factor in homophobia. The best evidence is the level of brutality of gay hate crimes; the degree of violence suggests that there is a deep fear and hatred at work. Why such hatred of somebody you don't even know? The answer must lie within oneself.

Why Are People Homophobic?

What motivates people to be homophobic? A number of theories have been suggested. Because rigid, authoritarian personalities are more likely to be homophobic, it may be a function of personality type; for such people, anything that deviates from their view of "correct" behavior elicits disdain (K. T. Smith, 1971). Another common suggestion is that heterosexual people fear their own suppressed homosexual desires or are insecure in their own masculinity or femininity (Adams et al., 1996). Others believe that this explanation is too simplistic (Rosser, 1999). Perhaps people are simply ignorant about homosexuality and would change their attitudes with education. Most likely, all of these are true to some degree in different people (Herek, 1986).

Another factor that might contribute to homophobia is our confusion of sexual orientation with gender identity. Sexual orientation refers to who your sexual partners are; gender identity has to do with definitions of masculinity and femininity. When a man violates masculine gender roles, people often react negatively (Madon, 1997). Women are often given more flexibility in crossing gender lines, which perhaps explains why there is more acceptance of lesbianism in society today.

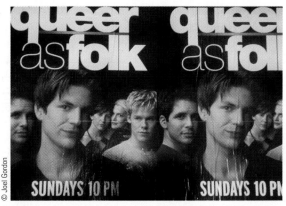

Queer as Folk, *a popular show about gay relationships that first aired in 1999, helped reduce some of the negative stereotypes about gay sexuality.*

How Can We Combat Homophobia and Heterosexism?

Heterosexism is widespread and subtle and therefore is very difficult to combat. Adrienne Rich (1983), a prominent scholar of lesbian studies, uses the term *heterocentrism* to describe the neglect of homosexual existence, even among feminists. Perhaps we can learn from the history of a similar term: ethnocentrism. Ethnocentrism refers to the belief that all standards of correct behavior are determined by one's own cultural background, leading to racism, ethnic bigotry, and even sexism and heterosexism. Although ethnocentrism is still rampant in American society, it is slowly being eroded by the passage of new laws, the media's spotlight on abuses, and improved education. Perhaps a similar strategy can be used to combat heterosexism.

Laws

Hate crimes legislation targets violence that is committed in response to a victim's identity, including sexual orientation. As of 2005, 29 states and the District of Columbia punish perpetrators of hate crimes motivated by sexual orientation and 7 of these states cover crimes motivated by gender identity (National Gay and Lesbian Task Force, 2005). However, the punishment varies from state to state. Hate crimes are harmful for many reasons, but especially because they provoke retaliatory crimes and cause community unrest (National Gay and Lesbian Task Force, 2001).

The Hate Crimes Statistics Act was reauthorized by Congress in 1996. This law requires the compilation of data on hate crimes so that there is a comprehensive picture of these crimes. In 1998 the Hate Crimes Right to Know Act was passed, which requires college campuses to report all hate crimes. However, it's important to point out that "monitoring" or "recording" hate crimes does not necessarily mean putting any resources into improving enforcement or prevention. But even laws protecting homosexuals from abuse can be thwarted by homophobia.

The Media

The representation of the gay, lesbian, and bisexual community is increasing in the media today (Draganowski, 2004). In 2000, Richard Hatch, a gay contestant on the first season of *Survivor*, claimed it was his minority membership and homosexuality that helped him win. Another show, *Will & Grace*, explored the relationship between gay and straight characters. Reality television shows, including *Real World* or *The Amazing Race*, have not been hesitant to use GLB cast members to improve ratings.

Many women discover their lesbianism through a close relationship with another woman.

Other television shows have helped bring homosexuality out of the closet. Examples include *Queer Eye for the Straight Guy*, *Queer Eye for the Straight Girl*, *Playing It Straight*, *Boy Meets Boy* (the latter two intersperse gay and straight men and have others guess who is gay), and *The L-Word* (the *Sex in the City* for lesbians). Although some of these shows have been controversial, they have also helped pave the way for GLBs on television, resulting in vastly different programming from just a few years ago. Before this, homosexuality was portrayed negatively, with images of GLBs as perverts or murderers, such as characters in movies such as *Basic Instinct* or *Silence of the Lambs*.

Another important development in the media is the explosion of gay fiction, nonfiction, plays, and movies that portray gay and lesbian life in America more realistically. Whereas once these types of media were shocking and hidden, now they appear in mainstream bookstores and movie theaters.

Education

Finally, an important step to stopping heterosexism is education. Homosexuality is still a taboo subject in schools, and most proposals to teach sexuality in general—never mind homosexuality in particular—encounter strong opposition by certain parent groups. No teacher would educate students about George Washington Carver, Malcolm X, or Martin Luther King without mentioning that they were black; why then teach students about Leonardo da Vinci, Walt Whitman, Oscar Wilde, Langston Hughes, or Gertrude Stein without mentioning that they were homosexual?

Review Question

Explain what researchers have found about people who are homophobic. How can we combat homophobia in society today?

DIFFERENCES AMONG HOMOSEXUAL GROUPS

Because homosexuality exists in almost every ethnic, racial, and religious group, many gays, lesbians, and bisexuals also belong to other minority groups. We will now discuss the unique situation of some of these groups.

Lesbianism: Facing Sexism Plus Homophobia

Research focusing on lesbian life and the lesbian community in particular lags far behind research on gay men. This is ironic, because many of the gains homosexuals made in the 1960s and 1970s were due to the close relationship between lesbians and the overall feminist movement. The lack of interest in lesbian studies may itself be a result of the lower value society puts on women and women's issues, but it may also be partially due to the fact that lesbians are more tolerated in society and often viewed as less "deviant."

Most of the writing and research about lesbian life in the United States is by lesbians themselves. Scholarship by lesbians tends to be strongly political, in part because lesbians have to deal with both sexism and heterosexism. Friction has arisen between the more radical lesbians and heterosexual feminists, with many lesbians seeing themselves as the vanguard of feminism and seeing heterosexist life as practically synonymous with male domination (Rich, 1983; Risman & Schwartz, 1988).

Overall, the research on lesbianism suggests that women's sexual identity is more fluid than men's (Diamond, 2005; Gallo, 2000). Many women do not fall neatly into homosexual–heterosexual categories. Maybe this is because society is less threatened by lesbian sexuality than by gay sexuality.

Other interesting findings include: lesbian and bisexual women have lower rates of preventive care (yearly physical examinations) than heterosexual women (Mays et al., 2002); they are more likely to be overweight, smoke cigarettes, have high rates of alcohol consumption; and they report higher levels of depression and antidepressant use than heterosexuals (Case et al., 2004; see the Sexbyte on page 349). Some research suggests that much of this hinges on the amount of personal acceptance from their parents. Lesbians who felt that their mothers were accepting of their sexual orientation had higher self-esteem and lower rates of smoking and alcohol consumption than those whose mothers were not accepting (LaSala, 2001).

Interestingly, although you might think lesbian women are more economically disadvantaged than their female heterosexual peers due to their stigmatized sexual orientation, research has found that lesbian workers earn more than their heterosexual female peers (Peplau & Fingerhut, 2004). Overall, lesbians who feel supported and accepted have higher levels of self-esteem and well-being (Beals & Peplau, 2005).

The lesbian community is a vibrant one. Bars, coffeehouses, bookstores, sports teams, political organizations, living cooperatives, media, and lesbian-run and -owned businesses often represent a political statement about the ways in which women can live and work together. A number of lesbian musicians—including k.d. lang, Melissa Etheridge, Tracy Chapman, and members of Tribe 8—sing of issues important to the lesbian community and yet have strong crossover appeal to the heterosexual community. Many lesbian magazines are dedicated to lesbian fiction, erotica, current events, and photography.

Lesbian and feminist journals provide a forum for the lively and argumentative debates among lesbian scholars. For example, pornography has been the subject of an ongoing dispute among lesbian (and feminist) writers. Some are antiporn, seeing most sexually explicit materials as debasing portrayals of women, whereas the "anti–antiporn" group argues that suppressing expressions of sexuality—even ones we disagree with—is a dangerous practice and limits female and lesbian sexual expression, just as new forms of that expression are beginning to appear (Henderson, 1991).

Review Question

Explain why the research on lesbianism lags far behind the research on gay men, and describe some of the research that has been done.

SEX Talk

Question: Are bisexuals really equally attracted to both sexes?

It depends on the bisexual. Some are more attracted to one sex than the other, whereas others say that they have no preference at all (F. Klein, 1978). Masters and Johnson (1979) found that both heterosexuals and homosexuals have at least some "cross-preference" fantasies; so perhaps if social pressures were not as strong as they are, many more people would be bisexual to some degree.

Bisexuality: Just a Trendy Myth?

Although we have been discussing bisexuality throughout this chapter, bisexuality has really emerged more recently as a separate identity from lesbian, gay, or heterosexual identities, and we are still learning more each year (Ryan & Futterman, 2001). Social and political bisexual groups began forming in the 1970s, but it wasn't until the late 1980s that an organized bisexual movement achieved visibility in the United States (Herek, 2002).

We do know that people who identify as bisexual often first identified as heterosexuals, and their self-labeling generally occurs later in life than either gay or lesbian self-labeling (Weinberg et al., 1994). It is interesting to note that for many years few people noticed the absence of research on bisexuality. This absence stemmed from the fact that researchers believed that sexuality was composed of only two opposing forms of sexuality: heterosexuality and homosexuality (Herek, 2002; Rust, 2000).

Homosexuals have tended to see bisexuals either as on their way to becoming homosexual or as people who want to be able to "play both sides of the fence," being homosexual in the gay community and heterosexual in straight society. Heterosexuals have tended to lump bisexuals in with homosexuals. Sexuality scholars have suggested that bisexuality is: a myth, or an attempt to deny one's homosexuality; identity confusion; or an attempt to be "chic" or "trendy" (Rust, 2000). Some studies claim that bisexuals are men and women who are ambivalent about their homosexual behavior (Carey, 2005; Rieger et

Sheryl Swoopes, the three-time Olympic gold medalist and reigning WNBA MVP, came out as a lesbian publicly in 2005. Swoopes said that she was tired of living in the closet and wanted to be open about her life, her wife, and their son. Ironically, a photo of a pregnant, married Swoopes had been used in promotional materials a few years back in an attempt to put a heterosexual face on the WNBA (Granderson, 2005).

al., 2005). To study this, researchers have measured genital arousal patterns in response to images of men and women and have found that those who identify as bisexual often show physical attraction patterns that differ from their stated desires (Rieger et al., 2005). Bisexuals themselves have begun to speak of **biphobia,** which they suggest exists in both the straight and gay and lesbian communities. Like homosexuals, bisexuals experience hostility, discrimination, and violence in response to their sexual orientation (Herek, 2002). This hostility may come not only from heterosexuals, but from homosexuals as well.

Many bisexuals see themselves as having the best of both worlds. As one bisexual put it, "The more I talk and think about it, and listen to people, I realize that there are no fences, no walls, no heterosexuality or homosexuality. There are just people and the electricity between them" (quoted in Spolan, 1991). In our society, fear of intimacy is expressed through either homophobia if you are heterosexual or **heterophobia** if you are gay or lesbian; no matter what your sexual orientation, one gender or another is always taboo—your sexual intimacy is always restricted (Klein, 1978). From that perspective, bisexuality is simply lack of prejudice and full acceptance of both sexes.

More people in American society exhibit bisexual behavior than exclusively homosexual behavior (F. Klein, 1990). In **sequential bisexuality,** the person has sex exclusively with one gender, followed by sex exclusively with the other; **contemporaneous bisexuality** refers to having sexual partners of both sexes during the same time period (Paul, 1984). Numbers are very hard to come by because bisexuality itself is so hard to define. How many encounters with both sexes are needed for a person to be considered bisexual? One? Fifty? And what of fantasies? It is difficult to determine what percentage of people are bisexual because many who engage in bisexual behavior do not self-identify as bisexual (Weinberg et al., 1994).

Some people come to bisexuality through intimate involvement with a close friend of the same sex, even if they have not had same-sex attractions before. Others have come to it through group sex or swinging, in which, in the heat of passion, a body is a body and distinctions between men and women easily blur. The new bisexual movement may succeed in breaking through the artificial split of the sexual world into homosexuals and heterosexuals. Perhaps we fear the fluid model of sexuality offered by bisexuals because we fear our own cross-preference encounter fantasies and do not want to admit that most of us, even if hidden deep in our fantasies, are to some degree attracted to both sexes.

Minority Homosexuality: Culture Shock?

Special problems confront homosexuals who are members of racial or ethnic minorities in the United States. Homosexuality is not accepted by many ethnic groups, and yet the gay community does not easily accommodate expressions of ethnic identity. Minority homosexual youths have been found to experience greater psychological distress than nonminority homosexual youths (Diaz et al., 2001). Many end up feeling torn between the two communities (Nagel, 2003). As one gay Asian American put it, "While the Asian-American community supports my Asian identity, the gay community only supports my being a gay man; as a result I find it difficult to identify with either" (Chan, 1989).

Gay African Americans can find their situation particularly troubling, as they often have to deal with the heterosexism of the African American community and the racism of the homosexual and straight communities. In the African American community, the strong disapproval of homosexuality has prevented black politicians and church leaders from taking a firm stand in combating AIDS, even though black Americans are at higher risk than whites for contracting the disease (Quimby & Friedman, 1989).

Some progress is being made, however. Books such as *In the Life, a Black Gay Anthology* (Beam, 1986) and its sequel, *Brother to Brother: New Writings by Black Gay Men* (Hemphill, 1991), have raised the issue in public. Many feminist and lesbian anthologies, such as *Home Girls: Black Feminist Anthology* (B. Smith, 1983), and most lesbian and feminist journals include writings explicitly by minority lesbians. As we discussed earlier in this chapter, there have also been some recent magazines published that are dedicated to minority gays and lesbians.

It is also worth pointing out that research has found that although many African American lesbians report positive relationships and pleasant feelings about their sexual relationships, more than half also report feeling guilty about these relationships (Wyatt, 1998). This is consistent with the aforementioned research noting the prevalence of psychological distress in homosexual minorities.

Review Question

Describe some of the problems that confront minority homosexual and bisexual youths.

Same-Sex Behavior in Prison

Homosexual behavior varies greatly in prisons. Sexual contact between inmates, although prohibited, still occurs in prisons today; however, research has found that the majority of this sexual activity is consensual (Saum et al., 1995). Those who engage in such behavior usually claim that they are not homosexuals and plan to return to heterosexual relationships exclusively once they are released. This **situational homosexuality** is also found in other places where men must spend long periods of time together, such as on ships at sea.

situational homosexuality
Homosexuality that occurs because of a lack of heterosexual partners.

Many people think that the majority of homosexual contacts in prisons are rapes. In fact, very few men report being raped in prison (Saum et al., 1995). Still, it depends on what we mean by "rape"; a man who is scared for his life and provides sexual services to a more powerful man for protection may feel coerced by his circumstances (see Chapter 17). On the other hand, same-sex attachments in prison can be strong and jealously guarded; for example, same-sex activity has been found to be the leading cause of inmate homicide in U.S. prisons (Nacci & Kane, 1983). Inmates speak of loving their inmate partners, and relations can become extremely intimate, even among those who return to a heterosexual life on release.

HOMOSEXUALITY IN RELIGION AND THE LAW

Religion has generally been considered a bastion of antihomosexual teachings and beliefs, and these beliefs have often helped shape laws that prohibit homosexual behaviors. We will now discuss both of these powerful influences.

Homosexuality and Religion

There has been a great deal of negativity surrounding homosexuality in religion, and changes in social attitudes toward homosexuality over the last 30 years have provoked conflict over homosexual policies in many religious denominations. Traditionally, both Judaism and Christianity have strongly opposed homosexual behavior.

Although there is still hostility within many organized religions toward homosexuals, religious scholars have begun to promote a more liberal attitude, including the ordination of gay and lesbian clergy and marriage or commitment ceremonies.

Some Christian religions that are more on the liberal side include the United Church of Christ and the Unitarian Universalist Association. These churches have welcomed gay, lesbian, and bisexual members; worked for equal rights; and ordained gay, lesbian, and bisexual clergy. They generally view homosexuality as neither a sin nor a choice, and they believe that it is unchangeable. One of the most accepting churches, the Metropolitan Community Churches, promotes itself as the world's largest organization with a primary, affirming ministry to gays, lesbians, bisexuals, and transgendered persons (Metropolitan Community Churches, 2005).

Mainline Christian religions, such as Presbyterians, Methodists, Lutherans, and Episcopalians, have more conflict over the issue of sexual orientation, resulting in both liberal and conservative views. In 2003, the Reverend Susan Andrews became the first female ever elected as the Presbyterian moderator. Andrews believes that the church is ready to lift the ban on having gays and lesbians ordained. Also in 2003, the Episcopal Church named its first openly gay bishop (D. Johnson & Nelson, 2003). Most of the more conservative views, including the idea that homosexuality can be changed through prayer and counseling, come from older members and those living in the southern part of the United States. The conservative churches, such as Catholics, Southern Baptists, and the Assemblies of God, view homosexuality as a sin and work to restrict gay, lesbian, and bisexual rights.

Where Do I Fit In?

Coming out experiences are different for everyone. Some people have really good and empowering experiences, whereas others struggle and experience tremendous negativity. Following is one woman's account of coming to terms with her sexual identity.

The story of my "coming-out" isn't spectacular in any way—I'm an ordinary person with a pretty ordinary life. From the time I was around age 7 or 8, I knew my feelings for other girls were "different." At first I thought the feelings I felt were some strange type of jealousy, but then realized it was attraction. Attraction is a pretty heavy concept for kids in the sixth and seventh grade anyway, but attraction to same-sex peers was just plain overwhelming.

I developed crushes on female classmates but felt so ashamed and awful that I would cry myself to sleep at night. I desperately wanted to make myself normal like the other girls. Girls and boys were pairing off into couples and kissing at middle-school parties, and kids who didn't participate were called "faggot" and "dyke," words that terrified me because I suspected they had something to do with who I was. . . . I searched the library for books about girls like me but never found one. I was a voracious reader, so I figured out that if girls like me weren't in any books, then there must not be any other girls like me out there. I worried that maybe I was the only one.

My freshman year of high school I felt like I was on a roller coaster—I realized I was a lesbian but had no idea where to go from there. During my freshman and sophomore years, I went to parties with friends, but I rarely drank. What if I lost control and told someone who I really was inside? . . . By the middle of my sophomore year, I couldn't take it anymore. I didn't want to be different, or hated, or bashed—I wanted to be invisible. I wrote notes to my mother, my father, and my best male friend, and hid them where they wouldn't find the notes for a day or so. I swallowed a bottle of Tylenol 4 with codeine, curled up in an out-of-the way bathroom stall at school while everyone else was at an assembly, and waited to die. A student found me unconscious and got the school nurse.

Sometimes life gets worse before it gets better, and for me, it did. . . . I met a guy who agreed to tutor me. He was soft-spoken and funny and was friends with my friends. He had a brother who was gay, and everyone made comments suggesting maybe he was gay too. . . . One afternoon, he asked me if I wanted to go to his house to study for an exam. We started studying in his bedroom, and things seemed to be going fine until he started trying to kiss me. I told him to stop, but he wouldn't listen. Then he raped me. . . . When it was over, I got in my car, drove away, and pulled over to throw up about a block from his house. It was the first time I had ever had sex. He returned to school bragging that he had "nailed" me, thus confirming his heterosexuality once and for all. . . . I hesitate to include this chapter of my life, because I don't want my life to be held up as "proof" that lesbians are women who have been abused by men.

There is also controversy over sexual orientation in Jewish synagogues throughout the United States. Although Orthodox Jews believe that homosexuality is an abomination forbidden by the Torah, conservative Jews are more likely to welcome all sexual orientations. However, many synagogues refuse to consider gays or lesbians as rabbis. Reform Jews tend to be the most accepting toward gay, lesbian, and bisexual members.

There is also no real consensus about gay and lesbian relationships among the various Buddhist sects in the United States. Buddhism differs from traditional Christianity in that it views behaviors as helpful/nonhelpful (whereas Christianity views behaviors as good/evil) and looks at whether there was intent to help or not. As a result of this, Buddhism encourages relationships that are mutually loving and supportive.

Recently, religious scholars, both homosexual and heterosexual, have begun to promote arguments based on religious law and even scripture for a more liberal attitude toward homosexuality. For example, some Jewish scholars have argued that because ho-

I was always a lesbian. The fact that I happened to be raped didn't change that in any way. I don't hate men now, and I didn't then. And I don't hate the person who raped me, either. I can finally recognize the role that homophobia played in shaping who he was and how he behaved. The only reason I have included this is because I want people who read this to realize that homophobia doesn't just hurt gay people. It hurts straight people, too—straight people like the guy who raped me because he wanted people to stop calling him a "faggot."

College was an amazing time for me. For the first time in my life, I was surrounded by gay people. I wasn't alone anymore, and it felt incredibly liberating. By my junior year, I knew that I wanted to come out, once and for all, but I was terrified that it would kill my parents, literally. I wanted their love and approval so badly, and all I ever wanted to be was the "perfect" daughter. This is where I feel fate/God/karma intervened, and it changed my life forever, in countless ways: My mom was diagnosed with terminal cancer, and was given 6 months to live. I was crushed—I couldn't imagine life without her. But as strange as this sounds, her diagnosis was a gift to both of us, because I realized I could finally tell her I was a lesbian. Why? Because I knew it wouldn't kill her—she was already dying, and it had nothing to do with my sexual orientation. No one could possibly blame me. Shortly after she was diagnosed, I picked up the phone and called her. I said, "Mom, I have something to tell you and it's really difficult . . . I'm gay." There was a pause, and then she started crying. She completely lost it on the phone and after an hour or so

she calmed down and told me she loved me and supported me, no matter what. From that day until the day she died, I told my mother everything. We talked for hours on the phone every day, trying to make up for lost time, both past and future. I came out to everyone in my life—friends, professors, classmates—and began living my life as the person I had always been inside. . . .

Once I decided to be out in every aspect of my life, everything in my life began to fall in place. I am now in a committed relationship of four years, and we have a 2-year-old son through adoption. . . . We struggled with homophobia during the adoption process of our son because of state laws prohibiting gay and lesbian adoption, but with persistence and with help from other gay couples who have adopted, we were able to bring our son into our family. We live our lives as an openly lesbian couple, and our son knows that he has a Mama and a Mommy that sleep in the same bed. Our families are incredibly supportive, and we have a loving circle of extended family and friends. Life is pretty good for me now, and I am comfortable with my life as a lesbian. . . .

As comfortable as I am with myself and my life, I try not to let myself become complacent, because I realize that the coming-out journey won't be any easier for the next generation if I don't work to change the way gay and lesbian people are perceived and treated today by living myself proudly, openly, and without shame.

SOURCE: Author's files.

mosexual orientation is not a free choice but an unalterable feature of the personality, it is immoral to punish someone for it (Kahn, 1989–90).

Homosexuality and the Law

Throughout history, laws have existed in the Western world that prohibited homosexual behavior, even on pain of death. In the United States, sodomy has been illegal since colonial days, and it was punishable by death until the late 18th century. Fellatio was technically legal until the early 20th century, although it was considered to be "loathsome and revolting" (Murphy, 1990). All 50 states outlawed homosexual acts until 1961.

As we discussed earlier in this chapter, in 2003 the Supreme Court overturned the Texas antisodomy law (which made consensual sex between same sex couples illegal). Prior to 2003, under Texas homosexual conduct law, for ex-

Lesbians, gay men, and bisexual people who also belong to other minority groups must deal with the prejudices of society toward both groups—as well as each group's prejudices toward each other.

ample, individuals who engaged in "deviate sexual intercourse" with a person of the same sex (even if the partner was consenting) were charged with a misdemeanor punishable by up to $500 in fines (LAMBDA, 2001).

Many gay, lesbian and bisexual employees are discriminated against on the job, yet they have little legal recourse. Homosexuals are often denied equal housing rights through exclusionary zoning, rent control, and rent stabilization laws. Even in long-term, committed, same-sex couples, partners are routinely denied the worker's compensation and healthcare benefits normally extended to a spouse or dependents. In addition, gay and lesbian couples are denied tax breaks, Social Security benefits, and rights of inheritance, all of which are available to married heterosexual couples. Some gay and lesbian couples have even resorted to legally adopting their partners in order to extend benefits they would otherwise be denied (Harvard Law Review, 1990).

Why Do Laws Discriminate Against Homosexuals?

Why are homosexuals in the United States so routinely denied the rights that the rest of the country takes for granted? What is the justification for denying homosexuals protection against housing discrimination, job discrimination, and invasions of their sexual privacy?

When it comes to sexual orientation, a liberal–conservative split exists in government as well. Some of those who are appointed to guard our rights in this country—judges and the legal community—hold predominantly negative views of gays, lesbians, and bisexuals. The efforts of local, grass-roots gay organizations, as well as the national efforts of groups like the LAMBDA Legal Defense and Education Fund, may yet break through the wall of legal inaction that prevents homosexuals from fighting the discrimination and victimization they experience in the United States.

Review Question

Explain the changes in social attitudes about homosexuality in various religions. What laws have been instituted to protect homosexual rights?

BEYOND OUR ASSUMPTIONS: A FINAL COMMENT

When the American Psychiatric Association (APA) decided in 1973 to remove homosexuality from its list of official mental diseases, many psychiatrists were outraged. They demanded a vote of the full APA membership. Think about that. Is that how questions of science should be decided—by a vote? But the whole question of homosexuality had become so politicized, so emotional, that the psychiatrists could not even see the implications of what they were doing (Bayer, 1981).

For 100 years or so, homosexuality was considered a sickness. Only when scientists dropped that assumption did they make real progress in understanding homosexuality. The enormous complexity of the human brain allows highly flexible human behavior patterns in almost every aspect of life, and human sexuality is not an exception to that rule.

Theories of sexual orientation change as society changes. Our society is grappling with its acceptance of new forms of sexual relationships. Only time will tell whether that yields increased tolerance or intolerance for people of all sexual orientations.

Chapter Review

ACTIVE SUMMARY

1. Sexual (a) _____ refers to the gender(s) that a person is attracted to (b) _____, physically, (c) _____, and romantically. Heterosexuals are predominantly attracted to members of the other sex; homosexuals to members of the same sex; and (d) _____ are attracted to both men and women.

2. Alfred (a) _____ introduced a 7-point sexual orientation scale based mostly on people's sexual behaviors, whereas other researchers suggest that people's (b) _____ and fantasies, more than their behaviors, are the most important determinants of sexual orientation. The (c) _____ sexual orientation grid (KSOG) includes the elements of time, fantasy, social and (d) _____ behavior, and self-identification.

3. The (a) _____ of gay, lesbian, and bisexual behavior in the United States has remained constant over the years. Scholars generally agree that there are between 3% and 4% of males who are predominantly (b) _____, 1.5% to 2% of women who are predominantly lesbian, and about 2% to 5% are (c) _____.

4. Several (a) _____ to explain the various sexual orientations have been proposed. These include the biological, (b) _____, and sociological theories. These theories can be divided into (c) _____ (there is an innate difference between homosexuals and heterosexuals) and (d) _____ (homosexuality is caused by social roles that have developed in cultures at different times).

5. (a) _____ theories claim that differences in sexual orientation are caused by genetics, hormones, birth order, or simple physical traits. (b) _____ theories focus on a person's upbringing and personal history to find the origins of homosexuality. These theories include the (c) _____, gender-role nonconformity, peer-interaction, and behavioral theories of homosexuality. The (d) _____ theories explain how social forces produce homosexuality in a society.

6. Same-sex activity was common before the 19th century, and homosexual (a) _____ was taxed by the state. (b) _____ was not treated with concern or much interest by either early Jews or early (c) _____. The church's (d) _____ to homosexuality lasted well through the 13th century. By 1300, however, the new intolerance of differences resulted in homosexuality being punishable by (e) _____ almost everywhere. This view, from the late Middle Ages, has influenced the Western world's view of (f) _____ for the last 700 years. In the 19th and early 20th centuries, physicians and scientists began to suggest that homosexuality was not a sin but a(n) (g) _____.

7. Same-sex sexual behavior is found in every (a) _____, and its prevalence remains about the same no matter how permissive or (b) _____ that culture's (c) _____ is toward it. Many homosexuals and bisexuals struggle with (d) _____, prejudice, laws that do not recognize their same-sex unions, lack of spousal (e) _____ for their partners, and families who may (f) _____ them. Even so, many gay and lesbian couples live together in (g) _____, happy unions.

8. Someone who is gay or lesbian must first (a) _____ his or her sexual identity to him- or herself, and undergo a process known as (b) _____ _____. The average age of coming out is about (c) _____ for both men and women, even though there are some youths who remain (d) _____ into late adolescence and even adulthood.

9. Women are more likely to discover their (a) _____ through a close relationship with another woman, whereas (b) _____ are more likely to discover their homosexuality through (c) _____ social/sexual contacts. (d) _____ couples have a double dose of relationship-enhancing influences, which may contribute to the higher levels of relationship (e) _____ among lesbian couples, whereas gay men have a double dose of (f) _____-_____ influences.

10. (a) _____ has found that arousal and orgasm in homosexuals are physiologically no different than in (b) _____ couples. However, gay and lesbian couples tend be slower, more relaxed, and less (c) _____ with each other during (d) _____ than heterosexuals.

11. Children who grow up with one or two gay and/or lesbian (a) _____ do as well emotionally, (b) _____, socially, and sexually as do children from (c) _____ parents.

12. (a) _____ is an irrational fear of homosexuals and homosexuality, and (b) _____ is the presumption of heterosexuality and the social (c) _____ used to promote it. Hate crimes, also known as (d) "_____ crimes," are motivated by hatred of someone's religion, sex, race, sexual orientation, disability, or ethnic group. Many states (e) _____ perpetrators of hate crimes, but the way they are punished varies from state to state. One of the best ways to stop heterosexism is through (f) _____.

13. (a) _____ is less threatened by lesbian sexuality, and perhaps this is the reason that women's sexual identity is more (b) _____ than men's. Overall, lesbian and (c) _____ women have been found to have lower rates of (d) _____ care than heterosexual women.

14. **(a)** _____ often identify first as heterosexuals, and their self-labeling generally occurs **(b)** _____ in life than either gay or lesbian self-labeling. **(c)** _____ is a fear of bisexuals.

15. Minority **(a)** _____ youths have been found to experience greater **(b)** _____ distress than **(c)** _____ homosexual youths.

16. Some **(a)** _____ have become more accepting of homosexuals. Laws that prohibited homosexual behavior have existed throughout history in the **(b)** _____ world, even on pain of death. In the United States prior to new legislation, **(c)** _____ had been illegal since colonial days. A number of American states have proposed laws over the last few years to **(d)** _____ homosexual rights.

Critical Thinking Questions

1. If you are not gay, lesbian, or bisexual, imagine for a moment that you are. Whom do you think you would approach first to talk about the issues surrounding this discovery? Would you feel comfortable talking with your friends? Parents? Siblings? Teachers? Why, or why not?

2. Suppose that one of your good friends, Tim, comes to you tomorrow and tells you that he thinks he is bisexual. You have seen Tim date only women and had no idea he was interested in men. What kinds of questions do you ask him? After reading this chapter, what can you tell him about the current research on bisexuality?

3. If a person fantasizes only about engaging in same-sex behavior but never has actually done so, would he or she be homosexual? Why, or why not?

4. Where do you fall on Kinsey's continuum? What experiences in your life contribute to your Kinsey ranking, and why?

5. What theory do you think best explains the development of sexual orientation? What features do you feel add to the theory's credibility?

6. Do you think same-sex couples should be allowed to marry each other? Why, or why not? Should they be allowed to have children? Why, or why not?

CHAPTER RESOURCES

Check It Out

Bullough, V. L. (Ed). (2002). **Before Stonewall: Activists for gay and lesbian rights in historical context.** Binghamton, NY: Harrington Park Press.

This collection of biographies illuminates the lives of the courageous individuals involved in the early struggle for gay and lesbian civil rights in the United States. Authored by many activists themselves, this book examines the lives of risk takers and trendsetters in gay and lesbian history.

A Home at the End of the World (2004; 1 hour, 37 minutes; Rated R)

This movie follows the lives of Bobby (Colin Farrell) and Jonathan (Dallas Roberts), two childhood friends who meet in an Ohio school. Bobby and Jonathan are inseparable from the moment they meet. For Jonathan, the unconventional Bobby is a connection to a larger world. For Bobby, Jonathan's family—and in particular Jonathan's mother Alice (Sissy Spacek)—represents a kind of stability that he hasn't known. As they grow up, the boys grow apart only to reunite in New York where, together with the free-spirited Clare (Robin Wright Penn), they invent a new kind of family. *A Home at the End of the World* looks at love, commitment, and loyalty.

InfoTrac® College Edition

If your instructor ordered InfoTrac with this book, explore InfoTrac College Edition, your online library, for additional readings and review. Go to: **www.thomsonedu.com,** and enter these search terms:

sexual orientation	gay gene	gender identity	coming out
homophobia	homosexuality and media	gay rights movement	civil unions
same-sex marriage	bisexual	lesbian	

Web Resources

***SexualityNow* Companion Website**
Go to **http://thomsonedu.com/carroll** for practice quiz questions, interactive activities, Internet links, critical thinking exercises, discussion forums, and more. You can also access sites from the Wadsworth Psychology Study Center **(http://psychology.wadsworth.com)** or you can connect directly to the following sites:

GLBTQ
An encyclopedia of gay, lesbian, bisexual, transgender, and queer culture. Contains information about GLBTQ culture, including arts, literature, history, and current rulings on same-sex marriage, civic unions, and domestic partnerships.

National Gay and Lesbian Task Force
The National Gay and Lesbian Task Force (NGLTF) is a national organization that works for the civil rights of gay, lesbian, bisexual, and transgendered people, with the vision and commitment to building a powerful political movement. Their website contains press releases and information on many GLBT issues, including affirmative action, domestic partnerships, and same-sex marriage.

Gay and Lesbian Association of Retiring Persons
The Gay and Lesbian Association of Retiring Persons (GLARP) is an international, nonprofit membership organization that was launched to enhance the aging experience of gays and lesbians. Their website provides retirement-related information and services. GLARP works to establish retirement communities offering independent and assisted living for gays and lesbians in the United States and abroad.

Healthy Lesbian, Gay, and Bisexual Students Project
This recently developed website works to strengthen the ability of the nation's schools to prevent risk to lesbian, gay, bisexual, and questioning students. The

site contains information about workshops, training, and issues affecting LGB students today.

LAMBDA Legal Defense and Education Fund
The LAMBDA Legal Defense and Education Fund is a national organization that works for recognition of the civil rights of lesbians, gay men, bisexuals, the transgendered, and people with HIV and AIDS. Their website contains information on affirmative action, civil unions, aging lesbian and gay men, transgendered, and youth issues. It also contains complete legal briefs and information on landmark cases.

Parents, Families, and Friends of Lesbians and Gays
Parents, Families, and Friends of Lesbians and Gays (PFLAG) is a national organization that works to promote the health and well-being of gay, lesbian, bisexual, and transgendered persons, as well as their families and friends. Through education, support, and dialogue, PFLAG provides opportunities to learn more about sexual orientation and helps to create a society that is respectful of human diversity.

Services and Advocacy for Gay, Lesbian, Bisexual, and Transgendered Elders (SAGE)
SAGE is the world's oldest and largest organization devoted specifically to meeting the needs of aging GLBT persons. Goals include improving the quality of health care and social services and building safe assisted senior living housing for LGBT elders. Through education and advocacy, this organization strives to combat ageism and homophobia.

SexualityNow

Go to **www.thomsonedu.com** to link to **SexualityNow,** your online study tool. First take the **Pre-Test** for this chapter to get your **Personalized Study Plan,** which will identify topics you need to review and direct you to online resources. Then take the **Post-Test** to determine what concepts you have mastered and what you still need work on.

Videos in SexualityNow
For additional information on topics discussed in this chapter, check out the videos in **SexualityNow** on the following topics:
- **Coming Out as a Lesbian**—Listen to one woman describe coming out as a lesbian at age 38 and how it affected her family and children.
- **Trying Not to Be Gay**—Hear a gay man describe his struggle to come to terms with his attraction to men.
- **Discovering Bisexuality**—Hear a woman describe how she gradually realized that she was bisexual.
- **Hating People for the People They Love**—See how complicated the attitudes toward gay and lesbian people actually are in Dr. Greg Herek's research.
- **Coming Out in the Workplace**—Interviews with men and women who describe their experiences being "out" in the workplace.
- **Don't Ask, Don't Tell**—A look at the ongoing debate about gays in the military.

12 Pregnancy and Birth

Sexuality ⬤ Now Go to www.thomsonedu.com to link to
SexualityNow, your online study tool.

*M*ost parents, sooner or later, must confront the moment when their child asks, "Where did I come from?" The answer they give depends on the parent, the child, the situation, and the culture. Every culture has its own traditional explanations for where babies come from. The Australian Aborigines, for instance, believe that babies are created by the mother earth and, therefore, are products of the land. The spirit of children rests in certain areas of the land, and these spirits enter a young woman as she passes by (Dunham et al., 1992). Women who do not want to become pregnant either avoid these areas or dress up like old women to fool the spirits. In Malaysia, the Malay people believe that because man is the more rational of the two sexes, babies come from men. Babies are formulated in the man's brain for 40 days before moving down to his penis for eventual ejaculation into a woman's womb.

In American culture, we take a more scientific view of where babies come from, and so it is important to understand the biological processes involved in conceiving a child, being pregnant, and giving birth. In this chapter we will begin to explore issues related to this incredible journey, including fertility, infertility, options for infertile couples, pregnancy, and childbearing.

FERTILITY

The biological answer to the question, "Where did I come from?" is that we are created from the union of an ovum and a spermatozoon. You may recall from the sexual anatomy and physiology chapters that fertilization and conception are dynamic processes that result in the creation of new life, a process so complex it is often referred to as "the incredible journey."

Conception: The Incredible Journey

Our bodies are biologically programmed to help pregnancy occur in many different ways. For instance, a woman's sexual desire is usually at its peak during her ovulation and just prior to her menstruation (Wilcox et al., 2004). During ovulation, a **mucus plug** in the cervix disappears, making it easier for sperm to enter the uterus, and the cervical mucus changes in consistency (becoming thinner and stretchy), making it easier for sperm to move through the cervix. The consistency of this mucus also creates wide gaps, which vibrate in rhythm with the tail motion of normal sperm, helping to quickly move the healthy sperm and detain abnormal sperm. The cervical mucus also helps filter out any bacteria in the semen. Finally, the female orgasm helps push semen into the uterus; once there, the orgasmic, muscular contractions of the vagina and uterus help pull sperm up toward the Fallopian tubes (pregnancy can certainly still occur, however, without the woman having an orgasm). The consistency of the ejaculated semen also helps. Almost immediately after ejaculation, semen thickens to help it stay in the vagina. Twenty minutes later, when the sperm has had a chance to move up into the uterus, it becomes thin again.

With all the help our bodies are programmed to give, the process of getting pregnant may appear rather easy; however, this is not always the case. The process of becoming pregnant is complex, and things can and do go wrong. For example, the female's immune system itself begins to attack the semen immediately after ejaculation, thinking it is unwanted bacteria. But although many sperm are killed by the woman's immune system,

mucus plug
A collection of thick mucus in the cervix that prevents bacteria from entering the uterus.

Sneak Peek

"When you see the babies and hold them, there's no feeling like that."—*A 57-Year-Old Woman's Successful* In Vitro *Fertilization*

Sexuality ● Now

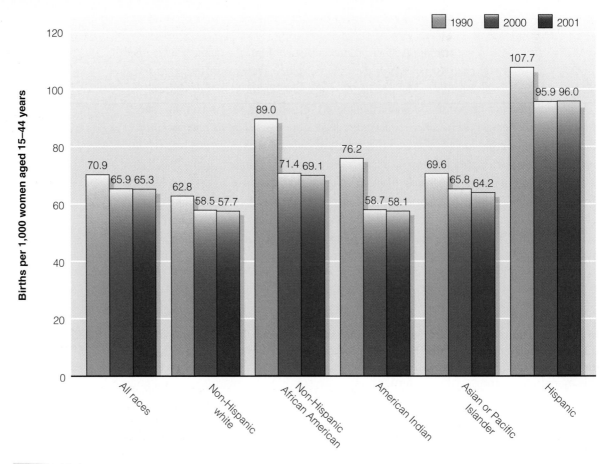

Figure 12.1

Number of births per 1,000 women between the ages of 15 and 44 years old by ethnicity. In the United States, minority women have more births than non-minority women.

Source: Ventura et al., 2003.

spontaneous abortion
A natural process whereby the body expels a developing embryo.

zygote
The single cell resulting from the union of a male and female gamete; the fertilized ovum.

this process is usually not a threat to conception. When a fertile woman engages in intercourse, 30% of the time she becomes pregnant, although a significant number of these pregnancies end in **spontaneous abortion** (Zinaman et al., 1996).

Because the ovum can live for up to 24 hours and the majority of sperm can live up to 72 hours in the female reproductive tract, pregnancy may occur if intercourse takes place either a few days before or after ovulation (A. J. Wilcox et al., 1995). Although most sperm die within 72 hours, a small number, less than 1%, can survive up to 7 days in the female reproductive tract (Ferreira-Poblete, 1997). Throughout their trip into the Fallopian tubes, the sperm haphazardly swim around, bumping into things and each other. When (and if) they reach the jellylike substance that surrounds the ovum, they begin wriggling violently. Although it is not clear how the sperm locate the ovum, preliminary research indicates that the ovum releases chemical signals that indicate its location (Palca, 1991).

Several sperm may reach the ovum, but only one will fertilize it. The sperm secretes a chemical that bores a hole through the outer layer of the ovum and allows the sperm to penetrate for fertilization. The outer layer of the ovum immediately undergoes a physical change, making it impossible for any other sperm to enter. This entire process takes about 24 hours. Fertilization usually occurs in the ampulla (the funnel-shaped open end of the Fallopian tube; see Figure 12.2); after fertilization, the fertilized ovum is referred to as a **zygote.**

As we discussed in Chapter 3, the sperm carry the genetic material from the male. Each sperm contains 23 chromosomes, including the X or Y sex chromosome, which will

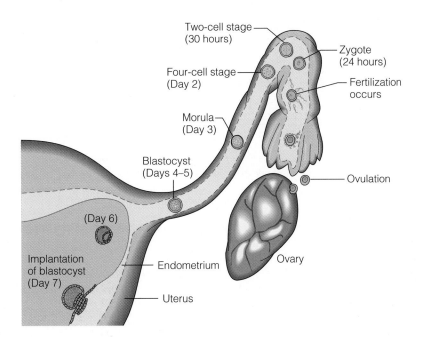

Two-cell stage
(30 hours)

Zygote
(24 hours)

Four-cell stage
(Day 2)

Fertilization
occurs

Morula
(Day 3)

Blastocyst
(Days 4–5)

Ovulation

(Day 6)

Implantation
of blastocyst
(Day 7)

Endometrium

Ovary

Uterus

Figure 12.2
After ovulation, the follicle moves through the Fallopian tube until it meets the spermatozoon. Fertilization takes places in the wide outer part of the tube. Approximately 24 hours later, the first cell division begins. For some 3 or 4 days, the fertilized ovum remains in the Fallopian tube, dividing again and again. When the fertilized ovum enters the uterus, it sheds its outer covering in order to be able to implant in the wall of the uterus.

determine whether the fetus is male or female. Other information is determined by both the male and female genes, including eye and hair color, skin color, and weight.

Approximately 12 hours after the genetic material from the sperm and ovum join together, the first cell division begins. At this point, the collection of cells is referred to as a **blastocyst.** The blastocyst will divide in two every 12 to 15 hours, doubling in size. As this goes on, the cilia in the Fallopian tube gently push the blastocyst toward the uterus. Fallopian tube muscles also help to move the blastocyst by occasionally contracting.

Approximately 3 to 4 days after conception, the blastocyst enters the uterus. For 2 to 3 days it remains in the uterus and absorbs nutrients secreted by the endometrial glands. On about the 6th day after fertilization, the uterus secretes a chemical that dissolves the hard covering around the blastocyst, allowing it to implant in the uterine wall (R. Jones, 1984). Implantation involves a series of complex interactions between the lining of the uterus and the developing embryo, and this usually occurs 5 to 8 days after fertilization. To facilitate implantation, the endometrium must have been exposed to the appropriate levels of estrogen and progesterone. Most of the time, implantation takes place in the upper portion of the uterus, and once this occurs the woman's body and the developing embryo begin to exchange chemical information. Hormones are released into the woman's bloodstream (these can be detected through pregnancy tests). If implantation does not occur, the blastocyst will degenerate and the potential pregnancy will be terminated.

It is fascinating that a woman's body allows the blastocyst to implant when so many of her body's defenses are designed to eliminate foreign substances. Apparently there is some weakening of the immune system that allows for an acceptance of the fertilized ovum (Nilsson, 1990). Some women do continually reject the fertilized ovum and experience repeated miscarriages. We will discuss this in greater detail later in this chapter.

After implantation, the blastocyst divides into two layers of cells, the ectoderm and endoderm. A middle layer, the mesoderm, soon follows. These three layers will develop into all the bodily tissues. From the 2nd through the 8th weeks, the developing human is referred to as an **embryo** (EMM-bree-oh; although it may also be referred to as a "pre-embryo" prior to the embryonic stage). Soon a membrane called the **amnion** begins to grow over the developing embryo, and the amniotic cavity begins to fill with amniotic fluid. This fluid supports the fetus and protects it from shock, as well as assists in fetal lung development. The **placenta,** which is the portion that is attached to the uterine wall, supplies nutrients to the developing fetus, aids in respiratory and excretory func-

blastocyst
The hollow ball of embryonic cells that enters the uterus from the Fallopian tube and eventually implants.

embryo
The developing organism from the 2nd to the 8th week of gestation.

amnion
A thin, tough, membranous sac that encloses the embryo or fetus.

placenta
The structure through which the exchange of materials between fetal and maternal circulations occurs.

Personal Voices

Where Did I Come From?

Do you remember where you thought babies came from as a child? How old were you? Did you talk to your friends about your ideas of where babies came from? What did they say?

Psychologist Anne Bernstein interviewed children between the ages of 3 and 12 to examine their ideas about sex and childbirth. She found that even when adults provided children with the straight facts, the story of human reproduction was often distorted and understood in different ways. Here is a sample of children's ideas about where babies come from. Notice how their thinking about pregnancy and birth changes as they age.

3-year-olds

You go to a baby store and buy one.

It just grows inside Mommy's tummy. It's there all the time. Mommy doesn't have to do anything. She just waits until she feels it.

4-year-olds

To get a baby to grow in your tummy, you just make it first. You put some eyes on it. Put the head on, and hair, some hair, all curls. You make it with head stuff you find in the store that makes it for you. Well, the Mommy and Daddy make the baby and then they put it in the tummy and then it goes quickly out.

God makes Mommies and Daddies with a little seed. He puts it down . . . on the table . . . then it grows bigger. The people grow together. He makes them eat the seed, then they grow to be people.

Daddies don't have babies because sometimes they have to work and it might come out when they're working, and they'll have to work with it in the tummy. But when there's a baby in the tummy, they have to go to the doctor right away, see. So they don't grow babies.

8-year-olds

[The father] puts his penis right in the place where the baby comes out, and somehow it comes out of there. It seems like magic sort of, 'cause it just comes out. Sometimes I think the father pushes, maybe.

The father gives the rest of the egg to the mother. When the man sticks his penis into the vagina. Because the mother just has half of it. It's like a egg has two parts. It's just like—we had a big salami, which is whole, and we cut it in half, and we just go like that.

Well, first a man and a woman have to like each other and be with each other a lot. They have to sleep with each other sometimes, and then—after a long time the woman starts getting a little bit big, starts getting big around here. Then in about six months she has a baby and the baby comes out of here [she points first to her abdomen and then to her crotch].

12-year-olds

Well, they have sexual intercourse. Then the man, he puts his penis in the lady's vagina and sperm comes out, and they go, if the lady's had her period and if her egg is in her ovary, a sperm will go into her egg, and it will fertilize it, and that becomes a baby.

The man and the woman have sexual intercourse. The man's sperm goes into the woman's egg and starts a baby. Lots of sperm go and only one gets through, and the egg gets fertilized.

The male injects sperm into the female's womb, and an egg forms, and there you have a baby. Well, an egg is fertilized, and it grows into a fetus, which after nine months of living in the womb, emerges as a baby.

SOURCE: Adapted from Bernstein, 1994.

---

umbilical cord
The long, ropelike structure that connects the fetus to the placenta.

fraternal twins
Two offspring developed from two separate ova fertilized by different spermatozoa.

dizygotic
Pertaining to or derived from two separate zygotes.

tions, and secretes hormones necessary for the continuation of the pregnancy. The **umbilical cord** connects the fetus to the placenta. By the 4th week of pregnancy the placenta covers 20% of the wall of the uterus, and at 5 months the placenta covers half of the uterus (R. Jones, 1984). Toward the end of pregnancy, approximately 75 gallons of blood will pass through the placenta daily.

The majority of women deliver a single fetus. However, in 2 out of every 100 couples there is a multiple birth. This can happen in two ways. Sometimes two ova are released by the ovaries, and if both are fertilized by sperm, **fraternal twins** (nonidentical) result. These twins are **dizygotic,** and they can be either of the same or different sex. Two-thirds of all twins are fraternal and are no more closely genetically related than any two siblings. The tendency to have fraternal twins may be inherited from the mother, and older women (over the age of 30) seem to have fraternal twins more often than younger women (due to erratic ovulation and an increased possibility of releasing more than one ovum).

Identical twins occur when a single zygote completely divides into two separate zygotes. This process produces twins who are genetically identical and are referred to as **monozygotic** twins. They often look identical and are always of the same sex. In rare cases, the zygote fails to divide completely, and two babies may be joined together at some point in their bodies; these are known as **conjoined twins,** often popularly referred to as Siamese twins. In some instances, many ova are released and fertilized, and **triplets** or **quadruplets** may result.

Recently, the number of multiple births has been increasing as more older women become pregnant and fertility drug use, which can stimulate the release of ova, becomes widespread (Garber, 2003). We will discuss this more later in this chapter.

Early Signs of Pregnancy

If the zygote does implant, most women experience physical signs very early that alert them to their pregnancy. The most common early indicator is missing a period, although some women notice some "spotting" that occurs during the pregnancy (anything more than this is often referred to as irregular bleeding and it may indicate a possible miscarriage). Other physical signs include breast tenderness, frequent urination, and **morning sickness** (see Table 12.1).

It is estimated that between 50% and 80% of all pregnant women experience some form of nausea, vomiting, or both, during pregnancy (Atanackovic et al., 2001). This sickness is due to the increase in estrogen and progesterone during pregnancy, which may irritate the stomach lining. It is often worse in the morning because there is no food in the stomach to counter its effects, although it can happen at any point during the day. Researchers now believe that morning sickness may protect the fetus from food-borne illness and chemicals in certain foods during the first trimester, which is the most critical time in development (Boyd, 2000). The lowest rates of morning sickness are found in cultures without animal products as a food staple. Some women also develop food aversions, the most common of which are to meat, fish, poultry, and eggs—all foods that can carry harmful bacteria.

In rare cases, **pseudocyesis** (sue-doe-sigh-EE-sis), or false pregnancy, occurs. This is a condition in which a woman believes she is pregnant when she is not. Her belief is so strong that she begins to experience several of the signs of pregnancy. She may miss her period, experience morning sickness, and gain weight.

Although the majority of cases of pseudocyesis have a psychological basis, there are some that have physical causes. For instance, a tumor on the pituitary gland may cause an oversecretion of prolactin, which in turn can cause symptoms such as breast fullness

Francis Leroy, Biocosmos/Photo Researchers, Inc.

As the head of the spermatozoon enters the ovum, the ovum prevents penetration by another spermatozoon.

identical twins
Two offspring developed from a single zygote that completely divides into two separate, genetically identical zygotes.

monozygotic
Pertaining to or derived from one zygote.

conjoined twins
Twins who are born physically joined together.

triplets
Three offspring having coextensive gestation periods and delivered at the same birth.

quadruplets
Four offspring having coextensive gestation periods and delivered at the same birth.

Review Question

Explain the process of conception, and describe how the human body is programmed to help pregnancy occur.

morning sickness
The nausea and vomiting that some women have when they become pregnant; typically caused by the increase in hormones. Can occur at any point in the day.

pseudocyesis
A condition in which a woman experiences signs of pregnancy, even though she is not pregnant.

SEX Talk

Question: *Will guys ever be able to become "pregnant"?*

It is possible that today's techniques will enable a man to carry a pregnancy to term in the near future. An embryo would have to be implanted into a man's abdomen with the placenta and attached to an internal organ. Hormonal treatment would be necessary in order to sustain the pregnancy. In addition, the father would have to undergo a cesarean section birth. There may not be many men standing in line to carry a pregnancy, however, because the hormones needed to maintain the pregnancy can cause breast enlargement and penile shrinkage.

TABLE 12.1   Pregnancy Signs

Physical Sign	Time of Appearance	Other Possible Reasons
Period late/absent	Entire pregnancy	Excessive weight gain or loss, fatigue, hormonal problems, stress, breast feedings, going off birth control pills
Breast tenderness	1–2 weeks after conception	Use of birth control pills, hormonal imbalance, period onset
Increased fatigue	1–6 weeks after conception	Stress, depression, thyroid disorder, cold or flu
Morning sickness	2–8 weeks after conception	Stress, stomach disorders, food poisoning
Increased urination	6–8 weeks after conception	Urinary tract infection, excessive use of diuretics, diabetes
Fetal heartbeat	10–20 weeks and then throughout entire pregnancy	None
Backaches	Entire pregnancy	Back problems
Frequent headaches	May be entire pregnancy	Caffeine withdrawal, dehydration, eyestrain, birth control pills
Food cravings	Entire pregnancy	Poor diet, stress, depression, period onset
Darkening of nipples	Entire pregnancy	Hormonal imbalance
Fetal movement	16–22 weeks after conception	Bowel contractions, gas

couvade
A condition in which the father (or other relative) experiences the symptoms of pregnancy and/or childbirth without an actual pregnancy.

Review **Question**

Identify four signs of pregnancy, and explain why they occur.

human chorionic gonadotropin (hCG)
The hormone that stimulates production of estrogen and progesterone to maintain pregnancy.

false negative
Incorrect result of a medical test or procedure that wrongly shows the lack of a finding.

false positive
Incorrect result of a medical test or procedure that wrongly shows the presence of a finding.

radioimmunoassay (RIA) blood test
Blood pregnancy test.

ectopic pregnancy
The implantation of the fertilized egg outside the uterus, such as in the Fallopian tubes or abdomen.

due date
The projected birth date of a baby.

and morning sickness. Pseudocyesis has been found to be more common in women who believe childbearing is central to their identity, have a history of infertility and/or depression, or have had a miscarriage (Whelan & Stewart, 1990). Although expectant fathers (and other relatives) have also been found to experience pseudocyesis, it is more typical for them to experience a related condition called **couvade** (coo-VAHD). Men with this condition experience the symptoms of their pregnant partners, including nausea, vomiting, increased or decreased appetite, diarrhea, and/or abdominal bloating.

Pregnancy Testing: Confirming the Signs

If you have had sexual intercourse without using birth control or have experienced any of the signs of pregnancy, it is a good idea to take a pregnancy test. Over-the-counter pregnancy tests can be purchased in drugstores, but sometimes tests are less expensive or even free in university health centers.

Pregnancy tests measure for a hormone in the blood called **human chorionic gonadotropin (hCG;** corr-ee-ON-ick go-nad-oh-TRO-pin**),** which is produced during pregnancy. The hormone hCG is manufactured by the cells in the developing placenta and can be identified in the blood or urine 8 to 9 days after ovulation. The presence of hCG helps build and maintain a thick endometrial layer and so prevents menstruation. Peak levels of hCG are reached in the 2nd and 3rd months of pregnancy and then drop off.

Home pregnancy tests can be inaccurate if taken too soon after conception, and some women who postpone pregnancy tests until after the 12th week may have a **false negative** pregnancy test because the hCG levels are too low to be detected by the test. If you are using an at-home test, be sure you know how soon after ovulation it can be used. Many tests today can detect hcG levels even before a period is late. **False positive** test results may occur in the presence of a kidney disease or infection, an overactive thyroid gland, or large doses of aspirin, tranquilizers, antidepressants, or anticonvulsant medications (Hatcher et al., 1998).

Of all pregnancy tests, **radioimmunoassay (RIA;** ray-dee-oh-im-mue-noh-ASS-say**) blood tests** are the most accurate. RIA tests can detect hCG within a few days after conception and are also useful for monitoring the progress of a pregnancy that may be in jeopardy. The levels of hCG rise early in pregnancy, and if a woman's hormones do not follow this pattern, a spontaneous abortion or an **ectopic pregnancy** may have occurred. We will discuss both of these later in this chapter.

After a woman's pregnancy is confirmed, her healthcare provider helps her to calculate a **due date.** Most physicians date the pregnancy from the first day of the last menstrual period rather than the day of ovulation or fertilization. The standard for due date calculation is called the **Naegeles** (nay-GEL-lays) **rule**—subtract 3 months from the first day of the last period and add 7 days for a single birth (Mittendorf et al., 1990; for example, if the last period began on August 1, subtract 3 months and add 7 days, which means that the due date would be May 8). This rule works most effectively with women who have standard 28-day menstrual cycles.

Naegeles rule
A means of figuring the due date by subtracting 3 months from the first day of the last menstrual period and adding 7 days.

Review Question

Explain how pregnancy tests work.

SEX Talk

Question: I have missed my period now for 2 months in a row. Does this mean that I am pregnant? What should I do?

If you have been engaging in sexual intercourse, there is certainly a chance that you are pregnant. However, there are several reasons for missing your period, including stress, losing weight, active participation in sports, or changes in eating patterns, as well as certain diseases. In any case, it is a good idea to see a gynecologist or your school nurse for an evaluation.

sex byte

Parents who smoke cigarettes around the time of conception have a lower chance of conceiving male children (Fukuda et al., 2002).

Sex Selection: Myth and Modern Methods

There are more male babies born every year than female; however, the ratio of male to female children has decreased significantly during the last few years. As we discussed in Chapter 3, although more males are conceived, a higher percentage of male fetuses spontaneously abort or die before birth than female fetuses (Fukuda et al., 2002; Mizuno, 2000).

Throughout time, many couples have searched for ways to choose the gender of their child. A variety of techniques have been proposed by different cultures at different times. Aristotle believed that if a couple had sexual intercourse in the north wind, they would have a male child, and if intercourse took place in the south wind, they would have a female. Hippocrates believed that males formed on the right side of the uterus and females on the left; and so, to conceive a daughter, a woman was advised to lie on her left side directly after intercourse. The ancient Greeks thought that if a man cut or tied his left testicle, a couple would not have girls because male sperm were thought to be produced in the right testicle (Dunham et al., 1992). Although some of these suggestions sound absurd today, many people in many cultures still hold myths of how to choose and how to know the gender of their child (see Human Sexuality in a Diverse World, "Is It a Boy or a Girl?").

Reasons for wanting to choose a child's sex vary; although some couples simply prefer a male or female child, others desire to choose the gender of their children for medical reasons. For example, certain inherited diseases are more likely to affect one gender (such as hemophilia, which affects more males).

Modern-day methods of gender selection were popularized by Shettles and Rorvik (1970) in their groundbreaking book *Your Baby's Sex: Now You Can Choose.* According to these authors, by taking into account the characteristics of the female (X) and male (Y) sperm, couples can use timing and pH level adjustments to the vaginal environment (douches) to increase the concentration of X or Y sperm.

Because Y sperm swim faster and thrive in an alkaline environment, Shettles and Rorvik recommended that to have a boy, a couple should have intercourse close to ovulation (to allow the faster-swimming Y sperm to get there first) and douche with a mixture of baking soda and water. Because X sperm tender to live longer and thrive in an acidic environment, for a girl, a couple should time intercourse 2 to 3 days prior to ovulation and douche with a mixture of vinegar and water.

Other formulas for gender selection include various dieting routines or "microsorting" (also known as "spinning"; separating the X and Y sperm followed by artificial insemination). But microsorting comes at a cost—approximately $3,500 per trial. The re-

sex byte

Researchers have begun to attempt to clone a human embryo using immature eggs incubated in a lab (Khamsi, 2005). Cells from these embryos may be used to create stem cell "lines" that can be used as a type of repair system in the body, replenishing other defective cells.

Human Sexuality in a Diverse World

Is It a Boy or a Girl?

Throughout the world, people have relied on folk wisdom to predict the sex of their baby. Here are some examples:

It's a Girl!

Baby sits on the left side of the womb (Nyinba, Nepal).

Mother puts her left foot first crossing the threshold (Bihar, India).

Baby sits low in the belly (Lepchas, Himalayas, and Bedouin tribes).

Mother is grumpy with women (Dinka, Africa).

Fetus moves slow and gentle (Dustin, North Borneo, and Egypt).

Mother first feels the baby when she is outside (Serbs, Yugoslavia).

Mother dreams of human skulls (Maori, New Zealand).

Mother dreams of a headkerchief (Egypt).

Mother craves spicy foods (Nyinba, Nepal).

Mother's face has yellow spots (Poland).

Baby "plays in stomach" before sixth month (Nyinba, Nepal).

It's a Boy!

Baby sits on the right side of the womb (Nyinba, Nepal).

Mother puts her right foot first crossing the threshold (Bihar, India).

Baby sits high in the belly (Lepchas, Himalayas, and Bedouin tribes).

Mother is grumpy with men (Dinka, Africa).

Fetus moves fast and rough (Dustin, North Borneo, and Egypt).

Mother first feels baby move when at home (Serbs, Yugoslavia).

Mother dreams of huisa feathers (Maori, New Zealand).

Mother dreams of a handkerchief (Egypt).

Mother craves bland foods (Nyinba, Nepal).

Mother looks well (Poland).

Baby first "plays in stomach" after sixth month (Nyinba, Nepal).

SOURCE: Dunham et al., 1992.

---

ported likelihood of conceiving a male is between 50% and 70% and a female is between 50% to 90% (Pozniak, 2002). Another technique involves genetic embryo testing and implantation of only those embryos that are the desired sex (Stein, 2004). However, there are no 100% reliable methods of gender selection at this time.

During the 16th or 17th week of pregnancy, a procedure called **amniocentesis** (am-nee-oh-sent-TEE-sis) can determine, among other things, the chromosomal sex of the fetus. Some **amniotic fluid** is extracted from the womb using a needle and is evaluated for chromosomal abnormalities (chromosomal abnormalities can also be checked with other procedures, which we will talk about later in this chapter). An amniocentesis is advised for women who will be 35 or older at the time of delivery because they are at a higher risk for chromosomal abnormalities. This test is also important in the early discovery of sex-linked abnormalities.

However, amniocentesis also raises many moral, sociological, and ethical issues about gender selection. For example, controversy surrounds whether or not parents should be able to choose the gender of a child through selective abortion. Some believe that in these cases, if a couple is carrying a boy and want a girl, they should not be allowed to terminate the pregnancy.

There are several places around the world where parents go to extremes to ensure the birth of a male baby. In India, for example, males are valued more than females because of their ability to care for and financially support aging parents. Female offspring, on the other hand, move into a husband's home after marriage and are unavailable to help care for their parents.

Early testing can now determine fetal gender, and this has led to the practice of **female infanticide** in India (VanBalen & Inhorn, 2003). India has the lowest ratio of girls to boys in the world, and one study found that 80% of girl babies in rural India were killed within minutes of birth ("India: Girl Children Increasingly Unwanted," 2002). Poor families often cannot afford to have girls because parents are expected to provide dowries for their daughters at marriage. Others believe that female infanticide is better

amniocentesis
A procedure in which a small sample of amniotic fluid is then analyzed to detect chromosomal abnormalities in the fetus or to determine the sex of the fetus.

amniotic fluid
The fluid in the amniotic cavity.

female infanticide
The killing of female infants; practiced in some countries that value males more than females.

than letting a female suffer throughout her life (women are given fewer opportunities and treated as second-class citizens). The following case is from a family in India:

> Lakshmi already had one daughter, so when she gave birth to a second girl, she killed her. For the three days of her second child's short life, Lakshmi admits, she refused to nurse her. To silence the infant's famished cries, the impoverished village women squeezed the milky sap from an oleander shrub, mixed it with castor oil, and forced the poisonous potion down the newborn's throat. The baby bled from the nose, then died soon afterward. Murdering girls is still sometimes believed to be a wiser course than raising them. "Instead of suffering the way I do, I thought it was better to get rid of her." (A. Jones, 1999)

Many girls in India die in suspicious circumstances. Some are fed dry, unhulled rice that punctures their windpipes; others are smothered with a wet towel or strangled (A. Jones, 1999).

In Chapter 3, we discussed the strong preference for males that exists in the People's Republic of China. Males can continue the family name and are also expected to care for their parents in old age. Even so, in China, government regulations on family size have led to the practice of both female and male infanticide. An excerpt from a publication about infanticide in China describes the horror of this practice:

> The Huang family already had three children when the mother became pregnant again. "Family Planning" officials seized the house and ordered the father to kill his newborn son, whom he instead attempted to hide. Officials found the baby and drowned him in a rice paddy, in front of his parents. (Saini, 2002, p. 25)

Review Question

Explain the methods for gender selection, and define and discuss infanticide.

ASSISTED REPRODUCTION

Almost every culture places a great deal of importance on the ability to have children. Rice was originally thrown at couples after marriage, in fact, because onlookers hoped that the great fertility of the rice plant would be transferred to the married couple. The same is true of the baby's breath plant, which was traditionally used in a bride's bouquet. Today many couples—gay, lesbian, and heterosexual—use assisted reproduction.

Fertility rates naturally decline with increasing age, beginning as early as 30 and then decreasing more quickly after age 40 (Swisher et al., 1998). Fertility is something most of us take for granted. However, being able to conceive is not always easy for couples. **Infertility** is defined as the inability to conceive (or impregnate) after 1 year of regular sexual intercourse without the use of any form of birth control (if a woman is over the age of 35, usually infertility is diagnosed after 6 months of not being able to conceive). About 1 out of every 5 couples in the United States of reproductive age is infertile (Berkow et al., 2000). This percentage of couples is much higher than the 8% to 10% average in developed countries (Prevost, 1998). Although decreasing fertility also affects gay and lesbian couples, unless these couples use a surrogate or a friend as a donor, they must often use assisted reproduction to achieve a pregnancy.

infertility
The inability to conceive (or impregnate).

The number of couples seeking assisted reproduction treatment is increasing each year. Fertility problems can be traced 70% of the time to one of the partners (40% of the time the female, and 30% of the time the male). In 20% of cases there is a combined problem, and in 10% the reason is unknown (Afek, 1990). Historically, women have been blamed for infertility problems, and up until the last few years, men were not even considered a possible part of the problem.

Infertility has a strong impact on a couple's well-being (Forti & Krausz, 1998). Emotional reactions to infertility can include depression, anxiety, anger, self-blame, guilt, frustration, and fear. Because the majority of people have no experience dealing with infertility, many of those who find out they are infertile isolate themselves and try not to think about it. Overall, women tend to have more emotional reactions to infertility and are more willing to confide in someone about their infertility than are men (Hjelmstedt et al., 1999). Childbearing in the United States is part of what defines be-

motherhood mandate

The belief that something is wrong with a woman if she is not involved in caregiving or childcare.

ing female, and so women who are infertile often feel less valued than fertile women. The term **motherhood mandate** refers to the idea that something is wrong with a woman if she does not play a central role in caregiving and childcare (Riggs, 2005). As one woman reports:

> I can't emphasize how devastating infertility is to one who has spent a lifetime basing her self-esteem on "what I can do." When you can't have children, the most natural and important aspect of life—none of your previous accomplishments seem important. They are overshadowed by this supreme failure. (Mahlstedt, 1987, p. 131)

Infertile couples usually seek professional help, although research indicates that women are often more committed than their partners to finding a solution to the infertility. Support groups for persons experiencing infertility are often very helpful. One of these groups, RESOLVE: The National Infertility Association (see Web Resources for more information about this organization), offers resources for couples struggling with infertility. RESOLVE helps couples see that they are not alone and provides a safe and healthy environment in which to discuss relevant issues.

The most common causes of female infertility include ovulation disorders, blocked Fallopian tubes, endometriosis (see Chapter 4), structural uterine problems, or excessive uterine fibroids. Causes for male infertility include a lack of sperm production and reduced or malformed sperm production. Infertility can also be caused by past infections with gonorrhea, chlamydia, or pelvic inflammatory disease (Hatcher et al., 2004), which is one of the reasons college students are encouraged to have regular medical checkups and women are encouraged to have regular Pap smears. If a sexually transmitted infection (STI) is treated early, there is less chance that it will interfere with fertility.

For some men and women who experience reproductive problems, changing lifestyle patterns, reducing stress, avoiding rigorous exercise, and maintaining a recommended weight may restore fertility. For other couples, new medical interventions offer new possibilities. It is also important to keep in mind that some infertile couples experience spontaneous pregnancies, usually when the stress of "getting pregnant" is reduced (Isaksson & Tiitinen, 1998). Many mind–body programs that teach relaxation techniques have been designed for women struggling with infertility. Programs include meditation and yoga to help participants reduce stress and many of these programs have helped infertile women become pregnant (Petersen, 2004).

Assisted Reproductive Options

Problems with infertility and gay and lesbian couples' desire to parent have given rise to artificial means of conception. Reproductive technologies that have been developed in the last few years enable some couples to have children even when one of them is infertile or they are the same gender. These technologies, although exciting, may also contribute to the further anguish and stress for the couple, particularly if the methods fail.

Review Question

Define assisted reproduction, and describe some of the emotional effects of infertility.

sex byte

Preliminary research has found that a mother's exposure to the flu during pregnancy may increase the chances that her offspring will develop schizophrenia later in life (Brown et al., 2004).

Timeline: The History of Assisted Reproduction

1677	1827	1934	1937	1945
Human sperm is first viewed under a microscope.	Ovum is discovered.	Progesterone is discovered by scientist who goes on to win the Nobel Prize in chemistry.	*New England Journal of Medicine* discusses the concept of IVF techniques.	*British Medical Journal* discusses artificial insemination using donor sperm.

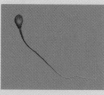

Dr. Denni Kunkel/Getty Images

Derek Berwin/Getty Images

Many of these options are very time consuming and expensive (see Table 12.2), and they do not guarantee success.

There has been a tremendous increase in the number of babies born through assisted reproduction. In fact, in 2002 a total of 45,751 babies resulted from reproductive technologies, which was a 120% increase over the 20,840 that were born in 1996 (Assisted Reproductive Technology, 2002). Many technologies are available to the couples, although deciding which treatment to use depends on factors such as the duration of infertility, a woman's age, and chances of conceiving without treatment. We will explore these options in more detail shortly.

As assisted reproductive procedures have become more common, many ethical and legal issues have also emerged (see Sex in Real Life, "Ethical, Legal, and Moral Issues Involved in Reproductive Technology"). In addition, infants born through assisted reproductive techniques have been found to have lower birth weights and increased prematurity (Kelly-Vance et al., 2004). There is also evidence that pregnancies achieved through assisted reproductive techniques are more at risk for miscarriage (Wang et al., 2004).

Fertility Drugs

As we discussed in Chapters 4 and 5, sperm production and ovulation are a result of a well-balanced endocrine system (pituitary, hypothalamus, and gonads). Some women and men have hormonal irregularities that may interfere with the process of ovulation or sperm production. Although we do not always know why these hormonal problems develop, many problems can be treated with fertility drugs. The results from these drugs have been encouraging.

Because all of the fertility drugs for women work to increase ova production, there is an increased possibility of multiple births and a condition known as "ovarian hyperstimulation syndrome." This has raised concern about the possible correlation between the use of fertility drugs and the development of breast or ovarian cancer. Although some studies have found a weak link between the two (Burmeister & Healy, 1998), others have found a moderate link (Brinton et al., 2005) or no association (Hollander, 2000).

Surgery

Cervical, vaginal, or endometrial abnormalities that prevent conception may be corrected surgically (Ruiz-Velasco et al., 1997). Scar tissue, cysts, tumors, or adhesions, as well as blockages inside the Fallopian tubes, may be surgically removed. The use of diagnostic techniques such as **laparoscopy** (la-puh-RAH-ske-pee) and **hysteroscopy** (hiss-stare-oh-OSK-coe-pee) are also common. In men, surgery may be required to remove any blockage in the vas deferens or epididymis, or repair a **varicocele** (VA-ruh-coe-seal).

laparoscopy
A procedure that allows a direct view of all the pelvic organs, including the uterus, Fallopian tubes, and ovaries; also refers to a number of important surgeries (such as tubal ligation or gall bladder removal) involving the laparoscope.

hysteroscopy
Visual inspection of the uterine cavity with an endoscope.

varicocele
An unnatural swelling of the veins in the scrotum.

1973	1978	1983	1984
IVF is first attempted in the United States. First IVF pregnancy is reported in Australia but does not produce a child. 	Louise Brown, the first IVF baby, is born in Cambridge, England. 	First IVF baby is born in the United States. Sperm Bank of California is opened to allow donations for unmarried women. First baby conceived with donor ova is born in Australia.	First baby developed from a frozen embryo is born in Australia.

TABLE 12.2   The Costs of Assisted Reproduction Tests, Treatments, and Adoption*

	Procedure	Fees
Diagnostic procedures	Initial visit, interview, physical exam (female)	$200, plus any lab work ordered
	Initial visit, interview, physical exam (male)	$100–150, plus any lab work ordered
	Semen analysis	$75–125 per test
	Sperm antibody test	$75–150 per test
	Various hormonal blood tests (male and female)	$75–100 per test
	Testicular biopsy	$800–2,000 depending on whether performed in physician's office or hospital
	Endometrial biopsy	$250 for physician's and laboratory charges
Corrective surgical procedures	Donor insemination (DI)	$225 per insemination, plus sperm
	Laparoscopy (diagnostic) or laparoscopic surgery (reparative)	$8,000–8,500 for surgeon, anesthesiologist, and outpatient hospital charges
	Major surgery for removal of tubal blockages, adhesions	$5,000 or more for surgeon, assistant surgeon, anesthesiologist charges, plus $7,000 or more for hospital charges, depending on length of stay, time in operating room, medications, and so on
	Vasectomy reversal	$2,500–6,000
	Varicocele surgery	$1,500–4,000
Fertility/pregnancy procedures	Fertility drug treatment	$1,500–2,500 per cycle for drug and monitoring
	Donor insemination (DI)	$225 per insemination, plus sperm
	IVF (in vitro fertilization)	$8,000–10,000 per attempt, depending on procedures and individual program
	GIFT (gamete intra-Fallopian tube transfer)	$8,000–10,000 per attempt
	ZIFT (zygote intra-Fallopian transfer)	$8,000–10,000 per attempt
	ICSI (intracellular sperm injection)	$1,000–2,000 per attempt
	Frozen embryo transfer	$1,000 per attempt
Adoptions	Independent adoption	$8,000–30,000, depending on birth mother's and newborn's needs for living, counseling, and medical costs, plus $3,000–4,000 for attorney's fees and other legal costs
	Agency adoption	Varies from several hundred dollars for some types of public agency adoptions to thousands of dollars for some private agency and international adoptions
	Surrogate arrangements	From about $12,000 for an arrangement based on the independent adoption model to $50,000 or more when fees for surrogate and agency services are added

*Only 15 states mandate insurance coverage for infertility treatments (Arkansas, California, Connecticut, Hawaii, Illinois, Louisiana, Maryland, Massachusetts, Montana, New Jersey, New York, Ohio, Rhode Island, Texas, and West Virginia). In these states, only certain treatments and procedures are covered.

Timeline: The History of Assisted Reproduction

1987	1988		1991	1992
Embryo transfer procedure is patented.	After a surrogate mother refuses to give up custody of baby she carried, the New Jersey Supreme Court gives custody of "Baby M" to the genetic father and his wife, and the surrogate is given visitation rights.		A 42-year-old woman becomes a surrogate mother for her daughter after becoming pregnant with the daughter's embryo.	Intracytoplasmic sperm injection (ICSI) for male infertility is introduced.

Ethical, Legal, and Moral Issues Involved in Reproductive Technology

Many of the reproductive technologies raise ethical, legal, and moral questions with which many scientists and researchers are grappling. Should we be allowed to artificially join the ovum and sperm outside of the uterus? Should gay and lesbian couples use reproductive technologies to become parents? Should stem cell research and embryo cloning continue? Will this one day give rise to the manipulation of certain traits or genes in the creation of a "perfect" baby?

In addition, all of these procedures are very expensive. Expensive technologies produce very expensive children. Does expensive mean "better"? Does this set up higher expectations for these children? Will people be disappointed if their expensive children are difficult in the future? Why are people willing to risk their life savings on having biologically related children when there are children waiting to be adopted?

In addition to these ethical and moral questions, several legal questions have arisen. What should be done with embryos that are fertilized and frozen for later use if a couple separates? Whose property are they? Should they be equitably distributed to both partners? Should they simply be disposed of? Also, because this field is so lucrative, some physicians have been known to perform expensive infertility procedures that may not be necessary.

What do you think about these reproductive techniques? Should a woman be able to "rent" her uterus for the development of someone else's child? Should fertilization be allowed to occur in a petri dish?

Artificial Insemination

Artificial insemination is the process of introducing sperm into a woman's reproductive tract without sexual intercourse. This is a popular option for both heterosexual and homosexual couples. Ejaculated sperm, collected through masturbation, can come from a partner or from a sperm donor. The sperm is then specially treated and washed, and the healthy sperm are extracted. Several samples may be collected from men with a low sperm count to increase the number of healthy sperm. Once washed, sperm can be deposited in the vagina, cervix, uterus (intrauterine), or Fallopian tubes (intratubal).

Men who decide to undergo sterilization or who may become sterile because of surgery or chemotherapy can collect sperm prior to the procedure. Sperm can be frozen for up to 10 years in a **sperm bank.** A vial of sperm from a sperm bank usually costs be-

artificial insemination
Artificially introducing sperm into a woman's reproductive tract.

sperm bank
A storage facility that holds supplies of sperm for future use.

1996	1998	2000	2001	2002
Policy is drawn up by the American Society for Reproductive Medicine on what to do with abandoned embryos. First baby born that was conceived with intracellular sperm injection (ICSI)	First embryonic stem cells isolated.	Preimplantation genetic diagnosis (PGD) is used to select an embryo to create child who can serve as a bone marrow donor to save a sibling.	Congress allocates $900,000 to promote embryo adoption.	Society for Assisted Reproductive Technology study determines that there are 400,000 frozen embryos stored at IVF facilities in the United States.

SOURCE: AFP, American Society for Reproductive Medicine, BBC, Blood lines/PBS, Canadian Broadcast. Co., Christian Medical Association, Fertility & Sterility, Monash IVF.

Will You Father My Child?

My life is not according to plan. I expected that after college, I would get a good job, find a great guy, fall in love, get married, and have 3 kids while establishing a rewarding career—all before the age of 30. In the real world, I have a successful career that I truly enjoy; I've been in love more than once but never married and have no children. At 43 years old I was faced with the biggest decision of my life—having a child on my own. This is something I have discussed with friends and family over the years as a possibility but always hoped it wouldn't be necessary. Although I felt nervous, I also was really excited about my decision. I had tremendous support and encouragement from family, friends, and even my gynecologist.

Michele A. Lewis

Anonymous sperm donation did not appeal to me. I really wanted to know the father; his personality, sense of humor, looks, intelligence, athleticism, and medical history. I did some research into sperm banks and sperm donation and was actually pleasantly surprised at the amount of information each sperm bank provides (such as height, weight, hair color, eye color, ethnicity, education, occupation, family medical history). In many ways, it felt like an online dating service—but still wasn't the route I wanted to take.

Over the years I have floated the idea of fathering a child for me to numerous male friends of mine. I had several interested parties, although my list became much shorter when it came time for the donation. The man I chose has been a friend for a long time (we dated briefly many years ago), he is married with children of his own and is a good father. He is good looking, intelligent, funny, driven, athletic, tall, well-built, and kind. We have agreed to keep his identity secret and that he will not play a role in the child's life—emotionally or financially. We will remain good long-distance friends, and I will always be thankful for his generosity.

My gynecologist referred me to a very successful fertility clinic. I went through a battery of fertility tests and the test results were favorable for a woman my age. The entire process took about a year and the year was full of excitement as well as anguish and disappointment. I estimate that the treatments cost about $30,000 altogether, and my insurance company covered about half these costs, which is pretty good.

After a comprehensive workup, I started fertility drugs. When those didn't work, a combination of fertility drugs was used. After a few months my physician recommended IVF. I was put on a series of drugs which produced several ova and when the time was right, I was scheduled for ova retrieval. I was put under general anesthesia for the retrieval, which took about 45 minutes. The doctor used a needle through my vagina to retrieve the four ova that were available. The lab takes the ova and immediately attempts to fertilize them. Four embryos resulted, but only three survived to be frozen. Unfortunately I was unable to complete the transfer on that cycle because of a uterine polyp that developed that had to be surgically removed. The three embryos were frozen for possible use later on.

After I healed from the outpatient polyp surgery my doctor and I decided to do a new full IVF cycle. Everything seemed like to be going perfectly—the ova retrieval and fertilization resulted in three embryos and all three were transferred to my uterus (the transfer happened three days after the ova retrieval). I was sure I was pregnant and when my period started again I was devastated. Afterwards the doctor counseled me that it was highly unlikely that my eggs would work and that I should consider egg donation or adoption unless I had unlimited funds and the stamina to keep trying. I said I would look into both options but wanted to transfer my frozen embryos as soon as possible.

The transfer took place that cycle. This time my optimism took a negative turn when I became premenstrual. In fact I was so certain it failed that I didn't even bother with a home pregnancy test before going to the doctor for testing on the 12th day. To my surprise, while the nurse was drawing my blood, the urine test showed positive. The nurse and I both started crying for joy. My doctor said I was his oldest patient to get pregnant with her own eggs. As happy and relieved as I was, I tried to keep my joy in check—knowing that miscarriage and genetic abnormalities were not uncommon for someone my age. So I viewed each check-up and test as clearing a hurdle. Even so, the smile didn't leave my face for nine months.

On February 15th I delivered a healthy baby girl. The labor was normal and lasted approximately 22 hours. The father, my mother, sister, and my girlfriend were all there to help me through the delivery. All in all, I feel like I hit the jackpot. Even though life is very different for me today, it is better than I could have ever imagined.

SOURCE: Author's files.

tween $180 and $250. Some couples buy several vials from the same donor so that off-spring can have the same donor father.

A donor may be found through one of the many sperm banks throughout the United States and abroad, usually from an online donor catalog (see Web Resources at the end of this chapter for more information). Once a donor is chosen, the sperm bank will typically send sperm to the physician who will be performing the insemination procedure, but in some cases the sperm is sent directly to the buyer. Prior to the artificial insemination procedure, the doctor often prescribes fertility drugs to increase the chances that there will be healthy ova present when the sperm is introduced.

In Vitro Fertilization

Another reproductive technology is **in vitro fertilization (IVF),** or the creation of a **test-tube baby.** In 1978, Louise Brown, the first test-tube baby, was born in England. Since that time, thousands of babies have been conceived in this fashion. The name is a bit deceiving, however, because these babies are not *born* in a test tube; rather, they are *conceived* in a petri dish, which is a shallow circular dish with a loose-fitting cover.

Many of the women who use this method have Fallopian tube blockage, which prevents fertilization in their tubes. Fertility drugs are usually used before the procedure to help the ovaries release multiple ova, and between four and six ova are retrieved (with the use of microscopic needles inserted into the abdominal cavity). Natural-cycle IVF, in which no fertility drugs are used and immature ova are collected from the ovaries, has also been used (Marcus, 2003). In fact, natural-cycle IVF has been used since the early beginnings of the procedure and was used when Louise Brown was conceived.

After collection, the ova are put into a petri dish and mixed with washed sperm. Once fertilization has occurred, the zygotes are transferred to the woman's uterus, where they should develop normally. Implantation problems with IVF are the biggest hurdle to overcome; it is estimated that only 5% to 30% implant (D. Wells et al., 2002). To increase the chances of implantation, typically several embryos are introduced at one time, which increases the possibility of multiple births. A pregnancy with multiple fetuses may lead to several negative health consequences for both the mother and child, including hypertension, miscarriage, cesarean delivery, low birthweight, and prematurity (Davies, 2005). We will discuss some of these complications later in this chapter.

Preimplantation genetic diagnosis (PGD) can identify embryos that contain gene defects or missing chromosomes (Johannes, 2004; Sher et al., 2005). It is estimated that by 2004, approximately PGD-screened 1,500 babies were born worldwide. A PGD screening costs between $4,000 and $5,000.

in vitro fertilization (IVF)
A procedure in which a woman's ova are removed from her body, fertilized with sperm in a laboratory, and then surgically implanted back into her uterus.

test-tube baby
A slang term for any zygote created by mixing sperm and egg outside a woman's body.

Gamete Intra-Fallopian Tube Transfer

Although **gamete intra-Fallopian tube transfer (GIFT)** is similar to IVF in that ova and sperm are mixed in an artificial environment, the main difference is that with GIFT both the ova and sperm are placed in the Fallopian tube *prior* to fertilization. Fertilization is allowed to occur naturally in the Fallopian tube, rather than in an artificial environment; fertility drugs and sperm washing are also used. This process has resulted in much higher implantation rates.

gamete intra-Fallopian tube transfer (GIFT)
A reproductive technique in which the sperm and ova are collected and injected into the Fallopian tube prior to fertilization.

Zygote Intra-Fallopian Tube Transfer

Similar to both IVF and GIFT, the **zygote intra-Fallopian tube transfer (ZIFT)** procedure allows ova and sperm to meet outside the body, where fertilization occurs. Directly following fertilization, the embryo is placed in the woman's Fallopian tube, allowing it to travel to the uterus and implant naturally. Fertility drugs and sperm washing are also used. This procedure has been found to yield higher implantation rates than IVF but not higher than GIFT.

zygote intra-Fallopian tube transfer (ZIFT)
A reproductive technique in which the sperm and ova are collected and fertilized outside the body, and the fertilized zygote is then placed into the Fallopian tube.

Zonal Dissection

Sometimes ova are resistant to fertilization due to problems with the enzyme in the head of the sperm, which is supposed to break down the hard outer covering of the ovum and allow fertilization. Zonal dissection involves drilling a microscopic hole in the ovum with a very small needle, making a small slit in the side of the jellylike coating, or using a chemical to dissolve the outer shell. Unfortunately, one drawback to this procedure is that several sperm may enter the ovum and cause developmental problems in the resulting embryo.

Intracellular Sperm Injections

Intracytoplasmic sperm injection (ICSI)
Fertility procedure that involves mechanically injecting a sperm into the center of an ovum.

© The Record/Corbis Sygma

Intracytoplasmic sperm injection (ICSI) was first introduced in 1992, with the first successful baby delivered in 1996 (Li et al., 1997). In 2005, ICSI was the most common form of infertility treatment used in Australia (Persson, 2005). This technology involves injecting a single sperm into the center of an ovum under a microscope. It was developed to help couples who could not use IVF due to low sperm counts or sperm motility. Usually ejaculated sperm are used, but sperm can also be removed from the epididymis or the testes (Van Steirteghem et al., 1998).

Results have been promising so far (pregnancy rates of approximately 52%), but there have been some difficulties (Simpson & Lamb, 2001). The ovum can be damaged during the procedure, and research indicates that ICSI may lead to an increased risk of genetic defect, which may be due to the fact that ICSI eliminates many of the natural barriers to conception, increasing the transmission of abnormal genes (Al-Shawaf et al., 2005). Scientists do not know how nature chooses one sperm for fertilization, and choosing one randomly may not be appropriate, though physicians usually try to pick one that appears vigorous and healthy.

Oocyte and Embryo Transplants

Some women may not be able to produce healthy ova due to ovarian failure or age-related infertility. For these women, oocyte (egg) and embryo donation have been successful. Live birth rates for oocyte and embryo donation range from 25% to 35% (Sauer et al., 1995). An embryo transplant involves artificial insemination of a donor's ovum with the male partner's sperm. After fertilization has occurred, the embryo is transferred to the female partner's uterus. To be successful, it is imperative that fertility drugs be used to synchronize both women's menstrual cycles. Preliminary research shows that ovum donation offers even higher success rates than natural conception (Remohi et al., 1997).

Surrogate Parenting

surrogate parenting
Use of a woman who, through artificial insemination or in vitro fertilization, gestates a fetus for another woman or man.

For women who have healthy ova but cannot sustain a pregnancy to term, **surrogate parenting** is an option. The couple's sperm and ovum are combined, and the zygote is implanted in another woman, called a gestational carrier. One gestational carrier relates her experiences:

> It's wonderful being a carrier. It's not easy, but it's wonderful. You feel all the emotions, it's like a roller coaster. You try to help the parents cope; but, at the same time, you're trying to deal with your own emotions. I feel very proud when I see the little one I carried—I love watching him with his parents; it's so overwhelming sometimes. They gave him life; I sustained that life and gave birth to him. It's wonderful. A very good high; I could burst with pride sometimes just watching him. (Author's files)

surrogate mother
A woman who donates her ovum (which is fertilized by the father's sperm) and then carries the zygote to term.

Women who can neither sustain a pregnancy nor produce their own ova may arrange to have another woman's ova fertilized by the father's sperm. The woman who carries the fetus is called a **surrogate mother.** At birth, the child is given to the noncarrying woman and her partner.

Other Options

Other options for infertility involve the freezing of embryos and sperm for later fertilization. This can be beneficial for men and women who are diagnosed with illnesses (such as cancer) whose treatment might interfere with their ability to manufacture healthy sperm or ova (recall Lance Armstrong's story in Chapter 5, Sex in Real Life, "Testicular Cancer," on page 151). Sperm can be frozen and stored in liquid nitrogen for many years through a process called **sperm cryopreservation.**

The sperm can be collected from the testis, epididymis, or from an ejaculate. The effectiveness of the sperm, once thawed, is variable, and sometimes the sperm do not survive the thawing process. **Embryo cryopreservation** is also possible; but, like sperm, not all embryos can survive the freezing and thawing process.

Recently, researchers in several countries have been experimenting with **ova cryopreservation.** Originally the intention was to thaw and fertilize frozen ova for IVF or ICSI. Large numbers of immature ova can be retrieved from unstimulated ovaries, whereas mature ova can be retrieved only after the use of fertility drugs (Hardy et al., 2002). The practice of ova freezing has been difficult because the ova seem to be vulnerable to chromosomal damage by freezing (Gosden, 2005; Wininger & Kort, 2002). If this procedure is successful, women who choose to delay childbearing until later in life could store ova while they are young. It could also give women who must undergo radiation and/or chemotherapy for cancer an option to save ova for a later pregnancy (Roberts & Oktay, 2005). At this time, only sperm and embryos are routinely frozen for use later on.

sperm cryopreservation
The freezing of sperm for later use.

embryo cryopreservation
The freezing of embryos for later use.

ova cryopreservation
The freezing of ova for later use.

Review Question
Identify and explain at least five of the assisted reproductive options available.

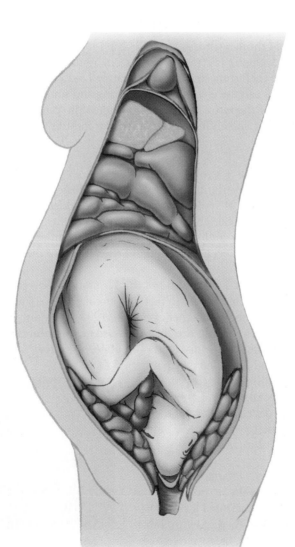

Figure 12.3
The fetus in place in the uterus.

Question: Do physicians ever mix up ova or embryos during embryo transplants? How do they know whose is whose?

Embryos are rarely mixed up because collection requirements are strictly followed. However, even using these methods, accidents can happen. In late 1998, there was a case of African-American and white twin boys born to a white couple who had undergone an embryo transplant in New York. In 2002, African-American twins were born to a white couple. Both of these were the result of embryo mix-ups during implantation. In many such cases, the offspring are returned to the biological parents if possible, and the birthing parents are given visitation rights. What is really interesting about these cases is that the main reason physicians knew there was a mix-up was because of skin color. How many cases go undetected when skin color isn't a giveaway?

A HEALTHY PREGNANCY

trimester
A term of three months; pregnancies usually consist of three trimesters.

Pregnancy is divided into three periods called **trimesters.** Throughout these trimesters important fetal development occurs as a pregnant woman's body changes and adjusts to these developments. We will now explore these changes.

The Prenatal Period: Three Trimesters

Although you would think a trimester would be a 3-month period, because pregnancies are dated from the woman's last menstrual period, a full-term pregnancy is actually 40 weeks, and therefore each trimester is approximately 12–15 weeks long. Throughout the pregnancy, physicians can use electronic monitoring and **sonography,** or **ultrasound,** to check on the status of the fetus. We will now discuss the physical development of the typical, healthy mother and child in each of these trimesters.

sonography
Electronic monitoring; also called ultrasound.

ultrasound
The use of ultrasonic waves to monitor a developing fetus; also called sonography.

First Trimester

The first trimester includes the first 13 weeks of pregnancy (1 to 13 weeks). It is the trimester in which the most important embryonic development takes place. When a woman becomes pregnant, her entire system adjusts. Her heart pumps more blood, her weight increases, her lungs and digestive system work harder, and her thyroid gland grows. All of these changes occur to encourage the growth of the developing fetus.

Prenatal Development   By the end of the 1st month of pregnancy, the fetal heart is formed and begins to pump blood. In fact, the circulatory system is the first organ system to function in the embryo (Rischer & Easton, 1992). In addition, many of the other major systems develop, including the digestive system, beginnings of the brain, spinal cord, nervous system, muscles, arms, legs, eyes, fingers, and toes. By 14 weeks the liver, kidneys, intestines, and lungs have begun to develop. In addition, the circulatory and urinary systems are operating, and the reproductive organs have developed. By the end of the first trimester, the fetus weighs ½ ounce and is approximately 3 inches long.

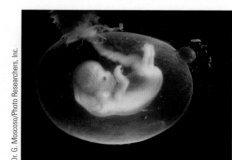

An embryo at 7 to 8 weeks. This embryo is approximately 1 inch long.

Changes in the Pregnant Mother During the first few weeks of pregnancy, a woman's body adjusts to increased levels of estrogen and progesterone. As we saw in Table 12.1, this can cause fatigue, breast tenderness, constipation, increased urination, and nausea and/or vomiting. Some women experience nausea and vomiting so severe during pregnancy that they must be hospitalized due to weight loss and malnutrition (S.W. Simpson et al., 2001). Specific food cravings are normal, as is an increased sensitivity to smells and odors.

Although some women feel physically uncomfortable because of all these changes, many also feel excited and happy about the life growing within them. The final, confirming sign of pregnancy—a fetal heartbeat—can be a joyous moment that offsets all the discomforts of pregnancy. The fetal heartbeat can usually be heard through ultrasound by the end of the first trimester.

Since its introduction in 1950, ultrasound has become a very useful tool in obstetrics. It can capture images of the embryo for measurement as early as 5½ weeks into the pregnancy, and a heartbeat can be seen by 6 weeks. Fetal heartbeat can also be heard through a stethoscope at approximately 9 to 10 weeks and after a heartbeat is either seen or heard, the probability of miscarriage drops significantly. Ultrasounds help to confirm a pregnancy, rule out abnormalities, indicate gestational age, and confirm multiple pregnancies. Newer three-dimensional and even four-dimensional ultrasounds have been introduced and will become more mainstream in the next few years.

Second Trimester

The second trimester includes the second 15 weeks of pregnancy (weeks 14 to 28). The fetus looks noticeably more human.

Prenatal Development   The fetus grows dramatically during the second trimester and by the end of the trimester is 13 inches long. He or she has developed tooth buds and reflexes, such as sucking and swallowing. Though the gender of the fetus is determined at conception, it is not immediately apparent during development. If the baby is positioned correctly during ultrasound, gender may be determined as early as 16 weeks, although most of the time it is not possible until 20 to 22 weeks.

During the second trimester, the mother will often feel the fetus moving around inside her uterus. Soft hair, called **lanugo** (lan-NEW-go), and a waxy substance, known as **vernix,** both cover the fetus's body. These may develop to protect the fetus from the constant exposure to the amniotic fluid. By the end of the second trimester, the fetus will weigh about 1¾ pounds. If birth takes place at the end of the second trimester, the baby may be able to survive with intensive medical care. We discuss premature birth later in this chapter.

lanugo
The downy covering of hair over a fetus.

vernix
Cheesy substance that coats the fetus in the uterus.

Changes in the Pregnant Mother   During the second trimester, nausea begins to subside as the body adjusts to the increased hormonal levels. Breast sensitivity also tends to decrease. However, fatigue may continue, as well as an increase in appetite, heartburn, edema (ankle or leg swelling), and a noticeable vaginal discharge. Skin pigmentation changes can occur on the face. As the uterus grows larger and the blood circulation slows down, constipation and muscle cramps bother some women. Internally, the cervix turns a deep red, almost violet color, due to an increased blood supply.

As the pregnancy progresses, the increasing size of the uterus and the restriction of the pelvic veins can cause more swelling of the ankles. Increased problems with varicose veins and hemorrhoids may also occur. Fetal movement is often felt in the second trimester, sometimes as early as the 16th week. Usually women can feel movement earlier in their second or subsequent pregnancies because they know what fetal movement feels like.

The second trimester of pregnancy is usually the most positive time for the mother. The early physiological signs of pregnancy such as morning sickness and fatigue lessen, and the mother-to-be finally feels better physically. This improvement in physical health also leads to positive psychological feelings including excitement, happiness, and a sense of well-being. Many women report an increased sex drive during the second trimester, and for many couples, it is a period of high sexual satisfaction.

As the developing fetus begins to move around, many women feel reassured after anxiously wondering whether the fetus was developing at all. In fact, many women report that the kicking and moving about of the developing fetus is very comforting. Finally, the transition to maternity clothes often results in more positive feelings, probably because it is now obvious and public knowledge that the woman is pregnant.

Neil Bromhall/Photo Researchers, Inc.

At 5 months, the fetus is becoming more and more lively. It can turn its head, move its face, and make breathing movements. This fetus is approximately 9 inches long.

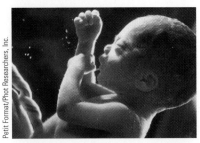

The fetus at 9 months, ready for birth.

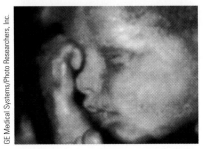

Newer ultrasound technology allows a developing fetus to be viewed in three dimensions and in real-time motion.

Braxton-Hicks contractions
Intermittent contractions of the uterus after the third month of pregnancy.

colostrum
A thin, yellowish fluid, high in protein and antibodies, secreted from the nipples at the end of pregnancy and during the first few days after delivery.

Review Question

Trace prenatal development and changes in the pregnant mother throughout the three trimesters of pregnancy.

sex byte

Healthy babies who are born to girls 15 years old or younger have three to four times higher risk of dying from sudden infant death syndrome (SIDS) before they turn 1 year old than do babies born to older mothers (Phipps et al., 2002).

Third Trimester

The third trimester includes the final weeks of pregnancy (weeks 28 to 40) and ends with the birth of a child.

Prenatal Development   By the end of the 7th month, the fetus begins to develop fat deposits. She or he can react to pain, light, and sounds. Some fetuses develop occasional hiccups or begin to suck their thumb. If a baby is born at the end of the 7th month, there is a good chance of survival. In the 8th month, the majority of the organ systems are well developed, although the brain continues to grow. By the end of the 8th month, the fetus is 15 inches long and weighs about 3 pounds. During the third trimester, there is often stronger and more frequent fetal movement, which will slow down toward the 9th month (because the fetus will have less room to move around). At birth, an infant on average weighs 7½ pounds and is 20 inches long.

Changes in the Pregnant Mother   Many of the symptoms from the second trimester continue, with constipation and heartburn increasing in frequency. Backaches, leg cramps, increases in varicose veins, hemorrhoids, sleep problems, shortness of breath, and **Braxton-Hicks contractions** often occur. At first these contractions are scattered and relatively painless (the uterus hardens for a moment and then returns to normal). In the 8th and 9th months, the Braxton-Hicks contractions become stronger. A thin, yellowish liquid called **colostrum** (kuh-LAHS-trum) may be secreted from the nipples as the breasts prepare to produce milk for breast-feeding. Toward the end of the third trimester, many women feel an increase in apprehension about labor and delivery; impatience and restlessness are common.

The Father's Experience

For men, pregnancy can be a time of joy and anticipation—but also of stress and anxiety. Feelings about parenting in combination with the many changes their partners are undergoing can all add to men's feelings of vulnerability.

In the United States today, fathers are allowed and encouraged to participate in the birth. However, this was not always the case. At one time, fathers were told to go to the waiting room and sit until the baby was born. In some other cultures, such as in Bang Chan, Thailand, the father aids in the actual birth of his child (Dunham et al., 1992). The role of the father in pregnancy varies among cultures. Some fathers are required to remain on a strict diet during the course of the pregnancy or to cater to their partner's food cravings at all times.

SEX Talk

Question: Do men ever feel left out because the woman gets all the attention while she is pregnant?

Some do. However, it is important to keep in mind that both mothers- and fathers-to-be share the pregnancy experience, both the excitement and the fears. Many years ago, male involvement in pregnancy and birth ended once a sperm fertilized the ovum. Today, many physicians recommend that fathers be included in many aspects of the pregnancy experience. They can go to the monthly obstetrician appointments with their partner, help out with their partner's special diet needs by preparing and eating healthy foods with her, read as many books as possible on pregnancy, talk to friends who have children about their experiences, talk to the baby while it is still in the womb, help shop for necessary baby items, take childbirth classes with their partner, and coach the mother through the birth itself. Overall, probably the most important thing that parents-to-be can do is to be open and honest about their feelings and communicate with each other.

There are many things a pregnant woman can do to be healthy during her pregnancy, including participating in physical exercise, getting good nutrition, and avoiding drugs and alcohol. Women often maintain sexual interest during pregnancy, although it may begin to wane during the third trimester.

Exercise and Nutrition

How much exercise should a woman get during pregnancy? Many physicians strongly advise light exercise during pregnancy; it has been found to result in a greater sense of well-being, shorter labor, and fewer obstetric problems (Wang & Apgar, 1998). However, although participation in ongoing exercise throughout pregnancy can enhance birth weight, severe exercise can result in a low-birth-weight baby (Pivarnik, 1998). Most healthcare providers agree that a woman's exercise routine should not exceed prepregnancy levels. If a woman exercised vigorously prior to her pregnancy, keeping up with a moderate amount of exercise during the pregnancy is fine.

Although it is true that pregnant women are "cardiovascularly challenged" early in pregnancy, it is a myth that too much exercise may cause a miscarriage or harm the developing fetus. Hundreds of pregnant women learned this prior to the legalization of abortion when they tried to exercise excessively or punch their abdomens in an unsuccessful attempt to dislodge the fertilized ovum. The implanted embryo is difficult to dislodge.

However, there are certain sports that should be avoided during pregnancy, such as water skiing, scuba diving, vigorous racquet sports, contact sports, and horseback riding, because these may cause injuries in both the mother and her fetus. Water exercise may be the best form of exercise for a pregnant woman because it causes fewer maternal and fetal heart rate changes and lower maternal blood pressure than land exercise (Katz, 1996). This is primarily due to a water-induced increase in circulating blood volume.

Physical stresses, such as prolonged standing, long work hours, and heavy lifting, can also affect a pregnancy. These stresses can reduce blood flow to the uterus, resulting in lower birth weights and prematurity (Clapp, 1996). It is also very important to drink lots of water during pregnancy because water is an essential nutrient and important for all bodily functions.

SEX Talk

Question: I've heard women say that if the average baby weighs about 7 pounds, then they will gain no more than 10 pounds during pregnancy. Is that safe? How small a weight gain is considered healthy? What about anorexics and bulimics?

It is estimated that a pregnant woman of average size should gain between 31 and 40 pounds throughout a pregnancy. Underweight women should gain between 36 and 40 pounds, whereas overweight women should gain between 26 and 30 pounds (Bracero & Byrne, 1998). This accounts for the fetus, amniotic fluid, placenta, breasts, and muscle and fat increases. Gaining less than this is not healthy for either the developing baby or the mother—and may actually predispose a baby to obesity later in life (because fetuses learn to restrict calories in the womb, but when nutrition is readily available, overeating is likely). In addition, too little weight gain during pregnancy has also been found to be related to a higher blood pressure in offspring once they reach early childhood (P. M. Clark et al., 1998). Anyone who has an eating disorder should consult with her healthcare provider before getting pregnant to determine an appropriate weight gain. If the nutritional requirements cannot be met, a woman should postpone pregnancy.

Nutritional requirements during pregnancy call for extra protein, iron, calcium, folic acid, and vitamin B$_6$ (found in foods such as milk, yogurt, beef, legumes, and dried fruits). In addition, it is important for a woman to increase her caloric intake during pregnancy. Failure to follow these nutritional requirements may result in low-birth-weight children or even spontaneous abortion.

Research indicates that poor nutrition during pregnancy may also have long-term consequences for the infant's risk of cardiovascular disease, hypertension, and diabetes (Godfrey et al., 1996). Fetuses who are forced to adapt to a limited supply of nutrients permanently "reprogram" their physiology and metabolism (Barker, 1997). In fact, in areas where food sources are limited, such as Sri Lanka or Bangladesh, the incidence of low-birth-weight deliveries ranges from 25% to 50% (compared to fewer than 7% in the United States; Gopalan, 1996). In addition, the majority of children in these areas suffer from mild to moderate forms of growth retardation.

During the second trimester, a woman is advised to increase her caloric intake by 300 calories per day, and protein requirements increase. For vegetarians, it is necessary to increase consumption of vegetables, whole grains, nuts, seeds, and also include a protein supplement to help ensure adequate protein intake. An increase in calcium is also needed to help with bone calcification of the growing fetus. Because a woman's blood volume increases as much as 50% during pregnancy, iron may be diluted in the blood; thus many pregnant women are advised to take prenatal vitamins, which include iron supplements.

Drugs and Alcohol

There are several substances that physicians recommend to avoid during pregnancy, including caffeine, nicotine, alcohol, marijuana, and other drugs (the accompanying Human Sexuality in a Diverse World, "Avoid the Sun?," describes activities that women in other cultures are told to avoid). All of these substances can cross the placenta, enter into the developing fetus's bloodstream, and cause physical or mental deficiencies. **Fetal alcohol syndrome (FAS),** a condition associated with alcohol intake, occurs when a woman drinks heavily during pregnancy, producing an infant with irreversible physical and mental disabilities. Even women who drink very little put their developing babies at risk. Presently, experts agree that there is no safe level of alcohol use during pregnancy.

It is estimated that 11% of U.S. women smoke cigarettes throughout their pregnancy (Centers for Disease Control and Prevention, 2004c). Smoking during pregnancy

Human Sexuality in a Diverse World

Avoid the Sun?

In the United States, most physicians recommend that pregnant women avoid substances such as alcohol, tobacco, and drugs and certain dangerous activities such as scuba diving and horseback riding. However, in other cultures, there are several additional activities that are avoided. These include:

• Lying too long in the sun, which may cause the baby to melt (Ibo, Nigeria).
• Eating hot food or drinking hot liquid, which may scald the fetus (East Africa).
• Sitting in front of a door for an extended period, which may cause the baby to have a big mouth and to cry too much (Java, Indonesia).

• Sleeping on one's back, which may cause the umbilical cord to wrap around the baby's neck (Bariba, People's Republic of Benin).
• Hanging the washing out, which may cause the umbilical cord to become knotted (Navajo Indians, United States).
• Gazing at the eclipse of the moon, which may cause a baby to be born with a cleft palate (Aztecs, Mexico).

SOURCE: Adapted from Dunham et al., 1992, p. 41.

has been associated with spontaneous abortion, low birth weight, prematurity, and low iron levels (Martin et al., 2005; Pandey et al., 2005). In addition, it increases the risk of vascular damage to the developing baby's brain and has been found to interfere with a male's future ability to manufacture sperm (Storgaard et al., 2003). Fathers, friends, relatives, and strangers who smoke around a pregnant woman jeopardize the future health of a developing baby.

Pregnancy in Women Over 30

Until the late 1980s, the majority of women had their first child in their early or mid-20s. Today, more and more women are delaying childbearing because of educational or career goals. Over the last few years, it has become common for women to delay having children until they are 35 or older (Tough et el., 2002). In the United States, from 1970 to 1990 the proportion of first births increased 100% among women 30 to 39 years old and 50% among women who were 40 to 44 years old (Bianco et al., 1996). In 2000, 13% of all U.S. births were to women 35 and older (J. A. Martin et al., 2001).

Delayed pregnancy does carry some risks, which include an increase in spontaneous abortion, first-trimester bleeding, low birth weight, increased labor time and rate of **cesarean (si-ZAIR-ee-un) section (c-section),** and chromosomal abnormalities (Tough et al., 2002). The likelihood of a chromosomal abnormality increases each year in women over 30 and in men over 55. Remember that a woman is born with a set number of follicles that will develop into ova. As she ages, so do her follicles. There is also a sharp decline in the ability to get pregnant after the age of 40 (Feinman, 1997). On any day of her menstrual cycle, the probability that a woman who is younger than 27 years old will get pregnant is twice as high as it is for a woman who is over the age of 35 (Dunson et al., 2002).

Because of this, women over 40 have a higher chance of achieving pregnancy from ovum donation than they do using their own aged ova (Lim & Tsakok, 1997). Even so, the use of assisted reproductive technologies by older women has raised some interesting questions. In the mid-1990s, Arceli Keh, who had been married for 16 years and had no children, lied about her age at an infertility clinic in order to be considered for embryo transplants. She claimed she was 50 years old when she entered the program. Because of her age, she underwent an extensive medical workup before entering the oocyte donation program. All medical tests supported the fact that her chronological age was 50 years old. Although the first embryo transfer resulted in a miscarriage at 8 weeks, the next transfer resulted in a pregnancy. During her first obstetric visit at 13 weeks, she informed her physician that she was really 10 years older than the age she had given previously. Soon it was revealed that her true age was 63 years at the time of the embryo transplant. She underwent a cesarean section at 38 weeks and delivered a healthy 6 pound, 4 ounce baby girl. The media provided extensive coverage, and many people questioned both the woman's and the clinic's ethics.

Older men are also becoming fathers, but with much less media coverage. Tony Randall became a first-time father in 1997 at the age of 77, but it did not result in the public debate that Arceli Keh's case did. Oftentimes, late fatherhood is seen as a sign of masculinity for a man, but late motherhood is viewed with more skepticism and condemnation. Why do you think this might be?

Sex During Pregnancy

In some cultures, sex during pregnancy is strongly recommended because it is believed that the father's semen is necessary for proper development of the fetus (Dunham et al., 1992). In the United States, many women continue to have satisfying sexual relations during pregnancy. In an uncomplicated pregnancy, sexual intercourse during pregnancy is safe for most mothers and the developing child up until the last several weeks of pregnancy. During a woman's first pregnancy, sexual interest is often decreased because of physical changes, including nausea and fatigue. Fluctuations in men's sexual interest during the pregnancy are very normal as well. Some men fear injury to the fetus during

Review Question

Explain the importance of avoiding drugs and alcohol during pregnancy.

sex byte

Men who use recreational drugs have been found to have more abnormalities in their sperm compared to those who do not, leading to an increase in birth defects in their offspring (Pollard, 2000).

cesarean section (c-section)
A surgical procedure in which the woman's abdomen and uterus are surgically opened and a child is removed; used when vaginal birth may endanger a mother and/or child.

Review Question

Discuss the reasons women are delaying pregnancy more often these days. What are the risks?

New research on brain physiology has found that when a baby gazes and smiles at its mother, activity in the mother's brain region associated with emotion processing increases (Nitschke et al., 2004). This brain region may be responsible for maternal attachment.

Review Question

Discuss the changes in women's sex interest during pregnancy.

sexual activity. Others report increases in sexual desire and find their pregnant partner particularly sexy and attractive.

Orgasm during pregnancy is also safe in an uncomplicated pregnancy, but occasionally it may cause painful uterine contractions. Cunnilingus can also be safely engaged in during pregnancy, although changes in vaginal aroma and discharge may make couples uncomfortable. As we discussed in Chapter 10, air should never be blown into the vagina of a pregnant woman because it could cause an air embolism, which could be fatal.

Sexual interest and satisfaction usually begins to subside as the woman and fetus grow during the third trimester (Gokyildiz & Beji, 2005). The increasing size of the abdomen puts pressure on many of the internal organs and also makes certain sexual positions difficult. During the first and part of the second trimester, the male-on-top position is used most often during sexual intercourse. However, later in pregnancy, the side-by-side, rear-entry, and female-on-top positions are used more frequently because they take the weight and pressure off the uterus. The main reasons that the frequency of sexual activity declines are physical discomfort, fear of fetal injury, awkwardness, or physician recommendation.

PROBLEMS IN THE PREGNANCY

The majority of women go through their pregnancy without any problems. However, understanding how complex the process of pregnancy is, it should not come as a surprise that occasionally something goes wrong. We will now discuss some of these problems.

Ectopic Pregnancy

Most zygotes travel through the Fallopian tubes and end up in the uterus. In an ectopic pregnancy, the zygote implants outside of the uterus (see Figure 12.4). Ninety-seven percent of ectopic pregnancies occur when the fertilized ovum implants in the Fallopian

Figure 12.4
In an ectopic pregnancy, the fertilized ovum implants outside the uterus. In most cases, it remains inside the Fallopian tube.

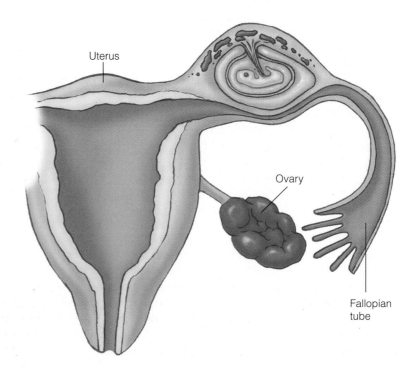

Uterus

Ovary

Fallopian tube

tube. These are called tubal pregnancies. The remaining 3% occur in the abdomen, cervix, or ovaries. Approximately 2% (1 in 50) of all U.S. pregnancies are ectopic, and this number has been steadily increasing in the past 2 decades. This is primarily due to increases in the incidence of pelvic inflammatory disease caused by chlamydia infections (Tay et al., 2000).

Prior to the 19th century, half of all women with an ectopic pregnancy died. But then doctors began surgical intervention and as a result, by the end of the 20th century only 5% of women with ectopic pregnancy died (Sepilian & Wood, 2004). Today the survival rate is increasing, even though the rates of ectopic pregnancy are increasing as well.

What contributes to the likelihood of an ectopic pregnancy? Research indicates that smokers may be at increased risk for ectopic pregnancies. Nicotine has been found to change the tubal contractions and muscular tone of the Fallopian tubes, which may lead to tubal inactivity, delayed ovum entry into the uterus, and changes in the tubes' ability to transport the ovum (Handler et al., 1989). Sexually transmitted infections may also cause ectopic pregnancies (Ankum et al., 1996).

The effects of ectopic pregnancy can be quite serious. Because the Fallopian tubes, cervix, and abdomen are not designed to support a growing fetus, when a growing fetus implants in one of these places, it can cause a rupture, causing internal hemorrhaging and possibly death. Symptoms of ectopic pregnancy include abdominal pain (usually on the side of the body that has the tubal pregnancy), cramping, pelvic pain, vaginal bleeding, nausea, dizziness, and fainting (Tay et al., 2000). Future reproductive potential is also affected by ectopic pregnancy. A woman who has experienced an ectopic pregnancy is at higher risk for developing another ectopic in future pregnancies (Sepilian & Wood, 2004). Today physicians can monitor pregnancies through ultrasound and HCG levels, and many ectopic pregnancies can be treated without surgery (Wiseman, 2003).

Spontaneous Abortion

A spontaneous abortion, or **miscarriage,** is a natural termination of a pregnancy before the time that the fetus can live on its own. Approximately 10% of all diagnosed pregnancies end in miscarriage, and 20% to 40% of pregnancies end before a pregnancy diagnosis is made. Miscarriages can also occur during the second and third trimesters of pregnancy, although the percentage drops dramatically after the first trimester. A miscarriage can be very difficult emotionally for both the woman and her partner, although research has found that men experience less intense emotional symptoms for a shorter period of time (Abboud & Liamputtong, 2003).

miscarriage
A pregnancy that terminates on its own; also referred to as a spontaneous abortion.

In a significant number of miscarriages, there is some chromosomal abnormality (Christiansen, 1996), which is more common in older women (Bulletti et al., 1996). The body somehow knows that there is a problem in the developing fetus and rejects it. In other cases, in which there are no chromosomal problems, the uterus may be too small, too weak, or abnormally shaped, or the miscarriage may be caused by maternal stress, nutritional deficiencies, excessive vitamin A, drug exposure, or pelvic infection.

Symptoms of miscarriage include vaginal bleeding, cramps, and lower back pain. Usually a normal menstrual period returns within 3 months after a miscarriage, and future pregnancies may be perfectly normal. However, some women experience continual spontaneous abortions, often due to anatomic, endocrine, hormonal, genetic, and/or chromosomal abnormalities (Bick et al., 1998), and problems with defective sperm (Carrell et al., 2003). Tests are being developed to try to predict when a spontaneous abortion will occur.

Chromosomal Abnormalities

We have already discussed amniocentesis, which identifies chromosomal abnormalities in the 16th to 17th weeks of pregnancy. But many women elect to undergo a **chorionic villus sampling (CVS) test,** which can be done between the 10th and 15th weeks. In this procedure, a sliver of tissue from the chorion (the tissue that develops into the placenta) is removed and checked for chromosomal abnormalities.

chorionic villus sampling (CVS)
The sampling and testing of the chorion for fetal abnormalities.

TABLE 12.3	Mother's Age and Risk of Chromosomal Abnormality

Statistics give you an idea of how a mother's age can affect her chances of having a baby with chromosomal abnormalities.

Age of Mother	Risk of Any Chromosomal Abnormality
20	1 in 526
25	1 in 476
30	1 in 384
35	1 in 192
40	1 in 66
45	1 in 21
49	1 in 8

SOURCE: Data based on information in Hook, 1981, and Hook et al., 1983.

maternal-serum alpha-fetoprotein screening (MSAFP)
A blood test used during early pregnancy to determine neural tube defects such as spina bifida or anencephaly.

spina bifida
A congenital defect of the vertebral column in which the halves of the neural arch of a vertebra fail to fuse in the midline.

anencephaly
Congenital absence of most of the brain and spinal cord.

Down syndrome
A problem occurring on the 21st chromosome of the developing fetus that can cause mental retardation and physical challenges.

Rhogam
A drug given to mothers whose Rh is incompatible with the fetus; prevents the formation of antibodies that can imperil future pregnancies.

Down syndrome, a chromosomal defect, can cause mental retardation and the characteristics of slanted eyes and flat face.

There are drawbacks to CVS, however. Some CVS tests will result in a false positive because the sample may have a different chromosomal composition than the fetus. In addition, there is an increased risk of miscarriage and limb reduction/deformities with this test. However, the risk to fetal limbs is reduced when CVS is performed after 9 weeks gestation. As a result, CVS at most institutions is performed after the 10th week (Mastroiacovo, 1992). Overall, the CVS test is viewed as the "gold standard" sampling method for genetic testing because it can be performed earlier in pregnancy than other tests (Brambati & Tului, 2005).

Another test, the **maternal-serum alpha-fetoprotein screening (MSAFP),** is used to detect defects such as **spina bifida** (SPY-na BIF-id-uh) or **anencephaly** (an-en-SEH-fuh-lee). MSAFP is a simple blood test done between the 16th and 18th weeks of pregnancy. However, due to this test's high frequency of false positive test results, second screenings are recommended. Finally, a blood sample can also be collected from the umbilical cord anytime after 18 weeks of pregnancy, and a chromosome analysis can be done (Berkow et al., 2000). All of these tests allow healthcare providers to detect fetal abnormalities.

The risk of chromosomal abnormalities increases as a woman ages, and chromosomal abnormalities can result in many different problems (see Table 12.3). Sometimes physicians are certain of where the chromosomal problem lies and how it will manifest itself; at other times, they just don't know. The most common chromosomal abnormality appears in the 21st chromosome and is known as **Down syndrome.** In Down syndrome, an extra chromosome has been added to the 21st chromosome; although most of us have 46 chromosomes (23 from each parent), a person with Down syndrome has 47. Down syndrome occurs in 1 out of every 1,000 live births.

Down syndrome is often blamed on ova that have aged. For that reason, older parents are at greater risk for Down syndrome children than younger parents. But it can also be due to deficient sperm. It is estimated that 25% of Down syndrome cases can be traced to defective sperm. A child with Down syndrome often exhibits low muscle tone, a flat facial profile, slanted eyes, mental retardation, and an enlarged tongue. There are also many long-term health concerns including increased risk of congenital heart defects, respiratory infections, Alzheimer's, and leukemia (National Down Syndrome Society, 2005). In 2005, a study on over 38,000 U.S. women found that a first-trimester screening test, combining a blood test with an ultrasound, can detect Down syndrome 11 weeks after conception (Malone et al., 2005). This test was based on research from a $15 million, 8-year study published in 2005. Although research has been in progress on first-trimester testing (Nicolaides et al., 2005; Orlandi et al., 2005), testing for Down syndrome typically had involved waiting for a CVS (10th- to 15th-week) or amniocentisis (16th- to 17th-week) test.

Rh Incompatibility

The Rh factor naturally exists on some people's red blood cells. If your blood type is followed by "+," you are "Rh positive," and if not, you are "Rh negative." This is important when you are having a blood transfusion or when pregnant.

A father who is Rh positive often passes on his blood type to the baby. If the baby's mother is Rh negative, any of the fetal blood that comes into contact with hers (which happens during delivery, not pregnancy) will cause her to begin to manufacture antibodies against the fetal blood. This may be very dangerous for any future pregnancies. Because the mother has made antibodies to Rh-positive blood, she will reject the fetal Rh-positive blood, which can lead to fetal death. After an Rh-negative woman has delivered, she is given **Rhogam** (row-GAM), which prevents antibodies from forming and ensures that her future pregnancies will be healthy. Rhogam is also given if an Rh-negative pregnant woman has an amniocentesis, miscarriage, or abortion.

Toxemia

In the last 2 to 3 months of pregnancy, 6% to 7% of women experience **toxemia** (tock-SEE-mee-uh), or **preeclampsia** (pre-ee-CLAMP-see-uh). Symptoms include rapid weight gain, fluid retention, an increase in blood pressure, and protein in the urine. If toxemia is allowed to progress, it can result in **eclampsia,** which involves convulsions, coma, and, in approximately 15% of cases, death. Eclampsia is a leading cause of maternal and fetal death in the United States today (Lipstein et al., 2003). These conditions, which occur primarily in women who neglect good prenatal care, are relatively rare in women with good medical care. Overall, African American women are at higher risk for eclampsia (MacKay et al., 2001).

One study found that the longer a woman has a monogamous relationship before she conceives, the less likely she is to develop preeclampsia and eclampsia (D. A. Clark, 1994). It has been suggested that longer relationships will produce a female immune response to certain chemicals in the sperm that may lead to complications with preeclampsia. Women whose mother experienced preeclampsia are more likely to experience preeclampsia in their own pregnancies, and male offspring from mothers with preeclampsia are twice as likely to father children through a preeclampsia pregnancy as are men who were born from a normal pregnancy (Seppa, 2001).

toxemia
A form of blood poisoning caused by kidney disturbances.

preeclampsia
A condition of hypertension during pregnancy, typically accompanied by leg swelling and other symptoms.

eclampsia
A progression of toxemia with similar, but worsening, conditions.

Review Question

Discuss the various problems that can occur in pregnancy, and explain how these problems might develop.

CHILDBIRTH

The average length of a pregnancy is 9 months, but a normal birth can occur 3 weeks before or 2 weeks after the due date. It is estimated that only 4% of American babies are born exactly on the due date predicted (Dunham et al., 1992). Early delivery may occur in cases in which the mother has exercised throughout the pregnancy, the fetus is female, or the mother has shorter menstrual cycles (R. Jones, 1984).

No one really knows why, but there is also a seasonal variation in human birth. More babies are born between July and October (meaning that more conceptions occur during the late fall and early winter). It has been hypothesized that this evolved because of the increased food supply available during the late summer and early fall months (although perhaps more couples engage in sexual intercourse to keep warm in the cold winter months!). There are also more babies born between the hours of 1 and 7 A.M., and again this is thought to have evolved because of the increased protection and decreased chances of predator attacks (R. Jones, 1984).

We do not know exactly what starts the birth process. It appears that in fetal sheep there is a chemical in the brain that signals it is time for birth (Palca, 1991). Perhaps this may also be true in humans, but the research is still incomplete.

SEX Talk

Question: What determines how long a woman will be in labor? Why do they say a woman's first baby is hardest? A friend of mine was in labor for 36 hours!

Usually, first labors are the most difficult. Second and subsequent labors are usually easier and shorter because there is less resistance from the birth canal and the surrounding muscles. Overall, the biggest differences are in the amount of time it takes for the cervix to fully dilate and the amount of pushing necessary to move the baby out of the birth canal. The first labor usually takes anywhere between 8 and 14 hours, whereas second and subsequent labors usually take anywhere between 4 and 9 hours. However, labor can, and often does, last up to 24 hours. We do not really know why some women have easier labors than others. Perhaps it could be due to diet and/or exercise during the pregnancy.

Preparing for Birth

As the birth day comes closer, many women (and men too!) become anxious, nervous, and excited about what is to come. This is probably why the tradition of baby showers started. These gatherings enable women (and more recently, men) to gather and discuss the impending birth. People often share their personal experiences and helpful hints. This ritual may help couples to prepare themselves emotionally and to feel more comfortable.

Increasing knowledge and alleviating anxiety about the birth process are the main concepts behind the **Lamaze** method of childbirth. In Lamaze, women and their partners are taught what to expect during labor and delivery and how to control the pain through breathing and massage. Tension and anxiety during labor have been found to increase pain, discomfort, and fatigue. Many couples feel more prepared and focused after taking these courses.

A few weeks before delivery, the fetus usually moves into a "'head down" position in the uterus. This is referred to as **engagement.** Ninety-seven percent of fetuses are in this position at birth (Nilsson, 1990). If a baby's feet or buttocks are first **(breech position),** the physician may either try to rotate the baby prior to birth or recommend a cesarean section. We will discuss this later in the chapter.

Birthplace Choices

In nonindustrialized countries, nearly all babies are born at home; worldwide, approximately 80% of babies are (Dunham et al., 1992). For low-risk pregnancies, home birth has been found to be as safe as a hospital delivery (Johnson & Daviss, 2005). Oftentimes, home births are done with the help of a **midwife.** Proponents of home birthing argue that it has been the medical establishment that has moved delivery into hospitals as a way of making money and controlling women's bodies. Even so, in the United States today, the majority of babies are born in hospitals. A relatively recent development is the concept of birthing centers within hospital settings. These centers provide very comfortable rooms, often complete with soothing music, a television, cheery colors, a shower, and a Jacuzzi. Some also provide a bed for the father-to-be.

Inducing the Birth

Inducing birth involves using techniques to artificially start the birth process. Usually this is in the form of drugs given in increasing doses to mimic the natural contractions of labor, although induced contractions can be more painful and prolonged than natural labor. Birth can occur anywhere from a few hours to several days after induction begins, depending on a woman's prior birth history. Over the last few years, there has been a tremendous increase in childbirth induction. In fact, labor induction is one of the fastest growing medical procedures in the United States (MacDorman et al., 2002). In 1998, induction was used in 19% of all U.S. births, which was more than twice the number from 1989.

A woman may need to have her pregnancy induced for several medical reasons, including being 1 or more weeks past her due date or to avoid having a cesarean section because the baby is growing too large. Induction may also be performed when a woman's labor is not progressing (i.e., her amniotic fluids have broken, but her contractions have stopped). Some women elect to have an induction prior to their due date for nonmedical reasons, including anything from wanting to avoid birth on a certain day (such as Halloween) or to accommodate a woman or her partner's work schedule. Most hospitals require a woman to be at least 39 weeks pregnant before induction is an option. Non-Hispanic white, college-educated, U.S.-born women have the highest rates of labor induction (MacDorman et al., 2002).

Birthing Positions

Although women can assume a variety of positions during childbirth, in the United States the majority of hospitals have a woman in the semireclined position with her feet up in stirrups. Some feminist health professionals claim that this position is easier for the

---

Lamaze
A prepared childbirth method in which couples are provided information about the birth process and are taught breathing and relaxation exercises to use during labor.

engagement
When the fetus moves down toward the birth canal prior to delivery.

breech position
An abnormal and often dangerous birthing position in which the baby's feet, knees, or buttocks emerge before the head.

midwife
A person who assists women during childbirth.

doctor rather than for the woman and that it is the most ineffective and dangerous position for labor. Recently, women have been given more freedom in deciding how to position themselves for childbirth in the United States. A woman on her hands and knees or in the squatting position allows her pelvis and cervix to be at its widest. In addition, the force of gravity can be used to help in the birth process.

In different areas of the world, positions for birth vary. Rope midwives in rural areas of the Sudan hang a rope from the ceiling and have the mother grasp the rope and bear down in a squatting position. In Bang Chan, Thailand, a husband cradles his pregnant wife between his legs and digs his toes into her thighs. This toe pressure is thought to provide relief from her pain (Dunham et al., 1992).

A recent controversial development in birthing is the underwater birth, which originated in Russia. A woman is seated in a warm bath or Jacuzzi and is allowed to give birth underwater. It is thought that the warmth of the water makes labor less painful for the woman and less traumatic for infants. Because the baby gets its oxygen from the mother until the umbilical cord is cut, proponents claim there is little danger to the baby. One study from Italy reviewed 1,575 underwater births and found that water birthing provided many advantages over traditional delivery, such as shorter first stage of labor, lower episiotomy rates, and reduced anesthesia use during labor (Thoni et al., 2005). However, other studies have not supported this research and have found that there are increased risks to both the baby and the mother (Pinette et al., 2004).

Stages of Childbirth

Birth itself takes place in three stages: **cervical effacement** and **dilation,** expulsion of the fetus, and expulsion of the placenta. The beginning of birth is usually marked by an expulsion of the mucus plug from the cervix. This plug protects the fetus from any harmful bacteria that might enter the vagina during pregnancy. Sometimes women experience "false labor," in which contractions are irregular and do not dilate the cervix. In "real labor," contractions will be regular and get closer together over time. In a typical birth process, the process is divided into three stages.

Stage One

In the United States, if the birth process is taking too long, physicians may administer the drug Pitocin to speed up labor. In Bolivia, however, certain groups of people believe that nipple stimulation helps the birth move quicker. So if a birth is moving too slowly, a woman's nipples may be massaged. Biologically, nipple stimulation leads to a release of oxytocin, which is a natural form of pitocin. This is why many midwives in the U.S. also practice nipple stimulation during childbirth.

In some Guatemalan societies, long and difficult labors are believed to be due to a woman's sins, and so she is asked to confess her sins. If this does not help speed up labor, her husband is asked to confess. If neither of these confessions helps, the father's loincloth is wrapped around the woman's stomach to assure her that he will not leave her once the baby is born (Dunham et al., 1992).

The first stage of labor can last anywhere from 20 minutes to 24 hours and is longer in first births. When true labor begins, the Braxton-Hicks contractions increase. The cervix begins dilation (opening up) and effacement (thinning out) to allow for fetal passage (this phase is called early labor). Throughout the first stage of labor the entrance to the cervix (the os) increases from 0 to 10 centimeters to allow for the passage of the fetus.

Toward the end of this stage, the amniotic sac usually ruptures (however, this may happen earlier in some women). Contractions may last for about 30 to 60 seconds with intervals of between 5 and 20 minutes, and the cervix usually dilates to 4 to 5 centimeters. Couples are advised to time the contractions and the interval between contractions and report these to their healthcare provider. When they are about 5 minutes apart, the healthcare provider will advise the couple to come to the hospital.

The contractions will eventually begin to last longer (1 minute or more), become more intense, and increase in frequency (every 1 to 3 minutes). Dilation of the cervix

Review Question

Describe the emotional and physical preparation necessary for the birth of a child, childbirth induction, and the various birthing positions.

cervical effacement
The stretching and thinning of the cervix in preparation for birth.

dilation
The expansion of the opening of the cervix in preparation for birth.

transition
The last period in labor, in which contractions are strongest and the periods in between contractions are the shortest.

endorphins
Neurotransmitters, concentrated in the pituitary gland and parts of the brain, that inhibit physical pain.

fetal distress
Condition in which a fetus has an abnormal heart rate or rhythm.

episiotomy
A cut made with surgical scissors to avoid tearing of the perineum at the end of the second stage of labor.

continues from 4 to 8 centimeters (this phase is called active labor). The contractions that open the os can be very painful, and nurses will usually monitor the progress of cervical dilation.

The last phase in stage one is called **transition,** which for most women is the most difficult part of the birth process. Contractions are very intense and long and have shorter periods in between, and the cervix dilates from 8 to 10 centimeters. The fetus moves into the base of the pelvis, creating an urge to push; however, the woman is advised not to push until her cervix is fully dilated. Many women feel exhausted by this point.

The woman's body produces pain-reducing hormones called **endorphins,** which may dull the intensity of the contractions. Should a woman feel the need for more pain relief, she can also be given various pain medications. However, she may become drowsy or nauseated and/or the drugs may affect the fetus. In the past several years, there has been a movement away from the use of drugs during delivery. Women are being encouraged to incorporate methods of relaxation, breathing, hypnosis, and acupuncture.

The fetus is monitored for signs of **fetal distress,** such as slowed heart rate or lack of oxygen. This is done either through the woman's abdomen by a sensor or by accessing the fetus's scalp through the cervix. Fetal monitoring can determine whether or not the fetus is in any danger that would require a quicker delivery or a cesarean section.

SEX Talk

Question: Is it safe to use drugs to lessen the pain of labor and birth?

Although some women believe in a "natural" childbirth (one without pain medications), other women want to use them. The search for a perfect drug to relieve pain, one that is safe for both the mother and her child, has been a long one. Every year, more and more progress is made. Medication is often recommended when labor is long and complicated, the pain is more than the mother can tolerate or interferes with her ability to push, forceps are required during the delivery, or when a mother is so restless and agitated that it inhibits labor progress. In all cases, the risks of drug use must be weighed against the benefits.

The most commonly used pain medications include analgesics (pain relievers) and anesthetics (which produce a loss of sensation). Which drug is used depends on the mother's preference, past health history, present condition, and the baby's condition. An epidural block (an anesthetic) is increasingly popular for the relief of severe labor pain. However, how well a pain medication works depends on the mother, the dosage, and other factors. We do know that the use of some drugs, including epidurals, can increase labor time and may be associated with other risk factors. However, newer lower dosage epidurals have been found to produce fewer side effects and are better tolerated by women (Neruda, 2005).

Stage Two

After the cervix has fully dilated, the second stage of birth, the expulsion of the fetus, begins. Contractions are somewhat less intense, lasting about 60 seconds and spaced at 1- to 3-minute intervals.

Toward the end of this stage of labor, the doctor may perform an **episiotomy** (ee-pee-zee-AH-tuh-mee) to reduce the risk of a tearing of the tissue between the vaginal opening and anus as the fetus emerges. Today episiotomies are very controversial, and the debate centers around several issues. Those who support the practice argue that it can speed up labor, prevent tearing during a delivery, protect against future incontinence, and promote quicker healing. Those who argue against the practice claim that it increases infection, pain, and healing times, and may increase discomfort when intercourse is resumed (Hartmann et al., 2005).

Although the use of routine episiotomy is gradually decreasing, it is estimated that episiotomies are done in over 40% of U.S. births (Allen & Hanson, 2005; Scott, 2005).

Other Western nations do far fewer, with seemingly few problems. Racial differences in episiotomy rates have found that overall, white women undergo episiotomies more frequently than black women (Goldberg et al., 2002).

As the woman pushes during contractions, the top of the head of the baby soon appears at the vagina, which is known as **crowning.** Once the face emerges, the mucus and fluid in the mouth and nostrils are removed by suction. The baby emerges and, after the first breath, usually lets out a cry. After the baby's first breath, the umbilical cord, which supplies the fetus with oxygen, is cut; this is painless for the mother and child. Eye drops are put into the baby's eyes to prevent bacterial infection.

Directly following birth, many physicians and midwives place the newborn directly on the mother's chest to begin the bonding process. However, sometimes the father may be the first to hold the child, or the nurses will perform an **Apgar** test (Finster & Wood, 2005). A newborn with a low Apgar score may require intensive care after delivery.

Stage Three

During the third stage of labor, the placenta (sometimes referred to as the "afterbirth") is expelled from the uterus. Strong contractions continue after the baby is born in order to push the placenta out of the uterus and through the vagina. Most women are not aware of this process because of the excitement of giving birth. The placenta must be checked to make sure all of it has been expelled. If there was any tearing or an episiotomy was performed, this will need to be sewn up after the placenta is removed. Usually this stage lasts about 30 minutes or so.

In parts of Kenya, the placenta of a female baby is buried under the fireplace, and the placenta of a male baby is buried by the stalls of baby camels. This practice is thought to forever connect the children's future to these locations. Some cultures bury their placentas, whereas others hang the placentas outside the home to show that a baby indeed arrived!

🛡 PROBLEMS DURING BIRTHING

For most women, the birth of a newborn baby proceeds without problems. However, a number of problems can arise, including premature birth, breech birth, cesarean section delivery, and stillbirth.

Premature Birth: The Hazards of Early Delivery

The majority of babies are born late rather than early. Birth that takes place before the 37th week of pregnancy is considered **premature birth.** About 8% of births in the United States are premature. Prematurity increases the risk of birth-related defects and infant mortality (Palca, 1991). However, research into pediatrics has led to tremendous improvements in the survival rates of premature infants. Today infants born at 24 weeks' gestation have a greater than 50% chance of survival (Welty, 2005). Unfortunately, more than half of these infants who survive develop complications and long-term effects of prematurity, such as developmental difficulties.

Birth may occur prematurely for several reasons, including early labor or early rupture of the amniotic membranes or because of a maternal or fetal problem. It is common for women who have had one premature birth to have subsequent premature births. Approximately 50% of all twin births are premature, and delivery of multiple fetuses occurs about 3 weeks earlier, on average, than single births. In 2004 the world's smallest surviving premature baby was born, weighing in at 8.6 ounces (her twin sister weighed 1 pound, 4 ounces; Huffstutter, 2004). These twins were delivered via caesarean section in the 26th week of pregnancy due to medical problems experienced by their mother. Other factors that may lead to premature birth include smoking during pregnancy, alcohol or drug use, inadequate weight gain or nutrition, heavy physical labor during the pregnancy, infections, and teenage pregnancy.

crowning
The emergence of a baby's head at the opening of the vagina at birth.

Apgar
Developed by Virginia Apgar, M.D., this system assesses the general physical condition of a newborn infant for five criteria: (A) activity/muscle tone, (P) pulse rate, (G) grimace and reflex irritability, (A) appearance/skin color, (R) respiration.

Review Question

Trace the three stages of birth from the loss of the mucus plug to the expulsion of the placenta.

sex byte

Pregnant women who eat large amounts of black licorice may increase their odds of having a premature baby (mainly due to the chemical component in the licorice; Strandberg, 2002).

premature birth
Any infant born before the 37th week of pregnancy.

Figure 12.5
In 3% to 4% of births, the fetus is in
the breech position, with feet and
buttocks against the cervix.

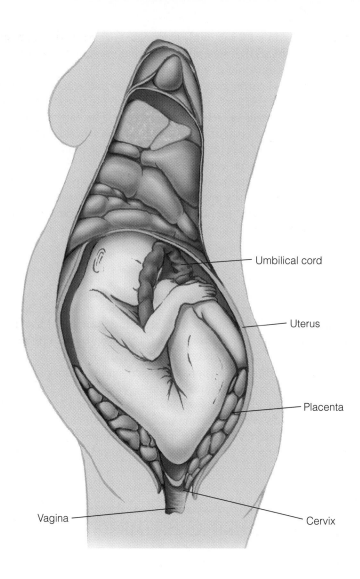

Umbilical cord

Uterus

Placenta

Cervix

Vagina

In many mammals, it is common for the mothers to eat the placenta after delivery, a process known as placentophagia (pla-sen-tuh-FAY-gee-uh). Although this does not sound very appetizing to us, it does serve two very important purposes. The placenta is rich in progesterone, which, once digested, is quickly released into the bloodstream, causing progesterone levels to temporarily stabilize. This stabilization of progesterone has been hypothesized as a way to decrease the incidence of postpartum depression (R. Jones, 1984). In addition, in animals, eating the placenta also avoids attracting predators.

Breech Birth: Feet First Into the World

In 97% of all births, the fetus emerges in the head-down position. However, in 3% to 4% of cases, the fetus is in the breech position, with the feet and buttocks against the cervix (see Figure 12.5). Interestingly, about half of all fetuses are in this position before the 7th month of pregnancy, but most rotate before birth (R. Jones, 1984). Sometimes doctors are aware of the position of the fetus prior to delivery and can try to change the fetus's position for normal vaginal delivery. However, if this is not possible, or if it is discovered too late into delivery, labor may take an unusually long time. A skilled midwife or physician often can flip the baby or deliver it safely even in the breech position. However, in the United States today, a cesarean section will often be performed to ensure the health and well-being of both the mother and her child (Ghosh, 2005).

Cesarean Section (C-Section) Delivery

A cesarean section (c-section) involves the delivery of the fetus through an incision in the abdominal wall. From 1970 to 1988, the rate of cesarean sections increased from 5% to close to 25% (Stein, 2003) for several reasons: women were waiting longer to have children, which increased labor complications; the procedure became easier and safer to perform than it was several years before; and doctors performed cesarean sections to reduce the risks associated with vaginal delivery due to their fear of malpractice suits.

One of the biggest concerns about cesarean section surgery has to do with possible pelvic floor injuries that can cause possible urinary or sexual problems later in life (Stein,

2002). Many hospitals are working with physicians to decrease the number of cesarean births; so far, these programs have been successful. In the United States today, approximately 21% of babies are born by cesarean section.

C-sections are needed when the baby is too large for a woman to deliver vaginally, the woman is unable to push the baby out the birth canal, the placenta blocks the cervix (**placenta previa**), the cervix does not dilate to 10 centimeters, or the baby is in fetal distress. If a doctor decides that a cesarean is necessary, the woman is moved to an operating room and is given either a general anesthestic or an epidural. The operation usually lasts between 20 and 90 minutes, and the woman will likely stay in the hospital longer than those who deliver vaginally. Women who have c-section births can get pregnant again and, although a woman may be able to deliver her next baby vaginally after a c-section (this referred to as a VBAC, or "vaginal birth after cesarean"), some choose to have another c-section for a variety of reasons, including to avoid the pain of vaginal labor or the risk of uterine rupture.

Stillbirth: Sad Circumstance

A fetus that dies after 20 weeks of pregnancy is called a **stillbirth** (prior to 20 weeks, it is called a miscarriage). There are many causes for a stillbirth, including umbilical cord accidents, problems with the placenta, birth defects, infections, and maternal diabetes or high blood pressure (Incerpi et al., 1998). Oftentimes the fetal loss is completely unexpected, as half of all stillbirths occur in pregnancies that appeared to be without problems (Pasupathy & Smith, 2005). It is estimated that 14% of fetal deaths occur during labor and delivery, whereas 86% occur before labor even begins (Fretts et al., 1992). In most cases, a woman goes into labor approximately 2 weeks after the fetus has died; if not, her labor will be induced. Some ethnic differences have been noted: higher rates of stillbirth have been found in African-American and interracial couples (Getahun et al., 2005).

The frequency of stillbirths has been decreasing over the last few years in the United States, due in part to better treatment of certain maternal medical conditions. Many women are advised to do "kick checks" beginning in the 26th week of pregnancy. If a woman notices that her fetus is kicking fewer than 6 times in an hour or has stopped moving or kicking, fetal monitoring can be done to check on the status of the fetus. This practice has reduced the frequency of fetal death.

POSTPARTUM PARENTHOOD

The majority of women and men are excited about being parents. However, many couples are not prepared for the many physical and emotional changes that occur after the child is born. They may also find changes in their sex lives because of the responsibility and exhaustion that often accompanies parenthood.

More Physical Changes for the Mother

Many women report painful contractions for a few days after birth. These contractions are caused by the secretion of oxytocin, which is produced when a woman breast-feeds and is responsible for the shrinking of the uterus. The uterus returns to its original size about 6 weeks postpartum: in breast-feeding women, the uterus returns to its original size quicker than in non–breast-feeding women. A bloody discharge persists for a week or so after delivery. It soon turns yellow-white and lasts for 10 days in mothers who breast-feed and up to a month or so in women who do not.

Women may experience an increase in frequency of urination, which can be painful if an episiotomy was performed or natural tearing occurred. Women may be advised to take sitz baths, in which the vagina and perineum are soaked in warm water to reduce the pain and to quicken the healing process. Until the cervix returns to its closed position, full baths are generally not advised.

placenta previa
A condition in which the placenta is abnormally positioned in the uterus so that it partially or completely covers the opening of the cervix.

stillbirth
An infant who is born dead.

Review Question

Define and discuss prematurity, breech birth, cesarean section delivery, and stillbirth.

Sneak Peek

"I like children, I love playing with children, but I've never felt the need to have a baby."— *Deciding Whether to Have Children*

Sexuality Now

sex byte

As of 2002, 35 states have "safe surrender" laws that allow parents to anonymously give up their baby (Weibley, 2002). These laws were instituted to decrease the likelihood of teenage parents leaving a newborn in a trash can or somewhere unattended to die.

Postpartum Psychological Changes

Although the majority of women feel excitement after the birth of a baby, many also feel exhausted. Minor sadness is a common complication of childbearing (Howard et al., 2005). However, for some, it is a very difficult time with endless crying spells, and anxiety. In severe cases, this is referred to as **postpartum depression.** Physical exhaustion, physiological changes, and an increased responsibility of child rearing all contribute to these feelings, coupled with postpartum hormonal changes (including a sudden drop in progesterone). Partner support has been found to decrease postpartum depression (Misri et al., 2000). Men have also been found to experience some degree of postpartum depression after the birth of a baby. In the most severe cases, mental disturbances, called **postpartum psychosis,** occur; and, in rare cases, women have killed or neglected their babies after delivery.

Some ethnic and racial differences have been found in the rates of postpartum depression, with African American and Hispanic mothers reporting more postpartum depression than white mothers (Howell et al., 2005; see Figure 12.6). Although the majority of studies on postpartum depression have studied only heterosexual mothers, newer studies are beginning to evaluate the frequency of postpartum depression in lesbian mothers. Reduced social support and homophobia may put lesbian mothers more at risk for depression, although the planning of pregnancy and shared responsibilities may offer some protection in lesbian couples (Ross, 2005). More research is needed in this area.

Sexuality for New Parents

Although most physicians advise waiting until 6 weeks postpartum before resuming intercourse, in an uncomplicated vaginal delivery (with no tears or episiotomy), intercourse can safely be engaged in 2 weeks after delivery. This period is usually needed to ensure that no infection occurs and that the cervix has returned to its original position. If an episiotomy was performed, it may take up to 3 weeks for the stitches to dissolve. Mothers can participate in intercourse at this time if there is no pain during penetration. By 6 weeks postpartum the majority of women resume intercourse, although it may take until 12 weeks postpartum for orgasm to resume (Connolly et al., 2005). Cesarean section incisions usually take approximately 2 weeks to heal, and sexual intercourse is safe after this time. To reduce the risk of infection, it is best to avoid cunnilingus until a woman is certain she has no cuts or lacerations as a result of the delivery.

Directly after delivery, many women report slower and less intense excitement stages of the sexual response cycle and a decrease in vaginal lubrication (Masters & Johnson, 1966). However, at 3 months postpartum, most women return to their original levels of desire and excitement. Research has also shown that women who breast-feed often report higher levels of sexual interest. It is important to remember that women who have just given birth experience an increase in tension, fatigue, and physical discomfort, and many do not feel like having sexual intercourse. However, this does not mean women do not want affection. Men also experience similar feelings and may lose their erections during the first few sexual attempts after a baby is born. This may occur out of fear of hurting their partner, general anxiety, or conflicts involved in viewing the birth process.

In her book Down Came the Rain: My Journey Through Postpartum Depression, *Brooke Shields details her struggle with infertility and depression.*

postpartum depression
A woman's clinical depression that occurs after childbirth.

postpartum psychosis
The rare occurrence of severe, debilitating depression or psychotic symptoms in the mother after childbirth.

Review Question

Describe the physical and emotional changes that women experience after the birth of a child.

Figure 12.6
In one study of 655 U.S. women, African American and Hispanic women more commonly reported postpartum depressive symptoms than white women. Rates of postpartum depression remained higher for both African American and Hispanic women after controlling for factors such as history of depression, social support, household management, and infant behavior.
Source: Howell et al., 2005.

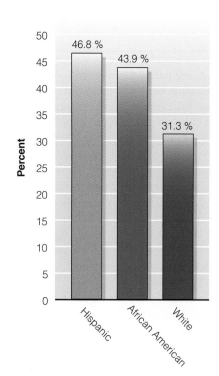

Racial and ethnic differences in postpartum depression

46.8 % Hispanic
43.9 % African American
31.3 % White

Breast-Feeding the Baby

Within an hour after birth, the newborn baby usually begins a rooting reflex, which signals hunger. The baby's sucking triggers the flow of milk from the breast. This is done through receptors in the nipples, which signal the pituitary to produce prolactin, a chemical necessary for milk production. Another chemical, oxytocin, is also produced, which, as we mentioned before, helps increase contractions in the uterus to shrink the uterus to its original size. In the first few days of breast-feeding, the breasts release a fluid called colostrum, which is very important in strengthening the baby's immune system. This is one of the reasons that breast-feeding is recommended to new mothers.

© Stockbyte/Picturequest

sexbyte

A breast-feeding woman is better able to handle different stressors than a non–breast-feeding woman; this may be because breast-feeding reduces the amount of stress-related hormones and buffers a woman's stress response (Azar, 2002).

There have been many benefits to breast-feeding reported over the years. It has been found to provide antibodies to strengthen an infant's immune system; strengthen cognitive development; and reduce allergies, asthma, tooth decay, respiratory infections, and diarrhea (Daniels & Adair, 2005; Khadivzadeh & Parsai, 2005). In addition, the body-to-body contact during breast-feeding has been found to decrease stress and improve mood for both mother and child (Groer, 2005).

For some women, however, breast-feeding is not possible. Time constraints and work pressures may also prevent breast-feeding. In poor countries, a child who is bottle-fed is more likely to die than a breast-fed one (Dunham et al., 1992). This is probably due to unsterilized bottles, water, and equipment often being used. For the most part, however, under sanitary conditions bottle feeding is perfectly safe.

Some women who want to breast-feed but who also wish to return to work use a breast pump. This allows a woman to express milk from her breasts that can be given to her child while she is away. Breast milk can be kept in the refrigerator or freezer, but it must be heated prior to feeding. The majority of U.S. states have laws that allow women to breast-feed in public and to express breast milk while at work in certain areas (LaLeche League, 2005).

There have been some heated debates about when a child should be **weaned** from breast-feeding. The American Academy of Pediatrics recommends exclusive breast-feeding (no other fluids or food) for 6 months and then continued breast-feeding for a minimum of 1 year, whereas the World Health Organization recommends exclusive breast-feeding for the first 4 to 6 months of life and continued breast-feeding until at least the age of 2.

wean
To accustom a baby to take nourishment other than nursing from the breast.

Breast-feeding advocates believe that American women wean their children too early. At 6 months of age, only 29% of American women are still breast-feeding their children (Taveras et al., 2003). This is probably due to several factors, but one of the biggest is cultural expectations. The question is: If there were no cultural taboos against breast-feeding, how long would a woman nurse? Research has found that the natural age of weaning is $2\frac{1}{2}$ years, with a maximum of 6 to 7 years (Dettwyler & Stuart-Macadam, 1995). In fact, all other primates breast-feed their infants for years, not months.

Throughout this chapter we have explored many issues related to fertility, infertility, pregnancy, and childbearing. In the next chapter we will begin to look at limiting fertility through contraception and abortion.

Review Question

Identify and explain the benefits of breast-feeding.

Chapter Review

ACTIVE SUMMARY

1. Our bodies are **(a)** _____ programmed to help pregnancy occur: a woman's sexual desire peaks at **(b)** _____, female orgasm helps push **(c)** _____ into the uterus, and semen **(d)** _____ after ejaculation.

2. **(a)** _____ can happen when intercourse takes place a few days before or after ovulation, and the entire process of **(b)** _____ takes about 24 hours. The fertilized ovum is referred to as a(an) **(c)** _____. After the first cell division, it is referred to as a blastocyst. From the 2nd to the 8th week, the developing human is called a(an) **(d)** _____.

3. Early signs of pregnancy include missing a(an) **(a)** _____, breast tenderness, frequent urination, and morning sickness. Pregnancy tests measure for a(an) **(b)** _____ in the blood known as human **(c)** _____ gonadatropin (hCG).

4. During the 16th or 17th week of pregnancy, **(a)** _____ can be done to **(b)** _____ the fetus for **(c)** _____ abnormalities.

5. Female and male **(a)** _____ has been practiced throughout the **(b)** _____, especially in areas where females are less valued in society and where there are governmental **(c)** _____ on family size.

6. **(a)** _____ is the inability to conceive (or impregnate) after 1 year of **(b)** _____ sexual intercourse without the use of any form of birth control. One out of every **(c)** _____ U.S. couples is **(d)** _____.

7. Couples interested in assisted reproduction have many options today, including **(a)** _____ drugs; surgery to correct cervical, vaginal, or endometrial abnormalities and blockage in the vas deferens or epididymis; artificial **(b)** _____; in vitro fertilization; GIFT; ZIFT; zonal dissection; intracellular **(c)** _____ injections; oocyte or embryo **(d)** _____; surrogate parenting; and cryopreservation.

8. Pregnancy is divided into three **(a)** _____-month periods called **(b)** _____. In the first trimester, the most important **(c)** _____ development takes place. In the **(d)** _____ trimester, the fetus grows dramatically, and by the end of this trimester is 3 inches long.

9. The mother often feels the fetus moving around inside her **(a)** _____ during the **(b)** _____ trimester. By the end of this trimester, the fetus is approximately 13 inches long and weighs about 2 pounds. The second trimester of pregnancy is usually the most **(c)** _____ time for the mother.

10. By the end of the **(a)** _____ month, the fetus is 15 inches long and weighs about 3 pounds. **(b)** _____-_____ contractions begin, and **(c)** _____ may be secreted from the nipples.

11. A woman's exercise routine should not exceed **(a)** _____ levels. Exercise has been found to result in a(an) **(b)** _____ sense of well-being, shorter labor, and fewer **(c)** _____ problems. Certain sports should be avoided during pregnancy, such as water skiing, scuba diving, vigorous **(d)** _____ sports, contact sports, and horseback riding.

12. Under- and overweight women are at greater risk of **(a)** _____ pregnancy outcome, and they are **(b)** _____ to gain or lose weight **(c)** _____ to pregnancy.

13. Drugs and alcohol can cross the **(a)** _____, enter into the developing fetus's bloodstream, and cause physical or mental **(b)** _____. **(c)** _____ occurs when a woman drinks heavily during pregnancy, producing an infant with irreversible physical and **(d)** _____ disabilities.

14. Delaying pregnancy has some risks, including increase in spontaneous **(a)** _____, first-trimester bleeding, low birth weight, **(b)** _____ labor time, increased rate of c-sections, and **(c)** _____ abnormalities.

15. Sexual **(a)** _____ during pregnancy is safe for most mothers and the developing child up until the last several **(b)** _____ of pregnancy, and **(c)** _____ is safe but occasionally may cause painful uterine **(d)** _____.

16. In a(an) **(a)** _____ pregnancy, the zygote implants outside the uterus, usually in the **(b)** _____ tube. This may be due to increased STIs and **(c)** _____.

17. The majority of **(a)** _____ occur during the **(b)** _____ trimester of pregnancy. The most common reason for miscarriage is a fetal **(c)** _____ abnormality.

18. The risk of chromosomal abnormality increases as **(a)** _____ age increases. The most common **(b)** _____ abnormality is **(c)** _____ syndrome.

19. An Rh-negative woman must be given **(a)** _____ directly after childbirth, abortion, or miscarriage so that she won't produce **(b)** _____ and to ensure that her future pregnancies are healthy. **(c)** _____ is a form of blood poisoning that pregnant women can develop; symptoms include weight gain, fluid retention, an increase in **(d)** _____ pressure, and/or protein in the urine.

20. Increasing knowledge and alleviating (a) _____ about the birth process are the main concepts behind the (b) _____ method of childbirth. Worldwide, the majority of (c) _____ are born at home, although most U.S. babies are born in (d) _____.

21. (a) _____ itself takes place in three stages: cervical effacement and (b) _____, expulsion of the fetus, and expulsion of the placenta. The first stage of labor can last anywhere from 20 minutes to 24 hours and is longer in first births. (c) _____, the last stage in stage one, is the most difficult part of the birth process. The second stage of birth involves the expulsion of the fetus. In the third stage of labor, strong (d) _____ continue and push the placenta out of the uterus and through the vagina.

22. The (a) _____ of babies are born late, but if birth takes place before the (b) _____ week of pregnancy, it is considered (c) _____. Premature birth may occur early for several reasons, including early labor, early rupture of the amniotic membranes, or a maternal or fetal problem.

23. A(An) (a) _____ section involves the delivery of the fetus through an incision in the abdominal wall. C-sections are needed when the baby is too (b) _____ for a woman to deliver vaginally, the woman is unable to push the baby out the (c) _____ canal, there is placenta previa or placental separation from the baby prior to birth, or if the baby is in (d) _____ distress.

24. The most common cause of (a) _____ is a failure in the baby's (b) _____ supply, (c) _____, or lungs.

25. Following delivery, the (a) _____ returns to its original size in about 6 (b) _____. Many women report painful (c) _____, caused by the hormone (d) _____, for a few days after birth. Breast-feeding women's uteruses return to the original size quicker than those of non–breast-feeding women.

26. The (a) _____ of women feel both excitement and exhaustion after the birth of a child. However, for some, it is a very (b) _____ time of depression, crying spells, and anxiety. In severe cases, a woman might experience (c) _____ depression or postpartum (d) _____.

27. Although most physicians advise waiting until 6 weeks postpartum before resuming (a) _____, in an uncomplicated vaginal delivery (with no tears or episiotomy), intercourse can safely be engaged in 2 weeks after delivery. Many women report slower and less intense excitement stages of the sexual (b) _____ cycle and a decrease in vaginal lubrication directly after delivery; however, at 3 months (c) _____, most women return to their original levels of (d) _____ and excitement.

28. In the first few days of breast-feeding, the breasts release a fluid called (a) _____, which is very important in strengthening the baby's (b) _____ system. The American Academy of Pediatrics recommends breast-feeding for at least (c) _____ year, whereas the World Health Organization recommends breast-feeding for up to (d) _____ years or longer.

Critical Thinking Questions

1. If gender preselection were possible, would you want to determine the gender of your children? Why or why not? If you did choose, what order would you choose? Why?

2. Do you think assisted reproductive techniques should be used on women over 50? Over 60? Do you think older moms can make good mothers? What about older dads?

3. If women can safely deliver at home, should they be encouraged to do so with the help of a midwife, or should they be encouraged to have children in the hospital? If you have children, where do you think you would want them to be born?

4. At what age do you think a child should be weaned? Should a woman breast-feed a child until he or she is 6 months old? Two years old? Four years old? How old?

5. In 2001, a woman ran an ad in a school newspaper at Stanford University offering $15,000 for a sperm donation from the right guy. She required the guy be intelligent, physically attractive, and over six feet tall. The year before an ad ran in the same newspaper from a couple who offered $100,000 for eggs from an athletically gifted female student. Would you have answered either of these ads? Why or why not?

Check It Out

Douglas, A. (2002). ***The mother of all pregnancy books: The ultimate guide to conception, birth, and everything in between*** (U.S. ed.). New York: Wiley.

This book is funny, entertaining, and packed with tons of nuts-and-bolts information. Unique and innovative, this book is packed with tools readers won't find anywhere else, including charts highlighting the risks of using various over-the-counter drug products during pregnancy and tables summarizing the functions of important nutrients during pregnancy. The book features a glossary of pregnancy-related terms, a sample birth plan, a set of emergency childbirth procedures, and updated information on infertility, high-risk pregnancy, pain relief during labor, episiotomy, circumcision, pregnancy, and infant loss.

Nine Months (1995; 1 hour, 43 minutes; Rated PG-13)

In this movie, an aging bachelor (Hugh Grant) can't decide whether to commit to the woman he loves (Julianne Moore). When she becomes pregnant, he still can't make up his mind about fatherhood, which causes tension in the relationship. There's a lot of comedy involving Grant's best friend (Tom Arnold), an ultra-married and child-ridden suburbanite who makes fatherhood look tough. Robin Williams has a funny cameo as a foreign doctor.

InfoTrac® College Edition

If your instructor ordered InfoTrac with this book, explore InfoTrac College Edition, your online library, for additional readings and review. Go to: **www.thomsonedu.com,** and enter these search terms:

amniocentesis	assisted reproductive technologies	fetus
fetal alcohol syndrome	pregnancy	miscarriage
morning sickness	postpartum depression	multiple birth(s)
surrogate motherhood		

Web Resources

SexualityNow Companion Website
Go to **http://thomsonedu.com/carroll** for practice quiz questions, interactive activities, Internet links, critical thinking exercises, discussion forums, and more. You can also access sites from the Wadsworth Psychology Study Center **(http://psychology.wadsworth.com)** or you can connect directly to the following sites:

American Society for Reproductive Medicine (ASRM)
The ASRM is an organization devoted to advancing knowledge and expertise in reproductive medicine, infertility, and assisted reproductive technologies. Links to a variety of helpful websites are available.

BirthStories
This interesting website contains true birth stories from a variety of women, including first-time moms, veteran moms, and births after a pregnancy loss. It also has information on birthing, breast-feeding, and newborns.

Childbirth
This website contains information about fertility, childbirth complications, pregnancy, labor, epidurals, cesarean sections, newborns, ectopic pregnancies, postpartum care, and a whole lot more.

International Council on Infertility Information Dissemination (INCIID)
This website provides detailed information on the diagnosis and treatment of infertility, pregnancy loss, family-building options, and helpful fact sheets on various types of fertility treatments and assisted reproductive techniques. Information on adoption and childfree lifestyles is also included.

RESOLVE
RESOLVE: The National Infertility Association, was established in 1974. It works to promote reproductive health, ensure equal access to fertility options for men and women experiencing infertility or other reproductive disorders, and provide support services and physician referral and education.

Sperm Bank Directory
A national directory of sperm cryobanks. Provides information on cryopreservation, sperm donation, and donor sperm. There are also links to sperm banks throughout the country, some of which include online donor catalogs.

StorkNet
This website provides a week-by-week guide to a woman's pregnancy. For each of the 40 weeks of pregnancy, there is information about fetal development, what types of changes occur within the pregnant body, and suggested readings and links for more information.

SexualityNow   **Sexuality ⓘ Now**

Go to **www.thomson.edu.com** to link to **SexualityNow,** your online study tool. First take the **Pre-Test** for this chapter to get your **Personalized Study Plan,** which will identify topics you need to review and direct you to online resources. Then take the **Post-Test** to determine what concepts you have mastered and what you still need work on.

Videos in SexualityNow

For additional information on topics discussed in this chapter, check out the videos in **SexualityNow** on the following topics:

- **Deciding Whether to Have Children**—Two couples describe how they decided whether or not to have children.
- **A 57-Year-Old Woman's Successful In Vitro Fertilization**—Learn the factors considered for whether in vitro fertilization is possible for women, no matter what their age is.

13 Contraception and Abortion

Sexuality ⚫ Now Go to www.thomsonedu.com to link to SexualityNow, your online study tool.

*D*o you ever want to have a child? You may have an exact plan about when you'd like to experience a pregnancy in your life. Or perhaps you have already decided you won't have any children. For many couples, deciding how to plan, and also how to avoid, pregnancies are important issues in their lives. The majority of pregnancies that occur each year in the United States are not planned (Forrest, 1994); they occur because no contraception was used (some others are due to contraceptive failure).

In deciding which contraceptive method to use, couples need to consider a variety of issues, including their sexual behavior, reproductive goals, and each partner's health and safety (J. L. Schwartz & Gablenick, 2002). This is further complicated by the fact that an ideal method for one person may not be an ideal method for another; and an ideal method for one person at one time in his or her life may not be an ideal method as he or she enters into different life stages. For example, some women might not want to remember to take a pill every day, whereas others might not want to interrupt sex to insert a contraceptive device. Because some methods are more expensive than others, cost can influence which method a couple uses. Having a wide variety of choices available is important to allow couples to choose and change methods as their contraceptive needs change.

In the early 1950s, a tremendous increase in reproductive and contraceptive research occurred in the United States, resulting in a new selection of modern birth control methods. These choices are made even more complex by disputes about the effectiveness of different methods, their side effects, and the increased use of some methods, such as condoms, in the prevention of AIDS and other sexually transmitted infections (STIs). These factors make knowledge about contraception even more important.

It probably won't surprise you to learn that many college students take great risks when it comes to **contraception,** even though they are intelligent and know about birth control. Researchers don't really know why this is, but many factors increase one's motivation to use contraception, including the ability to communicate with a partner, cost of the method, effectiveness rates, the frequency of sexual intercourse, the motivation to avoid pregnancy, the contraceptive method's side effects, and one's openness about sexuality. In this chapter, we explore the array of contraceptive methods available today, investigate their strengths and weaknesses, and also discuss emergency contraception and abortion.

contraception
Prevention of pregnancy by abstinence or the use of certain devices or surgical procedures to prevent ovulation, fertilization, or implantation.

CONTRACEPTION: HISTORY AND METHOD CONSIDERATIONS

Although many people believe that contraception is a modern invention, its origins actually extend back to ancient times. We will now explore contraception throughout history, both within the United States and cross-culturally.

Contraception in Ancient Times

People have always tried to invent ways to control fertility. The ancient Greeks used magic, superstition, herbs, and drugs to try and control their fertility, and the Egyptians tried fumigating the female genitalia with certain mixtures; inserting a tampon into the vagina that had been soaked in herbal liquid and honey; and inserting a mixture of crocodile feces, sour milk, and honey (Dunham et al., 1992). Another strategy was to insert objects into the vagina that could entrap or block the sperm. Such objects include vegetable seed pods (South Africa), a cervical plug of grass (Africa), sponges soaked with

Figure 13.1
The percentage of women who experience an unintended pregnancy using each birth control method during first year of typical use.
Source: Hatcher et al., 2004.

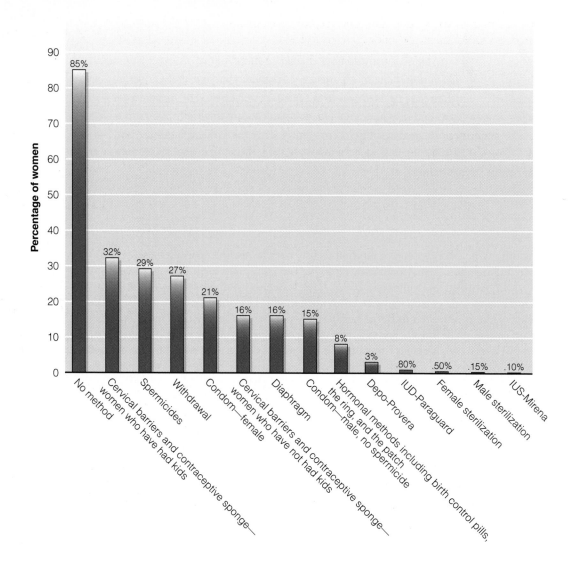

alcohol (Persia), and empty pomegranate halves (Greece). These methods may sound far-fetched to us today, but they worked on many of the same principles as modern methods. In the accompanying Human Sexuality in a Diverse World, "Herbal Lore and Contraception," we discuss some of these methods.

Contraception in the United States: 1800s and Early 1900s

In the early 1800s, several groups in the United States wanted to control fertility in order to reduce poverty. However, contraception was considered a private affair, to be discussed only between partners in a relationship. As we learned in Chapter 1, Anthony Comstock worked with Congress in 1873 to pass the Comstock Laws, which prohibited the distribution of all obscene material; this included contraceptive information and devices. Even medical doctors were not allowed to provide information about contraception (although a few still did). Margaret Sanger, the founder of Planned Parenthood, was one of the first people to publicly advocate the importance of contraception in the United States.

Contraception Outside the United States

Contraception throughout the world has always been affected by social and economic issues, knowledge levels, religion, and gender roles. For example, the high value placed on large family size in India has led to low rates of contraceptive usage (Nath & Nayar, 2004). This is in contrast to high contraceptive use in Hong Kong, where family planning groups urge couples to have only one or two children (Ng & Ma, 2004). Contraceptive misinformation and myths can also decrease contraceptive use. For example, in South Africa many believe that contraception is unnecessary if a person is engaging in sex infrequently (Nicholas, Daniels, & Hurwitz, 2004).

Contraceptive knowledge levels are also very important when it comes to contraceptive use. It is estimated that over 90% of teenage women in many countries in Asia, North Africa, Latin America, and the Caribbean report knowing about contraception, whereas women in sub-Saharan Africa have very low contraceptive knowledge levels (Blanc & Way, 1998).

Religion is another important factor when it comes to contraceptive use. Many predominantly Catholic regions and countries, such as Latin America, Ireland, France, and Poland, have limited contraceptive devices available. Many residents of these countries often do not agree with Church contraceptive teachings, however. One study in Brazil, which contains one of the highest concentrations of Catholics, found that 88% of participants did not follow the Church's contraceptive teachings (de Freitas, 2004). Countries that do have strong religious affiliations often promote the use of natural methods of contraception, such as withdrawal or natural family planning (Leyson, 2004).

Gender roles and power differentials also contribute to contraceptive use. Outside the United States, many women are often not involved in contraception decision making, and contraceptive use is thought to reduce a man's masculinity. For example, in Israel, Jewish religious law teaches that men should not "spill their seed" and therefore opposes contraceptive methods that may damage sperm, such as vasectomy, withdrawal, condoms, or spermicides (Shtarkshall & Zemach, 2004). Methods that do not harm sperm, such as oral contraceptives, IUDs, and even diaphragms are acceptable.

TABLE 13.1	History of Contraceptives in the United States

Year	Event
1839	Goodyear begins mass-production of condoms.
1925	Diaphragms available.
1960	First birth control pill available.*
1962	First IUD (Lippes Loop) available.
1970	Dalkon Shield IUD available (withdrawn in 1975).**
1982	Contraceptive sponge available (withdrawn in 1994 and reintroduced in 2005).
1984	Copper-releasing IUD available.
1988	Prentif cervical cap available (withdrawn in 2005).
1990	Norplant available (withdrawn in 2002).
1992	Depo-Provera available.
1994	Reality female condom available.
1995	Polyurethane condoms available.
1996	Jadelle 2-rod implant available (not marketed).
1998	Preven emergency contraception available (withdrawn in 2004).
1999	Plan B emergency contraception available.
2000	Lunelle injectable available (withdrawn in 2002).
2000	Mifepristone available for early abortion.
2000	Mirena IUS available.
2002	Ortho Evra contraceptive patch available.
2002	Lea's Shield cervical barrier available (not marketed).
2002	Vasclip available (not marketed until 2003).
2003	FemCap available (not marketed).
2003	Essure permanent sterilization device available.
2003	Seasonale 3-month birth control available.
2003	NuvaRing available.
2004	Implanon single-rod implant available (to be marketed soon).
2005	Today contraceptive sponge reintroduced.

*This timeline does not include the oral contraceptive pills that followed the first pill that was available. A variety of different pills have been introduced with major improvements including lower hormone levels.
**IUDs introduced after the Dalkon Shield are not included in this timeline.

Human Sexuality in a Diverse World

Herbal Lore and Contraception

In many places around the world, herbs are used as contraception. For example, American women in Appalachia drink tea made from Queen Anne's lace directly following sexual intercourse to prevent pregnancy (Rensberger, 1994). They are not alone. Many women from South Africa, Guatemala, Costa Rica, Haiti, China, and India rely on herbal contraceptives (L. Newman & Nyce, 1985). Newer hormonal methods of birth control have reduced fertility around the world, but nonhormonal methods such as natural family planning and herbal methods continue to be used. Some of the tested herbs have been found to have high success rates for contraceptive ability (Chaudhury, 1985).

A common herbal contraceptive in Paraguay is known as *yuyos*. Many different types of *yuyos* are taken for fertility regulation (Bull & Melian, 1998). The herbs are usually soaked in water and drunk as tea. Older women teach younger women how to use these herbs, but problems sometimes occur when herbal methods are used improperly. Remember that this method works only when using a mix of herbs that have been found to offer contraceptive protection. Drinking herbal tea from the grocery store isn't going to protect you in the same way!

Failure rates from herbal contraceptives are higher than from more modern methods, but many do work better than using nothing at all. What is it that makes the herbal methods effective? We don't know, but perhaps some future contraceptive drugs may come from research into plant pharmaceuticals.

Men are primarily responsible for birth control decisions in Japan, where many women do not discuss birth control with their husband (Hatano & Shimazaki, 2004). In fact, many Japanese women express shock over the liberal views that many American woman hold about birth control pill usage. In Kenya, married couples report low condom usage because condoms in marriage signify unfaithfulness on the part of the husband (Brockman, 2004). In Puerto Rico, women are uncomfortable asking their male partners to wear condoms. In some countries, contraception is the responsibility of both men and women. For example, in Germany, contraception is a joint decision between men and women, and it is estimated that 95% of sexually active people report using contraception (Lautmann & Starke, 2004).

Scandinavian countries are regarded as some of the most progressive with respect to contraceptive usage. In fact, Finland has been rated as a "model country" in contraceptive use because a variety of contraceptive methods are easily available and students can obtain contraception from school health services (Kontula & Haavio-Mannila, 2004). In the Netherlands and Norway, contraceptive use is high, and many couples use contraception prior to their first sexual intercourse (Drenth & Slob, 2004). In many of these countries, birth control is free and easily accessible (Trost & Bergstrom-Walan, 2004).

Choosing a Method of Contraception

Several methods of contraception, or **birth control,** are currently available. Prior to the availability of any contraceptive method, the United States **Food and Drug Administration (FDA)** must formally approve the method. Let's explore the FDA approval process and individual lifestyle issues that may affect contraceptive method choice.

FDA Approval Process

The FDA is responsible for approving all prescription medications in the United States. To get approval, a pharmaceutical company must submit a new drug application (NDA) to the FDA showing that the drug is safe in animal tests and that it is reasonably safe to proceed with human trials of the drug.

There are a total of three phases to the approval process. In Phase 1, the drug is introduced to approximately 20 to 80 healthy volunteers to collect information on the drug's effectiveness. In Phase 2, several hundred people with the medical disease or condition the drug will be treating are enrolled to evaluate how the drug works and determine what the side effects and risks of the drug are (in clinical trials volunteers are often given the drugs for free and perhaps even paid for their time). In Phase 3 trials, the study is expanded, hundreds to thousands of people are enrolled in the study, and information is collected to extrapolate to the general public. It is estimated that it takes 10 to 14 years to develop a new contraceptive drug (F. Stewart & Gabelnick, 2004). Throughout this process, animal trials are maintained to look at long-term side effects of the proposed drugs.

Lifestyle Issues

As we discussed earlier, no single method of birth control is best for everyone—the best one for you is one that you and your partner will use correctly every time you have sexual intercourse. Choosing a contraceptive method is an important decision and one that must be made with your lifestyle in mind. Important issues include your own personal health and health risks; the number of sexual partners you have; frequency of sexual intercourse; your risk of acquiring an STI; how responsible you are; the cost of the method; and the method's advantages and disadvantages.

Female sterilization, oral contraceptives, and the condom are the most widely used methods among whites, African Americans, and Latinos in the United States (Mosher et al., 2004). However, white women are more likely to use birth control pills, whereas black and Hispanic women are more likely to rely on female sterilization (see Figure 13.2).

In the following sections, we'll discuss barrier, hormonal, chemical, intrauterine, natural, permanent, ineffective, and emergency methods of contraception. For each of

Review Question

Explain what we know about the history of contraception and contraception outside the United States.

birth control
Another term for contraception.

Food and Drug Administration (FDA)
The agency in the U.S. federal government that has the power to approve and disapprove new drugs.

Review Question

Explain the FDA approval process and identify two important lifestyle issues to consider when choosing a contraceptive method.

Method of contraception by race/ethnicity

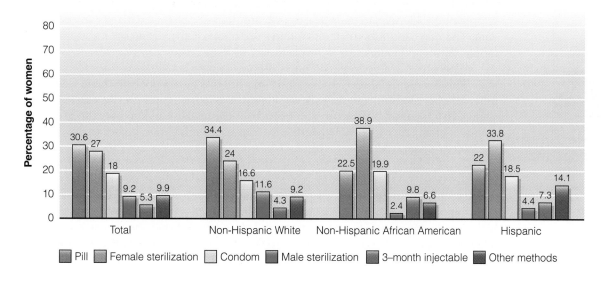

Figure 13.2

Method of contraception among women aged 15 to 44, currently using contraception, by race/ethnicity, in 2002.
Source: U.S. Department of Health and Human Services, 2005

these methods, we will cover how they work, their **effectiveness rates,** cost, advantages and disadvantages, and cross-cultural patterns of usage. Figure 13.1 illustrates the typical use effectiveness rates of the various contraceptive methods (effectiveness rates are often calculated by evaluating the percentage of women who experience an unintended pregnancy during the first year of typical use). Higher effectiveness rates are often representative of **perfect use.**

effectiveness rates
Estimated rates of the number of women who do not become pregnant each year using each method of contraception.

perfect use
Refers to the probability of contraceptive failure for a perfect user of each method.

BARRIER METHODS: CONDOMS AND CAPS

Barrier methods of contraception work by preventing the sperm from entering the uterus. These methods include condoms, the diaphragm, the contraceptive sponge, and the cervical barriers.

Condoms

Penile coverings have been used as a method of contraception since the beginning of recorded history. In 1350 B.C., Egyptian men wore decorative sheaths over their penises. Eventually, sheaths of linen and animal intestines were developed. In 1844, the Goodyear Company improved the strength and resiliency of rubber, and by 1850, rubber (latex) **condoms** were available in the United States (McLaren, 1990). Female condoms became available in 1994, whereas polyurethane (paul-lee-YUR-ith-ain) (nonlatex) condoms were launched in the United States in 1994 and in the United Kingdom and Italy in 1997. Polyurethane condoms can be used by those with latex allergies. However, for people who do not have a latex allergy, healthcare providers generally recommend using latex condoms because latex condoms tend to have lower rates of slippage and breakage.

Condom use in the United States has increased tremendously during the past decade. With the advent of AIDS in the 1980s, condoms became popular not only for their contraceptive abilities but also for the protection they provide from STIs. Condoms are one of the most inexpensive and cost-effective contraceptive methods, providing not only high effectiveness rates but also added protection from STIs and HIV

condom
A latex, animal membrane, or polyurethane sheath that fits over the penis and is used for protection against pregnancy and sexually transmitted infections; polyurethane female condoms, which protect the vaginal walls, are also available.

When using a condom, space should always be left in the top so that the force of the ejaculate does not break the condom.

Female condoms, made of polyurethane, have been available since 1994.

(Warner, Hatcher, & Steiner, 2004). A new line of sexual health products called Elexa was marketed by Trojan in late 2005. Elexa includes condoms, warming gels, and a vibrating ring. The ring is a one-time-use vibrator that can be used with or without a condom. The ring continues to vibrate for up to 20 minutes, increasing the pleasurable sensations during intercourse for the woman.

In 1994, the Reality Vaginal Pouch, a polyurethane female condom, became available. This condom is about 7 inches long and has two flexible polyurethane rings. The inner ring serves as an insertion device, and the outer ring lies on the outside of the vagina. In China, couples report a preference for the female condom over the male condom (Xu et al., 1998), possibly because feelings of sensitivity are higher than when using male condoms (because it is made of polyurethane).

Costs for latex male condoms range from $10 to $15 per dozen; polyurethane and lambskin condoms cost approximately $20 per dozen; all of these are usually less expensive at family planning clinics. Female condoms cost approximately $2 each, so they are fairly expensive to use. In some countries, such as Africa, where the cost is prohibitively high, women have been known to wash and reuse female condoms. There is some evidence that the female condom can be used more than once if it is properly disinfected, washed, dried, and relubricated (Potter et al., 2003), though they are made to be used only once.

How They Work

The male condom ("rubber" or "prophylactic") is placed on an erect penis prior to vaginal penetration. Condoms must be put on before there is any vaginal contact by the penis because sperm may be present in the urethra. After being rolled onto the penis, a half-inch empty space is left at the tip of the condom to allow room for the ejaculatory fluid (see photo on page 411). To prevent tearing the condom, the vagina should be well lubricated. Although some condoms come prelubricated, if extra lubrication is needed, water, contraceptive jelly or cream, or K-Y jelly should be used. Hand or body lotion, petroleum jelly (e.g., Vaseline), baby oil, massage oil, or vegetable oil should never be used, as they may damage the latex and cause the condom to break (because polyurethane condoms are nonlatex, they are not damaged by these products).

To avoid the possibility of semen leaking out of the condom, withdrawal must take place immediately after ejaculation, while the penis is still erect, and the condom should be grasped firmly at the base to prevent its slipping off into the vagina during withdrawal. Condom users should always remember to check expiration dates, pull back the foreskin on an uncircumcised penis before putting a condom on, pinch the reservoir tip to leave a half-inch space in the condom for ejaculation, and use only water-based lubricants.

SEX Talk

Question: Do some men have problems maintaining an erection when they use a condom?

Some men do report that they have more difficulties maintaining an erection when they use a latex condom. Some couples complain that wearing a condom is like "taking a shower with a raincoat on," or that it decreases sensitivity during sexual intercourse. For men, adding two or three drops of a lubricant, such as K-Y jelly, into the condom before rolling it on to the penis can improve penile sensitivity. Many women also report that putting a small amount of a lubricant into their vagina prior to intercourse helps increase their pleasure and sensitivity while using a condom. Lubricated condoms may help maintain erections by increasing sensitivity, as will polyurethane and lambskin condoms. It's also important to note that men who experience problems with premature ejaculation often find that condoms can help maintain erections.

SEX in Real Life

Nonoxynol-9: Harmful or Helpful?

Over the years, public health experts have recommended using condoms containing the spermicide nonoxynol-9 (N-9) to decrease the possibility of pregnancy. Although N-9 is an effective spermicide, several studies have raised red flags about its effectiveness and safety when it comes to protection from sexually transmitted infections. Research has found that spermicides containing nonoxynol-9 do not effectively protect against many sexually transmitted infections, including gonorrhea, chlamydia, or HIV infection (Boonstra, 2005; Workowski & Levine, 2002). In fact, HIV transmission was found to be higher in a population using N-9 than in another population using a placebo (Boonstra, 2005). This may be due to the fact that N-9 may cause irritation of the cervix, vagina, and rectum, which may aid in the transmission of sexually transmitted infections. In fact, N-9 did not protect women from gonorrhea and chlamydial infections any better than if condoms were used alone (Roddy et al., 2002), and it increased the risk of acquiring a urinary tract infection (Handley et al., 2002).

Because of these studies, the U.S. Centers for Disease Control concluded that N-9 was ineffective against HIV (Workowski & Levine, 2002). The World Health Organization also concluded that N-9 was only "moderately effective" for pregnancy prevention (World Health Organization, 2001). In 2002, Planned Parenthood Federation of America decided to cease production of their self-branded line of condoms that included N-9.

Concern over the use of N-9 has spurred development of new products, microbicides, which can reduce the risk of sexually transmitted infections. Scientists have identified over 60 substances as possible microbicides; 45 of these are in animal trials, 17 are in human testing phases, and 5 are in the final stages of testing (see FDA approval process on page 410). It is possible that microbicides will be available as early as 2010 (INFO Project, 2005).

There are many different types of male condoms on the market, including lubricated, colored, spermicidal, reservoir tip, and ribbed texture condoms. For protection from STIs, the most effective condoms are rubber (latex) and contain a spermicide called **nonoxynol-9,** although there is some controversy over this spermicide (see the accompanying Sex in Real Life, "Nonoxynol-9: Harmful or Helpful?").

The female condom is inserted into the vagina prior to penile penetration. The inner ring is squeezed between the thumb and middle finger, making it long and thin, and then inserted into the vagina. Once this is done, an index finger inside the condom can push the inner ring up close to the cervix. The outer ring remains outside the vagina. During intercourse, the penis is placed within the condom, and care should be taken to make sure it does not slip between the condom and the vaginal wall. It's important that the vagina is well-lubricated so that the female condom stays in place. Female and male condoms should never be used together, because they can adhere to each other and cause slippage or breakage.

nonoxynol-9
A spermicide that has been used to prevent pregnancy and protect against sexually transmitted infections.

Effectiveness

Latex condoms are between 85% (typical use) and 98% (perfect use) effective. If used properly and in conjunction with spermicidal jelly, this method approaches 100% effectiveness (Hatcher et al., 2004). Polyurethane condoms have equivalent levels of contraceptive protection to latex condoms, whereas female condoms have a 79% (typical use) to 95% (perfect use) effectiveness rate.

Latex and polyurethane condoms have been found to be effective barriers against the transmission of herpes, chlamydia, gonorrhea, and HIV. Although lambskin condoms block sperm, they may have microscopic holes big enough for the transmission of certain viruses. Research has found that the pores in lambskin condoms may be large enough to permit passage of HIV, hepatitis B virus, and herpes (Hatcher et al., 2004).

Some couples worry that condoms will break. All condoms made in the United States are tested and must meet very stringent quality control requirements. Studies

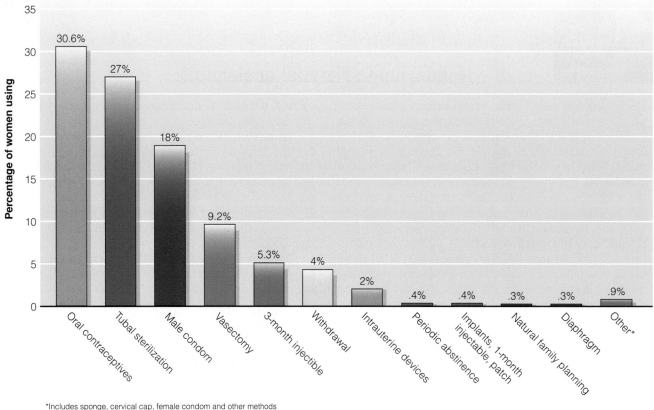

Figure 13.3
Contraceptive method choice among U.S. women, in 2002.
Source: Adapted from Alan Guttmacher Institute (2005b). Contraceptive use. Retrieved August 13, 2005, from http://www.agi-usa.org/pubs/fb_contr_use.html

Figure 13.4
Women's choice of contraceptive method worldwide, in 1999.
Adapted from *Sharing Responsibility: Women, Society, and Abortion Worldwide*, Chart 2.4, p. 15. Reproduced with permission of The Alan Guttmacher Institute.

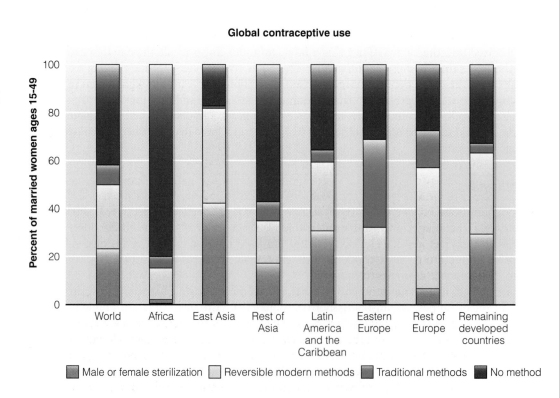

Global contraceptive use

SEX in Real Life

What to Use With Condoms

*C*ondoms can be made out of latex, polyurethane, or lambskin. Latex condoms should always be used with a water-based lubricant. Following are products that should be used with condoms and products that should be avoided when using latex condoms. All types of lubricants, including oil-based lubricants, can be safely used with polyurethane condoms.

FOR USE WITH ALL CONDOMS
Aloe-9
Water-based lubricants (including products such as AquaLube, AstroGlide, K-Y Jelly, N-R lubricating jelly, Touch, and Wet)
glycerin
Gynoll II
spermicide
saliva
water
silicone lubricant

DO NOT USE WITH LATEX CONDOMS
baby oil
yeast infection medication
cold creams
hand and body lotions
massage oil
Vaseline
vegetable or mineral oils
suntan oil and lotion
whipped cream
rubbing alcohol

SOURCE: Planned Parenthood Federation of America, 2004. Retrieved November 2, 2005, from http://www.plannedparenthood.org/bc/condom.htm

have demonstrated that when used correctly (without common errors in use, such as not leaving room at the top of the condom for the ejaculate), the overall risk of condom breakage is very low (Hatcher et al., 2004). Using a condom after the expiration date is the leading cause of breakage. However, if a condom does break while you are using it, the best thing to do is to insert a spermicidal jelly or cream into the vagina immediately.

As we discussed earlier, using certain products with latex condoms may cause them to tear (see the accompanying Sex in Real Life, "What to Use With Condoms"). These also include creams for vaginal infections (such as Monistat™ and Vagisil™). Exposure to heat can also cause a condom to break when used. This is why it's not a good idea to carry a condom in your pocket or wallet for an extended period of time.

Advantages

Barrier methods of birth control, including latex condoms, offer the most protection from STIs, including the virus that causes AIDS. In addition, condoms encourage male participation in contraception, are inexpensive (depending on how sexually active the couple is), do not require a prescription, may reduce the incidence of premature ejaculation, reduce **postcoital drip,** and have no medical side effects. Lubricated condoms may also make intercourse more pleasurable by reducing friction. Overall, polyurethane condom users report more sensitivity than do latex condom users (Hollander, 2001).

postcoital drip
A vaginal discharge (dripping) that occurs after sexual intercourse.

Disadvantages

Because a couple must interrupt foreplay to put the condom on, intercourse is less spontaneous. In addition, some people feel a reduced sensation or develop a slight allergic reaction to a specific type of condom or lubricant. Some condoms are available only in a single size, whereas others come in a variety of sizes and shapes. If a condom is too large, it may slip and be ineffective. Polyurethane condoms have also been found to be more difficult to put on than latex, and tend to slip or bunch up during sexual intercourse (Hollander, 2001).

Disadvantages of the female condom include the fact that they can be difficult to use, uncomfortable, and may slip during sexual intercourse. Users might find insertion "noisy" or difficult (Lie, 2000). Second-generation female condoms have been developed but have not yet gotten FDA approval. Female condoms can also be expensive. Manufacturers have looked for ways to reduce the cost while also addressing issues of slippage and other concerns. One second-generation condom, the *Reddy* female condom, uses a sponge to stabilize the condom and prevent slipping (J. L. Schwartz & Gabelnick, 2002).

Cross-Cultural Use

Condoms are popular in many countries throughout the world, including Australia, Canada, Croatia, Czech Republic, Greece, Hong Kong, India, Iran, Italy, Japan, Ireland, and Germany. In fact, German couples will often avoid intercourse when no condom is available (Lautmann & Starke, 2004), and in Ireland men have been known to make their own condoms out of plastic wrap when they cannot find a condom (Kelly, 2004; something that is not recommended by your author, by the way). Condoms are also very popular in Japan, where nearly 80% of couples using contraception choose them (Hatano & Shimazaki, 2004).

In many other countries, however, condoms are not widely used. This may be due to embarrassment, lack of availability, or religious prohibition. In Botswana, for example, many couples are embarrassed to purchase condoms (Mookodi, Ntshebe, & Taylor, 2004), and a similar attitude is found in Brazil, especially among women (de Freitas, 2004). However, these attitudes are slowly changing due to increased condom availability. In Costa Rica, where religious prohibitions discourage condom use, men report not wanting to use condoms and prohibit their partners from using protection as well (Arroba, 2004).

The Diaphragm

Overall, female barrier methods, including the **diaphragm** (DIE-uh-fram), have not been widely used or accepted (J. L. Schwartz & Gabelnick, 2002). The number of women using diaphragms dropped from 5% in 1988 to 2% in 1995, and to nearly zero in 2002 (Alan Guttmacher Institute, 2005a). However, the diaphragm works well to block the cervical entrance and protect it from early cervical changes associated with cancer (Hatcher et al., 2004; Moench et al., 2001).

Today, diaphragms are made of either latex or silicone and come in several different sizes and shapes that must be fitted by a healthcare provider. Like latex condoms, latex diaphragms should not be used with oil-based lubricants because these can damage the latex (see Sex in Real Life on page 415). In the United States, diaphragms range in cost from $20 to $35, the accompanying spermicidal cream or jelly costs approximately $13 per tube, and there is also a charge for an office visit. Again, all of this tends to be less expensive at family planning clinics.

How It Works

The diaphragm is a barrier method of contraception, and it must be used with a spermicidal jelly to ensure that sperm do not live if they should get past the barrier. Diaphragms come in a variety of different sizes and shapes, and they must be prescribed by a physician or other healthcare provider to ensure a proper fit over the cervix.

Prior to insertion, the diaphragm rim is covered with spermicidal jelly, and 1 tablespoon of the jelly is put into the dome of the diaphragm. Although healthcare providers generally advise women to insert more spermicidal jelly if a second intercourse will take place, the evidence to support this practice is weak (Hatcher et al., 2004). The diaphragm is folded in half and inserted into the vagina while a woman is standing with one leg propped up, squatting, or lying on her back (see Figure 13.5). The diaphragm is pushed downward toward the back of the vagina, while the front rim is tucked under the

diaphragm
A birth control device consisting of a latex dome on a flexible spring rim; used with spermicidal cream or jelly.

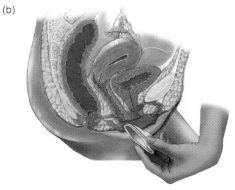

(a)

(b)

(c)

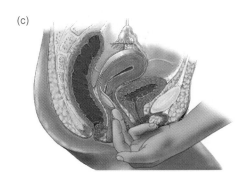

(d)

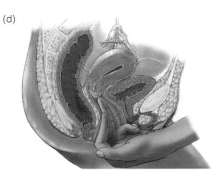

Figure 13.5
Instructions for proper insertion of a diaphragm.

pubic bone. The diaphragm can be inserted by the woman or her partner, and insertion may take place immediately prior to sexual intercourse or up to 6 hours before.

Once a diaphragm is in place, a woman should not be able to feel it; if she does, it is improperly inserted. The diaphragm must be checked to ensure it is properly placed on the cervix. This is done by inserting two fingers into the vagina and feeling for the diaphragm covering the cervix.

After intercourse, the diaphragm must be left in place for at least 6 to 8 hours, but never more than 24 hours. To remove the diaphragm, a finger is hooked over the front of the diaphragm rim, and then it is pulled down and out of the vagina. The diaphragm must be washed with soap and water and replaced in its container. If properly cared for, diaphragms can last for several years. However, if a woman loses or gains more than 10 pounds or experiences a pregnancy (regardless of how the pregnancy was resolved—through birth, miscarriage, or **abortion**), she must have her diaphragm refitted by her healthcare provider.

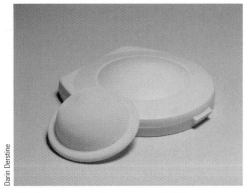

Darin Derstine

Diaphragms come in a variety of different shapes and sizes and must be fitted by a healthcare provider.

abortion
Induced termination of a pregnancy before fetal viability.

SEX Talk

Question: *Is it okay to borrow someone else's diaphragm if I can't find mine?*

Absolutely not. The diaphragm works by creating a suction on the cervix, which prevents sperm from entering the uterus. To get this suction, a healthcare provider must measure the cervix and prescribe the right size diaphragm for each individual woman. If you use someone else's diaphragm, it may be the wrong size and thus ineffective. Also, because of the risk of acquiring an STI, it is not a good idea to share diaphragms.

Effectiveness

Effectiveness rates for the diaphragm range from 84% (typical use) to 94% (perfect use). Correct and consistent use has been found to be an important factor in effectiveness rates. It is estimated that half of diaphragm users who become pregnant were using the method incorrectly (Hatcher et al., 2004). Women who have not had children have been found to have higher effectiveness rates than those women who have given birth.

Advantages

The diaphragm can be inserted prior to sexual activity, which increases spontaneity. In addition, the spermicidal cream or jelly provides some protection from STIs and **pelvic inflammatory disease** (PID), and it also reduces the risk of cervical dysplasia and/or cancer (Hatcher et al., 2004). The diaphragm does not affect hormonal levels and is relatively inexpensive. In addition, although it does not require partner involvement, men can be involved in the insertion of the diaphragm if desired.

Disadvantages

A physician fitting and prescription are necessary to use the diaphragm. In addition, a woman must be taught insertion and removal techniques and be comfortable touching her genitals. The diaphragm has also been found to increase the risk of toxic shock syndrome, urinary tract infection, and postcoital drip (Hatcher et al., 2004). It may also move during different sexual positions and become less effective or develop a foul odor if left in place too long. An allergic reaction to the spermicide may also develop.

Cross-Cultural Use

Because diaphragm use is low in the United States, it shouldn't come as any surprise that it also has low usage rates outside the United States. This is possibly due to the necessity of physician fitting, availability of spermicidal cream or jelly, cost, and the necessity of touching the genitals. Many women in other cultures are not comfortable touching the vagina or inserting anything into it (in fact, tampon use is also much lower in countries outside the United States). A shortage of physicians to fit diaphragms may also inhibit their use. There are exceptions to low usage however. The diaphragm remains a popular contraceptive method in Australia (Coates, 2004).

The Contraceptive Sponge

Although the Today **contraceptive sponge** was approved by the FDA in 1983, it was pulled off the market in 1995 because of stringent new government safety rules that had to do with the manufacturing plant. In late 2005 the sponge was reintroduced and available over the counter in the United States. The one-size-fits-all sponge covers the cervix and contains spermicide. A box of three sponges costs approximately $13.

How It Works

Contraceptive sponges work in three ways: as a barrier, blocking the entrance to the uterus; absorbing sperm; and deactivating sperm. Prior to vaginal insertion, the sponge is moistened with water, which activates the spermicide. It is then folded in half and inserted deep into the vagina (see Figure 13.6). Like the diaphragm, the sponge must be checked to make sure it is covering the cervix. Intercourse can take place immediately after insertion or at any time during the next 24 hours and can occur as many times as desired without adding additional spermicidal jelly or cream. However, the sponge must be left in place for 6 hours after intercourse. For removal, a cloth loop on the outside of the sponge (Today sponge) or die-cut slots (Protectaid sponge) are grasped to gently pull

pelvic inflammatory disease (PID)
Widespread infection of the female pelvic organs.

contraceptive sponge
Polyurethane sponge impregnated with spermicide, inserted into the vagina for contraception.

The Today contraceptive sponge was back on the market in late 2005 in the United States.

Darin Derstine

Personal Voices

What Do You Think About Your Method of Birth Control?

College students were asked about their contraceptive methods. Here are some of their personal stories and their opinions of their method.

Female: I recently tried the hormonal patch. It was relatively new, and I wanted to see what it was all about. I always had trouble remembering to take my pill at the right time, and I figured that it would be much easier to only have to remember once a week instead of seven times a week. The excitement didn't last for very long. The patch got in the way of so many things. My boyfriend felt that it got in the way when he touched me. It bothered me because it stuck so hard and the glue and pieces of fuzz from clothing were hard to remove. After only 5 months of using the patch I decided that taking a pill every day wasn't so bad.

Male: My girlfriend uses birth control pills. She did put on some weight, but I didn't mind. The pill doesn't seem to affect her sexual desires, and she doesn't have many side effects. I try to help as much as I can by reminding her to take it and paying for it each month. If she forgets to take it, we use condoms.

Female: When I first started having sex I also used a number of different types of backup (just in case the pill didn't work). I used condoms, but they were a hassle, and my boyfriend at the time didn't like using them, so we tried spermicides. First we used film, and that was okay, and then we used jelly. I think that was the best. It came in pre-filled tubes, and it was just like putting in a tampon. So easy, and we didn't have to wait for it to dissolve. It was so cool, I could even carry it in my purse and no one knew the difference.

Male: I used to use nothing but the pull-out method. BAD BAD BAD!! That was the worst thing that I ever did, talk about stress! I was not educated about different birth control methods, and my girlfriend at that time informed me that if I just pulled out that she wouldn't get pregnant. I thought she knew what she was talking about so I believed her. I use condoms with all my partners. I definitely don't want to get an STI and want to be sure my partners don't get pregnant until I'm ready.

Female: We use birth control pills because a child at this time would definitely not be good!

Male: My girlfriend and I have been using a diaphragm for about a year now. We like it because she can put it in early and we don't have to be bothered during sex. I don't mind her using it at all.

Male: I'm not in a relationship right now, but I have been having casual sex with a few different partners. I hate to say it, but I've just hoped they are on the pill because I don't use condoms. I know I should worry about infections, but since the sex is never planned, I just hope they know what they are doing.

Female: I'm on birth control pills, and I love them. I do not use condoms while on it, even though I know I should. The only problem I've found with the pill is that at first I gained a little weight, but if I really tried to eat healthy, I was fine. The pill is definitely good for a long-term committed relationship.

Male: My girlfriend just got one of the patches, and she put it on her stomach. Sometimes it bothers me a little when I rub it during sex, but really I don't care. I try to remind her to change it, and so far it's been working out well.

Female: I have been on the pill for 5 years and have had no problems. I like it because it is easy and the side effects are small. Occasionally I might forget to take it, but never more than one night, and then my boyfriend and I use a condom. He doesn't mind, because like me, kids are not high on our list of priorities right now.

SOURCE: Author's files.

the sponge out of the vagina. Like the diaphragm, the sponge can be inserted and removed by either the woman or her partner.

Effectiveness

Effectiveness rates for the sponge range from 75% (typical use) to 89% (perfect use). Like the diaphragm, these rates depend on the user, and failure rates are higher in women who have had children (Hatcher et al., 2004).

Figure 13.6
Instructions for proper insertion of a
contraceptive sponge.

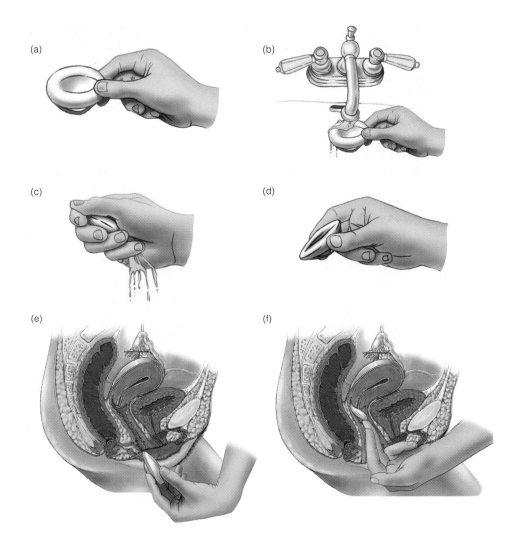

Advantages

Contraceptive sponges can be purchased without a prescription. Once inserted, sexual intercourse can take place as many times as desired during a 24-hour period. The sponge can be also be put in prior to sexual intercourse, which may increase sexual spontaneity. Sponges do not affect hormonal levels, are disposable, and do not require routine cleaning. In addition, although they do not require partner involvement, men can be involved in the insertion of the contraceptive sponge if desired.

Disadvantages

The contraceptive sponge may increase the risk of toxic shock syndrome and urinary tract infections. Unlike the diaphragm, the sponge cannot be left in place during a woman's menstrual period. Other disadvantages include required touching of the genitals, which may be uncomfortable for some women; a foul odor if left in place too long; possible spermicide-caused allergic reaction in the woman or her partner; high expense if used frequently; and difficulty for some couples to insert and remove. In addition, some men can feel the sponge inside and may find it uncomfortable.

Cross-Cultural Use

As we've discussed, the Today contraceptive sponge is available in Canada and many parts of Europe. However, there is little research on the cross-cultural use of the contraceptive sponge. We do know that for years women in France have been using vaginal sponges that have been dipped in various chemicals to avoid pregnancy. These sponges are washed and used over and over. This practice is not recommended, however, because of the risk of infection and toxic shock syndrome. As with diaphragms, sponges tend to have low usage rates in other cultures, which may be due to such factors as the lack of availability of spermicidal cream or jelly or the necessity of touching the genitals.

The Cervical Barriers

Cervical barriers are thimble-shaped, silicone devices that are inserted into the vagina and fit over the cervix. Like the diaphragm and sponge, cervical barriers block sperm from entering the uterus. As of 2005, there were two cervical barriers available in the United States—the **FemCap** and **Lea's Shield.** Both of these devices must be fitted by a healthcare provider. Lea's Shield has a one-way valve that allows the flow of cervical fluids and air, and is a one-size-fits-all method. The FemCap is available in three sizes— small for women who have never been pregnant, medium for women who have been pregnant but have not had a vaginal delivery, and large for women who have had a vaginal delivery of a full-term baby. Both cost between $15 and $75, depending on where they are purchased, and the necessary spermicide costs anywhere from $8 to $10.

> **cervical barrier**
> A plastic or rubber cover for the cervix that provides a contraceptive barrier to sperm.
>
> **FemCap**
> Reusable silicone barrier vaginal contraceptive that comes in three sizes.
>
> **Lea's Shield**
> Reusable silicone barrier vaginal contraceptive that contains a one-way valve.

How They Work

Cervical barriers work by blocking the entrance to the uterus and deactivating sperm through the use of spermicidal cream or jelly. After insertion, a woman must check to see that the barrier is covering her cervix. The barriers should be left in place for 8 hours after the last intercourse. Both cervical barriers have straps to aid in removal. Women should not use the barriers during menstruation because they can increase the risk of toxic shock. After use, the devices should be washed with soap and water and allowed to air dry.

Effectiveness

Effectiveness rates for typical use of both the FemCap and Lea's Shield are approximately 86% in women who have never had children (Cates & Stewart, 2004). Typical effectiveness rates are lower for women who have had children. At this time there are no perfect use effectiveness rates for the cervical barrier methods.

Advantages

Cervical barriers can be left in place for up to 48 hours, and can be inserted earlier and left in longer than a diaphragm. They do not affect hormonal levels, are immediately effective, and not permanent. In addition, they are made of silicone and users do not experience latex-related allergies. Partner involvement is possible, but not necessary, with these methods. Finally, Lea's Shield has a one-way release valve to reduce the risk of toxic shock syndrome.

Disadvantages

The use of cervical barriers may increase a woman's risk of toxic shock syndrome, cause abnormal Pap smears, increase the risk of urinary tract infections, increase vaginal odors, cause cervical damage, and increase postcoital drip. In addition, in the United States they must be fitted by a healthcare provider, may be felt by the male partner during sexual intercourse, may dislodge during penile thrusting, and may cause discomfort (Cates & Stewart, 2004).

Cross-Cultural Use

Cervical barriers are widely used in England and in some countries, including Germany, Austria, Switzerland, and Canada, Lea's Shield has been available over the counter since 1993 (Long,

(a) The FemCap is a silicone cup shaped like a sailor's hat that fits securely over the cervix. (b) Lea's Shield is a silicone cup with a one-way valve and a loop for easier removal.

Review Question

Identify five barrier methods of birth control, providing information on how the methods work, effectiveness rates, advantages and disadvantages, and cross-cultural use.

sex byte

It is estimated that over 80% of American women born since 1945 have used birth control pills at some point in their lives, whereas 95% of French women and 4% of Japanese women have used birth control pills (Blackburn, Cunkelman, & Zlidar, 2000).

oral contraceptive
The "pill"; a preparation of synthetic female hormones that blocks ovulation.

combination birth control pill
An oral contraceptive containing synthetic estrogen and progesterone.

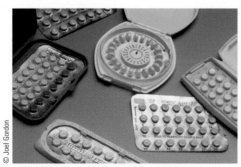

A variety of birth control pills are available, and a healthcare provider can prescribe the one that's best for you.

© Joel Gordon

HORMONAL METHODS FOR WOMEN: THE PILL, THE PATCH, AND MORE

Hormonal contraceptive methods contain synthetic hormones and include pills, patches, hormonal rings, subdermal implants, and injections (Economidis & Mishell, 2005). By changing hormonal levels, production of ova can be interrupted, and fertilization and implantation can be also be prevented. Hormonal methods have been found to be effective, safe, reversible, and acceptable to most women. However, for protection against STIs, condoms must also be used. Also, women who use hormonal methods of contraception should always inform their healthcare providers about their contraceptive use, especially in the event of surgery.

Combined-Hormone Methods

Combined-hormonal methods use a blend of hormones (including estrogen and progesterone) to suppress ovulation and thicken the cervical mucus to prevent sperm from joining the ovum. Combined-hormone methods include most birth control pills, injections, vaginal rings, and patches. Some birth control pills are progestin-based methods and do not include estrogen. We will discuss progestin-only methods later in this chapter. Here we'll concentrate on combined-hormonal methods.

Birth Control Pills

Margaret Sanger was the first to envision **oral contraceptives** (the birth control pill, or simply "the pill"). Many researchers had been working with chemical methods to inhibit pregnancy in animals, but they were reluctant to try these methods on humans because they feared that increasing hormones could cause cancer. The complexity of a woman's body chemistry and the expense involved in developing the pill inhibited its progress. Finally, in 1960, the birth control pill was federally approved as a contraceptive method.

At first, the pill was much stronger than it needed to be. In the search for the most effective contraception, more estrogen was seen as more effective. However, within 3 to 4 years, physicians realized that many women were experiencing negative side effects due to the high dosage of estrogen, so they lowered the amount of estrogen. Today's birth control pills have less than half the dose of estrogen the first pills had. After 40 years on the market, oral contraceptives still remain the most popular contraceptive method not only in the United States but around the world (Freeman, 2002; Lie, 2000). In addition, birth control pills are the most extensively studied type of medication in the history of medicine (Hatcher et al., 2004).

Combination birth control pills, which contain synthetic estrogen and a type of progesterone, are the most commonly used contraceptive method in the United States. They require a physician's prescription and cost between $12 and $25 per month at the pharmacy (less in family planning clinics).

In Chapter 4 we discussed menstrual manipulation and menstrual suppression. Birth control pills have typically been designed to mimic an average menstrual cycle, which is why a woman takes them for 21 days and then has 1 week off, in which she will usually start a period. Originally, this 3-week-on/1-week-off regimen was developed to convince women that the pill was "natural," which pill makers believed would make the product more acceptable to potential users and reassure them that they were not pregnant every month (Clarke & Miller, 2001; Thomas & Ellertson, 2000). As we discussed in Chapter 4, the bleeding that women experience while on the pill is medically induced and has no physiological benefit (J. L. Schwartz et al., 1999).

Monthly withdrawal bleeding while on oral contraceptives may soon become obsolete altogether. Some healthcare providers have begun the practice of "bicycling" (back-to-back use of two packs of active pills without only placebo pills at the end of the second pack) or "tricycling" (back-to-back-back use of three packs of active pills with placebo pills only after the third pack; Hatcher & Nelson, 2004). In 2003 the FDA approved a new continuous 84-day active pill with a 7-day placebo pill regimen called Seasonale. Users of Seasonale have only 4 periods a year, compared to the usual 13. Seasonale and other birth control pill manipulation routines may be attractive options for women who experience heavy bleeding and cramping with their periods each month. Research has found that 60% of women report a preference for no period while taking oral contraceptives (Lie, 2000).

How They Work   The hormones estrogen, progesterone, lutenizing hormone (LH), and follicle stimulating hormone (FSH) fluctuate during a woman's menstrual cycle. These fluctuations control the maturation of an ovum, ovulation, the development of the endometrium, and menstruation (see Chapter 4). The synthetic hormones replace a woman's own natural hormones but in different amounts. The increase in estrogen and progesterone prevent the pituitary gland from sending hormones to cause the ovaries to begin maturation of an ovum. Hormone levels while on the pill are similar to when a woman is pregnant, and this is what interferes with ovulation. Birth control pills also work by thickening the cervical mucus (which inhibits the mobility of sperm) and by reducing the buildup of the endometrium.

Combination birth control pills can either be **monophasic** or **multiphasic.** Monophasic pills contain the same amount of hormones in each pill, whereas multiphasic pills vary the hormonal amount. Traditionally, birth control pills have always been taken on either a 21-day or 28-day regimen and started on the 1st or 5th day of menstruation or on the 1st Sunday after menstruation. **Start days** vary depending on the pill manufacturer. The majority of manufacturers recommend a Sunday start day, which enables a woman to avoid menstruating during a weekend. Each pill must be taken every day, at approximately the same time. This is important because they work by maintaining a certain hormonal level in the bloodstream. If this level drops, ovulation may occur (see the accompanying Sex in Real Life, "What to Do If You Forget," for more information). The last seven pills in a 28-day regimen are **placebo pills** and, because they contain no hormones, a woman usually starts menstruating while taking them.

Women who take birth control pills usually have lighter menstrual periods because the pills decrease the buildup of the endometrium. Menstrual discomfort, such as cramping, is also reduced. Because oral contraception also increases menstrual regularity, some women with irregular periods are advised to take birth control pills to regulate their periods even if they do not need contraception. Contraceptive pill users may also experience slight breast enlargement due to increases in estrogen. Research has found that 30% of women who take birth control pills experience increased breast size and/or breast tenderness (Hatcher & Nelson, 2004).

Because different pills contain different dosages of estrogen and progesterone, a healthcare provider needs to determine the sensitivity of a woman's endocrine system to prescribe the appropriate level of hormones. There is no one type of pill that is better for everyone, based on side effects or effectiveness rates.

Before starting a regime of birth control pills, a woman must first have a full medical examination. Women with a history of circulatory problems, strokes, heart disease, breast or uterine cancer, hypertension, diabetes, and undiagnosed vaginal bleeding are generally advised not to take oral contraceptives (Hatcher et al., 2004). Although migraine headaches have typically been a contraindication for using birth control pills, some women may experience fewer migraines while using birth control pills, especially if used continuously without placebo pills (Hatcher et al., 2004). If a woman can use birth control pills, physicians usually begin by prescribing a low-dose estrogen pill, and they increase the dosage if **breakthrough bleeding** or other symptoms occur.

Triphasil (TRY-fay-sill) **pills** were introduced in the 1990s and have been growing in popularity. They contain three different sets of pills for the month. Each week, the hormonal dosage is increased, rather than keeping the level at the consistently high lev-

monophasic
Describes oral contraceptives containing stable levels of hormones during the entire month; the doses and types of hormones do not vary.

multiphasic
Describes oral contraceptives that contain varying levels of hormones during the month; each week the hormonal dosage is changed.

start day
The actual day that the first pill is taken in a pack of oral contraceptives.

placebo pills
In a pack of 28-day oral contraceptives, the seven pills at the end; these pills are sugar pills and do not contain any hormones; they are used to help a woman remember to take a pill every day.

breakthrough bleeding
Slight blood loss that occurs from the uterus when a woman is taking oral contraceptives.

triphasil pill
A type of multiphasic oral contraceptive with three different types of pills, each of which contains a different hormonal dosage.

SEX in Real Life

What to Do If You Forget

IF . . . THEN . . .

You forget one or two active combination pills with more than 20 mcg of estrogen OR one active combination pill with 20 mcg or less of estrogen . . . *Take them as soon as you remember. Take the next pill at the usual time (this means you may take two pills in 1 day). Finish that series, and start the next pack on time.*

If during the first 2 weeks you forget three or more active combination pills with more than 20 mcg of estrogen OR two or more active combination pills with 20 mcg or less of estrogen . . . *Take them as soon as you remember. Take the next pill at the regular time. Use a backup method for 7 days after the pills are skipped. Call your healthcare provider if you do not get your period.*

If during the 3rd week, you forget three or more active combination pills with more than 20 mcg of estrogen OR two or more active combination pills with 20 mcg or less of estrogen . . . *Use a backup method for 7 days after the pills are skipped. Take one active pill as soon as you remember. Take the next pill at the usual time. Continue tak-*

ing one active pill every day until you finish the active pills in the pack. Throw away any placebo pills. Start a new pack the next day. You may not have your period this month, but this is expected. Call your clinician if you do not get your period 2 months in a row.

You forget any of the seven placebo pills . . . *Throw away the pills you missed. Take one of the remaining sugar pills in the 4th week. Start the next pack on time.*

You forget to take your progestin-only pill for more than 3 hours past your regular time . . . *Take it as soon as you remember. Take the next pill at the usual time. Continue to take the rest of the pack on schedule. Use a backup method of birth control for 48 hours after taking the late pill. Start the next pack on time.*

You are still not sure what to do about the pills you have missed. . . . *Use a backup method anytime you have vaginal intercourse. Take one active pill each day until you can talk with your clinician.*

SOURCE: Planned Parenthood (http://www.plannedparenthood.org/bc/pill_schedule. html). Reprinted with permission from Planned Parenthood Federation of America, Inc. © 2000 PPFA. All rights reserved.

els like monophasic pills. When it was first introduced, many physicians liked this pill because it seemed to follow a woman's natural cycle. However, many women who use triphasil pills report an increase in breakthrough bleeding due to the fluctuating hormone levels.

Because the hormones in birth control pills are similar to those during pregnancy, it is not surprising that many women experience signs of pregnancy. These signs may include nausea, increase in breast size, breast tenderness, water retention, headaches, increased appetite, fatigue, depression, decreased sexual drive, and high blood pressure (Hatcher et al., 2004; see Chapter 12). Symptoms usually disappear within a couple of months, once a woman's body becomes used to the hormonal levels.

Physicians should reevaluate a woman on birth control pills after 3 months to see whether she is experiencing any problems, in which case a different dosage may be indicated. If a woman using the pill experiences abdominal pain, chest pain, severe headaches, vision or eye problems, and severe leg or calf pain, she should contact her physician immediately. In addition, a woman who takes birth control pills should always inform her physician of her oral contraceptive use, especially if she is prescribed other medications or undergoes any type of surgery. Certain drugs may have negative interactions with oral contraceptives (see the accompanying Sex in Real Life, "Drugs and Herbs That Interact With Oral Contraception").

Finally, over the last few years there has been a very vocal debate about whether oral contraceptive use increases a woman's risk of developing breast cancer (Fowke et al., 2004). But research has found that using birth control pills, even when begun at a young age, has little, if any, effect on the development of breast cancer (Hatcher et al., 2004). In addition, even birth control pill users with a family history of breast cancer do not

Drugs and Herbs That Interact With Oral Contraceptives

Many over-the-counter (nonprescription) drugs, prescription medications, and herbal supplements may lower the effectiveness of the pill, and the pill may interfere with another drug's effectiveness. When you take medications, you should always let your healthcare provider know that you are on birth control pills. Drugs that interact with oral contraceptives include the following:

In addition, women who take oral contraceptives should avoid Orlistat (drug developed to block fat absorption) because it has been shown to reduce absorption of oral contraceptives. Women should also avoid eating more than 10 to 50 gm a day of black licorice, which may increase blood pressure and water retention while on oral contraceptives.

SOURCE: Hatcher et al., 2004.

Drug	Effect
Acetaminophen (Tylenol)	Decreases effect of pain relief.
Alcohol (beer, wine, mixed drinks, etc.)	Increases effect of alcohol.
Anticoagulants (Heparin, Coumadin, aspirin)	Decreases anticoagulant effect. Aspirin may be less effective when used with oral contraceptives.
Antibiotics (Amoxicillin, Tetracycline, Ampicillin)	May decrease effectiveness of oral contraceptives.
Antidepressants (Prozac, Paxil)	Increases blood levels of antidepressant.
Antifungal medications (Grisactin)	Can cause breakthrough bleeding and spotting.
Barbiturates (Seconal, Nembutal)	Decreases effectiveness of oral contraceptives.
Vitamin C	May increase estrogen side effects in daily doses of 1,000 mg or more.
St. John's wort (Hypericum)	Decreases effectiveness of oral contraceptives.
Caffeine	May reduce caffeine metabolism.

have an increased risk for breast cancer. Furthermore, birth control pills may offer some protection from ovarian and endometrial cancers, and may reduce the risk of breast and uterine fibroids and/or cysts (Deligeoroglou et al., 2003; Hatcher et al., 2004).

Effectiveness Effectiveness rates for combination birth control pills range from 92% (typical use) to 99.7% (perfect use). To be effective, the pill must be taken every day, at the same time of day.

Advantages If used correctly, oral contraceptives have one of the highest effectiveness rates; do not interfere with spontaneity; reduce the flow of menstruation, menstrual cramps, and premenstrual syndrome; increase menstrual regularity; and reduce the likelihood of ovarian cysts, uterine and breast fibroids, and facial acne. Oral contraceptives also provide important degrees of protection against ovarian and endometrial cancers, pelvic inflammatory disease, and benign breast disease (Hatcher et al., 2004). In addition, use of oral contraceptives may increase sexual enjoyment because fear of pregnancy is reduced and they are convenient and easy to use. The pill offers rapid reversibility, and the majority of women who go off the pill return to ovulation within 2 weeks (Hatcher et al., 2004).

Disadvantages Oral contraceptives must be taken daily, offer no protection from STIs, and put all the responsibility for contraception on the female. They can be expensive and their effectiveness is decreased when certain other medications are used. In addition, they may also contribute to increased risk of STIs because birth control users tend to be poor users of condoms. Women who are overweight may experience lower effectiveness rates using oral contraceptives (Holt et al., 2004). In addition, women who smoke cigarettes should not use birth control pills. Heavy smokers who take birth control pills have been found to increase their risk of heart attacks (Rosenberg et al., 2001).

Cross-Cultural Use   Birth control pills have been used by more than 100 million women throughout the world (Hatcher & Nelson, 2004), and in many countries—including Australia, Argentina, Austria, Botswana, Brazil, Canada, Costa Rica, Cuba, Denmark, Finland, France, Germany, Hong Kong, Italy, Mexico, the Netherlands, Norway, Puerto Rico, Spain, Sweden, Switzerland, and the United Kingdom—they are the most popular contraceptive method (Francoeur & Noonan, 2004). In Costa Rica, Hong Kong, and Mexico, birth control pills are available over the counter without a prescription (Arroba, 2004; Ng & Ma, 2004).

In some countries, birth control pills are used, but they are not the most popular contraceptive choice. This would include countries such as the Czech Republic, Korea, China, Greece, India, Israel, Kenya, Nepal, Russia, Turkey, and Japan. In Russia, birth control pills are thought to be unsafe and unreliable (Kon, 2004). Prior to the pill's approval in 1999, it was not available for contraceptive use in Japan (Goto et al., 1999). Approval didn't come easy, and the restrictions on pill use are strict. For example, contraceptive pill users in Japan are required to have gynecological exams every 3 months and are expected to pay for all of their contraceptive pill expenses (with no insurance coverage). As in the United States, when safety reports about contraceptive pill use are issued, usage rates tend to decrease outside the United States.

SEX Talk

Question: Last week I lost my pack of birth control pills and did not have time to go to the student health center. My roommate let me take a few of her pills. Is this okay?

This is not a good idea. Because there are many different types of pills, with different levels of hormones in them, your roommate may not be taking the same kind of pill. Also, with the new triphasil pills, if you took someone else's pills and they were not the same, you could be at risk of getting pregnant. The best idea would be to make time to refill your own prescription and use another method of contraception until you start a new pack of pills.

Hormonal Ring

NuvaRing is a hormonal method of birth control that was introduced in 2003. It is a small plastic ring that is inserted into the vagina once a month and releases a constant dose of estrogen and progesterone. The amount of hormones released into the bloodstream with the NuvaRing is lower than in both oral contraceptives and the patch (Hatcher & Nelson, 2004; we will talk more about the patch later in this chapter). Each ring costs approximately $30 to $35, and the initial office visit often costs between $35 and $125.

How It Works   Like birth control pills, NuvaRing works by inhibiting ovulation, increasing cervical mucus, and rendering the uterus inhospitable to implantation (Hatcher & Nelson, 2004). The ring is inserted deep inside the vagina, and moisture and body heat activate the release of hormones. Each ring is left in place for 3 weeks and then taken out for 1 week. During this last week a woman will usually begin her period.

Effectiveness   The NuvaRing has not been available long enough to have documented typical use rates. However, it is a very effective method of birth control, and perfect use effectiveness rates are generally around 99.7% (Hatcher & Nelson, 2004).

NuvaRing
A small plastic contraceptive ring that is inserted into the vagina once a month and releases a constant dose of estrogen and progestin.

Effectiveness rates may be lower when other medications are taken, when the unopened package is exposed to high temperatures or direct sunlight, or when the ring is left in the vagina for over 3 weeks.

Advantages Like other hormonal methods of birth control, the NuvaRing has a high effectiveness rate; does not interfere with spontaneity; reduces the flow of menstruation, menstrual cramps, and premenstrual syndrome; and increases menstrual regularity (Hatcher & Nelson, 2004). It also provides lower levels of hormones than some of the other combined-hormone methods. In addition, NuvaRing may also offer some protection from ovarian and endometrial cancer and ovarian cysts. Fertility is quickly restored when the ring is removed.

The NuvaRing is inserted deep into the vagina; moisture and heat cause it to time-release hormones that inhibit ovulation.

Disadvantages A woman using NuvaRing must be comfortable touching her genitals and placing the ring inside her vagina. The NuvaRing offers no protection against STIs and may cause a variety of side effects, including breakthrough bleeding, weight gain or loss, breast tenderness, nausea, mood changes, changes in sexual desire, increased vaginal irritation, and discharge. However, many of these side effects dissipate with regular use. Because this method is new, there are no data on extended use.

Cross-Cultural Use We don't know a lot about NuvaRing use outside the United States. The necessity of touching the genitals may lead to lower usage rates throughout the world. Even so, NuvaRing has been used safely and effectively outside the United States, and research has found that it has been well tolerated (Bjarnadottir et al., 2002; Mulders & Dieben, 2001).

Hormonal Patch

The **Ortho Evra patch** is a hormonal method of birth control that was introduced in 2002. It is a thin, peach-colored patch that sticks to the skin and time-releases hormones into the bloodstream. The Ortho Evra patch costs about $30 to $35 per month, and the initial office visit often costs between $35 and $125.

Ortho Evra patch
A thin, peach-colored patch that sticks to the skin and time-releases synthetic estrogen and progestin into the bloodstream to inhibit ovulation, increase cervical mucus, and render the uterus inhospitable; also referred to as the "patch."

How It Works Like birth control pills and the NuvaRing, the Ortho Evra patch uses synthetic estrogen and progestin to inhibit ovulation, increase cervical mucus, and render the uterus inhospitable to implantation. Although we used to believe that the patch contained similar levels of estrogen as oral contraceptives, in late 2005 the FDA updated labeling for the Ortho Evra contraceptive patch to inform users that the patch exposes them to higher levels of estrogen than most birth control pills (U.S. Food and Drug Administration, 2005). This is important for women who might have certain risk factors, including potential blood clots.

The Ortho Evra patch is placed on the buttock, stomach, or upper torso once a week for 3 weeks. No patch is used during the 4th week; this is when a woman will usually have her period. It works best if the patch is changed on the same day of the week for 3 weeks in a row. A woman can maintain an active lifestyle with the patch in place—she can swim and shower without worrying that the patch will fall off.

The Ortho Evra patch is worn on the buttock, abdomen, or upper torso for 3 weeks each month.

Effectiveness Like NuvaRing, the patch has not been available long enough to generate typical use effectiveness rates. However, it is similar to NuvaRing, with perfect use effectiveness rates around 99.7% (Hatcher & Nelson, 2004). However, it may be less effective in women who weigh more than 198 pounds (Hatcher & Nelson, 2004). As with other hormonal methods, certain medications, such as antibiotic and seizure drugs, can decrease effectiveness. Heat, humidity, and exercise have not been found to interfere with adhesion or effectiveness rates (Zacur et al., 2002), nor have saunas, water baths, or swimming (Burkman, 2002).

Advantages Like other hormonal methods of birth control, the Ortho Evra patch has a high effectiveness rate; does not interfere with spontaneity; reduces menstrual flow, menstrual cramps, and premenstrual syndrome; and increases menstrual regularity (Hatcher & Nelson, 2004). The patch may also offer some protection against ovarian and endometrial cancer and ovarian cysts. The patch has over a 90% perfect dosing level because it is applied to the skin (Burkman, 2002).

Disadvantages The Ortho Evra patch offers no protection from STIs and may cause a variety of side effects, including breakthrough bleeding, weight gain or loss, breast tenderness (especially in the first 3 months of use), nausea, mood changes, changes in sexual desire, skin changes or irritation, and a change in vision. Some women may not be able to use their contact lenses because of these changes. In addition, some women report that they dislike the fuzz and lint that the patch collects from their clothing, and that it is nearly impossible to conceal the patch from a partner. Because this method is new, there are no data on extended use.

Cross-Cultural Use We don't know a lot about Ortho Evra's use outside the United States because it is so new. However, early estimates have found that approximately 2 million women worldwide use the contraceptive patch (Bestic, 2005).

Progestin-Only Methods

Progestin-only birth control methods do not contain estrogen. The methods can be used by women who cannot take estrogen or by women who are breast-feeding. They work by changing a woman's menstrual cycle, which may result in changes in menstrual flow and frequency of periods, as well as an increase in breakthrough bleeding. Over time, users of progestin-only methods report having no periods at all. Progestin-only methods may also lead to slight weight gains (approximately 4 to 5 pounds over 5 years of use), feelings of bloatedness, and/or breast tenderness. These problems are typically the most frequent reason for discontinuing usage.

Minipills

Earlier in this chapter we discussed combined-hormone pills, which work by inhibiting ovulation and thickening cervical mucus. **Minipills,** or **POPs (progestin-only pills),** work the same way, but they can be used by women who smoke or are breast-feeding and have fewer side effects than combined-hormone pills.

Minipills are more expensive and slightly less effective (92% for typical use; 99.7% for perfect use) than combination pills, require obsessive regularity in pill-taking, and can cause irregular bleeding (Hatcher, 2004). Women who get pregnant while taking minipills have a higher rate of ectopic pregnancy compared to women taking combined-hormone pills. In addition, minipills are less likely to be stocked by pharmacies.

Subdermal Implants

Subdermal contraceptive implants time-release a constant dose of progestin and typically are used for up to 5 years. **Norplant** was the first such method introduced in the United States, in 1990. However, due to multiple lawsuits and court battles, the manufacturer announced in 2002 that it would stop production of Norplant. As of 2005, Norplant implants are no longer available for new users but current users can continue using it until it expires.

An improved version of Norplant—called Jadelle—was approved by the FDA in 1996 but has not been marketed in the United States. Jadelle consists of two silicone cylinders that are implanted in a woman's forearm through a small incision. The implantation procedure takes about 10 minutes and is usually performed in a healthcare provider's office. Jadelle can be left in place for 5 years, after which the cylinders must be surgically removed. Fertility is restored as soon as the cylinders are removed.

progestin-only birth control method
Contraceptive hormonal method that does not contain estrogen and works by changing a woman's menstrual cycle.

minipills or POP (progestin-only pill)
A type of birth control pill that contains only synthetic progesterone and no estrogen.

subdermal contraceptive implant
Contraceptive implant that time-releases a constant dose of progestin to inhibit ovulation.

Norplant
A hormonal method of birth control using doses that are implanted in a woman's arm and that can remain in place for up to 5 years.

Other hormonal implants are being researched today. A single-rod progesterone implant, Implanon, was approved by the FDA in 2004. The single-rod system has been found to provide a more stable release of hormones than Norplant (Bennink, 2000; J. E. Edwards & Moore, 1999).

How They Work   The implants are often inserted during the first 7 days of a woman's menstrual cycle and contain time-released hormones (synthetic progestin) that suppress ovulation, thicken cervical mucus, and render the endometrium inhospitable to the zygote.

Effectiveness   Subdermal implants have been found to be 99.95% effective in the first year of use; effectiveness rates decrease consistently after the third year. Also, women who weigh more than 154 pounds generally absorb lower hormonal concentrations, which may increase the chances of pregnancy.

Advantages   Women who are unable to use oral contraceptives may be able to safely use subdermal implants. They are a highly effective, long-lasting, easily reversible contraceptive method with a rapid onset of protection. They require a simple implantation procedure; have no estrogen side effects; decrease menstrual flow, cramping, and risk of endometrial cancer; and increase spontaneity.

Disadvantages   Insertion and the implants' costs are estimated at $500 or more, depending on the physician's fees. Women using implants may experience irregular bleeding or other menstrual problems, arm pain, bleeding from the injection site, headaches or vision problems, dizziness, cramping, nausea, weight gain or loss, hair growth or loss, and general weakness (Hatcher, 2004). Additional side effects may include skin rash or acne, visible injection site and cylinders, painful removal procedures, and possible scars after removal (when protective scar tissue grows around the implants). In the future, scientists hope to develop self-dissolving cylinders so that removal is unnecessary.

Similar to oral contraceptives, subdermal implants' contraceptive effectiveness can be affected by the use of other drugs. In addition, these methods offer no protection from STIs.

Cross-Cultural Use   Prior to FDA approval in the United States, Norplant had been used throughout Europe, Latin America, and Asia. In several countries today, implants are one of the most popular contraceptive choices. In South Africa, 27% of women use implants (Nicholas, Daniels, & Hurwitz, 2004).

Hormonal Injectables

Depo-medroxyprogesterone acetate (DMPA, or **Depo-Provera;** DEP-poe PRO-vair-uh) was approved for use in the United States in 1992 and today is the most popular form of nonoral contraceptive (Hatcher et al., 2004). Depo-Provera is injected into the muscle of a woman's arm or buttock once every 3 months, and each injection costs $30 to $125. Depo-Provera begins working within 24 hours after the injection, and fertility resumes approximately 10 months after the last injection (Hatcher et al., 2004; Kaunitz et al., 1998).

In 2004, the FDA issued a "black box warning" that long-term use of Depo may result in the loss of bone density (U.S. Food and Drug Administration, 2004). This was a concern for female adolescents because they develop most of their bone mass between the ages of 15 to 19 and losing bone density could put a woman at risk for bone fractures or osteoporosis later in life. However, newer research has found that bone loss is reversible after a woman stops using Depo-Provera (Scholes et al., 2005).

Other injectable contraceptive devices have been available in several countries over the past few years. Noristerat, a long-acting drug, provides circulating levels of hormones to suppress ovulation and to make the endometrium inhospitable to the ovum.

Depo-Provera
Depo-medroxyprogesterone, an injectable contraceptive that prevents ovulation and thickens cervical mucus.

How It Works   Depo-Provera is an injectable form of contraception that contains synthetic progesterone, and it works chiefly by preventing ovulation and thickening cervical mucus. Supporters of Depo-Provera cite the fact that it does not contain estrogen (like some birth control pills), so it can be used by lactating and postpartum women or those who have adverse reactions to estrogen.

Effectiveness   Similar to oral contraceptives, Depo-Provera has a 97% (typical use) to 99.7% (perfect use) effectiveness rate (Hatcher, 2004).

Advantages   Depo-Provera is a highly effective method of birth control, and one injection lasts for 3 months. It is only moderately expensive, reversible, does not contain estrogen, and does not restrict spontaneity. Users of Depo-Provera often notice decreased cramping and pain during menstruation, and lighter periods. In fact, 30% to 50% of users have no menstrual periods at all (Hatcher, 2004). Depo use also reduces the risk of endometrial and ovarian cancer (Hatcher, 2004).

Disadvantages   Women who use Depo-Provera must schedule office visits every 3 months for their injections, and they often experience irregular bleeding and spotting. Other potential side effects include fatigue, dizzy spells, weakness, headaches, appetite increase (it is estimated that a woman will gain an average of 5.4 pounds in the first year of Depo use), and a decrease in bone density (Hatcher, 2004). Use may increase risk of cervical, liver, and/or breast cancers, and Depo-Provera cannot be used by women with a history of liver disease, breast cancer, or unexplained vaginal bleeding or blood clots. A return to fertility may take approximately 10 months after discontinuing the injections.

Cross-Cultural Use   Depo-Provera has been approved for use in more than 80 countries, including Botswana, Denmark, Finland, Great Britain, France, Sweden, Mexico, Norway, Germany, New Zealand, South Africa, and Belgium (Hatcher et al., 2004; Francoeur & Noonan, 2004). It has not been approved for contraceptive use in Australia, although it has been used for many years for other medical treatments (Coates, 2004). It has not been widely used in a variety of countries, including Brazil, Canada, China, Columbia, Croatia, Cuba, Czech Republic, Ireland, Japan, Kenya, and Spain (Francoeur & Noonan, 2004). Low usage rates may be due to a lack of marketing or religious prohibition.

CHEMICAL METHODS FOR WOMEN: SPERMICIDES

Spermicides come in a variety of forms, including creams, suppositories, gels, foams, foaming tablets, capsules, and films. They are relatively inexpensive and available without a prescription. Nonoxynol-9 is a spermicide that has been used for many years. It is available over the counter in many forms (creams, gels, suppositories, film, and condoms with spermicide) and can be used alone or in conjunction with another contraceptive method. However, as you saw from Sex in Real Life on page 413, there has been some controversy surrounding the use of nonoxynol-9.

Over the years, spermicides have become less popular as more effective contraceptive methods have been developed, but because spermicides can help prevent STIs, their popularity has been increasing again. Women need a product that can protect from both pregnancy and STIs. Scientists are actively pursuing approximately 60 products, called **microbicides** (my-crow-BISS-sides), that have been proven effective in protecting against HIV and other STIs, although none are currently available. It is anticipated that over the next few years there will be several new microbicides introduced (we will discuss these more in Chapter 15). Today in the United States, the cost for most spermicides ranges from $5 to $10. They are generally less expensive in clinics.

spermicide
Chemical method of contraception, including creams, gels, foams, suppositories, and films, that works to reduce the survival of sperm in the vagina.

microbicide
Chemical that works by inhibiting sperm function, are effective against HIV and other STIs, and are not harmful to the vaginal or cervical cells.

How They Work

Spermicides contain two components: one is an inert base such as jelly, cream, foam, or film that holds the spermicide close to the cervix; and the second is the spermicide itself. Foam, jelly, cream, and film are usually inserted into the vagina with either an applicator or a finger. **Vaginal contraceptive film (VCF),** produced in England, is now available over the counter in the United States. The film is 2 inches square, contains nonoxynol-9, and comes in packages of 12. To use, the film is wrapped around the index finger and inserted up into the vagina.

Suppositories are inserted in the vagina 10 to 30 minutes before intercourse to allow time for the outer covering to melt. It is important to read manufacturer's directions for spermicide use very carefully. Douching and tampon use should be avoided for 6 to 8 hours following the use of spermicides, as they interfere with effectiveness rates.

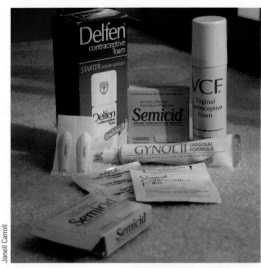

Spermicides are chemical methods of contraception, available without a prescription.

vaginal contraceptive film (VCF)
Spermicidal contraceptive film that is placed in the vagina.

Effectiveness

Effectiveness rates for spermicides range from 71% (typical use) to 82% (perfect use). Foam is generally considered more effective than jelly, cream, film, or suppositories. However, the most successful type of spermicide is one that a couple feels comfortable with and uses consistently.

Advantages

Spermicides can be purchased without a physician's prescription, and they are simple to use. In addition, spermicides provide lubrication during intercourse, a partner can participate in inserting them but does not have to be involved, and there are no serious medical side effects.

Disadvantages

Spermicides must be used each time a couple engages in sexual intercourse, which may be expensive depending on frequency of intercourse. In addition, there is an increase in postcoital drip, some couples may be allergic or have an adverse reaction, spermicides often have an unpleasant taste, and they may cause vaginal skin irritations or an increase in urinary tract infections (Hatcher et al., 2004).

Cross-Cultural Use

Spermicides are widely used in some countries, including Argentina, Australia, Colombia, Costa Rica, Cuba, and many European and Scandinavian countries (Francoeur & Noonan, 2004). However, in many other countries, including Botswana, Brazil, Canada, China, Hong Kong, Japan, Kenya, and Puerto Rico, spermicides are not widely used, probably due to the relatively high cost or an unwillingness to touch the genitals.

Review Question

Identify the chemical methods of birth control, providing information on how the methods work, effectiveness rates, advantages and disadvantages, and cross-cultural use.

INTRAUTERINE METHODS FOR WOMEN: IUDS AND IUSS

As of 2004, there was only one **intrauterine device (IUD)** available in the United States, the ParaGard Copper T (the Progestasert IUD was discontinued in 2001). The ParaGard Copper T can be left in place for 12 years. In 2000, the FDA approved the Mirena, an **intrauterine system (IUS).** This IUS is different from traditional IUDs because it contains a synthetic female hormone, progestin, which is time-released into the uterus. It can be kept in place for up to 5 years.

intrauterine device (IUD)
Small, plastic contraceptive device that is inserted into a woman's uterus.

intrauterine system (IUS)
Small, plastic contraceptive device that is inserted into a woman's uterus and contains a synthetic female hormone, progestin, which is time-released into the uterus.

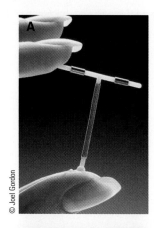

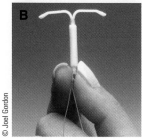

(a) The Copper T is a T-shaped IUD made of flexible plastic; it contains copper and can be left in place for up to 12 years. (b) The Mirena is a T-shaped IUS made of flexible plastic; it continuously releases a small amount of progestin and can be left in place for up to 5 years.

GyneFix, the newest IUD, contains a flexible row of copper beads instead of a rigid plastic frame like other IUDs (see photo). It is attached to the uterine wall by a nylon thread, which makes it less likely to be expelled. The GyneFix is awaiting FDA approval in the United States, although it has been used in China, Latin America, Asia, and Africa for many years.

The majority of IUD and IUS users today are women aged 35 or older. In the 1970s, approximately 10% of women using contraceptives in the United States used an intrauterine device (Hatcher et al., 1988). However, after that time, an increase in the number of problems associated with IUDs led to fewer types on the market, negative attitudes toward them, and a decrease in the number of IUD users. The Dalkon Shield was a popular type of IUD up until 1975, when the A. H. Robins Company recommended that it be removed from all women who were using them. At that time, women who had IUDs experienced many problems, including severe pain, bleeding, and pelvic inflammatory disease (PID), which even led to sterility in some cases. The problems with the Dalkon Shield were primarily caused by the multifilament string that allowed bacteria to enter into the uterus through the cervix. In the United States, the cost for an IUD can range from $150 to $300, plus physician fees.

How They Work

IUDs and IUSs have been found to create a low-grade infection in the uterus, which may interfere with sperm mobility and block sperm from passing into the Fallopian tubes and joining with an ovum. The IUS also time-releases progesterone into the lining of the uterus, which alters the lining, making implantation difficult.

IUDs/IUSs must be inserted by a healthcare provider, typically midcycle, when the cervix is softer. A string hangs down from the cervix, and the woman must check for the string once a month to make certain the IUD/IUS is still in place. Some men have reported that they can feel this string during intercourse. Because of the risk of pelvic inflammatory disease and sterility, IUDs/IUSs are not recommended for college-aged students who have not had children. Some IUDs can be left in place for up to 12 years, whereas others need to be changed yearly. It is recommended that the Mirena IUS be replaced every 5 years.

Effectiveness

Both of the intrauterine contraceptives provide some of the highest overall effectiveness rates, ranging from 99.2% to 99.9%. These rival the rates of tubal sterilization (Grimes, 2004), which we will discuss later in this chapter. Typically the Mirena IUS has a higher effectiveness rate than the Copper T (Grimes, 2004). Effectiveness also depends on the age of the woman and her past pregnancy history. A woman who has never been pregnant is more likely to expel the IUD/IUS through her cervix.

Figure 13.7
Insertion of an IUD.

Uterus

Cervix

Vagina

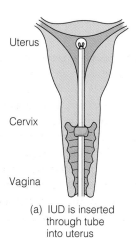

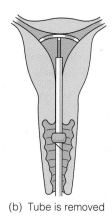

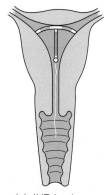

(a) IUD is inserted through tube into uterus

(b) Tube is removed

(c) IUD in place

Advantages

IUDs/IUSs are the least expensive method of contraception over time, and they do not interfere with spontaneity. In addition, they have long-lasting contraceptive effects. The Mirena IUS decreases menstrual flow because the progesterone reduces the endometrial buildup—20% of women using the Mirena will have no bleeding at all after 1 year of use (Dubuisson & Mugnier, 2002). The GyneFix IUD also has been found to reduce menstrual flow and cramping.

Disadvantages

IUDs/IUSs offer no protection from STIs, carry the risk of uterine perforation, may cause irregular bleeding patterns and spotting, and require painful insertion and removal procedures. The ParaGuard IUD also can increase the amount of menstrual flow and the severity of menstrual cramping. Because of this, approximately 4% to 14% of IUD users have their IUD removed in the first year of use (Stanback & Grimes, 1998).The IUD/IUS may also be expelled from the uterus and may create partner discomfort, and women with several sexual partners who use the IUD/IUS are at increased risk of pelvic inflammatory disease (Masters et al., 1994). It is anticipated that the GyneFix, once approved, will have much lower expulsion rates.

Cross-Cultural Use

IUDs are a popular contraceptive throughout the world. It is estimated that more than 25 million Copper T IUDs have been used in 70 countries (Grimes, 2004). In many countries, such as Turkey, China, Nigeria, England, Russia, and Korea, the IUD is the most frequently used form of contraception (Francoeur & Noonan, 2004). The Mirena IUS has been available in Europe for over 10 years, and it is estimated that at least 3 million women have used it throughout the world. In some countries, including China, Mexico, and Egypt, IUDs are inserted directly after the delivery of a baby (Grimes, 2004). Other countries with high IUD/IUS usage include Cuba, Finland, Turkey, Nepal, and the United Kingdom. Low usage has been report in countries such as Hong Kong, Korea, Ireland, Israel, Japan, and Kenya (Grimes, 2004). Overall, usage rates may vary based on media reports and how much the device is marketed in certain countries. For example, in Europe increases in IUD use may be a result of adverse publicity about birth control pills.

Review Question

Identify the intrauterine methods of birth control, providing information on how the methods work, effectiveness rates, advantages and disadvantages, and cross-cultural use.

NATURAL METHODS FOR WOMEN AND MEN

Natural methods of contraception do not alter any physiological function. They include natural family planning and fertility awareness, withdrawal, and abstinence.

Natural Family Planning and Fertility Awareness

With **natural family planning (NFP;** or the **symptothermal method**), a woman charts her menstrual periods by taking a daily **basal body temperature (BBT)** and checking cervical mucus to determine when she ovulates. During ovulation, she abstains from sexual intercourse. Although this may also be referred to as the **rhythm method,** generally the rhythm method does not involve monitoring the signs of ovulation.

When charting is used in conjunction with another form of birth control such as condoms, it is referred to as **fertility awareness.** In 2002, CycleBeads began a media campaign in hopes of increasing women's interest in natural family planning. CycleBeads are a series of color-coded beads that enable a woman to keep track of her menstrual cycle and avoid sexual intercourse on fertile days. To avoid pregnancy during that time, the woman and her partner would abstain from sex or use a different method of birth control.

natural family planning (NFP)
A contraceptive method that involves calculating ovulation and avoiding sexual intercourse during ovulation and at unsafe times.

symptothermal method
A contraceptive method that involves monitoring both cervical mucus and basal body temperature to determine ovulation.

basal body temperature (BBT)
The body's resting temperature used to calculate ovulation in the symptothermal method of contraception.

rhythm method
A contraceptive method that involves calculating the period of ovulation and avoiding sexual intercourse around this time.

fertility awareness
Basal body temperature charting used in conjunction with another method of contraception.

To use CycleBeads, a woman moves a ring over a series of color-coded beads that represent her fertile and low-fertility days. The color of the beads lets her know whether she is on a day when she is likely to be fertile.

How They Work

With natural family planning, a woman takes her BBT every morning before she gets out of bed and records it on a basal body temperature chart. Changes in hormonal levels cause body temperature to rise 0.4° to 0.8°F (0.2 to 0.4°C) immediately before ovulation, and it remains elevated until menstruation begins. A woman using this method monitors her cervical mucus, which becomes thin and stretchy during ovulation to help transport sperm. At other times of the month, cervical mucus is thicker. After 6 months of consistent charting, a woman will be able to estimate the approximate time of ovulation, and she can then either abstain from sexual intercourse or use contraception during her high-risk times (usually this period is between 1 and 2 weeks). Most women who use this method are spacing their pregnancies and are not as concerned about preventing pregnancies.

The rhythm method involves abstaining from intercourse midcycle, when ovulation is probable, but usually does not include BBT or cervical mucus charting. Ovulation kits, available in drugstores, can help women who desire pregnancy to determine their fertile days. Researchers at Duke University are working on a "hydration detection" device that would allow a woman to monitor the water content of her cervical secretions through a small vaginal probe (Jennings, Arevalo, & Kowal, 2004). Increases in cervical secretions would indicate possible ovulation, and a woman using this method would avoid intercourse or use contraception.

Effectiveness

Effectiveness rates for natural family planning range from 75% (typical use) to 99% (perfect use). The majority of failures with this method are due to couples engaging in intercourse too close to ovulation. In addition, a woman may ovulate earlier or later than usual because of diet, stress, or alcohol use. This method is best suited for those needing to space pregnancies, rather than for those who want to avoid pregnancy.

Advantages

Natural family planning is an acceptable form of birth control for those who cannot use another method for religious reasons. It is also inexpensive, teaches couples about the menstrual cycle, may encourage couples to communicate more about contraception, can involve the male, and has no medical side effects. It also helps women if they eventually want to get pregnant, because they know when they ovulate. Couples who use natural family planning use a variety of sexual expressions when they cannot engage in vaginal intercourse.

Disadvantages

Natural family planning provides no protection from STIs and restricts spontaneity. In addition, this method has low effectiveness rates, takes time and commitment to learn, and requires several cycles of records before it can be used reliably. In addition, women who have irregular cycles may have difficulty in interpreting their charts.

Cross-Cultural Use

What makes natural family planning so popular in many areas outside the United States is the fact that it is inexpensive and involves little assistance from physicians. Natural family planning may also be the only form of acceptable contraception in Catholic countries such as Ireland, Brazil, and the Philippines. In the Philippines natural family planning and the rhythm method are thought to improve a couple's relationship because they need to work together to use the method (Leyson, 2004). Societal issues and marketing may also affect the use of this method. For example, cultural resistance to condom use has increased the popularity of natural family planning

Review Question

Describe how natural family planning works, and provide effectiveness rates, advantages and disadvantages, and cross-cultural use.

in Kenya, where it is the most commonly used contraceptive method (Brockman, 2004). Today, many women's groups from the United States travel to developing countries to teach natural family planning.

Withdrawal

Withdrawal, or **coitus interruptus,** was the most popular method of birth control in the mid-1800s. Although the National Survey of Family Growth (see Chapter 2) estimated that only 2.9% of their sample used withdrawal, most researchers believe this was an underestimate (Kowal, 2004b). Because many couples don't consider withdrawal a legitimate contraceptive method, they may not report using it (Kowal, 2004b).

coitus interruptus
A contraceptive method involving withdrawal of the penis from the vagina prior to ejaculation.

How It Works

Withdrawal does not require any advance preparation. A couple engages in sexual intercourse; prior to ejaculation, the male withdraws his penis from the vagina. The ejaculate does not enter the uterus.

Effectiveness

Effectiveness rates for withdrawal range from 73% (typical use) to 96% (perfect use). Originally, scientists believed that high failure rates with this method were due to sperm contained in the preejaculatory fluid. However, newer research suggests that preejaculatory fluid has no sperm in it (Kowal, 2004b). Pregnancy can occur, however, if sperm remains in the urethra from a previous ejaculation and is not released during urination.

Advantages

Withdrawal is another acceptable method of birth control for those who cannot use another method for religious reasons. In addition, it may be a good method for couples who do not mind becoming pregnant, it is free, doesn't require any devices, and it is better than not using any method at all.

Disadvantages

Withdrawal provides no protection from STIs and has low effectiveness rates. In addition, withdrawal may contribute to premature ejaculation in some men and may be extremely stressful for both men and their partners. It can be a difficult method for a man to use because it requires him to withdraw the penis just before orgasm. Many men experience a mild to extreme "clouding of consciousness" just before orgasm when physical movements become involuntary (Kowal, 2004b). This method also requires trust from the female partner.

Cross-Cultural Use

Withdrawal is a popular contraceptive method throughout the world. It is one of the most frequently used methods in Austria, the Czech Republic, Greece, Ireland, and Italy (Francoeur & Noonan, 2004). In the Czech Republic, over 40% of women report using withdrawal as their contraceptive method (Zvěřina, 2004). Overall, it is a popular contraceptive method for couples with limited contraceptive choices or for those who are reluctant to use modern methods of contraception. In other countries, such as Germany, withdrawal remains very unpopular.

Abstinence

Abstinence (or not engaging in sexual intercourse at all) has probably been the most important factor in controlling fertility throughout history. However, over the last few years, there is some uncertainty about what "abstinence" really means. Although some would define abstinence as refraining from all sexual behaviors, including masturbation,

Review Question

How effective is withdrawal as a form of birth control? What are the advantages and disadvantages of this method?

others might define it as abstaining from sexual intercourse or specific types of sexual contact (Kowal, 2004a). Most experts would define abstinence as refraining from engaging in sexual intercourse. With this definition, abstinence can be considered the only 100% effective method of contraception. Couples may choose abstinence to prevent pregnancy, to protect against STIs, or for other reasons such as illness or disease.

PERMANENT (SURGICAL) METHODS

Although a man is fertile for most of his life, a healthy woman may be able to get pregnant until the age of 50 to 51 (Pollack, Carignan, & Jacobstein, 2004). Women who no longer wish to have children but are still fertile may look for long-term protection from pregnancy. **Sterilization** has been found to be one of the safest and most effective methods of contraception (Pollack, Carignan, & Jacobstein, 2004). In 1995, there were 693,000 tubal sterilizations and 494,000 vasectomies (Pollack, Carignan,& Jacobstein, 2004; see Figure 13.2 for more information about ethnicity and sterilization statistics).

The primary difference between sterilization and other methods of contraception is that sterilization is usually irreversible and requires surgery. Although some people have been able to have their sterilizations reversed, this can be very expensive and time consuming. The majority of people who request sterilization reversals do so because they have remarried and desire children with their new partners.

Female Sterilization

Female sterilization, or **tubal sterilization** (also referred to as getting one's "tubes tied"), is the most widely used method of birth control in the world (Church & Geller, 1990). Between 1994 and 1996, over 2 million tubal sterilizations were performed, half of which were done directly following childbirth (MacKay et al., 2001). In a tubal sterilization, a physician may sever or block both Fallopian tubes so that the ovum and sperm can not meet. Blocking the tubes can be done with **cauterization,** a ring, band, or clamp (which pinches the tube together), or **ligation.** The procedure is often done under general anesthesia. Recently, some of these procedures have been done using clips or silicone plugs instead of severing the tubes, which may enable physicians to reverse the operation in the future. However, at the present time, female sterilization is considered irreversible. The majority of women who undergo sterilization are happy with their decision, except for women aged 30 or younger. These women are more likely to regret the decision later in their lives (Alan Guttmacher Institute, 1999a).

Sterilization procedures can be done during **outpatient surgery** or directly following childbirth in a hospital. The sterilization procedure is generally done with the use of a **laparoscope** through a small incision either under the navel or lower in the abdomen. After this is done, a woman continues to ovulate, but the ovum does not enter the uterus. The costs for female sterilization vary, but generally range from $2,000 to $5,000.

As with any other surgery, potential risks exist. A woman may feel side effects from the anesthesia or experience bleeding, infection, or possible injury to other organs during the procedure. In a few cases, the surgery is unsuccessful and must be repeated. On the positive side, however, tubal sterilization has been found to substantially reduce the

sterilization
Surgical contraceptive method that causes permanent infertility.

tubal sterilization
A surgical procedure in which the Fallopian tubes are cut, tied, or cauterized, for permanent contraception.

cauterization
A sterilization procedure that involves burning or searing the Fallopian tubes or vas deferens for permanent sterilization.

ligation
A sterilization procedure that involves the tying or binding of the Fallopian tubes or vas deferens.

outpatient surgery
Surgery performed in the hospital or doctor's office, after which a patient is allowed to return home; inpatient surgery requires hospitalization.

laparoscope
A tiny scope that can be inserted through the skin and allows for the viewing of the uterine cavity.

Figure 13.8
Essure is a permanent method of contraception.

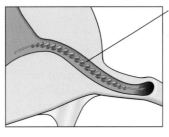 Essure is inserted into the Fallopian tube

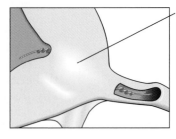 Body tissue grows into the Essure micro-insert, blocking the Fallopian tube

risk of ovarian cancer (Pollack, Carignan, & Jacobstein, 2004). Overall, research has shown that women who undergo tubal sterilization maintain their levels of sexual interest and desire and have more positive than negative sexual effects (Costello et al., 2002).

In 2003, the FDA approved Essure, a nonincision, permanent birth control method for women. Essure is a tiny, springlike device that is threaded into the Fallopian tubes. This creates tissue growth around the device, which blocks fertilization. This process generally takes 3 months from the time Essure is placed in the tubes, so it doesn't offer immediate birth control. A woman using this method must undergo testing to make sure that the Fallopian tubes are fully blocked.

Male Sterilization

Male sterilization, or **vasectomy,** blocks the flow of sperm through the vas deferens (see Chapter 5). Typically, this procedure is simpler, less expensive, and safer than a tubal sterilization (Pollack, Carignan, & Jacobstein, 2004). After a vasectomy, the testes continue to produce viable sperm cells, but with nowhere to go, they die and are absorbed by the body. Semen normally contains approximately 98% fluid and 2% sperm, and after a vasectomy, the man still ejaculates semen, but the semen contains no sperm (there is no overall change in volume or texture of the semen after a vasectomy). All other functions, such as the manufacturing of testosterone, erections, and urination, are unaffected by a vasectomy procedure. In the United States there are approximately 500,000 vasectomies performed each year (Barone et al., 2004).

The surgery for a vasectomy is done on an outpatient basis in a physician's office. The physician makes two small incisions about ¼ to ½ inch long in the scrotum. The vas deferens is then clipped or cauterized under local anesthesia, which usually takes approximately 20 minutes. Immediately following a vasectomy, enough sperm remains for 20 more ejaculations, and so sperm counts are taken 2 to 3 months later to check sterility (Pollack, Carignan, & Jacobstein, 2004). The cost for the procedure varies widely, depending on where it is done. Overall, costs range between $300 and $700. Vasectomy does have some risk involved, including swelling, bruising, and possible internal bleeding or infection.

A less invasive alternative to vasectomy, the Vasclip, was approved by the FDA in 2002 but not marketed until 2003. The Vasclip is a locking plastic band that is placed over the vas deferens, effectively closing the tube. This permanent method eliminates cutting, suturing, or cauterizing the vas deferens and results in less swelling and infection than a vasectomy.

Effectiveness

Tubal sterilizations are effective immediately, whereas vasectomies require semen analysis for 2 months after the procedure to ensure no viable sperm remains. Effectiveness for both procedures ranges from 99% to 99.9%.

sex byte

It is estimated that 50% to 80% of men who undergo a vasectomy develop antisperm antibodies, which may play a role in the decreased fertility rates of men undergoing vasectomy reversals (Pollack, Carignan, & Jacobstein, 2004).

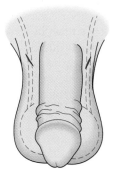
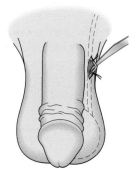
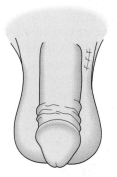

(a) Possible incision sites

(b) Incision on one side of the testicle and right and left vas are cut

(c) Incision closed

Figure 13.9
In a vasectomy, each vas deferens is clipped, cut, or cauterized. A vasclip uses a flexible plastic clip to block the vas deferens.

Advantages

Sterilization is a highly effective permanent method of contraception. It offers a quick recovery, few long-term side effects, and does not interfere with spontaneity,

Disadvantages

Sterilization requires surgery, can be expensive, provides no protection from STIs, and must be considered irreversible.

Cross-Cultural Use

Sterilization is a popular contraceptive method throughout the world. In Brazil sterilization is a popular choice in midlife, with over 42% of women undergoing surgical sterilization (de Freitas, 2004). Sterilization procedures are also common in Australia, Canada, China, Colombia, and Cuba (Francoeur & Noonan, 2004). A 1999 governmental ruling in Costa Rica has led to a waiting list for female sterilization. This ruling made female sterilization available on demand in Costa Rica, without doctor or spousal consent (Arroba, 2004). In Sweden, both male and female sterilization are free upon request to people over the age of 25 (Trost & Bergstrom-Walan, 2004). Typically, female sterilization is more prevalent in the majority of countries. However, this isn't true in China, where male sterilization techniques, including a new reversible sterilization surgery, are more popular (Ruan & Lau, 2004).

In countries where family planning clinics are sparse, many women travel long distances to be sterilized. As we have discussed, access to and promotion of a certain method also contribute to its popularity. In many countries, sterilization is the only method of nonnatural contraception available.

Review Question

Differentiate between male and female permanent methods of birth control, and provide advantages and disadvantages of each. How popular are these procedures outside the United States?

sex byte

So many children were killed in the deadly tsunami of 2004 that several state governments in India offer free sterilization reversals (M. Cohen, 2005). Although these procedures are not always successful, many women have undergone reversals and are hopeful they will be able to get pregnant again.

INEFFECTIVE METHODS AND EMERGENCY CONTRACEPTION

Many couples use ineffective methods in an attempt to avoid pregnancy, and some experience unplanned pregnancies. Emergency contraception can be used when a couple fails to use contraception or uses ineffective methods.

Unreliable Birth Control

Sometimes couples rely on methods of contraception that are ineffective. They may keep their fingers crossed, hoping that they won't get pregnant. Two ineffective methods that some couples rely on include douching and breast-feeding.

Douching

Douching involves using a syringe-type instrument to inject a stream of water (which may be mixed with other chemicals) into the vagina. In the mid-1800s, douching was actually recommended by physicians as a contraceptive. What we realize today, however, is that by the time a woman gets up to douche after intercourse, most of the sperm are already up in her cervix (Cates & Raymond, 2004). Many physicians recommend that women don't douche at all because it has been found to lead to a higher degree of pelvic infections and STIs. Some women may believe that they need to douche in order to be clean (see the Sex in Real Life feature on page 127 of Chapter 4).

Breast-Feeding

In Chapter 12, we discussed how breast-feeding can delay a woman's fertility after childbirth. However, this is an unreliable method of birth control because it is not known when ovulation will resume. Although she may not experience menstruation during this time, ovulation may still occur. Research has found that breast-feeding provides more than 98% protection from pregnancy in the first 6 months after giving birth (Kennedy & Trussell, 2004). However, as a woman begins to wean her child from breast-feeding, her fertility returns.

Emergency Contraception

In 1974, a Canadian professor, Albert Yuzpe, was the first to develop an emergency hormonal contraceptive; his plan has been referred to as the **Yuzpe regimen.** Yuzpe used a high dose of combination birth control pills to inhibit pregnancy after unprotected intercourse. This practice became the standard for **emergency contraception (EC;** also referred to as "morning after" contraception, or ECPs—emergency contraceptive pills). Emergency contraception is designed to prevent pregnancy after unprotected vaginal intercourse—in case of unanticipated sexual intercourse, contraceptive failure, or sexual assault. It is estimated that half of the women who seek emergency contraception did not use any contraception, 35% had trouble with a condom or other barrier method, and the remaining 10% missed a birth control pill, experienced a rape, or were not able to use withdrawal (F. Stewart, Trussell, & VanLook, 2004). The typical user of emergency contraception is single, without children, and between the ages of 15 and 25.

Two types of emergency contraception have been approved by the FDA. Plan B, a progestin-only method, was approved in 1999. Preven, a combination of estrogen and progestin, was approved in 1998, but the manufacturer ceased its production in 2004. Some physicians have also adapted standard oral contraceptives for emergency contraceptive use and copper IUD insertion within 5 days of unprotected intercourse (F. Stewart, Trussell, & VanLook, 2004).

When a woman is given emergency contraception within 72 hours of unprotected intercourse, her risk of pregnancy is reduced by 75% (Trussell, 2004), and there is some evidence that this may be effective up to 120 hours after unprotected intercourse (Ellertson et al., 2003). The earlier these methods are begun after unprotected sexual intercourse, the higher the effectiveness rates. IUD insertion has a 99% effectiveness rate (F. Stewart et al., 2004). The IUD insertion method is used much less frequently than ECPs, mainly because women who need emergency treatment often are not appropriate IUD candidates (F. Stewart et al., 2004). Emergency hormonal contraception costs approximately $25 plus the cost of an office visit and lab tests.

Emergency contraception has been available worldwide for over 2 decades (Wertheimer, 2000). Although a prescription is necessary to obtain emergency contraception in the United States, it is available over the counter in many other countries. In fact, women in 37 countries, including Denmark, Finland, France, Israel, Norway, Portugal, South Africa, Sweden, and the United Kingdom, can obtain emergency contraception over the counter, and in France EC is free (F. Stewart, Trussell, & VanLook, 2004).

It has been recommended that EC be available over the counter in the United States as well, although this has been very controversial. The schism became very clear in 2005, when the FDA postponed indefinitely a decision on whether emergency contraception should be available without a prescription—a ruling that came after clinical and scientific evidence had shown that the drug was safe and effective (Neergaard, 2005). Some proponents of emergency contraception argued that the FDA let politics overrule science. The FDA expressed concern over the drug getting into the hands of younger teenagers.

Hormonal emergency contraception methods have several side effects, including nausea, vomiting, cramping, breast tenderness, headaches, and abdominal pain (these side effects are less common in women who take Plan B, because it has no estrogen). Sometimes the nausea and vomiting can be so severe that an additional hormonal dosage is necessary. The majority of these symptoms disappear within 1 to 2 days after treatment. Overall, women who use ECPs are satisfied with the method and would recommend it to other women in similar situations (Harvey et al., 1999).

Other methods of emergency contraception include early abortion procedures (also called **menstrual extraction**). This procedure involves the removal of uterine contents

Yuzpe regimen
Original plan for emergency hormonal contraception using high doses of combination birth control pills to inhibit pregnancy after unprotected intercourse.

emergency contraception (EC)
Contraception that is designed to prevent pregnancy after unprotected vaginal intercourse.

menstrual extraction
Removal of the contents of the uterus prior to a positive pregnancy test.

Review Question

What options are available for emergency contraception? How do these methods work?

prior to a positive pregnancy test. Menstrual extraction has a high likelihood of incomplete abortion and physicians recommend waiting until at least 7 weeks' gestation. Today various drugs are used to induce early abortion. We will discuss these drugs later in this chapter.

CONTRACEPTION IN THE FUTURE

It is estimated that half of all unintended pregnancies occur because of contraceptive failures (F. Stewart & Gabelnick, 2004). Researchers and scientists continue to look for contraceptive methods with little or no side effects that are easy to use. They have also tried to include beneficial effects, such as reduced acne or water retention, to encourage usage (F. Stewart & Gabelnick, 2004). A consistent concern has been finding a method that can offer high effectiveness rates and protection from STIs and HIV/AIDS (Hatcher et al., 2004).

What's Ahead for Men

Historically, birth control has been considered a female's responsibility, and that may be why the condom and vasectomy are the only birth control methods available to men. Many feminists claim that the lack of research into male methods of birth control has to do with the fact that birth control research is done primarily by men. As a result, women are responsible for using birth control and must suffer through the potential side effects.

Others claim that there are few male methods because men produce 1 billion sperm for each ovum a woman produces. It is easier to interfere with one ovum, once a month, than billions of sperm at each ejaculation. They also argue that because men are constantly producing sperm from puberty to old age, chemical means of stopping sperm production may in some way harm future sperm production. Chemical contraception may also interfere with testosterone production, which is responsible for the male sexual drive.

It's interesting to realize that even though there are fewer male contraceptive methods available, an estimated one-third of the world's couples use these methods (F. Stewart & Gabelnick, 2004). In the future, men may have more options. Some possibilities include hormonal and nonhormonal drug treatments, including **gossypol** and anticancer drug injections. Both gossypol and the anticancer drugs work to reduce the quantity of sperm produced. However, sperm production has not been found to increase to original levels after discontinuation.

Researchers at the University of Kansas were awarded an $7.9 million grant from the National Institutes of Health in 2005 for the development of a male contraceptive pill (MSNBC, 2005). This pill would be taken weekly or monthly. Researchers at the University of Massachusetts are also working to develop a male birth control pill that would interfere with a sperm's ability to swim (A. Davis, 2005).

Weekly injections of testosterone have also been found to decrease sperm production. Side effects may include increased aggression, acne, weight gain, depression, and fatigue. Researchers are also experimenting with longer-acting formulas that can be injected every 3 or 4 months instead of weekly.

Scientists are also looking for vaccines that would cause infertility until pregnancy is desired (F. Stewart & Gabelnick, 2004). **Immunocontraceptives** are vaccines that suppress testicular function and would eliminate sperm and testosterone production. Unfortunately, vaccines such as these would effectively destroy sexual desire as well. It may be several years before we know whether vaccines will be a valid contraceptive option.

Finally, other research programs are looking into agents that can act in the epididymis. Because this is where sperm mature, scientists are hoping to inhibit sperm maturation in the epididymis (J. L. Schwartz & Gabelnick, 2002).

gossypol
An ingredient in cottonseed oil that, when injected or implanted, may inhibit sperm production.

immunocontraceptives
Vaccines designed to suppress testicular function and eliminate sperm and testosterone production.

What's Ahead for Women

Women report that they want contraceptives that are simpler to use and more suited to their lifestyles. This has given way to the longer-acting methods, such as the contraceptive patch and hormonal ring. In the future, these products may have even longer effectiveness periods. In addition, it is likely that contraceptive pills that eliminate monthly periods, such as Seasonale, will become more popular in the coming years. Other birth control pills that do not contain estrogen are also being investigated.

Many contraceptive developments are underway today. International pharmaceutical companies are working to find new and improved methods. There are now condoms that are ecologically sound and able to dissolve in water. Manufacturers are developing spermicides in a range of flavors to offset their current unpleasant taste. Disposable diaphragms coated with spermicide and contraceptive nasal sprays may soon be available.

The Ovès contraceptive cap, a silicone barrier method that is inserted into the vagina and covers the cervix, is available in the United Kingdom. The cap can be worn for 3 days and is completely disposable after use. The Ovès cap costs approximately $6, but is not available in the United States at this time.

Another immunocontraceptive is being studied that would inhibit the function of human chorionic gonadotropin (hCG; see Chapter 12) and interrupt a woman's ability to become pregnant (J. L. Schwartz & Gabelnick, 2002). However, this method is a challenge to researchers because it has also been found to interrupt other hormones.

Natural methods of contraception are also being studied. Saliva and urine tests can help natural planning by allowing a woman to determine whether she is ovulating. The Persona monitor is a handheld device that uses data from thousands of women along with chemical information obtained from the woman using the monitor. Test sticks are dipped in urine 8 days a month to determine safe days for intercourse. Currently this method is too expensive for routine use. Temporary sterilization techniques are also being evaluated. Although we still have a long way to go in making better methods available for controlling whether pregnancy occurs, many improvements are in the works and may be available in the near future.

Financial factors, political pressure, and legal concerns hold back most of the contraceptive research today. Private funding is often difficult because such large amounts are necessary for most research. Unfortunately, the threat of individual lawsuits (such as the Dalkon Shield situation discussed on page 432) has effectively scared most big pharmaceutical companies away from contraceptive research (J. L. Schwartz & Gabelnick, 2002).

Review Question

What does the future hold for contraception options?

Review Question

Describe why there have been fewer birth control options for men, and what the future holds for male contraception.

ABORTION

In the United States, abortion has become the moral issue of the times. It is one of the most popular questions that Supreme Court nominees are asked during judicial hearings. In addition, abortion leads many people to question the role that the government should play in their lives. Although we'll discuss the moral debate in more detail, the fact is, each year 46 million abortions are performed worldwide; 20 million of these procedures are considered unsafe (Alan Guttmacher Institute, 1999d).

The Abortion Debate

The abortion debate has been very emotional and sometimes even violent. Many on both sides of the issue have strongly held opinions. **Pro-life supporters** believe that human life, and therefore personhood, begins at conception, and so an embryo, at any stage of development, is a person. Pro-life supporters believe that aborting a fetus is murder and that the government should make all abortions illegal. One pro-life supporter states:

> [A woman] has the right to control her body by using birth control, but once a baby is created it's out of her hands; she has no right to kill what God has created: it's in her body, but it is separate, put there by an act of will. (Parsons et al., 1990, p. 110)

pro-life supporter
Individual who believes that abortion should be illegal or strictly regulated by the government.

On the other side of the issue, pro-choice supporters believe that the embryo has the capacity to become a full-fledged human life. **Pro-choice supporters** differ on when they believe personhood begins. For some, it may be in the second trimester of pregnancy, and for others, the third trimester. However, because not everyone agrees that personhood begins at conception, they believe that it is a woman's choice whether or not to have an abortion, and they strongly believe that the government should not interfere with her decision. One pro-choice supporter explains:

> Everybody should be able to control their own lives, to choose what happens to them, and every woman has the right to decide what's best for her; she must be able to choose abortion because having a child changes your life completely, and she has to decide if she wants her life to change. (Parsons et al., 1990, p. 110)

The abortion debate often polarizes people into pro-life and pro-choice camps, with each side claiming moral superiority over the other. Overall, although many people have strong opinions about abortion, few invest a significant amount of time and effort to support their cause (Kaysen & Stake, 2001). College students have generally been viewed as fairly liberal in their attitudes about abortion, but studies have found a normal distribution of abortion attitudes (Carlton et al., 2000; Reisberg, 1999). Some students are pro-choice, some are pro-life, and many are somewhere in between. No gender differences in attitudes about abortion have been found; however, there are some ethnic variations. African Americans tend to be more pro-choice than their white counterparts (Gay & Lynxwiler, 1999).

Historical Perspectives

Abortion has been practiced in many societies throughout history; in fact, there are few large-scale societies in which it has not been practiced (see Chapter 1). Aristotle argued that abortion was necessary as a backup to contraception. He believed that a fetus was not alive until certain organs had been formed; for males, at 40 days after conception, and for females, 90 days. In early Roman society, abortions were also allowed, but husbands had the power to determine whether or not their wives would undergo abortion.

For most of Western history, religion determined general attitudes toward abortion, and both Judaism and Christianity have generally condemned abortion and punished those who used it. Still, throughout recorded history, abortions were performed. Many women died or were severely injured by illegal surgical abortions performed by semi-skilled practitioners. Although it was little discussed publicly, abortion was apparently quite common; the Michigan Board of Health estimated in 1878 that one-third of all pregnancies in that state ended in abortion (D'Emilio & Freedman, 1988).

In 1965 all 50 states banned abortion, although there were exceptions that varied by state (for instance, to save the mother's life, in cases of rape or incest, or fetal deformity). Those who could not have a legal abortion either had the baby or had to acquire an illegal abortion. These illegal abortions, known as **back-alley abortions,** were very dangerous because they were often performed under unsanitary conditions and often resulted in multiple complications, sometimes ending in death. See the accompanying Personal Voices, "An Illegal Abortion," for one woman's account. In 1967 abortion laws in England were liberalized and many American women traveled to England for an abortion. By 1970, "package deals" appeared in the popular media advertising round-trip airfare, airport transfers, passport assistance, lodging, meals, and the procedure itself (Gold, 2003).

In 1973 the Supreme Court ruled in the *Roe v. Wade* decision that women have a constitutionally protected right to have an abortion in the early stages of pregnancy. In the first trimester of pregnancy, a woman can choose abortion without the state interfering. In the second trimester, a state can regulate abortion to protect a woman's health; and, in the third trimester, the potential fetal life enables the state to limit or ban abortion except in cases in which a woman's life or health would be at risk. This decision was enacted to help limit government from controlling a woman's body and ensure the right to privacy.

In 1992, the Supreme Court upheld the right to an abortion in the *Planned Parenthood of Southeastern Pennsylvania v. Casey* decision but also gave states the right to design re-

strictions for women who choose to have an abortion. The most common restrictions include waiting periods, mandatory counseling, parental involvement requirements, and public funding limitations.

In July 1994, the Supreme Court upheld a decision (*Madison v. Women's Health Center, Inc.*) barring antiabortion demonstrators from getting within 36 feet of an abortion clinic. This ruling was sparked by the fatal shooting of Dr. David Gunn outside of his abortion clinic in Pensacola, Florida (Word, 2003). Fewer doctors perform surgical abortions today than in the early years after the *Roe v. Wade* decision, probably due to increased death threats.

Because of the controversy over abortion, medical schools have been targeted to eliminate surgical abortion training in residency programs. Even so, U.S. medical schools have worked to maintain this teaching. As of 1996, there are standard requirements for the inclusion of abortion training as a part of obstetrics and gynecology residency programs (Almeling et al., 2000). Even so, many physicians opt not to perform surgical abortion, and this, coupled with the fact that there are fewer abortion clinics today, has decreased the availability of surgical abortion.

Overall, Louisiana has the most restrictive abortion laws. Louisiana has attempted to ban all abortions except in cases of rape, incest, or life endangerment, and has imposed many restrictions on abortion (Henshaw, 1998). New York, California, and Washington State have fought the hardest to protect their abortion laws. Today pressure exists in the United States to reverse the Supreme Court's decision in *Roe v. Wade* and make abortion illegal. This bitter battle between the pro-choice and pro-life factions can be seen in picketing and demonstrations outside abortion clinics.

Review **Question**

Trace the status of abortion throughout history. How is abortion viewed today?

Legal Versus Illegal Abortions

Since the legalization of abortion in the United States in 1973, the number of women's deaths from abortion have declined dramatically—even though the actual number is difficult to determine because so many abortion-related deaths were not noted on death certificates (Gold, 1990). Pro-choice supporters believe this is directly due to easier accessibility of abortion. They believe that the legalization of abortion ensured sanitary conditions and immediate treatment for infections.

On the other hand, pro-life supporters believe that prior to *Roe v. Wade*, women were more careful about becoming pregnant. Because abortion was not a legal right, many women used birth control consistently, and if they got pregnant, they gave birth. The legalization of abortion, according to the pro-life camp, has caused women and men to become irresponsible about sexuality and contraceptive use. By making abortion illegal, pro-life supporters believe that people will become more responsible about contraception and may delay sexual activity.

Review Question

Differentiate between legal and illegal abortion.

SEX Talk

Question: In the future, is abortion going to be illegal?

The Supreme Court may eventually overturn the *Roe v. Wade* decision. Should this happen, each state will be able to determine its own abortion policies. It is anticipated that if *Roe* is overturned, many states will quickly ban abortion or enforce existing bans. Some states have put into effect antichoice measures, further restricting a woman's right to choose (National Abortion Rights Action League, 2003a; this would include restrictions such as waiting periods or parental/spousal notification policies). These changing restrictions often work to block access to abortion at the state level. In the meantime, if justices appointed by President George W. Bush are pro-life, it is very possible that *Roe* will be overturned.

Why Do Women Have Abortions?

Many people claim that women have abortions because they do not use contraception. However, studies indicate that 54% of women who had an abortion had been using a contraceptive method the month they became pregnant (R. K. Jones, Darroch, & Henshaw, 2002a). Some of these women were using methods incorrectly or inconsistently. In fact, only 8% of women who have abortions never have used any contraception.

Women who have abortions do so for a variety of reasons. The majority report that a baby would interfere with other responsibilities, such as educational or career goals. Other reasons include an inability to financially provide for a child; difficulties in the relationship with the father; not wanting people to know they are sexually active; pressure from their partners or families; fetal deformity; risks to mother's health; having several children already; and rape or incest. From this research, the only thing that is clear is that there is no simple answer to the question of why a woman decides to have an abortion. The decision-making process is difficult and has no easy answers.

How do you feel about these reasons? Do any of these circumstances seem more justified than others? Do you feel that there are legitimate reasons for aborting a fetus?

Review Question

Identify some of the reasons a woman might choose to have an abortion.

Abortion Procedures

Abortion is one of the most common surgical procedures in the United States, and the majority of procedures are performed in specialized abortion clinics today (Henshaw & Finer, 2003). However, this has not always been the case. After *Roe v. Wade* in 1973, most abortions were performed in hospitals. The move away from hospitals and into clinics has reduced the cost of an abortion. Surgical abortion procedures involve risks, the most serious of which include **uterine perforation, cervical laceration,** severe hemorrhaging, infection, and anesthesia-related complications. These risks are greater when general anesthesia is used. In fact, the risk of death during a general anesthesia abortion is two to four times greater than during one with local anesthesia (Tietze, 1983).

uterine perforation
Tearing a hole in the uterus.

cervical laceration
Cuts or tears on the cervix.

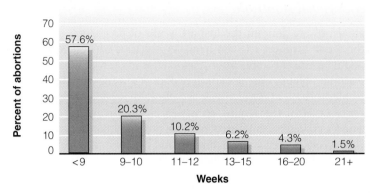

Figure 13.10
Current abortion statistics for the United States.
Reproduced with permission of The Alan Guttmacher Institute from *Physicians for Reproductive Choice and Health* and The Alan Guttmacher Institute (AGI) *An Overview of Abortion in the U.S.,* New York: AGI, 2003, Microsoft® Powerpoint® presentation.

(a)

Abortions by gestational age

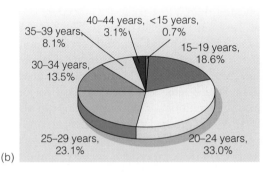

(b)

Abortions by client age

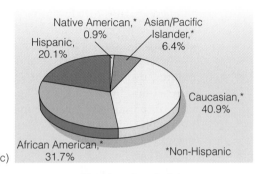

(c)

Abortions by ethnicity

Abortions can be performed as either first- or second-trimester procedures. **First-trimester abortions** are done before 14 weeks of gestation, and they are simpler and safer than those done after this time. **Second-trimester abortions,** or late abortions, are those done between 14 and 21 weeks.

First-Trimester Surgical Abortion

A first-trimester abortion (**vacuum aspiration,** or suction abortion) is usually performed on an outpatient basis, using local anesthesia. This is the most common type of abortion procedure in the United States today and accounts for 88% of all abortions (F. H. Stewart, Ellertson, & Cates, 2004). In this procedure, a woman lies on an examining table with her feet in stirrups, and a speculum is placed in her vagina to view the cervix. Local anesthesia is injected into the cervix, which numbs it slightly. **Dilation rods** are used to open the cervix and usually cause mild cramping of the uterus. Following dilation, a **cannula** is inserted into the cervix and is attached to a **vacuum aspirator,** which empties the contents of the uterus.

A first-trimester abortion usually takes between 4 and 6 minutes. After it is completed, most clinics require a woman to stay in the clinic, hospital, or doctor's office for a few hours. Once home, she is advised to rest, not to lift heavy objects, to avoid sexual intercourse, not to douche or use tampons for at least 2 weeks, and not to take baths; all of these activities increase the risk of hemorrhaging and infection. She will also experience bleeding and perhaps cramping, as she would during a normal period. Her menstrual period will return within 4 to 6 weeks.

There are several potential risks associated with a first-trimester abortion, including excessive bleeding, possible infection, and uterine perforation. However, because these risks are much lower than for a second-trimester procedure, most physicians advise women who are considering abortions to have a first-trimester procedure.

first-trimester abortion
Termination of pregnancy within the first 14 weeks of pregnancy.

second-trimester abortion
Termination of pregnancy between the 14th and 21st weeks of pregnancy.

vacuum aspiration
The termination of a pregnancy by using suction to empty the contents of the uterus.

dilation rods
A series of graduated metal rods that are used to dilate the cervical opening during an abortion procedure.

cannula
A tube, used in an abortion procedure, through which the uterine contents are emptied.

vacuum aspirator
A vacuum pump that is used during abortion procedures.

Second-Trimester Surgical Abortion

Although 88% of abortions are done in the first 14 weeks of pregnancy, approximately 11% occur during the second trimester (Elam-Evans et al., 2002). There may be several reasons for this, including medical complications, fetal deformities that were not revealed earlier, divorce or marital problems, miscalculation of date of last menstrual period, financial or geographic problems (such as not living near a clinic that offers the procedure), or a denial of the pregnancy until the second trimester. Second-trimester abortions are riskier than first-trimester procedures and involve more potential problems.

Between 13 and 16 weeks of pregnancy, a **dilation and evacuation (D&E)** is the most commonly used procedure. The procedure is similar to a vacuum aspiration, but it is done in a hospital under general anesthesia. Dilators, such as **laminaria** (lam-in-AIR-ree-uh), may be used to help begin the dilation process and may be inserted into the cervix 12 to 24 hours prior to the procedure. When a woman returns to the hospital, she may first be given intravenous pain medication and local anesthesia, which is injected into the cervix. The dilators are removed, and the uterus is then emptied with suction and various instruments. This procedure is more complicated than a first-trimester procedure because the fetus is larger. Generally, a D&E takes between 15 and 30 minutes. The risks associated with this type of abortion include increased pain, blood loss, and cervical trauma.

In the late part of the second trimester, some physicians may use **induced labor procedures,** including **saline** or **prostaglandin,** instead of a D&E. In these cases, a needle is injected into the amniotic sac, and amniotic fluid is removed. Then an equal amount of saline or prostaglandin can be injected into the amniotic sac. Prostaglandins can also be used orally to induce labor (Wiseman, 2003). When prostaglandins are used, uterine contractions force the fetus out of the uterus. Usually, after a saline or prostaglandin injection, the fetus is delivered within 19 to 22 hours. Both of these procedures are very painful emotionally and physically. Complications may include nausea, diarrhea, cervical problems, and uterine rupture; and the risk of death from a second-trimester abortion procedure is 25 times greater than from an abortion in the first trimester (Tyler, 1981). Overall, D&E procedures are safer, less painful, quicker, and less expensive than induced labor procedures.

A **hysterotomy** (hiss-stur-ROT-oh-mee) is a second-trimester abortion procedure that may be used if either of the aforementioned methods is contraindicated or if the woman's life is in immediate danger. In this procedure, the abdominal cavity is opened up to remove the fetus, similar to a cesarean section. This is done under general anesthesia and requires a hospital stay of between 5 and 7 days. Because it is a major operation, the possible risks are much greater and include problems with general anesthesia, prolonged recovery, and possible death. These risks have significantly reduced the use of this procedure. Another procedure that is rarely used today is a hysterectomy, which is a removal of the fetus and uterus.

dilation and evacuation (D&E)
A second-trimester abortion procedure that involves cervical dilation and vacuum aspiration of the uterus.

laminaria
Seaweed used in second-trimester abortion procedures to dilate the cervix. Used dried, it can swell three to five times its original diameter.

induced labor procedure
Using artificial means, such as drugs, to start labor.

saline abortion
A second-trimester abortion procedure in which amniotic fluid is removed and replaced with a saline solution, which causes premature delivery of the fetus.

prostaglandin
Oral or injected drug taken to cause uterine contractions.

hysterotomy
A second-trimester abortion procedure that involves a surgical removal of the fetus through the abdomen.

Review Question

Differentiate between first- and second-trimester surgical abortion procedures.

SEX Talk

Question: How much does an abortion cost?

The average cost for a first-trimester surgical abortion is $372 (Henshaw & Finer, 2003). These fees usually include an examination, laboratory tests, anesthesia, the procedure, and a follow-up examination. In a private physician's office, this procedure is more expensive. The average cost of an early medical abortion, using drugs (such as RU-486), is $490. A second-trimester abortion can run much higher, depending on whether the procedure is done in a private clinic or hospital.

Medical Abortion

A medical abortion involves the use of medicine to end a pregnancy. A woman works closely with a healthcare provider when taking these medications. Today two drugs have been used for medical abortion, Mifepristone (RU-486) and Methotrexate.

Although both drugs have been used in the United States for other medical purposes, neither had been approved for use in pregnancy termination. When one of these drugs is used in conjunction with a prostaglandin (Misoprostol), the uterus will contract and expel the contents.

Mifepristone was first approved for use in pregnancy termination in France in 1988. It was then approved in the United Kingdom in 1991, and in Sweden in 1992. The political climate in the United States during the early 1990s convinced RU-486's manufacturer not to seek approval in the United States (Planned Parenthood Federation of America, 2004). At about this same time, the Bush administration ruled that Mifepristone could not be brought into, or used in, the United States (Aguillaume & Tyrer, 1995). In an attempt to have this decision overruled, a woman named Leona Benten brought RU-486 into the United States in 1992, and the drug was immediately seized. The Supreme Court quickly upheld the confiscation (Talbot, 1999).

In 1994, the Clinton administration requested a reevaluation of the import ban from the FDA, and at the same time RU-486's manufacturer donated research rights to the United States Population Council, one of the world's leading laboratories for contraceptive development (Planned Parenthood Federation of America, 2004). The Population Council found that RU-486 was not only safe but highly effective as well. Based on this research, the FDA Advisory Committee recommended that Mifepristone be approved. However, it wasn't until 2000 that Mifepristone was formally approved for use in the United States.

A woman taking Mifepristone will usually begin bleeding within 4 to 5 hours, and bleeding will continue for up to 13 days, whereas a woman taking Methotrexate may continue bleeding for 4 weeks or more. Mifepristone is often more popular because it involves a shorter duration of bleeding; however, a physician will decide which method would work best for the patient. A medical abortion involves two or three office visits, testing, and exams, and costs $350 to $650.

The advantages of medical abortion include the fact that no anesthesia is used and women often report feeling more in control (F. H. Stewart, Ellertson, & Cates, 2004). Because the abortion is more like a miscarriage, some women report it feels more natural. The disadvantages include the fact that the woman must be prepared to undergo a surgical abortion if necessary. There has also been some concern over the increased risk of bacterial infection using Mifepristone (Centers for Disease Control, 2005a; Day & Bisset, 2004).

Mifepristone® (RU-486) Although **Mifepristone** (MYFE-priss-tone; **RU-486**) has only been FDA-approved in the United States since 2000, it has been used in several European countries for more than a decade. RU-486 is an antiprogestin, which blocks the development of progesterone, causing a breakdown.

Three RU-486 pills are taken, and 2 days later a woman takes an oral dose of prostaglandin (typically Misoprostol). This causes uterine contractions that expel the fertilized ovum. Effectiveness rates range between 95% and 97%. RU-486 can safely and effectively be used to terminate a pregnancy up until 63 days (9 weeks) from a woman's last menstrual period (F. H. Stewart, Ellertson, & Cates, 2004). There are some potential side effects, however, which include nausea, cramping, vomiting, and uterine bleeding for anywhere from 1 to 3 weeks (F. Stewart et al., 2004). The prolonged bleeding and the length of time to expulsion (days compared with minutes) make RU-486 less appealing than a vacuum aspiration abortion. However, with RU-486, surgery is unnecessary (unless there are complications), and there is no possibility of uterine perforation.

Methotrexate **Methotrexate** (METH-oh-trecks-ate) can also be used as an early option for nonsurgical abortion. It was approved by the FDA in 1953 as a breast cancer drug and is also used to treat psoriasis and rheumatoid arthritis. Methotrexate is often given in the form of an injection; and, when it is used in combination with Misoprostol, it has been found to cause a drug-induced miscarriage (Bygdeman & Danielsson, 2002). Methotrexate works by stopping the development of the developing cells of the zygote, and the prostaglandin is used to contract the uterus to expel the pregnancy. As with Mifepristone, Methotrexate can safely and effectively be used to terminate a pregnancy up to 63 days past a woman's last menstrual period.

Mifepristone
Drug used in medical abortion procedures; it blocks development of progesterone, which causes a breakdown in the uterine lining; also referred to as RU-486.

RU-486
Drug used in medical abortion procedures; it blocks development of progesterone, which causes a breakdown in the uterine lining; also referred to as Mifepristone.

Methotrexate
Drug used in medical abortion procedures; when taken, it stops the development of the zygote.

Review Question

Describe how Mifepristone and Methotrexate work to end a pregnancy.

sex byte

African American women are 3 times more likely and Hispanic women are 2½ times more likely than white women to have an abortion (Jones, Darroch, & Henshaw, 2002a).

Question: If you had an abortion, could that make you infertile later on?

Women who undergo an abortion can become pregnant and give birth later on in their life without complications (P. L. Frank, 1991). However, repeated abortions may create an incompetent cervix and could cause future miscarriages. Also, there are rare cases of unexpected complications of abortion that can lead to infertility or even hysterectomy, such as uterine perforation or severe infection. Women who use medical abortions may have less risk to future fertility because these are nonsurgical abortion options.

Reactions to Abortion

In the late 1980s, President Ronald Reagan asked Surgeon General Dr. C. Everett Koop to prepare a report on the physical aftereffects of women who have undergone elective abortions. The Surgeon General reported that scientific studies had documented that physiological health consequences—including infertility, incompetent cervix, miscarriage, premature birth, and low birth weight—are no more frequent among women who experience abortion than they are among the general population of women. The Surgeon General's findings do not support claims by pro-life advocates who state that there are severe physiological symptoms associated with abortion.

Women's Reactions

The decision to have an abortion is a difficult one. Terminating an unintended pregnancy or an intended pregnancy with a deformed fetus can be very painful. The physiological and psychological effects vary from person to person, and they depend on many factors.

Physiological Symptoms   Physiological reactions to abortion depend on the type of procedure used. After an early abortion, many women report increased cramping, heavy bleeding with possible clots, and nausea. These symptoms may persist for several days, but if any of these are severe, a physician should be seen for an evaluation. Severe complications are much more frequent in late abortion procedures and, as we discussed, include hemorrhaging, cervical laceration, uterine perforation, and infection (F. H. Stewart, Ellertson, & Cates, 2004). Of these complications, uterine perforation is the most serious, although the risk of occurrence is small. Although some people believe that early abortion is a risky procedure, studies have shown that the death rate from an abortion before 9 weeks is 1 in 260,000.

In 2002, many pro-life groups attempted to dissuade women from choosing abortion by citing the notion that abortion causes breast cancer. In some states, such as Texas, warnings about breast cancer are required when undergoing abortion procedures. In Mississippi, a woman undergoing an abortion must sign a form indicating she has been informed of the increased risk of breast cancer (Meckler, 2004). However, after a review of research, the National Cancer Institute (2003) has stated that there is no relationship between abortion and breast cancer, and the American Cancer Society, World Health Organization, and the National Institutes of Health have all agreed.

Psychological Symptoms   How a woman feels after an abortion has a lot to do with how her society views abortion. For example, a woman who underwent an illegal abortion in the 1960s might have felt an incredible sense of guilt and shame because abortion was illegal and therefore viewed as "bad." Psychological reactions also vary among women, as the story in the accompanying Personal Voices, "Having an Abortion: Stacy's Story," indicates. Overall, we know the most about psychological symptoms after surgical abortion and very little about reactions to medical abortions. Reactions may be very

Having an Abortion: Stacy's Story

My boyfriend, Jeff, and I had been sexually active for about two years and were using condoms for protection. However, one night after a party, we had been drinking and forgot to use a rubber. About three weeks later, my period was late. . . . When I found out my pregnancy test was positive, I couldn't stop crying. We talked about our options, but deep down I knew what would happen. I would not be able to keep this baby.

When it was time for the procedure, Jeff drove me there. I did my best to be brave, but honestly I didn't feel brave that day. I was in a group of about five other girls; they talked to us about exactly what would happen in the procedure and what instruments they would be using. We had to talk about ourselves and how we felt about our decision. The nurse asked me if I was sure about my decision to have an abortion. Neither Jeff nor I felt that we could handle a baby at that point in our life.

Soon afterward, we went into the preparation room. I was given some medicine to make me kind of drowsy, but I still was aware of what was going on. After about an hour, a nurse came and took me into the exam room. There they put me on a table and helped put my feet in stirrups. The doctor stuck something in me to open me up and then started this vacuum thing. I don't remember going to the recovery room. I just remember lying there, feeling like I was in shock. Finally, a nurse came to me with a list of people I could call for counseling. She told me that she really felt I should talk with someone about the abortion. . . . I remember feeling extremely faint when I started to walk. Jeff was there, and I just started crying again when I saw him.

Jeff was great. He didn't leave my side—taking care of me and getting me whatever I needed. The next morning I was still in a daze. Jeff was really concerned because I wouldn't talk to him. All I could do was lie there.

Today when I see babies, I wonder what mine would have looked like. What would he or she be like? It seems so long ago that all of this happened, but I still feel the guilt. I don't know how I finally decided to talk to someone, but it was really good for me. It was painful at first, but I'm still working on it.

SOURCE: Author's files.

similar, but this will be an area of research that will continue to grow as interest in medical abortion increases.

The majority of evidence from scientific studies indicates that most women who undergo surgical abortion have very few psychological side effects later on (Adler et al., 1992; Zolese & Blacker, 1992). In fact, relief is the more prominent response for the majority of women. However, although relief may be the immediate feeling, some researchers point out that there are actually three categories of psychological reactions to abortion. Positive emotions include relief and happiness; socially based emotions include shame, guilt, and fear of disapproval; and internally based emotions include regret, anxiety, depression, doubt, and anger, which are based on the woman's feelings about the pregnancy (Thorp et al., 2003). A woman may cycle through each of these reactions—feeling relief one minute, depression and/or guilt the next.

Some women experience intense, negative psychological consequences that include guilt, anxiety, depression, and regret. In 10% of these cases, these feelings are severe (Zolese & Blacker, 1992). Other possible negative psychological symptoms include self-reproach, increased sadness, and a sense of loss.

Certain conditions may put a woman more at risk for developing severe psychological symptoms. These include being young; not having family or partner support; being persuaded to have an abortion when a woman does not want one; having a difficult time making the decision to have an abortion; blaming the pregnancy on another person or on oneself; having a strong religious and moral background; having an abortion for medical or genetic reasons; having a history of psychiatric problems before the abortion; and having a late abortion procedure (Dagg, 1991; Mueller & Major, 1989; Zolese & Blacker, 1992). In addition, women who decided to tell no one about their decision to abort, because they anticipated a lack of support, were found to have more negative psychological symptoms following the procedure (Major et al., 1990).

Thus, although discovering an unplanned pregnancy and deciding to abort are very stressful decisions, in the majority of cases the emotional aftermath does not appear to be severe (Burnell & Norfleet, 1987; Major et al., 1985; Mueller & Major, 1989). Still, it is very beneficial for a woman (and her partner) who is contemplating an abortion to discuss this with a counselor or nurse. When looking for a reliable abortion clinic, check with someone you trust. In the last 5 years, several "fake" abortion clinics have been set up; although these appear to provide full health care for women, they only provide a pregnancy test and strong antiabortion information.

Men's Reactions

A woman's choice to have an abortion forces a couple to reevaluate their relationship and ask themselves some difficult questions. Do we both feel the same about each other? Is this relationship serious? Where is this relationship going? Keeping the lines of communication open during this time is very important. Some studies claim that abortion causes couples to break up, but there is also evidence that if couples can communicate about their thoughts, feelings, and fears while facing an unplanned pregnancy, an abortion may actually bring them closer. The male partner's involvement makes the abortion experience less traumatic for the woman; in fact, women whose partners support them and help them through the abortion show more positive responses after abortion (Adler et al., 1990; Moseley et al., 1981). Women who have no support from their partners or who make the decision themselves often experience greater emotional distress. In some cases, women have been found to conceal abortion decisions from their partners, and rates of domestic violence have been found to be high in this group (Woo, Fine, & Goetzl, 2005).

Some people believe that abortion is a difficult decision only for the woman because she is the one who carries the pregnancy. However, men also have a difficult time with the decision to abort, and they often experience sadness, a sense of loss, and fear for their

Personal Voices

Searching for Comfort

This poem was written by a male college student whose girlfriend was undergoing an abortion procedure. His pain and suffering is something that professionals often do not help men with.

Here the poor boy lies in wait,
Knowledge uncertain, only fear,
Demons torment through the silence,
Pain his beloved shall endure.
Searching for comfort in a sea of fire,

Finding only shame and sorrow.
Darkness captures another soul,
Leaving hatred in its wake.
Relief found only in departure,
Quickly subsiding to misconceptions,
Desire to prolong this union,
We have left only ourselves to heal.

Source: Author's files.

partner's well-being. Many men feel isolated and angry at both themselves and their partners. What makes it even more difficult for most men is that they often do not discuss the pregnancy with anyone other than their partner. Their own feelings are buried under the desire to help their partner get through it. Oftentimes they will become very rational, intellectual, and claim "the best thing to do is . . ." These are emotional defenses used to cover their underlying anxiety.

The frequent lack of counseling services for men at abortion facilities is further evidence to the men that they should be able to deal with their feelings on their own. Attending counseling, either with their partners or alone, can be very helpful for these men. The accompanying Personal Voices, "Searching for Comfort," includes a poem that was given to one of the authors by a male student whose girlfriend was undergoing an abortion, written while he was in the waiting room.

Question: *My friend had an abortion 2 months ago, but she still seems very depressed. How long does this last?*

It is hard to say how long the psychological reactions to abortion will last; it depends on the person. Some women feel sad for a few days, whereas others may feel sad for much longer. It would be helpful for your friend to talk things over with either a school counselor or healthcare provider.

Teens and Abortion

Each year in the United States, 1 million teenagers become pregnant, and 85% of these pregnancies are unintended (Alan Guttmacher Institute, 1999c). Many states have passed laws that control teenagers' access to abortion. For instance, some states require **parental notification** or **parental consent.** However, studies have shown that in states without mandatory parental consent or notice requirements, 75% of minors involve one or both parents (Henshaw & Kost, 1992). Those who do not usually have strong reasons for not doing so, and these laws make it difficult for many of them to obtain an abortion. Some states offer a **judicial bypass option,** in which a minor can obtain consent from a judge rather than from her parents.

Cross-Cultural Aspects of Abortion

Close to 4 of every 10 pregnancies throughout the world are unplanned, and 2 in 10 are terminated by abortion (Alan Guttmacher Institute, 1999b). The lowest abortion rates are in Spain, Ireland, Netherlands, and Belgium, whereas the highest rates in the world are in Romania, Cuba, Vietnam, and India (see Figure 13.11). Some countries do not have reliable reporting of abortion rates, and unofficial estimates are compiled. This is the case in India, where unofficial estimates put the annual number of abortions at over 6 million (Ertelt, 2004). Abortion is often used as a contraceptive method in India. In Russia, the average woman undergoes 4 or 5 abortions in her lifetime (Kon, 2004).

Whether or not a woman will have an abortion depends on whether her country's laws permit or prohibit the procedure. It is estimated that 25% of women live in countries with significant abortion restrictions (see Figure 13.12). Only a handful of countries, including Canada, Cuba, Puerto Rico, China, Singapore, Vietnam, South Africa, and many of the Scandinavian countries, permit abortion without restriction (Rahman, Katzive, & Henshaw, 1998). However, many other countries impose restrictions such as allowing abortion only to save a woman's life (including countries such as Brazil, Mexico, Egypt, Iran, Nepal, Sri Lanka, Ireland, and many areas within sub-Saharan Africa).

Review Question

Identify some physiological and psychological reactions to abortion, and discuss the research on men and abortion.

parental notification
Abortion legislation that requires the notification of the parents of a minor prior to an abortion procedure.

parental consent
Abortion legislation that requires the consent of the parents of a minor prior to an abortion procedure.

judicial bypass option
Abortion legislation that allows for a judge to bypass parental consent or notification for a minor to acquire an abortion.

Review Question

Describe the laws that have been imposed in an attempt to decrease abortion in adolescent populations.

sex byte

Compared with adolescents in France, Canada, Great Britain, and Sweden, U.S. adolescents have lower levels of contraceptive use and higher rates of abortion (Alan Guttmacher Institute, 2001).

Figure 13.11

Figure 13.11
Percentage of pregnancies aborted worldwide.
Source: From *Sharing Responsibility: Women, Society and Abortion Worldwide*, New York, 1999, p. 28. Reproduced with permission of The Alan Guttmacher Institute.

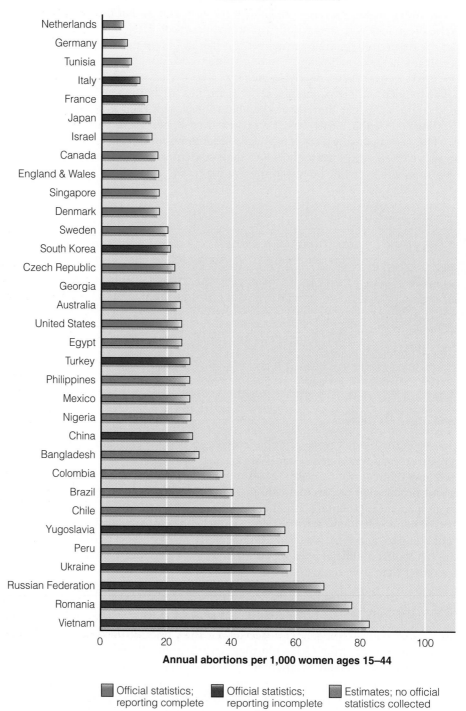

Global abortion statistics

Annual abortions per 1,000 women ages 15–44

Official statistics; reporting complete

Official statistics; reporting incomplete

Estimates; no official statistics collected

In countries where abortion laws are severely restrictive, some countries allow abortions in cases of rape (such as Brazil and Mexico). A few countries require permission of other family members, such as in Turkey, where a woman cannot have an abortion without the consent of her husband. Still other countries prohibit abortion altogether, even to save a woman's life, although legal appeals to save a woman's life may be successful in many of these countries (Rahman, Katzive, & Henshaw, 1998).

Medical abortion has been widely used outside the United States. In fact, Mifepristone has been used for over a decade in France, Great Britain, and Sweden (Jones & Henshaw, 2002). In Germany, women using medical abortion report satisfac-

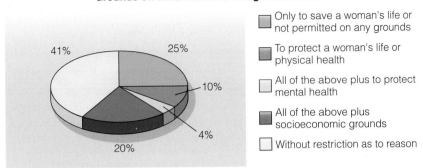

Grounds on which abortion is legal worldwide

- Only to save a woman's life or not permitted on any grounds
- To protect a woman's life or physical health
- All of the above plus to protect mental health
- All of the above plus socioeconomic grounds
- Without restriction as to reason

41%   25%   10%   4%   20%

Figure 13.12

Grounds on which abortion is legal worldwide. It was projected that there will be 1.38 billion women between the ages of 15 and 24 in 1999. *Source:* From *Sharing Responsibility: Women, Society and Abortion Worldwide,* New York, 1999, p. 28. Reproduced with permission of The Alan Guttmacher Institute.

tion and lower levels of initial anxiety than those using surgical abortion (Hemmerling, Siedentopf, & Kentenich, 2005).

Although many safe and legal abortions occur, approximately 20 million unsafe abortions take place each year (K. Singh & Ratnam, 1998). Unsafe abortion methods include taking drugs, inserting objects into the vagina, flushing the vagina with certain liquids, or having the abdomen vigorously massaged (Tietze & Henshaw, 1986). Deaths from unsafe abortion practices are highest in Africa, where there are 680 deaths per 100,000 abortions (Alan Guttmacher Institute, 1999d).

Abortion remains a controversial procedure in the United States as well as in the rest of the world. Both sides of the issue battle from what they believe are basic principles: one side from a fetus's right to be born, the other from a woman's right to control her own body. The pendulum of this debate continues to swing back and forth. For example, in the early 1970s, the right-to-choose group won an important victory with *Roe v. Wade;* in the early 1990s, the right-to-life group scored a victory with the decision that a state can limit access to abortion.

Current politics may influence whether *Roe v. Wade* is one day overturned. Although new developments like medical abortion may take the fight out of the abortion clinics and into women's homes, the only real certainty about the future of abortion is that it will remain one of the most controversial areas of American public life.

Review Question

Describe what we know about abortion outside the United States.

Chapter Review

ACTIVE SUMMARY

1. (a) _____ is not a modern invention. The ancient Greeks and Egyptians used a variety of techniques to try to control their (b) _____. Several groups began to explore controlling fertility in the early 1800s, and Margaret Sanger was one of the first people to advocate the importance of (c) _____ _____.

2. Contraception throughout the world has always been affected by social and economic issues, (a) _____ _____, (b) _____, and gender (c) _____. Outside the United States, many women are often not (d) _____ in contraceptive decision making, and contraceptive use is thought to reduce a man's (e) _____. Scandinavian countries are regarded as some of the most (f) _____ with respect to contraceptive (g) _____. Finland has been rated as a(an) (h) _____ country in contraceptive use.

3. The (a) _____ has approved several methods of contraception, but no method is best for (b) _____. These include (c) _____, hormonal, chemical, (d) _____, natural, permanent, and (e) _____ methods.

4. The (a) _____ is responsible for approving all prescription medicine in the United States. A pharmaceutical company must submit proof that the drug is (b) _____ for human use. It is estimated that it takes (c) _____ to (d) _____ years to develop a new (e) _____ drug.

5. Issues that must be considered when choosing a contraceptive method include: personal (a) _____; number of sexual (b) _____; (c) _____ of sexual intercourse; risk of acquiring a(n) (d) _____; responsibility of (e) _____; method cost; and (f) _____ advantages and disadvantages.

6. (a) _____ methods of birth control work by preventing the sperm from (b) _____ the uterus. Barrier methods include the (c) _____, diaphragm, FemCap, (d) _____, and the contraceptive sponge. Male condoms can be made of (e) _____, polyurethane, or lambskin. Female condoms are made of (f) _____.

7. (a) _____ methods work by changing hormone levels to interrupt ovulation. Combined-hormonal methods include most birth control pills, (b) _____, vaginal rings, and patches, whereas (c) _____-_____ methods include subdermal implants, injectables, and (d) _____.

8. (a) _____ birth control pills contain synthetic estrogen and a type of (b) _____. The increase in estrogen and progesterone prevents the (c) _____ gland from sending hormones to cause the (d) _____ to begin maturation of an ovum.

9. Other hormonal contraceptive options include a monthly injection of synthetic hormones, including estrogen and progestin; (a) _____ _____, a small plastic ring that releases a constant dose of estrogen and progestin and is changed once a month; the Ortho Evra (b) _____, which sticks to the skin and time-releases synthetic estrogen and progestin into the bloodstream. All of these work by inhibiting (c) _____, increasing cervical mucus, and/or rendering the uterus inhospitable to implantation.

10. (a) _____-_____ methods include minipills, Norplant, and Depo-Provera. (b) _____ is a subdermal contraceptive implant, whereas (c) _____-_____ is a progestin-only injectable contraceptive that works by preventing (d) _____ and thickening cervical mucus. Norplant was withdrawn from the market in 2005.

11. (a) _____ methods of contraception include spermicides such as creams, jellies, foams, suppositories, and films. (b) _____ work by reducing the survival of (c) _____ in the vagina.

12. IUDs and IUSs create a low-grade (a) _____ in the uterus, which may interfere with sperm (b) _____ and block sperm from passing into the Fallopian tubes and joining with an ovum. The (c) _____ devices also time-release (d) _____ into the lining of the uterus.

13. NFP involves charting (a) _____ periods by taking a daily basal body temperature (BBT) and checking (b) _____ mucus in order to determine ovulation. (c) _____ is avoided during ovulation. In the rhythm method, there is often no monitoring of the signs of ovulation. (d) _____ awareness involves charting in conjunction with another form of birth control.

14. (a) _____ is a method of contraception in which the man withdraws his (b) _____ from the vagina prior to (c) _____.

15. Couples may choose (a) _____ to prevent pregnancy, to protect against STIs, or for other reasons such as illness or disease. It is estimated that reported usage rates of this method are (b) _____ because many couples don't consider it a(n) (c) _____ method.

16. Tubal (a) _____ is the most widely used method of birth control in the world. In this procedure, a physician may sever or block both (b) _____ tubes so that the ovum and sperm cannot meet. A(An) (c) _____ blocks the flow of sperm through the vas deferens, and although the testes will continue to produce viable sperm cells, the cells die and are (d) _____ by the body.

17. Unreliable birth control methods include wishing, (a) _____, douching, and breast-feeding. The (b) _____ regimen involves using a high dose of (c) _____ _____ _____ as emergency contraception. Plan B was approved as emergency contraception in 1999, and it must be given within (d) _____ hours of unprotected intercourse. It may be effective for up to (e) _____ hours after unprotected intercourse. An IUD may also be implanted as a form of emergency contraception. Emergency contraception has been available worldwide for over (f) _____ decades.

18. Outside the United States, (a) _____ has been considered a female's responsibility, and that may be why the (b) _____ and vasectomy are the only birth control methods available to men. Many (c) _____ claim the lack of male methods is because most of those doing the contraceptive research are men, whereas others claim that most methods are for women because it's easier to interfere with one ovum a(n) (d) _____ than thousands of sperm a day.

19. There are many new contraceptive methods on the horizon, and many of these will be (a) _____ to use, more (b) _____-_____, and have higher effectiveness rates. (c) _____ are also being studied.

20. The (a) _____ debate has been very emotional and even violent. Many on both sides of the issue have strongly held (b) _____. There are (c) _____-_____ supporters and (d) _____-_____ supporters.

21. Abortion has been practiced in many (a) _____ throughout history; in fact, there are few large-scale societies where it has not been practiced. Before abortion was (b) _____, illegal abortions were common. For most of Western history, (c) _____ determined general attitudes toward abortion.

22. In 1973, the court case (a) _____ v. (b) _____ gave women a constitutionally protected right to have an abortion in the early stages of (c) _____. In the first trimester of pregnancy, a woman has a right to choose abortion without

the **(d)** _____ interfering. In the second trimester, a state can regulate abortion to protect a woman's health; and, in the third trimester, the potential fetal life enables the state to limit or ban abortion except in cases in which a woman's **(e)** _____ or health would be at risk.

23. The majority of surgical abortion procedures today are performed in **(a)** _____ abortion clinics, which is much less expensive than having it done in a **(b)** _____. The most serious risks of a surgical abortion include uterine **(c)** _____, cervical laceration, severe **(d)** _____, infection, and anesthesia-related complications.

24. Surgical abortions can be either first- or second-trimester **(a)** _____. First-trimester abortions are done before 14 weeks of **(b)** _____ and are simpler and **(c)** _____ than later procedures. **(d)** _____-trimester abortions are done between 14 and 21 weeks.

25. A(An) **(a)** _____ aspiration abortion is the most common type of surgical abortion procedure in the United States. There are several **(b)** _____ risks associated with this type of abortion, including excessive bleeding, possible infection, and uterine perforation. A woman may have a second-trimester abortion for several reasons, and a(an) **(c)** _____ and evacuation is the most commonly used procedure.

26. Medical abortion involves the use of **(a)** _____ to end a pregnancy. Today Mifepristone and Methotrexate are used, along with **(b)** _____. _____ is used more often since it involves a(an) **(c)** _____ duration of bleeding. A physician determines which drug will work best. Women report that medical abortions feel more **(d)** _____; however, a woman undergoing a medical abortion must be prepared to undergo a **(e)** _____ abortion if the procedure is unsuccessful.

27. Women who have **(a)** _____ do so for many reasons, including the belief that a baby would interfere with other responsibilities; an inability to **(b)** _____ provide for a child; difficulties in the relationship with the father; not wanting people to know they are **(c)** _____ active; pressure from their partners or families; fetal **(d)** _____; risks to mother's health; having several children already; and rape or incest.

28. **(a)** _____ reactions to surgical abortion depend on the type of procedure used. Early abortion procedures often result in **(b)** _____, heavy bleeding with possible clots, and nausea. Severe **(c)** _____ are much more frequent in late abortion procedures and include hemorrhaging, cervical laceration, uterine perforation, and **(d)** _____. The majority of women undergoing abortion have very few **(e)** _____ side effects later on, although there are certain conditions that

may put a woman more at risk for developing severe psychological symptoms.

29. The abortion experience is less **(a)** _____ when a male partner is involved. Women whose **(b)** _____ support them and help them through the abortion show more **(c)** _____ responses afterward. Women who have no support from their partners often experience greater **(d)** _____ distress. We know less about a woman's psychological reactions after a(an) **(e)** _____ abortion.

30. Many **(a)** _____ have a difficult time with the decision to abort and experience sadness, a sense of loss, and fear for their **(b)** _____ well-being. Many hold their feelings in and do not discuss the **(c)** _____ with anyone other than their partner.

31. It is estimated that **(a)** _____ of every 10 pregnancies throughout the world are unplanned, and **(b)** _____ in 10 end in an abortion. Whether or not a woman will have an abortion depends on whether her country's **(c)** _____ permit or prohibit the procedure. In Russia, the average woman undergoes **(d)** _____ or **(e)** _____ abortions in her lifetime.

Critical Thinking Questions

1. If you found out tomorrow that you (or your partner) were 6 weeks pregnant, what would your options be? Where would you go for help, and whom would you talk to? What would your biggest concerns be?

2. Suppose a good friend of yours, Sylvia, tells you that she is 10 weeks pregnant, and she and her boyfriend have decided that she will have an abortion. She knows that you are taking the sexuality course and asks you about her abortion options. What can you tell her?

3. What method of contraception do you think would work best for you at this time in your life? In 5 years? In 10 years? Why?

4. Do you think women who use herbal contraceptives should be taught about newer, more modern methods of birth control? What if the methods they are using are working for them?

CHAPTER RESOURCES

Check It Out

Tone, Andrea. (2001). **Devices & desires: A history of contraceptives in America.** New York: Hill and Wang.

In this book, Tone, a historian at Georgia Institute of Technology, discusses the history of contraception and the demand for contraceptives in the United States. Starting with Victorian times, she traces contraception through the Comstock Act, Margaret Sanger's work, and other milestones. She discusses the issues that surrounded the early birth control pill, such as health risks and religious objections, and the development of several other birth control methods.

Vera Drake (2004; 2 hours, 5 minutes; Rated R)

Vera Drake (Imelda Staunton), beloved wife of Stan (Phil Davis) and mother of Sid (Daniel Mays) and Ethel (Alex Kelly), spends her days cleaning houses for money and looking in on elderly and sick neighbors out of the kindness of her heart. But Vera performs another duty that her family doesn't know about—she helps women terminate their pregnancies. When tragedy befalls a young client of Vera's, the truth comes out, forcing her family to see their mother in an entirely different light. This is a very heavy and honest portrayal of Vera's life and experiences.

InfoTrac® College Edition

If your instructor ordered InfoTrac with this book, explore InfoTrac College Edition, your online library, for additional readings and review. Go to: **www.thomsonedu.com,** and enter these search terms:

abortion	birth control	contraception
condom	contraceptive methods	contraceptive testing
male contraceptive	sexual abstinence	sterilization

SexualityNow Companion Website

Go to **http://thomsonedu.com/carroll** for practice quiz questions, interactive activities, Internet links, critical thinking exercises, discussion forums, and more. You can also access sites from the Wadsworth Psychology Study Center **(http://psychology.wadsworth.com)** or you can connect directly to the following sites:

Planned Parenthood Federation of America

Planned Parenthood Federation of America is the world's largest voluntary reproductive healthcare organization. Founded by Margaret Sanger in 1916 as America's first birth control clinic, Planned Parenthood believes that women have the right to choose when or whether to have a child, that every child should be wanted and loved, and that women should be in charge of their own destinies. This website offers information on birth control, emergency contraception, STIs, safer sex, pregnancy, abortion, and other health-related concerns.

Alan Guttmacher Institute

The Alan Guttmacher Institute (AGI) is a nonprofit organization focused on sexual and reproductive health research, policy analysis, and public education. AGI publishes special reports on topics pertaining to sexual and reproductive health and rights. The Institute's mission is to protect the reproductive choices of all women and men in the United States and throughout the world.

Birthcontrol.Com

This Canadian website sells innovative contraceptive products from around the world. Sponges, condoms, spermicides, and barrier methods of contraception, including the Ovès contraceptive cap, can be found, all at relatively inexpensive prices.

National Abortion Federation

The National Abortion Federation (NAF) is the professional association of abortion providers in the United States and Canada. NAF members provide the broadest spectrum of abortion expertise in North America. Members include some 400 nonprofit and private clinics, women's health centers, Planned Parenthood facilities, and private physicians, as well as nationally and internationally recognized researchers, clinicians, and educators at major universities and teaching hospitals, who together care for more than half of the women who choose abortion each year in the United States.

National Abortion Rights Action League

NARAL is a pro-choice league that strives to help find workable answers to ultimately reduce the need for abortions. NARAL believes that ignoring limited access to contraception, reproductive health care, and sex education while taking away a woman's right to choose will only result in more unintended pregnancies and more abortions.

National Right to Life

The National Right to Life Committee was founded in response to the U.S. Supreme Court's 1973 decision in *Roe v. Wade*. Since its official beginning the National Right to Life Committee has grown to represent over 3,000 chapters in all 50 states and the District of Columbia. NRLC publishes a monthly newspaper, the *National Right to Life News,* and has an internal Political Action Committee and Educational Trust Fund. The goal of the National Right to Life Committee is to restore legal protection to human life.

Global Campaign for Microbicides

The Global Campaign for Microbicides is an international effort to build support among policymakers, opinion leaders, and the general public for the development of microbicides. The campaign works to accelerate product development, facilitate widespread access and use, and protect the needs and interests of users, especially women. The website contains information about current research and availability of microbicides.

Go to **www.thomsonedu.com** to link to **SexualityNow,** your online study tool. First take the **Pre-Test** for this chapter to get your **Personalized Study Plan,** which will identify topics you need to review and direct you to online resources. Then take the **Post-Test** to determine what concepts you have mastered and what you still need work on.

Videos in SexualityNow

For additional information on topics discussed in this chapter, check out the videos in **SexualityNow** on the following topics:

- **Virtual Safer-Sex Kit**—Learn the relative benefits and risks of each contraceptive device and safer sex aid depicted.
- **Emergency Contraception: The Debate About the Morning-After Pill**—The FDA's dilemma about how to make Plan B over-the-counter but still prevent young teens from obtaining it on their own.

14 Challenges to Sexual Functioning

Sexuality ▣ Now Go to www.thomsonedu.com to link to **SexualityNow,** your online study tool.

Healthy sexuality depends on good mental and physical functioning. Challenges to sexual functioning include anxiety, sexual dysfunctions, illness, disease, and disability. However, learning to adapt to these challenges is very important in maintaining a positive view of sexuality. In this chapter, we will discuss the various sexual dysfunctions, treatments, disabilities, diseases, and illnesses and how these may challenge one's sexual functioning.

It is important to point out that our knowledge about male sexual functioning has advanced far ahead of our knowledge about female sexual functioning. Widespread interest in female sexual dysfunction is fairly recent in the United States and due in part to the success of Viagra. In 2001 the International Society for the Study of Women's Sexual Health (ISSWSH) was established to help foster communication and research into women's sexual health (see Web Resources at the end of this chapter for more information).

In Chapter 10 we discussed the sexual response cycle—a series of physiological and psychological changes that occur in the body during sexual behavior. These sexual response cycle models help physicians and therapists identify how dysfunction, disease, illness, and disability affect sexual functioning. Over the last few years there has been some concern that these models do not apply equally to men and women (Tiefer, 2000). In this chapter we will look at these issues and how sexual dysfunctions occur, treatments used, and how illness and disability can interfere with sexual functioning.

© Roy McMahon/Corbis

Although our sexual response changes as we age, many older couples still enjoy an active, satisfying sex life.

 ## SEXUAL DYSFUNCTIONS: DEFINITIONS, CAUSES, AND TREATMENT STRATEGIES

What constitutes a sexual dysfunction? Not being able to get an erection one night? Experiencing difficulties having an orgasm during sexual intercourse? Having no sexual desire for your partner? Do sexual dysfunctions have to happen for extended periods of time, or do they happen only once in a while? There are many types of sexual dysfunctions, and they can happen at any point during sexual activity.

Sexual dysfunctions are classified by the *Diagnostic and Statistical Manual (DSM)*, the major diagnostic system used in U.S. research and therapy. The *DSM* is occasionally updated, with the last text revision in 2000 (referred to as the *DSM IV-TR;* American Psychiatric Association, 2000). The *DSM* provides diagnostic criteria for the most common sexual dysfunctions including description, diagnosis, treatment, and research findings.

Before we discuss the sexual dysfunctions, it's important to differentiate between common problems with sexual functioning and true sexual dysfunctions. Common sexual problems include things such as insufficient foreplay, lack of enthusiasm for sex, and/or the inability to relax. These problems often occur infrequently and may or may not interfere with overall sexual functioning. Most of us have experienced a problem that has interfered with our sexual functioning at one point or another, but the problem went away without treatment. Even "normal" couples report periodic problems with sexual functioning (E. Frank et al., 1978). A sexual dysfunction is characterized by a disturbance in the sexual response that typically doesn't go away by itself—in fact, it may get worse over time.

One more point is in need of clarification before moving on—as you will soon realize, the DSM classification system for sexual dysfunctions appears rather heterosexist in that often the criteria for diagnosis revolves around an inability to engage in vaginal in-

Personal Voices

What Do College Students Think About Sexual Problems?

College students were asked whether they had ever had a sexual experience in which they, or their partner, had trouble with sexual functioning. Many said they had experienced problems and had trouble talking to their partners about it. As you read the following accounts, notice how the women often feel responsible for their partner's sexual problems. Why do you think this is? What about the men's attitudes? How can women be taught to feel less responsible and guilty? How can men learn to feel less pressure to perform?

Female: *Being in college, you find yourself stressed more than anything. Therefore, sex isn't always the first thing on my list, but it is for my partner. It's hard to get turned on when you are stressed out. The best sex we have is on the weekend after a relaxing night out with friends.*

Female: *My boyfriend has problems getting an erection after a long night of drinking. I was crying and all upset because I thought he was cheating on me and didn't care about me or wasn't attracted to me anymore.*

Female: *My boyfriend has trouble becoming aroused. We never really talked about it, but it really bothered him. At first I thought it was me, but I realized later that it was his problem, and it can't be all my fault. He went on Viagra and that worked for him.*

Female: *My boyfriend has a tendency to orgasm after only a few minutes. This has gone on for quite a while, and we finally talked about it. He told me he just got too excited, and maybe we could slow down a bit.*

Female: *I have trouble reaching orgasm. It affects our relationship in a way that I get nervous when we reach that point, so it's even harder to get the orgasm. Makes me feel like I have done something wrong.*

Female: *This happens all the time with my boyfriend. Sometimes I'm wet and he can't get it up, or he can get it up and I can't get wet. We talk about it all the* time, *but it doesn't really affect our relationship, because we still have sex, just not as often. We do other things to sexually stimulate each other.*

Male: *The first time I ever tried to have sex I was unable to have an erection. I was really embarrassed, but my partner was very understanding.*

Male: *I always feel so much pressure during sexual intercourse. Men are supposed to be able to provide orgasms for their partners, and I tend to focus so much on this that I lose my erection. This is both disappointing and frustrating for me. The more frustrated I get, the more likely the erection won't come back.*

Male: *I have had a couple of times where I couldn't get an erection or my partner couldn't get turned on or sex hurt her. We have always had good communication skills so we can talk about it. It never hurt our relationship but probably made it stronger by talking about it. We still have a great sex life.*

Male: *I had too much to drink one time, and I didn't feel much of anything during sex. She was really upset and felt like it was her fault, so I had to convince her it really wasn't. I now know how to "read" the signs when sexual activity may be involved, so I drink much, much less. It helps because she sees I am making an effort to acknowledge how she feels, and we both end up happy with the result.*

Male: *My girlfriend was diagnosed with vulvar vestibulitis. Our sex life was great prior to the diagnosis but then she lost her sexual interest, and sex became really painful. I understood sex hurt, but she cut me off from everything, totally. Slowly our relationship disintegrated into a friendship with quite a bit of resentment and confusion.*

Source: Author's files.

tercourse. This implies that only heterosexuals experience sexual dysfunction because gay men and lesbian women do not engage in vaginal sexual intercourse. The truth is that we all—gay, straight, and bisexual—experience sexual dysfunctions. The definition of "penetration" may not always refer to penile–vaginal penetration—it can include anal, oral, or digital penetration. In this chapter, we will refer to an inclusive definition of sexual dysfunction.

A sex therapist's first task in evaluating a new client is to ascertain whether a dysfunction exists, and if so, whether the dysfunction is psychological, physiological, or mixed. This is not always an easy task because psychological and physiological factors can overlap. Let's take a look at some of these factors.

Psychological Factors in Sexual Dysfunction

Psychological factors that can interfere with sexual functioning include unconscious fears, ongoing stress, anxiety, depression, guilt, anger, fear of infidelity, partner conflict, fear of intimacy, dependency, abandonment, and/or loss of control, all of which may impair the ability to respond sexually. As we discussed in Chapter 10, the various pressures and time commitments of two-career families may often lead to an absence of sexual intimacy. Problems may also arise from the desire to have children, commitment demands, the children leaving home, or guilt about past sexual relationships.

We also know that anxiety plays an important role in developing and maintaining sexual dysfunctions. Both **performance fears** and an excessive need to please a partner interfere with sexual functioning (Bancroft et al., 2005; Kaplan, 1974; Masters & Johnson, 1970). When anxiety levels are high, physiological arousal may be impossible. Therefore, sex therapy usually begins by overcoming performance fears, feelings of sexual inadequacy, and other anxieties. Therapy may also treat emotional factors such as depression, anger, or guilt.

Men and women with sexual dysfunction also tend to underreport their own levels of sexual arousal (Barlow, 1986). A man who has trouble maintaining an erection may begin thinking, "I'm a failure," or "I can't have an erection," and his anxiety leads him to avoid sex and dampens his sexual desire. Distractions, shifts in attention, or preoccupation during sexual arousal may interfere with the ability to become aroused, as can **spectatoring.** We will talk about treatment for psychological factors more later in this chapter.

Physical Factors in Sexual Dysfunction

The prevalence of sexual dysfunction increases with age (Araujo et al., 2004; R. W. Lewis et al., 2004). This is mainly due to physical factors such as disease, disability, illness, and the use of many commonly used drugs. Prescription drugs may cause a loss of sexual desire, erectile or ejaculatory problems, and/or orgasm problems in women. **Psychotropic drugs** often lead to sexual dysfunction (Feliciano & Alfonso, 1997). Lowering the drug dosage or changing medications may result in a reversal of these difficulties. Nonprescription drugs such as tobacco, alcohol, marijuana, LSD, and cocaine may also cause sexual dysfunction. We will talk about treatment for physical factors more later in this chapter.

Categorizing the Dysfunctions

Sexual dysfunctions are categorized as either primary or secondary, and situational or global. A **primary sexual dysfunction** is one that has always existed, whereas a **secondary sexual dysfunction** is one in which a dysfunction developed after a period of adequate functioning. A **situational sexual dysfunction** is a dysfunction that occurs during certain sexual activities or with certain partners (for instance, a man who can get an erection with his girlfriend but not his wife; or a woman who can have orgasms during masturbation but not during oral sex). A **global sexual dysfunction** is a dysfunction that occurs in every situation, during every type of sexual activity, and with every sexual partner.

It is important to clarify these differences, for they may affect treatment strategies. For instance, primary problems tend to have more biological or physiological causes, whereas secondary problems tend to have more psychological causes. Sex therapists further categorize dysfunctions as those of sexual desire, sexual arousal, orgasm, or pain disorders (most sex therapists use the *DSM-IV-TR* to help in their diagnosing). Each of these may be primary or secondary, situational or global. See Table 14.1 for an overview of sexual dysfunctions.

sex byte

New research in brain chemistry has found that anti-inflammatory drugs, such as acetaminophen (Tylenol), ibuprofen (Advil), or aspirin, used during a woman's pregnancy may affect an offspring's sexual desire and functioning later in life (Amateau & McCarthy, 2004).

performance fears
The fear of not being able to perform during sexual behavior.

spectatoring
Acting as an observer or judge of one's own sexual performance.

psychotropic medications
Medications prescribed for psychological disorders, such as depression.

Review Question

Explain how sexual dysfunctions are classified, and what factors have been found to interfere with sexual functioning.

primary sexual dysfunction
A sexual dysfunction that has always existed.

secondary sexual dysfunction
A sexual dysfunction that occurs after a period of normal sexual functioning.

situational sexual dysfunction
A sexual dysfunction that occurs only in specific situations.

global sexual dysfunction
A sexual dysfunction that occurs in every sexual situation.

TABLE 14.1   The Sexual Dysfunctions

Sexual Desire Disorders	Symptoms: Sexual Interest
Hypoactive Sexual Desire Disorder	*Primary*—Lifelong diminished or absent feelings of sexual interest or desire; absent sexual thoughts and/or fantasies *Secondary*—Acquired diminished or absent feelings of sexual interest or desire; diminished or absent sexual thoughts and/or fantasies
Sexual Aversion Disorder	*Primary*—Lifelong persistent or recurrent extreme aversion to, and avoidance of, all genital sexual contact with a sexual partner *Secondary*—Acquired persistent or recurrent extreme aversion to, and avoidance of, all genital sexual contact with a sexual partner
Sexual Arousal Disorders	**Symptoms: Physiological Arousal**
Female Sexual Arousal Disorder	*Primary*—Lifelong diminished or absent lubrication response of sexual excitement *Secondary*—Acquired diminished or absent lubrication response of sexual excitement
Male Erectile Disorder	*Primary*—Lifelong diminished or absent ability to attain or maintain, until completion of the sexual activity, an adequate erection *Secondary*—Acquired diminished or absent ability to attain or maintain, until completion of the sexual activity, an adequate erection
Orgasm Disorders	**Symptoms: Orgasm Difficulties**
Female Orgasmic Disorder	*Primary*—Lifelong delay or absence of orgasm following normal sexual excitement *Secondary*—Acquired delay or absence of orgasm following normal sexual excitement
Male Orgasmic Disorder	*Primary*—Lifelong absence of orgasm in men *Secondary*—Acquired diminished ability to orgasm or markedly decreased orgasmic intensity from any type of stimulation
Premature Ejaculation	*Primary*—Lifelong pattern of ejaculating with minimal sexual stimulation before, on, or shortly after penetration and before the person wishes it *Secondary*—Acquired pattern of ejaculating with minimal sexual stimulation before, on, or shortly after penetration and before the person wishes it
Sexual Pain Disorders	**Symptoms: Genital Pain**
Dyspareunia	*Primary*—Lifelong recurrent or persistent genital pain associated with sexual intercourse, in either a male or female *Secondary*—Acquired recurrent or persistent genital pain associated with sexual intercourse, in either a male or female
Vaginismus	*Primary*—Lifelong pattern of recurrent or persistent involuntary spasms of the outer third of the vagina that interferes with sexual intercourse *Secondary*—Acquired pattern of recurrent or persistent involuntary spasms of the outer third of the vagina that interferes with sexual intercourse
Other Sexual Dysfunctions Due to a General Medical Condition	**Presence of Sexual Dysfunction That Is Due to the Physiological Effects of a General Medical Condition**

SOURCE: Reprinted with permission from the *Diagnostic and Statistical Manual of Mental Disorders, Fourth Edition, Text Revision.* Copyright © 2000 by the American Psychiatric Association.

Treating Dysfunctions

multimodal
Using a variety of techniques.

Treatment of most sexual dysfunctions begins with a medical history and workup to identify any physiological causes. In addition to a medical history and exam, it is also important to evaluate any past sexual trauma or abuse that may cause or contribute to the dysfunction. After identifying causes for a sexual dysfunction, the next step is to determine a plan of treatment. Such treatment may be **multimodal,** involving more than one type of therapy. Different types of therapies have different success rates. The highest success rates for treatment of sexual dysfunctions range from about 60% in those with primary erectile disorder to 97% in premature ejaculation; rates of about 80% have been reported in treatment of orgasmic disorder in women.

Much of the current clinical research today focuses on developing new drugs to treat dysfunctions (even though a number of dysfunctions may be caused by or worsened by

Women and Sexual Dysfunction

Masters and Johnson's sexual response cycle (see Chapter 10) and the *DSM* medical classification for sexual dysfunction (see Table 14.1) have long been used as the model for sexual dysfunction. However, many feminists are concerned about the applicability of these models to female sexuality. In 2000, Leonore Tiefer and colleagues proposed a "new view" of women's sexual problems that included a proposed revision in the classification system for female sexual dysfunction.

According to Tiefer and colleagues, sexual dysfunctions occur when there is "discontent or dissatisfaction with any emotional, physical, or relational aspect of sexual experience." Here are a few of the proposed factors that may interfere with female sexual functioning.

1. Lack of vocabulary to describe experiences.
2. Lack of information about human sexual biology and life-stage changes.
3. Lack of information about how gender roles influence men's and women's sexual expectations, beliefs, and behaviors.
4. Inadequate access to information and services for contraception and abortion, STI prevention and treatment, sexual trauma, and domestic violence.
5. Anxiety or shame about one's body, sexual attractiveness, or sexual responses.
6. Lack of interest, fatigue, or lack of time due to family and work obligations.
7. Inhibition of sexual pleasure due to past experiences of physical, sexual, or emotional abuse. (Tiefer, 2000)

The success of Viagra, approved by the FDA in 1998 to treat erectile disorders in men, sent pharmaceutical companies scrambling to find similar products for female sexual arousal disorder. In order to build a market for such a product, companies require a clearly defined medical diagnosis with measurable criteria in order to help design clinical trials (Moynihan, 2003). A study published in 1999 found that 43% of women between the ages of 18 and 59 experienced sexual dysfunction (Laumann et al., 1999). After publication, this statistic was prominently featured everywhere and soon was being misquoted as: "43% of all women over the age of 18 have sexual dysfunctions."

Sexologists have expressed serious reservations about the statistics in the study, based on the "yes" or "no" answers that 1,500 women gave to having experienced seven types of sexual problems (Laumann et al., 1999). If a woman answered yes to just one of the seven sexual problems (such as "Have you ever experienced low sexual desire?"), she was counted as having a sexual dysfunction (Moynihan, 2003). Measurement of sexual problems in men has always focused on easily measurable erections: if a man can't get one, he has an erectile disorder and can be prescribed any number of treatment options. Measuring sexual dysfunctions in women is much less obvious, and researchers and therapists have long struggled with establishing criteria and definitions.

This search for the "female Viagra" led researchers at Procter & Gamble to develop the Intrinsa testosterone patch for women. The Intrinsa patch was to be applied to the abdomen twice a week and would have been the first treatment approved by the FDA for the treatment of female sexual dysfunction. However, concerns over the safety of the drug caused the FDA to delay approval (Roylance, 2004). Many women's health advocates and sexologists were relieved to hear the news of Intrinsa's lack of FDA approval because they felt that a medical intervention would ignore the sociocultural issues that might be contributing to the lower levels of sexual interest. At this time, however, there are several other drugs being studied to treat female desire and arousal problems, some of which could be reviewed by the FDA in 2006.

Today, many sexologists believe that there has been an "overmedicalization" of female sexuality. They believe that female sexuality has become "orgasm" centered and has lost sight of other important factors for women, including relationship and social issues (Lavie-Ajayi, 2005). Reduced sexual arousal and desire is normal in both women and men and not necessarily a sexual dysfunction. Many physicians may jump to prescribing medications for these problems instead of evaluating other aspects of a client's life.

Leonore Tiefer believes that this overmedicalization of female sexuality has also resulted in promotion of genital sexuality, ignoring all other aspects of sexuality (Tiefer, 1996, 2002). Others argue that drug companies are sponsoring research on female sexual dysfunction so that they can create a medical disorder to label a "dysfunction," in order to develop a drug to cure it (Moynihan, 2003).

other medications). As we discussed in Chapter 13, the Food and Drug Administration (FDA) plays a major role in the approval of all new drugs in the United States. Many drug therapies used today for sexual dysfunctions, such as Wellbutrin or Viagra, were originally approved by the FDA to treat other diseases. There is also a brisk business in health supplements to aid in sexual functioning, including aphrodisiacs (see Sex in Real Life, "What Is an Aphrodisiac?" on page 467).

Review Question

Differentiate between primary/secondary and situational/global sexual dysfunctions, and explain how the treatment of sexual dysfunction is approached.

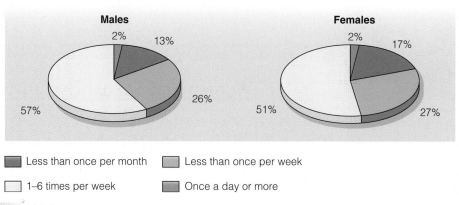

Figure 14.1
How frequently have you had sex in the last 12 months?
Data from The Global Study of Sexual Attitudes and Behaviors, funded by Pfizer, Inc. (© 2002 Pfizer, Inc.)

Since its introduction in 1998, Viagra has been represented by many spokespeople. Professional baseball player Rafael Palmeiro was a controversial spokesperson because many believed that Pfizer (Viagra's manufacturer) was trying to appeal to a younger audience—Palmeiro was only 37 at the time and never admitted to erectile problems.

hypoactive sexual desire (HSD)
Diminished or absent sexual interest or desire.

sexual aversion
Persistent or recurrent extreme aversion to and avoidance of all genital sexual contact.

We will discuss illness and physical causes later in this chapter, but now let us turn to the symptoms and possible causes of various sexual dysfunctions and the current therapies used to treat them.

SEXUAL DESIRE DISORDERS

The *DSM-IV-TR* has two categories of sexual desire disorders, **hypoactive sexual desire (HSD)** and **sexual aversion.** Although there appear to be fewer cases of male hypoactive sexual desire than female, these lower reports may be because men feel less comfortable discussing the problem. Although there are no overall statistics available for prevalence of sexual aversion, researchers believe the condition is relatively rare (Heiman, 2002).

Sexual desire disorders are considered by many therapists to be the most complicated sexual dysfunction to treat. As we discussed previously, treatment first involves a medical workup to identify any physiological causes. A psychological evaluation will explore any past sexual trauma or abuse that may interfere with sexual desire. Intensive psychotherapy can be done to identify and resolve these causes and can also explore the motivations for avoiding intimacy. The client may also be assigned homework exercises to help identify these motivations.

Hypoactive Sexual Desire

When someone has hypoactive sexual desire (HSD), there are diminished or absent feelings of sexual interest in, or desire for, sexual activity (Heiman, 2002). However, a person with a HSD can still function sexually even though he or she often does not feel interested in sex. Studies have found that 33% of women and 16% of men report a lack of sexual interest (Laumann et al., 1999). A large multicultural study on sexual dysfunction found that the prevalence of hypoactive sexual desire increased as women aged—10% of women under the age of 49 reported hypoactive sexual desire, whereas 22% of women between the ages of 50 and 65 and 47% of women between the ages of 66 and 74 reported diminished interest or desire (R. W. Lewis et al., 2004).

HSD may be manifested in several different ways. There may be a lack of sexual fantasies, a reduction of or absence in initiating sexual activity, or a decrease in self-stimulation. Primary HSD, the less common type, is diagnosed when a person has a lifelong pattern of complete disinterest in sex. Secondary HSD, which is more common, refers to a problem in which desire was normal for a certain period of time but then diminished.

Human Sexuality in a Diverse World

Treating Sexual Dysfunction in Other Cultures

Sex therapy in the United States has been criticized for its adherence to Western sexual attitudes and values, with an almost total ignorance of cultural differences in sexual dysfunction and therapy. Our view of sex tends to emphasize that activity is pleasurable (or at least natural), both partners are equally involved, couples need and want to be educated about sex, and communication is important to have good sexual relationships (Lavee, 1991; So & Cheung, 2005). It is important to recognize, however, that these ideas might not be shared outside the United States or within different ethnic groups—therefore Masters and Johnson's classic therapy model might less acceptable to these groups.

Sexual goals are different among cultural groups with an egalitarian ideology than among those without (Lau et al., 2005). An egalitarian ideology views mutual sexual pleasure and communication as important, whereas nonegalitarian ideologies view heterosexual intercourse as the goal and men's sexual pleasure as more important than women's (Reiss, 1986). Double standards of sexual pleasure are common, for example, in many Portuguese, Mexican, Puerto Rican, and Latino groups. Some Asian groups also often have strong cultural prohibitions about discussing sexuality. So U.S. values such as open communication, mutual satisfaction, and accommodation to a partner's sexuality may not be appropriate in working with people from these cultures.

In cultures where low female sexual desire is not viewed as a problem, hypoactive sexual desire wouldn't be viewed as a sexual dysfunction; it would be an acceptable part of female sexuality. In some Muslim groups, for example, the only problems that exist are those that interfere with men's sexual activity (Lavee, 1991).

Approaches to sexual dysfunction also differ outside the United States. Some cultures believe in supernatural causes of sexual dysfunction (such as the man being cursed by a powerful woman or being given the evil eye; So & Cheung, 2005). Malay and Chinese men who experience ED tend to blame their wives for the problem, whereas Indian men attribute their problem to fate (Low et al., 2002). However, Asian culture has also produced the Tantric ceremonial sexual ritual, which might be viewed as therapy for sexual dysfunction.

Tantric sex involves five exercises (Voigt, 1991). First, a couple begins by developing a private ritual to prepare them to share sexual expression: the lighting of candles; using perfume, lotions, music, a special bed or room; certain lighting patterns; massage; reciting poetry together; or meditating. Then they synchronize their breathing by lying together and "getting in touch" with each other. Direct eye contact is sustained throughout the ritual. (Couples often say that they feel uncomfortable using eye contact, but with practice it becomes very powerful.)

Next, "*motionless* intercourse" begins, in which the couple remains *motionless* at the peak of the sensual experience. For many couples, this may be during the time of initial penetration. Initially, this motionlessness may last only a few minutes, building up to increasingly longer periods. The final aspect of the Tantric ritual is to expand the sexual exchange without orgasm, resulting in an intensification of the sexual–spiritual energy. (This is similar to Masters and Johnson's technique of delaying orgasm to enjoy the physical sensations of touching and caressing.)

Psychological causes for HSD may include a lack of attraction to one's partner, fear of intimacy and/or pregnancy, marital or relationship conflicts, religious concerns, depression, and other psychological disorders. HSD can also result from negative messages about female sexuality while growing up, treating sex as a chore, a concern over loss of control, or a negative body image (Heiman & LoPiccolo, 1992). Anorexia, sexual coercion, and abuse have all been found to be associated with HSD (J. F. Morgan et al., 1999). In one study of survivors of sexual assault, more than half had long-lasting problems with sexual desire (Becker et al., 1986).

HSD in both men and women may also be due to biological factors such as hormonal problems, medication side effects, and illness. Chronic use of alcohol, marijuana, and/or cocaine have also been implicated in HSD (Abel, 1985).

Treating Hypoactive Sexual Desire

Treatment of hypoactive sexual desire disorder depends on many factors, including the individual and his or her relationship. Sex and marital therapy have both been found to be effective, although they may not be as effective in couples experiencing relationship difficulties on top of the sexual dysfunction. Cognitive-behavioral therapy, a form of psychotherapy that emphasizes the importance of how a person thinks and the effect these thoughts have on a person's feelings and behaviors, has offered promising results. These types of therapy are brief (the average number of sessions a client receives is 16), highly instructional, and structured.

Pharmacological (drug) treatment may also be used. Although there are no drugs *proven* to increase sexual desire in men or women, there is evidence that testosterone may be helpful in those who have low testosterone levels (Heiman, 2002). Some studies have found that low testosterone levels in women contribute to decreased desire, arousal, and/or orgasm (Talakoub et al., 2002). Preliminary research has found that women who undergo testosterone replacement therapy have less sexual distress and an increase in sexual functioning. However, possible side effects include unwanted facial hair, weight gain, acne, and a loss of head hair (Munarriz et al., 2002; Shifren et al., 2000). Other studies have found that testosterone levels in women have little to do with overall sexual desire and functioning (S. R. Davis et al., 2005). Because testosterone is largely responsible for male sexual desire, low male sexual desire has historically been treated with testosterone injections. However, the majority of men who experience low sexual desire have normal levels of testosterone (Wespes & Schulman, 2002).

Sometimes it is not one partner's level of desire that is the problem but the **discrepancy in desire** between the partners. Many couples experience differences in their levels of desire—one partner may desire sex more often than the other. One partner may desire sex only once a month, whereas the other may desire sex once a day. Often, the partner with a lower level of desire will show up at a therapist's office and not the partner with higher desire (R. C. Rosen & Leiblum, 1987). If the partner with the lower level of desire was paired with someone with an equal level of sexual desire, there would be no problem. People experiencing low levels of sexual desire may turn to **aphrodisiacs** for help (see the accompanying Sex in Real Life, "What Is an Aphrodisiac?").

Sexual Aversion

Unlike HSD, in which a person might be able to engage in sexual activity even though he or she has little or no desire to do so, a person with a sexual aversion reacts with strong disgust or fear to a sexual interaction. Men and women with sexual aversion seek to avoid any genital contact, and some women may even avoid gynecological examinations (Kingsberg & Janata, 2003). In primary sexual aversion, a man or woman has a negative response to sexual interactions from his or her earliest memory to the present; and, in a secondary sexual aversion, there was a period of pleasurable and desirable sexual activity before the aversion started.

Overall, sexual aversion affects more women than men, and it is frequently associated with a history of childhood sexual trauma or abuse (Kingsberg & Janata, 2003). This is especially true if the sexual abuse was forced, abusive, guilt-producing, or pressured. A history of anorexia has also been found to be associated with sexual aversion (J. F. Morgan et al., 1999).

Treating Sexual Aversion

Treatment of sexual aversion is difficult, mainly because most men and women would rather not discuss sexuality and are resistant to seeking help. If they do seek help, the most common treatment involves discovering and resolving the underlying conflict. Generally, cognitive-behavioral therapy is most successful at helping to uncover the relationship issues or events from early childhood that contribute to the symptoms of sexual aversion. Treatment often includes goal setting and the completion of homework assignments, both individually and with a partner. It is important that therapy moves at the client's pace and time is taken to work through his or her issues.

discrepancy in desire
Differences in levels of sexual desire in a couple.

aphrodisiac
A substance that increases, or is believed to increase, a person's sexual desire.

Review Question

Identify the sexual desire disorders, and describe the treatment(s).

What Is an Aphrodisiac?

Throughout history, people from primitive—and not so primitive—cultures have searched for the "ultimate" aphrodisiac to enhance sexual interest and performance. Oysters, for example, have been reported to increase sexual desire, although this has never been proven. The idea that oysters are an aphrodisiac may have originated from their resemblance to male testicles—or even to female ovaries. Ancient people believed that food with the shape or qualities of the genitals possessed aphrodisiac qualities; seeds of all kinds were associated with fertility and desire. In various cultures, carrots, cucumbers, chili peppers, rhino horns, and various seafood, as well as eggs and poppy seeds, were thought to increase sexual desire. The market for so-called aphrodisiacs in some countries has added to the decline of some endangered species, such as the rhinoceros, valued for its horn.

There are no proven aphrodisiacs, but it is possible that if a person thinks something will increase his or her sexual desire, it just might do so. Just *believing* something will increase desire may cause it to work. Here are some of the most popular substances that have been thought to increase sexual desire, and a few that we know act in reverse, *decreasing* sexual desire (also known as anaphrodisiacs). Note that several of these substances are both! Overall, to increase

In Bangkok, Thailand, a vendor is pushing cobra blood to improve sexual drive. Customers choose their own snake, and then the snake is split open with a razor blade. An incision is made in the major artery of the snake, and all the blood is drained into a wine glass. The blood is then mixed with warm whiskey and a dash of honey. Users believe it helps their sex drive.

sexual desire, rely on regular exercise, a healthy diet, candlelight, the use of scents, romantic music, and whatever else enhances your personal sexual arousal.

Alcohol: Although some people believe that alcohol increases their sexual desire, in actuality in low doses it merely decreases anxiety and inhibitions. In large amounts, alcohol can impair sexual functioning.

Amyl nitrate: Amyl nitrate (also called "snappers" or "poppers") is thought to increase orgasmic sensations. It is inhaled from capsules that are "popped" open for quick use. Amyl nitrate causes a rapid dilation of arteries that supply the heart and other organs with blood, which may cause warmth in the genitals. Amyl nitrate may dilate arteries in the brain, causing euphoria or giddiness, and relax the sphincter muscle to ease penetration during anal sex. Side effects include severe dizziness, migraine headaches, and fainting. (Amyl nitrate is used by cardiac patients to reduce heart pain.)

Cocaine: Thought to increase frequency of sexual behavior, sexual desire, and orgasmic sensations. In actuality, cocaine may reduce inhibitions, possibly leading to risky sexual behaviors. Long-term use can result in depression, addiction, and increased anxiety.

Ginseng: An herb that has been thought to increase sexual desire. It has not been found to have any specific effects on sexuality.

Marijuana: Reduces inhibitions and may improve mood. No proven effect on sexual desire.

Spanish fly: Consists of ground-up beetle wings (cantharides) from Europe and causes inflammation of the urinary tract and dilation of the blood vessels. Although some people find the burning sensation arousing, Spanish fly may cause death from its toxic side effects.

Yohimbine: From the African Yohimbe tree. Injections have been found to increase sexual arousal and performance in lab animals. It has been prescribed by physicians to increase the frequency of physiological arousal.

Anaphrodisiacs: Alcohol, cocaine, and tobacco. Although some people use street drugs, such as Ecstasy, to increase sexual desire, the majority of these drugs can result in decreased sexual functioning.

SEXUAL AROUSAL DISORDERS

The *DSM-IV-TR* has two categories of sexual arousal disorders, female **sexual arousal disorder** and male **erectile disorder.** Sexual arousal disorders occur even when the client reports adequate focus, intensity, and duration of sexual stimulation. The disorder may be primary, or more commonly, secondary in that it only occurs with a certain partner or specific sexual behavior.

sexual arousal disorder
Diminished or absent lubrication response of sexual excitation.

erectile disorder
Diminished or absent ability to attain or maintain, until completion of the sexual activity, an adequate erection.

SEX in Real Life

Sex Therapy

ex therapy, which was originally developed by Masters and Johnson (1970), is often recommended for the treatment of sexual dysfunctions. Their original program consisted of a 2-week intensive treatment program that required a couple to go to Masters and Johnson's clinic in St. Louis. Two therapists, a man and woman, would meet with individual couples daily and help establish better communication patterns, provide information about sex, and teach specific sexual techniques.

Because many of the therapies for sexual dysfunction required the presence of a willing and cooperative partner, Masters and Johnson originally provided a sexual surrogate for a person seeking therapy without a sexual partner. The surrogate was a trained professional who would work with the patient and teach him or her sexual skills to use with future sexual partners. This practice was discontinued because of questions raised about ethics, values, psychological effects, and use in normal sexual relations. Critics of this practice claimed that surrogates were merely acting as prostitutes and that this was not beneficial for patients. Further, it has been found to be more beneficial to treat other issues

in single men with sexual dysfunctions, such as their assertiveness, knowledge, and attitudes about sex.

Today, sex therapists prescribe a number of exercises to clients. Homework and exercises are used to increase awareness and to improve communication. Sexual intercourse as a part of therapy is usually reserved for the end of treatment in order to remove any demands for sexual performance. If one partner refuses to cooperate in therapy, the other partner can still be treated with education, self-exploration, body awareness, fantasy, and masturbation training. Also today, numerous books on sexual dysfunction are available, allowing partners to improve sexual functioning at home.

That Masters and Johnson's work is still the model for treatment of sexual dysfunction in the United States today is rather surprising, given that treatments for other psychological disorders have changed dramatically over the years. Changes have occurred in the duration of sex therapy (weekly instead of daily) and the number of therapists (one therapist instead of a male–female team). In addition, partners need not travel to the Masters and Johnson clinic to receive treatment.

Female Sexual Arousal Disorder

Female sexual arousal disorder (FSAD) is an inability to either obtain or maintain an adequate lubrication response of sexual excitement. Prevalence rates for FSAD increase with age and show that lubrication insufficiency is common after the age of 50 (R. W. Lewis et al., 2004). Some women who experience FSAD also experience problems related to desire or orgasmic disorders (Heiman, 2002). Physiological factors in FSAD include decreased blood flow and lubrication in the vulva; psychological factors include fear, guilt, anxiety, and depression. Women who experience female sexual arousal disorder have been found to have a lower sensitivity to touch compared to women without FSAD (Frohlich & Meston, 2005). Further research is needed to determine how this sensitivity might play a role in the development or maintenance of FSAD.

persistent sexual arousal syndrome
An excessive and unremitting level of sexual arousal.

A new category of female sexual arousal has been proposed, in which a woman experiences persistent sexual arousal (referred to as **persistent sexual arousal syndrome**). The opposite of FSAD, a woman's complaint is usually an excessive and unremitting arousal (Leiblum & Nathan, 2002). More research is needed to shed more light on this disorder.

Treating Female Sexual Arousal Disorder

There have been few studies evaluating the efficacy of treatments for FSAD (Heiman, 2002). Since the release of Viagra for men in 1998, research into drug treatments for FSAD has focused on finding a similar drug for women. In 2004, the FDA voted not to approve a new product for women called Intrinsa (see Sex in Real Life, "Women and Sexual Dysfunction," on page 462). Clinical trials of Viagra to treat FSAD have shown that although it can increase vasocongestion and lubrication, it provides little overall benefit in the treatment of female sexual arousal disorder (Basson et al., 2002).

A few pilot studies have been done on a variety of other **vasoactive agents** to help reduce FSAD, including VasoMax, or phentolamine. Oral phentolamine has been found to increase female sexual arousal, resulting in higher levels of lubrication and pleasurable effects in the vagina (Rubio-Aurioles et al., 2002). Herbal products, including Zestra, a botanical massage oil formulated to increase female arousal and pleasure, and Avlimil, a nonprescription daily supplement, have been successful at increasing female sexual arousal (Ferguson et al., 2003).

Other topical creams are now on the market, such as Viacreme, which is an amino-acid based cream that contains menthol. When applied to the clitoris, Viacreme can increase blood flow by dilating clitoral blood vessels. Although herbal products do not require FDA approval, more research is needed to assess their possible effects and complications (Islam et al., 2001). Studies are under way to test other agents to increase female sexual arousal, including the aphrodisiac **yohimbine** (yo-HIM-bean; Meston & Worcel, 2002).

In 2000, the EROS clitoral therapy device was approved by the FDA for the treatment of FSAD. The device has a small plastic cup that is placed over the clitoris before sex. The cup is attached to a vacuum pump that draws blood into the clitoris, leading to clitoral engorgement. This engorgement increases vaginal lubrication, sexual arousal, and desire. There have not yet been large-scale studies evaluating the benefits of using the EROS-CTD.

Because women are often more focused on the emotional aspects, rather than the genital aspects, of lovemaking, treating sexual arousal disorder with pharmaceuticals is not always a complete success. The most effective treatment may be a combination of drugs and psychological therapy (Brotto, 2004; Heiman, 2002; Millner, 2005). Couples therapy has also been found to be effective.

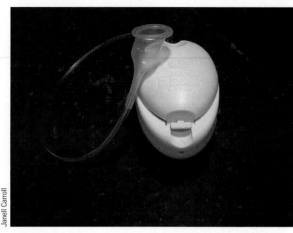

The EROS-CTD is a handheld device that increases blood flow to the clitoris. The plastic cup is placed directly over the clitoris.

vasoactive agent
Medication that causes dilation of the blood vessels.

yohimbine
Produced from the bark of the African yohimbe tree; often used as an aphrodisiac.

Review Question

Identify female sexual arousal disorder, and describe the possible treatment(s).

sex byte

A new generation of sex toys hit the market in 2005, aimed at increasing sexual desire and arousal in couples who are away from each other. The "Sinulator" allows couples to control each other's sex toys via the Internet. Partners can vary the speed or movement of the toys from their control devices, even if they live in different states.

SEX Talk

Question: Is erectile disorder hereditary?

No, erectile disorder itself is not hereditary. However, certain diseases, such as diabetes, may be inherited and can lead to an erectile disorder or other sexual dysfunctions. It is important to catch these diseases early so that medical intervention can decrease any possible sexual side effects.

Male Erectile Disorder

Erectile disorder (ED) is defined as the persistent inability to obtain or maintain an erection sufficient for satisfactory sexual performance (Fink et al., 2002). It is estimated that close to 30 million men in the United States experience ED (Lue, 2000). The prevalence of ED increases with age—12% of men younger than 59 experience ED, whereas 22% of men aged 60 to 69, and 30% of men over the age of 69 experience ED (Bacon et al., 2003).

We know that normal erectile function involves neurological, endocrine, vascular, and muscular factors. Psychological factors including fear of failure and performance anxiety may also affect erectile functioning. Anxiety has been found to have a cyclical effect on erectile functioning: if a man experiences a problem getting an erection one night, the next time he tries to have intercourse he remembers the failure and becomes anxious. This anxiety, in turn, interferes with his ability to have an erection.

Problems in any of these areas can lead to ED, although the majority of cases are caused by a combination of factors (Fink et al., 2002). Unfortunately, when a physician identifies a physical problem (such as hypertension), he or she might not continue to explore the psychological factors. Or if a psychological problem is found first (such as a recent divorce), the physician might not perform a medical evaluation. Overall, EDs in younger men (20 to 35 years old) are more likely to be psychologically based, whereas EDs in older men (60 and older) are more likely to be due to physical factors (Lue, 2000).

To diagnose the causes of erectile disorder, sex therapists can use tests such as the **nocturnal penile tumescence (NPT) test.** Men normally experience two or three erections a night during stages of rapid eye movement (REM) sleep. If these erections do not occur, it is a good indication that there is a physiological problem; if they do occur, erectile problems are more likely to have psychological causes. The NPT requires a man to spend at least three nights in a sleep laboratory hooked up to several machines, but newer devices allow him to monitor his sleep erections in the privacy of his own home. RigiScan, a portable diagnostic monitor, measures both rigidity and tumescence at the base and tip of the penis. Stamp tests and other at-home devices are also used. A stamp test uses perforated bands resembling postage stamps, which are placed on the base of the penis prior to retiring for the night. In the morning, if the perforations have ripped, this indicates that the man had normal physiological functioning while sleeping.

Treating Male Erectile Disorder

Of all the sexual dysfunctions, there are more treatment options for male erectile disorder than for any other sexual dysfunction. A tremendous amount of research has been dedicated to finding causes and treatment options for ED. Depending on the cause, treatment for ED includes psychological treatment, pharmacological treatment (drugs), hormonal and intracavernous injections, vascular surgery, vacuum constriction devices, and prosthesis implantation (Dinsmore, 2005; Fink et al., 2002). The success rate for treating male erectile disorder (ED) ranges from 50% to 80% (Lue, 2000). Research has found that 3 years after treatment, men show significant improvement in the ability to maintain erections during stimulation and in duration of foreplay (DeAmicis et al., 1985).

Psychological Treatment   The primary psychological treatments for ED include **systematic desensitization** and sex therapy that includes education, **sensate focus,** and communication training (Heiman, 2002). These treatments can help reduce feelings of anxiety and can evaluate issues that are interfering with erectile response. Relationship therapy can also help explore issues in a relationship that might contribute to erectile dysfunction, such as unresolved anger, bitterness, or guilt.

Pharmacological Treatment   In 1998 the FDA approved the use of Viagra (sildenafil citrate), the first oral medication for ED (Fink et al., 2002). Viagra can be used in a variety of ED cases—those that are **psychogenic** (sike-oh-JEN-nick), illness-related, or those that have physical causes (Heiman, 2002). Two newer drugs, Cialis and Levitra, which are similar to Viagra, were recently approved by the FDA.

All of these drugs produce muscle relaxation in the penis, dilation of the arteries supplying the penis, and an inflow of blood—which can lead to penile erection. They do not increase a man's sexual desire and will not produce an erection without adequate sexual stimulation. Typically, a man must take Viagra about 1 hour before he desires an erection, and Cialis and Levitra often work within 15 to 30 minutes. Erections can last up to 4 hours, although Cialis can aid in erections for up to 36 hours.

There are several side effects with these medications, including headaches, a flushing in the cheeks and neck, nasal congestion, indigestion, and vision changes. In 2005, the FDA called for revised labeling of all erectile drugs, outlining possible vision side effects (Kaufman, 2005). Users of erectile drugs have an increased risk of vision problems, including changes in color vision and possible total vision loss. These vision problems are due to a blockage of blood flow to the optic nerve. Cialis users also may experience an increase in back pain, which will go away within 48 hours of using the drug. Critics of pharmacological treatment for ED point out that drug use focuses solely on an erection and fails to take into account the multidimensional nature of male sexuality (B. W. McCarthy & Fucito, 2005).

---

nocturnal penile tumescence (NPT) test
A study done to evaluate erections during sleep that helps clarify the causes of erectile dysfunction.

sexbyte

The shape of a bicycle seat can affect penile blood flow—a narrow saddle seat has been found to result in significant reduction in penile blood flow, which, over time, may lead to an erectile disorder (Jeong et al., 2002).

SneakPeek

"In the process of becoming aroused, all of a sudden it would be over. And I didn't understand that at all."—*Erectile Dysfunction: Clark*

Sexuality Now

systematic desensitization
A treatment method for sexual dysfunction that involves neutralizing the anxiety-producing aspects of sexual situations and behavior by a process of gradual exposure.

sensate focus
A series of touching experiences that are assigned to couples in sex therapy to teach nonverbal communication and reduce anxiety.

psychogenic
Relating to psychological causes.

Yohimbine, a substance that is produced in the bark of African yohimbe trees, has been found to improve erections and is most successful in cases with nonphysical causes (Ernst & Pittler, 1998). It works by stimulating the parasympathetic nervous system, which is linked to erectile functioning. Side effects include dizziness, nervousness, irritability, and an increased heart rate and blood pressure.

Hormonal Treatments   Hormonal treatment may help improve erections in men who have hormonal irregularities (such as too much prolactin or too little gonadal hormones; Lue, 2000). Excessive prolactin can interfere with adequate secretion of testosterone and can cause erectile dysfunction. A man with low testosterone levels can be prescribed testosterone therapy either through injections, patches, gels, or creams. These therapies will not improve erectile functioning in a man with normal hormone levels.

A testosterone patch is applied directly to the scrotum, whereas gels and creams can be applied to other parts of the body such as the arms or stomach. AndroGel, a clear, colorless, odorless gel, was approved by the FDA in 2000 for the treatment of low testosterone (Morley & Perry, 2000). It is applied daily and is absorbed into the skin. Some men prefer this type of application over a painful injection or patch. Side effects are rare but include headaches, acne, depression, gynecomastia, and hypertension. None of these testosterone preparations should be used by men with prostate cancer because they can exacerbate this condition.

Intracavernous Injections   **Intracavernous** (in-truh-CAV-er-nuss) **injections** are a relatively new development in the treatment of ED (Lue, 2000). Men and their partners are taught to self-inject these preparations directly into the corpora cavernosa (see Chapter 5) while the penis is gently stretched out. The injections cause the blood vessels to relax and as a result, blood flow to the penis is increased. The majority of patients report very minor pain from these injections. However, each time a man desires an erection, he must use this injection. The higher the dosage of medication, the longer the erection will last.

Priapism, a possible side effect of treatment, occurs in 4% to 8% of men who use these injections. Other side effects are more related to the injection than to the drug itself and may include pain, bleeding, and/or bruising (Israilov et al., 2002). Another treatment method that works to increase blood flow to the penis involves the insertion of prostaglandin pellets directly into the opening of the penis. The prostaglandin is then absorbed by the penis and works similar to intracavernous injections. Typically an erection will occur within 20 minutes and will last for an hour and a half.

Vacuum Constriction Devices   **Vacuum constriction devices,** which use suction to induce erections, have become more popular in the last several years, in part because they are less invasive and safer than injections. One such device, the ErecAid System, involves putting the flaccid penis into a vacuum cylinder and pumping it to draw blood into the corpora cavernosa (similar to the one Austin Powers was caught with in *International Man of Mystery*). To keep the blood in the penis, a constriction ring is rolled onto the base of the penis after it is removed from the vacuum device. This ring is left on the penis until the erection is no longer desired. When it is removed, the man will lose his erection. Side effects include possible bruising and, in rare cases, testicular entrapment in the vacuum chamber (Lue, 2000). Overall, these devices can be expensive, bulky and noisy, and they reduce spontaneity, which some couples find unappealing.

Surgical Treatments   Surgical intervention has increased as a treatment for erectile dysfunction. In some cases, physicians perform **revascularization** to improve erectile functioning; in other cases, **prosthesis** (pross-THEE-sis) **implantation** may be recommended. Acrylic implants for erectile dysfunction were first used in 1952, but they were replaced by silicone rubber in the 1960s and then by a variety of synthetic materials in the 1970s. Today there are two main types of implants: **semirigid rods,** which provide a permanent state of erection but can be bent up and down; and inflatable devices that become firm when the man pumps them up (J. McCarthy & McMillan, 1990). Sexual intercourse may safely be engaged in 4 to 8 weeks after

intracavernous injection
A treatment method for erectile dysfunction in which vasodilating drugs are injected into the penis for the purpose of creating an erection.

priapism
A condition in which erections are long lasting and often painful.

vacuum constriction device
Treatment device for erectile dysfunction used to pull blood into the penis.

revascularization
A procedure used in the treatment of vascular erectile dysfunction in which the vascular system is rerouted to ensure better blood flow to the penis.

prosthesis implantation
A treatment method for erectile dysfunction in which a prosthesis is surgically implanted into the penis.

semirigid rod
Flexible rod that is implanted into the penis during prosthetic surgery.

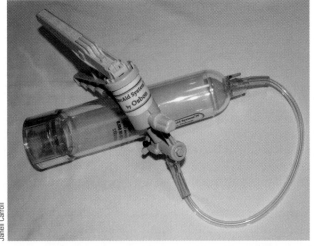

Janell Carroll

Vacuum constriction devices, such as the ErecAid, are often used in the treatment of ED. A man places his penis in the cylinder and vacuum suction increases blood flow to the penis.

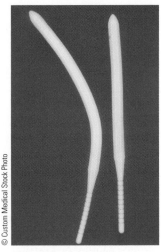

© Custom Medical Stock Photo

These semirigid prostheses are surgically implanted in the penis and can enable a man with erectile dysfunction to penetrate during sexual activity.

Review Question

Identify male erectile disorder, and describe the possible treatments.

surgery. After prosthesis implantation, a man is still able to orgasm, ejaculate, and impregnate (J. McCarthy & McMillan, 1990).

Sexual satisfaction after a prosthesis implantation has been found to be related to several factors, such as a man's relationship with his partner and feelings about his own masculinity (Kempeneers et al., 2004). Between 10% and 20% of patients remain dissatisfied, dysfunctional, or sexually inactive even after prosthetic surgery (J. McCarthy & McMillan, 1990). In some cases, if a man has psychological factors that contribute to his erectile difficulties, these issues are likely to resurface once a prosthesis is implanted.

SEX Talk

Question: A couple of guys I know have some Viagra, and they have been trying to get me to take it. Is it safe to use this drug if you don't have ED?

Although Viagra was first marketed to older men, today it is being marketed to younger men. It is estimated that the fastest growing group of users are between the ages of 18 and 45 (Delate et al., 2004). Even so, Viagra's manufacturer, Pfizer, does not suggest the use of this drug just for kicks. All Viagra users should undergo a clinical evaluation with a physician to evaluate their erectile condition and past medical history. Truth be told, however, it's fairly easy to get Viagra without a prescription these days, and more and more college students are reporting they have tried Viagra as a "recreational" drug. In 1999, Ben Affleck spoke up about his recreational use of Viagra and said that he was told it would make you feel "like you were 14 and jerking off six times a day" (Keller, 1999). Even so, Affleck told *Playboy Magazine* that he suffered serious side effects after using Viagra including an increased heart rate, dizziness, and uncontrollable sweating.

sex byte

The newest ED drug, Cialis, is referred to in the French media as "le weekend," because the drug can be taken on a Friday night and last until early Sunday (Japsen, 2003).

ORGASM DISORDERS

Every individual reaches orgasm differently and has different wants and needs to build sexual excitement. Some people need very little stimulation, others need a great deal of stimulation, and some never reach orgasm. The *DSM-IV-TR* has three categories of

orgasmic disorders: female orgasmic disorder, male orgasmic disorder, and **premature ejaculation.** Recently there has been some talk about a new subcategory of orgasmic disorders that takes into consideration the effects of medications on orgasm. We will discuss this more shortly.

Female Orgasmic Disorder

Historically, this female sexual dysfunction was referred to as "frigidity," which had negative implications about the woman. *DSM-IV-TR* defines female orgasmic disorder as a delay or absence of orgasm following a normal phase of sexual excitement. This is a common complaint among women, and studies have found that 24% of women have female orgasmic disorder (Laumann et al., 1994). Remember though, that the DSM definition does not indicate that orgasm must occur during sexual intercourse. In fact, the majority of women are unable to orgasm during sexual intercourse. If a woman is unable to orgasm during all sexual activities after a normal phase of sexual excitement, she may be experiencing orgasmic disorder. Some women who take certain psychotropic drugs, including many types of antidepressants, experience delayed or absent orgasms (Meston & Frohlich, 2000).

Primary orgasmic disorder describes a condition in which a woman has never had an orgasm. Secondary orgasmic disorder refers to a condition in which a woman was able to have orgasms previously but later has trouble reaching orgasm. Situational orgasmic disorder refers to a condition in which a woman can have orgasms only with one type of stimulation.

Women with orgasmic disorders, compared with orgasmic women, have more negative attitudes about masturbation, believe more myths about sexuality, and possess greater degrees of sex guilt (M. P. Kelly et al., 1990). They also have more difficulties in asking their partners for direct clitoral stimulation, discussing how slow or fast they want to go, or how hard or soft stimulation should be. Some women worry about what their partners might think if they made sexual suggestions or feel uncomfortable receiving stimulation (such as cunnilingus or manual stimulation) without stimulating their partners at the same time. Distracting thoughts, such as "his hand must be falling asleep" or "he can't be enjoying this" can increase existing anxiety and interfere with orgasm (Birnbaum et al., 2001; M. P. Kelly et al., 1990).

If the woman displays no physical problems, most cases of orgasmic difficulties are presumed to be psychogenic (Andersen, 1981). Several psychological issues have been found to interfere with orgasmic response, including a lack of sex education and fear or anxiety related to sexuality (Kelly et al., 1990).

Physical factors can also cause female orgasmic disorder. Severe chronic illness and disorders such as diabetes, neurological problems, hormonal deficiencies, and alcoholism can all interfere with orgasmic response. Certain prescription drugs can also impair this response.

Treating Female Orgasmic Disorder

Today, the majority of treatment programs for orgasmic disorder involve a combination of different treatment approaches, such as homework assignments, sex education, communication skills training, cognitive restructuring, desensitization, and other techniques (M. P. Kelly et al., 1990). The most effective treatment for female orgasmic disorder was developed by LoPiccolo & Lobitz (1972) and involves teaching a woman to masturbate to orgasm.

On a psychological level, masturbation also helps increase the pleasurable anticipation of sex. Education, self-exploration, communication training, and body awareness are also included in masturbation training for orgasmic problems. Masturbation exercises begin with a woman examining her body and vulva with mirrors. Then she is instructed to find which areas of her body feel the most pleasurable when touched and to stroke them. If this does not result in orgasm, a vibrator is used. As a woman progresses through these stages, she may involve her sexual partner so that the partner is able to learn which areas are more sensitive than others.

Although masturbation training is the most effective treatment for female orgasmic disorder, some therapists do not incorporate it into their treatment for a variety of reasons (including patient or therapist discomfort). Interestingly, improving orgasmic responsivity does not always increase sexual satisfaction. Women often prefer and engage in sexual intercourse over masturbation because it provides more intimacy and closeness, even though masturbation may be a better means of reaching orgasm (Jayne, 1981).

Two additional treatments involve systematic desensitization and **bibliotherapy.** Both of these have been found to be helpful in cases in which there is a great deal of sexual anxiety. In systematic desensitization, events that cause anxiety are recalled into imagination, and then a relaxation technique is used to dissipate the anxiety. With enough repetition and practice, eventually the anxiety-producing events lose the ability to create anxiety. Both masturbation training and systematic desensitization have been found to be effective; however, masturbation training has higher effectiveness rates (Heiman & Meston, 1997).

Bibliotherapy has also been found to be helpful for not only orgasmic dysfunctions, but other dysfunctions as well. It can help a person regain some control and understand the problems she is experiencing. Although the results may be short-lived, bibliotherapy has been found to improve sexual functioning (van Lankveld et al., 2001).

SEX Talk

Question: *I seem to have problems achieving orgasm with my partner, yet I am able to with the help of a vibrator. Are there different levels of orgasms? Sometimes it is so deep and complete and emotional; other times it is very satisfying but not to the tips of my toes! Is this normal? I would love to be able to achieve the same satisfaction with my partner as I can by myself or with a vibrator.*

There are different levels of sexual satisfaction that result from orgasms. Orgasms differ based on stress, emotions, thoughts, physical health, menstrual cycles, sexual position, and method of stimulation. However, Masters and Johnson did find that masturbation usually evoked more powerful orgasms than intercourse. In order to experience these orgasms with your partner, you might try masturbating together or using a vibrator with your partner.

Male Orgasmic Disorder

Male orgasmic disorder is relatively rare, with only 8% of men reporting problems reaching orgasm (Laumann et al., 1994). It is defined as a delay or absence of orgasm following a normal phase of sexual excitement. As we discussed previously, many men who take psychotropic medications experience problems with orgasm.

Treating Male Orgasmic Disorder

Male orgasmic disorder is uncommon and is rarely treated by sex therapists (Heiman, 2002). Treatment options include psychotherapy and if necessary, changing medications. As we discussed earlier, psychotropic medications can cause a delayed or absent orgasm. If this is the case, changing medications can often improve orgasmic functioning.

Premature Ejaculation

Defining premature ejaculation (PE) has always been difficult for professionals (Renshaw, 2005). Does it depend on how many penile thrusts take place before orgasm, how many minutes elapse between actual penetration and orgasm, or whether a man reaches orgasm prior to his partner? All of these definitions are problematic because they involve individual differences in sexual functioning and also make the assumption that females always reach orgasm during sexual intercourse.

Although the time it takes to ejaculate may vary based on a man's age, sexual experience, health, and stress level, premature ejaculation usually refers to a man reaching orgasm just prior to, or directly following, penetration (Grenier & Byers, 2001). If the couple believes there is a problem, then it is often treated like one. However, in some cultures premature ejaculation may not be viewed as a problem because only male pleasure is considered important in sexual encounters.

Research has found that worldwide, premature ejaculation is the most prevalent sexual dysfunction (Jannini & Lenzi, 2005). In the United States, estimates are that close to 30% of men report experiencing PE in the last year (Laumann et al., 1994). Although we don't know exactly what causes premature ejaculation, some evolutionary theorists claim that PE may actually provide a biological advantage in that a male will be able to mate quickly, decreasing his chances of being killed or pushed away. Masters and Johnson (1970) originally proposed that PE develops when a man's early sexual experiences are rushed because of the fear of being caught or discovered. These fears, they believed, could condition a man to ejaculate rapidly. Others have pointed out that PE occurs in men who are unable to accurately judge their own levels of sexual arousal, which would enable them to use self-control and avoid rapid ejaculation (H. S. Kaplan, 1989). Like other erectile problems, premature ejaculation has been found to be associated with depression, anxiety, drug and alcohol abuse, and personality disorders.

Treating Premature Ejaculation

Premature ejaculation is often treated in a variety of ways. Today, popular methods include behavioral cognitive therapy and pharmaceutical treatments (Wylie & Ralph, 2005). Two behavioral techniques are also popular, including the **squeeze technique** and the **stop–start technique.** Both involve stimulating the penis to the point just prior to ejaculation. Usually a man practices these techniques alone during masturbation and then with a partner (Heiman, 2002).

With the squeeze technique, sexual intercourse or masturbation is engaged in just short of orgasm and then stimulation is stopped. The man or his partner puts a thumb on the frenulum and the first and second fingers on the dorsal side of the penis (see Figure 14.2). Pressure is applied for 3 to 4 seconds, until the urge to ejaculate subsides. With the stop–start technique, stimulation is simply stopped until the ejaculatory urge subsides. Stimulation is then repeated up until that point, and this process is repeated over and over. These techniques must be used for 6 to 12 months or whenever necessary to control premature ejaculation. For a man to gain some control over his erection often takes 2 to 10 weeks, and within several months, he can have excellent control.

It is believed that these techniques may help a man get in touch with his arousal levels and sensations. Suggested effectiveness rates have been as high as 98%, although

squeeze technique
A technique in which the ejaculatory reflex is reconditioned using a firm grasp on the penis.

stop–start technique
A technique in which the ejaculatory reflex is reconditioned using intermittent pressure on the glans of the penis.

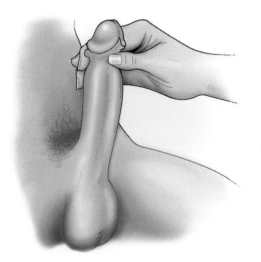
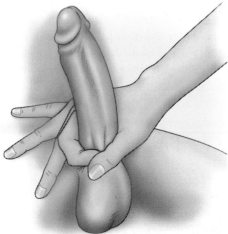

Figure 14.2
The squeeze technique is often recommended in the treatment of premature ejaculation. Pressure is applied either at the top or to base of the penis for several seconds until the urge to ejaculate subsides.

it is unclear how this effectiveness is being measured (Masters & Johnson, 1970). In addition, many studies fail to mention whether or not the treatment permanently solves the problem or if periodic repetition of the techniques is necessary. Directly following treatment for premature ejaculation, men showed significant gains in length of foreplay, satisfaction with sexual relationships, and increased mate acceptance (DeAmicis et al., 1985). However, these improvements were not maintained 3 years later, and the frequency and desire for sexual contact, duration of sexual intercourse, and marital satisfaction all decreased.

As discussed, physicians have been exploring pharmaceutical treatments for PE (Wylie & Ralph, 2005; Renshaw, 2005). Earlier we discussed how certain medications can cause a delay or absence of orgasm. Many of these drugs are being evaluated to see whether they can increase the time needed to ejaculate.

Retarded Ejaculation

retarded ejaculation
Condition in which ejaculation is impossible or occurs only after strenuous efforts.

Retarded (or inhibited) **ejaculation** refers to a situation in which a man may be entirely unable to reach orgasm during certain sexual activities or may only be able to ejaculate after prolonged stimulation (for 30 to 45 minutes; it is also sometimes referred to as absent ejaculation). Therapists distinguish between primary and secondary retarded ejaculation in diagnosing and treating this sexual dysfunction. Primary retarded ejaculation, which is rare, occurs when a man has never been able to ejaculate during any type of sexual activities. A secondary problem occurs when a man could ejaculate without delay at one time but develops a problem later on.

Retarded ejaculation may be due to both physical and psychological factors. It may also be situational (e.g., he may be able to have an orgasm during masturbation but not during oral sex). Psychological factors include a strict religious upbringing, unique or atypical masturbation patterns, fear of pregnancy, or ambivalence over sexual orientation. Retarded ejaculation may also be caused by diseases, injuries, or medications. Recent research suggests that men with retarded ejaculation get erections quickly, but arousal is slow to catch up (R. Rosen, 1994).

Treating Retarded Ejaculation

Although psychological factors have been primarily implicated in retarded ejaculation, we still do not really understand what causes this problem, which makes treatment difficult. In many cases, psychotherapy is used to help work through some of these issues as a part of treatment. One 43-year-old man shared with me his lifelong problem in reaching orgasm with his partner. He had been sexually abused as a child for many years by an uncle who was a few years older than he. During this abuse, the uncle tried to make him reach orgasm. However, the boy learned to withhold the orgasmic response, much to the dismay of the uncle. Later on in life, this pattern continued even though he was not consciously trying to do so.

To treat retarded ejaculation, the man is instructed to use situations in which he is able to achieve ejaculation to help him during those where he is not. For example, if a man can ejaculate during masturbation while fantasizing about being watched during sexual activity, he is told to use this fantasy while he is with his partner. Gradually, the man is asked to incorporate his partner into the sexual fantasy and to masturbate while with the partner. Finally, he is to allow the partner to masturbate him to orgasm. Retarded ejaculation can be very difficult to treat.

Review Question

Identify the various orgasmic disorders, and describe the treatments.

PAIN DISORDERS

Genital pain disorders can occur at any stage of the sexual response cycle. Although pain disorders are more frequent in women, they also occur in men. *DSM-IV-TR* has two categories of pain disorders, **vaginismus** (vadg-ih-NISS-muss), which occurs in women, and **dyspareunia** (diss-par-ROON-ee-uh), which can affect both men and women.

vaginismus
Involuntary spasms of the muscles around the vagina in response to attempts at penetration.

dyspareunia
Genital pain associated with intercourse.

Vaginismus

The **pubococcygeus** (pub-oh-cock-SIGH-gee-us) **muscle** surrounds the entrance to the vagina and controls the vaginal opening. Vaginismus involves involuntary contractions of this muscle, which can make penetration during sexual intercourse virtually impossible. Forced penetration can be very difficult and may cause a woman severe pain. Vaginismus may be situation-specific, meaning that a woman may be able to allow penetration under certain circumstances but not in others (say, during a pelvic exam but not during sexual intercourse; LoPiccolo & Stock, 1986).

The muscle contractions that occur during vaginismus are in reaction to anticipated vaginal penetration. One woman had been in a relationship with her partner for more than 3 years, but they had never been able to engage in penile–vaginal intercourse because she felt as if her vagina "was closed up" (Author's files). Penetration of her vagina with her partner's fingers was possible and enjoyable, but once penile penetration was attempted, her vagina closed off. She also shared that she had been forced to engage in sex with her stepfather for several years of her early life.

Vaginismus is common in women who have been sexually abused or raped, and it is often present along with other sexual difficulties such as sexual aversion and/or difficulties becoming aroused. Women who experience vaginismus often experience dyspareunia, or painful intercourse, as well (Heiman, 2002).

pubococcygeus muscle
A muscle that surrounds and supports the vagina.

Treating Vaginismus

People who experience any of the pain disorders often believe that they have to live with the problem. As a result, they do not seek help. However, medical evaluations and counseling can help isolate possible causes and solutions. Women who are experiencing vaginismus should consult with a physician and bring their partner as well. A physical examination will check for any physical problems that may be contributing to the pain.

After the diagnosis is confirmed, one of the most effective treatments is the use of **dilators.** After a physician instructs a woman to use these dilators, they can be used at home and inserted by the woman or her partner. The size of the dilators is slowly increased, and they can even be left in place overnight if necessary. These dilators help to open and relax the vaginal muscles. If these procedures are successful, penile or digital penetration can be attempted. In some cases, however, it may be necessary to use a dilator on a regular basis just prior to penetration. It is estimated that between 75% and 100% of women who use this technique are able to experience sexual intercourse by the end of treatment (Heiman, 2002).

It is also helpful for couples to become educated about vaginismus and sexuality to reduce their anxiety or tension. If a history of sexual abuse or rape exists, it is important to work through the trauma prior to beginning work with the dilators, or treatment for vaginismus may be unsuccessful.

dilators
A graduated series of metal rods used in the treatment of vaginismus.

Dyspareunia and Vulvodynia

Dyspareunia may occur prior to, during, or after sexual intercourse and may involve only slight pain, which does not interfere much with sexual activity. However, when it is extreme, it may make sexual intercourse difficult, if not impossible. It is estimated that close to 15% of women experience pain during sexual intercourse (Laumann et al., 1999). Contrary to popular belief, men can also experience dyspareunia, which may cause pain in the testes or penis, either during or after sexual intercourse.

A number of things may cause such pain, from physical problems to allergies or infections. Psychological problems can also cause dyspareunia, and so a full diagnosis from a health professional is imperative. In Chapter 4 we discussed vulvodynia, which can be another cause of dyspareunia. **Vulvar vestibulitis** (vess-tib-u-LITE-is) **syndrome,** a type of vulvodynia, is considered one of the most common causes of dyspareunia today (Bergeron et al., 1997). In another study, almost 20% of women were found to experience chronic vulvar pain, yet 40% of these women never sought treatment for the pain

vulvar vestibulitis syndrome
Syndrome that causes pain and burning in the vaginal vestibule and often occurs during sexual intercourse, tampon insertion, gynecological exams, bicycle riding, and wearing tight pants.

SEX Talk

Question: Every time I have sexual intercourse, the pain in my vagina is so intense, I almost feel like I should stop having sex altogether. Could this have anything to do with the fact that I was forced to have sex with my brother for several years while I was growing up?

The pain you experience during sexual intercourse may be due to the sexual abuse you experienced as an adolescent, as well as stress, fear, and anxiety. You should consider talking to a counselor to help clarify what is contributing to this pain and also have a full medical evaluation. It is also possible that you may have a condition known as vulvodynia, which causes chronic vulval pain and soreness (see Chapter 4). In the meantime, try engaging in other sexual activities besides intercourse to relieve the anxiety that is associated with penetration through the anticipation of pain.

(National Vulvodynia Association, 2003). Women with vulvodynia report poor sexual functioning and significant pain during sexual intercourse (Masheb et al., 2004).

Dyspareunia in men is caused by the same physiological and psychological factors as in females. It can also be due to Peyronie's disease (which we discussed in Chapter 5). Severe cases can cause curvature in the penis, which can make sexual intercourse impossible.

Treating Dyspareunia and Vulvodynia

Like vaginismus, dyspareunia should be evaluated medically prior to treatment. Several physical and psychological issues can contribute to painful intercourse. If there is a physical problem, such as an infection, medical treatment will usually result in a lessening or total elimination of the pain. As we discussed earlier in this chapter, women suffering from dyspareunia should also be evaluated for vulvodynia prior to any treatment for their sexual dysfunction. Treatment for vulvar vestibulitis, including psychotherapy, biofeedback and surgery, have resulted in significant reduction in dyspareunia after treatment and in follow-up studies (Binik et al., 2002). Psychological causes of dyspareunia, such as performance anxieties or a fear of intimacy, must be treated through counseling or psychotherapy.

A controversy arose in 2005 over whether dyspareunia should be classified as a *sexual* pain disorder. Some researchers believe that it should be classified as a pain disorder, rather than a sexual dysfunction (Binik, 2005). This discussion will continue and may affect how dyspareunia is diagnosed and treated in the future.

Review Question

Identify and describe the genital pain disorders, and describe the treatments available.

SEX Talk

Question: Why do women fake orgasms rather than honestly telling their partners what they are doing wrong?

Faking orgasms often occurs as a result of a dysfunction. To a man or woman who experiences orgasmic disorder or retarded ejaculation, faking an orgasm may seem the best way to end the sexual activity or to please the partner. However, such deceptions are not healthy in a committed relationship, and partners are generally advised to discuss any sexual problems they have instead of covering them up. A woman (or a man) may have a difficult time communicating sexual needs and desires. So, instead of talking to her partner about what sexually excites her, she hopes that he knows how to do it. She may feel too embarrassed or vulnerable to tell him what to do. In this society, we expect men to know exactly what turns a woman on. However, what feels best to one woman may not feel good to another, and what feels good may change over time. Many variables can also interfere with sexual pleasure, such as stress, fatigue, anxiety, or depression. It is important that couples communicate so that they can make their sex lives satisfying for both partners.

sex byte

Researchers have recently discovered a condition known as sleep sex, which causes people to commit sexual acts in their sleep. Similar to sleepwalking, in which a person walks in his or her sleep, sleep sex involves a person either making sexual sounds, engaging in violent masturbation, or making unwanted violent sexual advances on his or her partner (Guilleminault et al., 2002). Treatment involves medication, combined with psychotherapy.

ILLNESS, DISABILITY, AND SEXUAL FUNCTIONING

We all need love, and we all need touching and contact with others. Yet somehow we have grown to think that sexuality is the privilege of the healthy. We tend to exclude ill or disabled people from our visions of the sexual, and so we deny them a basic human right (see the nearby Personal Voices, "I Want Sex—Just Like You"). If you were suddenly disabled or developed a chronic illness, would you lose your desire to be regarded by another as sexy and desirable?

Healthcare providers often rely on the International Classification of Diseases (ICD), an official system of identifying various illnesses. Several of these illnesses and their treatments can interfere with a person's sexual desire, physiological functioning, or both. Sexual functioning involves a complex physiological process, which can be impaired by pain, immobility, changes in bodily functions, or medications (Levay et al., 1981). More often, though, the problems are psychological. Sudden illness causes shock,

SEX in Real Life

"I Want Sex—Just Like You"

For years, because of my cerebral palsy and certain other physical difficulties, I doubted my ability to give and receive pleasure in sexual intercourse. For a long time I did not want to ask my doctors about sex because I felt that a negative answer would make me regard myself as nonhuman—such is the value our society places on sexuality. . . .

Finally, since I was extremely hazy about what physical movements were involved in coitus, I decided to go to a movie. After the first two minutes I got the idea down pat and saw that I was perfectly capable of performing. My self-image skyrocketed. I, just like other women, had something sexual to offer a man!

There are various reasons why sexuality of the handicapped was avoided for so long and why it makes many professionals intolerably uncomfortable. First, most physical disabilities alter the looks of the person—deformities, bizarre head and arm motions, drooling, and poor eye-contact. Few professionals are able to see their patients as sexually desirable, and there is even the subtly expressed attitude that there is something a bit wrong with anyone who is sexually attracted to a disabled person. You can imagine what such an attitude does to the self-esteem of the handicapped person—"Anyone who wants me must be nuts!"

The couple too disabled to have sex by themselves must decide whether they want to forgo sex or whether they want to make love in spite of needing help to do so. There are many reasons for making love—recreation, bribery, consolation, procreation, the desire for one-on-one attention, religious experience. Some of the reasons are more amenable than others to third-party participation. But I feel strongly that no couple who wants to have sex should be denied the necessary help to do so, and that, if they live in a health-care facility, it is the duty of the health-care professional to provide such help.

Initial access to potential partners is extremely limited, in large part due to my distorted speech. Opportunities to meet are few, and when they do exist, men who are not trained to work with handicapped people tend to shy away from me. Somehow I hardly think the father of young children who held me in his arms as he helped me into the YWCA swimming pool was making plans to have me as a future bed partner. Even if I did get to know a guy well enough so that the moment for sex drew near, there would be the problem of birth control. An able-bodied woman can have herself fitted with a diaphragm with very little failure, and furthermore she can insert the device herself at the opportune time. . . .

Intellectually I know that sexually I can perform—the movie proved it. Yet at what might be called the subintellectual level I doubt my body's ability to give another pleasure. Rarely does my body give me pleasure. When I tell it to do something as often as not it does exactly the opposite, or else it flares out in wild, tantrumlike motions. How could my body possibly conform to the wishes of an expectantly excited lover? This is the question I still ask myself.

Source: Sutherland, 1987, pp. 25, 27.

anger, resentment, anxiety, and depression, all of which can adversely affect sexual desire and functioning. Many illnesses cause disfiguration and force a person to deal with radical changes in body image; after removal of a limb, breast, testicle, or the need to wear an external bag to collect bodily waste, many people wonder: How could anyone possibly find me sexually attractive?

Serious illness often puts strains on loving relationships. A partner may be forced to become nurse, cook, maid, and caretaker as well as lover. The caretaker of an ill person may worry that the sick partner is too weak or fragile for sex or be too concerned with his or her illness to want sexual contact. Still, many couples do enjoy loving, full relationships (see Personal Voices, "Stories of Love Among the Disabled," on page 488).

A majority of the research on the sexuality of the disabled has been done on men, and physicians are more likely to talk to their male patients about sexual issues than their female ones. Healthcare workers often assume that female patients do not want to have sex or that they are interested only in whether or not they can still do it; yet the little research that exists on gender differences in the sexuality of the disabled has found that disabled women have more sexual difficulties than disabled men (Fine & Asch, 1988).

Another common assumption is that all patients are heterosexual, and so, for example, disabled lesbians may be given contraceptive advice without being asked if they need it (O'Toole & Bregante, 1992). Heterosexual women looking for information about sexuality and their particular disability may find little, and lesbians may find none at all.

The real questions that sick people and their partners have about their sexuality are too often ignored by medical professionals. They may be questions of mechanics, such as "What positions can I get into now that I have lost a leg?"; questions of function, "Will my genitals still work now that I have a spinal-cord injury?"; questions of attractiveness, "Will my husband still want me now that I have lost a breast?"; even questions of appropriateness, "Should I allow my mentally ill teenage daughter to pursue a sex life when she may not understand the consequences?" We will now review a sample of physical and mental challenges that confront people and also some of the sexual questions and problems that can arise.

Cardiovascular Problems: Heart Disease and Stroke

Heart disease, including **hypertension, angina,** and **myocardial infarction (MI),** is the number one cause of death in the United States. A person with heart disease—even a person who has had a heart transplant—can return to a normal sex life shortly after recovery. Most cardiologists allow intercourse as soon as the patient feels up to it, although they usually recommend that heart transplant patients wait from 4 to 8 weeks to give the incision time to heal. However, researchers have found that the frequency of sexual intercourse after MIs does decrease. Why does this occur?

One reason is fear. Many patients (or their partners) fear that their damaged (or new) heart is not up to the strain of intercourse or orgasm. This fear can be triggered by the fact that, when a person becomes sexually excited, his or her heartbeat and respiration increase, and he or she may break out into a sweat (these are also signs of a heart attack). Some people with heart disease actually do experience some angina during sexual activity. Although not usually serious, these incidents may be frightening. Research has found that although sexual activity can trigger a MI, this risk is extremely low (Muller et al., 1996). In fact, except for patients with very serious heart conditions, sex puts no more strain on the heart than walking up a flight or two of stairs. (See Chapter 10, page 320, for a personal account of sex after a cardiac incident.)

Not all problems are psychological, however. Because achieving an erection is basically a vascular process, involving the flow of blood into the penis, some forms of heart disease can result in erectile difficulties (in fact, many men who have had a MI report having had erectile difficulties before their heart attack). Some heart medications also can dampen desire or cause erectile problems, or, less often, women may experience a decrease in lubrication (see Table 14.2). Sometimes, adjusting medications can help couples who are experiencing such problems.

Review Question

Explain how physical illness and its treatment can interfere with sexual desire, physiological functioning, or both.

hypertension
Abnormally high blood pressure.

angina
Chest pains that accompany heart disease.

myocardial infarction (MI)
A cutoff of blood to the heart muscle, causing damage to the heart; also referred to as a heart attack.

TABLE 14.2   Specific Drugs and Symptoms of Sexual Problems

	Type of Drug	Possible Problems in Women	Possible Problems in Men
Antihypertensive (blood pressure) medications	Aldomet	Reduced sexual desire, impaired orgasm	Reduced sexual desire, erectile and ejaculatory problems, impaired orgasm
	Catapres, Inderal, Minipress	Reduced sexual desire	Reduced sexual desire, erectile problems
	Lopressor	Reduced sexual desire	Reduced sexual desire, Peyronie's disease
Tranquilizers	Barbiturates	Reduced sexual desire	Reduced sexual desire, erectile problems
	Valium, Xanax	Reduced sexual desire, impaired orgasm	Reduced sexual desire, ejaculatory problems, impaired orgasm
Antidepressants	Clomipramine (Anafranil)	Reduced sexual desire, impaired orgasm	Reduced sexual desire, ejaculatory problems, impaired orgasm
	Desyrel		Erectile problems, priapism
	Elavil	Reduced sexual desire	Reduced sexual desire, erectile and ejaculatory problems, testicular swelling
	SSRIs (Prozac, Paxil, Zoloft)	Reduced sexual desire	Reduced sexual desire
Antipsychotics	Mellaril	Reduced sexual desire, menstrual problems	Reduced sexual desire, ejaculatory problems, priapism, gynecomastia
	Stelazine	Menstrual problems	Erectile and ejaculatory problems, priapism, gynecomastia
	Thorazine	Menstrual problems	Erectile and ejaculatory problems, priapism
Ulcer Medications	Tagamet	Reduced sexual desire	Reduced sexual desire
	Xantac	Reduced sexual desire	Reduced sexual desire, erectile problems
Other Drugs	Antabuse (treats alcoholism)		Erectile problems
	Naproxen (anti-inflammatory)		Erectile and ejaculatory problems
	Alkeran (cancer therapy)	Reduced sexual desire, menstrual problems	Reduced sexual desire, erectile problems, gynecomastia

After a heart attack or other heart problems, it is not uncommon to have feelings of depression, inadequacy (especially among men), or loss of attractiveness (especially among women; Schover & Jensen, 1988). In addition, after a heart attack, the patient's partner often assumes the responsibility of enforcing the doctor's orders: "Don't smoke!" "Don't eat fatty foods!" "Don't drink alcohol!" "Don't get so excited!" "Don't put so much salt on that!" "Get some exercise!" This is hardly a role that leads to good feelings and sexual desire. Any combination of these factors may lead one or both partners to avoid sex. Consequently, distance in the relationship may grow, and the couple may drift apart just when they need each other most (Sandowski, 1989).

Strokes, also called cerebral vascular accidents (CVAs), happen when blood is cut off from part of the brain, usually because a small blood vessel bursts. Although every stroke is different depending on what areas of the brain are damaged, some common results are **hemiplegia** (he-mi-PLEE-jee-uh), **aphasia** (uh-FAY-zhee-uh), and other cognitive, perceptual, and memory problems. As with other types of brain injury (such as those caused by automobile accidents), damage to the brain can affect sexuality in a number of ways.

In most cases of stroke, sexual functioning itself is not damaged, and many stroke victims do go on to resume sexual activity. The problems that confront a couple with normal functioning are similar to those with cardiovascular disease: fear of causing another stroke, worries about sexual attractiveness, and the stresses and anxieties of having to cope with a major illness. However, a stroke can also cause physiological changes that affect sexuality. Some men find that after a stroke their erections are crooked because the nerves controlling the erectile tissue on one side of the penis are affected. Hemiplegia can result in spasticity (jerking motions) and reduced sensation on one side of the body. Paralysis can also contribute to a feeling of awkwardness or unattractiveness. In addition, aphasia can affect a person's ability to communicate or understand sexual cues.

Some stroke victims also go through periods of **disinhibition,** in which they exhibit behavior that, before the stroke, they would have been able to suppress. Often this includes **hypersexuality,** in which the patient may make lewd comments, masturbate in public, disrobe publicly, or make inappropriate sexual advances (Larkin, 1992). Others

stroke
Occurs when blood is cut off from part of the brain, usually because a small blood vessel bursts.

hemiplegia
Paralysis of one side of the body.

aphasia
Defects in the ability to express and/or understand speech, signs, or written communication, due to damage to the speech centers of the brain.

disinhibition
The loss of normal control over behaviors such as expressing sexuality or taking one's clothes off in public.

hypersexuality
Abnormally expressive or aggressive sexual behavior, often in public; the term usually refers to behavior due to some disturbance of the brain.

may experience **hyposexuality,** in which they show decreased sexual desire, or they may experience ED. Sexual intervention programs have been designed for use in rehabilitation hospitals, and they can be of great help in teaching couples how to deal with the difficulties of adjusting to life after a stroke.

Cancer

Cancer is one of the most dreaded diseases, can involve almost any organ of the body, and has a reputation of being invariably fatal. In fact, cure rates have increased dramatically, and some cancers are now more than 90% curable. Still, cancer can kill, and a diagnosis of cancer is usually accompanied by shock, numbness, and gripping fear. Also, as in other illness, partners may need to become caretakers, and roles can change. For these reasons, cancer can lead to a decrease in sexual desire and activity, even when it attacks nonsexual organs. Sexual dysfunctions are often high among cancer survivors (Auchincloss, 1991).

For example, surgery is required for a number of cancers of the digestive system, and it can lead to **ostomies** (OST-stome-mees). People with cancer of the colon often need to have part or all of the large intestine removed; the rectum may be removed as well. A surgical opening, called a **stoma** (STOW-mah), is made in the abdomen to allow waste products to exit the body. This is collected in a bag which, for many patients, must be worn at all times (others can take it off periodically). Ostomy bags are visually unpleasant and may emit an odor, and the adjustment to their presence can be very difficult for some couples. Having a new opening on the body to eliminate bodily wastes is itself a hard thing to accept for many people, but most people eventually adjust to it and, barring other problems related to their disease, go on to live healthy and sexually active lives. One woman wondered how an ostomy would change her self-image:

> I had to go through a total reevaluation of my physical appearance. I couldn't ever imagine myself attracting somebody in a bikini or in any of those normal, stereotypical ways. I would eventually have to confront the reality that I was having this ostomy, and if I was to develop any kind of an intimate relationship with anybody, that was going to have to be dealt with. So I had to look deeper down beyond the flesh. (Register, 1987, pp. 38–39)

Cancer can affect sexual functioning in other ways as well. Physical scars, the loss of limbs or body parts, changes in skin texture when radiation therapy is used, the loss of hair, nausea, bloatedness, weight gain or loss, and acne are just some of the ways that cancer and its treatment can affect the body and one's body image. In addition, the psychological trauma and the fear of death can lead to depression, which can inhibit sexual relations. Perhaps the most drastic situations, however, occur when cancer affects the sexual organs themselves.

Breast Cancer

In American society, breasts are a focal part of female sexual attractiveness, and women often invest much of their feminine self-image in their breasts. For many years, a diagnosis of breast cancer usually meant that a woman lost that breast; **mastectomy** was the preferred treatment. **Simple mastectomies** meant that the breast tissue alone was removed, whereas radical mastectomies involved the removal of the breast along with other tissues and lymph nodes. As we discussed in Chapter 4, the numbers of mastectomies have decreased today, and many women are opting for lumpectomies. These are often coupled with chemotherapy, radiation therapy, or both. Still, some women must undergo radical mastectomies and must contend not only with having cancer, but also with an altered image of their sexual identity.

There might be very little time to prepare oneself psychologically for the loss of a breast. One woman who had a mastectomy years ago reported: "It all happened so fast. I was told on Friday, and on Monday it [the breast] was off" (Sandowski, 1989, p. 166). A woman who loses a breast may worry that her partner will no longer find her attractive or desirable. Some go so far as to wear their bras when making love or to avoid looking in mirrors when nude.

In order to wear the clothes they are used to wearing, many woman missing a breast (or both breasts) will wear a prosthesis. Other women choose to undergo breast reconstruction, in which tissue and fat from other parts of the body are molded into the shape of a breast and implanted under a fold of skin, or fluid-filled implants are added. Years ago, reconstructed breasts were not very satisfactory, but recent advances in reconstructive techniques can create a much more natural-looking breast. Surgery can also create a realistic looking nipple, although some women are satisfied with just the form of a breast (Sandowski, 1989).

There is no reason that a mastectomy should interfere with normal sexual functioning. The most important factor in resuming a normal sexual life is the encouragement and acceptance from the woman's sexual partner, assuring her that she is still sexually attractive and desirable.

Pelvic Cancer and Hysterectomies

Cancer can also strike a woman's vagina, uterus, cervix or ovaries. Women with these cancers experience negative changes in all stages of the sexual response cycle and with their sex lives in general (Gamel et al., 2000). Some women who have been diagnosed with cervical cancer initiate sexual intercourse as a way to "say goodbye" to their sex lives because they believe they will never have a sex life after cancer treatment (Zegwaard et al., 2000). A woman's feelings about her cancer treatment and her social support network are both important in sexual recovery from these treatments.

Cancer of the reproductive organs may result in a hysterectomy. In a total hysterectomy, the uterus and cervix (which is part of the uterus) are removed; in a radical hysterectomy, the ovaries are also removed (**oophorectomy;** oh-uh-for-RECT-toe-mee), along with the Fallopian tubes and surrounding tissue. Hysterectomies are also performed for conditions other than cancer. In fact, they are done so often that hysterectomy is the most common medical procedure performed in the United States today (Kuppermann et al., 2004). Many critics began to claim that American surgeons were much too quick to remove a woman's uterus; in France, for example, doctors performed fewer than one-fifth the number of hysterectomies as in the United States. Because of this criticism, the number of hysterectomies performed in the United States has been dropping.

Physicians may neglect to discuss the sexual implications of losing a uterus with their patients because they know that the uterus does not directly influence sexuality and they assume that the woman feels the same way. Yet many women believe that their uterus is needed for normal sexual functioning and worry that removal will affect their sexual desire or their ability to have normal relations. Research has found that women who undergo hysterectomies often have low blood flow responses to the vagina, which suggests possible nerve damage (Maas et al., 2004). Other studies have found that sexual functioning improved after hysterectomy (Rhodes et al., 1999).

A hysterectomy can affect sexual functioning and pleasure in a number of different ways. The ovaries produce most of a woman's estrogen and progesterone; so, when they are removed, hormonal imbalances follow. Even with hormone replacement therapy, reduced vaginal lubrication, mood swings, and other bodily changes can occur. Also, many women find the uterine contractions of orgasm very pleasurable, and when the uterus is removed, they lose that aspect of orgasm. In some cases, part of the woman's upper vagina may be removed, and the vagina may then be shorter, making intercourse uncomfortable or painful.

Some women experience depression and the disruption of intimate relationships after a hysterectomy. In part, how a woman feels about her hysterectomy reflects other needs in her life. Older women who are through with childbearing may find it less disturbing; in fact, some women are happy to be free of menstrual periods and the need for contraception (especially if the hysterectomy was for reasons other than cancer). Other women may feel a profound sense of loss because they may have wanted to bear children

An advertising campaign by The Breast Cancer Fund parodied the fact that society routinely represents women's breasts as only sexual in nature, whereas breast cancer is treated with secrecy.

oophorectomy
The surgical removal of the ovaries.

or because they are mourning the loss of a cherished part of their body and female identity. Sexual partners must be sensitive to how the woman tries to work out her new relationship to her sexuality. Over time, the adjustment to these changes often improves.

Prostate Cancer

Almost all men will experience a normal enlargement of the prostate gland if they live long enough (see Chapter 5). Prostate cancer is one of the most common cancers in men over 50. When prostate cancer is diagnosed or if the normal enlargement of the prostate progresses to the point at which it affects urination, a **prostatectomy** (pross-tuh-TECK-toe-mee; sometimes along with a **cystectomy**) must be performed. In the past, a prostatectomy involved cutting the nerves necessary for erection, resulting in erectile dysfunction. Newer techniques, however, allow more careful surgery, and fewer men suffer ED as a result.

One result of prostatectomy may be **incontinence,** sometimes necessitating an **indwelling catheter.** Many couples fear that this means the end of their sex life because removing and reinserting the catheter can lead to infection. However, the catheter can be folded alongside the penis during intercourse or held in place with a condom (Sandowski, 1989). For men who experience erectile dysfunction from the surgery, penile prostheses or intracavenous injections are possible. As in all surgeries of this kind, the man must also cope with the fear of disease, concern about his masculinity and body image, concern about the reactions of his sexual partner, and the new sensations or sexual functioning that can accompany prostate surgery.

It is well documented that sexual dysfunctions can occur as a result of any type of cancer or cancer treatment (Sheppard & Wylie, 2001). Men with prostate cancer report higher levels of sexual problems than men from the general population (Jakobsson et al., 2001). However, because prostate cancer treatment is often aimed at a cure, many of these sexual problems remain after treatment. It's important that sexual functioning be evaluated after treatment for prostate cancer.

Testicular Cancer

Cancer of the penis or scrotum is rare, and cancer of the testes is only slightly more common. Still, the sexual problems that result from these diseases are similar to those from prostate cancer. Testicular cancer is most common in men who are in their most productive years. Research has found that although sexual problems are common after treatment for testicular cancer, there is considerable improvement 1 year after diagnosis (van Basten et al., 1999).

In Chapter 5 we discussed testicular cancer, and, although the surgical removal of a testicle (orchiectomy) due to cancer usually does not affect the ability to reproduce (as the remaining testicle produces enough sperm and, usually, adequate testosterone), some men do experience psychological difficulties. This is mainly due to feelings that they have lost part of their manhood or fears about the appearance of their scrotum. The appearance of the scrotum can be helped by inserting a testicular prosthesis that takes the place of the missing testicle. In some rare cases, cancer of the penis may necessitate a partial or total **penectomy** (pee-NECK-toe-mee). In a total penectomy, the man's urethra is redirected downward to a new opening that is created between the scrotum and anus. Even with a penectomy, some men can have orgasms by stimulating whatever tissue is left where the penis was, and the ejaculate leaves the body through the urethra (Schover & Jensen, 1988).

Chronic Illness and Chronic Pain

Many people born with chronic diseases, or those who develop them later in life, suffer for many years with their condition. They must learn to make adjustments in many parts of their lives, including their sexual behaviors. Chronic pain from illnesses such as arthritis, migraine headaches, and lower back pain can make intercourse difficult or impossible at times. One woman describes the results of her painful condition:

prostatectomy
The surgical removal of the prostate gland.

cystectomy
The surgical removal of the bladder.

incontinence
Lack of normal voluntary control of urinary functions.

indwelling catheter
A permanent catheter, inserted in the bladder, to allow the removal of urine in those who are unable to urinate or are incontinent.

penectomy
The surgical removal of the penis.

Review Question

Explain how the various cancers in women and men can psychologically and physiologically interfere with sexual functioning.

It is difficult to express sensual pleasures—intercourse, touching, holding, hand-holding, hugging—when my body hurts. I often feel pain when trying new positions, which is also affected by my limited range of motion. My husband was afraid to try new things and positions sometimes because of the fear he might physically hurt me. I was afraid of trying new things because I might hurt myself or cry out in pain and spoil the mood or feel embarrassed. (Kohler et al., 1990, p. 95)

Still, with gentle, caring lovemaking and an avoidance of those positions that are too painful or stressful, many people report that sexual activity actually provides them some respite from their pain.

Respiratory Illnesses

Other conditions that affect sexual functioning are the respiratory illnesses, including **chronic obstructive pulmonary disease (COPD),** asthma, and tuberculosis. These diseases affect sexual functioning not only because they may make physical exertion difficult, but also because perceptual and motor skills can be impaired. The 20 million people who have COPD learn to take medicine before sexual activity, slow down their pace of lovemaking, and use positions that allow the partner with COPD to breathe comfortably.

chronic obstructive pulmonary disease (COPD)
Disease of the lung that affects breathing.

Many other chronic illnesses call for special types of sexual counseling and understanding. In order to understand the challenges that chronic illness poses to sexual functioning, we will now review a sample of such conditions and examine the types of sexual challenges they present.

Diabetes

Diabetes is caused by the inability of the pancreas to produce insulin, which is used to process blood sugar into energy, or by the inability of the body to use the insulin produced. Diabetes may affect children (type I diabetes), who must then depend on insulin injections for the rest of their lives, or it may appear later (type II diabetes) and may then be controlled through diet or oral medication. Diabetes is a serious condition that can ultimately lead to blindness, renal failure, and other problems.

Diabetes is often used to demonstrate the effects of disease on sexuality because diabetics tend to exhibit multiple and complex sexual difficulties. In fact, sexual problems (especially difficulty in getting an erection for men and vaginitis or yeast infections in women) may be one of the first signs of diabetes. A large number of men in the later stages of diabetes have penile prostheses implanted. Women with Type I diabetes, aside from some problems with vaginal lubrication, do not seem to have significantly more problems than unaffected women. However, women with Type II diabetes show loss of desire, difficulties in lubrication, less satisfaction in sex, and difficulty reaching orgasm (Schover & Jensen, 1988).

Differentiating between how much of a person's sexual difficulty is due to underlying physiological problems and how much is due to psychological issues is often difficult. Depression, fear of erectile disorder, lack of sexual response, anxiety about the future, and the life changes that diabetes can bring all can dampen sexual desire. Sexual counseling is an important part of diabetes treatment. From a sexual standpoint, Viagra may be helpful for men with diabetes who are experiencing ED, enabling them to successfully engage in sexual intercourse again (Fink et al., 2002).

Multiple Sclerosis

Multiple sclerosis (MS) involves a breakdown of the myelin sheath that protects all nerve fibers, and it can be manifested in a variety of symptoms, such as dizziness, weakness, blurred or double vision, muscle spasms, spasticity, and loss of control of limbs and muscles. Symptoms can come and go without warning, but MS is progressive and worsens over time. MS often strikes people between the ages of 20 and 50, at a time when they are establishing sexual relationships and families (M. P. McCabe, 2002).

Multiple sclerosis can affect sexual functioning in many ways. Between 60% and 80% of men with MS experience ED problems (M. P. McCabe, 2002), whereas women with MS may have lack of vaginal lubrication, altered feelings during orgasm, or difficulty experiencing orgasm. Both men and women may become hypersensitive to touch, experiencing even light caresses as painful or unpleasant. Fatigue, muscle spasms, and loss of bladder and bowel function can also inhibit sexual contact. Sexual counseling, penile prostheses in men, and artificial lubrication in women can help overcome some of these difficulties. Sexual dysfunctions may increase as the disease progresses (Dupont, 1996).

Alcoholism

Alcohol is the most common type of chemical dependency in the United States and western Europe; about one-third of American families have at least one problem drinker in the family, and alcohol is the third leading cause of death in the United States. Ethyl alcohol is a general nervous system depressant that has both long- and short-term effects on sexual functioning. It can impair spinal reflexes and decrease serum testosterone levels, which can lead to erectile dysfunction. Paradoxically, even as serum testosterone levels drop, luteinizing hormone (LH) levels can increase, leading to increased libido (George & Stoner, 2000).

Long-term alcohol abuse can have drastic consequences. **Hyperestrogenemia** (high-per-ess-troh-jen-EE-mee-uh) can result from the liver damage due to alcoholism, which, combined with lower testosterone levels, may cause feminization, gynecomastia (which we discussed in Chapter 5), testicular atrophy, sterility, ED, and the decreased libido seen in long-term alcoholic males. In women, liver disease can lead to decreased or absent menstrual flow, ovarian atrophy, loss of vaginal membranes, infertility, and miscarriages. Alcohol can affect almost every bodily system; after a while, the damage it causes, including the damage to sexual functioning, can be irreversible, even if the person never drinks alcohol again.

Alcoholism also has a dramatic impact on families. It often coexists with anger, resentment, depression, and other familial and relationship problems. Some people become abusive when drunk, whereas others may withdraw and become noncommunicative. For both sexes, problem drinking may lead them into a spiral of guilt, lowered self-esteem, and even to thoughts of suicide. Recovery is a long, often difficult process, and one's body and sexuality need time to recover from periods of abuse.

Spinal Cord Injuries

The spinal cord brings impulses from the brain to the various parts of the body; damage to the cord can cut off those impulses in any areas served by nerves below the damaged section. Therefore, to assess the dysfunctions that result from a spinal cord injury (SCI; or a spinal tumor), a physician must know exactly where on the spine the injury occurred and how extensively the cord has been damaged (Benevento & Sipski, 2002). Though some return of sensation and movement can be achieved in many injuries, most people are left with permanent disabilities. In more extreme cases, SCI can result in total or partial **paraplegia** (pah-ruh-PLEE-jee-uh) or total or partial **quadriplegia** (kwa-druh-PLEE-jee-uh). In these cases, the person is rendered extremely dependent on his or her partner or caretaker.

Men are four times more likely than women to experience SCI. If the injury is above a certain vertebra and the cord is not completely severed, a man may still be able to have an erection through the body's reflex mechanism, although it may be difficult to maintain as he will not be able to feel skin sensations in the penis. Injuries to the lower part of the spine are more likely to result in erectile difficulties in men, but they are also more likely to preserve some sensation in the genitals. Men without disabilities maintain erections in part through psychic arousal, such as thoughts and feelings and fantasies about the sex act; but, with SCI, psychic arousal cannot provide continuing stimulation. Most men with SCI who are capable of having erections are not able to climax or ejaculate, which involves a more complex mechanism than an erection (Benevento & Sipski, 2002).

hyperestrogenemia
Having an excessive amount of estrogens in the blood.

paraplegia
Paralysis of the legs and lower part of the body, affecting both sensation and motor response.

quadriplegia
Paralyis of all four limbs.

Women with SCI remain fertile and can bear children, and so they must continue to use contraception. However, women with SCI can also lose sensation in the genitals and with it the ability to lubricate during sexual activity. In one survey, 52% were able to achieve an orgasm after SCI, but half said that the orgasm felt different from before (Kettl et al., 1991). Some women (and men) report experiencing "phantom orgasm," a psychic sensation of having an orgasm without the corresponding physical reactions. Also, skin sensation in the areas unaffected by the injury can become greater, and new erogenous zones can appear (Brown et al., 2005; Ferreiro-Velasco et al., 2005). The breasts, for example, may become even more sexually sensitive in women who retain sensation there.

Sexual problems develop over time as the full impact of their situation takes effect. Although men with SCI resume sexual activity within a year of their injury, their frequency of sexual activity decreases after the injury. Ninety-nine percent of men with SCI reported sexual intercourse as their favorite sexual activity before SCI, and only 16% report this after injury (Alexander et al., 1993). Many men and women enjoy a variety of sexual activities after SCI, including kissing, hugging, and touching.

Rehabilitation from SCI is a long, difficult process. Still, with a caring partner, meaningful sexual contact can be achieved. Men incapable of having an erection can still use their mouths and sometimes their hands. If vaginal penetration is desired, couples can consider a penile prosthesis or use the technique of "stuffing," in which the flaccid penis is pushed into the vagina. Newer treatment methods including prosthesis implantation, vacuum erection devices, and the injection of vasoactive drugs have all been used in men with SCI. However, men with SCI have higher rates of complications with prosthetic implants (Kabalin & Kessler, 1988) and may not be able to use other treatment methods, such as the vacuum pump or injections, because of limited mobility. Research has found that Viagra can significantly improve erections in men with spinal cord injury (Fink et al., 2002).

AIDS and HIV

In other chapters we discussed the influence that AIDS has had on the sexual behaviors and attitudes of people in the United States. Because HIV can be passed to others through sexual activity, millions of Americans have changed their sexual lifestyles to include safer sex practices. But what of those who discover that they are HIV-positive or have developed AIDS? Although we will discuss HIV and AIDS in depth in Chapter 15, here we will review how the knowledge about HIV and the virus itself affect sexual functioning.

Caught up in the tragedy of their situation, their fear of infecting others, and often their shame, some people cease all sexual activity. Others limit their sexual contact to hugging, kissing, and caressing. Although people with HIV often experience sexual dysfunction (Catalan & Meadows, 2000), the existence of HIV in the bloodstream need not mean the end of one's sexual life. HIV-positive people need to be careful and considerate with their partners, avoiding exchange of body fluids and accidental infection. However, there is ample opportunity for loving, sexual relations while maintaining safety.

Wearing a condom reduces (although it does not eliminate) the risk of sexually transmitting the virus during oral, vaginal, or anal sex (Schover & Jensen, 1988). Mutual massage, mutual masturbation, the use of vibrators or other sex toys, and kissing without the exchange of saliva are all safe practices if care is taken (for example, the ejaculate of an infected partner should not come into contact with skin if the skin has cuts or abrasions; Sandowski, 1989). Sexuality can be very important to those infected with HIV, for in the midst of the world's fear and rejection, sexuality reaffirms that they are loved, cared for, and accepted by their partners.

Mental Illness and Retardation: Special Issues

People with psychiatric disorders have sexual fantasies, needs, and feelings, and they have the same right to a fulfilling sexual expression as do others. However, historically they have either been treated as asexual, or their sexuality has been viewed as illegitimate, warped, or needing external control (Apfel & Handel, 1993). Yet a sudden or drastic change in sexual habits may be a sign of mental illness or a sign that a mentally ill person is getting worse (or better, depending on the change). Therefore, understanding the sexual problems of the psychiatric patient can be quite complex (Schover & Jensen, 1988).

People with **schizophrenia,** for example, can be among the most impaired and difficult psychiatric patients. **Neuroleptics,** antipsychotic drugs such as Thorazine and Haldol, can cause increased or decreased desire for sex; painful enlargement of the breasts, reproductive organs, or testicles; difficulty in achieving or maintaining an erection; delayed or retrograde ejaculation; and changes, including pain, in orgasm.

Yet, outside of the effects of neuroleptics, people with schizophrenia have been found to grapple with the same sexual questions and dysfunctions as other people. The same is true of people with **major depression** and other **affective disorders.** They may experience hyposexuality when depressed or hypersexuality in periods of mania. Both can also occur as a result of antidepressant medications. Otherwise, their sexual problems do not differ significantly from those of people without major psychiatric problems (Schover & Jensen, 1988).

Sexual issues among the mentally ill are neglected in psychiatric training, and physicians who treat the mentally ill have often been more interested in controlling and limiting patients' sexual behavior than they have been in treating sexual dysfunction. For years, the mentally retarded population has been kept from having sexual relationships, and those who are institutionalized are often discouraged from masturbating. It is as if an otherwise healthy adult is supposed to display no sexual interest or activity at all. Educators have designed special sexuality education programs for the mentally retarded and developmentally disabled to make sure that they express their sexuality in a socially approved manner (Monat-Haller, 1992). But to deny people with psychiatric problems or retardation the pleasure of a sexual life is cruel and unnecessary.

Many people with mental disabilities (and physical disabilities) must spend long periods of their lives—sometimes their entire lives—in institutions, which makes devel-

schizophrenia
Any of a group of mental disorders that affect the individual's ability to think, behave, or perceive things normally.

neuroleptics
A class of antipsychotic drugs.

major depression
A persistent, chronic state in which the person feels he or she has no worth, cannot function normally, and entertains thoughts of or attempts suicide.

affective disorders
A class of mental disorders that affect mood.

Personal Voices

Stories of Love Among the Disabled

*A*ndy: *For a while, sure I felt bad [about breaking up with previous partner], but I went on and picked myself up, and I feel this [relationship with Carol] will be better for me. It's doing me a lot of good so far, and I hope she feels that way. For me, I don't want to lose her.*

Carol: *I'm looking for the same thing he's looking for—security. I thought I had it in the past, but I didn't. [Security is] being with each other and having the ability to talk to one another.*

Al: *She means everything to me. As soon as I get my divorce—put this in the book—I'll marry her.*

Bev: *No matter how good or bad the situation is, he's there for me, loving me—letting me know he loves me. Like everything else, you have to find your own way of intimacy. There's nothing that I can give to Al that he can't give back to me. It's mutual.*

Earl: *Some people don't look at it [an older person's sex life] as [important and healthy]. "Oh, that dirty, dirty old man!" [He's 65, she's 33.] I'm sick and tired of listening to that "dirty old man" talk! I think it's wrong when they say that. What the man needs is love, just like I'm giving Gina. Love makes me feel happier. But a lot of people don't understand it because not only am I older—I'm handicapped. I say to hell with that! Handicap or no handicap, we're all human. We're all human.*

Gina: *Above all, he has an inner strength in him that has reflected on me and gotten through to me so that I'm more able to cope with life. He has a much better inner strength than I have seen in any other person. I can talk with him about anything and everything under the sun, and he can make me feel so much better and so much more at ease.*

SOURCE: Stehle, 1985.

oping a sex life difficult. Institutions differ greatly in the amount of sexual contact they allow; some allow none whatsoever, whereas others allow mutually consenting sexual contact, with the staff carefully overseeing the patients' contraceptive and hygienic needs (Trudel & Desjardins, 1992). Whether people with severe mental illness can consent to mutual sex in an institutional setting is a difficult question (Kaeser, 1992).

Another aspect of institutional life involves the sexual exploitation of patients with mental illness or mental retardation. This is well known but seldom discussed by those who work in such institutions. About half of all women in psychiatric hospitals report having been abused as children or adolescents, and many are then abused in a hospital or other institutional setting. Children who grow up with developmental disabilities are between four and ten times more likely to be abused than children without those difficulties (Baladerian, 1991). Therefore, it is difficult to separate the sexual problems of retardation, developmental disability, and psychiatric illness from histories of sexual abuse (Apfel & Handel, 1993; Monat-Haller, 1992).

Review Question

Explain how the chronic illnesses, such as diabetes, multiple sclerosis, alcoholism, spinal cord injuries, AIDS/HIV, and mental illness, can psychologically and physiologically interfere with sexual functioning.

GETTING THE HELP YOU NEED

People who are ill or disabled have the same sexual needs and desires as everyone else. In the past, these needs have too often been neglected, not because the disabled themselves were not interested in sexuality but because physicians and other healthcare professionals were uncomfortable learning about their sexual needs and discussing these needs with their patients. Fortunately, that is beginning to change, and now sexuality counseling is a normal part of the recuperation from many diseases and injuries in many hospitals. It is important for all of us to learn that the disabled are just like everybody else and simply desire to be treated like anyone else.

If you are experiencing problems with sexual functioning, illness, or disability, it is important to seek help as soon as possible. Often, when the problems are ignored, they lead to bigger problems down the road. If you are in college and have a student counseling center available to you, this may be a good place to start looking for help. Request a counselor who has received training in sexuality or ask to be referred to one who has.

Today, many therapists receive specific training in sexuality. One of the best training organizations in the United States is the American Association of Sexuality Educators, Counselors, and Therapists (AASECT). This organization offers certification programs in human sexuality for counselors, educators, and therapists and can also provide information on those who are certified as therapists or counselors.

Review Question

Explain how the sexual needs of people who are ill or disabled have been neglected over the years.

Chapter Review

ACTIVE SUMMARY

1. **(a)** _____ sexuality depends on good mental and physical functioning. Sexual **(b)** _____ and dysfunctions are common, and **(c)** _____ plays an important role in developing and maintaining sexual **(d)** _____.

2. Therapists use the sexual response cycle to help **(a)** _____ how sexual dysfunction, disease, illness, and disability affect sexual **(b)** _____. Many feminists believe that the sexual response cycle may not fully **(c)** _____ female sexual functioning. Therapists use the *DSM-IV-TR* to **(d)** _____ sexual dysfunction. Today our knowledge about male sexual functioning has been far **(e)** _____ of our knowledge about female sexual functioning.

3. A sex **(a)** _____ first must determine whether a problem is psychological or physiological, and often these two can

(b) _____. **(c)** _____ causes include unconscious fears, ongoing stress, anxiety, **(d)** _____, guilt, anger, fear of infidelity, partner conflict, fear of intimacy, dependency, abandonment, or loss of control. **(e)** _____ causes for sexual dysfunction include disease, disability, illness, and many commonly used drugs. Nonprescription drugs such as **(f)** _____, alcohol, marijuana, LSD, and cocaine can also cause sexual dysfunctions.

4. Sexual dysfunctions can be primary or **(a)** _____ and situational or **(b)** _____. Research has found that **(c)** _____ problems have more biological or physiological causes, whereas **(d)** _____ problems tend to have more psychological causes. **(e)** _____ problems occur during certain sexual activities or with certain partners, whereas global problems occur in every situation, during every type of sexual activity, and with every sexual partner. Sex therapists further categorize **(f)** _____ as those of sexual desire, sexual arousal, orgasm disorders, and pain disorders.

5. Sexual **(a)** _____ disorders include hypoactive sexual desire and sexual aversion. In HSD there is a low or **(b)** _____ desire for sexual activity. Secondary HSD is more common than primary HSD. Psychological causes for HSD include a lack of **(c)** _____ to one's partner, fear of intimacy and/or pregnancy, marital or relationship conflicts, **(d)** _____ concerns, depression, and other psychological disorders. HSD can also result from **(e)** _____ messages about female sexuality while growing up, treating sex as a chore, a concern over a loss of control, or a negative body image. There are fewer cases of male hypoactive sexual desire than female. **(f)** _____-_____ therapy and medications to increase testosterone have been found to be beneficial in the treatment of HSD.

6. Sexual **(a)** _____ disorder involves an actual fear or **(b)** _____ associated with sexual activity, and it affects more women than men. This condition is often caused by past **(c)** _____ abuse. The most common treatment for sexual aversion involves discovering and resolving the underlying conflict that is **(d)** _____ to the sexual aversion.

7. Sexual **(a)** _____ disorders include female sexual arousal disorder and male **(b)** _____ disorder. FSAD is an inability to either obtain or maintain an adequate lubrication response of sexual excitement; it can have both physiological and psychological causes. Several **(c)** _____ are being evaluated in the treatment of FSAD. The EROS-CTD is available to women who are diagnosed with FSAD.

8. **(a)** _____ disorder is defined as the persistent inability to obtain or maintain an erection sufficient for satisfactory sexual performance. It can be caused by neurological, endocrine, vascular, or **(b)** _____ factors, and often there is a combination of these factors at play. Of all the sexual dysfunctions, there are more treatment options for male erectile disorder than for any other sexual dysfunction. Treatment options include psychological treatment (including systematic **(c)** _____ and sex therapy); psychopharmacological, hormonal, and intracavernous injections; transurethral therapy; vascular surgery; vacuum constriction devices; and prosthesis implantation. The treatment of ED has changed considerably since **(d)** _____ became available.

9. **(a)** _____ disorders include female orgasmic disorder, male orgasmic disorder, and premature ejaculation. Female orgasmic disorder is a(an) **(b)** _____ or absence of orgasm following a normal phase of sexual excitement. There are both **(c)** _____ factors (such as chronic illness, diabetes, neurological problems, hormonal deficiencies, or **(d)** _____) and psychological factors (such as a lack of sex **(e)** _____, fear or anxiety, or psychological disorders) that may interfere with a woman's ability to reach orgasm. The majority of **(f)** _____ programs for orgasmic disorder involve a combination of different treatment approaches, such as homework assignments, sex education, communication skills training, cognitive restructuring, desensitization, and other techniques.

10. **(a)** _____ orgasmic disorder is relatively rare and involves a delay or absence of orgasm following a normal phase of sexual excitement. **(b)** _____ medications have been found to interfere with orgasmic ability. Treatment options include **(c)** _____ and, if necessary, changing **(d)** _____.

11. Premature **(a)** _____ refers to a condition in which a man reaches orgasm just prior to, or directly following, penetration. This condition is primarily caused by **(b)** _____ factors. Premature ejaculation is often treated with two techniques, the **(c)** _____ and the **(d)** _____ techniques.

12. **(a)** _____ ejaculation refers to a situation in which a man may be entirely unable to reach orgasm during certain sexual activities or may be able to ejaculate only after **(b)** _____ intercourse. Retarded ejaculation can be caused by both psychological and physical factors. In many cases, **(c)** _____ is used to help work through some of these issues as a part of treatment.

13. The genital pain disorders include **(a)** _____ and **(b)** _____. Vaginismus involves involuntary contractions of the **(c)** _____ muscles, which can make vaginal **(d)** _____ virtually impossible. One of the most effective treatments for vaginismus includes the use of **(e)** _____.

14. **(a)** _____ is pain prior to, during, or after sexual intercourse; it can occur in men and women. Vulvar **(b)** _____ _____ is considered one of the most common causes of dyspareunia today. Dyspareunia should be evaluated **(c)** _____ to determine if there are any medical problems contributing to the pain.

15. Other problems can interfere with sexual functioning. **(a)** _____ orgasms often occurs as a result of a dysfunction, and generally the dysfunction should be discussed with sexual partners. **(b)** _____ _____ is a condition in which a person commits sexual acts in his or her sleep. Peyronie's disease is not a sexual dysfunction in and of itself, but it can cause sexual **(c)** _____.

16. Bibliotherapy, **(a)** _____, relaxation training, and **(b)** _____ also show some promise in the treatment of sexual dysfunction. Much of the current clinical research today focuses on developing new **(c)** _____ to treat dysfunctions.

17. Physical illness and its treatment can interfere with a person's **(a)** _____ desire, physiological functioning, or both. Cardiovascular problems, including **(b)** _____ and my-

ocardial infarctions, strokes, and **(c)** _____ can all affect sexual functioning. There can be physical problems that interfere with physiological functioning, or there can be **(d)** _____ problems or fear of sexual activity that can interfere with sexual functioning.

18. **(a)** _____ illnesses, such as diabetes, multiple sclerosis, muscular dystrophy, and **(b)** _____ can also negatively affect sexual functioning. Spinal cord injuries, mental illness and retardation, and infection with HIV and AIDS all present specific **(c)** _____ to sexual functioning. People who are ill or **(d)** _____ have the same sexual needs and desires that healthy people do.

19. People who are experiencing sexual **(a)** _____, illness, disease, or disability should seek **(b)** _____ as soon as possible in order to avoid the development of further **(c)** _____.

Critical Thinking Questions

1. Suppose that one night you discover that you are having trouble reaching orgasm with your partner. What do you do about it? When it happens several times, what do you do? Who would you feel comfortable talking to about this problem?

2. If you were suddenly disabled or developed a chronic illness, would you lose your desire to love and be loved, to touch and be touched, to be regarded by another as sexy and desirable?

3. Do you think insurance plans should cover Viagra? Do you think college students without erectile disorder should take Viagra? Why, or why not?

4. Do you think that drug companies could convince us that a dysfunction exists when there is none? Should researchers be doing more work to uncover the causes of female sexual dysfunction, even if the pharmaceutical companies are paying for this research? Why, or why not?

5. Although women may be diagnosed with persistent sexual arousal syndrome, there is no companion diagnosis for men. Why do you think this is? Do you think there should be such a diagnosis for men? Why, or why not?

CHAPTER RESOURCES

Check It Out

Metz, M. E., & McCarthy, B. E. (2004). **Coping with premature ejaculation: How to overcome premature ejaculation, please your partner and have great sex.** Oakland, CA: New Harbinger.

Metz and McCarthy use a biopsychosocial approach to aid in the understanding and treatment of premature ejaculation, which they claim is the easiest sexual dysfunction to treat. They review the physiological, neurological, and medical aspects of sex and sexual dysfunction, and uncover myths about male sexual functioning. They also focus on the important role that sexual partners can play in the treatment of premature ejaculation and suggest ways to improve relationship communication.

Something's Gotta Give (2003; 2 hours, 8 minutes; Rated PG-13)

Harry Langer (Jack Nicholson) is an aged music industry executive who, because of his fear of getting old, prefers younger women. His current girlfriend, Marin (played by Amanda Peet), brings him to the home of her mother (Erica, played by Diane Keaton) for a weekend, where things turn awkward. Harry suffers a heart attack there. Left in the care of Erica and his doctor (Keanu Reeves), a love triangle starts to take shape. This movie explores aging, challenges to sexuality, and relationships.

InfoTrac® College Edition

If your instructor ordered InfoTrac with this book, explore InfoTrac College Edition, your online library, for additional readings and review. Go to: **www.thomsonedu.com,** and enter these search terms:

erectile dysfunction   erectile disorder   dyspareunia
premature ejaculation   sexual arousal disorder   female sexual dysfunction

Web Resources

SexualityNow Companion Website
Go to **http://thomsonedu.com/carroll** for practice quiz questions, interactive activities, Internet links, critical thinking exercises, discussion forums, and more. You can also access sites from the Wadsworth Psychology Study Center **(http://psychology.wadsworth.com)** or you can connect directly to the following sites:

International Society for the Study of Women's Sexual Health (ISSWSH)
The ISSWSH is a multidisciplinary, academic, and scientific organization whose purposes are: (1) to provide opportunities for communication among scholars, researchers, and practitioners about women's sexual function and sexual experience, (2) to support the highest standards of ethics and professionalism in research, education, and clinical practice of women's sexuality, and (3) to provide the public with accurate information about women's sexuality and sexual health.

Disability Resources
This website offers information on sexuality for people with disabilities and for parents of children with disabilities. General disability information can be found, as well as disability-specific information.

Female Sexual Dysfunction—ALERT
This website, founded by Leonore Tiefer, a sex therapist and activist, challenges the myths promoted by the pharmaceutical industry and calls for research on the many causes of women's sexual problems. The pharmaceutical industry wants women to think that sexual problems are simple and offers drugs as magic fixes. A variety of links to sexual health organizations are available.

Masters and Johnson's Therapy Program
Masters and Johnson's therapy program website provides information on relational and sex therapy, trauma-based disorders, eating disorders, sexual compulsivity, and dissociative disorders. A question-and-answer section of the site answers the most frequently asked questions about sex therapy and the treatment of various disorders.

Dr. Carne's Resources for Sex Addiction & Recovery
Dr. Patrick Carne is a pioneer in the field of sexual addiction. This website offers information, research, and assistance for sex addiction and recovery. The site includes information on sexual addiction, sexual anorexia, Internet addiction, and 12-step groups. Several online tests are available for sexual addiction (gay and straight), Internet sexual addiction, and betrayal bonds.

The Sexual Health Network
The Sexual Health Network is dedicated to providing easy access to sexuality information, education, mutual support, counseling, therapy, health care, products, and other resources for people with disabilities, illness, or natural changes throughout the life cycle and those who love them or care for them.

SexualityNow   Sexuality Now

Go to **www.thomsonedu.com** to link to **SexualityNow,** your online study tool. First take the **Pre-Test** for this chapter to get your **Personalized Study Plan,** which will identify topics you need to review and direct you to online resources. Then take the **Post-Test** to determine what concepts you have mastered and what you still need work on.

Videos in SexualityNow
For additional information on topics discussed in this chapter, check out the videos in **SexualityNow** on the following topics:
- **Erectile Dysfunction: Clark**—Hear how various factors affect Clark's erectile dysfunction, including physical symptoms, depression, and cultural expectations.
- **Sex Patch for Women**—Acting on the brain, this sex patch slowly releases testosterone in the skin, allowing women to experience sexual desire and improve the quality of their sex lives.
- **Sex Devices for Women**—Hear how the 43% of women between the ages of 18 and 59 who have sexual dysfunction may experience sexual desire and arousal again with these aids.
- **Herbal Sexual Enhancements: Do They Work?**—Learn how the effectiveness of sexual enhancements is unproven and their safety is unknown.

15 Sexually Transmitted Infections and HIV/AIDS

Sexuality Now Go to www.thomsonedu.com to link to **SexualityNow,** your online study tool.

*I*t is estimated that roughly 22% of the U.S. population (or just over 65 million people) are living with an incurable sexually transmitted infection (STI). The Centers for Disease Control and Prevention estimate that there are approximately 19 million STI infections each year and half of these are among men and women between the ages of 15 and 24 years old (Weinstock et al., 2004). Although there are more than 25 infections spread primarily through sexual activity, in this chapter we will limit our discussion to pubic lice, scabies, gonorrhea, syphilis, chlamydia, vaginal infections, herpes, human papillomavirus, viral hepatitis, and the human immunodeficiency virus. We will explore attitudes, incidence, diagnosis, symptoms, treatment, and the prevention of STIs.

ATTITUDES AND THE STI EPIDEMIC

The sudden appearance of a new disease has always elicited fear about the nature of its **contagion.** Cultural fears about disease and sexuality in the early 20th century gave way to many different theories about casual transmission (Brandt, 1985). At the turn of the 20th century, physicians believed that STIs could be transmitted on pens, pencils, toothbrushes, towels, and bedding. In fact, during World War I, the United States Navy removed doorknobs from its battleships, claiming that they were responsible for spreading sexual infections.

Sexually transmitted infections have historically been viewed as symbols of corrupt sexuality (P. A. Allen, 2000). When compared with other illnesses, such as cancer or diabetes, attitudes about STIs have been considerably more negative, and many people believe that people so afflicted "got what they deserved." This has been referred to as the **punishment concept** of disease. In order to acquire an STI, it was generally believed, one must break the silent moral code of sexual responsibility. Those who become ill therefore have done something bad, for which they are being punished.

Kopelman (1988) suggests that this conceptualization has endured because it serves as a defense mechanism. By believing that a person's behavior is responsible for acquiring an STI, we believe ourselves to be safe by not engaging in whatever that behavior is. For example, if we believe that herpes happens only to people who have more than 10 sexual partners, we may limit our partners to 2 or 3 to feel safe. Whether we are safe, of course, depends on whether our beliefs about the causes of transmission are true or not. Negative beliefs and stigma about STIs persist today. One study found that many people who are diagnosed with STIs experience "self-stigmatization," which is an acceptance of the negative aspects of stigma (feeling inadequate and ashamed; Fortenberry et al., 2002). These negative feelings can also interfere with the act of getting tested at all.

College students are often apprehensive about getting tested for STIs, especially when they think they might be positive. One study found that social stigma and negative consequences of testing often cause college students to delay or avoid getting tested for STIs (Barth et al., 2002). Students report that they would feel "embarrassed" and worried that other people perceive them as "dirty." This is probably why in one study, many students said they would "rather not know" if they had an STI (Barth et al., 2002).

College students often act as though they are invincible; they may believe that although others may get STIs, it will not happen to them. In fact, the majority of young people believe that they are not at risk for contracting an STI (Ku et al., 2002). Yet, we know that college students are a part of the population that is most at risk for contracting an STI. This is because college students engage in many high-risk sexual be-

contagion
Disease transmission by direct or indirect contact.

punishment concept
The idea that people who had become infected with certain diseases, especially STIs, had done something wrong and were being punished.

SEX in Real Life

High-Risk Sexual Behaviors

High-risk sexual behaviors are those practices that increase the risk of acquiring a sexually transmitted infection. Following are some of these high-risk behaviors. Drinking alcohol and engaging in sexual activity under the influence of alcohol often increases the risk of acquiring an STI because alcohol can increase the likelihood that a person will participate in high-risk sexual activity.

Engaging in safer-sex behaviors can decrease the risk of acquiring an STI. Safer sex behaviors include knowing your partner's STI history, being in a monogamous sexual relationship, using condoms and barriers for all sexual activity, and avoiding alcohol use (see Chapter 10, Sex in Real Life, "Safer-Sex Behavior Guidelines," on page 323).

- Unprotected sexual intercourse without the use of a male or female condom unless this occurs in a long-term, single-partner, monogamous relationship in which both partners have been tested for STIs
- Engaging in oral sex with a male or female partner without using a condom or dental dam unless this occurs in a long-term, single-partner, monogamous relationship in which both partners have been tested for STIs
- Engaging in sexual intercourse prior to age 18
- Having multiple sex partners
- Engaging in sexual intercourse with a partner who has multiple sex partners
- Engaging in anal sex without a condom
- Engaging in sexual activity with a partner who has anal sex with multiple sex partners
- Engaging in oral sex with a partner who has multiple sex partners
- Engaging in sexual activity with a partner who has ever injected drugs
- Engaging in sex work or sexual activity with a partner who has ever engaged in sex work
- Engaging in sexual activity with a partner who has a history of STIs
- Engaging in sexual activity with a partner with an unknown STI history

---

haviors that put them at risk, such as having multiple partners and not always using condoms (see the accompanying Sex in Real Life, "High-Risk Sexual Behaviors," for more information).

The truth is that young adults are disproportionately affected by STIs, and the incidence of STIs continues to grow in this population (vonSadovszky et al., 2002). Studies have found 40% of sexually active young women have had an STI (Bunnell et al., 1999) and two-thirds of all STIs occurred in individuals under 25 years old (Hatcher et al., 2004). More frightening still is that adolescents are more biologically at risk for developing an STI (Santelli et al., 1999). Research has found that the cervix of a teenage girl is more vulnerable to certain STIs than the cervix of an adult woman (Centers for Disease Control and Prevention, 2005d). Even so, adolescent females often do not believe they are at risk for contracting a sexually transmitted infection (Ethier et al., 2003).

Review Question

Define the punishment concept of disease, and explain how it might protect a person from the fear of contracting an STI.

SEX Talk

Question: How did STIs start? I have heard it was from having sex with animals. Is this true?

Everyone has different theories on how STIs started. Some claim that it was a punishment for being sexually active; others thought that it was a result of promiscuity. We know that sexually transmitted infections are caused by bacteria and viruses. A person who comes into contact with these bacteria and viruses is at risk of developing an STI. We do not know where these different infectious agents came from, just as we do not know where the common cold virus or the flu originated.

All states (and the District of Columbia) require that syphilis, gonorrhea, chancroid, chlamydia, the human immunodeficiency virus (HIV), and the acquired immune deficiency syndrome (AIDS) be reported to public health centers. In addition, many states require reporting cases of genital herpes and genital warts. Reporting these infections helps to identify disease trends and communities that may be at high risk. However, because many states offer anonymous HIV testing and non–FDA-approved home tests may be used, it is nearly impossible to know the actual total of HIV infections in the United States.

Overall, women tend to be more susceptible to gonorrhea, chlamydia, and HIV, although the spread of syphilis and genital warts is usually shared equally between the sexes (although the prevalence of HIV was higher in men in the late 1980s, women are still more susceptible if they have sexual intercourse with an infected male partner). Studies have found that women are at greater risk for long-term complications from STIs because the tissue of the vagina is much more fragile than the skin covering the penis. In addition, many more women are **asymptomatic;** therefore, they do not know that they are infected. Some infections, such as herpes and HIV, also have properties of **latency.** A person can have the virus that causes the disease but not have symptoms, and tests may even show up negative. As a result, the person may be unaware that he or she is infecting others.

STIs can adversely affect pregnancy as well. In fact, certain untreated STIs, such as syphilis, gonorrhea, chlamydia, herpes, hepatitis B, and HIV, can cause problems such as miscarriage, stillbirth, early onset of labor, premature rupture of the amniotic sac, mental retardation, and fetal or uterine infection (Centers for Disease Control and Prevention, 2005d). From 30% to 40% of preterm births and infant deaths are due to STIs (Goldenberg et al., 1999). Some STIs, like syphilis, can cross the placenta and infect a developing fetus, whereas other STIs, such as gonorrhea, chlamydia, and herpes, can infect a newborn as he or she moves through the vagina during delivery. HIV can cross the placenta, infect a newborn at birth, or, unlike other STIs, can be transmitted during breast-feeding (Arias et al., 2003).

Bacterial STIs can be treated during pregnancy with antibiotics, and if treatment is begun immediately there is less chance the newborn will become infected. Viral infections cannot be treated, but antiviral medications can be given to pregnant women to lessen the symptoms of these infections (Centers for Disease Control and Prevention, 2005d). If there are active vaginal lesions or sores from an STI, a healthcare provider may recommend a cesarean section delivery. Women who do not know their partner's STI history should always use latex condoms during pregnancy.

asymptomatic
Without recognizable symptoms.

latency
A period in which a person is infected with an STI but does not test positive for it.

Question: How can you know whether your partners have any STIs before becoming sexual with them?

You should ask your partner, prior to any sexual involvement, whether or not he or she has had or currently has an STI. You can also check his or her genitals prior to engaging in sex. Look for open sores or scarring on the penis, lips, vulva, or anus. You can also get tested for STIs to determine whether or not you have been exposed. But keep in mind that many STIs do not have any symptoms and that there is no way to know for sure whether or not your partner has an STI. Making sure you are both tested, prior to sexual behavior, is the best bet.

There are also some racial/ethnic differences in STIs. Though STIs occur in all racial and ethnic groups, African Americans have higher rates of most STIs than whites and Hispanics. Gonorrhea and syphilis are as much as 44 times higher in African Americans than whites. These differences may partially be due to the fact that African

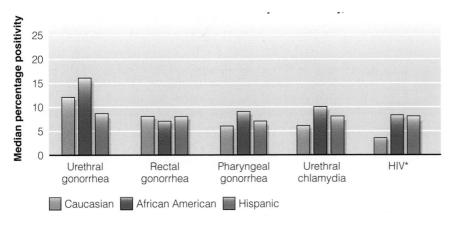

Figure 15.1
Test positivity for gonorrhea, chlamydia, and HIV among men who have sex with men, by race/ethnicity, United States, 2004.
Source: Centers for Disease Control and Prevention, 2005d.

*Excludes persons previously known to be HIV-positive.

Americans are more likely to be treated in public clinics, which are more likely to report STIs. Even so, this can't explain all of these ethnic and racial differences in STI rates. Other factors, such as access to health care, the ability to seek help, poverty, and sexual practices are also responsible for some of the rate disparities (Laumann & Youm, 2001).

Over the last several decades the rates of HIV infection have declined in men who have sex with men (MSM). However, there have been increased rates of gonorrhea, syphilis, and chlamydia reported in HIV-infected MSM (Centers for Disease Control and Prevention, 2005d). Researchers believe that STI increases in men who have sex with men are due to several factors, including a decreased fear of acquiring HIV; an increase in high-risk sexual behaviors, including oral sex; a lack of knowledge about STIs; increased Internet access to sexual partners; and the increased use of Viagra as a recreational drug (which would increase and prolong erection; Ciesielski, 2003). See Figure 15.1 for more information on STIs in men who have sex with men.

Although there have been few studies that have examined the incidence of STIs in women who have sex with women (WSW), we do know that several STIs can be transmitted during vulva-to-vulva sex, including hepatitis C (Fethers et al., 2000); herpes (Johnson et al., 1992); trichomoniasis (Kellock & O'Mahony, 1996); human papillomavirus (O'Hanlan & Crum, 1996); and HIV (Troncoso et al., 1995). In addition, bacterial vaginosis (BV) was found to be more common in WSW (Fethers et al., 2000). Overall, however, lesbian couples are more likely to have fewer sexual partners and engage in less penetrative sex, which reduces their risk of STI infection. Bisexual women, on the other hand, are more likely to have multiple partners and an increased risk of STI infection (Koh et al., 2005; Morrow & Allsworth, 2000). Compared to heterosexuals and bisexuals, lesbians are less likely to obtain regular STI testing or yearly pelvic exams, probably because they believe they are both less at risk and do not need contraception (Bauer & Welles, 2001).

For those who do need contraception, birth control methods offer varying levels of protection from sexually transmitted infections. In 1993, the FDA approved labeling contraceptives for STI protection. Barrier methods, such as condoms, diaphragms, or contraceptive sponges, can decrease the risk of acquiring an STI. Although contraceptive-using African American women in the United States have been found to use effective birth control methods, they do not typically use methods that protect against the spread of disease (Wyatt et al., 2000).

As we discussed in Chapter 13, although we used to believe that nonoxynol-9 (N-9) spermicide was the most effective at reducing the risk of acquiring an STI, today there is good evidence that N-9 does not protect against STIs and may, in fact, increase the rate of genital ulceration, causing a higher risk of STI infection (Boonstra, 2005; Richardson, 2002; Wilkinson et al., 2002b). (See Chapter 13 for more information on nonoxynol-9.) N-9 may also increase the risk for HIV transmission during both vaginal and anal sex (Jain et al., 2005). The intrauterine device

TABLE 15.1	Rates of Sexually Transmitted Infections, United States, 2004*	

STI	Rate of Infection
Syphilis (primary and secondary only)	7,980
Gonorrhea	330,132
Chancroid	30
Chlamydia	929,462
Estimated number of total AIDS cases in adults and children through 2004	944,306
Herpes	296,000
Human papillomavirus	316,000
Trichomoniasis (female only)	221,000
Other vaginitis	3,602,000

*The rates for syphilis, gonorrhea, chancroid, chlamydia, and AIDS were taken from the Centers for Disease Control and Prevention's database of nationally reported sexually transmitted infections—however, this does not include all cases because many go unreported. The rates for herpes, human papillomavirus, trichomoniasis, and other vaginitis are not reported nationally, so the statistics shown here represent U.S. visits to healthcare providers for these sexually transmitted diseases.
Sources: Centers for Disease Control and Prevention, 2004b, 2005b, 2005d; UNAIDS, 2005b.

Review Question

Explain how age, gender, and racial/ethnic differences may affect STI rates. How do contraceptive methods and nonoxynol-9 affect the transmission of STIs?

sex byte

It has been found that approximately 25% of men and 40% of women infected with gonorrhea are also infected with chlamydia (Cates, 2004).

(IUD) offers no protection against STIs and increases the risk of pelvic inflammatory disease (PID) in those at risk for STIs (Steen & Shapiro, 2004).

Condoms are the most effective contraceptive method for reducing the risk of acquiring an STI. For example, one study found that there was a significant decrease in the incidence of bacterial STIs in Thailand after a 100% condom policy was instituted for its prostitutes (Steen, 2001). Condoms do have limitations, however; they cannot always protect the vulva or parts of the penis or scrotum that are not covered.

The role of oral contraceptives in preventing STIs is complicated. The increased hormones change the cervical mucus and the lining of the uterus, which can help prevent any infectious substance from moving up into the genital tract. In addition, the reduced buildup of the endometrium decreases the possibility of an infectious substance growing (because there is less nutritive material for bacteria to survive). However, oral contraceptives may also cause the cervix to be more susceptible to infections because of changes in the vaginal environment.

Sexually transmitted infections can be caused by several different agents, some of which are bacterial, others viral. The causal agents are important in treating STIs. The most effective way of avoiding STI transmission is to abstain from oral, vaginal, and anal sex or to be in a long-term, mutually monogamous relationship with someone who is free from STIs.

SEX Talk

Question: Can STIs be transmitted through oral sex?

If there are open sores on the penis or vulva, it is possible that an STI may be transmitted to the mouth through oral sex. If there are active cold sores on the mouth or lips and a person performs oral sex, it is possible to transmit the virus to the genitals. Oral sex with a partner infected with gonorrhea or chlamydia may cause an infection in the throat. As for the AIDS virus, some researchers have found that oral sex is an unlikely method of transmission for the virus (Kohn et al., 2002), whereas others have found that HIV transmission through oral sex is possible (Centers for Disease Control and Prevention, 2003a).

Ectoparasitic Infections: Pubic Lice and Scabies

Ectoparasitic infections are those that are caused by parasites that live on the skin's surface. The two ectoparasitic infections that are sexually transmitted are pubic lice and scabies.

Pubic Lice

pubic lice
A parasitic STI that infests the pubic hair and can be transmitted through sexual contact; also called crabs.

Pubic lice (or "crabs") are a parasitic STI; the lice are very small, wingless insects that can attach themselves to pubic hair with their claws. They feed off the tiny blood vessels just beneath the skin and are often difficult to detect on light-skinned people. Under closer observation, it is possible to see the movement of their legs. They may also attach themselves to other hairy parts of the body, although they tend to prefer pubic hair. When not attached to the human body, pubic lice cannot survive more than 24 hours. However, they reproduce rapidly, and the female cements her eggs to the sides of pubic hair. The eggs hatch in 7 to 9 days, and the newly hatched nits (baby pubic lice) reproduce within 17 days.

Incidence   Pubic lice are common and regularly seen by health clinics and various healthcare providers. Although there are no mandated reporting laws, pubic lice affect millions of people worldwide.

Symptoms   The most common symptom is a mild to unbearable itching, which often increases during the evening hours. This itching is thought to be a result of an allergic reaction to the saliva that the lice secrete during their feeding. People who are not allergic to this saliva may not experience any itching.

Diagnosis   The itching usually forces a person to seek treatment, though some people detect the lice visually first. Diagnosis is usually made fairly quickly because the pubic lice and eggs can be seen with the naked eye.

Treatment   To treat pubic lice, it is necessary to kill both the insects and their eggs. In addition, the eggs must be destroyed on sheets and clothing. Healthcare providers can prescribe Kwell ointment, which comes in a shampoo or cream. The cream must be applied directly to the pubic hair and left on for approximately 12 hours, whereas the shampoo can be applied and directly rinsed off. There are also some fairly effective over-the-counter products that can be purchased in drugstores; however, these products are usually not as effective as Kwell. Sheets and all articles of clothing should be either dry cleaned, boiled, or machine washed in very hot water. As with the other STIs, it is important to tell all sexual partners to be checked for lice because they are highly contagious.

The Wellcome Medical Photo Library, London

Pubic lice attach to pubic hair and feed off the tiny blood vessels beneath the skin.

SEX Talk

Question: Can crabs be spread through casual contact, such as sleeping on the same sheets or sharing clothes? What if someone with crabs sat on my couch and I sat down right after them?

If you slept in the bed of a person who was infected with pubic lice, or wore the same clothes without washing them, there is a chance that you could become infected. Although crabs are usually spread through sexual contact, it is possible to acquire them if you share towels, linens, articles of clothing, combs and brushes, or toilet seats with a person who is infected. They can also be transferred while sharing a bed, even if there is no sexual contact.

Scabies

Scabies is an ectoparasitic infection of the skin with the mite *Sarcoptes scabiei*. It is spread during skin-to-skin contact, both during sexual and nonsexual contact. The mites can live for up to 48 hours on bedsheets and clothing and are impossible to see with the naked eye.

Incidence   Infection with scabies occurs worldwide and among all races, ethnic groups, and social classes. Like pubic lice, there are no mandated reporting laws, but scabies affects millions of people worldwide (Schleicher & Stewart, 1997).

Symptoms   Usually the first symptoms include a rash and intense itching. The first time a person is infected, the symptoms may take between 4 and 6 weeks to develop. If a person has been infected with scabies before, the symptoms usually develop more quickly.

Diagnosis   A diagnosis can usually be made on examination of the skin rash. A skin scraping can be done to confirm the diagnosis. However, it is easy to miss a scabies infection, as there are usually fewer than 10 mites on an entire body during infestation (Centers for Disease Control and Prevention, 2005b).

scabies
A parasitic STI that affects the skin and is spread during skin-to-skin contact, both during sexual and nonsexual contact.

Review Question

Identify the sexually transmitted infections that are caused by ectoparasites. Explain the incidence, symptoms, diagnosis, and treatment of these infections.

gonorrhea
A bacterial STI that causes a puslike discharge and frequent urination in men; many women are asymptomatic.

Treatment Topical creams are available to treat scabies. All bedsheets, clothing, and towels must be washed in hot water, and all sexual partners should be treated. Usually itching continues for 2 to 3 weeks after infection, even after treatment.

Bacterial Infections: Gonorrhea, Syphilis, Chlamydia, and More

Some sexually transmitted infections are caused by bacteria, including gonorrhea, syphilis, chlamydia, chancroid, and a variety of vaginal infections.

Gonorrhea

Gonorrhea (the "clap" or "drip") is caused by the bacterium *Neisseria gonorrhoeae*, which can survive only in the mucous membranes of the body. These areas, such as the cervix, urethra, mouth, throat, rectum, and even the eyes, provide moisture and warmth that help the bacterium survive. *Neisseria gonorrhoeae* is actually very fragile and can be destroyed by exposure to light, air, soap, water, or a change in temperature, and so it is nearly impossible to transmit gonorrhea nonsexually. The only exception to this is the transmission of gonorrhea from a mother to her baby as the baby passes through the vagina during delivery. Transmission of gonorrhea occurs when mucous membranes come into contact with each other; this can occur during sexual intercourse, oral sex, vulva-to-vulva sex, and anal sex.

Incidence Gonorrhea is the second most commonly reported infectious disease in the United States (chlamydia, which we will discuss shortly, is the first). Gonorrhea rates have dropped significantly over the last 30 years. In fact, there were over 1 million new cases of gonorrhea each year from 1976 to 1980 but only 330,000 cases in 2004 (Centers for Disease Control and Prevention, 2005d). Each year, there are between 600,000 and 1 million new cases. Overall, U.S. gonorrhea rates have been declining, and today the highest rates of gonorrhea are among those 25 years old and younger (Fortenberry, 2002). Racial differences have been found, and African Americans account for close to 80% of all gonorrhea cases (Maldonado, 1999). There have also been differences in gonorrhea rates in different parts of the United States. For example, rates are highest in parts of the South and lowest in the North (see Figure 15.2).

Symptoms The majority of women who are infected with gonorrhea are asymptomatic and do not know that they are carrying the disease; however, they are still able to infect their partners. In women, the cervix is the most common site of infection, and a pus-filled cervical discharge may develop. If there are any symptoms, they develop within 3 to 5 days and include an increase in urinary frequency, abnormal uterine bleeding, and bleeding after sexual intercourse, which results from an irritation of the cervix. The cervical discharge can irritate the vaginal lining, causing pain and discomfort. Urination can be difficult and painful. (This is different from the pain caused by a urinary tract infection—see Chapter 4). If left untreated, gonorrhea can move up into the uterus and Fallopian tubes, and may lead to pelvic inflammatory disease (PID, which we'll discuss later in this chapter).

Approximately 25% of infected men are asymptomatic, although they are still able to transmit the disease to their partners (Cates, 2004). When a man experiences symptoms, these would include **epididymitis** (epp-pih-did-ee-MITE-us), urethral discharge, painful urination, and an increase in the frequency and urgency of urination. Symptoms usually appear between 2 and 6 days after infection.

Rectal gonorrhea, which can be transmitted to men and women during anal intercourse, may cause bloody stools and a puslike discharge. If left untreated, gonorrhea can move throughout the body and settle in various areas, including the joints, causing swelling, pain, and pus-filled infections.

epididymitis
An inflammation of the epididymis in men, usually resulting from STIs.

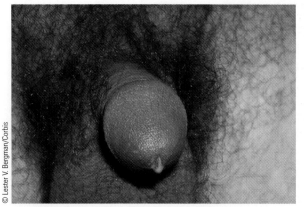

The majority of men infected with gonorrhea experience symptoms and will seek out treatment. However, this may not happen until they have already infected others.

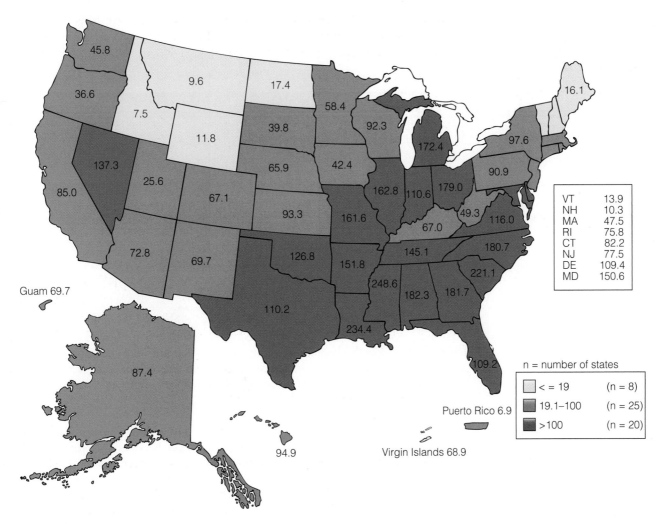

Figure 15.2
Gonorrhea rates per 100,000 population by state, United States and outlying areas, 2004.
Source: Centers for Disease Control and Prevention, 2005d.

VT	13.9
NH	10.3
MA	47.5
RI	75.8
CT	82.2
NJ	77.5
DE	109.4
MD	150.6

Guam 69.7

Puerto Rico 6.9

Virgin Islands 68.9

n = number of states

	< = 19	(n = 8)
	19.1–100	(n = 25)
	>100	(n = 20)

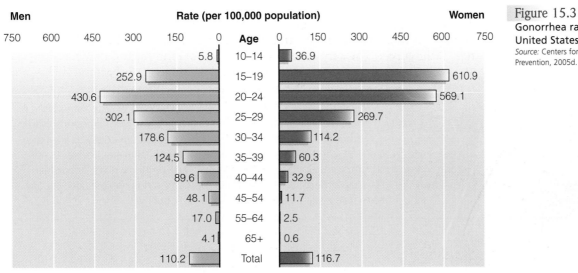

Men **Rate (per 100,000 population)** **Women**

Men	Age	Women
5.8	10–14	36.9
252.9	15–19	610.9
430.6	20–24	569.1
302.1	25–29	269.7
178.6	30–34	114.2
124.5	35–39	60.3
89.6	40–44	32.9
48.1	45–54	11.7
17.0	55–64	2.5
4.1	65+	0.6
110.2	Total	116.7

Figure 15.3
Gonorrhea rates by age and sex, United States, 2004.
Source: Centers for Disease Control and Prevention, 2005d.

Figure 15.4

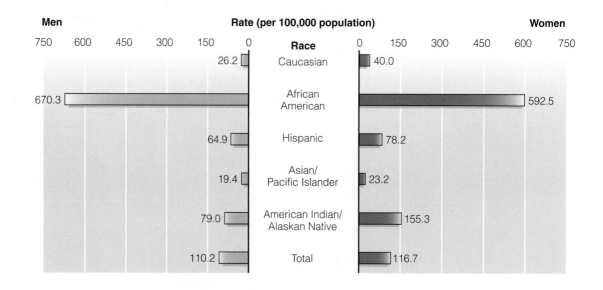

Figure 15.4
Gonorrhea rates by race/ethnicity and sex, United States, 2004.
Source: Centers for Disease Control and Prevention, 2005d.

Men Rate (per 100,000 population)	Race	Women
26.2	Caucasian	40.0
670.3	African American	592.5
64.9	Hispanic	78.2
19.4	Asian/ Pacific Islander	23.2
79.0	American Indian/ Alaskan Native	155.3
110.2	Total	116.7

gonococcus bacterium
The bacterium that causes gonorrhea (*Neisseria gonorrhoeae*).

Review Question

Explain the incidence, symptoms, diagnosis, and treatment of gonorrhea.

sex byte

The human papillomavirus, trichomoniasis, and chlamydia account for 88% of all new STI cases among 15- to 24-year-olds (Weinstock, Berman, & Cates, 2004).

Diagnosis   Testing for gonorrhea involves collecting a sample of the discharge from the cervix, urethra, or another infected area with a cotton swab. The discharge is incubated to allow the bacteria to multiply. It is then put on a slide and examined under a microscope for the presence of the **gonococcus bacterium.** Recently DNA testing using a person's urine has become the gold standard for gonorrhea testing (Hawthorne, Farber, & Bibbo, 2005).

Treatment   Gonorrhea can be treated effectively with antibiotics, either orally or via injection. However, some strains of gonorrhea have become resistant to certain antibiotics and other drugs must be used (Schwebke, 1991). Many sex partners of persons who test positive for gonorrhea are not treated, which can lead to reinfection and further infection of others (Golden et al., 2005).

Every once in awhile the Centers for Disease Control and Prevention locate a few cases of drug-resistant gonorrhea in the United States. Most recently this occurred in Michigan, when several drug-resistant cases of gonorrhea were reported to the CDC (Macomber et al., 2005). This had also happened in the 1980s, when gonorrhea became resistant to penicillin (the most common drug treatment at the time). Although uncommon, it is not unheard of for strains of infectious diseases to mutate and become drug resistant over time.

SEX Talk

Question: What STIs do gynecologists check for during a regular exam?

During a woman's yearly visit, healthcare providers perform a Pap testing, which is designed to evaluate the cervical cells. Although it is possible that some STIs, such as cervical warts and herpes, may show up during Pap testing, many will not. If you think that you may have been exposed to any STIs, it is important for you to ask your healthcare provider to perform specific tests to screen for these. Specific tests can be run for syphilis, gonorrhea, chlamydia, herpes, genital warts, or HIV. All sexually active young people (under the age of 25) should have a chlamydia test performed annually (Couldwell, 2005).

Syphilis

syphilis
A bacterial STI that is divided into primary, secondary, and tertiary stages.

Syphilis is caused by an infection with the bacterium *Treponema pallidum*. Like *Neisseria gonorrhoeae*, these bacteria can live only in the mucous membranes of the body. The bacteria enter the body through small tears in the skin and are able to replicate themselves.

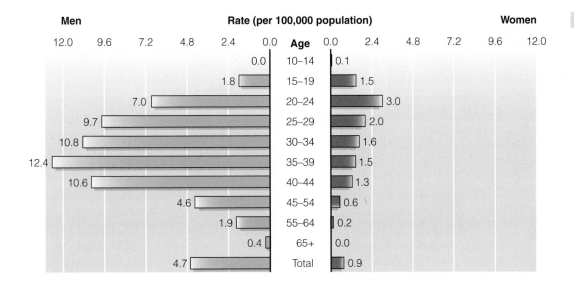

Figure 15.5
Primary and secondary
syphilis rates by age and
sex, United States, 2004.
Source: Centers for Disease Control
and Prevention, 2005d.

Syphilis is transmitted during sexual contact, and it usually first infects the cervix, penis, anus, lips, or nipples. **Congenital syphilis** may also be transmitted via the placenta during the first or second trimester of pregnancy.

congenital syphilis
A syphilis infection acquired by an infant from the mother during pregnancy.

Incidence Syphilis rates decreased in 1990, and in 2000 were the lowest since reporting began in 1941. However, rates began to increase again in 2002, mostly among men who were having sex with men (Centers for Disease Control and Prevention, 2005d). In 2004 there were 7,980 cases of primary and secondary syphilis reported (see Table 15.1 and Figure 15.5).

Like gonorrhea, syphilis rates differ geographically, with lower rates in the Midwest and higher rates in the South. There are also racial and ethnic variations, with higher rates in African Americans (see Figure 15.6 for more information on syphilis and race/ethnic groups).

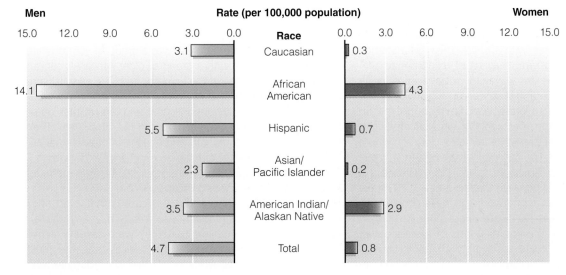

Figure 15.6
Primary and secondary syphilis rates by race/ethnicity and sex, United States, 2004.
Source: Centers for Disease Control and Prevention, 2005d.

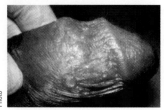

The chancre, which appears on the underside of the penis in this photo, is the classic painless ulcer of syphilis.

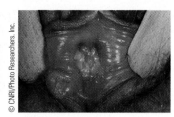

Typical syphilis chancre on a woman's labia.

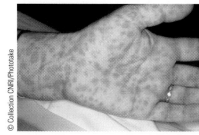

A secondary syphilis infection produces rashes on the palms and/or soles of the feet, as well as a generalized body rash.

chancre
A small, red-brown sore that results from syphilis infection; the sore is actually the site at which the bacteria entered the body.

Symptoms   Infection with syphilis is divided into three stages. The first stage of infection, primary or early syphilis, occurs anywhere from 10 to 90 days after infection (typically this happens within 2 to 6 weeks). During this stage, there may be one or more small, red-brown sores, called chancres, that appear on the vulva, penis, vagina, cervix, anus, mouth, or lips. The **chancre** (SHANK-ker), which is a round sore with a hard raised edge and a sunken center, is usually painless and does not itch. If left untreated, the chancre will heal in 3 to 8 weeks. However, during this time the person can still transmit the disease to other sexual partners.

Once the chancre disappears, the infected person enters into the second stage, secondary syphilis, which begins anywhere from 3 to 6 weeks after the chancre has healed. During this stage, the syphilis invades the central nervous system. The infected person develops reddish patches on the skin that look like a rash or hives. There may also be wartlike growths in the area of infection (Brown & Frank, 2003). If the rash develops on the scalp, hair loss can also occur. The lymph glands in the groin, armpit, neck, or other areas enlarge and become tender. Additional symptoms at this stage include headaches, fevers, anorexia, flulike symptoms, and fatigue.

In the third and final stage of the disease, tertiary or late syphilis, the disease goes into remission. The rash, fever, and other symptoms go away, and the person usually feels fine. He or she is still able to transmit the disease for about 1 year, but after this time the person is no longer infectious. Left untreated, however, tertiary or late syphilis can cause neurological, sensory, muscular, and psychological difficulties and is eventually fatal. Syphilis causes more severe symptoms and progresses much more quickly in patients who have been diagnosed with HIV (Gregory et al., 1990).

Diagnosis   Anyone who develops a chancre should immediately go to a healthcare provider to be tested for the presence of the syphilis-causing bacteria. This diagnosis can be made in several ways. A culture can be taken from one of the lesions and microscop-

SEX in Real Life

The Lost Children of Rockdale County

In 1996, in a small suburb of Atlanta, a school nurse reported an increasing number of teenagers who were infected with syphilis. This was a strange occurrence because, as you may recall, experts had predicted that syphilis was on its way to virtual elimination in the United States. The number of teenagers testing positive for syphilis continued to grow, and slowly public health workers realized that the infected teens were all interacting sexually together. First six white females (four of whom were under the age of 16), two white males (both 17 years old), and two African-American males (ages 19 and 16) were diagnosed with syphilis (Rothenberg et al., 1998). By piecing together the social networks of these adolescents, researchers realized that the sexual interactions had begun at least 1 year before the first diagnosis of syphilis (when STIs occur, researchers use social network tools to help them understand recent outbreaks). Upon investigation, researchers found that underground experimental sex and drug/alcohol use in a group of teenagers in Rockdale

County was wildly spreading syphilis among the participants (Loftus, 2001).

The center of the outbreak was a group of young white girls who often met with a group of older African-American and white boys at one of the teens' homes. The parents were usually working or out of the home. During the sexual interactions the girls would have oral, anal, and vaginal intercourse with many of the boys, often in front of the other teens. Then they would all swap partners and engage in other sexual behaviors. Oftentimes the girls would experience a "sandwich," which involved giving a boy oral sex while being penetrated anally and vaginally by two other boys.

What is interesting about this case is that even after some of the girls were diagnosed with STIs, many of their parents refused to believe that they were sexually active (Loftus, 2001). They convinced themselves that they must have become infected from some other way. Many experts believe that the parents' and teens' "disconnect" may not be that rare today, especially when talking about sex.

ically examined. Today the most common tests used for the detection of syphilis are blood tests. These tests check for the presence of antibodies, which develop once a person is infected with the bacteria. During late syphilis, blood tests may be negative or weakly positive even if the infection exists (Lowhagen, 1990). If a person thinks that he or she may have been exposed to syphilis but tests negative, he or she should engage only in safer-sex activity and consult with his or her healthcare provider immediately.

Treatment   Although there have been several different treatments for syphilis over the years, penicillin is the treatment of choice today (Centers for Disease Control and Prevention, 2002a). The dosage and length of treatment depend on the stage of illness and severity of symptoms. Antibiotics may cause a temporary increase in fever or symptoms, which subsides in a few hours. Follow-up examinations may be done in 6 to 12 months if necessary. Many physicians today recommend HIV tests and counseling for patients who have syphilis.

Chlamydia and Nongonococcal Urethritis

Chlamydia is the common name for infections caused by a bacterium called *Chlamydia trachomatis*. Risk factors for chlamydia are similar to those for other STIs and include multiple sexual partners, a partner who has had multiple sexual partners, being under age 25, inconsistent use of barrier contraceptives (such as condoms), and a history of STIs. Chlamydia can be transmitted during vaginal intercourse, oral, or anal sex.

The bacterium that causes chlamydia can also cause epididymitis and **nongonococcal urethritis (NGU)** in men. In fact, chlamydia has been found to cause 50% of all cases of NGU (Kassler & Cates, 1992). NGU may also be caused by the trichomoniasis or herpes organism; however, 40% of the cases of NGU seem to have no direct cause (Baldassare, 1991).

Incidence   Chlamydia is the most commonly reported infectious disease in the United States and is also the most commonly diagnosed bacterial STI in the developed world (Gilson & Mindel, 2001; see Figure 15.7). In 2004 there were 929,462 new cases of chlamydia reported, although experts believe that the majority of cases went unreported (Centers for Disease Control and Prevention, 2005d). It is estimated there are closer to 2.8 million new cases of chlamydia each year (Weinstock et al., 2004). Chlamydia affects all socioeconomic and ethnic groups and is highest among African Americans (see Figure 15.8). Chlamydia rates are also higher in younger women than in younger men (see Figure 15.7). However, this may be because screening programs have been primarily aimed at women. Chlamydia infection in men is underdiagnosed, and ex-

chlamydia
A bacterial STI; although often asymptomatic, it is thought to be one of the most damaging of all the STIs.

nongonococcal urethritis (NGU)
Urethral infection in men that is usually caused by an infection with chlamydia.

Review Question

Explain the incidence, symptoms, diagnosis, and treatment of syphilis.

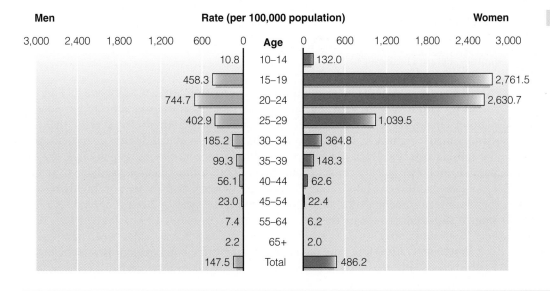

Men						Rate (per 100,000 population)		Age						Women
3,000	2,400	1,800	1,200	600	0		0		600	1,200	1,800	2,400	3,000	
					10.8		10–14	132.0						
				458.3			15–19						2,761.5	
			744.7				20–24						2,630.7	
				402.9			25–29			1,039.5				
					185.2		30–34	364.8						
					99.3		35–39	148.3						
					56.1		40–44	62.6						
					23.0		45–54	22.4						
					7.4		55–64	6.2						
					2.2		65+	2.0						
					147.5		Total		486.2					

Figure 15.7
Chlamydia rates by age and sex, United States, 2004.
Source: Centers for Disease Control and Prevention, 2005d.

Figure 15.8
Chlamydia rates by race/ethnicity
and sex, United States, 2004.
Source: Centers for Disease Control
and Prevention, 2005d.

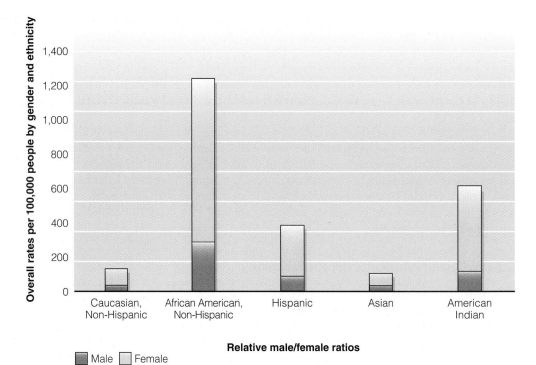

Relative male/female ratios

■ Male □ Female

A baby exposed to a chlamydial infection in the birth canal
during delivery may develop
an eye infection. Symptoms
include a bloody discharge
and swollen eyelids.

sexbyte

Male circumcision has been found to
reduce the risk of acquiring chlamydia
infection in female sexual partners
(Castellsague et al., 2005).

perts claim that if men were routinely screened, the rates for men and women would be more similar (Ku et al., 2002). Lesbians also are at risk for chlamydia, although it is most common in heterosexual populations (K. M. Freund, 1992).

Symptoms   In approximately 75% of women and 50% of men, chlamydia is asymptomatic (Centers for Disease Control and Prevention, 2005d). Those who do have symptoms usually develop them within 1 to 3 weeks after becoming infected. Even without symptoms, chlamydia is very contagious, which explains why rates are increasing.

Female symptoms can include burning during urination, pain during sexual intercourse, and pain in the lower abdomen. In most women, the cervix is the site of infection with chlamydia, and so cervical bleeding or spotting may occur. Some women do experience a vaginal discharge; however, this is rare and is more likely an indication of another STI (K. M. Freund, 1992). Male symptoms may include a discharge from the penis, burning sensation during urination, burning and itching around the opening of the penis, and a pain or swelling in the testicles. Men may also experience epididymitis (Baldassare, 1991).

In women, the bacteria can move up from the uterus to the Fallopian tubes and ovaries, leading to PID. In fact, infection with chlamydia is thought to be one of the agents most responsible for the development of PID (Terán et al., 2001). Women who are infected with cervical chlamydia and who undergo an elective (or possibly spontaneous) abortion or vaginal birth are also at increased risk of developing pelvic inflammatory disease (Boeke et al., 2005).

Diagnosis   Because chlamydia testing is not routine, women who have had unprotected sexual intercourse with several partners should ask their healthcare provider to perform chlamydia tests during their yearly physical examinations, even if they are asymptomatic. A healthcare provider will culture the cervical discharge and examine the cells microscopically or use a blood test. Blood tests are easier, more reliable, less expensive, and offer quicker results (Schachter, 1999). Urine tests are available to screen for chlamydia in men. The Centers for Disease Control and Prevention highly recommends annual screenings for all women between the ages of 20 and 25 and for older women with multiple sex partners.

Treatment   Antibiotics are used to treat chlamydia, but, like gonorrhea, chlamydia has become highly resistant. Antibiotics are usually taken for a certain period of time

Vaccines for Sexually Transmitted Infections?

A vaccine is a preparation that contains disease-causing organisms, or parts of organisms, that cause a person to have immunity against the disease. Our bodies' immune response to the organisms causes the development of antibodies, which prevent future infections. Many successful vaccines, including smallpox and polio, have been developed throughout history.

As of 2005, the hepatitis A and B vaccinations were the only vaccine available for the prevention of STI complications (Mays et al., 2004). Vaccinations for hepatitis B are administered at birth and are recommended for children throughout the United States, whereas vaccinations for hepatitis A are recommended only in certain areas (Centers for Disease Control and Prevention, 2005c). There are currently a variety of STI vaccines in different stages of development, the most promising of which targets two types of human papillomavirus that have been found to cause 60% to 70% of cervical cancers (Brody, 2005; Harper et al., 2004; Koutsky et al., 2002). In research trials, this vaccination has been found to be 100% effective, and experts are hopeful that it will be available to the public sometime in 2006. After the HPV vaccine is approved for use, a panel of experts at the Centers for Disease Control and Prevention will determine whether it will be a mandatory childhood vaccination (Stein, 2005).

However, there is some controversy over the vaccines for sexually transmitted infections. One involves who should be vaccinated. In the case of the HPV vaccine, should this be given only to girls, because boys are not at risk for developing cervical cancer? Or should boys be given the vaccination because they help spread HPV? Experts believe that both boys and girls should be given the vaccination.

Another controversy involves the fact that STI vaccines will need to be given early in a child's life, well before the child is sexually active. In fact, the ideal group to be immunized with the HPV vaccine are non–sexually active girls and boys between the ages of 9 and 15 (Taira et al., 2004). Some healthcare advocates believe that the HPV vaccine should be used aggressively to decrease the incidence of cervical cancer (Stein, 2005). However, many conservatives believe that vaccinating young children will promote sexual promiscuity (Phung, 2005; Rubin, 2005; Stein, 2005).

The majority of parents of adolescents find STI vaccination for their children very acceptable (Liddon et al., 2005; Zimet et al., 2005). When parents were asked about the potential for accepting vaccines for genital herpes, the human immunodeficiency virus (HIV), the human papillomavirus (HPV), and gonorrhea for their 8- to 17-year-olds, more than 70% of parents approved (Mays et al., 2004). The HIV vaccination was the most acceptable, followed by vaccines for genital herpes, gonorrhea, and HPV (Mays et al., 2004). Research has also found that the majority of college students would be willing to get STI vaccinations if they were available (Boehner et al., 2003).

The search for STI vaccinations continues today. The National Institute of Allergy and Infectious Diseases has been sponsoring a study for the development of a vaccine for genital herpes, and research on vaccinations for other sexually transmitted infections, including gonorrhea, hepatitis C, and HIV, is ongoing (Harding, 2005; Hoshino et al., 2005; Oxman et al., 2005; Stanberry et al., 2005; Sternberg, 2004a). Later in this chapter we'll discuss the failure of the first AIDS vaccine to pass clinical trials in 2003. As of 2005, there were over 50 AIDS vaccine trials in progress (Chase, 2005).

(usually at least 7 to 10 days). An infected person's sexual partners over the 3 months prior to the diagnosis should be referred to a healthcare provider for treatment, whether or not they are experiencing symptoms. This is necessary to avoid reinfection, further complications, and the spread of chlamydia to others (Gilson & Mindel, 2001). Follow-up examinations are necessary only if a healthcare provider suspects a reinfection (Centers for Disease Control and Prevention, 2002a).

Chancroid

Although a **chancroid** (SHANK-kroyd) may look similar to a syphilis chancre, the difference lies in its soft edges compared with the hard edges of a syphilis sore. Chancroids are sexually transmitted through the *Hemophilus ducreyi* bacterium.

Incidence This STI is relatively rare in the United States (see Figure 15.1), but worldwide 7 million cases occur each year (Steen, 2001). The reported cases of chancroid in the United States were approximately 5,000 in 1987, but only 30 in 2004

Review Question

Explain the incidence, symptoms, diagnosis, and treatment of chlamydia.

chancroid
A bacterial STI characterized by small bumps that eventually rupture and form painful ulcers.

Personal Voices

"What Would You Do if Your Partner Told You He or She Had an STI?"

College students were asked about sexually transmitted infections. Many shared their experiences and what they would do if they found out someone they were interested in had an STI. Most said they would want to know well before the relationship became sexual but were unsure exactly how early in a relationship they would want to be told. Here are some of their thoughts.

Female: *My friend got genital warts from her first partner. When she dates she lets the guys know after a few weeks. Unfortunately, most run.*

Male: *If I ever dated someone and found out she had an STI, I think it would depend on the STI and how much I cared about her.*

Female: *If I were to meet someone and she told me that she had an STI, I'm not sure I'd stay. How much I like her would influence my decision.*

Male: *My girlfriend told me she had HPV before we became sexual. As hard as we tried to be safe, I was diagnosed with HPV a few months later. It was a difficult time, but I just was so glad that she had told me about it before we were having sex. At this point, we're fine with it and neither of us has frequent outbreaks.*

Female: *I have genital warts and I have had sex with partners without telling them about it. Sometimes it's just really hard to talk about and if I don't have an outbreak, I figure there's no reason to freak them out.*

Male: *If I met a girl that I liked and found out that she had an STI, I would probably stop whatever relationship we had. I would definitely not have any type of sexual contact with that person.*

Female: *If I was dating someone I was crazy about and he told me he had herpes, I would definitely not have sex with him. I wouldn't hold it against him though.*

Male: *I wouldn't break up with her, but I would definitely do a lot of research to make sure our sexual relationship was as safe as possible.*

Female: *If I was dating someone who told me he had an STI, I would be turned off. I would be afraid of catching it if we had sex. I really want to have children, and STIs can affect getting pregnant. I would end the relationship.*

Male: *I just started dating someone and I really like her. Telling her that I had [genital] herpes was the hardest thing I've ever had to do, but I wanted her to know before we started having sex. She was ok with it and really happy I told her. We use condoms and she does not have herpes.*

Female: *My current boyfriend has HPV, but he never knew it because warts never showed on his penis. I got a wart on my labia, and I found out he gave it to me. At first I was angry because I thought he cheated, but now I realized it could be dormant on a guy and he might not have symptoms.*

Male: *I think STIs are disgusting, and I think I would be clinically depressed for the rest of my life if I ever did get one. I am really "skeeved out" by the thought of an STI. For me, dating someone with an STI would be very difficult. Let's face it, relationships are difficult enough without STIs!*

SOURCE: Author's files.

(Centers for Disease Control and Prevention, 2005d). However, this bacterial infection is underreported, and many clinics do not have screening kits.

The majority of cases diagnosed in the United States involve a person who has traveled to a country where the disease is more common. Chancroid is one of the most prevalent STIs in many poor countries, such as those in Africa, Asia, and the Caribbean (Trees & Morse, 1995). In places where chancroid is common, the incidence in women is 25 times higher than in men (Trees & Morse, 1995) and higher in men who have multiple sexual partners (Crowe, 2002). Uncircumcised men are also more at risk than circumcised men (D. S. Lewis, 2000). Chancroid has also been found to be associated with HIV transmission and is common in areas with high rates of HIV.

Symptoms   Both women and men infected with chancroid develop a small lesion or several lesions at the point of entry. Four to 7 days after infection, a small lump appears and ruptures within 2 or 3 days, forming a shallow ulcer. These ulcers are painful, with ragged edges, and may persist for weeks and even months (D. A. Lewis, 2000). The infection may spread to the lymph nodes of the groin, which can cause swelling and pain.

Diagnosis   Diagnosis is often difficult, mainly because of difficulties culturing *Hemophilus ducreyi*, the responsible bacteria (Schulte et al., 1992). As a result, chancroid may be significantly underdiagnosed. A fluid sample from the ulcers is collected to examine for the presence of *Hemophilus ducreyi*.

Treatment   Chancroids are treated with antibiotics. Counseling about HIV and testing are often recommended because chancroids can increase the risk of HIV infection. Regular follow-ups are advisable until the ulcer is completely healed. All recent sexual contacts should be contacted for testing and treatment.

Review Question

Explain the incidence, symptoms, diagnosis, and treatment of chancroid.

Vaginal Infections

There are several common vaginal infections that may also be associated with sexual intercourse, including trichomoniasis, hemophilus, bacterial vaginosis, and candidiasis. All of these may cause a vaginal discharge, vulvar itching, and irritation and/or vaginal odor.

Trichomoniasis (trick-oh-mun-NYE-iss-sis; also called trich, or TV) is a form of vaginitis that is caused by *Trichomonas vaginalis*. Women can contract trichomoniasis from an infected man or woman, whereas a man usually contracts it only from an infected woman. Even though the actual number of women seeking healthcare visits for trichomoniasis is fairly low (see Table 15.1), experts estimate that there are 7.4 million new cases of trichomoniasis every year (Centers for Disease Control and Prevention, 2005). The organism is acquired through sexual activity, and symptoms usually appear anywhere from 3 to 28 days after infection.

trichomoniasis
A vaginal infection that may result in discomfort, discharge, and inflammation.

The most common symptom for women is an increase in vaginal discharge, which may be yellowish or green-yellow, frothy, and foul-smelling; it may cause a burning or itching sensation in the vagina. Some women are asymptomatic or have minimal symptoms (Centers for Disease Control and Prevention, 2002a). In men, the most common site of infection is the urethra, although trichomoniasis infection is often asymptomatic. If there are symptoms, there may be a slight increase in burning on the tip of the penis, mild discharge, or slight burning after urination or ejaculation.

The most common treatment for trichomoniasis is metronidazole (Flagyl), which can cause side effects such as nausea, headaches, loss of appetite, diarrhea, cramping, and a metallic taste in the mouth. Anyone taking this medication should not drink alcohol until 24 hours after treatment. It is recommended that all partners should be treated, and sex should be avoided until after treatment.

Bacterial vaginosis (BV) is the most common vaginal infection in women of childbearing age (Schwebke, 2000). Symptoms may include an increase in vaginal discharge and a fishy odor to the discharge. However, approximately half of infected women are asymptomatic. BV occurs when there is an overabundance of certain types of bacteria that are present normally in the vagina (Holzman et al., 2001). Overall, multiple sex partners, douching, and low concentrations of beneficial vaginal bacteria have been found to increase a woman's susceptibility to BV. In addition, research has found that occurrences of BV are more common in the first week of the menstrual cycle (Keane et al., 1997). Bacterial vaginosis rates vary by race and ethnicity—from 6% in Asians, 9% in Caucasians, 16% in Hispanics, and 23% in African Americans (Centers for Disease Control and Prevention, 2005d).

bacterial vaginosis (BV)
Bacterial infection that can cause vaginal discharge and odor but is often asymptomatic.

Women with BV have been found to have an increased risk of endometriosis and PID. Treatment is generally metronidazole or clindamycin, either orally or vaginally. As we discussed earlier, alcohol should be avoided during the course of treatment. Treatment of male sex partners has not been found to be beneficial in the treatment of BV.

vulvovaginal candiasis
A vaginal infection that causes a heavy discharge; also referred to as a yeast infection.

yeast infection
Vaginal infection that causes an increase in vaginal discharge, burning, and itching and may be sexually transmitted; also referred to as vulvovaginal candiasis.

Vulvovaginal candiasis (can-DIE-ass-sis; yeast infections, also called moniliasis or candidiasis) can be very troubling to women who are prone to them. **Yeast infections** can be difficult to get rid of, and recurrences are common. The infections are caused by a variety of different fungi, but one of the most common is *Candida albicans*. This fungus is normally present in the vagina, but it multiplies when the pH balance of the vagina is disturbed because of antibiotics, regular douching, pregnancy, oral contraceptive use, diabetes, or careless wiping after defecation (yeast is present in fecal material, and so it is important to make sure it does not come into contact with the vulva). Although yeast infections are not sexually transmitted, if a woman experiences multiple infections, her partner should be evaluated and treated with topical antifungal creams (Wilson, 2005). Men are less likely to have problems with yeast infections because the penis does not provide the warm and moist environment that the vagina does.

A yeast infection often causes burning, itching, and an increase in vaginal discharge. The discharge may be white, thin, and watery, and may include thick white chunks. It is estimated that 75% of women will experience a yeast infection at least once in their life, and 40% to 45% will have two or more yeast infections (Wilson, 2005).

Treatment includes either an antifungal prescription or over-the-counter drugs (such as Monistat, Gyne-Lotrim, or Mycelex), which are applied topically on the vulva and are inserted into the vagina. However, research has shown that a widespread use of these over-the-counter antifungal medications has caused a large increase in recurrent infections (MacNeill & Carey, 2001). Perhaps this is because many women misdiagnose their symptoms; one study found that 67% of women who thought they had a yeast infection were wrong (Crow, 1999). Misuse of over-the-counter drugs can contribute to medication-resistant strains of yeast.

Plain yogurt may provide relief to women suffering from a yeast infection. The yogurt can be applied to the outside of the vulva, and a tampon can be dipped into the yogurt and inserted into the vagina. Eating one cup of yogurt daily can also sometimes reduce recurrences. **Lactobacillus,** a type of "good" bacteria found in the vagina of healthy women, is also present in yogurt and can help the vagina to produce more of it.

Lactobacillus
Bacterium in the vagina that helps maintain appropriate pH levels.

Review Question

Differentiate among the common vaginal infections, including trichomoniasis, hemophilus, bacterial vaginosis, and vulvovaginal candiasis. Explain symptoms and treatments for each.

SEX Talk

Question: I have a vaginal discharge that is yellowish white, but there is no odor. I think it's a yeast infection because it's kind of itchy. Should I use an over-the-counter cream?

Remember that having a discharge doesn't always mean that you have a vaginal infection. Normal vaginal discharge can range from white to slightly yellow, and it varies throughout the menstrual cycle. If it is thick, chunky, clearly yellow to green, or smells fishy, get it checked out by your healthcare provider. Many women mistake bacterial vaginosis for a yeast infection. Like a yeast infection, bacterial vaginosis can sometimes be triggered by the use of antibiotics or the use of feminine hygiene products. Over-the-counter medications for yeast infections, which fight fungus, are ineffective against bacterial vaginosis.

Pelvic Inflammatory Disease

In Chapter 13 we discussed pelvic inflammatory disease (PID), an infection of the female genital tract, including the endometrium, Fallopian tubes, and the lining of the pelvic area. Here we look at the role of STIs in the development of pelvic inflammatory disease. Pelvic inflammatory disease can be caused by many different agents, but the two that have been most often implicated are *Chlamydia trachomatis* and *Neisseria gonorrhoeae* (J. Ross, 2001). It is estimated 10% to 20% of women with gonorrhea or chlamydia develop PID (Centers for Disease Control and Prevention, 2005d). Long-term complications of PID include ectopic and tubal pregnancies, chronic pelvic pain, and infertility. About 20% of women with PID become infertile, 20% develop chronic pelvic pain, and 10% who conceive have an ectopic pregnancy (Metters et al., 1998; J. Ross, 2001).

Although the exact rates of PID are unknown, it has been estimated that there are 1 million U.S. cases of PID each year, and 1 out of every 7 women of reproductive age is found to have at least one episode of PID by the age of 35 (Handsfield, 1992). However, many cases of PID remain unrecognized, either because it is asymptomatic or because the healthcare system or the patient misses it (Centers for Disease Control and Prevention, 2005d). Women who are diagnosed with PID tend to be young, be unmarried, have multiple sexual partners, have had an STI in the past, engage in sexual intercourse at a young age, be members of a minority group (Cates et al., 1990), and/or use douches (Aral et al., 1991).

Symptoms of PID include acute pelvic pain, fever of 101° or higher, and an abnormal vaginal discharge. Treatment for PID includes antibiotics for 14 days, which effectively eliminates the symptoms of PID (Ross, 2001). If the symptoms continue or worsen, hospitalization may be necessary. Sexual partners should be evaluated if they engaged in sexual contact 60 days prior to the PID diagnosis to rule out infections with gonorrhea and chlamydia (Centers for Disease Control and Prevention, 2002a).

Viral Infections: Herpes, Human Papillomavirus, and Hepatitis

Sexually transmitted infections can also be caused by viruses. Once a virus invades a body cell, it is able to reproduce itself, so a person will have the virus for the rest of his or her life. Viruses can live in the body, and, although a person may not experience symptoms, he or she is still infected with the virus. We will now discuss herpes, human papillomavirus, and viral hepatitis, and later in this chapter we will explore the human immunodeficiency virus and AIDS.

Herpes

Herpes (herpes simplex, herpes genitalis) is caused by an infection with the herpes simplex virus (HSV). Typically the virus prefers to infect the mouth and face (**herpes simplex I,** or HSV-1), or the genitals (**herpes simplex II,** or HSV-2), where it causes sores to appear. HSV-1 and HSV-2 are usually transmitted through different routes; however, once infected, the signs and symptoms they cause can overlap (Whitley & Roizman, 2001). If the virus infects a less preferred site, such as an HSV-1 infection of the genitals or an HSV-2 infection of the mouth and face, the symptoms are usually less severe.

HSV-1 and HSV-2 are contained in the sores that the virus causes, but they are also released between outbreaks from the infected skin (often referred to as "**viral shedding**"). Because of this, the virus can be transmitted even when the infected partner doesn't have any active symptoms (Wald et al., 2000). A person who engages in unprotected sexual activity (vaginal intercourse or anal sex) with a partner who is infected with HSV-2 will most probably become infected with a genital HSV-2 infection. A person who receives oral sex from a person infected with HSV-1 will most likely become infected with a genital HSV-1 infection.

It is possible for people who are infected with HSV to reinfect themselves on another part of their body. For instance, if a woman with HSV-1 touches an open lesion and then rubs another mucosal area, such as the mouth or genitals, she may **autoinoculate** herself. She could also transmit HSV to her partner's genitals in this manner.

Pregnant mothers can pass the herpes virus on to their infants in several ways. The most common method of infection is during delivery. However, transmission can also occur while the baby is in the uterus or directly following birth.

Incidence   The herpes simplex virus II is one of the most common STIs in the United States today, with as many as 1 million people becoming infected each year (Weinstock et al., 2004). It is estimated that approximately 45 million people, age 12 and older, have genital herpes (Centers for Disease Control and Prevention, 2005d). However, infection rates are higher than reported because the majority of people with genital herpes have not been diagnosed (Centers for Disease Control and Prevention, 2002a).

Review Question

Explain what pelvic inflammatory disease is, and identify causes, symptoms, and long-term risks.

herpes
A highly contagious viral infection that causes eruptions of the skin or mucous membranes.

herpes simplex virus (HSV)
The virus that causes herpes.

herpes simplex I (HSV-I)
A viral infection that causes cold sores on the face or lips.

herpes simplex II (HSV-2)
A viral infection that is sexually transmitted and causes genital ulcerations.

viral shedding
The release of viral infections between outbreaks from infected skin.

autoinoculate
To cause a secondary infection in the body from an already existing infection.

We do know that rates of genital herpes are higher in women, mainly due to the fact that male-to-female routes of transmission are more efficient than female-to-male routes. It is estimated that 1 in 4 women and 1 in 5 men have genital herpes (Centers for Disease Control and Prevention, 2005d). Herpes is also more common among African Americans (46%) than among Caucasians. Oral herpes is fairly common today. In fact, by the age of 5, it is estimated that more than 35% of African American children and 18% of Caucasian children are infected with HSV-1 (Whitley & Roizman, 2001). This is probably a result of kissing from HSV-1–infected relatives and friends.

Symptoms   The first symptoms of herpes usually appear within 4 days after infection, but they can appear anywhere from 2 to 12 days later. However, the majority of those infected with HSV-1 and HSV-2 do not experience any noticeable symptoms (Whitley & Roizman, 2001). If a person does develop HSV sores, the first occurrence is generally the most painful. Overall, women tend to have more severe symptoms with HSV-2 than men.

At the onset, there is usually a tingling or burning feeling in the affected area, which can grow into an itching and a red, swollen appearance of the genitals (this period is often referred to as the **prodromal phase**). The sores usually last anywhere from 8 to 10 days, and the amount of pain they cause can range from mild to severe. Pain is usually most severe at the onset of the infection and improves thereafter. Depending on the amount of pain, urination may be difficult. Small blisters may appear externally on the vagina or penis. The blisters, which are usually red and sometimes have a grayish center, will eventually burst and ooze a yellowish discharge. As they begin to heal, a scab will form over them. Other symptoms of HSV include a fever, headaches, pain, itching, vaginal or urethral discharge, and general fatigue. These symptoms peak within 4 days of the appearance of the blisters. A few patients with severe symptoms require hospitalization.

The frequency and severity of recurrent episodes of herpes depend on several things, including the amount of infectious agent, the severity of the infection, the type of herpes, and the timing of treatment (Kroon, 1990). Over time the frequency of recurrent outbreaks diminishes (Centers for Disease Control and Prevention, 2005d).

Psychological reactions to herpes outbreaks can include anxiety, guilt, anger, frustration, helplessness, a decrease in self-esteem, and depression (Dibble & Swanson, 2000). Persons with supportive partners and social relationships tend to do better psychologically. In addition, those who receive psychological support services experience a greater reduction in recurrent episodes of herpes and an improvement in their emotional health (Swanson et al., 1999). Physical and emotional stress may increase the likelihood of recurrent episodes. People who have been infected with the herpes virus are advised to get plenty of sleep, to eat and exercise properly, and to reduce alcohol intake, cigarette smoking, and stress.

Recent research reveals that people who are infected with HSV-2 are at greater risk for acquiring HIV if they engage in unprotected sexual intercourse with someone who is HIV-positive, because the herpes blisters facilitate the transmission of HIV (Centers for Disease Control and Prevention, 2005d).

prodromal phase
The tingling or burning feeling that precedes the development of herpes blisters.

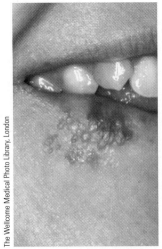

This is a typical patch of HSV-1 blisters, which often appear on the lips or mouth.

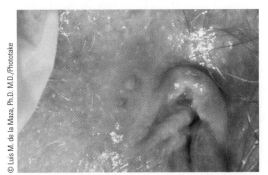

HSV-2 infection in women can cause blisters on the vulva, vagina, or anyplace the virus entered the body.

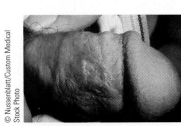

Here HSV-2 blisters appear on the penis.

Diagnosis   The presence of blisters caused by the herpes virus is often enough to diagnose the disease. Oftentimes, however, healthcare providers will take a scraping of the blisters to evaluate for the presence of HSV (Whitley & Roizman, 2001). No tests for the detection of HSV-1 or HSV-2 are 100% accurate because tests depend on the amount of infectious agent and the stage of the disease. Success rates for detecting HSV-2 antibodies vary from 80% to 98%, and there are high false negative results, mainly due to the fact that tests are performed too early.

Treatment   There is no cure for infection with the herpes virus. Once infected, a person will always carry the virus in his or her body. The standard therapy for HSV infection today is antiviral drugs (Balfour, 1999). Aciclovir, Valacyclovir, Famciclovir, and Penciclovir are all antiviral drugs that shorten the duration of outbreaks, prevent complications, and reduce viral shedding (Corey et al., 2004; Sacks et al., 2005). Topical, oral, or injected antiviral drugs can all be given, depending on the site of infection. Patients with frequent outbreaks are often put on suppressive or antiviral therapy to suppress or reduce the frequency of recurrences (Wald, 1999; Whitley & Roizman, 2001). Antiviral therapy can significantly reduce sexual transmission of the virus (Patel, 2004).

Natural remedies for herpes outbreaks include applying an ice pack to the affected area during the prodromal phase and applying cooling or drying agents such as witch hazel. Increasing intake of foods rich in certain amino acids, such as L-lysine, which includes fish or yogurt, and decreasing the intake of sugar and nuts (which are high in arginine) may also help reduce recurrences (Griffith et al., 1987; Vukovic, 1992). Lysine can also be purchased from the vitamin section of any drugstore.

A vaccine for genital herpes (HSV-2), Simplirix, developed by SmithKline Beecham, has so far proved effective (Weibley, 2001). Although not yet approved by the FDA, this vaccine appears to be effective only for women who have not already been infected with HSV-2 and have never had HSV-1, but unfortunately this vaccine has not shown effectiveness in men. Other vaccines for HSV are currently in clinical trials, and these will be available to a wider percentage of people.

Review Question

Explain the incidence, symptoms, diagnosis, and treatment of the herpes simplex virus, and differentiate between HSV-1 and HSV-2.

SEX Talk

Question: Because herpes is not curable, when people are in their "downtime" between flare-ups, can they still transmit it?

Although many people believe that the herpes virus cannot be transmitted if there are no active lesions, there is now evidence that it can be transmitted even in the absence of active lesions (Boselli et al., 2005; Whitley & Roizman, 2001). Herpes simplex viruses are often asymptomatic, and therefore men and women who are infected with HSV-2 should always use condoms so that they do not infect their partners.

Human Papillomavirus

The majority of college students know very little about the **human papillomavirus (HPV;** Lambert, 2001). The fact is that there are over 30 types of the human papillomavirus (HPV) that can infect the genital tract (Centers for Disease Control and Prevention, 2004a). Some of these viruses are called "high risk" because they may cause abnormal Pap tests and increase the potential for certain kinds of cancers (on the cervix, anus, vagina, vulva, or penis). There is ample evidence that almost all cervical cancers can be attributed to HPV infection (Peyton et al., 2001). Other types of the virus are called "low risk" and can cause genital warts (*condyloma acuminata*, venereal warts), which are similar to warts that appear on other parts of the body. The human papillomavirus can be transmitted through sexual intercourse, oral sex, vulva-to-vulva sex, or anal sex.

human papillomavirus (HPV)
A sexually transmitted viral infection that can cause genital warts and/or cervical cancer.

genital wart
Wartlike growth on the genitals; also called venereal wart, condylomata, or papilloma.

Warts that appear on the penis are usually flesh-colored and may have a bumpy appearance.

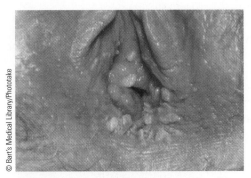

Here genital warts appear on the outside of the vulva.

Incidence   As of 2004, there were 20 million people infected with genital HPV in the United States (Centers for Disease Control and Prevention, 2004a). It is estimated that at least 50% of sexually active men and women will acquire HPV at some point in their life (Centers for Disease Control and Prevention, 2004a).

Several factors have been found to be related to HPV infection, including early age of first intercourse (before the age of 16; J. A. Kahn et al., 2002) and having more than two sexual partners within the past year (Peyton et al., 2001). Research has found that Hispanic women are at higher risk for HPV than are non-Hispanic white women (Peyton et al., 2001). In 2002, experts proposed comprehensive screening guidelines that recommended testing all women every 2 years for HPV to decrease rates of cervical cancer (Mandelblatt et al., 2002).

Symptoms   Many people who are infected with HPV are asymptomatic, but those who develop symptoms do so as late as 6 weeks to 9 months after infection (Centers for Disease Control and Prevention, 2004a). It is estimated that 10% of HPV infections lead to **genital warts** (Koutsky, 1997). Genital warts are usually flesh colored and may have a bumpy surface. Warts develop in women on the vagina, vulva, or cervix, and in men on the penile shaft, head, scrotum, and rarely, the urethra (Krilov, 1991). Warts can also appear on the anus in both men and women. In some areas, warts may grow together and have a cauliflowerlike appearance. These lesions are generally asymptomatic; and, unless the warts are large, many people do not notice them and unknowingly infect other sexual partners. Because of the contagious nature of genital warts, approximately 65% of sexual partners of people with cervical warts develop warts within 3 to 4 months of contact (Krilov, 1991).

HPV can also cause a foul-smelling discharge, which may cause some itching and pain. Children who are infected with HPV at birth are at risk of developing viral growths in the respiratory tract, which can cause respiratory distress and hoarseness (Fletcher, 1991).

Diagnosis   A healthcare provider may be able to detect warts upon visual inspection. If not, a high-risk detection kit can also be performed to aid in diagnosis. A healthcare provider may also soak the infected area with acetic acid (white vinegar), which turns the skin of the warts white and makes them easier to see under magnification. An examination of the cervix under magnification (called colposcopy) can also be used. Biopsies are also done to check for HPV. Although HPV may show up on Pap testing, 80% to 90% of the time, it does not (Kassler & Cates, 1992).

Finally, the FDA approved an HPV DNA test in 2003 that can identify 13 of the high-risk types of HPV associated with cervical cancer. Cells are collected during a woman's Pap testing and sent to a lab for analysis. Healthcare providers recommend that women who have more than one sexual partner should ask their medical provider for an HPV DNA test. At this time, there are no specific HPV tests for men.

Treatment   Because warts can grow and multiply, it is important to seek treatment immediately. Using condoms and avoiding multiple sexual partners can reduce the chances of acquiring genital warts. If genital warts are left untreated, they may resolve on their own, remain unchanged, or increase in number or size (Centers for Disease Control and Prevention, 2002a). Genital warts can be treated in several ways, and no treatment method is superior to another or best for all patients with HPV. Important factors for a healthcare provider to consider when deciding treatment options include the number and size of the warts, patient preference, treatment costs, convenience, and side effects.

Treatment alternatives include chemical topical solutions (to destroy external warts), cryotherapy (freezing the warts with liquid nitrogen), electrosurgical interventions (removal of warts using a hot wire loop), or laser surgery (high-intensity lasers to destroy the warts). It may be necessary to try several treatment methods, and repeat applications are common (Centers for Disease Control and Prevention, 2002a).

Although the majority of sexual partners of those infected with HPV are already infected with HPV, if they are not infected, an infected person should use condoms during sexual intercourse for at least 6 months following treatment (Lilley & Schaffer, 1990). Some couples decide to use condoms long term because of the possibility of transmitting the virus when no warts are present. Newer research indicates, however, that over time most HPV infections are cleared up by the immune system. The Centers for Disease Control and Prevention have reported that the majority of HPV infections in women resolve within 1 year (Centers for Disease Control and Prevention, 2005d). Persistent infections are usually caused by specific types of HPV, which may also be related to the development of cervical cancer.

Women who have been diagnosed with **cervical dysplasia** are encouraged to have pelvic exams and Pap tests at least once a year. Some studies indicate that folic acid (vitamin B) may help to keep HPV in check in women who have been diagnosed with genital warts. It is not known exactly how folic acid may help reduce the effects of HPV, but it is thought that it helps to strengthen the cervical cells. Folic acid can be found in green leafy vegetables, yeast breads, and liver. Researchers are exploring ways to prevent HPV—clinical trials that test the safety and efficacy of developed HPV vaccines are already underway (Kahn & Bernstein, 2005; see Sex in Real Life, "Vaccines for Sexually Transmitted Infections?" on page 507).

cervical dysplasia
Disordered growth of cells in the cervix, typically diagnosed upon Pap testing.

Review Question

Explain the incidence, symptoms, diagnosis, and treatment of human papillomavirus.

Viral Hepatitis

Viral hepatitis is an infection that causes impaired liver function. The three main types of viral hepatitis include hepatitis A (HAV), hepatitis B (HBV), and hepatitis C (HCV). Hepatitis A is transmitted through fecal–oral contact and is often spread by food handlers but can also be spread through anal–oral contact. In the United States, hepatitis A is the most frequent vaccine-preventable disease (Centers for Disease Control and Prevention, 2005e). Hepatitis B is predominantly spread during high-risk sexual behaviors (see Sex in Real Life, "High-Risk Sexual Behaviors," on page 495; Kellerman et al., 2003). Although hepatitis C can be spread through sexual behavior, it is mostly caused by illegal intravenous drug use or unscreened blood transfusions.

viral hepatitis
A viral infection; three main types of viral hepatitis include hepatitis A (HAV), hepatitis B (HBV), and hepatitis C (HCV).

Incidence One-third of Americans have evidence of a past infection with hepatitis A (Centers for Disease Control and Prevention, 2005e; see Figure 15.9 for more information on hepatitis infection rates). Although 10,609 HAV cases were reported in 2001, because of underreporting researchers estimated this number was closer to 45,000 (Centers for Disease Control and Prevention, 2005e). Historically rates for HAV have varied by ethinicity, with higher rates in Native Americans and Alaskan Natives. However, this was probably due to increased contact with people from countries with higher HAV rates (such as Mexico and Central America) and socioeconomic and living conditions.

There are approximately 1.25 million people infected with hepatitis B in the United States, and another 78,000 become infected every year (Centers for Disease Control and Prevention, 2005d). A total of 3.9 million Americans have been infected with hepatitis C, and close to 70% are chronically infected (Centers for Disease Control and Prevention, 2005e).

Figure 15.9
Percent of people in the United States ever infected with hepatitis A, B, or C.
Source: Centers for Disease Control and Prevention, 2003c.

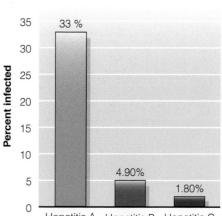

Symptoms Symptoms of hepatitis A usually occur within 4 weeks after a person is infected and include fatigue, abdominal pain, loss of appetite, and diarrhea. Hepatitis A has no chronic long-term infection. Symptoms of hepatitis B usually occur anywhere from 6 weeks to 6 months after infection, although infection with hepatitis B is usually asymptomatic. Possible symptoms may include nausea, vomiting, jaundice, headaches, fever, a darkening of the urine, moderate liver enlargement, and fatigue. It is estimated that 15% to 25% of those infected with hepatitis B will die from chronic liver disease (Centers for Disease Control and Prevention, 2005e). Finally, most people infected with hepatitis C are asymptomatic or have a mild illness and develop this illness within 8 to 9 weeks. The Centers for Disease Control and Prevention estimate that between 75% and 85% of those infected with hepatitis C will develop a chronic liver infection.

Diagnosis   Blood tests are used to identify viral hepatitis infections.

Treatment   At this time there are three drugs licensed for hepatitis; these drugs have been found to be effective (Marcellin et al., 2003). These therapies have been designed to reduce viral load by interfering with the life cycle of the virus and also causing the body to generate an immune response against the virus (Guha et al., 2003). Healthcare providers generally recommend bed rest and adequate fluid intake so that a person doesn't develop dehydration. Usually after a few weeks an infected person feels better, although this can take longer in persons with severe infections.

Vaccines are available for the prevention of both hepatitis A and B, and persons at high risk of contracting either of these should have the vaccine. High-risk individuals include healthcare workers who may be exposed to blood products, intravenous drug users and their sex partners, people with multiple sexual partners, people with chronic liver disease, and housemates of anyone with hepatitis (Centers for Disease Control and Prevention, 2005e; K. Miller & Graves, 2000). Men who have sex with men should also be vaccinated against HAV and HBV (C. Diamond et al., 2003). A vaccine for hepatitis C is urgently needed, and research is ongoing to find one.

HUMAN IMMUNODEFICIENCY VIRUS (HIV) AND ACQUIRED IMMUNE DEFICIENCY SYNDROME (AIDS)

Although the **human immunodeficiency virus (HIV)** is a viral infection, there are several factors that set it apart from other STIs and also shed some light on why the **acquired immune deficiency syndrome (AIDS)** debate has become so politically charged. HIV/AIDS appeared at a time when modern medicine was believed to be well on its way to reducing epidemic disease (D. Altman, 1986). In addition, AIDS was first identified among gay men and, as of 1995, the largest number of cases in this country were gay and bisexual men and intravenous drug users.

Because of this early identification, the disease was linked with "socially marginal" groups in the population (D. Altman, 1986; Kain, 1987). The media gave particular attention to the lifestyle of "victims" and implied that social deviance has a price. One study found that 1 in 5 people believed that people who got AIDS through sex or drugs got what they deserved (Valdiserri, 2002). Although the stigma of HIV/AIDS decreased in the 1990s, in 1999, nearly 1 in 5 American adults said they "fear" a person with AIDS (Herek et al., 2002). We will talk more about public attitudes about AIDS later in this chapter.

AIDS is caused by a viral infection with the human immunodeficiency virus (HIV), a virus primarily transmitted through body fluids, including semen, vaginal fluid, breast milk, and blood. During vaginal or anal intercourse, this virus can enter the body through the rectum, vagina, penis, or mouth. It is also possible to transmit the virus during intravenous drug use by sharing needles. Oral sex may also transmit the virus, although it is difficult to measure the risk associated with oral sex because few people engage exclusively in oral sex. Even so, the research has consistently shown that the risk is lower than that of unprotected vaginal or anal sex (Kohn et al., 2002; E. D. Robinson & Evans, 1999). Kissing has been found to be low-risk for transmitting HIV, especially when there are no cuts in the mouth or on the lips.

Like the herpes virus, HIV never goes away; it remains in the body for the rest of a person's life. However, unlike the herpes virus, an untreated HIV infection is often fatal. After a person is infected, the virus may remain dormant for awhile and cause no symptoms. This is why some people who are infected may not realize that they are. However, a blood test can be taken to reveal whether or not someone is HIV-positive. Even a person who does not know that he or she has been infected can transmit the virus to other people immediately after infection.

HIV attacks the **T-lymphocytes** (tee-LIM-foe-sites; **T-helper cells**) in the blood, leaving fewer of them to fight off infection. When there is a foreign invader in our blood-

ReviewQuestion

Explain the incidence, symptoms, diagnosis, and treatment of hepatitis. Differentiate between HAV, HBV, and HCV.

human immunodeficiency virus (HIV)
The retrovirus responsible for the development of AIDS; can be transmitted during vaginal or anal intercourse.

acquired immune deficiency syndrome (AIDS)
A condition of increased susceptibility to opportunistic diseases; results from an infection with HIV, which destroys the body's immune system.

sex byte

In 2004, an estimated 5 million people became newly infected with HIV worldwide, and 640,000 of them were under the age of 15 (Kaiser Family Foundation, 2005a).

T-lymphocyte (T-helper cell)
Type of white blood cell that helps to destroy harmful bacteria in the body.

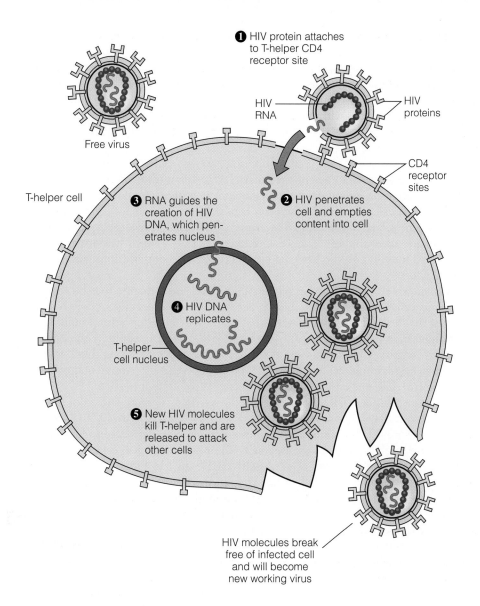

❶ HIV protein attaches to T-helper CD4 receptor site

HIV RNA

HIV proteins

Free virus

CD4 receptor sites

T-helper cell

❸ RNA guides the creation of HIV DNA, which penetrates nucleus

❷ HIV penetrates cell and empties content into cell

❹ HIV DNA replicates

T-helper cell nucleus

❺ New HIV molecules kill T-helper and are released to attack other cells

HIV molecules break free of infected cell and will become new working virus

Figure 15.10
HIV attacking a T-helper cell. (1) The protein on the surface of HIV fits the CD4 receptor of the T-helper cell. (2) HIV RNA enters the T-helper cell and uses the cell's machinery to create HIV DNA. (3) HIV DNA enters the nucleus, where it (4) replicates and (5) forms new HIV molecules that destroy the cell and go looking for new T-helper cells.

stream, antibodies develop that are able to recognize the invader and destroy it. However, if the antibodies cannot do this or if there are too many viruses, a person will become ill. These antibodies can be detected in the bloodstream anywhere from 2 weeks to 6 months after infection, which is how the screening test for HIV works. The immune system also releases many white blood cells to help destroy invaders.

HIV attaches itself to the T-helper cells and injects its infectious RNA into the fluid of the helper cell. The RNA contains an enzyme known as **reverse transcriptase** (trans-SCRIPT-ace), which is capable of changing the RNA into DNA. The new DNA takes over the T-helper cell and begins to manufacture more HIV (see Figure 15.10).

The attack on the T-helper cells causes the immune system to be less effective in its ability to fight disease, and so many **opportunistic diseases** infect people with AIDS that a healthy person could easily fight off (we will discuss these diseases later in this chapter). No one knows exactly why some people acquire the virus from one sexual encounter whereas others may not be infected even after repeated exposure. It appears that a person is more at risk for acquiring HIV who already has another STI (Gilson & Mindel, 2001; Hader et al., 2001).

It is unknown where exactly HIV came from, although scientists have many different theories. None of these theories has been proven, however. In the early 1980s, a number of gay men, mostly in Los Angeles and New York City, began coming down with rare forms of pneumonia and skin cancer. Physicians began calling the disease GRID, for

reverse transcriptase
A chemical that is contained in the RNA of HIV; it helps to change the virus's DNA.

opportunistic disease
Disease that occurs when the immune system is depressed; often fatal.

Review Question

Explain how HIV is transmitted and how the virus affects the body.

"gay-related immunodeficiency syndrome." It was hypothesized that there was a new infectious agent causing the disease, that the immune system was being suppressed by a drug that the infected persons were using, or that perhaps a sexual lubricant was involved. Many physicians felt that this infectious agent would quickly be isolated and wiped out. Today, it is anticipated that the AIDS virus will continue to infect people for the next several decades without a cure.

Incidence

Since the first reported case of AIDS in 1981, 1.5 million people in the United States have become infected with HIV, including more than 500,000 who have died (UNAIDS, 2005b). Worldwide, there are between 36.7 million and 45.3 million people living with HIV (see Table 15.2). One-third of these HIV-infected people throughout the world are under the age of 25 (S. Sternberg, 2002). Since it was first recognized in 1981, over 25 million people have died from HIV/AIDS complications worldwide (UNAIDS, 2005c).

As mentioned earlier in this chapter, all 50 U.S. states require that HIV and AIDS cases be reported to local or state health departments. These statistics help to track the spread of the illness. Some were fearful that mandatory HIV reporting would deter men and women from being tested. Yet, with more HIV-infected people living longer without progressing to AIDS, it may be important to begin documenting these cases. Some states have begun using codes to keep HIV-positive people anonymous and confidential; but doing this does not ensure that every person is counted only once.

The transmission of HIV has also shifted over time. The proportion of newly diagnosed heterosexual AIDS cases rose from 3% in 1985 to 31% in 2003 (Kaiser Family Foundation, 2005b). Individuals don't always know whether their partner is putting them at risk for HIV, and this is especially the case for women (Hader et al., 2001). Women are the fastest-growing group with AIDS in the United States (UNAIDS, 2005c). It is estimated that half of the people now infected with HIV worldwide are women (UNAIDS, 2005c). As we have discussed, the vaginal tissue is thinner than penile tissue and easily traumatized during sexual intercourse, making infection more likely if the penetrative partner has the infection.

The increase in infections in women is also due to the continued spread of AIDS in women in sub-Saharan Africa. Overall, women have been found to be 17 times more likely to be infected by their partners than they are to give the infection (Padian et al., 1991); yet, it is men who drive the spread of the virus (Schoofs & Zimmerman, 2002). Generally this is due to the fact that men have more sexual partners than women, and they also have more control over whether or not a condom is used (see Figure 15.11 for more information about the percentage of women living with HIV/AIDS globally).

An infected mother can also transmit HIV to her fetus. It is estimated that approximately 750,000 children have become infected with HIV worldwide, and most of these are through mother-to-child transmission (Newell, 2005). Although infection may be possible through breast-feeding, it is more likely that transmission takes place during pregnancy through the placenta or through the birth canal during delivery (Newell, 2005). Fortunately, due to improvements in obstetric care, rates of maternal–infant transmission have decreased. Today HIV tests are routinely offered to pregnant women; and if a test is positive, medications can be used to reduce **viral load,** and a planned cesarean section can be done to reduce the risk of transmission to the infant during delivery.

Teens are also affected by HIV and AIDS. At least half of all new HIV infections are among those under the age of 25 (Centers for Disease Control and Prevention, 2004b; Kaiser Family Foundation, 2005b). An HIV diagnosis in children is not always a death sentence, however;

viral load
The amount of viral particles in a sample of blood. A person with high viral load usually develops AIDS faster than a person with a low viral load.

TABLE 15.2	Global Summary of HIV/AIDS*	
Number of people living with HIV/AIDS in 2005	Total	40.3 million (36.7–45.3 million)
	Adults	38 million (34.5–42.6 million)
	Women	17.5 million (16.2–19.3 million)
	Children under 15 years	2.3 million (2.1–2.8 million)
People newly infected with HIV in 2005	Total	4.9 million (4.3–6.6 million)
	Adults	4.2 million (3.6–5.8 million)
	Children under 15 years	700,000 (630,000–820,000)
AIDS deaths in 2005	Total	3.1 million (2.8–3.6 million)
	Adults	2.6 million (2.3–2.9 million)
	Children under 15 years	570,000 (510,000–670,000)

*Numbers presented here are averages; ranges are provided in parentheses.
SOURCE: UNAIDS, 2005b.

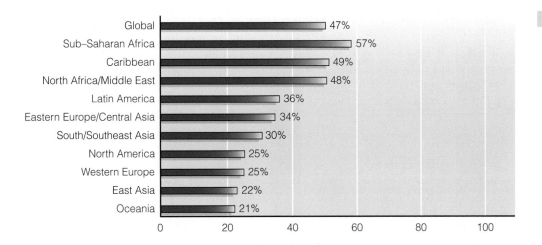

Figure 15.11
Women as a percent of adults living with HIV/AIDS by region, end of 2004.
Source: Centers for Disease Control and Prevention, 2004; Kaiser Family Foundation, 2005a.

there are children who were born with HIV who have survived and are living through adulthood.

AIDS is most dramatically affecting African Americans and continues to disproportionately affect minority communities. In the United States, 71% of the new AIDS cases are diagnosed among racial and ethnic minorities (Kaiser Family Foundation, 2005a). African Americans have the highest rates of AIDS, followed by Latinos, American Indian/Alaskan Natives, Caucasians, and Asian/Pacific Islanders (UNAIDS, 2005b). There are a variety of reasons for these racial differences, including late identification of HIV infection in African Americans, less access to healthcare and HIV therapy, and a lack of health insurance (Maldonado, 1999).

Review Question

Identify the various routes of transmission for HIV, and identify the groups with the highest rates of infection today.

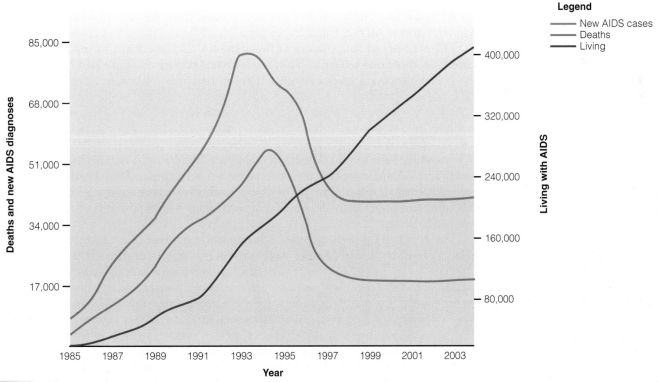

Figure 15.12
Estimated new AIDS cases, deaths among people with AIDS, and people living with AIDS in the United States, 1985–2003.
Source: Centers for Disease Control and Prevention, 2004b; HIV/AIDS Policy Fact Sheet, September 2005, Henry J. Kaiser Family Foundation, www.kff.org. Reprinted with permission. The Kaiser Family Foundation, based in Menlo Park, California, is a nonprofit, independent national health care philanthropy and is not associated with Kaiser Permanente or Kaiser Industries.

Kaposi's sarcoma is the most common cancer affecting untreated people with AIDS.

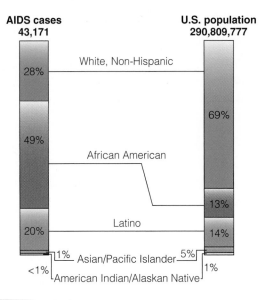

AIDS cases 43,171		U.S. population 290,809,777
28%	White, Non-Hispanic	69%
49%	African American	13%
20%	Latino	14%
1%	Asian/Pacific Islander	5%
<1%	American Indian/Alaskan Native	1%

Figure 15.13
Estimated AIDS diagnoses and U.S. population by race/ethnicity, 2003.
Source: Centers for Disease Control and Prevention, 2004b; Kaiser Family Foundation, 2005b.

Knowledge and Attitudes About AIDS

College students are at risk for HIV because of high rates of sexual activity, multiple sexual partners, lack of protection during sexual activity, and sexual activity that takes place after a couple has been drinking (LaBrie et al., 2002). Knowledge levels among college students are generally high; on the other hand, students also tend to overestimate their knowledge about AIDS. Higher knowledge levels about AIDS in the United States have not been found to be consistently correlated with behavior changes or the practice of safer sex (Caron et al., 1992).

Public attitudes about AIDS may incorporate a mixture of the fear of casual contact and homophobia (see Chapter 11). There are three aspects of AIDS that make it different from other infections. First is the fear of transmission; even though one may know that it is not casually transmitted, the fear of catching AIDS is worrisome to most. Second, there is an issue of the social worth of the individuals who have been diagnosed with the disease. There is an illusion that membership in a particular group other than those most at risk conveys protection. Finally, society's inability to comprehend the magnitude of this illness has left many people feeling isolated and frightened.

Although fewer people hold negative attitudes about people with AIDS today, research has found AIDS remains a stigmatized condition in the United States (Herek et al., 2002). Earlier in this chapter we mentioned that many Americans hold negative opinions of those infected with STIs—today we find that many people are also afraid and uncomfortable around someone with AIDS and have many mistaken beliefs about how AIDS is transmitted.

Symptoms

HIV infection results in a gradual deterioration of the immune system through the destruction of T-helper lymphocytes (Friedman-Kien & Farthing, 1990). For those who are not being treated, this decline in T-helper lymphocytes takes an average of 3 years in those who are emotionally depressed and more than 5 years in those who are nondepressed (B. Bower, 1992).

The average HIV-positive person who is not on any type of treatment will develop AIDS within 8 to 10 years. Flulike symptoms such as fever, sore throat, chronic swollen lymph nodes in the neck or armpits, headaches, and fatigue may appear. After this period, an infected person will seem to recover, and all symptoms will disappear. Later symptoms may include significant weight loss, severe diarrhea that persists for over 1 month, night sweats, **oral candidiasis,** gingivitis, oral ulcers, and persistent fever (Friedman-Kien & Farthing, 1990). In addition, a person might experience persistent dizziness, confusion, and blurring of vision or hearing.

In general, the rates of HIV opportunistic illnesses (also referred to as HIV infection diseases) are similar in men and women with a few exceptions (cervical cancer may develop as an AIDS-defining condition in women; Hader et al., 2001). The deterioration of the immune system makes it easier for opportunistic diseases to develop. One of these is **pneumocystis carinii pneumonia (PCP),** a type of pneumonia that was uncommon prior to 1980. Other opportunistic diseases include **toxoplasmosis, cryptococcosis,**

Review Question

Explain what we know about the public's knowledge levels and attitudes about AIDS.

oral candidiasis
An infection in the mouth caused by the excess growth of a fungus that naturally occurs in the body.

pneumocystis carinii pneumonia (PCP)
A rare type of pneumonia; an opportunistic disease that often occurs in people with AIDS.

toxoplasmosis
A parasite that can cause headache, sore throat, seizures, altered mental status, or coma.

cryptococcosis
An acute or chronic infection that can lead to pulmonary or central nervous system infection.

cytomegalovirus, and **Kaposi's sarcoma (KS).** KS is a rare type of blood vessel cancer that occurs in homosexual men but is rarely seen in other populations. Lesions from KS frequently occur around the ankle or foot, or they may be on the tip of nose, face, mouth, penis, eyelids, ears, chest, or back. Without treatment, two-thirds of male patients with AIDS develop KS lesions on the head and neck (Alkhuja et al., 2001). Other STIs may appear or progress quickly, such as genital warts or syphilis, which may be resistant to treatment.

cytomegalovirus
A virus that can lead to diarrhea, weight loss, headache, fever, confusion, or blurred vision.

Kaposi's sarcoma (KS)
A rare form of cancer that often occurs in people with AIDS.

Review **Question**

Identify the various symptoms and opportunistic diseases that develop as a result of HIV and AIDS.

SEX Talk

Question: *When someone is diagnosed as having HIV, is there a chance they will never develop AIDS? If not, about how long until they get AIDS?*

Before the advent of antiviral therapy, there was a median incubation period from the time of HIV infection to onset of AIDS symptoms of approximately 8 to 10 years (Osmond, 1998). Some people did get sick immediately after infection, and those who were taking medication lived longer without developing symptoms. However, at this point, research indicates that almost all people who are infected with HIV and do not receive treatment will develop AIDS at some point in their lives. However, with treatment a person may never develop AIDS.

Diagnosis

Tests for HIV can either identify the virus in the blood, or more commonly, detect whether the person's body has developed antibodies to fight HIV. The most widely used test for antibodies is the **ELISA (enzyme-linked immunoabsorbent assay).** To check for accuracy, if an ELISA test result is positive, a second test, known as the **Western Blot,** is used. These tests can determine the presence or absence of HIV antibodies. If there are none, the test results are negative, indicating that the person is probably not infected with HIV. It takes some time for the body to develop antibodies, and so there is a period in which a person is infected with HIV but the test will not reveal it. If the test is positive, antibodies are present in the body, and the person has HIV. It should be noted that **false negative** and **false positive** test results are also possible.

Probably the biggest development in diagnosis in the last few years has been the development of rapid HIV testing. Both the ELISA and Western Blot HIV tests require as much as 2 weeks before a result is possible. The OraQuick Rapid HIV Antibody test was the first FDA-approved, noninvasive HIV antibody test. This test detects the presence of antibodies to HIV and requires only a drop of blood. Test results are available within 20 minutes. An oral version of this test, called the OraQuick Advance Antibody Device, has also been approved by the FDA. The oral test collects antibodies from the blood vessels in mucous membranes in the mouth (it does *not* collect saliva). Unfortunately, both of these rapid tests must be used by trained professionals and because effectiveness rates for these tests are lower than for blood tests, those who test positive are encouraged to follow up with an AIDS blood test.

In late 2005 the Food and Drug Administration began hearing arguments for at-home AIDS testing (Harris, 2005). This debate began in 1987, when the first application for an at-home AIDS test was submitted. The controversy revolves around the lack of counseling and support after using an at-home test. If approved for at-home use, these AIDS tests may come with a 24-hour hotline number.

ELISA (enzyme-linked immunoabsorbent assay)
The screening test used to detect HIV antibodies in blood samples.

Western Blot
A test used to confirm a positive ELISA test; more accurate than the ELISA test, but too expensive to be used as the primary screening device for infection.

false negative
A negative test result that occurs in a person who is positive for the virus.

false positive
A positive test result that occurs in a person who is negative for the virus.

Review **Question**

Explain how a person is diagnosed with HIV infection.

Treatment

Since 1995, there has been a tremendous decrease in HIV- and AIDS-related deaths, primarily because of the development of **highly active antiretroviral therapy (HAART;** Katz et al., 2002). HAART is the combination of three or more HIV drugs, often referred to as "drug cocktails." This development, in conjunction with the development of

highly active antiretroviral therapy (HAART)
The combination of three or more HIV drugs.

HIV RNA testing (which allows healthcare providers to monitor the amount of virus in the bloodstream), has allowed for better control of HIV and has slowed the disease progression. However, HAART therapy is the standard of care only in North America and Europe, where approximately 1.6 million of the 38 million HIV-positive people live (D. Brown, 2002b). Fewer than 1% of HIV-positive men and women in sub-Saharan Africa are on HAART therapy. We will talk more about cross-cultural differences in treatment shortly.

The life expectancy of children infected with HIV at birth has increased substantially since the introduction of highly active antiretroviral therapy ("Trends in HIV/AIDS Diagnoses," 2005). Whereas in the past the infection progressed rapidly until death, today children are surviving with HIV longer than earlier in the epidemic (Abrams et al., 2001).

Before starting treatment for HIV infection, a person should be given both a viral load test and **CD4+ T cell count.** These tests can determine how much HIV is in a person's system and also estimate the T-helper white blood cell count (which can show how well a person's immune system is controlling the virus). A baseline CD4+ cell count will also give a healthcare provider a starting measure to compare to later viral load estimates after a person has started drug therapy. This will enable the healthcare provider to see whether the drug combinations are effective.

HAART therapy for HIV is complicated and can involve taking 25 or more pills a day at various times during the day. Some drugs must be taken on an empty stomach, while others must be taken just after eating. Some people on HAART therapy miss pills due to oversleeping, traveling, feeling too sick, or simple forgetting (Chesney, 2000). Once a person starts this type of drug therapy, it is very important that the dosages are taken every day at the same time (unlike other medications that require an 80% adherence, HIV drugs require a near-perfect adherence to dosing schedules; Mannheimer et al., 2002). Missed dosages can cause a drug resistance, which will destroy the drug's effectiveness. A missed dose could also cause the virus to survive and mutate into a resistant strain that will not respond to drug therapy. Some people on HAART therapy set timers to remember to take their pills at the right time. HAART therapy is also expensive, usually ranging from $10,000 to $15,000 a year (Cox, 2000). A person who begins drug therapy will most probably continue it for his or her entire life.

There are side effects to HAART therapy. These include problems such as fatigue, nausea, fever, nightmares, headaches, diarrhea, changes in a person's fat distribution, elevated cholesterol levels, the development of diabetes, decreased bone density, liver problems, and skin rashes. Two to eight weeks after starting HAART therapy, a person should have his or her viral load test redone. This will enable a healthcare provider to see how effective the drugs are. After this initial test, a person should have a viral load test every 3 to 4 months and a CD4+ T cell count every 3 to 6 months to make sure the drugs are still effective. If the viral load is still detectable 4 to 6 months after starting treatment, the drug therapy should be changed. How fast the viral load decreases depends on several factors, including baseline CD4+ T cell count, whether the person has any AIDS-related illnesses, and how closely the person has followed the drug therapy protocol.

Many healthcare providers believe that after a patient has been diagnosed with HIV, it is important that he or she receive psychological counseling to provide information on the virus, promote a healthier lifestyle, reduce the risk of transmission to others, help him or her learn coping strategies, and abstain from high-risk behaviors. Without this intervention, it is possible that people who are diagnosed with HIV will become depressed and may even attempt suicide (Ickovics et al., 2001).

Research has found that depressed men in the early stages of AIDS infection suffer a more rapid decline in their physical health and die earlier than do nondepressed men (Antoni et al., 2002). Being optimistic, having social support, and engaging in a diversion of attention (e.g., "keeping busy") have also been found to confer a mental health benefit on HIV-positive men and women (J. M. Johnson & Endler, 2002). Studies have shown that friends generally provide more social support to people with HIV/AIDS than do family members (Serovich et al., 2000). This is especially true for those who became infected with HIV through same-sex activity or drug use.

Question: What are the chances of actually finding a cure for AIDS?

The current thinking is that there will never be a cure for AIDS. Because HIV has the ability to become latent in the cells of the body, total eradication may be impossible as well. Many research studies are being done all over the world, and scientists are searching for vaccines, treatments, and cures. Because the virus is so complex and because it constantly reproduces and changes itself, finding a cure is very difficult. There is a much greater chance of finding a vaccine to immunize people against AIDS than of finding a cure for people who are already infected.

Although HAART therapy has significantly decreased deaths from HIV/AIDS, these effects are less pronounced in elderly people. Today those who are diagnosed with HIV after age 60 have a shorter survival rate than those who are diagnosed earlier (Butt et al., 2001). These elderly HIV-positive patients are also more likely to be male and African American or Hispanic, and the majority are men who are having sex with men or intravenous drug users. There are many reasons why survival times might be shorter in elderly patients, including the belief that HIV doesn't occur in older people or a lack of education about symptoms or the disease, all of which can lead to failure to be tested or seek care.

Review Question

Explain HAART therapy, and describe how it works. What other factors are important in the treatment of HIV and AIDS?

Question: If two people are free of the AIDS virus and have anal sex, could they then get AIDS from each other?

If neither partner is infected with HIV, there is no way they can transmit the virus to each other—or to anyone else—regardless of their sexual behaviors.

Prevention

In order to prevent the further spread of AIDS, people's behavior must change. Many programs have been started to achieve this goal, including educational programs, advertising, and mailings. In 2003, Viacom (which owns CBS, Black Entertainment Television, Nickelodeon, and MTV) and the Kaiser Foundation began a multimedia AIDS awareness and educational campaign. Public service announcements about AIDS were increased on radio stations, and many television programs agreed to address HIV/AIDS in upcoming episodes. A variety of television shows have also included the topic of HIV/AIDS in their programming (such *The Parkers* and *One on One*).

At the beginning of the AIDS crisis, gay men made big strides in changing their behavior. There were dramatic decreases in high-risk behaviors such as unprotected anal and oral sex. In the early 1980s, approximately 40% of gay men reported engaging in risky sex, but by 1987 this number fell to 10% (Staver, 1992). Today the availability of HAART has not been found to result in an increase in high-risk sexual behaviors among heterosexual men or women. However, in men who have sex with men, HAART therapy has been strongly associated with a failure to use condoms (DiClemente et al., 2001) and an increase in risky sexual behavior (M. H. Katz et al., 2002; Stephenson et al., 2003). HIV-negative men who have sex with men are engaging in more unprotected anal sex (Wolitski et al., 2001) and worrying less about contracting AIDS since the introduction of HAART therapy (Elford et al., 2000).

Microbicides: New Barriers Against HIV

*A*lthough you probably have never heard about microbicides, they are one of the most promising new developments in the fight against STIs (Trager, 2003). Microbicides are chemical substances that can significantly reduce STI transmission when applied vaginally or rectally. They come in many forms, such as creams, gels, suppositories, lubricants, and dissolving film (Gottemoeller, 2001). Microbicides work by killing microbes, or pathogens that are present in semen or vaginal fluids. These products can be used by couples trying to avoid a pregnancy and an STI, and also by couples who are infected with STIs but are trying to become pregnant.

Some traditional spermicides have antimicrobial properties, including nonoxynol-9 (N-9; see Chapter 13 for more information). Although N-9 has been at the forefront of the fight against STIs, we now know that frequent use of N-9 spermicide has been found to cause irritation of the cervix and vagina, which may actually help in the transmission of HIV (Gayle, 2000). In fact, HIV transmission has been found to be higher in a population using N-9 than in a population using a placebo (Van Damme et al., 2002). Other studies showed that 15 minutes after N-9 was applied rectally, severe peeling and scaling of the inside layer of the rectal epithelium occurred, leaving the skin more exposed to STI infection (Maguire, 2002). Because of this, N-9 is no longer recommended as a microbicide.

Condoms have always been our number one defense against STIs; however, their use must be negotiated with a partner, and because of this they aren't used as often as they should be (remember that in Chapter 13 we learned that almost 20% of young women believe that they don't have the right to tell their partner they won't have intercourse without using condoms; Rickert et al., 2002). Microbicides can be used by one partner without negotiation, and studies have shown that microbicides are more accepted than condoms. In fact, 90% of men in one study said they would not object to their partners using these products (Callahan, 2002). Microbicides could help to reduce the number of HIV infections by 2.5 million over 3 years (DePineres, 2002).

As of early 2006, microbicides were not yet available to the public. Much of the research is being done by smaller companies because of reduced funding. A phase-three trial (we discussed how FDA approval works in Chapter 13) must enroll thousands of participants and can cost up to $46 million (Alliance for Microbicide Development, 2001). Larger pharmaceutical companies have stayed away from the development of microbicides mainly because they will be low cost and over the counter, which doesn't give the companies much incentive to develop them (Gottemoeller, 2001).

Many schools are beginning to include HIV education in their classes. These programs provide students with information about risky sexual behaviors, facts about AIDS, and prevention strategies. Different educational programs emphasize different messages. One may discourage sexual activity, whereas a second provides information about condom use, and a third stresses monogamy. All are similar in that the goal is to change behavior and increase self-responsibility. However, these programs have not progressed without controversy. People disagree about when these programs should start, how explicit they should be, and whether or not such education will increase sexual promiscuity.

Once a diagnosis of HIV has been made, it is important to inform all past sexual contacts to prevent the spread of the disease. Because the virus can remain in the body for several years before the onset of symptoms, some people may not know that they have the virus and are capable of infecting others.

It seems reasonable that before we can determine what will reduce high-risk behaviors that contribute to increases in HIV and AIDS, we need to know the behaviors in which people are engaging. Yet data on sexual practices are lacking in the United States. As you remember from Chapter 2, many of our assumptions about current sexual behaviors are based on the Kinsey studies from the 1940s and 1950s. We know very little about current rates of high-risk behaviors, such as anal intercourse, extramarital or teenage sexuality, and homosexuality. The National Health and Social Life Survey helped shed some light on these behaviors, and two ongoing surveys, the Behavioral Risk Factor Surveillance Survey (BRFSS) and the Youth Risk Behavior Surveillance Survey (YRBS), continue to collect and monitor information about risk behaviors at the state level (see Chapters 2 and 8 for more information about these studies).

In 2003, after years of hard work, the first AIDS vaccine (AIDSVAX) was found to be ineffective in FDA clinical trials (see Chapter 13 for more information about the FDA approval process; also see Sex in Real Life, "Vaccines for Sexually Transmitted Infections?" on page 507). In 2005, the National Institute of Allergy and Infectious Diseases granted more than $300 million to establish a new center for HIV/AIDS vaccine development (Markel, 2005). Ongoing national and international trials are taking place for the development of an HIV vaccine. As of 2005, there were two ongoing trials for a therapeutic HIV vaccine that helps delay the progression of the disease rather than preventing the onset of the disease. Unfortunately the development of an HIV vaccine could take years. The polio vaccine took 47 years to produce, and it is anticipated that the HIV vaccine may take just as long (Markel, 2005). Researchers will continue to work on the development of an AIDS vaccine.

Families and AIDS

Families and friends of people with AIDS often do not receive the same social support as do families and friends of people with other devastating illnesses, such as cancer or Alzheimer's disease. There is a great social stigma attached to AIDS, and many caregivers find that they have to deal with this pain on their own. Children whose parents become infected with the AIDS virus often have difficulties sorting through their own personal feelings about this.

Today, with the help of HAART therapies, many parents with HIV are living longer (see Figure 15.12). This has brought up many new issues, such as disclosure (when and how to tell family members) and adjusting to having a parent with HIV. Research has found that the majority of parents living with AIDS have discussed their illness with their family members (Rotheram-Borus et al., 1997). Overall, mothers are more likely to disclose their HIV status earlier than fathers, and they disclose more often to their daughters than their sons (Lee & Rotheram-Borus, 2002). Adolescents who were told their parents had AIDS engaged in more high-risk sexual behaviors and had more emotional distress than adolescents who were uninformed (Lee & Rotheram-Borus, 2002; Rotheram-Borus et al., 1997). Many people with HIV-positive family members find it helpful to become involved in AIDS-related activities such as a support group. The names of several organizations are provided at the end of this chapter.

GLOBAL ASPECTS OF AIDS*

The United Nations Program on HIV/AIDS estimates that unless improvements are made in treatment and prevention, from 2000 to 2020, 68 million people in the 45 most heavily affected countries will die of AIDS. The global total of young people living with HIV/AIDS could experience a 70% increase by 2010 (Summers et al., 2002). What makes the global numbers even more threatening is that 95% of those infected with HIV have no access to treatment, mostly because of financial and cultural reasons (Kreinin, 2001). Other problems may also interfere with access to treatment, including transportation issues and possible drug confiscation to sell for profit in other markets.

Children are grossly affected by the AIDS epidemic. In fact, it is estimated that every minute a child becomes infected with HIV and another child dies of an AIDS-related illness (UNAIDS, 2005b). By 2005, an estimated 15 million children had lost at least one parent to AIDS worldwide; but by 2010 it is estimated that there will be 18 million children who have lost a parent to AIDS *in sub-Saharan Africa alone* (UNAIDS, 2005b). The number of children who have been orphaned throughout the world due to AIDS is equivalent to the total number of children under the age of 5 living in the United States.

*Much of the material in this section was taken from the *AIDS Epidemic Update: December, 2005*, published by Joint United Nations Programme on HIV/AIDS.

sexbyte

Since 1981, AIDS has killed more than 23 million people, an estimated 40 million people are living with HIV, and close to 5 million were newly infected with HIV in 2005 (UNAIDS, 2005b).

Review Question

Identify the various prevention efforts that have been launched in the face of AIDS.

Review Question

Identify and explain some of the important issues that face the family of a person with AIDS.

Sneak Peek

"Now they don't want me anymore."—
AIDS in Africa

Sexuality Now

Asia and the Pacific

Over 8.3 million people are living with HIV in Asia and the Pacific (UNAIDS, 2005b). Much of the current increases are due to the rising numbers in India (where close to 5 million are living with HIV) and China (where over 1 million reported people are living with HIV). Chinese companies have begun developing generic versions of anti-retroviral drugs, which are much cheaper than the imported name-brand drugs. In Asia, there has been a constant increase in HIV infection among intravenous drug users, with more than half of all intravenous drug users infected in Nepal, southern China, and northeastern India (Sharma, 2001). The most serious HIV epidemics in China have occurred among specific populations, such as IV drug users, sex workers, and their partners. Many of these populations are poorly educated about HIV and AIDS.

Cambodia is another country that has been hard hit by the AIDS epidemic. It is estimated that close to 3% of the entire adult population is infected with HIV, although these numbers have slowly been dropping (UNAIDS, 2005b). Educational efforts in Cambodia have been aimed at prostitutes, who are being encouraged to use condoms consistently.

Indonesia has experienced a sharp increase in the number of intravenous drug users, which has helped to fuel the spread of HIV. It is estimated that if the pattern of drug use continues, intravenous drug users will account for over 80% of all HIV infections in Indonesia.

New HIV infections in Thailand have been dropping over the last 10 years, and many hail Thailand's response to AIDS as a success story (UNAIDS, 2005b). This may be because government officials in Thailand began copying antiretroviral drugs for their AIDS patients, which made the drugs much more accessible for those with HIV/AIDS (T. Rosenberg, 2001). In addition, Thailand has instituted a "100% condom use" program targeted at the prostitution industry (Sharma, 2001). Interestingly, because Thailand is the world's largest rubber exporter, Thailand has been considering tackling the AIDS epidemic by recycling stockpiled rubber into condoms (Noikorn, 2001).

In India, it was estimated that as of 2005, 5.1 million people were infected with HIV, but due to underreporting, this number may be much higher (UNAIDS, 2005b). A large proportion of HIV infections is occurring in married women whose husbands frequent sex workers. Both prostitution and IV drug use have helped fuel the epidemic in India.

Europe and Central Asia

Portions of Europe and central Asia have the world's fastest-growing number of HIV and AIDS cases (Kelly & Amirkhanian, 2003). As of 2005, there were approximately 1.6 million adults and children living with HIV in this area (UNAIDS, 2005b). The Russian Federation has the largest AIDS epidemic in all of Europe, which is mainly fueled by IV drug use and prostitution. It is estimated that three-quarters of new HIV infections occur in 15- to 29-year-olds. An increase in media coverage in the Russian Federation has helped bring some attention to the increasing numbers of HIV infection (Sternberg, 2004b). This has been due, in part, to a global effort with a variety of U.S. media groups, including Viacom and the Kaiser Family Foundation.

Sub-Saharan Africa

The majority of the world's HIV-positive people live in sub-Saharan Africa, where close to 60% of the global number of people are living with HIV (and where only 10% of the world's total population lives; UNAIDS, 2005b; see Figure 15.14). In much of sub-Saharan Africa, HIV knowledge levels are low and women have lower knowledge levels than men (UNAIDS, 2005b). Among young people, it is estimated that three-quarters of those already infected live in sub-Saharan Africa (Summers et al., 2002). If these facts haven't blown your mind yet, read on: a 15-year-old in Botswana has an 80% chance of dying from AIDS (Piot, 2000); because of AIDS, the average life span in Swaziland is

In South Africa, an HIV-positive Muppet was added to the cast of Sesame Street. Her name is Kami, which is derived from the Tswana word for acceptance.

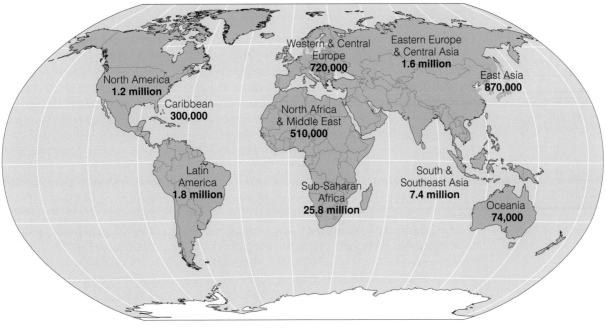

Total: 40.3 million

Figure 15.14

Estimated numbers of adults and children living with HIV as of the end of 2005.

Source: Based on World Health Organization data, UNAIDS, 2005a.

now 33 years and is expected to drop to 27 years by the year 2010 (the average life span was 58 years before the AIDS epidemic); and more than 25% of the total population in Swaziland is infected with HIV.

In 2002, South Africa's *Sesame Street* unveiled an HIV-positive muppet character, a 5-year-old girl who was orphaned when her parents died of AIDS. Her name is Kami, and she is now a regular part of the *Sesame Street* lineup in South Africa. Kami's character was designed to help children in South Africa understand AIDS and teach them it's okay to play with HIV-positive children.

One of the biggest problems in many parts of Africa is that because of cost, only a small percent of the many people with HIV are receiving HAART therapy. In addition, millions of infected men and women are not being treated for opportunistic diseases. The South African government does not provide HAART therapy drugs to its citizens dying of AIDS. One of the biggest obstacles is President Thabo Mbeki, who doesn't believe that HIV causes AIDS. Even so, some groups have tried to get HAART therapy to those who need it. Some employers in South Africa have begun providing HAART therapy free of charge to their employees, whereas some drug manufacturers, such as Pfizer, have offered to give AIDS drugs to South Africans for free.

Other problems that have helped fuel the AIDS crisis involve the nature of male–female sexual relationships. This was one woman's experience getting HIV tested in Zambia:

> Kasune Zulu's doctor refused to perform an HIV test until she had obtained the consent of her husband. When the results came back positive, she was excommunicated from her local church after her husband reported that she wasn't being submissive. Even traditional counselors in many African societies told her to stop making trouble and obey the man she married. (Schoofs & Zimmerman, 2002, p. D4)

Dangerous cultural myths exist in some parts of South Africa. Groups of HIV-positive men believe that sex with a young virgin will cure them of AIDS (Sidley, 2002). As a result, dozens of babies in South Africa have been raped by HIV-positive men, and the crime is increasing. In 2002, a 9-month-old baby was raped by a group of HIV-positive men and reconstructive surgery was necessary to repair her vagina (Sidley, 2002).

sex byte

In Kenya, it is a common practice to pass wives down from one HIV-infected brother to another (Steinhauer, 2001).

Latin America and the Caribbean

There are close to 2 million adults and children living with HIV in Latin America, and another 300,000 in the Caribbean (UNAIDS, 2005b). Brazil accounts for half of the total HIV cases in Latin America. Typically this is due to IV drug use and unsafe sex practices between both heterosexual and homosexual couples. Men who have sex with men have the highest levels of HIV infection, followed by female sex workers (UNAIDS, 2005b). There is some indication that safer sex practices, including increased condom use, are increasing in these areas.

The Brazilian government can afford to treat AIDS and pay for the expensive therapy because it manufactures generic copies of the expensive drugs. This is possible because many drugs (including many antiretroviral drugs) are not patented in countries outside the United States. As a result, these countries can make their own copies of the drugs or import generics (T. Rosenberg, 2001).

Healthcare workers in Brazil are working hard to teach AIDS patients how to use antiretroviral therapy and the importance of taking the pills on time. This has been a tremendous additional weight on the shoulders of healthcare professionals, many of whom are already working overtime.

The Middle East and North Africa

There are a total of 510,000 people estimated to be living with HIV and AIDS in the Middle East and North Africa, although it has been difficult to collect actual numbers (UNAIDS, 2005b). Intravenous drug use, the sharing of needles, men having sex with men, prostitution, and low condom usage have all helped to fuel the outbreak of HIV infection. The country affected the most in this area is Sudan. Although Sudan has increased efforts at educating the public about HIV and AIDS, one study found that only 5% of women knew that condom use could protect them from HIV infection, and more than two-thirds of the women had never heard of a condom (UNAIDS, 2005b).

Other Issues

The majority of HIV-infected people in the hardest hit areas outside the United States do not have access to HAART therapy because of the expense or other reasons. It is estimated that about 250,000 people in the developed world are on HAART therapy (D. Brown, 2002b). Bringing HAART therapy to poor countries has been controversial. Some argue that people dying from AIDS should have access to all drugs, regardless of their ability to pay for them (as we discussed earlier, HAART therapy costs range from $10,000 to $15,000 per year in the United States—although many U.S. companies make the medications available for less in some countries). Others argue that money is more wisely spent on AIDS education and prevention rather than on triple-therapy drugs for those already infected. Opponents also argue that there is little expertise in administering the drugs in poor countries, and this could cause an increase in resistant strains of HIV (D. Brown, 2002b).

SEX Talk

Question: *If a person has been diagnosed with an STI, does he or she need to use condoms for the rest of his or her life?*

It would be a good idea to talk to your healthcare provider about this. Often, if you have been diagnosed with herpes, genital warts, or HIV, healthcare providers will advise wearing condoms during sexual activity to decrease the risk of transmission to your sexual partner(s). The answer to this question really depends on the particular STI and whether or not it is curable.

Recent research suggests that, in developing countries, counseling is being increasingly recognized as an important part of care for people with AIDS and their families. Providing education and information has also gained popularity. In some countries, home-based health care is also being established to remove some of the burden from the hospitals, increase quality health care, and reduce costs.

Review Question

Explain how the incidence and transmission of HIV and AIDS differ outside the United States.

PREVENTING STIS AND AIDS

You might be feeling pretty overwhelmed with all this new information about STIs. It's important not to lose sight of the fact that there is much that you can do to help prevent a sexually transmitted infection. If you are sexually active, one of the most important things you can do is to get yourself tested. When you get into a sexual relationship, make sure your partner is also tested. Today's experts recommend full testing for STIs for sexually active men and women, including HIV testing (L. A. Johnson, 2005).

You can also make sure that you carefully choose your sexual partners and use barrier methods such as condoms to reduce your chances of acquiring an STI. Unless you are in a monogamous relationship, it's important to avoid high-risk sexual behaviors (see Sex in Real Life, "High-Risk Sexual Behaviors," on page 495). In addition, it's also important to be sure you are knowledgeable about STIs. Knowledge and education are powerful tools in decreasing the frequency of STIs.

Early Detection

If you already have a sexually transmitted infection, early detection and management of the infection are important and can help lessen the possibility of infecting others. Be sure to notify your sexual partners as soon as a positive diagnosis is made to help reduce the chances that someone else will become infected. As we discussed earlier in this chapter, many college students are apprehensive about getting tested for STIs, especially when they think they might be positive. It's important to be proactive in these matters and seek testing and treatment if you think you may have become infected. Many of the bacterial STIs can be treated with antibiotics. However, delaying treatment may result in more long-term consequences to your health, such as PID or infertility (for you or your partner).

Talking About STIs

Talking about STIs isn't always easy to do, and although people might not always respond positively to such a discussion, it is important. Honesty, trust, and communication are key elements to any successful relationship. In order to begin a conversation about STIs, choose a time when you can be alone and uninterrupted. Sometimes it's a little easier to start by bringing up the importance of honesty in relationships. You could talk about what you've learned in this class and how it's made you think about your current and future health. Talk about any infections, diseases, and past behaviors that may have put you or your partner at risk. Suggest STI testing and the importance of monogamy in your relationship. Chapter 10 includes a book recommendation about negotiating safer sex behaviors in intimate relationships (see page 325). This book discusses STI communication and the difficulties involved in such conversations.

Overall, as we discussed at the beginning of this chapter, it's important that we continue to try to break the silence about sexually transmitted infections and work to reduce the negative beliefs and stigma associated with these infections. Only then can we help encourage responsibility and safe behaviors.

Review Question

In what ways can we help to prevent STIs and AIDS?

Chapter Review

ACTIVE SUMMARY

1. STIs have historically been viewed as symbols of **(a)** _____ sexuality, which is why there has been a "punishment concept" of disease. College students are at a(an) **(b)** _____ risk of acquiring STIs because they engage in many behaviors that put them at higher risk, such as having **(c)** _____ partners and engaging in **(d)** _____ sexual intercourse.

2. The majority of STIs occur in those under **(a)** _____ years old; adolescents have a(an) **(b)** _____ biological **(c)** _____ for developing an STI.

3. All states require that syphilis, gonorrhea, chlamydia, HIV, AIDS, and chancroid be **(a)** _____ to public health centers. In addition, many states **(b)** _____ reporting cases of **(c)** _____ and HPV.

4. Women are at **(a)** _____ risk for long-term complications from STIs because of the fragility of the female **(b)** _____ tract. More women are **(c)** _____ and are more susceptible to gonorrhea, chlamydia, and HIV, although the spread of syphilis and genital warts is usually **(d)** _____ between the sexes. African Americans have higher rates of most STIs than Caucasians, even though STIs occur in all **(e)** _____ and ethnic groups.

5. HIV infection has **(a)** _____ in men who have sex with men, although there have been increases in the rates of gonorrhea, syphilis, and **(b)** _____ in HIV-infected MSM. Women who have sex with women can become infected with **(c)** _____, herpes, trichomoniasis, and **(d)** _____ .

6. Nonoxynol-9 has been found to increase the rate of genital **(a)** _____, causing a higher risk of STI **(b)** _____. **(c)** _____ are the most effective contraceptive method for **(d)** _____ the risk of acquiring an STI.

7. **(a)** _____ infections are those that are caused by parasites that live on the skin's surface and include pubic lice and **(b)** _____. Treatment is with **(c)** _____ creams to kill the parasites and their **(d)** _____.

8. The majority of women who are infected with **(a)** _____ are asymptomatic, whereas men are **(b)** _____. Testing for gonorrhea involves collecting a sample of the **(c)** _____ from the cervix, urethra, or another **(d)** _____ area with a cotton swab. Gonorrhea can be treated effectively with **(e)** _____. Antibiotics are usually administered orally, but in severe cases intramuscular injections may be necessary.

9. **(a)** _____ usually first infects the cervix, penis, anus, lips, or **(b)** _____. It can also infect a baby during birth.

Syphilis has decreased over the last few years in the United States and may soon be eliminated. Infection with syphilis is divided into **(c)** _____ stages: primary or early syphilis, secondary syphilis, and **(d)** _____ or late syphilis. **(e)** _____ are the treatment of choice today.

10. **(a)** _____ is the most frequently reported infectious disease in the United States and the most commonly diagnosed **(b)** _____ STI in the developed world. The majority of men and women with a chlamydia infection are **(c)** _____. Antibiotics are the treatment of choice today for chlamydia.

11. **(a)** _____ is relatively rare in the United States but is one of the most **(b)** _____ STIs in many developing countries. Once infected, women and men often develop small **(c)** _____ where the infected entered the body. The infection may spread to the lymph nodes of the groin, which can cause **(d)** _____ and pain. Chancroids are treated with antibiotics.

12. **(a)** _____ infections include trichomoniasis, hemophilus, bacterial vaginosis, and candiasis. The majority of women have symptoms, whereas the majority of men are asymptomatic. **(b)** _____ is caused by bacteria; and, although the majority of women are asymptomatic, some may experience a vaginal **(c)** _____, soreness, itching, and burning. Treatment includes oral antibiotics or vaginal **(d)** _____.

13. Bacterial **(a)** _____ (BV) is the most common cause of vaginal discharge and odor. Women with BV have been found to have an increased risk of **(b)** _____ and pelvic inflammatory disease. VVC is caused by a(an) **(c)** _____ that is normally present in the vagina, but it multiplies when the pH balance of the vagina is disturbed. Treatment includes either a(an) **(d)** _____ prescription or over-the-counter drugs.

14. **(a)** _____ infections include HSV, HPV, viral hepatitis, and HIV. Herpes is caused by either HSV-1 or HSV-2; however, once a person is infected, the symptoms can overlap. **(b)** _____ is one of the most common STIs in the United States. The virus can be transmitted even when a person does not have symptoms. Although the majority of genital herpes cases are caused by an infection with HSV-2, more are being caused by HSV-1. If a person does develop HSV sores, the **(c)** _____ occurrence is generally the most **(d)** _____. Recurrences of HSV are much less frequent with genital HSV-1 infection than with HSV-2. Once infected, a person will **(e)** _____ carry the virus in his or her body. The standard therapy for HSV infection today is **(f)** _____ drugs.

15. There are over 100 types of HPV, and 30 of these are sexually transmitted. Almost all (a) _____ disease can be attributed to HPV infection. Many people who are infected with HPV are asymptomatic, whereas others develop symptoms as late as 6 weeks to 9 months after infection. The majority of (b) _____ partners of people with cervical warts develop warts within 3 to 4 months of contact. (c) _____ warts can be treated in several ways, and no treatment method is superior to another or best for all patients with HPV. Women who have been diagnosed with genital warts are encouraged to have (d) _____ exams and Pap testing at least once a year.

16. Viral hepatitis is an infection that causes impaired (a) _____ function. There are three types of viral hepatitis: hepatitis A (HAV), hepatitis B (HBV), and hepatitis C (HCV). HAV infection is usually (b) _____, whereas infection with HBV and HCV is asymptomatic. (c) _____ tests are used to identify viral hepatitis infections. There is no specific treatment for infection with hepatitis A or hepatitis B. The majority of those infected with hepatitis C will become carriers of the infection, even though there may be no symptoms. (d) _____ are available for the prevention of both HAV and HBV, and research on a vaccine for hepatitis C is in progress.

17. Pelvic (a) _____ disease (PID) is an infection of the female genital tract, including the endometrium, Fallopian tubes, and the lining of the pelvic area. Today, (b) _____ is the leading cause of PID; 1 out of every (c) _____ women of reproductive age are found to have at least one episode of PID by the age of 35. Treatment for PID includes (d) _____.

18. (a) _____ is caused by an infection with the human immunodeficiency virus and is primarily transmitted through body fluids, including semen, vaginal fluid, and (b) _____. HIV attacks the (c) _____ cells in the blood, and antibodies can be detected in the bloodstream anywhere from 2 weeks to 6 months after infection. The attack on the T-helper cells causes the immune system to be less effective in its ability to fight disease, and so many infected people develop (d) _____ diseases. Women are the fastest growing U.S. group with AIDS, and heterosexual transmission is the most common way a woman is infected with HIV. AIDS is most dramatically affecting African Americans and continues to disproportionately affect (e) _____ communities throughout the world. College students are at risk for HIV because of high rates of sexual activity, multiple sexual partners, lack of (f) _____ during sexual activity, and sexual activity that takes place after a couple has been drinking.

19. Later symptoms of untreated AIDS may include significant weight loss, severe diarrhea, night sweats, oral (a) _____, gingivitis, oral ulcers, and persistent fever. The deterioration of the (b) _____ system makes it easier for opportunistic diseases to develop, including PCP, toxoplasmosis, cryptococcosis, cytomegalovirus, and Kaposi's sarcoma. Life expectancies for women with AIDS has been found to be (c) _____ shorter than men's, and infected women have a higher rate of cervical (d) _____ than do non–HIV-infected women.

20. Tests for HIV can either look for the virus itself or for (a) _____ that the body has developed to fight HIV. One of the biggest developments in diagnosis has been the development of (b) _____ HIV testing. These tests detect the presence of antibodies to HIV and require either a drop of (c) _____ or (d) _____ _____. Research continues to look for (e) _____ AIDS tests.

21. The development of highly active antiretroviral therapy has significantly reduced the number of deaths from HIV/AIDS. However, (a) _____ therapy is much more common in North America and Europe. (b) _____ dosages can cause a drug resistance or could cause the virus to survive and mutate into a (c) _____ strain that will not respond to drug therapy. An HIV-infected man or woman must undergo drug therapy for (d) _____.

22. (a) _____ and educational programs have begun to help reduce the spread of AIDS. Educational programs, advertising, mailings, public service announcements, and television shows all have helped to increase (b) _____ levels about HIV/AIDS. Many (c) _____ are beginning to include AIDS education in their (d) _____.

23. Families and friends of people with AIDS often do not receive the same (a) _____ support as do families and friends of people with other devastating diseases. Today, with the help of HAART (b) _____, many parents with HIV are living longer, and this has brought up issues of (c) _____ and (d) _____ to having a parent with HIV.

24. The worldwide total number of people living with HIV is over 38 million, and by far the (a) _____ of people infected with HIV have no access to (b) _____, mostly because of financial and cultural reasons. (c) _____ have also been affected by the AIDS epidemic; in fact, one child becomes an orphan every 14 seconds. Ninety percent of these orphans live in (d) _____ Africa.

25. There are ways to (a) _____ yourself from becoming infected with a(an) (b) _____. If you do become infected, early (c) _____ can reduce long-term (d) _____. Although it's not always easy to talk to a sexual partner about STIs, it's important to do so. We need to continue to break the (e) _____ about sexually transmitted infections and work to reduce the negative beliefs and (f) _____ associated with these infections.

ANSWERS

1. (a) corrupt; (b) increased; (c) multiple; (d) unprotected. 2. (a) 25; (b) higher; (c) risk; 3. (a) reported; (b) require; (c) HSV. 4. (a) greater; (b) reproductive; (c) asymptomatic; (d) equal; (e) racial. 5. (a) declined; (b) chlamydia; (c) hepatitis C; (d) HPV. 6. (a) ulceration; (b) infection; (c) Condoms; (d) reducing. 7. (a) Ectoparasitic; (b) scabies; (c) topical; (d) larvae. 8. (a) gonorrhea; (b) symptomatic; (c) discharge; (d) infected; (e) antibiotics. 9. (a) Syphilis; (b) nipples; (c) three; (d) tertiary; (e) Antibiotics. 10. (a) Chlamydia; (b) bacterial; (c) asymptomatic. 11. (a) Chancroid; (b) prevalent; (c) lesions; (d) swelling. 12. (a) Vaginal; (b) Hemophilus; (c) discharge; (d) suppositories. 13. (a) vaginosis; (b) endometriosis; (c) fungus; (d) antifungal. 14. (a) Viral; (b) HSV-2; (c) first; (d) painful; (e) always; (f) sexual; 15. (a) cervical; (b) Genital; (d) pelvic. 16. (a) liver; (b) symptomatic; (c) Blood; (d) Vaccines. 17. (a) inflammatory; (b) chlamydia; (c) 7; (d) antibiotics. 18. (a) AIDS; (b) blood; (c) T-helper; (d) opportunistic; (e) minority; (f) protection. 19. (a) candidiasis; (b) immune; (c) significantly; (d) dysplasia. 20. (a) antibodies; (b) rapid; (c) blood; (d) oral fluids; (e) home. 21. (a) HAART; (b) Missed; (c) resistant; (d) life. 22. (a) Prevention; (b) knowledge; (c) schools; (d) classes. 23. (a) social; (b) therapies; (c) disclosure; (d) adjusting. 24. (a) majority; (b) treatment; (c) Children; (d) sub-Saharan. 25. (a) protect; (b) STI; (c) detection; (d) consequences; (e) silence; (f) stigma.

Critical Thinking Questions

1. How will reading this chapter affect your own sexual practices? What material has made the biggest impact on you, and why?

2. Suppose that your best friend has never heard of chlamydia, and you now know that it occurs most frequently in those under the age of 25. What can you tell your friend about the symptoms, long-term risks, diagnosis, and treatment of chlamydia? Should he or she be worried?

3. Suppose that one late night when you are talking to a group of friends, the topic of sexually transmitted infections comes up. In your argument to encourage your friends to use condoms, what can you say about the asymptomatic nature of STIs? The properties of latency? How women are more at risk? How do you think your friends will respond?

4. Do you think the United States should provide HAART therapy to AIDS-infected men and women in sub-Saharan Africa who cannot afford it? Or should the United States provide sexuality education on AIDS prevention and to those who do not have the virus? How would the money be best spent, and why?

5. Have you ever dated someone with an STI? If so, when did you find out about it? How did you feel? Did it affect your sex life? How so?

6. If scientists developed a vaccine for STIs, would you take it? Why, or why not?

CHAPTER RESOURCES

Check It Out

Stine, G. J. (2005). **AIDS update: An annual overview of acquired immune deficiency syndrome.** San Francisco, CA: Benjamin Cummings.

This book presents an annual overview of the acquired immune deficiency syndrome and includes a balanced review of the latest information and most important aspects of HIV infection, HIV disease, and AIDS. More important, it places this information within a biological, medical, social, and legal framework so that students can understand the AIDS epidemic today. Information on anti-HIV therapy, testing, opportunistic infections, and cross-cultural aspects is included.

Philadelphia (1993; 2 hours, 5 minutes; Rated PG-13)

Although released in 1993, this film is a classic and contains excellent acting by Tom Hanks. Andrew Beckett (Tom Hanks), a gay lawyer infected with AIDS, is fired from his conservative law firm in fear that they might contract AIDS from him. Andrew then sues his former law firm with the help of Joe Miller (Denzel Washington), a homophobic lawyer. During the court battle, Miller sees that Beckett is no different from anyone else on the streets of Philadelphia, sheds his homophobia, and helps Beckett with his case before AIDS overcomes him. This movie explores the fear and societal implications of sexually transmitted infections.

 InfoTrac® College Edition

If your instructor ordered InfoTrac with this book, explore InfoTrac College Edition, your online library, for additional readings and review. Go to: **www.thomsonedu.com,** and enter these search terms:

chlamydia	pelvic inflammatory disease	gonorrhea
genital herpes	genital warts	HIV
HAART	AIDS	HPV

SexualityNow Companion Website

Go to **http://thomsonedu.com/carroll** for practice quiz questions, interactive activities, Internet links, critical thinking exercises, discussion forums, and more. You can also access sites from the Wadsworth Psychology Study Center (**http://psychology.wadsworth.com**) or you can connect directly to the following sites:

American Social Health Association

The American Social Health Association provides information on sexually transmitted infections. The website contains support, referrals, resources, and in-depth information about sexually transmitted infections.

Centers for Disease Control and Prevention

The Centers for Disease Control and Prevention's division of STI prevention provides information about sexually transmitted infections, including surveillance reports and disease facts. The CDC's division of HIV/AIDS prevention provides information about HIV and AIDS, including surveillance reports and facts about the infection.

Herpes.org

Herpes.org is an online resource for people with herpes and the human papillomavirus. The website provides information about the infections, what nonprescription and prescription treatments work, and where to find medical help and medication.

IWannaKnow.org

This website, maintained by the American Social Health Association, is designed to provide information about sexually transmitted infections. It includes facts on various STIs, symptoms, and treatments, as well as information on hepatitis infections, tattooing, and body piercings.

Joint United Nations Program on HIV and AIDS

The Joint United Nations Program on HIV and AIDS provides monitoring and evaluation of AIDS research and also provides access to various links and information about AIDS. Information on AIDS scenarios for the future, antiretroviral therapy, and HIV/AIDS in children and orphans is available.

SexualityNow   Sexuality Now

Go to **www.thomsonedu.com** to link to **SexualityNow,** your online study tool. First take the **Pre-Test** for this chapter to get your **Personalized Study Plan,** which will identify topics you need to review and direct you to online resources. Then take the **Post-Test** to determine what concepts you have mastered and what you still need work on.

Videos in SexualityNow

For additional information on topics discussed in this chapter, check out the videos in **SexualityNow** on the following topics:

- **AIDS in Africa**—Describes HIV/AIDS as related to gender, poverty, stigma, education, and justice.
- **HIV/AIDS: Orel**—Listen to Orel describe how strong social support and pursuing personal interests helps to mitigate the effects of HIV/AIDS.

16 Varieties of Sexual Expression

Sexuality ●● Now Go to www.thomsonedu.com to link to SexualityNow, your online study tool.

*H*uman sexuality can be expressed in many different ways. We tend to celebrate individual and cultural differences in most aspects of human life—in what people eat, how they dress, or how they dance, for example. Yet we have been less tolerant of sexual diversity, and we have historically considered such behavior "deviant" or "perverted." More modern views of sexuality, however, do not categorize people as "deviant" versus "normal" but see sexual behavior as a continuum.

For example, the sexual world is not really split into those who become sexually excited from looking at others naked or having sex and those who do not; most people get aroused to some degree from visual sexual stimuli. Some people get more aroused than others, and at the upper limits are those who can get aroused only when watching sexual scenes; such people have taken a normal behavior to an extreme. In this chapter we will explore variations of sexual behavior, including differences in sexual desire and the paraphilias.

WHAT IS "TYPICAL" SEXUAL EXPRESSION?

Some medical and sexuality texts still categorize certain kinds of behavior as sexual deviance. Many undergraduate texts discuss these behaviors in chapters titled abnormal, unusual, or atypical sexual behavior. Yet how exactly do we decide whether a behavior is "normal"? What is "typical" sexual activity? Where do we draw the line? Do we call it "atypical" if 5% of sexually active people do it? Ten percent? Twenty-five percent?

Sexual behaviors increase and decrease in popularity; oral sex, for example, was once considered a perversion, but now the majority of couples report that they engage in it at least occasionally. Perhaps, then, we should consider as "deviant" only behaviors that may be harmful in some way. Yet masturbation was once believed to lead to mental illness, acne, and stunted growth, and now it is considered a normal, healthy part of sexual expression. If many of these desires exist to some degree in all of us, then the desire itself is not atypical, just the degree of the desire.

Social value judgments, not science, primarily determine which sexual behaviors are considered "normal" by a society. For example, in 1906, Krafft-Ebing defined sexual deviance as "every expression of (the sexual instinct) that does not correspond with the purpose of nature—i.e., propagation" (J. C. Brown, 1983, p. 227). Certainly, most people would not go so far today. Freud himself stated that the criterion of normalcy was love and that defenses against "perversion" were the bedrock of civilization because perversion trivializes or degrades love (A. M. Cooper, 1991). Note that Freud's objections to perversion are not medical, as they were to most other mental disturbances, but moral.

Even "modern" definitions can contain hidden value judgments: "The sexually variant individual typically exhibits sexual arousal or responses to inappropriate people (e.g., minors), objects (e.g., leather, rubber, garments), or activities (e.g., exposure in public, coercion, violence)" (Gudjonsson, 1986, p. 192). "Appropriate" or "inappropriate" people, objects, or activities of sexual attention differ in different times, in different cultures, and for different people.

Despite these objections, certain groups of behaviors are considered the most common deviations from conventional heterosexual or homosexual behavior. The people who engage in these activities may see them as unproblematic, exciting aspects of their sexuality, or they may be very troubled by their behavior. Society may see the behavior as either solely the business of the individual in the privacy of his or her bedroom (e.g.,

Personal Voices

What Is "Kinky"?

College students were asked what the phrase "kinky sex" meant to them and how they would feel if their partner asked them to engage in "kinky" sex. Where, exactly, do most college students draw the line in the bedroom?

Male: *Kinky includes anything that involves going beyond what you're used to. I feel that if you act out of character, you are kinky. I have certain things that turn me on and certain things that don't. For example, I don't think anal sex is that outrageous but my girlfriend does.*

Female: *I'm not afraid to share details about my sex life, and I like to learn and experience different types of sexual activities. This is abundantly clear to anyone who comes in my room and sees the whip and handcuffs hanging off the bedpost. For me, something is kinky if it gets you excited because you feel you are being deviant by doing it.*

Male: *If somebody asked me to be "kinky," I might tie them up or something. I think assuming a dominating* position in the bedroom could be interesting. As for drawing the line, I remember one person telling me about "skat." This involves sexual arousal and the actual act of sex being performed using human feces (including orally). Yeah, I'd draw the line way before that.

Female: *If my partner asked me to try something new, or kinky, I would probably consider it. It's fun to experiment with some new behaviors . . . it brings a lot of spontaneity to the bedroom. I would draw the line at behaviors that made me feel uncomfortable. I would also become concerned if my partner liked behaviors that are aggressive or inflict pain. But as a general rule of thumb: anything that we both consent to is fair game.*

Male: *If a girl decided to give a guy a blow job but threw in the twist of putting ice in her mouth while she did it, that might be classified as kinky. Most people are brought up on the idea that sex in general or other sexual acts are performed under certain universal guidelines or standards.*

SOURCE: Author's files.

Review Question

Explain how a society determines what are "normal" and "abnormal" sexual behaviors.

sexual excitement from shoes or boots) or as a sign that the person is mentally ill (e.g., having sex with animals) or as dangerous and illegal (e.g., sex with underage children). In this chapter, we explore sexual behaviors that are fairly rare, theories of why people are attracted to unusual sexual objects, and how therapists have tried to help those who are troubled by their sexual desires.

sex byte

The risk of getting caught for engaging in a sexual offense is low. In fact, one pedophilia expert estimated there is only a 3% risk of being caught (Salter, 2003).

SEX Talk

Question: If I fantasize about watching other people having sex or if I get turned on by being spanked, does that mean I have a paraphilia?

A strong and varied fantasy life is the sign of healthy sexuality, and acting out fantasies in a safe sexual situation can add excitement to one's sex life. Problems may arise when: the fantasy or desire becomes so prominent or preoccupying that you are unable to function sexually in its absence; sexual play is taken to the point of physical or psychological injury; you feels extreme levels of guilt about the desire; or your compulsion to perform a certain type of sexual behavior interferes with everyday life, disrupts your personal relationships, or risks getting you in trouble with the law. Under any of these circumstances, it is advisable to see a qualified sex therapist or counselor.

PARAPHILIAS: MOVING FROM EXOTIC TO DISORDERED

The word **paraphilia** (pear-uh-FILL-ee-uh) is derived from the Greek "para" (besides) and "philia" (love or attraction). In other words, paraphilias are sexual behaviors that involve a craving for an erotic object that is unusual or different. According to the *DSM IV-TR*, the essential features involved in a paraphilia are recurrency and intensity of the sexual behavior that involves a nonhuman object or the suffering or humiliation of oneself or one's partner, a child, or a nonconsenting person (American Psychiatric Association, 2000). This behavior causes significant distress and interferes with a person's ability to work, interact with friends, and other important areas. To be diagnosed with a paraphilia, a person must be experiencing symptoms for 6 months or more. For some paraphiliacs, the fantasy or presence of the object of their desire is necessary for arousal and orgasm, whereas in others, the desire occurs periodically or exists separately from their other sexual relationships.

Research has shown that there are no "classic" profiles of a paraphiliac (Scheela, 1995). Individuals who engage in paraphiliac behavior are a heterogeneous group with no true factors that set them apart from nonparaphiliacs, with the exception of gender—the majority of paraphiliacs are men. Other than this, paraphiliacs come from every socioeconomic bracket, every ethnic and racial group, and from every sexual orientation (Seligman & Hardenburg, 2000). Although there are similar ranges of intelligence between paraphiliacs and nonparaphiliacs, there is some evidence that paraphiliacs have lower scores of overall general intelligence (Cantor et al., 2005). It is estimated that half of those who engage in paraphiliac behavior are married, and the majority report sexual problems and dysfunctions in their marital sexual relationships (S. B. Levine et al., 1990).

Although there are no classic profiles that fit all paraphilias, there are some factors that have been found to be related to the development of a paraphilia. Research has found that many paraphiliacs have grown up in a dysfunctional family and have experienced significant family problems during childhood that contribute to the poor social skills and distorted views of sexual intimacy often seen in paraphiliacs (Seligman & Hardenburg, 2000). This is not to say that everyone who grows up in such a household will develop a paraphilia; rather, it may be a related factor. The severity of paraphilias varies; someone with a mild case might use disturbing sexual fantasies during masturbation, whereas someone with a severe case may engage in unwanted sexual behavior with a child or may even murder.

Paraphilias are similar to many impulse-control disorders, such as substance abuse, gambling, and eating disorders (A. Goodman, 1993). Many paraphiliacs feel conflicted over their behavior, and they develop tension and a preoccupation with certain behaviors. They repeatedly try to suppress their sexual behaviors but are unable to do so (Seligman & Hardenburg, 2000). At some point, erotic arousal and sexual pleasure override their negative feelings (Golden, 2001).

Many people find lingerie exciting, or enjoy watching sexual scenes, or enjoy being lightly bitten or scratched during sex. For many paraphiliacs, however, the lingerie itself becomes the object of sexual attention, not a means of enhancing the sexuality of the partner. For this reason, some have suggested that the defining characteristic of paraphilia is that it replaces a whole with a part, that it allows the person to distance himself or herself from complex human sexual contact and replace it with the undemanding sexuality of an inanimate object, a scene, or a single action (L. J. Kaplan, 1991).

Motivations for paraphiliac behaviors vary (see Table 16.1). Some paraphiliacs claim that their behaviors provide meaning to their lives and give them a sense of self (A. Goodman, 1993), whereas others say the behaviors relieve their depression and loneliness and/or help them express rage (S. B. Levine et al., 1990). Many violent or criminal paraphiliacs have little ability to feel empathy for their victims and may convince themselves that their victims enjoy the experiences, even though the victims do not consent to them (Seligman & Hardenburg, 2000).

paraphilia
Clinical term used to describe types of sexual expressions that are seen as unusual and potentially problematic. A person who engages in paraphilias is often referred to as a paraphiliac or a sexual offender.

Sneak Peek

"In bondage, her life can literally be in my hands with rope, fire play, or more extreme kinds of S&M."—*Bondage and S&M*

Sexuality Now

TABLE 16.1	Paraphilia Typology
Paraphilia	**Behaviors**
Naïve experimenter	Limited number of exploratory paraphiliac behaviors; uses no force or threat
Undersocialized exploiter	Sexually isolated, unskilled; seeks self-aggrandizement and intimacy; behaviors are long-standing
Pseudo-socialized exploiter	Has good social skills; often suffered abuse; has rationalized behaviors; feels little guilt or remorse; seeks sexual pleasure
Sexually aggressive	Angry and aggressive; wants to dominate and humiliate others; often has coexisting problems with substances and impulse control; long-lasting disorder
Sexually compulsive	Repressed family background; engages in repetitive and compulsive behaviors for anxiety reduction; no direct physical contact with victims
Disturbed impulsive	Severely troubled family; emotional and cognitive difficulties; often misuses substances; is impulsive
Group-influenced	Motivated by peer pressure and a desire for approval and admiration

Source: O'Brien & Bera, 1986.

fetishist
One who focuses intensely on an inanimate object or body part (the *fetish*) for the arousal of sexual desire.

Research on paraphilias has been drawn mostly from clinical and incarcerated samples, which are almost certainly not representative of the population as a whole. The number of people who live comfortably with uncommon sexual habits is hard to determine because people tend to be reluctant to admit to their sexual inclinations, even in confidential questionnaires, especially if they seem unusual. What is known is that people who do have paraphilias usually have more than one (American Psychiatric Association, 2000).

Paraphiliacs are often portrayed as sick, perverted, or potential sex offenders. There is thus an attempt to draw a clear line between paraphiliacs and "normal" people; yet the line is rarely that clear. Certainly, there are paraphiliac behaviors that can be dangerous or can threaten others. Men who expose themselves to young girls, people who violate corpses, strangers who rub against women on buses, or adults who seduce underage children must not be allowed to continue their behavior. There can even be legal problems with the paraphilias that are not in themselves dangerous; some **fetishists** resort to stealing the object of interest to them, and occasionally a voyeur will break into people's homes. Also, paraphiliacs are often compulsive masturbators, even up to 10 times a day or more, which can make it difficult to hold certain jobs, for example. A number of therapies have been developed to help these people; but, as you will see, it is very difficult to change a person's arousal patterns.

Other people live comfortably with their paraphilias. It's important for us to differentiate between paraphilias that are consensual (those that involve a partner's consent) and nonconsensual (those that do not involve a partner's consent). A man who has a fetish for lingerie, for example, may find a partner who very much enjoys wearing it for him. As you will see from Thomas Sargent's description of his rubber fetish in Personal Voices, "The Story of a Rubber Fetishist," on page 543, the behavior brings him comfort, excitement, and a sense of well-being, and he has no desire to see his fetish go away.

SEX Talk

Question: Don't women also engage in these behaviors? Why are paraphilias more common in men?

No one really knows, although theories abound. Perhaps, some researchers suggest, paraphilias are developed visually, and the male tends, for some biological reason, to be more sexually aroused by visual stimuli than the female. Maybe cultural variables give men more sexual latitude in expressing what excites them. It could also have something to do with the way we look at it; women may express their paraphilias in different, less obvious ways than men. There could also be power differentials that contribute to higher rates in men.

Paraphilias Throughout the World

Although there has not been much research documenting the incidence, expression, and treatment of paraphilias outside the United States, there have been limited studies. The majority of information available concerns pedophilia, transvestism, and transsexualism. A limited amount of research exists on other paraphilias, such as sadomasochism. Below, we explore what we do know about paraphilias in a variety of countries.

Brazil

In Chapter 9 we discussed the conservative and religious background of many Brazilians, so it shouldn't come as any surprise that there is not a great deal of acceptance for paraphiliac behaviors. Although there are no legal restrictions against transvestism, researchers estimate that there are few who engage in this practice (de Freitas, 2004). Transsexualism is viewed negatively, and it is against the law to undergo sexual reassignment surgery (SRS). In fact, both the patient and surgeon would be charged with a felony if SRS were to take place (de Freitas, 2004). Because of this, some transsexuals travel to Europe to undergo SRS. We do know that throughout history zoophilia has been found to occur in Brazil, and it has been found to be more common in both men and those living in rural areas (de Freitas, 2004).

China

China has very strict policies against behaviors it deems inappropriate, and paraphilias certainly fall into this category. Sex offenders in China are often charged with "hooliganism," which is a term that includes a wide range of uncivil and sexually unrestrained behavior (Ruan & Lau, 2004). China has very severe penalties for those who engage in such behaviors, and harsh punishments are common. For example, one review reported that the Chinese government enforced the death penalty for certain sexual crimes, including forced sex and pedophilia (Ruan & Lau, 2004).

Germany

Although transvestites are considered deviant in Germany, they don't get much attention (Lautmann & Starke, 2004). Transsexuals, however, are often treated with disdain. Even so, new laws established in 2002 have provided two possibilities of gender change for transsexuals. In the first, often referred to as the "small solution," a transsexual changes his or her name without changing gender. To do so, he or she would need expert opinions from two people, confirming that he or she has been transsexual for at least 3 years. A "major solution" involves sexual reassignment surgery, which is widely available in Germany. This would lead to legal recognition of gender reassignment on official documents, including passports and birth certificates.

Denmark

Denmark, and many of the Scandinavian countries, have much more liberal attitudes about sexuality, so it shouldn't come as any surprise that they are more likely to see criminal behavior and press appropriate charges. Denmark has high sex crime reporting and treatment of offenders rates (Graugaard et al., 2004). In reaction to increased rates of child sexual abuse, Denmark opened a center for the treatment of sexually abused children at the University Hospital in Copenhagen in 2000, and today many groups actively educate professionals and the lay public about child sexual abuse (Graugaard et al., 2004).

Czech Republic

Paraphiliacs in the Czech Republic have many more opportunities for communication and contact with other paraphiliacs than they did in when they were under communist control (Zvěřina, 2004). This would include clubs, magazines, newspapers, and the Internet. Sadomasochism and fetishes are the most common paraphilias in the Czech Republic (Zvěřina, 2004). Sexual offenders who are charged with crimes are referred for counseling and treatments, which are covered under national health insurance plans.

Japan

Sadism and masochism are well-known in Japanese art and literature (Hatano & Shimazaki, 2004). Thousands of S&M magazines are sold each month, and many nightclubs cater to the S&M subculture. Like China, Japan has strict laws and punishments for people who engage in child sexual abuse. In 1999, Japan enacted a Child Prostitution and Child Pornography Prohibition Law that prohibits sexual activity with minors and enforces strict punishments for those charged with these behaviors (Hatano & Shimazaki, 2004).

Hong Kong

Although transvestism is not illegal in Hong Kong, a transvestite will be arrested if his or her appearance or behaviors disrupts the peace (Ng & Ma, 2004). Transvestites and transsexuals are often eyed with suspicion and treated differently than nonparaphiliacs. Transsexuals are allowed to undergo sexual reassignment surgery, but they are not legally recognized and must continue to use their chromosomal sex (Ng & Ma, 2004). This often leads to a reduction in social rights, such as tax deductions and child adoptions.

SOURCE: Francoeur & Noonan, 2004.

Review Question

Define paraphilia, and explain the factors that have been found to be related to the development of paraphilias.

Why should he want to put it to an end just because some other people find it distasteful, perverted, or abnormal? In what sense is such a person sick?

For this reason, paraphilias have become very controversial. Some theorists suggest that the term describes a society's value judgments about sexuality and not a psychiatric or clinical category (Silverstein, 1984). In fact, some theorists deny that terms like paraphilia really describe anything at all. Robert J. Stoller, a famous psychoanalytic theorist, objected to the idea of trying to create psychological explanations that group people by their sexual habits (Stoller, 1996).

Theories About Where Paraphilias Begin

Many researchers have theorized as to why and how paraphilias develop, but very little consensus has been reached. Paraphilias are undoubtedly complex behavior patterns, which may have biological, psychological, or social origins—or aspects of all three.

Biological Theories

Biological researchers have found that a number of conditions can initiate paraphiliac behavior. Men without previous paraphilias began to display paraphiliac behavior when they developed temporal lobe epilepsy, brain tumors, and disturbances of certain areas of the brain (Kreuter et al., 1998; G. Simpson et al., 2001). This does not mean that everyone with a paraphilia has one of these diseases. Researchers have found that some paraphiliacs have differences in brain structure and brain chemistry and possible lesions in certain parts of the brain (Kennet, 2000). Researchers have also been studying whether higher levels of certain hormones, such as testosterone, may contribute to the development of a paraphilia (Giotakos et al., 2005). However, at most these are factors that may lead some people to be more likely to develop a paraphilia, and they do not explain the majority of paraphiliac behaviors.

Psychoanalytic Theory

Psychoanalytic thought suggests that paraphilias can be traced back to the difficult time the infant has in negotiating his way through the Oedipal crisis and castration anxiety. This can explain why paraphilias are more common among men because both boys and girls identify strongly with their mothers, but girls can continue that identification, whereas boys must, painfully, separate from their mothers to establish a male identity.

Louise Kaplan, a psychoanalyst, suggests that every paraphilia involves issues of masculinity or femininity; as she writes, "[E]very male perversion entails a masquerade or impersonation of masculinity and every female perversion entails a masquerade or impersonation of femininity" (1991, p. 249). For example, a man who exposes himself in public may be coping with castration anxiety by evoking a reaction to his penis from women. The exhibitionist in this view is "masquerading" as a man to cover up feelings of nonmasculinity; he is saying, in effect, "Let me prove that I am a man by showing that I possess the instrument of masculinity." He even needs to demonstrate that his penis can inspire fear, which may be why exhibitionists disproportionately choose young girls, who are more likely to display a fear reaction (Kline, 1987). This confirms to the exhibitionist the power of his masculinity.

On the other hand, voyeurs, who are excited by looking at others nude or having sex, may be fixated on the experience that aroused their castration anxieties as children—the sight of genitals and sexuality (Kline, 1987). Looking allows the person to gain power over the fearful and hidden world of sexuality while safe from the possibility of contact. The visual component of castration anxiety occurs when the boy sees the power and size of the father's genitals and the lack of a penis on his mother or sisters. The act of looking initiates castration anxiety, and in the voyeur, the looking has never ceased. Yet looking itself cannot really relieve the anxiety permanently, and so the voyeur is compelled to peep again and again.

Peggy Beauregard

Janell Carroll

Young children often cross-dress as the other sex; however, the majority of them will not become cross-dressers.

Developmental Theories

Freud suggested that children are polymorphously perverse; that is, at birth we have a general erotic potential that can be attached to almost anything. We learn from an early age what sexual objects society deems appropriate for us to desire, but society's messages can get off track. For example, advertising tries to "sexualize" its products—we have all seen shoe commercials, for example, that emphasize the long, sexy legs of the model while focusing on the shoes she wears. Some boys may end up focusing on those shoes as objects of sexual fantasy, which can develop into a fetish.

A theory that builds on similar ideas is John Money's (1984, 1986, 1990) **lovemaps.** Money suggests that the auditory, tactile, and (especially) the visual stimuli we experienced during childhood sex play form a template in our brain that defines our ideal lover and ideal sexual situation. If our childhood sex play remains undisturbed, development goes on toward heterosexual desires. If, however, the child is punished for normal sexual curiosity or if there are traumas during this stage, such as sexual abuse, the development of the lovemap can be disrupted in one of three ways.

In **hypophilia** (high-po-FILL-ee-uh), negative stimuli prevent the development of certain aspects of sexuality, and the genitals may be impaired from full functioning. Overall, females are more likely to experience hypophilia than men, resulting in an inability to orgasm, vaginal pain, or lubrication problems later in life. A lovemap can also be disrupted to cause a condition called **hyperphilia** (high-per-FILL-ee-uh)**,** in which a person defies the negative sexual stimulus and becomes overly sexually active, even becoming compulsively sexual (we discuss hypersexuality later in this chapter). Finally, a lovemap can be disrupted when there is a paraphilia and a *substitution* of new elements into the lovemap. Because normal sexual curiosity has been discouraged or made painful, the child redirects erotic energy toward other objects that are not forbidden, such as shoes, rubber, or just looking; in other cases, the child turns his or her erotic energy inward and becomes excited by pain or humiliation.

Once this lovemap is set, it becomes very stable, which explains why changing it is so difficult. For example, Money (1984) suggests that sexual arousal to objects may arise when a parent makes a child feel shame interest in an object. For example, a boy may be caught with his mother's panties in the normal course of curiosity about the woman's body, but when he is severely chastised, the panties become forbidden, dirty, promising of sexual secrets, and he may begin to seek them out. The development of a lovemap is similar to a big bowl of Jell-O. When you first make Jell-O, it's fluid and moves around in the dish. If you put fruit in the Jell-O, it moves around as well. However, once the Jell-O is set, it becomes very difficult to take a piece of the fruit out without leaving a big gaping hole. Like the Jell-O that is firmly set after time, a lovemap is difficult to change.

Another theory about how these fixations occur is the idea of **courtship disorders** (K. Freund & Blanchard, 1986; K. Freund et al., 1983, 1984). Organizing paraphilias into "courtship" stages suggests that the paraphiliac's behavior becomes fixed at a preliminary stage of mating that would normally lead to sexual intercourse. Thus, a person becomes fixated on a particular person, object, or activity and does not progress to typical mating behaviors.

Behavioral Theories

Behaviorists suggest that paraphilias develop because some behavior becomes associated with sexual pleasure through conditioning (G. D. Wilson, 1987). For example, imagine that a boy gets an enema. While receiving it, the boy has an erection, either by coincidence or because he finds the stimulus of the enema pleasurable (it becomes a reinforcement). Later, remembering the enema, he becomes excited and masturbates. As he repeats his masturbatory fantasy, a process called **conditioning** occurs, whereby sexual excitement becomes so associated with the idea of the enema that he has trouble becoming excited in its absence.

You can imagine how similar situations could lead to other types of fetishes: A boy lies naked on a fur coat, or takes a "horse" ride on his aunt's long black leather boots, or

lovemap
Term coined by John Money to refer to the template of an ideal lover and sexual situation we develop as we grow up.

hypophilia
Lack of full functioning of the sexual organs due to missing stages of childhood development.

hyperphilia
Compulsive sexuality due to overcompensating for negative reactions to childhood sexuality.

courtship disorder
A theory of paraphilias that a person's paraphilia stems from being stuck in a preliminary stage of normal courtship progression.

conditioning
In behaviorism, the process whereby a person associates a particular behavior with a positive response; for example, if food repeatedly is served to a dog right after the sound of a bell, the dog will salivate at the sound of the bell even when no food is served.

puts on his sister's panties, or spies on a female houseguest through the bathroom key-hole. All of these behaviors become positively reinforced and thus are more likely to be repeated.

Sociological Theories

Another way of looking at the causes of paraphilias is to examine the ways society encourages certain behaviors. Feminists, for example, argue that in societies that treat women as sexual objects anyway, it is a natural development to replace the woman with another, inanimate sexual object. When men and their sexual organs are glorified, some men may need to reinforce their masculinity by exposing themselves and evoking fear.

American society is ruled by images, saturated with television, movies, commercials, advertisements, and magazines; and most of these images have highly charged sexual imagery (Collins, 2005). The result, some argue, is a world where the image takes the place of the reality, where it becomes common to substitute fantasies for reality. Surrounded by media, the society experiences things vicariously, through reading about it or seeing it rather than actually doing it. In such a climate, representations of eroticism may be easily substituted for sex itself, and so paraphilias become common.

Describing the Paraphilias

Paraphilias have been grouped into a number of major categories by researchers and clinicians. We will review some of the more common types of paraphilias, including: fetishism; sadism and masochism; exhibitionism and voyeurism; transvestic fetishism; and pedophilia.

Fetishism

A fetish is an inanimate object or a body part not usually associated with the sex act that becomes an individual's primary or exclusive focus of sexual arousal and orgasm. The fetishist (FEH-tish-ist) can develop a sexual response to an object, such as shoes, boots, panties, or bras; to a fabric, such as leather, silk, fur, or rubber; or to a body part, such as feet, buttocks, or hair (Wasserman, 2001). As with most paraphilias, the majority of fetishists are male. The strength of the preference for the object varies from thinking about or holding the object to a need to use it during all sexual acts. In the absence of the object, a male with a fetish may experience erectile dysfunction (American Psychiatric Association, 2000).

Many people enjoy using lingerie or even rubber or other fabrics as part of their lovemaking without becoming dependent on them for arousal. The fetishist, on the other hand, needs the presence or the fantasy of the object in order to achieve arousal and sometimes cannot achieve orgasm in its absence. Some fetishists integrate the object of their desire into their sexual life with a partner; for others it remains a secret fetish, with hidden collections of shoes, or panties, or photographs of a body part, over which they masturbate in secret, ever fearful of discovery.

Many fetishists see their sexual habits as a major part of their life, a source of their sense of identity; yet because fetishism is often regarded by society as shameful, they may be embarrassed to admit to their sexual desires. It is therefore rare to find a person who is open about their fetish and even has a sense of humor about it, as Sargent does in his description of his rubber fetish in the accompanying Personal Voices, "The Story of a Rubber Fetishist."

Different cultures hold up different body parts, objects, colors, or smells as symbols of attraction and sexuality for mating (see Chapter 7, page 194, for more information about Attraction in Different Cultures). Fetishism is symbol selection gone awry, in which the person becomes sexually attracted to the symbol itself, instead of what it represents. Put another way, for the fetishist, the object—unlike the living, breathing person—can stand for pure eroticism without the complication of having to deal with another person's feelings, wants, and needs. It can be a refuge from the complexity of interpersonal sexual relations. In that sense, all the paraphilias we discuss can be seen as a

Review Question

Differentiate between how the biological, psychoanalytic, developmental, behavioral, and sociological theories explain paraphilias.

sex byte

After the 2005 hurricanes in Florida, convicted sex offenders were banned from using public hurricane shelters (because many were located in schools; Koch, 2005). During the aftermath of the hurricane, convicted sex offenders were offered temporary housing in prisons.

Personal Voices

The Story of a Rubber Fetishist

I am a rubber fetishist and professional therapist, in that order. This combination has given me a special view of unusual sexual practices both through my own personal experience and as a result of the large number of other individuals whom I have encountered professionally and personally.

I have four clear vignettes of memory associated with my early delight with rubber which I present either because they stimulate me in the telling or because they may be important to a therapist or client. One is of a woman with long dark hair playing with my penis by stroking it with soft rubber panties and moving her long hair gently and playfully over it. The whole image is intense and all involving. It is loving, fun, sexually exciting (I have no image of the state of my penis), secure, and safe. For me, rubber most often provides all of these experiences in one simultaneous concert of sensations. A second image is that of a moment of pleasant security when I pull back the bed covers far enough to place my hand gently on the rubber sheet . . . to exchange the upset of a forgotten and unpleasant encounter with an adult for the quiet tranquility of the soft rubber and its loving associations. A third image is sliding under the cotton sheet to enjoy the rubber after I have been "tucked in" at night and then engaging in what my mother called "bounding up and down," still my favorite form of stimulation with my face and whole body gently moving over the rubber, skillfully massaging my penis between the rubber and my stomach. The fourth image is of a birthday. The rubber was in the form of solid rubber animals, smooth and rubber smelling but rather hard and of little sexual use. By the time I was three I was a full-blown rubber fetishist. No raincoat, bathing cap, or pair of baby panties was (or is) safe from me. My pediatrician was warm and kind about it, and I appreciate the impact of his support on my life. I had no inkling of being weird, no guilt, in contrast with many of my fellow fetishists at the hands of their professionals. I hoped that I wouldn't outgrow it, and I didn't. . . . Simply stated, my life involved rubber as a central element from my earliest years and still does as I enter my sixties. Neither my mother nor professionals stimulated any guilt.

I had one encounter with a psychiatrist regarding my fetish. He told me that if I felt guilty (discovering that I was unusual seemed like guilt) I could either lay the guilt to rest or the rubber. Keeping both could be emotionally disruptive. . . . For me, of course, I chose to keep the rubber.

In my own presentations of my rubber fetish I do not fail to enjoy some good laughs at myself. This is because I take myself seriously, seriously enough to laugh at things that are absurd. For example, I have received disapproving looks from women wearing rubber raincoats who thought I was looking at them, and from men who mistook my absorbed gaze as sexual attraction to them. . . . Or the small department store that always had a supply of various kinds of rubber coats (if I don't have a particular size or color, I must [get one]). The salesman took me to a private loft upstairs where there were hundreds of rubber coats. I do not know if someone there shared my fetish, but it was my idea of heaven. I took lots of time, so the salesman asked if it was all right if he left me alone. All right? I went around my heaven with a delightful erection and sampled the softness of the rubber against my penis. Every coat in the collection. Then I took a few and laid them on a flat surface and made love to them. It was incredible. It's all silly, and fun.

Laughter, particularly at the self, dislodges the judgments and fears that are associated with most sexual behaviors because it provides a new perspective. The fetishes offer the therapist the opportunity to dislodge the seriousness which entrenches a distressed perspective, and discover the effectiveness of these approaches even to serious sexual difficulty and offenses. It is also effective. At best, a six-foot man looks ridiculous in ten-inch heels and knows it. If the therapist can't laugh, the message is clear to the client that it is as weird as he thought.

SOURCE: From Thomas Sargent, "Fetishism," *Journal of Social Work and Human Sexuality,* 1988, pp. 27–42. Reprinted by permission of The Haworth Press, Inc.

---

type of fetishism; pain and humiliation, or women's clothes, or looking at people having sex can each be a substitute for interpersonal sexuality.

Sadism and Masochism

Sadism refers to the intentional infliction of physical or psychological pain on another person in order to achieve sexual excitement. The *DSM-IV-TR* describes sadism as a condition in which a person has sexual fantasies, urges, or behaviors that involve an

Review Question

Explain fetishism, and identify the most common fetish items.

sadism
Focus on administering pain and humiliation as the preferred or exclusive method of sexual arousal and orgasm.

Sadomasochists often use props, like leather clothes, studs, chains and nipple clips, to symbolize their dominance or submission.

masochism
Focus on receiving pain and humiliation as the preferred or exclusive method of sexual arousal and orgasm.

sadomasochism
The sexual activities of partners in which one takes a dominant, "master" position, and the other takes a submissive, "slave," position.

dominant
Describes the active role in sadomasochistic sexuality.

submissive
Describes the passive role in sadomasochistic activity.

flagellation
Striking a partner, usually by whipping.

caning
Beating someone with a rigid cane.

birching
Whipping someone using the stripped branch of a tree.

scatophagia
The ingestion of feces, often as a sign of submission.

urolagnia
The ingestion of urine, often as a sign of submission.

infantilism
Treating the submissive partner as a baby, including dressing the person in diapers in which he or she is forced to relieve himself or herself.

infliction of pain, suffering, or humiliation to enhance or achieve sexual excitement. Sadistic fantasies or acts may include restraint, blindfolding, strangulation, spanking, whipping, pinching, beating, burning, electrical shocks, torture, and in some cases, killing (American Psychiatric Association, 2000).

The term is named after Donatien Alphonse François de Sade (1740–1814), known as the Marquis de Sade. De Sade was sent to prison for kidnapping and terrorizing a beggar girl and then later for tricking some prostitutes into eating "Spanish fly," supposedly an aphrodisiac, but which caused such burning and blistering that one threw herself out a window (see Chapter 14 for more information about Spanish fly and other aphrodisiacs). While in prison, de Sade wrote novels describing such tortures as being bound hand and foot, suspended between trees, set upon by dogs, almost being eviscerated (cut open), and so on. De Sade believed that the highest form of sexual activity for women was pain, not pleasure, because pleasure could be too easily faked. Marquis De Sade spent much of his life in prison and died in a lunatic asylum (Bullough, 1976).

Masochism (MASS-oh-kiz-um), the achievement of sexual pleasure through one's own physical pain or psychological humiliation, was named after another novelist, Leopold Baron Von Sacher-Masoch (1836–1895). Sacher-Masoch believed that women were created to subdue men's "animal passions," and he describes the whippings he himself experienced at the hands of his mistresses (Bullough, 1976). Masochism involves the act of being humiliated, beaten, bound, or made to suffer (American Psychiatric Association, 2000).

Sadism and masochism both associate sexuality and pain, and most people who practice one are also involved with the other. Therefore, the phenomenon as a whole is often referred to as **sadomasochism** (say-doe-MASS-oh-kiz-um), or S&M. Because sadomasochism encompasses a wide variety of behaviors, the number of people who engage in it depends on how one defines it. In their survey, Janus & Janus (1993) found that 14% of men and 11% of women report some personal experience with S&M.

Freud and his followers made sadomasochism central to their theories about adult sexuality. Freud believed that to some degree we all feel ambivalent about the ones we love and even, at times, feel the desire to hurt them. But we also feel guilty about it, especially in early childhood, and the guilt we feel is satisfied by turning that hurt on ourselves. Later psychoanalytic theorists believed that the goal of masochism was not pain or punishment itself, but rather relinquishing the self to someone else in order to avoid responsibility or anxiety for sexual desires. To these theorists, we all engage in some sadistic and some masochistic behaviors in our love relationships.

Sexual responses to pain exist, to some degree, in many sexual relationships. Kinsey and his colleagues (1953), for example, found that about half the men and women in his sample experienced erotic response to sexual biting, and 24% of men and 12% of women had some erotic response to sadomasochistic stories. Another study found that 25% of men and women reported occasionally engaging in sadomasochistic behavior (Rubin, 1990). For example, some couples use bondage as a variation on their lovemaking without any other strong sadomasochistic elements (Comfort, 1987).

The paraphiliac sadomasochist takes these natural sadomasochistic tendencies to an extreme. S&M involves the use of physical pain, psychological humiliation, or both as part of sexuality. In most S&M encounters, one partner plays the **dominant** role ("master") and the other the **submissive** ("slave"). Overall, bondage and restraint are the most common expressions of S&M, although spanking and exposure to urine and feces may also be involved (Seligman & Hardenburg, 2000).

A variety of techniques are commonly used to physically dominate the submissive partner. Tying the submissive partner up or using restraints to render him or her helpless is often referred to as "bondage and discipline" (B&D). B&D is often accompanied by **flagellation, caning, birching,** or other painful or shocking stimuli on the skin such as the use of hot wax, ice, or biting. Psychological techniques can include sensory deprivation (through the use of face masks, blindfolds, earplugs), humiliation (being subject to verbal abuse or being made to engage in embarrassing behaviors such as boot-licking, **scatophagic** (scat-oh-FAJ-ick) behavior, **urolagnia** (yur-oh-LOG-nee-uh), or acting like a dog), forced cross-dressing, or **infantilism** (American Psychiatric Association, 2000;

Gosselin, 1987; Moser, 1988). This is accompanied by verbal descriptions of what is to come and why the person deserves it, increasing in intensity over time to eventual sexual climax. Note that the pain is used as part of a technique to enhance sexuality—the pain itself is not exciting. If the submissive partner were beat up on his or her way home from a sexual encounter, he or she would not find the resultant pain in any way exciting.

S&M does not generally result in any lasting physical damage, as the encounter is usually a carefully scripted sexual ritual, with both sides knowing how far they can go and what roles to play. Partners often have an agreed on "exit phrase" that serves as a signal to end the role playing. Still, sometimes S&M can go too far and result in accidental injury or even death. Though a small number of people are nonconsensual, criminal sadists who derive joy in hurting or killing others, they bear little relation to the subculture of sadomasochists who use S&M as a mutual sexual activity.

People can participate in S&M to different degrees. For some couples, S&M is an occasional diversion in their lovemaking. Others pursue it outside of a committed relationship; for example, most big cities have newspapers with advertisements for sadomasochistic services, in which a **dominatrix** will offer her services to submissive males. Many report that executives and politicians and other men with power are among their biggest clients. For these men, the opportunity to absolve themselves of decision making and put their sexual lives completely in the hands of a dominant woman is very exciting.

A sadomasochistic subculture exists for those who have adopted S&M as a lifestyle (see the accompanying Personal Voices, "Vanilla's Okay, But I Prefer Rocky Road"). Partners meet in S&M clubs, read S&M newsletters and magazines, and join organizations (such as the Eulenspiegel Society, the Society of Janus, or the lesbian S&M group SAMOIS). Specialty shops cater to S&M advocates, selling restraints, whips, and leather clothing. The sadomasochistic encounter, which is really a kind of drama or performance, is enhanced by both sides knowing their roles and dressing the part.

Much of S&M is about playing roles, usually with appropriate attitude, costuming, and scripted talk (Hoff, 2003). The S&M encounter is carefully planned, and the dominant partner is usually very careful not to actually hurt the submissive partner while "torturing" him or her. A "safe word" is usually agreed on so that the submissive partner can signal if he or she is in real distress. *The Master's and Mistress' Handbook*, a guide to S&M encounters, offers a set of rules on how to torture one's partner without really causing harm:

> Remember that a slave may suddenly start to cough or feel faint. If masked and gagged, choking or lack of oxygen may result in serious consequences within seconds. . . . Never leave a bound and gagged slave alone in a room. . . . It is essential that gags, nostril tubes, enema pipes, rods and other insertions should be scrupulously clean and dipped into mild antiseptic before use. . . . Never use cheap or coarse rope. This has no "give" and can quickly cause skin-sores. (Quoted in Gosselin, 1987, pp. 238–239)

Sadomasochistic subcultures exist among gays, lesbians, and heterosexuals. In heterosexual S&M, power relations between the sexes are often overturned, with the female being the dominant partner and the male submissive. The sadomasochistic drama is used to explore the nature of social relations by using sex as a means to explore power (Truscott, 1991). Both heterosexual and homosexual S&M practitioners derive sexual excitement from playing with power relations, from either being able to dominate another completely or to give in completely to another's will.

The S&M subculture takes symbols of authority and dominance from the general culture, such as whips, uniforms, and handcuffs, and uses them in a safe erotic drama in which scripted roles take the place of "real self." It even mocks these symbols of authority by using them for erotic pleasure. R. F. Baumeister (1988) suggests that sadomasochism is a reaction to modern society itself. Noting that sexual masochism proliferated when Western culture became highly individualistic, Baumeister suggests that it relieves the submissive partner of a sense of responsibility for the self by placing one's behavior completely under someone else's control (which may be why many businessmen pay a dominatrix to humiliate them). For the sadistic partner, it relieves the sense of interaction and sensitivity usual to some degree in sexual intercourse; the personhood of the submissive partner is ignored, and he or she can become a vehicle for the pleasure of the dominant partner.

dominatrix
A woman, often a prostitute, who humiliates and dominates submissive men.

© Joel Gordon

A dominatrix engages in S&M behavior and offers her services to submissive males.

Review Question

Differentiate between sadism and masochism, and explain sadomasochistic behaviors.

Personal Voices

Vanilla's Okay, But I Prefer Rocky Road

Following is a personal account written by Jillian G., a 21-year-old college student who became interested in masochistic behavior when she was 6 years old.

As an American, I enjoy my constitutional rights. As a child of the 80s, I really enjoy The Breakfast Club. As a human, I can't help but love Oreos. I'm just like you. But I'm also a masochist; and as a masochist, I enjoy being tied up and spanked.

When a Dominant puts me over his knee and spanks me, first gently, then harder, with escalating force—it's an amazing feeling. At first I feel the warmth of his hand and legs and perhaps I feel his pulse picking up despite his composed expression. Then the pain sets in, and that's all I can think of; that shocking, delicious pain and the knowledge that I could stop it if I really wanted to, but I don't want to. The experience is too wonderful; the spanking itself, the warmth my reddening skin gives off, the intermittent kneading after every ten slaps or so. Now, he changes to a paddle, wood or leather for preference; adding to the shock of pain the surprise of sudden coolness against my hot skin, the flat firmness contrasting the soft contours of his hand. Everything else fades away. Maybe there are others in the dark watching this little tableau, maybe I had a fight with a friend and it's been haunting me, maybe my foot has fallen asleep—at this moment none of that matters. My world consists solely of the spanker, my body and the wonderful sensations.

I realized I was a submissive by the time I turned 6 years old. When I was 11, roaming the stacks of my local library I found a copy of Exit to Eden—a romantic novel set on an island resort devoted to sadistic and masochistic fantasies. That's how I learned that I was a masochist and that's how I learned there were other people like me.

There are a lot of people in the psychological community and the community at large who would say

that wanting what I want and doing what I do means that there's something wrong with me, that something happened to me when I was a child to pervert my sexual behavior. But they're wrong; this is who I am. Though I can and do, on occasion, enjoy what is known as "vanilla sex," I just prefer "rocky road."

I became an active member in the "scene," or the sadomasochism community, when I turned 21. Before then I'd tried a few Internet fetish dating sites, with very limited success. I enjoy myself and life more now then I ever did when I repressed my "deviant" desires. Like any interest that isn't totally mainstream, it's easier to become more comfortable with yourself once you socialize with your peers. I joined The Eulenspiegel Society, an organization concerned mainly with safety, education and socializing within the BDSM (bondage/discipline/sadism/masochism) community. I met some great friends, learned a terrific amount of stuff about the scene and myself; and became more confident and assertive in my everyday life—a great lesson I learned there was just because I'm submissive doesn't mean I'm submissive to YOU. Another terrific factor of being out and about "in the scene" is I can casually ask someone what they're "into." After stumbling through explanations to several boyfriends about wanting to be tied up and spanked, it's a really amazing, really freeing experience to be able to be so open so easily.

Writing this has been freeing, as well; I've been given the opportunity to give you a first-hand account from the other side; I'm not a psychologist, but I do know myself. And there's nothing sick or wrong about what I do. People like me follow the same basic tenets as you do—actually, we're known for it: "Safe, Sane and Consensual" has always been our motto. It's just that where you say potato, we say kinky sex.

SOURCE: Author's files.

Exhibitionism and Voyeurism

Visual stimuli are basic aspects of sexuality; most sexually active people enjoy looking at the nude bodies of their partners, and such things as lingerie and the act of undressing one's partner can enhance the sexual nature of the human form. The enormous industry of adult magazines and books, the almost obligatory nude scene in modern movies, the embarrassment most people feel when seen naked inappropriately, and even the common nighttime dream of being caught naked in public all show the fundamental psychological power of visual sexual stimuli.

For some people, looking at nudity or sexual acts, or being seen naked or engaging in sex, become the paramount activities of sexuality. The person who becomes sexually aroused primarily from displaying his (or, more rarely, her) genitals, nudity, or sexuality to strangers is an **exhibitionist;** the person whose primary mode of sexual stimulation is to watch others naked or engaging in sex is called a **voyeur.** Langevin and Lang (1987) review a number of studies that show that there is a close connection between exhibitionism and voyeurism; most exhibitionists engaged in voyeuristic habits before beginning to expose themselves.

exhibitionist
A person who exposes his or her genitals to strangers as a preferred or exclusive means of sexual arousal and orgasm.

voyeur
One who observes people undressing or engaging in sex acts without their consent as a preferred or exclusive means of sexual arousal and orgasm.

Exhibitionism   Exhibitionism involves exposing the genitals to a stranger (American Psychiatric Association, 2000). As such, this behavior is nonconsensual. The exhibitionist (or "flasher"), who is usually male, achieves sexual gratification from exposing his genitals in public or to unsuspecting people. What excites the exhibitionist is not usually the nudity itself but the lack of consent of the victim as expressed in his or her shocked or fearful reaction. True exhibitionists would not get the same sexual charge being naked on a nude beach, for example, where everyone is naked.

Exhibitionists usually have erections while exposing themselves, and they masturbate either then and there or later, while thinking about the reactions of their victims. Usually exhibitionism begins in the teen years and decreases as a man ages; however, it may worsen in times of stress or disappointment (American Psyciatric Association, 2000; Seligman & Hardenburg, 2000).

Exhibitionism is legally classified as "indecent exposure" and accounts for up to one-third of all sex convictions in the United States, Canada, and Europe (Langevin & Lang, 1987). However, it's important to keep in mind that exhibitionists have a witness to their crimes, unlike some of the other paraphilias (such as voyeurism). As such, there is a higher likelihood of being caught. Although overall rates of exhibitionism are difficult to determine, between 33% and 35% of women in a United States college sample (D. J. Cox, 1988) and in a similar Hong Kong sample (D. J. Cox et al., 1982) reported being subjected to a male exhibitionist, most commonly in their early adolescence.

Although female exhibitionism is rare, it is interesting how much more acceptable it is for a woman to expose her body in U.S. society. Few people would complain about this woman exposing her breasts in public.

Many exhibitionists do not desire actual sexual activity with the victim. Research has failed to confirm any personality characteristics that might be common to exhibitionists except that the behavior is compulsive and very difficult to stop (Rabinowitz et al., 2002). Many exhibitionists have normal dating and sexual histories, are married and have normal sexual relations with their spouses, and do not seem to engage in their behavior instead of heterosexual intercourse (Langevin & Lang, 1987). Others tend to be shy and withdrawn and to marry their first girlfriend. If you are approached by a flasher, the best option would be to quietly walk away.

Exhibitionism in women is rare, although cases of it are reported in the literature (Grob, 1985; Rhoads & Boekelheide, 1985). Rhoads and Boekelheide (1985) suggest that the female exhibitionist may desire to feel feminine and appreciated, and seeing men admire her naked body reinforces her sense of sexual value and femininity. Perhaps, then, exhibitionism in women just takes a different form than in men. Another factor may be that women have much more opportunity to expose their bodies in social settings without being arrested. Even sophisticated eveningwear often exposes the woman's cleavage, and short skirts and women's bathing suits (such as thong-style suits) cover very little. Women, therefore, have more legitimate ways to expose their bodies than men do. This type of exposure may be enough for female exhibitionists.

Obscene Telephone Callers   The exhibitionist must have the courage to confront his victims in person; the telephone allows a more anonymous kind of contact for the timid paraphiliac. **Scatolophilia** (scat-oh-low-FILL-ee-uh), the technical name for obscene telephone calling, is a form of exhibitionism in which a person, almost always male, calls women and becomes excited as the victims react to his obscene suggestions. Most scatolophiliacs masturbate either during the call or afterward. Like exhibitionism, scatophilia is nonconsensual, and the scatolophiliac becomes excited by the victim's reactions of fear, disgust, or outrage.

scatolophilia
Sexual arousal from making obscene telephone calls.

Most scatolophiliacs have problems in their relationships and suffer from feelings of isolation and inadequacy. For many, scatolophilia is the only way they can express themselves sexually (Holmes, 1991). Scatolophiliacs often have coexisting paraphilias, such as exhibitionism or voyeurism (Price et al., 2002).

Personal Voices

Reactions to an Obscene Telephone Caller

The following personal account is from a 28-year-old woman, who was sharing a house with two roommates.

One day I noticed several messages on my phone machine. Many of these were very explicit and perverted. The guy who left them knew my name and said he was watching me, following all my moves, and had seen me taking a shower before. The whole time he kept breathing heavily. I was very scared, because I didn't know who this person was, whether he was hiding in the bushes, or how he could know who I was.

His calls became more frequent and persisted for months. Each time he called he was very disgusting— saying things about pussy, vaginas, breasts, nipples, wanting to fuck me. He described what he thought it would be like to have sex with me—in fact, he also threatened to rape me. It was really disgusting. I was so scared and would cry all the time. I felt as if he were everywhere, because I didn't know who he was. The police told me to be careful about where I went and whom I talked to.

He called at all different times of the day. He'd tell me what I had worn on particular days and knew what I looked like. I felt his closeness. . . . I felt as though I was a threat to the safety of my roommates, who were frightened as well. My Dad brought over a shotgun

and slept in the house one night. Actually that was the night that this guy told me he was going to come over and rape me.

The phone company eventually traced the incoming calls to a specific phone number. It turned out it was a family number, and one of the kids living at home was making the calls. He was about 19 and the grocery clerk at the store that I shopped at. Every time I went there and checked out, he saw what I was wearing and also took all of the information off my checks. The arrest was made. He admitted to harassing about six other women over the phone. The charges that were filed against him were called harassment by communication. We began the trial, and although it was hard to go over everything that happened again, I felt that everyone I interacted with respected and believed in me, which made me feel stronger.

In the end, the guy was found guilty, sentenced to community service, had to go to therapy 2 to 3 times a week, and pay a fine of $500. One month later, he started calling again. I couldn't believe it! I called the police, and he was picked up and thrown in jail again.

In thinking about this now, I just wish that I hadn't waited so long to call the police the first time. I endured a whole month of his calls before I called the police. This guy's phone calls totally took away the trust and compassion I had for other people.

SOURCE: Author's files.

The obscene telephone caller may boast of sexual acts he will perform on the victim, may describe his masturbation in detail, may threaten the victim, or may try to entice the victim to reveal aspects of her sexual life or even perform sexual acts such as masturbating while he listens on the phone. Some callers are very persuasive; many have great success in talking women into performing sexual acts while posing as product representatives recalling tampons or douches, as the police, or even as people conducting a sexual survey. (Please note: no reputable sexuality researchers conduct surveys over the phone. If you receive such a call, do not answer any sexually explicit questions.) Others threaten harm to the victim or her family if she does not do what he asks (obscene callers often know the victim's address, if only from the phone book). Some will get a woman's phone number while observing her writing a check at a place like the supermarket and then will frighten her more because he knows her address, appearance, and even some of her food preferences (Matek, 1988; see the accompanying Personal Voices, "Reactions to an Obscene Telephone Caller").

Currently, thousands of phone lines have been established in which a person can pay to have sexually explicit phone conversations. Perhaps these lines may lessen the need of obscene callers to contact unsuspecting victims. However, new and potentially more intrusive types of obscene calls may be just around the corner. Recently, the first picture phones have been put into general use; these phones have a screen that transmits the picture of the person calling. The picture phone may initiate a whole new type of obscene telephone call.

SEX Talk

Question: *What should I do if I receive an obscene telephone call?*

You should react calmly and not exhibit the reactions of shock, fright, or disgust that the caller finds exciting. Do not slam the phone down; simply replace it gently in the cradle. An immediate ring again is probably a callback; ignore it, or pick up the phone and hang up quickly without listening. Sometimes a gentle suggestion that the person needs psychological help disrupts the caller's fantasy. Persistent callers can be discouraged by suggesting that you have contacted the police. If you do get more than one call, notify the telephone company. Caller ID has been helpful in reducing the rates of obscene phone calls.

Voyeurism Voyeurs, or those who engage in **scopophilia,** are people whose main means of sexual gratification is watching unsuspecting persons undressing, naked, or engaging in sexual activity. Some would argue that we are a voyeuristic society; our major media—newspapers, television, movies, advertisements—are full of sexual images that are intended to interest and arouse us. Magazines and movies featuring nude women or couples are very popular. Even television shows display far more nudity and sexuality than would have been allowed in movies just a few years ago. In modern society, it seems, we have all become casual voyeurs to some degree.

Clinical voyeurs, however, are those for whom watching others naked or viewing erotica is a compulsion. Voyeurs are often called "Peeping Toms," a revealing term because implicit in it are two important aspects of voyeurism. First, a "peeper" is one who looks without the knowledge or consent of the person being viewed, and true voyeurs are excited by the illicit aspect of their peeping. Second, the voyeur is usually male. Though it is becoming more acceptable for women in society to read magazines such as *Playgirl,* which show nude men, or to spend an evening watching male strippers such as the Chippendales, clinically speaking there are very few "Peeping Janes."

The typical voyeur is a heterosexual male who begins his voyeuristic behaviors before the age of 15 (Seligman & Hardenburg, 2000). **Primary voyeurism** is apparently rare. More often, voyeurism is mixed in with a host of other paraphiliac behaviors (Langevin & Lang, 1987). In one study, fewer than 2% of voyeurs said that voyeurism was their only paraphilia (G. Abel et al., 1988). Still, voyeurs are generally harmless and are satisfied just with peeping, although they certainly can scare an unsuspecting person who sees a strange man peering in the window. In a few cases, however, voyeurism can lead to more and more intrusive sexual activity, including rape (Holmes, 1991). Voyeurs, when caught, are usually not charged with a sex crime but with trespassing or sometimes breaking and entering. Therefore, how many actually get in trouble with the law is difficult to determine.

Many voyeurs satisfy some of their urges by renting pornographic videos or going to live sex shows. For most voyeurs, however, these are ultimately unsatisfying, for part of the excitement is the knowledge that the victim does not know or approve of the fact that the voyeur sees them. Like exhibitionists, voyeurs tend to be immature, sexually frustrated, poor at developing relationships, and chronic masturbators (Holmes, 1991). Some voyeurs have turned to voyeuristic webcam sites that capture unsuspecting sexual activity and broadcast it live over the Internet (Griffiths, 2000).

Although it technically refers to a single couple copulating in front of others, **troilism** (TROY-ill-iz-um) has come to mean any sex sessions involving multiple partners. Troilism is not new; in 1631, Mervyn Touchet, the Second Earl of Castlehaven, was ex-

scopophilia
The psychoanalytic term for voyeurism, literally "the love of looking."

primary voyeurism
Voyeurism as the main and exclusive paraphilia.

troilism
Any sex sessions involving multiple partners, typically witnessed by others.

ecuted in England for ordering his servants to have sex with his wife while he watched. The fact that they were servants and thus beneath his station was as damaging to him as the actual act (Bullough, 1976). Janus & Janus (1993) found that 14% of men and 8% of women in their survey had engaged in group sex.

Troilism may involve aspects of voyeurism, exhibitionism, and, sometimes, latent homosexual desires; an observer who gets excited, for example, by watching his wife fellate another man may be subconsciously putting himself in his wife's place. Some troilists install ceiling mirrors, video cameras, and other means to capture the sexual act for viewing later on. Others engage in sharing a sexual partner with a third party while they look on, or they engage in swinging (see Chapter 9). Many couples experiment with group sex, but to the troilist, engaging in or fantasizing about such sexual activity is the primary means of sexual arousal.

Transvestic Fetishism

In Chapter 3 we discussed the concept of transgenderism. Typically, a transvestite (TV) obtains sexual pleasure from dressing in the clothing of the other sex (see Table 16.2). As the accompanying Personal Voices, "A Cross-Dresser and His (Her?) Wife" illustrates, a transgendered person typically feels a sense of comfort, whereas a TV typically feels sexual arousal (Seligman & Hardenburg, 2000). Both may be comfortable being the gender they are and not in search of sex reassignment surgery.

True transvestism is often referred to as **transvestic fetishism** (trans-VESS-tick FEH-tish-iz-um) to emphasize the fact that the cross-dresser has an erotic attraction to the clothing he or she wears. Clothes are, in all cultures, symbols of sexual identity and gender roles. Many transvestites are not comfortable with the gender roles that society forces on them because of their biological gender, and many men feel that cross-dressing liberates them from the expectations society puts on them.

A true transvestite is almost always a heterosexual male (Docter, 1988), although perhaps this is because cross-dressing for women is much more acceptable in our society. For example, in the United States, women often wear traditionally male clothing such as pants, suits, or ties, and they are free to wear pink, blue, or whatever colors they choose. Drag kings (straight and gay women who dress up as men) are generally less noticeable than their male counterparts.

Male transvestites are more common in society because men have limited ability to explore female gender roles in our society (Dzelme & Jones, 2001), although this is slowly changing. Recently your author saw a T-shirt in the men's section of a department store that said "Real Men Wear Pink!" However, although it is more common for a man to wear a wide range of colors today, it is still generally not acceptable for him to wear a dress. Imagine what students at your university would say if a male student wore a dress to class. In fact, the entertainment industry is the only area in which society approves of men cross-dressing (Bullough & Bullough, 1993). For example, cross-dressing has been depicted in popular movies, such as *Big Momma's House*, *White Chicks*, or the classic *Mrs. Doubtfire*.

Transvestites differ from transsexuals in that they do not desire to change their biological gender. Their differences also seem to begin early in life; one study found that transsexuals, but not transvestites, lacked interest in playing with other boys while young, and transvestites, but not transsexuals, cross-dressed very early in life (Bullough et al., 1983). A small number of transvestites will go to great lengths to feminize their appearance, employing electrolysis (hair removal), taking hormones, or even getting surgical implants to simulate female breasts. But even most of these transves-

Review Question

Differentiate between exhibitionism and voyeurism, and explain the variations of these behaviors.

transvestic fetishism
A paraphilia in which the preferred or exclusive method of sexual arousal or orgasm is through wearing the clothing of the other sex.

TABLE 16.2	Transgendered Behaviors
Term	Definition
Female impersonator	A role played by a professional male actor who dresses in women's clothing for a variety of reasons
Drag queen	A role played by a professional actor, typically a gay man, who dresses in flamboyant women's clothing to perform for a variety of reasons
Gender dysphoric	Having one's gender identity inconsistent with one's biological sex
Cross-dresser	Living full or part time in the other gender's role and deriving psychosocial comfort in doing so
Transgendered	Engaging in both masculine and feminine behaviors, dress, and/or stereotypic behaviors
Transvestite	Dressing in the clothing of the other gender and deriving sexual pleasure from doing so
Fetishistic transvestite	Wearing the clothing of the other sex as the preferred or exclusive method of sexual arousal or orgasm
Transsexual	Feeling trapped in the body of the wrong gender; sometimes this will lead to undergoing sexual reassignment surgery

Personal Voices

A Cross-Dresser and His (Her?) Wife

Elayne (alter ego of Wayne): Last night I sat in a car with two cross-dressers and held hands. Although we talked only about petty things, we touched. I can express my inner self as Wayne, but when I'm being Elayne, a few more bricks disappear. When I looked into Diane's eyes [another cross-dresser], she looked right back into mine, but earlier, when I talked to [her as] Ed, he couldn't look at me. We spoke to the side of each other. But Diane and I didn't speak to each other, we spoke within each other.

I knew there was something different about me from the time I was six years old and I put on my sister's silk pajamas. They felt so good, but I was scolded and scoffed at. I grew up in a very conservative, redneck area of Iowa where "women were women and men were men." All through my childhood I wore black and white or muted plaid. When I was given crayons, I dared use only the black and white ones. I was so afraid of using color and being perceived as different.

I looked all over for information on cross-dressing. I finally found something in Ann Landers—she told a wife that it was okay for her husband to wear her clothes. When I read that, I knew that there were others like me. I still have that column—it has turned yellow!

When I am dressed as Elayne, my son Ryan and I sometimes go for a ride through the woods and farms on our bicycles, and I'm sure most of the people who see us assume I'm his mother. I've always dressed around the kids. When they get older, maybe they'll tell their friends. I won't hide my cross-dressing. I won't flaunt it either.

I don't feel particularly masculine. I tend to see men as hairy and fuzzy and bulky and aggressive. . . . Why should women have all the experiences in life? I fantasized about having a baby and being pregnant, especially when Kaye was. If it were possible, I'd like to have a child. I'd be first in line to be the prototype mother–father! I'd like to have breasts and have a baby suckle at my nipple. Kaye has beautiful, wonderful breasts. It's fun for her to lie on her back on top of me, and I can put my arms around her and feel the fantasy. She becomes part of me.

Kaye (Elayne/Wayne's wife): Sometimes I find Elayne too pretty and overpowering. Sometimes I feel I'm

Elayne and his/her daughter.

married to two people. I like them both. They have different auras. Elayne is a different kind of outgoing. If I'm feeling good about myself, I find Elayne easier to take.

When I first heard about this cross-dressing, I thought it was no big deal. What's so strange about that? I even assisted him in making a dress. At first I just thought he likes to wear women's clothes because they're prettier. Now I see it's also because it enables him to get into a different space where he is more conscious of the feminine side of himself and can make it more accessible. I don't think cross-dressers should be seen any differently from artists or people who set fads.

I think Wayne's cross-dressing has been, for the most part, a good learning experience for the children. It could make them more accepting of other people. Ryan climbs trees, but he also works with needlepoint. Sometimes I wonder if there'll be a backlash from the community if Elayne becomes more and more open. . . .

Wayne, not Elayne, is my bed partner most of the time. He is gentle, though Elayne is even gentler. We both like to play the passive role. He prefers when I initiate and when I'm on top. He'll often wear a nightgown to bed. It's no big deal. I like the feeling of pantyhose in bed. It doesn't matter who wears them!

SOURCE: From *Transformations* by Marriette Pathy Allen, 1989, Dutton Books. Reprinted by permission of the Carol Mann Agency.

Cross-dressing is often depicted in movies like *Big Momma's House, in which Martin Lawrence dressed up as a woman.*

tites would stop at sex reassignment surgery because they enjoy heterosexual intercourse and being men.

Many theorists believe that transvestism evolves from an early childhood experience, such as a male masturbating with or in some item of female clothing (Stayton, 1996). Some TVs report childhood experiences of being punished or humiliated by women and being forced to dress as a woman (Maxmen & Ward, 1995). This behavior soon develops into a sexual experience with the male getting physically aroused while holding, touching, or wearing the item of clothing.

Some transvestites then move beyond the sexual arousal and begin to feel less anxious and stressed when around the particular item of clothing (Stayton, 1996). Cross-dressing may allow these men to relax, freed from the societal pressures of being male. Most transvestites began cross-dressing at a very young age and began masturbating while wearing women's clothing during adolescence (Dzelme & Jones, 2001). Male transvestites display more pre-adult feminine behaviors, such as preferring the company of girls, being called a sissy, or having female hobbies than do a nontransvestite control group (Buhrich & McConaghy, 1985).

Many transvestites are very secretive about their habits, fearing that others will censure or ridicule them. Many have private collections of female clothes, and married transvestites may even hide their habit from their wives, although the majority do tell. This secrecy makes it difficult to determine how common transvestism actually is. Janus and Janus (1993) report that 6% of the men and 3% of the women in their survey reported some personal experience with cross-dressing.

It's not uncommon for transvestites to marry and raise families, which can cause problems if their spouses do not know of their habit. The majority of partners of transvestites know about the cross-dressing behavior and are accepting of it (Reynolds & Caron, 2005). Most had learned of their partner's habit early in the relationship and tolerated or even supported it to some degree, although some expressed resentment and fear of public exposure. However, the majority characterized their marriage as happy and described their husbands as loving and good fathers. Some women married to transvestites fully support their husband's feminine identity, seeing "her" as a separate partner and friend from "him." In some families, the male's transvestism is completely open, and the children know about it and even help Daddy pick out clothes or do his nails (Allen, 1989).

Transvestism is usually harmless, and most transvestites are not anxious to seek out therapy to stop their behavior. Many times treatment is sought only when a TV's partner is upset or the cross-dressing causes stress in the relationship (Dzelme & Jones, 2001). The majority of female partners of transvestites do not understand the male's need to dress in women's clothing (Dzelme & Jones, 2001), even though they are accepting of the behavior. In any case, transvestism is usually so firmly fixed in a man's personality that eradication is neither possible nor desirable. The goal of therapy is to cope with the anxieties and guilt of the transvestite and the way he relates interpersonally and sexually with his partner and family (Peo, 1988). In the past few years, transvestite support groups have been organized in cities all over the country.

Review Question

Differentiate between transvestism and transsexualism, and explain the development of transvestism.

SEX Talk

Question: Aren't transvestites, deep down, really homosexual?

No. Some male homosexuals enjoy dressing as females, and some may derive a certain sexual satisfaction from it. Most heterosexual transvestites are not at all interested in sex with men. They seem all absorbed by women; they want to look, act, and behave like women and get a strong sexual attraction from women's clothes. Some like it when men approach them when they are cross-dressed, but only because it affirms their abilities to pass as women.

20th Century Fox/The Kobal Collection

Pedophilia

Pedophilia (pee-doh-FILL-ee-uh ; meaning "love of children") has been called many things throughout history: child-love, cross-generational sex, man/child (or adult/child) interaction, boy-love, pederasty, and Greek love (Bullough, 1990). The variety of terms shows how differently adult–child sexual interactions have been viewed in different periods of history. In Chapter 17 we will discuss child sexual abuse and incest, whereas here we will concentrate our attention on pedophilia.

Pedophilia is one of the most common paraphilias and is most likely to be seen in treatment due to its harmful and illegal nature (O'Grady, 2001). However, even though many people consider sexual contact between adults and children to be one of the most objectionable of crimes today, in many periods of history and in different cultures today, various types of child–adult sexual contact have been seen as acceptable (see Chapter 1 for more information about Greek pederasty, or Chapter 11 for more information on the Sambian culture). Even so, pedophilia is illegal in every country in the world (O'Grady, 2001).

What exactly constitutes such contact in a society may be unclear. For example, as recently as the 1980s, a girl in the state of New Mexico could get married at age 13. If a 30-year-old man marries a 13-year-old girl and has legal, consensual marital intercourse with her, is it pedophilia? What if they have consensual sex but are not married? Why should a piece of paper—a marriage certificate—make a difference in our definition?

Throughout most of history, a girl was considered ready for marriage and an adult sexual relationship as soon as she "came of age," that is, at menarche. It was common for much older men to be betrothed to very young women, and such marriages were seen as proper. For example, Saint Augustine decided to get married in order to try to curb his sexual promiscuity, and so he was betrothed to a prepubertal girl. Although intercourse was not permitted until she reached puberty, such early marriages were apparently common (Bullough, 1990). In England in the 18th to 19th centuries, 12 was considered the age of consent. In the 18th century as well, adult–child sex (especially same-sex pairings) were accepted in China, Japan, parts of Africa, Turkey, Arabia, Egypt, and the Islamic areas of India (Ames & Houston, 1990).

To some degree or another, then, what legally constitutes pedophilia is a matter of the laws in different societies. Yet, clinically speaking, pedophilia refers to sexual activity with a prepubescent child (below the age of 13). (Many times these behaviors are also referred to as child sexual abuse. Attraction to postpubertal boys and girls is called **ephebephilia** (ef-fee-be-FILL-ee-uh), but it is not usually considered pathological. In fact, it has been shown that heterosexual males in almost all cultures are attracted to younger females, and homosexual males are attracted to younger or younger-appearing males (O'Grady, 2001). Pedophiles are often 16 years old or older and at least 5 years older than their victims (American Psychiatric Assocation, 2000).

Pedophiles often report an attraction to children of a particular age range, most often 8- to 10-year-olds in those attracted to girls, and slightly older in those attracted to boys (attraction to prepubescent girls is more common; Murray, 2000). Some pedophiles are unable to function sexually with an adult, whereas others also maintain adult sexual relationships (Seligman & Hardenburg, 2000). Many pedophiles believe that pedophilia will be like homosexuality, in that once it was unacceptable and today it is more acceptable (O'Grady, 2001).

Pedophiliac behavior is often obsessive (O'Grady, 2001). Pedophiles are usually obsessed with their fantasies, and these fantasies tend to dominate their lives. They are also predators—they know which child they like, and they work hard to get the trust and support from the parents or caretakers first. Pedophiles are good at winning the trust of parents. In fact, parents often trust the pedophile so much that they often take the pedophile's word over their own child's (O'Grady, 2001).

Many pedophiles threaten their victims and tell them they must keep their sexual activity secret. One therapist tells of a patient who had been repeatedly threatened by her assailant:

> . . . as a young teen, she and a friend were raped repeatedly by a friend of their parents. It went on for years. He would rape the girls in front of each other and threatened the

pedophilia
Sex with children as a preferred or exclusive mode of sexual interaction in an adult; child molestation. People who engage in this behavior are called pedophiles, or sexual offenders.

ephebephilia
Attraction to children who have just passed puberty; also called hebephilia.

lives of both of them if they told. They didn't. They were both afraid of him and convinced they wouldn't be believed anyway, given his high standing in the community and his friendship with their parents. There is a song she still hates, she tells me, because he used to sing it as he undressed them. (Salter, 2003, p. 13)

In the United States, an adult who has sexual contact with a boy or girl under the age of consent (see Table 17.1, on page 569, for more information about the age of consent) to whom he or she is not married is guilty of child sexual abuse. A child sexual abuser may or may not be a pedophile; a person may sexually abuse a child because an adult is not available, because children are easier to seduce than adults, out of anger, or because of other sexual, psychological, or familial problems.

Girls are twice as likely as boys to be victims of pedophiliac behavior (Murray, 2000). In one study, 44% of pedophiles chose only girls, 33% chose only boys, and 23% abused both boys and girls (Murray, 2000). Boys are less likely to reject sexual advances and to report their sexual advances to authorities than girls, and they will take the initiative in sexual encounters with adults more often than girls will (Brongersma, 1990). This may be the reason that violence is less common in sexual contact between men and boys than between men and girls.

Some pedophiles only look at children and never touch, whereas others engage in a variety of different sexual acts with their victims, with the most common behavior being fondling and exhibitionism, rather than penetration (Miranda & Fiorello, 2002). In the majority of cases, pedophiles do not require penetration (Murray, 2000). As we discussed earlier, pedophiles often have a lack of empathy and believe that their behavior does not cause any negative psychological or physical consequences for their victims (Miranda & Fiorello, 2002).

Unfortunately, some pedophiles, realizing the chance of the child reporting the act, kill their victims. After one such murder of a young New Jersey girl named Megan Kanka in July 1994, her parents spearheaded "Megan's Law," which was signed into state law in October 1994. This law made it mandatory for authorities in New Jersey to tell parents when a convicted child molester moved into the neighborhood and increased penalties for child molesters. In 1996, Megan's Law became federal law. See the accompanying Sex in Real Life, "Megan's Law," for more information.

Female pedophiles also exist, although they often abuse children in concert with another person, usually their male partner. They may act to please their adult sexual partners rather than to satisfy their own pedophilic desires. Although less common, female pedophiles have been found to have a higher incidence of psychiatric disorders than male pedophiles (Chow & Choy, 2002).

A number of small organizations in Western countries, usually made up of pedophiles and ephebephiles, argue that man–boy love should be legalized, usually under the pretense of guarding "the sexual rights of children and adolescents" (Okami, 1990). In America, the North American Man–Boy Love Association (NAMBLA) supports the abolition of age-of-consent laws. NAMBLA believes that there is a difference between those who simply want to use children for sexual release and those who develop long-lasting, often exclusive, and even loving relationships with a single boy. Suppe (1984) agrees that pederasty among postpubescent boys need not necessarily be harmful (which is not to deny that it often may be).

On the other hand, those who work with sexually abused children vehemently deny the claim, pointing to children whose lives were ruined by sex with adults. The accompanying Personal Voices, "Pedophilia: An Autobiography," tells the story of one pedophiliac, a physician, who established emotional and intimate relationships with young boys before being caught and sentenced to a prison term.

Several factors may go into pedophilic behavior (Murray, 2000). Pedophiles have been described as having had arrested psychological development, which makes them childlike with childish emotional needs. They may also have low self-esteem and poor social relations with adults, may be trying to overcome their own humiliations and pains from their childhood, or may exaggerate the social male role of dominance and power over a weaker sexual partner. Conditions such as alcoholism may lessen the barriers to having sex with children. In one study, pe-

© Les Stone/Corbis

Many media images sexualize childhood and associate sexuality with extreme youth. This may encourage pedophiliac fantasies.

Megan's Law

In 1994, 7-year-old Megan Kanka was lured into her neighbor's home in Hamilton Township, New Jersey, by the promise of a puppy. There she was raped, strangled, and suffocated by a two-time convicted sexual offender. Shortly thereafter, the governor of New Jersey, Christie Todd Whitman, signed the toughest sex offender registration act in the country, known as "Megan's Law." In 1996 Megan's Law became federal law and mandated that every community have access to information about the presence of convicted sex offenders in their neighborhoods. In 1994, a federal statute known as the Jacob Wetterling Crimes Against Children and Sexually Violent Offender Registration Program was passed, which also requires all states to create registration programs for convicted sex offenders (Trivits & Reppucci, 2002).

Today, all 50 states require that convicted sex offenders register on their release from prison into the community and require the listing (with the offenders' names, addresses, photographs, crimes, and sometimes physical descriptions) to be made available to the public. Although all require sex offenders to register, the statutes vary in what information is made available and for how long (Trivits & Reppucci, 2002). In some states, sexual offenders must register for the rest of their lives.

Many convicted sex offenders have protested the law, claiming that it violates their constitutional rights; however, the government has decided that the safety of children is a higher priority than the privacy of convicted sex offenders. Critics also argue that these listings encourage violent behavior directed at the offenders, although studies have found that the actual incidence of such events is low (Klaas, 2003; J. Miller, 1998). In addition, some argue that having such lists creates instant mailing lists for those who wish to connect with other offenders (Sommerfeld, 1999).

Some states continue to add regulations to their sex offender registry laws. For example, in 2005, certain towns in New York, Florida, and New Jersey banned convicted child molesters from being within 2,500 feet of any school, daycare center, playground, or park (Koch, 2005). Other

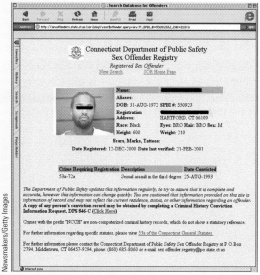

Newsmakers/Getty Images

All 50 states require convicted sex offenders to register upon their release to the community. Sexual offender registry profiles often contain personal information including name, address, date of birth, offense, and physical description.

states use electronic monitoring in addition to their online registries. For example, Florida, Alabama, New Jersey, Missouri, Ohio, and Oklahoma all passed laws requiring electronic monitoring (ankle bands that monitor the offender's whereabouts).

Unfortunately, the registries may have given many parents and caregivers a false sense of security. Of the 551,000 sex offenders that were registered in 2005, 100,000 were missing or had failed to supply a current address (Koch, 2005). In addition, sex offender registries contain only those offenders who have been convicted of sexual offenses and not all who commit such crimes. Nonetheless, many of these new laws and tracking devices may help to discourage sexual offenders from engaging in these behaviors.

---

dophiles were asked why they engaged in sex with children. The most common response was that the children didn't fight it, followed by a lack of sexual outlets with adults, intoxication, and victim-initiation of sexual behavior (Pollack & Hashmall, 1991).

Over the years, research has found that being a victim of sexual abuse in childhood is one of the most frequently reported risk factors for becoming a pedophile (Glasser et al., 2001; Langstrom et al., 2000). It is estimated that 35% of pedophiles were sexually abused as children (Keegan, 2001). Studies have also found that the choice of gender and age of victims often reflect the pattern of past sexual abuse in the pedophile's life (Pollock & Hashmall, 1991). Although past sexual abuse is a risk factor, it's important

Personal Voices

Pedophilia: An Autobiography

The following is an account by Dr. Silva (not his real name), a physician incarcerated for having sex with a minor.

I believe that I was born a pedophile because I have had feelings of sexual attraction toward children and love for them as long as I can remember. I was not traumatized into this age orientation nor, certainly, did I ever make a conscious decision to be attracted in this way. Just as homosexuals and heterosexuals discover their sexual orientation, I discovered my age orientation as I grew, and I have been aware of it from a young age.

My developing experience with sex was occurring when I was 14 and 15 years old, and it was during this time that we in my peer group were befriended by a neighborhood man, about 25, who was known to "like boys." He drove us around and treated us to snacks and movies. At times, we went to his apartment, in pairs or as a group, where he took us individually into his bedroom to fellate us. I once spent the night with him. His mother and sister, with whom he lived, barely reacted to my presence there in the morning, as if it were not unusual for him to appear in the morning with a boy. While I enjoyed the oral sex he performed on me, the overall experience was unfulfilling. I was disappointed that he did not feel the emotional bond for me that I expected after such an intimate encounter. I felt satisfied physically but used. Subsequent experiences with him became acceptable once I adjusted my expectations and sought only sexual gratification.

In my second semester in medical school, I befriended Peter, a fellow medical student whose family lived in a nearby town. He invited me to meet his family and see the town. I will never forget the first time I met his brother Allen, who was 11 or 12 at the time. I loved the whole family, but what I felt for Allen was stronger than anything I had ever known before. During one of the earliest [visits to Peter's family], I had the opportunity to share a single bed with Allen. In future encounters he was wide awake and actively participated in our sexual relationship, which went on during the next two years and even later when I returned to visit. My relationship with him was the first true pedophilic/pedosexual relationship. After our sexual activity ceased, we maintained a close friendship that endures to this day.

In my fourth semester at medical school, I moved into a boarding house. Other students lived there with the host family, which consisted of a mother and three sons, ages 11, 12, and 13; the boys certainly were a fac-

tor in my choice. Thirteen-year-old John showed much interest in me. We became excited and it was not long before we had our clothes off and began fondling each other. By now it was clear to me that I loved children, especially boys, and was happiest when I was in their company. What I took pleasure in most was seeing them happy and developing healthy in mind and body. So, I encouraged their interests if I felt these interests were healthy, or I exposed them to experiences that I thought would contribute to their educational or cultural edification.

It was in this period that I became friends with Eric, just about to turn 9, whose family recently had moved onto our street. I had been dating Cathy [at the time], a foreign-born peer female who lived in my city and worked near our house. I enjoyed a good relationship, sexual and otherwise, with Cathy for about six months. Before we broke up, my relationship with Eric had become sexual and more pleasing than that with Cathy, and also she and I had been growing apart emotionally. I began to feel that I was maintaining our relationship for the sake of appearances and that young males were my true love—especially Eric.

Eric and I had become increasingly close. What made our relationship so beautiful and precious was the way in which it developed so gradually and so naturally. Most of the time, he just came over to my house and lay down with me for a few moments. One special time was a morning that he was on his way to school. He climbed into my room through my window, as he frequently did, removed his bookbag, and lay down next to me. We embraced for a few moments until we were satisfied and it was time for him to get to school. Not a word was spoken; all of our communication was physical on that occasion. Clearly, it was not sex that attracted me to him but, rather, our great emotional bond, which made sex so gratifying. Sex was a small but incredibly beautiful part of our relationship. The vast majority of the time we engaged in many other recreational and constructive activities.

The demise of our relationship began when his mother suspected some friends of mine were using marijuana in his presence. Eric was told we could no longer be friends. The next time I came over, she told me he did not want to see me anymore. Not long afterwards, he moved out of the country with his family. It still hurts me to think about him, and I do not think I will ever fully recover.

Source: From *Pedophilia: Biosocial Dimensions* by Donald C. Silva, 1990. Reprinted by permission Springer-Verlag.

to point out that the majority of male victims of child sexual abuse do not become pedophiles (Salter et al., 2003). Pedophiles have high **recidivism** (re-SID-iv-iz-um) rates, and for some unknown reason these rates are higher in homosexual men (Murray, 2000). The recidivism rate is the main impetus for legislation such as Megan's Law (M. A. Alexander, 1999).

One more thing before we move on to discuss other paraphilias. The Internet has been a two-edged sword when it comes to pedophilia. On the one hand it has helped pedophiles find each other and talk about their behaviors. This can validate their behaviors because they are no longer feeling isolated, as though they are the only person who engages in child sex behaviors. Pedophiles are also able to gather information and can actually share images with each other. Internet chat rooms are a popular place for pedophiles to hang out today (O'Grady, 2001). There, pedophiles can befriend others in the chat room and act like one of the nonoffender participants. On the other hand, the Internet has also become a powerful tool to combat pedophilia, both in the online reporting of sex offenders and the ability of law officials to go undercover and seek out pedophiles online (Trivits & Reppucci, 2002; see the Sexbyte on page 558).

Other Paraphilias

People can be sexually attracted to almost anything. An article in the *Journal of Forensic Sciences* tells of a man who was erotically attracted to his tractor; he wrote poetry to it, he had a pet name for it, and his body was found after he was asphyxiated by suspending himself by the ankles from the tractor's shovel in order to masturbate (O'Halloran & Dietz, 1993). However, there are a number of other paraphilias that are relatively more common, although all are rare, and we will now review a sample of them.

Frotteurism **Frotteurism** (frah-TOUR-iz-um; or frottage) involves a man rubbing his genitals against a woman's thighs or buttocks in a crowded place (such as a subway) where he can claim it was an accident and get away quickly. In some cases, he may fondle a woman's breasts with his hand while he is rubbing up against her. This is similar to **toucheurism,** which is the compulsive desire to touch strangers with one's hands for sexual arousal. This desire, usually in men, finds expression on buses, trains, in shopping malls, while waiting in line, at crowded concerts, anywhere where bodies are pressed together. There have also been cases of frotteurism or toucheurism among doctors or dentists who rub against or touch their patients. Frotteurism, however, does not usually appear in isolation but as one of a number of paraphilias in an individual (Langevin & Lang, 1987).

Zoophilia **Zoophilia** (zoo-uh-FILL-ee-uh; also referred to as **bestiality),** or sexual contact with animals, is rare, although Kinsey and his colleagues (1948, 1953) found that one man out of every 13 engages in this behavior. Contact between people and animals has been both practiced and condemned since earliest times.

Studies of people who engage in sex with animals have found that a male dog is the most popular animal sex partner for both men and women (Miletski, 2002). Sexual behaviors included masturbating the animal, submitting to anal sex performed by the animal, or active or passive oral sex with the animal (Miletski, 2002).

Necrophilia Tales of **necrophilia** (neck-row-FILL-ee-uh), or having sex with corpses, have been found even in ancient civilizations. The Egyptians prohibited embalmers from taking immediate delivery of corpses of the wives of important men for fear that the embalmers would violate them (Rosman & Resnick, 1989). More recently, the legends of the vampires imply necrophilia in the highly sexual approaches of the "undead." The stories of Sleeping Beauty, Snow White, and Romeo and Juliet all convey a sense of the restorative powers of loving the dead and thereby bringing the corpse back to life.

Rosman and Resnick (1989) suggest that necrophiliacs desire a partner who is unresisting and unrejecting; to find one, many seek out professions that put them in con-

---

recidivism
A tendency to repeat crimes, such as sexual offenses.

Review Question

Explain pedophilia and the behaviors that pedophiles engage in. What factors have been found to be related to the development of pedophiliac behavior?

frotteurism
The act of compulsively rubbing against strangers for sexual arousal; also referred to as frottage.

toucheurism
The act of compulsively touching strangers with the hands to achieve sexual arousal.

sexbyte

Frotteurism is most common in people between the ages of 15 and 25 years old and decreases as a person ages (Seligman & Hardenburg, 2000).

zoophilia
The sexual attraction to animals in fantasy or through sexual contact as a preferred or exclusive means of sexual arousal and orgasm.

bestiality
A paraphilia that involves engaging in sexual relations with an animal.

necrophilia
The sexual attraction to dead bodies in fantasy or through sexual contact as a preferred or exclusive means of sexual arousal and orgasm.

---

tact with corpses. They identify three types of genuine necrophilia: necrophiliac fantasy, in which a person has persistent fantasies about sex with dead bodies without actually engaging in such behavior; "regular" necrophilia, which involves the use of already-dead bodies for sexual pleasure; and necrophiliac homicide, in which the person commits murder to obtain a corpse for sexual pleasure. However, necrophilia is extremely rare and accounts for only a tiny fraction of murders.

An infamous case of necrophiliac homicide was that of serial killer Jeffrey Dahmer. Dahmer, who admitted to killing 17 men and having sex with their corpses, also mutilated their bodies, tried to create a "shrine" out of their organs that he thought would give him "special powers," and ate their flesh. In keeping with Rosman and Resnick's claim that necrophiliacs desire a partner who is unresisting and unrejecting, Dahmer bored holes into his victims' skulls while they were alive and poured in acid or boiling water, trying to create "zombies" who would fulfill his every desire.

On the other hand, Dahmer also had sex with his victims while they were alive; perhaps he was an **erotophonophiliac,** which is someone who gets sexual excitement from the act of murder itself. Dahmer admitted his deeds but claimed he was insane. A jury found him sane and guilty, and he was sentenced to life in prison with no chance of parole; he was killed by another inmate in 1994.

Other Paraphilias A number of other behaviors fall under the rubric of paraphilias, most of which are rare. The accompanying Sex in Real Life, "Other Paraphilias," lists a number of terms and their descriptions.

Assessing and Treating Paraphilias

Although the majority of paraphiliacs do not seek treatment and are content with balancing the pleasure and guilt of their paraphilia, others find their paraphilia to be an unwanted disruption to their lives. Their sexual desires may get in the way of forming relationships, may get them into legal trouble, or may become such a preoccupation that

erotophonophiliac
A person who derives sexual excitement from murdering others.

Review Question

Define frotteurism, zoophilia, and necrophilia, and identify factors that have been found to be related to the development of these paraphilias.

SEX in Real Life

Other Paraphilias

Each term that follows refers to an object or practice that a person is compulsively responsive to and dependent on for sexual arousal and orgasm. Often these behaviors are addictively repetitious.

Acrotomophilia and apotemnophilia: Having either a partner who is an amputee, or imagining oneself being an amputee.

Asphyxiophilia or hypoxyphilia (also known as autoerotic asphyxiation): Decreasing the flow of oxygen to the brain. Many who engage in this practice use a rope or noose around their neck and try to hang themselves at the moment of orgasm. This is very dangerous, and one estimate is that 31% of adolescent suicides in a 10-year period were actually due to autoerotic asphyxiation that accidentally (or intentionally) went too far (Sheehan & Garfinkel, 1988).

Autonepiophilia: Impersonating a baby in diapers and being treated as one by partner.

Coprophilia and urophilia: Being smeared with or ingesting feces or urine.

Formicophilia: The sensations produced by insects, frogs, or snails creeping or crawling on the genitals.

Gerontophilia: Having a partner who is elderly.

Hyphephilia: The feel of a certain type of texture, such as skin, hair, fur, or leather.

Klismaphilia: Receiving an enema.

Mysophilia: Self-degradation by smelling, chewing, or utilizing sweaty or soiled clothes or menstrual items, such as used tampons.

Narratophilia: Using erotic or obscene talk, such as the pay-sex phone lines.

Olfactophilia: The smells of certain body parts, especially sexual and hairy areas.

Stigmatophilia: Being with a partner who is pierced or tattooed.

SOURCE: Adapted from Holmes, 1991; Money, 1984.

they dominate their lives. For these people, a number of therapeutic solutions have been tried, with varying success.

Assessment

The first step in treating a person with a paraphilia of some sort is to assess the nature and scope of the problem. This can be done through self-report, through behavioral observation, or by physiological tests or personality inventories (Seligman & Hardenburg, 2000). Self-reports may not be reliable, however; individuals under court order to receive treatment for pedophilia may be highly motivated to report that the behavior has ceased. Also, people are not necessarily the best judge of their own desires and behavior; some may truly believe they have overcome their sexual desires when in fact they have not. The second technique, behavioral observation, is limited by the fact that it cannot assess fantasies and desires; also, most people can suppress these behaviors for periods of time.

Physiological tests may be a bit more reliable. The most reliable technique for men is probably **penile plethysmography,** which is often used with male sex offenders. For example, a pedophile can be shown films of nude children and the plethysmograph can record his penile blood volume. If he becomes excited at the pictures, then he is probably still having pedophilic desires and fantasies. A similar test is also available to test the sexual response of female offenders. However, both of these physiological tests have been found to be of limited use in this population (Seligman & Hardenburg, 2000).

Personality inventories, such as the **Minnesota Multiphasic Personality Inventory (MMPI),** can help establish personality patterns and determine whether there are additional psychological disorders (Seligman & Hardenburg, 2000). Other psychological inventories for depression and anxiety are often also used.

penile plethysmography
A test performed by measuring the amount of blood that enters the penis in response to a stimulus, which can indicate how arousing the stimulus is for the male.

Minnesota Multiphasic Personality Inventory (MMPI)
Psychological test used to assess general personality characteristics.

Treatment Options

Treatment for paraphilias is generally multifaceted and may include group, individual, and family therapy, medication, education, and/or self-help groups (Seligman & Hardenburg, 2000; see Table 16.3). Overall, treatment is aimed at the reduction or elimination of the paraphiliac symptoms, relapse prevention, and increasing victim empathy (d'Amora & Hobson, 2003).

Whatever the technique, the most important goal of therapy must be to change a person's behavior. If behavior can be changed, even if fantasies and inner emotional life are not altered, then at least the person will not be harming others or himself or herself. That is why behavioral techniques have been the most commonly used and most successful of the paraphilia treatments.

Therapy to resolve earlier childhood trauma or experiences that help maintain the paraphiliac behaviors is also helpful (H. Kaplan et al., 1994). This therapy can help increase self-esteem and social skills, which are often lacking in paraphiliacs. Positive behaviors can be encouraged by teaching paraphiliacs how to improve their social skills, allowing them to meet more men or women as potential sexual partners. To change emotions and thoughts, counseling, modeling (taking after a positive role model), or feedback can be used to change a person's attitudes toward the sexual object. In empathy training, which is useful when there is a victim, the person is taught to increase his or her compassion by putting him- or herself in the same situation as the victim. Incarcerated sex offenders may be exposed to relapse prevention therapies, which focus on controlling the cycle of troubling emotions, distorted thinking, and fantasies that accompany their activities (Goleman, 1992). These techniques can be used in either group psychotherapy or individual counseling sessions. Group therapy has been found to be an important tool in reducing isolation, improving social skills, and reducing shame and secrecy (Seligman & Hardenburg, 2000).

Yet most find their desires difficult to suppress, and for them aversion therapy is one of the most common treatment strategies (Seligman & Hardenburg, 2000). In aversion therapy, the undesirable behavior is linked with an unpleasant stimulus. For example, the person might be shown pictures of nude boys or asked to fantasize about exposing himself to a girl, while an unpleasant odor, a drug that causes nausea, or an electric shock is administered. This technique has had some success (Hawton, 1983; Little & Curran,

TABLE 16.3   Paraphilia Treatment Options

Treatment for paraphilias may often involve several different approaches. Overall, the goal of treatment is to reduce or eliminate the paraphiliac behaviors, reduce or eliminate the chances of relapse, and increase personal feelings of self-esteem as well as victim empathy. Although many sexual offenders are mandated by courts to go to therapy, those who seek out therapy on their own have been found to be more motivated and successful in their treatment. Although many convicted sex offenders will reduce their paraphiliac behavior after treatment, some may not. Those who are engaging in high levels of paraphiliac behavior and/or those with multiple psychological disorders are often less successful in therapy. Following are the various treatment options for paraphilias.

Type of Therapy	Therapeutic Methods
Individual	One-on-one therapy with a psychologist or counselor; work on improving self-esteem and social skills. Often uses modeling, empathy, and social skills training, controlling the cycle of troubling emotions, distorted thinking, and fantasies that accompany their activities.
Group	A form of psychotherapy in which a therapist works with multiple paraphiliacs with similar conditions. The interactions between the members of the group are analyzed and considered to be therapeutic.
Family	Treatment of more than one member of a family in the same session. Family relationships and processes are explored and evaluated for their potential role in the paraphiliac's behavior.
Cognitive behavioral	Combination of cognitive and behavior therapy. Works to help weaken the connections between certain situations and emotional/physical reactions to them (including depression, self-defeating, or self-damaging behaviors), while also examining how certain thinking patterns help contribute to behavior. Emphasizes relaxation and improving emotional health.
Systematic desensitization	A technique used in behavior therapy to treat behavioral problems involving anxiety. Clients are exposed to threatening situations under relaxed conditions until the anxiety reaction is extinguished.
Aversion	A behavior-modification technique that uses unpleasant stimuli in a controlled fashion to change behavior in a therapeutic way. An example would be a pedophile who is given an electric shock or a nausea drug while looking at naked pictures of children.
Shame aversion	A behavior-modification technique that uses shame as the unpleasant stimuli to change behavior in a therapeutic way. An example would be an exhibitionist that is asked to expose himself in front of an audience.
Orgasmic reconditioning	A behavioral technique that involves reprogramming a person's fantasies. An example would be to have a paraphiliac masturbate and when orgasm is inevitable, he would switch his fantasy to a more desired one, hoping thereby to increasingly associate orgasm and, later, erection with the desirable stimulus.
Satiation	A behavioral technique in which a person masturbates to a conventional fantasy and then immediately masturbates again to an undesirable fantasy. The decreased sex drive and low responsiveness of the second attempt makes the experience less exciting than usual, and eventually the behavior may lose its desirability.
Pharmacotherapy	Medications may be used to improve symptoms, delay the progression, or reduce the urge to act on paraphiliac behaviors. A variety of medications have been used, including antidepressants and testosterone-suppressing drugs.
Surgical	Procedures such as castration are used to stop the paraphiliac behavior.
Chemotherapy	Using medication to either decrease sexual drive or to treat psychological pathologies that are believed to underlie the paraphiliac behavior.

shame aversion
A type of aversion therapy in which the behavior that one wishes to extinguish is linked with strong feelings of shame.

systematic desensitization
A technique by which a person learns to relax while experiencing arousal or anxiety-provoking stimuli.

orgasmic reconditioning
A sex therapy technique where a person switches fantasies just at the moment of masturbatory orgasm in order to try to condition himself or herself to become excited by more conventional fantasies.

satiation therapy
A therapy to lessen excitement to an undesired stimulus by masturbating to a desired stimulus and then immediately masturbating again, when desire is lessened, to an undesired stimulus.

1978), although its effectiveness decreases over time. In **shame aversion,** the unpleasant stimulus is shame; for example, an exhibitionist may be asked to expose himself in front of an audience.

Although removing the behavior itself may protect any victims, the person who still fantasizes about the behavior or has the same underlying attitude that led to it (such as fear of women) may not really be that much better off. The psychological underpinnings of the paraphilia also must be changed. In **systematic desensitization** (Wolpe, 1958), the person is taught to relax and then taken through more and more anxiety-provoking or arousing situations until eventually the person learns to relax during even the most extreme situations (Hawton, 1983).

A number of therapies incorporate masturbation to try to reprogram a person's fantasies. In **orgasmic reconditioning,** the paraphiliac masturbates; just as he feels orgasm is inevitable, he switches his fantasy to a more desired one, hoping thereby to increasingly associate orgasm and, later, erection with the desirable stimulus. Similarly, in **satiation therapy** the person masturbates to a conventional fantasy and then right away masturbates again to the undesirable fantasy (Marshall, 1979). The decreased sex drive and low responsiveness of the second attempt makes the experience less exciting than usual, and eventually the behavior may lose its desirability.

In addition to these behavioral therapies, pharmacotherapy (drug therapy) has become more popular in the last several years (Chopin-Marcé, 2001). Several drugs have been found to reduce the urges to act out on paraphiliac behaviors and can maintain a reduction in undesirable behavior even when drug therapy is stopped (Terao & Nakamura, 2000). Testosterone-suppressing drugs (antiandrogen) have been used to treat paraphilias in men. These drugs can produce castration levels of testosterone for up to 5 years (Reilly et al., 2000). The research does show that certain drugs can lead to a significant decrease in deviant sexual fantasies, urges, and behaviors (Keegan, 2001).

Antidepressants have also been found to be effective. In fact, many therapists believe that the compulsive nature of many paraphilias is related to a psychological condition known as **obsessive-compulsive disorder** (OCD). Because of these similarities, treatment options for sexual paraphilias have begun to evaluate the use of serotonin reuptake inhibitors (SSRIs; these antidepressant drugs have been successful in the treatment of OCD; Abouesh & Clayton, 1999). SSRIs have been found to reduce deviant sexual fantasies, urges, and behaviors (Keegan, 2001). See Table 16.4 for more information about treatment based on the severity of the paraphilia.

Surgery has also been used in the treatment of paraphilias. Castration may not be the answer to the violent or pedophilic offender; some use foreign objects on their victims, and so the inability to achieve erection is not necessarily an impediment to their activity. Others cite the fact that although castration may cause a decrease in testosterone, it does not always result in a decrease in sex drive (Santen, 1995). To the degree that such crimes are crimes of aggression, rather than of sex, castration may not address the underlying cause.

Ultimately, there is no certain way of changing a person's sexual desires. For many paraphiliacs whose desires are socially or legally unacceptable, life is a struggle to keep their sexuality tightly controlled. As we mentioned earlier, recidivism rates for paraphiliacs are generally high, so long-term treatment is often necessary (Rabinowitz et al., 2002; McGrath, 1991). Those who do best are motivated and committed to treatment (as opposed to being mandated by the court to appear in therapy), seek treatment early, and have normal adult sexual outlets (Seligman & Hardenburg, 2000). Those with less treatment success often have multiple psychological disorders, low empathy levels, and a high frequency of paraphiliac behavior (H. Kaplan et al., 1994).

TABLE 16.4	Paraphilia Treatment Plans and Severity of Behaviors

Keegan (2001) has established a treatment plan for paraphilias, taking into consideration the severity of the behaviors, ranging from mild to catastrophic. The aims of this treatment are to suppress deviant sexual fantasies, urges, and behaviors, with a mild impact on sexual drive at levels two and three. A moderate reduction in sexual drive occurs at levels three and four, and a severe reduction in sexual drive at levels four and five. Finally, in level six, there is a complete or near-complete reduction in sex drive.

Level	Treatment Plan
One	Regardless of the severity of the paraphilia, cognitive-behavioral treatment and relapse-prevention treatment is given.
Two	*Mild cases:* Pharmacological treatment would start with antidepressants.
Three	*Mild to moderate cases:* If antidepressants are not effective in 4 to 6 weeks, a small dose of an antiandrogen would be added.
Four	*Most moderate and some severe cases:* Full antiandrogen or hormonal treatment would be given orally.
Five	*Severe cases and some catastrophic cases:* Antiandrogen or hormonal treatment would be given intramuscularly every 2 weeks.
Six	*Severe and catastrophic cases:* A complete suppression of androgens and sex drive would be sought by intramuscular injections weekly.

Source: Keegan, 2001.

obsessive-compulsive disorder
A psychological disorder in which a person experiences recurrent and persistent thoughts, impulses, or images that are intrusive and inappropriate and that cause marked anxiety and repetitive behaviors.

Review Question

Identify and discuss the treatments for the paraphilias.

VARIATIONS IN SEXUAL FREQUENCY

Another variation of human sexuality is sexual frequency. Although there is a great range in frequency of sexual contact in the general population (see Chapter 10), some argue that certain people cross over the line from a vigorous sex life to an obsessed sex life. On the other side are those who, for various reasons, seem to have little or no sex drive at all.

Hypersexuality: Does Obsession Imply Addiction?

Sexuality, like drugs, alcohol, gambling, and all other behaviors that bring a sense of excitement and pleasure, should involve some degree of moderation. Yet for some people, the need for repeated sexual encounters, which often end up being fleeting and unfulfilling, becomes almost a compulsion (Bancroft & Vukadinovic, 2004; Golden, 2001). An addiction involves an uncontrollable craving and compulsive need for a specific object. A typical sexual addict is a married man whose obsession with masturbation increases to an obsession with pornography, prostitute visits, and multiple sexual affairs (Keane, 2004).

In the past, derogatory terms, mostly for women, were used to describe these people; an example is **nymphomaniac.** Terms for men were more flattering and included **Don Juanism, satyriasis,** or, in other cases, "studs." Perhaps nowhere else is the double standard between the sexes so blatant—women who enjoy frequent sexual encounters are considered "whores" or "sluts," whereas men who enjoy similar levels of sexual activity have been admired. However, on some college campuses across the United States, men who engage in sex with many partners are often referred to as "man whores" or male "sluts" (Author's files).

"Sexual addiction," also called compulsive sexual behavior, sexual compulsivity, sexual dependency, sexual impulsivity, and hypersexuality, has become a popular and controversial topic of discussion, in part due to the book *Out of the Shadows: Understanding Sexual Addiction* by Patrick Carnes (2001). Carnes's argument is that people who engage in many of the paraphilias we have discussed, not just hypersexuality, are really sexual addicts whose need for constant sexual encounters is similar to any addictive behavior. Sex and orgasm are mood-altering, just as drugs are, and the addict will often sacrifice family, friends, work, health, and values in order to maintain the sexual behavior. Many sexual addicts have concurrent addictions, including drugs, alcohol, gambling, food, or shopping (Carnes, 2003). Carnes estimated that between 17 million and 37 million Americans have sexual addictions (Hagedorn & Juhnke, 2005).

According to Carnes, a sexual addict goes through four cycles repeatedly: a preoccupation with thoughts of sex; ritualization of preparation for sex (such as primping oneself and going to bars); compulsive sexual behavior over which the addict feels he or she has no control; and despair afterward as the realization hits that he or she has again repeated the destructive sequence of events. Sexual addiction can even be dangerous, as it may result in STIs, injury, or suicide.

nymphomaniac
A term used to describe women who engage in frequent or promiscuous sex; usually used pejoratively.

satyriasis, or Don Juanism
Terms used to describe men who engage in frequent or promiscuous sex.

SEX in Real Life

Internet Sexual Addiction

The convenience of the Internet has helped shape compulsive patterns of online use, especially in the area of sexuality (Boies et al., 2004; Young et al., 2000). Today, men and women can search online for information about sex, engage in online chats, and buy sexual products and materials. Some of these Internet activities may be potentially addictive, especially those that involve sexually related Internet crimes, such as cyberstalking (Griffiths, 2001). It's not hard to understand how an addiction might develop when we learn that about 200 new sex-related sites are added to the Internet every day, and sex on the Internet generates 1 billion dollars each year (Carnes, 2003).

A person who has an Internet sexual addiction routinely spends significant amounts of time in chat rooms and instant messaging with the intent of getting sex; feels preoccupied with using the Internet to find online sexual partners; discusses personal sexual fantasies not typically expressed offline; masturbates while engaging in online chats; ob-

sesses about the next opportunity to engage in online sex; moves from cybersex to phone sex or face-to-face meetings; hides online chat sessions from others; feels guilty; and has decreasing interest in real-life sexual partners (Griffiths, 2001). Men and women with low self-esteem, a distorted body image, an untreated sexual dysfunction, or a prior diagnosed sexual addiction are more at risk for developing an Internet sexual addiction (Young et al., 2000), and those who seek out Internet pornography have been found to have higher levels of loneliness, compared to those who do not (Yoder et al., 2005).

Many paraphiliacs turn to the Internet as a "safe" outlet for their sexual fantasies and urges. Psychotherapy and support groups often offer the most help for those with Internet sexual addictions. More research is needed into this new and growing problem. Reesearch has shown that there is a small minority of men and women who experience significant disturbances caused by their online sexual activity (Griffiths, 2000).

Many have criticized the idea of sexual addiction, however. They argue that terms such as "sexual addiction" are really disguised social judgments. Sexual addiction may be nothing more than an attempt to "repathologize" sexual behaviors (Keane, 2004). Before the sexual freedom of the 1960s, those who engaged in promiscuous sex were often considered physically, mentally, or morally sick. Some scholars suggest that there has been an attempt to return to a pathological model of sexuality using the concept of addiction (Irvine, 1995). In "sex-positive" cultures, where sex is seen as healthy and acceptable, having sex frequently, even several times every night, is seen as normal.

Although little systematic research has been done on sexual addiction, a number of psychologists have argued that sexual addiction is a real phenomenon that describes the behavior of a certain subgroup of people in both the heterosexual and homosexual communities (Pincu, 1989). Clinicians have found that sexual addicts tend to have a low opinion of themselves, distorted beliefs, a desire to escape from unpleasant emotions, difficulty coping with stress, a memory of an intense "high" that they experienced at least once before in their life (and that they are looking for again), and an uncanny ability to deny that they have a problem, even when it severely disrupts their lives (Earle & Crow, 1990). In response, a number of self-help groups have been organized, including Sexaholics Anonymous, Sex Addicts Anonymous, Sex and Love Addicts Anonymous, and Co-Dependents of Sexual Addicts.

SEX Talk

Question: I think about sex a lot—it seems like it is almost all the time. I also like to have sex as often as I can. Do I have sex addiction?

Probably not. Thinking about sex is a universal human pastime, especially when a person is younger and just beginning to mature as a sexual being. Sexual addiction becomes a problem when people find their sexual behavior becoming dangerous or uncomfortable. People who find that they cannot stop themselves from engaging in behaviors that put them at physical risk, that they find immoral, that make them feel extremely guilty, or that intrude on their ability to do other things in their life should probably seek counseling—but that is true whether or not the behavior is sexual.

Hyposexuality: Lacking Desire and Avoiding Sex

On the other side of the spectrum are those who have lost their sexual desire or never had it in the first place. People with hyposexuality have low sexual fantasies or desire for sexual activity. In Chapter 14 we discussed sexual aversion disorder, in which a person cannot engage in sex, feeling disgust, aversion, or fear when confronted by a sexual partner (American Psychiatric Association, 2000). People with such conditions are different from those who choose celibacy as a sexual lifestyle, which we discussed in Chapter 10; in contrast to those who choose to be celibate, people with hyposexuality often have low sexual desire or lack sexual desire altogether. Their problems may be due to substance abuse, hormonal disturbances, or psychological causes, and various therapies may be recommended, depending on the cause.

Review Question

Discuss the variations in sexual frequency.

◆ VARIATIONS, DEVIATIONS, AND WHO GETS TO DECIDE?

What criteria should we use to decide whether or not a sexual behavior is "normal"? The number of people who engage in it? What a particular religion says about it? Popular opinion? Should we leave it up to the courts or psychiatrists? Stoller (1991) suggests that we are all perverse to some degree. Why should some people be singled out as being *too* perverse, especially if they do no harm to anyone else?

Perhaps the need we feel to brand some sexual behaviors as perverse is summed up by S. B. Levine and colleagues (1990, p. 92), who write, "Paraphiliac images often involve arousal without the pretense of caring or human attachment." We tend to be uncomfortable with sex for its own sake, separate from ideas of love, intimacy, or human attachment, which is one reason that masturbation was seen as evil or sick for so many years.

Paraphilias are still labeled "perversions" by law and often carry legal penalties. Because even consensual adult sexual behavior, such as anal intercourse, is illegal in some states, it is not surprising that paraphilias are as well. Yet these laws also contain contradictions; for example, why is it illegal for men to expose themselves, yet women are not arrested for wearing a see-through blouse? We must be careful deciding that some sexual behaviors are natural and others are unnatural or some normal and others abnormal. Those that we call paraphilias may simply be part of human sexual diversity, unproblematic unless they cause distress, injury, or involve an unconsenting or underage partner.

Chapter Review

ACTIVE SUMMARY

1. People celebrate individual differences for most aspects of human life, with the exception of sexual (a) _____. Sexual behavior can be viewed as a continuum, but social value (b) _____, rather than science, determine which sexual behaviors are considered acceptable in society. Attitudes about which behaviors are (c) _____ vary over time, and there are (d) _____ variations.

2. (a) _____ are recurrent, intense sexually arousing fantasies, sexual urges, or behaviors that involve a craving for a(an) (b) _____ object for 6 months or more, that involves a nonhuman object, the suffering or humiliation of oneself or one's partner, or children or other nonconsenting persons. This behavior causes significant (c) _____ and interferes with a person's ability to work, (d) _____ with friends, and other important areas.

3. (a) _____ come from every socioeconomic bracket, every ethnic and racial group, and every sexual orientation. The factors that have been found to be related to the development of a paraphilia include gender, growing up in a(an) (b) _____ family or experiencing family problems during childhood, and past (c) _____ abuse.

4. Several theories attempt to explain the development of paraphilias. The (a) _____ theories claim physical factors are responsible for the development of paraphiliac behavior. (b) _____ theorists suggest that the causes can be traced back to problems during the Oedipal crisis and with castration anxiety. Developmental theories claim that a person forms a template in his or her brain that (c) _____ his or her ideal lover and sexual situation, and this can be disrupted in several ways. Paraphilias may also be due to courtship disorders in which the behavior becomes fixed at a preliminary stage of (d) _____ that would normally lead to sexual intercourse. (e) _____ suggest that paraphilias develop because a behavior becomes associated with sexual pleasure through conditioning. Sociologists look at the ways in which society shapes and encourages certain behaviors.

5. Some of the most common paraphilias include fetishism, (a) _____, masochism, exhibitionism, voyeurism, transvestism, and pedophilia. A(An) (b) _____ is an inanimate object or a body part (not usually associated with the sex act) that becomes the primary or exclusive focus of sexual arousal and orgasm in an individual. Sadism refers to the intentional infliction of physical or psychological pain on another person in order to achieve sexual excitement. A masochist derives sexual pleasure through his or her own physical (c) _____ or psychological humiliation. (d) _____ is the most common of all reported sexual offenses, and it involves a person becoming sexually aroused primarily from displaying his (or, more rarely, her) genitals. Voyeurs' main means of sexual gratification are in watching unsuspecting persons undressing, naked, or engaging in sexual activity.

6. (a) _____ (also called transvestic fetishism) is another type of paraphilia in which a person obtains sexual pleasure from dressing in the clothing of the other sex. The biggest difference between a cross-dresser and a transvestite is the fact that the TV feels sexual pleasure during (b) _____, whereas a cross-dresser usually does not. Most of the time, neither desires sexual (c) _____ surgery.

7. (a) _____ refers to a persistent and intense need to engage in sexually arousing fantasies, sexual urges, or behaviors involving sexual activity with a prepubescent child. Pedophiles most often report an attraction to (b) _____ of a particular age range. Many choose children because they are available and vulnerable; some pedophiles are unable to function

sexually with an adult. The **(c)** _____ has been both helpful and detrimental in the elimination of pedophilia: pedophiles use it to find each other and talk about their behaviors, but it has also helped to **(d)** _____ pedophiles.

8. Treatment for paraphilias first involves a(an) **(a)** _____. This can be done through self-report, behavioral observation, physiological tests, or personality inventories. Overall, the most important goal of therapy must be to **(b)** _____ a person's behavior. Treatments for paraphilias may include group, individual, and **(c)** _____ therapy, medication, education, and/or self-help groups. Behavioral methods are most common; techniques include **(d)** _____ therapy, shame aversion, systematic desensitization, orgasmic reconditioning, and satiation therapy. Pharmacological and surgical interventions, such as testosterone-suppressing drugs, antidepressants, and **(e)** _____ are also used.

9. Hypersexuality and hyposexuality are two variations in sexual behavior. Some have called hypersexuality a sexual **(a)**

_____ because it involves compulsive sexual behavior. **(b)** _____ argues that people who engage in many of the paraphilias are really sexual **(c)** _____ whose need for constant sexual encounters is similar to any addictive behavior.

10. It is difficult to determine how to decide whether a sexual **(a)** _____ is normal or abnormal. Much of **(b)** _____ feels uncomfortable with the idea of sex for its **(c)** _____ sake, separate from love, intimacy, and **(d)** _____ attachment.

ANSWERS

1. (a) diversity; (b) judgments; (c) acceptable; (d) cultural. 2. (a) Paraphilias; (b) erotic; (c) distress; (d) interact. 3. (a) Paraphilias; (b) dysfunctional; (c) sexual. 4. (a) biological; (b) Psychoanalytic; (c) defines; (d) mating; (e) Behaviorists. 5. (a) sadism; (b) fetish; (c) pain; (d) Exhibitionism. 6. (a) Transvestism; (b) cross-dressing; (c) reassignment. 7. (a) Pedophilia; (b) children; (c) Internet; (d) identify. 8. (a) assessment; (b) change; (c) family; (d) aversion; (e) chemotherapy. 9. (a) addiction; (b) Carnes; (c) addicts. 10. (a) behavior; (b) society; (c) own; (d) human.

Critical Thinking Questions

1. How do you decide whether a sexual behavior is "normal"? What is your definition of "typical" sexual activity, and where do you draw the line for yourself?

2. Do you think people should be allowed to engage in any sexual behaviors they choose, as long as they don't hurt anyone? Explain.

3. If the majority of people feel that the behavior of Dr. Sargent (the rubber fetishist) is distasteful, perverted, or abnormal, should we as a society make him stop doing it? Do you think he is sick? Do you think he needs help to stop this behavior? Why, or why not?

4. Which theory do you think best explains why a paraphilia might develop? What aspects of this theory make the most sense to you, and why?

5. Suppose that tonight when you are walking by yourself, you are approached by a middle-aged man who flashes you and begins stroking his erect penis. What do you think you would be thinking as he stands in front of you stroking his penis? What do you do? Whom do you tell?

6. Do you think a pedophile's address and photograph should be made public so that neighbors can be aware of his or her crimes against young children? How long should this information be listed? For 1 year? 5 years? 10 years? The rest of his or her life? Explain.

CHAPTER RESOURCES

Check It Out

Carnes, P. (2001). **Out of the shadows: Understanding sexual addiction.** Center City, MN: Hazelden Information and Education.

This breakthrough work, the first to describe sexual addiction, is still the standard for recognizing and overcoming sexual addiction. Dr. Patrick Carnes outlines how to identify a sexual addict, recognize the way others may unwittingly become complicit or codependent, and change the patterns that support the addiction.

The Woodsman (2004; 1 hour, 27 minutes; Rated R)

Walter (Kevin Bacon) returns to his hometown after 12 years in prison as a convicted sexual offender. Shunned by his family, his only contact is his brother-in-law (Benjamin Bratt), who eyes him suspiciously. He moves into an apartment across the street from an elementary school and gets a job at a lumberyard. At work, he meets Vickie (Kyra Sedgwick), a tough-talking woman who doesn't judge him for his past. He lives in fear of being discovered, and one day a coworker outs him and fighting breaks out. A local police officer (David Alan Grier) keeps a close eye on Walter. After befriending a young girl in a neighborhood park, Walter must also grapple with his own reawakened demons. An excellent, award-winning film that captures the many emotions involved in sexual offenses.

InfoTrac® College Edition

If your instructor ordered InfoTrac with this book, explore InfoTrac College Edition, your online library, for additional readings and review. Go to: **www.thomsonedu.com,** and enter these search terms:

cross-dressing   paraphilia   sexual addiction

transvestites   voyeurism   exhibitionism

Web Resources

SexualityNow Companion Website

Go to **http://thomsonedu.com/carroll** for practice quiz questions, interactive activities, Internet links, critical thinking exercises, discussion forums, and more. You can also access sites from the Wadsworth Psychology Study Center (**http://psychology.wadsworth.com**) or you can connect directly to the following sites:

Association for the Treatment of Sexual Abusers

The Association for the Treatment of Sexual Abusers is a nonprofit, interdisciplinary organization founded to foster research, facilitate information exchange, further professional education, and provide for the advancement of professional standards and practices in the field of sex offender evaluation and treatment.

Center for Sex Offender Management

The Center for Sex Offender Management's (CSOM) goal is to enhance public safety by preventing further victimization through improving the management of adult and juvenile sex offenders in the community. The Center is sponsored by the Office of Justice Programs, U.S. Department of Justice, in collaboration with the National Institute of Corrections, State Justice Institute, and the American Probation and Parole Association.

Sex Addicts Anonymous

Sex Addicts Anonymous (SAA) is a fellowship of men and women who share their experience, strength, and hope with each other so they may overcome their sexual addiction and help others recover from sexual addiction or dependency.

Silent Lambs

Silent Lambs is a website dedicated to reducing the ability of churches to adopt a "code of silence" when it comes to child sexual abuse that occurs within the church. This website has a variety of links and helpful information; a variety of videos and transcripts are available from recent clergy sexual abuse cases.

Vegan Erotica

VeganErotica.com manufactures handcrafted vegan bondage gear, whips, belts, harnesses, and other vegan leather (a.k.a. "pleather") items. Vegan condoms and other sex products are also available. All products are 100% vegetarian and do not contain animal products, nor were they tested on animals.

National Sex Offender Public Registry

The National Sex Offender Public Registry, coordinated by the Department of Justice, is a cooperative effort between the state agencies hosting public sexual offender registries and the federal government. This website's search tool has a number of search options that allow a user to submit a single national query to obtain information about sex offenders. All state registries are available through this website.

Go to **www.thomsonedu.com** to link to **SexualityNow,** your online study tool. First take the **Pre-Test** for this chapter to get your **Personalized Study Plan,** which will identify topics you need to review and direct you to online resources. Then take the **Post-Test** to determine what concepts you have mastered and what you still need work on.

Videos in SexualityNow

For additional information on topics discussed in this chapter, check out the videos in **SexualityNow** on the following topics:

• **Bondage and S&M**—Check your ideas about bondage, domination, and sadomasochism against these couples who engage in these practices.

17

Power and Sexual Coercion

Sexuality ● Now Go to www.thomsonedu.com to link to **SexualityNow**, your online study tool.

Power is an aspect of all sexual relationships. Sexual relationships are healthy when power is shared and when the relationship empowers the partners. In sexuality, however, as everywhere in human life, power can also be used to degrade and oppress. For example, the act of seduction is usually an interaction between each partner's power, which is partly what makes dating and sexual anticipation so exciting. On the other hand, coercive sexuality involves the clash of personal power, with one partner overpowering the other.

Physically or psychologically forcing sexual relations on another person is usually referred to as rape. Sexual contact with a minor by an adult is called child sexual abuse and, in some societies, is also considered rape. There are also instances in which a person with more power entices, pressures, or encourages another person with less power into sexual activities, ranging from an unwanted glance or word to actual sexual contact. This is sexual harassment. This chapter will begin with rape and sexual assault and will go on to explore other ways that power can be misused in relationships.

SEX Talk

Question: Why do people rape?

There are several theories as to why rape exists in our society. Feminists argue that the nature of the relationships between the sexes fosters rape. Others argue that it exists because of the rapist's psychopathology. Still others claim it is because of how women dress, act, or behave. Today, most theorists agree that rape is a crime of power in which sex is used as a weapon.

RAPE AND SEXUAL ASSAULT: INCIDENCE, THEORIES, AND ATTITUDES

For most mammals, penile penetration of a female by a male is done only when the female is in estrus, or "heat" as it is commonly called. However, forced penetration is common in a wide variety of animal species (Lalumière et al., 2005b); for instance, male orangutans often engage in forced mating and vicious biting of the female. Humans can have sexual intercourse at any point in the menstrual cycle, which means other motivations determine when intercourse might take place. However, in humans, male and female desire for sexual contact may not coincide.

Defining Rape and Sexual Assault

rape
Forced sexual behavior with an individual without that person's consent.

The line that separates **rape** from other categories of sexual activity can be blurry because of the fine distinctions between forced and consensual sex, as well as societal patterns of female passivity and male aggression (LaFree, 1982). For instance, societal and cultural rules often dictate that men, not women, should initiate sexual activity. These beliefs about how sex is supposed to be can make defining rape a difficult task.

Typically we define rape as forced sexual intercourse (force can be physical or psychological), and sexual assault as victimization that include unwanted sexual behavior.

That said, it's also important to point out that every state has its own legal definitions of rape and sexual assault. For example, in order for a rape to occur in North Carolina there must be penile–vaginal intercourse, whereas in other states, such as Arkansas and New Jersey, a rape can include penetration with a hand, finger, or object (American Prosecutors Research Institute, 2003b). Lack of consent, force or threat of force, and vaginal penetration are typically included in the definition of rape and sexual assault. Ejaculation is not a necessary part of the definition; however, there are states that require the exchange of semen in order for a crime to be established (American Prosecutors Research Institute, 2003b).

Regardless of state definitions, many women do not consider an assault rape if there was no penis involved (Bart & O'Brien, 1985). This is because many women view rape as something that is done by a penis (intercourse, fellatio, sodomy) rather than something done to a vagina (digital penetration, cunnilingus, touching). However, research has shown us that a woman subjected to such assaults still experiences a trauma quite similar to that of a woman who is forced to endure penile penetration. A nonpenile sexual attack has also been referred to as **sexual assault** and is defined as the unwanted touching of an intimate part of another person, including the genitals, buttocks, and/or breasts, for sexual arousal. Sexual assault also includes sexual penetration (vaginal, oral, anal) as well (Searles & Berger, 1987). This would include rape that occurs to both females and males.

sexual assault
Coercion of a nonconsenting victim to have sexual contact.

Recently there has been a debate about the appropriate term for a person who has experienced a rape. Although the word *victim* emphasizes the person's lack of responsibility for the incident, it may also imply that the person was a passive recipient of the attack. The term *victim* can also become a permanent label. Some prefer the term *survivor*, which implies that the person had within her- or himself the strength to overcome and to survive the rape. It also confirms that the person made important decisions—for example, not to fight and possibly be killed—during the assault and thus was not com-

---

TABLE 17.1 Age of Consent

Many countries, and states within the United States, have legal ages of consent. The age of consent is how old a person must be to be considered capable of legally giving informed consent to engage in sexual acts with another person. It is considered a crime for a person to engage in sexual behavior with someone below the age of consent. Many countries and states provide ages of consent for male–male and female–female sex. In some countries there is no information on specific ages for certain behaviors.

Country	Male–Female Sex	Male–Male Sex	Female–Female Sex
Queensland, Australia	16	18	16
Austria	14	18	14
Bahamas	16	18	18
Botswana	16 for females 14 for males	Illegal for all ages	No information
Denmark	15	15	15
Hong Kong	16	21	No information
Croatia	14	14	14
India	16	Illegal for all ages	Illegal for all ages
Italy	14	14	14
Kenya	16	Illegal for all ages	Illegal for all ages
Madagascar	21	21	21
Puerto Rico	14	Illegal for all ages	Illegal for all ages
Saudia Arabia	No age minimum but must be married	Illegal for all ages	Illegal for all ages
South Africa	16	19	19
Swaziland	18	Illegal for all ages	Illegal for all ages
U.S.A.—California	18	18	18
U.S.A.—Connecticut	16	16	16
U.S.A.—Illinois	17	17	17
U.S.A.—New Hampshire	16	18	18
U.S.A.—Pennsylvania	16	16	16

Source: "Legal age of consent." (1998–2000). Retrieved November 30, 2005, from http://www.ageofconsent.com/ageofconsent.htm

pletely passive. However, for clarity, in this chapter we will use the term *victim* to refer to a person who has survived a rape.

Incidence of Rape

The United States Department of Justice reported 72,240 rapes and 44,650 attempted rapes in 2003 (U.S. Department of Justice–Office of Justice Programs, 2005). This translates into someone being sexually assaulted every 2½ minutes in the United States (Rape, Abuse, & Incest National Network, 2005). Although the incidence of reported rape and attempted rape has decreased over the last few years (see Figure 17.1, where you'll notice the 1992–2002 average rape incidence was much higher), these numbers are still a cause for concern, especially because rape rates are significantly underreported. There is also a seasonal variation in rape, with the highest percentage occurring during the summer, and the lowest percentage in December (U.S. Department of Justice–Federal Bureau of Investigation, 2004). Although rape prevalence in industrialized nations is estimated to be between 21% and 25%, among nonindustrialized nations the prevalence is between 43% and 90% (Rozee, 2005).

Rape is prevalent on U.S. college campuses. It is estimated that approximately 3% of women experience a completed and/or attempted rape during a typical college year (Fisher et al., 2000). The majority of the offenders are acquaintances of the victim (B. S. Fisher et al., 2005; see Figure 17.2). Verbal sexual coercion is also prevalent on college campuses (DeGue & DiLillo, 2005). Sanday (1990) refers to verbal sexual coercion as "working a yes out." Some men have been found to use nonphysical methods of coercion to obtain sexual contact with an unwilling partner, such as continual arguments, verbal pressure, and/or deceit (DeGue & DiLillo, 2005). Men who use verbal sexual coercion have been found to believe in more rape myths[*], report more hostility toward women, and have more sexual partners than men who do not use such coercion (DeGue & DiLillo, 2005).

It is difficult, however, to assess the actual number of rapes because rape has been one of the most underreported crimes in the United States (U.S. Department of Justice–Office of Justice Programs, 2002). However, rape victims are significantly more likely to report a rape today than they were a few years ago (National Crime Victimization Survey, 2004).

---

[*]Martha Burt (1980) proposed the concept of rape myths, which she defined as false beliefs about rape, rape victims, and/or rapists. Myths would include "Only bad girls get raped," "Men can't be raped," or "Women ask for rape."

Rape, injury, and reporting in the United States, 1992-2002

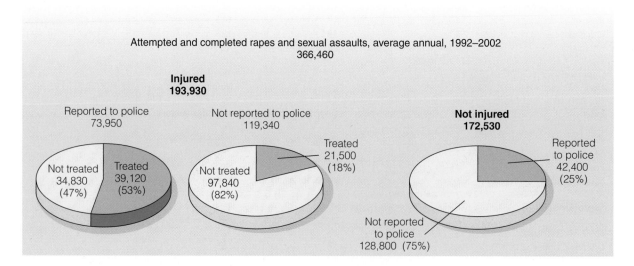

Figure 17.1
Most rapes and sexual assaults are not reported to police, and injuries sustained during a rape are often left untreated.
Source: U.S. Department of Justice–Office of Justice Programs, 2002.

In fact, close to half of all rapes are reported today (Rape, Abuse & Incest National Network, 2005).

Why are many women unlikely to report rape? Some do not report it because they do not think it was rape, they believe they did something to put themselves at risk, they feel shame and humiliation, or fear their report won't be taken seriously (U.S. Department of Justice–Office of Justice Programs, 2002). Others fear no one will believe them or that no legal action will be taken.

Characteristics of Rapists

Who is it that rapes? What is your image of a "rapist"? A man in an alley? Someone who cannot control himself sexually? A drunk college student? A psychopath? What drives a man to commit rape? Anger? Frustration? Even today, the question of why men rape is still largely unanswered.

Research has shown that rapists are primarily young, between the ages of 15 and 30, single (Amir, 1971; D. E. H. Russell, 1984), and tend to reduce their rape behavior as they get older (Kantrowitz & Gonzalez, 1990). Antisocial personality patterns and high levels of impulsivity and aggression are common in men who rape (Giotakos et al., 2005; Lalumière et al., 2005d), and many rapists have experienced overwhelmingly negative early interpersonal experiences, most of which were with their fathers (McCormack et al., 2002). Sexist views about women are common, and rape myth acceptance, low self-esteem, and political conservatism have also been found (S. Peterson & Franzese, 1987). There are also correlations found between rapists and past sexual abuse (Stevenson & Gajarsky, 1992) and between the use of violent and degrading pornography and a negative view of women (Millburn et al., 2000). However, despite the assumption that rapists are psychologically disturbed individuals, research does not support the assumption that they are very different from "normal" men (Cornett & Shuntich, 1991).

Convicted rapists are not the only ones who are attracted to the idea of forcing a woman to engage in sex. In a classic study about the potential to rape, 356 college-age males were asked, "If you could be assured that no one would know and that you could in no way be punished for forcing a woman to do something she really didn't want to do (rape), how likely, if at all, would you be to commit such acts?" Sixty percent indicated that under the right circumstances, there was some likelihood that they would use force, or rape, or both (Ceniti & Malamuth, 1984). This study is dated, however, so it is difficult to know whether the results would be significantly different today. Your author is hopeful that it would be.

Theories About Rape

What drives someone to rape another person? We will discuss the most prominent theories of why rape occurs, including rapist psychopathology, victim precipitation, feminist, sociological, and evolutionary theories.

Rapist Psychopathology: A Disease Model

Modern ideas about why rape occurs evolved first from psychiatric theories, which suggested that men rape because of mental illness, uncontrollable sexual urges, or alcohol intoxication. This theory of **rapist psychopathology** suggests that it is either disease or intoxication that forces men to rape and that if they did not have these problems, they would not rape.

According to this theory, the rape rate can be reduced by finding these sick individuals and rehabilitating them. The theory makes people feel safer because it suggests that only sick individuals rape, not "normal" people. However, research consistently fails to identify any significant distinguishing characteristics of rapists (Fernandez & Marshall,

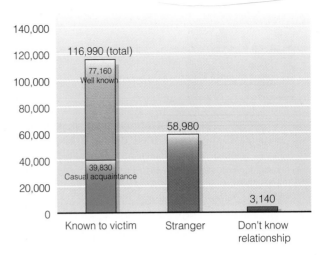

Figure 17.2

Number of rapes/sexual assaults by relationship to offender, 2003.

Source: U.S. Department of Justice–Office of Justice Programs, 2003.

Review Question

Describe the problems that have been encountered in attempting to identify the actual number of rapes.

sex byte

Two main forms of ambiguous communication are related to sexual victimization—token resistance (when a woman says "no" but means "yes"), and compliance (when a woman says "yes" but means "no"; Krahé et al., 2000).

Review Question

Identify what researchers have found about the characteristics of rapists.

rapist psychopathology

A theory of rape that identifies psychological issues in a rapist that contribute to rape behavior.

Date-Rape Drugs

The term "date-rape drug" is slang for any drug that may be used during a sexual assault. This would include Rohypnol (also called roofies, Forget Pill, or Mind Eraser), gamma hydroxybutyric acid (GHB; also called Liquid Ecstasy, Georgia Home Boy, or Easy Lay), and Ketamine (also called Special K, Kit Kat, or Cat Valium). Today experts refer to rapes using these drugs as "drug-facilitated sexual assault." The effects of these drugs are similar to those of Valium, but they are much more powerful. The drugs go to work quickly, and the time they last varies. If a person has been drinking alcohol when the drugs were ingested, the drug effects will last longer. Side effects of these drugs may include drowsiness, memory problems, lower blood pressure, sleepiness, problems talking, dizziness, and/or impaired motor functions. With higher doses, convulsions, vomiting, loss of consciousness, and coma and/or death can occur. In late 2005, reports circulated about fatal levels of GHB given to women at Colorado fraternity parties ("Date Rape Drug Served," 2005).

Rohypnol is illegal in the United States, but is legal in several countries and has been smuggled into the United

These and similar coasters include test patches that can show the presence of date-rape drugs in a drink.

AP Photo/Eric Risberg

States. Rohypnol comes in tablet form and is typically placed in a drink, where it quickly dissolves. Once dissolved, the tablets are undetectable—there is no taste or color change to the liquid. Ketamine is a white powder that easily dissolves in a drink, whereas GHB can come in tablet, liquid, or powder form. Ketamine and GHB are both legal and used for different medical purposes. The effects of these drugs usually begin within 30 minutes, peak within 2 hours, and can last a total of 8 hours. An individual may feel nauseous, hot or cold, and dizzy within 10 minutes after ingesting these drugs.

You can protect yourself from drug-facilitated sexual assault by never accepting drinks from other people, opening your drinks yourself, and by never leaving your drink unattended. If you think you have been drugged, it's important to go to a police station or hospital as soon as possible. A urine test can check for the presence of the drugs. These drugs can leave your body within 12 to 72 hours, so it's important to get a urine test as soon as possible. For more information about date-rape drugs, check the website listings at the end of this chapter.

2003). Having psychological or alcohol problems does not predispose a person to be a rapist. In fact, men who rape are often found to be nearly "normal" in every other way. Perhaps it is easier to see rapists as somehow sick than realize that the potential to rape exists in many of us.

Theories of rapist psychopathology were very common until the 1950s, when feminist researchers began to refocus attention on rape's effect on the victim rather than on the offender. However, there are still those who accept psychopathological theories today. In fact, college students often report that this theory helps to explain stranger rape but doesn't help us to understand date or acquaintance rape (Cowan, 2000).

Victim Precipitation Theory: Blaming the Victim

victim precipitation theory
A theory of rape that identifies victim characteristics or behaviors that contribute to rape.

Victim precipitation theory explores the ways victims make themselves vulnerable to rape, such as how they dress, act, or where they walk (Wakelin, 2003). By focusing on the victim and ignoring the motivations of the attacker, many have labeled this a "blame the victim" theory.

The victim precipitation theory of rape shifts the responsibility from the person who knowingly attacked to the innocent victim (Sawyer et al., 2002): "She was walking home too late at night," "She was drunk," "She was wearing too much makeup," or "She was flirting." The theory also serves to distance people from the reality of rape and lulls

What to Do If You Are Raped

1. Know that it was not your fault. When a woman is raped, she often spends a long time trying to figure out exactly what she did to put herself at risk for a rape. This is probably because women have always been told to "be careful," "watch how you dress," or "don't drink too much." In reality, a rape might happen anywhere and at any time. No one asks to be raped.

2. Talk to a rape crisis counselor. Some women like to talk to a rape crisis counselor before going to the hospital or police. This is very helpful because counselors can often give you advice. Besides this, they are knowledgeable about rape and the aftermath of symptoms. Many hospitals have on-site counselors, usually volunteers from Women Organized Against Rape. Talking to a counselor also helps give the victim back her sense of control (see the Web Resources at the end of this chapter).

3. Go to a hospital for a medical examination. An immediate medical evaluation is imperative. If there is a nurse or healthcare provider on campus, you can see either of them, but it is better to go to a local emergency room in order to have a thorough physical examination. Medical evaluations are important for two reasons: to check for STIs that may have been transmitted during the rape and to check for the presence of date-rape drugs. Because some of the STIs take time to show up positive on a culture, it is important to be retested in the following weeks. Recently, some women have requested AIDS

tests postrape, although infection with HIV also takes time to show up. If a woman was not using birth control or has reason to suspect that she may have become pregnant, the hospital can administer the morning-after pill (see Chapter 12 for more information about the morning-after pill). Also, if you think you might have been drugged, you can also have a urine test to check for the drug's presence. Try not to urinate before having this test.

4. Do not throw away any evidence of the rape. Do not shower before you go to the hospital. If you decide to change your clothes, do not wash or destroy what you were wearing. If anything was damaged in the assault, such as glasses, jewelry, or book bags, keep these too. Put everything in a plastic bag, and store it in a safe place. It is necessary to preserve the evidence of the rape, which will be very important if you decide to press charges against the rapist.

5. Decide whether you want to file a police report. You have a choice of filing either a formal or informal report. This is something that you will need to sort through and decide. A rape crisis counselor can be very helpful in this decision process.

6. Decide whether you want to press charges. Although you do not need to decide this right away, you will need to think about it as soon as possible. It is important to review this decision with a lawyer experienced in rape cases.

them into the false assumption that it could not happen to them or someone close to them because they would not act like "those other women." If we believe bad things happen to people who take risks, then we are safe if we do not take those risks. In the majority of rapes, however, women are not engaging in risky behavior. College students often report that the victim precipitation theory explains date-rape cases better than stranger-rape cases (Cowan, 2000).

In Susan Brownmiller's (1975) classic work on gender and rape, she argues that rape forces a woman to stay in at night, to monitor her behavior, and to look to men for protection. This attitude also contributes to a rape victim's guilt because she then wonders: "If I hadn't worn what I did, walked where I walked, or acted as I did, maybe I wouldn't have been raped." Overall, men are more likely than women to believe in the victim precipitation theory and to view sexual coercion as acceptable (Auster & Leone, 2001; Proto-Campise et al., 1998).

Feminist Theory: Keeping Women in Their Place

Feminist theorists contend that rape and the threat of rape are tools used in our society to keep women in their place. This fear keeps women in traditional sex roles, which are subordinate to men's. Feminist theorists believe that the social, economic, and political separation of the genders has encouraged rape, which is viewed as an act of domination

sex byte

Women who live away from their parents report higher rates of sexual aggression than women who live with their parents (Buddie & Testa, 2005). This may be due in part to the fact that women who live away from their parents report higher rates of binge drinking and more sexual partners.

feminist theory
A theory of rape that contends that rape is a tool used in society to keep a woman in her place.

of men over women (Murnen et al., 2002). Sex-role stereotyping—which reinforces the idea that men are supposed to be strong, aggressive, and assertive, whereas women are expected to be slim, weak, and passive—encourages rape in our culture (Murnen et al., 2002).

Sociological Theory: Balance of Power

Sociological theory and feminist theory have much in common; in fact, many feminist theorists are sociologists. Sociologists believe that rape is an expression of power differentials in society (Martin, 2003). When men feel disempowered by society, by changing sex roles or by their jobs, overpowering women with the symbol of their masculinity (a penis) reinforces, for a moment, men's control over the world.

Sociologists explore the ways people guard their interests in society. For example, the wealthy class in a society may fear the poorer classes, who are larger in number and envy the possessions of the upper class. Because women have been viewed as "possessions" of men throughout most of Western history, fear of the lower classes often manifested itself in a belief that lower-class males were "after our wives and daughters." During the slavery period in the United States, for example, it was widely believed that, if given the chance, black males would rape white women, whereas white males did not find black women attractive. Yet the truth was just the opposite; rape of white women by black males was relatively rare, whereas many white slave masters routinely raped their black slaves. Once again, this supports the idea that rape is a reflection of power issues rather than just sexual issues.

Evolutionary Theory: Product of Evolution

Finally, a controversial theory on the origins of rape comes out of evolutionary theory. Randy Thornhill and Craig Palmer, authors of *Natural History of Rape: Biological Bases of Sexual Coercion,* propose that rape is rooted in human evolution (Thornhill & Palmer, 2000). According to evolutionary theory, men and women have developed differing reproductive strategies, wherein men desire frequent mating in order to spread their seed, whereas women are designed to protect their eggs and be more selective in choosing mates (see Chapter 2 for more information about evolutionary theory). Rape has developed as a consequence of these differences in reproductive strategies. The majority of rapists are male, Thornhill and Palmer assert, because men are designed to impregnate and spread their seed.

As you might guess, this theory is controversial, and many feminists and sociologists alike are upset about ideas proposed in this theory (Brownmiller, 2000; Roughgarden, 2004). However, controversial or not, it's an interesting argument for us to consider when discussing theories on the development of rape.

Gender Differences in Attitudes About Rape

Researchers have used many techniques to measure attitudes about rape and rape victims, such as questionnaires, written vignettes, mock trials, videotaped scenarios, still photography, and newspaper reports. Gender research has found that overall, men are less empathetic and sensitive than women toward rape, and they attribute more responsibility to the victim (Nagel et al., 2005; B. H. White & Kurpius, 2002; Workman & Freeburg, 1999). Men believe more rape myths (see the footnote about Burt's 1980 research on page 570), and they also believe that a woman is signaling sexual availability when the woman thinks her behavior is simply friendly or even neutral (B. E. Johnson et al., 1997; Saal et al., 1989). Women rate a rape as more justified and see the victim as more responsible for the rape when the woman was seen as "leading a man on" (Muehlenhard & MacNaughton, 1988). Some women believe that if they "led a man on," they gave up their right to refuse sex (Muehlenhard & Schrag, 1991).

However, there is some hope in changing these attitudes about rape. One longitudinal study found that all men experienced a decline in negative rape attitudes over the

4 years they were in college (Pamm, 2001). This may be due in part to rape education workshops, which have been found to decrease rape myths (Klaw et al., 2005).

Ethnic Differences in Attitudes About Rape

Although the majority of the research has examined gender differences in attitudes about rape, there is also research on ethnicity differences in rape attitudes. Overall, ethnic minorities have been found to have more traditional attitudes toward women, which has been found to affect rape attitudes (Fischer, 1987). For example, among college students, non-Hispanic whites are more sympathetic than African Americans to women who have been raped (Nagel et al., 2005). However, African Americans are more sympathetic than either Hispanic (Fischer, 1987) or Japanese American college students (Yamawaki & Tschanz, 2005). Asian American students have the least sympathy for women who have been raped, and are more likely to hold a rape victim responsible for the rape and excuse the rapist (J. Lee et al., 2005; Yamawaki & Tschanz, 2005).

Researchers suggest that these differences are due to variations in cultural gender roles and conservative attitudes about sexuality. It's important to keep in mind that within these ethnic groups, there are also gender differences in attitudes about rape, with women more supportive of rape victims than men.

Rape in Different Cultures

The United States has the highest rate of reported rapes in the world. In 1990, women in the United States were 8 times more likely to report being raped than were European women, 26 times more likely than Japanese, and 46 times more likely than Greek women (Mann, 1991). However, the incidence of rape varies depending on how each culture defines rape; one culture might accept sexual behavior that is considered rape in another culture.

Throughout history rape has been accepted as a punishment in some cultures. Among the Cheyenne Indians, a husband who suspected his wife of infidelity could put her "out to field," where other men were encouraged to rape her (Hoebel, 1954). In the Marshall Islands of the Pacific Ocean, women were seen as the property of the males, and any male could force sexual intercourse upon them (Sanday, 1981). In Kenya, the Gusii people view intercourse as an act in which males overpower their female partners and cause them considerable pain. In fact, if she has difficulty walking the next morning, the man is seen as a "real man" and will boast of his ability to make his partner cry (Bart & O'Brien, 1985). In 2002, an 11-year-old Pakistani boy was found guilty of walking unchaperoned with a girl from a different tribe. His punishment involved the gang raping of his 18-year-old sister, which was done to shame his family. The gang rape took place in a mud hut while hundreds of people stood by and laughed and cheered (Tanveer, 2002).

Rape has also been used for initiation purposes. In East Africa, the Kikuyu used to have an initiation ritual in which a young boy was expected to rape to prove his manhood (Broude & Greene, 1976). Until he did this, he could not engage in sexual intercourse or marry a woman. In Australia, among the Arunta, rape serves as an initiation rite for girls. After the ceremonial rape, she is given to her husband, and no one else has access to her (Broude & Greene, 1976).

Child rape is also common in some places around the globe. In Chapter 15 we discussed the South African myth about curing AIDS through sex with a virgin child (Posel, 2005). It is estimated that sexual violence against children, including infant rape, has increased 400% over the past decade in South Africa (Dempster, 2002). Some studies have found that 1 million women and children are raped in South Africa each year (Meier, 2002).

There are many cultural beliefs and societal issues that are responsible for the high rape rates in South Africa, including the fact that South African women have a difficult time saying no to sex; many men believe they are entitled to sex and believe that women enjoy being raped (Meier, 2002). South Africa has the highest reported rape rates in the

Review Question

Discuss gender and ethnicity differences in rape attitudes and how these attitudes might be changed.

sexbyte

"Persecutory" rape occurs in the context of a political conflict (Dunkley, 2005). This would include rape that occurs during times of war, when men are indifferent to the fate of women they view as enemies (Hynes, 2004; Lalumière et al., 2005c). Although men are also raped during wartime, women are more frequently targeted (Borchelt, 2005).

sexbyte

A female born in South Africa has a greater chance of being raped in her lifetime than of learning to read (Dempster, 2002).

Rapex, a new antirape condom that will cost 20 cents, is worn by women. The South African inventor, shown here, hopes that women in South Africa will insert the device as a part of their daily security routine. During a rape, metal barbs in the condom will hook onto the skin of the penis and immediately disable a man, allowing the woman to get away. The barbs must be surgically removed, so a rapist will need to seek medical attention, enabling the police to identify him.

© Mike Hutchings/Reuters/Corbis

world (and probably a higher unreported rape rate), and experts have been looking for ways to help deter men from committing rape (Dixon, 2005). Because of this, in 2005, an antirape female condom was unveiled in South Africa (Dixon, 2005; see photo above). This device is controversial: some believe that it puts the responsibility for the problem on the shoulders of South African women, whereas others believe that the device may help lessen the climbing rape rates in South Africa.

In Asian cultures there are often more conservative attitudes about sex; because of this, there is often more tolerance for rape myths (M. A. Kennedy & Gorzalka, 2002). Research by Sanday (1981) indicates that the primary cultural factors that affect the incidence of rape in a society include relations between the sexes, the status of women, and male attitudes in the society. Societies that promote male violence have higher incidences of rape because men are socialized to be aggressive, dominating, and to use force to get what they want.

RAPE ON CAMPUS

A study done in 2000 looked at sexual coercion on college campuses across the United States and found that 2% of women reported they had been raped, whereas 1% reported they were victims of an attempted rape—meaning that 35 women are raped or experience an attempted rape for every 1,000 college students each year (B. S. Fisher et al., 2000). As we discussed earlier, the majority of these women knew the person who sexually victimized them; the majority were ex-boyfriends, classmates, friends, and/or coworkers (B. S. Fisher et al., 2000).

In Chapter 7 we discussed stalking in intimate relationships. Some women report being stalked on campus, either physically, or through notes and e-mails (see Figure 17.3). Overall, a total of 8% to 16% of women and 2% to 7% of men report being stalked at some point in their lives (Dennison & Thomson, 2005). What's interesting is that college-aged men and women often have differing definitions for stalking, and typically, men are not as quick to define unwanted attention and interest as stalking (Hills & Taplin, 1998). Stalking is a serious problem, especially given that 81% of women who have been stalked by a lover were also physically assaulted by that lover, whereas 31% were sexually assaulted by him (Tjaden & Thoennes, 1998).

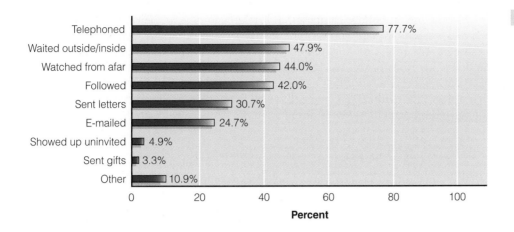

Figure 17.3
Percentages of stalking behaviors on college campuses.
Source: B. S. Fisher et al., 2000; Stalking Resource Center, 2000.

Because the majority of women know their assailants on college campuses, it won't come as any surprise that few feel comfortable reporting or pressing charges. Studies have found that although two-thirds of the women talked to someone else about the incident, the majority told only a friend (B. S. Fisher et al., 2000). In 1990, the United States passed the Student Right-to-Know and Campus Security Act, which requires colleges with federal student aid programs to provide campus crime statistics upon request (Fisher et al., 2000).

Alcohol and Rape

Alcohol use is one of the strongest predictors of acquaintance rape on college campuses (Koss, 1988; Loiselle, 2004), where half of all rape cases involve the use of alcohol by the rapist, victim, or both (Abbey, 2002; Abbey et al., 2001; Hensley, 2002; Marx et al., 1999).

For men, alcohol seems to "sexualize" the environment around them. Cues that might be taken as neutral if the men were not drunk (such as a certain woman talking to them or dancing with them) may be seen as an indication of sexual interest (Abbey et al., 2005). In addition, alcohol increases the chances of engaging in risky sexual behaviors (O'Hare, 2005).

For women, alcohol may lead to increased teasing and flirting, which sends ambiguous messages. Like alcohol use in men, women under the influence of alcohol engage in risky sexual behaviors (Maisto et al., 2004; O'Hare, 2005; see Chapter 15 for a discussion of high-risk sexual behaviors). Muehlenhard and Cook (1988) found that 43% of college women reported regretting sexual intercourse they engaged in while intoxicated. For a woman, being drunk is one of the strongest risk factors for being sexually victimized (B. S. Fisher et al., 2000). Women who get drunk are more likely to be viewed as "loose" or sexually "easy" (Parks & Scheidt, 2000). These views help put blame on the women who have been raped. Unfortunately, when a woman experiences a rape while drunk she is more likely to blame herself and often will not label the attack as a rape even when it clearly was (L. G. Hensley, 2002).

ReviewQuestion

Explain what we know about rape on campus.

Alcohol can sexualize the environment for men. A man who has been drinking may believe that a woman is signaling that she is available when she is acting friendly.

SEX Talk

Question: *What if you are drunk and she is too, and when you wake up in the morning she says you raped her?*

Claims of rape must be taken seriously. This is why men and women should be very careful in using alcohol and engaging in sexual activity. The best approach would be to delay engaging in sexual activity if you have been drinking. This way, you will not find yourself in this situation.

Alcohol use on college campuses, as it relates to rape, is viewed very differently for men and women. A man who is drunk and is accused of rape is seen as less responsible because he was drinking ("Lighten up; he was so smashed he didn't even know what he was doing"); a woman who has been drinking is seen as more responsible for her behavior ("Can you believe her? She's had so much to drink that she's flirting with everyone—what a slut!"; Richardson & Campbell, 1982; Scully & Marolla, 1983). In court, women who have been drinking or were drunk are more likely to be discredited.

Fraternities and Rape

Many fraternities may create a ripe environment for rape.

Initially, Greek organizations were established to help students join together to participate in social issues that they felt were largely ignored by their respective universities (Bryan, 1987). Today, however, many fraternities and sororities operate primarily for socializing. It is estimated that 10% of college rapes happen in fraternities (B. S. Fisher et al., 2000).

Although rape does occur in residence halls and off-campus apartments, there are several ways in which fraternities create a riper environment for rape. Many fraternities revolve around an ethic of masculinity. Values that the members see as important include competition, dominance, willingness to drink alcohol, and sexual prowess. There is considerable pressure to be sexually successful, and the members gain respect from other members through sex (P. Y. Martin & Hummer, 1989). The emphasis on masculinity, secrecy, and the protection of the group often provides a fertile environment for coercive sexuality (Adams-Curtis & Forbes, 2004).

Some fraternities have begun to institute educational programs for their members. Others invite guest speakers from **rape crisis centers** to discuss the problem of date rape. Until members of fraternities learn to use peer pressure against those who violate the rights of women, rape will certainly continue to be a problem.

rape crisis centers
Organizations that offer support services to victims of sexual assault, their families, and friends. Many offer information, referrals, support groups, counseling, educational programs, and workshops.

SEX Talk

Question: I am in a fraternity, and last semester there was a rape by one of my brothers. All of the members supported him when he said he did not do it, even though everyone knew he did. Why did they support him and not the woman?

This is a very difficult question to answer because it involves a group process in which these men agree to support each other "no matter what." There is a considerable amount of fear in telling the truth because the members of the fraternity will be angry and may even kick out the guy who tells or supports the woman. However, it appears that more and more fraternities are beginning to turn this peer pressure around. Some have even sponsored workshops for the fraternity members to teach them the laws and definitions of rape. Unfortunately, when a fraternity stands behind a rapist, they are silently encouraging his behavior.

Athletes and Rape

Male athletes have been found to be disproportionately overrepresented as assailants of rape by women surveyed (Locke & Mahalik, 2005; Sawyer et al., 2002). In addition, athletes who participate on teams that produce revenue have higher rates of sexually abusive behavior than athletes on teams that don't produce revenue (Koss & Gaines, 1993; McMahon, 2004). Researchers suggest that perhaps it is the sense of privilege that contributes to a view of the world in which rape is legitimized. Playing sports may also help connect aggression and sexuality.

Some researchers suggest that it may be this need to be aggressive and tough while playing sports that helps create problems off the field (Boeringer, 1999; T. J. Brown et al., 2002). One male athlete explains:

You can be the nicest guy, but when you step on that mat, you've gotta flip a switch. You've gotta go nuts, and you've gotta become an animal. Within the rules, but you've gotta go out there and you've gotta be so intense. You have to just break that guy. (McMahon, 2004, p. 10).

Many male athletes may also have a distorted view of women, which often revolves around views expressed in the locker room. Locker room talk often includes derogatory language about women (including the use of words such as "sluts" or "bitches" to describe women), whereas those athletes who are not playing well are referred to as "girls" (McMahon, 2004).

Studies have also been done on female athletes, who often believe they are less at risk than female nonathletes (McMahon, 2004). When asked about the potential for a female athlete to be raped, one woman said:

I think it would be a shock to a female athlete—because, we feel that we're so tough. . . . I always am kidding around that like, I could sit on a guy and knock the wind out of him and the idea of a guy taking advantage of me seems . . . well, that could never happen. . . . I work out all the time, I'm so strong. . . . I'm not some little girl. I'm tough. (McMahon, 2004, p. 16).

Compared to female nonathletes, female athletes are more likely to blame the victim for a rape and believe that some women who are raped have put themselves in a bad situation (McMahon, 2004). Overall, female athletes have more negative attitudes about date rape than male athletes (Holcomb et al., 2002).

Sneak Peek

"He said that if I would tell anyone what happened he'd come after my 5-year-old sister. So I knew . . . that I wasn't going to tell a soul."—*Rape and Posttraumatic Stress Disorder*

Sexuality ◉ Now

Review Question

Explain what we know about alcohol, fraternities, and athletes on campus and the role each plays in rape on campus.

EFFECTS OF RAPE

Rape is an emotionally, physically, and psychologically shattering experience for the victim. Immediately after a rape, many victims report feeling numb and disorganized. Some deny that the rape occurred at all, to avoid the pain of dealing with it. Others express self-blame, disbelief, anger, vulnerability, and increased feelings of dependency. As time goes by, the healing process begins, and feelings may shift to self-pity, sadness, and guilt. Anxiety attacks, nightmares, and fear slowly begin to decrease, although the incident is never forgotten. Women with a history of sexual abuse, including rape, have a lower health-related quality of life and more psychological symptoms than those who have no history of sexual abuse (L. M. Dickinson et al., 1999). Some women never return to prior functioning levels and must create an entirely new view of themselves.

Rape Trauma Syndrome

Researchers Burgess and Holmstrom (1974) coined the term **rape trauma syndrome (RTS),** which describes the effects of rape. RTS is a two-stage stress response pattern characterized by physical, psychological, behavioral, and/or sexual problems, and it occurs after forced, nonconsenting sexual activity. Although not all victims respond to rape in the same manner, what follows is a description of what typically occurs.

During the first stage of RTS, the **acute phase,** most victims fear being alone, strangers, or even their bedroom or their car if that is where the rape took place. Other emotional reactions to rape include anger (at the assailant, the rape, healthcare workers, family, one's self, court), anxiety, depression, confusion, shock, disbelief, incoherence, guilt, humiliation, shame, and self-blame (Frazier, 2000). A victim may also experience wide mood fluctuations. Difficulties with sleeping, including recurrent nightmares, are common. This phase begins immediately following the assault, may last from days to weeks, and involves several stress-related symptoms. A man or woman who has been raped may also experience **post-traumatic stress disorder (PTSD).**

The majority of victims eventually talk to someone about the rape (B. S. Fisher et al., 2003). However, in one study, half of the women who were raped waited years before telling anyone (Monroe et al., 2005). Most of the time a victim will talk to friends

rape trauma syndrome (RTS)
A two-stage stress response pattern that occurs after a rape.

acute phase
First stage of the rape trauma syndrome, in which a victim often feels shock, fear, anger, or other related feelings.

posttraumatic stress disorder
A psychiatric disorder that can occur following the experience or witnessing of life-threatening events such as a violent personal assault like rape. People who suffer from PTSD often relive the experience through nightmares and flashbacks, have difficulty sleeping, and feel detached or estranged, and these symptoms can be severe enough and last long enough to significantly impair the person's daily life.

During the first stage of rape trauma syndrome, victims may feel depressed, confused, angry, guilty, or humiliated. Talking to a counselor can be very helpful in working through these feelings.

or family members rather than to the police. Younger victims are more likely to tell someone than older victims, perhaps because older victims blame themselves more for the rape and may fear that others, too, will blame them. Some victims initially tell someone right after the rape and then, because of negative reactions from support persons, halt their disclosure and never mention it again (Ahrens, 2002).

Depression often follows a rape, and some victims report still feeling depressed 8 to 12 months postrape. Women who have been raped are more likely to experience depression than women who never experience sexual abuse (Cheasty et al., 2002). Several factors have been found to be related to the development of a significant depression after a rape, including having a history of prior psychological problems or prior victimization and a tendency to self-blame (Frazier, 2000).

Sometimes depressive feelings are so severe that victims' thoughts turn to suicide. In fact, research has found an association between rape and attempted suicide (Bridgeland et al., 2001). Poverty, prior depression, and prior sexual assaults also increase feelings of depression, anxiety, and overall problems associated with the rape (Cheasty et al., 2002).

Emotional reactions also vary depending on whether or not the victim knew his or her assailant. Women who report being raped by strangers experience more anxiety, fear, and startle responses, whereas those raped by acquaintances usually report more depression and guilt and a decrease in self-confidence (Sorenson & Brown, 1990). A woman who knew her assailant may have initially trusted him and agreed to be with him, and so after the rape she may wonder how she could have had such bad judgment, why she did not see it coming, and she may feel a sense of betrayal (see the accompanying Personal Voices, "Acquaintance Rape").

There are also many physical symptoms experienced by men and women who have been raped. Some of these include general body soreness, bruises, difficulties with swallowing and throat soreness if there was forced oral sex (in women), genital itching or burning, rectal bleeding and/or pain, STI symptoms, and eating disorders. In women, the emotional stress of the rape may also cause menstrual irregularities. However, some of these symptoms (nausea and menstrual irregularities) are also signs of pregnancy, which is why a pregnancy test is of utmost importance after a victim has been raped.

Recent research reveals that there is a higher incidence of pregnancy in women who have been raped than in women who engage in consensual unprotected sexual intercourse (Gottschall & Gottschall, 2003). We do know that women who are in prime fertile ages are overrepresented in rape victim statistics. This, in conjunction with the fact that women who are ovulating may be more physically attractive to rapists, may contribute to the higher pregnancy rates (Gottschall & Gottschall, 2003; the hormones involved in ovulation, which we discussed in Chapter 4, often make a woman appear more attractive). A young, healthy woman will have a higher chance of pregnancy than an older woman. Many rape victims are also concerned about the risk of acquiring HIV from their assailants (Salholz et al., 1990).

Long-term reorganization, stage two of RTS, involves restoring order in the victim's lifestyle and reestablishing control. Many victims report that changing some aspect of their lives, such as changing their address or phone number, helped them to gain control. Symptoms from both stages can persist for 1 to 2 years after the rape (Nadelson et al., 1982), although Burgess and Holmstrom (1979) found that 74% of rape victims recovered within 5 years. Recovery is affected by the amount and quality of care that the victim received after the rape. Positive crisis intervention and the support of others decrease the symptoms of the trauma.

In the past, many researchers have argued that rape is a violent crime, not a sexual one. "Desexualizing" rape, or taking the sexual aspect out of it, has deemphasized postrape sexual concerns (Wakelin, 2003). Rape is indeed both a violent and a sexual crime, and the majority of victims report experiencing sexual problems postrape, even though these problems may not be lifelong (Becker et al., 1986; Holmstrom & Burgess, 1978).

long-term reorganization
The second stage of the rape trauma syndrome, which involves a restoration of order in the victim's lifestyle and reestablishment of control.

Personal Voices

Acquaintance Rape

ollowing is a letter written by an 18-year-old college student who had been raped by an acquaintance. It is written to the man who raped her. Notice the lack of trust and vulnerability she expresses.

Once I called you a friend. Not anymore. Once I trusted you. You broke that trust by using it to get what you wanted. You are a thief. You stole something of mine. Something that had been very special to me. So special, that it was something I had reserved only for someone I loved. I will never forget that night. I will never forget how I said "NO" and you didn't listen, didn't care, and didn't stop. I will never forget the fact that you raped me. When you took my body, you took every ounce of trust I had in me too. Because of what you did, I'm distrustful and suspicious of every male's intentions. Imagine being so frightened that when you catch
someone simply looking at you, the hair on the back of your neck stands up and you wonder, what does he want? Imagine freaking out if a guy accidentally touches you. Imagine being afraid to let a guy hold your hand or put his arm around you for fear he'll want more. Imagine always thinking that if he wants it, he'll TAKE it.

You've made me feel so violated, isolated, sad, and angry. More scared than anything though. Every man I meet will pay for what you did. I pay for what you did. Sometimes I wonder "why me?" It doesn't seem fair. Fifteen minutes of self-gratification for you, but God only knows how many months of pain, suffering and fear I have already had to, and will have to, endure.

SOURCE: Author's files.

Changes in sexual behaviors and sexual difficulties can persist for a considerable period after the rape (Campbell, Sefl, & Ahrens, 2004). It can take weeks, months, or even years to work through sexual difficulties such as fear of sex, desire and arousal disorders, and specific problems with sexual behaviors such as sexual intercourse, genital fondling, and oral sex. Counseling can be helpful for women suffering from postrape sexual difficulties. It is not uncommon for a woman to seek help for a sexual problem, such as anorgasmia (lack of orgasm) and, during the course of therapy, reveal an experience with rape that she had never discussed.

Review Question

Describe rape trauma syndrome and the long- and short-term aspects of rape.

Question: Do women who are raped eventually have a normal sex life?

Although it may take anywhere from a few days to months, most rape victims report that their sex lives get back to what is normal for them. However, research indicates that lesbian women may have more difficulties with sexual problems postrape. Counseling, a supportive partner, and emotional support are extremely helpful.

Silent Rape Reaction

Some victims never discuss their rape with anyone and carry the burden of the assault alone. Burgess and Holmstrom (1974) call this the **silent rape reaction,** and in many ways, it is similar to RTS. Feelings of fear, anger, and depression and physiological symptoms still exist; however, they remain locked inside. In fact, those who take longer to confide in someone usually suffer a longer recovery period (L. Cohen & Roth, 1987).

The silent rape reaction occurs because some victims deny and repress the incident until a time when they feel stronger emotionally. This may be months or even years later. A student of mine, who had been raped 3 years earlier, was taking a course in psy-

silent rape reaction
A type of rape trauma syndrome in which a victim does not talk to anyone after the rape.

Review Question

Describe the silent rape reaction and the long-term effects of this reaction.

chology and noticed with frustration that as she read each chapter of the textbook, she would become extremely anxious when she saw the word *therapist*. When she explored why this produced anxiety, she realized that she could read the word only as *the rapist*, and it frightened her. Perhaps her subconscious was letting her know that she was finally ready to work through the repressed experience. Slowly the memories of the rape came back, as did all of the pain and sorrow from the attack. After 2 months in counseling, she had worked through the memories sufficiently to feel that she was on her way to resolving her feelings about the rape.

Rape of Partners and Other Special Populations

Although we have learned from the research that there are certain groups more at risk for rape and sexual assault, we also know that there are special populations who are also at risk, including spouses, lesbians, older women, women with disabilities, and prostitutes.

Marital Rape

As of 1993, marital rape is considered a crime in all 50 states, even though it may be treated differently in various states. For example, in some states, such as Arizona, Connecticut, and Idaho, there must be force or the threat of force in order for it to be considered marital rape (American Prosecutors Research Institute, 2003a). It has been estimated that 10% to 14% of all married women are raped by their husbands, although this number is much higher in battered women (Russell & Howell, 1983; Yllo & Finkelhor, 1985).

Overall, college-aged women are consistently more likely than college-aged men to view marital rape as a serious crime (Auster & Leone, 2001). Another study found that college students rated married women more responsible for rape when they were dressed seductively (Whatley, 2005). However, both men and women report that marital rape is less a violation of the victim's rights and less psychologically damaging to the victims compared to other types of rape (Simonson & Subich, 1999).

Although their symptoms are similar to those who are victims of nonmarital rape, many of these women report feeling extremely betrayed and may lose the ability to trust others, especially men. In addition, there is often little social support for wives who are raped, and those who stay with their husbands often endure repeated attacks. Unfortunately, marital rape may be one of the least discussed types of rape.

Lesbians

Rape is a common experience in both heterosexual and lesbian women. Like heterosexual women, lesbian women also experience rape trauma syndrome following a rape. However, for many lesbians, it is very difficult to assimilate the experience of rape into their own self-image (Orzek, 1988). Many lesbians may also be "feminist-identified" in most areas of their lives, and the rape may force them to reexamine the patriarchal society and their feelings about men. Some lesbians may have never experienced sexual intercourse with a man and may be unaccustomed to dealing with the fear of pregnancy, let alone the extreme feelings of being violated and abused.

Older Women

Many people believe that rape only happens to younger women. It is difficult to think about our mothers or grandmothers being raped. The stereotype that only young, attractive women are raped prevents our thinking about the risk of rape for older women. Although it is true that younger women are more at risk for rape, older women are also raped (Ball, 2005; Burgess & Morgenbesser, 2005; Jeary, 2005). Older women are likely to be even more traumatized by rape than younger women because many have very conservative attitudes about sexuality, have undergone physical changes in the genitals (lack of lubrication and/or thinning of the walls of the vagina) that can increase the severity of physical injury, and have less social support after a rape, which reinforces and intensifies their sense of vulnerability (Burgess & Morgenbesser, 2005).

© Matthew Alan/Corbis

Older women are also victims of rape and may experience increased trauma due to declining physical health and more conservative attitudes about sexuality.

Women With Disabilities

Women with disabilities, regardless of their age, race, ethnicity, sexual orientation, or socioeconomic class, are assaulted, raped, and abused at a rate two times greater than women without disabilities (Cusitar, 1994; Sobsey, 1994). They may be more vulnerable because of their diminished ability to fight back. In addition, mentally handicapped persons may have a more difficult time reading the preliminary cues that would alert them to danger. The impact of a rape may be very intense for these people because of a lack of knowledge about sexuality, loss of a sense of trust in others, and the lack of knowledgeable staff who can effectively work with these victims. In many cases, women with severe mental disabilities who have been sexually assaulted may not realize that their rights have been violated and, therefore, may not report the crime. Because of these factors, the intensity and length of time of RTS is usually prolonged.

Prostitutes

Studies have found that between 68% and 70% of female prostitutes have been victims of rape (Farley & Barkan, 1998; Silbert, 1998). Because a prostitute's job is to provide sex in exchange for payment, the question of consent is often difficult to judge. Also, because of the general disapproval of prostitution, a prostitute who reports rape is often treated with disdain. People tend not to believe that she was raped or may think that she is angry because she was not paid. Many prostitutes who are raped begin to question their involvement in prostitution. Believing and trusting her experience and performing a comprehensive medical checkup are imperative.

SEX Talk

Question: Why do prostitutes care if they are raped? Don't they just sell it anyway? I thought it was just like another customer who refused to pay.

Prostitutes agree on a price in exchange for sexual activity. When a man has an agreement with a prostitute and then rapes her—which would be forceful and against her will—this simply reinforces the idea that every man has the right to a woman's body. Rape does not have anything to do with the availability of sex. These men are taking what they believe is theirs, using force and doing it without the woman's consent. Prostitutes also take an enormous risk in their profession because rapists know that there is little chance that any retribution will follow.

How Partners React to Rape

When a man or woman's sexual partner is raped, the partner often feels anger, frustration, and intense feelings of revenge (M. E. Smith, 2005). Many partners express a strong desire to "kill him" (the rapist), "make him pay," and the like. In addition, some partners experience a sense of loss, guilt, self-blame, and jealousy. Emotional reactions to the rape may affect a man's or woman's feelings about his or her partner and view of men in the world (M. E. Smith, 2005). In cases of acquaintance rape, a man or woman may lose trust in his or her partner, feeling that because the partner knew the assailant, she may have expressed sexual interest in him. Often, these reactions further isolate the victim and reinforce her feelings of guilt.

All in all, rape places a great deal of stress on a relationship. Couples often avoid dealing with rape entirely, believing that talking about it would be too stressful. Many men feel uncomfortable sharing their feelings about a rape because they worry about burdening their partners. However, open communication is extremely beneficial and should be encouraged. Even though dealing with a rape in a relationship can be traumatic, it has been found that women who have a stable and supportive partner recover from a rape more quickly than those who do not.

Review Question

Describe the effects of rape in special populations, including: married partners, lesbians, older women, women with disabilities, prostitutes, and partners of women who have been raped.

WHEN MEN ARE RAPE VICTIMS

Can a man be raped? Each year in the United States, more than 14,000 men report being victims of rape or attempted rape (Rennison, 2001; this means that 5% of all reported rapes are reported by men). However, male rape is even more underreported than female rape (Wiwanitkit, 2005). Typically, men who are raped are viewed more negatively than women who have been raped (I. Anderson, 2004). Like women, long-term effects of rape are common in men, and can include depression, anger, anxiety, self-blame, and increased vulnerability (J. Walker et al., 2005).

SEX Talk

Question: Technically, can a man really be raped?

Some people think that it is impossible for a woman to rape a man because he just would not get an erection. Even though men are anxious, embarrassed, or terrorized during a rape, they are able to have erections. Having an erection while being raped may be confusing and humiliating, just as an orgasm is for females. In fact, for some it may be the most distressing aspect of the assault (Sarrel & Masters, 1982). Women who rape men can also use dildos, hands, or other objects to penetrate the anus. In addition, men can be orally or anally raped by men and forced to perform various sexual behaviors.

Rape of Men by Women

Students often laugh at the idea that a man could be raped by a woman because they believe the myth that men are always willing to have sex, and so a woman would never need to rape a man. However, the myth actually serves to make male rape more humiliating and painful for many men. One study found that 1 in 33 men report having experienced an attempted or completed rape in their lifetime (Hensley, 2002).

Female rapists have been found to engage in a wide range of sexually aggressive behaviors, including forced sex and the use of verbal coercion (P. B. Anderson & Savage, 2005). In a study of male college students, 34% reported coercive sexual contact: 24% from women, 4% from men, and 6% from both sexes (Struckman-Johnson & Struckman-Johnson, 1994). The majority of male rapes by women use psychological or pressured contact, such as verbal persuasion or emotional manipulation, rather than physical force. Although the majority of college men had no or very mild negative reactions to the unwanted female contact, 20% of the men experienced strong negative reactions. Because men who are raped by women are often unwilling to define themselves as victims, many do not report these rapes even though physical and psychological symptoms are common (P. B. Anderson & Savage, 2005).

Rape of Men by Men

In 2000 a high school football team in Yucca Valley, California was found guilty of participating in a bizarre "hazing" incident. New team players were treated aggressively, shoved, abused, and even anally penetrated with a large stick. Many of the athletes claimed that this hazing was a tradition that helps increase team bonding. Do you think that forcing the new players to submit to anal penetration with a wooden object constitutes rape? Many people did.

Research estimates that 1 out of 6 men have experienced unwanted sexual contact with an older person by the age of 16, and 1 in 4 report sexual victimization in childhood (Finkelhor et al., 1990; Lisak et al., 1996). However, once again, this is probably an underrepresentation of the true incidence, because the rape of men by men is infrequently reported to the police (Hodge & Canter, 1998). The sexual assault of boys is most commonly performed by older men who are outside of the family structure (e.g., a babysitter, teacher, or mother's boyfriend; Finkelhor & Browne, 1985; Finkelhor et al., 1990). Later in this chapter we will discuss the sexual abuse of male children.

It has been said that the incidence of male rape in the gay community is low because of the greater access to consensual sex in gay bars, bookstores, and the like, and that it is more difficult to overpower another male than a female (Russell, 1984). Some feminists would argue that rape is a **misogynist's** (muh-SAH-juh-nist) act of hatred toward women, and that this is why the incidence in the gay community is lower.

misogynist
A person who hates women.

Hickson and colleagues (1994) found that in a sample of 930 gay men, close to 30% claimed they had been sexually assaulted at some point in their lives. Close to one-third of the victims had been sexual with the perpetrator prior to the sexual assault. The victims reported forced anal and oral sex and masturbation to ejaculation. The most common type of activity in the sexual assault of men by men is anal penetration followed by oral penetration (N. Groth & Burgess, 1980). Getting the victim to ejaculate is important in male rape by men. Many male assailants either masturbate or perform fellatio on the victim to the point of orgasm. The assailant may believe that if the victim has an orgasm, he will be less likely to report the attack or that it proves that the victim really "wanted it."

As in the case of female rape, male rape is an expression of power, a show of strength and masculinity that uses sex as a weapon. Many victims of male rape question their sexual orientation and feel that the rape makes them less of a "real man." The risk of suicide in men who have been raped has been found to be higher than in women (Holmes & Slap, 1998). Also, unlike women, some male rape victims may increase their subsequent sexual activity to reaffirm their manhood.

Prison Rape

In 2003, President Bush signed off on the Prison Rape Elimination Act, a federal law that reduces tolerance for prison sexual assault, mandates the collection of national data on the incidence of prison rape, and provides funding for research and program development. This law has helped reduce prison rape and support those who have been raped in prison. Studies have found that approximately 18% of prison inmates report sexual threats from other prisoners, whereas 8.5% report sexual assaults in prison (Hensley et al., 2005).

Although prison rape occurs most frequently in the male population, it also occurs between female inmates using a variety of different objects to penetrate the vagina or anus. Women who are in U.S. prisons are often victims of sexual harassment, molestation, coercive sexual behaviors, and forced sexual intercourse, with the majority of this abuse being perpetuated by prison staff (Struckman-Johnson & Struckman-Johnson, 2002). Female inmates also experience sexual pressure in their interactions with other female inmates (Alarid, 2000). Some researchers have pointed out that incarcerated women are viewed as "bad girls" and because of this they are viewed as sexually easy (Struckman-Johnson & Struckman-Johnson, 2002). The majority of women who are raped in prison never report the crime for fear of retaliation.

Men in prison learn avoidance techniques that women use in society—physical modesty, no eye contact, no accepting of gifts, and tempering of friendliness (Bart & O'Brien, 1985). Prison rape has been found to be an act of asserting one's own masculinity in an environment that rewards dominance and power (Peeples & Scacco, 1982). Sex, violence, and conquest are the only avenues open to men in the restrictive confines of prison. To rape another man is seen as the "ultimate humiliation" because it forces the victim to assume the role of a woman. The victim becomes the "property" of his assailant, who will, in turn, provide protection in return for anal or oral sex. However, the rapist often will "sell" sexual favors from his man to other inmates in exchange for cigarettes or money.

Like rape in other populations, prison rape has been found to have a significant role in the development of posttraumatic stress disorder (Kupers, 2001). Inmates who have been raped also experience rape trauma syndrome. As mentioned previously, the acute phase is characterized by feelings of fear, anxiety, anger, and guilt, as well as numerous physical problems. Because these men and women must continue to interact with their

Review Question

Differentiate between the various types of rape against men, and describe the effects of these types of rape.

assailants, long-term reorganization may take longer to work through. In addition, oftentimes there are no rape crisis services for those who have been raped in prison and little sympathy from prison employees.

REPORTING, AVOIDING, AND TREATING RAPISTS

As we learned earlier in the chapter, the majority of rape victims do not report the rape to the police. We will now explore reporting statistics and reasons for nonreporting; and the process of telling the police, pressing charges, and going to court. We also will look at rape avoidance strategies and rapist treatment.

Reporting a Rape

It is estimated that about 1 in 7 rapes is reported (Resnick et al., 2005); the likelihood of reporting is increased if the assailant was a stranger, if there was violence, or if a weapon was involved (U.S. Department of Justice–Office of Justice Programs, 2002). This probably has to do with the fact that victims are clearer about intent under these conditions.

Gender differences in reporting are also common. Women are less likely to report a rape if it does not fit the stereotypical rape scenario, whereas men are less likely to report if it jeopardizes their masculine self-identity (Pino & Meier, 1999). Women who report their rapes to the police have been subsequently found to have a better adjustment and fewer emotional symptoms than those who do not report (L. Cohen & Roth, 1987).

It is also important for a victim to write out exactly what happened in as much detail as possible. When did the rape occur? Where was the victim? What time was it? Who was with the victim? What did the rapist look like? What was he or she wearing? Exactly what happened? Was alcohol involved? Was anyone else present? The victim should keep this for his or her own records, for if he or she decides to press charges it will come in handy. Over time memories fade, and the victim can lose the important small details.

Telling the Police

On college campuses, campus police are often notified before the local police. Campus police may be able to take disciplinary action, such as fines or dismissal if the assailant is a student, but they are not able to press formal charges. Pressing charges with the local police may be important for two reasons. First, it alerts the police to a crime and thus may prevent other women from being victimized. Second, if the victim decides to take legal action, he or she will need to have a formal report from the local police (not the campus police).

Although police officers have become more sensitive to the plight of rape victims in the past few years, some victims still report negative experiences (Monroe et al., 2005). Society's victim-precipitated view of rape also affects the attitudes of the police. To make sure that a crime did indeed occur, police must interrogate each case completely, which can be very difficult for a victim who has just been through a traumatic experience. Still, many report that taking such legal action makes them feel back in control, that they are doing something about their situation.

Pressing Charges

The decision to press official charges is a very difficult one that takes much consideration. It has often been said that a rape victim goes through a second rape because he or she seems to be put on trial more than the accused rapist. Court proceedings take up a great deal of time and energy, and they create considerable anxiety.

Victims of rape report that they pressed charges because they were angry, to protect others, or they wanted justice to be served. Reasons for refusing to press charges include being afraid of revenge, wanting to just forget, feeling sorry for the rapist, or feeling as though it would not matter anyway because nothing would be done. Victims of rape can also file a civil lawsuit and sue the assailant for monetary damages. Civil lawsuits are generally easier to prove than criminal lawsuits (Wagner, 1991).

Going to Court

If a victim is undecided about whether or not to press charges, it may be helpful to sit in on a rape trial. Rape trials can be extremely difficult for all involved. However, the purpose of sitting in is not to scare a person but to prepare oneself. It is not easy to proceed with legal action, so it can be really helpful to gather support from friends and family.

During court proceedings, the line of questioning of rape victims is often different from that in other crimes (see the accompanying Sex in Real Life, "Questioning the Victim: Was He Asking for It?"). Should a victim decide to proceed with legal action, he or she must also be prepared for the possibility that the rapist may be found not guilty. Victims must consider how this would affect them and their recovery. One victim reported that she was so unprepared for a verdict of not guilty that, when it happened, she completely fell apart (Author's files).

Review Question

Explain the process of telling the police, pressing charges, and going to court. What are some of the problems a rape victim might experience along the way?

SEX in Real Life

Questioning the Victim: Was He Asking for It?

Imagine a man who has been mugged going through the same type of cross-examination as a woman who has been raped:

"Mr. Henke, you were held up at gunpoint on the corner of Locust and 12th?"

"Yes."

"Did you struggle with the mugger?"

"No, I did not."

"Why not?"

"I saw he had a gun!"

"You decided to comply rather than to fight him?"

"Yes."

"Did you scream for help?"

"No. I was worried he might kill me!"

"Mr. Henke, have you ever given away money?"

"Yes."

"And you did so willingly?"

"What are you getting at?"

"Well, the way I see it, Mr. Henke, you've given money away in the past. Maybe you just wanted someone to take your money forcibly."

"Yeah . . . sure."

"OK, what time did this mugging occur?"

"About 11:30 P.M."

"What were you doing out on the street that late?"

"Walking home."

"From where?"

"I had been out at a bar entertaining clients."

"So you were drinking?"

"Yes."

"What were you wearing?"

"A suit. I was still in my work clothes."

"An expensive suit?"

"Yeah, actually it was, I am a successful businessman, you know. I have to wear nice clothes."

"In other words, Mr. Henke, you were walking around the city streets late at night, under the influence of alcohol, in an expensive suit that advertised your wealth, right? If we didn't know better, Mr. Henke, we might even think that you were asking for this to happen, mightn't we?"

Power and Sexual Coercion   **587**

Avoidance Strategies

Rape is the only violent crime in which we expect a person to fight back. If a woman does not struggle, we question whether or not she wanted to have sex. Only with visible proof of a struggle (bruises and cuts) does society seem to have sympathy. Some victims of rape have said that, at the time of the rape, they felt frozen with fear, that it was impossible to move because they just could not believe what was happening to them. One victim explains:

> Did you ever see a rabbit stuck in the glare of your headlights when you were going down a road at night? Transfixed—like it knew it was going to get it—that's what happened. (Brownmiller, 1975, p. 358)

How does a person know when to fight back? What should his or her strategies be? If you are confronted with a potential or attempted rape, the first and best strategy is to try to escape. However, this may not be possible if you are in a deserted area, if there are multiple attackers, or if your attacker has a weapon. If you cannot escape, effective strategies include verbal strategies such as screaming, dissuasive techniques ("I have my period," or "I have herpes"), empathy (listening or trying to understand), negotiation ("Let's discuss this"), and stalling for time. However, if the rapist does not believe the victim, these techniques may cause more harm than good.

Prentky and colleagues (1986) asserts that the safest strategy is to attempt to talk to the attacker and try to make yourself a real person to him ("I'm a stranger; why do you want to hurt me?"). Self-defense classes can help a person to feel more confident in his or her ability to fight back. One study found that women who had taken a self-defense class felt more prepared and less scared during the rape than women who had never taken such a class (Brecklin & Ullman, 2005).

Review Question

Explain some of the strategies given for avoiding a rape. When might these strategies cause more harm than good?

Treating the Rapist

Can men who rape be treated so that they lose their desire to rape? Many different therapies have been tried, including shock treatment, psychotherapy, behavioral treatment, support groups, and the use of Depo-Provera, a drug that can diminish a man's sex drive. The idea behind Depo-Provera is that if the sex drive is reduced, so too is the likelihood of rape. So far these treatments have yielded inconclusive results. Many feminists argue that because violence, not sexual desire, causes rape, taking away sexual desire will not decrease the incidence of rape. For many men in treatment, the most important first step is to accept responsibility for their actions.

Many programs have been developed to decrease myths about rape and increase knowledge levels. All-male programs have been found to significantly reduce the belief in rape myths (Foubert & Marriott, 1997). In another study evaluating posteducation outcomes, among the 20% of men who indicated a possible likelihood of raping before participating in an educational program, 75% reported less likelihood of raping after the program (Foubert & McEwen, 1998). However, although attitudes about rape myths appear to change after these programs, research has yet to show that these attitude changes result in changes in sexually coercive behavior (Foubert, 2000). Treatments for high-risk rapists (those who are repeat offenders) have not been found to be overwhelmingly successful (Lalumière et al., 2005a).

Review Question

Explain some of the therapies that have been used in the treatment of rapists.

SEXUAL ABUSE OF CHILDREN

child sexual abuse
Sexual contact with a minor by an adult.

So far we have been talking about forced sexual relations between adults. But what happens when the coercive behavior involves children? **Child sexual abuse** is defined as sexual behavior that occurs between an adult and a minor. One important characteristic of child sexual abuse is the dominant, powerful position of the adult or older teen that allows him or her to force a child into sexual activity. The sexual activity can include inappropriate touch, removing a child's clothing, genital fondling, masturbation, digital penetration with fingers or sex toys, oral sex, vaginal and/or anal intercourse (Valente, 2005). These behaviors are all illegal because the child is not old enough or mature enough to consent to this behavior.

As straightforward as this seems, the definition of child sexual abuse can become fuzzy. For instance, do you consider sexual play between a 13-year-old brother and his 7-year-old sister sexual abuse? How about an adult male who persuades a 14-year-old female to fondle his genitals? Or a mother who caresses her 2-year-old son? How about a 14-year-old-boy who willingly has sex with a 25-year-old woman? How would you define the sexual abuse of children? Personal definitions of sexual abuse affect how we perceive those who participate in this behavior (Finkelhor, 1984).

Many researchers differentiate between child sexual abuse, which usually involves nonrelatives; pedophilia, which involves a compulsive desire to engage in sex with a particular age of child; and **incest,** which is sexual contact between a child or adolescent who is related to the abuser. There are several types of incest, including father–daughter, father–son, brother–sister, grandfather–grandchild, mother–daughter, and mother–son. Incest can also occur between stepparents and stepchildren or aunts and uncles and their nieces and nephews. Sexual activity between a child and someone who is responsible for the child's care (such as a babysitter) may also be considered incest, though definitions for incest vary from state to state.

Because most children look to their parents for nurturing and protection, incest involving a parent, guardian, or someone else the child trusts can be extremely traumatic. The incestuous parent exploits this trust to fulfill sexual or power needs of his or her own. The particularly vulnerable position of children in relation to their parents has been recognized in every culture. The **incest taboo**—the absolute prohibition of sex between family members—is universal (Herman, 1981).

Sociologists suggest that social restrictions against incest may have originally formed to reduce role conflicts (Henslin, 2005). A parent who has a sexual relationship with his or her child will have one role (i.e., parent) that conflicts with another (i.e., lover), which can interfere with responsibilities. We must also understand, however, that definitions of incest vary cross-culturally. A tribal group in tropical Africa called the Burundi believe that a mother causes her son's erectile dysfunction by allowing the umbilical cord to touch his penis during birth (Henslin, 2005). To rectify this situation, the mother must engage in sexual intercourse with the son. Although this practice may sound crazy to us, the culture of the Burundi supports this practice. The incest taboo still exists in this culture, but this practice is not viewed as incestuous behavior.

In the United States, we typically believe that father–daughter incest is the most common type, but research has shown that today the most common offenders are uncles and male first cousins (Henslin, 2005). Sibling incest also occurs and is more likely to occur in families in which there is a dominating father, a passive mother, and a dysfunctional home life (Phillips-Green, 2002). Many siblings play sex games with each other while growing up, and there is some disagreement over whether this sex play between siblings is traumatic. Some believe that it is not traumatic unless there is force or exploitation, whereas others believe that it may lead to long-term difficulties in both interpersonal and sexual relationships (Cyr et al., 2002; Daie et al., 1989).

Although the majority of offenders are male, some women do engage in incest. Mother–son incest is more likely to be subtle, including behaviors that may be difficult to distinguish from normal mothering behaviors (including genital touching; R. J. Kelly et al., 2002). Men who have been sexually abused by their mothers often experience more trauma symptoms than do other sexually abused men.

Finally, it's also important to mention that the increased time that children spend unsupervised on the Internet has given rise to a new type of child sexual abuse (Seymour et al., 2000). Online sexual predators lurk in chat rooms and post sexually explicit material on the Internet in hopes of making contact with children. Aggressive predators will dedicate much time to the development of relationships with vulnerable children and will try to alienate these children from their families. Some predators have even bought plane tickets for children to set up meetings (Seymour et al., 2000).

incest
Sexual contact between persons who are related or have a caregiving relationship.

incest taboo
The absolute prohibition of sex between family members.

Review Question

Define child sexual abuse, and differentiate it from incest and pedophilia.

Incidence of Child Sexual Abuse

Accurate statistics on the prevalence of child sexual abuse are difficult to come by for many reasons: some victims are uncertain about the precise definition of sexual abuse, or they might be unwilling to report, and/or uncomfortable about sex and sexuality in general (Ephross, 2005: Finkelhor, 1984). The overall reported incidence has been increasing over the past 30 years. In the Kinsey and colleagues (1953) study of 441 females, 9% reported sexual contact with an adult before the age of 14. By the late 1970s and early 1980s, reports of child sexual abuse were increasing dramatically; 1,975 cases were reported in 1976, 22,918 in 1982 (Finkelhor, 1984), and 130,000 by 1986 (Jetter, 1991). It is estimated that 1 out of every 4 girls and 1 out of every 10 boys experiences sexual abuse as a child (Fieldman & Crespi, 2002; Valente, 2005).

Perhaps the increase in the incidence of child sexual abuse is a reflection of the changing sexual climate (in which there is less tolerance for such behavior), rather than an actual increase in the number of sexual assaults on children. The women's movement and the child protection movement both have focused attention on child sexual abuse issues (Finkelhor, 1984). Women's groups often teach that child sexual abuse is due to the patriarchal social structure and must be treated through victim protection. The child protection movement views the problem as one that develops out of a dysfunctional family and is treated through family therapy.

The reported incidence of child sexual abuse in other countries is much lower than in the United States (Finkelhor, 1984). However, note that the rate in the United States increased as the sexual climate changed. The incidence in other countries may be similar to the United States, but the United States may be more receptive to reports of abuse or may define child sexual abuse differently.

Recently there has been some doubt about the credibility of child sex abuse reporting. Would a child ever "make up" a story of sexual abuse? Research has shown that false reports occur in fewer than 10% of reported cases (Besharov, 1988). This is important because a child's report of sexual abuse remains the single most important factor in diagnosing abuse (Heger et al., 2002).

Review Question

Discuss the incidence of child sexual abuse, and explain some of the reasons why the incidence may be increasing.

Victims of Child Sexual Abuse

Although research is limited because of sampling and responding rates, we do know that the median age for sexual abuse of both girls and boys is around 8 or 9 years old (Feinauer, 1988; Finkelhor et al., 1990). Boys are more likely to be sexually abused by strangers (40% of boys, 21% of girls), whereas girls are more likely to have family members as assailants (29% of girls, 11% of boys; Finkelhor et al., 1990).

Finkelhor proposes three reasons why the reported rates of male sexual abuse may be lower than those for females: (1) boys grow up believing that they must be self-reliant and may feel that they should be able to handle the abuse; (2) male sexual abuse gets entwined with the stigma of homosexuality, because the majority of offenders are male; and (3) because boys often have more freedom than girls in our society, they may have a great deal to lose by reporting a sexual assault (1984, pp. 156–157).

Reactions to abuse vary. Many victims are scared to reveal the abuse, either because of shame, fear of retaliation, belief that they themselves are to blame, or fear that they will not be believed. Some incest victims try to get help only if they fear that a younger sibling is threatened. When they do get help, younger victims are more likely to go to a relative for help, whereas older victims may run away or enter into early marriages to escape the abuse (J. L. Herman, 1981). Victims of incest with a biological father delay reporting the longest, whereas those who have been victims of stepfather or live-in partners have been found to be more likely to tell someone more readily (Faller, 1989).

Review Question

Describe what the research has shown with respect to victims of child sexual abuse and incest.

How Children Are Affected

There have been conflicting findings regarding the traumatic effects of sexual abuse. Some studies indicate that children are not severely traumatized by sexual abuse (Fritz et al., 1981), whereas more recent studies indicate that it may have long-lasting effects that may lead to other psychological problems, including antisocial behavior, drug abuse, and prostitution. Groth (1978) suggests that sexual abuse is the most traumatic when it exists over a long period of time, the offender is a person who is trusted, penetration occurs, and there is aggression.

Keep in mind that what follows is a discussion of what is typically experienced by a victim of childhood sexual abuse or incest. As we have discussed before, it is impossible to predict what a child's experience will be; the reaction of each child is different. There are a few factors that make the abuse more traumatic, including the intensity of the sexual contact and how the sexual abuse is handled in the family. If a family handles the sexual abuse in a caring and sensitive manner, the effects on the child are often reduced.

Psychological and Emotional Reactions

Sexual abuse can be devastating for a child and often causes feelings of betrayal, powerlessness, fear, anger, self-blame, low self-esteem, and problems with intimacy and relationships later in life (Valente, 2005). Children who hide their sexual abuse often experience shame and guilt and fear the loss of affection from family and friends (Seymour et al., 2000). They also feel frustrated about not being able to stop the abuse.

Whether or not they tell someone about their sexual abuse, many victims experience psychological symptoms such as depression, increased anxiety, nervousness, emotional problems, and personality and intimacy disorders. Similar to reactions of rape victims, depression is the most prevalent emotional symptom, which may be higher in victims who are abused repeatedly (Cheasty et al., 2002). Guilt is usually severe, and many children blame themselves for the sexual abuse (Valente, 2005). Victims of sexual abuse are also more likely than nonabused children to commit suicide (Valente, 2005).

Victims may also try to cut themselves off from a painful or unbearable memory, which can lead to what psychiatrists refer to as a **dissociative disorder.** In its extreme form, dissociative disorder may result in **dissociative personality disorder (DPD),** in which a person maintains two or more distinct personalities. Although it has long been a controversial issue in psychology (McNally, 2003), there is research to support the claim that some abuse victims are unable to remember past abuse. In one study of incest victims, 64% were found to partially repress their abuse, whereas 28% severely repressed it (Herman & Schatzow, 1987). Some experts claim that although the memories are classified as bad, disgusting, and confusing, many times they are not "traumatic." Because of this, the memories are simply forgotten, and not repressed (McNally et al., 2004; McNally et al., 2005). This issue continues to be controversial even though many victims of sexual abuse often report an inability to remember details or the entirety of the abuse.

Women who were sexually abused as children have higher rates of personality disorders and post-traumatic stress disorder than those who experienced sexual abuse later in life (McLean & Gallop, 2003). Antisocial behavior and promiscuous sexual behavior are also related to a history of childhood sexual behavior (Valente, 2005). The most devastating emotional effects occur when the sexual abuse is done by someone the victim trusts. In a study of the effects of sexual abuse by relatives, friends, or strangers, it was found that the stronger the emotional bond and trust between the victim and the assailant, the more distress the victim experienced (Feinauer, 1989).

Long-Term Effects

It is not uncommon for children who are sexually abused to display what Finkelhor and Browne (1985) refer to as **traumatic sexualization.** Children may begin to exhibit compulsive sex play or masturbation and show an inappropriate amount of sexual knowledge. When they enter adolescence they may begin to show promiscuous and compulsive sexual behavior, which may lead to sexually abusing others in adulthood (Valente, 2005). These children have learned that it is through their sexuality that they get attention from adults. Children who have been sexually abused are also more vulnerable to revictimization later in life (Valente, 2005).

Children who are sexually abused have been found to experience sexual problems in adulthood. The developmentally inappropriate sexual behaviors that they learned as

sexbyte

It is estimated that about 50% of all victims of sexual abuse suffer from some form of memory loss (Maltz, 2001).

dissociative disorder
Psychological disorder involving a disturbance of memory, identity, and consciousness, usually resulting from a traumatic experience.

dissociative personality disorder (DPD)
A dissociative disorder in which a person develops two or more distinct personalities.

Review Question

Discuss victims' psychological and emotional reactions to child sexual abuse.

traumatic sexualization
A common result of sexual abuse in which a child displays compulsive sex play or masturbation and shows an inappropriate amount of sexual knowledge.

children can contribute to a variety of sexual dysfunctions later in life (Najman et al., 2005). Research has found that a large proportion of patients who seek sex therapy have histories of incest, rape, and other forms of sexual abuse (Maltz, 2002).

Eating disorders are also common. Recent research reveals a connection between eating disorders and sexual abuse (Wonderlich et al., 2001). In one study sexually abused children were found to eat less when they were emotionally upset and were more likely than nonabused children to desire a thinner body type (Wonderlich, 2000). The obsessions about food become all-consuming and may temporarily replace the original trauma of the sexual abuse. When these patients discussed their past sexual abuse, they were often able to make significant changes in their eating patterns.

Children who are sexually abused also commonly develop problems such as drug and alcohol addiction or prostitution. In fact, victims of sexual abuse have been found to have higher rates of alcohol and drug use, even as early as age 10 (Valente, 2005). Finkelhor and Browne (1985) hypothesized that because of the stigma that surrounds the early sexual abuse, the children believe they are "bad," and the thought of "badness" is incorporated into their self-concept. As a result, they often gravitate toward behaviors that society sees as deviant.

It is not unusual for adults who had been abused as children to confront their offenders later in life, especially among those who have undergone some form of counseling or psychotherapy to work through their own feelings about the experience. They may feel a strong need to deal with the experience and often get help to work through it. The accompanying Personal Voices, "Confronting the Incest Offender," is a letter written by an 18-year-old incest victim to her father. She had been sexually assaulted by him throughout her childhood, and this was the first time that she had confronted him.

Review Question

Identify and discuss the effects of childhood sexual abuse.

Characteristics of Child Sexual Abusers

Many of us would like to believe that sexual abusers are identifiable by how they look. They are not. Sexual abusers look like nice people. Yet there are things that distinguish abusers from those who do not abuse children. Research comparing child molesters to nonmolesters has shown us that molesters tend to have poorer social skills, lower IQs, unhappy family histories, lower self-esteem, and less happiness in their lives (Finkelhor et al., 1990; Hunter et al., 2003; Langevin et al., 1988; Milner & Robertson, 1990). The majority of abusers are heterosexual males (Valente, 2005). As surprising as it may seem, many abusers have strict religious codes yet still violate sexual norms. In one study, for example, an incest offender who had been having sexual interactions with his daughter for 7 years was asked why he had not had vaginal intercourse with her. He replied: "I only had anal sex with her because I wanted her to be a virgin" (Dwyer & Amberson, 1989, p. 112).

Denying responsibility for the offense and claiming they were in a trancelike state is also common. The majority of offenders are also very good at manipulation, which they develop to prevent discovery by others. One man told his 13-year-old victim, "I'm sorry this had to happen to you, but you're just too beautiful," demonstrating the typical abuser's trait of blaming the victim for the abuse (Vanderbilt, 1992, p. 3). Ironically, those who abuse children also often report disdain for other sex offenders (Dwyer & Amberson, 1989).

The Development of a Sexual Abuser

Three prominent theories—learning, gender, and biological—propose factors that make abuse more likely. Proponents of learning theories believe that what children learn from their environment or those around them contributes to their behavior later in life. Many child sex abusers were themselves sexually abused as children. Many reported an early initiation into sexual behavior that taught them about sex at a young age. Many learned that such behavior was how adults show love and affection to children.

Proponents of gender theories identify gender as an important aspect in the development of an abuser—sexual abusers are overwhelmingly male (Finkelhor et al., 1990).

Personal Voices

Confronting the Incest Offender

The following letter was written by an 18-year-old female college student to her father. She had just begun to recall past sexual abuse by her father and was in counseling working on her memories. She decided to confront her father with this letter.

Dad: I can't hide it any longer! I remember everything about when I was a little girl. For years I acted as if nothing ever happened; it was always there deep inside but I was somehow able to lock it away for many years. But Daddy, something has pried that lock open, and it will never be able to be locked away again. I remember being scared or sick and crawling into bed with my parents only to have my father's hands touch my chest and rear. I remember going on a Sunday afternoon to my father's office, innocently wanting to spend time with him, only to play with some machine that vibrated.

I remember sitting on my father's lap while he was on the phone. I had a halter top on at the time. I remember wondering what he was doing when he untied it then turned me around to face him so he could touch my stomach and chest. I remember many hugs, even as a teenager, in which my father's hand was on my rear. I remember those words, "I like what is underneath better," when I asked my father if he liked my new outfit. But Daddy, more than anything, I remember one night when mom wasn't home. I was scared so I crawled into bed with my father who I thought was there to protect me. I remember his hands caressing my still undeveloped breast. I remem-

ber his hand first rubbing the top of my underwear then the same hand working its way down my underwear. I remember thinking that it tickled, but yet it scared me.

Others had never tickled me like this. I felt frozen until I felt something inside me. It hurt, and I was scared. I said stop and started shaking. I remember jumping out of bed and running to my room where I cried myself to sleep. I also remember those words I heard a few days later, "I was just trying to love you. I didn't mean to hurt you. No one needs to know about this. People would misunderstand what happened."

You don't have to deal with the memories of what this has done to my life, my relationships with men, my many sleepless nights, my days of depression, my feelings of filth being relieved through making myself throw up and the times of using—abusing—alcohol in order to escape. You haven't even had to see the pain and confusion in my life because of this. I have two feelings, pain and numbness. You took my childhood away from me by making me lock my childhood away in the dark corners of my mind. Now that child is trying to escape, and I don't know how to deal with her.

I felt it was only fair that you know that it is no longer a secret. I have protected you long enough. Now it is time to protect myself from all of the memories. Daddy, I must tell you, even after all that has happened, for some reason I'm not sure of, I still feel love for you—that is, if I even know what love is.

SOURCE: Author's files.

Males often are not taught how to express affection without sexuality, which leads to needing sex to confirm their masculinity, being more focused on the sexual aspect of relationships, and being socialized to be attracted to mates that are smaller (Finkelhor, 1984). Keep in mind that the incidence of female offenders may be lower because of lower reporting rates for boys and/or because society accepts intimate female interaction with children as normal (Groth, 1978). Although we used to think that about 4% of offenders were female (D. E. H. Russell, 1984), newer studies have found that these numbers may be significantly higher. In one study, a review of 120,000 cases of child sexual abuse, 25% of cases were found to involve a female offender (Boroughs, 2004).

Proponents of biological theories suggest that physiology contributes to the development of sexual abusers (see Chapter 16). One study found that male offenders had normal levels of the male sex hormone testosterone but elevated levels of other hormones (Lang et al., 1990). There have also been reports of neurological differences between incest offenders and non–sex-criminal offenders that are thought to contribute to violence (Langevin et al., 1988).

Review Question

Explain what the research tells us about sexual abusers and the development of such behavior.

ReviewQuestion

Describe the most effective treatments for victims and perpetrators of childhood sexual abuse.

ReviewQuestion

Identify some ways in which society can help prevent childhood sexual abuse.

intimate partner violence
A pattern of coercive behavior designed to exert power and control over a person in an intimate relationship through the use of intimidation, threats, or harmful or harassing behavior.

Treating Child Sexual Abuse

We know that sexual abuse can have many short- and long-term consequences—for victims as well as abusers. As a result, it is important to help victims of child sexual abuse to heal and help abusers learn ways to eliminate their abusive behaviors.

Helping the Victims Heal

Currently, the most effective treatments for victims of child sexual abuse include a combination of cognitive and behavioral psychotherapies, which teach victims how to understand and handle the trauma of their assaults more effectively. Many victims of sexual abuse also have difficulties developing and maintaining intimate relationships. Being involved in a relationship that is high in emotional intimacy and low in expectations for sex is beneficial (W. Maltz, 1990). Learning that they have the ability to say no to sex is very important and usually develops when they establish relationships based first on friendship, rather than sex. Many times the partners of victims of sexual abuse are confused; they do not fully understand the effects of abuse in the lives of their mates, and so they may also benefit from counseling (L. Cohen, 1988).

Treating Abusers

In Chapter 16 we discussed treatment for pedophilia. The treatment of child sexual abusers is similar in that the primary goal is to decrease the level of sexual arousal to inappropriate sexual objects—in this case, children. This is done through behavioral treatment, psychotherapy, or drugs. Other goals of therapy include teaching sexual abusers to interact and relate better with adults; assertiveness skills training; empathy and respect for others; increasing sexual education; and evaluating and reducing any sexual difficulties that they might be experiencing with their sexual partners (Abel et al., 1980). Because recidivism is high in these abusers, it is also important to find ways to reduce the incidence of engaging in these behaviors (Firestone et al., 2005).

Preventing Child Sexual Abuse

How can we prevent child sexual abuse? One program that has been explored is the "just say no" campaign, which teaches young children how to say no to inappropriate sexual advances by adults. This program has received much attention. How effective is such a strategy? Even if we can teach children to say no to strangers, can we also teach them to say no to their fathers or sexually abusive relatives? Could there be any negative effects of educating children about sexual abuse? These are a few questions that future research will need to address.

Increasing the availability of sex education has also been cited as a way to decrease the incidence of child sexual abuse. Children from traditional, authoritarian families that have no sex education are at higher risk for sexual abuse. Education about sexual abuse—teaching that it does not happen to all children—may help children to understand that it is wrong. Telling children where to go and whom to talk to is also important.

Another important factor in prevention is adequate funding and staffing of child welfare agencies. Social workers may be among the first to become aware of potentially dangerous situations. Physicians and educators must also be adequately trained to identify the signs of abuse.

⊘ INTIMATE PARTNER VIOLENCE

Intimate partner violence (IPV, which may also be referred to as domestic violence) is found among all racial, ethnic, and socioeconomic classes, and it is estimated that more than 2 million people—1.5 million women and 834,732 men—are victims of IPV each year (Gazmararian et al., 2000; Tilley & Brackley, 2005; Tjaden & Thoennes, 2000;

Tonelli, 2004). The numbers of unreported IPV incidents are much higher. In fact, a national study found that 29% of women and 22% of men had experienced intimate partner violence in their lifetime (Coker et al., 2002). Many women and men are killed by their violent partners—76% of IPV homicide victims were women, whereas 24% were men (Fox & Zawitz, 2004).

Victims of IPV experience both physical and psychological symptoms, and the symptoms depend on both the frequency and severity of the violence (J. C. Campbell et al., 2002). Common psychological symptoms, similar to those experienced by victims of other coercive sexual behaviors, include depression, antisocial behavior, increased anxiety, low self-esteem, and a fear of intimacy (Tjaden & Thoennes, 2000). Physical symptoms may include headaches, back pain, broken bones, gynecological disorders, and stomach problems.

Defining Intimate Partner Violence and Coercion

Intimate partner violence is coercive behavior that uses threats, harassment, or intimidation. It can involve physical (shoving, hitting, hair-pulling), emotional (extreme jealousy, intimidation, humiliation), or sexual (forced sex, physically painful sexual behaviors) abuse. Some offenders even are violent toward pets, especially pets

Personal Voices

Why Women Stay

Following is an essay written by a woman who lived with an abusive spouse. Notice the degree of manipulation and power he used to make her stay.

One of the most difficult emotional decisions to understand is why, at the first sign of aggression or mistreatment, a woman does not or cannot leave a man who abuses her. It sounds straightforward and easy, but is it?

Let me begin by saying that abusive relationships do not start with violence. Women do not enter into a relationship saying, "It's okay to hurt me." Even abusive relationships usually start romantically, sharing love and trust, building dreams together, and often having children—just as in a normal relationship.

Often, the spouse's controlling behavior is not seen immediately but develops slowly over time. When a woman realizes how damaging her relationship is, she often has really made an emotional commitment and developed a sense of loyalty to her partner. The bonds between the couple have been built over time and do not suddenly cease to exist. Once abuse enters the relationship, her emotional ties are a great source of turmoil. I know when I took my marriage vows, I meant "for better or for worse." But when "until death do us part" suddenly became a frightening reality, I was faced with some terrifying decisions.

There are myriad and complex reasons for staying in an abusive relationship. Many women have no other source of financial support or housing. We ask them to leave their homes behind, cloaked only by the tempo-

rary safety of darkness, to hide in community shelters (when there is room) or to live in the streets. How many people would choose to take their children from their home, with no guarantee of food or shelter? How realistic are the options that we insist are the "obvious solutions" to this problem?

The fear of retaliation and further victimization by the abuser is another serious concern. Once, when I tried to leave, my ex-husband took my dachshund puppy and beat him against the wall. He told me to remember those cries because if I ever left him or tried to get help, those cries would haunt me because they would be cries of my young niece. At that moment, I knew he was capable of every horrible threat he had ever made and my life was in grave danger.

Abuse by an intimate partner, either emotional or physical, is a commonly unrecognized cause of illnesses and injury among women. Recent estimates reveal that from 2 million to 4 million women are battered by their "significant other" each year. How long can we continue to ignore this horrifying crime? We must realize that your actions, or lack of action, can have a huge impact on a woman's life. Be aware that by not asking a woman about it, you could be closing your eyes to the fact that this woman will most likely return home, only to be beaten again and again.

SOURCE: From G. Bundow, 1992, "Resident Forum: Why Women Stay," *Journal of the American Medical Association*, Vol. 267, p. 23. Reprinted with permission.

that are close to the victim. Generally there is a pattern of abuse, rather than a single isolated incident.

As the accompanying Personal Voices, "Why Women Stay" indicates, many women in abusive relationships claim their relationship started off well. They believe the first incidence of violence is a one-time occurrence that won't happen again. They often excuse their partner's behavior and accept their partner's apologies. In time, the abuser convinces his partner that it is really *her* fault that he became violent and if *she* changes it won't happen again.

Most women in this situation begin to believe that the problems are indeed their fault, so they stay in the abusive relationship. Many actually believe that it's safer in the relationship than outside of it. Things that may make it more difficult for a woman to leave include issues such as finances, low self-esteem, fear, or isolation.

This type of violence and abuse also occurs among college students. One 21-year-old college student talks about her relationship:

No one could understand why I wanted my relationship with Billy to work. After all, no relationship is perfect. He didn't mean to slam me that hard. Why would he want to leave bruises on me? Look at him. He's a big guy. Anyone can tell he might have trouble seeing his own strength. He means well. He gives the best hugs, like a big sweet bear. He always says he's sorry. He loves me and tells me this in letters all the time. He thinks I'm sweet, pretty, and kind. Maybe my friends are just jealous. After all, he is a really good-looking guy. I know a lot of girls who want him. He tells me girls throw themselves at him every day. Why would he lie? (Author's files)

sex byte

One study on violence in college dating relationships found that men and women who had shoved, punched, or physically abused a sibling were more likely to engage in intimate partner violence later in life (Noland et al., 2004). As siblings compete with one another for family resources, they use violence as a form of manipulation and control and then carry these behaviors into future intimate relationships.

Personal Voices

Domestic Violence in Lesbian Relationships

I met my girlfriend at a party that a friend hosted. She was intelligent, beautiful, and had a wonderful sense of humor. Our relationship developed rapidly and the closeness we shared was something I had never experienced before. It is difficult to remember exactly when the abuse began because it was subtle. She criticized me because she didn't like my cooking, and she occasionally called me names when we argued. I didn't think much about it because she had recently lost custody of her daughter to her ex-husband because of her sexual orientation and was angry, irritable, and depressed. She often threatened suicide and attempted it during an argument that we had and then blamed me for calling 911 for help. Despite the stress she was experiencing, she was very supportive of me when my family "disowned" me after I came out to them. When I bought my first car, she insisted I put it in her name. Although we had periods of profound happiness, our arguments increased in frequency as did her drinking and drug use. I kept telling myself that things would get better but they never did. She continually accused me of being unfaithful (I wasn't) and even once raped me after claiming I had flirted with a supermarket cashier. The first time she hit me I grabbed her wrist and twisted her arm to keep from being hit again. My response frightened me so much I suggested we see a couple's counselor, and she agreed.

Couple counseling was not helpful, and although things felt worse, our therapist said that was normal so we persevered. I began scrutinizing my own behavior believing that if I could only do things better or differently, our life together would improve. It wasn't until she pulled a knife on me that I realized that it wasn't going to change for the better . . . it was only going to get worse. I called a crisis line and the counselor suggested that what I was experiencing was domestic violence. That had actually never occurred to be because we were both women. Leaving her was the hardest thing I have ever done.

It's still difficult to think of my situation as domestic violence but with the help of my counselor and support group, I am learning that women can be violent to other women, that anger, stress, depression, alcohol and drugs do not cause violence, that violence is a choice the abuser makes, and finally, that I am not to blame.

SOURCE: National Coalition of Anti-Violence Programs, 1998.

Intimate partner violence in same-sex relationships looks similar to IPV in heterosexual relationships. However, in same-sex relationships there are additional issues that may arise, including being "outed" if a partner tries to get help or leave the relationship. Outing when a person is not ready could result in employment or social issues (National Coalition of Anti-Violence Programs, 1998). One lesbian survivor of intimate partner violence tells her story in the accompanying Personal Voices, "Domestic Violence in Lesbian Relationships."

Preventing Intimate Partner Violence

Several factors have been found to be related to IPV, including a history of IPV in the offender's family and excessive alcohol use (Leonard, 2005; Lipsky et al., 2005). Educational programs can help educate the public about intimate partner violence. Safe housing for victims of IPV can also reduce the likelihood of future abuse. Today there are thousands of battered women's shelters across the United States. These shelters provide women with several important things, including information and a safe haven. Often these centers have 24-hour hotlines that can help women who are struggling with issues related to domestic violence (see the Web Resources at the end of this chapter for other hotline options). Increasing the availability of safe houses and counseling and education is imperative. In addition, increasing the availability of services for gay, lesbian, bisexual, transgendered, elderly, and disabled women and men will help ensure that help is available for all who may need it.

© Joel Gordon

Intimate partner violence in lesbian relationships looks similar to IPV in heterosexual relationships.

 ## SEXUAL HARASSMENT

Sexual harassment is a very broad term that includes anything from jokes, unwanted sexual advances, a "friendly" pat, an "accidental" brush on a person's body, or an arm around a person (Cammaert, 1985). It can also include unwanted sexual attention online (Barak, 2005). Because of the wide variety of actions that fall under this definition, many people are confused about what exactly constitutes sexual harassment.

In the United States, the courts recognize two types of sexual harassment, including **quid pro quo harassment** and **hostile environment harassment.** Quid pro quo (meaning "this for that") harassment occurs when a person is required to engage in some type of sexual conduct in exchange for a certain grade, employment, or other benefit. For example, a teacher or employer might offer you a better grade for engaging in sexual behavior. Another type of sexual harassment involves being subjected to unwelcome repeated sexual comments or visually offensive material that creates a hostile work environment and interferes with work or school. For example, a student or employee might repeatedly tell sexual jokes or send them via the Internet.

It may seem that sexual harassment is not as shocking as other forms of sexual coercion, but the effects of harassment on the victim can be traumatic and often cause long-term difficulties. Fitzgerald and Ormerod claim that "there are many similarities between sexual harassment and other forms of sexual victimization, not only in the secrecy that surrounds them but also in the [myth] that supports them" (1991, p. 2). Severe or chronic sexual harassment can cause psychological side effects similar to rape and sexual assault, and in extreme cases it has been known to contribute to suicide. In 1996, the family of one woman who worked for the Postal Service was awarded $5.5 million when their daughter committed suicide as a result of repeated sexual harassment at work (Employment Practices Solutions, 1996).

Incidence and Reporting of Harassment

It is estimated that 25% to 30% of college students report experiences of sexual harassment (Mènard et al., 2003). Sexual harassment on campus usually involves sexist comments, jokes, or touching, and the majority of students do not report it (Mènard et al., 2003). Federal law prohibits the sexual harassment of college students, and victims of

Review Question

Describe what we know about the development of intimate partner violence and how it relates to sexual and physical abuse.

sexual harassment
Unwanted sexual attention from someone in school or the workplace; also includes unwelcome sexual jokes, glances, or comments, or the use of status and/or power to coerce or attempt to coerce a person into having sex.

quid pro quo harassment
A type of sexual harassment that involves submission to a particular type of conduct, either explicitly or implicitly, in order to get education or employment.

hostile environment harassment
A type of sexual harassment that occurs when an individual is subjected to unwelcome repeated sexual comments, innuendoes, or visually offensive material or touching that interferes with school or work.

sexual harassment can sue their schools for damages for sexual harassment (Hogan, 2005).

In the United States, sexual harassment has increased in the past few years, probably in relation to the increase in women in the workforce. Because of sexual harassment, women are nine times more likely than men to quit a job, five times more likely to transfer, and three times more likely to lose their jobs (Parker & Griffin, 2002). Although the majority of people who are sexually harassed are female, it can also happen to men. Same-sex harassment also occurs (Foote & Goodman-Delahunty, 2005).

As we have discussed, many victims of sexual harassment never say anything to authorities, although they may tell a friend. This may be in part because women are socialized to keep harmony in relationships. Others verbally confront the offender or leave their jobs in order to get away from it. Assertiveness is the most effective strategy, either by telling someone about it or confronting the offender. Many fear, however, that confronting a boss or teacher who is harassing them could jeopardize their jobs or their grades. Also, although these strategies increase the chances that the behavior will stop, they do not guarantee it. If you are being sexually harassed by someone in a university setting, the best advice is to talk to a counselor or your advisor about it. Remember that you are protected by federal law. Colleges and universities today will not tolerate the sexual harassment of any student, regardless of gender, ethnicity, religion, or sexual orientation.

Women and men think differently about sexual harassment. In one study, females were more likely than males to experience sexual harassment and to perceive it as harmful (Hand & Sanchez, 2000). Researchers have found that a behavior might be interpreted as sexual harassment by a woman, whereas it's interpreted as flattering to a man (Lastella, 2005).

Preventing Sexual Harassment

The first step in reducing the incidence of sexual harassment is to acknowledge the problem. Too many people deny its existence. Because sexual harassers usually have more power, it is difficult for victims to come forward to disclose their victimization. University officials and administrators need to work together to provide educational opportunities and assistance for all students, staff, and employees. Establishing policies for dealing with these problems is necessary. Workplaces also need to design and implement strong policies against sexual harassment.

Education, especially about the role of women, is imperative. As our society continues to change and as more and more women enter the workforce, we need to prepare men for this adjustment. Throughout history, when women have broken out of their traditional roles, there have always been difficulties. Today, we need research to explore the impact of women on the workforce.

Throughout this chapter we have explored how power can be used in sexual relationships to degrade and oppress. Rape, the sexual abuse of children, incest, intimate partner violence, and sexual harassment are problems in our society today. The first step in reducing these crimes is to acknowledge the problems and not hide them. Education, especially about the role of women, is necessary; without it, these crimes will undoubtedly continue to escalate.

sexbyte

Cross-cultural studies on attitudes about sexual harassment have found that students from individualist countries (such as the United States, Canada, Germany, and the Netherlands) are less accepting of sexual harassment, whereas students from collectivist countries (such as Ecuador, Pakistan, the Phillippines, Taiwan, and Turkey) are more accepting (Sigal et al., 2005).

Review Question

Define sexual harassment, explain its effects, and identify strategies to prevent it.

ACTIVE SUMMARY

1. Physically or psychologically **(a)** _____ sexual relations on another person is usually referred to as rape. Sexual **(b)** _____ refers to sexual penetration (vaginal, oral, anal) as well as **(c)** _____ sexual touching.

2. On the average, a rape occurs every **(a)** _____ minutes in the United States. Actual incidence rape rates are difficult to determine because forcible rape is one of the most **(b)** _____ crimes in the United States. Women do not report rape for several reasons, including that they do not think that they were really raped, they **(c)** _____ themselves, they fear no one will believe them, they worry that no legal action will be taken, or they feel shame and/or **(d)** _____. However, today more and more women are reporting their rapes.

3. Four theories that explain why rape occurs are the rapist psychopathology, victim precipitation, feminist, and sociological theories. The rapist psychopathology theory suggests that either **(a)** _____ or intoxication forces men to rape. Victim precipitation theory shifts the responsibility from the person who knowingly attacked to the innocent **(b)** _____. Feminists believe that rape and the threat of rape are **(c)** _____ used in our society to keep women in their place. The social, economic, and political separation of the genders has also encouraged rape, which is viewed as an act of **(d)** _____ of men over women. Finally, **(e)** _____ believe that rape is an expression of power differentials in society. When men feel disempowered by society, by changing sex roles or by their jobs, overpowering women with the symbol of their masculinity (a penis) reinforces, for a moment, men's control over the world.

4. There are also strong **(a)** _____ differences in attitudes toward rape. Men have been found to be less empathetic and sensitive toward rape than women and to attribute more responsibility to the **(b)** _____ than women do, especially those men who often view **(c)** _____. During a man's college years, he will experience a decline in negative rape attitudes. Rape awareness **(d)** _____ can also help decrease the acceptability of rape myths.

5. The United States has the highest rate of reported rapes in the world. In some cultures, rape is accepted as a(an) **(a)** _____ for women or is used for initiation purposes. Rape has also been used during times of war as a(an) **(b)** _____. This is referred to as **(c)** _____ rape. The rape of **(d)** _____ is also common in some places around the globe.

6. Almost a(an) **(a)** _____ of college women report that they were forced to have sexual intercourse at some point in their lives. The majority of these women **(b)** _____ the person who sexually victimized them. Some women also report being **(c)** _____ on campus, either physically or through notes and e-mails. Because many of these women know their attackers, **(d)** _____ feel comfortable reporting or pressing charges.

7. **(a)** _____ use is one of the strongest predictors of acquaintance rape on college campuses. **(b)** _____ of all rape cases involve alcohol consumption by the rapist, victim, or both. Alcohol use on college campuses, as it **(c)** _____ to rape, is viewed very **(d)** _____ for men and women.

8. Fraternities tend to tolerate and may actually **(a)** _____ the sexual coercion of women, because they tend to **(b)** _____ large parties with lots of **(c)** _____ and little university supervision. The ethic of **(d)** _____ also helps foster an environment that is ripe for rape.

9. Male **(a)** _____ have been found to be disproportionately overrepresented as assailants of rape by women surveyed. Many athletes have been found to **(b)** _____ the world in a way that helps to **(c)** _____ rape, and many feel a sense of privilege. Female athletes have been found to be more likely than nonathletes to believe in the **(d)** _____-_____-_____ theory of rape, and believe that some women put themselves in a(an) **(e)** _____ situation.

10. Rape is an emotionally, **(a)** _____, and psychologically shattering experience for the victim. Rape **(b)** _____ syndrome is a two-stage stress response pattern characterized by physical, psychological, behavioral, and/or sexual problems. Two stages, the acute and long-term **(c)** _____, detail the symptoms that many women feel after a rape. Rape can cause **(d)** _____ difficulties that can persist for a considerable period after the rape. Some victims have a silent rape reaction because they never report or talk about their rape.

11. The effects of rape are **(a)** _____ in special populations, including rape between **(b)** _____ partners, lesbians, older women, women with disabilities, and prostitutes. Partners of women who have been raped also experience **(c)** _____ symptoms. All in all, rape places a great deal of stress on a(an) **(d)** _____.

12. Men can be raped by women and also by other men. The majority of male rapes by women use psychological or **(a)** _____ contact, such as verbal **(b)** _____ or emotional manipulation, rather than physical force. The true incidence is unknown because the rape of men by men is **(c)** _____ reported to the police. Male rape is an expression of **(d)** _____, a show of strength and masculinity, that uses sex as a weapon. Rape also occurs in prison.

13. (a) _____ are primarily from younger age groups and tend to reduce their rape behavior as they get older. They have also been found to have experienced overwhelmingly (b) _____ early interpersonal experiences, most of which were with their (c) _____; have sexist views about women; accept myths about rape; have low self-esteem; and be (d) _____ conservative.

14. Different therapies for rapists include (a) _____ treatment, psychotherapy, behavioral treatment, support groups, and the use of medications. Many programs have been developed to (b) _____ myths about rape and increase (c) _____ levels. All-male programs have been found to significantly reduce the belief in rape (d) _____.

15. The likelihood that a rape will be reported increases if the assailant was a(an) (a) _____, if there was violence, or if a weapon was involved. Women who report their rapes to the police have been found to have a better (b) _____ and fewer emotional symptoms than those who do not report. Some victims refuse to press charges because they are afraid of (c) _____, want to just forget, feel sorry for the rapist, or feel as though it would not matter anyway because (d) _____ will be done.

16. (a) _____ refers to sexual contact between a child or adolescent and a parent, stepparent, uncle, cousin, or caretaker. Child sexual abuse can include undressing, inappropriate (b) _____, oral and genital stimulation, and vaginal or anal penetration. The most common incest offenders are (c) _____.

17. The overall reported incidence of child sexual abuse has been (a) _____ over the past 30 years. This may be because of the (b) _____ sexual climate rather than an actual increase in the number of sexual (c) _____ on children.

18. The (a) _____ age for sexual abuse of both girls and boys is around 8 or 9 years old, and many victims are (b) _____ to reveal the abuse. Victims of incest with a(an) (c) _____ father delay reporting the longest, whereas those who have been victims of stepfathers or live-in partners tell more (d) _____.

19. Children who (a) _____ their sexual abuse often experience shame and (b) _____ and fear the (c) _____ of affection from family and friends. They also have low self-esteem and feel frustrated about not being able to stop the abuse.

20. Whether or not they tell someone about their sexual abuse, many (a) _____ experience psychological symptoms such as depression, increased anxiety, nervousness, emotional problems, low self-esteem, and personality and intimacy disorders. (b) _____ is usually severe, and many females develop a tendency to (c) _____ themselves for the sexual abuse. Men and women who have been sexually abused may not be able to (d) _____ the abuse. The most devastating emotional effects occur when the sexual abuse is done by someone the victim (e) _____.

21. Research comparing child molesters to nonmolesters has shown that molesters tend to have poorer (a) _____ skills, lower IQs, unhappy family histories, lower (b) _____, _____, and less happiness in their lives. As surprising as it may seem, many abusers have strict (c) _____ codes, yet still violate sexual norms. Three prominent theories that propose factors that make abuse more likely are (d) _____, gender, and biological theories.

22. Currently, the most effective treatments for victims of sexual abuse include a combination of (a) _____ and behavioral psychotherapies. Many victims of sexual abuse also have difficulties developing and maintaining (b) _____ relationships. Goals for therapy of child sex abusers include decreasing sexual (c) _____ to inappropriate sexual objects, teaching them to interact and relate better with adults; assertiveness skills training; empathy and respect for others; increasing sexual education; and evaluating and (d) _____ any sexual difficulties that they might be experiencing with their sexual partners.

23. Increasing the availability of sex (a) _____ can also help decrease child sexual (b) _____. Adequate funding and staffing of child (c) _____ agencies may also be helpful.

24. Women are (a) _____ times more likely to experience violence from a partner or ex-partner than from a stranger. Intimate partner violence is (b) _____ behavior that is done through the use of threats, harassing, or intimidation. It can be (c) _____, emotional, or sexual. When intimate partner violence occurs in gay or lesbian relationships, one fear is being (d) _____ if a partner tries to get help or leave the relationship.

25. Sexual harassment includes anything from (a) _____, unwanted sexual advances, a(an) (b) _____ pat, an "accidental" brush on a person's body, or an arm around a person. Severe or chronic sexual harassment can cause (c) _____ side effects similar to rape and sexual assault, and in extreme cases it has been known to contribute to (d) _____. It is estimated that (e) _____ to (f) _____ of college students report experiences with sexual harassment.

26. The first step in (a) _____ the incidence of sexual harassment is to acknowledge the problem. Too many people deny its existence. Because sexual harassers usually have more (b) _____, it is difficult for victims to come (c) _____ to disclose their victimization.

Critical Thinking Questions

1. If a woman is raped who was alone and drunk at a bar dancing very seductively with several different men, do you think she is more to blame than a woman who was raped in the street by an unknown assailant? Explain.

2. In 2003, a woman accused Kobe Bryant of the Los Angeles Lakers of rape. Do you think professional athletes make poor decisions with women who flock to them? Do you think a woman would cry rape without just cause? Why, or why not?

3. Do you consider a 17-year-old male who has sexual intercourse with his 14-year-old girlfriend sexual abuse? How would you define the sexual abuse of children?

4. In 2003, Max Factor heir Andrew Luster, who had jumped bond for rape and sexual assault, was captured and sentenced to over 120 years in prison for rape. His personal worth at the time was around $30 million. Why do you think such a person would rape? Using the theories presented in this chapter, explain what factors might have led to these behaviors.

5. In a handful of divorce cases, one spouse accuses the other of child sexual abuse. Do you think that these accusations originate from a vengeful ex-spouse wanting custody, or do you think it might be easier to discuss the sexual abuse once the "bonds of secrecy" have been broken, as they typically are during divorce?

CHAPTER RESOURCES

Check It Out

Maltz, W. (2001). **The sexual healing journey: A guide for survivors of sexual abuse.** New York: HarperCollins.

This how-to, personal therapy book gives concrete details on what constitutes abuse and shatters the myths surrounding double standards. In addition to identifying the many types of abuse, Maltz demonstrates how the abuse in a person's unconscious mind may lead to sexual dysfunction. She carefully deconstructs the common negative sexuality that often acts as a defense mechanism and attempts to replace it with a healthy, positive approach to sex. This book can help victims of sexual abuse along the road to healing.

The Accused (1988; 1 hour, 51 minutes; Rated R)

A dated but classic movie that is based on a real-life gang rape that occurred in 1983 at a bar in New Bedford, Massachusetts. Sarah Tobias (Jodie Foster) is raped by three men at the local bar, while a group of male onlookers cheer and lead the rapists on. The district attorney, Kathryn Murphy (Kelly McGillis), wants to prove that although Sarah had been dancing provocatively while in the bar, she was not at fault, and the men responsible should be brought to justice. Kathryn Murphy goes after both the rapists and the men who cheered them on. A disturbing portrayal of gang rape and the court case that follows.

InfoTrac® College Edition

If your instructor ordered InfoTrac with this book, explore InfoTrac College Edition, your online library, for additional readings and review. Go to: **www.thomsonedu.com,** and enter these search terms:

child sexual abuse	cyberstalking	rape
date rape	rape and culture	sexual scripts
sexual harassment	domestic violence	intimate partner violence

SexualityNow **Companion Website**
Go to **http://thomsonedu.com/carroll** for practice quiz questions, interactive activities, Internet links, critical thinking exercises, discussion forums, and more. You can also access sites from the Wadsworth Psychology Study Center **(http://psychology.wadsworth.com)** or you can connect directly to the following sites:

Adult Survivors of Child Abuse
Designed specifically for adult survivors of physical, sexual, and/or emotional child abuse or neglect, ASCA offers an effective support program. This website's mission is to reach out to as many survivors of child abuse as possible and it offers information on individual and group support groups.

American Women's Self-Defense Association
The American Women's Self-Defense Association (AWSDA) began with the realization that women's self-defense need were not being met. Founded in 1990, AWSDA is an educational organization dedicated to furthering women's awareness of self-defense and rape prevention.

National Violence Against Women Prevention Research Center
The National Violence Against Women Prevention Research Center provides information on current topics related to violence against women and its prevention. The website contains statistics and information on many topics, including evaluations of college sexual assault programs across the nation.

Rape, Abuse & Incest National Network
The Rape, Abuse & Incest National Network (RAINN) is the nation's largest anti–sexual assault organization. RAINN operates the National Sexual Assault Hotline at 1-800-656-HOPE and carries out programs to prevent sexual assault, help victims, and ensure that rapists are brought to justice. Their website includes statistics, counseling resources, prevention tips, news, and more.

Men Can Stop Rape
Men Can Stop Rape (MCSR) is a nonprofit organization that works to increase men's involvement and efforts to reduce male violence. MCSR empowers male youth and the institutions that serve them to work as allies with women in preventing rape and other forms of men's violence. MCSR uses education and community groups to build men's capacity to be strong without being violent.

Security on Campus
Security on Campus is a nonprofit organization that works to make campuses safe for college and university students. It was cofounded in 1987 by Connie and Howard Clery, following the murder of their daughter at Lehigh University. Jeanne Clery was a freshman when she was beaten, raped, and murdered by another student in her dormitory room. Security on Campus educates students and parents about crime on campus and assists victims in understanding laws pertaining to these crimes.

Male Survivor
Male Survivor works to help people better understand and treat adult male survivors of childhood sexual abuse. Information about male sexual abuse and a variety of helpful links are available.

Northwest Network of Bi, Trans, Lesbian and Gay Survivors of Abuse
The Northwest Network provides support and advocacy for bisexual, transsexual, lesbian, and gay survivors of abuse. Information about sexual abuse and a variety of helpful links are available.

Go to **www.thomsonedu.com** to link to **SexualityNow,** your online study tool. First take the **Pre-Test** for this chapter to get your **Personalized Study Plan,** which will identify topics you need to review and direct you to online resources. Then take the **Post-Test** to determine what concepts you have mastered and what you still need work on.

Videos in SexualityNow
For additional information on topics discussed in this chapter, check out the videos in **SexualityNow** on the following topics:
- **Rape and Posttraumatic Stress Disorder**—Learn how the effects of rape affect this woman's life in the 10 years since it happened.
- **Gang-Rape in Pakistan**—Hear how a Pakistani woman challenged the existing power structures after being gang-raped.
- **Does He Treat You Right?**—Listen to a woman voice concern about the way her friend's boyfriend treats her.

18 Sexual Images and Selling Sex

Sexuality◑Now Go to www.thomsonedu.com to link to
SexualityNow, your online study tool.

*O*ur lives today are full of visual media: magazines, newspapers, book covers, CD and DVD packaging, cereal boxes and food products—even medicines are adorned with pictures of people, scenes, or products. Advertisements peer at us from magazines, billboards, buses, matchbook covers, and anywhere else that advertisers can buy space. Television, movies, computers, and other moving visual images surround us almost everywhere we go, and we will only depend on them more as information technology continues to develop. We live in a visual culture whose images we simply cannot escape.

We begin this chapter with a brief history of erotic representations. Next we take a look at how erotic representations are presented to us every day in books, television, advertising, and other media. Only then do we turn to the graphic sexual images of pornography. We will also explore how sex itself is sold today, from lap dances in strip clubs to prostitution. Along the way ask yourself: What influence do sexual representations and selling sex have on us? What are they trying to show us about ourselves? How do they subtly affect the way we think about men, women, and sexuality?

EROTIC REPRESENTATIONS IN HISTORY

Human beings have been making representations of themselves and the world around them since ancient times. Many of the earliest cave drawings and animal bone sculptures have been representations of the human form, usually scantily dressed or naked. Often the poses or implications of the art seem explicitly erotic. Yet it is hard to know to what degree these images were considered erotic by preliterate people, for early erotic art was also sacred art whose purpose was to represent those things most important to early people—the search for food and the need to reproduce (Lucie-Smith, 1991). However, by the dawn of the great ancient civilizations such as Egypt, people were drawing erotic images on walls or pieces of papyrus just for the sake of eroticism (Manniche, 1987). Since that time, human beings have been fascinated with representations of the human form naked or engaged in sexually explicit behavior; in turn, many governments have been equally intent on limiting or eradicating those images.

Erotic representations have appeared in most societies throughout history, and they have been greeted with different degrees of tolerance. Ancient cultures often created public erotic tributes to the gods, including temples dedicated to phallic worship. India's sacred writings are full of sexual accounts, and some of the most explicit public sculptures in the world adorn its temples. Greece is famous for the erotic art that adorned objects like bowls and urns. When archaeologists in the 18th and 19th centuries uncovered the Roman city of Pompeii, buried in a volcanic blast in 79 A.D., they were startled and troubled to find that this jewel of the Roman Empire, which they had so admired, was full of brothels, had carved phalluses protruding at every street corner, and had private homes full of erotic **frescoes** (FRESS-cohs; Kendrick, 1987). Authorities hid these findings for years by keeping the erotic objects in locked museum rooms and publishing pictures of the city in which the phalluses were made to taper off like candles.

Not all sexual representations are explicit, and many of our greatest artists and writers included sexual components in their creations. The plays of Shakespeare, though hardly shocking by today's standards, do contain references to sexuality and sexual intercourse. The art of Michelangelo and Leonardo da Vinci also included graphic nudity

fresco
A type of painting done on wet plaster so that the plaster dries with the colors incorporated into it.

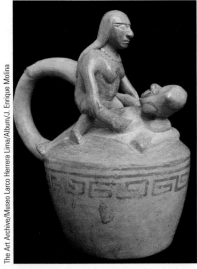

Early erotic art was often public art. The city of Pompeii included large, erect phalluses on street corners, and erotic frescoes adorned many people's homes.

without being titillating. Still, in their day, these pictures caused controversy: in the 16th century, for example, priests painted loincloths over nude pictures of Jesus and the angels. What people in one society or one period in history see as obscene, another group—or the same group later—can view as great art.

Review Question

Explain how erotic representations have appeared throughout history.

The Development of Pornography

Most sexual representations created throughout history had a specific purpose, whether it was to worship the gods, to adorn pottery, or later, to criticize the government or religion. Very little erotic art seems to have been created simply for the purpose of arousing the viewer, as much of modern erotic art is. So most of history's erotic art cannot be considered "pornographic" in the modern sense (L. Hunt, 1993).

Pornography, which tends to portray sexuality for its own sake, did not emerge as a distinct, separate category until the middle of the 18th century. For most of history, sexuality itself was so imbedded in religious, moral, and legal contexts that it was not thought of as a separate sphere of life (Kendrick, 1987). Explicit words and pictures (along with other forms of writing, such as political writings) were controlled in the name of religion or in the name of politics, not in the name of public **decency** (L. Hunt, 1993). For example, **obscenity** was illegal among the Puritans (punishable originally by death and later by boring through the tongue with a hot iron) because it was an offense against God. That is why before the 19th century, **hard-core** sexual representations were extremely rare.

Another strong influence on the development of pornography was the development of the printing press and the mass availability of the printed word (sexually explicit books were printed within 50 years of the invention of movable type in the Western world). For most of history, written or printed work was available only to a small elite because only they could afford it and, more important, only they could read.

The most famous pornographic work of the 18th century was John Cleland's *Memoirs of a Woman of Pleasure* (better known as *Fanny Hill*), first published in 1748. Cleland made no pretenses of being political or philosophical, and his book contains neither humor nor satire; his work was aimed at sexually arousing the reader. Before Cleland, most sexually explicit books were about prostitutes because these women did "unspeakable" things (that could be described in graphic detail) and because they could end up arrested, diseased, and alone, thereby reinforcing society's condemnation of their actions. In fact, the word *pornography* literally means "writing about harlots."

Cases like *Fanny Hill* teach us that to really understand the meaning of "pornography," we must understand the desire of the government and other groups to control it and suppress it. In other words, the story of pornography is not just about publishing erotic material but also about the struggle between those who try to create it and those who try to stop them. Both sides must be included in any discussion of pornography; without those who try to suppress it, pornography just becomes erotic art. In fact, the term **erotica,** often used to refer to sexual representations that are not pornographic, really just means pornography that a particular person finds acceptable. One person's pornography can be another person's erotica. As we shall see in this chapter, the modern arguments about pornography are some of the most divisive in the country, pitting feminists against feminists, allying some of the most radical feminist scholars with fundamentalist preachers of the religious right, and pitting liberals against liberals and conservatives against conservatives in arguments over the limits of free speech.

But sexually explicit representations are not the only sexual images in our society. Sexuality is present in almost all of our **media,** from the model sensuously sipping a bottle of beer to the offhand sexual innuendos that are a constant part of television sitcoms. In fact, the entertainment media seems to be almost obsessed by sexual imagery; Michel Foucault, French philosopher and historian of sexuality, has called it a modern compulsion to speak incessantly about sex. Before we discuss the sexually explicit representations of "pornography" with the heated arguments they often inspire, let us turn to the erotic images that present themselves to us in the popular media every day.

pornography
Any sexually oriented material that is created simply for the purpose of arousing the viewer.

decency
Conformity to recognized standards of propriety, good taste, and modesty—as defined by a particular group (standards of decency differ among groups).

obscenity
A legal term for materials that are considered offensive to standards of sexual decency in a society.

hard-core
Describes explicit, genitally oriented sexual depictions; more extreme than soft-core, which displays sexual activity without explicit portrayals of genital penetration.

erotica
Sexually oriented media that are considered by a viewer or society as within the acceptable bounds of decency.

media
All forms of public communication.

Review Question

Describe the development of pornography.

Over the last 25 years, representations in the **mass media** have become more explicitly erotic. Many of the images we see today are explicitly or subtly sexual. Barely clothed females and shirtless, athletic males are so common in our ads that we scarcely notice them anymore. Some even feature full nudity. The majority of movies, even those directed at children, have sexual scenes that would not have been permitted in movie theaters even 20 years ago. The humor in television sitcoms has become more and more sexual, and nudity has begun to appear on prime-time network television shows. In addition, graphic depictions of sexuality, which until recently could only be found in adult bookstores and theaters, are now available at neighborhood video stores.

We like to believe that we are so used to the media that we are immune to its influences. Does sex (or violence) on television, for example, really influence how promiscuous (or violent) our society becomes? Do the constant sexual stereotypes paraded before us in commercials and advertisements really help shape our attitudes toward gender relations? Does constant exposure to sexual images erode family life, encourage promiscuity, and lead to violence against women, as some conservative and feminist groups claim? Also, if we find out that sex and violence in the media do have an effect on how we behave, what should we do about it?

Erotic Literature: The Power of the Press

Although the portrayal of sexuality is as old as art itself, pornography and censorship are more modern concepts, products of the mass production of erotic art in society. Throughout Western history, reactionary forces (usually the clergy) often censored nudity in public art, especially when it featured religious figures. For example, on the walls of Michelangelo's Sistine Chapel, clerics painted over the genitals of nudes with loincloths and wisps of fabric. Still, because there was no way to mass produce these kinds of art, the Church's reactions varied on a case-by-case basis.

Pornography in the modern sense began to appear when printing became sophisticated enough to allow fairly large runs of popular books, beginning in the 16th century. Intellectuals and clergy were often against this mass production of books. They worried that if everybody had books and could learn about things for themselves, why would anyone need teachers, scholars, or theologians? Religious and secular intellectuals quickly issued dire warnings about the corrupting effects of allowing people direct access to knowledge and established censorship mechanisms. By the 17th century, the Church was pressuring civic governments to allow them to inspect bookstores, and soon forbidden books, including erotica, were being removed; such books then became rarer and more valuable, and a clandestine business arose in selling them. It was this struggle between the illicit market in sexual art and literature and the forces of censorship that started what might be called a pornographic subculture, one that still thrives today.

Today, erotic literature of almost any kind is readily available. The sexual scenes described in the average romance novel today would have branded it as pornographic only a few decades ago. One would think that such books would be the main targets of people trying to censor sexually explicit materials. Yet most censorship battles over sexually explicit material involve images rather than written word.

Although the early court cases that established the American legal attitudes toward pornography in the United States were often about books (especially about sending them through the mail), modern debates about pornography tend to focus more on explicit pictures and movies. Still, it was the erotic novel that first established pornographic production as a business in the Western world and provoked a response from religious and governmental authorities.

Television and Film: Stereotypes, Sex, and the Decency Issue

The advent of television has only increased our dependence on visual media, and it is probably no exaggeration to say that television is the single strongest influence on the modern American outlook toward life. It is estimated that teenagers watch 3 hours of television each day and one in four teens says that television influences his or her behavior (Henry J. Kaiser Family Foundation, 2003; Roberts et al., 2005). Parents believe that sexual content on television influences teenage sexual behavior (Kunkel et al., 2005).

Television allows us to have the world delivered to us in the comfort of our home. But the world we see on TV is only a small slice of the real world; television, like the movies, edits and sanitizes the world it displays. For example, although literally hundreds of acts of sexual intercourse are portrayed or suggested on television shows and in the movies every day, we rarely see a couple discuss or use contraception, discuss the morality of their actions, contract a sexually transmitted infection, worry about AIDS, experience erectile dysfunction, or regret the act afterward. Most couples fall into bed shortly after initial physical attraction and take no time to build an emotional relationship before becoming sexually active. Values and morals about sexuality seem nonexistent.

In an attempt to capture viewers back from cable and satellite stations, the major television networks have been *increasing* the sexual content of their programming (Kunkel et al., 2005). Television talk shows have also become decidedly more graphic in their content. As the number of talk show hosts has increased, so has competition for provocative guests, and a good sexual confession—men who cross-dress, mothers who sleep with their teenage sons' best friends, women who leave their spouses for other women, teenage prostitutes—are guaranteed at least to catch some attention. The HBO hit *Sex in the City* broke new ground by having four women openly discussing their sexuality. Popular nightly dramas such as *Laguna Beach* and *Desperate Housewives* both use sex to entice viewers.

Television magazine shows that imitate news reports but concentrate on two or three stories (e.g., *48 Hours*) often search for stories with lurid content, and if there is a sexual scandal or a rape accusation in the news, they are sure to feature it. Even the "hard" news shows, such as the networks' evening news reports, have turned a corner in their willingness to use graphic descriptions of sexual events. News shows, after all, also need ratings to survive, and one way to interest audiences is to report legitimate news stories that have a sexual content in a graphic and provocative way. These news reports deliver the sexually explicit information with the implicit message that they disapprove of it; but they still deliver it.

Television and movie producers believe that "sex sells," and so they fill their programming with it. In 2005, *Sex on TV4*, a biennial study of sexual content on television, analyzed over 1,000 hours of programming including all genres of television shows. Overall, 70% of the shows studied included some sexual content; and shows averaged 5 sexual episodes per hour (Kunkel et al., 2005). These numbers were up from 1998, when 56% of shows included sexual content, and 3.2 sexual episodes occurred every hour. During prime-time programming, 77% of shows included sexual content and averaged close to 6 sexual episodes per hour (Kunkel et al., 2005; see Figures 18.1, 18.2, and 18.3). This study also found that only 11% of prime-time network shows made references to sexual risks or responsibilities, and this percentage has remained virtually the same since 1998 (Kunkel et al., 2005). Interestingly, approximately 53% of sexual scenes that included intercourse were between couples with an established relationship; 20% were between couples who have met but who have no relationship; 15% were between couples who have just met; and in 12% of cases it was unclear what the couple's relationship is (Kunkel et al., 2005).

The AIDS epidemic was a key factor in opening up the way news organizations speak about sexuality (for example, the word *condom*

Vince Bucci/AFP/Getty Images

Although now in reruns, the HBO hit "Sex in the City" broke new ground by openly discussing the sex lives of four single women living in New York City.

Percentage of television shows with sexual content

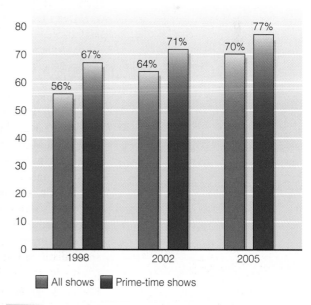

Figure 18.1

Percentage of television shows with sexual content over time, 1998–2005.

Source: From "Sex on TV4, A Kaiser Family Foundation Report," (#7398), Chart 1, Nov. 2005, The Henry J. Kaiser Family Foundation. The Kaiser Family Foundation, based in Menlo Park, California, is a nonprofit, independent national health care philanthropy and is not associated with Kaiser Permanente or Kaiser Industries.

Figure 18.2

Percentage of television shows with sexual content over time, 1998–2005, by type of content.

Source: From "Sex on TV4, A Kaiser Family Foundation Report," (#7398), Chart 1, Nov. 2005, The Henry J. Kaiser Family Foundation. The Kaiser Family Foundation, based in Menlo Park, California, is a nonprofit, independent national health care philanthropy and is not associated with Kaiser Permanente or Kaiser Industries.

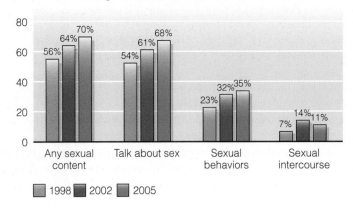

Percentage of shows with sexual content over time

■ 1998 ■ 2002 ■ 2005

Figure 18.3

Percentage of television shows in 2005 with sexual content, by show type.

Source: From "Sex on TV4, A Kaiser Family Foundation Report," (#7398), Chart 1, Nov. 2005, The Henry J. Kaiser Family Foundation. The Kaiser Family Foundation, based in Menlo Park, California, is a nonprofit, independent national health care philanthropy and is not associated with Kaiser Permanente or Kaiser Industries.

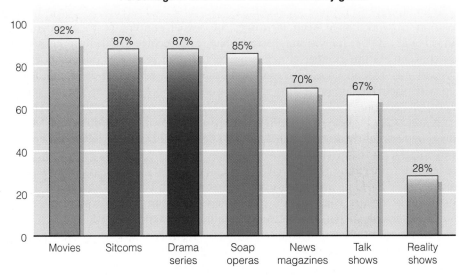

Percentage of shows with sexual content by genre

Review Question

Explain how television uses sex to attract viewers and increase their ratings.

would never have appeared on a major news network before AIDS). Another landmark came in 1998 when news broke of a sex scandal between then-President Bill Clinton and Monica Lewinsky. The Clinton–Lewinsky story was one of the biggest of the decade and was covered by most evening news shows in explicit detail. This story broke precedent and allowed the networks to use language and sexual references that would have been unthinkable just a few years before.

The new frankness on television can, of course, be used to transmit important sexual information and help demystify sexuality through educational programming. Shows such as *Talk Sex with Sue Johanson* on Oxygen and other shows have helped educate the public about sex. However, the vast majority of sexual references are made to titillate, not inform, and much of the sex portrayed on television is provided in an artificial and unrealistic light (Kunkel et al., 2005).

Television, Film, and Minority Sexuality

As sexually explicit as the visual media have become, they have generally had a very poor track record in their portrayals of certain sexual behaviors, such as same-sex behavior, and certain minorities, such as the elderly, the disabled, and racial and ethnic minorities. Today popular shows such as *Six Feet Under*, *Queer Eye for the Straight Guy*, and the *L Word* help lesbian and gay men become more mainstream on television.

Unfortunately, the sexual lives of ethnic and racial minorities have historically been neglected by the major media. African Americans complained for many years that television and movies tend to portray them as criminals, drug pushers, or pimps; only recently have black actors begun appearing in stable television roles and sitcoms. African American filmmakers such as Spike Lee continue to release movies showing African American sexual life from the African American perspective, and the popularity of black film stars such as Will Smith, Denzel Washington, and Jamie Foxx have broken the barriers and encouraged movies with African American romantic leads.

Although the roles for African Americans have improved, today other minorities, such as Asian Americans, Latinos, and Native Americans, are less common, and they are rarely portrayed as romantic leads. Even in films that feature minority populations, such as *Dances with Wolves* and *The Last of the Mohicans*, a white actor plays the romantic lead. Can you even think of a movie (outside of kung fu movies) in which an Asian man is the romantic lead?

Some progress has been made, however. *The Golden Girls* is a classic sitcom that showed that older women also have sexual desires, make sexual jokes, and engage in sexual behaviors. So although there have been a few steps in the right direction, we are still a long way from seeing a representative sample of realistic portrayals of minority sexuality in movies and television.

Television, Film, and Gender

Television offers its viewers sexual information both explicitly (through such things as news, documentaries, and public service announcements) and implicitly (through the ways it portrays sexuality or gender relations in its programming; Gunter & McAleer, 1990). One implicit message of television programming, almost since its inception, has been that men are in positions of leadership (whether they are chief legal counsel or the head of the family), whereas women, even if they are high-ranking, are sexual temptations for men. Even today, the stereotyping of women is often extreme in television commercials, which we consider in the section on advertising. Although the types of portrayals of women's roles are changing and improving on television today, men still outnumber women in major roles, and the traditional role of woman as sex object still predominates on television.

Many gender stereotypes persist on television. The only place they often don't show up is on soap operas. Because soap operas are aimed at women, they tend to portray women as more competent than other programming does (Geraghty et al., 1992). Yet even soap operas send subtle messages about keeping women in their place; women who are more sexually active and independent of men tend to be portrayed as evil or unsympathetic.

Fortunately, some gender stereotypes on other television shows are changing. Men are now being shown as single or stay-at-home dads, and there is a tendency to mock the old "macho man" stereotypes on shows such as *The Family Guy*. Shows like *Alias*, *CSI*, and *Law & Order* regularly feature women in leading roles and have helped establish the new television woman: forceful, working outside the home, and dealing with the real-life problems of balancing social life, personal issues, and work. These women are smart, motivated, and self-confident. Gender stereotypes have also been changing with the increasing popularity of reality television shows, such as *Survivor* and *Fear Factor*. Shows like these portray the majority of females as strong, independent, and self-confident women who are willing to take risks.

Television and Children

Earlier we mentioned the number of hours that teenagers watch television. Although most watch 3 hours per day, during a typical school day, teenagers spend 4 hours and 41 minutes in front of a screen of some type (TV Turnoff Network, 2005). By the time today's youths are 70 years old, they will have spent about 7 years of their lives watching television! Television viewing begins early: 2- to 5-year-olds spend almost 28 hours a week watching television and teenagers about 22 hours. Every year the typical American youth spends approximately 900 hours in front of the television, and 1,023 hours in school (TV Turnoff Network, 2005).

Review Question

Explain how the sexual lives of minorities have been neglected by the major media.

sex byte

In 15% of all television scenes with sexual intercourse, the couples have just met (Kunkel et al., 2005).

Review Question

In what ways do television and movies influence our perceptions of gender?

Generation M

The face of media is quickly changing all around us. Today we can hear music from devices smaller than our finger and Internet through our cell phones. Newer cars have optional built-in television monitors on seat backs, and today's cell phones download e-mails and take digital pictures. Today's adolescents spend an average of 6½ hours per day using media, including television, movies, Internet, video, cell phones, iPods, MP3 players, GameCubes, and PlayStations (Rideout et al., 2005). What is the effect of all this media on the lives of young people today?

In 2005, the Henry J. Kaiser Family Foundation released *Generation M: Media in the Lives of 8–18-Year-Olds,* the results of a study that included responses to anonymous questionnaires from over 2,000 8- to 18-year-olds. In addition, 700 adolescents were asked to keep private journals detailing their use of various media. Thirty-nine percent of adolescents were found to have their own cell phone, and 55% owned their own video game player. Following are other interesting findings from this important study. On average, adolescents between the ages of 8 to 18 were found to:

- Watch 4 hours of television each day
- Listen to 1¾ hours of music each day
- Use the computer for recreational use 1 hour each day
- Play video games for 50 minutes per day
- Read recreational material for 43 minutes a day

In the average home in America, 80% get cable or satellite and 55% of these also get premium cable channels, such as HBO. What is interesting, however, is the number of adolescents who have access to this material in their bedrooms. Fifty-three percent of 8- to 18-year-olds report

there are no rules about television watching (Rideout et al., 2005). The study also found that in the average adolescent bedroom:

- 68% have a television
- 54% have a DVD/VCR
- 49% have a video game console
- 31% have a computer
- 65% have an MP3, iPod, CD player, or tape player

Gender differences were found: boys were twice as likely as girls to play video games, but girls spent more time listening to music than boys. As for the overall types of music listened to by both girls and boys, rap and hip-hop were the clear favorites (60% of Caucasians, 70% of Hispanics, and 81% of African Americans reported this genre of music as their favorite; Rideout et al., 2005). Ethnic differences revealed that African American youths spent more time watching television than Hispanic or Caucasian Americans.

Adolescents' increased access to computers and the Internet gives them much greater access to information. Many adolescents report that their parents are unaware of what they see online (Cameron et al., 2005). In addition, instant messaging has become one of the most popular computer activities in this age group (Rideout et al, 2005). Because research has shown that the exposure to sexuality in the media has been found to be related to adolescent sexual behavior (Pardun et al., 2005), the content of these media is worth exploring. This generation of adolescents is certainly a media generation, but now the question for researchers is: what long-term impact will this have on adolescents?

SOURCE: Rideout et al., 2005.

Figure 18.4

Percentage of 7th- to 12th-graders who have engaged in certain behaviors without the knowledge of their parents.

Source: From "Generation M: Media in the Lives of 8–18 Year-Olds," (#7251), p. 20. The Henry J. Kaiser Family Foundation, March 2005. Reprinted with permission from the Henry J. Kaiser Family Foundation. The Kaiser Family Foundation, based in Menlo Park, California, is a nonprofit, independent national health care philanthropy and is not associated with Kaiser Permanente or Kaiser Industries.

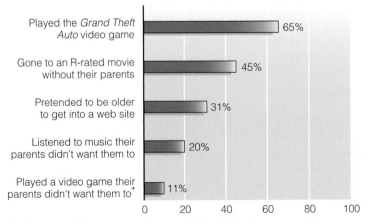

Percentage of 7th- to 12th-graders who say they have ever...

- Played the *Grand Theft Auto* video game — 65%
- Gone to an R-rated movie without their parents — 45%
- Pretended to be older to get into a web site — 31%
- Listened to music their parents didn't want them to — 20%
- Played a video game their parents didn't want them to* — 11%

*Among all 8- to 18-year-olds

Researchers have begun to ask serious questions about the impact of all this television watching, especially because television is so inundated with sexuality and sexual stereotypes. For example, children are very concerned with gender roles, and they often see the world in terms of "boy's" behavior and "girl's" behavior. As we discussed in Chapter 3, children are taught early to behave in gender-appropriate ways, and they quickly begin to tease other children who do not follow these stereotypes (such as effeminate boys). Still, research shows that when children are exposed to books or films that portray nonstereotyped gender behaviors, their gender stereotypes are reduced (Comstock & Paik, 1991).

Historically, many children's shows lacked positive female role models and offered stereotyped portrayals of men and women. For example, although *Sesame Street* has had a human cast of mixed ethnicities and genders and even a number of female muppets, its most notable muppet figures (from Kermit to Bert and Ernie to Big Bird to the Count) have all been male. It was only with the introduction of Zoe in 1993 that a female muppet managed to gain a high profile.

Television executives argue that boys will not watch cartoons with a female lead, but girls will watch cartoons with a male lead, and so it makes more economic sense to produce cartoons featuring males. The result is that it is hard for young girls to find good gender role models in cartoons. It is understandable that researchers have found that more television viewing is correlated with greater sexual stereotyping in certain groups of children (Gunter & McAleer, 1990). However, today the situation is improving, with *Blue's Clues* (Blue is a girl), *Dora the Explorer,* and *Bob the Builder* (Wendy, Bob's sidekick, is more handy than Bob).

One might also wonder what effect television has on the developing sexuality of children and adolescents. We know that sex is a common theme on many television programs today. How does this affect the sexual behavior of teens? Research has shown that increasing sexual content on television is related to early sexual initiation in adolescents (Collins et al., 2004). Teens who watch a lot of television are likely to believe their peers are sexually active. One study found that the more hours of television teens watched, the more likely they were to perceive their peers as being sexually active (Eggermont, 2005).

Review Question

Identify and explain how television has been found to socialize children from a young age.

Question: *Most kids today know all about sex at an early age. So why are people so uptight about showing nudity on television? What do they think it will do to their kids?*

Even in a society like ours, which has begun to discuss sex more openly, it is still a difficult subject for children to understand. Many parents believe that it is their job to introduce the topic to their children, to explain it to them, and to teach their children whatever values the parents believe are appropriate. This may be undermined when children see fairly uncensored sexuality on television, which is usually shown without any discussion of values and without any way to address the children's questions about what they are seeing. In the accompanying Sex in Real Life, "Generation M," we talk about research on the media consumption habits of children and teenagers.

The Movement Against the Sexualization of the Visual Media

The irony is that networks have turned to sex to increase their ratings, yet the constant presence of sexual themes on television is beginning to turn viewers away. The majority of Americans want stronger regulation of sexual content and profanity (Kunkel et al., 2005).

Portrayal of sexuality in movies has also long been a source of controversy. There was no control over motion picture content until the 1930s, when the industry began

How Do Movies Rate?

Have you ever wondered how movies get the ratings they do? Ratings are assigned by the Motion Picture Association of America (MPAA) to advise audiences about the age-appropriateness of movies (Federman, 2002). The producer submits a film for rating by a select group of 8 to 13 MMPA members, who view the film and assign a rating. After a rating is assigned, the producer can decide to keep that rating, edit and resubmit the film for a revised rating, or release the film without a rating (NR). Today ratings include:

G = General audiences
PG = Parental guidance suggested; not suitable for children
PG-13 = Parents strongly cautioned; film inappropriate for children under the age of 13
R = Restricted
NC-17 = No one under 17 admitted

These categories—and, for that matter, the whole rating system—are controversial. First, the criteria change over time; what is allowed in many PG-13 movies today probably would have earned an R rating not too long ago, and many of today's R movies would have been called pornographic. Also, rating standards seem to focus on sexuality and ignore excessive violence; there is little problem showing a body being blown to bits, but a couple cannot be shown making love.

Research has found that 84% of parents use film ratings in deciding what movies they will let their children watch (Federman, 2002). However, studies have also found that these ratings systems tend to attract the very audience that the MPAA is trying to discourage. A film with a PG-13 or an R rating is viewed as more attractive to young viewers than one with a G rating (Federman, 1997). But perhaps this applies to only half of the young population: more recent research has found that boys are more likely to avoid G-rated movies and seek PG-13 and R films, whereas girls show no statistically significant differences in their desire for a certain rating (Federman, 2002).

---

policing itself with The Motion Picture Code (see the accompanying Sex in Real Life, "How Do Movies Rate?"). But the rating system has not stopped the movies from trying to be as sexually explicit as they can within their rating categories. Hollywood seems to try to push the limits of the R rating as far as possible, and a number of directors have had to cut sexually explicit scenes out of their movies. In fact, some movies are made in two or three versions; the least sexually explicit version is for release in the United States, a more explicit copy is released in Europe (where standards are looser), and a third, even more explicit version, is released on DVD.

A backlash does seem to be developing, and Hollywood has been reducing the sexual explicitness of its general release movies. Michael Medved (1992), a noted movie critic, argued in his book *Hollywood vs. America* that the movie and television industries are out of touch; too dedicated to violence, profanity, and sex; and do not really understand what consumers want to see on television and in the movies. He claimed that G- and PG-rated movies actually make more money than R-rated movies.

However, some of the shows boycotted by groups such as the American Family Association get high ratings for the very reasons that they are boycotted: because they are willing to deal with complex issues such as abortion and homosexuality in a frank and honest (if sometimes sensationalistic) manner. It will be interesting to see whether advertisers are scared away by these groups or continue to sponsor provocative and controversial programs.

Advertising: Sex Sells and Sells

Advertising is a modern medium, and its influence pervades modern life. There is practically no area free from its effects, from mass media to consumer products and even to nature itself—billboards obscure our views from highways, and planes drag advertising banners at our beaches. People proudly wear advertisements for soft drinks or fashion designers on their shirts, sneakers, or hats, not realizing that they often spend more for such clothing, paying money to help the company advertise!

According to estimates, children see up to 40,000 advertisements on television every year (TV Turnoff Network, 2005). Studies have shown that advertising has a profound effect on the way children think about the world (forming a mind-set of "products I want to have," for example), and it influences the way they begin to form their ideas of sexuality and gender roles (Durkin, 1985; Gunter & McAleer, 1990).

Advertising and Gender Role Portrayals

In his groundbreaking book *Gender Advertisements*, Erving Goffman (1976) used hundreds of pictures from print advertising to show how men and women are positioned or displayed to evoke sexual tension, power relations, or seduction. Advertisements, Goffman suggested, do not show actual portrayals of men and women but present clear-cut snapshots of the way we *think* they behave. Advertisements try to capture ideals of each sex: men are shown as more confident and authoritative, whereas women are more childlike and deferential (Belknap & Leonard, 1991). Since Goffman's book was published, advertisements have become more blatantly sexual, and analyzing the gender role and sexual content of advertisements has become a favorite pastime of those who study the media.

Although studies indicate that advertising is becoming less sexist today, gender differences still exist (Wolin, 2003). Studies of television commercials, for example, still show differences between the way men and women are portrayed. Men are pictured in three times the number of occupational categories as women, and women are more likely than men to be in commercials that feature the home. Male spokespersons are also commonly used for female products; however, female spokespersons are rarely used to advertise male products (Peirce, 2001).

As you flip through popular magazines today, it's obvious that advertising companies are trying to put more women into ads in positions of authority and dominance. Men are also being shown in traditionally female roles, such as cuddling babies or cooking. However, the naked body is still a primary means of selling products, and even if gender roles are becoming more egalitarian, portrayals of sexuality are still blatant.

Advertising and Portrayals of Sexuality

The purpose of advertising is threefold—to get your attention, to get you physiologically excited, and to associate that excitement with the product being advertised. The excitement can be intellectual, emotional, physical (sports, for example), or visual (fast-moving action, wild colors); but when you think of "getting excited," what immediately comes to mind? Well, that is what comes to the mind of advertising executives also, and so ads often use sexual images or suggestions to provoke, to entice—in short, to *seduce*.

Sexuality (especially female sexuality) has been used to sell products for decades. In an analysis comparing magazine advertisements in 1964 with advertisements in 1984, Soley and Kurzbard (1986) found that although the percentage of advertisements portraying sexuality did not change, sexual illustrations had become more overt and visually explicit by 1984. By the late 1990s, a variety of advertisers, including Calvin Klein and Abercrombie & Fitch, were challenging the limits with advertising campaigns that featured graphic nudity or strong sexual implications. Although Abercrombie was forced to withdraw many of its catalogs because of public outcry, today clothing manufacturers and perfume companies constantly try to out-eroticize each other. Today ads with nudity and sexual innuendo are commonplace.

Not all portrayals of sexuality are this blatant, however. Some are suggestive, such as sprays of soda foam near the face of an ecstatic looking woman, models posing with food or appli-

A recent advertising campaign for the Pirelli fashion collection featured Naomi Campbell and Tyson Beckford naked, wearing only sneakers.

© Handout/Reuters/Corbis

Review Question

Explain how gender roles have been portrayed in various types of advertising.

Calvin Klein was one of the first to use nudity and sex in its advertising.

Calvin Klein Jeans
Tarnished Denim

© Joel Gordon

ances placed in obviously phallic positions, models posed in sexual positions even if clothed, or ads that show women and, less often, men whose faces are contorted in sexual excitement. Some authors even claim that advertisements have tried to use **subliminal** sexuality—pictures of phalluses or breasts or the word *sex* worked into advertisements so they cannot be seen without extreme scrutiny (J. Levine, 1991). Whether these strategies work is a matter of much debate, but Calvin Klein's ads were so provocative that news reports about them appeared in newspapers and on television news shows—and that is just what advertisers want most for their ads and the products they represent, for people to talk and think about them.

subliminal
Existing or functioning below the threshold of consciousness, such as images or words, often sexual, that are not immediately apparent to the viewer of an advertisement, intended to excite the subconscious mind and improve the viewer's reaction to the ad.

Review Question

Explain how sexuality has been portrayed in various types of advertising.

Other Media: Music Videos, Virtual Reality, and More

There are other forms of media that we have not discussed. Because sexuality pervades our lives, it also pervades our art and our media. Today sex-advice columns run in many newspapers and magazines across the country. There are also thousands of "900 number" telephone lines offering sexual services of various kinds across the country. People call the number and pay a certain amount per minute (or use their credit cards for a flat fee) and can talk either to other people who have called in on a party line or to professionals who will discuss sex or play the part of the caller's sexual fantasy. These phone lines cater to men and women (though more commonly to men) and to heterosexuals and homosexuals. Even cell phones are now capable of receiving pornographic images and video clips (see the accompanying Sex in Real Life, "Portable Pornography").

We have discussed the power of the Internet throughout this text, but we mention it here once again because the Internet allows for completely unregulated interaction be-

SEX in Real Life

Portable Pornography

You've probably heard people complain that "porn is everywhere today." Although it's a bit of an exaggeration, pornography *has* been creeping into a variety of new places, including cell phones and video iPods. Analysts believe that in the next few years these will become popular devices for accessing pornography because they are small and easy to conceal (Hall, 2005; Regan, 2005), and many of today's cell phones have high-resolution screens and increased memory capabilities that enable them to play videos.

In Europe, cell phone pornography brings in over $100 million a year (Regan, 2005). What makes porn manufacturers optimistic about cell phone porn is that many U.S. consumers are willing to spend extra money for cell phone content. In fact, ringtone sales topped $450 million in the United States in 2005 (Regan, 2005). Consumers are willing to spend money on a variety of other content, including interactive games, downloadable music, sports and weather, instant messaging, and other services.

© Corbis

The major wireless telecommunication carriers are devising a ratings system to prepare for the onslaught of cell phone pornography (this rating system will be similar to the movie rating system—see the Sex in Real Life, "How Do Movies Rate?" on p. 612). Companies such as Hotphones, Pornforyourphone, Voooyeur, Xobile, and Vivid Entertainment have all been working on pornographic content for cell phones. Xobile now offers 2-minute pornographic video clips for 44 cents each (Regan, 2005). Another company, Dirty-Text, Inc., offers pornographic text messaging to cell phones for a fee (Korzeniowski, 2005).

At the same time, other companies are scrambling to develop cell phone blocks for under-age cell phone users. Over the next few years, it will be interesting to keep an eye on these developments. Experts predict that by 2009, sales of portable pornography will reach $200 million in the United States (Hall, 2005; Regan, 2005) and will probably top $2.5 billion worldwide (Korzeniowski, 2005).

tween millions of people. The Internet has generated whole new forms of communications; and, as new forms of media are developed, sexual and gender issues are arising there, too. Literally thousands of sexually explicit conversations, art works, and computer games go zipping through the Internet between the users of computer networks every day. Today anyone with access to a computer, from 10-year-olds to college professors, can have virtually unlimited access to explicit sexual materials on the web.

Computer technology has been taken even one step further: virtual reality (VR). In VR, pictures generated by computer are projected into goggles put over the eyes, and as the head and eyes move, the picture moves accordingly. The user is given the illusion of actually being in the scene before him or her. Recently, enterprising VR producers have been making sexually explicit VR movies that are coordinated with "stimulators" (vibrators) attached to sensors at the groin; one can actually feel as though one is acting in the pornographic scene while the computer responds to the user's own physical states of excitement and stimulates the user to orgasm. Certainly, new forms of media will present challenges to those who want to regulate or control the public's access to sexually explicit materials.

Review Question

Explain how advances in technology have provided people with greater access to sexual content.

GRAPHIC IMAGES: PORNOGRAPHY AND THE PUBLIC'S RESPONSE

Pornography has always aroused passions, but the debate over pornography is particularly active today because pornography is so widely available. People can buy books or magazines at a local store, rent a movie at the video store, tune into a certain channel on cable or satellite TV, or view images on the Internet. Throw in arguments from free-speech advocates, antiporn (and anti-antiporn) feminists, religious groups, presidential commissions, the American Civil Liberties Union, and a powerful pornography industry, and you can begin to see the extent of the fights that have developed over this issue.

Question: I've heard that men and women who are looking for child pornography often use the Internet. What kind of images do they look for? How often do they get caught?

Although the distribution of child pornography is illegal and banned by federal law in all 50 states, the crimes still occur. Research has found that from 2000 to 2001 an estimated 1,713 nationwide arrests were made for Internet-related crimes involving the possession of child pornography (Wolak et al., 2005). Those who were arrested all had access to minor children, either by living with them, through a job, or in organized youth activities. The majority were Caucasian (91%), older than 25 (86%), and unmarried (Wolak et al., 2005). When law officials reviewed the child pornography that offenders had in their possession, they found 83% had images of 6- to 12-year-olds; 39% had images of 3- to 5-year-olds; and 19% had images of children under the age of 3. These images contained children involved in a range of sexual behaviors including oral sex, genital touching, and penetration (Wolak et al., 2005).

Defining Obscenity: "Banned in Boston"

We begin this section by reviewing the disputes over the legal and governmental definitions of pornography as they have been argued in presidential commissions and in the highest courts in the country. Then we look at how those same debates are discussed among the scholars and activists who try to influence the country's policies toward pornography. We also examine the basic claim of modern opponents of pornography:

sex byte

Annual worldwide revenues generated from pornography are estimated to range from $31 billion to $75 billion (Korzeniowski, 2005).

that pornography is harmful in its effects on individuals and society as a whole. Finally, we examine the public's attitudes toward pornography.

Court Decisions

The First Amendment to the Constitution of the United States, enacted in 1791, includes the words: "Congress shall make no law . . . abridging the freedom of speech, or of the press." Ever since, the court system has struggled with the meaning of those words, for it is obvious that they cannot be taken literally; we do not have the right to make false claims about other people, lie in court under oath, or, in the most famous example, "yell 'fire' (falsely) in a crowded theater," even though that limits our freedom of speech.

Court cases in the United States have established the following three-part definition of obscenity that has determined how courts define pornography. For something to be obscene it must (1) appeal to the **prurient** (PRURE-ee-ent) interest; (2) offend contemporary community standards; and (3) lack serious literary, artistic, political, or scientific value.

prurient
Characterized by lascivious thoughts; used as criterion for deciding what is pornographic.

Personal Voices

I Want to Be a Porn Star!

Alan and Chris are a typical couple, although Alan is 8 years older than Chris. One evening while out with buddies at a strip club, Alan was asked whether he would like to have the chance to appear in a porn video. Following, he and Chris talk about this experience.

Alan: It's not like I've always wanted to be a porn star. Of course I've wondered what the lifestyle would be like, and how I would perform if I were one.

One night we learn that a famous porn star, Ginger Lynn, is dancing at a local strip club. We go to see her, and after her dance she offers to sign autographs. She also mentions that she is sponsoring a competition to earn a chance to star in an adult porno film with her. I was intrigued and decided to approach her to ask her about it. After speaking with her for a while about the opportunity she took some information from me and told me that she would call me.

I'll never forget my telephone conversation with my girlfriend later that night: "Hi babe, guess what? I'm gonna be a porn star!" The conversation didn't go so well after that, but we got past it.

After a battery of tests to check for STIs, I flew out west to make my porn debut a few months later. I was given $700 to pay for travel expenses and my "services." My head was spinning on the plane because I was consumed by anticipation, excitement,

Bert Loewenherz/Getty Images

nervousness, and fear. I was mostly worried about my relationship with my girlfriend. I knew that she was having a hard time understanding why I wanted to do this. To be honest, I wasn't even sure why I wanted to do it. I guess I looked at it as the opportunity of a lifetime. But I still questioned it. Was I trying to prove something?

It is hard to explain the feelings I had when I first arrived to the set where the filming would take place. There were many people walking around freely observing the sex scenes while they were being filmed. The people there were all very courteous and professional. Each of us was taken aside and asked about what types of scenes and sex acts we were willing to participate in. The producers stressed that we should not participate in anything we were uncomfortable with.

The days on the set were long. There were about a dozen each males and females participating, and each of us had to do a minimum of three scenes, each scene lasting about an hour. The male performers were encouraged to take a Viagra pill for insurance after consulting the onsite doctor.

On this first day I participated in two scenes. The first involved an oral sex competition with seven girls and seven guys. The guys serviced the girls first while the girls were blindfolded. We had to kneel and perform cunnilingus on each girl for three minutes. By a

But these criteria are not without critics. Important questions remain about topics such as the definitions of community standards and prurient interest, and who gets to decide. Some argue that the criteria of prurience, offensiveness, and community standards turn moral fears into legal "harms," which are more imaginary than real, and so we end up with arbitrary discussions of what is "prurient" and which speech has "value" (I. Hunter et al., 1993). On the other hand, antiporn feminists argue that pornography laws were made to reflect a male preoccupation with "purity" of thought and insult to moral sensibilities and to ignore the true harms of pornography: the exploitation of women (which we'll explore shortly; R. J. Berger et al., 1991).

Review Question

Explain how courts define pornography and obscenity.

Presidential Commissions

Although presidential commissions date back to George Washington, they became more popular in the 20th century (Rosenbaum, 2005). As of 2005, a total of 46 presidential commissions had been established, examining issues such as bioethics, chemical warfare, and terrorist attacks. These commissions issued detailed reports and recommended

show of fingers in the air the girls were asked to "score" the guys on a scale of 1 to 10. There was a cash prize for the guy with the highest score.

The second scene was much like the first only it involved the guys seated on the couches and the girls on their knees. I was blindfolded and each of the seven girls came around and gave me oral sex for three minutes each. When each of the girls had given action to each of us, we removed our blindfolds to watch the grand finale—our ejaculations. During all the scenes the cameramen moved around freely filming video and taking still photos.

My third scene was filmed on the final day of shooting. I was to be dominated by two women. We participated in a kinky threesome the likes of which I have never known. The women performed oral sex on each other and on me. We switched positions repeatedly, and there was much groping and licking. The scene lasted for about an hour, but the time seemed to go by very quickly. At one point I was lying down and one girl was sitting on my face while the other was sucking on my cock.

The experience was very interesting. Although I was glad to have the experience I did not find that it was an appealing career for me to pursue, and I have been troubled by the potential aftermath of my participation. I realize that I might lose my relationship with Chris because of my participation in this event. I have often wondered if jealousy would drive her to cheat on me. I also wonder if she'll think more about it and decide to let me go because she is so unhappy that I would partake in such an undertaking.

Chris: When I think of Alan's experience my thoughts go back and forth. There are some days that I am glad that he went; after all, this was a once in a lifetime opportunity for him. But then there are days when just thinking about my boyfriend having any sexual contact with other women makes me sick to my stomach.

What was I thinking to let him go? I still don't know, but I do know that I love him, and he still loves me. I think that after all of this our relationship has become much stronger, and I feel like he appreciates me more than before. That's not saying that he didn't before, but now I feel as if he goes as far out of his way as he can to show me that he appreciates me. If he were to have the opportunity to go again he would have to make a choice between going and me, because I want him to only want me. I never had to tell him that, he already knows. But I don't think that he really wants to go again. He tells me that he is glad that he had the opportunity to go, but it's not his thing (and I cannot tell you how happy I was to hear that!). I hope that over time this whole experience will be nothing more than that, just another experience in my relationship with him. Someday soon, it will be a thing in our past, because we are moving on together toward a bright future.

Author's Note: Chris and Alan's relationship ended about a year after Alan's adult film experience. The porn video was troubling to Chris and difficult for her to come to terms with. Alan felt guilty but was still happy for the opportunity to be involved in the video. In the end, they decided to go their separate ways.

Source: Author's files.

changes in public policy. Even though presidential commissions often do not lead to an adoption of new policies, they do help educate Americans about important issues. Now we'll explore two of the commissions on pornography.

1970 Commission on Obscenity and Pornography   In 1967, President Lyndon Johnson set up a commission to study the impact of pornography on American society. The commission was headed by a behavioral scientist who brought on other social scientists, and although the commission also included experts in law, religion, broadcasting, and publishing, its findings were based on empirical research, and much of its $2 million budget was used to fund more scientific studies (Einsiedel, 1989). The commission (which used the terms *erotica* or *explicit sexual material* rather than *pornography*), studied four areas: pornography's effects, traffic and distribution of pornography, legal issues, and positive approaches to cope with pornography (R. J. Berger et al., 1991).

The 1970 Commission operated without the benefit of the enormous research on pornography that has appeared in the last 30 years, and so it has been criticized for such things as not distinguishing between different kinds of erotica (for example, violent versus nonviolent); for including homosexuals, exhibitionists, and rapists all under the same category of "sex offenders"; and for relying on poor empirical studies. Still, although calling for more research and better designed and funded studies in the future, the Commission did perform the most comprehensive study of the evidence up until that time and concluded that no reliable evidence was found to support the idea that exposure to explicit sexual materials is related to the development of delinquent or criminal sexual behavior among youths or adults, so adults should be able to decide for themselves what they will or will not read (Einsiedel, 1989).

In other words, the Commission recommended that the state stop worrying so much about pornography, which it saw as a relatively insignificant threat to society. The U.S. Senate was not happy with the Commission's conclusions and condemned them.

The 1986 Attorney General's Commission on Pornography (the "Meese Commission")   In 1985, President Ronald Reagan appointed Attorney General Edwin Meese to head a new commission that he expected to overturn the 1970 Commission's findings. In fact, the official charter of the Meese Commission was to find "more effective ways in which the spread of pornography could be contained" (R. J. Berger et al., 1991, p. 25) and so already assumed that pornography is dangerous or undesirable and needs containment. Whereas the 1970 Commission focused on social science, the Meese Commission listened to experts and laypeople through public hearings around the country, most of whom supported restricting or eliminating sexually graphic materials. Virtually every claim made by antipornography activists was cited in the report as fact with little or no supporting evidence, and those who did not support the Commission's positions were treated rudely or with hostility (R. J. Berger et al., 1991).

The Meese Commission divided pornography into four categories: violent pornography, "degrading" pornography (e.g., anal sex, group sex, homosexual depictions), nonviolent/nondegrading pornography, and nudity. The Commission used a selection of scientific studies to claim that the first two categories are damaging and may be considered a type of social violence, and that they hurt women most of all. Overall, the Meese Commission came to the opposite conclusions of the 1970 Commission and made a number of recommendations:

- Antipornography laws were sufficient as they were written, but law enforcement efforts should be increased at all levels.
- Convicted pornographers should forfeit their profits and be liable to have property used in production or distribution of pornography confiscated, and repeat offenses against the obscenity laws should be considered felonies.
- Religious and civic groups should picket and protest institutions that peddle offensive materials.
- Congress should ban obscene cable television, telephone sex lines, and child pornography in any form.

sex byte

Pornography has become more popular among both college-aged men and women today; however, men have been found to use pornography more than women (Seidman, 2004). Men are also more likely to use porn while they are alone and masturbate, whereas women are more likely to watch porn with a partner without masturbation (Seidman, 2004).

Reaction to the Meese Commission was immediate and strong. Many of the leading sexuality researchers cited by the Commission in support of its conclusions condemned the report and accused the Commission of intentional misinterpretation of their scientific evidence. The Moral Majority, the religious right, and conservative supporters hailed the findings as long overdue. Women's groups were split on how to react to the report. On the one hand, the report used feminist language and adopted the position that pornography damages women. Antiporn feminists saw in Meese a possible ally to get pornography banned or at least restricted and so supported the Meese Commission's conclusions, if not its spirit. Other women's groups, however, were very wary of the Commission's antigay postures and conservative bent, and they worried that the report would be used to justify wholesale censorship.

Review Question

Discuss and differentiate between the two commissions on pornography, and explain the findings of each.

SEX Talk

Question: *I've watched pornography, and I'm just curious about condom use. Are there any rules about using condoms on the sets of pornographic movies?*

Male and female adult film actors are not legally required to wear condoms during filming. Some production companies may require condoms, but producers argue that what sells best is "real" sex without without condoms (Madigan, 2004). Actors are required to undergo monthly testing for sexually transmitted infections, but as you learned from Chapter 15, many infections may not show up in testing until many weeks after a person becomes infected. Some states have begun exploring legislation to require condom use during filming. In fact, in 2004 the California Assembly warned the pornographic-film industry that condoms must be worn or they will write a law to require it (Madigan, 2004).

The Pornography Debates: Free Speech and Censorship

The religious conservative opposition to pornography is based on a belief that people have an inherent human desire to sin and that pornography reinforces that tendency and so undermines the family, traditional authority, and the moral fabric of society (R. J. Berger et al., 1991). Unless strong social standards are kept, people will indulge themselves in individual fulfillment and pleasure, promoting material rather than spiritual or moral values (Downs, 1989). Users of pornography become desensitized to shocking sexual behaviors, and pornography teaches them to see sex as simple physical pleasure rather than a part of a loving, committed relationship. This leads to increased teen pregnancy rates, degradation of females, and rape; in this, at least, the religious conservative antipornography school agrees with the antiporn feminists.

Nowhere has the issue of pornography been as divisive as among feminist scholars, splitting them into two general schools. The antipornography feminists see pornography as an assault on women that silences them, renders them powerless, reinforces male dominance, and indirectly encourages sexual and physical abuse against women. The other side, which includes groups such as the Feminist Anticensorship Taskforce (FACT), argues that censorship of sexual materials will eventually (if not immediately) be used to censor such things as feminist writing and gay erotica and would therefore endanger women's rights and freedoms of expression (Cowan, 1992). Some who argue against the antipornography feminists call themselves the "anti-antiporn" contingent, but for simplicity's sake we will refer to them simply as the "anticensorship" group.

In 2005, Jenna Jameson, one of the most successful female porn stars in the world, recorded "moan tones" to sell as downloadable ringtones for cell phones.

AP Photo/Amy Sussman via Jennifer Graylock

Review Question

Identify the two schools of thought regarding the pornography debate.

Antipornography Arguments

One of the scholars who has written most forcefully and articulately against pornography is Catherine MacKinnon (1985, 1987, 1993). MacKinnon argues that pornography cannot be understood separately from the long history of male domination of women and that it is in fact an integral part and a reinforcing element of women's second-class status. According to MacKinnon, pornography is less about sex than power. She argues that pornography is a discriminatory social practice that institutionalizes the inferiority and subordination of one group by another, the way segregation institutionalized the subordination of blacks by whites.

MacKinnon suggests that defending pornography on First Amendment terms as protected free speech is to misunderstand the influence of pornography on the every-day life of women in society. She suggests thinking of pornography itself as a violation of a woman's right not to be discriminated against, guaranteed by the Fourteenth Amendment. Imagine, she suggests, if the thousands of movies and books produced each year by the pornographic industry were not showing women, but rather Jews, African Americans, the handicapped, or some other minority splayed naked, often chained or tied up, urinated and defecated on, with foreign objects inserted into their orifices, while at the same time physical assaults and sexual assaults against that group were epidemic in society (as they are against women). Would people still appeal to the First Amendment to prevent some kind of action?

Other feminists take this argument a step further and claim that male sexuality is by its nature subordinating; Andrea Dworkin (1981, 1987), for example, is uncompromising about men and their sexuality. Dworkin, like MacKinnon, sees pornography as a central aspect of male power, which she sees as a long-term strategy to elevate men to a superior position in society by forcing even strong women to feign weakness and dependency. Even sexuality reflects male power: Dworkin sees every act of intercourse as an assault, because men are the penetrators and women are penetrated.

Because pornography is harmful in and of itself, such authors claim, it should be controlled or banned. Although they have not had much success passing such laws in the United States, their strong arguments have set the agenda for the public debate over pornography.

Review Question

Identify and explain the antipornography arguments.

Anticensorship Arguments

A number of critics have responded to the arguments put forth by people like MacKinnon and Dworkin (Kaminer, 1992; Posner, 1993; Wolf, 1991). First, many argue that a restriction against pornography cannot be separated from a restriction against writing or pictures that show other oppressed minorities in subordinate positions. Once we start restricting all portrayals of minorities being subordinated, we are becoming a society ruled by censorship. Many Hollywood movies, television shows, and even women's romance novels portray women as subordinate or secondary to men; are all of those to be censored, too? MacKinnon seems to make little distinction between *Playboy* and movies showing violent rape; are all sexual portrayals of the female body or of intercourse harmful to women?

Also, what about lesbian pornography, in which the models and the intended audience are female, and men almost wholly excluded? Many of these portrayals are explicitly geared toward resisting society's established sexual hierarchies; should they also be censored (Henderson, 1991)? Once sexually explicit portrayals are suppressed, anticensorship advocates argue, so are the portrayals that try to challenge sexual stereotypes.

A more complicated issue is the antiporn group's claim that pornography harms women. One response is to suggest that such an argument once again casts men in a more powerful position than women and, by denying women's power, supports the very hierarchy it seeks to dismantle. But the question of whether it can be demonstrated that pornography actually harms women is a difficult one.

Review Question

Identify and explain the anticensorship arguments.

Studies on Pornography and Harm

Both sides of the pornography debate produce reams of studies that support their side; the Meese Report and antiporn feminists such as MacKinnon and Dworkin produce papers showing that pornography is tied to rape, assault, and negative attitudes toward women, and others produce studies showing that pornography has no effects or is secondary to more powerful forces (W. A. Fisher & Barak, 1991). More recent experts argue that pornography is linked to failed relationships and negative attitudes about women (Paul, 2005). Who is right?

SEX Talk

Question: *I agree that in many cases pornography is degrading to women, but I still find it turns me on. How can I find something to be disgusting intellectually and yet still find it sexually arousing?*

Sexuality, as we have emphasized, is a complicated, often confusing part of life. Sexual arousal has physiological, psychological, and social aspects to it that combine in different ways in different people, which is what makes studying sexuality so interesting. Pornography often tries to bypass the brain and shoot right for the groin, in the sense that it shows sexuality in its most obvious, raw, and uncreative forms. There is no reason to feel guilty that pictures of sexual situations are arousing to you. However, if you want to avoid looking at pictures that are demeaning to women, you may want to search out erotic materials that treat the sexes with greater equality. Erotic videos, pictures, and magazines that treat both sexes with respect, often produced by women, are now widely available, and you may find them just as stimulating.

Society-Wide Studies

In 1969, J. Edgar Hoover, Director of the F.B.I., submitted evidence to the Presidential Commission on Obscenity and Pornography claiming that police observation had led him to believe that:

> A disproportionate number of sex offenders were found to have large quantities of pornographic materials in their residences . . . more, in the opinion of witnesses, than one would expect to find in the residences of a random sample of non-offenders of the same sex, age, and socioeconomic status, or in the residences of a random sample of offenders whose offenses were not sex offenses. (Quoted in I. Hunter et al., 1993, p. 226)

Correlations like these have been used since the early 19th century to justify attitudes toward pornography (I. Hunter et al., 1993). Such claims are easily criticized on scientific grounds because a "witness's opinion" cannot be relied on (and there has never been a study that has reliably determined the amount of pornography in the "average" nonoffender or non–sex offender's home). Better evidence is suggested in the state-by-state studies (Baron & Straus, 1987; J. E. Scott & Schwalm, 1988). Both groups of researchers found a direct nationwide correlation between rape and sexually explicit magazines: rape rates are highest in those places with the highest circulation of sex magazines.

On the other hand, Denmark, which has no laws against pornography at all, and Japan, in which pornography is sold freely and tends to be dominated by rape and bondage scenes, have low rates of reported rape, relative to the United States (Posner, 1993). In a study of four countries over 20 years, Kutchinsky (1991) could find no increase in rape relative to other crimes in any of the countries, even as the availability of pornography increased dramatically. Baron (1990), the same researcher who found that rape rates correlated with explicit magazines, did a further study, which showed that gender equality was higher in states with higher circulation rates of sexually explicit magazines. This may be because those states are generally more liberal. Women in societies that forbid or repress pornography (such as Islamic societies) tend to be more oppressed than those in societies where it is freely available. All in all, the effects of pornography on a society's violence toward women are far from clear.

Individual Studies

Several laboratory studies have sought to determine the reactions of men exposed to different types of pornography. In most cases, men are shown pornography, and then a test is done to determine whether their attitudes toward women, sex crimes, and the like are altered. Although little evidence indicates that nonviolent, sexually explicit films provoke antifemale reactions in men (Padgett et al., 1989), many studies have shown that violent or degrading pornography does influence attitudes. Viewing sexual violence and degradation increases fantasies of rape, the belief that some women secretly desire to be raped, acceptance of violence against women, insensitivity to rape victims, desire for sex without emotional involvement, the treatment of women as sex objects, and desire to see more violent pornography (R. J. Berger et al., 1991; W. A. Fisher & Barak, 1991; Linz, 1989).

On the other hand, these studies take place under artificial conditions (would these men have chosen to see such movies if not in a study?), and feelings of sexual aggression in a laboratory may not mirror a person's activities in the real world. It is also unclear how long such feelings last and whether they really influence behavior (Kutchinsky, 1991). Other studies show that men's aggression tends to increase after seeing any violent movie, even if it is not sexual, and so the explicit sexuality of the movies may not be the important factor (Linz & Donnerstein, 1992).

What Is Harm?

Lahey (1991) argues that the attempt to determine the effects of viewing pornography misses the point because once again the focus is on men and their reactions; is it not enough that women feel belittled, humiliated, and degraded? The voice of women is silent in pornography studies. The questions focus on whether pornography induces sexual violence in men. Pornography, Lahey (after MacKinnon and Dworkin) argues, harms women by teaching falsehoods about women (that they enjoy painful sex, are not as worthy as men, secretly desire sex even when they refuse it, and do not know what they really like); it harms women's self-esteem; and it harms women by reproducing itself in men's behavior toward women.

Certainly, there is an argument to be made that certain kinds of sexually explicit materials contribute little to society and cause much pain directly and indirectly to women. Many who defend sexually explicit materials that show consensual sex abhor the violent and degrading pornography that is the particular target of feminist ire. Whether the way to respond to such materials is through new laws (which may do little to stop its production; for example, child pornography, which is illegal, flourishes in the United States; Wolak et al., 2005) or through listening to the voices of women, who are its victims, is an open question.

Online Pornography

The online pornography industry is quickly growing and was worth approximately $1 billion in 2003 (Griffiths, 2003). Many of the online buying features available through websites today (such as real-time credit card processing) were developed by the pornography industry (Griffiths, 2003). This is not surprising, because research has found that 69% of U.S. Internet spending is for sex-related products (Griffiths, 2003). The accessibility, anonymity, and ease of use have all contributed to the growing popularity of the Internet. Some view pornographic images online, visit sexually oriented chat rooms, or may engage in sexual activities with an anonymous person online (Schneider, 2000a).

Many men and women visit online sexual websites, although typical users are male (Cooper et al., 1999; Paul, 2005). Females do visit sexual websites; however, they are more likely to visit sexually oriented chat rooms, whereas male users more likely to view online porn (Schneider, 2000a).

Online sex users can be either *recreational users* (those who enter sites out of curiosity or for entertainment), *at-risk users* (those who are increasingly drawn to usage of online sexually oriented materials), or *compulsive users* (those who spend over 11 hours per week engaging in online sexual activities; Cooper et al., 1999). Research has found that approximately 83% of online sex users are recreational users; 11% are at-risk users, and 6% are compulsive users (Cooper et al., 1999). Individuals who engage in compulsive online sex often experience changes in their intimate relationships. In fact, one study found 68% of users lost interest in sex with their partner (Schneider, 2000b). Partners

Review Question

Describe the studies that have been done examining pornography and harm.

sex byte

Men who watch pornographic videos containing images of naked men with a woman have been found to have higher quality sperm than men who watch similar videos containing only women (Kilgallon & Simmons, 2005). Researchers suggest this is due to a perceived sperm competition, wherein a male produces higher quality sperm when there is a threat of a female choosing another male.

and children of users also experience psychological side effects as well, including depression and loneliness (Paul, 2005).

Users of online pornography also report a desensitization to pornography over time. One 30-year-old user explains:

> In the last couple of years, the more porn I've viewed, the less sensitive I am to certain porn that I used to find offensive. The sheer quantity of porn on the 'net has done this. It's so easy to click on certain things out of curiosity in the privacy of your own home and the more you see them, the less sensitized you are. I used to only be into softcore porn showing the beauty of the female body. Now I'm into explicit hardcore. (Schneider, 2000)

It will be interesting to see what happens to online pornography over the next few years. There is a tremendous draw to online porn because it reduces embarrassment and allows individuals to watch and buy pornography in the privacy of their own home. But we know that accessing online pornography, visiting sexually oriented chat rooms, and engaging in sexual activity can potentially escalate into more intense usage and have serious consequences, including potential job and partner loss (Paul, 2005; Schneider, 2000a).

What the Public Thinks About Pornography

It is not only scholars and activists who disagree about pornography; the general public seems profoundly ambivalent about it as well. The majority want to ban violent pornography and feel that such pornography can lead to a loss of respect for women, acts of violence, and rape. Female erotica and soft-core pornography are generally not viewed as negatively. One of the biggest producers of female erotica is Candida Royalle, who had previously been an adult film actress. Royalle is the founder of Femme Productions, which has produced over sixteen soft-core pornography videos for women and couples.

Unlike many other businesses today, America's pornography industry continues to do well. One study found that the porn industry generated $10 billion in 1998 alone (Wilborn, 2002). Video and computer technology continues to open doors to millions and millions of customers throughout the world. Even so, pornography is a difficult, controversial problem in American society. By arguing that sex is the only part of human life that should not be portrayed in our art and media, the core conflict over sexuality is revealed: people seem to believe that although sexuality is a central part of human life, it should still be treated differently than other human actions, as a category unto itself.

Sneak Peek

"My best friend is an exotic dancer. I think it's a degrading way to earn a living, but she says it's just like any other job."—*My Best Friend Is an Exotic Dancer*

Sexuality Now

Review Question

Discuss public attitudes toward pornography.

SELLING SEX

Thus far we have explored how sexual images have been used to sell everything from blue jeans to perfume and how sex has been used in television and films to increase viewership and ratings. We also looked at pornography's history, its growing presence on the Internet, and the public's response to it. Now we will turn our attention to the selling of sex through prostitution.

Defining Prostitution

Researchers have found the study of prostitution a challenge, because the exact size of the population is unknown, making a representative sample difficult to come by (Shaver, 2005). Also, because prostitution is illegal, many prostitutes are hidden, so their behaviors cannot be measured.

Defining prostitution is not easy. The U.S. legal code is ambiguous about what constitutes prostitution; for instance, some state penal codes define prostitution as the act of hiring out one's body for sexual intercourse, whereas other states define prostitution as sexual intercourse in exchange for money or as any sexual behavior that is sold for profit. Some consider erotic dancers and models to be a form of prostitution (Dalla, 2002).

SEX in Real Life

Am I a Prostitute?

Dictionaries also have different definitions for prostitution. For example, the *Oxford English Dictionary* defines prostitution as "offering of the body to indicate lewdness for hire," whereas the *American Heritage Dictionary* defines a prostitute as "a person who solicits and accepts payment for sexual intercourse." Take a moment to read over the scenarios in the accompanying Sex in Real Life, "Am I a Prostitute?" Based on the first definition, Sue, Will, and Tim are prostitutes; but, by the second definition, only Sue could be considered a prostitute. For our purposes in this chapter, we define prostitution as the act of a male or female engaging in sexual activity in exchange for money or other material goods.

Over the course of time, prostitutes have been called many slang terms, such as "whores," "hookers," "sluts," or "hustlers." Some other terms often used when discussing prostitution include a **pimp,** who may act as a protector and business manager for many prostitutes; and a **madam,** who is in charge of managing a home, **brothel,** or group of prostitutes. A **john** is a person who hires a prostitute, and a **trick** is the service that the prostitute performs (although recently *trick* has come to mean the same as *john*). Historically, most prostitutes worked in brothels, although with the exception of certain areas of Nevada, few brothels remain in the United States. However, brothels are still widespread in the Asian world.

Sociological Aspects of Prostitution

Society has created social institutions such as marriage and the family in part to regulate sexual behavior. However, it is also true that throughout history, people have had sexual relations outside these institutions. Prostitution has existed, in one form or another, as long as marriage has, which has led some to argue that it provides a needed sexual release. Whether a society should recognize this by allowing legal, regulated prostitution, however, raises a number of controversial social, political, economic, and religious questions.

Some sociologists suggest that prostitution developed out of the **patriarchal** nature of most societies. In a society in which men are valued over women and men hold the reins of economic and political power, some women exploit the only asset that cannot be taken away from them—their sexuality. Other sociologists used to claim that women actually benefited from prostitution because, from a purely economic point of view, they get paid for giving something away that is free to them. Kingsley Davis, one of the most famous sociologists of this century, wrote:

> The woman may suffer no loss at all, yet receive a generous reward, resembling the artist who, paid for his work, loves it so well that he would paint anyway. Purely from the angle of economic return, the hard question is not why so many women become prostitutes, but why so few of them do. (As quoted in Benjamin, 1961, p. 876)

Review Question

Identify the factors that sociologists believe helped foster the development of prostitution.

Who Becomes a Prostitute?

It is estimated that there are as many as 2 million prostitutes working in the United States today, some full time and some part time. Although there are more female prostitutes with male clients than all other forms combined, there are also gay, lesbian, and straight male prostitutes (Goode, 1994; Perkins & Bennett, 1985).

What motivates a man or woman to sell sex for money? Is it the money? Is it fear? Is it necessity? The majority of prostitutes say that their primary and maybe even sole motivation for prostituting is for the money (Rio, 1991). Prostitutes can make more money, on average, than their peers who work conventional jobs.

Many prostitutes say that the major drawback to their job is having to engage in sex with their clients. It is a myth that women become prostitutes because they love sex or because they are "sex addicts." Those involved in the prostitution subculture say that if a prostitute enjoys sexual intercourse with clients, it "gets in her way" (Goode, 1994) because she may lose sight of the importance of client pleasure, or she might want to spend more time with a particular client, which could reduce her income. One prostitute said:

> I would say that nothing could prompt me to have an orgasm or even become excited with a john. . . . I doubt that I would be able to manage it. . . . I will always pretend to be excited, and to come at the moment he comes, but if I really got excited I would be all involved with myself, and the timing would be thrown off, and actually he wouldn't have a good time as if I were faking it. It's funny to think of, but he gets more for his money if it's a fake than if he were to get the real thing. (Wells, 1970, p. 139)

The majority of prostitutes do not enjoy their work. In fact, one study found that 89% of female prostitutes reported wanting to escape from prostitution (Farley et al., 2003). Most prostitutes work full time, with 49% of their clients repeat customers, including some long-term customers (M. Freund et al., 1989). A regular customer visits the prostitute at least once a week, and some have sexual encounters two or three times each week with the prostitute or spend several hours at a hotel (or one of their homes) together.

SEX Talk

Question: Do prostitutes enjoy having sex?

Having sex with whom? Eighty percent of prostitutes have sexual lives outside of their professional lives (Savitz & Rosen, 1988). As for sex with clients, some prostitutes report that they enjoy both sexual intercourse and oral sex, although the majority do not. Some do experience orgasms in their interactions with clients, but again, the majority do not. In fact, in Masters and Johnson's early research on sexual functioning, they included prostitutes (see Chapter 2) but found that the pelvic congestion in prostitutes, which resulted from having sex without orgasms, made them poor subjects for their studies.

Female Prostitutes

In the United States, most female prostitutes are young. The average age of entry into female prostitution is 14 years old (Dittmann, 2005). One study found that 75% of prostitutes were younger than 25 (Potterat et al., 1990). The majority of female prostitutes are single (Medrano et al., 2003).

pseudofamily

A type of family that develops when prostitutes and pimps live together; rules, household responsibilities, and work activities are agreed on by all members of the family.

Typically, female prostitutes live in an apartment or home with several other prostitutes and one pimp. This is known as a **pseudofamily** (Romenesko & Miller, 1989). The pseudofamily operates much like a family does; there are rules and responsibilities for all family members. The pimp is responsible for protecting the prostitutes, whereas the prostitutes are responsible for bringing home the money. Other household responsibilities are also agreed on. When the female ages and/or the male tires of her, she may be traded like a slave or simply disowned.

Psychological problems are more common in prostitutes than nonprostitutes and more common in older prostitutes (de-Schampheleire, 1990). There are dangers associated with a life of prostitution—stressful family situations and mistreatment by clients or pimps. To deal with these pressures, many prostitutes turn to drugs or alcohol, although many enter prostitution to enable them to make enough money to support their preexisting addictions. One study found that 95% of prostitutes used drugs, including crack, heroin, alcohol, and marijuana (Dalla, 2002). One prostitute said: "It would take a real strong person to prostitute without drugs." Many women who become prostitutes have

Human Sexuality in a Diverse World

Female Prostitution in Australia

*L*ee is a 37-year-old prostitute in Sydney, Australia. She also raises a family at home. Here she talks about her life of prostitution.

I began prostituting when I was nineteen and met some working ladies. I was intrigued by what they were doing and saw the money they had and what they could do with it. . . .

I've made $2,000 in one week, which is very good money. I charge $20 minimum, short time, just for straight sex. That's ten minutes, which will not sound very long to most people, but when you consider that the average male only needs two or three minutes in sex—I had some guys finishing even before they get on the bed. I make all my clients wear a condom and I've put the condom on them and by the time I've turned around to get on the bed they've already blown it. In most of these cases it's the guys who are most apologetic and feel they have fallen down on the job.

I always check my clients both for any disease or body lice. If I am at all wary of a client I always get another girl to double-check. I go to the doctor once a week and get a report within ten minutes. There are some girls who will take anybody and don't use any protection, and they don't know how to check a client properly anyway. Girls on drugs are less careful than they should be, and in the parlors condoms are generally not insisted on.

Clients ask for a range of different sexual activities. It can range from good old-fashioned straight-out sex to swinging from the chandeliers. Apart from bondage and discipline there are some weird requests such as golden showers, spankings and whippings, and the guy who wants a girl to shit on a glass-top table with him underneath the table. There's money to be made in these things but I won't do them because it's my own individual choice.

As for a typical day for me, I get up between seven and seven-thirty and have the usual argument with getting kids off to school. I do my housework like any other housewife. I have pets, and I have a normal home. I eat, sleep and breathe like any normal human being. I enjoy cooking a lot. I keep my business quite separate from my home life, and the kids don't know what I do, my husband doesn't want to know about it and I don't want to discuss it with him. Work is work. I go to work to work and when I go home and close the doors on the house that's it. My occupation is not all that different from any nine-to-five worker except the hours are better, I'm my own boss, and the pay's better.

Source: Perkins & Bennett, 1985, pp. 71–85.

drug addictions and use the prostitution as a way to help pay for their drugs (Potterat et al., 1998).

Entry into prostitution is often a gradual process (Goode, 1994). At first, the activity may bother them; but, as time goes by, they become accustomed to the life and begin to see themselves and the profession differently. In the accompanying Human Sexuality in a Diverse World, "Female Prostitution in Australia," one woman shares her feelings about her work.

Predisposing Factors

Some common threads run through the lives of many prostitutes. The most common factor, according to researchers, is an economically deprived upbringing (Goode, 1994). However, because high-class prostitutes, who often come from wealthy backgrounds, are less likely to be caught and arrested, research studies may concentrate too much on poorer women.

Early sexual contact with many partners in superficial relationships has also been found to be related to prostitution. Prostitutes are also more often victims of sexual abuse, initiate sexual activity at a younger age, and experience a higher frequency of rape. Intrafamilial violence and past physical and sexual abuse are also common (Earls & David, 1990; Simons & Whitbeck, 1991). Overall, black women who have a history of emotional or physical abuse have been found to be more likely to engage in prostitution than white or Hispanic women with similar abuse (Medrano et al., 2003).

Sexually abused children who run away from home have been found to be more likely to become prostitutes than those who do not run away (Seng, 1989). Perhaps these experiences also affect a woman's decreasing sense of self-esteem. Parents of prostitutes often report experiencing stress due to a history of failed intimate relationships, economic problems, and unstable relationships. In addition, many prostitutes grow up in poor neighborhoods, which provide easy access to prostitution careers because active prostitution circles are common.

Keep in mind that though these factors contribute to a predisposition to prostitution, they do not *cause* a woman to become a prostitute. For example, we know that many prostitutes have had no early sex education either in school or from their family; however, this does not mean that the lack of sex education *caused* them to become prostitutes. Many different roads lead to a life of prostitution.

Types of Female Prostitution

Female prostitutes can solicit their services either in the street, bars, hotels, brothels, massage parlors, as **call girls** or **courtesans,** or out of an **escort agency** (Perkins & Bennett, 1985). These types of prostitutes differ with respect to the work setting, prices charged, and safety from violence and arrest. Streetwalkers make up about 20% of all prostitutes; bar girls, 15%; massage-parlor prostitutes, 25%; hotel prostitutes, 10%; brothel prostitutes, 15%; and call girls, 15% (C. P. Simon & Witt, 1982).

Streetwalkers   Also called street prostitutes, streetwalkers are the most common type of prostitute. To attract customers, they dress in tight clothes and high heels and may work on street corners or transportation stops (Riccio, 1992). This type of prostitution is considered the most dangerous type because streetwalkers are often victims of violence, rape, and robbery (Dalla, 2002; Romero-Daza et al., 2003). For this reason, they usually have a pimp for protection (we will discuss pimps in greater detail shortly).

Streetwalkers generally approach customers and ask them questions such as, "Looking for some action?" or "Do you need a date?" If the client is interested, the prostitute will suggest a price, and they will go to a place where the service can be provided (an alley, car, or cheap hotel room). Typically, streetwalkers are looking to make as much money as possible, and they will try to "hustle" to make more (by suggesting more expensive types of sexual activity).

call girl
A higher-class female prostitute who is often contacted by telephone and may either work by the hour or the evening.

courtesan
A prostitute who often interacts with men of rank or wealth.

escort agency
An agency set up to arrange escorts for unaccompanied males; sexual services are often involved.

Bar Prostitutes Also called bar girls, bar prostitutes work in bars and hustle patrons for drinks and sexual activity. Because they usually work for the bar owner, they try to build up a client's bar bill. Unlike streetwalkers, bar girls have more protection from violence and police arrests. Bar prostitutes typically hand over 40% to 50% of their nightly earnings to the bar manager.

Hotel Prostitutes Prostitutes may be referred to hotel patrons by a bellboy or hotel manager. They keep 40% to 50% of the money they charge clients, and the hotel manager keeps the rest.

Brothel Prostitutes Brothel prostitutes work out of a home or apartment that is shared by a group of prostitutes. A madam or pimp generally runs the house. Brothels offer more protection for prostitutes than the street.

In the United States, Nevada is the only state with counties in which brothels are legal. Prostitutes carry identification cards and are routinely examined for STIs. When a customer walks into a brothel in Nevada, he may be given a "menu" of choices. From this menu he picks an appetizer (such as a hot bath or a pornographic video) and a main course (such as the specific sexual position). Then he can choose a woman from a **lineup,** and the couple go into a private room.

The typical rate is $2 per minute, with more exotic services being more expensive. Usually conventional sexual intercourse costs $30 to $40, and oral sex may cost $50 or more. Prostitutes inspect the client's genitals for signs of sexually transmitted infections and collect payment. The brothel prostitute keeps between 50% and 60% of her earnings, and the rest goes to the brothel owner.

Massage Parlor Prostitutes Some prostitutes are masseuses who also provide sexual services. The owners of the massage parlor act as though they are unaware of this sexual activity. The most common service offered in massage parlors is fellatio or fellatio accompanied by sexual intercourse (Perkins & Bennett, 1985). Prices in massage parlors are typically higher than those charged by streetwalkers, and security guards provide additional protection. However, the trade-off is that a parlor keeps more of the profit earned for working in their establishment.

Escorts Escort services, agencies that provide prostitutes who serve as escorts, operate in ways similar to massage parlors, except that escort services do not have to take the responsibility for sexual activity because it does not occur on their premises. Prices for an escort vary widely and are dependent on location and hours worked.

Call Girls and Courtesans Higher-class prostitution involves both call girls and courtesans (Dalla, 2002). In 1993, Heidi Fleiss, the "Hollywood Madam," was arrested for prostitution activities with Hollywood actors and executives. Today call girls are often contacted by telephone, and they may work by the hour or the evening. Some call girls charge $1,000 or more a night (Perkins & Bennett, 1985). Courtesans are also elite prostitutes, and many would argue that they are not prostitutes at all, even though they exchange sex for very expensive gifts.

Other Types of Prostitutes Other, less common types of prostitutes include **bondage and discipline (B&D) prostitutes** who engage in sadomasochistic services, using such things as leather, whips, and/or chains. Women who specialize in B&D will advertise with pseudonyms like Madam Pain or Mistress Domination (Perkins & Bennett, 1985). B&D prostitutes may have dungeons, complete with whips, racks, and leg irons, and wear black leather, studded belts, and masks. Many do not have sexual intercourse with their clients at all but simply inflict pain or humiliation, which the client finds pleasurable. B&D prostitutes can make good money because few prostitutes choose to specialize in this area.

Lesbian prostitutes also exist, but we know little about them. Lesbian prostitutes tend to be older, and many take a younger woman on as a paid sexual partner (Perkins & Bennett, 1985). Lesbian prostitutes often have only one client at any given time.

---

lineup
The lining up of prostitutes in a brothel so that when clients enter a brothel, they can choose the prostitute they want.

© Corbis Sygma

In a classic movie from 1990, Julia Roberts played a prostitute in Pretty Woman. *Unfortunately, prostitution in the movies is much more glamorous than it is in real life. In this movie, Richard Gere (a millionaire) hires Roberts as a prostitute and falls in love with her.*

bondage and discipline (B&D) prostitute
A prostitute who engages in sadomasochistic sexual services.

Review Question

Describe what the research has found about female prostitutes, and differentiate among the various types of female prostitutes.

Male Prostitutes

Male prostitutes who service women are referred to as **gigolos** (JIG-uh-lows). Traditionally, gigolos are young men who are hired by older women to have an ongoing sexual relationship. Male prostitutes who service other men are referred to as hustlers or "boys." Some male prostitutes service both men and women. In the accompanying Personal Voices, "Male Prostitution," one man discusses his work.

Male prostitutes who have sex with men may be otherwise heterosexual. For example, some bodybuilders hustle gay men for extra money (A. M. Klein, 1989). Ironically, many of these heterosexual, masculine bodybuilders are homophobic, which causes many conflicts between their attitudes and behaviors. Approximately 50% of male prostitutes are homosexual, and 25% each are bisexual or heterosexual (Pleak & Meyer-Bahlburg, 1990). Like women, men tend to enter into the life of prostitution early, usually by the age of 16 (with a range from 12 to 19; Cates & Markley, 1992). The majority of male prostitutes are between the ages of 16 and 29 and white (D. J. West, 1993). Like the pimp for female prostitutes, many male prostitutes also have mentors, or "sugardaddies."

When male prostitutes are asked what types of sexual behavior they engage in with their clients, 99% say that they perform fellatio, either alone or in combination with other activities; 80% say that they engage in anal sex, and 63% participate in **rimming** (Morse et al., 1992). In addition, many reported other activities including **water sports** and/or sadomasochistic behavior.

Predisposing Factors

Like females, males become prostitutes mainly for the money. However, many factors predispose a man to become a prostitute. Early childhood sexual experience (such as coerced sexual behavior), combined with a homosexual orientation, increases the chances of choosing prostitution (Earls & David, 1989). Male prostitutes often experience their first sexual experience at a young age (approximately 12 years old) and have

gigolo
A man who is hired to have a sexual relationship with a woman and receives financial support from her.

rimming
Oral stimulation of the anus.

water sports
Sexual services that involve urinating on or inside one's sexual partner.

Personal Voices

Male Prostitution

*S*tephen is an 18-year-old male prostitute who has been working on the streets since he was 16 or 17 years old. He identifies himself as gay and has sex primarily with male clients.

I only prostitute occasionally—about once or twice a week—but I used to do it nearly every day. I usually work for about two hours at a time until someone picks me up.

I got involved in prostitution because I knew I could make the money. It's taken as quite a common thing to do with the people I hang around with. None of us like it but it's easy money. I don't do it that much anymore but it's there if I need it. I'd like to stop but who's going to pay for the food? There's nothing else I can do to get an income.

The usual procedure is quite simple. I just go to the park, take a seat and wait. Normally I don't have to

wait too long—up to an hour at most. When a customer comes along we work out what's going to happen. We normally go to his place—sometimes mine. We do it, I get paid, he leaves his card or phone number and goes. Normally the whole thing usually takes about an hour and I usually see the guy again—in the next few weeks. But overall there is little preparation involved.

I don't mind doing this. It can be fun at times. You get to make a lot of money, working very small hours—normally everything goes well. If I thought there were better alternatives around (and there aren't), I'd take them, but at the present moment in time I don't mind.

SOURCE: Perkins & Bennett, 1985, pp. 196–199.

older partners. Male prostitutes also have fewer career aspirations than do nonprostitutes and are more likely to view themselves as addicted to either drugs or alcohol (Cates & Markley, 1992). More than 50% of male prostitutes report using alcohol and a variety of drugs with their clients and commonly accept drugs or alcohol as a trade for sex (Morse et al., 1992).

Like female prostitutes, male street prostitutes have more psychopathology than nonprostitute peers (P. M. Simon et al., 1992), which may have to do with their dangerous and chaotic environments. They are more suspicious, mistrustful, hopeless, lonely, and often lack meaningful interpersonal relationships (Leichtentritt & Arad, 2005). These feelings may develop out of the distrust that many have for their clients; clients may refuse to pay for services, hurt them, and/or force them to do things that they do not want to do. In fact, more than half of male prostitutes report that they are afraid of violence while they are hustling (Scott et al., 2005). The majority live alone, with no partner. This may be due to the type of lifestyle they lead or to the sense of hopelessness they carry with them. Although many would like to stop prostituting, they feel that they would not be able to find other employment (P. M. Simon et al., 1992).

Types of Male Prostitution

Male prostitutes, like females, may engage in street hustling, bar hustling, and escort prostitution (Luckenbill, 1984). The differences between these types of prostitution are in income potential and personal safety.

Street and Bar Hustlers Male street and bar hustlers solicit clients on the street or in parks that are known for the availability of the sexual trade. The majority of male prostitutes begin with street hustling, especially if they are too young to get into bars. Male prostitutes, like female prostitutes, ask their clients if they are "looking for some action."

Due to increasing fear and danger on the streets, many street hustlers eventually move into bars. One male prostitute explains:

> You got a lot of different kinds of assholes out there. When someone pulls up and says "get in," you get in. And you can look at their eyes, and they can be throwing fire out of their eyes, and have a knife under the seat. You're just in a bad situation. I avoid it by not hustling in the street. I hustle in the bars now. (Luckenbill, 1984, p. 288)

Male prostitutes also report that bar hustling enables them to make more money than street hustling because they get to set their own prices. The average price for a bar trick ranges from $50 to $75.

Escorts A natural progression after bar hustling is escort prostitution, which involves finding someone who arranges clients but also takes a share of the profits. Each date that is arranged for an escort can bring from $150 to $200, and the prostitute usually keeps 60% for himself. However, escort services are not always well-run or honest operations, and problems with escort operators may force a male prostitute to return to bar hustling. Compared with other types of male prostitutes, however, escort prostitutes are least likely to be arrested.

Call Boys Like call girls, **call boys** keep a small group of clients with whom they have sex occasionally to earn money. Many of these prostitutes have had experience working both on the street and in bars, but they leave to go into business for themselves.

Transsexual and Transvestite Prostitutes Transsexual and transvestite prostitution is more common among male-to-female transsexuals than female-to-male (Perkins & Bennett, 1985). Some male transvestite prostitutes adopt an exaggerated female appearance and work beside female prostitutes (Elifson et al., 1993a), luring unsuspecting clients who do not always realize he is male. Most are homosexual males, but some are **she-males.** After being on hormonal therapy prior to sex reassignment surgery, they develop breasts but also still have a penis.

call boy
A higher-class male prostitute who is often contacted by telephone and may work by either the hour or the evening.

she-male
A slang term that refers to a male who has been on hormones for sex reassignment but has not undergone surgery; she-males often have both a penis and breasts.

Review Question

Describe what the research has found about male prostitutes, and differentiate among the various types of male prostitutes.

Adolescent Prostitutes

What we know about adolescent prostitution is disheartening. For adolescents who run away from home, prostitution offers a way to earn money and to establish their autonomy. Many of these adolescents have been sexually abused and have psychological problems (Gibson-Ainyette et al., 1988; S. J. Thompson, 2005). Adolescent prostitution can have long-term psychological and sociological effects on the adolescents and their families (Landau, 1987).

It is estimated that between 750,000 and 1,000,000 minors run away from home each year in the United States and that more than 85% eventually become involved in prostitution (Landau, 1987). Others prostitute while living at home. See the accompanying Personal Voices, "Adolescent Prostitution," for one adolescent's account.

Pimps look for scared adolescent runaways at train and bus stations and lure them with promises of friendship and potential love relationships. A pimp will approach a runaway in a very caring and friendly way, offering to buy her a meal or give her a place to stay. At first, he makes no sexual demands whatsoever. He buys her clothes and meals and does whatever it takes to make her feel indebted to him. To him, all of his purchases

Personal Voices

Adolescent Prostitution

The following is an account from Lynn, a 13-year-old adolescent prostitute.

It was freezing cold that Friday afternoon as I stood on the street corner looking for buyers. The harsh wind made the temperature feel as though it were below zero, and I had been outdoors for almost two and a half hours already. I was wearing a short fake fur jacket, a brown suede miniskirt and spike heels. Only a pair of very sheer hose covered my legs, and I shook as I smiled and tried to flag down passing cars with male drivers. The cold bit at my skin, but if I had come out dressed in jeans and leg warmers, I'd have never gotten anywhere. After all, I was selling myself, and the merchandise had to be displayed.

Finally, a middle-aged man in an expensive red sports car pulled up to the curb. He lowered the car window and beckoned me over to him with his finger. I braced myself to start my act. Trying as hard as I could to grin and liven up my walk, I went over to his car, rested my chest on the open window ledge and said, "Hi ya, Handsome."

He answered, "Hello, Little Miss Moffet. How'd you like Handsome to warm you up on a cold day like this?" I wished that I could have told him that I wouldn't like it at all. That even the thought of it made me sick to my stomach. He had called me Little Miss Moffet—they always made some remark about my age because I'm so young. Being thirteen has been a strong selling point for me. In any case, I hid my feelings and tried to look enthusiastic. They all want a happy girl who they think wants them. So with the broadest smile I could man-

age, I answered, "There's nothing I'd like better than to be with you, Sir." I started to get into his car, but he stopped me, saying, "Not so fast, Honey, how much is this going to cost me?" I hesitated for a moment. I really wanted twenty dollars, but it had been a slow day and I had a strong feeling that this guy wasn't going to spring for it, so I replied, "Fifteen dollars, and the price of the hotel room."

We had sex in the same run-down dirty hotel that I always take my tricks to. It doesn't cost much, and usually that's all that really matters to them. Being with that guy was horrible, just like it always turns out to be. That old overweight man sweated all over me and made me call him Daddy the whole time. He really smelled bad too, once he got started. He may have thought that he was kissing me, but actually he just slobbered on my body. He kept calling me Marcy, and later he explained that Marcy was his youngest daughter.

Once he finished with me, the guy seemed in a big hurry to leave. He dressed quickly, and just as he was about to rush out the door, I yelled out, "But what about my money?" He pulled a ten-dollar bill out of his back pocket and laid it on the dresser, saying only, "Sorry, kid, this is all I've got on me right now."

At that moment I wished that I could have killed him, but I knew that there was nothing I could do. The middle-class man in the expensive red sports car had cheated his 13-year-old hooker. That meant that I had to go back out on the street and brave the cold again in order to find another taker.

Source: Landau, 1987, pp. 25–26.

are a debt she will one day repay. As soon as the relationship becomes sexual and the girl has professed her love for the pimp, he begins asking her to "prove" her love by selling her body. The girl may agree to do so only once, not realizing the destructive cycle she is beginning. This cycle is based on breaking down her self-esteem and increasing her feelings of helplessness. Male adolescents may enter into the life of prostitution in similar ways. Some may choose a life of prostitution to meet their survival needs or to support a drug habit.

Outside the United States, adolescent prostitution is prevalent in many countries, such as Brazil and Thailand. Female adolescents in Brazil are drawn to prostitution primarily for financial and economic reasons (Penna-Firme et al., 1991). (See Personal Voices "Sexual Trafficking" on page 639.) In Thailand, some parents sell their daughter's virginity for money or act as their managers and arrange jobs for them. One Thai prostitute said:

> I started to work when I was fourteen years old. I worked at a "steakhouse," an entertainment place which was half a nightclub and half a restaurant. During this time, I went out with customers only when I wanted to. I had worked there for about one year before I met one man who took me to a brothel. This man was a friend of a friend. He said he would like to show me the beach. He took us four girls. He did not take us to the beach but to a brothel and he sold us to the owner. Every day I had to receive fifteen men. If I did not obey the owner or did not get many men, I got beaten. I could finally escape from that brothel because one man helped me. (Pheterson, 1989, p. 64)

Other Players in the Business

Prostitutes are not the only people involved in the business. Other players include pimps, clients, and the government.

The Pimp

Review Question

Define and describe a pimp.

Pimps play an important role in prostitution, although not all prostitutes have pimps. In exchange for money, a pimp offers the prostitute protection from both clients and the police. Many pimps take all of a prostitute's earnings and manage the money, providing her with clothes, jewels, food, and sometimes a place to live. A pimp recruits prostitutes and will often manage a group of prostitutes, known as his "stable." His women are known by each other as "wives-in-law" (Ward et al., 1994).

Many pimps feel powerful within their peer group and enjoy the fact that their job is not particularly stressful for them. Pimps often require that their prostitutes make a certain amount of money (Dalla, 2002). In addition, a pimp often has several women working for him, many of whom he is involved with sexually.

The Client

As we discussed earlier, clients of prostitutes are often referred to as "johns," "tricks," or even "kerb crawlers" (Brooks-Gordon & Geisthorpe, 2003). The term *trick* has also been used to describe the behavior requested by the client. This term originated from the idea that the client was being "tricked" out of something, mainly his money (Goode, 1994).

What motivates people to go to prostitutes? An abnormally high sex drive? Variety in their sexual lives? Sigmund Freud believed that some men preferred sex with prostitutes because they were incapable of sexual arousal without feeling that their partner was inferior or a "bad" woman. Carl Jung went a step further and claimed that prostitution was tied to various unconscious **archetypes,** such as the "Great Mother." This archetype includes feelings of hatred and sexuality, which are connected to mother figures. This in turn leads men to have impersonal sex with partners whom they do not love or to whom they have no attraction.

There is much confusion about clients and the reasons they visit prostitutes (Brooks-Gordon & Geisthorpe, 2003). What we do know is that the majority of clients of prostitutes are male (Monto, 2001); and they visit prostitutes for a variety of reasons: for guaranteed sex, to eliminate the risk of rejection, for greater control in sexual encounters, for

archetypes
Ancient images that Carl Jung believed we are born with and influenced by.

Review Question

Describe what the research has found about adolescent prostitutes.

companionship, to have the undivided attention of the prostitute, because they have no other sexual outlets, because of physical or mental handicaps, and for adventure, curiosity, or to relieve loneliness (Jordan, 1997; McKeganey & Bernard, 1996; Monto, 2000). They may also be turned on by engaging in the illicit or risky sex with prostitutes (Monto, 2001). Married men sometimes seek out prostitutes when their wives will not perform certain behaviors, when they feel guilty about asking their wives to engage in an activity, or when they feel the behaviors are too deviant to discuss with their wives (Jordan, 1997).

When men who were arrested for prostitution were asked which sexual behaviors they engaged in with a prostitute, 81% had received fellatio, 55% had engaged in sexual intercourse, while others engaged in a little of both, or manual masturbation (i.e., hand jobs; Monto, 2001). Clients from this study also reported that they believed that oral sex had a lower risk of STI or AIDS transmission than other sexual behaviors.

Sadomasochistic behavior, with the woman as dominant and the man submissive, is the most common form of "kinky" sexual behavior requested from prostitutes (Goode, 1994). Other commonly requested behaviors from prostitutes include clients dressing as women, masturbating in front of nude clients, and rubber fetishes. One prostitute recalled a job in which she was paid $300 to dress up in a long gown and urinate in a cup while her client masturbated, and another was asked to have sex with a client in his daughter's bed (Dalla, 2002).

Clients may also seek out prostitutes because they are afraid of emotional commitments and want to keep things uninvolved; to build up their egos (many prostitutes fake orgasm and act very sexually satisfied); because they are starved for affection and intimacy; or because they travel a great deal or work in heavily male-populated areas (such as in the armed services) and desire sexual activity.

Kinsey found that clients of prostitutes are predominantly white, middle-class, married men who are between the ages of 30 and 60 (Kinsey et al., 1948). More recent research supports Kinsey's findings—the majority of men who visit prostitutes are middle-aged and unmarried (or unhappily married; Monto & McRee, 2005). They also tend to be regular or repeat clients: almost 100% go monthly or more frequently, and half of these go weekly or more frequently (M. Freund et al., 1991). "Regulars" often pay more than new customers and are a consistent source of income (Dalla, 2002).

Male clients are most often solicited in their car on street corners in areas where female prostitution is common, but solicitation can also happen in hotels or transportation stops (Riccio, 1992). Of the clients who seek male prostitutes, almost 75% also go to female prostitutes for sex (Morse et al., 1992). Anal sex and oral sex are the two most popular sexual behaviors requested from male prostitutes (M. Freund et al., 1991).

The majority of clients are not concerned with the police because law enforcement is usually directed at prostitutes rather than clients. However, today more and more police are turning to the clients in order to stop prostitution. Some authorities have gone so far as videotaping license plates and enrolling clients in "John school" to stop their behaviors (B. Fisher et al., 2002).

The Government: Prostitution and the Law

Prostitution is illegal in every state in the United States, except for certain counties in Nevada. However, even though it is illegal, it still exists in almost every large U.S. city. In general, the government could address the issue of prostitution in two ways. Prostitution could remain a criminal offense, or it could be legalized and regulated. If prostitution were legalized, it would be subject to government regulation over such things as licensing, location, health standards, and advertising.

The biggest roadblock to legalized prostitution in the United States is that prostitution is viewed as an immoral behavior by the majority of people (Rio, 1991). Laws that favor legal prostitution would, in effect, be condoning this immoral behavior. Overall, however, the strongest objections to legalized prostitution are reactions to streetwalking. Today, the majority of Americans believe that the potential benefits of legalized prostitution should be evaluated.

Those who feel that prostitution should be legalized believe that this would result in lower levels of sexually transmitted infections (because prostitutes could be routinely

sex byte

The National Health and Social Life Survey found a substantial discrepancy between men's and women's interest in fellatio. Although 45% of men reported receiving fellatio very appealing, only 17% of women found giving it appealing (Monto, 2001). Not surprisingly, fellatio is the most requested sexual behavior from prostitutes (Monto, 2001).

Review Question

Identify the factors that research has found motivate people to use prostitutes.

checked for STIs) and less disorderly conduct. Another argument in favor of legalization is that if prostitution were legal, the government would be able to collect taxes on the money earned by both prostitutes and their pimps. Assuming a 25% tax rate, this gross income would produce $20 billion each year in previously uncollected taxes.

When college students were asked how they felt about the legalization of prostitution, those who scored high on scales of feminist orientation were more likely to view prostitution as an exploitation and subordination of women; they were also less likely to believe that women engage in prostitution for economic needs; and they believed that prostitution should not be legalized (Basow & Campanile, 1990). Overall, women are more likely than men to believe that prostitution should not be legalized and to see prostitution as exploitation and subordination of women (see the accompanying Personal Voices, "Prostitution," for some college students' views).

In Nevada, where prostitution is legal (only in registered brothels, however, not as streetwalking), the overwhelming majority of people report that they favor legalized prostitution. Ordinances for prostitution in Nevada vary by county, with each county responsible for deciding whether prostitution is legal throughout the county, only in certain districts, or not at all.

For instance, there are no legal brothels in Reno or Las Vegas, perhaps because these cities enjoy large conventions and because many men attend these conventions without their wives. City officials felt that if a convention was held in a town with legalized prostitution, many wives might not want their husbands to attend; thus, there would be a decrease in the number of convention participants. Even so, there are several brothels near Reno and Las Vegas and also several that are close to state borders. Usually, these

Personal Voices

Prostitution

College students were asked how they felt about prostitution and whether or not they thought prostitution should be legal. Following are some of their answers.

Female: *Prostitution should be illegal, because it's not healthy and morally wrong.*

Male: *I think prostitution should be legalized. If people want to pay to get laid, and other people are willing to make a career out of it, they should be allowed to. If prostitution was going to be legalized, there should be some rules and regulations and some way to make sure that everyone who is involved is clean and safe to have sex with.*

Female: *Prostitution should be legal simply because there will always be hookers, so why not tax them? Also, legalizing will decrease STI rates.*

Male: *I think everyone can do what they want. It's kinda gross, but if someone wants to sell themselves for money, that's fine with me. I wouldn't ever come near them.*

Female: *Prostitution is disgusting. I don't think anyone should sell themselves, and I don't think anyone should be able to buy sex.*

Male: *Prostitution is one of the dangerous professions because it can spread STIs. I think it should be illegal because it endangers the welfare of the prostitutes and those who go to them.*

Female: *Prostitution should be illegal, because sex should be something special.*

Male: *Prostitution could be legal under certain circumstances. If prostitutes were being safe (and could be prosecuted if not), there wouldn't be a problem.*

Female: *When people prostitute to make money for drug addictions, this is wrong. If they do it to make money for their kids, then it's not right, but I can understand it more.*

Male: *Sex should be an intimate expression of love between two people, not merely a way to make money or have an orgasm.*

SOURCE: Author's files.

are the largest of all the Nevada brothels. Brothels are locally owned small businesses that cater to both local and tourist customers. Although prostitution in Nevada is not a criminal offense, there are laws against enticing people into prostitution, such as pimping or advertising for prostitutes (H. Reynolds, 1986).

Crackdowns on prostitution in other areas of the United States (where prostitution is not legal) often result in driving it further underground. This is exactly what happened in New York City in the 1980s. After law officials cracked down on prostitution in Manhattan, many brothels moved to Queens. Some of the prostitutes began operating out of "massage parlors" or private homes, which were supported through drug money.

There are many groups in the United States and abroad that are working for the legalization of prostitution. In San Francisco in 1973, an organization called COYOTE ("Call Off Your Old Tired Ethics") was formed by an ex-prostitute named Margo St. James to change the public's views of prostitution. Today, COYOTE is regarded as the best-known prostitutes' rights group in the United States. COYOTE's mission is to repeal all laws against prostitution, to reshape prostitution into a credible occupation, and to protect the rights of prostitutes. Members argue that contrary to popular belief, not all prostitution is forced—some women voluntarily choose to prostitute, and so prostitution should be respected as a career choice.

Delores French, a prostitute, author, president of the Florida COYOTE group, and president of HIRE ("Hooking Is Real Employment") argues that:

> A woman has the right to sell sexual services just as much as she has the right to sell her brains to a law firm when she works as a lawyer, or to sell her creative work to a museum when she works as an artist, or to sell her image to a photographer when she works as a model, or to sell her body when she works as a ballerina. Since most people can have sex without going to jail, there is no reason except old fashioned prudery to make sex for money illegal. (Quoted in Jenness, 1990, p. 405)

Review Question

Identify and explain the pros and cons of legalized prostitution.

PROSTITUTION: EFFECTS AND CULTURAL DIFFERENCES

No discussion of prostitution can be complete without examining sexually transmitted infections, life after prostitution, and prostitution in other cultures.

Prostitution and Sexually Transmitted Infections

Most prostitutes are knowledgeable about STIs and AIDS. They try to minimize their risks by using condoms, rejecting clients with obvious STIs, and routinely taking antibiotics. However, although female prostitutes often do feel they are at risk of infection with STIs or AIDS with clients, they usually do not feel this way with their husbands or boyfriends (Dorfman et al., 1992). Condoms are used less frequently with their own sexual partners than with clients. Among homosexual male prostitutes, receptive anal intercourse without a condom is the most common mode of HIV transmission (Elifson et al., 1993a), whereas among female prostitutes, intravenous drug use is the most common mode of HIV transmission.

Many opponents of legalized prostitution claim that legalization would lead to increases in the transmission of various STIs. However, STI transmission and prostitution have been found to have less of a relationship than you might think. Rates of STIs in Europe were found to *decrease* when prostitution was legalized and to *increase* when it was illegal (Rio, 1991). This is probably because when prostitution is legal, restrictions can be placed on the actual practice and medical evaluations are often required. Many prostitutes take antibiotics sporadically to reduce the risk of STIs; however, this practice has led some strains of STIs to become resistant to many antibiotics. Long-term use of antibiotics diminishes their effectiveness in an individual. Also, viral STIs, such as AIDS and herpes, are not cured by antibiotics.

sex byte

Over 60% of prostitutes experience violence while involved in prostitution (Valera, 2000).

Male prostitutes have sex with multiple partners, are exposed to blood and semen, frequently practice high-risk sexual behaviors, and may continue prostituting even after they find out they are HIV-positive. In addition, many have been infected with other STIs, which may make HIV transmission easier (Morse et al., 1991).

Outside the United States, increasing prostitutes' condom use and knowledge about AIDS has been an important task. There has been a lot of attention to AIDS transmission among prostitutes in Africa, for example. In Nigeria, AIDS prevention programs, which include health education, condom promotion and distribution, and a sexually transmitted infection treatment clinic, resulted in two-thirds of prostitutes using condoms (E. Williams et al., 1992). In Somalia, the prevalence of HIV in nonprostitute populations is 16 per 1,000; and, in prostitutes, 30 per 1,000 (Corwin et al., 1991). Men and nonprostitute women knew more about AIDS and preventive information than female prostitutes. In Zaire, 99% of prostitutes reported hearing of AIDS, but only 77% knew that sex was the predominant mode of transmission (Nzila et al., 1991). Seventy-five percent of prostitutes had at least one sexually transmitted disease, and 35% were HIV-positive.

Life After Prostitution

Potterat and colleagues (1990) found that female prostitutes stay in the life for a relatively short time, usually 4 or 5 years. Some feel ready to leave, whereas others are forced out because of a deteriorating physical appearance or because of addiction to drugs or alcohol. Life after prostitution is often grim because most prostitutes have little money and few skills (which is why they turned to prostitution in the first place; Farley et al., 2003). In addition, there is usually little to show for the years they spent prostituting. Some seek psychotherapy as a way to handle leaving prostitution, and others spend a great deal of time in and out of prison for shoplifting or robbery.

Research has found that many prostitutes are raped and physically assaulted as a result of their work. One study found that between 60% and 75% of female prostitutes were raped, whereas 70% to 95% were physically assaulted (U.S. Department of State, 2005). Overall, 68% qualified for a diagnosis of posttraumatic stress disorder. As a result, some resort to suicide as a way out.

Even so, there is a lot of disagreement about whether or not mandatory treatment programs should exist for prostitutes. If a person voluntarily chooses to engage in prostitution and he or she does not feel it is a problem, should the government require that he or she undergo treatment? Even if it were possible to make prostitutes stop prostituting, few resources are available for them to establish a similarly salaried occupation (Rio, 1991). We need to evaluate how to best help a prostitute if he or she decides to stop prostituting. Also, because we have learned that the backgrounds of many prostitutes include a history of sexual abuse, familial violence, and alcohol abuse, perhaps we can offer intervention early on to help these people find alternative ways to make a living.

Prostitution in Other Cultures

Prostitution exists all over the globe. We will now explore how different countries handle prostitution and the different problems they encounter. In the accompanying Human Sexuality in a Diverse World, "In Their Own Words," three women discuss their experiences of prostitution.

During World War II it is estimated that 200,000 women from Japan, Korea, China, the Philippines, Indonesia, Taiwan, and the Netherlands were taken by the Imperial Japanese Army from their hometowns and put in brothels for Japanese soldiers (Kakuchi, 2005). In 1993, Japan finally admitted to having forced women to prostitute themselves as **comfort girls,** and now these women are demanding to be compensated for the suffering they were forced to endure. In 2005, the Women's Active Museum on War and Peace in Tokyo was opened to honor the women who worked as sex slaves during World War II.

In the Philippines, many women were similarly forced into prostitution and were called **hospitality girls.** Although hospitality girls are a thing of the past, today women may freely choose to prostitute and may informally work when they need extra money

Review Question

Explain what has been found about STI knowledge and condom usage in prostitutes.

Review Question

Identify and explain the issues that arise after a prostitute stops prostituting.

comfort girl
A woman in Japan or the Philippines during World War II who was forced into prostitution by the government to provide sex for soldiers; also called hospitality girl.

hospitality girl
A prostitute in Japan or the Philippines who was forced into prostitution by the government to provide sex for soldiers; also called comfort girl.

or have lost their jobs. These women do not see themselves as prostitutes and may have other jobs in addition to sporadic prostitution. The majority of police in the Philippines believe that prostitution is shameful for women (Guinto-Adviento, 1988).

A group named GABRIELA (General Assembly Binding Women for Reforms, Integrity, Equality, Leadership, and Action) has formed in the Philippines in an attempt to fight prostitution, sexual harassment, rape, and battering of women. There are more than 100 women's organizations that belong to GABRIELA, which supports the economic, health, and working conditions of women. GABRIELA operates free clinics for prostitutes and also provides seminars and activities to educate the community about prostitution (West, 1989).

Human Sexuality in a Diverse World

In Their Own Words

*P*rostitutes the world over have different opinions, attitudes, and concerns about prostitution. Here are several comments from prostitutes from different countries.

Frau Eva, Vienna, Austria: I have been in the business for eleven years and I founded the Austrian Association of Prostitutes. We organized in order to have a voice with public authorities. Austria, like West Germany, is a federation of states. Prostitution policies differ from one state to another.

In Vienna there are toleration zones and toleration times for prostitution. Prostitution is allowed only when it is dark outside and only in the police-controlled neighborhoods. Also, prostitution is allowed only in houses where no one lives, not even the prostitutes themselves, and only in areas where no kindergartens or schools or churches are nearby and where it is not too settled. Registration with the police is required, including registration of your work place. If you decide to deregister, it takes five years to get a letter of good conduct, something required for various jobs such as nursing or driving a taxi. The registration includes a photo, just like with criminals.

Prostitutes have to carry a little book when they're working that records weekly required medical checks. If you are shown to be sick, then your book is confiscated and you are not allowed to work. The police can demand to see your book anytime. At present prostitutes throughout Austria are also required to get a monthly AIDS test. If they fail to comply, they are fined up to the equivalent of $7,000 or given a prison sentence. There is no real choice of doctor because the AIDS test is free only when done by a state-designated agency.

Mae, Bangkok, Thailand: Talking about the situation of prostitutes we might distinguish three main types: one is forced prostitutes, the second is so-called free prostitutes, and the third is migrant prostitutes abroad. Most of the first type who are forced are from the country-side and mostly they are deceived by agents or sold by their parents. The agents usually deceive them and say that they will be working in a restaurant or somewhere else other than prostitution. Often they are kept in a house of prostitution and not allowed to go out; they are given no freedom and many times little or no earnings. They will be beaten if they don't receive guests or if they don't obey the owner. And they have to work very hard; they have to receive at least ten to fifteen guests a day. The living condition is awfully bad. Many women have to sleep in one small room without enough air circulation; they get only two meals a day and not enough medical care. You can get away from the forced condition only by running away or when your body is not fit to work anymore.

Yolanda, Zurich, Switzerland: I'm a mother of four children. I have three children at school and one at home, plus I have my mother at home. I have been divorced for fourteen years, I raised the children all by myself, and I had to move very often because people discovered that I was a prostitute. So I'm not even entitled to my own private home. I have to pay three thousand francs rent in order to be left alone—yes, as soon as they know that you are a prostitute, they charge more; you are discriminated against. This is true for all women who are prostitutes. But we are the oldest profession of the world and everybody knows that. So it is time for all of us to stand up for our rights. We are people just like all other people. We have our profession, we make a living. A normal woman can buy what she wants, but we prostitutes cannot act as we want. We should be able to act as the others do! I also have a friend. We have a very good relationship. He comes and sees the children. I give my children love. They have parents. I didn't have that love when I was child but believe me, I am giving my children plenty of love.

SOURCE: Pheterson, 1989, pp. 62–83.

Prostitution has long been a part of the cultural practices in Thailand. Many countries, including the United States, Japan, Taiwan, South Korea, Australia, and Europe, organize "sex tours" to Thailand. Prostitution is endorsed by both men and women in Thailand mainly because of the prevailing belief that men have greater sex drives than women (Taywaditep et al., 2004). In fact, college students in Thailand often report that prostitution protects "good women" from being raped (Taywaditep et al., 2004). It is estimated that there are between 500,000 and 700,000 female sex workers and between 5,000 and 8,000 male sex workers in Thailand—working "direct" (in brothels or massage parlors) or "indirect" (available for dates and also offering sex for their customers). Direct sex workers make between $2 and $20 for a service, whereas indirect sex workers make between $20 and several hundred dollars (Taywaditep, 2004). Sex workers in Thailand are required to participate in the governmental STI monitoring system, which has helped decrease STI prevalence.

Thailand has instituted a "100% condom use" program targeted at the prostitution industry (Sharma, 2001). Although HIV infections have been decreasing in Thailand, the World Health Organization estimates that prostitution will be the key factor in future HIV transmission. These numbers are high because Thai men do not generally wear condoms. Some maintain that they are immune from AIDS, and prostitutes are too afraid to ask their clients to wear condoms. Prostitution is so prevalent in Thailand that Thai men view a trip to a prostitute almost in the same regard as going to the store for milk. It has also been suggested that because many Thais are Buddhists, they believe in reincarnation and hope that they will not be a prostitute in their next life. This belief in reincarnation often reduces the fear of death.

In Amsterdam, Holland, there is a strip known as the red-light district. The red-light district is crowded with sex shops, adult movie and live theater shows, and street and window prostitutes. These prostitutes are called "window" prostitutes because they sit behind a window and sell their bodies. There are approximately 200 such windows in the red-light district, which is one of the biggest tourist attractions in Amsterdam. Travel services run tours through the red-light district, although these tourists do not generally use the prostitutes' services. Prostitution in Amsterdam is loosely regulated by authorities. Prostitutes pay taxes, get regular checkups, and participate in government-sponsored health and insurance plans (McDowell, 1986).

In Cuba, male and female prostitutes who solicit tourists are known as *jineteros* (Espín et al., 2004). *Jineteros* exchange sex for clothing or other luxuries brought over from other countries. In Havana, teenagers offer sex to older tourists in exchange for a six-pack of cola or a dance club's cover charges. Female prostitutes in Cuba also ply the tourist trade.

In New Zealand, prostitution is not illegal, but several laws exist to restrict solicitation to certain places. This is a description of one prostitute from Dunedin, New Zealand:

> Lynne, a 24-year-old, strolled into the sex industry from a normal childhood in a rural town in Southland. She has worked as an escort and in massage parlours for the last five years and would like nothing more than to "retire" and buy her own home in her old town. The trouble is the money is very, very good and it is hard for her to turn her back on such a highly paid job. Besides, once you have worked in the business it is not easy to find a job elsewhere. How do you tell a prospective employer where you have worked for the last five years when you have no reference? How do you explain your range of skills in relating to people? ("Working Girls," 1992, p. 21)

"Window prostitutes" in Amsterdam, Holland, solicit customers in the red-light district, where prostitution is legal.

In a beach resort in Thailand, young prostitutes wait for a buyer.

Personal Voices

Sexual Trafficking

Worldwide, thousands of women and children are sold into sexual trafficking or sexual slavery every year (U.S. Department of State, 2005). This involves recruiting, obtaining, and transporting individuals by use of force or coercion for the purpose of forcing them into involuntary acts, such as prostitution. Typically young and vulnerable individuals are targeted and given a promise of marriage, employment, education, or simply a better life. They often give up their passports in return, which makes them dependent on their "owner."

Although sexual trafficking and sexual slavery are illegal in the United States, the government believes that between 600,000 and 800,000 people are trafficked across international borders every year—80% of whom are female and 50% are children (U.S. Department of State, 2005). Today many governmental groups are working to eliminate sex trafficking. In fact, in 2004, the U.S. government gave $82 million in antitrafficking assistance to foreign governments (U.S. Department of State, 2005).

Following is one young woman's testimony before the U.S. Senate Foreign Relations Committee in 2000:

> When I was 14, a man came to my parents' house in Veracruz, Mexico, and asked me if I was interested in making money in the United States. He said I could make many times as much money doing the same things that I was doing in Mexico. At the time, I was working in a hotel cleaning rooms and I also helped around my house by watching my brothers and sisters. He said I would be in good hands, and would meet many other Mexican girls who had taken advantage of this great opportunity. My parents didn't want me to go, but I persuaded them.
>
> A week later, I was smuggled into the United States through Texas to Orlando, Florida. It was then the men told me that my employment would consist of having sex with men for money. I had never had sex before, and I had never imagined selling my body.
>
> And so my nightmare began. Because I was a virgin, the men decided to initiate me by raping me again and again, to teach me how to have sex. Over the next three months, I was taken to a different trailer every 15 days. Every night I had to sleep in the same bed in which I had been forced to service customers all day.
>
> I couldn't do anything to stop it. I wasn't allowed to go outside without a guard. Many of the bosses had guns. I was constantly afraid. One of the bosses carried me off to a hotel one night, where he raped me. I could do nothing to stop him.
>
> Because I was so young, I was always in demand with the customers. It was awful. Although the men were supposed to wear condoms, some didn't, so eventually I became pregnant and was forced to have an abortion. They sent me back to the brothel almost immediately.
>
> I cannot forget what has happened. I can't put it behind me. I find it nearly impossible to trust people. I still feel shame. I was a decent girl in Mexico. I used to go to church with my family. I only wish none of this had ever happened. (Polaris Project, 2005)

Although prostitution exists all over the world, it is dealt with differently in each culture. We have much to learn from the way that other cultures deal with prostitution. There are many places throughout the world where young girls are forced into sexual slavery against their will (see the accompanying Personal Voices, "Sexual Trafficking"). In 2003, the Bush administration established a task force to help fight these practices in 165 countries throughout the world.

Throughout this chapter we have explored erotic representations in books, television, advertising, other media, and how sex is used to sell products. We have also examined the sale of sex itself through prostitution and strip bars. There are many effects to living in a society so saturated with sexual representations, and these effects certainly help shape our opinions and thoughts about men, women, and sexuality today.

Review Question

Describe what is known about prostitution outside the United States.

Strip Clubs

There are many occupations within the sex industry, including prostitution, porn acting, erotic writing, and dancing. Erotic dancing has typically been looked down upon, and strippers are often viewed as "deviant" and "bad" (Sweet & Tewksbury, 2000). What would make a woman want to take off her clothes for money? Women who strip for money have been found to have: an early physical maturity and early sexual experiences, early departure from home, an average level of education, a lack of father figure in the home prior to adolescence, and a history of "exhibitionistic" behavior (Thompson & Harred, 1992). Although there is a stereotype that strippers are uneducated, research has shown that today's strippers are typically high school graduates and many have attended college (Sweet & Tewksbury, 2000).

I asked students about strip clubs and their thoughts about such clubs. Here are some of the answers to the question: "Have you ever been to a strip club? If so, what did you think of the club?" As you read through the following answers, notice how many women talk about visiting strip clubs mainly on special occasions (such as an engagement or wedding shower), whereas the men are more likely to visit female strip clubs for no particular occasion.

Female: *The dancers at male strip clubs are always very nice because they love seeing girls in the club.*

Male: *Watching a lap dance is hysterical and much more humorous when you see an old guy trying to get the dancer's attention. The dancers are all about money.*

Female: *I thought it was hysterical to see how far some dancers go to get money.*

Male: *The dancers were only nice to us to get money. They would act like they liked me, but I didn't want to give them any money.*

Female: *The guys at the male strip clubs are always so muscular and just beautiful.*

Male: *I question the psychological health of using your body as a pseudo-sexual object for money.*

Female: *It is amusing. A nice break from the stresses of the world because it is so carefree in the club. The dancers all appear to really like what they do.*

Male: *Some of the female dancers are really young, around our age.*

Female: *The male dancers are all so beautiful and in shape. They are always so nice to us since we don't try to take advantage of them.*

Male: *I was shocked because the strip club I went to was in a shopping center with a grocery store. The chairs we sat in were lawn chairs. The place was dark and dimly lit.*

Female: *The men were all ugly and greasy.*

Male: *It was a little uncomfortable since I didn't know what to do with my hands during the lap dances.*

SOURCE: Author's files.

© Gary Houlder/Corbis

Active Summary

1. (a) _____ representations have existed in almost all (b) _____ at almost all times; they have also been the subject of (c) _____ by religious or governmental powers.

2. (a) _____ emerged as a separate category of erotic art during the (b) _____ century. The (c) _____ press made it more readily available. The (d) _____ novel first established pornography production as a business in the Western world, and it provoked a response of censorship from (e) _____ and governmental authorities.

3. Television and, to a lesser extent, movies have become the (a) _____ media in the United States, and they contain enormous amounts of sexually (b) _____ material. Certain groups have begun to organize to change the content of (c) _____ programming.

4. Advertising has commercialized (a) _____ and uses an enormous amount of sexual (b) _____ to sell products. (c) _____ are becoming more sexually (d) _____ in the general media in the United States.

5. (a) _____ is one of the most difficult issues in public life in America. Feminists, conservatives, and the religious right argue that pornography is (b) _____, violates the rights of women, corrupts children, and should be banned or severely restricted. (c) _____ and critics of banning pornography argue that creating a definition of pornography that protects art and literature is impossible, that people have the right to read whatever materials they want in their own homes, and that censorship is a slippery slope that leads to further (d) _____. The (e) _____ is split between these positions.

6. The online pornography industry is quickly growing. The accessibility, (a) _____, and ease of use have all contributed to the growing popularity of the Internet. Some view online pornography, visit sexually oriented (b) _____ rooms, or may engage in sexual activities with an anonymous person (c) _____. Online sex users can be either (d) _____ *users* (those who enter sites out of curiosity or for entertainment), (e) _____ *users* (those who are increasingly drawn to usage of online sexually oriented materials), or (f) _____ *users* (those who spend over 11 hours per week engaging in online sexual activities). Users of online pornography also report a(an) (g) _____ to pornography over time.

7. It is often difficult to (a) _____ prostitution, and many (b) _____ terms have been developed. According to (c) _____, society has created social institutions to (d) _____ sexual behavior. Prostitution may have developed out of a(an) (e) _____ society.

8. Many prostitutes claim their sole motivation for prostituting is the (a) _____. However, many also claim the major (b) _____ of their job is engaging in (c) _____ with their clients.

9. There are several different types of female prostitutes, including streetwalkers; bar, hotel, and (a) _____ prostitutes; call girls; and courtesans. (b) _____ are considered to have the most dangerous job because they are often victims of violence, rape, and robbery. Bondage-and-discipline and (c) _____ prostitutes also exist.

10. Male prostitutes are often referred to as hustlers, (a) _____, or "boys." There are different types of male prostitutes. They may engage in street or (b) _____ hustling or escort prostitution or may work as (c) _____ boys. Straight, gay, bisexual, transvestite, and transsexual prostitutes exist. The majority of males begin in street prostitution and may eventually move into bar and (d) _____ prostitution.

11. Of the estimated 750,000 to 1,000,000 minors who (a) _____ _____ from home each year, more than 85% eventually become involved in prostitution in order to make money. Many of them have been (b) _____ abused and have psychological problems. Outside of the United States, adolescent prostitution is (c) _____.

12. Pimps play an important role in prostitution. They offer (a) _____, recruit other prostitutes, may manage a group of prostitutes, and try to keep prostitutes (b) _____ to make money. Successful pimps can make a great deal of money and often feel (c) _____ in their role as a pimp.

13. Clients go to prostitutes for a variety of reasons, including (a) _____ sex, to eliminate the risk of rejection, for companionship, to have the (b) _____ attention of the prostitute, because they have no other sexual outlets, for adventure or (c) _____, or to (d) _____ loneliness.

14. Many people believe that prostitution should be (a) _____ so that it can be subjected to government (b) _____ and taxation. However, others think that it would be (c) _____ to legalize prostitution.

15. Different groups, such as (a) _____, have organized to change the public's views of (b) _____ and to change the laws against it. These groups are also (c) _____ outside the United States.

16. Prostitutes are at high risk for acquiring STIs and (a) _____. Overall, they are knowledgeable about these risks and use (b) _____ some of the time. STIs have been found to decrease when prostitution is (c) _____ and to (d) _____ when it is illegal.

17. Female prostitutes stay in the life for a relatively **(a)** _____ time; some feel ready to leave, whereas others are **(b)** _____ out because of a deteriorating physical appearance or because of addiction to drugs or alcohol. **(c)** _____ have few skills after a life of prostitution, and there is usually little to show for the years they spent prostituting. Some seek **(d)** _____, and others spend a great deal of time in and out of prison for shoplifting or robbery.

18. Prostitution exists all over the world. **(a)** "_____ girls" were forced into prostitution in **(b)** _____ during World War II. "Hospitality girls" were used for the same purposes in **(c)** _____.

19. Prostitution has long been a part of the **(a)** _____ practices in Thailand. Prostitution is **(b)** _____ and supported by both men and women in Thailand mainly because of the prevailing belief that men have **(c)** _____ sex drives than women. College students in Thailand often report that prostitution protects "good women" from being **(d)** _____. Sex workers in Thailand are required to be under a governmental **(e)** _____ monitoring system, which has helped **(f)** _____ STI prevalence.

Critical Thinking Questions

1. Why do you think teenage boys care more about movie ratings than girls do? Is it socialization or biology?

2. When you read through one of your favorite magazines and see the various advertisements that use sex to sell their products, what effect do these ads have on you? Do you think there are any effects of living in a society so saturated with sexual images? Why, or why not?

3. Do you think that sex or violence on television influences how promiscuous and/or violent our society becomes? Do the sexual stereotypes paraded before us in commercials and advertisements shape our attitudes toward gender relations? What do you think can be done about this?

4. What television shows did you watch as a child? What messages about gender, sexuality, and relationships did you learn from these shows? Would you let your own child watch these shows today? Why, or why not?

5. Would you ever want to go to a strip club? If so, what would be your reasons for going? For not going? If you have been, what types of reactions did you have?

CHAPTER RESOURCES

Check It Out

Paul, P. (2005). **Pornified: How pornography is transforming our lives, our relationships, and our families.** New York: Times Books.

Pamela Paul interviewed more than 100 people—80 of them young, straight men—to find out the impact of pornography on today's relationships. In *Pornified*, Paul explores how pornography can harm intimate relationships, distracting men from their partners and detracting from their sexual skills. She discusses how women face new forms of social pressure—from men and women—not to dislike pornography because to do so now, Paul believes, would be seen as limiting women's sexual self-expression. She also explores the prevalence of pornography in teenagers' lives today and the power of the Internet—including our increased access to pornography. Overall, Paul believes that pornography should be discouraged and proposes that the government should work to decrease consumer demand.

Born Into Brothels: Calcutta's Red Light Kids (2004; 1 hour, 35 minutes; Rated R)

Filmmakers Zana Briski and Ross Kauffman chronicle the lives of impoverished children in Sonagachi (Calcutta's red light district) in this moving documentary. In the film, they enlist a group of children of prostitutes to teach them about photography. As the children learn to take their own photos, the filmmakers struggle to help them have a chance for a better life away from the miserable poverty and potential for a life of prostitution. The film is a heartbreaking look at prostitution and poverty.

InfoTrac® College Edition

If your instructor ordered InfoTrac with this book, explore InfoTrac College Edition, your online library, for additional readings and review. Go to: **www.thomsonedu.com,** and enter these search terms:

censorship and sex   erotica   pornography
prostitution   sex workers

Web Resources

SexualityNow Companion Website
Go to **http://thomsonedu.com/carroll** for practice quiz questions, interactive activities, Internet links, critical thinking exercises, discussion forums, and more. You can also access sites from the Wadsworth Psychology Study Center **(http://psychology.wadsworth.com)** or you can connect directly to the following sites:

STORM: Sex Trade Opportunities for Risk Minimization
STORM is a harm reduction advocacy, education, direct services, and activist organization for individuals and issues involving the sex trade. Their website contains harm reduction information and strategies offered by current or former sex workers with the intent of minimizing the possible risks faced by the sex worker.

Coalition Against Trafficking in Women (CATW)
Founded in 1988, CATW was the first international, nongovernmental organization to focus on human sex trafficking, especially in women and children. CATW promotes women's human rights by working internationally to combat sexual exploitation in all its forms. Their website contains links to a variety of valuable sources, including worldwide information on sex trafficking.

GABRIELA Network, USA (GABNet)
The GABRIELA (General Assembly Binding women for Reform, Integrity, Equality, Leadership, and Action) Network is a United States–based multiracial, multiethnic women's solidarity organization that works on issues that impact women and children of the Philippines but have their roots in decisions made in the United States. Its objectives are to inform and educate people of the United

States on the impact of global and U.S. policy decisions on women of the Philippines. The Purple Rose Campaign, spearheaded by GABRIELA, addresses the issue of sex trafficking of Filipino women and children.

Henry J. Kaiser Family Foundation
The Kaiser Foundation conducts original survey research on a wide range of topics related to health policy and public health, as well as major social issues, including sexuality. In 2005 the Kaiser Foundation published *Sex on TV4,* the fourth study on sex on television. The goal of Kaiser's surveys is to better understand the public's knowledge, attitudes, and behaviors. Some Foundation surveys are conducted in partnership with other organizations, such as research institutions, universities, and media outlets.

Prostitution Research and Education
Prostitution Research and Education, sponsored by the San Francisco Women's Centers, develops research and educational programs to document the experiences of people in prostitution through research, public education, and arts projects. Links are provided to fact sheets about prostitution, arguments for and against legalization, outreach programs for those who want to leave the business, information on female slavery outside the United States, and many other important topics.

Victims of Pornography
Victims of Pornography is a website aimed to educate and create awareness that there are real victims of pornography. The site includes news, letters from men, women, and children who have been involved with pornography, and links to advocacy and outreach groups.

SexualityNow   Sexuality Now

Go to **www.thomsonedu.com** to link to **SexualityNow,** your online study tool. First take the **Pre-Test** for this chapter to get your **Personalized Study Plan,** which will identify topics you need to review and direct you to online resources. Then take the **Post-Test** to determine what concepts you have mastered and what you still need work on.

Videos in SexualityNow
For additional information on topics discussed in this chapter, check out the videos in **SexualityNow** on the following topics:
• **My Best Friend Is an Exotic Dancer**—Listen to how two friends resolve their differing opinions about one's part-time job.

References

Abbey, A. (2002). Alcohol-related sexual assault: A common problem among college students. *Journal of Studies on Alcohol, 63*(2), 118–130.

Abbey, A., Zawacki, T., & Buck, P. O. (2005). The effects of past sexual assault perpetration and alcohol consumption on men's reactions to women's mixed signals. *Journal of Social & Clinical Psychology, 24*(2), 129–155.

Abbey, A., Zawacki, T., Buck, P. O., Clinton, A., & McAuslan, P. (2001). Alcohol and sexual assault. *Alcohol Research and Health, 25*(11), 43–57.

Abboud, L. N., & Liamputtong, P. (2003). Pregnancy loss: What it means to women who miscarry and their partners. *Social Work in Health Care, 36*(3), 37–62.

Abel, E. L. (1985). *Psychoactive drugs and sex.* New York: Plenum.

Abel, G., Becker, J., & Skinner, L. (1980). Aggressive behavior and sex. *Psychiatric Clinics of North America, 3,* 133–135.

Abel, G., et al. (1988). Multiple paraphiliac diagnoses among sex offenders. *Bulletin of the American Academy of Psychiatry & Law, 2,* 153–168.

Abouesh, A., & Clayton, A. (1999). Compulsive voyeurism and exhibitionism: A clinical response to paroxetine. *Archives of Sexual Behavior, 28*(1), 23–30.

Abrams, E. J., Weedon, J., Bertolli, J., Bornschlegel, K., Cervia, J., Mendez, H., et al. (2001). Aging cohort of perinatally human immunodeficiency virus-infected children in New York City: New York City pediatric surveillance of disease consortium. *Pediatric Infectious Disease Journal, 20*(5), 511–517.

Ackers, M. L., Parekh, B., Evans, T. G., Berman, P., Phillips, S., Allen, M., & McDougal, J. S. (2003). Human immunodeficiency virus seropositivity among uninfected HIV vaccine recipients. *Journal of Infectious Diseases, 187*(6), 879–886.

Adair, L. S., & Gordon-Larsen, P. (2001). Maturational timing and overweight prevalence in U.S. adolescent girls. *American Journal of Public Health, 91*(4), 642–645.

Adam, B. D. (1987). *The rise of a gay and lesbian movement.* Boston: Twayne.

Adams, H. E., Wright, L. W., Jr., & Lohr, B. A. (1996). Is homophobia associated with homosexual arousal? *Journal of Abnormal Psychology, 105,* 440–445.

Adams, K. E. (2004). What's "normal": Female genital mutilation, psychology, and body image. *Journal of the American Women's Association, 59*(3), 168–170.

Adams-Curtis, L. E., & Forbes, G. B. (2004). College women's experiences of sexual coercion: A review of cultural, perpetrator, victim, and situational variables. *Trauma, Violence & Abuse, 5*(2), 91–122.

Add Health. (2002). Add Health and Add Health 2000: A national longitudinal study of adolescent health. Retrieved June 14, 2002, from www.cpc.unc.edu/addhealth

Adler, N. E., David, H. P., Major, B. N., et al. (1992). Psychological factors in abortion. *American Psychologist, 47,* 1194–1204.

Adler, N. E., David, H. P., Major, B. N., Roth, S. H., Russo, N. F., & Wyatt, G. E. (1990). Psychological responses after abortion. *Science, 248,* 41–44.

Afek, D. (1990). Sarah and the women's movement: The experience of infertility. *Women and Therapy, 10,* 195–203.

Afifi, W. A. (1999). Harming the ones we love. *Journal of Sex Research, 36*(2), 198–206.

Aghajanian, S., Berstein, L., & Grimes, D. A. (1994). Bartholin's duct abscess and cyst: A case-control study. *South Medicine Journal, 87*(1), 26–29.

Agocha, V. B., & Cooper, M. L. (1999). Risk perceptions and safer sex intentions. *Personality and Social Psychology Bulletin, 25*(6), 746–759.

Aguillaume, C. J., & Tyrer, L. B. (1995). Current status and future projections on the use of RU-486. *Contemporary OB/GYN, 40*(6), 23–40.

Ahmed, J. (1986). Polygyny and fertility differentials among the Yoruba of western Nigeria. *Journal of Biosocial Sciences, 18,* 63–73.

Ahrens, C. E. (2002). Silent and silenced: The disclosure and non-disclosure of sexual assault. *Dissertation Abstracts,* University of Illinois at Chicago, #0-493-62204-7.

Ainsworth, M. D. S., Blehar, M. C., Waters, E., & Wall, S. (1978). *Patterns of attachment: A psychological study of the strange situation.* Hillsdale, NJ: Erlbaum.

Ako, T., Takao, H., Yoshiharo, M., Osamu, I., & Yutaka, U. (2001). Beginnings of sexual reassignment surgery in Japan. *International Journal of Transgenderism.* Retrieved June 1, 2003, from http://www.symposion.com/ijt/ijtvo05no01_02.htm

Alan Guttmacher Institute. (1999). Sharing responsibility: Women, society and abortion worldwide. Retrieved September 2, 2005, 2005 from http://www.guttmacher.com/pubs/sharing.pdf

Alan Guttmacher Institute. (1999a). Facts in brief: Contraceptive use. Retrieved August 22, 2001, from http://www.agi-usa.org/pubs/fb_contr-use.html

Alan Guttmacher Institute. (1999b). Facts in brief: Induced abortion worldwide. Retrieved on September 9, 2003, from http://www.agi-usa.org/pubs/fb_0599.html

Alan Guttmacher Institute. (1999c). Facts in brief: Teen sex and pregnancy. Retrieved September 9, 2003, from http://www.agi-usa.org/pubs/fb_teen_sex.pdf

Alan Guttmacher Institute. (1999d). Sexually transmitted disease surveillance. Unpublished tabulations of the 1988–1994 National Health and Nutrition Examination Surveys. Atlanta, GA: Centers for Disease Control and Prevention.

Alan Guttmacher Institute. (2001a). Can more progress be made? Teenage sexual and reproductive behavior in developed countries. Executive summary. Retrieved January 14, 2003, from http://www.agi-usa.org/pubs/euroteens_summ.pdf

Alan Guttmacher Institute. (2001b). Facts in brief: Teenage sexual and reproductive behavior, developed countries. Retrieved August 26, 2003, from http://www.agi-usa.org/pubs/fb_teens.html

Alan Guttmacher Institute. (2001c). State-level policies on sexuality, STD education. Retrieved August 26, 2003, from http://www.agi-usa.org/pubs/ib_5-01.html

Alan Guttmacher Institute. (2002a). Facts in brief: Contraceptive use. Retrieved January 14, 2003, from www.agi-usa.org/pubs/fb_contr_use.html

Alan Guttmacher Institute. (2002b). *In their own right: Addressing the sexual and reproductive health needs of American men.* Retrieved July 26, 2002, from http://guttmacher.org/pubs/exs_men.html

Alan Guttmacher Institute. (2003). State facts about abortion: 2003. Retrieved August, 28, 2005, from http://www.guttmacher.org/statecenter/sfaa.html

Alan Guttmacher Institute. (2004). State facts about abortion, 2003. Retrieved August 21, 2005, from http://www.guttmacher.org/pubs/sfaa.html

Alan Guttmacher Institute. (2004, February 19). U.S. teenage pregnancy statistics: Overall trends by race and ethnicity. Retrieved May 30, 2005, from http://www.guttmacher.org/pubs/state_pregnancy_trends.pdf

Alan Guttmacher Institute. (2005a). Contraceptive use. Retrieved August 13, 2005, from http://www.agi-usa.org/pubs/fb_contr_use.html

Alan Guttmacher Institute. (2005b). Facts in brief: Contraceptive use. Retrieved September 1, 2005 from http://www.guttmacher.com/pubs/fb_contr_use.html

Alanis, M. C., & Lucidi, R. S. (2004, May). Neonatal circumcision: A review of the world's oldest and most controversial operation. *Obstetrical & Gynecological Survey, 59*(5), 379–395.

Alarid, L. F. (2000). Sexual orientation perspectives of incarcerated bisexual and gay men: The county jail protective custody experience. *Prison Journal, 80*(1), 80–95.

Alavi, A. K. (2001). Little white lies: Racialized images of the phallus in the U.S. *Dissertation Abstracts*, Georgia State University, #0-493-36368-4.

Albert, A., & Porter, J. R. (1988). Children's gender-role stereotypes: A sociological investigation of psychological models. *Sociological Forum, 3,* 184–210.

Albrecht, H. (2003). Making sense of AIDSVAX. *AIDS Clinical Care, 15*(4), 42.

Alexander, C. J., Sipski, M. L., & Findley, T. W. (1993). Sexual activities, desire, and satisfaction in males pre- and post-SCI. *Archives of Sexual Behavior, 22,* 217–228.

Alexander, M. A. (1999). Sexual offender treatment efficacy revisited. *Sexual Abuse: A Journal of Research and Treatment, 11,* 101–116.

Alexander, M. G., & Fisher, T. D. (2003). Truth and consequences: Using the bogus pipeline to examine sex differences in self-reported sexuality. *The Journal of Sex Research, 40,* 27–35.

Alkhuja, S., Mnekel, R., Patel, B., & Ibrahimbacha, A. (2001). Stidor and difficult airway in an AIDS patient. *AIDS Patient Care and Sexually Transmitted Diseases, 15*(6), 293–295.

Allen, B. P. (1995). Gender stereotypes are not accurate. *Sex Roles, 32*(9–10), 583–600.

Allen, D. J., & Oleson, T. (1999). Shame and internalized homophobia in gay men. *Journal of Homosexuality, 37*(3), 33–34.

Allen, L. (2005). Increased frequency in cohabitating couples raises new legal concerns. Retrieved September 17, 2005, from http://www.lawyers.com/lawyers/A~1026044~LDS/COHABITATING+lEGAL+CONCERNS.html

Allen, M. P. (1989). *Transformations.* New York: Dutton.

Allen, M., Emmers-Sommer, T. M., & Crowill, T. L. (2002). Couples negotiating safer sex behaviors: A meta-analysis of the impact of conversation and gender. In M. Allen & R. Preiss (Eds.), *Interpersonal communication research.* Mahwah, NJ: Erlbaum.

Allen, P. L. (2000). *The wages of sin: Sex and disease, past and present.* Chicago: University of Chicago Press.

Allen, R. E., & Hanson, R. W. (2005). Episiotomy in low-risk vaginal deliveries. *Journal of the American Board of Family Practitioners, 18*(1), 8–12.

Alliance for Microbicide Development. (2001). The National Institutes of Health spent $34 million in microbicide research, USAID spent $5 million and CDC less than $3 million in FY 2000. Retrieved May 25, 2003, from http://www.microbicide.org/

Allport, S. (1997). *A natural history of parenting.* New York: Random House.

Almerling, R., Tews, L., & Dudley, S. (2000). Abortion training in the U.S. obstetrics and gynecology residency programs, 1998. *Family Planning Perspectives, 32*(6). Retrieved November 11, 2005, from http://www.agi-usa.org/pubs/journals/3226800.html

Aloni, M., & Bernieri, F. J. (2004). Is love blind? The effects of experience and infatuation on the perception of love. *Journal of Nonverbal Behavior, 28*(4), 287–295.

Al-Shawaf, T., Zosmer, A., Dirnfeld, M., & Grudzinskas, G. (2005). Safety of drugs used in assisted reproduction techniques. *Drug Safety, 28*(6), 513–528.

Althaus, F. (1997). Most Japanese students do not have intercourse until after adolescence. *Family Planning Perspectives, 29*(3), 145–147.

Althaus, F. (2001). Levels of sexual experience among U.S. teenagers have declined for the first time in three decades. *Family Planning Perspectives, 33*(4), 180–182.

Altman, C. (2000). Gay and lesbian seniors: Unique challenges of coming out in later life. *SIECUS Report, 4,* 14.

Altman, D. (1986). *AIDS in the mind of America.* New York: Anchor Press, Doubleday.

Alzate, H. (1985). Vaginal eroticism: A replication study. *Archives of Sexual Behavior, 14,* 529–537.

Alzate, H., & Hoch, Z. (1986). The "G spot" and "female ejaculation": A current appraisal. *Journal of Sex and Marital Therapy, 12,* 211–220.

Amador, J., Charles, T., Tait, J., & Helm, H. (2005). Sex and generational differences in desired characteristics in mate selection. *Psychological Reports, 96*(1), 19–25.

Amateau, S. K., & McCarthy, M. M. (2004). Induction of PGE_2 by estradiol mediates developmental masculinization of sex behavior. *Nature Neuroscience, 7*(6), 1–8.

Amato, P. (1996). Explaining the intergenerational transmission of divorce. *Journal of Marriage and the Family, 58,* 628–640.

Amato, P. R., Johnson, D. R., & Booth, A. (2003). Continuity and change in marital quality between 1980 and 2000. *Journal of Marriage and the Family, 65*(1), 1–22.

American Academy of Pediatrics. (1999). Circumcision Policy Statement (RE 9850), *Pediatrics, 103,* 686–693.

American Cancer Society. (2001). Probability of developing invasive cancer over selected age intervals, 1995–1997. Retrieved September 8, 2002, from http://cancer.org/downloads/STT/F+F2001.pdf

American Cancer Society. (2002). *Cancer facts and figures: 2002.* Atlanta, GA: Author.

American Cancer Society. (2003a). *Cancer facts and figures: 2003.* Atlanta, GA: The American Cancer Society.

American Cancer Society. (2003b). How to perform a breast self-exam. Retrieved October 7, 2005, from http://www.cancer.org/docroot/CRI/content/CRI_2_6x_How_to_perform_a_breast_self_exam_5.asp?sitearea=

American Cancer Society. (2005a). Estimated new cancer cases for selected cancer sites by state, U.S., 2005. Retrieved March 21, 2005, from http://www.cancer.org/docroot/PRO/content/PRO_1_1_Cancer_Statistics_2005_Presentation.asp

American Cancer Society. (2005b). Estimated new cancer cases for selected cancer sites by State, U.S., 2005. Retrieved March 21, 2005, from http://www.cancer.org/downloads/stt/Estimated_New_Cancer_Cases_for_Selected_Cancer_Sites_by_State,_US,_2005.pdf

American Cancer Society. (2005c). Overview: Testicular cancer: How many men get testicular cancer? Cancer reference information. Retrieved April 10, 2005, from http://www.cancer.org/docroot/CRI/content/CRI_2_2_1x_How_Many_People_Get_Testicular_Cancer_41.asp?sitearea=

American Cancer Society. (2005d). Overview: Testicular cancer: Survival rates cancer reference information. Retrieved April 10, 2005, from http://www.cancer.org/docroot/CRI/content/CRI_2_2_6x_Survival_Rates_41.asp?sitearea=

American Cancer Society. (2005e). What are the key statistics about prostate cancer? Retrieved April 10, 2005, from http://www.cancer.org/docroot/CRI/content/CRI_2_4_1X_What_are_the_key_statistics_for_prostate_cancer_36.asp?sitearea=

American Prosecutors Research Institute. (2003a). How is spousal rape treated? Retrieved October 17, 2005, from http://www.ndaa-apri.org/pdf/vaw_spousal_rape.pdf

American Prosecutors Research Institute. (2003b). State definitions of penetration for sex crimes. Retrieved October 17, 2005, from http://www.ndaa-apri.org/pdf/vaw_sex_acts.pdf

American Psychiatric Association. (1994). *Diagnostic and statistical manual of mental disorders* (4th ed.). Washington, DC: Author.

American Psychiatric Association. (2000). *Diagnostic and statistical manual of mental disorders* (4th ed., Text. Rev.). Washington, DC: Author.

American Psychological Association. (1998). Hate crimes today: An age-old foe in modern dress. APA position paper. Retrieved May 21, 2003, from http://www.apa.org/pubinfo/hate/

American Society of Reproductive Medicine. (2005). Patient fact sheets. Retrieved November, 4, 2005, from http://www.asrm.org/Patients/FactSheets/fact.html

Ames, M. A., & Houston, D. A. (1990). Legal, social, and biological definitions of pedophilia. *Archives of Sexual Behavior, 19,* 333–342.

Amir, M. (1971). *Patterns in forcible rape.* Chicago: University of Chicago Press.

Anderson, C. A., Carnagey, N. L., & Eubanks, J. (2003). Exposure to violent media: The effects of songs with violent lyrics on aggressive thoughts and feelings. *Journal of Personality and Social Psychology, 84*(5), 960–971.

Anderson, F. D., & Hait, H. (2003). A multicenter, randomized study of an extended cycle oral contraceptive. *Contraception, 68*(2), 89–96.

Anderson, I. (2004). Explaining negative rape victim perception: Homophobia and the male rape victim. *Current Research in Social Psychology, 10*(4), 43–57.

Anderson, P. B., & Savage, J. S. (2005). Social, legal, and institutional context of heterosexual aggression by college women. *Trauma, Violence, & Abuse, 6*(2), 130–140.

Anderton, D., & Emigh, R. (1989). Polygynous fertility: Sexual competition vs. progeny. *American Journal of Sociology 94*(4), 832–855.

Angier, N. (1999). *Woman: An intimate geography.* New York: Anchor Books.

Ankum, W. M., Hajenius, P. J., Schrevel, L. S., & Van der Veen, F. (1996). Management of suspected ectopic pregnancy. Impact of new diagnostic tools in 686 consecutive cases. *Journal of Reproductive Medicine, 41*(10), 724–728.

Antoni, M. H., Cruess, D. G., Klimas, N., Maher, K., Cruess, S., Kumarr, M., et al. (2002). Stress management and immune system reconstitution in symptomatic HIV-infected gay men over time. *American Journal of Psychiatry, 159*(1), 143–144.

Apfel, R. J., & Handel, M. H. (1993). *Madness and loss of motherhood.* Washington, DC: American Psychiatric Press.

Aral, S. O., Mosher, W. D., & Cates, W. (1991). Self-reported pelvic inflammatory disease in the U.S., 1988. *Journal of the American Medical Association, 266,* 2570–2573.

Araujo, A. B., Mohr, B. A., & McKinley, J. B. (2004). Changes in sexual function in middle-aged and older men: Longitudinal data from the Massachusetts male aging study. *Journal of the American Geriatrics Society, 52*(9), 1502–1509.

Archer, D. F., Bigrigg, A., Smallwood, G. H., Shangold, G. A., Creasy, G. W., & Fisher, A. C. (2002). Assessment of compliance with a weekly contraceptive patch among North American women. *Fertility and Sterility, 77* (2 Suppl. 2), 527–531.

Arevelo, M., Jennings, V., & Sinai, I. (2002). Efficacy of a new method of family planning: The standard days method. *Contraception, 65,* 333–338.

Arias, R. A., Munoz, L. D., & Munoz-Fernandez, M. A. (2003). Transmission of HIV-1 infection between trophoblast placental cells and T-cells take place via an LFA-1-mediated cell to cell contact. *Virology, 307*(2), 266–277.

Aries, P. (1962). *Centuries of childhood: A social history of family life.* New York: Vintage Books.

Armesto, J. C. (2001). Attributions and emotional reactions to the identity disclosure of a homosexual child. *Family Process, 40*(2), 145–162.

Armstrong, M. L., Roberts, A. E., Owen, D. C., & Koch, J. R. (2004). Toward building a composite of college student influences with body art. *Issues in Comprehensive Pediatric Nursing, 27,* 277–295.

Aron, A., Fisher, H., Mashek, D. J., Strong, G., Li, H., & Brown, L. (2005). Reward, motivation, and emotion systems associated with early-stage intense romantic love. *Journal of Neurophysiology, 94,* 327–337.

Arroba, A. (2004). Costa Rica. In R. T. Francoeur & R. J. Noonan (Eds.), *The Continuum international encyclopedia of sexuality* (pp. 227–240). New York/London: Continuum International.

Assisted Reproductive Technology. (2002). Assisted reproductive technology report, Centers for Disease Control and Prevention. Retrieved October 5, 2005, from http://www.cdc.gov/reproductivehealth/ART02/nation.htm

Atanackovic, G., Wolpin, J., & Koren, G. (2001). Determinants of the need for hospital care among women with nausea and vomiting of pregnancy. *Clinical and Investigative Medicine, 24*(2), 90–94.

Athenstaedt, U., Haas, E., & Schwab, S. (2004). Gender role self-concept and gender-typed communication behavior in mixed-sex and same-sex dyads. *Sex Roles, 50*(1–2), 37–52.

Auchincloss, S. (1991). Sexual dysfunction after cancer treatment. *Journal of Psychosocial Oncology, 9*(1), 23–42.

Auster, C. J., & Leone, J. M. (2001). Late adolescents' perspectives on marital rape. *Adolescence, 36,* 141–152.

Auster, C. J., & Ohm, S. C. (2000). Masculinity and femininity in contemporary American Society. *Sex Roles, 43*(7–8), 499–528.

Austoni, E., Colombo, F., Romano, A. L., Guarneri, A., Goumas, I. K., & Cazzaniga, A. (2005). Soft prosthesis implant and relaxing albugineal incision with saphenous grafting for surgical therapy of Peyronie's disease. *European Urology, 47*(2), 223–230.

Auvert, B., Bure, A., Lagarde, E., Kahindo, M., Chege, J., Rutenberg, N., et al. (2001). Male circumcision and HIV infection in four cities in sub-Saharan Africa. *AIDS, 15*(Suppl. 4), 531–540.

Auvert, B., Taljaard, D., Lagarde, E., Sobngwi-Tambekou, J., Sitta, R., & Puren, A. (2005). Randomized, controlled intervention trial of male circumcision for reduction of HIV infection risk: The ANRS 1265 trial. *Public Library of Science, 2*(11), e298.

Auvert, B., Taljaard, D., Lagarde, E., Sobngwi-Tambekou, J., Sitta, R., & Puren, A. (2005). Randomized, controlled intervention trial of male circumcision for reduction of HIV infection risk: The ANRS 1265 trial. *Public Library of Science, 2*(11), e298.

Aviram, I. (2005). Online infidelity: Aspects of dyadic satisfaction, self-disclosure, and narcissism. Retrieved May 9, 2005, from http://jcmc.indiana.edu/vol10/issue3/aviram.html

Awad, G., & Saunders, E. (1989). Adolescent child molesters: Clinical observations. *Child Psychiatry and Human Development, 19,* 195–206.

Azam, S. (2000). What's behind retro virginity? The Toronto Star Life Story. Retrieved December 29, 2002, from http://www.psurg.com/star2000.html

Azar, B. (2002). The postpartum cuddles: Inspired by hormones? *Monitor on Psychology, 33*(9), 54–56.

Bacon, C. G., Mittleman, M. A., Kawachi, I., et al. (2003). Sexual function in men older than 50 years of age: Results from the health professionals follow-up study. *Annals of Internal Medicine, 139,* 161–168.

Bailey, A., & Hurd, P. (2005). Finger length ratio correlates with physical aggression in men but not in women. *Biological Psychology, 68*(3), 215–222.

Bailey, B. P., Gurak, L. J., & Konstan, J. A. (2003). Trust in cyberspace. In J. Ratner (Ed.), *Human factors and Web development* (2nd ed, pp. 311–321). Mahwah, NJ: Erlbaum.

Bailey, J. M., Nothnagel, J., & Wolfe, M. (1995). Retrospectively measured individual differences in childhood sex-typed behavior among gay men. *Archives of Sexual Behavior, 24*(6), 613–623.

Bailey, J. M., & Pillard, R. C. (1993). A genetic study of male sexual orientation. *Archives of General Psychiatry 50*(3), 240–241.

Bailey, J. M., Pillard, R. C., Neale, M. C., & Agvei, Y. (1993). Heritable factors influence sexual orientation in women. *Archives of General Psychiatry, 50*(3), 217–223.

Bailey, R. C., Muga, R., Poulussen, R., & Abicht, H. (2002). The acceptability of male circumcision to reduce HIV infections in Nyanza Province Kenya. *AIDS Care, 14*(1), 27–40.

Bain, J. (2001). Testosterone replacement therapy for aging men. *Canadian Family Physician, 47,* 91–97.

Baldassare, J. S. (1991). Update on the management of sexually transmitted diseases. *Philadelphia Medicine, 87,* 230–233.

Balfour, H. H. (1999). Antiviral drugs. *New England Journal of Medicine, 340,* 1255–1268.

Ball, H. (2005). Sexual offending on elderly women: A review. *Journal of Forensic Psychiatry & Psychology, 16*(1), 127–138.

Bancroft, J. (1996). Sex research in the U.S. *Journal of Sex Research, 33*(4), 327–328.

Bancroft, J. (1999). Sexual science in the 21st century: Where are we going? *Journal of Sex Research, 36*(3), 226–230.

Bancroft, J., Herbenick, D., Barnes, T., Hallam-Jones, R., Wylie, K., & Janssen, E. (2005). The relevance of the dual control model to male sexual dysfunction: The Kinsey Institute/BASRT collaborative project. *Sexual & Relationship Therapy, 20*(1), 13–30.

Bancroft, J., & Vukadinovic, Z. (2004). Sexual addiction, sexual compulsivity, or what? Toward a theoretical model. *Journal of Sex Research, 41*(3), 225–234.

Bandura, A. (1969). *Principles of behavior modification.* Austin, TX: Holt, Rinehart & Winston.

Barak, A. (2005). Sexual harassment on the Internet. *Social Science Computer Review, 23*(1), 77–92.

Barbach, L. (1982). *For each other: Sharing sexual intimacy.* New York: Penguin Group.

Barker, D. J. (1997). Maternal nutrition, fetal nutrition, and disease in later life. *Nutrition, 13*(9), 807–813.

Barker, D. J., & Barker, M. J. (2002). The body as art. *Journal of Cosmetic Dermatology, 1*(2), 88.

Barker, O. (2002, Feb. 8). Many manly fingers are sporting engagement rings. *USA Today.*

Barlett, N. H., Vasey, P. L., & Bukowski, W. M. (2000). Is gender identity disorder in children a mental disorder? *Sex Roles, 43*(11–12), 753–785.

Barlow, D. H. (1986). Causes of sexual dysfunction: The role of anxiety and cognitive interference. *Journal of Consulting and Clinical Psychology, 54,* 140–148.

Barner, J. M. (2003). Sexual fantasies, attitudes, and beliefs: The role of self-report sexual aggression for males and females. *Dissertation Abstracts International, 64*(4-B), 1887 (#0419–4217).

Baron, J., & Siepmann, M. (2000). Techniques for creating and using Web questionnaires in research and teaching. In M. H. Birbaum (Ed.), *Psychological experiments on the Internet* (pp. 235–265). San Diego, CA: Academic Press.

Baron, L. (1990). Pornography and gender equality: An empirical analysis. *The Journal of Sex Research, 27,* 363–380.

Baron, L., & Straus, M. A. (1987). Four theories of rape: A macrosociological analysis. *Social Problems, 34,* 467–489.

Baron, N. S. (2004). See you online: Gender issues in college student use of instant messaging. *Journal of Language & Social Psychology, 23*(4), 397–423.

Barone, M. A., Johnson, C. H., Luick, M. A., Teutonico, D. L., & Magnani, R. J. (2004). Characteristics of men receiving vasectomies in the U.S., 1998–1999. *Perspectives on Sexual and Reproductive Health, 36*(1).

Bart, P. B., & O'Brien, P. H. (1985). *Stopping rape: Successful survival strategies.* New York: Pergamon Press.

Barth, K. R., Cook, R. L., Downs, J. S., Switzer, G. E., & Fischoff, B. (2002). Social stigma and negative consequences: Factors that influence college students' decision to seek testing for STIs. *Journal of American College Health, 50*(4), 153–160.

Bartoi, M. G., & Kinder, B. N. (1998). Effects of child and adult sexual abuse on adult sexuality. *Journal of Sex and Marital Therapy, 24,* 75–90.

Bartsch, R. A., Burnett, T., Diller, T. R., & Rankin-Williams, E. (2000). Gender representation in television commercials: Updating an update. *Sex Roles, 43*(9–10), 735–743.

Baslington, H. (2002). The social organization of surrogacy: Relinquishing a baby and the role of payment in the psychological detachment process. *Journal of Health Psychology, 7*(1), 57–71.

Basow, S. A., & Campanile, F. (1990). Attitudes toward prostitution as a function of attitudes toward feminism in college students: An exploratory study. *Psychology of Women Quarterly, 14,* 135–141.

Basson, R., Berman, J., Burnett, A., Derogaris, L., & Ferguson, D. (2000). Report of the international consensus development conference on female sexual dysfunction: Definitions and classifications. *Journal of Urology, 163,* 888–893.

Basson, R., McInnes, R., Smith, M., Hodgson, G., & Koppiker, N. (2002). Efficacy and safety of sildenafil citrate in women with sexual dysfunction associated with female sexual arousal disorder. *Journal of Women's Health and Gender-Based Medicine, 11*(4), 367–377.

Batabyal, A. A. (2001). On the likelihood of finding the right partner in an arranged marriage. *Journal of Socio-Economics, 30*(3), 273–281.

Bauer, G. R., & Welles, S. L. (2001). Beyond assumptions of negligible risk: STDs and women who have sex with women. *American Journal of Public Health, 91*(8), 1282–1287.

Baum, M. (2004). Introduction to "Olfaction, Sex, and Behavior" [Special issue]. *Hormones & Behavior, 46*(3), 217–218.

Baum, N. (2003). The male way of mourning divorce: When, what, and how. *Clinical Social Work Journal, 31*(1), 37–50.

Baumeister, L. M., Flores, E., & Marin, B. V. (1995). Sex information given to Latina adolescents by parents. *Health Education Research, 10*(2), 233–239.

Baumeister, R. F. (1988). Masochism as escape from self. *Journal of Sex Research, 25,* 28–59.

Baumer, E. P., & South, S. J. (2001). Community effects on youth sexual activity. *Journal of Marriage and Family, 63*(2), 540–555.

Bayer, R. (1981). *Homosexuality and American psychiatry: The politics of diagnosis.* New York: Basic Books.

Beach, S. R., & Tesser, A. (1988). Love in marriage: A cognitive accountology of love. In R. J. Sternberg & R. J. Barnes (Eds.), *Psychology of love* (pp. 330–355). New Haven, CT: Yale University Press.

Beals, K. P., & Peplau, L. A. (2005). Identity support, identity devaluation, and well-being among lesbians. *Psychology of Women Quarterly, 29*(2), 140–148.

Beam, J. (1986). *In the life: A black gay anthology.* Los Angeles, CA: Alyson Publications.

Bearman, P., & Brueckner, H. (1999). Promising the future: Virginity pledges and the transition to first intercourse. *American Journal of Sociology, 106,* 859–912.

Becker, G., Landes, E., & Michael, R. (1977). An economic analysis of marital stability. *Journal of Political Economy, 85,* 1141–1187.

Becker, J. V., et al. (1986). Level of postassault sexual functioning in rape and incest victims. *Archives of Sexual Behavior, 15,* 37–50.

Belknap, P., & Leonard II, W. M. (1991). A conceptual replication and extension of Erving Goffman's study of gender advertisements. *Sex Roles, 25,* 103–118.

Bell, A. P., & Weinberg, M. S. (1978). *Homosexualities: A study of diversity among men and women.* New York: Simon & Schuster.

Bell, A. P., Weinberg, M. S., & Hammersmith, S. K. (1981). *Sexual preference: Its development in men and women.* Bloomington: Indiana University Press.

Bem, D. (1996). Exotic becomes erotic: A development theory of sexual orientation. *Psychological Review, 103*(2), 320–336.

Bem, S. L. (1974). The measurement of psychological androgyny. *Journal of Consulting and Clinical Psychology, 42,* 155–162.

Bem, S. L. (1977). On the utility of alternative procedures for assessing psychological androgyny. *Journal of Consulting and Clinical Psychology, 45,* 196–205.

Bem, S. L. (1981). Gender schema theory: A cognitive account of sex-typing. *Psychological Review, 88,* 354–364.

Bem, S. L. (1987). Masculinity and femininity exist only in the mind of the perceiver. In J. M. Reinisch, L. A. Rosenblum, & S. Stephanie (Eds.), *Masculinity/femininity: Basic perspectives* (pp. 304–311). New York: Oxford University Press.

Bem, S. L. (1989). Genital knowledge and gender constancy in preschool children. *Child Development, 60,* 649–662.

Benevento, B. T., & Sipski, M. L. (2002). Neurogenic bladder, neurogenic bowel, and sexual dysfunction in people with spinal cord injury. *Physical Therapy, 82*(6), 601–612.

Benjamin, H. (1961). *Encyclopedia of sexual behavior.* New York: Hawthorn Books.

Bennett, N. E., Bloom, D. A., & Craig, E. H. (1992). American marriage patterns in transition. In S. J. South & S. E. Tolnay (Eds.), *The changing American family: Sociological and demographic perspectives* (pp. 89–108). Boulder, CO: Westview.

Bennett, S., & Assefi, N. (2005). School-based teenage pregnancy prevention programs: A systematic review of randomized controlled trials. *Journal of Adolescent Health, 36*(1), 72–81.

Bennink, H. J. (2000). The pharmacokinetics and pharmacodynamics of Implanon, single-rod etonorgestrel contraceptive implant. *European Journal of Contraception and Reproductive Health Care, 5*(Suppl. 2), 12–20.

Benokraitis, N. V. (1993). *Marriages and families.* Englewood Cliffs, NJ: Prentice Hall.

Berenbaum, S. A., & Snyder, E. (1995). Early hormonal influences on childhood sex-typed activity and playmate preferences. *Developmental Psychology, 31*(1), 31–43.

Berger, G., Hank, L., Rauzi, T., & Simkins, L. (1987). Detection of sexual orientation by heterosexuals and homosexuals. *Journal of Homosexuality, 13,* 83–100.

Berger, R. J., Searles, P., & Cottle, C. E. (1991). *Feminism and pornography.* New York: Praeger.

Bergeron, S., Binik, Y. M., Khalife, S., & Pagidask (1997). Vulvar vestibulitis syndrome. A critical review. *Clinical Journal of Pain, 13,* 27–42.

Berglund, A., Migaard, L., & Rylander, E. (2002). Vulvar pain, sexual behavior and genital infections in young population: A pilot study. *Acta Obstetricia et Gynecologica Scandinavica, 81*(8), 738–742.

Bergmann, M. S. (1987). *The anatomy of living.* New York: Fawcett Columbine.

Bergstrand, C., & Williams, J. B. (2000). Today's alternative marriage styles: The case of swingers. *The Electronic Journal of Human Sexuality, 3.* Retrieved August 27, 2002, from http://ejhs.org/volume3/swing/ body.htm

Berkey, B. R., Perelman-Hall, T., & Kurdek, L. A. (1990). The multidimensional scale of sexuality. *Journal of Homosexuality, 19,* 67–87.

Berkow, R., Beers, M. H., Fletcher, A. J., & Bogin, R. M. (Eds). (2000). *Merck manual of medical information* (Home Ed.). Whitehouse Station, NJ: Merck & Co.

Bernstein, A. (1994). *Flight of the stork: What children think (and when) about sex and family building.* Indianapolis, IN: Perspectives Press.

Berrill, K. T., & Herek, G. M. (1990). Primary and secondary victimization in anti-gay hate crimes. *Journal of Interpersonal Violence, 5,* 401–413.

Besharov, D. (1988). *Protecting children from abuse and neglect: policy and practices.* Springfield, IL: Charles C Thomas.

Bestic, L. (2005). When a patch works. Retrieved August 30, 2005, from http://www.timesonline.co.uk/article/0,,8124-1716899,00.html

Bianchi, S. M., Milkie, M. A., Sayer, L. C., & Robinson, J. P. (2000). Is anyone doing the housework? Trends in the gender division of household labor. *Social Forces, 29*(1), 191–229.

Bianco, A., Stone, J., Lynch, L., Lapinski, R., Berkowitz, G., & Berkowitz, R. L. (1996). Pregnancy outcome at age 40 and older. *Journal of Obstetrics & Gynecology, 87*(6), 917–922.

Bick, R. L., Maden, J., Heller, K. B., & Toofanian, A. (1998). Recurrent miscarriage: Causes, evaluation, and treatment. *Medscape Women's Health, 3*(3), 2.

Bidwell, R. J., & Deisher, R. W. (1991). Adolescent sexuality: Current issues. *Pediatric Annals, 20,* 293–302.

Bieber, I., et al. (1962). *Homosexuality: A psychoanalytic study.* New York: Basic Books.

Bigelow, B. J. (1977). Children's friendship expectations: A cognitive developmental study. *Child Development, 48,* 246–253.

Bigner, J. J., & Jacobsen, R. B. (1989). Parenting behaviors of homosexual and heterosexual fathers. *Journal of Homosexuality, 18,* 173–186.

Bigner, J. J., & Jacobsen, R. B. (1992). Adult response to child behavior and attitudes toward fathering: Gay and nongay fathers. *Journal of Homosexuality, 23,* 99–112.

Binik, Y. (2005). Should dyspareunia be retained as a sexual dysfunction in DSM-V? A painful classification decision. *Archives of Sexual Behavior, 34*(1), 11–21.

Binik, Y. M., Reissing, E., Pukall, C., Flory, N., Payne, K., & Khalife, S. (2002). The female sexual pain disorders: Genital pain or sexual dysfunction? *Archives of Sexual Behavior, 31*(5), 425–429.

Birnbaum, G., Glaubman, H., & Mikulincer, M. (2001). Women's experience of heterosexual intercourse. *Journal of Sex Research, 38*(3), 191–194.

Biro, R. M., Lucky, A. W., Simbartl, L. A., Barton, B. A., Daniels, S. R., Striegel-Moore, R., et al. (2003). Pubertal maturation in girls and the relationship to anthropometric changes: Pathways through puberty. *Journal of Pediatrics, 142*(6), 643–646.

Bishop, E. P., & Myricks, N. (2004). Sex reassignment surgery: When is a "he" a "she" for the purpose of marriage in the United States? *American Journal of Family Law, 18*(1), 30–36.

Bittles, A. H., Mason, W. M., & Greene, J. (1991). Reproductive behavior and health in consanguineous marriages. *Science, 252*(5007), 789–794.

Bjarnadottir, R. I., Tuppurainen, M., & Killick, S. R. (2002). Comparison of cycle control with a combined contraceptive vaginal ring and oral levonorgestrel/ethinyl estradiol. *American Journal of Obstetrics and Gynecology, 186*(3), 389–395.

Blackburn, R. D., Cunkelman, A., & Zlidar, V. M. (2000). Oral contraceptives—An update. *Population Reports, 28*(1),1–16, 25–32.

Blagojevic, M. (1989). The attitudes of young people towards marriage: From the change of substance to the change of form. *Marriage and Family Review, 14*(1–2), 217–238.

Blair, A. (2000) Individuation, love styles and health-related quality of life among college students. *Dissertation Abstracts International,* University of Florida, #0-599-91381-9.

Blair, C. D., & Lanyon, R. I. (1981). Exhibitionism: Etiology and treatment. *Psychological Bulletin, 89*(3), 439–463.

Blake, K. U., Gurrin, L. C., Beilin, L. J., Stanley, F. J., Kendall, G. E., Landau, L., et al. (2002). Prenatal ultrasound biometry related to subsequent blood pressure in childhood. *Journal of Epidemiology and Community Health, 56*(9), 713–718.

Blakemore, J. E. (2003). Children's beliefs about violating gender norms: Boys shouldn't look like girls, and girls shouldn't act like boys. *Sex Roles, 48*(9–10), 411–419.

Blanc, A. K. & Way, A. A. (1998). Sexual behavior and contraceptive knowledge and use among adolescents in developing countries. *Studies in Family Planning, 29,* 106–116.

Blanchard, R. (2004). Quantitative and theoretical analyses of the relation between older brothers and homosexuality in men. *Journal of Theoretical Biology, 230*(2), 173–187.

Blinn-Pike, L. (1999). Why abstinent adolescents report they have not had sex: Understanding sexually resilient youth. *Family Relations: Interdisciplinary Journal of Applied Family Studies, 48*(3), 295–301.

Block, J. (1983). Differential premises arising from differential socialization of the sexes: Some conjectures. *Child Development, 54,* 1335–1354.

Block, J. D. (1999). *Sex over 50.* Paramus, NJ: Reward Books.

Blow, A. J., & Hartnett, K. (2005). Infidelity in committed relationships: A methodological review. *Journal of Marital and Family Therapy, 31*(2), 183–216.

Blum, R. W., Beuhring, T., Shew, M. L., Bearinger, L. H., Sieving, R. E., & Resnick, M. D. (2000). Adolescent risk behaviors. *American Journal of Public Health, 90,* 1879–1885.

Blumstein, H. (2001). Bartholin gland disease. Retrieved September 9, 2002, from http://www.emedicine.com/emeg/topic54.htm

Blumstein, P., & Schwartz, P. (1983). *American couples.* New York: William Morrow.

Bly, R. (1992). *Iron John: A book about men.* New York: Vintage Books.

Boehmer, U. (2002). Twenty years of public health research: Inclusion of lesbian, gay, bisexual and transgender populations. *American Journal of Public Health, 92*(7), 1125–1131.

Boehner, C. W., Howe, S. R., Bernstein, D., & Rosenthal, S. L. (2003). Viral sexually transmitted vaccine acceptability among college students. *Journal of the American Sexually Transmitted Disease Association, 30*(10), 774–778.

Boeke, A. J., van Bergen, J. E., Morre, S. A., & van Everdingen, J. J. (2005). The risk of pelvic inflammatory disease associated with urogenital infection with chlamydia trachomatis: Literature review. *Ned Tijdschr Geneeskd, 149*(16), 878–884.

Boekeloo, B. O., & Howard, D. E. (2002). Oral sexual experience among young adolescents receiving general health examination. *American Journal of Health Behavior, 26*(4), 306–314.

Boeringer, S. (1999). Associations of rape-supportive attitudes with fraternal and athletic participation. *Violence Against Women, 5*(1), 81–90.

Bogaert, A. (1996). Volunteer bias in human sexuality research: Evidence for both sexuality and personality differences in males. *Archives of Sexual Behavior, 25*(2), 125–140.

Bogaert, A. F. (2004). The prevalence of male homosexuality: The effect of fraternal birth order and variations in family size. *Journal of Theoretical Biology, 230*(1), 33–37.

Bogaert, A. F., Bezeau, S., Kuban, M., & Blanchard, R. (1997). Pedophilia, sexual orientation and birth order. *Journal of Abnormal Psychology, 106*(2), 331–335.

Boies, S. C., Knudson, G., & Young, J. (2004). The Internet, sex, and youths: Implications for sexual development. *Sexual Addiction & Compulsivity, 11,* 343–363.

Bolso, A. (2005). Orgasm and lesbian sexuality. *Sex Education, 5*(1), 29–48.

Bolton, F. G., & MacEachron, A. E. (1988). Adolescent male sexuality: A developmental perspective. *Journal of Adolescent Research, 3,* 259–273.

Bonaccorsi, L., Marchiani, S., Muratori, M., Forti, G., & Baldi, E. (2004*). Journal of Cancer Research and Clinical Oncology, 130*(1), 604–614.

Boonstra, H. (2002a). Emergency contraception: Steps being taken to improve access. *The Guttmacher Report, 5*(5), 10–13.

Boonstra, H. (2002b). Legislators craft alternative vision of sex education to counter abstinence-only drive. *Guttmacher Report, 5*(2). Retrieved May 25, 2003, from http://www.agi-usa.org/journals/toc/ gr0502toc.html

Boonstra, H. (2002c, April). Teen pregnancy: Trends and lessons learned. *Issues Brief, Alan Guttmacher Institute, 1,* 1–4.

Boonstra, H. (2004). *Abstinence promotion and the U.S. approach to HIV/AIDS prevention overseas.* New York: The Alan Guttmacher Institute.

Boonstra, H. (2005, May). Condoms, contraceptives and nonoxynol-9: Complex issues obscured by ideology. *The Guttmacher Report on Public Policy, 8*(2), pp. 4–7.

Borchelt, G. (2005). Sexual violence against women in war and armed conflict. A. Barnes (Ed.), *Handbook of women, psychology, and the law* (pp. 293–327). New York: Wiley.

Born, L., & Steiner, M. (2001). Current management of premenstrual syndrome and premenstrual dysphoric disorder. *Current Psychiatry Reports, 3*(6), 463–469.

Bornstein, D. (Ed.). (1979). *The feminist controversy of the Renaissance.* Delmar, NY: Scholars' Facsimiles & Reprints.

Boroughs, D. S. (2004). Female sexual abusers of children. *Children & Youth Services Review, 26*(5), 481–487.

Boselli, F., Choissi, G., Bortolamasi, M., & Callinelli, A. (2005). Prevalence and determinants of genital shedding of herpes simplex virus among women attending Italian colposcopy clinics. *European Journal of Obstetrics and Reproductive Biology, 118*(1), 86–90.

Boswell, J. (1980). *Christianity, social tolerance, and homosexuality: Gay people in western Europe from the beginning of the Christian era to the fourteenth century.* Chicago: The University of Chicago Press.

Bouchard, C., Brisson, J., Fortier, M., Morin, C., & Blanchette, C. (2002). Use of oral contraceptive pills and vulvar vestibulitis. *American Journal of Epidemiology, 156*(3), 254–261.

Bower, B. (1992). Depression, early death noted in HIV cases. *Science News, 142,* 53.

Bower, H. (2001). The gender identity disorder in the DSM-IV classification: A critical evaluation. *Australian and New Zealand Journal of Psychiatry, 35*(1), 1–8.

Bowser, B. (2001). Social class in black sexuality. In R. Satow (Ed.), *Gender and social life* (pp. 120–124). Needham Heights, MA: Allyn & Bacon.

Boxer, D. (1996). Ethnographic interviewing as a research tool in speech act analysis: The case of complaints. In S. M. Gass & J. Neu (Eds.), *Speech acts across cultures* (pp. 217–239). New York: de Gruyter.

Boyd, L. (2000). Morning sickness shields fetus from bugs and chemicals. *RN, 63*(8), 18–20.

Boyle, G. J., Goldman, R., Svoboda, J. S., & Fernandez, E. (2002). The acceptability of male circumcision to reduce HIV infections in Nyanza Province, Kenya. *AIDS Care, 14*(1), 27–40.

Bracero, L. A., & Byrne, D. W. (1998). Optimal maternal weight gain during singleton pregnancy. *Gynecology and Obstetric Investigation, 46*(1), 9–16.

Brambati, B., & Tului, L. (2005). Chorionic villus sampling and amniocentesis. *Current Opinions in Obstetrics & Gynecology, 17*(2), 197–201.

Brandt, A. M. (1985). *No magic bullet: A social history of venereal disease in the United States.* New York: Oxford University Press.

Brawer, M. K. (1999). Prostate cancer: Epidemiology and screening. *Prostate Cancer and Prostatic Disease, 2*(S1), 2–6.

Breast Cancer Coalition. (2002). Breast cancer coalition: Facts about breast cancer in the U.S., year 2002. Retrieved September 11, 2002, from http://www.natlbcc.org

Brecher, E. M., & Brecher, J. (1986). Extracting valuable sexological findings from severely flawed and biased population samples. *Journal of Sex Research, 22,* 6–20.

Brecher, E., & the Editors of Consumer Reports Books. (1984). *Love, sex and aging.* Boston: Little, Brown.

Brecklin, L. R., & Ullman, S. E. (2005). Self-defense or assertiveness training and women's responses to sexual attacks. *Journal of Interpersonal Violence, 20*(6), 738–762.

Bren, L. (2001, November–December). Alternatives to hysterectomy: New technologies, more options. *FDA Consumer Magazine.*

Brener, N., Lowry, R., Kann, L., Kolbe, L., Lehnherr, J., Janssen, R., & Jaffe, H. (2002). Trends in sexual risk behaviors among high school students: United States, 1991–2001. *Morbidity and Mortality Weekly Report, 51*(38), 856–859.

Bretschneider, J. G., & McCoy, N. L. (1988). Sexual interest and behavior in healthy 80 to 102 year olds. *Archives of Sexual Behavior, 17,* 109–129.

Brett, K. M., & Cooper, G. S. (2003). Associations with menopause and menopausal transition in a nationally representative U.S. sample. *Maturitas, 45*(2), 89–97.

Breuss, C. E., & Greenberg, S. (1981). *Sex education: Theory and practice.* Belmont, CA: Wadsworth.

Bridgeland, W. M., Duane, E. A., & Stewart, C. S. (2001). Victimization and attempted suicide among college students. *College Student Journal, 35*(1), 63–76.

Bridges, L. J., & Moore, K. A. (2002). *Religious involvement and children's well-being: What research tells us (and what it doesn't).* Washington, DC: ChildTrends Research Brief.

Brienza, J. (1998). Hate crimes against gays hurt body and soul. *Trial, 34*(10), 95–98.

Bright, C. (2004). Deconstructing reparative therapy: An examination of the processes involved when attempting to change sexual orientation. *Clinical Social Work Journal, 32*(4), 471–481.

Bright, S. (2005). Checking out: The suicide of a radical hedonist. Retrieved February 13, 2005, from http://www.salon.com/weekly/binintro960805.html

Brindis, C. D., Driscoll, A. K., Biggs, M. A., & Valerrama, L. T. (2002). *Fact sheet on Latino youth: Sexual behavior.* San Francisco, CA: Center for Reproductive Health Research and Policy, Department of Obstetrics, Gynecology and Reproductive Health Sciences and the Institute for Health Policy Studies.

Brinton, L. A., & Schairer, C. (1997). Postmenopausal hormone-replacement therapy: Time for a reappraisal? *New England Journal of Medicine, 336*(25), 1821–1822.

Brinton, L. A., Moghissi, K. S., Scoccia, B., Westhoff, C. L., & Lamb, E. J. (2005). Ovulation induction and cancer risk. *Fertility & Sterility, 83*(2), 261–274.

Brockman, N. (2004). Kenya. In R. T. Francoeur & R. J. Noonan (Eds.), *The Continuum international encyclopedia of sexuality* (pp. 679–691). New York/London: Continuum International.

Brody, J. E. (2005). Getting to know a virus, and when it can kill. Retrieved November 25, 2005, from http://www.cluw.org/CCPW/JaneBrody.htm

Brongersma, E. (1990). Boy-lovers and their influence on boys: Distorted research and anecdotal observations. *Journal of Homosexuality, 20,* 145–173.

Brooks-Gordon, B., & Geisthorpe, L. (2003). What men say when apprehended for kerb crawling: A model of prostitutes' clients' talk. *Psychology, Crime and Law, 9*(2), 145–171.

Brooks-Gunn, J., & Furstenberg, F. F. (1989). Adolescent sexual behavior. *American Psychologist, 44,* 249–257.

Brooks-Gunn, J., & Furstenberg, F. F. (1990). Coming of age in the era of AIDS: Puberty, sexuality, and contraception. *Milbank Quarterly, 68,* 59–84.

Brotto, L. A. (2004). Genital and subjective sexual arousal in women: Effects of menopause, sympathetic nervous system activation, and arousal disorder. *Dissertation Abstracts International, 64*(11-B), #0419-4217.

Broude, G. J., & Greene, S. J. (1976). Cross-cultural codes on twenty sexual attitudes and practices. *Ethnology, 15,* 409–428.

Brown, A. S., Begg, M. D., Gravenstein, S., Schaefer, C. A., Wyatt, R. J., Bresnahan, M., Babulas, V. P., & Susser, E.S. (2004). Serologic evidence of prenatal influenza in the etiology of schizophrenia. *Archives of General Psychiatry, 61*(8), 774–780.

Brown, B. B., Dolcini, M. M., & Leventhal, A. (1997). Transformations in peer relationships at adolescence: Implications for healthrelated behavior. In J. Schulenberg, J. L. Maggs, & K. Hurrelmann (Eds.), *Health risks and developmental transitions during adolescence* (pp. 161–189). Cambridge, U.K.: Cambridge University Press.

Brown, D. (2002a, November 27). New turn in AIDS epidemic. *Hartford Courant,* p. A1.

Brown, D. (2002b, April 23). WHO urges global drug treatment of HIV. *Washington Post,* p. A2.

Brown, D. L., & Frank, J. E. (2003). Diagnosis and management of syphilis. *American Family Physician, 68*(2), 283–290.

Brown, D. J., Hill, S. T., & Baker, H. W. (2005). Male fertility and sexual function after spinal cord injury. *Progress in Brain Research, 152,* 427–439.

Brown, J. C. (1983). Paraphilias: Sadomasochism, fetishism, transvestism and transsexuality. *British Journal of Psychiatry, 143,* 227–231.

Brown, M. S., & Brown, C. A. (1987). Circumcision decision: Prominence of social concerns. *Pediatrics, 80,* 215–219.

Brown, T. J., Sumner, K. E., & Nocera, R. (2002). Understanding sexual aggression against women: An examination of the role of men's athletic participation and related variables. *Journal of Interpersonal Violence, 17*(9), 937–952.

Brownmiller, S. (1975). *Against our will: Men, women, and rape.* New York: Simon & Schuster.

Brownmiller, S. (2000). Rape on the brain: A review of Randy Thornhill and Craig Palmer. Retrieved December 5, 2005, from http://www.susanbrownmiller.com/html/review-thornhill.html

Brückner, H., & Bearman, P. (2005). After the promise: The STD consequences of adolescent virginity pledges. *Journal of Adolescent Health, 36*(4), 271–278.

Brumberg, J. J. (1997). *The body project: An intimate history of American girls.* New York: Vintage Books.

Bryan, W. A. (1987). Contemporary fraternity and sorority issues. *New Directions for Student Services, 40,* 37–56.

Buddie, A. M., & Testa, M. (2005). Rates and predictors of sexual aggression among students and nonstudents. *Journal of Interpersonal Violence, 20*(6), 713–724.

Buhrich, N., & McConaghy, N. (1985). Preadult feminine behaviors of male transvestites. *Archives of Sexual Behavior, 14,* 413–419.

Bulcroft, R., & Bulcroft, K. (1991). The nature and functioning of dating in later life. *Research on Aging 13*(2), 244–260.

Bull, S. S., & Melian, L. M. (1998). Contraception and culture: The use of Yuyos in Paraguay. *Health Care for Women International, 19*(1), 49–66.

Bulletti, C., Flaigni, C., & Giacomucci, E. (1996). Reproductive failure due to spontaneous abortion and recurrent miscarriage. *Human Reproductive Update, 2*(2), 118–136.

Bullough, V. (1977). Sex education in medieval Christianity. *Journal of Sex Research, 13*(3), 185–196.

Bullough, V. (1994). *Science in the bedroom: The history of sex research.* New York: Basic Books.

Bullough, V. L. (1973). *The subordinate sex: A history of attitudes toward women.* Urbana: University of Illinois Press.

Bullough, V. L. (1976). *Sexual variance in society and history.* New York: Wiley.

Bullough, V. L. (1979). *Homosexuality: A history.* New York: New American Library.

Bullough, V. L. (1990). History in adult human sexual behavior with children and adolescents in Western societies. In J. Feierman (Ed.), *Pedophilia biosocial dimensions* (pp. 69–90). New York: Springer-Verlag.

Bullough, V. L. (1998). Alfred Kinsey and the Kinsey Report: Historical overview and lasting contributions. *Journal of Sex Research, 35*(2), 127–131.

Bullough, V. L. (2001). Transgenderism and the concept of gender. Retrieved May 24, 2003, from http://www.symposium.com/ijt/gilbert/bullough.htm

Bullough, V. L., & Bullough, B. (1993). *Crossdressing, sex, and gender.* Philadelphia: University of Pennsylvania Press.

Bullough, V. L., Bullough, B., & Smith, R. (1983). A comparative study of male transvestites, male to female transsexuals, and male homosexuals. *Journal of Sex Research, 19,* 238–257.

Bullough, V. L., & Weinberg, J. S. (1988). Women married to transvestites: Problems and adjustments. *Journal of Psychology and Human Sexuality, 1,* 83–104.

Bullough, V., & Bullough, B. (1987). *Women and prostitution: A social history.* Buffalo, NY: Prometheus Books.

Bumpass, L. L., & Lu, H. H. (2000). Trends in cohabitation and implications for children's family contexts in the U.S. *Population Studies, 54,* 29–41.

Bundow, G. L. (1992). Why women stay. *Journal of the American Medical Association, 267*(23), 3229.

Bunnell, R. E., Dahlberg, L., Rolfs, R., Ransom, R., Gersham, K., Farshy, C., et al. (1999). High prevalence and incidence of STDs in urban adolescent females despite moderate risk behaviors. *Journal of Infectious Diseases, 180*(5), 1624–1631.

Burbidge, M., & Walters, J. (1981). *Breaking the silence: Gay teenagers speak for themselves.* London, U.K.: Joint Council for Gay Teenagers.

Burch, B. (1998). Lesbian sexuality. *Psychoanalytic Review, 85*(3), 349–372.

Bürgel, J. C. (1979). Love, lust and longing: Eroticism in early Islam as reflected in literary sources. In Al-Sayyid-Marsot & A. Lutfi (Eds.), *Society and the sexes in medieval Islam.* Malibu, CA: Undena Publications.

Burgess, A. W., & Holmstrom, L. L. (1974). Rape trauma syndrome. *American Journal of Psychiatry, 131,* 981–986.

Burgess, A. W., & Holmstrom, L. L. (1979). *Rape: Crisis and recovery.* Bowie, MD: Robert J. Brady.

Burgess, A. W., & Morgenbesser, L. I. (2005). Sexual violence and seniors. *Brief Treatment & Crisis Intervention, 5*(2), 193–202.

Burkeman, O., & Younge, G. (2005). Being Brenda. Retrieved February 24, 2005, from http://www.godspy.com/life/Being-Brenda.cfm

Burkman, R. T. (2002). The transdermal contraceptive patch: A new approach to hormonal contraception. *International Journal of Fertility and Women's Medicine, 47*(2), 69–76.

Burleson, B. R., & Denton, W. H. (1997). The relationship between communication skill and marital satisfaction: Some moderating effects. *Journal of Marriage and Family, 59*(4), 884–894.

Burmeister, L., & Healy, D. L. (1998). Ovarian cancer in infertility patients. *Annals of Medicine, 30*(6), 525–526.

Burnell, G. M., & Norfleet, M. A. (1987). Women's self-reported response to abortion. *Journal of Psychology, 121,* 71–76.

Burt, M. (1980). Cultural myths and support for rape. *Journal of Personality and Social Psychology, 38,* 217–230.

Burton, A. (2002). Circumcision reduces cervical cancer risk. *Lancet Infectious Diseases, 2*(6), 320.

Burton, K. (2005). Attachment style and perceived quality of romantic partner's opposite-sex best friendship: The impact on romantic relationship satisfaction. *Dissertation Abstracts International, 65*(8-B), 4329, # 0419-4217.

Bushman, B., & Bonacci, A. M. (2002). Violence and sex impair memory for television ads. *Journal of Applied Psychology, 87*(3), 557–564.

Buss, D. (1989a). Conflict between the sexes: Strategic interference and the evocation of anger and upset. *Journal of Personality and Social Psychology, 56*(5), 735–747.

Buss, D. (1989b). Sex differences in human mate preferences: Evolutionary hypotheses tested in 37 cultures. *Behavioral and Brain Sciences, 12,* 1–49.

Buss, D. M. (1994). *The evolution of desire: Strategies of human mating.* New York: Basic Books.

Buss, D. M. (2003). The dangerous passion: Why jealousy is as necessary as love and sex. *Archives of Sexual Behavior, 32*(1), 79–80.

Buss, D. M., Shackelford, T. K., Kirkpatrick, L., & Larsen, R. J. (2001). A half century of mate preferences: The cultural evolution of values. *Journal of Marriage & the Family, 63*(2), 491–503.

Buston, K., & Wight, D. (2002). The salience and utility of school sex education to young women. *Sex Education, 2*(3), 233–250.

Butler, M. H., & Wampler, K. S. (1999). A meta-analytic update of research on the couple communication program. *American Journal of Family Therapy, 27*(3), 223.

Butt, A. A., Dascomb, K. K., DeSalvo, K. B., Bazzano, L., Kissinger, P. J., Szerlip, H. M., et al. (2001). Human immunodeficiency virus infection in elderly patients. *Southern Medical Journal, 94*(4), 397–400.

Buunk, B. (1987). Conditions that promote breakups as a condition of extradyadic involvements. *Journal of Social and Clinical Psychology 5*(3), 271–284.

Buunk, B. P., Angleitner, A., & Oubaid, V. (1996). Sex differences in jealousy in evolutionary and cultural perspective: Tests from the Netherlands, Germany, and the United States. *Psychological Science, 7*(6), 359–363.

Buysse, A. (1998). Safer sexual decision making in stable and casual relationships: A prototype approach. *Psychology and Health, 13,* 55–66.

Buysse, A., & Ickes, W. (1999). Communication patterns in laboratory discussions of safer sex. *Journal of Sex Research, 36*(2), 121.

Buysse, A., DeClerq, A., & Verhofstadt, L. (2000). Dealing with relational conflict: A picture in milliseconds. *Journal of Social and Personal Relationships, 17*(4–5), 574–597.

Bygdeman, M., & Danielsson, K. G. (2002). Options for early therapeutic abortion. *Drugs, 62*(17), 2459–2470.

Byrne, D., & Murnen, S. K. (1988). Maintaining loving relationships. In R. Sternberg & M. L. Barnes (Eds.), *Psychology of love* (pp. 293–310). New Haven, CT: Yale University Press.

Cabaret, A. S., Leveque, J., Dugast, C., Blanchot, J., & Grall, J. Y. (2003). Problems raised by the gynaecologic management of women with BRCA 1 and 2 mutations. *Gynecology, Obstetrics and Fertility, 31*(4), 370–377.

Cado, S., & Leitenberg, H. (1990). Guilt reactions to sexual fantasies during intercourse. *Archives of Sexual Behavior 19*(1), 49–63.

Cahill, S., South, K., & Spade, J. (2000). *Outing age: Public policy issues affecting gay, lesbian, bisexual and transgender elders.* Washington, DC: National Gay and Lesbian Task Force.

Cai, D., Wilson, S. R., & Drake, L. E. (2000). Culture in the context of intercultural negotiation: Individualism-collectivism and paths to integrative agreements. *Human Communication Research, 26*(4), 591–617.

Calderone, M. (1983). On the possible prevention of sexual problems in adolescence. *Hospital and Community Psychiatry, 34,* 528–530.

Caldwell, E. (2003). What's love got to do with it? Plenty, OSU studies find. Retrieved January 31, 2003, from http://www.eurekalert.org/pub_releases/2003-01/osum_wlg013003.php

Caliendo, C., Armstrong, J. L., & Roberts, A. E. (2005). Self-reported characteristics of women and men with intimate body piercings. *Journal of Advanced Nursing, 49*(5), 474–484.

Callahan, M. M. (2002). Safety and tolerance studies of potential microbicides following multiple penile applications. Annual Conference on Microbicides, May 12–15, 2002, Antwerp, Belgium.

Cameron, K. A., Salazar, L. F., Bernhardt, J. M., Burgess-Whitman, N., Wingood, G. M., & DiClemente, R. J. (2005). Adolescents' experience with sex on the web: Results from online focus groups. *Journal of Adolescence, 28*(4), 535–540.

Cammaert, L. (1985). How widespread is sexual harassment on campus? Special issue, Women in groups and aggression against women. *International Journal of Women's Studies, 8,* 388–397.

Campbell, J. C., Webster, D., Koziol-McLain, J., Block, C., Campbell, D., Curry, M. A., et al. (2002). Intimate partner violence and physical health consequences. *Archives of Internal Medicine, 162*(10), 1157–1163.

Campbell, R., & Wasco, S. M. (2005). Understanding rape and sexual assault: 20 years of progress and future directions. *Journal of Interpersonal Violence, 20*(1), 127–131.

Campbell, R., Sefl, T., & Ahrens, C. E. (2004). The impact of rape on women's sexual health risk behaviors. *Health Psychology, 23*(1), 67–74.

Campenni, C. E. (1999). Gender stereotyping of children's toys: A comparison of parents and nonparents. *Sex Roles, 40*(1–2), 121–138.

Camperio-Ciani, A., Corna, F., & Capiluppi, C. (2004). Evidence for maternally inherited factors favouring male homosexuality and promoting female fecundity. *Proceedings: Biological Sciences, 271*(1554), 2217–2221.

Can taking the pill dull a woman's sexual drive forever? (2005, May 27). Retrieved August 21, 2005, from http://www.newscientist.com/article/mg18625015.600.html

Canli, T., Desmond, J. E., Zhao, Z., & Gabrieli, J. (2002). Sex differences in the neural basis of emotional memories. *Proceedings of the National Academy of Sciences, 99,* 10789–10794.

Cantor, J. M., Blanchard, R., Paterson, A. D., & Bogaert, A. (2002). How many gay men owe their sexual orientation to fraternal birth order? *Archives of Sexual Behavior, 31*(1) 63–71.

Cantor, J. M., Blanchard, R., Robichaud, L., & Christensen, B. (2005). Quantitative reanalysis of aggregate data on IQ in sexual offenders. *Psychological Bulletin, 131*(4), 555–568.

Carcopino, X., Shojai, R., & Boubli, L. (2004). Female genital mutilation: Generalities, complications and management during obstetrical period. *Journal of Gynecology, Obstetrics, & Biological Reproduction, 33*(5), 378–383.

Carey, B. (2004, November 9). Long after Kinsey, only the brave study sex. Retrieved April 2, 2005, from http://query.nytimes.com/gst/abstract.html?res=FA0D11F638580C7A8CDDA80994DC404482

Carey, B. (2005a). Straight, gay or lying? Bisexuality revisited. Retrieved July 5, 2005, from http://www.thetaskforce.org/downloads/07052005NYTBisexuality.pdf

Carey, B. (2005b). Watching new love as it sears the brain. Retrieved May 31, 2005, from http://www.nytimes.com/2005/05/31/health/psychology/31love.html

Carlton, C. L., Nelson, E. S., & Coleman, P. K. (2000). College students' attitudes toward abortion and commitment to the issue. *Social Science Journal, 37*(4), 619–625.

Carnes, P. (2001). *Out of the shadows: Understanding sexual addiction.* Center City, MN: Hazelden Information Education.

Carnes, P. (2003). Understanding sexual addiction. *SIECUS Report, 31*(5), 5–7.

Caron, S. L., Davis, C. M., Wynn, R. L., & Roberts, L. W. (1992). America responds to AIDS, but did college students? Differences between March, 1987, and September 1988. *AIDS Education and Prevention, 4,* 18–28.

Carr, R. R., & Ensom, M. H. (2002). Fluoxetine in the treatment of premenstrual dysphoric disorder. *Annuals of Pharmacotherapy, 36*(4), 713–717.

Carrell, D. T., Wilcox, A. L., Lowry, L., Peterson, C. M., Jones, K. P., Erickson, L., et al. (2003). Elevated sperm chromosome aneuploidy and apoptosis in patients with unexplained recurrent pregnancy loss. *Obstetrics and Gynecology, 101*(6), 1229–1235.

Carrier, J. M. (1989). Gay liberation and coming out in Mexico. *Journal of Homosexuality, 17,* 225–252.

Carroll, J. (2002). The stuff that dreams are made of. Unpublished manuscript.

Carvajal, S. C., Parcel, G. S., & Basen-Engquist, K. (1999). Psychosocial predictors of delay of first sexual intercourse by adolescents. *Health Psychology, 18*(5), 443–452.

Case, P., Austin, S. B., Hunter, D., Manson, J., Malpeis, S., Willett, W., & Spiegelman, D. (2004). Sexual orientation, health risk factors, and physical functioning in the nurses' health study II. *Journal of Women's Health, 13*(9), 1033–1047.

Cass, V. C. (1979). Homosexual identity formation: A theoretical model. *Journal of Homosexuality, 4,* 219–235.

Cass, V. C. (1984). Homosexual identity formation: Testing a theoretical model. *The Journal of Sex Research, 20,* 143–167.

Casteels, K., Wouters, C., VanGeet, C., & Devlieger, H. (2004). Video reveals self-stimulation in infancy. *Acta Paediatrics, 93*(6), 844–846.

Castellsague, X., Peeling, R. W., Franceschi, S., deSanjose, S., Smith, J. S., Albero, G., Diaz, M., Herroro, R., Munoz, N., & Bosch, F. X. (2005). Chlamydia trachomatis infection in female partners of circumcised and uncircumcised adult men. *American Journal of Epidemiology,* Epub ahead of print. Retrieved September 24, 2005, from http://www.ncbi.nlm.nih.gov/entrez/query.fcgi?cmd=Retrieve&db=pubmed&dopt=Abstract&list_uids=16177149&query_hl=15

Catalan, J., & Meadows, J. (2000). Sexual dysfunction in gay and bisexual men with HIV infection: Evaluation and treatment. *AIDS Care, 12*(3), 279–286.

Catania, J. A., Binson, D., Van Der Straten, A., & Stone, V. (1995). Methodological research on sexual behavior in the AIDS era. *Annual Review of Sex Research, 6,* 77–125.

Catania, J. A., Coates, T. J., Kegeles, S. M., et al. (1989). Implications of the AIDS risk-reduction model for the gay community: The importance of perceived sexual enjoyment and help-seeking behaviors. In V. M. Mays, G. W. Albee, & S. F. Schneider (Eds.), *Primary prevention of AIDS: Psychological approaches* (pp. 242–261). Newbury Park, CA: Sage.

Catania, J. A., McDermott, L. J., & Pollack, L. M. (1986). Questionnaire response bias and face-to-face interview sample bias in sexuality research. *Journal of Sex Research, 22,* 52–72.

Catania, J. A., & White, C. B. (1982). Sexuality in an aged sample: Cognitive determinates of masturbation. *Archives of Sexual Behavior, 11,* 237–245.

Cates, J. A., & Markley, J. (1992). Demographic, clinical, and personality variables associated with male prostitution by choice. *Adolescence, 27,* 695–706.

Cates, W. (1999). Estimates of the incidence and prevalence of STDs in the U.S.: American Social Health Association. *Sexually Transmitted Diseases, 26*(4 Suppl.), S2–S7.

Cates, W. (2004). Reproductive tract infections. In R. A. Hatcher et al. (Eds.), *Contraceptive technology* (18th Rev. ed., pp. 191–220). New York: Ardent Media.

Cates, W., & Raymond, E. G. (2004). Vaginal spermicides. In R. A. Hatcher et al. (Eds.), *Contraceptive technology* (18th Rev. ed., pp. 355–363). New York: Ardent Media.

Cates, W., & Stewart, F. (2004). Vaginal barriers. In R. A. Hatcher et al. (Eds.), *Contraceptive technology* (18th Rev. ed., pp. 365–389). New York: Ardent Media.

Cates, W., Rolfs, R. T., & Aral, S. O. (1990). STDs, PID, and infertility: An epidemiologic update. *Epidemiology Review, 12,* 199–220.

Ceniti, J., & Malamuth, N. (1984). Effects of repeated exposure to sexually violent or nonviolent stimuli on sexual arousal to rape or nonrape depictions. *Behavior Research and Therapy, 22,* 535–548.

Centers for Disease Control and Prevention. (1991). Advance report on final divorce statistics, 1988. *National Center for Health Statistics 39*(12).

Center on Addiction and Substance Abuse. (2002, February). Substance use and risky sexual behavior: Attitudes and practices among adolescents and young adults. Retrieved September 30, 2002, from www.casa.columbia.org

Centers for Disease Control and Prevention. (2002a). Sexually transmitted diseases: Treatment guidelines, 2002. *Morbidity and Mortality Weekly Report, 51*(RR-6). Retrieved November 22, 2005, from http://www.cdc.gov/std/treatment/TOC2002TG.htm

Centers for Disease Control and Prevention. (2002b). Teenagers in the United States: Sexual activity, contraceptive use, and childbearing. Series 23(24). Retrieved June 1, 2005, from http://www.cdc.gov/nchs/data/series/sr_23/sr23_024FactSheet.pdf

Centers for Disease Control and Prevention. (2003). AIDS Cases in Adolescents and Adults, by Age—United States, 1994–2000. *AIDS/HIV Surveillance Supplemental Report, 9*(1). Retrieved on May 25, 2003, from http://www.cdc.gov/hiv/stats/hasrsuppVol9No1.htm

Centers for Disease Control and Prevention. (2003a). Can I get HIV from oral sex? Retrieved November 22, 2005, from http://www.cdc.gov/hiv/pubs/faq/faq19.htm

Centers for Disease Control and Prevention. (2003b). Viral hepatitis A, B, and C in the United States. Retrieved November 22, 2005, from http://www.cdc.gov/ncidod/diseases/hepatitis/resource/dz_burden02.htm

Centers for Disease Control and Prevention. (2004a). Genital HPV infection: CDC fact sheet. Retrieved November 22, 2005, from http://www.cdc.gov/std/HPV/STDFact-HPV.htm

Centers for Disease Control and Prevention. (2004b). HIV/AIDS surveillance report. Retrieved November 22, 2005, from http://www.cdc.gov/hiv/stats/2004SurveillanceReport.pdf

Centers for Disease Control and Prevention. (2004c, October 8). Smoking during pregnancy United States—1990–2002, *Morbidity and Mortality Weekly Report, 53*(39), 911–915.

Centers for Disease Control and Prevention. (2005a). Clostridium sordellii toxic shock syndrome after medical abortion with mifepristone and intravaginal misoprostol—United States and Canada, 2001–2005. *Morbidity & Mortality Weekly Report, 54*(29), 724.

Centers for Disease Control and Prevention. (2005b). Parasitic disease information: Scabies. Retrieved November 22, 2005, from http://www.cdc.gov/ncidod/dpd/parasites/scabies/factsht_scabies.htm

Centers for Disease Control and Prevention. (2005c). Recommended childhood and adolescent immunization schedule—United States. *Morbidity and Mortality Weekly Report, 53*(51, 52), Q1–Q3.

Centers for Disease Control and Prevention. (2005d). Sexually transmitted disease surveillance, 2004. Retrieved November 25, 2005, from http://www.cdc.gov/std/stats/04pdf/2004SurveillanceAll.pdf

Centers for Disease Control and Prevention. (2005e). Viral hepatitis. National Center for Infectious Diseases. Retrieved November 22, 2005, from http://www.cdc.gov/ncidod/diseases/hepatitis/

Chan, C. S. (1989). Issues of identity development among Asian-American lesbians and gay men. *Journal of Counseling and Development, 68,* 16–20.

Chase, M. (2005, January 25). Merck plans to start phase II of AIDS-vaccine human trials. *Wall Street Journal,* p. D3.

Chaudhury, R. R. (1985). Plant contraceptives translating folklore into scientific application. In D. B. Jelliffe & E. F. Jelliffe (Eds.), *Advances in international maternal and child health* (pp. 107–114). Oxford, U.K.: Claredon Press.

Cheasty, M., Clare, A. W., & Collins, C. (2002). Child sexual abuse: A predictor of persistent depression in adult rape and sexual assault victims. *Journal of Mental Health, 11*(1), 79–84.

Cheng, W., & Warren, M. (2001). She knows more about Hong Kong than you do isn't it: Tags in Hong Kong conversational English. *Journal of Pragmatics, 33,* 1419–1439.

Chesney, M. A. (2000). Factors affecting adherence to antiretroviral therapy. *Clinical Infectious Diseases, 30,* 5171–5176.

Chevan, A. (1996). As cheaply as one: Cohabitation in the older population. *Journal of Marriage and the Family, 58,* 656–667.

Chia, M., & Abrams, D. (1997). *The multiorgasmic man: Sexual secrets every man should know.* San Francisco: HarperCollins.

Chick, D., & Gold, S. R. (1987–88). A review of influences on sexual fantasy: Attitudes, experience, guilt, and gender. *Imagination, Cognition, and Personality, 7,* 61–76.

Chilman, C. S. (1983). *Adolescent sexuality in a changing American society.* New York: Wiley.

Chilman, C. S. (1986). Some psychosocial aspects of adolescent sexual and contraceptive behaviors in a changing American society. In J. B. Lancaster & B. A. Hamburg (Eds.), *School-age pregnancy and parenthood: Biosocial dimensions* (pp. 191–217). New York: DeGruyter.

Chivers, M. L., & Bailey, J. M. (2000). Sexual orientation of female-to-male transsexuals: A comparison of homosexuals and non-homosexuals. *Archives of Sexual Behavior, 29*(3), 259–279.

Chlebowski, R. T., Chen, Z., Anderson, G. L., Rohan, T., Aragaki, A., Lane, D., Dolan, N. C., Paskett, E. D., McTiernan, A., Hubbell, F. A., Adams-Campbell, L. L., & Prentice, R. (2005). Ethnicity and breast cancer: Factors influencing differences in incidence and outcome. *Journal National Cancer Institute, 97*(6), 439–448.

Chodorow, N. (1978). *The reproduction of mothering: Psychoanalysis and the sociology of gender.* Berkeley: University of California Press.

Choi, N. (2004). Sex role group differences in specific, academic, and general self-efficacy. *Journal of Psychology: Interdisciplinary & Applied, 138*(2), 149–159.

Chollar, S. (2000). Are monthly periods obsolete? Retrieved June 16, 2000, from http://my.webmd.com/ content/article/1689.50764

Chopin-Marcé, M. J. (2001). Exhibitionism and psychotherapy: A case study. *International Journal of Offender Therapy & Comparative Criminology, 45*(5), 626–633.

Chow, E. W., & Choy, A. L. (2002). Clinical characteristics and treatment response to SSRI in a female pedophile. *Archives of Sexual Behavior, 31*(2), 211–215.

Christensen, A., & Shenk, J. L. (1991). Communication, conflict, and psychological distance in nondistressed, clinic, and divorcing couples. *Journal of Consulting and Clinical Psychology 59*(3), 458–463.

Christianson, A. (2005). A re-emergence of reparative therapy. *Contemporary Sexuality, 39*(10), 8–17.

Christie-Mizell, C. (2003). Racial variation in the effects of sons versus daughters on the disruption of the first marriage. *Journal of Divorce and Remarriage, 38*(3–4), 41–60.

Church, C. A., & Geller, J. (1990). Voluntary female sterilization: Number one and growing. *Population Reports—Series J*(39), 2–31.

Ciesielski, C. A. (2003). STDs in men who have sex with men: An epidemiologic review. *Current Infectious Diseases Report, 5*(2), 145–152.

Cindoglu, D. (1997). Virginity tests and artificial virginity in modern Turkish medicine. *Women's Studies International Forum, 20*(2), 253–261.

Clapp, J. F. (1996). Morphometric and neurodevelopmental outcome at age five years of the offspring of women who continued to exercise regularly throughout pregnancy. *Journal of Pediatrics, 129*(6), 856–863.

Clark, A. M., Ledger, W., Galletly, C., Tomlinson, L., Blaney, F., Wang, X., & Norman R.J. (1995). Weight loss results in significant improvement in pregnancy and ovulation rates in anovulatory obese women. *Human Reproduction, 10,* 2705–2712.

Clark, D. A. (1994). Does immunological intercourse prevent pre-eclampsia? *The Lancet, 344,* 969–970.

Clark, J. (2005). The big turnoff. *Psychology Today, 38*(1), 17–19.

Clark, M. S., & Reis, H. T. (1988). Interpersonal processes in close relationships. *Annual Review of Psychology, 39,* 609–672.

Clark, P. M., Atton, C., Law, C. M., Shiell, A., Godfrey, K., & Barker, D. J. (1998). Weight gain in pregnancy, triceps skinfold thickness, and blood pressure in offspring. *Obstetrics and Gynecology, 91*(1), 103–107.

Clarke, A. K., & Miller, S. J. (2001). The debate regarding continuous use of oral contraceptives. *Annals of Pharmacotherapy, 35,* 1480–1484.

Class of 1978. (1983–1984). An investigation of remarriages in Hongkou district, Shanghai. *Chinese Sociology and Anthropology 16*(1–2), 117–127.

Coates, J. (1986). *Women, men and language.* New York: Longman.

Coates, R. (2004). Australia. In R. T. Francoeur & R. J. Noonan (Eds.), *The Continuum international encyclopedia of sexuality* (pp. 27–41). New York/London: Continuum International.

Cochran, S. D., & Mays, V. M. (2000). Lifetime prevalence of suicide symptoms and affective disorders among men reporting samesex sexual partners: Results from NHANES III. *American Journal of Public Health, 90*(4), 573–578.

Cohan, C., & Kleinbaum, S. (2002). Toward a greater understanding of the cohabitation effect. *Journal of Marriage and Family, 64*(1), 180–193.

Cohen, A. B., & Tannenbaum, I. J. (2001). Lesbian and bisexual women's judgments of the attractiveness of different body types. *Journal of Sex Research, 38*(3), 226–232.

Cohen, K. M., & Savin-Williams, R. C. (1996). Developmental perspectives on coming out to self and others. In R. C. Savin-Williams & K. M. Cohen (Eds.), *The lives of lesbians, gays, and bisexuals: Children to adults* (pp. 113–151). Fort Worth, TX: Harcourt Brace.

Cohen, L. (1988). Providing treatment and support for partners of sexual-assault survivors. *Psychotherapy, 25,* 94–98.

Cohen, L., & Roth, S. (1987). The psychological aftermath of rape: Long-term effects and individual differences in recovery. *Journal of Social and Clinical Psychology, 5,* 525–534.

Cohen, M. (2005, July 23–24). Hidden tragedies of the tsunami. Retrieved July 23, 2005, from http://www.thestandard.com.hk/stdn/std/others/print.htm

Cohen-Bendahan, C., van de Beek, C., & Berenbaum, S. (2005). Prenatal sex hormone effects on child and adult sex-typed behavior: Methods and findings. *Neuroscience & Biobehavioral Reviews, 29*(2), 353–384.

Cohen-Ketteris, P. T., & Gooren, L. J. G. (1999). Transsexualism: A review of etiology, diagnosis and treatment. *Journal of Psychosomatic Research, 46*(4), 315–333.

Coker, A. L., Davis, K. E., Arias, I., Desai, S., Sanderson, M., Brandt, H. M., et al. (2002). Physical and mental health effects of intimate partner violence for men and women. *American Journal of Preventive Medicine, 23*(4), 260–268.

Colapinto, J. (2001). *As nature made him: The boy who was raised as a girl.* New York: HarperCollins.

Coleman, E. (1982). Developmental stages of the coming-out process. *American Behavioral Scientist, 25,* 469–482.

Coleman, E. (2002). Masturbation as a means of achieving sexual health. *Journal of Psychology and Human Sexuality, 14*(2–3), 5–16.

Coleman, M., & Ganong, L. H. (1985). Love and sex role stereotypes: Do macho men and feminine women make better lovers? *Journal of Personality & Social Psychology, 49*(1), 170–176.

Coleman, M., Ganong, L., & Fine, M. (2000). Reinvestigating remarriage: Another decade of progress. *Journal of Marriage and Family, 62*(4), 1288–1308.

Coleman, P. (2002). *How to say it for couples.* New York: Prentice Hall Press.

Coles, R., & Stokes, G. (1985). *Sex and the American teenager.* New York: Harper & Row.

Collaborative Group on Hormonal Factors in Breast Cancer. (2001). Familial breast cancer. *The Lancet, 358*(9291), 1389–1399.

Collier, J. F., & Rosaldo, M. Z. (1981). Politics and gender in simple societies. In S. Ortner & H. Whitehead (Eds.), *Sexual meanings* (pp. 275–329). Cambridge, U.K.: Cambridge University Press.

Collins, P. H. (1998). The tie that binds: Race, gender and U.S. violence. *Ethnic and Racial Studies, 21*(5), 917–939.

Collins, P. H. (2000). It's all in the family. *Women and Language, 23*(2), 65–69.

Collins, R. (1988). *Sociology of marriage and the family.* Chicago: Nelson-Hall.

Collins, R. (2005). Sex on television and its impact on American youth: Background and results from the RAND television and adolescent sexuality study. *Child & Adolescent Psychiatric Clinics of North America, 14*(3), 371–385.

Collins, R. L., Elliott, M. N., Berry, S. H., Kanouse, D. E., Kunkel, D., Hunter, S. B., & Miu, A. (2004). Watching sex on television predicts adolescent initiation of sexual behavior. *Pediatrics, 114*(3), 280–289.

Coltrane, S., & Messineo, M. (2000). The perpetuation of subtle prejudice: Race and gender imagery in 1990s television advertising. *Sex Roles, 42*(5–6), 363–389.

Comfort, A. (1987). Deviation and variation. In G. D. Wilson (Ed.), *Variant sexuality: Research and theory* (pp. 1–20). Baltimore: Johns Hopkins University Press.

Comfort, A., & Rubenstein, J. (1992). *The new joy of sex: A gourmet guide to lovemaking in the nineties.* New York: Simon & Schuster.

Comstock, G., & Paik, H. (1991). *Television and the American child.* San Diego, CA: Academic Press.

Conkright, L., Flannagan, D., & Dykes, J. (2000). Effects of pronoun type and gender role consistency on children's recall and interpretation of stories. *Sex Roles, 43*(7–8), 481–497.

Connolly, A., Thorp, J., & Pahel, L. (2005). Effects of pregnancy and childbirth on postpartum sexual function: A longitudinal prospective study. *International Urogynecological Journal of Pelvic Floor Dysfunction,* Epub ahead of print. Retrieved July 17, 2005, from http://www.ncbi.nlm.nih.gov/entrez/query.fcgi?cmd=Retrieve&db=pubmed&dopt=Abstract&list_uids=15838587&query_hl=53

Conway, A. M. (2005). Girls, aggression, and emotion regulation. *American Journal of Orthopsychiatry, 75*(2), 334–339.

Cooper, A. M. (1991). The unconscious core of perversion. In G. I. Fogel & W. A. Myers (Eds.), *Perversions and near-perversions in clinical practice: New psychoanalytic perspectives* (pp. 17–35). New Haven: Yale University Press.

Cooper, A., Putnam, D. E., Planchon, L., & Boies, S. C. (1999). Online sexual compulsivity: Getting tangled in the net. *Sexual Addiction & Compulsivity, 6*(2), 79–104.

Cooper, A., & Sportolari, L. (1997). Romance in cyberspace: Understanding online attraction. *Journal of Sex Education and Therapy, 22*(1), 7–14.

Corey, L., Wald, A., Patel, R. Sacks, S., Tyring, S., Warren, T., Douglas, J., Paavonen, J., Morrow, R., Beutner, K., Strachounsky, L., Mertz, G., Keene, O., Watson, H., Tait, D., & Vargas-Cortes, M. (2004). Once-daily Valacyclovir to reduce the risk of transmission of genital herpes. *The New England Journal of Medicine, 350*(1), 11–20.

Cornett, M., & Shuntich, R. (1991). Sexual aggression: Perceptions of its likelihood of occurring and some correlates of selfadmitted perpetration. *Perceptual & Motor Skills, 73,* 499–507.

Cornog, M. (2003). *The big book of masturbation: From angst to zeal.* San Francisco, CA: Down There Press.

Corwin, A. L., Olson, J. G., Omar, M. A., Razaki, A., et al. (1991). HIV-1 in Somalia: Prevalence and knowledge among prostitutes. *AIDS, 5,* 902–904.

Costello, C., Hillis, S. D., Marchbanks, P. A., Jamieson, D. J., & Peterson, H. B. (2002). The effect of interval tubal sterilization on sexual interest and pleasure. *Obstetrics and Gynecology, 100*(3), 511–518.

Couldwell, D. L. (2005). Management of unprotected sexual encounters. *The Medical Journal of Australia, 183*(10), 525–528.

Coulson, N. J. (1979). Regulation of sexual behavior under traditional Islamic law. In Al-Sayyid-Marsot & A. Lutfi (Eds.), *Society and the sexes in medieval Islam* (pp. 63–68). Malibu, CA: Undena Publications.

Covey, H. C. (1989). Perceptions and attitudes toward sexuality of the elderly during the Middle Ages. *The Gerontologist, 29,* 93–100.

Cowan, G. (1992). Feminist attitudes toward pornography control. *Psychology of Women Quarterly*, 165–177.

Cowan, G. (2000). Beliefs about the causes of four types of rape. *Sex Roles, 42*(9–10), 807–823.

Cox, D. J. (1988). Incidence and nature of male genital exposure behavior as reported by college women. *Journal of Sex Research, 24,* 227–234.

Cox, D. J., Tsang, K., & Lee, A. (1982). A cross cultural comparison of the incidence and nature of male exhibitionism among female college students. *Victimology: An International Journal, 7,* 231–234.

Cox, F. D. (2000). *The AIDS booklet* (6th ed.). New York: McGraw-Hill.

Cranberry and urinary tract infection. (2005). *Drug Therapy Bulletin, 43*(3), 17–19.

Crawford, I., Allison, K. W., Zamboni, B. D., & Sotot, T. (2002). The influence of dual-identity on the development of the psychosocial functioning of African-American gay and bisexual men. *Journal of Sex Research, 39*(3), 179–190.

Crawford, J. T., Leynes, P. A., Mayhorn, C. B., & Bink, M .L. (2004). Champagne, beer, or coffee? A corpus of gender-related and neutral words. *Behavior Research Methods, Instruments & Computers, 36*(3), 444–459.

Critelli, J. W., Myers, E. J., & Loos, V. E. (1986). The components of love: Romantic attraction and sex role orientation. *Journal of Personality, 54*(2), 354–370.

Crittenden, A. (2001). *The price of motherhood.* New York: Metropolitan Books.

Cross, S. E., & Madson, L. (1997). Models of the self: Self-constructs and gender. *Psychological Bulletin, 122,* 5–37.

Crow, S. M. (1999, January 15). Only a yeast infection? *Parents Magazine,* pp. 54–55.

Crowder, K. D., & Tolnay, S. E. (2000). A new marriage squeeze for black women: The role of racial intermarriage by black men. *Journal of Marriage and Family, 62*(3), 792–817.

Crowe, M. (2002). Chancroid. Retrieved March 24, 2003 from http://www.emedicine.com/derm/topic71.htm

Cullinan, K. (2003). Swaziland grapples with AIDS. Retrieved August 29, 2003, from http://www.csa.za.org/article/articleview/194/1/1/

Cummins, H. J. (2002, March 18). First comes love . . . then cohabiting, then maybe marriage. Retrieved June 21, 2002, from www.startribune.com/stories/389/2101335.html

Cusitar, L. (1994). *Strengthening the link: Stopping the violence.* Toronto: Disabled Women's Network.

Cyr, M., Wright, J., McDuff, P., & Perron, A. (2002). Intrafamilial sexual abuse. *Child Abuse and Neglect, 26*(9), 957–973.

Dade, L. R., & Sloan, L. R. (2000). An investigation of sex-role stereotypes in African Americans. *Journal of Black Studies, 30*(5), 676.

Dagg, P. K. B. (1991). The psychological sequelae of therapeutic abortion—denied and completed. *American Journal of Psychiatry, 148,* 578–585.

Daie, N., Wilztum, E., & Eleff, M. (1989). Longterm effects of sibling incest. *Journal of Clinical Psychiatry, 50,* 428–431.

Dailard, C. (2001a). Recent findings from the "ADD Health" Survey: Teens and sexual activity. *The Guttmacher Report, 4*(4). Retrieved August 26, 2003, from http://www.agi-usa.org/pubs/journals/gr040401.html

Dailard, C. (2001b). Sex education: Politicians, parents, teachers and teens. *The Guttmacher Report on Public Policy, 4*(1), 9–12.

Daley, A. (2004). Caring for women who have undergone genital mutilation. *Nursing Times, 100*(26), 32–35.

Dalla, R. L. (2002). Night moves: A qualitative investigation of street-level sex work. *Psychology of Women Quarterly, 26*(1), 63–74.

d'Amora, D., & Hobson, B. (2003). Sexual offender treatment. Retrieved March 31, 2003, from http://www.smith-lawfirm.com/Connsacs_offender_treatment.htm

Dancey, C. P. (1990). Sexual orientation in women: An investigation of hormonal and personality variables. *Biological Psychology, 30,* 251–264.

Daragahi, B., & Dubin, A. (2001). Can prenups be romantic? *Money, 30*(2), 30–38.

Dare, R. O., Oboro, V. O., Fadiora, S. O., Orji, E. O., Sule-Edu, A. O., & Olabode, T. O. (2004). Female genital mutilation: An analysis of 522 cases in South-Western Nigeria. *Journal of Obstetrics & Gynaecology, 24*(3), 281–283.

Darroch, J. D., & Singh, S. (1999). Why is teenage pregnancy declining? *The Roles of Abstinence, Sexual Activity and Contraceptive Use, Occasional Report No. 1.* New York: Alan Guttmacher Institute.

Date rape drug served at Colorado fraternity parties: One dose potentially fatal, investigation finds. (2005). Retrieved December 3, 2005, from http://www.thedenverchannel.com/news/5068195/detail.html

D'Augelli, A., Grossman, A., & Starks, M. (2005). Parents' awareness of lesbian, gay, and bisexual youths' sexual orientation. *Journal of Marriage & Family, 67*(2), 474–482.

Davey, C. L., & Davidson, M. J. (2000). The right of passage? The experiences of female pilots in commercial aviation. *Feminism & Psychology, 10*(2), 195–225.

Davidson, J. K., & Darling, C. A. (1986). The impact of college level sex education on sexual knowledge, attitudes, and practices: The knowledge/sexual experimentation myth revisited. *Deviant Behavior, 7,* 13–30.

Davidson, J. K., & Darling, C. A. (1993). Masturbatory guilt and sexual responsiveness among post-college-age women: Sexual satisfaction revisited. *Journal of Sex and Marital Therapy, 19,* 289–300.

Davidson, J., Moore, N., & Ullstrup, K. (2004). Religiosity and sexual responsibility: Relationships of choice. *American Journal of Health Behavior, 28*(4), 335–346.

Davies, M. (2004). Correlates of negative attitudes toward gay men: Sexism, male role norms, and male sexuality. *Journal of Sex Research, 41*(3), 259–266

Davies, M. F. (2001). Socially desirable responding and impression management in the endorsement of love styles. *Journal of Psychology: Interdisciplinary & Applied, 135*(5), 562–570.

Davies, M. J. (2005). Fetal programming: The perspective of single and twin pregnancies. *Reproduction, Fertility and Development, 17*(3), 379–386.

Davis, A. (2005). Male birth control pill underway. Retrieved February 5, 2005, from http://www.dailyfreepress.com/global_user_elements/printpage.cfm?storyid=852 859.

Davis, K. E., & Latty-Mann, H. (1987). Love styles and relationship quality: A contribution to validation. *Journal of Social & Personal Relationships, 4*(4), 409–428.

Davis, K. E., & Todd, M. J. (1982). Friendship and love relationships. *Advances in Descriptive Psychology, 2,* 79–122.

Davis, P., & Lay-Yee, R. (1999). Early sex and its behavioral consequences in New Zealand. *Journal of Sex Research, 36*(2), 135–145.

Davis, S. R., Davison, S. L., Donath, S., & Bell, R. J. (2005). Circulating androgen levels and self-reported sexual function in women. *Journal of the American Medical Association, 294*(1), 91–96.

Daw, J. (2002). Hormone therapy for men? *Monitor on Psychology, 33*(9), 53.

Day, M., & Bisset, S. (2004). Revealed: Two British women die after taking controversial new abortion pill. Retrieved September 3, 2005, from http://www.telegraph.co.uk/news/main.jhtml?xml=/news/2004/01/18/nabort18.xml&sSheet=/news/2004/01/18/ixhome.html

D.C. hosts world conference on sexual slavery. (2003). *Contemporary Sexuality, 37*(3), 9.

DeAmicis, L. A., Goldberg, D. C., LoPiccolo, J., Friedman, J., & Davies, L. (1985). Clinical follow-up of couples treated for sexual dysfunction. *Archives of Sexual Behavior, 14,* 467–489.

de Beauvoir, S. (1952). *The second sex.* New York: Vintage Books.

DeBellis, M. D., Keshavan, M. S., Beers, S. R., Hall, J., Frustaci, K., Masalehdan, A., et al. (2001) Sex differences in brain maturation during childhood and adolescence. *Cerebral Cortex, 11*(6), 552-557.

de Freitas, S. (2004). Brazil. In R. T. Francoeur & R. J. Noonan (Eds.), The Continuum complete international encyclopedia of sexuality (pp. 98–113). New York/London: Continuum International.

deGaston, J. F., Jensen, L., & Weed, S. (1995). A closer look at adolescent sexual activity. *Journal of Youth and Adolescence, 24*(4), 465–479.

DeGue, S., & DiLillo, D. (2005). "You would if you loved me": Toward an improved conceptual and etiological understanding of nonphysical male sexual coercion. *Aggression & Violent Behavior, 10*(4), 513–532.

DeLamater, J. (1987). A sociological approach. In J. H. Geer & W. T. O'Donohue (Eds.), *Theories of human sexuality* (pp. 237–253). New York: Plenum Press.

DeLamater, J. D. (1989). The social control of human sexuality. In K. McKinney & S. Sprecher (Eds.), *Human sexuality* (p. 30–62). Norwood, NJ: Ablex.

DeLange, J. (1995). Gender and communication in social work education: A cross-cultural perspective. *Journal of Social Work Education, 31*(1), 75–82.

Delate, T., Simmons, V. A., & Motheral, B. R. (2004). Patterns of use of sildenafil among commercially insured adults in the U.S.: 1998–2002. *International Journal of Impotence Research, 16*(4), 313–318.

Deligeoroglou, E., Michailidis, E., & Creatsas, G. (2003). Oral contraceptives and reproductive system cancer. *Annals of New York Academy of Science, 997,* 199–208.

Demarest, J., & Allen, R. (2000). Body image: Gender, ethnic, and age differences. *Journal of Social Psychology, 140*(4), 465–472.

D'Emilio, J., & Freedman, E. (1988). *Intimate matters: A history of sexuality in America.* New York: Harper & Row.

Demir, E., & Dickson, B. J. (2005). Fruitless splicing specifies male courtship behavior in Drosophila. *Cell, 121*(5), 785–794.

Dempster, C. (2002). Silent war on South African women. Retrieved April 10, 2003, from www.new.bbc.co.uk/hi/english/world/africa/newsid_190900011909220.stm

Dennerstein, L., Dudley, E., Guthrie, J., & Barrett-Connor, E. (2000). Life satisfaction, symptoms, and the menopausal transition. *Medscape Women's Health, 5*(4), E4.

Dennison, S. M., & Tomson, D. M. (2005). Criticisms of plaudits for stalking laws? What psycholegal research tells us about proscribing stalking. *Psychology, Public Policy, & Law, 11*(3), 384–406.

Denny, D., & Wiederman, M. W. (2004). A chorus of transgender voices. *Journal of Sex Research, 41*(4), 410–412.

DePineres, T. (2002). Reproductive health 2002: Update on contraception and medical abortion from the ARHD Annual Meeting. *Medscape Ob/Gyn and Women's Health, 7*(2). Retrieved May 20, 2003, from http://www.medscape.com/viewarticle/442100

Depner, C., & Ingersoll-Dayton, B. (1985). Conjugal social support. *Journal of Gerontology, 40,* 761–766.

de-Schampheleire, D. (1990). MMPI characteristics of professional prostitutes: A crosscultural replication. *Journal of Personality Assessment, 54,* 343–350.

DeSteno, D., Barlett, M. T., Braverman, J., & Salovey, P. (2002). Sex differences in jealousy: Evolutionary mechanism or artifact of measurement? *Journal of Personality and Social Psychology, 83*(5), 1103–116.

Dettwyler, K., & Stuart-Macadam, P. (1995). *Breastfeeding: Biocultural perspectives.* New York: Walter de Gruyter.

Deveny, K. (2003, June 30). We're not in the mood: How stress causes strife in the bedroom—and beyond. *Newsweek,* pp. 41–45.

Dholakia, R. R., Dholakia, N., & Kshetri, H. (2003). Gender and internet usage. Retrieved May 5, 2005, from http://ritim.cba.uri.edu/wp2003/pdf_format/Wiley-Encycl-Internet-Usage-Gender-Final.pdf

Diamond, C., Thiede, H., Perdue, T., Secura, G. M., Valleroy, L., Mackellar, D., Corey, L., & Seattle Young Men's Survey Team. (2003). Viral hepatitis among young men who have sex with men: Prevalence of infection, risk behaviors, and vaccination. *Sexually Transmitted Diseases, 30*(5), 424–432.

Diamond, L. M. (2000). Sexual identity, attractions, and behavior among young sexualminority women over a 2-year period. *Developmental Psychology, 36*(2), 241–250.

Diamond, L. M. (2005). A new view of lesbian subtypes: Stable versus fluid identity trajectories over an 8-year period. *Psychology of Women Quarterly, 29*(2), 119–128.

Diamond, M. (1993). Homosexuality and bisexuality in different populations. *Archives of Sexual Behavior, 22,* 291–310.

Diamond, M., & Diamond, G. H. (1986). Adolescent sexuality: Biosocial aspects and intervention. In P. Allen-Meares & D. A. Shore (Eds.), *Adolescent sexualities: Overviews and principles of intervention* (pp. 3–13). New York: Haworth Press.

Diaz, R. M., Ayala, G., Bein, E., Henne, J., & Marin, B. V. (2001). The impact on homophobia, poverty, and racism on the mental health of gay and bisexual Latino men. *American Journal of Public Health, 41*(6), 927–933.

Dibble, S. L., & Swanson, J. M. (2000). Gender differences for the predictors of depression in young adults with genital herpes. *Public Health Nursing, 17*(3), 187–194.

Dickinson, A. (2001, July 23). Take a pass on the postnup: The latest trend in marriage is to negotiate your divorce in advance. *Time, 148*(3), 73.

Dickinson, L. M., DeGruy, F. U. III, Dickinson, W. P., & Candib, L. M. (1999). Health related quality of life and symptom profiles of female survivors of sexual abuse. *Archives of Family Medicine, 8*(1), 35–43.

DiClemente, R. J., Funkhouser, E., Wingood, G., Fawal, H., Holmberg, S. D., & Vermund, S. H. (2001). Protease inhibitor combination treatment and decreased condom use among gay men. *Southern Medical Journal, 95*(4), 421–426.

diMauro, D. (1995). *Sexuality research in the United States: An assessment of the social and behavioral sciences.* New York: Social Science Research Council.

Dindia, K. (2000). Sex differences in self-disclosure, reciprocity of self-disclosure, and self-disclosure and liking: Three meta-analyses reviewed. In S. Petronio (Ed.), *Balancing the secrets of private disclosures* (pp. 21–35). Milwaukee, WI: Lea's Communication Series.

Dindia, K. (2003). Definitions and perspectives on relational maintenance communication. In D. J. Canary (Ed.), *Maintaining relationships through communication: Relational, contextual, and cultural variations* (pp. 1–73). Mahwah, NJ: Erlbaum.

Dinsmore, W. W. (2005). Available and future treatments for erectile dysfunction. *Clinical Cornerstone, 7*(1), 37–45.

Dion, K. L., & Dion, K. K. (1988). Romantic love: Individual and cultural perspectives. In R. J. Sternberg & R.J. Barnes (Eds.), *Psychology of love* (pp. 264–289). New Haven, CT: Yale University Press.

Dittmann, M. (2005). Getting prostitutes off the streets. *Monitor on Psychology, 35*(9), 71.

Dittmar, M. (2000). Age at menarche in a rural Aymara-speaking community located at high altitude in northern Chile. *Mankind Quarterly, 40*(4), 38–52.

Dixit, A. K., & Pindyck, R. S. (1994). *Investment under uncertainty.* Princeton, NJ: Princeton University Press.

Dixon, R. (2005). Controversy in South Africa over device to snare rapists. Retrieved October 19, 2005, from http://www.smh.com.au/news/world/controversy-in-south-africa-over-device-to-snare-rapists/2005/09/01/1125302683893.html

Dobel, C. (1999, September/October). Members only: The best sex I ever had. *Modern Maturity,* 104.

Docimo, S. G., Silver, R. S., & Cromie, W. (2000, November 1). The undescended testicle: Diagnosis and management. Retrieved April 10, 2005, from http://www.aafp.org/afp/20001101/2037.html

Docter, R. F. (1988). *Transvestites and transsexuals: Mixed views.* Los Angeles, CA: Delacorte.

Dolcini, M., Catania, J., Coates, T., Stall, R., Hudes, E., Gagnon, J., et al. (1993). Demographic characteristics of heterosexuals with multiple partners. *Family Planning Perspectives, 25,* 208–214.

Donnan, H. (1988). *Marriage among Muslims: Preference and choice in Northern Pakistan.* New York: E. J. Brill.

Dorfman, L. E., Derish, P. A., & Cohen, J. B. (1992). Hey girlfriend: An evaluation of AIDS prevention among women in the sex industry. *Health Education Quarterly, 19,* 25–40.

Dorgan, M. (2001, June 13). New divorce laws in China give rise to spying. *Hartford Courant,* A13.

Douglas, N., Kemp, S., Aggleton, P., & Warwick, I. (2001). The role of external professionals in education about sexual orientation—towards good practice. *Sex Education, 1*(2), 149–162.

Downs, D. A. (1989). *The new politics of pornography.* Chicago: The University of Chicago Press.

Doyle, R. (2005). Gay and lesbian census. *Scientific American, 292*(3), 28.

Draganowski, L. (2004). Unlocking the closet door: The coming out process of gay male adolescents. *Dissertation Abstracts International, 64*(11-B). (#0419-4217)

Drenth, J. J., & Slob, A. K. (2004). Netherlands and the autonomous Dutch Antilles. In R. T. Francoeur & R. J. Noonan (Eds.), *The Continuum international encyclopedia of sexuality* (pp. 725–751). New York/London: Continuum International.

Drew, P. E. (2004). Iran. In The International Encyclopedia of Sexuality. In R. T. Francoeur & R. J. Noonan (Eds.), *The Continuum international encyclopedia of sexuality* (pp. 554–568). New York/London: Continuum International.

Drexler, P., &Gross, L. (2005). *Raising boys without men: How maverick moms are creating the next generation of exceptional men.* New York: Rodale Books.

Druff, G. H. (2000). Eliminating monthly periods—weighing the risks. Retrieved July 16, 2002, from http://www.viahealth.org/push/womens_health/2000/Sept2000

Dubuisson, J., & Mugnier, E. (2002). Acceptability of the levonorgestrel-releasing intrauterine system after discontinuation of previous contraception. *Contraception, 66*(2), 121.

Duffy, J., Warren, K., & Walsh, M. (2001). Classroom interactions: Gender of teacher, gender of student and classroom subject. *Sex Roles, 45*(9–10), 579–593.

Dunham, C., Myers, F., McDougall, A., & Barnden, N. (1992). *Mamatoto: A celebration of birth.* New York: Penguin Group.

Dunkley, C. (2005). Rape as a method of torture. *British Journal of Guidance & Counselling, 33*(1), 142–143.

Dunn, M. E., & Trost, J. E. (1989). Male multiple orgasms: A descriptive study. *Archives of Sexual Behavior, 18,* 377–387.

Dunson, D. B., Colombo, B., & Baird, D. D. (2002). Changes with age in the level of duration of fertility in the menstrual cycle. *Human Reproduction, 17*(5), 1399–1403.

Dupont, S. (1996). Sexual function and ways of coping in patients with MS and their partners. *Sex and Marital Therapy, 11,* 359–372.

Durkin, K. (1985). *Television, sex roles, and children.* Milton Keynes, UK: Open University Press.

Dutton, D. G., & Aron, A. P. (1974). Some evidence for heightened sexual attraction under conditions of high anxiety. *Journal of Personality & Social Psychology, 30*(4), 510–517.

Dworkin, A. (1981). *Pornography: Men possessing women.* New York: Putnam.

Dworkin, A. (1987). *Intercourse.* New York: The Free Press.

Dwyer, S. M., & Amberson, J. I. (1989). Behavioral patterns and personality characteristics of 56 sex offenders: A preliminary study. *Journal of Psychology and Human Sexuality*, 2, 105–118.

Dzelme, K., & Jones, R. A. (2001). Male cross-dressers in therapy: A solution-focused perspective for marriage and family therapists. *American Journal of Family Therapy*, 29, 293–305.

Earle, R. H., & Crow, G. M. (1990). Sexual addiction: Understanding and treating the phenomenon. *Contemporary Family Therapy*, 12, 89–104.

Earls, C. M., & David, H. (1989). A psychosocial study of male prostitution. *Archives of Sexual Behavior*, 18, 401–419.

Eckstein, D., & Goldman, A. (2001). The couples' gender-based communication questionnaire. *Family Journal of Counseling and Therapy for Couples and Families*, 9(1), 62–74.

Economidis, M. A., & Mishell, D. R. (2005). Pharmacological female contraception: An overview of past and future use. *Expert Opinion on Investigational Drugs*, 14(4), 449–456.

Edwards, A. T. (1997). Let's stop ignoring our gay and lesbian youth. *Educational Leadership*, 54(7), 68–71.

Edwards, J. E., & Moore, A. (1999). Implanon: a review of clinical studies. *British Journal of Family Planning*, 4, 3–16.

Edwards, N. K. (2000, September). Works in progress: Women's transitional journeys in the realm of sexuality. *Dissertation Abstracts*, University of Minnesota, #0419-4217.

Edwards, R. (1998). The effects of gender, gender role, and values. *Journal of Language and Social Psychology*, 17(1), 52–72.

Edwards, R., & Hamilton, M. A. (2004). You need to understand my gender role: An empirical test of Tannen's model of gender and communication. *Sex Roles*, 50(7–8), 491–504.

Eggermont, S. (2005). Young adolescents' perception of peer sexual behaviours: The role of television viewing. *Child: Care, Health and Development*, 31(4), 459–468.

Egolf, B., Lasker, J., Wolf, S., & Potvin, L. (1992). The Roseto effect: A 50-year comparison of mortality rates. *American Journal of Public Health*, 82(8), 1089–1092.

Einsiedel, E. (1989). Social science and public policy: Looking at the 1986 commission on pornography. In S. Gubar & J. Hoff (Eds.), *For adult users only* (pp. 87–107). Bloomington: Indiana University Press.

Eisenberg, M. (2001). Differences in sexual risk behaviors between college students with same-sex and opposite-sex experience. *Archives of Sexual Behavior*, 30(6), 575–589.

Eisenhart, M. A., & Holland, D. C. (1992). Gender constructs and career commitment: The influence of peer culture on women in college. In T. L. Whitehead & B. V. Reid (Eds.), *Gender constructs and social issues* (pp. 142–180). Chicago: University of Illinois Press.

Eiser, J. R., & Ford, N. (1995). Sexual relationships or holiday: A case of situational disinhibition? *Journal of Social and Personal Relationships*, 12, 323–339.

Eisinger, F., & Burke, W. (2002). Breast cancer and breastfeeding. *Lancet*, 360(9328), 187–195.

Elam-Evans, L. D., Strauss, L. T., Herndon, J., Parker, W. Y., Whitehead, S., & Berg, C. J. (2002). Abortion surveillance—United States, 1999. *Morbidity & Mortality Weekly Report*, 51(SS-9), 1–9, 11–28.

Elford, J., Bolding, G., Maguire, M., & Sherr, L. (2000). Combination therapies for HIV and sexual risk behavior among gay men. *Journal of Acquired Immune Deficiency Syndrome and Human Retrovirology*, 23, 266–271.

Elias, M. (2001, August 23). Growing up with gay parents. *USA Today*, p. D2.

Elifson, K. W., Boles, J., Posey, E., Sweat, M., et al. (1993a). Male transvestite prostitutes and HIV risk. *American Journal of Public Health*, 83, 260–261.

Elifson, K. W., Boles, J., & Sweat, M. (1993b). Risk factors associated with HIV infection among male prostitutes. *American Journal of Public Health*, 83, 79–83.

Ellen-Rinsza, M., & Kirk, G. M. (2005). Common medical problems of the college student. *Pediatric Clinics of North America*, 52(1), 9–24.

Ellertson, C., Evans, M., Ferden, S., Leadbetter, C., Spears, A., Johnstone, K., & Trussell, J. (2003). Extending the time limit for starting the Yuzpe regimen of emergency contraception to 120 hours. *Obstetrics & Gynecology*, 101, 1168–1171.

Elliott, H. (2002). Premenstrual dysphoric disorder: A guide for the treating physician. *North Carolina Medicine Journal*, 63(2), 72–75.

Elliott, L., & Brantley, C. (1997). *Sex on campus*. New York: Random House.

Ellis, B., & Symons, D. (1990). Sex differences in sexual fantasy: An evolutionary psychology approach. *Journal of Sex Research*, 27, 527–555.

Ellis, H. (1910). *Studies in the psychology of sex* (Vols. I–VI). Philadelphia: F. A. Davis.

Ellis, L., Ames, M., Ashley, P. W., & Burke, D. (1988). Sexual orientation of human offspring may be altered by severe maternal stress during pregnancy. *The Journal of Sex Research*, 25, 152–157.

Ellis, L., Burke, D., & Ames, M. (1987). Sexual orientation as a continuous variable: A comparison between the sexes. *Archives of Sexual Behavior*, 16, 523–529.

Ellis, M. (1984). Eliminating our heterosexist approach to sex education. *Journal of Sex Education and Therapy*, 10, 61–63.

Eminem. (2000, May 23). Kill you. On *The Marshall Mathers LP*. Los Angeles, CA: Interscope Records.

Employment Practices Solutions. (1996). $5.5 million awarded in sexual harassment case. Retrieved October 25, 2005, from http://www.epexperts.com/print.php?sid=308

Eng, J., & Butler, W. (1997). *The hidden epidemic: Confronting STDs*. Washington DC: National Academy Press.

Engel, J. W., & Saracino, M. (1986). Love preferences and ideals: A comparison of homosexual, bisexual, and heterosexual groups. *Contemporary Family Therapy: An International Journal*, 8(3), 241–250.

Ensign, J., Scherman, A., & Clark, J. (1998). The relationship of family structure and conflict to levels of intimacy and parental attachment in college students. *Adolescence*, 33(131), 575–582.

Ephross, P. H. (2005). Group work with sexual offenders. In G. L. Greif (Ed.), *Group work with populations at risk* (pp. 253–266). New York: Oxford University Press.

Epps, J., & Kendall, P. C. (1995). Hostile attributional bias in adults. *Cognitive Therapy and Research*, 19, 159–178.

Epstein, C. F. (1986). Symbolic segregation: Similarities and differences in the language and non-verbal communication of women and men. *Sociological Forum*, 1, 27–49.

Epstein, C. F. (1988). *Deceptive distinctions: Sex, gender, and the social order*. New Haven, CT: Yale University Press.

Ericksen, J. A. (1999). *Kiss and tell: Surveying sex in the twentieth century*. Cambridge, MA: Harvard University Press.

Erikson, K. (1986). *Wayward Puritans*. New York: Macmillan.

Ernst, E., & Pittler, M. H. (1998). Yohimbine for erectile dysfunction. *Journal of Urology*, 19, 433–436.

Ersoy, B., Balkan, C., Gunay, T., & Egemen, A. (2005). The factors affecting the relation between the menarcheal age of mother and daughter. *Child: Care, Health & Development*, 31(3), 303–308.

Ertelt, S. (2004). India has six million abortions annually, figure could be higher. Retrieved December 12, 2004, from http://www.lifenews.com/nat1057.html

Espín, M. C., Llorca, M. D. C., Simons, B. C., Borrego, N. G., Cueto, G. M., Guerra, E. A., Rodríguez, B. T., et al. (2004). Cuba. In R. T. Francoeur & R. J. Noonan (Eds.), *The Continuum complete international encyclopedia of sexuality* (pp. 259–327844). New York/London: Continuum International.

Etaugh, C., & Liss, M. (1992). Home, school, and playroom: Training grounds for adult gender roles. *Sex Roles*, 26, 129–147.

Ethier, K. A., Kershaw, T., Niccolai, L., Lewis, J. B., & Ickovics, J. R. (2003). Adolescent women underestimate their susceptibility to sexually transmitted infections. *Sexually Transmitted Infections*, 79, 408–411.

Etzioni, R., Penson, D. F., Legler, J. M., Tommaso, D., Boer, R., Gann, P. H., et al. (2002). Overdiagnosis due to prostate-specific antigen screening. *Journal National Cancer Institute*, 94, 981–990.

Evans, C. (2004). Equality from state to state: Gay, lesbian, bisexual, and transgender Americans and state legislation. Retrieved July 3, 2005, from http://www.hrc.org/Content/ContentGroups/Publications1/Equality_State_by_State.pdf

Fabes, R., Martin, C., & Hanish, L. (2003). Young children's play qualities in same-, other-, and mixed-sex peer groups. *Child Development*, 74(3), 921–932.

Faderman, L. (1981). *Surpassing the love of men: Romantic friendship and love between women from the Renaissance to the present*. New York: William Morrow.

Faller, K. C. (1989). The role relationship between victim and perpetrator as a predictor of characteristics of intrafamilial sexual abuse. *Child and Adolescent Social Work Journal*, 6, 217–229.

Faludi, S. (1991). *Backlash: The undeclared war against American women*. New York: Crown.

Farah, M. (1984). *Marriage and sexuality in Islam*. Salt Lake City: University of Utah Press.

Farley, M., & Barkan, H. (1998). Prostitution, violence against women, and post-traumatic stress disorder. *Women & Health*, 27(3), 37–49.

Farley M., Cotton A., Lynne, J., et al. (2003). Prostitution and trafficking in nine countries: An update on violence and posttraumatic stress disorder. In M. Farley (Ed.), *Prostitution, trafficking and traumatic stress* (pp. 33–74). Binghamton, NY: Haworth Press.

Farr, C., Brown, J., & Beckett, R. (2004). Ability to empathise and masculinity levels: Comparing male adolescent sex offenders with a normative sample of non-offending adolescents. *Psychology, Crime & Law, 10*(2), 155–168.

Faulkner, A. H., & Cranston, K. (1998). Correlates of same-sex sexual behavior in a random sample of Massachusetts high school students. *American Journal of Public Health, 88*(2), 262–266.

Fay, R. E., Turner, C. F., Klassen, A. D., & Gagnon, J. H. (1989). Prevalence and patterns of same-gender sexual contact among men. *Science, 243,* 338–348.

Federal Interagency Forum on Aging-Related Statistics. (2004). Older Americans 2004: Key indicators of well being. Retrieved October 19, 2005, from http://www.agingstats.gov/chartbook2004/default.htm

Federman, J. (1997). National television violence study, vol. 2, executive summary. Retrieved May 23, 2003, from http://www.ccsp.ucsb.edu/execsum.pdf

Federman, J. (2002). Rating sex and violence in the media: Media ratings and proposals for reform. Retrieved May 23, 2003, from http://www.kff.org/content/2003/20030204a/FINAL_EX.PDF

Feeney, J. A., & Noller, P. (1990). Attachment style as a predictor of adult romantic relationships. *Journal of Personality & Social Psychology, 58*(2), 281–291.

Feinauer, L. (1988). Relationship of long term effects of childhood sexual abuse to identity of the offender: Family, friend, or stranger. *Women and Therapy, 7,* 89–107.

Feinauer, L. (1989). Comparison of long-term effects of child abuse by type of abuse and by relationship of the offender to the victim. *American Journal of Family Therapy, 17,* 46–48.

Feinberg, L. (1999). *Trans liberation: Beyond blue and pink.* Boston: Beacon Press.

Feinman, M. A. (1997). Infertility treatment in women over 40 years of age. *Current Opinions in Obstetrics and Gynecology, 9*(3), 165–168.

Feliciano, R., & Alfonso, C. A. (1997). Sexual side effects of psychotropic medication: Diagnosis, neurobiology, and treatment strategies. *International Journal of Mental Health, 26*(1), 79–89.

Ferguson, D. M., Steidle, C. P., Singh, G. S., Alexander, J. S., Weihmiller, M. K., & Crosby, M. G. (2003). Randomized placebo-controlled, double blind, crossover design trial of the efficacy and safety of Zestra for women with and without female sexual arousal disorder. *Journal of Sex and Marital Therapy, 29*(Suppl. 1), 33–44.

Ferguson, R. B. (2004). The associations among members' perceptions of intragroup relationship conflict, leader-member exchange quality, and leader gossiping behavior. *Dissertation Abstracts International, 64*(10-A). (#0419-4209)

Fernandez, Y. M., & Marshall, W. L. (2003). Victim empathy, social self-esteem, and psychopathology in rapists. *Sexual Abuse: Journal of Research and Treatment, 15*(1), 11–26.

Ferree, M. M., & Hess, B. B. (1985). *Controversy and coalition: The new feminist movement.* Boston: Twayne.

Ferreira-Poblete, A. (1997). The probability of conception on different days of the cycle with respect to ovulation: An overview. *Advances in Contraception, 13*(2–3), 83–95.

Ferreiro-Velasco, M. E., Barca-Buyo, A., de la Barrera, S. S., Montoto-Marques, A., Vazquez, X. M., & Rodriguez-Sotillo, A. (2005). Sexual issues in a sample of women with spinal cord injury. *Spinal Cord, 43*(1), 51–55.

Fethers, K., Marks, C., Mindel, A., & Estocourt, C. S. (2000). STI and risk behaviors in women who have sex with women. *Sexually Transmitted Infections, 76*(5), 345–349.

Fieldman, J. P., & Crespi, T. D. (2002). Child sexual abuse: Offenders, disclosure and school-based initiatives. *Adolescence, 37*(145), 151–160.

Fields, J. (2001a). Normal queers: Straight parents respond to their children's "coming-out." *Symbolic Interaction, 24*(2), 165–188.

Fields, J. (2001b). Risky lessons: Sexuality and inequality in school-based sex education. Doctoral dissertation, The University of North Carolina at Chapel Hill. *Dissertation Abstracts International,* #0-493-44513-7.

Fields, J., & Casper, L. M. (2001). America's families and living arrangements. *Current Population Reports.* Washington, DC: U.S. Census Bureau.

Finan, S. L. (1997). Promoting healthy sexuality: Guidelines for early through older adulthood. *Nurse Practitioner, 22*(12), 59–60, 63–64.

Fine, M., & Asch, A. (1988). Disability beyond stigma: Social interaction, discrimination, and activism. *Journal of Social Issues, 44,* 3–21.

Finer, L. B., & Henshaw, S.K. (2003). Abortion incidence and services in the United States in 2000. *Perspectives on Sexual and Reproductive Health, 35*(1), 6–15.

Fink, H. A., MacDonald, R., Rutks, I. R., & Nelson, D. B. (2002). Sildenafil for male erectile dysfunction: A systematic review and meta-analysis. *Archives of Internal Medicine, 162*(12), 1349–1360.

Finkelhor, D. (1980). Sex among siblings: A survey on prevalence, variety, and effects. *Archives of Sexual Behavior, 9,* 171–194.

Finkelhor, D. (1984). *Child sexual abuse: New theory and research.* New York: The Free Press.

Finkelhor, D., & Browne, A. (1985). The traumatic impact of child sexual abuse. *American Journal of Ortho-Psychiatry, 55,* 530–541.

Finkelhor, D., Hotaling, G., Lewis, I. A., & Smith, C. (1990). Sexual abuse in a national survey of adult men and women: Prevalence, characteristics, and risk factors. *Child Abuse and Neglect, 14,* 19–28.

Finster, M., & Wood, M. (2005). The Apgar score has survived the test of time. *Anesthesiology, 102*(4), 855–857.

Firestone, P., Nunes, K. L., Moulden, H., Broom, I., & Bradford, J. M. (2005). Hostility and recidivism in sexual offenders. *Archives of Sexual Behavior, 34*(3), 277–283.

Fischer, G. J. (1986). College student attitudes toward forcible date rape. *Archives of Sexual Behavior 15*(6), 457–466.

Fischer, G. J. (1987). Hispanic and majority student attitudes toward forcible date rape as a function of differences in attitudes toward women. *Sex Roles, 17*(1–2), 93–101.

Fisher, B. S., Cullen, F. T., & Daigle, L. E. (2005). The discovery of acquaintance rape: The salience of methodological innovation and rigor. *Journal of Interpersonal Violence, 20*(4), 493–500.

Fisher, B. S., Cullen, F. T., & Turner, M. G. (2000a). Are rapes and sexual assault part of college life? Retrieved April 10, 2003, from http://www.center4policy.org/violencem.html

Fisher, B. S., Cullen, F. T., & Turner, M. G. (2000b). *Sexual victimization of college women.* Washington, DC: U.S. Department of Justice, National Institute of Justice.

Fisher, B. S., Daigle, L. E., Cullen, F. T., & Turner, M. G. (2003). Reporting sexual victimization to the police and others: Results from a national-level study of college women. *Criminal Justice & Behavior, 30*(1), 6–38.

Fisher, B., Wortley, S., Webster, C., & Kirst, M. (2002). The socio-legal dynamics and implications of "diversion": The case study of the Toronto "John School" diversion programme for prostitution offenders. *Criminal Justice: International Journal of Policy and Practice, 2*(34), 385–410.

Fisher, W. A., & Barak, A. (1991). Pornography, erotica, and behavior: More questions than answers. *International Journal of Law and Psychiatry, 14,* 65–83.

Fitch, M.T. (2003). Levels of family involvement and gender role conflict among stay-at-home dads. *Dissertation Abstracts International Section A: Humanities & Social Sciences, 64*(2-A), #AA13080872.

Fitch, R. H., & Denenberg, V. H. (1998). A role for ovarian hormones in sexual differentiation of the brain. *Behavioral Brain Science, 21*(3), 311–327.

Fitzgerald, L. F., & Ormerod, A. J. (1991). Perceptions of sexual harassment: The influence of gender and academic context. *Psychology of Women Quarterly, 15,* 281–294.

Flacelière, R. (1962). *Love in ancient Greece.* New York: Crown.

Flanigan, C., Suellentrop, K., Albert, B., Smith, J., & Whitehead, M. (2005, September 15). Science says #17: Teens and oral sex. Retrieved September 17, 2005, from http://www.teenpregnancy.org/works/pdf/ScienceSays_17_OralSex.pdf

Fleischmann, A. A., Spitzberg, B. H., Andersen, P. A., Roesch, S. C., & Metts, S. (2005). Tickling the monster: Jealousy induction in relationships. *Journal of Social and Personal Relationships, 22*(1), 49–73.

Fletcher, J. L. (1991). Perinatal transmission of human papillomavirus. *American Family Physician, 43,* 143.

Flowers, R. B. (1998) *The prostitution of women and girls.* Jefferson, NC: McFarland.

Folbre, N. (1995). Sexual orientation showing up in paychecks. *Working Women, 20*(1), 15–16.

Foote, W. E., & Goodman-Delahunty, J. (2005). Harassers, harassment contexts, same-sex harassment, workplace romance, and harassment theories. In W. E. Foote & J. Goodman-Delahunty (Eds.), *Evaluating sexual harassment: Psychological, social, and legal considerations in forensic examinations* (pp. 27–45). Washington, DC: American Psychological Association.

Ford, C. S., & Beach, F. A. (1951). *Patterns of sexual behavior.* New York: Harper & Brothers.

Forrest, J. D. (1994). Epidemiology of unintended pregnancy and contraceptive use. *American Journal of Obstetrics & Gynecology, 170*(5), 1485–1489.

Forrest, K., Austin, D., Valdes, M., Guentes, E., & Wilson, S. (1993). Exploring norms and beliefs related to AIDS prevention among California Hispanic men. *Family Planning Perspectives, 25,* 111–117.

Forsé, M., Jaslin, J. P., Yannick, M., et al. (1993). *Recent social trends in France 1960–1990.* Frankfurt-am-Main, Germany: Campus Verlag.

Forstein, M. (1988). Homophobia: An overview. *Psychiatric Annals, 18*, 33–36.

Fortenberry, J. D. (2002). Unveiling the hidden epidemic of STDs. *Journal of the American Medical Association, 287*(6), 768–769.

Forti, G., & Krausz, C. (1998). Clinical review 100: Evaluation and treatment of the infertile couple. *Journal of Clinical Endocrinology Medicine, 83*(12), 4177–4188.

Foubert, J. D. (2000). The longitudinal effects of a rape: Prevention program on fraternity men's attitudes. *Journal of American College Health, 48*(4), 158–163.

Foubert, J. D., & Marriott, K. A. (1997). Effects of sexual assault peer education program on men's belief in rape myths. *Sex Roles, 36*, 257–266.

Foubert, J. D., & McEwen, M. K. (1998). An all-male rape prevention peer education program: Decreasing fraternity men's behavioral intent to rape. *Journal of College Student Development, 39*, 548–556.

Foucault, M. (1978). *The history of sexuality: An introduction.* New York: Vintage Books.

Foucault, M. (1987). *The history of sexuality: Volume 2, The use of pleasure.* London: Penguin Books.

Foucault, M. (1988). *The history of sexuality: Volume 3, The care of the self.* New York: Random House.

Fowers, B. J. (1998). Psychology and the good marriage. *American Behavioral Scientist, 41*(4), 516.

Fowke, J. H., Shu, X. O., Dai, W., Jin, F., Cai, W., Gao, Y. T., & Zheng, W. (2004). Oral contraceptive use and breast cancer risk. *Cancer Epidemiology Biomarkers & Prevention, 13*(8), 1308–1315.

Fox, J. A., & Zawitz, M. W. (2004). Homicide trends in the United States. Retrieved October 23, 2005, from www.ojp.usdoj.gov/bjs/homicide/homtrnd.htm

Frackiewicz, E. J. (2000). Endometriosis: An overview of the disease and its treatment. *Journal of the American Pharmaceutical Association, 40*(5), 645–657.

Francoeur, R. T., & Noonan, R. J. (Eds.). (2004). *The Continuum international encyclopedia of sexuality.* New York/London: Continuum International.

Frangou, E. M., Lawson, J., & Kanthan, R. (2005). Angiogenesis in male breast cancer. *World Journal of Surgical Oncology, 3*(1), 16.

Frank, E., & Anderson, C. (1989). The sexual stages of marriage. In M. Henslin (Ed.), *Marriage and family in a changing society* (pp. 190–195). New York: The Free Press.

Frank, E., Anderson, C., & Rubinstein, D. N. (1978). Frequency of sexual dysfunction in normal couples. *New England Journal of Medicine, 299*, 111–115.

Frank, P. L. (1991). The effect of induced abortion on subsequent pregnancy outcome. *British Journal of Obstetrics and Gynecology, 98*, 1015.

Frankel, L. (2002). "I've never thought about it": Contradictions and taboos surrounding American males' experiences of first ejaculation (semenarche). *Journal of Men's Studies, 11*(1), 37–54.

Franklin, K. (2000). Antigay behaviors among young adults. *Journal of Interpersonal Violence, 15*(4), 339–363.

Fraser, I. S. (2000). Forty years of combined oral contraception: Evolution of a revolution. *Medical Journal of Australia, 173*(10), 541–544.

Frazier, P. A. (2000). The role of attributions and perceived control in recovery from rape. *Journal of Personal and Interpersonal Loss, 5*(2/3), 203–225.

Freedman, M. (2001). For love and money. *Forbes, 167*(14), 202.

Freeman, S. (2002). Contraceptive efficacy and patient acceptance of Lunelle. *Journal of American Academic Nursing Practice, 14*(8), 342–346.

Freitas, S. L. G. (2004). Brazil. In R. T. Francoeur & R. J. Noonan (Eds.), *The Continuum complete international encyclopedia of sexuality* (pp. 98–113). New York/London: Continuum International.

Fretts, R.C., Boyd, M. E., Usher, R. H., & Usher, H. A. (1992). The changing pattern of fetal death, 1961–1988. *Obstetrics and Gynecology, 79*(1), 35–39.

Freud, S. (1953). Three essays on the theory of sexuality. In J. Strachey (Ed. & Trans.), *The standard edition of the complete psychological works of Sigmund Freud* (Vol. 7, pp. 130–243). London: Hogarth Press. (Original work published 1905)

Freund, K., & Blanchard, R. (1986). The concept of courtship disorder. *Journal of Sex and Marital Therapy, 12*, 79–92.

Freund, K., Scher, H., & Hucker, S. (1983). The courtship disorders. *Archives of Sexual Behavior, 12*, 369–379.

Freund, K., Scher, H., & Hucker, S. (1984). The courtship disorders: A further investigation. *Archives of Sexual Behavior, 13*, 133–139.

Freund, K. M. (1992). Chlamydial disease in women. *Hospital Practice*, 175–186.

Freund, M., Lee, N., & Leonard, T. (1991). Sexual behavior of clients with street prostitutes in Camden, New Jersey. *Journal of Sex Research, 28*, 579–591.

Freund, M., Leonard, T. L., & Lee, N. (1989). Sexual behavior of resident street prostitutes with their clients in Camden, New Jersey. *Journal of Sex Research, 26*, 460–478.

Friden, C., Hirschberg, A. L., Saartok, T., Backstrom, T., Leanderson, J., & Renstrom, P. (2003). The influence of premenstrual symptoms on postural balance and kinesthesia during the menstrual cycle. *Gynecological Endocrinology, 17*(6), 433–440.

Friedan, B. (1963). *The feminine mystique.* New York: Dell.

Friedl, K. (1993). Effects of anabolic steroids on physical health. In C. Yesalis (Ed.), *Anabolic steroids in sport and exercise* (pp. 107–150). Champaign, IL: Human Kinetics.

Friedland, G. (1988). AIDS and compassion. *Journal of the American Medical Association, 259*, 2898–2899.

Friedman, R. M. (1986). The psychoanalytic model of male homosexuality: A historical and theoretical critique. *The Psychoanalytic Review, 73*, 484–519.

Friedman-Kien, A. E., & Farthing, C. (1990). Human immunodeficiency virus infection: A survey with special emphasis on mucocutaneous manifestations. *Seminars in Dermatology, 9*, 167–177.

Friedrich, W. N. (1998). Behavioral manifestations of child sexual abuse. *Child Abuse and Neglect, 22*(6), 523–531.

Friedrich, W. N., Grambsch, P., Broughton, D., Kuiper, J., & Beilke, R. L. (1991). Normative sexual behavior in children. *Pediatrics, 88*, 456–464.

Fritz, G. S., Stoll, K., & Wagner, N. N. (1981). A comparison of males and females who were sexually molested as children. *Journal of Sex & Marital Therapy, 7*(1), 54–59.

Frohlich, P. F., & Meston, C. M. (2000). Evidence that serotonin affects female sexual functioning via peripheral mechanisms. *Physiology and Behavior, 71*(3–4), 383–393.

Frohlich, P. F., & Meston, C. M. (2005). Tactile sensitivity in women with sexual arousal disorder. *Archives of Sexual Behavior, 34*(2), 207–217.

Fuglo-Meyer, K. S. (2001, October). Epidemiology of female sexual function. Paper presented at Female Sexual Function Forum, Boston, MA.

Fukuda, M., Fukuda, K., Shimizo, T., Anderson, C. Y., & Byskov, G. (2002). Parental periconceptional smoking and male:female ratio of newborn infants. *Lancet, 359*(9315), 1407–1408.

Furnham, A., & Mak, T. (1999). Sex-role stereotyping in television commercials: A review and comparison of fourteen studies done on five continents over 25 years. *Sex Roles, 41*(5–6), 413–437.

Furstenberg, F. F., & Cherlin, A. J. (1991). *Divided families: What happens to children when parents part.* Cambridge, MA: Harvard University Press.

Fyfe, B. (1983). "Homophobia" or homosexual bias reconsidered. *Archives of Sexual Behavior, 12*, 549–554.

Gagnon, J. H. (1985). Attitudes and responses of parents to pre-adolescent masturbation. *Archives of Sexual Behavior, 14*, 451–466.

Gagnon, J. H. (2001). A comparative study of the couple in the social organization of sexuality in France and the United States—statistical data included. *Journal of Sex Research, 38*(1), 24–34.

Gaither, G. A. (2000). The reliability and validity of three new measures of male sexual preferences (Doctoral dissertation, University of North Dakota). *Dissertation Abstracts International, 61*, 4981.

Gaither, G. A., Sellbom, M., & Meier, B. P. (2003). The effect of stimulus content on volunteering for sexual interest research among college students. *Journal of Sex Research, 40*(3), 240–249.

Gallagher, M., & Waite, L. (2000). *The case for marriage.* New York: Doubleday.

Gallo, R. V. (2000). Is there a homosexual brain? *Gay and Lesbian Review, 7*(1), 12–16.

Gallup, G. G., Burch, B. S., & Platek, B. A. (2002). Does semen have antidepressant properties? *Archives of Sexual Behavior, 31*(3), 289–293.

Gamson, J. (1990). Rubber wars: Struggles over the condom in the United States. *Journal of the History of Sexuality, 1*, 262–282.

Garber, F. (2003). Multiple births on the rise in the U.S. Retrieved January 26, 2003, from http://www.medscape.com/viewarticle/447825?WebLogicSession= P1QPmqfn 5lg22ajOk9SH7z7GmmecyaLtmA8Eqv97m C9v0193O4YB|4011205724105262238/ 184161392/6/7001/7001/ 7002/7002/7001/-1

Gard, C. (2000). What is he/she saying? *Current Health, 26*(8), 18–20.

Garner, M. J., Turner, M. C., Ghadirian, P., & Krewski, D. (2005). Epidemiology of testicular cancer: An overview. *International Journal of Cancer*, published online ahead of print. Retrieved April 15, 2005, from http://www.ncbi.nlm.nih.gov/entrez/query.fcgi?cmd= Retrieve&db=pubmed&dopt=Abstract&list_ uids=15818625

Gass, G. Z., & Nichols, W. C. (1988). Gaslighting: A marital syndrome. *Contemporary Family Therapy 10*(1), 3–16.

Gates, G. J., & Sonenstein, F. L. (2000). Heterosexual genital sexual activity among adolescent males: 1998–1995. *Family Planning Perspectives, 32*(6), 295–304.

Gay, D., & Lynxwiler, J. (1999). The impact of religiosity on race variations in abortion attitudes. *Sociological Spectrum, 19*(3), 359–377.

Gay and Lesbian Alliance Against Defamation (GLAAD) (2000). Musical gay bashing doesn't sound so good. GLAAD Alert. Retrieved May 25, 2003, from http://www.glaad.org

Gayle, H. (2000). Letter to colleagues from Helene Gayle, M.D. Retrieved March 4, 2000, from http://www.cdc.gov/washington/testimony/ha030200.htm

Gazmararian, J. A., Petersen, R., Spitz, A. M., Goodwin, M. M., Saltzman, L. E., & Marks, J. S. (2000). Violence and reproductive health: Current knowledge and future research directions. *Maternal and Child Health Journal, 4*(2), 79–84.

Gebhard, P., & Johnson, A. (1979). *The Kinsey data: Marginal tabulations of the 1938–1963 interviews conducted by the Institute for Sex Research.* Philadelphia: W. B. Saunders.

Gebhard, P. H., Gagnon, J. H., Pomeroy, W. B., & Christenson, C. V. (1965). *Sex offenders: An analysis of types.* New York: Harper & Row.

Geer, J. H., & O'Donohue, W. T. (1987). A sociological approach. In J. H. Geer & W. T. O'Donohue (Eds.), *Theories of human sexuality* (pp. 237–253). New York: Plenum Press.

Gelbard, M. (1988). Dystrophic penile classification in Peyronie's disease. *Journal of Urology, 139,* 738–740.

Gemelli, R. J. (1996). *Normal child and adolescent development.* Arlington, VA: American Psychiatric Press.

GenderAIDS. (2003). Swaziland king's polygamy remarks condemned. Retrieved August 29, 2003, from http://archives.healthdev.net/gender-aids/msg00495.html

George, W. H., & Stoner, S. A. (2000). Understanding acute alcohol effects on sexual behavior. *Annual Review of Sex Research, 11,* 92–122.

Geraghty, C., et al. (1992). A woman's space: Women and soap opera. In F. Bonner, L. Goodman, & R. Allen (Eds.), *Imagining women* (pp. 221–236). United Kingdom: Polity Press.

Getahun, D. Ananth, C. V., Selvam, N., & Demissie, K. (2005). Adverse perinatal outcomes among interracial couples in the United States. *Obstetrics and Gynecology, 106*(1), 81–88.

Ghaziani, A. (2005). Breakthrough: The 1979 national march. *Gay & Lesbian Review Worldwide, 12*(2), 31–33.

Ghosh, M. K. (2005). Breech presentation: Evolution of management. *Journal of Reproductive Medicine, 50*(2), 108–116.

Gibson-Ainyette, I., Templer, D. I., Brown, R., & Veaco, L. (1988). Adolescent female prostitutes. *Archives of Sexual Behavior, 17,* 431–438.

Giles, G., English, D., McCredie, M., Borland, R., Boyle, P., & Hopper, J. (2003). Sexual factors and prostate cancer. *British Journal of Urology, 92*(3), 211–216.

Gilman, S. E., Cochran, S. D., Mays, V., Hughes, M., Ostrow, D., & Kessler, R. C. (2001). Risk of psychiatric disorders among individuals reporting same-sex sexual partners in the national comorbidity survey. *American Journal of Public Health, 91*(6), 933–940.

Gilmore, D. D. (1990). *Manhood in the making: Cultural concepts of masculinity.* New Haven, CT: Yale University Press.

Gilson, R. J., & Mindel, A. (2001). Sexually transmitted infections. *British Medical Journal, 322*(729S), 1135–1137.

Ginty, M. M. (2005). New pills launch debate over menstruation. Retrieved March 19, 2005, from http://www.womensenews.org/article.cfm/dyn/aid/1879/context/archive

Giotakos, O., Markianos, M., & Vaidakis, N. (2005). Aggression, impulsivity, and plasma sex hormone levels in a group of rapists, in relation to their history of childhood attention-deficit/hyperactivity disorder symptoms. *Journal of Forensic Psychiatry & Psychology, 16*(2), 423–433.

Glass, L. (1992). *He says, she says: Closing the communication gap between the sexes.* New York: Perigee Books.

Glasser, M., Kolvin, I., Campbell, D., Glasser, A., Leitch, I., & Farrelly, S. (2001). Cycle of child sexual abuse: Links between being a victim and becoming a perpetrator. *British Journal of Psychiatry, 179,* 482–494.

Glazer, H. I., Jantos, M., Hartmann, E. H., & Swencionis, C. (1998). Electromyograpic comparisons of pelvic floor in women with dyesthetic vulvodynia and asymptomatic women. *Journal of Reproductive Medicine, 43,* 959–962.

Glei, D. A. (1999). Measuring contraceptive use patterns among teenage and adult women. *Family Planning Perspectives, 31*(2), 73-81.

Glenn, N., & Marquardt, E. (2001). Hooking up, hanging out and hoping for Mr. Right: College women on mating and dating today. Retrieved October 19, 2005, from http://www.americanvalues.org/Hooking_Up.pdf

Globerman, S. (2005, March). Right test, wrong results: When little things can mean a lot. *O, The Oprah Magazine,* p. 116.

Godfrey, K., Robinson, S., Barker, D. J., Osmond, C., & Cox, V. (1996). Maternal nutrition in early and late pregnancy in relation to placental and fetal growth. *British Medical Journal, 312*(7028), 410–414.

Goffman, E. (1976). *Gender advertisements.* New York: Harper Colophon Books.

Gokyildiz, S., & Beji, N. K. (2005). The effects of pregnancy on sexual life. *Journal of Sex and Marital Therapy, 31*(3), 201–215.

Gold, J. C. (2004). Kiss of the yogini: "Tantric sex" in its South Asian contexts. *Journal of Religion, 84*(2), 334–336.

Gold, R. (1990). *Abortion and women's health, a turning point for Americans.* New York: Alan Guttmacher Institute.

Gold, R. B. (2003, March). Lessons from before Roe: Will past be prologue? Retrieved September 3, 2005, from http://www.agi-usa.org/pubs/ib_5-03.html

Gold, S. R., & Chick, D. A. (1988). Sexual fantasy patterns as related to sexual attitude, experience, guilt, and sex. *Journal of Sex Education and Therapy, 14,* 18–23.

Goldberg, J., Holtz, D., Hyslop, T., & Tolosa, J. (2002). Has the use of routine episiotomy decreased? Examination of episiotomy rates from 1983 to 2000. *Obstetrics & Gynecology, 99*(3), 395–400.

Golden, G. H. (2001). Dyadic-dystonic compelling eroticism: Can these relationships be saved? *Journal of Sex Education & Therapy, 26*(1), 50.

Golden, M. R., Whittington, W. L., Handsfield, H. H., Hughes, J. P., Stamm, W. E., Hogben, M., Clark, A., Malinski, C., Helmers, J., Thomas, K., & Holmes, K. (2005). Effect of expedited treatment of sex partners on recurrent or persistent gonorrhea or chlamydial infection. *The New England Journal of Medicine, 352*(7), 676–685.

Goldenberg, R. L., Andrews, W. W., & Yuan, A. C. (1999). Pregnancy outcomes related to STDs. In P. J. Hitchcock, H. T. Mackay, & J. N. Wasserheit (Eds.), *STDS and adverse outcomes to pregnancy* (pp. 1–27). Washington DC: ASM Press.

Goldman, J., & Bradley, G. L. (2001). Sexuality education across the lifecycle in the new millennium. *Sex Education, 1*(3), 197–217.

Goldstein, J. R. (1999). The leveling of divorce in the U.S. *Demography, 36,* 409–414.

Goleman, D. (1992, April 14). Therapies offer hope for sexual offenders. *The New York Times,* pp. C1, C11.

Golombok, S., & Tasker, F. (1996). Do parents influence the sexual orientation of their children? *Developmental Psychology, 32*(1), 3–12.

Goode, E. (1994). *Deviant behavior.* Englewood Cliffs, NJ: Prentice Hall.

Goode, E. (2001, July 17). A rainbow of differences in gays' children. *New York Times,* pp. 1–7.

Goodman, A. (1993). Diagnosis and treatment of sexual addiction. *Journal of Sex and Marital Therapy, 19*(3), 225–251.

Gooren, L. J., & Bunck, M. C. (2004). Transsexuals and competitive sports. *European Journal of Endocrinology, 151*(4), 425–429.

Gopalan, C. (1996). Current food and nutrition situation in south Asian and south-east Asian countries. *Biomedical Environmental Science, 9*(2–3), 102–116.

Gordon, B. N., & Schroeder, C. S. (1995). *Sexuality: A developmental approach to problems.* Chapel Hill, NC: Clinical Child Psychology Library.

Gordon, S. (1986). What kids need to know. *Psychology Today, 20,* 22–26.

Gosden, R. G. (2005). Prospects for oocyte banking and in-vitro maturation. *Journal of the National Cancer Institute Monograph, 34,* 60–63.

Gosselin, C. C. (1987). The sadomasochistic contract. In G. D. Wilson (Ed.), *Variant sexuality: Research and theory* (pp. 229–257). Baltimore: Johns Hopkins University Press.

Goto, A., Reich, M., & Aitkin, I. (1999). Oral contraceptives and women's health in Japan. *Journal of American Medical Association, 282*(22), 2173–2177.

Gottemoeller, M. G. (2001). Microbicides: Expanding the options for STD prevention. *SIECUS Report, 30*(1), 10–13.

Gottlieb, B., Beitel, L. K., & Trifiro, M. A. (2004). Androgen-insensitivity syndrome. Retrieved October 1, 2005, from http://www.genetests.org/servlet/access?id=8888890&key=xFHesh8I5L1gp&gry=INSERTGRY&fcn=y&fw=MPzN&filename=/glossary/profiles/androgen/details.html

Gottman, J., & Silver, N. (2000). *The seven principles for making marriage work.* New York: Crown.

Gottman, J. M. (1994). *Why marriages succeed or fail.* New York: Simon & Schuster.

Gottman, J. M. (1999). *The seven principles for making marriage work.* New York: Random House.

Gottman, J. M., Coan, J., Carrene, S., & Swanson, C. (1998). Predicting marital happiness and stability from newlywed interactions. *Journal of Marriage and the Family, 60,* 5–22.

Gottschall, J. A., & Gottschall, T. A. (2003). Are per-incident rape-pregnancy rates higher than per-incident consensual pregnancy rates? *Human Nature, 14*(1), 1–20.

Gould, S. J. (1981). *The mismeasure of man.* New York: Norton.

GPAC. (2000). Ohio court removes child from parents because of her gender. Retrieved May 30, 2003, from http://www.gpac.org

Granderson, L. Z. (2005). Three-time MVP "tired of having to hide my feelings." Retrieved October 26, 2005, from http://sports.espn.go.com/wnba/news/story?id=2203853

Graugaard, C., Eplov, L. F., Giraldi, A., Mohl, B., Owens, A., Risor, H., & Winter, G. (2004). Denmark. In R. T. Francoeur & R. J. Noonan (Eds.), *The Continuum complete international encyclopedia of sexuality* (pp. 329–344). New York/London: Continuum International.

Greeley, A. M. (1991). *Faithful attraction.* New York: Tom Doherty Associates.

Greely, A. (1994). Review of the Janus report on sexual behavior. *Contemporary Sociology, 23,* 221–223.

Green, C. A. (2004). Gender differences in the relationships between multiple measures of alcohol consumption and physical and mental health. *Alcoholism: Clinical & Experimental Research, 28*(5), 754–765.

Green, R. (1987). *The "sissy boy syndrome" and the development of homosexuality.* New Haven, CT: Yale University Press.

Green, R. (1988). The immutability of (homo)sexual orientation: Behavioral science implications for a constitutional (legal) analysis. *The Journal of Psychiatry and the Law, 16,* 537–575.

Green, R. J. (2000). Lesbians, gay men and their parents: A critique of LaSala and the prevailing clinical wisdom. *Family Process, 39*(2), 257–267.

Greenblat, C. S. (1989). Sexuality in the early years of marriage. In J. M. Henslin (Ed.), *Marriage and family in a changing society* (pp. 180–189). New York: The Free Press.

Greenwald, E., & Leitenberg, H. (1989). Longterm effects of sexual experiences with siblings and nonsiblings during childhood. *Archives of Sexual Behavior, 18,* 289–400.

Gregory, N., Sanchez, M., & Buchness, M. R. (1990). The spectrum of syphilis in patients with HIV infection. *Journal of the American Academy of Dermatology, 22,* 1061.

Greig, R. (2003). Ethnic identity development: Implications for mental health in African-American and Hispanic adolescents. *Issues in Mental Health Nursing, 24*(3), 317–331.

Grenier, G., & Byers, E. (2001). Operationalizing premature or rapid ejaculation. *Journal of Sex Research, 38*(4), 369–378.

Griffen, G. (1995). *Penis size and enlargement: Facts, fallacies, and proven methods.* Aptos, CA: Hourglass.

Griffith, R. S., Walsh, D. E., Myrmel, K. H., Thompson, R. W., & Behforooz, A. (1987). Success of L-lysine therapy in frequently recurrent herpes simplex infection. Treatment and prophylaxis. *Dermatologica, 175*(4), 183–190.

Griffiths, M. (2001). Sex on the Internet: Observations and implications for Internet sex addiction. *Journal of Sex Research, 38*(4), 333–343.

Griffiths, M. (2003). Internet abuse in the workplace and concern for employers and employment counselors. *Journal of Employment Counseling, 40*(2), 87–97.

Griffiths, M. D. (2000). Excessive Internet use: Implications for sexual behavior. *Cyberpsychology and Behavior, 3,* 537–552.

Griffitt, W., & Veitch, R. (1971). Hot and crowded: Influences of population density and temperature on interpersonal affective behavior. *Journal of Personality and Social Psychology, 17,* 92–98.

Grimes, D. A. (2004). Intrauterine devices (IUDs). In R. A. Hatcher et al. (Eds.), *Contraceptive technology* (18th Rev. ed., pp. 495–530). New York: Ardent Media.

Grob, C. S. (1985). Single case study: Female exhibitionism. *Journal of Nervous and Mental Disease, 173,* 253–256.

Groer, M. W. (2005). Differences between exclusive breastfeeders, formula-feeders, and controls: A study of stress, mood, and endocrine variables. *Biological Research for Nursing, 7*(2), 106–117.

Grosskurth, P. (1980). *Havelock Ellis: A biography.* New York: Alfred A. Knopf.

Groth, A. N. (1978). Patterns of sexual assault against children and adolescents. In A. W. Burgess, A. N. Groth, L. L. Holmstrom, & S. M. Sgroi (Eds.), *Sexual assault of children and adolescents.* Toronto: Lexington Books.

Groth, N., & Burgess, A. (1980). Male rape: Offenders and victims. *American Journal of Psychiatry, 137,* 806–810.

Gruber, A. J., & Pope, H. G. (2000). Psychiatric and medical effects of anabolic-androgenic steroid use in women. *Psychotherapy and Psychosomatics, 69*(1), 19–26.

Grunbaum, J. A., Kann, L., Kinchen, S. A., Williams, B., Ross, J. G., Lowry, R., & Kolbe, L. (2002). Youth risk behavior surveillance: United States, 2001. *Morbidity and Mortality Weekly Report, 51*(no. SS-4).

Gudjonsson, G. H. (1986). Sexual variations: Assessment and treatment in clinical practice. *Sexual and Marital Therapy, 1,* 191–214.

Guerrero, L. K., & Afifi, W. (1999). Toward a goal-oriented approach for understanding communicative responses to jealousy. *Western Journal of Communication, 63*(2), 216–248.

Guffey, M. E. (1999). *Business communication: Process & product* (3rd ed.). Belmont, CA: Wadsworth.

Guha, C., Shah, S. J., Ghosh, S. S., Lee, S. W., Roy-Chowdhury, N., & Roy-Chowdhury, J. (2003). Molecular therapies for viral hepatitis. *BioDrugs, 17*(2), 81–91.

Guilleminault, C., Moscovitch, A., & Poyares, D. (2002). Atypical sexual behavior during sleep. *Psychosomatic Medicine, 64,* 328–336.

Guinto-Adviento, M. L. (1988). The human factor in law enforcement: An exploratory study of the attitudes of policemen toward prostitution. *Philippine Journal of Psychology, 21,* 12–33.

Gunawan, M. H. (2001). Nonverbal communication: The "silent" cross-cultural contact with Indonesians. Retrieved September 29, 2005, from http://www.ialf.edu/kipbipa/papers/MuhamadHandiGunawan.doc

Gundersen, B. H., Melas, P. S., & Skar, J. E. (1981). Sexual behavior of preschool children: Teachers' observations. In L. L. Constantine & F. M. Martinson (Eds.), *Children and sex: New findings, new perspectives* (pp. 45–61). Boston: Little, Brown.

Gunter, B., & McAleer, J. L. (1990). *Children and television: The one-eyed monster?* London: Routledge, Chapman, Hall.

Hack, W. W., Meijer, R. W., Bos, S. D., & Haasnoot, K. (2003). A new clinical classification for undescended testis. *Scandinavian Journal of Nephrology, 37*(1), 43–47.

Hader, S. L., Smith, D. K., Moore, J. S., & Holmberg, S. D. (2001). HIV infection in women in the U.S.: Status at the millennium. *Journal of the American Medical Association, 285*(9), 1186–1192.

Hagedorn, W. B., & Juhnke, G. A. (2005). Treating the sexually addicted client: Establishing a need for increased counselor awareness. *Journal of Addictions & Offender Counseling, 25*(2), 66–86.

Hahlweg, K., Kaiser, A., Christensen, A., Fehm-Wolfsdorf, G., & Grother, T. (2000). Selfreport and observational assessment of couples' conflict. *Journal of Marriage and Family, 62*(1), 61.

Haldeman, D. C. (1994). The practice and ethics of sexual orientation conversion therapy. *Journal of Consulting Clinical Psychology, 62,* 221.

Halfon, N., McLearn, K. T., & Schuster, M. A. (2002). *Child rearing in America: Challenges facing parents with young children.* New York: Cambridge University Press.

Hall, C. T. (2004). FDA to issue abortion drug warning RU-486 caution partly in response to local teen's death. Retrieved September 3, 2005, from http://www.sfgate.com/cgi-bin/article.cgi?file=/c/a/2004/11/16/MNGCD9S8RJ1.DTL

Hall, P. (2005, December 14). Porta-porn: Smut finding it's way onto video iPods in a big way. *Hartford Courant,* p. D1.

Halpern, C. J., Udry, J. R., Suchindran, C., & Campbell, B. (2000a). Adolescent males' willingness to report masturbation. *Journal of Sex Research, 37*(4), 327–333.

Halpern, C. T., Joyner, K., Udry, J. R., & Suchindran, C. (2000b). Smart teens don't have sex (or kiss much either). *Journal of Adolescent Health, 26*(3), 213–225.

Halpern, C. T., Udry, J. R., & Suchindran, C. (1997). Testosterone predicts initiation of coitus in adolescent females. *Psychosomatic Medicine, 59*(2), 161–171.

Hamberg, K. (2000). Gender in the brain: A critical scrutiny of the biological gender differences. *Lakartidningen, 97,* 5130–5132.

Hamburg, B. A. (1986). Subsets of adolescent mothers: Developmental, biomedical, and psychosocial issues. In J. B. Lancaster & B. A. Hamburg (Eds.), *School-age pregnancy and parenthood: Biosocial dimensions* (pp. 115–145). New York: Aldine DeGruyter.

Hamer, D. H., et al. (1993). A linkage between DNA markers on the X chromosome and male sexual orientation. *Science, 261,* 321–327.

Hamilton, T. (2002). *Skin flutes and velvet gloves.* New York: St. Martin's Press.

Hammermeister, J., & Burton, D. (2004). Gender differences in coping with endurance sport stress: Are men from Mars and women from Venus? *Journal of Sport Behavior, 27*(2), 148–165.

Han, W. (2004, September 6). Campus connection: A look at the new twist on Internet dating, coming to a college near you. *Time, 164*(10).

Hand, J. Z., & Sanchez, L. (2005). Badgering or bantering? Gender differences in experience of, and reactions to, sexual harassment among U.S. high school students. *Gender & Society, 14*(6), 718–746.

Handler, A., Davis, F., Ferre, C., & Yeko, T. (1989). The relationship of smoking and ectopic pregnancy. *American Journal of Public Health, 79*, 1239–1242.

Handley, M. A., Reingold, A. L., Shiboskis, S. & Padian, N. S. (2002). Incidence of acute urinary tract infection in young women and use of male condoms with and without nonoxynol 9 spermicides. *Epidemiology, 13*(4), 431–436.

Handsfield, H. (1992). Recent development in STDs: Viral and other syndromes. *Hospital Practice*, 175–200.

Harding, A. (2005). Progress made toward gonorrhea vaccine. Retrieved November 25, 2005, from http://www.sabin.org/PDF/071905_02.pdf

Hardy, K., Wright, C., Rice, S., Tochataki, M., Roberts, R., Morgan, D., et al. (2002). Future developments in assisted reproduction in humans. *Reproduction, 123*(2), 171–183.

Hardy, S., & Raffaelli, M. (2003). Adolescent religiosity and sexuality: An investigation of reciprocal influences. *Journal of Adolescence, 26*(6), 731–739.

Harish, D., & Sharma, B. R. (2003). Medical advances in transsexualism and the legal implications. *American Journal of Forensic Medical Pathology, 24*(1), 100–105.

Harkless, L. E., & Fowers, B. J. (2005). Similarities and differences in relational boundaries among heterosexuals, gay men, and lesbians. *Psychology of Women Quarterly, 29*(2), 167–176.

Harlan, L. C., Potosky, A., Cilliland, F. D., Hoffman, R., Albertsen, P. C., Hamilton, A. S., Eley, J. W., Stanford, J. L., & Stephenson, R. A. (2001). Factors associated with initial therapy for clinically localized prostate cancer: Prostate cancer outcomes study. *Journal of the National Cancer Institute, 93*(24), 1864–1871.

Harlow, H. F. (1959). Love in infant monkeys. *Scientific American, 200*, 68–70.

Harper, D. M., Franco, E. L., Wheeler, C., Ferris, D. G., Jenkins, D., Schuind, A., Zahaf, T., Innis, B., Naud, P., DeCarvalho, N., Roteli-Martins, C., et al. (2004). Efficacy of a bivalent L1 virus-like particle vaccine in prevention of infection with human papillomavirus types 16 and 18 in young women: A randomized controlled trial. *Lancet, 364*, 1757–1765.

Harris, C. R. (2003). A review of sex differences in sexual jealousy, including self-report data, psychophysiological responses, interpersonal violence, and morbid jealousy. *Personality and Social Psychology Review, 7*(2), 102–128.

Harris, G. (2005). FDA to weigh at-home testing for AIDS virus. Retrieved November 21, 2005, from http://www.nytimes.com/2005/10/13/health/13aids.html?th=&emc=th&pagewanted=print

Hart, C. W. M., & Pilling, A. R. (1960). *The Tiwi of North Australia.* New York: Holt, Rinehart & Winston.

Hartmann, K., Viswanathan, M., Palmieri, R., Garlehner, G., Thorp, J., & Lohr, K. N. (2005). *Journal of the American Medical Association, 293*(17), 2141–2148.

Harvard Law Review. (1990). *Sexual orientation and the law.* Cambridge, MA: Harvard University Press.

Harvey, S. M., Beckman, L. J., Sherman, C., & Petitti, D. (1999). Women's experience and satisfaction with emergency contraception. *Family Planning Perspectives, 31*(5), 237–240, 260.

Haselton, M. G., & Buss, D. M. (2001). The affective shift hypothesis: The functions of emotional changes following sexual intercourse. *Personal Relationships, 8*(4), 357–369.

Hatano, Y., & Shimazaki, T. (2004). Japan. In R. T. Francoeur & R. J. Noonan (Eds.), *The Continuum international encyclopedia of sexuality* (pp. 636–678). New York/London: Continuum International.

Hatcher, R. (2004). Depo-Provera injections, implants, and progestin-only pills (minipills). In R. A. Hatcher et al. (Eds.), *Contraceptive technology* (18th Rev. ed., pp. 461–494). New York: Ardent Media.

Hatcher, R., & Nelson, A. (2004). Combined hormonal contraceptive methods. In R. A. Hatcher et al. (Eds.), *Contraceptive technology* (18th Rev. ed., pp. 361–460).

Hatcher, R. A., Guest, F., Stewart, F., Stewart, G., et al. (1988). *Contraceptive technology 1988–1989.* New York: Irvington.

Hatcher, R. A., Trussell, J., Stewart, F. H., Nelson, A. L., Cates, W., Guest, F., & Kowal, D. (2004). *Contraceptive technology* (18th Rev. ed.). New York: Ardent Media.

Hatcher, R. A., Trussell, J., Stewart, F., Stewart, G., et al. (1994). *Contraceptive technology.* New York: Irvington.

Hatfield, E. (1988). Passionate and companionate love. In R. J. Sternberg & R. J. Barnes (Eds.), *Psychology of love* (pp. 191–217). New Haven, CT: Yale University Press.

Hatfield, E., & Sprecher, S. (1986). Measuring passionate love in intimate relationships. *Journal of Adolescence, 9*(4), 383–410.

Hawkins, A. J., Nock, S. L., Wilson, J. C., Sanchez, L., & Wright, J. D. (2002). Attitudes about covenant marriage and divorce: Policy implications from a three-state comparison. *Family Relations, 51*(2), 166–176.

Haworth, A. (2002, September). Where sex is against the law. *Marie Claire*, pp. 108–116.

Hawthorne, C. M., Farber, P. J., & Bibbo, M. (2005). Chlamydia/gonorrhea combo and HR HPV DNA testing in liquid-based pap. *Diagnostic Cytopathology, 33*(3), 177–180.

Hawton, K. (1983). Behavioural approaches to the management of sexual deviations. *British Journal of Psychiatry, 143*, 248–255.

Hays, D., & Samuels, A. (1989). Heterosexual women's perceptions of their marriages to bisexual or homosexual men. *Journal of Homosexuality, 18*, 81–100.

Hays, W. (2003). Human pheromones: Have they been demonstrated? *Behavioral Ecology & Sociobiology, 54*(2), 89–97.

Hazan, C., & Shaver, P. (1987). Romantic love conceptualized as an attachment process. *Journal of Personality & Social Psychology, 52*(3), 511–524.

Heavey, C. L., Christensen, A., & Malamuth, N. M. (1995). The longitudinal impact of demand and withdrawal during marital conflict. *Journal of Consulting and Clinical Psychology, 63*(5), 797–801.

Heger, A., Ticson, L., Velasquez, O., & Bernier, R. (2002). Children referred for possible sexual abuse: Medical findings in 2384 children. *Child Abuse & Neglect, 26*(6–7), 645–659.

Heiman, J. (2002). Sexual dysfunction: Overview of prevalence, etiological factors, and treatments. *Journal of Sex Research, 39*(1), 73–79.

Heiman, J., & LoPiccolo, J. (1992). *Becoming orgasmic: A sexual and personal growth program for women.* New York: Simon & Schuster.

Heiman, J., & Meston, M. (1997). Empirically validated treatment for sexual dysfunction. *Annual Review of Sex Research, 8*, 148–194.

Hemmerline, A., Siedentopf, F., & Kentenich, H. (2005). Emotional impact and acceptability of medical abortion with mifepristone: A German experience. *Journal of Psychosomatic Obstetrics & Gynecology, 26*(1), 23–31.

Hemphill, E. (1991). *Brother to brother: New writings by black gay men.* Boston: Alyson.

Henderson, L. (1991). Lesbian pornography: Cultural transgression and sexual demystification. *Women and Language, 14*, 3–12.

Henderson-King, D. H., & Veroff, J. (1994). Sexual satisfaction and marital well-being in the first years of marriage. *Journal of Social and Personal Relationships, 11*, 509–534.

Hendrick, C., & Hendrick, S. S. (1989). Research on love: Does it measure up? *Journal of Personality & Social Psychology, 56*(5), 784–794.

Hendrick, C., & Hendrick, S.S. (2000). *Close relationships: A sourcebook.* Thousand Oaks, CA: Sage.

Henningsen, D. D. (2004). Flirting with meaning: An examination of miscommunication in flirting intentions. *Sex Roles, 50*(7–8), 481–489.

Henry J. Kaiser Family Foundation. (2000a). 1998 National Survey of Americans on Values. Retrieved May 20, 2001, from www.kff.org/content/archive/1441/values.pdf

Henry J. Kaiser Family Foundation. (2000b). *Sex education in America: A view from inside the nation's classrooms.* Menlo Park, CA: Chart Park.

Henry J. Kaiser Family Foundation. (2003). Sex on TV 3: Content and context. Executive summary. Retrieved May 23, 2003, from http://www.kff.org/content/2003/20030204a/FINAL_EX.PDF

Hensel, D. J., Fortenberry, J. D., Harezlak, J., Anderson, J. G., & Orr, D. P. (2004). A daily diary analysis of vaginal bleeding and coitus among adolescent women. *Journal of Adolescent Health, 34*(5), 392–394.

Henshaw, S. K. (1998). Abortion incidence and services in the United States, 1995–1996. *Family Planning Perspectives, 30*(6), 263–270, 287.

Henshaw, S. K., & Finer, L. B. (2003). The accessibility of abortion services in the United States, 2001. *Perspectives on Sexual and Reproductive Health, 35*(1), 16–24.

Henshaw, S. K., & Kost, K. (1992). Parental involvement in minors' abortion decisions. *Family Planning Perspectives, 24*, 200.

Hensley, C., Koscheski, M., & Tewksbury, R. (2005). Examining the characteristics of male sexual assault targets in a Southern maximum-security prison. *Journal of Interpersonal Violence, 20*(6), 667–679.

Hensley, C., Struckman-Johnson, C., & Eigenberg, H. (2000). The history of prison sex research. *The Prison Journal, 80*, 360–367.

Hensley, L. G. (2002). Treatment of survivors of rape: Issues and interventions. *Journal of Mental Health Counseling, 24*(4), 331–348.

Henslin, J. M. (2005). The sociology of human sexuality. In J. M. Henslin, *Sociology: A down-to-earth approach.* Online chapter retrieved November 30, 2005, from http://www.ablongman.com/html/henslintour/henslinchapter/ahead3.html

Herdt, G. (1981). *Guardians of the flutes: Idioms of masculinity.* New York: McGraw-Hill.

Herdt, G. (1988). Cross-cultural forms of homosexuality and the concept "gay." *Psychiatric Annals, 18*, 37–39.

Herdt, G. (1989). Introduction: Gay and lesbian youth, emergent identities, and cultural scenes at home and abroad. In G. Herdt (Ed.), *Gay and lesbian youth* (pp. 1–42). New York: Harrington Park Press.

Herdt, G. (1990). Mistaken gender: 5-Alpha reductase hermaphroditism and biological reductionism in sexual identity reconsidered. *American Anthropologist, 92*(2), 433–446.

Herek, G. (2002). Heterosexuals' attitudes toward bisexual men and women in the United States. *Journal of Sex Research, 39*(4), 264–274.

Herek, G., Cogan, J. C., & Gillis, J. (2002). Victim experiences in hate crimes based on sexual orientation. *Journal of Social Issues, 58*(2), 319–339.

Herek, G. M. (1984). Beyond "homophobia": A social psychological perspective on attitudes toward lesbians and gay men. In J. P. DeCecco (Ed.), *Homophobia: An overview* (pp. 1–21). New York: The Haworth Press.

Herek, G. M. (1986). The social psychology of homophobia: Toward a practical theory. *New York University Review of Law & Social Changes, 14*, 923–935.

Herek, G. M., Capitanio, J. P., & Widaman, K. F. (2002). HIV-related stigma and knowledge in the U.S., 1991–1999. *American Journal of Public Health, 92*, 371–377.

Herman, J., & Schatzow, E. (1987). Recovery and verification of memories of childhood sexual trauma. *Psychoanalytic Psychology, 4*, 1–14.

Herman, J. L. (1981). *Father–daughter incest.* Cambridge, MA: Harvard University Press.

Herman-Giddens, M. E., & Slora, E. J. (1997). Secondary sexual characteristics and menses in young girls seen in office practice. *Pediatrics, 99*(4), 505–513.

Heron, A. (1994). *Two teenagers in twenty: Writings by gay and lesbian youth.* Boston, MA: Alyson.

Hickman, S. E., & Muehlenhard, C. L. (1999). By the semi-mystical appearance of a condom: How young women and men communicate sexual consent in heterosexual situations. *Journal of Sex Research, 36*(3), 258–272.

Hicks, S. (2005). Is gay parenting bad for kids? Responding to the "very idea of difference" in research on lesbian and gay parents. *Sexualities, 8*(2), 153–168.

Hicks, T. V., & Leitenberg, H. (2001). Sexual fantasies about one's partner versus someone else. *Journal of Sex Research, 38*(1), 43–50.

Hickson, F. C. I., Davies, P. M., & Hunt, A. J. (1994). Gay men as victims of nonconsensual sex. *Archives of Sexual Behavior, 23*(3), 281–294.

Hills, A. M., & Taplin, J. L. (1998). Anticipated responses to stalking: Effect of threat and target-stalker relationship. *Psychiatry, Psychology & Law, 5*(1), 139–146.

Hilton, G. (2003). Listening to the boys: English boys' views on the desirable characteristics of teachers of sex education. *Sex Education, 3*(1), 33–45.

Hinshelwood, M. (2002). Early and forced marriage: The most widespread form of sexual exploitation of girls? Retrieved August 27, 2003, from http://www.kit.nl/ils/exchange_content/html/forced_marriage_-_sexual_healt.asp

Hirayama, H., & Hirayama, K. (1986). The sexuality of Japanese Americans. Special issue: Human sexuality, ethnoculture, and social work. *Journal of Social Work and Human Sexuality, 4*(3), 81–98.

Hirschfeld, M. (1910). *The transvestites: An investigation of the erotic desire to cross dress.* Amherst, NY: Prometheus Books.

Hirschfeld, M. (1932). *Sexual pathology.* New York: Emerson Books.

Hirschfeld, M. (1940). *Sexual knowledge.* New York: Emerson Books.

Hite, S. (1981). *The Hite report on male sexuality.* New York: Alfred Knopf.

Hjelmstedt, A., Andersson, L., Skoog-Syanberg, A., Bergh, T., Boivin, J., & Collins, A. (1999). Gender differences in psychological reactions to infertility among couples seeking IVF and ICSI treatment. *Acta Obstetricia et Gynecologica Scandinavica, 78*(1), 42–48.

Ho, G. Y., Bierman, R., Beardsley, L., Chang, C. J., Burk, R. D., et al. (1998). Natural history of cervicovaginal papillomavirus infection in young women. *New England Journal of Medicine, 338*(7), 423–428.

Hodge, S., & Canter, D. (1998). Victims and perpetrators of male sexual assault. *Journal of International Violence, 13*, 222–239.

Hoebel, E. A. (1954). *The law of primitive man.* Cambridge, MA: Harvard University Press.

Hoff, G. (2003). Power and love: Sadomasochistic practices in long-term committed relationships. *Dissertation Abstracts: Section B, 64*(1-B), #0419–4217.

Hofman, B. (2005). "What is next?": Gay male students' significant experiences after coming-out while in college. *Dissertation Abstracts International Section A: Humanities & Social Sciences, 65*(8-A), #0419–4209.

Hogan, H. (2005). Title IX requires colleges & universities to eliminate the hostile environment caused by campus sexual assault. Retrieved October 25, 2005, from http://www.securityoncampus.org/victims/titleixsummary.html

Holcomb, D. R., Savage, M. P., Seehafer, R., & Waalkes, D. M. (2002). A mixed-gender date rape prevention intervention targeting freshmen college athletes. *College Student Journal, 36*(2), 165–179.

Hollander, D. (2000, March/April). Fertility drugs do not raise breast, ovarian or uterine cancer risk. *Family Planning Perspectives, 32*(2), 100–103.

Hollander, D. (2001). Users give new synthetic and latex condoms similar ratings on most features. *Family Planning Perspectives, 33*(1), 45–48.

Holmes, R. (1991). *Sex crimes.* Newbury Park, CA: Sage.

Holmes, W., & Slap, G. (1998). Sexual abuse of boys: Definition, prevalence, correlates, sequelae, and management. *Journal of the American Medical Association, 280*, 1855–1862.

Holmstrom, L. L., & Burgess, A. W. (1978). *The victim of rape: Institutional reactions.* New York: Wiley.

Holmstrom, L. L., & Burgess, A. W. (1979). Rape: The husband's and boyfriend's initial reactions. *The Family Coordinator, 28*, 321–330.

Holt, V., Scholes, D., Wicklund, K. G., Cushing-Haugen, K. L., & Daling, J. R. (2004). Body mass index, weight, and oral contraceptive failure risk. *Obstetrics & Gynecology, 105*(1), 46–52.

Holzman, C., Leventhal, J. M., Qiu, H., Jones, N., & Wang, J. (2001). Factors linked to bacterial vaginosis in nonpregnant women. *American Journal of Public Health, 91*(10), 1664–1671.

Hook, E. B. (1981). Rates of chromosome abnormalities at different maternal ages. *Obstetrics & Gynecology, 58*, 282–285.

Hook, E. B., Cross, P. K., & Schreinemachers, D. M. (1983). Chromosomal abnormality rates at amniocentesis in born infants. *Journal of the American Medical Association, 249*(15), 2034–2038.

Hooker, E. (1957). The adjustment of the male overt homosexual. *Journal of Projective Techniques, 21*, 18–31.

Hooton, T. M. (2003). The current management strategies for community-acquired urinary tract infection. *Infectious Disease Clinics of North America, 17*(2), 303–332.

Horowitz, S. M., Weis, D. L., & Laflin, M. T. (2001). Differences between sexual orientation behavior groups and social background, quality of life, and health behaviors. *Journal of Sex Research, 38*(3), 205–219.

Hoshino, Y., Dalai, S., Wang, K., Pesnicak, L., Lau, T., Knipe, D. M., Cohen, J., & Straus, S. E. (2005). Comparative efficacy and immunogenicity of replication-defective, recombinant glycoprotein, and DNA vaccines for herpes simplex virus 2 infections in mice and guinea pigs. *Journal of Virology, 79*, 410–418.

Houran, J., & Lange, R. (2004). Expectations of finding a "soul mate" with online dating. *North American Journal of Psychology, 6*(2), 297–308.

Howard, L. M., Hoffbrand, S., Henshaw, C., Boath, L., & Bradley, E. (2005). Antidepressant prevention of postnatal depression. *The Cochrane Database of Systematic Reviews, 2*, art. no. CD004363.

Howell, E. A., Mora, P. A., Horowitz, C. R., & Leventhal, H. (2005). Racial and ethnic differences in factors associated with early postpartum depressive symptoms. *Obstetrics & Gynecology, 105*(6), 1442–1450.

Hu, Y., Wood, J., Smith, V., & Westbrook, N. (2004). Friendships through IM: Examining the relationship between instant messaging and intimacy. *Journal of Computer-Mediated Communication, 10*(1), art. 6.

Hudson, F. (1991). *Taking it lying down: Sexuality and teenage motherhood.* Hampshire, U.K.: MacMillan.

Huffstutter, P. J. (2004). Smallest surviving preemie will go home soon. Retrieved December 23, 2004, from http://www.latimes.come/news/nationworld/nation/la-na-baby22dec,0,3320847,print.story

Human Genome Project. (2003). How many genes are in the human genome? Retrieved October 1, 2005, from http://www.ornl.gov/sci/techresources/Human_Genome/faq/genenumber.shtml

Human Rights Watch. (2001). Hatred in the hallways. Retrieved May 14, 2003, from http://www.hrw.org/reports/2001

Hunt, L. (1993). Introduction: Obscenity and the origins of modernity, 1500–1800. In L. Hunt (Ed.), *The invention of pornography* (pp. 9–45). New York: Zone Books.

Hunt, M. (1974). *Sexual behavior in the 1970's.* New York: Dell.

Hunter, I., Saunders, D., & Williamson, D. (1993). *On pornography: Literature, sexuality and obscenity law.* New York: St. Martin's Press.

Hunter, J. A., Figueredo, A. J., Malamuth, N. M., & Becker, J. V. (2003). Juvenile sex offenders: Toward the development of a typology. *Sexual Abuse: Journal of Research & Treatment, 15*(1), 27–48.

Hurlbert, D. F. (1992). Factors influencing a woman's decision to end an extramarital sexual relationship. *Journal of Sex and Marital Therapy, 18*(2), 104–113.

Hutson J. M., & Hasthorpe S. J. (2005). Testicular descent and cryptorchidism: The state of the art in 2004. *Pediatric Surgery, 40*(2), 297–302.

Hutson, J. M., Baker, M., Terada, M., Zhou, B., & Paxton, G. (1994). Hormonal control of testicular descent and the cause of cryptorchidism. *Reproduction, Fertility and Development, 6*(2), 151–156.

Hutter, M. (1981). *The changing family: Comparative perspective.* New York: Wiley.

Hyde, J., & Oliver, M. B. (2000). Gender differences in sexuality: Results from metaanalysis. In C. B. Travis & J. W. White (Eds.), *Sexuality, society, and feminism* (pp. 57–77). Washington, DC: American Psychological Association.

Hyde, J. S., & Kling, K. C. (2001). Women, motivation and achievement. *Psychology of Women Quarterly, 25*(4), 364–378.

Hynes, H. P. (2004). On the battlefield of women's bodies: An overview of the harm of war to women. *Women's Studies International Forum, 27*(5–6), 431–445.

Ickovics, J. R., Hamburger, M. E., Vlahov, D., Schoenbaum, E. E., et al. (2001). Mortality, CD4 cell decline, and depressive symptoms among HIV-seropositive women. *Journal of the American Medical Association, 285*(111), 1466–1474.

Impett, E. A., Beals, K. P., & Peplau, L. A. (2001). Testing the investment model of relationship commitment and stability in a longitudinal study of married couples. *Current Psychology, 20*(4), 312–327.

India: Girl children increasingly unwanted. (1999). *Women's International Network News, 25*(3), 67–75.

Info Reports. (2005). Microbicides: New potential for protection. Retrieved September 1, 2005 from http://www.infoforhealth.org/inforeports/microbicides/index.shtml

Innamaa, A., & Nunns, D. (2005). The management of vulval pain syndromes. *Hospital Medicine, 66*(1), 23–26.

International Journal of Impotence Research. (2003). Penis enlargement: Current status. *International Journal of Impotence Research, 15*(7), S44–S45.

Irvine, J. (1990). *Disorders of desire, sex, and gender in modern American sexology.* Philadelphia: Temple University Press.

Irvine, J. (1995). Reinventing perversion: Sex addiction and cultural anxieties. *Journal of the History of Sexuality, 5*(3), 429–449.

Isaksson, R., & Tiitinen, A. (1998). Obstetric outcome in patients with unexplained infertility: Comparison of treatment-related and spontaneous pregnancies. *Acta Obstetricia et Gynecologica Scandinavica, 77*(8), 849–853.

Isay, R. A. (1989). *Being homosexual.* New York: Farrar, Straus, & Giroux.

Islam, A., Mitchel, J., Rosen, R., Phillips, N., Ayers, C., Ferguson, D., et al. (2001). Topical alprostadil in the treatment of female sexual arousal disorder. *Journal of Sex and Marital Therapy, 27*(5), 531–540.

Israilov, S., Niv, E., Livne, P. M., Shmeuli, J., Engelstein, D., Segenreich, E., & Baniel, J. (2002). Intracavernous injections for erectile dysfunction in patients with cardiovascular diseases and failure or contraindications for sildenafil citrate. *International Journal of Impotence Research, 14*(1), 38–43.

Iverson, J. S. (1991). A debate on the American home: The antipolygamy controversy, 1880–1890. *Journal of the History of Sexuality, 1,* 585–602.

Jaccard, J., Dittus, P. J., & Gordon, V. V. (1998). Parent–adolescent congruency in reports of adolescent sexual behavior and in communications about sexual behavior. *Child Development, 69*(1), 247–261.

Jaccard, J., Dittus, P. J., & Gordon, V. V. (2000). Parent–teen communication about premarital sex: Factors associated with the extent of communication. *Journal of Adolescent Research, 15*(2), 187–209.

Jackman, L. P., Williamson, D. A., Netemeyer, R. G., & Anderson, D. A. (1995). Do weight-preoccupied women misinterpret ambiguous stimuli related to body size? *Cognitive Therapy and Research, 19,* 341–355.

Jackson, G. (2002). Extramarital sex hazardous to health? Retrieved December 10, 2002, from http:www.cnn.con/2002/HEALTH/12/05/extramarital.sex.reut/index.html

Jackson, M. (1984). Sex research and the construction of sexuality: A tool of male supremacy? *Women's Studies International Forum, 7,* 43–51.

Jacquet, S. E., & Surra, C. A. (2001). Parental divorce and premarital couples: Commitment and other relationship characteristics. *Journal of Marriage and Family, 63*(3), 627–639.

Jain, J. K., Minoo, P., Nucatola, D. L., & Felix, J. C. (2005). The effect of nonoxynol-9 on human endometrium. *Contraception, 71*(2), 137–142.

Jakobsson, L., Loven, L., & Hallberg, I. (2001). Sexual problems in men with prostate cancer in comparison with men with benign prostatic hyperplasia and men from the general population. *Journal of Clinical Nursing, 10*(4), 573–583.

James, S. E. (1998). Fulfilling the promise: Community response to the needs of sexual minority youth and families. *American Journal of Orthopsychiatry, 68*(3), 447–455.

James, W. (1971). The reliability of reporting coital frequency. *Journal of Sex Research, 7,* 312–314.

Janeway, E. (1971). *Man's world, woman's place: A study in social mythology.* New York: W. Morrow.

Jannini, E. A., & Lenzi, A. (2005). Epidemiology of premature ejaculation. *Current Opinions in Urology, 15*(6), 399–403.

Janus, S. S., & Janus, C. L. (1993). *The Janus report on sexual behavior.* New York: Wiley.

Japsen, B. (2003). Viagra faces 1st rivals by year's end. Retrieved July 18, 2003, from http://www.webprowire.com/summaries/5357111.html

Jayne, C. (1981). A two-dimensional model of female sexual response. *Journal of Sex and Marital Therapy, 7,* 3–30.

Jeary, K. (2005). Sexual abuse and sexual offending against elderly people: A focus on perpetrators and victims. *Journal of Forensic Psychiatry & Psychology, 16*(2), 328–343.

Jemal, A., Murray, T. Ward, E., Samuels, A., Tiwari, R. C., Ghafoor, A., Feuer, E. J., & Thun, M. J. (2005). Cancer statistics, 2005. *CA: A Cancer Journal for Clinicians, 55,* 10–30.

Jenkins, D., & Johnston, L. (2004). Unethical treatment of gay and lesbian people with conversion therapy. *Families in Society, 85*(4), 557–561.

Jenness, V. (1990). From sex as sin to sex as work: COYOTE and the reorganization of prostitution as a social problem. *Social Problems, 37,* 403–420.

Jennings, V. H., Arevalo, M., & Kowal, D. (2004). Fertility awareness-based methods. In R. A. Hatcher et al. (Eds.), *Contraceptive technology* (18th Rev. ed., pp. 317–330). New York: Ardent Media.

Jensen, M. N. (1998). Heterosexual women have noisy ears. *Science News, 153*(10), 151–152.

Jeong, S. J., Park, K., Moon, J. D., & Ryu, S. B. (2002). Bicycle saddle shape affects penile blood flow. *International Journal of Impotence Research, 14,* 513–517.

Jetter, A. (1991). Faye's crusade. *Vogue,* 147–151, 202–204.

Johannes, L. (2004, November 23). A screening test for high-risk mothers. *Wall Street Journal,* pp. D1–D10.

Johansson, T., & Ritzen, E. M. (2005). Very long-term follow-up of girls with early and late menarche. *Endocrine Development, 8,* 126–136.

Johnson, A., Wadsworth, J., Wellings, K., Bradshaw, S., & Field, J. (1992). Sexual lifestyles and HIV risk. *Nature, 360,* 410–412.

Johnson, A. M. (2001). Popular belief in gender-based communication differences and relationship success. *Dissertation Abstracts,* University of Massachusetts, Amherst, #0-599-95739-5.

Johnson, B. E., Kuck, D. L., & Schander, P. R. (1997). Rape myth acceptance and sociodemographic characteristics: A multidimensional analysis. *Sex Roles, 36*(11–12), 693–707.

Johnson, C. B., Stockdale, M. S., & Saal, F. E. (1991). Persistence of men's misperceptions of friendly cues across a variety of interpersonal encounters. *Psychology of Women Quarterly, 15,* 463–475.

Johnson, D., & Nelson, M. (2003, August 18). Gays in church and state. *Newsweek,* p. 34.

Johnson, G. (2005). Same-sex marriage. Retrieved June 18, 2005, from http://www.glbtq.com/social-sciences/same_sex_marriage.html

Johnson, H. D. (2004). Gender, grade, and relationship differences in emotional closeness within adolescent friendships. *Adolescence, 39*(154), 243–256.

Johnson, J. (2001). *Male multiple orgasm: Step by step* (4th ed.) Jack Johnson Seminars.

Johnson, J., & Alford, R. (1987). The adolescent quest for intimacy: Implications for the therapeutic alliance. *Journal of Social Work and Human Sexuality* (Special issue: Intimate Relationships) 5, 55–66.

Johnson, J., Canning, J., Kaneko, T., Pru, J. K., & Tilly, J. L. (2004). Germline stem cells and follicular renewal in the postnatal mammalian ovary. *Nature, 428,* 145–150.

Johnson, J. M., & Endler, N. S. (2002). Coping with HIV: Do optimists fare better? *Current Psychology, 21*(1), 3–17.

Johnson, K. C., & Daviss, B. A. (2005). Outcomes of planned home births with certified professional midwives: Large prospective study in North America. *British Medical Journal, 330*(7505), 1416–1420.

Johnson, L. A. (2005). Experts urge routine HIV tests for all. Retrieved February 11, 2005, from http://abcnews.go.com/Health/wireStory?id=485527

Johnson, S. E. (1996). *Lesbian sex: An oral history.* Tallahassee, FL: Naiad Press.

Johnson, W. R. (2005). Maps of percentages of pregnancies aborted worldwide—by country. Retrieved September 1, 2005, from http://www.johnstonsarchive.net/policy/abortion/mapworldabrate.html

Joint United Nations Programme on HIV/AIDS and the World Health Organization. (2002). *AIDS Epidemic Update*. Geneva, Switzerland: UNAIDS.

Jones, A. (1999). Case study: Female infanticide. Retrieved September 1, 2003, from http://www.gendercide.org/case_infanticide.html

Jones, J. H. (1997). *Alfred C. Kinsey: A public/private life*. New York: W. W. Norton.

Jones, M. B., & Blanchard, R. (1998). Birth order and male homosexuality. *Human Biology, 70*(4), 775–788.

Jones, R. (1984). *Human reproduction and sexual behavior*. Englewood Cliffs, NJ: Prentice Hall.

Jones, R. K., Darroch, J .E., & Henshaw, S. K. (2002a). Contraceptive use among U.S. women having abortions in 2000–2001, *Perspectives on Sexual and Reproductive Health, 34*(6), 294–303.

Jones, R. K., Darroch, J.E., & Henshaw, S. K. (2002b). Patterns in the socioeconomic characteristics of women obtaining abortions in 2000–2001. *Perspectives on Sexual and Reproductive Health, 34*(5), 226–235.

Jones, R., Darroch, J., & Singh, S. (2005). Religious differentials in the sexual and reproductive behaviors of young women in the United States. *Journal of Adolescent Health, 36*(4), 279–288.

Jones, R. K., & Henshaw, S. K. (2002). Mifepristone for early medical abortion: Experiences in France, Great Britain and Sweden. *Perspectives on Sexual and Reproductive Health, 34*(3). Retrieved September 9, 2003, from http://www.agi-usa.org/pubs/journals/3415402.html

Jordan, J. (1997). User buys: Why men buy sex. *Australian and New Zealand Journal of Criminology, 30*, 55–71.

Jorgenson, C. (1967). *Christine Jorgenson: Personal biography*. New York: Erickson.

Joung, I. M., Stronks, K., & van de Mheen, H. (1995). Health behaviours explain part of the differences in self-reported health associated with partner/marital status in the Netherlands. *Journal of Epidemiology and Community Health, 49*(5), 482–488.

Joyner, K., & Udry, J. R. (2000). You don't bring me anything but down: Adolescent romance and depression. *Journal of Health and Social Behavior, 41*(4), 369–391.

Kaats, G. R., & Davis, K. E. (1971). Effects of volunteer biases in studies of sexual behavior and attitudes. *Journal of Sex Research, 7*, 26–34.

Kabalin, J. N., & Kessler, R. (1988). Infectious complications of penile prosthesis surgery. *Journal of Urology, 139*, 953–955.

Kaeser, F. (1992). Can people with severe mental retardation consent to mutual sex? *Sexuality and Disability, 10*, 33–42.

Kahla, P. B., Cassaro, S., Vladimir, F. G., Wayne, M. G., & Cammarata, A. (2005). Bilateral synchronous breast cancer in a male. *Mt. Sinai Journal of Medicine, 72*(2), 120–123.

Kahn, J. A., & Bernstein, D. I. (2005). Human papillomavirus vaccines and adolescents. *Current Opinions Obstetrics and Gynecology, 17*(5), 476–482.

Kahn, J. A., Rosenthal, S. L., Succop, P. A., Ho, G., & Burk, R. D. (2002). Mediators of the association between age of first sexual intercourse and subsequent HPV infection. *Pediatrics, 109*(1), 132–134.

Kahn, J. G., Brindis, C. D., & Glei, D. A. (1999). Pregnancies averted among U.S. teenagers by the use of contraceptives. *Family Planning Perspectives, 31*(1), 29–35.

Kahn, Y. (1989–90). Judaism and homosexuality: The traditionalist/progressive debate. *Journal of Homosexuality, 18*, 47–82.

Kaiser Family Foundation. (2004, Fall). Key facts: Tweens, teens, and magazines. Retrieved on December 24, 2004, from http://www.kff.org/entmedia/loader.cfm?url=/commonspot/security/getfile.cfm&PageID=47098

Kaiser Family Foundation. (2005a). HIV/AIDS policy fact sheet: The global HIV/AIDS epidemic. Retrieved September 25, 2005, from http://www.kff.org/hivaids/3030-05.cfm

Kaiser Family Foundation. (2005b).HIV/AIDS policy fact sheet: The HIV/AIDS epidemic in the United States. Retrieved September 25, 2005, from http://www.kff.org/hivaids/3029-05.cfm

Kakavoulis, A. (2001). Family and sex education: A survey of parental attitudes. *Sex Education, 1*(2), 163–174.

Kakuchi, S. (2005). New museum documents lives of Japan's "comfort women." Retrieved November 6, 2005, from http://www.womensenews.org/article.cfm?aid=2509

Kalisch, P. A., & Kalisch, B. J. (1984). Sex-role stereotyping of nurses and physicians on prime-time television: A dichotomy of occupational portrayals. *Sex Roles, 10*, 533–553.

Kallen, L. (1998). Men don't cry, women don't fume. *Psychology Today, 31*(5), 20.

Kaminer, W. (1992, November). Feminists against the first amendment. *Atlantic Monthly*, pp. 111–117.

Kantor, L. (1992). Scared chaste? Fear based educational curricula. *SIECUS Reports, 21*, 1–15.

Kantrowitz, B., & Gonzalez, D. (1990, July 23). Examining the mind of the rapist. *Newsweek*, pp. 46–53.

Kaplan, G. (1977). Circumcision: An overview. *Current Problems in Pediatrics, 1*, 1–33.

Kaplan, H., Sadock, B., & Grebb, J. (1994). *Synopsis of psychiatry* (7th ed.). Baltimore, MD: Williams and Wilkins.

Kaplan, H. S. (1974). *The new sex therapy*. New York: Bruner/Mazel.

Kaplan, H. S. (1979). *Sexual desire disorders: Dysfunctional regulation of sexual motivation*. New York: Brunner-Mazel.

Kaplan, H. S. (1989). *How to overcome premature ejaculation*. New York: Bruner- Routledge.

Kaplan, L. J. (1991). Women masquerading as women. In G. I. Fogel & W. A. Meyers (Eds.), *Perversions and near-perversions in clinical practice: New psychoanalytic perspectives* (pp. 127–152). New Haven, CT: Yale University Press.

Kaplowitz, P. B., Slora, E. J., Wasserman, R. C., Pedlow, S. E., & Herman-Giddens, M. E. (2001). Earlier onset of puberty in girls: Relation to increased body mass index and race. *Pediatrics, 2108*(2), 347–354.

Karniol, R. (2001). Adolescent females' idolization of male media stars as a transition into sexuality. *Sex Roles, 44*(1–2), 61–77.

Kaschak, E., & Tiefer, L. (Eds.). (2001). *A new view of women's sexual problems*. Binghamton, NY: Haworth Press.

Kassler, W. J., & Cates, W. (1992). The epidemiology and prevention of sexually transmitted diseases. *Urologic Clinics of North America, 19*, 1–12.

Katz, M. H., Schwarcz, S. K., Kellogg, T. A., Klausner, J. D., Dilley, J. W., Gibson, S., et al. (2002). Impact of highly active antiretroviral treatment on HIV seroincidence among men who have sex with men. *American Journal of Public Health, 92*(3), 388–395.

Katz, V. L. (1996). Water exercise in pregnancy. *Seminars in Perinatology, 20*(4), 285–291.

Kaufman, M. (2005). FDA investigates blindness in Viagra users. Retrieved November 15, 2005, from http://www.washingtonpost.com/wp-dyn/content/article/2005/05/27/AR2005052701246_pf.html

Kaunitz, A., Nelson, A., Wysocki, S., & Schnare, S. (1998). Frequent urination and Depo-Provera. Ask the experts. *Contraceptive Technology Update, 19*(12), 160–161.

Kayongo-Male, D., & Onyango, P. (1984). *The sociology of the African family*. London: Longman.

Kaysen, D., & Stake, J. (2001). From thought to deed: Understanding abortion activism. *Journal of Applied Social Psychology, 31*(11), 2378–2400.

Keane, H. (2004). Disorders of desire: Addiction and problems of intimacy. *Journal of Medical Humanities, 25*(3), 189–197.

Keegan, J. (2001). The neurobiology, neuropharmacology and pharmacological treatment of the paraphilias and compulsive sexual behavior. *Canadian Journal of Psychiatry, 46*(1), 26–33.

Keen, S. (1992). *Fire in the belly: On being a man*. New York: Bantam Doubleday.

Keller, J. (1999). Ben Affleck's Viagra tales. Retrieved July 20, 2003, from http://www.eonline.com/News/Items/0,1,5510,00.html

Keller, J. (2002). Blatant stereotype threat and women's math performance. *Sex Roles, 47*(3–4), 193–198.

Kellerman, S. E., Hanson, D. L., McNaghten, A. D., & Fleming, P. L. (2003). Prevalence of chronic hepatitis B and incidence of acute hepatitis B infection in human immunodeficiency virus-infected subjects. *Journal of Infectious Disease, 188*(4), 571–577.

Kellock, D., & O'Mahony, C. P. (1996). Sexually acquired metronidazole-resistant trichomoniasis in a lesbian couple. *Genitourinary Medicine, 72*, 60–61.

Kelly, J. A., & Amirkhanian, Y. A. (2003). The newest epidemic: A review of HIV/AIDS in Central and Eastern Europe. *International Journal of Sexually Transmitted Diseases, 14*(6), 362–371.

Kelly, J. B. (1989). Mediated and adversarial divorce: Respondents' perceptions of their processes and outcomes. *Mediation Quarterly, 24*, 71–88.

Kelly, M. P., Strassberg, D. S., & Kircher, J. R. (1990). Attitudinal and experiential correlates of anorgasmia. *Archives of Sexual Behavior, 19*, 165–177.

Kelly, R. J., Wood, J., Gonzalez, L., MacDonald, V., & Waterman, J. (2002). Effects of mother–son incest and positive perceptions of sexual abuse experiences on the psychosocial adjustment of clinic-referred men. *Child Abuse and Neglect, 26*(4), 425–441.

Kelly, T. P. (2004). Ireland. In R. T. Francoeur & R. J. Noonan (Eds.), *The Continuum international encyclopedia of sexuality* (pp. 569–580). New York/London: Continuum International.

Kelly-Vance, L., Anthis, K. S., & Needelman, H. (2004). Assisted reproduction versus spontaneous conception: A comparison of the developmental outcomes in twins. *Journal of Genetic Psychology, 165*(2), 157–168.

Kempeneers, P., Andrianne, R., & Mormont, C. (2004). Penile prosthesis, sexual satisfaction and representation of male erotic value. *Sexual & Relationship Therapy, 19*(4), 379–392.

Kendrick, W. M. (1987). *The secret museum: Pornography in modern culture*. New York: Viking.

Kennedy, A., Schulpher, M. J., Coulter, A., Dwyer, N., Rees, M., & Abrams, K. R. (2002). Effects of decision aids for menorrhagia on treatment choices, health outcomes and costs. *Journal of the American Medical Association, 288*(21), 2701–2708.

Kennedy, K. I., & Trussell, J. (2004). Postpartum contraception and lactation. In R. A. Hatcher et al. (Eds.), *Contraceptive technology* (18th Rev. ed., pp. 575–600). New York: Ardent Media.

Kennedy, M. A., & Gorzalka, B. B. (2002). Asian and non-Asian attitudes toward rape, sexual harassment and sexuality. *Sex Roles, 46*(7–8), 227–238.

Kennet, G. A. (2000). *Serotonin receptors and their function*. Bristol, U.K.: Tocris.

Kettl, P., et al. (1991). Female sexuality after spinal cord injury. *Sexuality and Disability, 9,* 287–295.

Khadivzadeh, T., & Parsai, S. (2005). Effect of exclusive breastfeeding and complementary feeding on infant growth and morbidity. *Eastern Mediterranean Health Journal, 10*(3), 289–294.

Khamsi, R. (2005, June 21). "Ripened eggs" used for cloning work: Immature human eggs could be a source of stem cells. Retrieved November 3, 2005, from http://www.nature.com/drugdisc/news/articles/050620-4.html

Kilgallon, S., & Simmons, L. (2005). Image content influences men's semen quality. *Biology Letters, 1*(3), 253–255.

Kim, K., & Smith, P. K. (1999). Family relations in early childhood and reproductive development. *Journal of Reproductive and Infant Psychology, 17*(2), 133–149.

King, B. M., & Lorusso, J. (1997). Discussions in the home about sex: Different recollections by parents and children. *Journal of Sex and Marital Therapy, 23*(1), 52–60.

King, V., & Scott, M. (2005). A comparison of cohabiting relationships among older and younger adults. *Journal of Marriage & Family, 67*(2), 271–285.

Kingsberg S. A., & Janata, J. W. (2003). Sexual aversion disorder. In S. Levine (Ed.), *Handbook of clinical sexuality for mental health professionals* (pp. 153–166). New York: Brunner-Routledge.

Kinkade, S., & Meadows, S. (2005). Does neonatal circumcision decrease morbidity? *The Journal of Family Practice, 54*(1), 81–82.

Kinnunen, L. H., Moltz, H., Metz, J., & Cooper, M. (2004). Differential brain activation in exclusively homosexual and heterosexual men produced by the selective serotonin reuptake inhibitor, fluoxetine. *Brain Research, 1024*(1–2), 251–254.

Kinsey, A., Pomeroy, W. B., & Martin, C. E. (1948). *Sexual behavior in the human male*. Philadelphia: Saunders.

Kinsey, A. C., Pomeroy, W., Martin, C. E., & Gebhard, P. (1953). *Sexual behavior in the human female*. Philadelphia: Saunders.

Kirby, D. (1992). Sexuality education: It can reduce unprotected intercourse. *SIECUS Report, 21,* 19–25.

Kirby, D. (1999). Reflections on two decades of research on teen sexual behavior and pregnancy. *Journal of School Health, 69*(3), 89–95.

Kirby, D. (2001, May). Emerging answers: Research findings on programs to reduce teen pregnancy. National Campaign to Prevent Teen Pregnancy.

Kirchofer, T. (1999). Developer targets gay retirees. Retrieved October 21, 2003, from www.djc.com/news/re10059682.html

Kirk, K., M., Bailey, J., Michael, M., & Nicholas, G. (1999). How accurate is the family history method for assessing siblings' sexual orientation? *Archives of Sexual Behavior, 28*(2), 129–138.

Kitazawa, K. (1994). Sexuality issues in Japan. *SIECUS Report,* 7–11.

Kito, M. (2005). Self-disclosure in romantic relationships and friendships among American and Japanese college students. *Journal of Social Psychology, 145*(2), 127–140.

Kitson, G. C. (1992). *Portrait of divorce: Adjustment to marital breakdown*. New York: Guilford Press.

Kjerulff, K. H., Erikson, B., & Langenberg, P. W. (1996). Chronic gynecological conditions reported by U.S. women: Findings from the National Health Interview Survey, 1984 to 1992. *American Journal of Public Health, 86,* 195–199.

Klaas, M. (2003). *Klaas Action Review Newsletter, 9*(1). Retrieved May 23, 2003, from http://www.pollyklaas.org/newsletter.htm

Klaw, E. L., Lonsway, K. A., Berg, D. R., Waldo, C. R., Kothari, C., Mazurek, C. J., & Hegeman, K. E. (2005). Challenging rape culture: Awareness, emotion and action through campus acquaintance rape education. *Women & Therapy, 28*(2), 47–63.

Klein, A. M. (1989). Managing deviance: Hustling, homophobia, and the bodybuilding subculture. *Deviant Behavior, 10,* 11–27.

Klein, F. (1978). *The bisexual option: A concept of one-hundred percent intimacy*. New York: Arbor House.

Klein, F. (1990). The need to view sexual orientation as a multivariable dynamic process: A theoretical perspective. In D. P. McWhirter, S. A. Sanders, & J. M. Reinisch (Eds.), *Homosexuality/heterosexuality: Concepts of sexual orientation* (pp. 277–282). New York: Oxford University Press.

Klein, M. (1988). *Your sexual secrets: When to keep them, when and how to tell*. New York: E. P. Dutton.

Kline, P. (1987). Sexual deviation: Psychoanalytic research and theory. In G. D. Wilson (Ed.), *Variant sexuality: Research and theory* (pp. 150–175). Baltimore: Johns Hopkins University Press.

Knobloch, S., Callison, C., Chen, L., Fritzsche, A., & Zillmann, D. (2005). Children's sex-stereotyped self-socialization through selective exposure to entertainment: Cross-cultural experiments in Germany, China, and the United States. *Journal of Communication, 55*(1), 122–138.

Knower, K. C., Kelly, S., & Harley, V. R. (2003). Turning on the male—SRY, SOX9 and sex determination in mammals. *Cytogenetic and Genome Research, 101*(3–4), 185–198.

Knox, D., Sturdivant, L., & Zusman, M. E. (2001). College student attitudes toward sexual intimacy. *College Student Journal, 35*(2), 241–243.

Knox, D., Zusman, M. E., Buffington, C., & Hemphill, G. (2000). Interracial dating attitudes among college students. *College Student Journal, 434*(1), 69–72.

Knox, D., Zusman, M. E., & Mabon, L. (1999). Jealousy in college student relationships. *College Student Journal, 33*(3), 328–329.

Koch, W. (2005). Despite high-profile cases, sex-offense crimes decline. Retrieved October 9, 2005, from http://www.usatoday.com/news/nation/2005-08-24-sex-crimes-cover_x.htm?POE=NEWISVA

Koci, A. F. (2004). Marginality, abuse and adverse health outcomes in women. *Dissertations Abstracts International,* 0419–4217.

Koenig, L. (2002). Review of HIV/AIDS. Personal Communication, March 23, 2003.

Koh, A. S., Gomez, C. A., Shade, S., & Rowley, E. (2005). Sexual risk factors among self-identified lesbians, bisexual women, and heterosexual women accessing primary care settings. *Sexually Transmitted Diseases, 32*(9), 563–569.

Kohl, J. V., & Francoeur, R. (2002). *The scent of eros: Mysteries of odor in human sexuality*. Lincoln, NE: iUniverse, Author's Choice Press.

Kohler, K., Schweikert-Stary, M. T., & Lubkin, I. (1990). Altered mobility. In I. M. Lubkin (Ed.), *Chronic illness impact and interventions* (pp. 86–110). Boston: Jones & Bartlett.

Kohn, C., Hasty, S., & Henderson, C. W. (2002, September 3). Study confirms infection from receptive oral sex occurs rarely. *AIDS Weekly,* 20–22.

Kon, I. S. (2004). Russia. In R. T. Francoeur & R. J. Noonan (Eds.), *The Continuum international encyclopedia of sexuality* (pp. 888–908). New York/London: Continuum International.

Kong, S. C. (2004). Kamasutra: A new, complete English translation from the Sanskrit text. *Herisons, 17*(3), 42–43.

Kontula, O., & Haavio-Mannila, E. (2004). Finland. In R. T. Francoeur & R. J. Noonan (Eds.), *The Continuum international encyclopedia of sexuality* (pp. 381–411). New York/London: Continuum International.

Kopelman, L. (1988). The punishment concept of disease. In C. Pierce & D. Vandeveer (Eds.), *AIDS, ethics, and public policy*. Belmont, CA: Wadsworth.

Kormann, K. U. (2001). Treatment of testicular cancer—Is quality management possible? *Onkologie, 24*(2), 177–179.

Korzeniowski, P. (2005). Adult entertainment on a cell phone near you. Retrieved November 5, 2005, from http://www.technewsworld.com/story/41140.html

Koss, M. P. (1988). Hidden rape: Sexual aggression and victimization in a national sample in higher education. In A. Burgess (Ed.), *Rape and sexual assault* (pp. 3–25). New York: Garland.

Koss, M. P., & Gaines, J. A. (1993). The prediction of sexual aggression by alcohol use, athletic participation and fraternity affiliation. *Journal of Interpersonal Violence, 8*(1), 94–108.

Kotchick, B. A., Dorsey, S., & Miller, K. S. (1999). Adolescent sexual risk-taking behavior in single-parent ethnic minority families. *Journal of Family Psychology, 13*(1), 93–102.

Kourtis, A. P., Bulterys, M., Nesheim, S. R., & Lee, F. K. (2001). Understanding the timing of HIV transmission from mother to infant. *Journal of the American Medical Association, 285*(6), 709–712.

Koutsky, L. (1997). Epidemiology of genital human papillomavirus infection. *American Journal of Medicine, 102*(Suppl. 5A), 3–8.

Koutsky, L. A., Ault, K. A., Wheeler, C., Brown, D., Barr, E., Alvarez, F., Chiacchierini, L., & Jansen, K. (2002). A controlled trial of a human papillomavirus type 16 vaccine. *The New England Journal of Medicine, 347*(21), 1645–1651.

Kowal, D. (2004a). Abstinence and the range of sexual expression. In R. A. Hatcher et al. (Eds.), *Contraceptive technology* (18th Rev. ed., pp. 305–309). New York: Ardent Media.

Kowal, D. (2004b). Coitus interruptus (withdrawal). In R. A. Hatcher et al. (Eds.), *Contraceptive technology* (18th Rev. ed., pp. 311–316). New York: Ardent Media.

Krahé, B., Scheinberger-Olwig, R., & Kolpin, S. (2000). Ambiguous communication of sexual intentions as a risk marker of sexual aggression. *Sex Roles, 42*(5–6), 313–337.

Krause, H. (1986). *Family law.* St. Paul, MN: West.

Kreider, R. M., & Fields, J. M. (2001). Number, timing and duration of marriages and divorces. *Current Population Reports.* Washington, DC: U.S. Census Bureau.

Kreinin, T. (2001). Help for the 36 million people with AIDS? *SIECUS Report, 29*(5), 4.

Kreuter, M., Dahllof, A. G., Gudjonsson, G., Sullivan, M., & Siosteen, A. (1998). Sexual adjustment and its predictors after traumatic brain injury. *Brain Injury, 12,* 349–368.

Krilov, L. (1991). What do you know about genital warts? *Medical Aspects of Human Sexuality, 25,* 39–41.

Kristof, N. (2005, February 16). Bush's sex scandal. Retrieved April 2, 2005, from http://query. nytimes.com/gst/abstract.html?res= F30710FE385E0C758DDDAB0894DD404482

Kristof, N. D. (1996, February 11). Who needs love! In Japan, many couples don't. *New York Times,* p. A1.

Kroon, S. (1990). Genital herpes—when and how to treat. *Seminars in Dermatology, 9,* 133–140.

Krstic, Z. D., Smoljanic, Z., Vukanic, D., Varinac, D., & Janiic, G. (2000). True hermaphroditism: 10 years' experience. *Pediatric Surgery International, 16*(8), 580–583.

Kruks, G. N. (1991). Gay and lesbian homeless/street youth: Special issues and concerns. *Journal of Consulting Clinical Psychology, 62,* 221.

Ku, L., St. Louis, M., Farshy, C., Aral, S. Turner, C., Lindberg, L. D., & Sonenstein, F. (2002). Risk behaviors, medical care, and chlamydial infection among young men in the U.S. *American Journal of Public Health, 92*(7), 1140–1144.

Ku, L., Sonenstein, F. L., Lindberg, L. D., Bradner, C. H., Boggess, S., & Pleck, J. H. (1998). Understanding changes in sexual activity among young metropolitan men: 1979–1995. *Family Planning Perspectives, 30*(6), 256–263.

Kulig, J. (1994). Sexuality beliefs among Cambodians: Implications for health care professionals. *Health Care for Women International, 15*(1), 69–76.

Kunin, C. M. (1997) *Urinary tract infections: Detection, prevention and management.* (5th ed.) Baltimore: Williams & Wilkins.

Kunkel, D., Beily, E., Eyal, K., Cope-Farrar, K., Donnerstein, E., & Fandrich, R. (2003). Sex on TV3. Retrieved July 26, 2003, from http://www.kff.org/content/2003/20030204a /Sex_on_TV_3_Full.pdf

Kunkel, D., Eyal, K., Finnerty, K., Biely, E., & Donnerstein, E. (2005). Sex on TV4. Retrieved November 9, 2005, from http://www.kff.org/entmedia/upload /Sex-on-TV-4-Full-Report.pdf

Kupers, T. A. (2001). Psychotherapy with men in prison. In G. R. Brooks & G. E. Good (Eds.), *The new handbook of psychotherapy and counseling with men: A comprehensive guide to settings, problems, and treatment approaches* (pp. 170–184). San Francisco, CA: Jossey-Bass.

Kuppermann, M., Varner, R. E., Summitt, R. L., Learman, L., Ireland, C., Vittinghoff, E., Stewart, A., Lin, F., Richter, H. E., Showstack, J., Hulley, S. B., & Washington, A. E. (2004). Effect of hysterectomy vs. medical treatment on the health-related quality of life and sexual functioning. *Journal of the American Medical Association, 291*(12), 1447–1455.

Kurdek, L. A. (1999). The nature and predictors of the trajectory of change in marital quality for husbands and wives over the first 10 years of marriage. *Developmental Psychology, 35,* 1283–1296.

Kurdek, L. A. (2001). Differences between heterosexual-nonparent couples and gay, lesbian, and heterosexual-parent couples. *Journal of Family Issues, 22*(6), 28–56.

Kutchinsky, B. (1991). Pornography and rape: Theory and practice? *International Journal of Law and Psychiatry, 14,* 47–64.

La Leche League. (2005). Summary of breastfeeding legislation in the U.S. as of 6/19/05. Retrieved November 4, 2005, from http://www. laleche-league.org/Law/summary.html

LaBrie, J. W., Schiffman, J., & Earleywine, M. (2002). Expectancies specific to condom use mediate the alcohol and sexual risk relationship. *Journal of Sex Research, 39*(2), 145–153.

Lacey, R. S., Reifman, A., Scott, J. P., Harris, S. M., & Fitzpatrick, J. (2004). Sexual-moral attitudes, love styles, and mate selection. *The Journal of Sex Research, 41*(2), 121–129.

Laflamme, D., Pomerleau, A., & Malcuit, G. (2003). A comparison of father's and mother's involvement in childcare and stimulation behaviors during freeplay with their infants at 9 and 15 months. *Sex Roles, 47*(11–12), 507–518.

LaFree, G. (1982). Male power and female victimization. *American Journal of Sociology, 88,* 311–328.

Lague, J. B. (2001, February). An introduction to "Couple assessment: Using the 16PF couple's counseling report." A three-part videotape series. *Dissertation Abstracts International,* #0419-4217, Azusa Pacific University.

Lahdenper, M., Lummaa, V., & Russell, A. F. (2004, November). Menopause: Why does fertility end before life? *Climacteric, 7*(4), 1–5.

Lahey, K. A. (1991). Pornography and harm—learning to listen to women. *International Journal of Law and Psychiatry, 14,* 117–131.

Lalumière, M. L., & Blanchard, R. (2000). Sexual orientation and handedness in men and women: A meta-analysis. *Psychological Bulletin, 126*(4), 575–593.

Lalumière, M. L., Harris, G. T., Quinsey, V., & Rice, M. E. (2005a). Clinical assessment and treatment of rapists. In M. L. Lalumière & G. Harris (Eds.), *Causes of rape: Understanding individual differences in male propensity for sexual aggression* (pp. 161–181). Washington, DC: American Psychological Association.

Lalumière, M. L., Harris, G. T., Quinsey, V., & Rice, M. E. (2005b). Forced copulation in the animal kingdom. In M. L. Lalumière & G. Harris (Eds.), *Causes of rape: Understanding individual differences in male propensity for sexual aggression* (pp. 31–58). Washington, DC: American Psychological Association.

Lalumière, M. L., Harris, G. T., Quinsey, V., & Rice, M. E. (2005c). Rape across cultures and time. In M. L. Lalumière & G. Harris (Eds.), *Causes of rape: Understanding individual differences in male propensity for sexual aggression* (pp. 9–30). Washington, DC: American Psychological Association.

Lalumière, M. L., Harris, G. T., Quinsey, V., & Rice, M. E. (2005d). Sexual interest in rape. In M. L. Lalumière & G. Harris (Eds.), *Causes of rape: Understanding individual differences in male propensity for sexual aggression* (pp. 105–128). Washington, DC: American Psychological Association.

LaMar, L., & Wiederman, M. W. (1998). "Not with him you don't!": Gender and emotional reactions to sexual infidelity during courtship. *Journal of Sex Research, 35*(3), 288–297.

LAMBDA. (2001). State-by-state map of sodomy laws. Retrieved October 15, 2003, from http://lambdalegal.org/cgi_bin/pages/ states/sodomy-map

Lambert, E. C. (2001). College students' knowledge of HPV and effectiveness of a brief educational intervention. *Journal of American Board of Family Practitioners, 14*(3), 178–183.

Lambert, L. (2004). A pill for all seasons. Retrieved March 19, 2005, from http://ppfa. org/pp2/portal/files/portal/webzine/ sexualityhealth/feas-041122-seasonale.xml

Lambert, T. A., Kahn, A., & Apple, K. (2003). Pluralistic ignorance and hooking up. *Journal of Sex Research, 40*(2), 129–133.

Lancaster, J. B. (1986). Human adolescence and reproduction: An evolutionary perspective. In J. B. Lancaster & B. A. Hamburg (Eds.), *School-age pregnancy and parenthood: Biosocial dimensions* (pp. 17–37). New York: Aldine DeGruyter.

Land, K. C. (2005, February 23). Personal communication.

Landau, E. (1987). *On the streets: The lives of adolescent prostitutes.* New York: Julian Messner.

Lang, R., Flor-Henry, P., & Frenzel, R. (1990). Sex hormone profiles in pedophilic and incestuous men. *Annals of Sex Research, 3,* 59–74.

Langevin, R., & Lang, R. A. (1987). The courtship disorders. In G. D. Wilson (Ed.), *Variant sexuality: Research and theory* (pp. 202–228). Baltimore: Johns Hopkins University Press.

Langevin, R., Wortzman, G., Dickey, R., Wright, P., et al. (1988). Neuropsychological impairment in incest offenders. *Annals of Sex Research, 1,* 401–415.

Langfeldt, T. (1981a). Processes in sexual development. In L. L. Constantine & F. M. Martinson (Eds.), *Children and sex: New findings, new perspectives* (pp. 37–44). Boston: Little, Brown.

Langfeldt, T. (1981b). Childhood masturbation: Individual and social organization. In L. L. Constantine & F. M. Martinson (Eds.), *Children and sex: New findings, new perspectives* (pp. 63–72). Boston: Little, Brown.

Langstrom, N., Grann, M., & Lindblad, F. (2000). A preliminary typology of young sex offenders. *Journal of Adolescence, 23,* 319–329.

Larkin, M. (1992). Reacting to patients with sexual problems. *Headlines, 3,* 2, 3, 6, 8.

Larsson, I., & Svedin, C. G. (2002). Sexual experiences in childhood: Young adults' recollections. *Archives of Sexual Behavior, 31*(3), 203–273.

LaSala, M. C. (2000). Lesbians, gay men and their parents: Family therapy for the coming out crisis. *Family Process, 39*(2), 257–266.

LaSala, M. C. (2001). The importance of partners to lesbians' intergenerational relationships. *Social Work Research, 25*(1), 27–36.

Lastella, D. D. (2005). Sexual harassment as an interpersonal dynamic: The effect of race, attractiveness, position power and gender on perceptions of sexual harassment. *Dissertation Abstracts International: Section B.,* #0419–4217.

Lau, J., Kim, J. H., & Tsui, H. Y. (2005). Prevalence of male and female sexual problems, perceptions related to sex and association with quality of life in a Chinese population. *International Journal of Impotence Research, 17*(6), 494–505.

Lauer, R. H., Lauer, J. C., & Kerr, S. T. (1990). The long-term marriage: Perceptions of stability and satisfaction. *International Journal of Aging and Human Development, 31*(3), 189–195.

Laumann, E., & Youm, Y. (2001). Racial/ethnic group differences in the prevalence of STDs in the U.S. In E. O. Laumann & R. T. Michael (Eds.), *Sex, love and health in America* (pp. 327–351). Chicago: University of Chicago Press.

Laumann, E. O., Gagnon, J., Michael, R., & Michaels, S. (1994). *The social organization of sexuality: Sexual practices in the United States.* Chicago: University of Chicago Press.

Laumann, E. O., Masi, C. M., & Zuckerman, E. W. (2000). Circumcision in the United States: Prevalence, prophylactic effects, and sexual practice. In E. O. Laumann and R. T. Michael (Eds.), *Sex, love and health in America: Private choices and public policies.* Chicago: University of Chicago Press.

Laumann, E. O., & Michaels, S. (Eds.). (2001). *Sex, love, and health in America* (pp. 197–238). Chicago: Chicago University Press.

Laumann, E. O., Paik, A., & Rosen, R. (1999). Sexual dysfunction in the United States. *Journal of the American Medical Association, 281,* 537–544.

Lautmann, R., & Starke, K. (2004). Germany. In R. T. Francoeur & R. J. Noonan (Eds.), *The Continuum international encyclopedia of sexuality* (pp. 450–466). New York/London: Continuum International.

Laval, J. D. (2002). Leiomyomata Uteri. Retrieved July 20, 2002, from http://www.medical-library.org/journals/secure/obgyn_review_p/secure/Leiomyomata%2OU

Lavee, Y. (1991). Western and non-Western human sexuality: Implications for clinical practice. *Journal of Sex and Marital Therapy, 17,* 203–213.

Lavie-Ajayi, M. (2005). "Because all real women do": The construction and deconstruction of "female orgasmic disorder." *Sexualities, Evolution & Gender, 7*(1), 57–72.

Lawhorn, B. A. (2005). Communication breakdown: Common workplace communication complaints. Retrieved September 3, 2005, from http://www.utexas.edu/staff/apsa/Gender_Communication.ppt#267,21,References

Lawlis, G., & Lewis, J. (1987, September). Relationship problems in adolescence. *Medical Aspects of Human Sexuality,* 62–67.

Lawrence, S. (2003). Older woman, younger man relationships. Retrieved June 10, 2005, from http://www.msnbc.msn.com/id/3679116/

Layton-Tholl, D. (1998). Extramarital affairs: The link between thought suppression and level of arousal. *Dissertation Abstracts,* Miami Institute of Psychology of the Caribbean Center for Advanced Studies, #AAT9930425.

Lazovich, D., Forster, J., Sorensen, G., Emmons, K., Stryker, J., Demierre, M. F., Hickle, A., & Remba, N. (2004). Characteristics associated with use or intention to use indoor tanning among adolescents. *Archives of Pediatric Adolescent Medicine, 158,* 918–924.

Lease, S. H. (2003). Testing a model of men's non-traditional occupational choices. *Career Development Quarterly, 51*(3), 244–259.

Leavy, W. (1993). Sex in black America: Reality and myth. *Ebony, 48*(10), 126–130.

Lee, J., Pomeroy, E. C., Yoo, S., & Rheinboldt, K. (2005). Attitudes toward rape: A comparison between Asian and Caucasian college students. *Violence Against Women, 11*(2), 177–196.

Lee, J. A. (1974). The styles of loving. *Psychology Today, 8,* 43–51.

Lee, J. A. (1988). Love-styles. In R. Sternberg & M. Barnes (Eds.), *The Psychology of Love.* New Haven, CT: Yale University Press.

Lee, J. A. (1998). Ideologies of lovestyle and sexstyle. In V. de Munck (Ed.), *Romantic love and sexual behavior* (pp. 33–76). Westport, CT: Praeger.

Lee, M. B., & Rotheram-Borus, M. J. (2002). Parents' disclosure of HIV to their children. *AIDS, 16*(16), 2201–2207.

Leiblum, S., & Nathan, S. (2002). Persistent sexual arousal syndrome in women: A not uncommon but little recognized complaint. *Sexual & Relationship Therapy, 17*(2), 191–200.

Leiblum, S., & Nathan, S. G. (2001). Persistent sexual arousal syndrome: A newly discovered pattern of female sexuality. *Journal of Sex and Marital Therapy, 27*(4), 365–380.

Leiblum, S. R., & Rosen, R. C. (1988). *Sexual desire disorders.* New York: Guilford Press.

Leichtentritt, R. D., & Arad, B. D. (2005). Young male street workers: Life histories and current experiences. *British Journal of Social Work, 35*(4), 483–509.

Leitenberg, H., Detzer, M. J., & Srebnik, D. (1993). Gender differences in masturbation and the relation of masturbation experience in preadolescence and/or early adolescence to sexual behavior and sexual adjustment in young adulthood. *Archives of Sexual Behavior, 22,* 87–98.

Leitenberg, H., & Henning, K. (1995). Sexual fantasy. *Psychological Bulletin, 117*(3), 469–496.

Leitzmann, M. F., Platz, E. A., Stampfer, M. J., Willett, W. C., & Giovannucci, E. (2004). Ejaculation frequency and subsequent risk of prostate cancer. *Journal of the American Medical Association, 291*(13), 1578–1586.

Leonard, K. E. (2005). Editorial: Alcohol and intimate partner violence: When can we say that heavy drinking is a contributing cause of violence? *Addiction, 100*(4), 422–425.

Lerner, H. (1998). *The mother dance: How children change your life.* New York: HarperCollins.

Leslie, G. R., & Korman, S. K. (1989). *The family in social context.* New York: Oxford University Press.

Levay, A. N., Sharpe, L., & Kugel, A. (1981). The effects of physical illness on sexual functioning. In H. Lief (Ed.), *Sexual problems in medical practice* (pp. 169–190). Chicago: American Medical Association.

LeVay, S. (1991). A difference in hypothalamic structure between heterosexual and homosexual men. *Science, 253,* 1034–1037.

Levesque, W. R. (2002, July 26). Airline security all aquiver over vibrating bag. *San Francisco Chronicle,* pp. A1–A19.

Levin, R. (2004). Smells and tastes—their putative influence on sexual activity in humans. *Sexual & Relationship Therapy, 19*(4), 452–462.

Levine, D. A., & Gemignani, M. L. (2003). Prophylactic surgery in hereditary breast/ovarian cancer syndrome. *Oncology, 17*(7), 932–941.

Levine, J. (1991). Search and find. *Forbes, 148,* 134–135.

Levine, J. (2002). *Harmful to minors: The perils of protecting children from sex.* Minneapolis: University of Minnesota Press.

Levine, R., Sato, S., & Hashimoto, T. (1995). Love and marriage in eleven cultures. *Journal of Cross-Cultural Psychology, 26*(5), 554–571.

Levine, R. J. (1999). Seasonal variation of semen quality and fertility. *Scandinavian Journal of Work and Environmental Health, 25*(Suppl. 1), 34–37.

Levine, S. B., Risen, C. B., & Althof, S. E. (1990). Essay on the diagnosis and nature of paraphilia. *Journal of Sex and Marital Therapy, 16*(2), 89–102.

Lewes, K. (1988). *The psychoanalytic theory of male homosexuality.* New York: Meridian.

Lewin, R. (1988). New views emerge on hunters and gatherers. *Science, 240*(4856), 1146–1148.

Lewis, D. A. (2000). Chancroid: From clinical practice to basic science. *AIDS Patient Care and STDs, 14*(1), 19–36.

Lewis, L., & Kertzner, R. M. (2003). Toward improved interpretation and theory building of African American male sexualities. *Journal of Sex Research, 40*(4), 383–399.

Lewis, M. (1987). Early sex role behavior and school age adjustment. In J. M. Reinish, L. A. Rosenblum, & S. A. Sanders (Eds.), *Masculinity/femininity: Basic perspectives* (pp. 202–226). New York: Oxford University Press.

Lewis, R. J., & Janda, L. H. (1988). The relationship between adult sexual adjustment and childhood experiences regarding exposure to nudity, sleeping in the parental bed, and parental attitudes toward sexuality. *Archives of Sexual Behavior, 17,* 349–362.

Lewis, R. W., Fugl-Meyer, K. S., Bosch, R., Fugl-Meyer, A., Laumann, E. O., Lizza, E., & Martin-Morales, A. (2004). Epidemiology/risk factors of sexual dysfunction. *The Journal of Sexual Medicine, 1*(1), 35.

Leyendecker, G., Kunz, G., Herbertz, M., Beil, D., Huppert, P., Mall, G., Kissler, S., Noe, M., & Wildt, L. (2004, December). Uterine peristaltic activity and the development of endometriosis. *Annals of the New York Academy of Sciences, 1034,* 338–355.

Leyson, J. F. (2004). Philippines. In R. T. Francoeur & R. J. Noonan (Eds.), *The Continuum international encyclopedia of sexuality* (pp. 825–845). New York/London: Continuum International.

Liben, L. S., & Bigler, R. S. (2002). The developmental course of gender differentiation. *Monographs of the Society of Research in Child Development, 67*(2), vii–147.

Liccardi, G., Gilder, J. A., D'Amato, M., & D'Amato, G. (2002). Drug allergy transmitted by passionate kissing. *Lancet, 359*(9318), 1700.

Liddon, N., Pulley, L., Cockerham, W. C., Lueschen, G., Vermund, S., & Hook, E. W. (2005). Parents'/guardians' willingness to vaccinate their children against genital herpes. *Journal of Adolescent Health, 37*(3), 187–193.

Lie, D. (2000). Contraception update for the primary care physician. Retrieved May 17, 2001, from http://www.medscape.com/medscape/CNO/200/AAFP/AAFP-06.html

Lilley, L. L., & Schaffer, S. (1990). Human papillomavirus: A sexually transmitted disease with carcinogenic potential. *Cancer Nursing, 13,* 366–372.

Lim, A. S., Tsakok, M. F. (1997). Age-related decline in fertility: A link to degenerative oocytes? *Fertility and Sterility, 68*(2), 265–271.

Limosin, F., & Ades, J. (2001). Psychiatric and psychological aspects of premenstrual syndrome. *Encephale, 27*(6), 501–508.

Linz, D. (1989). Exposure to sexually explicit materials and attitudes toward rape: A comparison of study results. *The Journal of Sex Research, 26,* 50–84.

Linz, D., & Donnerstein, E. (1992, September 30). Research can help us explain violence and pornography. *The Chronicle of Higher Education,* B3–B4.

Lippa, R. A. (2003). Handedness, sexual orientation, and gender-related personality traits in men and women. *Archives of Sexual Behavior, 32*(2), 103–114.

Lippa, R. A., & Tan, F. P. (2001). Does culture moderate the relationship between sexual orientation and gender-related personality trait? *Journal of Comparative Social Science, 35*(1), 65–87.

Lipsky, S., Caetono, R., Field, C. A., & Larkin, G. (2005). Psychosocial and substance-use risk factors for intimate partner violence. *Drug & Alcohol Dependence, 78*(1), 39–47.

Lipstein, H., Lee, C. C., & Crupi, R. S. (2003). A current concept of eclampsia. *American Journal of Emergency Medicine, 21*(3), 223–226.

Lisak, D., Hopper, J., & Song, P. (1996). Factors in the cycle of violence: Gender rigidity and emotional constriction. *Journal of Traumatic Stress, 9,* 721–743.

Lite, J. (2005). The pills puts brakes on sex drive. Retrieved August 21, 2005, from http://www.nydailynews.com/front/v-pfriendly/story/313514p-268163c.html

Litta, P., Cosmi, E., Sacco, G., Saccardi, C., Ciavattini, A., & Ambrosini, G. (2005, August 5). Hysteroscopic permanent tubal sterilization using a nitinol-dacron intratubal device without anaesthesia in the outpatient setting. *Human Reproduction,* Epub ahead of print. Retrieved August 9, 2005, http://www.ncbi.nlm.nih.gov/entrez/query.fcgi?cmd=Retrieve&db=pubmed&dopt=Abstract&list_uids=16085664&query_hl=11

Little, L. M., & Curran, J. P. (1978). Covert sensitization: A clinical procedure in need of some explanations. *Psychological Bulletin, 3,* 513–531.

Lloyd, T., Petit, M. A., Lin, H. M., & Beck, T. J. (2004). Lifestyle factors and the development of bone mass and bone strength in young women. *Journal of Pediatrics, 144*(6), 776–782.

Lock, J., & Steiner, H. (1999). Gay lesbian and bisexual youth risks for emotional, physical, and social problems: Results from a community-based survey. *Journal of American Academy of Child and Adolescent Psychiatry 38*(3), 297–305.

Locke, B. D., & Mahalik, J. R. (2005). Examining masculinity norms, problem drinking, and athletic involvement as predictors of sexual aggression in college men. *Journal of Counseling Psychology, 52*(3), 279–283.

Loftus, M. (2001). The lost children of Rockdale County: Teenage syphilis outbreak revisited. *SIECUS Report, 30*(1), 24–26.

Loiselle, M. M. (2004). The effect of alcohol on women's detection of risk in a date rape analogue. *Dissertation Abstracts International: Section B: The Sciences & Engineering, 65* (5-B), #0419–4217.

Long, V. E. (2003). Contraceptive Choices: New options in the U.S. market. *SIECUS Report, 31*(2), 13–18.

LoPiccolo, J., & Lobitz, W. C. (1972). The role of masturbation in the treatment of orgasmic dysfunction. *Archives of Sexual Behavior, 2,* 163–171.

LoPiccolo, J., & Stock, W. E. (1986). Treatment of sexual dysfunction. *Journal of Consulting and Clinical Psychology, 54,* 158–167.

Lopresto, C. T., Sherman, M. F., & Sherman, N. C. (1985). The affects of a masturbation seminar on high school males' attitudes, false beliefs, and behavior. *Journal of Sex Research, 21,* 142–156.

Lorber, J. (1994). *Paradoxes of gender.* New Haven, CT: Yale University Press.

Lorio, A. (2004). Assign gender when child can give input, experts say. *Urology Times, 32*(5), 27–30.

Lotery, H. E., McClure, N., & Galask, R. P. (2004). Vulvodynia. *Lancet, 363*(9414), 1058–1060.

Lott, A. J., & Lott, B. E. (1961). Group cohesiveness, communication level, and conformity. *Journal of Abnormal & Social Psychology, 62,* 408–412.

Lovejoy, F. H., & Estridge, D. (Eds.). (1987). *The new child health encyclopedia.* New York: Delacorte Press.

Low, W. Y., Wong, Y. L., Zulkifli, S. W., & Tan, H. (2002). Malaysian cultural differences in knowledge, attitudes and practices related to erectile dysfunction. *International Journal of Impotence Research, 14*(6), 440–445.

Lowhagen, G. B. (1990). Syphilis: Test procedures and therapeutic strategies. *Seminars in Dermatology, 9,* 152–159.

Lucie-Smith, E. (1991). *Sexuality in western art.* London: Thames & Hudson.

Luckenbill, D. F. (1984). Dynamics of the deviant scale. *Deviant Behavior, 5,* 337–353.

Lue, T. (2000). Erectile dysfunction. *New England Journal of Medicine, 342*(24), 1802–1813.

Lueptow, L. B., Garovich-Szabo, L., & Lueptow, M. B. (2001). Social change and the persistence of sex typing: 1974–1997. *Social Forces, 80*(1), 1–36.

Maas, C. P., ter Kuile, M. M., Laan, E., Tuynman, C. C., Weyenborg, P., Trimbos, J. B., & Kenter, G. G. (2004). Objective assessment of sexual arousal in women with a history of hysterectomy. *British Journal of Obstetrics and Gynaecology, 111,* 456–462.

Maccoby, E. E. (2002). Gender and group process: A developmental perspective. *Current Directions in Psychological Science, 11*(2), 54–58.

MacDorman, M. F., Mathews, T. J., Martin, J. A., & Malloy, M H. (2002). Trends and characteristics of induced labour in the U.S., 1989–1998. *Paediatric & Perinatal Epidemiology, 16*(3), 263–274.

Maciejewski, S. I. (2002). Cultural influence on reporting rape to police: A comparison of Japanese American women and European American women. *Dissertation Abstracts,* Alliant International University of San Francisco, #0-493-68263-5.

MacKay, A. P., Berg, C. J., & Atrash, H. K. (2001). Pregnancy-related mortality from preeclampsia and eclampsia. *Obstetrics and Gynecology, 97*(4), 533–538.

MacKay, A. P., Kieke, B. A., Koonin, L. M., & Beattie, K. (2001). Tubal sterilization in the United States 1994–1996. *Family Planning Perspectives, 33*(4), 161–165.

Mackay, J. (2000). *The Penguin atlas of human sexual behavior.* New York: Penguin.

MacKinnon, C. A. (1985, March 26). Pornography: Reality, not fantasy. *The Village Voice.*

MacKinnon, C. A. (1986). Pornography: Not a moral issue. (Special Issue: Women and the law.) *Women's Studies International Forum, 9,* 63–78.

MacKinnon, C. A. (1987). *Feminism unmodified: Discourses on life and law.* Cambridge, MA: Harvard University Press.

MacKinnon, C. A. (1993). *Only words.* Cambridge, MA: Harvard University Press.

Macklon, N., & Fauser, B. (2000). Aspects of ovarian follicle development throughout life. *Hormone Research, 52,* 161–170.

Macneil, S. (2004). It takes two: Modeling the role of sexual self-disclosure in sexual satisfaction. *Dissertation Abstracts International: Section B: The Sciences & Engineering, 65*(1-B), 481. (#0419–4217)

MacNeill, C., & Carey, J. C. (2001). Recurrent vulvovaginal candidiasis. *Current Women's Health Reports, 1*(1), 31–35.

Macomber, K. E., Boehme, M. S., Rudrik, J. T., Ganoczy, D., Crandell-Alden, E., Schneider, W. A., & Somsel, P. A. (2005). Drug-resistant Neisseria gonorrhoeae in Michigan. *Emergency Infectious Diseases, 11*(7), 1009–1015.

Macomber, K. E., Boehme, M. S., Rudrik, J. T., Ganoczy, D., Crandell-Alden, E., Schneider, W. A., & Somsel, P. A. (2005). Drug-resistant Neisseria gonorrhoeae in Michigan. *Emergency Infectious Diseases, 11*(7), 1009–1015.

Madigan, N. (2004). Man, 86, convicted under new law against Americans who go abroad to molest minors. Retrieved November 11, 2004, from http://travel2.nytimes.com/2004/11/20/national/20predator.html?ex=1129003200&en=8275e98301fbe992&ei=5070&n=Top%2fFeatures%2fTravel%2fDestinations%2fUnited%20States%2fRegions

Madigan, N. (2004). Sex-film industry threatened with condom requirement. Retrieved November 8, 2005, from http://www.aegis.com/news/ads/2004/AD041716.html

Madon, S. (1997). What do people believe about gay males? A study of stereotype content and strength. *Sex Roles, 37*(9–10), 663–686.

Magoha, G. A., & Magoha, O. B. (2000). Current global status of female genital mutilation: A review. *East African Medical Journal, 77*(5), 268–72.

Maguire, R. (2002). Effect of nonoxynol-9 on the human rectal mucosa. Annual Conference on Microbicides, May 12–15, 2002, Antwerp, Belgium.

Mah, K., & Binik, Y. (2005). Are orgasms in the mind or the body? Psychosocial versus physiological correlates of orgasmic pleasure and satisfaction. *Journal of Sex & Marital Therapy, 31*(3), 187–200.

Mahay, J., Laumann, E. O., & Michaels, S. (2001). Race, gender, and class in sexual scripts. In E. O. Laumann & S. Michaels (Eds.), *Sex, love, and health in America* (pp. 197–238). Chicago: Chicago University Press.

Mahlstedt, P. (1987). The crisis of infertility. In G. Weeks & L. Hof (Eds.), *Integrating sex and marital therapy: A clinical guide* (pp. 121–148). New York: Bruner/Mazel.

MaHood, J., & Wenburg, A. R. (1980). *The Mosher survey*. New York: Arno.

Maisto, S. A., Carey, M. P., Carey, K. B., Gordon, C. M., Schum, J., & Lynch, K. (2004). The relationship between alcohol and individual differences variables on attitudes and behavioral skills relevant to sexual health among heterosexual young adult men. *Archives of Sexual Behavior, 33*(6), 571–584.

Major, B., Cozzarelli, C., Sciacchitano, A. M., & Cooper, M. (1990). Perceived social support, self-efficacy, and adjustment to abortion. *Journal of Personality and Social Psychology, 59*, 452–463.

Major, B., Mueller, P., & Hildebrandt, K. (1985). Attributions, expectations, and coping with abortion. *Journal of Personality and Social Psychology, 48*, 585–599.

Maldonado, M. (1999). *HIV/AIDS: African Americans*. Washington DC: National Minority AIDS Council.

Malone, F. D., Canick, J. A., Ball, R. H., Nyberg, D. A., Comstock, C. H., Bukowski, R., Berkowitz, R. L., Gross, S. J., Wolfe, H. M., et al. (2005). First-trimester or second-trimester screening, or both, for Down's syndrome. *The New England Journal of Medicine, 353*(19), 2001–2011.

Maltz, D. W., & Borker, R. A. (1982). A cultural approach to male–female communication. In J. J. Gumperz (Ed.), *Language and social identity* (pp. 196–216). New York: Cambridge University Press.

Maltz, W. (1990, December). Adult survivors of incest: How to help them overcome the trauma. *Medical Aspects of Human Sexuality*, 38–43.

Maltz, W. (2001). *The sexual healing journey*. New York: HarperCollins.

Maltz, W. (2002). Treating the sexual intimacy concerns of sexual abuse survivors. *Sexual and Relationship Therapy, 17*(4), 321–327.

Maltz, W., & Boss, S. (2001). *Private thoughts: Exploring the power of women's sexual fantasies*. Novato, CA: New World Library.

Mandelblatt, J. S., Lawrence, W. F., Gaffikin, L., Limpahayom, K. K., Warakamin, S., King, J., et al. (2002). Costs and benefits of different strategies to screen for cervical cancer in less-developed countries. *Journal of the National Cancer Institute, 94*(19), 1469–1483.

Mann, J. (1991, March 29). Kuwaiti rape a doubly savage crime. *Washington Post*, p. C3.

Mannheimer, S., Friedland, G., Matts, J., Child, C., & Chesney, M. (2002). The consistency of adherence to antiretroviral therapy predicts biologic outcome for HIV-infected persons in clinical trials. *Clinical Infectious Disease, 34*(8), 1115–1121.

Manniche, L. (1987). *Sexual life in ancient Egypt*. London: KPI Ltd.

Manson, J. E. (2004, December). Your doctor is in. *Glamour*, p. 104.

Mantica, A. (2005). Better test for a stealthy cancer. *Prevention, 57*(3), 48–51.

Marcellin, P., Chang, T. T., Lim, S. G., Tong, M. J., Sievert, W., Shiffman, M. L., Jeffers, L., Goodman, Z., Wulfsohn, M. S., Xiong, S., Fry, J., & Brosgart, C. L. (2003). Adefovir dipivoxil for the treatment of hepatitis B e antigenpositive chronic hepatitis B. *New England Journal of Medicine, 348*(9), 808–816.

Marcus, A. D. (2003, March 6). Finding a cheaper way to make a baby. *Wall Street Journal*, pp. D1–D4.

Margulies, S. (2003). The psychology of prenuptial agreements. *Journal of Psychiatry & Law, 31*(4), 415–432.

Margulis, L., & Sagan, D. (1991). *Mystery dance: On the evolution of human sexuality*. New York: Summit Books.

Markel, H. (2005). The search for effective HIV vaccines. *The New England Journal of Medicine, 353*(8), 753–757.

Marklein, M. B. (2004, June 21). Gender-neutral comes to campus. Retrieved February 27, 2005, from http://www.usatoday.com/life/lifestyle/2004-06-21-lgbt-gender-neutral-housing_x.htm

Markoff, J. (2004, December 30). Internet use said to cut into TV viewing and socializing. *New York Times*, p. C5.

Marris, E. (2005). Is tattoo ink safe? Retrieved March 15, 2005, from http://www.nature.com/news/2005/050314/pf/050314-3_pf.html

Marshall, D., & Suggs, R. (1971). *Human sexual behavior: Variations in the ethnographic spectrum*. Englewood Cliffs, NJ: Prentice Hall.

Marshall, D. S. (1971). Sexual behavior on Mangaia. In D. S. Marshall & R. C. Suggs (Eds.), *Human sexual behavior*. New York: Basic Books.

Marshall, W. L. (1979). Satiation therapy: A procedure for reducing deviant sexual arousal. *Journal of Applied Behavior Analysis, 12*(3), 377–389.

Martin, H. P. (1991). The coming-out process for homosexuals. *Hospital and Community Psychiatry, 42*, 158–162.

Martin, J. (1999, June–July). Nipple piercing: Is it compatible with breastfeeding? *LEAVEN, 35*(3), 64–65.

Martin, J. A., Hamilton, B. E., & Ventura, S. J. (2001). *Births: Preliminary data for 2000. National Vital Statistics Reports*. Hyattsville, MD: National Center for Health Statistics.

Martin, P. Y., & Hummer, R. A. (1989). Fraternities and rape on campus (Special issue: Violence Against Women). *Gender and Society, 3*, 457–473.

Martin, R. P., Dombrowski, S. C., Mullis, C., Wisenbaker, J., & Huttunen, M. O. (2005, July 7). Smoking during pregnancy: Association with childhood temperament, behavior, and academic performance. *Journal of Pediatric Psychology*, Epub ahead of print. Retrieved July 17, 2005, from http://www.ncbi.nlm.nih.gov/entrez/query.fcgi?cmd=Retrieve&db=pubmed&dopt=Abstract&list_uids=16002482&query_hl=23

Martin, T. A. (2003). Power and consent: Relation to self—reported sexual assault and acquaintance rape. *Dissertation Abstracts International: Section B: The Sciences & Engineering, 64*(3-B), #0419–4217.

Martin, W. E. (2001). A wink and a smile: How men and women respond to flirting. *Psychology Today, 34*(5), 26–27.

Martineau, P. A., Al-Jassir, F., Lenczner, E., & Burman, M. (2004). Effect of the oral contraceptive pill on ligamentous laxity. *Clinical Journal of Sport Medicine, 14*(5), 281–286.

Martinson, F. M. (1981a). Eroticism in infancy and childhood. In L. L. Constantine & F. M. Martinson (Eds.), *Children and sex: New findings, new perspectives* (pp. 23–35). Boston: Little, Brown.

Marx, B. P., Gross, A., & Adams, H. E. (1999). The effect of alcohol on the responses of sexually coercive and non-coercive men to an experimental rape analogue. *Sexual Abuse: Journal of Research & Treatment, 11*(2), 131–145.

Masheb, R. M., Lozano-Blanco, C., Kohorn, E., Minkin, M. J., & Kerns, R. D. (2004). Assessing sexual function and dyspareunia and the female sexual function index in women with vulvodynia. *Journal of Sex and Marital Therapy, 30*(5), 315–324.

Mason, M. A., Fine, M. A., & Carcochan, S. (2001). Family law in the new millennium: For whose families? *Journal of Family Issues, 22*(7), 859–882.

Mason, M. A., & Goulden, M. (2004). Do babies matter? *Academe, 90*(6), 10–16.

Massa, G., Verlinde, F., DeSchepper, J., Thomas, M., Bourguignon, J. P, Craen, M., de Segher, F., Francois, I., Du Caju, M., Maes, M., & Heinrichs, C. (2005). Trends in age at diagnosis of Turner syndrome. *Archives of Disease in Childhood, 90*(3), 267–275.

Masters, W. H., & Johnson, V. E. (1966). *Human sexual response*. Boston: Little, Brown.

Masters, W. H., & Johnson, V. E. (1970). *Human sexual inadequacy*. Boston: Little, Brown.

Masters, W. H., & Johnson, V. E. (1979). *Homosexuality in perspective*. Boston: Little, Brown.

Masters, W. H., Johnson, V. E., & Kolodny, R. (1994). *Heterosexuality*. New York: HarperCollins.

Masters, W. H., Johnson, V. E., & Kolodny, R. C. (1982). *Human sexuality*. Boston: Little, Brown.

Masterton, G. (1987). *How to drive your woman wild in bed*. New York: Penguin Books.

Mastroiacovo, P., Botto, L. D., Cavalcanti, D. P., Lalatta, F., Selicomi, A., Tozzi, A. E., Baronciani, D., & Cigolotti, A. C. (1992). Limb anomalies following chorionic villus sampling: A registry based case-control study. *American Journal of Medical Genetics, 44*(6), 856–864.

Matek, O. (1988). Obscene phone callers. (Special issue: The sexually unusual: Guide to understanding and helping.) *Journal of Social Work and Human Sexuality, 7*, 113–130.

Mathes, E. W. (2005). Relationship between short-term sexual strategies and sexual jealousy. *Psychological Reports, 96*(1), 29–35.

Maticka-Tyndale, E. T., Herold, E. S., & Mewhinney, D. (1998). Casual sex on spring break: Intentions and behaviors of Canadian students. *Journal of Sex Research, 35*(3), 254–265.

Matsubara, H. (2001, June 20). Sex change no cure for torment. *Japan Times*.

Matsumoto, D. (1996). *Culture and psychology*. Pacific Grove, CA: Brooks/Cole.

Maugh, T. H. (2005). Study suggests shift in teen sex practices. Retrieved September 17, 2005 from http://www.latimes.com/news/nationworld/nation/la-sci-oralsex16sep16,1,4010701.story?coll=la-headlines-nation

Maurer, H. (1994, January). My sex life, chapter one. *Harper's Magazine, 288*(1724), 34.

Maxmen, J., & Ward, N. (1995). *Essential psychopathology and its treatment* (2nd ed.). New York: Norton.

Mays, R. M., Sturm, L. A., Zimet, G. D. (2004). Parental perspectives on vaccinating children against sexually transmitted infections. *Social Science & Medicine, 58*(7), 1405–1413.

Mays, V. M., Yancy, A. K., Cochran, S. D., Weber, M., & Fielding, J. E. (2002). Heterogeneity of health disparities among African-American, Hispanic and Asian American women. *American Journal of Public Health, 92*(4), 632–640.

McAdams, M. (1996). Gender without bodies. Retrieved September 3, 2005, from http://www.december.com/cmc/mag/1996/mar/mcadams.html

McCabe, M. P. (2002). Relationship functioning among people with MS. *Journal of Sex Research, 39*(4), 302–309.

McCabe, M. P., & Cummins, R. A. (1998). Sexuality and quality of life among young people. *Adolescence, 33*(132), 761–773.

McCabe, S. E. (2002). Gender differences in collegiate risk factors for heavy episodic drinking. *Journal of Studies on Alcohol, 63*(1), 49–56.

McCarthy, B. W., & Fucito, L. M. (2005). Integrating medication, realistic expectations, and therapeutic interventions in the treatment of male sexual dysfunction. *Journal of Sex and Marital Therapy, 31*(4), 319–328.

McCarthy, J., & McMillan, S. (1990). Patient/partner satisfaction with penile implant surgery. *Journal of Sex Education and Therapy, 16*, 25–37.

McCormack, J., Hudson, S. M., & Ward, T. (2002). Sexual offenders' perceptions of their early interpersonal relationships: An attachment perspective. *Journal of Sex Research, 39*(2), 85–93.

McDaniel, J. S., D'Augelli, A. R., & Purcell, D. (2001). The relationship between sexual orientation and risk for suicide. *Suicide and Life-Threatening Behavior, 31*(Suppl.), 84–105.

McDowell, B. (1986). The Dutch touch. *National Geographic, 170*, 501–525.

McGrath, R. (1991). Sex offender risk assessment and disposition planning. *International Journal of Offender Treatment and Comparative Criminology, 35*(4), 328–350.

McKeganey, N., & Bernard, M. (1996). *Sex work on the streets: Prostitutes and their clients.* Philadelphia, PA: Open University Press.

McKenna, K. Y., Green, A. S., & Smith, P. (2001). Demarginalizing the sexual self. *Journal of Sex Research, 38*(4), 302–402.

McLaren, A. (1990). *A history of contraception.* Cambridge, MA: Basil Blackwell.

McLean, L. M., & Gallop, R. (2003). Implications of childhood sexual abuse for adult borderline personality disorder and complex post traumatic stress disorder. *American Journal of Psychiatry, 160*(2), 369–371.

McLusky, D. (2005). Transsexual golfers can play in women's British open. Retrieved March 2, 2005, from http://www.bloomberg.com/apps/news?pid=10000102&sid=aKYeDa2UJ1fE&refer=uk

McMahon, S. (2004). Student-athletes, rape-supportive culture, and social change. Retrieved October 16, 2005, from http://sexualassault.rutgers.edu/pdfs/student-athletes_rape-supportive_culture_and_social_change.pdf

McNally, R. J. (2003). *Remembering trauma.* Cambridge, MA: Belknap Press/Harvard University Press.

McNally, R. J., Clancy, S. A., Barrett, H. M., & Parker, H. A. (2004). Inhibiting retrieval of trauma cues in adults reporting histories of childhood sexual abuse. *Cognition and Emotion, 18*(4), 479–493.

McNally, R. J., Clancy, S. A., Barrett, H. M., & Parker, H. A. (2005). Reality monitoring in adults reporting repressed, recovered, or continuous memories of childhood sexual abuse. *Journal of Abnormal Psychology, 114*(1), 147–152.

McNeely, C., Shew, M., Beuhring, T., Sieving, R., Miller, B., & Blum, R. (2002). Mothers' influence on the timing of first sex among 14- and 15-year olds. *Journal of Adolescent Health, 31*(3), 256–265.

McSwain, H., Shaw, C., & Hall, L. D. (2005). Placement of the Essure permanent birth control device with fluoroscopic guidance: A novel method for tubal sterilization. *Journal of Vascular and Interventional Radiology, 16*(7), 1007–1012.

Mead, M. (1988). *Sex and temperament in three primitive societies.* New York: Quill.

Meadows, M. (2000). Tampon safety. TSS now rare, but women still should take care. *FDA Consumer, 34*(2), 20–24.

Meadows, S. O., Land, K. C., & Lamb, V. L. (2005). Assessing Gilligan vs. Sommers: Gender-specific trends in child and youth well-being in the United States, 1985–2001. *Social Indicators Research, 70*, 1–52.

Meckler, L. (2004). Questions on states' abortion warnings: Unproven link to cancer cited. Retrieved November 11, 2005, from http://www.boston.com/news/nation/articles/2004/11/10/questions_on_states_abortion_warnings?mode=PF

MedlinePlus. (2004a). Androgen insensitivity syndrome. Retrieved October 3, 2005, from http://www.nlm.nih.gov/medlineplus/ency/article/001180.htm

MedlinePlus. (2004b). Congenital adrenal hyperplasia. Retrieved October 1, 2005, from http://www.nlm.nih.gov/medlineplus/ency/article/000411.htm

Medrano, M. A., Hatch, J. P., & Zule, W. A. (2003). Childhood trauma and adult prostitution behavior in a multiethnic heterosexual drug-using population. *American Journal of Drug and Alcohol Abuse, 29*(20), 463–486.

Medved, M. (1992). *Hollywood vs. America: Popular culture and the war on traditional values.* New York: HarperCollins.

Meier, E. (2002). Child rape in South Africa. *Pediatric Nursing, 28*(5), 532–535.

Meignant, M. (2004). France. In R. T. Francoeur & R. J. Noonan (Eds.), *The Continuum complete international encyclopedia of sexuality* (pp. 412–430). New York/London: Continuum International.

Mendick, H. (2005). A beautiful myth? The gendering of being/doing 'good at maths.' *Gender & Education, 17*(2), 203–220.

Meschke, L. L., Bartholomae, S., & Zentall, S. R. (2000). Adolescent sexuality and parent–adolescent processes: Promoting healthy teen choices. *Family Relations, 49*(2), 143–155.

Messenger, J. C. (1993). Sex and repression in an Irish folk community. In D. N. Suggs & A. W. Miracle (Eds.), *Culture and human diversity.* Pacific Grove, CA: Brooks/Cole.

Meston, C. M., & Frohlich, P. F. (2000). The neurobiology of sexual function. *Archives of General Psychiatry, 57*, 1012–1030.

Meston, C. M., Trapnell, P. D., & Gorzalka, B. B. (1996). Ethnic and gender differences in sexuality: Variations in sexual behavior between Asian and non-Asian university students. *Archives of Sex Behavior, 25*(1), 33–71.

Meston, C. M., & Worcel, M. (2002). The effects of yohimbine plus L–arginine glutamate on sexual arousal in post menopausal women with sexual arousal disorders. *Archives of Sexual Behavior, 31*(4), 323–332.

Metropolitan Community Churches. (2005). About us. Retrieved November 7, 2005, from http://www.mccchurch.org/AM/TextTemplate.cfm?Section=About_Us&Template=/CM/HTMLDisplay.cfm&ContentID=877

Metz, M. E., & Miner, M. H. (1998). Psychosexual and psychosocial aspects of male aging and sexual health. *Canadian Journal of Human Sexuality, 7*(3), 245–259.

Meyer, L. (1999, April 13). Hostile classrooms. *The Advocate, 32*(1).

Mhloyi, M. M. (1990). Perceptions on communication and sexuality in marriage in Zimbabwe. *Women and Therapy, 10*(3), 61–73.

Michael, R. T., Gagnon, J. H., Laumann, E. O., & Kolata, G. (1994). *Sex in America.* Boston, MA: Little, Brown.

Middlebrook, D. W. (1999). *Suits me: The double life of Billy Tipton.* New York: Houghton Mifflin.

Mihalik, G. (1988). Sexuality and gender: An evolutionary perspective. *Psychiatric Annals, 18*, 40–42.

Mikulincer, M., & Shaver, P. (2005). Attachment theory and emotions in close relationships: Exploring the attachment-related dynamics of emotional reactions to relational events. *Personal Relationships, 12*(2), 149–168.

Miletski, H. (2002). *Understanding bestiality and zoophilia.* Bethesda, MD: East-West.

Milhausen, R. R., & Herold, E. S. (1999). Does the sexual double standard still exist? Perceptions of university women. *Journal of Sex Research, 36*(4), 361–369.

Milinski, M., & Wedekind, C. (2001). Evidence for MHC-correlated perfume preferences in humans. *Behavioral Ecology, 12*(2), 140–149.

Millburn, M. A., Mather, R., & Conrad, S. D. (2000). The effects of viewing R-rated movie scenes that objectify women on perceptions of date rape. *Sex Roles, 43*(9–10), 645–664.

Miller, J. (1998). A review of sex offender legislation. *Kansas Journal of Law and Public Policy, 7*, 40–67.

Miller, K., & Graves, J. (2000). Update on the prevention and treatment of STDs. *American Family Physician, 61*, 379–386.

Millet, K. (1969). *Sexual politics.* New York: Granada.

Millett, G., Malebranche, D., Mason, B., & Spikes, P. (2005). Focusing "down low": Bisexual black men, HIV risk and heterosexual transmission. *Journal of the National Medical Association, 97*(7 Suppl.), 52S–59S.

Millman, R. B., & Ross, E. J. (2003). Steroid and nutritional supplement use in professional athletes. *American Journal of Addiction, 12*(Suppl. S), 48–54.

Millner, V. S. (2005). Female sexual arousal disorder and counseling deliberations. *Family Journal: Counseling & Therapy for Couples and Families, 13*(1), 95–100.

Milner, J., & Robertson, K. (1990). Comparison of physical child abusers, intrafamilial sexual child abusers, and child neglecters. *Journal of Interpersonal Violence, 5*, 37–48.

Misri, S., Kostaras, X., Fox, D., & Kostaras, D. (2000). The impact of partner support in the treatment of postpartum depression. *Canadian Journal of Psychiatry, 45*(6), 554–559.

Mitchell, K. J., Wolak, J., & Finkelhor, D. (2005). Police posing as juveniles online to catch sex offenders: Is it working? *Sexual Abuse: A Journal of Research and Treatment, 17*(3), 241–267.

Mittendorf, R., Williams, M. A., Berkey, C. S., & Cotter, P. F. (1990). The length of uncomplicated human gestation. *Obstetrics and Gynecology, 75*(6), 929–932.

Mizuno, R. (2000). The male/female ratio of fetal deaths and births in Japan. *Lancet, 356* (9231), 738.

Moaveni, A. (2003, June 11). Baghdad women kept under tight guard. *Hartford Courant,* p. A3.

Modan, B., Hartge, P., Hirsh-Yechezkel, G., Chetrit, A., Lubin, F., Beller, U., Ben-Baruch, G., Fishman, A., et al. (2001). Parity, oral contraceptives, and the risk of ovarian cancer among carriers and noncarriers of BRCA1 or BRCA2 mutation. *New England Journal of Medicine, 345*(4), 235–240.

Modern Maturity. (1999, September–October). AARP and *Modern Maturity* sexuality study, pp. 41–57.

Moench, T. R., Chipato, T., & Padian, N. S. (2001). Preventing disease by protecting the cervix: The unexplored promise of internal vaginal barrier devices. *AIDS, 15*(13), 1595–1602.

Monat-Haller, R. K. (1992). *Understanding and experiencing sexuality.* Baltimore: Brookes.

Money, J. (1955). Hermaphroditism, gender, and precocity in hyper-adrenocorticism: Psychologic findings. *Bulletin of the Johns Hopkins Hospital, 96,* 253–254.

Money, J. (1975). Ablatio penis: Normal male infant sex-reassigned as a girl. *Archives of Sexual Behavior, 4*(1), 65–71.

Money, J. (1984). Paraphilias: Phenomenology and classification. *American Journal of Psychotherapy, 38,* 164–179.

Money, J. (1986). *Venuses penuses: Sexology, sexophy, and exigency theory.* Buffalo, NY: Prometheus Books.

Money, J. (1987). Sin, sickness, or status? Homosexual gender identity and psychoneuroendocrinology. *American Psychologist, 42,* 384–399.

Money, J. (1990). Pedophilia: A specific instance of new phylism theory as applied to paraphiliac lovemaps. In J. Feierman (Ed.), *Pedophilia: Biosocial dimensions* (pp. 445–463). New York: Springer-Verlag.

Money J., & Norman, B. F. (1987). Gender identity and gender transposition: Longitudinal outcome study of 24 male hermaphrodites assigned as boys. *Journal of Sex and Marital Therapy, 13,* 75.

Monroe, L. M., Kinney, L., Weist, M., Dafeamekpor, D., Dantzler, J., & Reynolds, M. (2005). The experience of sexual assault: Findings from a statewide victim needs assessment. *Journal of Interpersonal Violence, 20*(7), 767–776.

Montgomery, M. (2005). Psychosocial intimacy and identity: From early adolescence to emerging adulthood. *Journal of Adolescent Research, 20*(3), 346–374.

Monto, M. A. (2000). Why men seek out prostitutes. In R. Weitzer (Ed.), *Sex for sale: Prostitution, pornography, and the sex industry* (pp. 67–83). New York: Routledge.

Monto, M. A. (2001). Prostitution and fellatio. *Journal of Sex Research, 38*(2), 140–146.

Monto, M. A., & McRee, N. (2005). A comparison of the male customers of female street prostitutes with national samples of men. *International Journal of Offender Therapy and Comparative Criminology, 49*(5), 505–529.

Mookodi, G., Ntshebe, O., & Taylor, I. (2004). Botswana. In R. T. Francoeur & R. J. Noonan (Eds.), *The Continuum international encyclopedia of sexuality* (pp. 89–97). New York/London: Continuum International.

Moore, M. (1994, October 8). Changing India: Arranged marriages persist with 90s twist. *The Washington Post.*

Moore, S. (1999). Barriers to safer sex: Beliefs and attitudes among male and female adult heterosexuals across four relationship groups. *Journal of Health Psychology, 4*(2), 149–163.

Morales, A. (2004). Andropause (or symptomatic late-onset hypogonadism): Facts, fiction and controversies. *Aging Male, 7*(4), 297–304.

Moreno-Garcia, M., Fernandez-Martinez, F. J., & Miranda, E. B. (2005). Chromosomal anomalies in patients with short stature. *Pediatric International, 47*(5), 546–549.

Morgan, J. F., Lacey, J. H., & Reid, F. (1999). Anorexia nervosa: Changes in sexuality during weight restoration. *Psychosomatic Medicine, 61,* 541–545.

Morgan, J. F., Murphy, H., Lacey, J. H., & Conway, G. (2005). Long term psychological outcome for women with congenital adrenal hyperplasia: Cross sectional survey. *British Medical Journal, 330*(7487), 340–342.

Morgan, S. P., & Rindfuss, R. (1985). Marital disruption: Structural and temporal dimensions. *American Journal of Sociology, 90*(5), 1055–1077.

Morley, J., & Perry, H. (2000). Androgen deficiency in aging men. *Journal of Laboratory and Clinical Medicine, 135*(5), 370–378.

Morris, R. J. (1990). Aikane: Accounts of Hawaiian same-sex relationships in the journals of Captain Cook's third voyage (1776–1780). *Journal of Homosexuality, 19,* 21–54.

Morrison, M., & Shaffer, D. (2003). Gender-role congruence and self-referencing as determinants of advertising effectiveness. *Sex Roles, 49*(5–6), 265–275.

Morrone, A., Hercogova, J., & Lotti, T. (2002). Stop genital mutilation. *International Journal of Dermatology, 41*(5), 253–263.

Morrow, K. M., & Allsworth, J. E. (2000). Sexual risk in lesbians and bisexual women. *Journal of Gay and Lesbian Medical Association, 4*(4), 159–165.

Morse, E. V., Simon, P. M., Balson, P. M., & Osofsky, H. J. (1992). Sexual behavior patterns of customers of male street prostitutes. *Archives of Sexual Behavior, 21,* 347–357.

Morse, E. V., Simon, P. M., Osotsky, H. J., Balson, P. M., & Gaumer, R. (1991). The male street prostitute. *Social Science Medicine, 32,* 535–539.

Mortenson, S. T. (2002). Sex, communication, values, and cultural values. *Communication Reports, 15*(1), 57–71.

Mosconi, A. M., Roila, F., Gatta, G., & Theodore, C. (2005). Cancer of the penis. *Critical Reviews in Oncology/Hematology, 53*(2), 165–178.

Moseley, D. T., Follingstad, D. R., & Harley, H. (1981). Psychological factors that predict reaction to abortion. *Journal of Clinical Psychology, 37,* 276–279.

Moser, C. (1988). Sadomasochism. Special issue: The sexually unusual: Guide to understanding and helping. *Journal of Social Work and Human Sexuality, 7,* 43–56.

Mosher, C. M. (2001). The social implications of sexual identity formation and the coming-out process: A review of the theoretical and empirical literature. *Family Journal, 9*(20), 164–174.

Mosher, W. D., Martinez, G. M., Chandra, W., Abma, J. C., & Willson, S. J. (2004, December). Use of contraception and use of family planning services in the United States: 1982–2002. *Advance Data from Vital and Health Statistics, No. 350.*

Moynihan, R. (2003). Who pays for the pizza? Redefining the relationships between doctors and drug companies. *British Medical Journal, 326,* 1189–1192.

MSNBC. (2005, June 23). Male birth control pill in the works. Retrieved June 22, 2005, from http://msnbc.msn.com/id/8300857/

Muehlenhard, C. L., & Cook, S. W. (1988). Men's self-reports of unwanted sexual activity. *Journal of Sex Research, 24,* 58–72.

Muehlenhard, C. L., & MacNaughton, J. S. (1988). Women's beliefs about women who "lead men on." *Journal of Social and Clinical Psychology, 7,* 65–79.

Muehlenhard, C. L., & Schrag, J. (1991). Nonviolent sexual coercion. In A. Parrot & L. Beckhofer (Eds.), *Acquaintance rape—The hidden crime* (pp. 115–128). New York: Wiley.

Mueller, P., & Major, B. (1989). Self-blame, selfefficacy, & adjustment of abortion. *Journal of Personality & Social Psychology, 57,* 1059–1068.

Muir, J. G. (1993, March 31). Homosexuals and the 10% fallacy. *The Wall Street Journal,* p. A14.

Mulders, T. M., & Dieben, T. O. (2001). Use of the novel combined contraceptive vaginal ring, NuvaRing, for ovulation inhibition. *Fertility and Sterility, 75*(5), 865–870.

Muller, J. E., Mittleman, M. A., Maclure, M., Sherwood, J. B., & Toffer, G. H. (1996). Triggering myocardial infraction by sexual activity. *Journal of the American Medical Association, 275*(18), 1405–1409.

Mullis, C. (2005, September 25). AIDS expert advocates circumcision as "vaccine." *Hartford Courant,* p. A6.

Mulvaney, B. M. (1994). Gender differences in communication: An intercultural experience. Paper prepared by the Department of Communication, Florida Atlantic University.

Munarriz, R., Talakoub, L., & Flaherty, E. (2002). Androgen replacement therapy with dehydroepiandrosterone for androgen insufficiency and female sexual dysfunction: Androgen and questionnaire results. *Journal of Sex & Marital Therapy, 28*(Suppl. 1), 165–173.

Munson, M. (1987). How do you do it? *On Our Backs 4*(1).

Murnen, S. K., Wright, C., & Kaluzny, G. (2002). If boys will be boys then girls will be victims? A meta-analytic review of the research that relates masculine ideology to sexual aggression. *Sex Roles, 46*(11–12), 359–375.

Murphy, L. R. (1990). Defining the crime against nature: Sodomy in the United States appeals courts, 1810–1940. *Journal of Homosexuality, 19,* 49–66.

Murray, J. (2000). Psychological profile of pedophiles and child molesters. *Journal of Psychology, 134*(2), 211–224.

Murray, S., & Dynes, W. (1999). Latin American gays: Snow Whites and snake charmers. *The Economist, 353*(8150), 82.

Mustanski, B. (2000). Semantic heterogeneity in the definition of "having sex" for homosexuals. Unpublished manuscript. Department of Psychology, Indiana University, Bloomington, IN.

Mustanski, B. (2001). Getting wired: Exploiting the internet for the collection of valid sexuality data. *Journal of Sex Research, 38*(4), 292–302.

Mydans, S. (2004). There she is,"Miss Spinster Thailand" and proud of it. *New York Times Online*. Retrieved November 21, 2004, from http://www.nytimes.com/2004/11/20/international/asia/20spinster.html?ex=1101998843&ei=1&en=46bfe43980442b95

Nacci, P. L., & Kane, T. R. (1983). The incidence of sex and sexual aggression in federal prisons. *Federal Probation, 47*, 31–36.

Nadelson, C. C., Notman, M. T., Zackson, H., & Gornick, J. (1982). A follow-up study of rape victims. *American Journal of Psychiatry, 139*, 1266–1270.

Nagel, B., Matsuo, H., McIntyre, K. P., & Morrison, N. (2005). Attitudes toward victims of rape: Effects of gender, race, religion, and social class. *Journal of Interpersonal Violence, 20*(6), 725–737.

Nagel, J. (2003). *Race, ethnicity and sexuality*. New York: Oxford University Press.

Najib, A., Lorberbaum, J. P., Kose, S., Bohning, D. E., & George, M. (2004). Regional brain activity in women grieving a romantic relationship breakup. *American Journal of Psychiatry, 161*(12), 2245–2256.

Najman, J. M., Dunne, M. P., Purdie, D. M., Boyle, F. M., & Coxeter, P. D. (2005). Sexual abuse in childhood and sexual dysfunction in adulthood: An Australian population-based study. *Archives of Sexual Behavior, 34*(5), 517–526.

Nanda, S. (2001). *Gender diversity: Crosscultural variations*. Prospect Heights, IL: Waveland Press.

Nannini, D. K., & Meyers, L. S. (2000). Jealousy in sexual and emotional infidelity. *Journal of Sex Research, 37*(2), 117–123.

Nardone, A. (2004, October). Don't sweat it. *Fitness*, p. 78.

Narod, S. A., Dube, M. P., Klijn, J., Lubinski, J., Lynch, H. T., Ghadirian, P., Provencher, D., Heimdal, K., Moller, P., Robson, M., Offit, K., Isaacs, C., Weber, B., Friedman, E., et al. (2002). Oral contraceptives and the risk of breast cancer in BRCA1 and BRCA2 mutation carriers. *Journal of National Cancer Institute, 94*(23), 1773–1779.

Narod, S. A., Sun, P., Ghadirian, P., Lynch, H., Isaacs, C., Garber, J., Weber, B., Karlan, B., Fishman, D., Rosen, B., Tung, N., & Neuhausen, S. L. (2001). Tubal ligation and risk of ovarian cancer in carriers of BRCA1 or BRCA2 mutations: A case-control study. *Lancet, 357*(9267), 843–844.

Nath, J. K., & Nayar, V. R. (2004). India. In R. T. Francoeur & R. J. Noonan (Eds.), *The Continuum international encyclopedia of sexuality* (pp. 516–532). New York/London: Continuum International.

National Abortion Rights Action League. (1989). *The voices of women. Abortion in their own words*. Washington, DC: Author.

National Abortion Rights Action League. (2003a). Abortion legislation. Retrieved September 9, 2003, from http://www.naral.org/legislation/index.cfm

National Abortion Rights Action League. (2003b). Retrieved May 20, 2003, from htttp://www.naral.org

National Cancer Institute. (2003). Abortion, miscarriage and breast cancer risk. Retrieved September 3, 2005, from http://cis.nci.nih.gov/fact/3_75.htm

National Center for Injury Prevention and Control. (2005). Intimate partner violence: Fact sheet. Retrieved October 17, 2005, from http://www.cdc.gov/ncipc/factsheets/ipvfacts.htm

National Coalition of Anti-Violence Programs. (1998, October 6). Annual report on lesbian, gay, bisexual, and transgender domestic violence. Retrieved May 23, 2003, from http://www.hrc.org/issues/hate_crimes/antiviolence.asp

National Council on Aging. (1998). Sex and aging. *Patient Care, 32*(20), 14–15.

National Crime Victimization Survey. (2004). Criminal victimization, 2004. Retrieved October 17, 2005, from http://www.ojp.usdoj.gov/bjs/abstract/cv04.htm

National Down Syndrome Society. (2005). Questions and answers about down syndrome. Retrieved November 4, 2005, from http://www.ndss.org/content.cfm?fuseaction=InfoRes.Generalarticle&article=194

National Gay and Lesbian Task Force. (2001). Hate crimes legislation and the first amendment. Retrieved October 15, 2003, from http://www.ngltf.org/statelocal/hcfirstamendment.htm

National Gay and Lesbian Task Force. (2003). Hate crime laws in the United States. Retrieved September 1, 2003, from http://www.ngltf.org/issues/maps.cfm?issueID=12

National Gay and Lesbian Task Force. (2005). Hate crimes. Retrieved November 4, 2005, from http://www.thetaskforce.org/theissues/issue.cfm?issueID=12

National Institute of Allergy and Infectious Diseases. (2004). Chlamydia. Retrieved September 20, 2005, from http://www.niaid.nih.gov/factsheets/stdclam.htm

National Institutes of Health. (2002). Major domains of research: National Institute of Health. Retrieved June 10, 2002, from www.nichd.nih.gov/publications/pubs/coun_despr.htm

National Survey of Adolescent Males. (2002). Retrieved June 14, 2002, from www.socio.com/srch/summary/nat5/dapplp4.htm

National Telecommunications and Information Administration and the U.S. Department of Commerce. (1999). Falling through the Net: Defining the digital divide: A report on the telecommunications and information technology gap in America. Retrieved June 1, 2002, from http://www.ntia.doc.gov/ntiahome/fttn99/contents.html

National Vulvodynia Association. (2003). National Vulvodynia Association announces results from first epidemiological study on chronic vulvar pain. Retrieved February 11, 2003, from http://www.nva.org/nva_newsletter/nva_news.html

Navarro, M. (2004, November 28). The most private of makeovers. *The New York Times*, Sec. 9, p. 1.

Nazario, B. (2003). First chewable contraceptive approved. Retrieved August 13, 2005, from http://aolsvc.health.webmd.aol.com/content/article/77/90376.htm?printing=true

Neal, J., & Frick-Horbury, D. (2001). The effects of parenting styles and childhood attachment patterns on intimate relationships. *Journal of Instructional Psychology, 28*(3), 178–183.

Nebehay, S. (2004). Cervical cancer epidemic in poor countries. Retrieved December 12, 2004, from http://www.reuters.co.uk/printerFriendlyPopup.jhtml?type=healthNews&storyID=7114888

Neergaard, L. (2005). Doctors are holding off on surgery for newborns of uncertain gender. Retrieved February 22, 2005, from http://www.cleveland.com/health/plaindealer/index.ssf?/base/news/110889699317860.xml

Neergaard, L. (2005, September 1). Leading FDA deputy resigns in protest. *Hartford Courant*, p. A9.

Neff, L., & Karney, B. (2005). To know you is to love you: The implications of global adoration and specific accuracy for marital relationships. *Journal of Personality & Social Psychology, 88*(3), 480–497.

Neisen, J. H. (1990). Heterosexism: Redefining homophobia for the 1990s. *Journal of Gay and Lesbian Psychotherapy, 1*, 21–35.

Nelson, R. (2005). Gottman's sound medical house model. Retrieved September 3, 2005, from http://www.psychpage.com/family/library/gottman.html

Neruda, B. (2005). Development and current status of combined spinal epidural anaesthesia [article in German]. *Anasthesiol Intensivemed Nofallmed Schmerzther, 40*(8), 4590–460.

New, J. F. H. (1969). *The Renaissance and Reformation: A short history*. New York: Wiley.

Newell, M. L. (2005). Current issues in the prevention of mother-to-child transmission of HIV-1 infection. *Transactions of the Royal Society of Tropical Medicine and Hygiene, 100*(1), 1–5.

Newman, L., & Nyce, J. (Eds.). (1985). *Women's medicine: A cross-cultural study of indigenous fertility regulation*. New Brunswick, NJ: Rutgers University Press.

Newport, F. (1998). Americans remain more likely to believe sexual orientation due to environment, not genetics. *The Gallup Poll Monthly, 394*(14–17).

Ng, E., & Ma, J. L. (2004). Hong Kong. In R. T. Francoeur & R. J. Noonan (Eds.), *The Continuum international encyclopedia of sexuality* (pp. 489–502). New York/London: Continuum International.

Nguyen, M. M., & Ellison, L. M. (2005). Testicular cancer patterns in Asian-American males: An opportunity for public health education to impact outcomes. *Urology, 66*(3), 606–609.

Nicholas, D. R. (2000). Men, masculinity and cancer. *Journal of American College Health, 49*(1), 27–33.

Nicholas, L. J., Daniels, P. S., & Hurwitz, M. B. (2004). South Africa. In R. T. Francoeur & R. J. Noonan (Eds.), *The Continuum international encyclopedia of sexuality* (pp. 909–932). New York/London: Continuum International.

Nichols, M. (1990). Lesbian relationships: Implications for the study of sexuality and gender. In D. McWhiter, S. A. Sanders, & J. Reinish (Eds.), *Homosexuality/heterosexuality: Concepts of sexual orientation* (pp. 350–364). The Kinsey Institute Series. New York: Oxford University Press.

Nichols, M. P. (1995). *The lost art of listening*. New York: Guilford.

Nichols, S. L. (1999). Gay, lesbian, and bisexual youth: Understanding diversity and promoting tolerance in schools. *The Elementary School Journal, 99*(5), 505.

Nickerson, A., & Nagle, R. (2005). Parent and peer attachment in late childhood and early adolescence. *Journal of Early Adolescence, 25*(2), 223–249.

Nicolosi, A., Correa Leite, M. L., Musicco, M., Arici, C., et al. (1994). The efficiency of male-to-female and female-to-male sexual transmission of the human immunodeficiency virus: A study of 730 stable couples. *Epidemiology, 5*(6), 570–555.

Nielson, A. C. (2000). A. C. Nielsen survey finds nearly two-thirds of U.S. population age 12 or older are online. Retrieved June 12, 2002, from http://acnielsen.com/news/american/us/2000?20000508.htm

Nilsson, L. (1990). *A child is born.* New York: Delacorte Press, Bantam Books.

Niolaides, K. H., Spencer, K., Avgidou, K., Faiola, S., & Falcon, O. (2005). Multicenter study of first-trimester screening for trisomy 21 in 75,821 pregnancies: Results and estimation of the potential impact of individual risk-orientated two-stage first-trimester screening. *Ultrasound Obstetrics and Gynecology, 25*(3), 221–226.

Nitschke, J. B., Nelson, E. E., Rusch, B. D., Fox, A. S., Oakes, T. R., & Davidson, R. J. (2004). Orbitofrontal cortex tracks positive mood in mothers viewing pictures of their newborn infants. *NeuroImage, 21*(2), 583–592.

Noikorn, W. (2001). Thailand mulls turning stockpiled rubber into condoms. Retrieved July 10, 2001, from http://www.thebody.com/cdc/news_updates/update.html.

Noland, V. J., Liller, K. D., McDermott, R. J., Coulter, M. L., & Seraphine, A. E. (2004). Is adolescent sibling violence a precursor to college dating violence? *American Journal of Health Behavior, 28*(Suppl. 1), S13–S23.

Noller, P. (1993, March–June). Gender and emotional communication in marriage: Different cultures or differential social power? *Journal of Language & Social Psychology, 12*(1–2), 132–152.

Nonnemaker, J., McNeely, C., & Blum, R. (2003). Public and private domains of religiosity and adolescent health risk behaviors: Evidence from the National Longitudinal Study of Adolescent Health. *Social Science & Medicine, 57*(11), 2049–2054.

North American Menopause Society. (2003). Menopause guidebook: Helping women make informed healthcare decisions through perimenopause and beyond. Cleveland, OH: North American Menopause Society.

Nour, N. M. (2004). Female genital cutting: Clinical and cultural guidelines. *Obstetrical & Gynecological Survey, 59*(4), 272–279.

Nzila, N., Laga, M., Thiam, M., Mayimona, K., et al. (1991). HIV and other sexually transmitted diseases among female prostitutes in Kinshasa. *AIDS, 5*, 715–721.

O'Brien, M. J., & Bera, W. H. (1986). Adolescent sexual offenders: Descriptive typology. *Preventing Sexual Abuse, 1*, 1–4.

Obrizzo, L. (2005, March 8). Personal communication.O'Connor, T. G., Thorpe, K., Dunn, J., & Golding, J. (1999). Parental divorce and adjustment in adulthood: Findings from a community sample. *Journal of Child Psychology and Psychiatry, 40*, 777–789.

Ogletree, S. M., & Ginsburg, H. J. (2000). Kept under the hood: Neglect of the clitoris in common vernacular. *Sex Roles, 43*(11–12), 917–927.

O'Grady, R. (2001). Eradicating pedophilia toward the humanization of society. *Journal of International Affairs, 55*(1), 123–140.

O'Halloran, R. L., & Dietz, P. E. (1993). Autoerotic fatalities with power hydraulics. *Journal of Forensic Sciences, 38*, 359–364.

O'Hanlan, K. A., & Crum, C. P. (1996). HPV associated cervical intraepithelial neoplasia following lesbian sex. *Obstetrics and Gynecology, 88*, 702–703.

O'Hare, T. (2005). Risky sex and drinking contexts in freshman first offenders. *Addictive Behaviors, 30*(3), 585–588.

Okami, P., Olmstead, R., & Abramson, P. R. (1997). Sexual experiences in early childhood: 18-year longitudinal data from the UCLA Family Lifestyles Project. *Journal of Sex Research, 34*(4), 339–347.

Okami, P., Olmstead, R., & Abramson, P. R. (1998). Early childhood exposure to parental nudity and scenes of parental sexuality ("primal scenes"): An 18-year longitudinal study of outcome. *Archives of Sexual Behavior, 27*(4), 361–384.

Okazaki, S. (2002). Influences of culture on Asian Americans' sexuality. *Journal of Sex Research, 39*(1), 34–41.

O'Neill, N., & O'Neill, G. (1972). *Open marriage: A new life style for couples.* New York: Evans.

Oner, B. (2001). Factors predicting future time orientation for romantic relationships with the opposite sex. *Journal of Psychology: Interdisciplinary & Applied, 135*(4), 430–438.

Onik, G., Mnarayan, P., Vaughan, D., Dineen, M., & Brunelle, R. (2002). Focal "nerve-sparing" cryosurgery for treatment of primary prostate cancer: A new approach to preserving potency. *Urology, 60*(1), 109–114.

Orenstein, R., & Wong, E. S. (1999, March 1). Urinary tract infections in adults. Retrieved March 22, 2005, from http://www.aafp.org/afp/990301/1225.html

Oriel, K. A., & Schrager, S. (1999). Abnormal uterine bleeding. *American Family Physician, 60*(5), 1371–1380.

Orlandi, F., Rossi, C., Orlandi, E., Jakil, M. C., Hallahan, T. W., Macri, V. J., & Krantz, D.A. (2005). First-trimester screening for tisomy-21 using a simplified method to assess the presence or absence of the fetal nasal bone. *American Journal of Obstetrics & Gynecology, 192*(4), 1107–1111.

Ornish, D. (1999). *Love and survival: The scientific basis for the healing power of intimacy.* New York, NY: Harper Paperbacks.

Orthoevra.com. (2005). Frequently asked questions. Retrieved August 6, 2005, from http://www.orthoevra.com/birth-control-patch/faqs.html#VI

Ortner, S., & Whitehead, H. (1981). Introduction: Accounting for sexual meanings. In S. Ortner & H. Whitehead (Eds.), *Sexual meanings* (pp. 1–27). Cambridge, UK: Cambridge University Press.

Orzek, A. M. (1988). The lesbian victim of sexual assault: Special considerations for the mental health professional. (Special issue: Lesbianism: Affirming nontraditional roles.) *Women and Therapy, 8*, 107–117.

Osmond, D. H. (1998, May). Epidemiology of disease progression in HIV. Retrieved November 23, 2005, from http://hivinsite.ucsf.edu/InSite?page=kb-03&doc=kb-03-01-04

O'Sullivan, C. (1991). Acquaintance gang rape on campus. In A. Parrot & L. Bechhofer (Eds.), *Acquaintance rape: The hidden crime* (pp. 140–156). New York: Wiley.

O'Toole, C. J., & Bregante, J. L. (1992). Lesbians with disabilities. *Sexuality and Disability, 10*, 163–172.

Oxman, M. N., Levin, M., Johnson, G. R., Schmader, M. D., Straus, W., Gelb, L., Arbeit, R., Simberkoff, M., Gershon, A., Davis, L., Weinberg, A., Boardman, K., Williams, H., et al. (2005). A vaccine to prevent herpes zoster and postherpetic neuralgia in older adults. *The New England Journal of Medicine, 352*(22), 2271–2284.

Padgett, V. R., Brislin-Slutz, J. A., & Neal, J. A. (1989). Pornography, erotica, and attitudes toward women: The effects of repeated exposure. *The Journal of Sex Research, 26*, 479–491.

Padian, N. S., Shiboski, S. C., & Jewell, N. P. (1991). Female to male transmission of HIV. *Journal of the American Medical Association, 266*, 1664.

Palca, J. (1991). Fetal brain signals time for birth. *Science, 253*, 1360.

Pamm, C. J. (2001). Effect of attitudes toward women and other attitudinal variables on the formation of rape callousness and sexual misconduct among African, European, and Asian-American college students at a prestigious northeastern university: A longitudinal study. University of Pennsylvania, *Dissertation Abstracts International, #0-493-257063.*

Pandey, M. K., Rani, R., & Agrawal, S. (2005). An update in recurrent spontaneous abortion. *Archives of Gynecology & Obstetrics, 272*(2), 95–108.

Pardun, C. J., L'Engle, K. L., & Brown, J. D. (2005). Linking exposure to outcomes: Early adolescents' consumption of sexual content in six media. *Mass Communication & Society, 8*(2), 75–1.

Parker, S. K., & Griffin, M. A. (2002). What is so bad about a little name calling? *Journal of Occupational Health Psychology, 7*(3), 195–210.

Parker-Pope, T. (2002a, June 25). Doctors push new efforts to eliminate women's periods. *Wall Street Journal,* p. D1.

Parker-Pope, T. (2002b, August 6). How eyerolling destroys a marriage. *Wall Street Journal,* p. D1.

Parker-Pope, T. (2002c, August 27). A new reason for teens to avoid sex: It could be harmful to their health. *Wall Street Journal.* Retrieved December 19, 2005, from http://www.aegis.com/news/ads/2002/AD021652.html

Parkin, D. M., Bray, F., Ferlay, J., & Pisani, P. (2005). Global cancer statistics, 2002. *CA: A Cancer Journal for Clinicians, 55*(2), 74–108.

Parkin, D. M., Pisani, P., & Ferlay, J. (1999). Estimates of the worldwide incidence of 25 major cancers in 1990. *International Journal of Cancer, 80*, 827–841.

Parks, K. A., & Scheidt, D. M. (2000). Male bar drinkers' perspective on female bar drinkers. *Sex Roles, 43*(11/12), 927–935.

Parsons, N. K., Richards, H. C., & Kanter, G. D. (1990). Validation of a scale to measure reasoning about abortion. *Journal of Counseling Psychology, 37*, 107–112.

Pasterski, V. L., Brain, C., Geffner, M. E., Hindmarsh, P., Brook, C., & Hines, M. (2005). Prenatal hormones and postnatal socialization by parents as determinants of male-typical toy play in girls with congenital adrenal hyperplasia. *Child Development, 76*(1), 264–279.

Pasupathy, D., & Smith, G. C. (2005). The analysis of factors predicting antepartum stillbirth. *Minerva Ginecology, 57*(4), 397–410.

Patel, R. (2004). Supporting the patient with genital HSV infection. *Herpes, 11*(3), 87–92.

Pattatucci, A. M. (1998). Molecular investigations into complex behavior: Lessons from sexual orientation studies. *Human Biology, 70*(2), 367–387.

Patterson, J., & Kim, P. (1991). *The day America told the truth.* New York: Plume/Penguin.

Paul, J. P. (1984). The bisexual identity: An idea without social recognition. *Journal of Homosexuality, 9*, 45–63.

Paul, P. (2005). *Pornified: How pornography is transforming our lives, our relationships and our families.* New York: Times Books.

Payer, P. J. (1991). Sex and confession in the thirteenth century. In J. E. Salisbury (Ed.), *Sex in the Middle Ages.* New York: Garland.

Pearlstein, T., & Yonkers, K. A. (2002). Review of fluoxetine and its clinical applications in premenstrual dysphoric disorder. *Expert Opinion in Pharmacotherapy, 3*(7), 979–991.

Pearson, J. C., Turner, L. H., & Todd-Mancillas, W. (1991). *Gender and communication* (2nd ed.). Dubuque, IA: William C. Brown.

Pearson, R., & Lewis, M. B. (2005). Fear recognition across the menstrual cycle. *Hormones & Behavior, 47*(3), 267–271.

Peck, S. (1978). *The road less traveled: A new psychology of love, traditional values and spiritual growth.* Oxford, England: Simon & Schuster.

Peele, S. (1988). Fools for love: The romantic ideal, psychological theory, and addictive love. In R. J. Sternberg & R. J. Barnes (Eds.), *Psychology of love* (pp. 159–188). New Haven, CT: Yale University Press.

Peele, S., & Brodsky, A. (1991). *Love and addiction.* Jersey City, NJ: Parkwest.

Peeples, E. H., & Scacco, A. M. (1982). The stress impact study technique: A method for evaluating the consequences of male-on-male sexual assault in jails, prisons, and other selected single-sex institutions. In A. M. Scacco (Ed.), *Male rape: A casebook of sexual aggressions* (pp. 241–278). New York: AMS Press.

Peirce, K. (2001). What if the Energizer Bunny were female? Importance in gender perceptions of advertising spokes-character effectiveness. *Sex Roles, 45*(11–12), 845–858.

Pelin, S. T. (1999). The question of virginity testing in Turkey. *Bioethics, 13*(3–4), 256–261.

Pelton, R. W. (1990). *Loony laws: That you never knew you were breaking.* New York: Walker.

Penna-Firme, T., Grinder, R. E., & Linhares-Barreto, M. S. (1991). Adolescent female prostitutes on the streets of Brazil: An exploratory investigation of ontological issues. *Journal of Adolescent Research, 6*, 493–504.

Peo, R. (1988). Transvestism. *Journal of Social Work and Human Sexuality, 7*, 57–75.

Peplau, L. A., & Conrad, E. (1989). Beyond nonsexist research: The perils of feminist methods in psychology. *Psychology of Women Quarterly, 13*, 381–402.

Peplau, L. A., & Fingerhut, A. (2004). The paradox of the lesbian worker. *Journal of Social Issues, 60*(4), 719–736.

Peplau, L. A., Garnets, L. D., & Spalding, L. R. (1998). A critique of Bem's "Exotic becomes erotic" theory of sexual orientation. *Psychological Review, 105*(2), 387–394.

Peplau, L. A., Rubin, W., & Hill, C. T. (1977). Sexual intimacy in dating relationship. *Journal of Social Issues, 33*(2), 86–109.

Perkins, R., & Bennett, G. (1985). *Being a prostitute: Prostitute women and prostitute men.* Boston: Allen & Unwin.

Perper, T. (1985). *Sex signals: The biology of love.* Philadelphia, PA: ISI Press.

Perrin, E. C. (2002). Technical report: Coparent or second-parent adoption by same-sex parents. *Pediatrics, 109*(2), 341–345.

Perrone, K. M., Webb, L., & Blalock, R. (2005). The effects of role congruence and role conflict on work, marital, and life satisfaction. *Journal of Career Development, 31*(4), 225–238.

Perrow, C., & Guillén, M. F. (1990). *The AIDS disaster.* New Haven, CT: Yale University Press.

Perry, B. (2000). Can some people read minds? *Science World, 57*(1), 16.

Person, E. S., Terestman, N., Myers, W. A., Goldberg, E., et al. (1992). Associations between sexual experiences and fantasies in a nonpatient population. *Journal of American Academy of Psychological Analysis, 20*, 75–90.

Persson, J. (2005). The ART of assisted reproductive technology. *Australian Family Physician. 34*(3), 119–122.

Petersen, A. (2004, November 23). Women struggling to get pregnant often are told: "Just relax." *Wall Street Journal*, p. D10.

Peterson, S., & Franzese, B. (1987). Correlates of college men's sexual abuse of women. *Journal of College Student Personnel, 28*, 223–228.

Petrie, T. A. (2001). Extending the discussion of eating disorders to include men and athletes. *Counseling Psychologist, 29*(5), 743–753.

Petrovic, J. E. (2002). Promoting democracy and overcoming heterosexism: And never the twain shall meet? *Sex Education, 2*(2), 145–154.

Peyton, C. L., Hunt, W. C., Hundley, R. S., Zhao, M., Wheller, C. M., Gravitt, P. E., & Apple, R. J. (2001). Determinants of genital human papillomavirus detection in a U.S. population. *Journal of Infectious Diseases, 183*(11), 1554–1565.

Pfizer. (2002). *Pfizer global study of sexual attitudes and behaviors.* Retrieved May 20, 2003, from http://pfizerglobalstudy.com

Phares, V., Steinberg, A. R., & Thompson, J. K. (2004). Gender differences in peer and parental influences: Body image disturbance, self-worth, and psychological functioning in preadolescent children. *Journal of Youth & Adolescence, 33*(5), 421–430.

Pheterson, G. (1989). *A vindication of the rights of whores.* Seattle: Seal Press.

Philadelphia, D. (2000). Let's remake a deal. *Time, 155*(16), p. 56.

Phillips, J., & Sweeney, M. (2005). Premarital cohabitation and marital disruption among white, black, and Mexican American women. *Journal of Marriage & Family, 67*(2), 296–314.

Phillips, K. A., & Castle, D. J. (2002). Body dysmorphic disorder. In J. Castle & K. A. Phillips (Eds.), *Disorders of body image* (pp. 101–120). Petersfield, U.K.: Wrightson.

Phillips-Green, M. J. (2002) Sibling incest. *The Family Journal, 10*(2), 195–202.

Phipps, M. G., Blume, J. D., & DeMonner, S. M. (2002). Young maternal age associated with increased risk of postneonatal death. *Obstetrics and Gynecology, 100*(3), 481–486.

Phung, T. M. (2005, September 18). STD vaccines in works, but for children. Retrieved September 18, 2005, from http://www.chicagotribune.com/features/health/chi-0509180282sep18,1,756443.story

Piaget, J. (1951). *Play, dreams, and imitation in children.* New York: Norton.

Pillard, R. C. (1991). Masculinity and femininity in homosexuality: "Inversion" revisited. In J. C. Gonsiorek & J. D. Weinrich (Eds.), *Homosexuality: Research implications for public policy* (pp. 32–43). Newbury Park, CA: Sage.

Pillard, R. C. (1998). Biologic theories of homosexuality. *Journal of Gay and Lesbian Psychotherapy, 2*(4), 75–76.

Pillard, R. C., & Bailey, J. M. (1998). Human sexual orientation has a heritable component. *Human Biology, 70*(2), 347–366.

Pincu, L. (1989). Sexual compulsivity in gay men: Controversy and treatment. *Journal of Counseling and Development, 68*, 63–66.

Pinette, M. G., Wax, J., & Wilson, E. (2004). The risks of underwater birth. *American Journal of Obstetrics and Gynecology, 190*(5), 1211–1215.

Pino, N. W., & Meier, R. F. (1999). Gender differences in rape reporting. *Sex Roles, 40*(11–12), 979–990.

Piot, P. (2000). Global AIDS epidemic: Time to turn the tide. *Science, 288*(5474), 2176–2188.

Pipher, M. (1994). *Reviving Ophelia: Saving the selves of adolescent girls.* New York: Ballantine Books.

Pivarnik, J. M. (1998). Potential effects of maternal physical activity on birth weight: Brief review. *Med Science Sports Exercise, 30*(3), 400–406.

Planned Parenthood Federation of America. (2004). Mifepristone: Expanding women's options for early abortion. Retrieved September 3, 2005, from http://www.plannedparenthood.org/pp2/portal/files/portal/medicalinfo/abortion/fact-early-abortion-mifepristone.xml

Planned Parenthood Federation of America. (2005). Abstinence-only "sex" education. Retrieved May 30, 2005, from http://www.plannedparenthood.org/pp2/portal/medicalinfo/teensexualhealth/fact-abstinence-education.xml

Plaud, J. J., Gaither, G. A., Hegstand, H. J., Rowan, L., Devitt, M. K. (1999). Volunteer bias in human psychophysiological sexual arousal research: To whom do our research results apply? *The Journal of Sex Research, 36*, 171–179.

Plaut, A., & Kohn-Speyer, A. C. (1947). The carcinogenic action of smegma. *Science, 105*, 392.

Pleak, R. R., & Meyer-Bahlburg, H. F. (1990). Sexual behavior and AIDS knowledge of young male prostitutes in Manhattan. *Journal of Sex Research, 27*, 557–587.

Plummer, K. (1989). Lesbian and gay youth in England. *Journal of Homosexuality, 17*, 195–223.

Plummer, K. (1991). Understanding childhood sexualities. *Journal of Homosexuality, 20*, 231–249.

Pogatchnik, S. (1995, November 26). Ireland legalized divorce. *Hartford Courant*, p. A1.

Polaris Project. (2005). Testimony of Rosa. Retrieved December 13, 2005, from http://www.humantrafficking.com/humantrafficking/features_ht3/Testimonies/testimonies_mainframe.htm

Pollack, A. E., Carignan, C. S., & Jacobstein, R. (2004). Female and male sterilization. In R. A. Hatcher et al. (Eds.), *Contraceptive technology* (18th Rev. ed., pp. 531–573). New York: Ardent Media.

Pollack, W. (1998). *Real boys: Rescuing our sons from the myths of boyhood.* New York: Henry Holt.

Pollard, I. (2000). Substance abuse and parenthood: Biological mechanisms—Bioethical challenges. *Women Health, 30*(3), 1–24.

Pollock, N. L., & Hashmall, J. M. (1991). The excuses of child molesters. *Behavioral Sciences and the Law, 9*, 53–59.

Polson, D. W., Adams, J., Wadsworth J., & Franks, S. (1988). Polycystic ovaries—a common finding in normal women. *Lancet, 1*, 870–872.

Pomerleau, A., Bolduc, D., Malcuit, G., & Cossette, L. (1990). Pink or blue: Environmental gender stereotypes in the first two years of life. *Sex Roles, 22*, 359–367.

Pomeroy, W. B. (1982). *Dr. Kinsey and the Institute for Sex Research.* New Haven, CT: Yale University Press.

Pomeroy, W. C. (1972). *Dr. Kinsey and the Institute for Sex Research*. New York: Harper & Row.

Popovic, M. (2005). Intimacy and its relevance in human functioning. *Sexual and Relationship Therapy, 20*(1), 31–49.

Porter, R. (1982). Mixed feelings: The Enlightenment and sexuality in eighteenth-century Britain. In P.-G. Goucé (Ed.), *Sexuality in eighteenth-century Britain* (pp. 1–27). Manchester, U.K.: Manchester University Press.

Posel, D. (2005). The scandal of manhood: "Baby rape" and the politicization of sexual violence in post-apartheid South Africa. *Culture, Health, & Sexuality, 7*(3), 239–252.

Posner, R. A. (1993). Obsession. *The New Republic, 209*, 31–36.

Postma, R., & Schroder, F. H. (2005). Screening for prostate cancer. *European Journal of Cancer, 41*(6), 825–833.

Pothen, S. (1989). Divorce in Hindu society. *Journal of Comparative Family Studies, 20*(3), 377–392.

Potosky, A. L., Legler, J., Albertsen, P. C., Stanford, J. L., Guilliland, F. D., Hamilton, A. S., et al. (2000). Health outcomes after prostatectomy or radiotherapy for prostate cancer. *Journal of National Cancer Institutes, 92*(19), 1582–1592.

Potter, B., Gerofi, J., Pope, M., & Farley, T. (2003). Structural integrity of the polyurethane female condom after multiple cycles of disinfection, washing, drying and relubrication. *Contraception, 67*(1), 65–72.

Potterat, J. J., Rothenberg, R. B., Muth, S. Q., Darrow, W. W., & Phillips-Plummer, L. (1998). Pathways to prostitution: The chronology of sexual and drug abuse milestones. *Journal of Sex Research, 35*(4), 333–340.

Potterat, J. J., Woodhouse, D. E., Muth, J. B., & Muth, S. Q. (1990). Estimating the prevalence and career longevity of prostitute women. *Journal of Sex Research, 27*, 233–243.

Poulson, R. L., Eppler, M. A., Satterwhite, T. N., Wuensch, K. L., & Bass, L. A. (1998). Alcohol consumption, strength of religious beliefs, and risky sexual behavior in college students. *Journal of American College Health, 46*(5), 227–233.

Pound, N., Javed, M. H., Ruberto, C., Shaikh, M., & DelValle, A. P. (2002). Duration of sexual arousal predicts semen parameters for masturbatory ejaculates. *Physiology and Behavior, 76*(4–5), 686–689.

Powell, K. C. (2000). Developmental challenges and barriers: How senior executive women cope with difficult situations in their careers. *Dissertation Abstracts International Section A: Humanities & Social Sciences, 59*(10-A), #0419-4209.

Pozniak, A. (2002). Pink versus blue: The things people do to choose the sex of their baby. Retrieved June 3, 2002, from http://abcnews.go.com/sections/living/DailyNews/choosingbabysex020603.html

Predrag, S. (2005). LGBT news and views from around the world. *Lesbian News, 30*(9), 19–21.

Prentice, A. (2001). Endometriosis. *British Medical Journal, 323*(7304), 93–96.

Preti, G., Wysocki, C. J., Barnhart, K. T., Sondheimer, S. J., & Leyden, J. J. (2003). Male axillary extracts contain pheromones that affect pulsatile secretion of luteinizing hormone and mood in women recipients. *Biology of Reproduction, 68*, 2107–2113.

Prevost, R. R. (1998). Recombinant follicle-stimulating hormone: New biotechnology for infertility. *Pharmacotherapy, 18*(5), 1001–1010.

Price, J. R. (2001). A state-by-state guide to adoption. Retrieved October 27, 2003, from http://www.adoptionfamilycenter.org/resources/states/bythenumbers.htm

Price, M., Kafka, M., Commons, M., Gutheil, T., & Simpson, W. (2002). Telephone scatologia: Comorbidity with other paraphilias and paraphilia-related disorders. *International Journal of Law & Psychiatry, 25*(1), 37–49.

Proto-Campise, L., Belknap, J., & Wooldredge, J. (1998). High school students' adherence to rape myths. *Violence Against Women, 4*, 308–328.

Prud'homme, A. (1991). What's it all about, Calvin? *Time, 138*, 44.

Pryke, S. (2005). The control of sexuality in the early British boy scouts movement. *Sex Education, 5*(1), 15–28.

Pryzgoda, J., & Chrisler, J. C. (2000). Definitions of gender and sex: The subtleties of meaning. *Sex Roles, 43*(7–8), 499–528.

Pubic hair transplants are big business in South Korea. (2005). Retrieved March 22, 2005, from http://www.ananova.com/news/story/sm_815503.html?menu=news.quirkies

Puente, S., & Cohen, D. (2003). Jealousy and the meaning (or nonmeaning) of violence. *Personality and Social Psychology Bulletin, 29*(4), 449–460.

Quadagno, D., Sly, D. F., & Harrison, D. F. (1998). Ethnic differences in sexual decisions and sexual behavior. *Archives of Sexual Behavior, 27*(1), 57–75.

Quam, J. K., & Whitford, G. S. (1992). Adaptation and age-related expectations of older gay and lesbian adults. *The Gerontologist, 32*(3), 367–374.

Quimby, E., & Friedman, S. R. (1989). Dynamics of black mobilization against AIDS in New York City. *Social Problems, 36*, 403–415.

Quindlen, A. (2005, February 21). The good enough mother. *Newsweek*, pp. 50–51.

Rabinowitz Greenberg, S. R., Firestone, P., Bradford, J., & Greenberg, D. M. (2002). Prediction of recidivism in exhibitionists: Psychological, phallometric, and offense factors. *Sexual Abuse: Journal of Research & Treatment, 14*(4), 329–347.

Rado, S. (1949, rev. 1955). An adaptional view of sexual behavior. *Psychoanalysis of behavior: Collected papers*. New York: Grune & Stratton.

Ragsdale, J. D. (1996). Gender, satisfaction level and the use of relational maintenance strategies in marriage. *Communication Monographs, 63*(4), 354–369.

Rahman, A., Katzive, L., & Henshaw, S. K. (1998). A global review of laws on induced abortion, 1985–1997. *International Family Planning Perspectives, 24*(2), 56–64.

Rahman, Q. (2005). Fluctuating asymmetry, second to fourth finger length ratios and human sexual orientation. *Psychoneuroendocrinology, 30*(4), 382–391.

Rancour-Laferriere, D. (1985). *Signs of the flesh*. New York: Mouton de Gruyter.

Rape, Abuse & Incest National Network. (2005). Statistics. Retrieved October 19, 2005, from http://www.rainn.org/statistics/index.html

Raskin, H., & Rogers, C. R. (1989). Personcentered therapy. In R. J. Corsini & D. Wedding (Eds.), *Current psychotherapies* (4th ed., pp. 155–196), Pacific Grove, CA: F. E. Peacock.

Rasmussen, P. R. (2005). The sadistic and masochistic prototypes. In P. R. Rasmussen (Ed.), *Personality-guided cognitive-behavioral therapy* (pp. 291–310). Washington, DC: American Psychological Association.

Raup, J. L., & Myers, J. E. (1989). The empty nest syndrome: Myth or reality? *Journal of Counseling and Development, 68*(2), 180–183.

Ravert, A. A., & Martin, J. (1997). Family stress, perception of pregnancy, and age of first menarche among pregnant adolescents. *Adolescence, 32*(126), 261–269.

Reed, D. (1998). Erotic Stimulus Pathway (ESP) model. In J. S. Greenberg, C. E. Bruess, & D. W. Haffner (Eds.), *Exploring the dimensions of human sexuality*. Sudbury, MA: Jones & Bartlett.

Reeves, T., & Bennett, C. (2003). The Asian and Pacific Islander population in the United States. Current population report, U. S. Census Bureau. Retrieved August 29, 2003, from http://www.census.gov/prod/2003pubs/p20-540.pdf

Regan, K. (2005). Mobile industry prepares for cell phone porn. Retrieved November 7, 2005, from http://www.technewsworld.com/story/46206.html

Regan, P. C., Levin, L., Sprecher, S., Christopher, F. S., & Cate, R. (2000). Partner preferences: What characteristics do men and women desire in their short-term sexual and long-term romantic partners? *Journal of Psychology and Human Sexuality, 12*(3), 1–21.

Register, C. (1987). *Living with chronic illness*. New York: Macmillan.

Reilly, D. R., Delva, N. J., & Hudson, R. W. (2000). Protocols for the use of cyproterone, medroxyprogesterone, & leuprolide in the treatment of paraphilia. *Canadian Journal of Psychiatry, 45*(6), 559–564.

Reingold, A. L. (1991). Toxic shock syndrome: An update. *American Journal of Obstetrics and Gynecology, 165*(4, Pt. 2), 1236.

Reips, U. D. (2000). The Web experiment method: Advantages, disadvantages, and solutions. In M. H. Birnbaum (Ed.), *Psychological experiments on the Internet* (pp. 89–114). San Diego, CA: Academic Press.

Reips, U. D., & Bachtiger, M. T. (2000). Are all flies drosophilae? Participant selection bias in psychological research. Unpublished manuscript.

Reisberg, L. (1999). Survey of freshmen finds a decline in support for abortion and casual sex. *Chronicle of Higher Education, 45*(21), A47.

Reisenzein, R. (1983). The Schachter theory of emotion: Two decades later. *Psychological Bulletin, 94*(2), 239–264.

Reisenzein, R. (1994). Pleasure-arousal theory and the intensity of emotions. *Journal of Personality and Social Psychology 67*(3), 525–539.

Reiss, I. L. (1982). Trouble in paradise: The current status of sexual science. *Journal of Sex Research, 18*, 97–113.

Reiss, I. L. (1986). *Journey into sexuality: An exploratory voyage*. Englewood Cliffs, NJ: Prentice Hall.

Reiter, E. O. (1986). The neuroendocrine regulation of pubertal onset. In J. B. Lancaster & B. A. Hamburg (Eds.), *School-age pregnancy and parenthood: Biosocial dimensions* (pp. 53–76). New York: Aldine DeGruyter.

Remez, L. (2000). Oral sex among adolescents: Is it sex or is it abstinence? *Family Planning Perspectives, 32*(6), 298–305.

Remez, L. (2000, November/December). Oral sex among adolescents: Is it sex or is it abstinence? *Family Planning Perspectives, 32*(6), 298–304.

Remohi, J., Ardiles, G., Garcia-Velasco, J. A., Gaitan, P., Simon, C., & Pellicer, A. (1997). Endometrial thickness and serum oestradiol concentrations as predictors of outcome in oocyte donation. *Human Reproduction, 12*(10), 2271–2276.

Rempel, J. K., & Baumgartner, B. (2003). The relationship between attitudes towards menstruation and sexual attitudes, desires, and behavior in women. *Archives of Sexual Behavior, 32*(2), 155–163.

Remsberg, K. E., Demerath, E. W., Schubert, C. M., Chumlea, C., Sun, S. S., & Siervogel, R. M. (2005). Early menarche and the development of cardiovascular disease risk factors in adolescent girls: The Fels longitudinal study. *Journal of Clinical Endocrinology & Metabolism,* published online ahead of print. Retrieved March 22, 2005, from http://jcem.endojournals.org/cgi/content/abstract/jc.2004-1991v1

Renaud, C. A., & Byers, E. S. (1999). Exploring the frequency, diversity, and content of university students' positive and negative sexual cognitions. *Canadian Journal of Human Sexuality, 8*(1), 17–30.

Rennison, C. M., & Rand, M. R. (2002). National Crime Victimization, Criminal victimization, 2002. Retrieved September 16, 2003, from http://www.rainn.org/ncvs_2002.pdf

Rennison, C. M., & Welchan, S. (2000). *Intimate partner violence.* Washington, DC: U.S. Department of Justice, Bureau of Justice Statistics.

Rensberger, B. (1994, July 25). Contraception the natural way: Herbs have played a role from ancient Greece to modern-day Appalachie. *Washington Post,* p. A3.

Renshaw, D. C. (2005). Premature ejaculation revisted—2005. *Family Journal: Counseling & Therapy for Couples and Families, 13*(2), 150–152.

Resnick, H., Acierno, R., Kilpatrick, D. G., & Holmes, M. (2005). Description of an early intervention to prevent substance abuse and psychopathology in recent rape victims. *Behavior Modification, 29*(1), 156–188.

Resnick, M. D., Bearman, P. S., Blum, R. W., Bauman, K. E., Harris, K. M., Jones, J., et al. (1997). Protecting adolescents from harm: Findings from the National Longitudinal Study on Adolescent Health. *Journal of the American Medical Association, 278*(10), 823–832.

Resnick, S. K. (1992, May/June). Weep for health. *Natural Health,* pp. 56, 58.

Reynolds, A. L., & Caron, S. L. (2005). How intimate relationships are impacted when heterosexual men cross-dress. *Journal of Psychology & Human Sexuality, 12*(3), 63–77.

Reynolds, H. (1986). *The economics of prostitution.* Springfield, IL: Charles C Thomas.

Reynolds, R. F., & Obermeyer, C. M. (2001). Age at natural menopause in Beirut, Lebanon: The role of reproductive and lifestyle factors. *Annals of Human Biology, 28*(1), 21–29.

Rhoads, J. M., & Boekelheide, P. D. (1985). Female genital exhibitionism. *The Psychiatric Forum,* Winter, 1–6.

Rhodes, G., Simmons, L., & Peters, M. (2005). Attractiveness and sexual behavior: Does attractiveness enhance mating success? *Evolution & Human Behavior, 26*(2), 186–201.

Rhodes, J. C., Kjerulff, K. H., Langenberg, P. W., & Guzinski, G. M. (1999). Hysterectomy and sexual functioning. *Journal of the American Medical Association, 282,* 1934–1941.

Riccio, R. (1992). Street crime strategies: The changing schemata of streetwalkers. *Environment and Behavior, 24,* 555–570.

Rich, A. (1983). Compulsory heterosexuality and lesbian existence. In A. Snitow, C. Stinsell, & S. Thompson (Eds.), *Powers of desire: The politics of sexuality* (pp. 177–205). New York: Monthly Review Press.

Richardson, B. A. (2002). Nonoxynol-9 as a vaginal microbicide for prevention of sexually transmitted infections. *Journal of American Medication Association, 287,* 1171–1172.

Richardson, D., & Campbell, J. L. (1982). The effect of alcohol on attributions of blame for rape. *Personality and Social Psychology Bulletin, 8,* 468–476.

Richer, S. (1990). *Boys and girls apart: Children's play in Canada and Poland.* Ottawa, Canada: Carleton University Press.

Richters, J., Hendry, O., & Kippax, S. (2003). When safe sex isn't safe. *Culture, Health & Sexuality, 5*(1), 37–52.

Rickert, V. I., Sanghvi, R., & Weimann, C. M. (2002). Is lack of sexual assertiveness among adolescent and young adult women a cause for concern? *Perspectives on Sexual and Reproductive Health, 34*(4), 178–183.

Rideout, V., Roberts, D. F., & Foehr, U. G. (2005). Generation M: Media in the lives of 8–18 year-olds. Retrieved November 7, 2005, from http://www.kff.org/entmedia/upload/Executive-Summary-Generation-M-Media-in-the-Lives-of-8-18-Year-olds.pdf

Ridge, R. D., & Reber, J. S. (2002). "I think she's attracted to me": The effect of men's beliefs on women's behavior in a job interview scenario. *Basic and Applied Social Psychology, 24*(1), 1–14.

Ridley, M. (2003). What makes you who you are: Which is stronger, nature or nurture? *Time Magazine, 161*(22). Retrieved July 4, 2003, from http://www.time.com/time/archive/preview/from_covers/0,10987,1101030602-454451,00.html

Rieger, G., Chivers, M. L., & Bailey, J. M. (2005). Sexual arousal patterns of gay men. *Psychological Science, 16*(8), 579–584.

Riggs, J. M. (2005). Impressions of mothers and fathers on the periphery of child care. *Psychology of Women Quarterly, 29*(1), 58.

Rio, L. M. (1991). Psychological and sociological research and the decriminalization or legalization of prostitution. *Archives of Sexual Behavior, 20,* 205–218.

Risman, B., & Schwartz, P. (1988). Sociological research on male and female homosexuality. *Annual Review of Sociology, 14,* 125–147.

Rittenhouse, C. A. (1991). The emergence of premenstrual syndrome as a social problem. *Social Problems, 38*(3), 412–425.

Roach, M. K. (2004). *The Salem witch trials: A day-by-day chronicle of a community under siege.* Lanham, MD: Taylor Trade.

Roan, A. (2004, December). Herbs and your sexual health. *Glamour,* p. 108.

Roberts, D. F., Foehr, U. G., & Rideout, V. (2005). Generation M: Media in the lives of 8–18 year-olds. Retrieved November 3, 2005, from http://www.kff.org/entmedia/upload/Generation-M-Media-in-the-Lives-of-8-18-Year-olds-Report.pdf

Roberts, J. E., & Oktay, K. (2005). Fertility preservation: A comprehensive approach to the young woman with cancer. *Journal of the National Cancer Institute Monograph, 34,* 57–59.

Roberts, S. J., Grindel, C. G., Patsdaughter, C. A., Demarco, R., & Tarmina, M. S. (2005). Lesbian use and abuse of alcohol results of the Boston lesbian health project II. *Substance Abuse, 25*(4), 1–9.

Robinson, E. D., & Evans, B. G. I. (1999). Oral sex and HIV transmission. *AIDS, 16*(6), 737–738.

Robinson, J., & Godbey, G. (1998). No sex please. We're college graduates. *American Demographics, 20*(2), 18–23.

Robinson, J. D. (2001). The thematic content categories of lesbian and bisexual women's sexual fantasies, psychological adjustment, daydreaming variables and relationships functioning. *Dissertation Abstracts,* California School of Professional Psychology–Los Angeles, #0-493-12701-1.

Robinson, J. D., & Parks, C. W. (2003). Lesbian and bisexual women's sexual fantasies, psychological adjustment, and close relationship functioning. *Journal of Psychology & Human Sexuality 15*(4), 85–203.

Roddy, R. E., Zekeng, L., Ryan, K. A., Tamoufe, U., & Tweedy, K. G. (2002). Effect of nonoxynol-9 on urogenital gonorrhea and chlamydial infection: A randomized controlled trial. *Journal of the American Medical Association, 287*(9), 1117–1122.

Rodriguez, I. (2004). Pheromone receptors in mammals. *Hormones & Behavior, 46*(3), 219–230.

Rogers, S. C. (1978). Woman's place: A critical review of anthropological theory. *Comparative Studies in Society and History, 20,* 123–162.

Rohner, R., & Veneziano, R. A. (2001). The importance of father love: History and contemporary evidence. *Review of General Psychology, 5*(4), 382–405.

Rome, E. (1998). Anatomy and physiology of sexuality and reproduction. In The Boston Women's Health Collective (Eds.), *The New Our Bodies, Ourselves* (pp. 241–258). Carmichael, CA: Touchstone Books.

Romenesko, K., & Miller, E. M. (1989). The second step in double jeopardy: Appropriating the labor of female street hustlers. (Special issue: Women and crime.) *Crime and Delinquency, 35,* 109–135.

Romero-Daza, N., Weeks, M., & Singer, M. (2003). "Nobody gives a damn if I live or die": Violence, drugs, and street-level prostitution in inner-city Hartford, Connecticut. *Medical Anthropology, 22*(3), 233–259.

Rosario, M., Meyer-Bahlburg, H., Exner, T. M., Gwadz, M., Keller, A. M., & Hunter, J. (1996). The psychosexual development of urban lesbian, gay and bisexual youths. *Journal of Sex Research, 33*(2), 113–117.

Rosario, M., Schrimshaw, E., & Hunter, J. (2004). Predictors of substance use over time among gay, lesbian, and bisexual youths. An examination of three hypotheses. *Addictive Behaviors, 29*(8), 1623–1631.

Rosen, R. (1994). Sexual dysfunction in the 1990's: Current research and theory. Paper delivered at the SSSS Midwest Meeting, May 26–29, 1994, Austin, Texas.

Rosen, R. C., & Leiblum, S. R. (1987). Current approaches to the evaluation of sexual desire disorders. *Journal of Sex Research, 23,* 141–162.

Rosenbaum, D. E. (2005, October 30). Commissions are fine, but rarely what changes the light bulb. Retrieved November 6, 2005, from http://www.nytimes.com/2005/10/30/weekinreview/30rosenbaum.html?fta=y

Rosenberg, L., Palmer, J. R., Rao, R. S., & Shapiro, S. (2001). Low-dose oral contraceptive use and the risk of myocardial infarction. *Archives of Internal Medicine, 161*(8), 1065–1070.

Rosenberg, T. (2001, January 28). Look at Brazil. *The New York Times Magazine*, pp. 26–63.

Rosenblatt, P. C., Karis, T. A., & Powell, R. D. (1995). *Multiracial couples.* Thousand Oaks, CA: Sage.

Rosenthal, R., & Rosnow, R. L. (1975). *The volunteer subject.* New York: Wiley.

Rosman, J. P., & Resnick, P. J. (1989). Sexual attraction to corpses: A psychiatric review of necrophilia. *Bulletin of the American Academy of Psychiatry and the Law, 17*, 153–163.

Ross, J. (2001). Pelvic inflammatory disease. *British Medical Journal, 322*(7287), 658–659.

Ross, L. E. (2005). Perinatal mental health in lesbian mothers: A review of potential risk and protective factors. *Women Health, 41*(3), 113–128.

Ross, M. W., Månsson, S., & Daneback, K. (2005). Biases in internet sexual health samples: Comparison of an internet sexuality survey and a national sexual health survey in Sweden. *Social Science & Medicine, 61*(1), 245–252.

Rosser, B. R. (1999). Homophobia: Description, development and dynamic of gay bashing. *Journal of Sex Research, 36*(2), 211.

Rossi, A. S. (1978). The biosocial side of parenthood. *Human Nature, 1*, 72–79.

Roth, N. (1991). "Fawn of my delights": Boy-love in Hebrew and Arabic verse. In J. E. Salisbury (Ed.), *Sex in the Middle Ages* (pp. 157–172). New York: Garland.

Rothenberg, R. B., Toomey, K. E., Potterat, J. J., Johnson, D., Schrader, M., & Hatch, S. (1998). Using social network and ethnographic tools to evaluate syphilis transmission. *Sexually Transmitted Diseases, 25*(3), 154–160.

Rotheram-Borus, M. J., Draimin, B. H., Reid, H. M., & Murphy, D. A. (1997). The impact of illness disclosure and custody plans on adolescents whose parents live with AIDS. *AIDS, 11*(9), 1159–1164.

Rothman, S. M. (1978). *Woman's proper place.* New York: Basic Books.

Roughgarden, J. (2004). A review of evolution, gender, and rape. *Ethology, 110*(1), 76.

Roylance, F. D. (2004, December 3). FDA panel urges delay in Intrinsa. *Hartford Courant*, p. A3.

Rozee, P. D. (2005). Rape resistance: Successes and challenges. In A. Barnes (Ed.), *Handbook of women, psychology, and the law* (pp. 265–279). New York: Wiley.

Ruan, F., & Lau, M. P. (2004). China. In R. T. Francoeur & R. J. Noonan (Eds.), *The Continuum international encyclopedia of sexuality* (pp. 182–209). New York/London: Continuum International.

Ruan, F. F., & Tsai, Y. M. (1988). Male homosexuality in contemporary mainland China. *Archives of Sexual Behavior, 17*, 189–199.

Rubin, L. (1990). *Erotic wars.* New York: Farrar, Straus, & Giroux.

Rubin, R. (2002, July 9). U.S. stops study on hormone therapy. *USAToday.*

Rubin, R. (2005, October 19). Injected into a controversy. Retrieved November 25, 2005, from http://www.usatoday.com/news/health/2005-10-19-cervical-cancer-injection_x.htm

Rubin, R. H. (2001). Alternative lifestyles revisited, or whatever happened to swingers, group marriages, and communes. *Journal of Family Issues, 22*(6), 711–728.

Rubin, Z. (1970). Measurement of romantic love. *Journal of Personality & Social Psychology, 16*(2), 265–273.

Rubin, Z. (1973). *Liking and loving: An invitation to social psychology.* Oxford, England: Holt, Rinehart & Winston.

Rubio-Aurioles, E., Lopez, M., Lipezker, M., Lara, C., Ramirez, A., Rampazzo, C., et al. (2002). Phentolamine mesylate in postmenopausal women with female sexual arousal disorder. *Journal of Sex and Marital Therapy, 28*(Suppl. 1), 205–215.

Rudd, J. M., & Herzberger, S. D. (1999). Brother–sister incest, father–daughter incest: A comparison of characteristics and consequences. *Child Abuse and Neglect, 23*(9), 915–928.

Rudolph, K., Caldwell, M. & Conley, C. (2005). Need for approval and children's well-being. *Child Development, 76*(2), 309–323.

Rudy, K. (2000). Queer theory and feminism. *Women's Studies, 29*(2), 195–217.

Rugh, A. B. (1984). *Family in contemporary Egypt.* Syracuse, NY: Syracuse University Press.

Ruiz-Velasco, V., Gonzalez, A. G., Pliego, S. L., & Alamillo, V. M. (1997). Endometrial pathology and infertility. *Fertility and Sterility, 67*(4), 687–692.

Russell, D. E. H. (1984). *Sexual exploitation: Rape, child sexual abuse, and workplace harassment.* Beverly Hills, CA: Sage.

Russell, D. E. H., & Howell, N. (1983). The prevalence of rape in the United States revisited. *Signs: Journal of Women in Culture and Society*, 688–695.

Russell, S. T., & Joyner, K. (2001). Adolescent sexual orientation and suicide risk: Evidence from a natural study. *American Journal of Public Health, 91*(8), 1276–1282.

Rust, P. C. R. (2000). *Bisexuality in the U.S.* New York: Columbia University Press.

Ryan, C. J., & Small, E. J. (2005). Progress in detection and treatment of prostate cancer. *Current Opinion in Oncology, 17*(3), 257–260.

Ryan, C., & Futterman, D. (2001). Social and developmental challenges for lesbian, gay, bisexual youth. *SIECUS Report, 29*(4), 5–18.

Saal, F. E., Johnson, C. B., & Weber, N. (1989). Friendly or sexy? It may depend on who you ask. *Psychology of Women Quarterly, 13*, 263–276.

Sabelli, H., Fink, P., Fawcett, J., & Tom, C. (1996). Sustained antidepressant effect of PEA replacement. *Journal of Neuropsychiatry and Clinical Neuroscience, 8*(2), 168–171.

Sabo, D. S., & Runfola, R. (1980). *Jock: Sports and male identity.* New York: Prentice Hall.

Sacks, S. L., Aoki, F., Martel, A., Shafran, S. D., & Lassonde, M. (2005). Clinic-initiated, twice-daily oral famciclovir for treatment of recurrent genital herpes: A randomized, double-blind, controlled trial. *Clinical Infectious Diseases, 41*(8), 1097–1104.

Saewyc, E. M., Bearinger, L. H., Blum, R. W., & Resnick, M. D. (1999). Does sexual orientation make a difference? *Family Planning Perspectives, 31*(3), 127–132.

Saewyc, E. M., Bearinger, L. H., Heinz, P. A., Blum, R. W., & Resnick, M. (1998). Gender differences in health and risk behaviors among bisexual and homosexual adolescents. *Journal of Adolescent Health, 23*(2), 181–188.

"Safer sex basics." (2005). Retrieved October 12, 2005, from http://sexuality.about.com/cs/safersex/a/safersexbasics.htm

Safir, M. P., Rosenmann, A., & Kloner, O. (2003). Tomboyism, sexual orientation, and adult gender roles among Israeli women. *Sex Roles, 48*(9–10), 401–410.

Sagarin, B. J., Becker, D., Guadagno, R. E., Nicastle, L. D., & Millevoi, A. (2003). Sex differences (and similarities) in jealousy. The moderating influence of infidelity experience and sexual orientation of the infidelity. *Evolution and Human Behavior, 24*(1), 17–23.

Saini, S. (2002). Born to die. *Humanist, 62*(4), 25–28.

Sakorafas, G. H. (2005). The management of women at high risk for the development of breast cancer: Risk estimation and preventative strategies. *Cancer Treatment Reviews, 29*(2), 79–89.

Salholz, E., Springen, K., DeLaPena, N., & Witherspoon, D. (1990). A frightening aftermath. *Newsweek, 116*, p. 53.

Salter, A. C. (2003). *Predators, pedophiles, rapists, and other sex offenders.* New York: Basic Books.

Salter, D., McMillan, D., Richards, M., Talbot, T., Hodges, J., Bentovim, A., et al. (2003). Development of sexually abusive behavior in sexually victimized males. *Lancet, 361*(9356), 471–476.

Samet, N., & Kelly, E. W. (1987). The relationship of steady dating to self-esteem and sex role identity among adolescents. *Adolescence, 22*(85), 231–245.

Sanday, P. R. (1981). The socio-cultural context of rape: A cross-cultural study. *Journal of Social Issues, 37*, 5–27.

Sanday, P. R. (1990). *Fraternity gang rape: Sex, brotherhood, and privilege on campus.* New York: New York University Press.

Sanders, S. A., & Reinisch, J. M. (1999). Would you say you "had sex" if . . . ? *Journal of the American Medical Association, 281*(3), 275–277.

Sandnabba, N. K., & Ahlberg, C. (1999). Parents' attitudes and expectations about children's cross-gender behavior. *Sex Roles, 40*(3–4), 249–263.

Sandowski, C. L. (1989). *Sexual concerns when illness or disability strikes.* Springfield, IL: Charles C. Thomas.

Sangrador, J. L., & Yela, C. (2000). "What is beautiful is loved": Physical attractiveness in love relationships in a representative sample. *Social Behavior & Personality, 28*(3), 207–218.

Santelli, J., DiClemente, R., Miller, K., & Kirby, D. (1999). Sexually transmitted diseases, unintended pregnancy and adolescent health promotion. *Adolescent Medicine: Prevention Issues in Adolescent Health Care, 10*, 87–108.

Santelli, J. S., Linberg, L. D., Abma, J., McNeely, C. S., & Resnick, M. (2000). Adolescent sexual behavior: Estimates and trends from four nationally representative surveys. *Family Planning Perspectives, 23*(4), 156–167.

Santen, R. J. (1995). The testis. In P. Felig, J. D. Baxter, & L. A. Frolman, (Eds.), *Endocrinology and metabolism* (3rd ed.). New York: McGraw-Hill.

Santos, P., Schinemann, J., Gabarcio, J., & da Graca, G. (2005). New evidence that the MHC influences odor perception in humans: A study with 58 Southern Brazilian students. *Hormones and Behavior, 47*(4), 384–388.

Sargent, T. (1988). Fetishism. *Journal of Social Work and Human Sexuality, 7*, 27–42.

Sarrel, P., & Masters, W. (1982). Sexual molestation of men by women. *Archives of Sexual Behavior, 11*, 117–131.

Sarrel, P. M. (1990). Sexuality and menopause. *Obstetrics & Gynecology, 75*(4 Suppl.), 26S–30S.

Sather, L. (2002). Effects of abstinence-only education on adolescent attitudes and values concerning premarital sexual intercourse. *Family and Community Health, 25*(2), 1–15.

Sati, N. (1998). Equivocal lifestyles. The Living Channel. Retrieved July 7, 2003, from http://www.glas.org/ahbab/Articles/arabia1.html

Sauer, M. V., Paulson, R. J., & Lobo, R. A. (1995). Pregnancy in women 50 or more years of age: Outcomes of 22 consecutively established pregnancies from oocyte donation. *Fertility and Sterility, 64*(1), 111–115.

Saum, C. A., Surratt, H. L., Inciardi, J. A., & Bennett, R. E. (1995). Sex in prison: Exploring the myths and realities. *Prison Journal, 75*(4), 413–431.

Savaya, R., & Cohen, O. (2003). Divorce among Moslem Arabs living in Israel: Comparison for reasons before and after the actualization of the marriage. *Journal of Family Issues, 24*(3), 338–351.

Savic, I., Berglund, H., & Lindstrom, P. (2005). Brain response to putative pheromones in homosexual men. *Proceedings of the National Academy of Sciences, 102*(20), 7356–7361.

Savin-Williams, R., & Diamond L. (2000). Sexual identity trajectories among sexual-minority youths: Gender comparisons. *Archives of Sexual Behavior, 29*(6), 607–627.

Savin-Williams, R. C., & Dube, E. M. (1998). Parental reactions to their child's disclosure of a gay/lesbian identity. *Family Relations, 47*, 7–13.

Savitz, L., & Rosen, L. (1988). The sexuality of prostitutes: Sexual enjoyment reported by "streetwalkers." *Journal of Sex Research, 24*, 200–208.

Sawyer, R. G., Thompson, E. E., & Chicorelli, A. M. (2002). Rape myth acceptance among intercollegiate student athletes. *American Journal of Health Studies, 18*(1), 19–25.

Sbarra, D., & Emery, R. (2005). The emotional sequelae of nonmarital relationship dissolution: Analysis of change and intraindividual variability over time. *Personal Relationships, 12*(2), 213–232.

Schachter, J. (1999). Which test is best for chlamydia? *Current Opinion in Infectious Diseases, 12*, 41–45.

Schachter, S., & Singer, J. (1962). Cognitive, social, and physiological determinants of emotional state. *Psychological Review, 69*(5), 379–399.

Schachter, S., & Singer, J. (2001). Cognitive, social, and physiological determinants of emotional state. In W. Parrott. (Ed.), *Emotions in social psychology: Essential readings* (pp. 76–93). New York: Psychology Press.

Scheela, R. A. (1995). Remodeling as metaphor: Sex offenders' perceptions of the treatment process. *Issues in Mental Health Nursing, 16*, 493–504.

Schleicher, S., & Stewart, P. (1997, June). Scabies: The mite that roars. *Emergency Medicine,* 54–58.

Schlichter, A. (2004). Queer at last? *GLW: A Journal of Lesbian and Gay Studies, 10*(4), 543–565.

Schmidhammer, S., Ramoner, R., Holtl, L., Bartsch, G., Thurnher, M., & Zelle-Rieser, C. (2002). An Escherichia coli–based oral vaccine against urinary tract infections potently activates human dendritic cells. *Urology, 60*(3), 521–526.

Schnarch, D. (1997). *Passionate marriage.* New York: Henry Holt.

Schneider, F., Habel, U., Kessler, C., Salloum, J. B., & Posse, S. (2000). Gender differences in regional cerebral activity during sadness. *Human Brain Mapping, 9*(4), 226–238.

Schneider, J. P. (2000a). Qualitative study of cybersex participants: Gender differences, recovery issues, and implications for therapists. *Sexual Addiction & Compulsivity, 7*(4), 249–278.

Schneider, J. P. (2000b). Effects of cybersex addiction on the family: Results of a survey. *Sexual Addiction & Compulsivity, 7*(1), 31–58.

Schneider, M. (1989). Sappho was a right-on adolescent: Growing up lesbian. *Journal of Homosexuality, 17*, 111–130.

Scholes, D., LaCroix, A. Z., Ichikawa, L., Barlow, W., & Ott, S. (2005). Change in bone mineral density among adolescent women using and discontinuing depot medroxyprogesterone acetate contraception. *Archives of Pediatrics & Adolescent Medicine, 159*, 139–144.

Schoofs, M., & Zimmerman, R. (2002, July 9). Sexual politics drive AIDS epidemic. *Wall Street Journal,* D4.

Schover, L., & Jensen, S. B. (1988). *Sexuality and chronic illness.* New York: Guilford Press.

Schulte, J. M., Martich, F. A., & Schmid, G. P. (1992). Chancroid in the United States, 1981–1990: Evidence for underreporting of cases. *Morbidity and Mortality Weekly Report, 992, 41*(no. SS-3), 57–61.

Schwartz, I. M. (1999). Sexual activity prior to coitus initiation: A comparison between males and females. *Archives of Sexual Behavior, 28*(1), 63–69.

Schwartz, J. L., Creinen, M. D., & Pymar, H. C. (1999). The trimonthly combination oral contraceptive regimen: Is it cost effective? *Contraception, 60*, 263–267.

Schwartz, J. L., & Gabelnick, H. L. (2002). Current contraceptive research. *Perspectives on Sexual and Reproductive Health, 34*(6), 310–316.

Schwebke, J. R. (1991, April). Syphilis in the 90's. *Medical aspects of human sexuality,* 44–49.

Schwebke, J. R. (2000). Bacterial vaginosis. *Current Infectious Disease Report, 2*(1), 14–17.

Scott, J., Minichiello, V., Mariño, R., Harvey, G. P., Jamieson, M., & Browne, J. (2005). Understanding the new context of the male sex work industry. *Journal of Interpersonal Violence, 20*(3), 320–342.

Scott, J. E., & Schwalm, L. A. (1988). Rape rates and the circulation rates of adult magazines. *Journal of Sex Research, 24*, 241–250.

Scott, J. R. (2005). Episiotomy and vaginal trauma. *Obstetrics and Gynecology Clinics of North America, 32*(2), 307–321.

Scully, D., & Marolla, J. (1983). *Incarcerated rapists: Exploring a sociological model.* Final Report for Department of Health and Human Services, NIMH.

Scully, D., & Marolla, J. (1984). Convicted rapists' vocabulary of motive: Excuses and justifications. *Social Problems, 31*, 530–544.

Scully, D., & Marolla, J. (1985). Riding the bull at Gilley's: Convicted rapists describe the rewards of rape. *Social Problems, 32*, 251–263.

Searles, P., & Berger, R. J. (1987). The current status of rape reform legislation. *Women's Rights Law Reporter, 10*, 25–44.

Seidman, E. L. (2004). The pornographic retreat: Contemporary patterns of pornography use and the psychodynamic meaning of frequent pornography use for heterosexual men. *Dissertation Abstracts International, 64*(8-B), #0419-4217.

Seidman, S. N., & Rieder, R. O. (1994). A review of sexual behavior in the U.S. *American Journal of Psychiatry, 151*, 330–341.

Seiffge-Krenke, I., Shulman, S., & Klesinger, N. (2001). Adolescent precursors of romantic relationships in young adulthood. *Journal of Social & Personal Relationships, 18*(3), 327–346.

Seligman, L., & Hardenburg, S. A. (2000). Assessment and treatment of paraphilias. *Journal of Counseling and Development, 78*(1), 107–113.

Seltzer, J. A. (2000). Families formed outside of marriage. *Journal of Marriage and Family, 62*(4), 1247.

Seng, M. J. (1989). Child sexual abuse and adolescent prostitution: A comparative analysis. *Adolescence, 24*, 665–675.

Sepilian, V., & Wood, E. (2004). Ectopic pregnancy. Retrieved July 19, 2005, from http://www.emedicine.com/med/topic3212.htm

Seppa, N. (2001) Study reveals male link to preeclampsia. *Science News, 159*(12), 181–182.

Serovich, J. M., Brucker, P. S., & Kimberly, J. A. (2000). Barriers to social support for persons living with HIV/AIDS. *AIDS Care, 12*(5), 651–663.

Sexuality Information and Education Council of the United States. (2004a). Guidelines for comprehensive sexuality education (3rd ed.). Retrieved September 22, 2005, from http://www.siecus.org/pubs/guidelines/guidelines.pdf

Sexuality Information and Education Council of the United States. (2004b). Sexuality education and abstinence-only-until-marriage programs in the states: An overview. Retrieved May 30, 2005, from http://www.siecus.org/policy/states/2004/analysis.html

Sexuality Information and Education Council of the United States. (2005a). Sexuality education: Public support for sexuality education. Retrieved June 1, 2005, from http://www.siecus.org/school/sex_ed/sex_ed0000.html

Sexuality Information and Education Council of the United States. (2005b). SIECUS applauds the introduction of the Responsible Education About Life Act. Retrieved May 30, 2005, from http://www.siecus.org/media/press/press0090.html

Seymour, A., Murray, M., Sigmon, J., Hook, M., Edmunds, C., Gaboury, M., et al. (Eds.). (2000). Retrieved May 22, 2003, from http://www.ojp.usdoj.gov/ovc/assist/nvaa2000/academy/welcome.html

Shafik, A. (1991). Testicular suspension: Effect on testicular function. *Andrologia, 23*(4), 297–301.

Shamloul, R. (2005). Treatment of men complaining of short penis. *Urology, 65*(6), 1183–1185.

Sharma, R. (2001). Condom use seems to be reducing number of new HIV/AIDS cases. *British Medical Journal, 323*(7310), 417–421.

Sharpsteen, D. J., & Kirkpatrick, L. A. (1997). Romantic jealousy and adult romantic attachment. *Journal of Personality & Social Psychology, 72*(3), 627–640.

Shaver, F. M. (2005). Sex work research: Methodological and ethical challenges. *Journal of Interpersonal Violence, 20*(3), 296–319.

Shaver, P., & Hazan, C. (1987). Being lonely, falling in love: Perspectives from attachment theory. *Journal of Social Behavior & Personality, 2*(2, Pt 2), 105–124.

Shaver, V. L., & Brown, M. L. (2002). Racial and ethnic disparities in the receipt of cancer treatment. *Journal of National Cancer Institutes, 94*(5), 334–357.

Sheehan, W., & Garfinkel, B. D. (1988). Case study: Adolescent autoerotic deaths. *Journal of the American Academy of Child and Adolescent Psychiatry, 27,* 367–370.

Sheppard, C., & Wylie, K. R. (2001). An assessment of sexual difficulties in men after treatment for testicular cancer. *Sexual and Relationship Therapy, 16*(1), 47–58.

Sher, G., Keskintepe, L., Fisch, J. D., Acacio, B. A., Ahlering, P., Batzofin, J., & Ginsburg, M. (2005). Soluble human leukocyte antigen G expression in phase I culture media at 46 hours after fertilization predicts pregnancy and implantation from day 3 embryo transfer. *Fertility & Sterility, 83*(5), 1410–1413.

Sherfey, J. (1972). *The nature and evolution of female sexuality.* New York: Random House.

Sherif, B. (2004). Egypt. In R. T. Francoeur & R. J. Noonan (Eds.), *The Continuum complete international encyclopedia of sexuality* (pp. 345–358). New York/London: Continuum International.

Sherr, L. (1990). Fear arousal and AIDS: Do shock tactics work? *AIDS, 4,* 361–364.

Sherris, J., Bingham, A., Burns, M. A., Girvin, S., Westley, E., & Gomez, P. I. (2005). Misoprostol use in developing countries: Results from a multicountry study. *International Journal of Gynecology & Obstetrics, 88*(1), 76–81.

Shettles, L., & Rorvik, D. (1970). *Your baby's sex: Now you can choose.* New York: Dodd, Mead.

Sheynkin, Y., Jung, M., Yoo, P., Schulsinger, D., & Komaroff, E. (2005). Increase in scrotal temperature in laptop computer users. *Human Reproduction, 20,* 452–455.

Shifren, J. L., Braunstein, G. D., Simon, J. A., Casson, P. R., Buster, J. E., Redmond, G. P., et al. (2000). Transdermal testosterone treatment in women with impaired sexual function after oophorectomy. *New England Journal of Medicine, 343*(10), 682–688.

Shilts, R. (2000). *And the band played on: Politics, people, and the AIDS epidemic.* New York: St. Martin's Press.

Shtarkshall, R. A., & Zemach, M. (2004). Israel. In R. T. Francoeur & R. J. Noonan (Eds.), *The Continuum international encyclopedia of sexuality* (pp. 581–619). New York/London: Continuum International.

Sidley, P. (2002). Doctor reprimanded for giving antiretroviral drug to baby who was raped. *British Medical Journal, 324*(7331), 191–193.

Sexuality Information and Education Council of the United States. (2001). Issues and answers: Fact sheet on sexuality education. *SIECUS Report, 29*(6).

Sigal, J., Gibbs, M. S., Goodrich, C., Rashid, T., Anjum, A., Hsu, D., Perrino, C., Boratrav, H., Carson-Arenas, A., et al. (2005). Cross-cultural reactions to academic sexual harassment: Effects of individualist vs. collectivist culture and gender of participants. *Sex Roles, 52*(3–4), 201–215.

Silbert, M. (1998). Compounding factors in the rape of street prostitutes. In A. W. Burgess (Ed.), Rape and sexual assault II. London: Taylor & Francis.

Sillars, A. L., & Wilmot, W. W. (1989). Marital communication across the lifespan. In J. F. Nussbaum (Ed.), *Lifespan communication: Normative processes* (pp. 225–254). Hillsdale, NJ: Erlbaum.

Silva, D. C. (1990). Pedophilia: An autobiography. In J. Feierman (Ed.), *Pedophilia: Biosocial dimensions* (pp. 464–487). New York: Springer-Verlag.

Silverman, B., & Gross, T. (1997). Use and effectiveness of condoms during anal intercourse. *Sexually Transmitted Diseases, 24,* 11–17.

Silverstein, C. (1984). The ethical and moral implications of sexual classification: A commentary. *Journal of Homosexuality, 9,* 29–38.

Simon, C. P., & Witt, A., (1982). *Beating the system: The underground economy.* Boston: Auburn House.

Simon, P. M., Morse, E. V., Osofsky, H. J., & Balson, P. M. (1992). Psychological characteristics of a sample of male street prostitutes. *Archives of Sexual Behavior, 21,* 33–44.

Simon, R. W. (2002). Revisiting the relationships among gender, martial status, and mental health. *American Journal of Sociology, 107*(4), 1065–1097.

Simon, R. W., & Marcussen, K. (1999). Marital transitions, marital beliefs, and mental health. *Journal of Health and Social Behavior, 430,* 111–125.

Simons, M. (1996, January 26). African women in France battling polygamy. *New York Times,* p. A1.

Simons, R. L., & Whitbeck, L. B. (1991). Sexual abuse as a precursor to prostitution and victimization among adolescent and adult homeless women. *Journal of Family Issues, 12,* 361–379.

Simonson, K., & Subich, L. M. (1999). Rape perceptions as a function of gender role traditionality and victim–perpetrator association. *Sex Roles, 40*(7–8), 617–634.

Simpson, G., Tate, R., Ferry, K., Hodgkinson, A., & Blaszczynski, A. (2001). Social, neuroradiologic, medical, and neuropsychologic correlates of sexually aberrant behavior. *Journal of Head Trauma Rehabilitation, 16*(6), 556–572.

Simpson, J. L., & Lamb, D. J. (2001). Genetic effects of intracytoplasmic sperm injection. *Seminars in Reproductive Medicine, 19*(3), 239–249.

Simpson, S. W., Howes, R. A., Goodwin, T. M., Robins, S. B. Buckwalter, J.G., Rizzo, A. A., et al. (2001). Psychological factors and hyperemesis gravidarum. *Journal of Women's Health and Gender-Based Medicine, 10*(5), 471–478.

Simsir, A., Thorner, K., Waisman, J., & Cangiarella, J. (2001). Endometriosis in abdominal scars. *American Surgeon, 67*(10), 984–987.

Singh, D., Vidaurri, M., Zambarano, R. J., & Dabbs, J. M. (1999). Lesbian erotic role identification: Behavioral, morphological, and hormonal correlates. *Journal of Personality and Social Psychology, 76*(6), 1035–1049.

Singh, K., & Ratnam, S. S. (1998). The influence of abortion legislation on maternal mortality. *International Journal of Gynaecology and Obstetrics, 63*(Suppl. 1), S123–129.

Skaletsky, H., Kuroda-Kawaguchi, T., Minx, P. J., Cordum, H. S., Hillier, L., & Brown, L. G. (2003). The male-specific region of the human Y chromosome is a mosaic of discrete sequence classes. *Nature, 423,* 825–827.

Skinner, B. F. (1953). *Science and human behavior.* New York: Macmillan.

Skolnick, A. (1992). *The intimate environment: Exploring marriage and the family.* New York: HarperCollins.

Smith, B. (1983). *Home girls: A black feminist anthology.* New York: Women of Color Press.

Smith, C. J., Khouri, R. K., & Baker, T. J. (2000). Initial experience with the Brava nonsurgical system of breast enhancement. *Plastic and Reconstructive Surgery, 105*(7), 2500–2512.

Smith, C. J., McMahon, C., & Shabsigh, R. (2005). Peyronie's disease: The epidemiology, aetiology and clinical evaluation of deformity. *British Journal of Urology International, 95*(6), 729–32.

Smith, K. T. (1971). Homophobia: A tentative personality profile. *Psychological Reports, 29,* 1091–1094.

Smith, M. E. (2005). Female sexual assault: The impact on the male significant other. *Issues in the Mental Health Nursing, 26*(2), 149–167.

Smith, Y. L. S., VanGoozen, S. H. M., & Cohen-Kettenis, D. T. (2001). Adolescents with gender identity disorder who were accepted or rejected for sexual reassignment surgery. *Journal of the American Academy of Child and Adolescent Psychiatry, 40*(4), 472–481.

Smythers, R. (1894). *Instruction and advice for the young bride.* New York: Spiritual Guidance Press.

So, H. W., & Cheung, F. M. (2005). Review of Chinese sex attitudes & applicability of sex therapy for Chinese couples with sexual dysfunction. *Journal of Sex Research, 42*(2), 93–102.

Sobel, J. D. (1997). Pathogenesis of urinary tract infection. Role of host defenses. *Infectious Disease Clinics of North America 1997, 11,* 531–549.

Sobsey, D. (1994). *Violence and abuse in the lives of people with disabilities.* Baltimore, MD: Paul H. Brookes.

Society for Adolescent Medicine. (1991). Society for adolescent medicine position paper on reproductive health care for adolescents. *Journal of Adolescent Health, 12,* 649–661.

Soley, L., & Kurzbard, G. (1986). Sex in advertising: A comparison of 1964 and 1984 magazine advertisements. *Journal of Advertising, 15,* 46–54.

Sommerfeld, J. (1999). Megan's Law expands to the Internet. Retrieved March 31, 2003, from http://www.msnbc.com/news/297969.asp?cp1=1

Sorenson, R. C. (1973). *Adolescent sexuality in contemporary America.* New York: World.

Sorenson, S., & Brown, V. (1990). Interpersonal violence and crisis intervention on the college campus. *New Directions for Student Services, 49,* 57–66.

Sotirin, P. (2000). All they do is bitch, bitch, bitch: Political and interactional features of women's office talk. *Women and Language, 23*(2), 19.

South, S. J. (1991). Sociodemographic differentials in mate selection preferences. *Journal of Marriage and the Family, 53,* 928–940.

South, S. J. (1993). Racial and ethnic differences in the desire to marry. *Journal of Marriage and the Family, 55,* 357–370.

South, S. J., Trent, K., & Shen, Y. (2001). Changing partners: Toward a macrostructural opportunity theory of marital dissolution. *Journal of Marriage and the Family, 63*(3), 743–755.

Spence, J. T. (1984). Gender identity and its implications for the concepts of masculinity and femininity. In T. B. Sonderegger (Ed.), *Psychology and gender* (pp. 59–95). Lincoln: University of Nebraska Press.

Spolan, S. (1991, March 22). Oh, by the way. *Philadelphia City Paper*, p. 7.

Sprecher, S. (2002). Sexual satisfaction in premarital relationships: Associations with satisfaction, love, commitment and stability. *Journal of Sex Research, 39*(3), 190–196.

Sprecher, S., Barbee, A., & Schwartz, P. (1995). "Was it good for you, too?" Gender differences in first sexual intercourse experiences. *Journal of Sex Research, 32*(1), 3–15.

Sprecher, S., Cate, R., & Levin, L. (1998). Parental divorce and young adults' beliefs about love. *Journal of Divorce & Remarriage, 28*(3–4), 107–120.

Sprecher, S., & Hendrick, S. (2004). Self-disclosure in intimate relationships: Associations with individual and relationship characteristics over time. *Journal of Social and Clinical Psychology, 23*(6), 857–877.

Sprecher, S., & Regan, P. (1996). College virgins: How men and women perceive their sexual status. *Journal of Sex Research, 33*(1), 3–16.

Sprecher, S., & Regan, P. (2002). Liking some things (in some people) more than others: Partner preferences in romantic relationships and friendships. *Journal of Social & Personal Relationships, 19*(4), 463–481.

Sprecher, S., & Toto-Morn, M. (2002). A study of men and women from different sides of earth to determine if men are from Mars and women are from Venus in their beliefs about love and romantic relationships. *Sex Roles, 46*(5–6), 131–147.

Stack, S., & Gundlach, J. H. (1992). Divorce and sex. *Archives of Sexual Behavior, 21*(4), 359–367.

Stalking Resource Center. (2000). The extent and nature of the sexual victimization of college women: A national-level analysis. Retrieved October 19, 2005, from http://www.ncvc.org/src/main.aspx?dbID=DB_NCWSV466

Stanback, J., & Grimes, D. (1998). Can intrauterine device removals for bleeding or pain be predicted at one-month follow-up visit? A multivariate analysis. *Contraception, 58*(6), 357–360.

Stanberry, L. R., Spruance, S. L., Cunningham, A., Bernstein, D., Mindel, A., Sacks, S., Tyring, S., Aoki, F., Slaoui, M., Denis, M., Vandepapeliere, P., & Dubin, G. (2005). Glycoprotein-D-adjuvant vaccine to prevent genital herpes. *The New England Journal of Medicine, 347*(21), 1652–1661.

Stanford, E. K. (2002). Premenstrual syndrome. Retrieved July 18, 2002, from http://www.medical-library.org/journals/secure/gynecol/secure/Premenstrual%20syndromes

Stanton, B., Li, X., Black, M., Galbraith, J., Kaljee, L., & Feigelman, S. (1994). Sexual practices and intentions among pre-adolescent and adolescent youths. *Pediatrics, 93,* 966–973.

Starkman, N., & Rajani, N. (2002). The case for comprehensive sex education. *AIDS Patient Care and STDs, 16*(7), 313–318.

Starling, K. (1999). How to bring the romance back. *Ebony, 54*(4), 136–137.

Starr, B., & Weiner, M. B. (1981). *Sex and sexuality in the mature years*. New York: Stein & Day.

Staver, S. (1992, November 9). Gay men may be relapsing into risky sex. *American Medical Association News,* 10.

Stayton, W. R. (1996). Sexual and gender identity disorders in a relational perspective. In F. W. Kaslow (Ed.), *Handbook of relational diagnosis and dysfunctional family patterns* (pp. 357–370). New York: Wiley.

Stearns, S. (2001). PMS and PMDD in the domain of mental health nursing. *Journal of Psychosocial Nursing and Mental Health Services, 39*(1), 16–27.

Steen, R. (2001). Eradicating chancroid. *Bulletin of the World Health Organization, 79*(9), 818–827.

Stehle, B. (1985). *Incurably romantic*. Philadelphia: Temple University Press.

Stein, J. H., & Reiser, L. W. (1994). A study of white, middle-class adolescent boys' responses to 'semenarche'. *Journal of Youth and Adolescence, 23*(3), 373–384.

Stein, R. (2003). Caesarean births hit high mark. Retrieved July 17, 2005, from http://www.washingtonpost.com/ac2/wp-dyn/A5920-2002Dec15?language=printer

Stein, R. (2004). A boy for you, a girl for me: Technology allows choice. Retrieved December 14, 2004, from http://www.washingtonpost.com/wp-dyn/articles/A62067-2004Dec13.html

Stein, R. (2005). Debate rages on use of cervical cancer vaccine. Retrieved November 25, 2005, from http://www.sfgate.com/cgi-bin/article.cgi?file=/c/a/2005/10/31/MNG2LFGJFT1.DTL

Steiner, M., Dunn, E., & Born, L. (2003). Hormones and mood: From menarche to menopause and beyond. *Journal of Affective Disorders, 74*(1), 67–83.

Steinhauer, J. (2001, June 27). U.N. united to combat AIDS but splits over how to do it. *New York Times,* p. 10.

Stephens, R. (1963). *The Muria of Africa*. New York: Random House.

Stephenson, J. M., Imrie, J., Davis, M. M., Mercer, C., Black, S., et al. (2003). Is use of antiretroviral therapy among homosexual men associated with increased risk of transmission of HIV infection? *Sexually Transmitted Diseases, 79*(1), 7–10.

Sternberg, R. (1985). A triangular theory of love. *Psychological Review, 93*(2), 119–135.

Sternberg, R. J. (1987). Liking versus loving: A comparative evaluation of theories. *Psychological Bulletin, 102*(3), 331–345.

Sternberg, R. J. (1998). *Cupid's arrow: The course of love through time*. New Haven, CT: Yale University Press.

Sternberg, R. J. (1999). *Love is a story*. New York: Oxford University Press.

Sternberg, S. (2002, July 7). The face of AIDS is young. Retrieved July 18, 2002, from http://www.usatoday.com/news/healthscience/health/aids/2002-07-17-aids-youth_x.htm

Sternberg, S. (2004a). After 20 years, AIDS vaccine still seems a distant dream. Retrieved November 25, 2005, from http://www.usatoday.com/news/health/2004-09-29-aids-usat_x.htm

Sternberg, S. (2004b, November 30). Imagine . . . a Russia without young people. Retrieved December 1, 2004, from http://www.usatoday.com/news/health/2004-11-30-aids-awareness_x.htm

Sternfeld, B., Swindle, R., Chawla, A. Long, S., & Kennedy, S. (2002). Severity of premenstrual symptoms in a health maintenance organization population. *Obstetrics & Gynecology, 99*(6), 1014–1024.

Stevenson, M., & Gajarsky, W. (1992). Unwanted childhood sexual experiences relate to later revictimization and male perpetration. *Journal of Psychology and Human Sexuality, 4,* 57–70.

Stewart, E. A. (2001). Uterine fibroids. *Lancet, 357*(9252), 293–298.

Stewart, F., & Gabelnick, H. L. (2004). Contraceptive research and development. In R. A. Hatcher et al. (Eds.), *Contraceptive technology* (18th Rev. ed., pp. 601–616). New York: Ardent Media.

Stewart, F., Trussell, J., VanLook, P. F. (2004). Emergency contraception. In R. A. Hatcher et al. (Eds.), *Contraceptive technology* (18th Rev. ed., pp. 575–600). New York: Ardent Media.

Stewart, F. H., Ellertson, C., & Cates, W. (2004). Abortion. In R. A. Hatcher et al. (Eds.), *Contraceptive technology* (18th Rev. ed., pp. 673–700). New York: Ardent Media.

Stewart, H. (2005). Senoritas and princesses: The quinceanera as a context for female development. *Dissertation Abstracts, 65*(7-A), 2770, #0419–4209.

Stewart, J. (1990). *The complete manual of sexual positions*. Chatsworth, CA: Media Press.

Stewart, S. T., Lenert, L., Bhatnagar, V., & Kaplan, R. M. (2005). Utilities for prostate cancer health states in men aged 60 and older. *Medical Care, 43*(4), 347–355.

Stockinger, P., Kvitsiani, D., Rotkopf, S., Tirian, L., & Dickson, B. J. (2005). Neural circuitry that governs Drosophila male courtship behavior. *Cell, 121*(5), 795–807.

Stoller, R. J. (1991). The term perversion. In G. I. Fogel & W. A. Myers (Eds.), *Perversions and near-perversions in clinical practice: New psychoanalytic perspectives* (pp. 36–58). New Haven, CT: Yale University Press.

Stoller, R. J. (1996). The gender disorders. In I. Rosen (Ed.), *Sexual deviation* (3rd ed., pp. 111–133). London: Oxford University Press.

Stoller, R. J., & Herdt, G. H. (1985). Theories of origins of male homosexuality. *Archives of General Psychiatry, 42,* 399–404.

Storgaard, L., Bonde, J. P., Ernst, E., Spano, M., Andersen, C. Y., Frydenberg, M., & Olsen, J. (2003). Does smoking during pregnancy affect sons' sperm counts? *Epidemiology, 14*(3), 278–286.

Storms, M. D. (1980). Theories of sexual orientation. *Journal of Personality and Social Psychology, 38,* 783–792.

Storms, M. D. (1981). A theory of erotic orientation development. *Psychological Review, 88,* 340–353.

Strandberg, T. E. (2002). Preterm birth and licorice consumption during pregnancy. *American Journal of Epidemiology, 156*(9), 803–805.

Strasburger, V. C. (1989). Adolescent sexuality and the media. *Pediatric Clinics of North America, 36,* 747–773.

Strassberg, D. S., & Lockerd, L. K. (1998). Force in women's sexual fantasies. *Archives of Sexual Behavior, 27*(4), 403–415.

Strathern, M. (1981). Self-interest and the social good: Some implications of Hagen gender imagery. In S. Ortner & H. Whitehead (Eds.), *Sexual meanings* (pp. 166–191). Cambridge, U.K.: Cambridge University Press.

Strine, T. W., Chapman, D. P., & Ahluwalia, I. B. (2005). Menstrual-related problems and psychological distress among women in the United States. *Journal of Women's Health, 14*(4), 316–323.

Strommen, E. F. (1989). "You're a what?": Family member reactions to the disclosure of homosexuality. *Journal of Homosexuality, 18*, 37–58.

Struckman-Johnson, C., & Struckman-Johnson, D. (1994). Men pressured and forced into sexual experience. *Archives of Sexual Behavior, 23*, 93–115.

Struckman-Johnson, C., & Struckman-Johnson, D. (2002). Sexual coercion reported by women in three midwestern prisons. *Journal of Sex Research, 39*(3), 217–227.

Studwell, K. (2004, March). Congressional briefing highlights sexual behavior research. *Psychological Science Agenda, 18*(3). Retrieved February 18, 2005, at http://www.apa.org/science/psa/mar4briefing.html

Suitor, J. J., & Carter, R. S. (1999). Jocks, nerds, babes and thugs: A research note on regional differences in adolescent gender norms. *Gender Issues, 17*(3), 87.

Sulak, P. J., Kuehl, T. J., Ortiz, M., & Shull, B. L. (2002). Acceptance of altering the standard 21-day/7-day oral contraceptive regimen to delay menses and reduce hormone withdrawal symptoms. *American Journal of Obstetrics and Gynecology, 186*(6), 1142–1149.

Summers, T., Kates, J., & Murphy, G. (2002). The global impact of HIV/AIDS on young people. *SIECUS Report, 31*(1), 14–23.

Suplicy, M. (1994). Sexuality education in Brazil. *SIECUS Report*, 1–6.

Suppe, F. (1984). Classifying sexual disorders: The diagnostic and statistical manual of the American Psychiatric Association. *Journal of Homosexuality, 9*, 9–28.

Sussman, N. M., & Tyson, D. H. (2000). Sex and power: Gender differences in computer-mediated interactions. *Computers in Human Behavior, 16*(4), 381–394.

Sutherland, P. (1987). I want sex, just like you. *The Village Voice, 32*(14), 25.

Swaab, D. F. (2004). Sexual differentiation of the human brain: Relevance for gender identity, transsexualism and sexual orientation. *Gynecological Endocrinology, 19*(6), 201–312.

Swaab, D. F., & Hofman, M. A. (1990). An enlarged suprachiasmatic nucleus in homosexual men. *Brain Research, 537*, 141–148.

Swanson, J. M., Dibble, S., & Chapman, L. (1999). Effects of psychoeducational interventions on sexual health risks and psychosocial adaptation in young adults with genital herpes. *Journal of Advanced Nursing, 29*(4), 840–851.

Sweet, N., & Tewksbury, R. (2000). What's a nice girl like you doing in a place like this? Pathways to a career in stripping. *Sociological Spectrum, 20*(3), 325–344.

Swisher, E. D., Wobster, R., & Armstrong, A. (1998). Age-related pregnancy rates in GIFT patients. *Mil Medicine, 163*(7), 449–450.

Szymanski, D. M., Chung, Y., & Balsam, K. (2001). Psychosocial correlates of internalized homophobia in lesbians. *Measurement and Evaluation in Counseling and Development, 34*(1), 27–39.

Taira, A. V., Neukermans, C. P., & Sanders, G. D. (2004). Evaluating human papillomavirus vaccination programs. Retrieved November 25, 2005, from http://www.cdc.gov/ncidod/EID/vol10no11/04-0222.htm

Takeuchi, S. A. (2000, June). If I don't look good, you don't look good? Toward a new matching theory of interpersonal attraction based on the behavioral and the social exchange principles. *Dissertation Abstracts International*, #0419-4209.

Talakoub, L., Munarriz, R., Hoag, L., Gioia, M., Flaherty, E., & Goldstein, I. (2002). Epidemiological characteristics of 250 women with sexual dysfunction who presented for initial evaluation. *Journal of Sex and Marital Therapy, 28* (Suppl. 1), 217–224.

Talbot, M. (1999). The little white bombshell. *New York Times Magazine*, pp. 39–43.

Tannahill, R. (1980). *Sex in history*. New York: Stein & Day.

Tannen, D. (1990). *You just don't understand: Women and men in conversation*. New York: Ballantine Books.

Tantleff-Dunn, S. (2001). Breast and chest size: Ideals and stereotypes through the 1990s. *Sex Roles, 45*(3–4), 231–242.

Tanveer, K. (2002, July 7). In Pakistan, gang rape as a tribal punishment. *The Hartford Courant*, A2.

Taveras, E. M., Capra, A. M., Braveman, P. A., Jensvold, N. G., Escobar, G. J., & Lieu, T. A. (2003). Clinician support and psychosocial risk factors associated with breastfeeding discontinuation. *Pediatrics, 112*(1), 108–115.

Tay, J. I., Moore, J., & Walker, J. J. (2000). Ectopic pregnancy. *British Medical Journal, 320*(7239), 916–920.

Taylor, C. (1986). Extramarital sex: Good for the goose? *Women and Therapy, 5*(2–3), 289–295.

Taylor, H. E. (2000). Meeting the needs of lesbian and gay young adults. *The Clearing House, 73*(4), 221.

Taywaditep, K. J., Coleman, E., & Dumronggittigule, P. (2004). Thailand. In R. T. Francoeur & R. J. Noonan (Eds.), *The Continuum complete international encyclopedia of sexuality* (pp. 1021–1053). New York/London: Continuum International.

Teachman, J. (2003). Premarital sex, premarital cohabitation and the risk of subsequent marital dissolution among women. *Journal of Marriage and Family, 65*(2), 444–455.

Teitelman, A. (2004). Adolescent girls' perspectives of family interactions related to menarche and sexual health. *Qualitative Health Research, 14*(9), 1292–1308.

Terán, S., Walsh, C., & Irwin, K. L. (2001). Chlamydia trachomatis infection in women: Bad news, good news, and next steps in prevention. *Journal of the American Medical Association, 56*(3), 100–104.

Terán, S., Walsh, C., & Irwin, K. L. (2002). Chlamydia infection in women: Bad news, good news, and next steps. *SIECUS Report, 30*(1), 17–23.

Terao, T., & Nakamura, J. (2000). Exhibitionism and low-dose trazodone treatment. *Human Psychopharmacology: Clinical & Experimental, 15*(5), 347–349.

Terry, J. (1990). Lesbians under the medical gaze: Scientists search for remarkable differences. *The Journal of Sex Research, 27*, 317–339.

Thakar, R., Ayers, S., Clarkson, P., Stanton, S., & Manyonda, I. (2002). Outcomes after total versus subtotal abdominal hysterectomy. *New England Journal of Medicine, 347*(17), 1318–1325.

Thomas, S. L., & Ellertson, C. (2000). Nuisance or natural and healthy: Should monthly menstruation be optional for women? *Lancet, 355*, 922–924.

Thomasset, C. (1992). The nature of woman. In C. Klapisch-Zuber (Ed.), *A history of women in the West, Volume II: Silences of the Middle Ages* (pp. 43–70). Cambridge, U.K.: Belknap Press.

Thompson, A. P. (1984). Emotional and sexual components of extramarital relations. *Journal of Marriage and the Family, 46*, 35–42.

Thompson, S. J. (2005). Factors associated with trauma symptoms among runaway/homeless adolescents. *Stress, Trauma and Crisis: An International Journal, 8*(2–3), 143–156.

Thompson, W. E., & Harred, J. L. (1992). Topless dancers. *Deviant Behavior, 13*, 291–311.

Thoni, A., Zech, N., & Moroder, L. (2005). Water birth and neonatal infections. Experience with 1575 deliveries in water. *Minerva Ginecol., 57*(2), 199-206.

Thorne, N., & Amrein, H. (2003). Vomeronasal organ: Pheromone recognition with a twist. *Current Biology, 13*(6), R220–R222.

Thornhill, R., & Palmer, C. T. (2000). *A natural history of rape: Biological bases of sexual coercion*. Boston: MIT Press.

Thornton, A., & Young-DeMarco, L. (2001). Four decades in attitudes toward family issues in the U.S.: The 1960s to the 1990s. *Journal of Marriage and Family, 63*(4), 1009.

Thorp, J. M., Hartmann, K. E., & Shadigian, E. (2003). Long-term physical and psychological health consequences of induced abortion: review of the evidence. *Obstetrical and Gynecological Survey, 58*(1), 67–79.

Thyen, U., Richter-Appelt, H., Wiesemann, C., Holterhus, P. M., & Hiort, O. (2005). Deciding on gender in children with intersex conditions: Considerations and controversies. *Treatments in Endocrinology, 4*(1), 1–8.

Tiefer, L. (1995). *Sex is not a natural act and other essays*. Boulder, CO: Westview Press.

Tiefer, L. (1996). The medicalization of sexuality: Conceptual, normative and professional issues. *Annual Review of Sex Research, 7*, 252–282.

Tiefer, L. (2000). A new view of women's sexual problems. *Electronic Journal of Human Sexuality* (3), 15. Retrieved May 24, 2005, from http://www.ejhs.org/volume3/newview.htm

Tiefer, L. (2001). A new view of women's sexual problems: Why new? Why now? *Journal of Sex Research, 38*(2), 89–96.

Tiefer, L. (2002). Beyond the medical model of women's sexual problems: A campaign to resist the promotion of "female sexual dysfunction." *Sexual & Relationship Therapy, 17*(2), 127–135.

Tietze, C. (1983). *Induced abortion: A world review, 1983*. New York: The Population Council.

Tietze, C., & Henshaw, S. K. (1986). *Induced abortion: A world review, 1986*. New York: Alan Guttmacher Institute.

Tilley, D. S., & Brackley, M. (2005). Men who batter intimate partners: A grounded theory study of the development of male violence in intimate partner relationships. *Issues in Mental Health Nursing, 26*(3), 281–297.

Timeline Science. (2005). Infertility treatment timeline. Retrieved November 4, 2005, from http://www.timelinescience.org/resource/students/inferty/inftimel.htm

Timmreck, T. C. (1990). Overcoming the loss of a love: Presenting love addiction and promoting positive emotional health. *Psychological Reports, 66*(2), 515–528.

Ting-Toomey, S., Gao, G., & Trubisky, P. (1991). Culture, face maintenance, and styles of handling interpersonal conflicts: A study in five cultures. *International Journal of Conflict Management, 2*(4), 275–296.

Tinklin, T., Croxford, L., Ducklin, A., & Frame, B. (2005). Gender and attitudes to work and family roles: The views of young people at the millennium. *Gender & Education, 17*(2), 129–143.

Tjaden, P., & Thoennes, N. (1998). *Stalking in America: Findings from the National Violence Against Women Survey*. National Institute of Justice and the Centers for Disease Control and Prevention.

Tjaden, P., & Thoennes, N. (2000). *Extent, nature, and consequences of intimate partner violence: Findings from the National Violence Against Women Survey*. Washington, DC: National Institute of Justice and the Centers for Disease Control and Prevention.

Todosijevic, J., Rothblum, E. D., & Solomon, S. E. (2005). Relationship satisfaction, affectivity, and gay-specific stressors in same-sex couples joined in civil unions. *Psychology of Women Quarterly, 29*(2), 158–166.

Tone, A. (2001). *Devices and desires: A history of contraceptives in America*. New York: Hill & Wang.

Tonelli, M. (2004). Teens and intimate partner violence. *Journal of Pediatric Adolescent Gynecology, 17*, 421–422.

Toto-Morn, M., & Sprecher, S. (2003). A cross-cultural comparison of mate preferences among university students: The United States vs. the People's Republic of China. *Journal of Comparative Family Studies, 34*(2), 151–170.

Tough, S. C., Newburn-Cook, C., Johnston, D. W., Svenson, L. W., Rose, S., & Belik, J. (2002). Delayed childbearing and its impact on population rate changes in lower birth weight, multiple birth, and preterm delivery. *Pediatrics, 109*(3), 399–403.

Towne, B., Czerwinski, S. A., Demerath, E. W., Blangero, J., Roche, A. F., & Siervogel, R. M. (2005). Heritability of age at menarche in girls from the Fels longitudinal study. *American Journal of Physical Anthropology*, published online ahead of print. Retrieved March 22, 2005, from http://www.ncbi.nlm.nih.gov/entrez/query.fcgi?cmd=Retrieve&db=pubmed&dopt=Abstract&list_uids=15779076

Trager, R. S. (2003). Microbicides. Raising new barriers against HIV infection. *Science, 299*(5603), 39.

Treas, J., & Giesen, D. (2000). Sexual infidelity among married and cohabiting Americans. *Journal of Marriage and Family, 62*(1), 48–61.

Treatment & Crisis Intervention, 5(2), 193–202.

Trees, D. L., & Morse, S. A. (1995). Chanchroid and *Haemophilus ducreyi*: An update. *Clinical Microbiology Review, 8*, 357–375.

Treloar, S. A., Heath, A. C., & Martin, N. G. (2002). Genetic and environmental influences on premenstrual symptoms in an Australian twin sample. *Psychological Medicine, 32*(1), 25–38.

Tremble, B., Schneider, M., & Appathurai, C. (1989). Growing up gay or lesbian in a multicultural context. In G. Herdt (Ed.), *Gay and lesbian youth* (pp. 253–267). New York: Harrington Park Press.

"Trends in HIV/AIDS diagnoses." (2005). Trends in HIV/AIDS diagnoses—33 states, 2001–2004. *Morbidity & Mortality Weekly Report, 54*(45), 1149–1153.

Trivits, L. C., & Reppucci, N. D. (2002). Application of Megan's Law to juveniles. *American Psychologist, 57*(9), 690–704.

Troiden, R. R. (1989). The formation of homosexual identities. In G. Herdt (Ed.), *Gay and lesbian youth* (pp. 43–73). New York: Harrington Park Press.

Troncoso, A. P., Romani, A., Carmnze, C. M., Macias, J. R., & Masini, R. (1995). Probable HIV transmission by female homosexuals. *Contact Medicina, 55*, 334–336.

Trost, J. E. (2004). Sweden. In R. T. Francoeur & R. J. Noonan (Eds.), *The Continuum international encyclopedia of sexuality* (pp. 984–994). New York/London: Continuum International.

Trost, J. E., & Bergstrom-Walan, M. (2004). Sweden. In R. T. Francoeur & R. J. Noonan (Eds.), *The Continuum international encyclopedia of sexuality* (pp. 824–845). New York/London: Continuum International.

Trudel, G., & Desjardins, G. (1992). Staff reactions toward the sexual behaviors of people living in institutional settings. *Sexuality and Disability, 10*, 173–188.

Trumbach, R. (1990). Is there a modern sexual culture in the west, or, did England never change between 1500 and 1900? *Journal of the History of Sexuality, 1*, 206–309.

Truscott, P. (1991). S/M: Some questions and a few answers. In M. Thompson (Ed.), *Leatherfolk: Radical sex, people, politics, and practice* (pp. 15–36). Boston: Alyson Publications.

Trussell, J. (2004). The essentials of contraception: Efficacy, safety, and personal considerations. In R. A. Hatcher et al. (Eds.), *Contraceptive technology* (18th Rev. ed., pp. 221–252). New York: Ardent Media.

Tucker, M. B., & Mitchell-Kernan, C. (1995). Trends in African-American family formation: A theoretical and statistical overview. In M. D. Tucker & C. Mitchell-Kernan (Eds.), *The decline of marriage among African-Americans* (pp. 3–26). New York: Russell Sage.

Turner, W. (2000). *A genealogy of queer theory*. Philadelphia: Temple University Press.

Turner's Syndrome Society (TSS). (2002). Turner's Syndrome Society: Resources and research. Retrieved September 11, 2002, from www.turner-syndrome-us.org

TV Turnoff Network. (2005). Facts and figures about our TV habit. Retrieved November 6, 2005, from http://www.tvturnoff.org/images/facts&figs/factsheets/FactsFigs.pdf

Twenge, J. M., Campbell, W., & Foster, C. (2003). Parenthood and marital satisfaction: A meta-analytic review. *Journal of Marriage & Family, 65*(3), 574–583.

Tyler, C. W. (1981). Epidemiology of abortion. *Journal of Reproductive Medicine, 26*, 459.

Tzeng, O. (1992). Cognitive/comparitive judgment paradigm of love. In O. Tzeng (Ed.), *Theories of love development, maintenance, and dissolution: Octagonal cycle and differential perspectives*, p. 133–149.

Uehling, D. T., Hopkins, W. J., Beierle, L. M., Kryer, J. V., & Heisey, D. M. (2001). Vaginal mucosal immunization in recurrent urinary tract infections: Extended phase II clinical trials. *Journal of Infectious Disease, 183* (Suppl. 1), 581–583.

Ugboma, H. A., Akani, C. I., & Babatunde, S. (2004). Prevalence and medicalization of female genital mutilation. *Niger Journal of Medicine, 13*(3), 250–253.

Uman, K. (2004). Cross-gender communication differences: Understanding them can help you be more effective. Retrieved September 3, 2005, from http://www.exe-coach.com/CrossGenderCommunication.html

UNAIDS. (1997, October 22). Health education does lead to safer sexual behavior. *UNAIDS Review Press Release*, Joint United Nations Programme on HIV/AIDS.

UNAIDS. (2004a). UNAIDS report on the global AIDS epidemic. Retrieved September 25, 2005, from http://www.unaids.org/bangkok2004/report_pdf.html

UNAIDS. (2004a). UNAIDS report on the global AIDS epidemic. Retrieved September 25, 2005, from http://www.unaids.org/bangkok2004/report_pdf.html

UNAIDS. (2004b). Sub-Saharan Africa. Retrieved November 22, 2005, from http://www.unaids.org/EN/Geographical+Area/By+Region/sub-saharan+africa.asp

UNAIDS. (2005a). Adults and children estimated to be living with HIV as of end 2005. Retrieved November 22, 2005, from http://www.unaids.org/NetTools/Misc/DocInfo.aspx?LANG=en&href=http://GVA-DOC-OWL/WEBcontent/Documents/pub/Topics/Epidemiology/Slides02/12-05/EpiCoreDec05Slide004_en.ppt

UNAIDS. (2005b). AIDS Epidemic Update: December, 2005. Retrieved November 22, 2005, from http://www.unaids.org/epi2005/doc/report_pdf.html

UNAIDS. (2005c, October 25). Children: The missing face of AIDS. October 25, 2005. Retrieved November 22, 2005, from http://www.unaids.org/html/pub/media/press-releases03/pr_unicef_25oct05_en_pdf.htm

U.S. Bureau of the Census. (1999). *Statistical Abstract of the United States: 1999* (119th ed.). Washington, DC: U.S. Government Printing Office.

U.S. Bureau of the Census. (2001). America's families and living arrangements: Population characteristics. Retrieved August 31, 2003, from http://www.census.gov/prod/2001pubs/p20-537.pdf

United States Census Bureau. (2001). Marital status history for people 15 years old and over by age, sex, race, and ethnicity. Retrieved October 12, 2005, from http://www.census.gov/population/www/socdemo/marr-div/p70-97-tab01.html

U.S. Department of Health and Human Services, Health Resources and Services Administration. (2005). *Women's health USA 2005*. Rockville, MD: Author.

U.S. Department of Health and Human Services. (1995). *Healthy people 2000: Midcourse review and 1995 revisions*. Washington, DC: U.S. Government Printing Office.

U.S. Department of Justice–Federal Bureau of Investigation. (2004). Crime in the United States, 2004: Forcible rape. Retrieved December 3, 2005, from http://www.fbi.gov/ucr/cius_04/offenses_reported/violent_crime/forcible_rape.html

U.S. Department of Justice–Office of Justice Programs. (2002). Rape and sexual assault: Reporting to police and medical attention, 1992–2000. Retrieved October 22, 2005, from http://www.ojp.usdoj.gov/bjs/pub/pdf/rsarp00.pdf

U.S. Department of Justice–Office of Justice Programs. (2003). Number of victimizations, by type of crime and relationship to offender. Retrieved October 22, 2005, from http://www.ojp.usdoj.gov/bjs/pub/pdf/cvus/current/cv0333.pdf

U.S. Department of Justice–Office of Justice Programs. (2005). Criminal Victimization in the United States, 2003 Statistical Tables. National Crime Victimization Survey. Retrieved December 3, 2005, from http://www.ojp.usdoj.gov/bjs/pub/pdf/cvus03.pdf

U.S. Department of State. (2005). Trafficking in persons report. Retrieved December 12, 2005, from http://www.state.gov/documents/organization/47255.pdf

U.S. Food and Drug Administration. (2004). Black box warning added concerning long-term use of Depo-Provera contraceptive injection. Retrieved November 3, 2005, from http://www.fda.gov/bbs/topics/ANSWERS/2004/ANS01325.html

U.S. Food and Drug Administration. (2005). FDA updates labeling for Ortho Evra contraceptive patch. Retrieved November 13, 2005, from http://www.fda.gov/bbs/topics/news/2005/NEW01262.html

U.S. Preventive Services Task Force (USPSTF). (2005). Screening for ovarian cancer: Recommendation statement. *American Family Physician, 71*(4), 759–763.

U.S. Supreme Court. (1973). *Roe v. Wade Supreme Court decision.* Retrieved September 9, 2003, from http://womenshistory.about.com/library/etext/gov/bl_roe_a.htm

U.S. Supreme Court. (1992, June 29). Planned Parenthood of Southeastern Pennsylvania v. Casey. *West's Supreme Court Report, 112,* 2791–2885.

U.S. Surgeon General. (2001). Press release. Retrieved July 12, 2002, from www.surgeongeneral.gov/news/pressreleases/pr_sexualhealth.htm

Upchurch, D. M., Aneshensel, C. S., Mudgal, J., & McNeely, C. S. (2001). Sociocultural contexts of time to first sex among Hispanic adolescents. *Journal of Marriage and Family, 63*(4), 1158.

Upchurch, D. M., Aneshensel, C. S., Sucoff, C. A., & Levy-Storms, L. (1999). Neighborhood and family contexts of adolescents' sexual activity. *Journal of Marriage and Family, 61*(4), 920–934.

Upchurch, D. M., Levy-Storms, L., et al. (1998). Gender and ethnic differences in the timing of first sexual intercourse. *Family Planning Perspectives, 30*(3), 121–128.

Urbaniak, G. C., & Kilmann, P. R. (2003). Physical attractiveness and the "nice guy paradox": Do nice guys really finish last? *Sex Roles, 49*(9–10), 413–425.

Ursus. (2004, December 7). Query: Pubic hair. *Canadian Medical Association Journal, 171*(12), 1569.

Valdiserri, R. O. (2002). HIV/AIDS stigma: An impediment to public health. *American Journal of Public Health, 92*(3), 341–343.

Valente, S. M. (2005). Sexual abuse of boys. *Journal of Child and Adolescent Psychiatric Nursing, 18*(1), 10–16.

Valera, R. J. (2000). Violence and post-traumatic stress disorder in a sample of inner city street prostitutes. *American Journal of Health Studies, 16*(3), 149–156.

Van Balen, F., & Inhorn, M. C. (2003). Son preference, sex selection, and the "new" new reproductive technologies. *International Journal of Health Services, 33*(2), 235–252.

van Basten, J. P., Van Driel, M. F., Hoekstra, H. J., Sleijfer, D. T., van de Wiel, H. B., Droste, J. H., et al. (1999). Objective and subjective effect of treatment for testicular cancer on sexual function. *British Journal of Urology, 84*(6), 671–678.

Van Damme, L., Ramjee, G., Alary, M., Vuylsteke, B., Chandeying, V., Rees, H., et al. (2002). Effectiveness of COL-1492, a N-9 vaginal gel on HIV-transmission in female sex workers. *Lancet, 360*(9338), 971–977.

Van Damme, L., Wright, A., Depraetere, K., Rosenstein, I., Vandersmissen, V., & Poulter, L. (2000). A phase I study of a novel potential intravaginal microbicide PRO2000, in healthy sexually inactive women. *Sexually Transmitted Infections, 76*(2), 126–130.

Van der Horst, C., Stuebinger, H., Seif, C., Melchior, D., Martinez-Portillo, F. J., & Juenemann, K. P. (2003). Priapism—etiology, pathophysiology and management. *International Brazilian Journal of Urology, 29*(5), 391–400.

Van de Ven, P., Campbell, D., & Kippax, S. (1997). Factors associated with unprotected anal intercourse in gay men's casual partnerships in Sydney, Australia. *AIDS Care, 9*(6), 637–649.

VandeWijgert, J., & Coggins, C. (2002). Microbicides to prevent heterosexual transmission of HIV: Ten years down the road. *BETA, 15*(2), 23–28.

Vanfossen, B. (1996). ITROWs women and expression conference. Institute for Teaching and Research on Women, Towson University, Towson, MD. Retrieved April 15, 2003, from http://www.towson.edu/itrow

van Lankveld, J., Everaerd, W., & Grotjohann, Y. (2001). Cognitive-behavioral bibliotherapy for sexual dysfunctions in heterosexual couples: A randomized waiting-list controlled clinical trial in the Netherlands. *Journal of Sex Research, 38*(1), 51–67.

Van Oss Marin, B., & Gomez, C. (1994). Latinos, HIV disease, and cultures. In P. Cohen, M. Sande, & P. Volberding (Eds.), *The AIDS knowledge base* (pp. 10.8–10.13). New York: Little, Brown.

van Steirteghem, A., Nagy, P., Joris, H., Janssenswillen, C., Staessen, C., Verheyen, G., et al. (1998). Results of intracytoplasmic sperm injection with ejaculated, fresh and frozen–thawed epididymal and testicular spermatozoa. *Human Reproduction, 13*(Suppl. 1), 134–142.

VanTilburg, M., Unterberg, M. L., & Vingerhoets, J. (2002). Crying during adolescence. *British Journal of Developmental Psychology, 20*(1), 77–87.

Ventura, S., Hamilton, B. E., & Sutton, P. D. (2003, February). Revised birth and fertility rates for the United States, 2000 and 2001. Retrieved September 8, 2005, from http://www.cdc.gov/nchs/data/nvsr/nvsr51/nvsr51_04.pdf

Verkasalo, P. K., Thomas, H. V., Appleby, P. N., Davey, G. K., & Key, T. J. (2001). Circulating levels of sex hormones and their relation to risk factors for breast cancer: A crosssectional study in 1092 pre- and postmenopausal women. *Cancer Causes and Control, 12*(1), 47–59.

Vigano, P., Parazzini, F., Somigliana, E., & Vercellini, P. (2004). Endometriosis: Epidemiology and aetiological factors. *Best Practice & Research Clinical Obstetrics & Gynaecology, 18*(2), 177–200.

Vincent, P. C., Peplau, L. A., & Hill, C. (1998). A longitudinal application of the theory of reasoned action to women's career behavior. *Journal of Applied Social Psychology, 28*(9), 761–778.

Voigt, H. (1991). Enriching the sexual experience of couples: The Asian traditions and sexual counseling. *Journal of Sex and Marital Therapy, 17,* 214–219.

VonSadovszky, V., Keller, M. L., & McKinney, K. (2002). College students' perceptions and practices of sexual activities in sexual encounters. *Journal of Nursing Scholarship, 34*(2), 133.

Von Sydow, K. (2000). Sexuality of older women: The effect of menopause, other physical and social and partner-related factors. *Arztl Fortbild Qualitatssich, 94*(3), 223–229.

Vukovic, L. (1992, November–December). Cold sores and fever blisters. *Natural Health,* 119–120.

Waal, F. B. M. (1995). Bonobo sex and society. *Scientific American,* 82–88. Retrieved July 4, 2003, from http://songweaver.com/info/bonobos.html

Wagner, E. (1991). Campus victims of date rape should consider civil lawsuits as alternatives to criminal charges or colleges' procedures. *The Chronicle of Higher Education,* August 7, B2.

Wakelin, A. (2003). Effects of victim gender and sexuality on attributions of blame to rape victims. *Sex Roles, 49*(9–10), 477–487.

Wald, A. (1999). New therapies and prevention strategies for genital herpes. *Clinical Infectious Diseases, 28* (Suppl. 1), S4–S13.

Wald, A., Zeh, J., Selke, S., Warren, T., Ryncarz, A. J., Ashley, R., et al. (2000). Reactivation of genital herpes simplex virus type-2 infection in asymptomatic seropositive persons. *New England Journal of Medicine, 342*(12), 844–850.

Waldner, L. K, Sikka, A., & Baig, S. (1999). Ethnicity and sex differences in university students' knowledge of AIDS, fear of AIDS, and homophobia. *Journal of Homosexuality, 37*(3), 117–118.

Walen, S. R., & Roth, D. (1987). A cognitive approach. In J. H. Geer & W. T. O'Donahue (Eds.), *Theories of human sexuality* (pp. 335–360). New York: Plenum Press.

Walker, B. W., & Ephross, P. H. (1999). Knowledge and attitudes toward sexuality of a group of elderly. *Journal of Gerontological Social Work, 31*(1–2), 85–87.

Walker, J., Archer, J., & Davies, M. (2005). Effects of rape on men: A descriptive analysis. *Archives of Sexual Behavior, 34*(1), 69–80.

Walker, M. C., Murphy, K. E., Pan, S., Yang, Q., & Wen, S. W. (2004). Adverse maternal outcomes in multifetal pregnancies. *British Journal of Obstetrics & Gynecology, 111*(11), 1294–1296.

Wallerstein, E. (1980). *Circumcision: An American health fallacy.* New York: Springer.

Walsh, P. C., Retik, A. B., Vaughan, E. D., & Wein, A. J. (Eds.). (1997). *Campbell's urology.* Philadelphia: W. B. Saunders.

Walters, J. (2005, January 2). No sex is safe sex for teens in America. Retrieved October 19, 2005, from http://observer.guardian.co.uk/international/story/0,6903,1382117,00.html

Wang, H., & Amato, P. R. (2000). Predictors of divorce adjustment: Stressors, resources and definitions. *Journal of Marriage and Family, 62*(3), 655–669.

Wang, J. X., Norman, R. J., & Wilcox, A. J. (2004). Incidence of spontaneous abortion among pregnancies produced by assisted reproductive technology. *Human Reproduction, 19*(2), 272–277.

Wang, T. W., & Apgar, B. S. (1998). Exercise during pregnancy. *American Family Physician, 57*(8), 1846–1852.

Ward, D., Carter, T., & Perrin, D. (1994). *Social deviance: Being, behaving, and branding.* Boston: Allyn & Bacon.

Wardle, L. D. (1999). Divorce reform at the turn of the millennium: Certainties and possibilities. *Family Law Quarterly, 33,* 783–900.

Wardle, L. D. (2001). Multiply and replenish: Considering same-sex marriage in light of state interests in marital procreation. *Harvard Journal of Law and Public Policy, 24*(3), 771–815.

Warne, G. L., & Kanumakala, S. (2002). Molecular endocrinology of sex differentiation. *Seminars in Reproductive Medicine, 20*(3), 169–179.

Warne, G. L., Grover, S., & Zajac, J. D. (2005). Hormonal therapies for individuals with intersex conditions: Protocol for use. *Treatments in Endocrinology, 4*(1), 19–29.

Warner, J. (2005, February 21). Mommy madness. *Newsweek,* pp. 42–49.

Warner, L., Hatcher, R. A., & Steiner, M. J. (2004). Male condoms. In R. A. Hatcher et al. (Eds.), *Contraceptive technology* (18th Rev. ed., pp. 331–353). New York: Ardent Media.

Warr, M. (1985). Fear of rape among urban women. *Social Problems, 32,* 238–250.

Warren, M. P., Brooks-Gunn, J., Fox, R. P., Holderness, C. C., Hyle, E. P., & Hamilton, W. G. (2002). Osteopenia in exercise-associated amenorrhea using ballet dancers as a model: A longitudinal study. *Journal of Clinical Endocrinology Metabolism, 87*(7), 3162–3168.

Warrington, M., & Younger, M. (2000). The other side of the gender gap. *Gender and Education, 12*(4), 493–508.

Wasserman, A. L. (2001). Development of the fetish interest scale: A measure of sexual interest using forced-choice and visual reaction time methodologies. *Dissertation Abstracts International,* Hahnemann University, December, #0419-4217.

Watkins, G., & Bessin, R. (2005). Praying mantids. Retrieved February 5, 2005, from http://www.uky.edu/Agriculture/Entomology/entfacts/trees/ef418.htm

Watkins, S. A. (2002). Demographic shifts change notional face of HIV/AIDS. *SIECUS Report, 31*(1), 10–12.

Waxman, H. (2004a). Abstinence-only education. Retrieved September 17, 2005, from http://www.democrats.reform.house.gov/investigations.asp?Issue=Abstinence-Only+Education

Waxman, H. (2004b). The content of federally funded abstinence—only education programs. Retrieved September 17, 2005, from http://www.democrats.reform.house.gov/Documents/20041201102153-50247.pdf

Wechsler, H., & Issac, N. (1992). "Binge" drinkers at Massachusetts colleges. *Journal of the American Medical Association, 267*(21), 2929–2931.

Weeks, G., & Hof, L. (1987). *Integrating sex and marital therapy.* New York: Brunner/Mazel.

Weibley, S. (2001). New vaccines may give sexuality education advocates the shot they need. *SIECUS Report, 30*(1), 27.

Weibley, S. (2002). States implement "safe surrender" laws for people who give up their babies. *SIECUS Report, 30*(3), 13–15.

Weigel, D. J., & Ballard-Reisch, D. S. (1999). The influence of marital duration on the use of relationship maintenance behaviors. *Communication Reports, 12*(2), 59–70.

Weinberg, M. S., Williams, C. J., & Pryor, D. W. (1994). *Dual attraction: Understanding bisexuality.* New York: Oxford University Press.

Weinstock, H., Berman, S., & Cates, W. (2004). Sexually transmitted diseases among American youth: Incidence and prevalence estimates. *Perspectives Sex Reproductive Health, 36*(1), 6–10.

Weinstock, H., Berman, S., & Cates, W. (2004, January/February). Sexually transmitted diseases among American youth: Incidence and prevalence estimates, 2000. *Perspectives on Sexual and Reproductive Health, 36*(1), 6–10. Retrieved October 19, 2005, from http://www.guttmacher.org/pubs/journals/3600604.html

Weiss, T. (2004, December 9). Face value: Interactive directory keeps students connected. *Hartford Courant,* p. D1.

Weitzman, G. D. (1999). What psychology professionals should know about polyamory: The lifestyles and mental health concerns of polyamorous individuals. Paper presented at the 8th Annual Diversity Conference. Retrieved June 11, 2005, from http://www.polyamory.org/~joe/polypaper.htm

Welch, L. (1992). *Complete book of sexual trivia.* New York: Citadel Press.

Wells, D., Escudero, T., Levy, B. Hirschhorn, K., Delhanty, J. D., & Munne, S. (2002). First clinical application of comparative genomic hybridization and polar body testing for pre-implantation genetic diagnosis of aneuploidy. *Fertility & Sterility, 78*(3), 543–549.

Wells, J. W. (1970). *Tricks of the trade.* New York: New American Library.

Welty, S. E. (2005). Critical issues with clinical research in children: The example of premature infants. *Toxicology and Applied Pharmacology,* Epub ahead of print. Retrieved July 19, 2005, from http://www.ncbi.nlm.nih.gov/entrez/query.fcgi?cmd=Retrieve&db=pubmed&dopt=Abstract&list_uids=16023161&query_hl=14

Werner-Wilson, R. J. (1998). Gender differences in adolescent sexual attitudes: The influence of individual and family factors. *Adolescence, 33*(131), 519–531.

Wespes, E., & Schulman, C. C. (2002). Male andropause: Myth, reality and treatment. *International Journal of Impotence Research, 14*(Suppl. 1), 593–598.

West, D. J. (1993). *Male prostitution.* Cambridge, U.K.: University of Cambridge Press.

West, L. (1989). Philippine feminist efforts to organize against sexual victimization. *Response to the Victimization of Women and Children, 12,* 11–14.

Westefeld, J. S., Buford, B., Taylor, S., & Maples, M. R. (2001). Gay, lesbian and bisexual college students: The relationship between sexual orientation and depression, loneliness, and suicide. *Journal of College Student Psychotherapy, 15*(3), 71–82.

Westermarck, E. (1972). *Marriage ceremonies in Morocco.* London, U.K.: Curzon Press.

Whalen, R. E., Geary, D. C., & Johnson, F. (1990). Models of sexuality. In D. P. McWhirter, S. A. Sanders, & J. M. Reinisch (Eds.), *Homosexuality/heterosexuality: Concepts of sexual orientation* (pp. 61–70). New York: Oxford University Press.

Whatley, M. A. (2005). The effect of participant sex, victim dress, and traditional attitudes on causal judgments for marital rape victims. *Journal of Family Violence, 20*(3), 191–200.

Whelan, C. I., & Stewart, D. E. (1990). Pseudocyesis—a review and report of six cases. *International Journal of Psychiatry in Medicine, 20,* 97–108.

Whincup, P. H., Gilg, J. A., Odoki, K., Taylor, S. J. C., & Cook, D. G. (2001). Age of menarche in contemporary British teenagers: Survey of girls born between 1982 and 1986. *British Medical Journal, 322*(7294), 1095–1097.

Whipple, B. (2000). Beyond the g spot. *Scandinavian Journal of Sexology, 3*(2), 35–42.

Whitam, F. L., Daskalos, C., Sobolewski, C. G., & Padilla, P. (1999). The emergence of lesbian sexuality and identity cross-culturally. *Archives of Sexual Behavior, 27*(1), 31–57.

Whitbeck, L. B., Yoder, K. A., Hoyt, D. R., & Conger, R. D. (1999). Early adolescent sexual activity: A developmental study. *Journal of Marriage and Family, 61*(4), 934–947.

White, B. H., & Kurpius, S. E. (2002). Effects of victim sex and sexual orientation on perceptions of rape. *Sex Roles, 46*(5–6), 191–200.

White, C. B. (1982). Sexual interest, attitudes, knowledge, and sexual history in relation to sexual behavior in the institutionalized aged. *Archives of Sexual Behavior, 11,* 11–21.

White, S. D., & DeBlassie, R. R. (1992). Adolescent sexual behavior. *Adolescence, 27,* 183–191.

Whitehead, H. (1981). The bow and the burden strap: A new look at institutionalized homosexuality in native North America. In S. Ortner & H. Whitehead (Eds.), *Sexual meanings* (pp. 80–115). Cambridge, U.K.: Cambridge University Press.

Whiteman, M. K., Staropoli, C. A., Benedict, J. C., Borgeest, C., & Flaws, J. A. (2003). Risk factors for hot flashes in midlife women. *Journal of Women's Health, 12*(5), 459–472.

Whiting, B., & Edwards, C. P. (1988). A cross-cultural analysis of sex differences in the behavior of children aged 3 through 11. In G. Handel (Ed.), *Childhood socialization* (pp. 281–297). New York: Aldine De Gruyter.

Whiting, B. B., & Whiting, J. W. (1975). *Children of six cultures: A psycho-cultural analysis.* Cambridge, MA: Harvard University Press.

Whitley, R. J., & Roizman, B. (2001). Herpes simplex virus infections. *Lancet, 357*(9267), 1513–1519.

Whitsel-Anderson, S. A. (2002). Body dissatisfaction in men. Dissertation Abstracts International, Indiana University, April, 2002, AAI3026622.

Wiederman, M. W. (1999). Volunteer bias in sexuality research using college student participants. *Journal of Sex Research, 36*(1), 59–66.

Wikan, U. (1977). Man becomes woman: Transsexualism in Oman as a key to gender roles. *Man, 12,* 304–391.

Wilborn, P. (2002, November 26). Porn industry stays profitable. *The Hartford Courant,* E4.

Wilcox, A. J., Weinberg, C. R., & Baird, D. D. (1995). Timing of sexual intercourse in relation to ovulation. Effects on the probability of conception, survival of the pregnancy, and sex of the baby. *New England Journal of Medicine, 333*(23), 1517–1521.

Wilcox, B., et al. (1996, November 18). Adolescent abstinence promotion programs: An evaluation of evaluations. Paper presented at the Annual Meeting of the American Public Health Association, November 17–21, 1996, New York.

Wilkinson, D., Ramjee, G., Tholandi, M., & Rutherford, G. (2002b). Nonoxynol-9 for preventing vaginal acquisition of STIs by women from men. *Cochrane Database System, 4,* CD003939.

Williams, C. W. (1991). *Black teenage mothers: Pregnancy and child rearing from their perspective*. Lexington, MA: Lexington Books.

Williams, E., Lamson, N., Efem, S., Weir, S., et al. (1992). Implementation of an AIDS prevention program among prostitutes in the Cross River State of Nigeria. *AIDS, 6*, 229–230.

Williams, J. E., & Best, D. L. (1994). Cross-cultural views of women and men. In W . J. Lonner & R. Malpass (Eds.), *Psychology and culture*. Boston: Allyn & Bacon.

Williams, S., & Kelly, F. (2005). Relationships among involvement, attachment, and behavioral problems in adolescence: Examining father's influence. *Journal of Early Adolescence, 25*(2), 168–196.

Williams, W. L. (1986). *The spirit and the flesh: Sexual diversity in American Indian culture*. Boston: Beacon Press.

Williams, W. L. (1990). Book review: P. A. Jackson, Male homosexuality in Thailand: An interpretation of contemporary Thai sources. *Journal of Homosexuality, 19*, 126–138.

Willis, M. T. (2001) Fewer periods: Experts challenge idea that women on the pill should menstruate. Retrieved July 16, 2002, from http://abcnews.go.com/sections/living/DailyNews/skipping_periods011030.html

Wilson, B., & Clark, S. (1992). Remarriages: A demographic profile. *Journal of Family Issues, 13*, 123–141.

Wilson, C. (2005). Recurrent vulvovaginitis candidiasis: An overview of traditional and alternative therapies. *Advanced Nurse Practitioner, 13*(2), 24–29.

Wilson, G. D. (1987). An ethological approach to sexual deviation. In G. D. Wilson (Ed.), *Variant sexuality: Research and theory* (pp. 84–115). Baltimore: Johns Hopkins University Press.

Wilson, P. (1994). Forming a partnership between parents and sexuality educators. *SIECUS Report, 22*, 1–5.

Wilson, S., & Medora, N. (1990). Gender comparisons of college students' attitudes toward sexual behavior. *Adolescence, 25*, 615–627.

Wininger, J. D., & Kort, H. I. (2002). Cryopreservation of immature and mature human oocytes. *Seminars in Reproductive Medicine, 20*(1), 45–49.

Wiseman, C., Peltzman, B., Halmi, K. A., & Sunday, S. R. (2004). Risk factors for eating disorders: Surprising similarities between middle school boys and girls. *Eating Disorders: The Journal of Treatment & Prevention, 12*(4), 315–320.

Wiseman, V. (2003). Personal Communication. July 17, 2003.

Wittchen, H. U., Becker, E., Lieb, R., & Krause, P. (2002). Prevalence, incidence and stability of premenstrual dysphoric disorder in the community. *Psychological Medicine, 32*(1), 119–132.

Wiwanitkit, V. (2005). Male rape, some notes on the laboratory investigation. *Sexuality & Disability, 23*(1), 41–46.

Wolak, J., Finkelhor, D., & Mitchell, K. J. (2005). Child pornography possessors arrested in internet-related crimes: Findings from the National Juvenile Online Victimization Study. Retrieved November 7, 2005, from http://www.missingkids.com/en_US/publications/NC144.pdf

Wolf, N. (1991). *The beauty myth: How images of beauty are used against women*. New York: W. Morris.

Wolitski, R. J., Valdiserri, R. O., Denning, P. H., & Levine, W. C. (2001). Are we headed for a resurgence of the HIV epidemic among men who have sex with men? *American Journal of Public Health, 91*(6), 883–888.

Wolpe, J. (1958). *Psychotherapy by reciprocal inhibition*. Stanford, CA: Stanford University Press.

Wonderlich, S. A., Crosby, R. D., Mitchell, J. E., Roberts, J. A., Haseltine, B., DeMuth, G., & Thompson, K. M. (2000). Relationship of childhood sexual abuse and eating disturbance in children. *Journal of the American Academy of Child & Adolescent Psychiatry, 39*(10), 1277–1283.

Wonderlich, S. A., Crosby, R. D., Mitchell, J. E., Thompson, K. M., Redlin, J., Demuth, G., & Smyth, J. (2001). Pathways mediating sexual abuse and eating disturbances in children. *International Journal of Eating Disorders, 29*(3), 270–279.

Woo, J., Fine, P., & Goetzl, L. (2005). Abortion disclosure and the association with domestic violence. *Obstetrics & Gynecology, 105*(6), 1329–1334.

Wood, E., Desmarais, S., & Gugula, S. (2002). The impact of parenting experience on gender stereotyped toy play of children. *Sex Roles, 47*(1–2), 39–49.

Wood, J. (1999). Gendered lives: Communication, gender, and culture. Belmont, CA: Wadsworth.

Wood, K. (2005). Masturbation as a means of achieving sexual health. *Culture, Health & Sexuality, 7*(2), 182–184.

Woodward, L., Fergusson, D. M., & Horwood, L. J. (2001). Risk factors and life processes associated with teenage pregnancy. *Journal of Marriage and Family, 63*(4), 1170–1185.

Woolf, L. M. (2002). Gay and lesbian aging. *SIECUS Report, 30*(2), 16–21.

Word, R. (2003). Former minister Paul Hill executed for shotgun slayings of abortion doctor, bodyguard. Retrieved September 9, 2003, from http://www.washingtonpost.com/ac2/wp-dyn/A21484-2003Sep3?language=printer

Working girls: Sex industry on legal tightrope. (1992, March 21). *Otago (New Zealand) Daily Times*, p. 21.

Workman, J. E., & Freeburg, F. W. (1999). An examination of date rape, victim dress, and perceiver variables within the context of attribution theory. *Sex Roles, 41*(3–4), 261–277.

Workowski, K. A., & Levine, W. C. (2002, May 10). Sexually transmitted diseases treatment guidelines. *Morbidity & Mortality Weekly, 51*(RR06), 1–8.

World Health Organization. (2001). Technical consultation on nonoxynol-9. Retrieved October 9, 2001, from http://www.conrad.org

Worth, H., Reid, A., & McMillan, K. (2002). Somewhere over the rainbow: Love, trust, and monogamy in gay relationships. *Journal of Sociology, 238*, 237–253.

Wright, K. (1994). The sniff of legend—human pheromones. Chemical sex attractants? A sixth sense organ in the nose? What are we animals? *Discover, 15*(4), 60.

Wu, Z., & Penning, M. (1997). Marital instability after midlife. *Journal of Family Issues, 18*, 459–478.

Wu, Z., & Schimmele, C. (2005). Repartnering after first union disruption. *Journal of Marriage & Family, 67*(1), 27–36.

Wurtele, S. K., Melzer, A. M., & Kast, L. C. (1992). Preschoolers' knowledge of, and ability to learn, genital terminology. *Journal of Sex Education and Therapy, 18*, 115–122.

Wyatt, G. (1998). *Stolen women: Reclaiming our sexuality, taking back our lives*. New York: Wiley.

Wyatt, G. E., Carmona, J. V., Loeg, T. B., Guthrie, D., Chin, D., & Gordon, W. (2000). Factors affecting HIV contraceptive decisionmaking among women. *Sex Roles, 42*(7–8), 495–521.

Wylie, K. R., & Ralph, D. (2005). Premature ejaculation: The current literature. *Current Opinions in Urology, 15*(6), 393–398.

Wylie, K., Hallam-Jones, R., & Harrington, C. (2004). Psychological difficulties within a group of patients with vulvodynia. *Journal of Psychosomatic Obstetrics & Gynaecology, 25* (3–4), 257–265.

Xu, J. S., Leeper, M. A., Wu, Y., Zhou. X. B., Xu., S. Y., Chen, T., Yang, X. L., & Shuang, L. Q. (1998). User acceptability of a female condom (Reality) in Shanghai. *Advances in Contraception, 14*(4), 193–199.

Yamawaki, N., & Tschanz, B. T. (2005). Rape perception differences between Japanese and American college students: On the mediating influence of gender role traditionality. *Sex Roles, 52*(5–6), 379–392.

Yang, Q., Rassmussen, S. A., & Friedman, J. M. (2002). Mortality associated with down's syndrome in the USA from 1983–1997. *Lancet, 359*, 1019–1025.

Yarab, P. E., & Allgeier, E. R. (1998). Don't even think about it: The role of sexual fantasies as perceived unfaithfulness in heterosexual dating relationships. *Journal of Sex Education and Therapy, 23*(3), 246–254.

Yesalis, C. E., & Bahrke, M. S. (2000). Doping among adolescent athletes. *Best Practice & Research Clinical Endocrinology & Metabolism, 14*(1), 25–35.

Yllo, K., & Finkelhor, D. (1985). Marital rape. In A. W. Burgess (Ed.), *Rape and sexual assault* (pp. 146–158). New York: Garland.

Yoder, V. C., Virden, T. B., & Amin, K. (2005). Internet pornography and loneliness: An association? *Sexual Addiction & Compulsivity, 12*(1), 19–44.

Yonkers, K. A. (1999). Medical management of premenstrual dysphoric disorder. *Journal of Gender-Specific Medicine, 2*(3), 55–60.

Young, K. S., Griffin-Shelley, E., Cooper, A., O'Mara, J., & Buchanan, J. (2000). Online infidelity. In A. Cooper (Ed.), *Cybersex: The dark side of the force* (pp. 59–74). Philadelphia, PA: Brunner Routledge.

Zacharias, P. (2005). Snap, crackle and profit—the story behind a cereal empire. *The Detroit News*. Retrieved February 5, 2005, from http://info.detnews.com/history/story/index.cfm?id=146&category=business

Zacur, H. A., Hedon, B., Mansourt, D., Shangold, G. A., Fisher, A. C., & Creasy, G. W. (2002). Integrated summary of Ortho Evra contraceptive patch adhesion in varied climates and conditions. *Fertility and Sterility, 77* (2 Suppl. 2), 532–535.

Zak, A., Collins, C., & Harper, L. (1998). Self-reported control over decision-making and its relationship to intimate relationships. *Psychological Reports, 82*(2), 560–562.

Zebrowitz, L. A., Collins, M.A., & Dutta, R. (1998). The relationship between appearance and personality across the life span. *Personality & Social Psychology Bulletin, 24*(7), 736–749.

Zegwaard, M. I., Gamel, C. J., Dugris, D. J., & Logmans, A. (2000). The experience of sexuality and information received in women with cervical cancer and their partners. *Verpleegkunde, 15*(1), 18–27.

Zelnik, M., & Kantner, J. F. (1980). Sexual activity, contraceptive use and pregnancy among metropolitan-area teenagers: 1971–1979. *Family Planning Perspectives, 12*(5), 230–237.

Zept, B. (2002). Does male circumcision prevent cervical cancer in women? *American Family Physician, 66*(1), 147–149.

Zheng, W., & Hart, R. (2002). The effects of marital and nonmarital union transition on health. *Journal of Marriage and Family, 64*(2), 420–433.

Zimet, G. D., Perkins, S. M., Sturm, L. A., Bair, R. M., Juliar, B. E., & Mays, R. M. (2005). Predictors of STI vaccine acceptability among parents and their adolescent children. *Journal of Adolescent Health, 37*(3), 179–186.

Zinaman, M. J., Clegg, E. D., Brown, C. C., O'Connor, J., & Selevan, S. G. (1996). Estimates of human fertility and pregnancy loss. *Journal of Fertility and Sterility, 65*(3), 503–509.

Zinn, M. B., & Eitzen, S. D. (1993). *Diversity in families*. New York: HarperCollins.

Zolese, G., & Blacker, C. V. R. (1992). The psychological complications of therapeutic abortion. *British Journal of Psychiatry, 160*, 742–749.

Zucker, K. J. (1990). Psychosocial and erotic development in cross-gender identified children. *Canadian Journal of Psychiatry, 35*, 487–495.

Zurbriggen, E. L., & Yost, M. R. (2004). Power, desire, and pleasure in sexual fantasies. *Journal of Sex Research, 41*(3), 288–300.

Zverina, J. (2004). Czech Republic. In R. T. Francoeur & R. J. Noonan (Eds.), *The Continuum international encyclopedia of sexuality* (pp. 320–328). New York/London: Continuum International.

Name Index

Subject Index